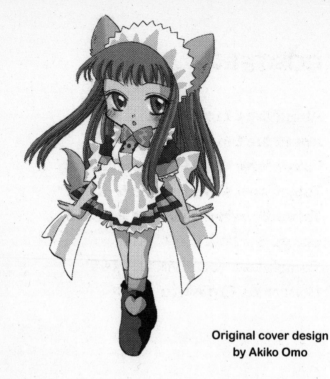

**Original cover design
by Akiko Omo**

Born on March 27th, Aries, Blood type O, from Ôsaka Prefecture. She won the 24th Nakayoshi New Faces Manga Award in 1997 with the manga *Usagi no Furasu Hoshi*, which made its debut in the January 1998 issue of *Run-Run*. Her featured works are *Super Doll Rika-Chan* and *Ichigo no Mori no Nemurihime*. She enjoys playing with her cat and wearing cute (weird?) clothes.

ABOUT THE STORY

TOKYO MEWMEW OMNIBUS

☆ICHIGO WAS AN ORDINARY JUNIOR-HIGH STUDENT, BUT ONE DAY SHE BECAME A MEW MEW, ONE OF THE WORLD'S CHAMPIONS OF JUSTICE! SHE'S TRYING TO SAVE THE EARTH FROM ALIENS WITH THE HELP OF HER FOUR MEW MEW COMPANIONS.

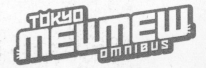

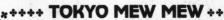

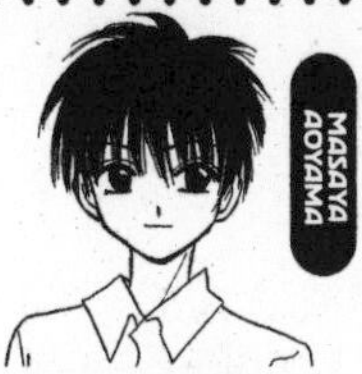
MASAYA AOYAMA

A PERFECT BOY, POPULAR, AND GOOD AT KENDO.

CAFÉ MEW MEW

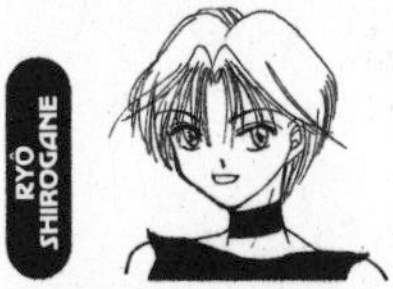
RYÔ SHIROGANE

A MYSTERIOUS RICH BOY.

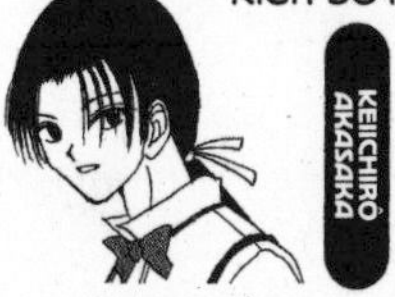
KEIICHIRÔ AKASAKA

SHIROGANE'S FRIEND, A CAFÉ WAITER.

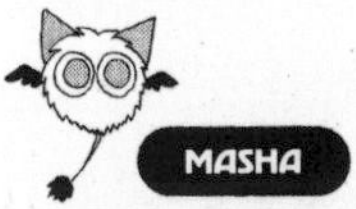
MASHA

ICHIGO'S PET ROBOT.

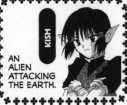

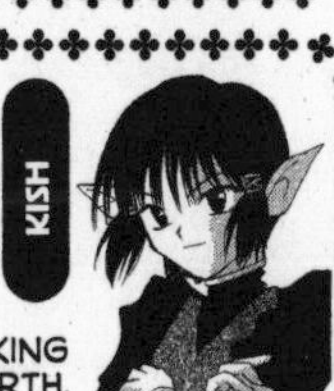
KISH

AN ALIEN ATTACKING THE EARTH.

TOKYO MEW MEW

◀BEFORE ▼AFTER

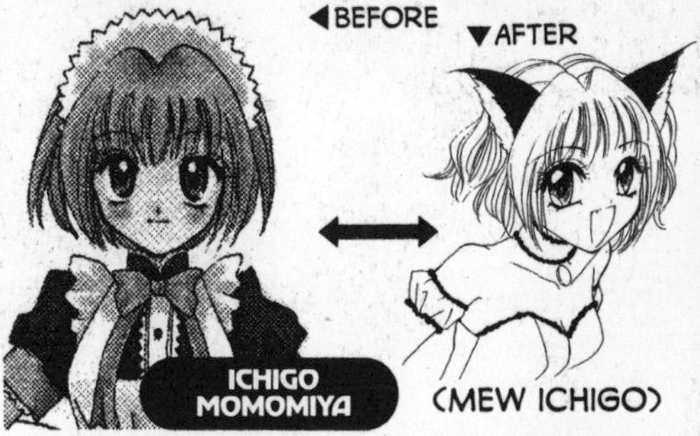
ICHIGO MOMOMIYA

(MEW ICHIGO)

A FIRST-YEAR JUNIOR-HIGH GIRL, IN LOVE WITH AOYAMA-KUN, AND INFUSED WITH IRIOMOTE WILDCAT DNA.

(MEW MINT)

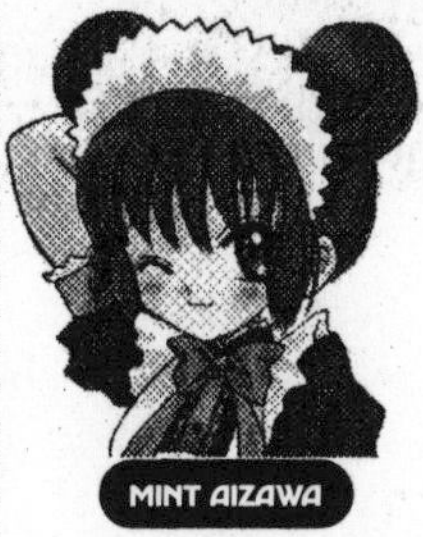
MINT AIZAWA

AN AFFLUENT, STRONG-MINDED GIRL.

(MEW LETTUCE)

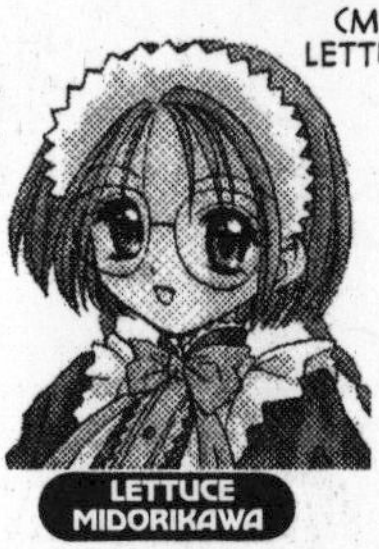
LETTUCE MIDORIKAWA

A NICE, QUIET GIRL.

(MEW PUDDING)

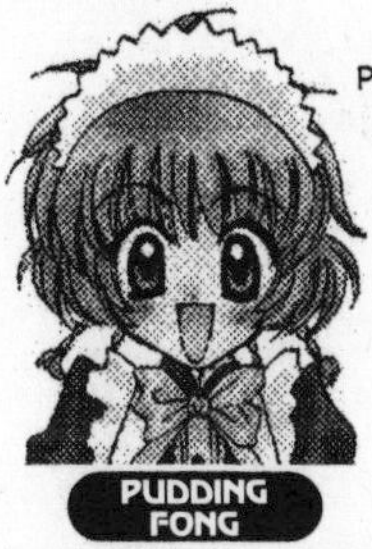
PUDDING FONG

A VERY SOCIAL AND MATERIALISTIC GIRL.

(MEW ZACRO)

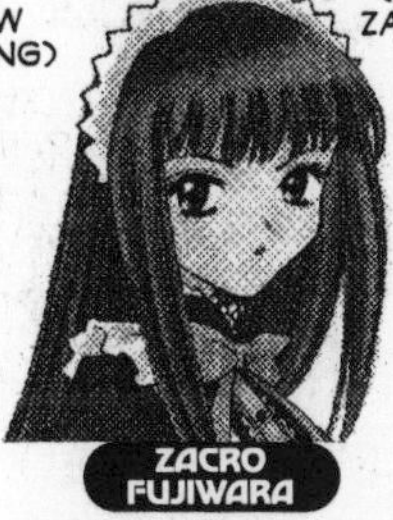
ZACRO FUJIWARA

A COOL GIRL, GORGEOUS AND A RETURNING STUDENT.

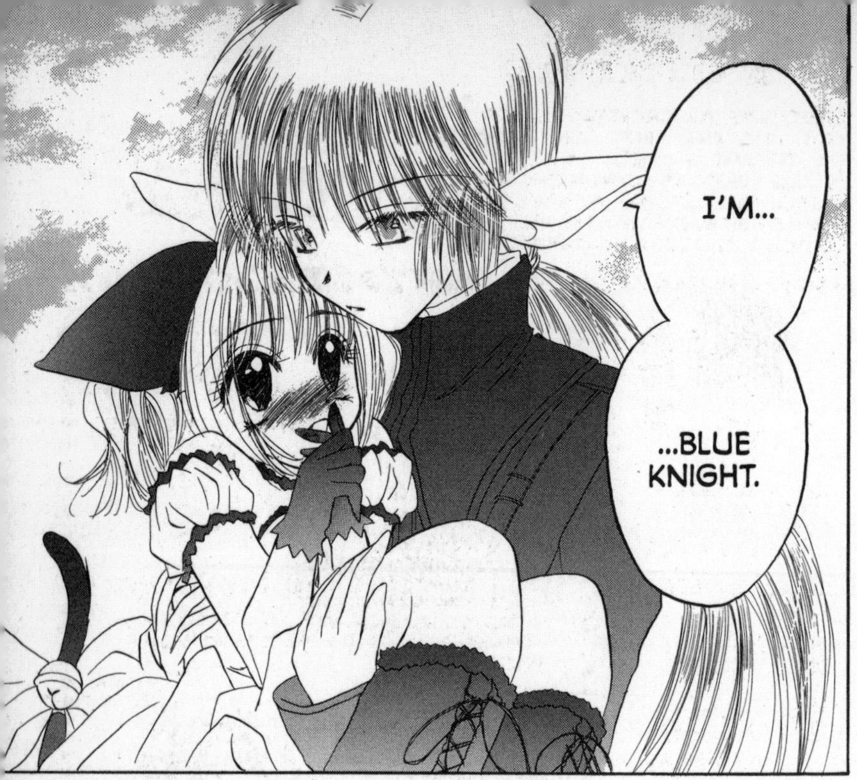
I'M...
...BLUE KNIGHT.

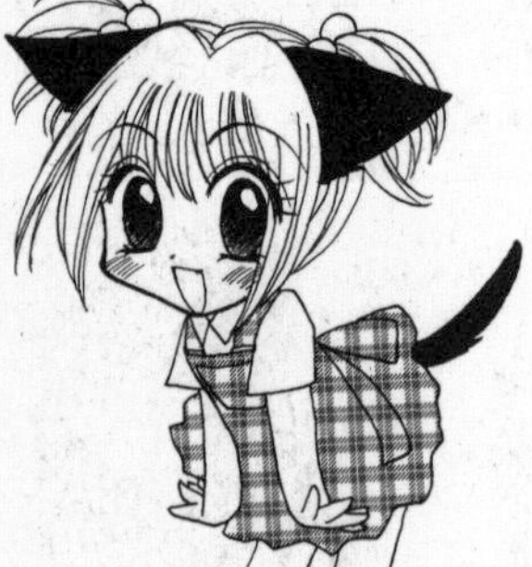

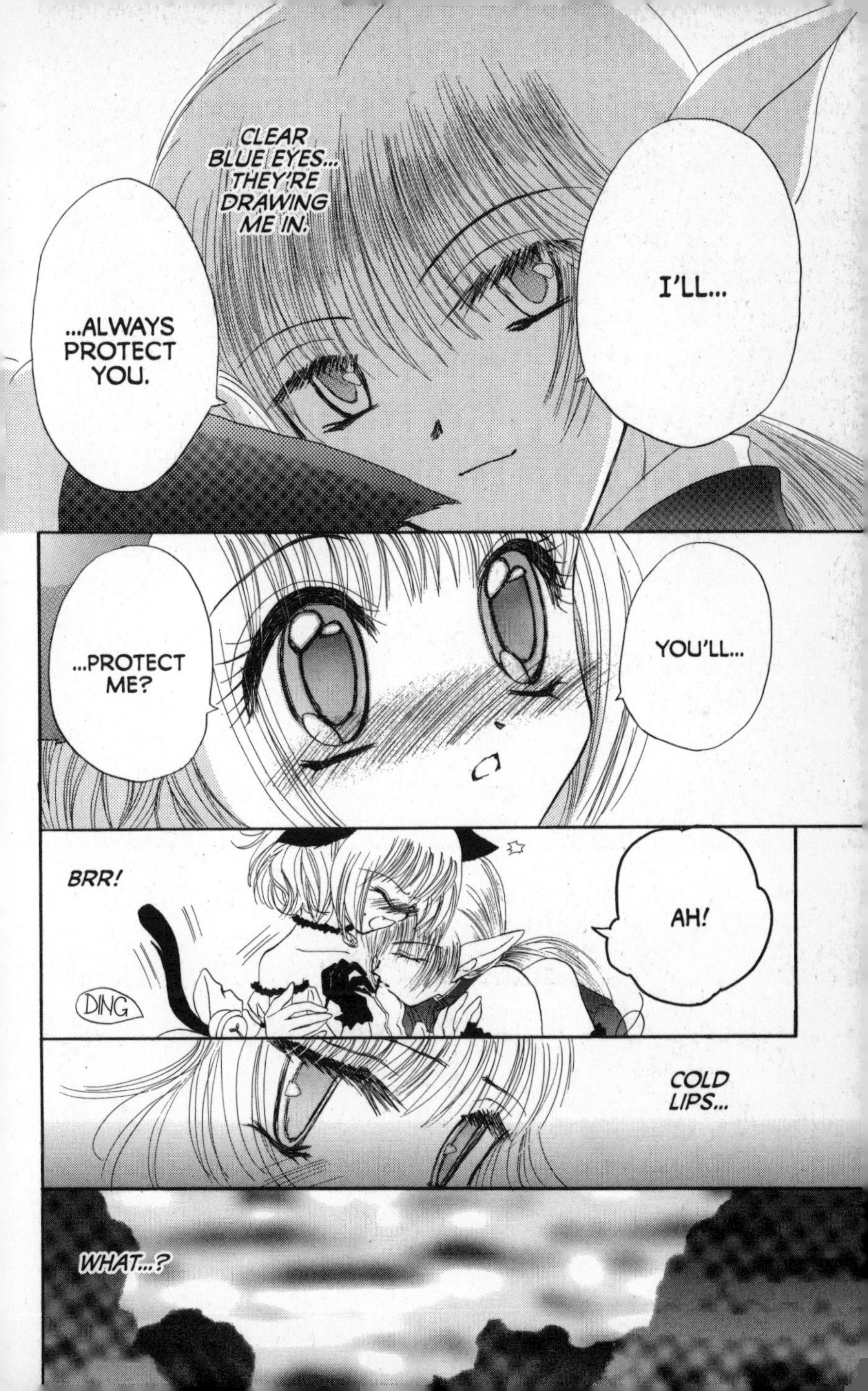
CLEAR BLUE EYES... THEY'RE DRAWING ME IN.
I'LL...
...ALWAYS PROTECT YOU.
YOU'LL...
...PROTECT ME?
AH!
BRR!
DING
COLD LIPS...
WHAT...?

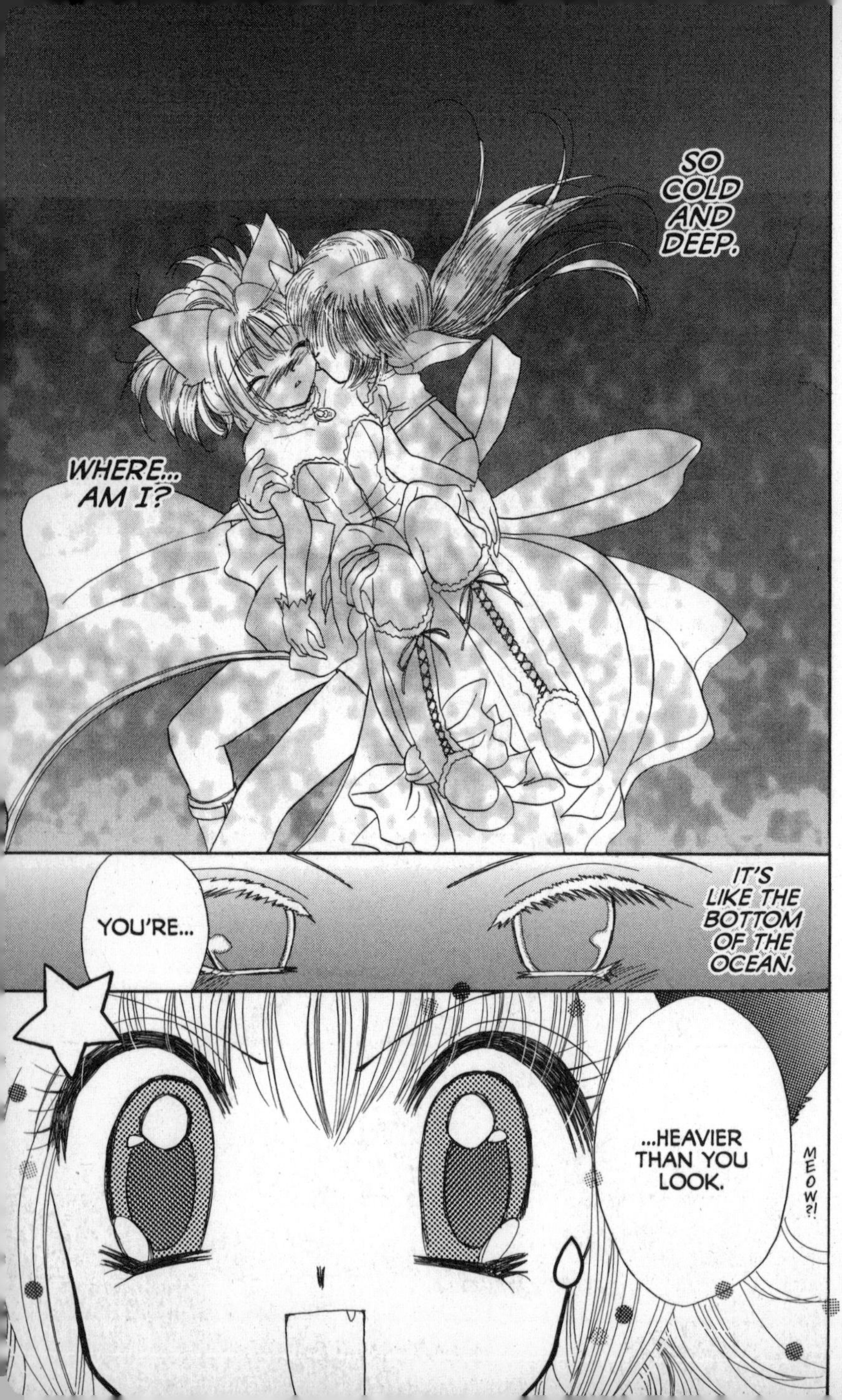
SO COLD AND DEEP.
WHERE... AM I?
IT'S LIKE THE BOTTOM OF THE OCEAN.
YOU'RE...
MEOW?!
...HEAVIER THAN YOU LOOK.

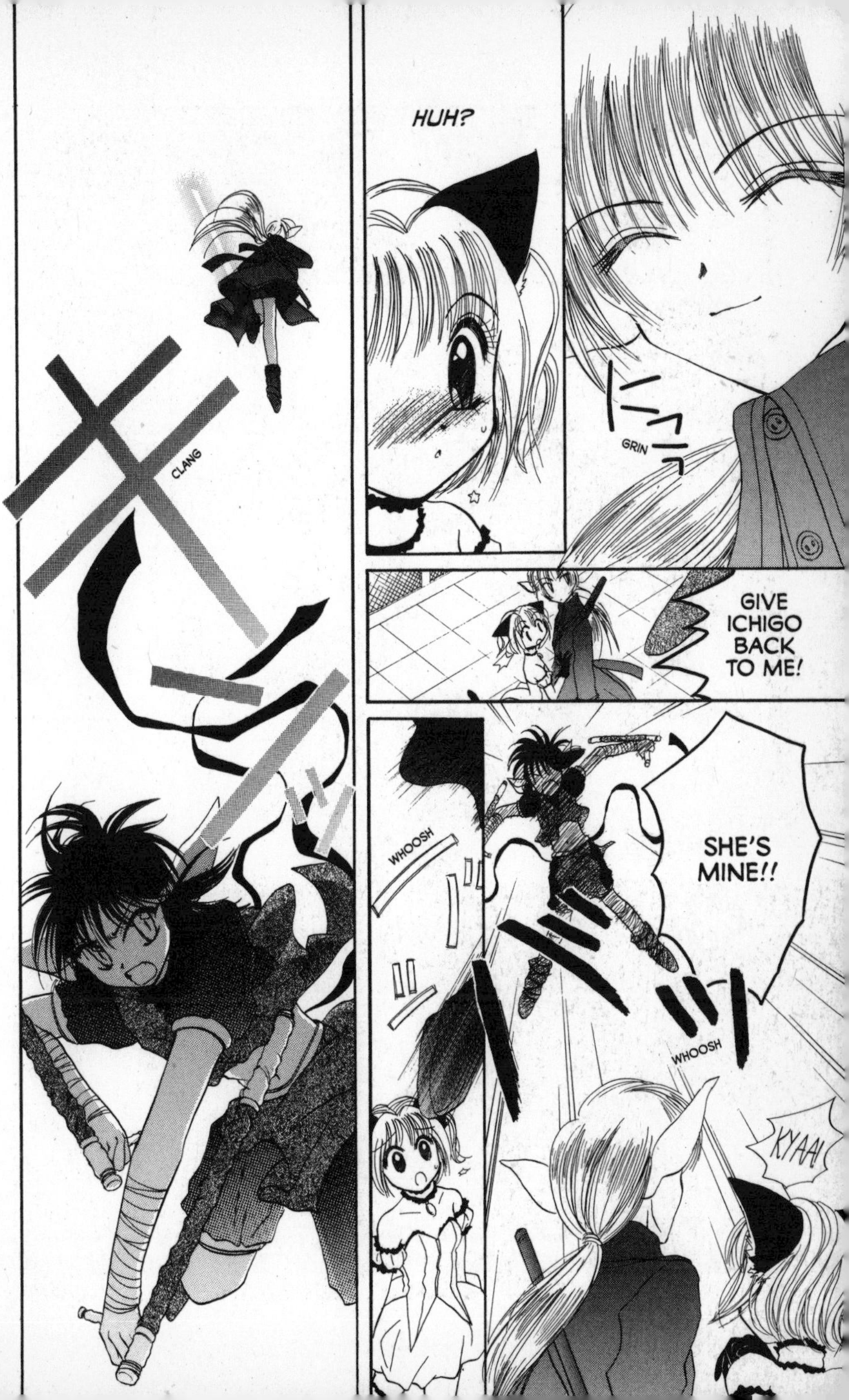
GRIN
HUH?
GIVE ICHIGO BACK TO ME!
SHE'S MINE!!
WHOOSH
WHOOSH
KYAA!
CLANG

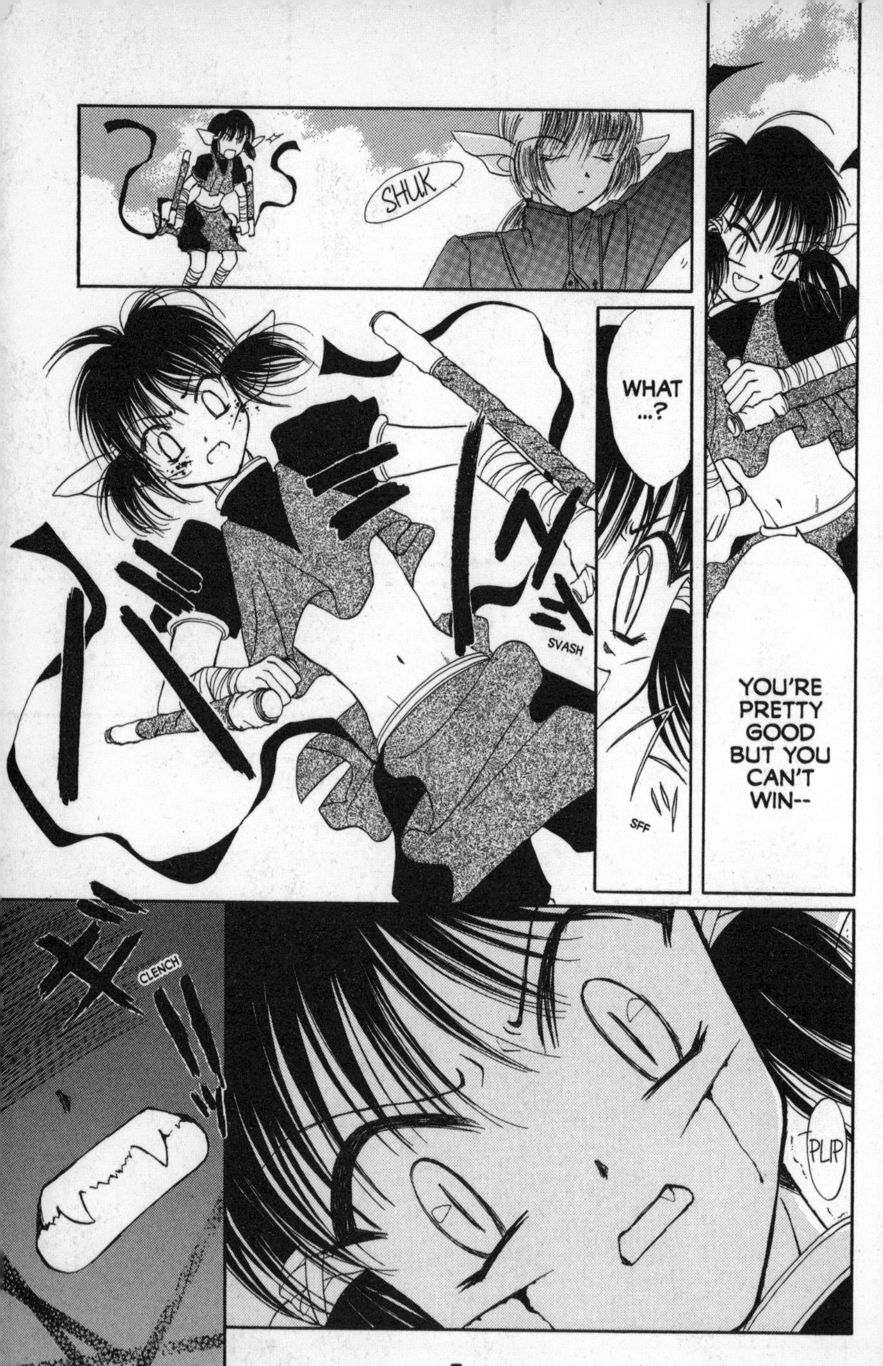
YOU'RE PRETTY GOOD BUT YOU CAN'T WIN--
SHUK
WHAT ...?
SFF
SVASH
PLIP
CLENCH

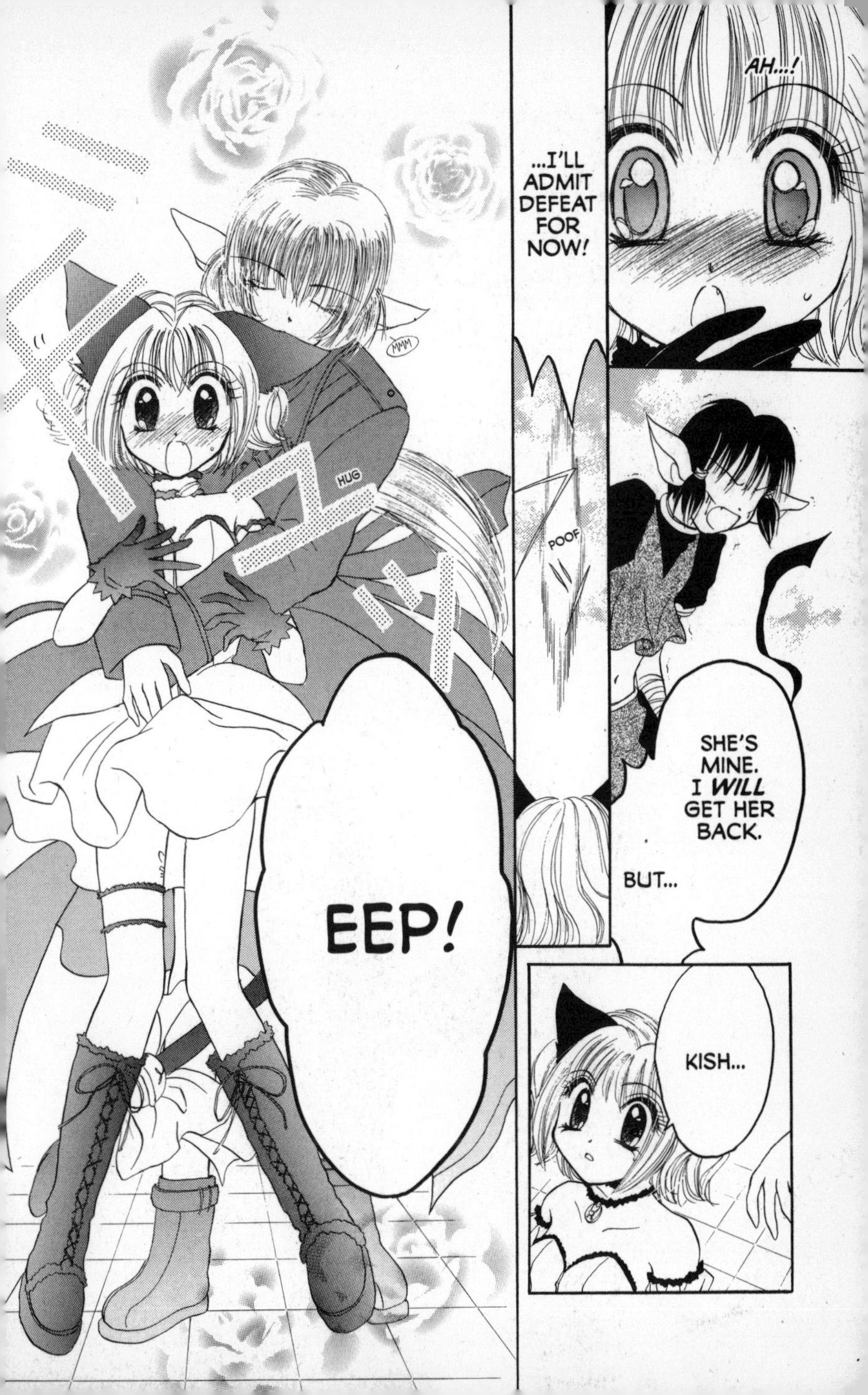
SHE'S MINE. I *WILL* GET HER BACK.
BUT...
...I'LL ADMIT DEFEAT FOR NOW!
POOF
AH...!
KISH...
EEP!
HUG
MMM

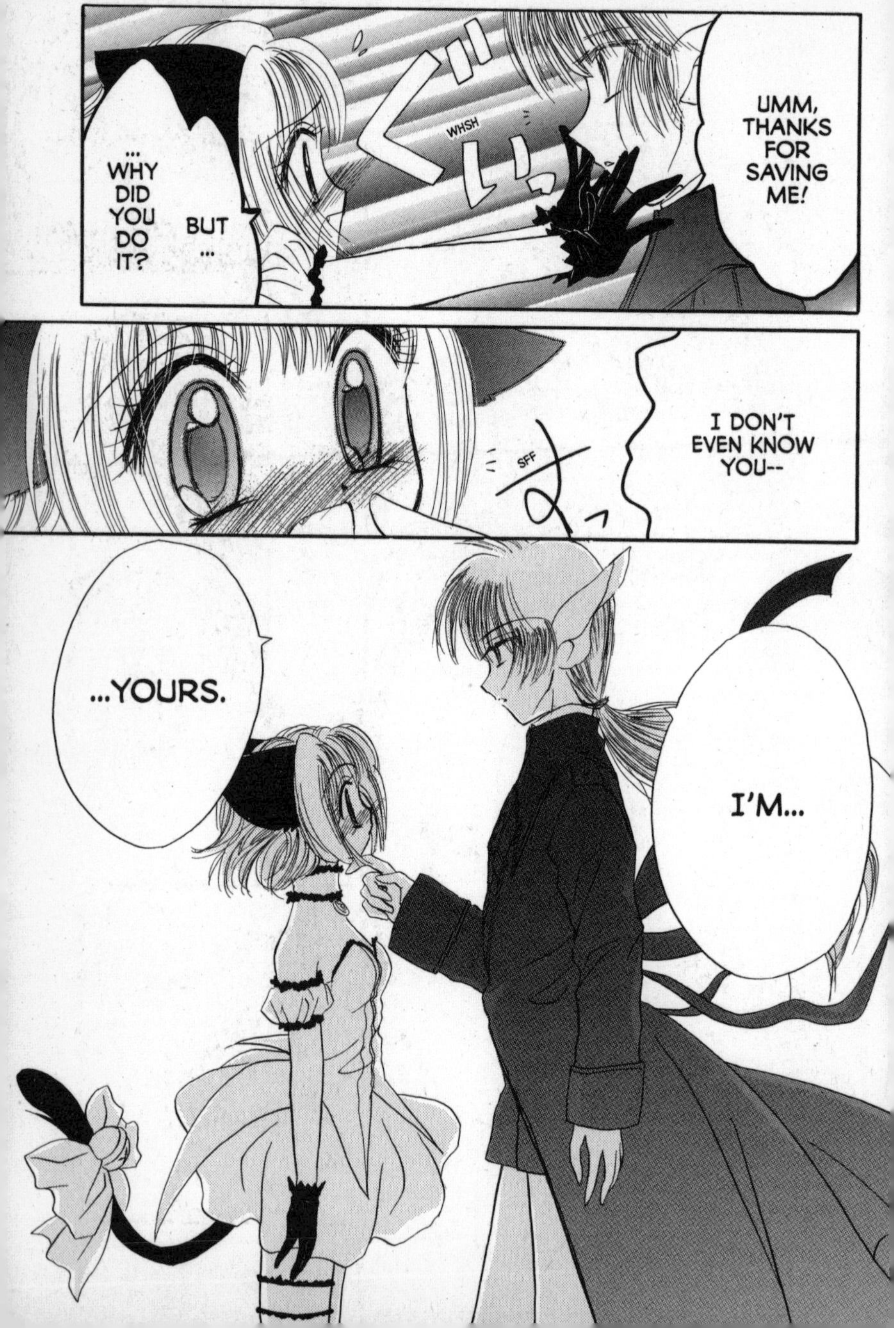
UMM, THANKS FOR SAVING ME!
WHSH
BUT ...
... WHY DID YOU DO IT?
I DON'T EVEN KNOW YOU--
SFF
I'M...
...YOURS.

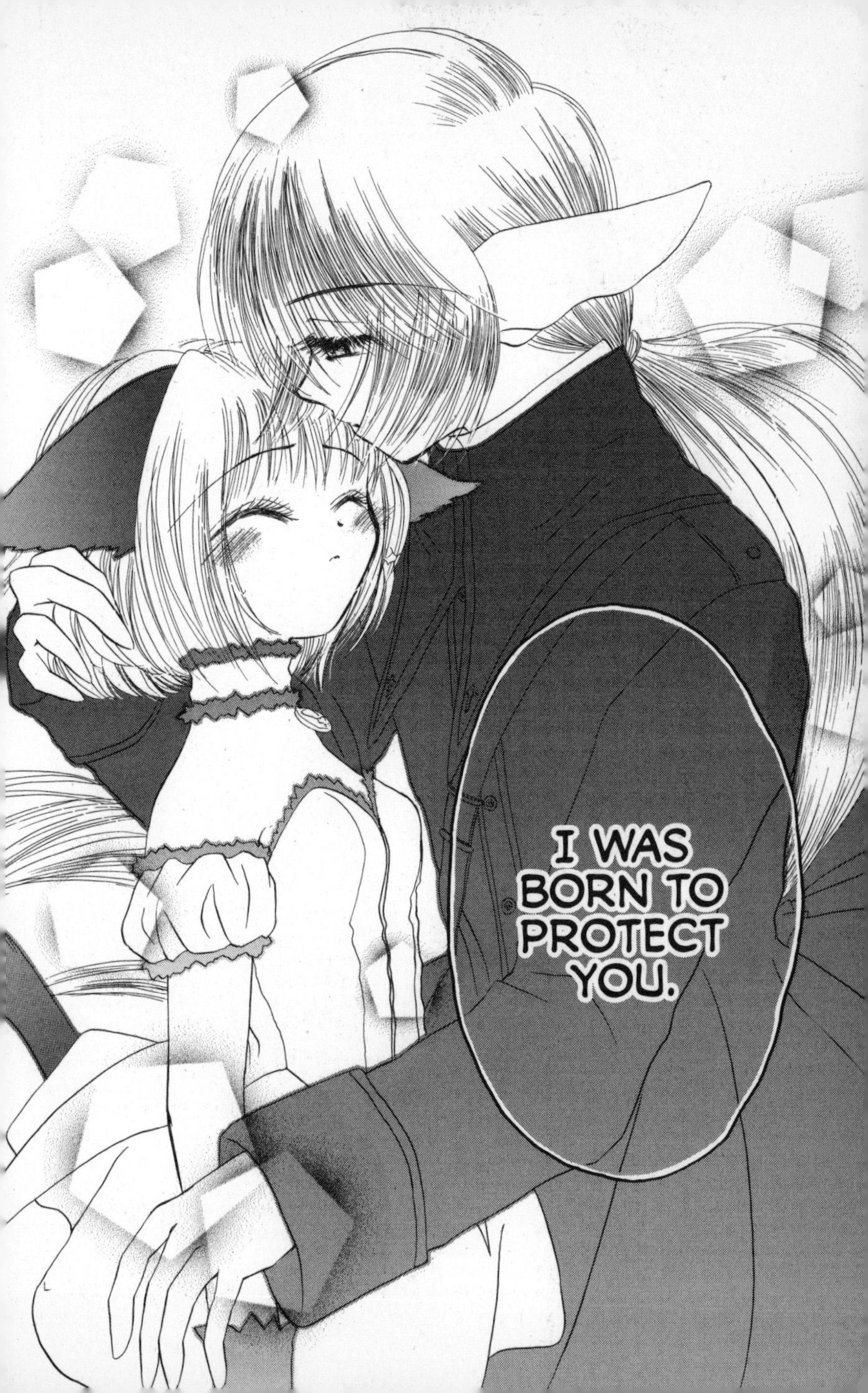
I WAS BORN TO PROTECT YOU.

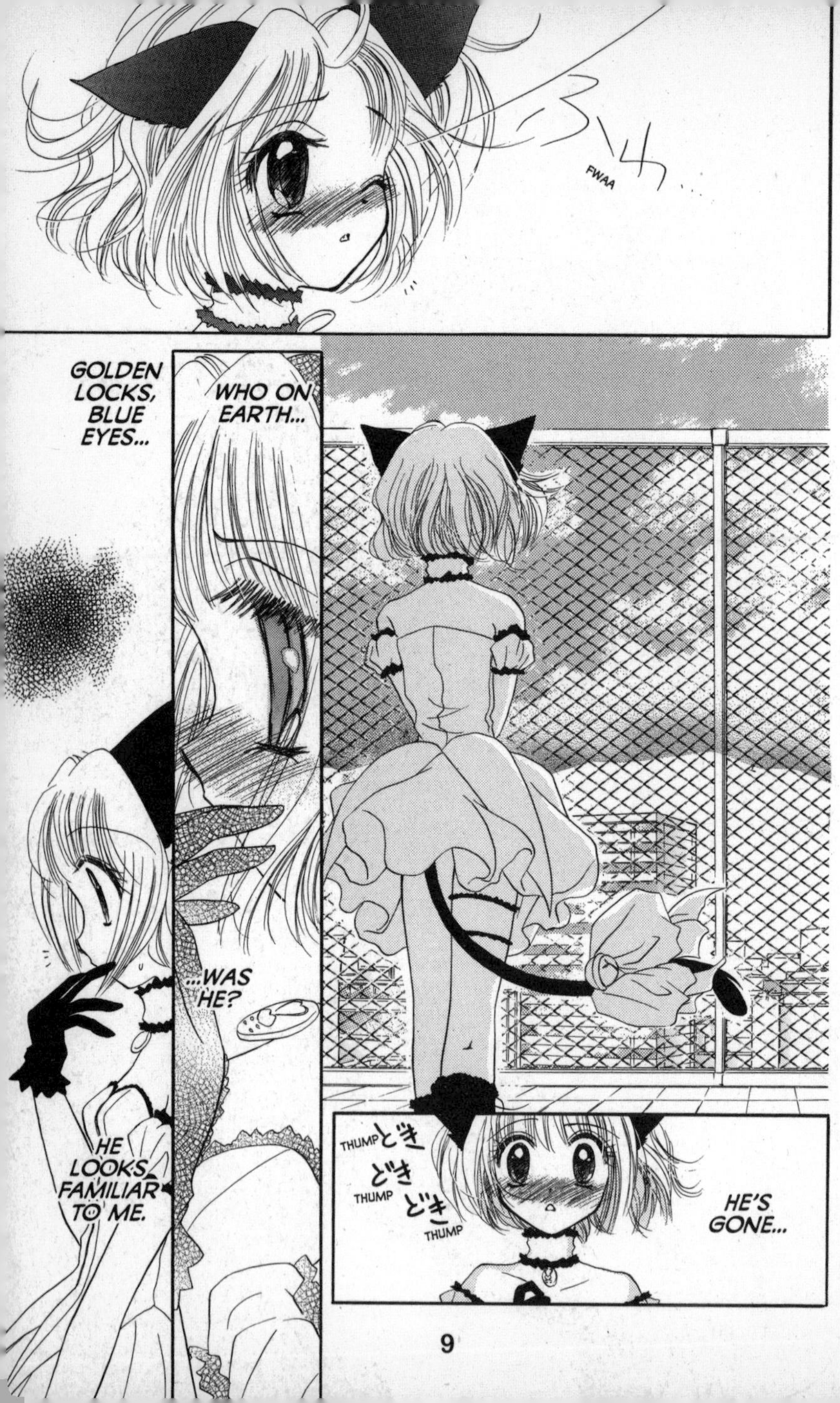
FWAA
THUMP どき
どき THUMP
どき THUMP
HE'S GONE...
WHO ON EARTH...
...WAS HE?
GOLDEN LOCKS, BLUE EYES...
HE LOOKS FAMILIAR TO ME.

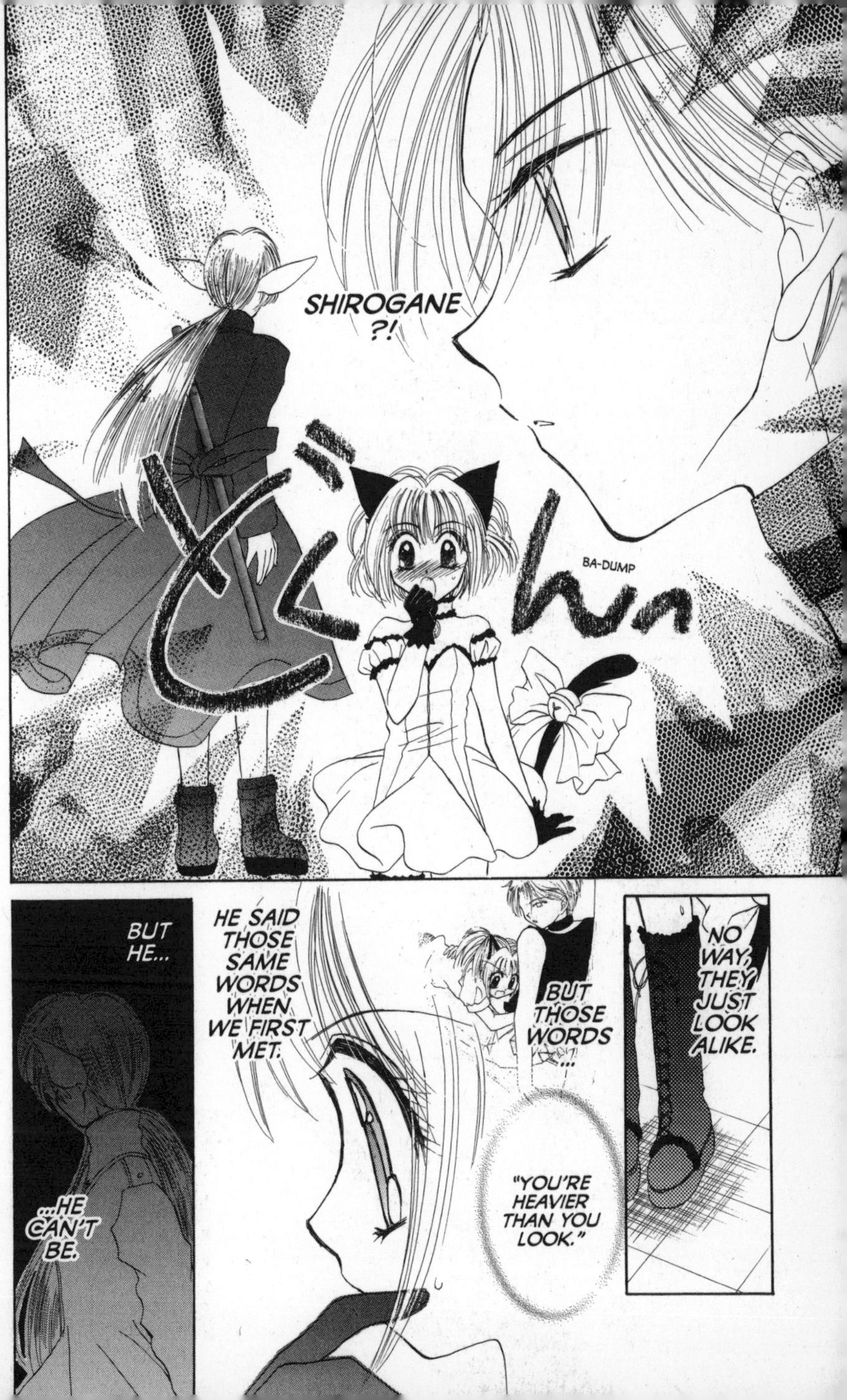
SHIROGANE ?!
BA-DUMP
NO WAY, THEY JUST LOOK ALIKE.
BUT THOSE WORDS ...
"YOU'RE HEAVIER THAN YOU LOOK."
HE SAID THOSE SAME WORDS WHEN WE FIRST MET.
BUT HE...
...HE CAN'T BE.

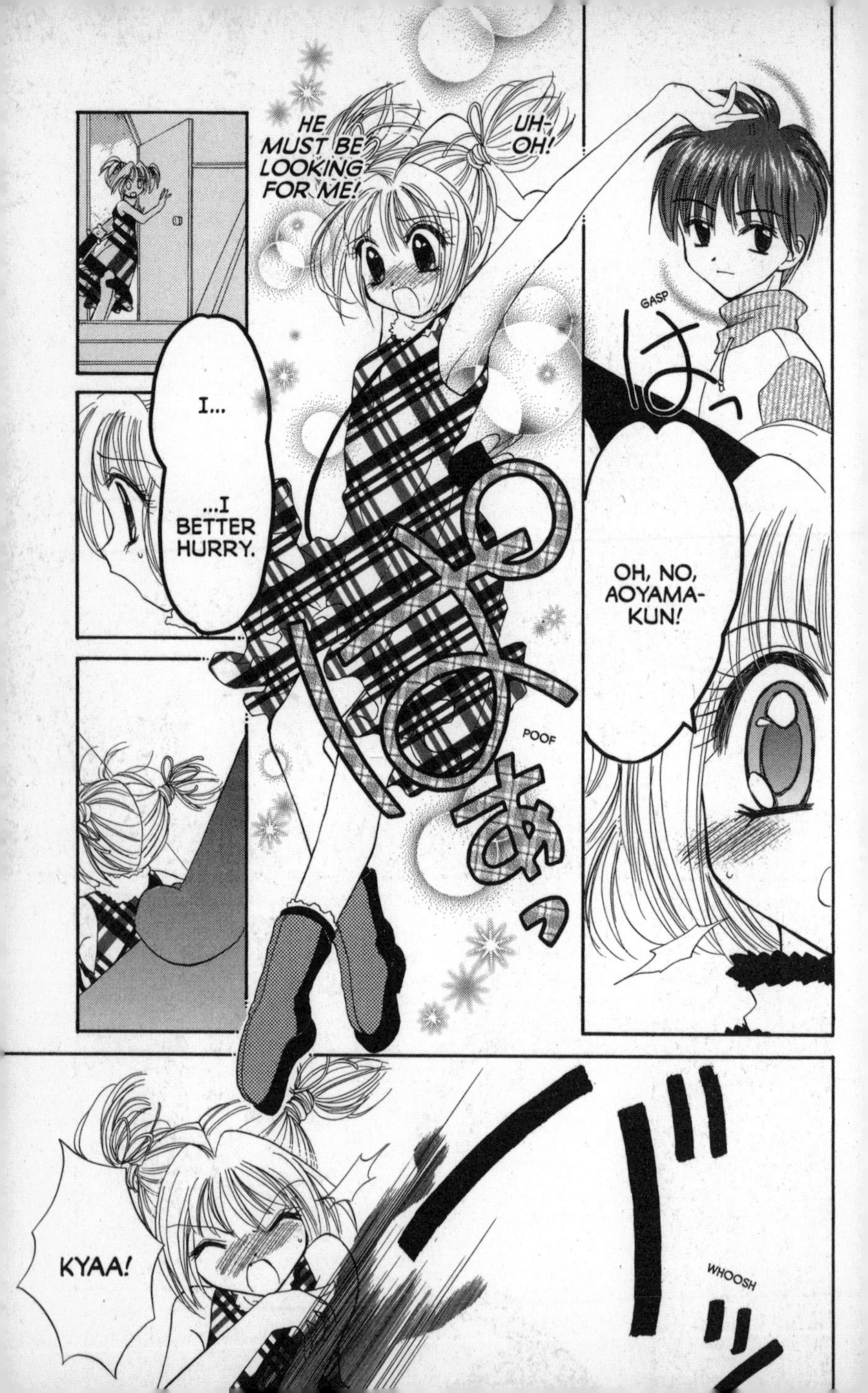

GASP
はっ
OH, NO, AOYAMA-KUN!
UH-OH!
HE MUST BE LOOKING FOR ME!
POOF
あっ
I...
...I BETTER HURRY.
WHOOSH
KYAA!

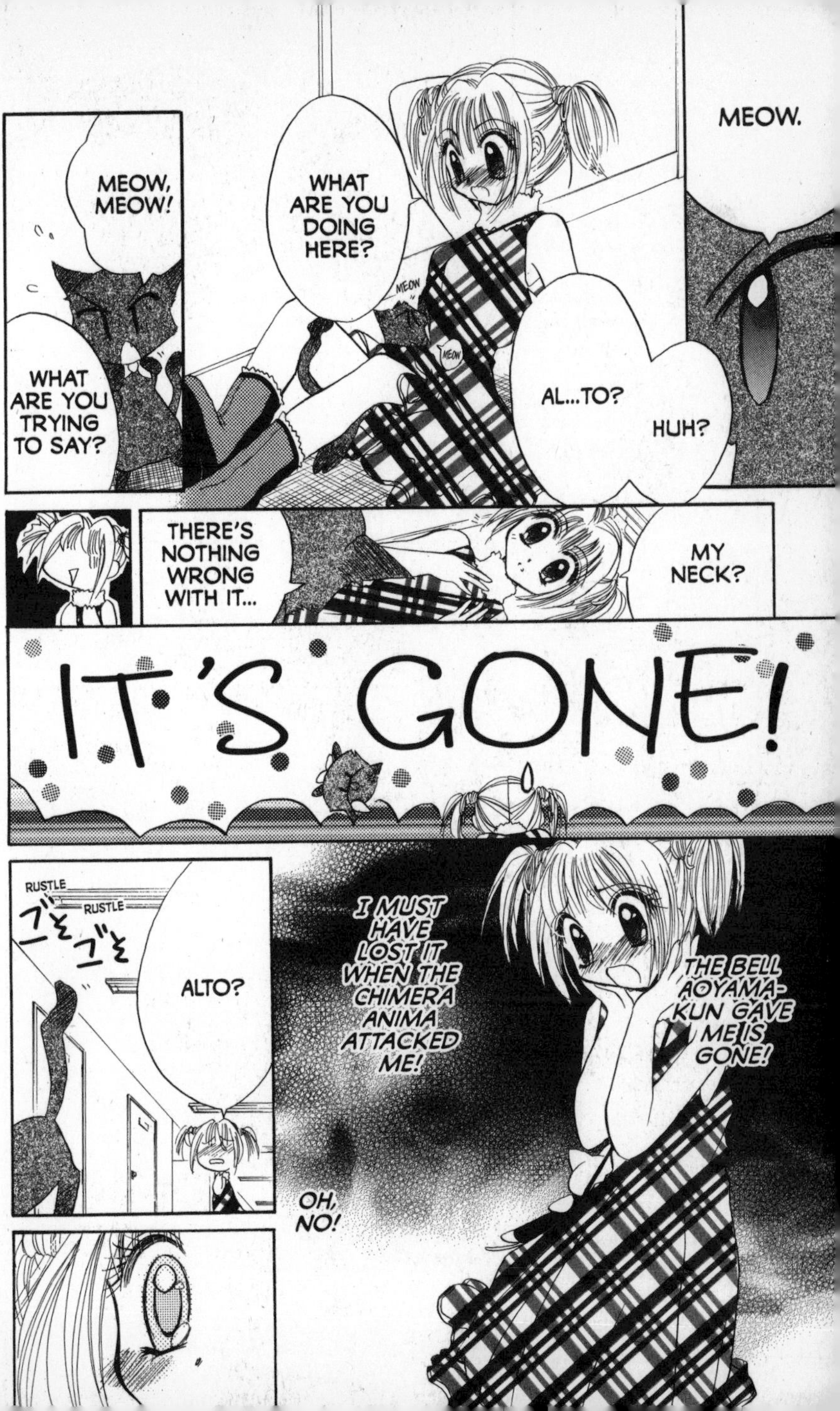
MEOW.
WHAT ARE YOU DOING HERE?
MEOW
MEOW
AL...TO?
HUH?
MEOW, MEOW!
WHAT ARE YOU TRYING TO SAY?
MY NECK?
THERE'S NOTHING WRONG WITH IT...
IT'S GONE!
THE BELL AOYAMA-KUN GAVE ME IS GONE!
I MUST HAVE LOST IT WHEN THE CHIMERA ANIMA ATTACKED ME!
OH, NO!
RUSTLE
RUSTLE
ごそごそ
ALTO?

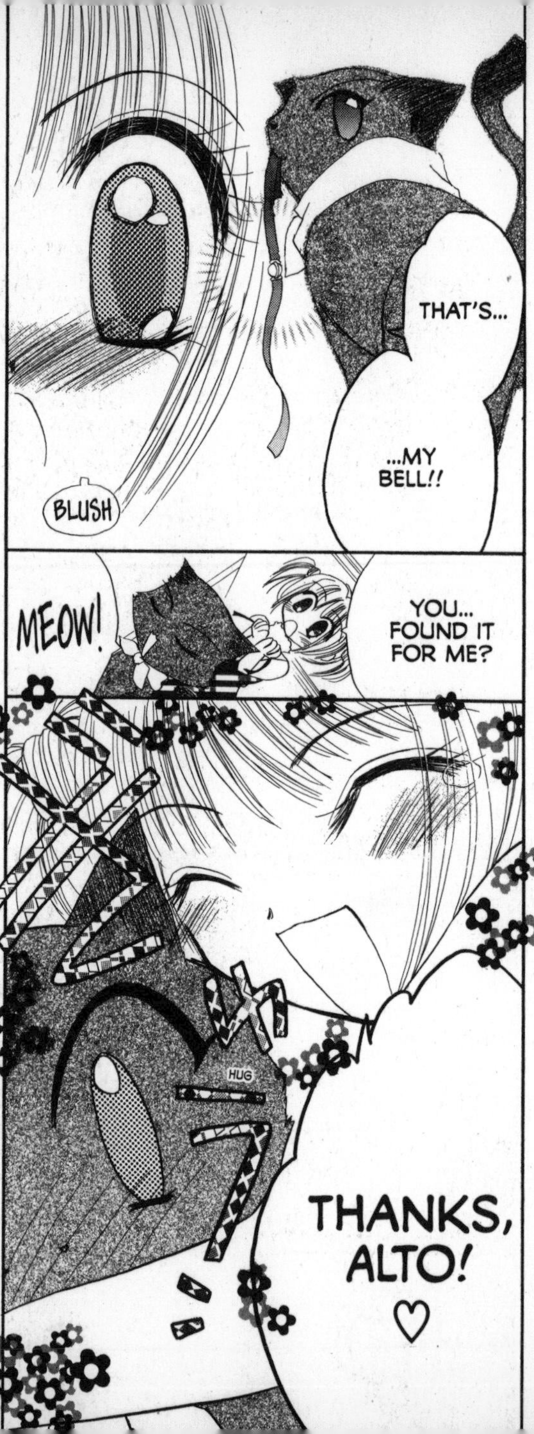
THAT'S...
...MY BELL!!
BLUSH
YOU... FOUND IT FOR ME?
MEOW!
THANKS, ALTO! ♡
HUG

Ikumi's Day

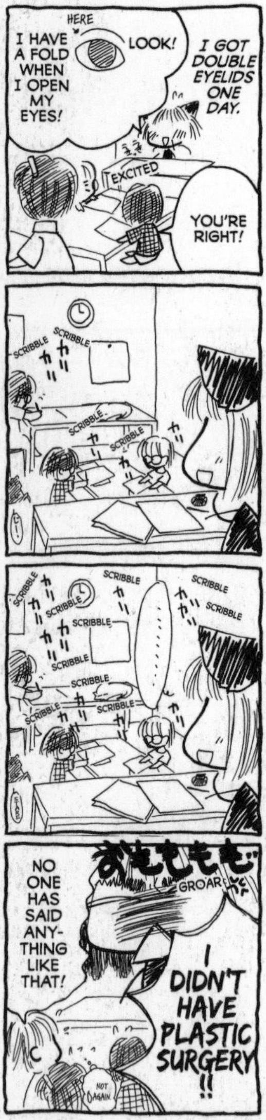
I GOT DOUBLE EYELIDS ONE DAY.
HERE
I HAVE A FOLD WHEN I OPEN MY EYES!
LOOK!
EXCITED
YOU'RE RIGHT!
SCRIBBLE
SCRIBBLE
SCRIBBLE
SCRIBBLE
SCRIBBLE
SCRIBBLE
SCRIBBLE
SCRIBBLE
SCRIBBLE
SCRIBBLE
SCRIBBLE
SCRIBBLE
SCRIBBLE
......
GROAR
I DIDN'T HAVE PLASTIC SURGERY!!
NO ONE HAS SAID ANYTHING LIKE THAT!
NOT AGAIN

↗ SHE'S UPSET THAT SHE GOT SNUBBED.

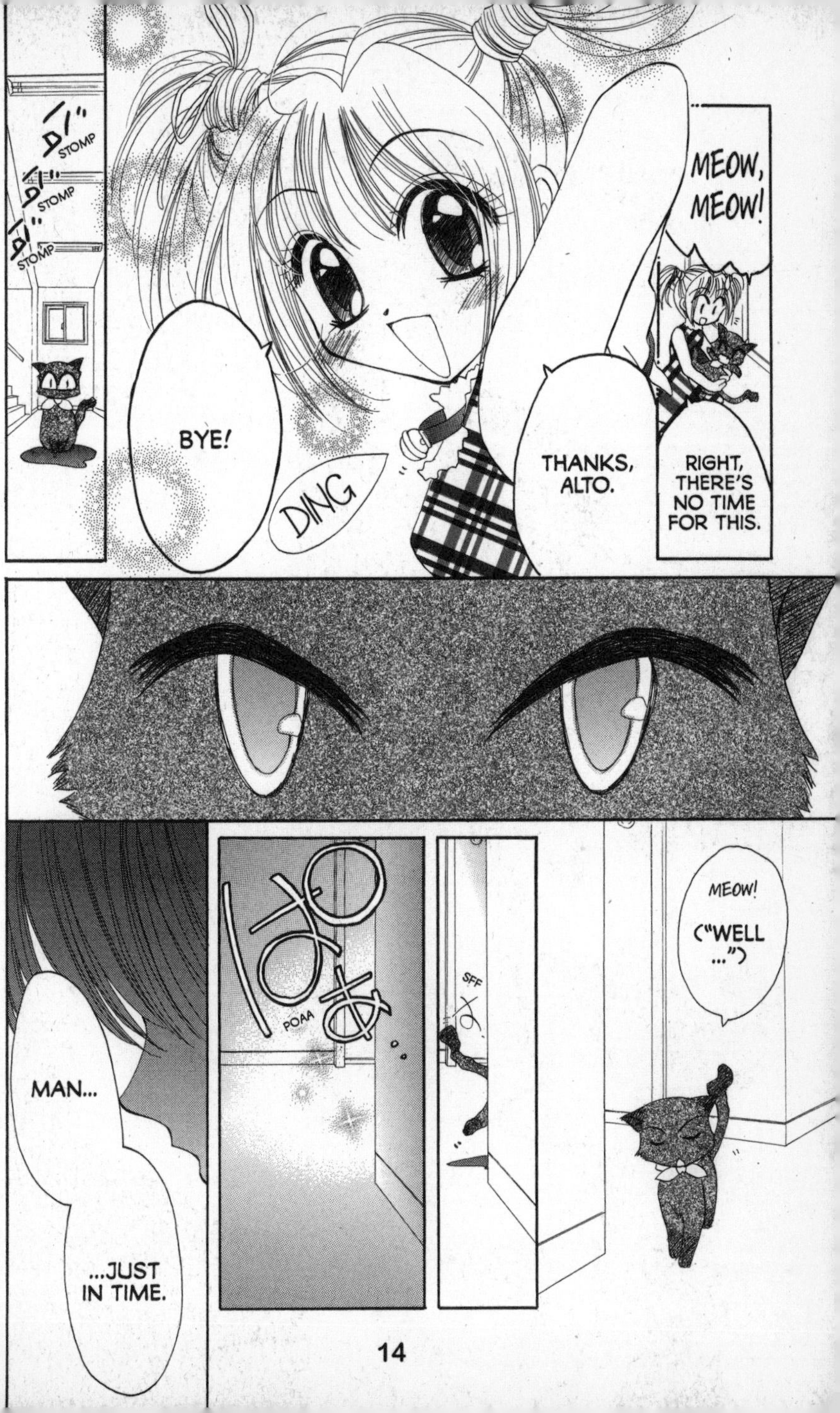
MEOW, MEOW!
RIGHT, THERE'S NO TIME FOR THIS.
THANKS, ALTO.
BYE!
DING
STOMP
STOMP
STOMP
MEOW!
("WELL ...")
SFF
POAA
MAN...
...JUST IN TIME.

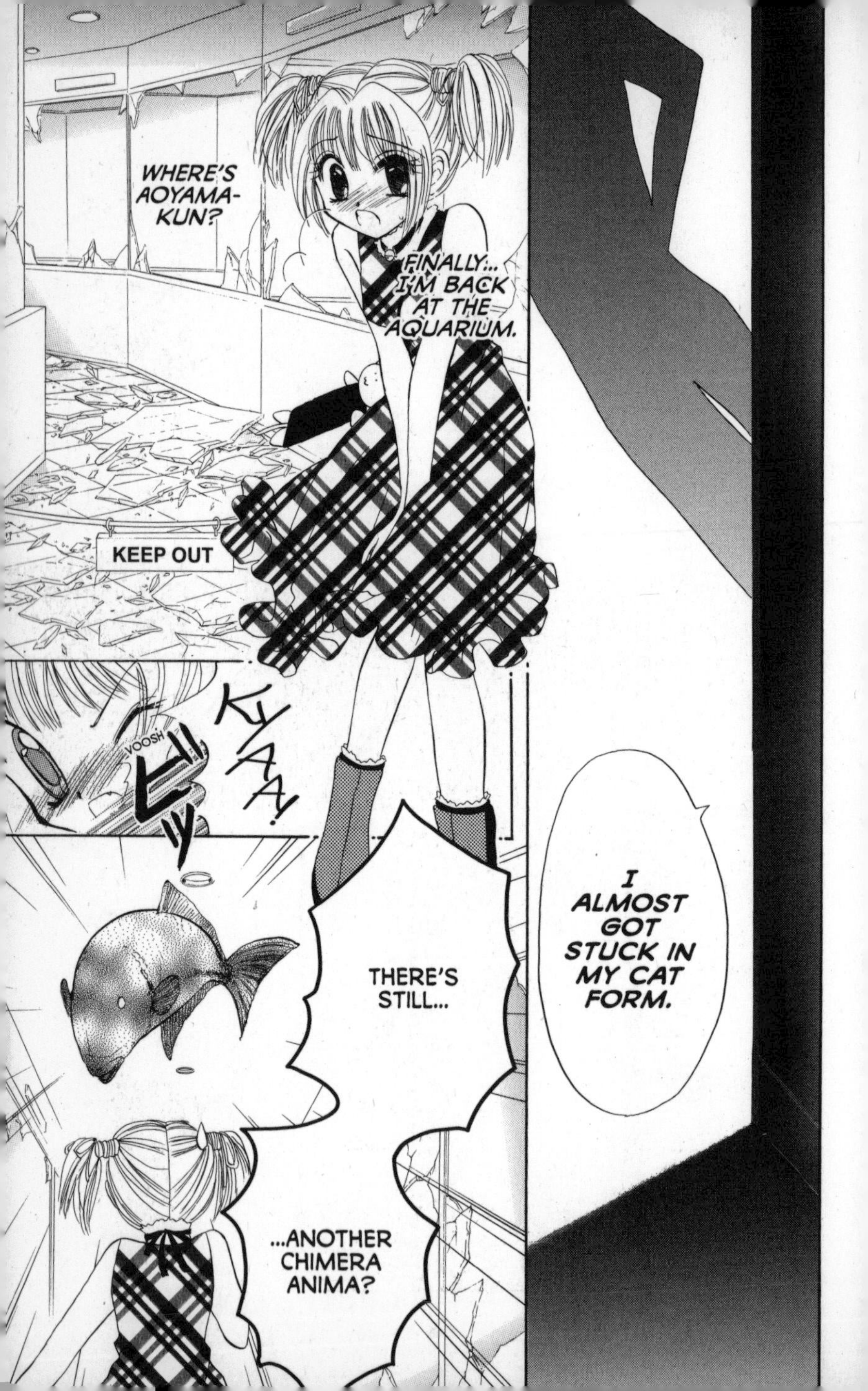

I ALMOST GOT STUCK IN MY CAT FORM.
FINALLY... I'M BACK AT THE AQUARIUM.
WHERE'S AOYAMA-KUN?
KEEP OUT
KYAAA!
ヒッ
VOOSH
THERE'S STILL...
...ANOTHER CHIMERA ANIMA?

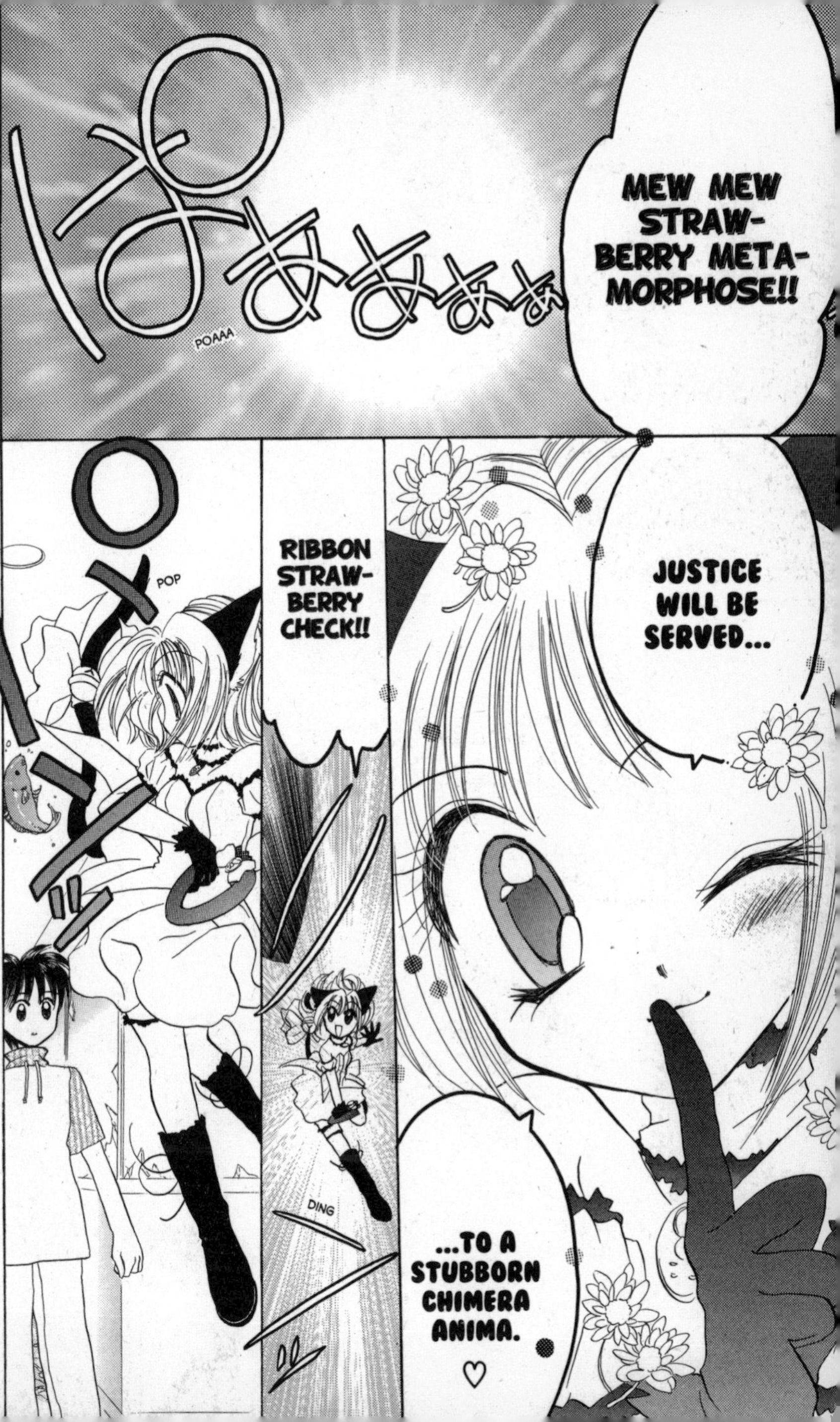
MEW MEW STRAW-BERRY META-MORPHOSE!!
POAAA
JUSTICE WILL BE SERVED...
...TO A STUBBORN CHIMERA ANIMA. ♡
RIBBON STRAW-BERRY CHECK!!
DING
POP

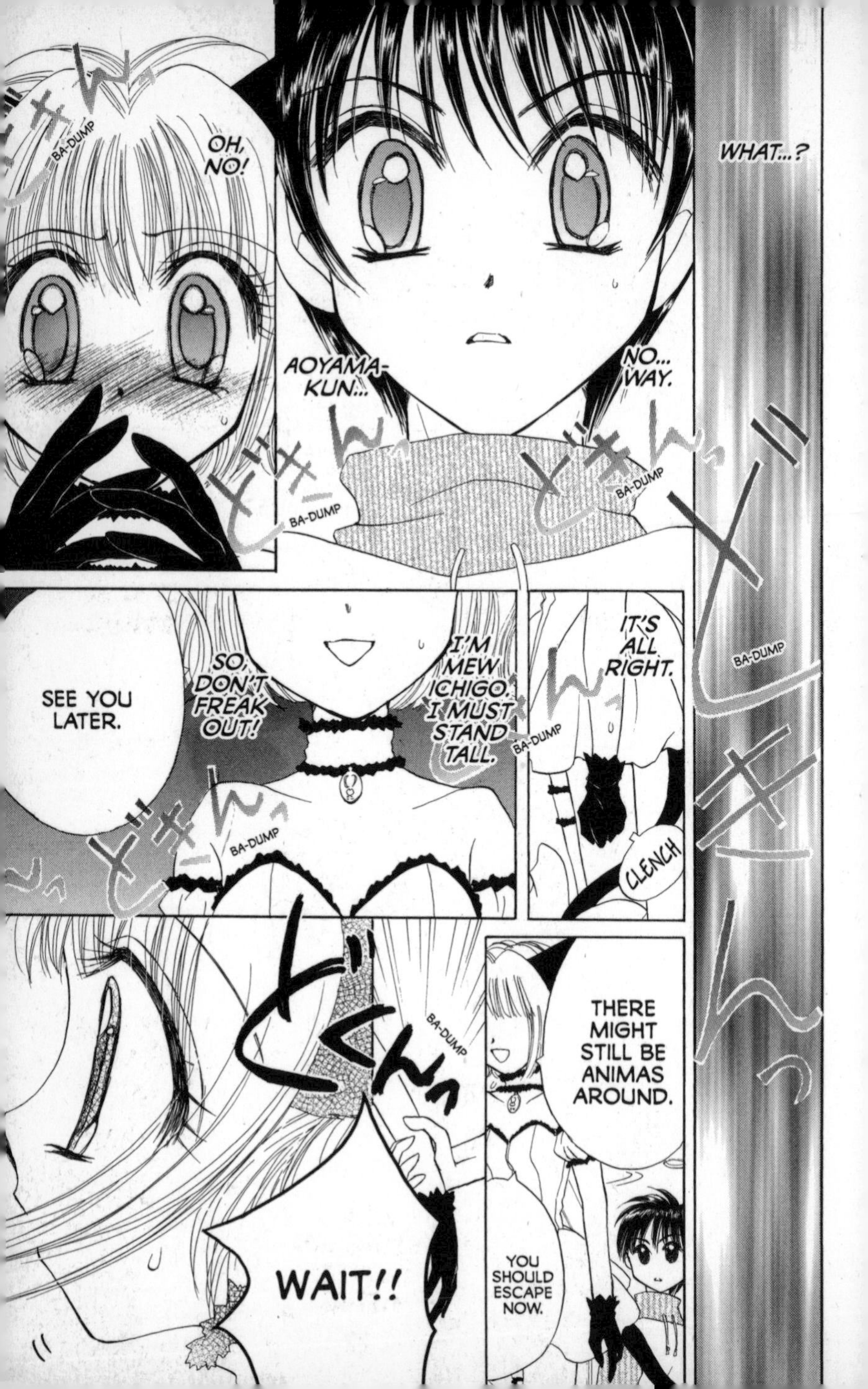
WHAT...?
BA-DUMP
NO... WAY.
AOYAMA-KUN...
BA-DUMP
BA-DUMP
OH, NO!
BA-DUMP
IT'S ALL RIGHT.
CLENCH
BA-DUMP
I'M MEW ICHIGO. I MUST STAND TALL.
SO, DON'T FREAK OUT!
SEE YOU LATER.
BA-DUMP
THERE MIGHT STILL BE ANIMAS AROUND.
YOU SHOULD ESCAPE NOW.
BA-DUMP
WAIT!!

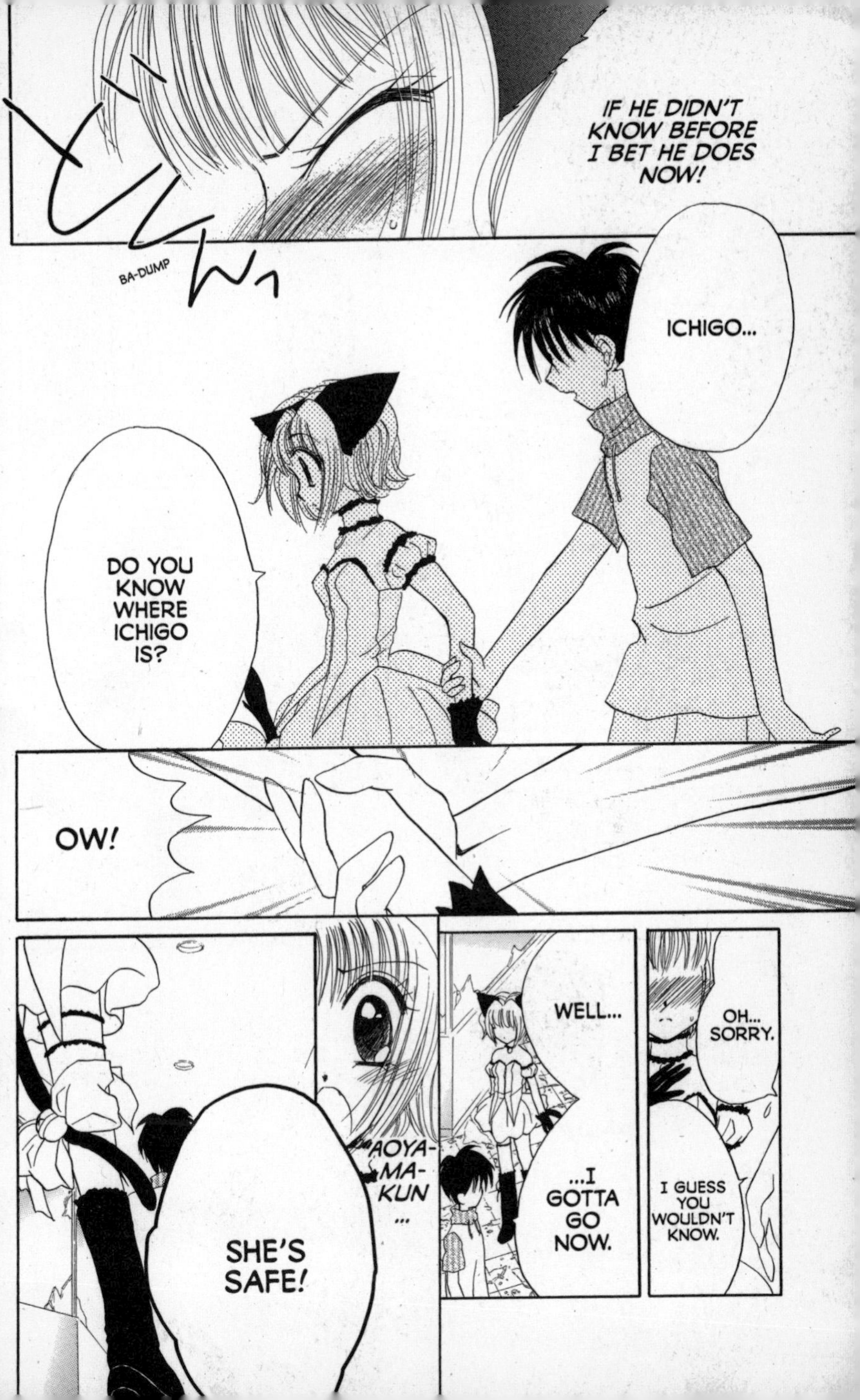
IF HE DIDN'T KNOW BEFORE I BET HE DOES NOW!
BA-DUMP
ICHIGO...
DO YOU KNOW WHERE ICHIGO IS?
OW!
OH... SORRY.
I GUESS YOU WOULDN'T KNOW.
WELL...
...I GOTTA GO NOW.
AOYAMA-KUN ...
SHE'S SAFE!

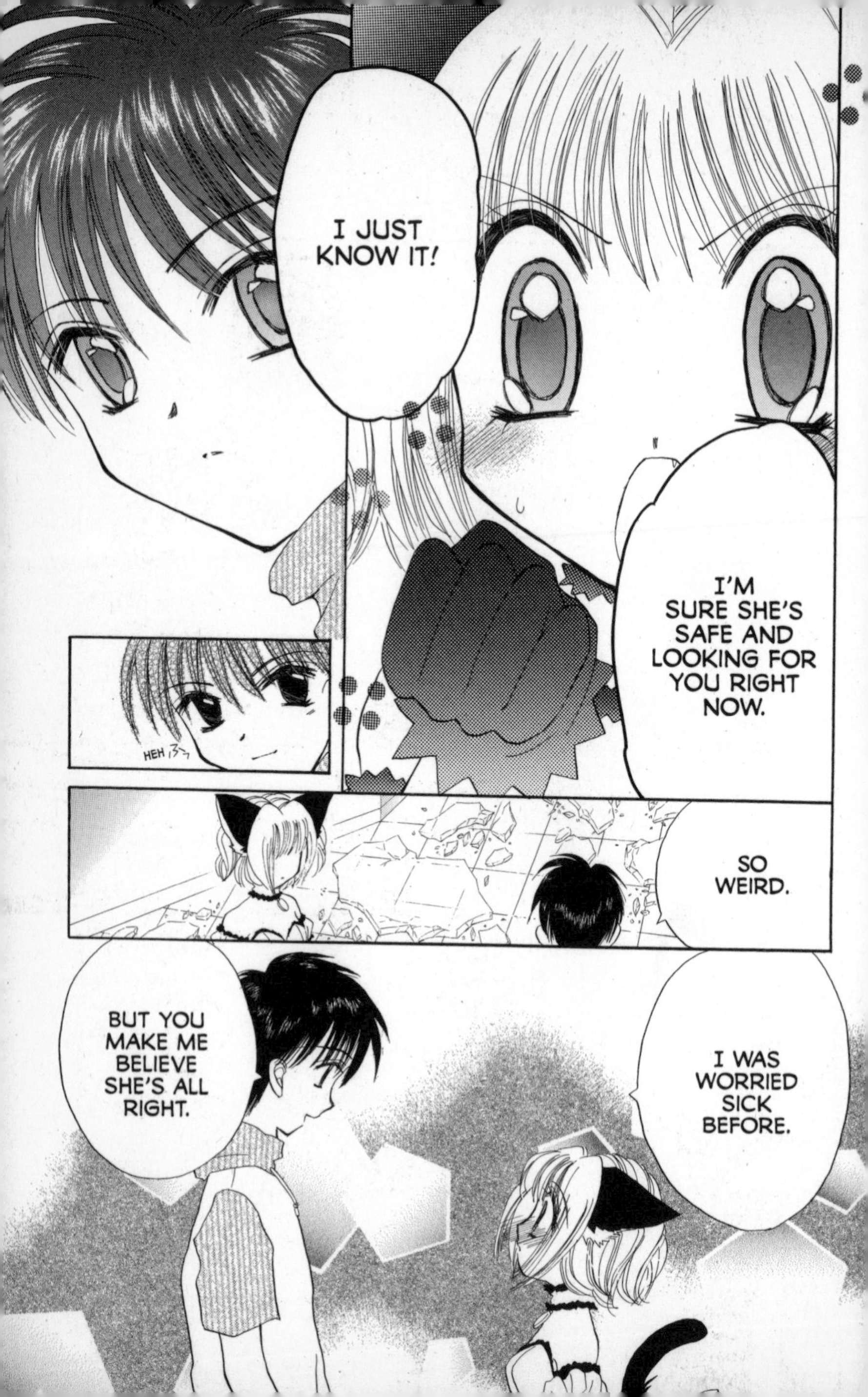
I'M SURE SHE'S SAFE AND LOOKING FOR YOU RIGHT NOW.
I JUST KNOW IT!
HEH
SO WEIRD.
I WAS WORRIED SICK BEFORE.
BUT YOU MAKE ME BELIEVE SHE'S ALL RIGHT.

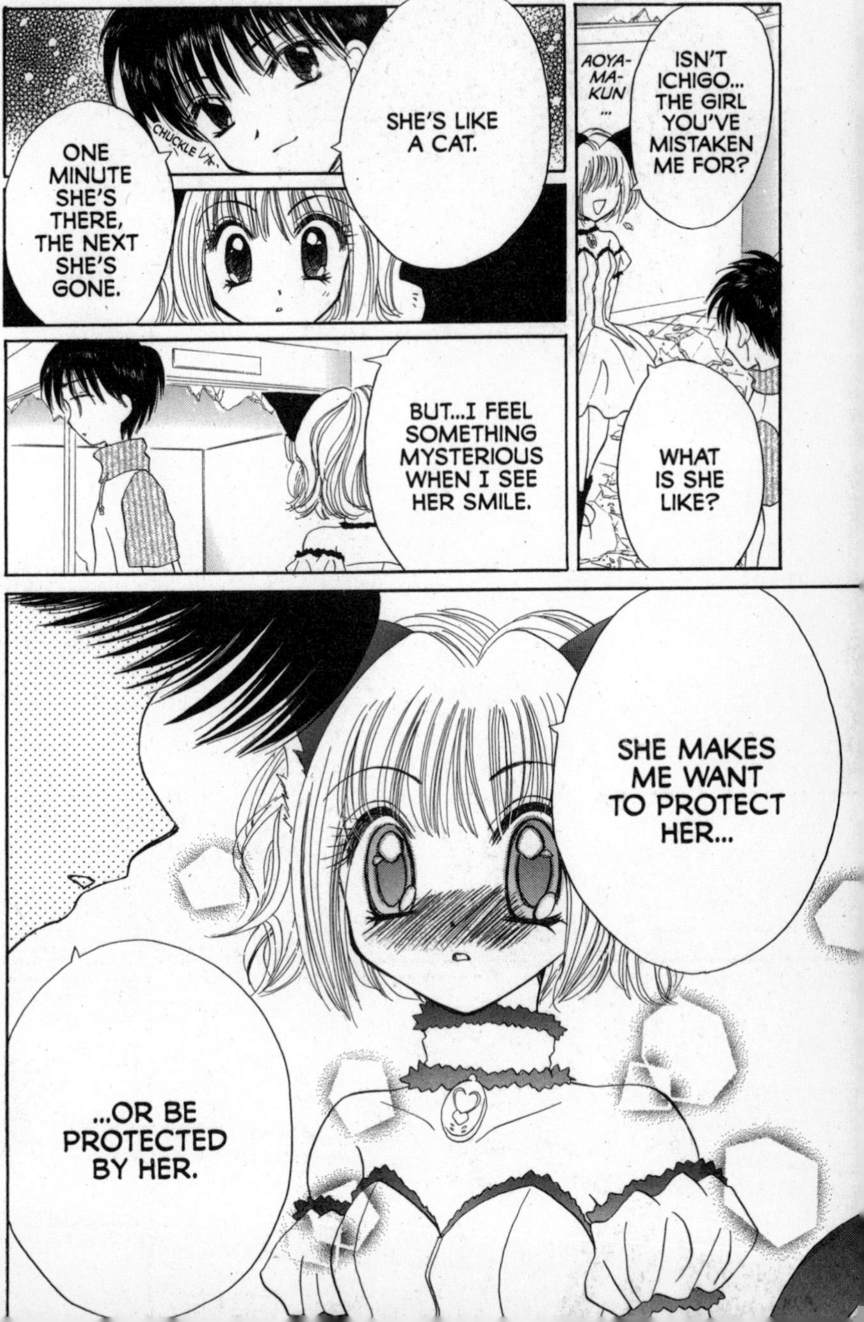
ISN'T ICHIGO... THE GIRL YOU'VE MISTAKEN ME FOR?
AOYAMA-KUN ...
WHAT IS SHE LIKE?
SHE'S LIKE A CAT.
CHUCKLE
ONE MINUTE SHE'S THERE, THE NEXT SHE'S GONE.
BUT...I FEEL SOMETHING MYSTERIOUS WHEN I SEE HER SMILE.
SHE MAKES ME WANT TO PROTECT HER...
...OR BE PROTECTED BY HER.

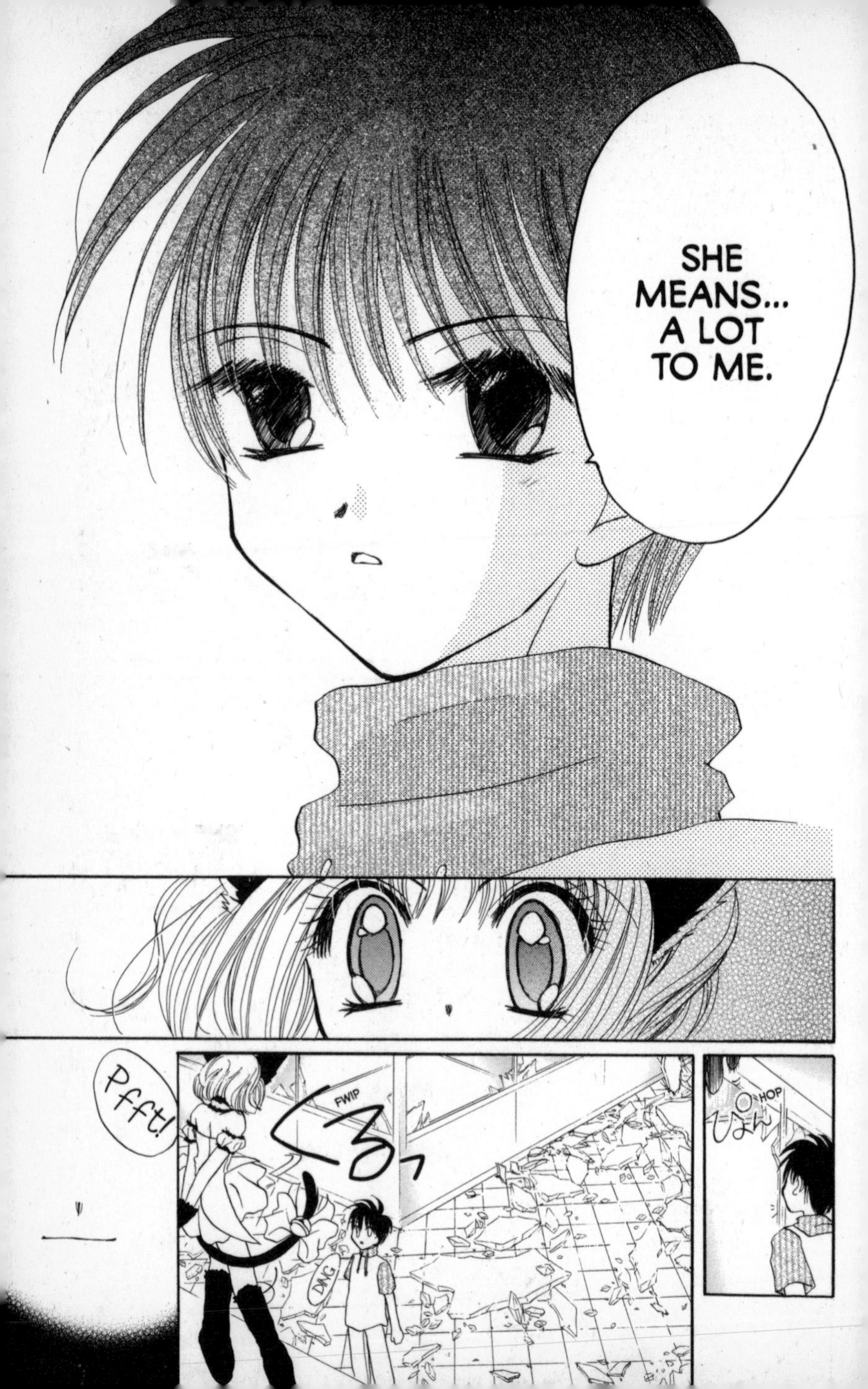
SHE MEANS... A LOT TO ME.
HOP
FWIP
Pfft!
DING

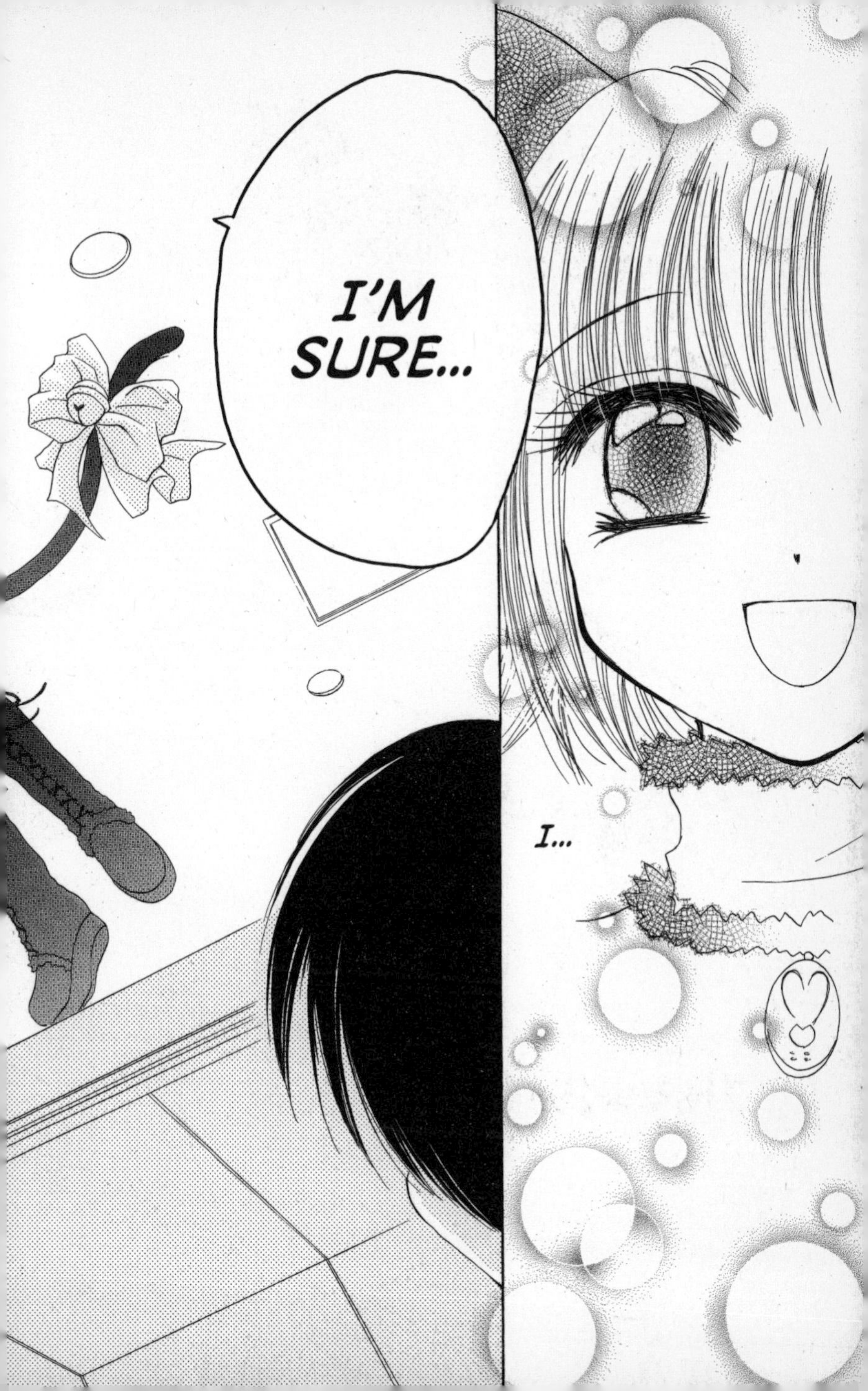
I'M SURE...
I...

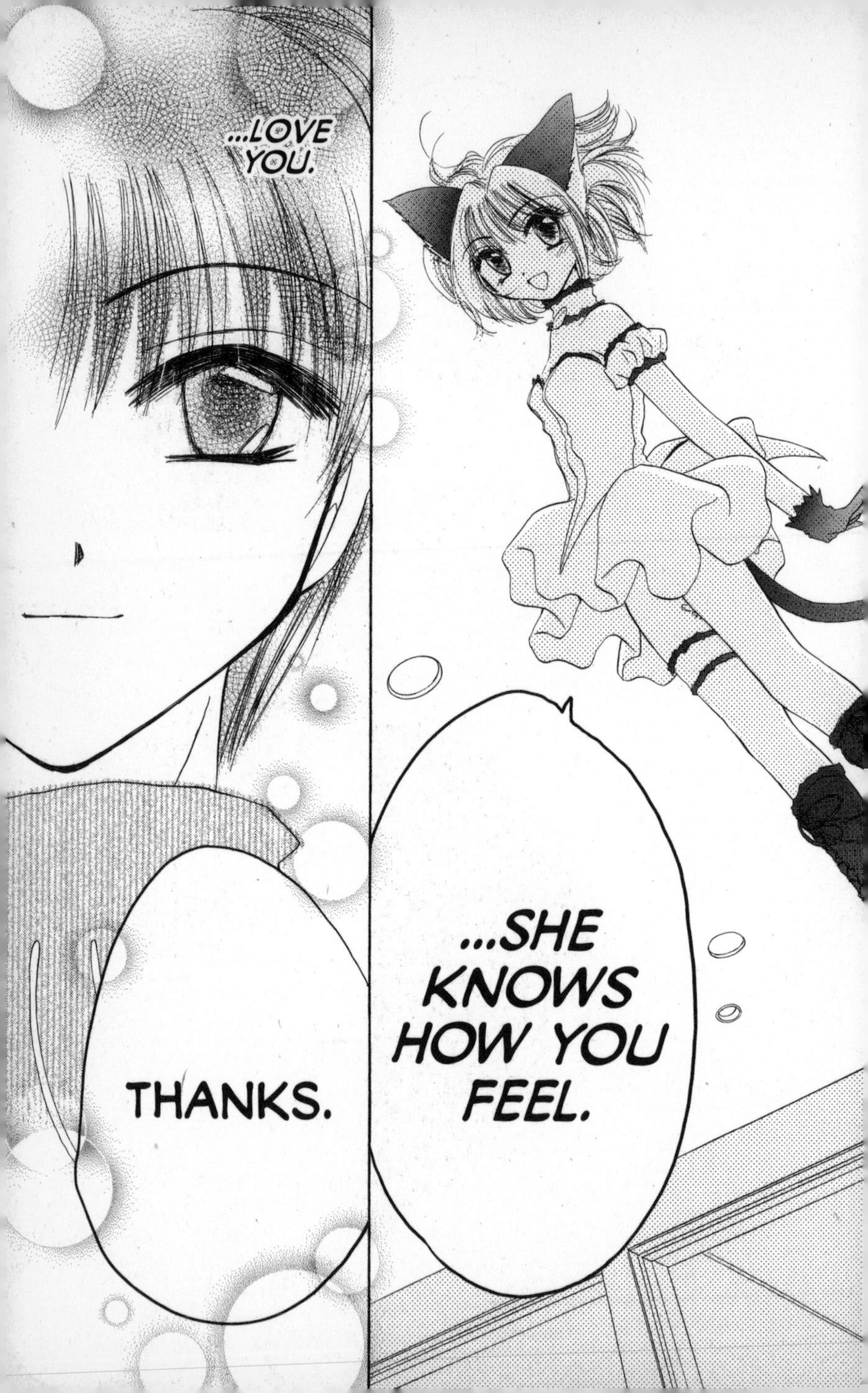
...SHE KNOWS HOW YOU FEEL.
...LOVE YOU.
THANKS.

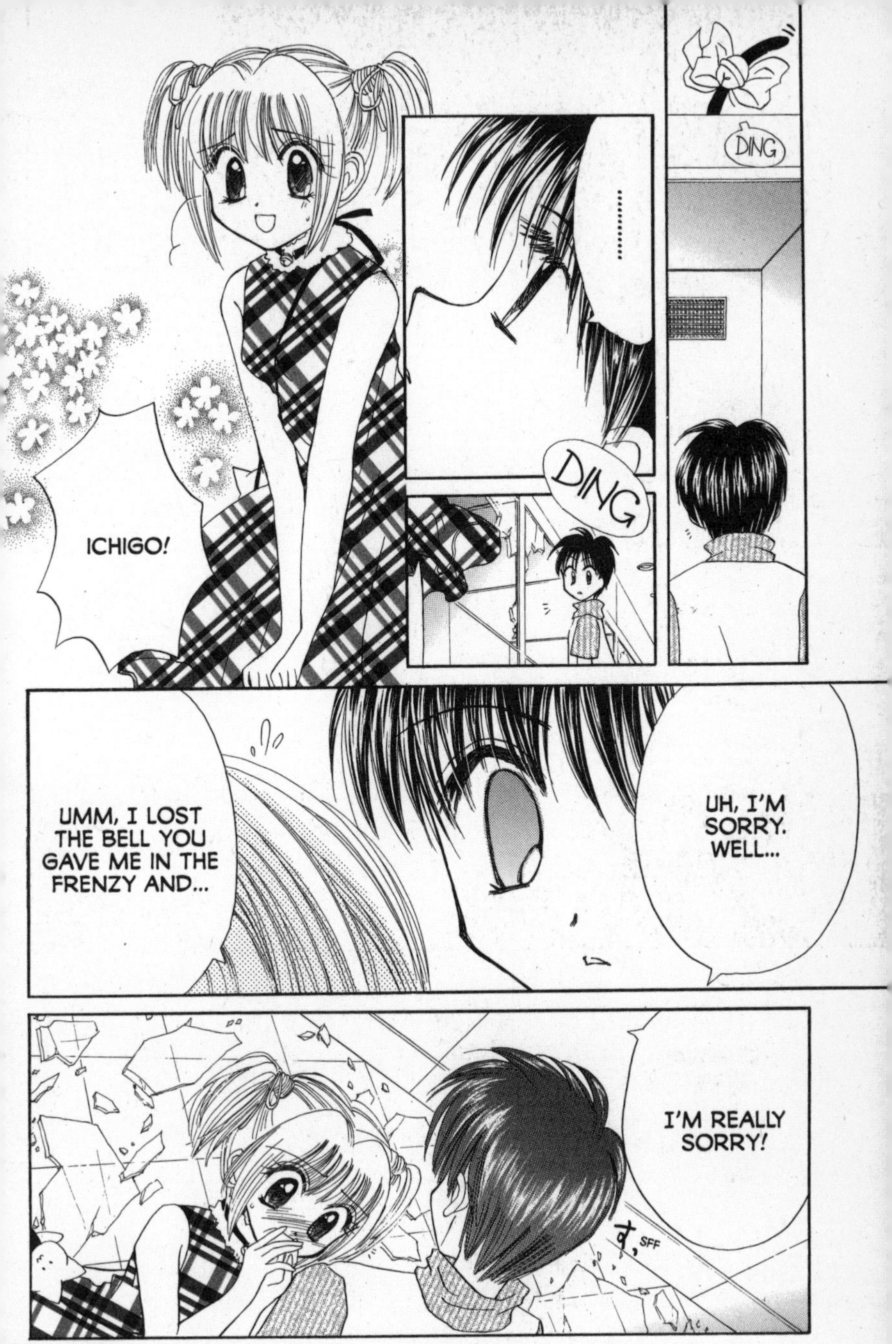
DING
....
DING
ICHIGO!
UH, I'M SORRY. WELL...
UMM, I LOST THE BELL YOU GAVE ME IN THE FRENZY AND...
I'M REALLY SORRY!
す, SFF

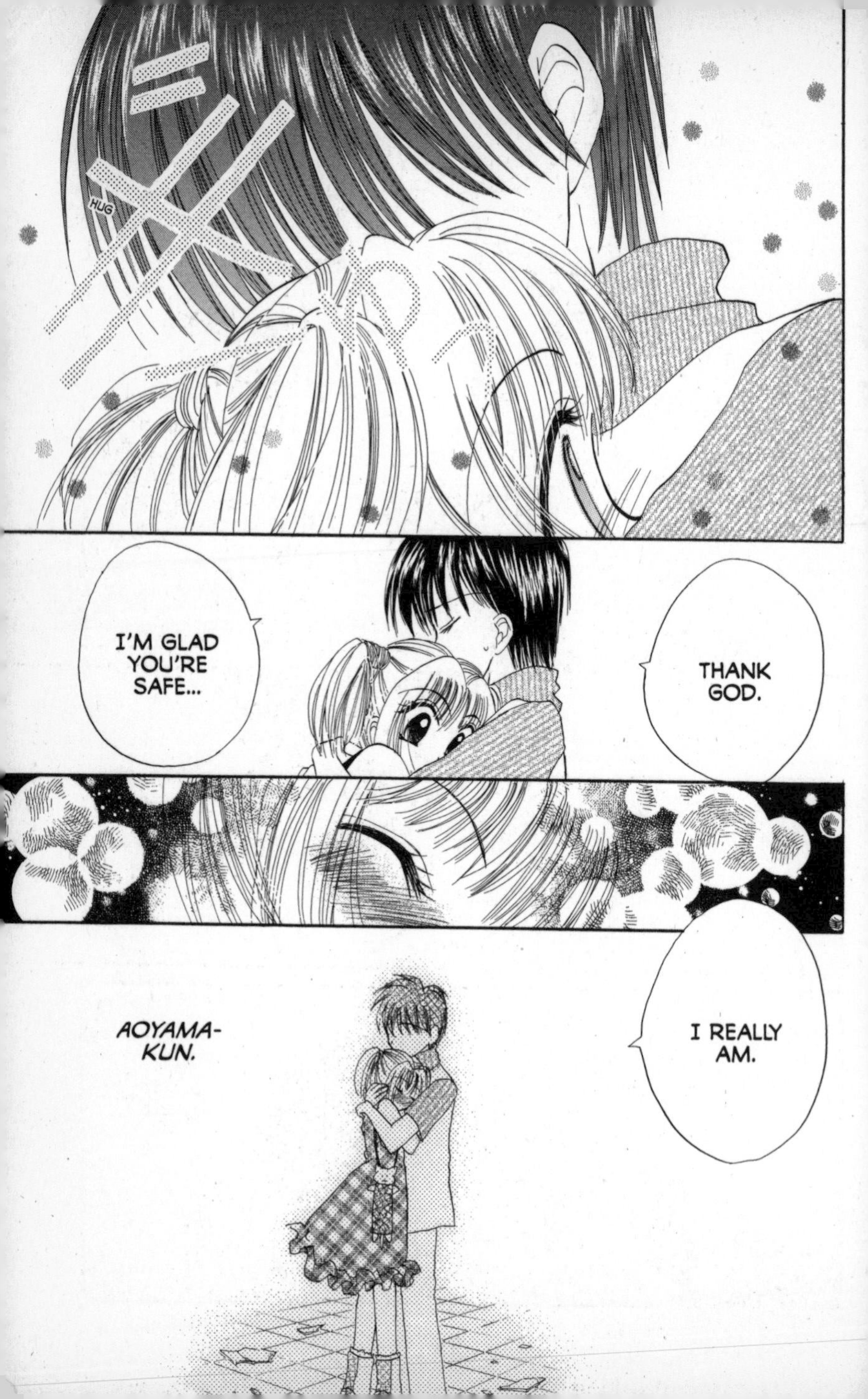
HUG
THANK GOD.
I'M GLAD YOU'RE SAFE...
I REALLY AM.
AOYAMA-KUN.

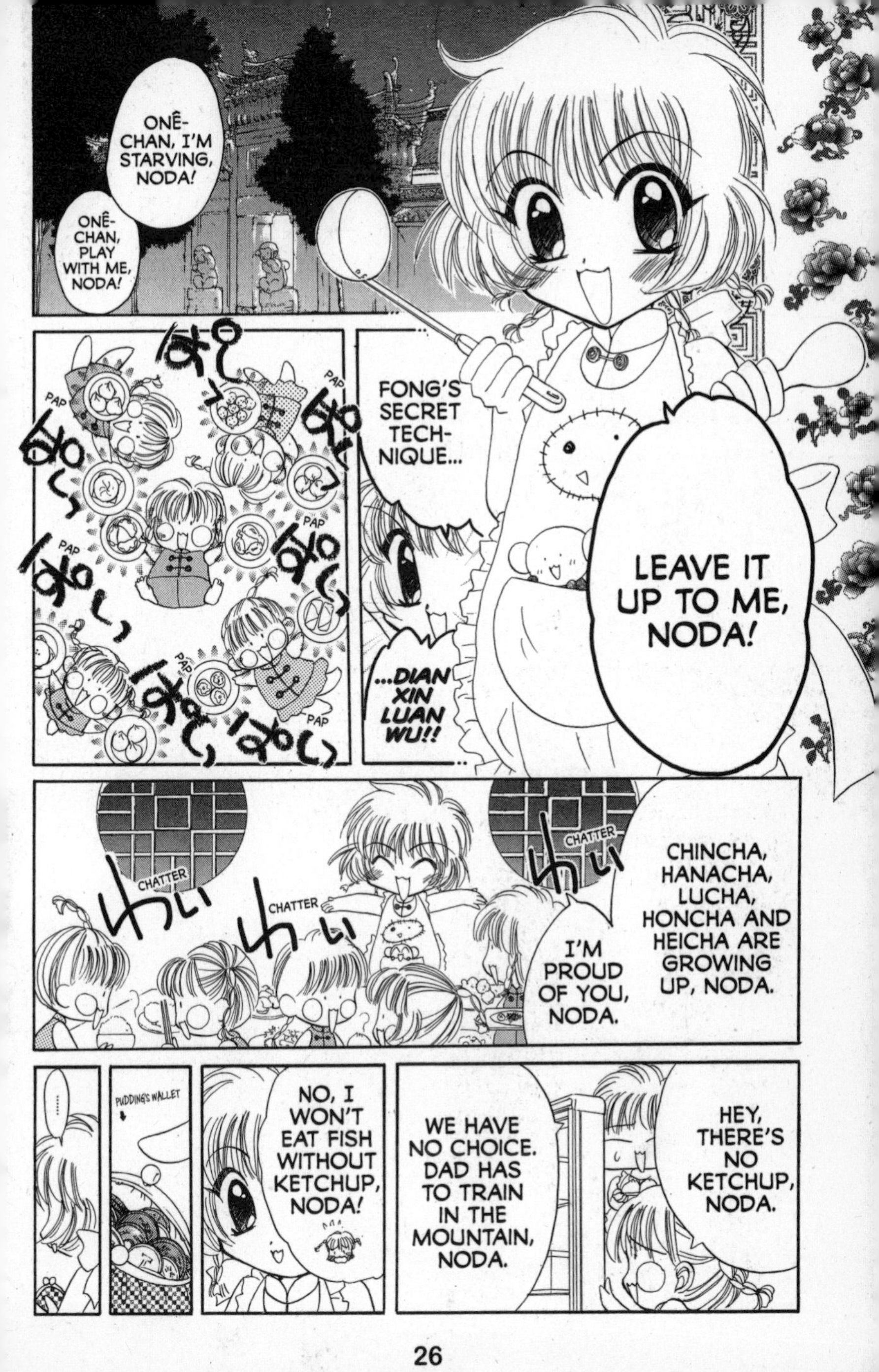
ONÊ-CHAN, I'M STARVING, NODA!
ONÊ-CHAN, PLAY WITH ME, NODA!
LEAVE IT UP TO ME, NODA!
FONG'S SECRET TECH-NIQUE...
...DIAN XIN LUAN WU!!
PAP
PAP
PAP
PAP
PAP
CHINCHA, HANACHA, LUCHA, HONCHA AND HEICHA ARE GROWING UP, NODA.
I'M PROUD OF YOU, NODA.
CHATTER
CHATTER
CHATTER
HEY, THERE'S NO KETCHUP, NODA.
WE HAVE NO CHOICE. DAD HAS TO TRAIN IN THE MOUNTAIN, NODA.
NO, I WON'T EAT FISH WITHOUT KETCHUP, NODA!
PUDDING'S WALLET
......

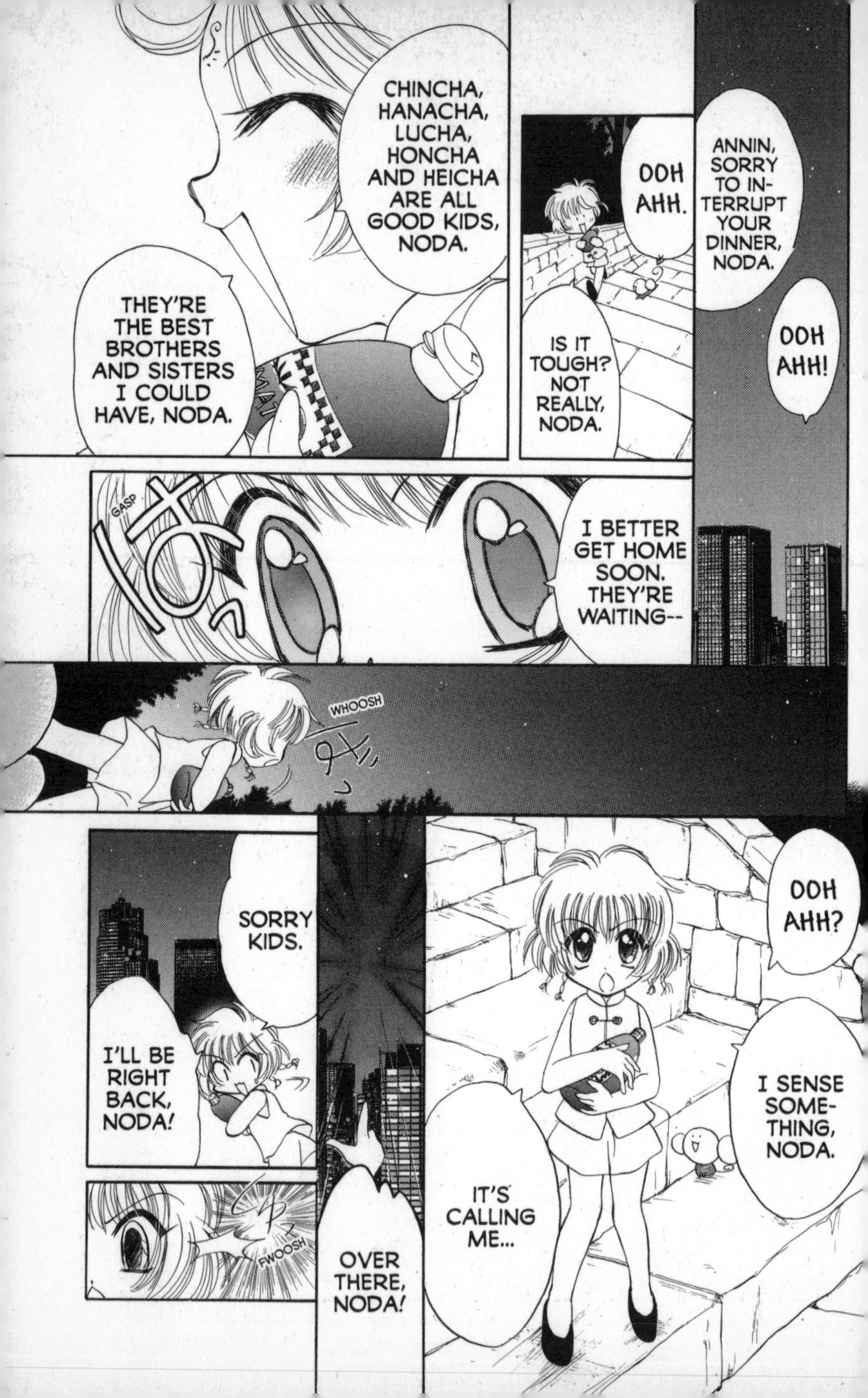
ANNIN, SORRY TO INTERRUPT YOUR DINNER, NODA.
OOH AHH!
OOH AHH.
IS IT TOUGH? NOT REALLY, NODA.
CHINCHA, HANACHA, LUCHA, HONCHA AND HEICHA ARE ALL GOOD KIDS, NODA.
THEY'RE THE BEST BROTHERS AND SISTERS I COULD HAVE, NODA.
I BETTER GET HOME SOON. THEY'RE WAITING--
GASP
WHOOSH
OOH AHH?
I SENSE SOMETHING, NODA.
IT'S CALLING ME...
OVER THERE, NODA!
SORRY KIDS.
I'LL BE RIGHT BACK, NODA!
FWOOSH

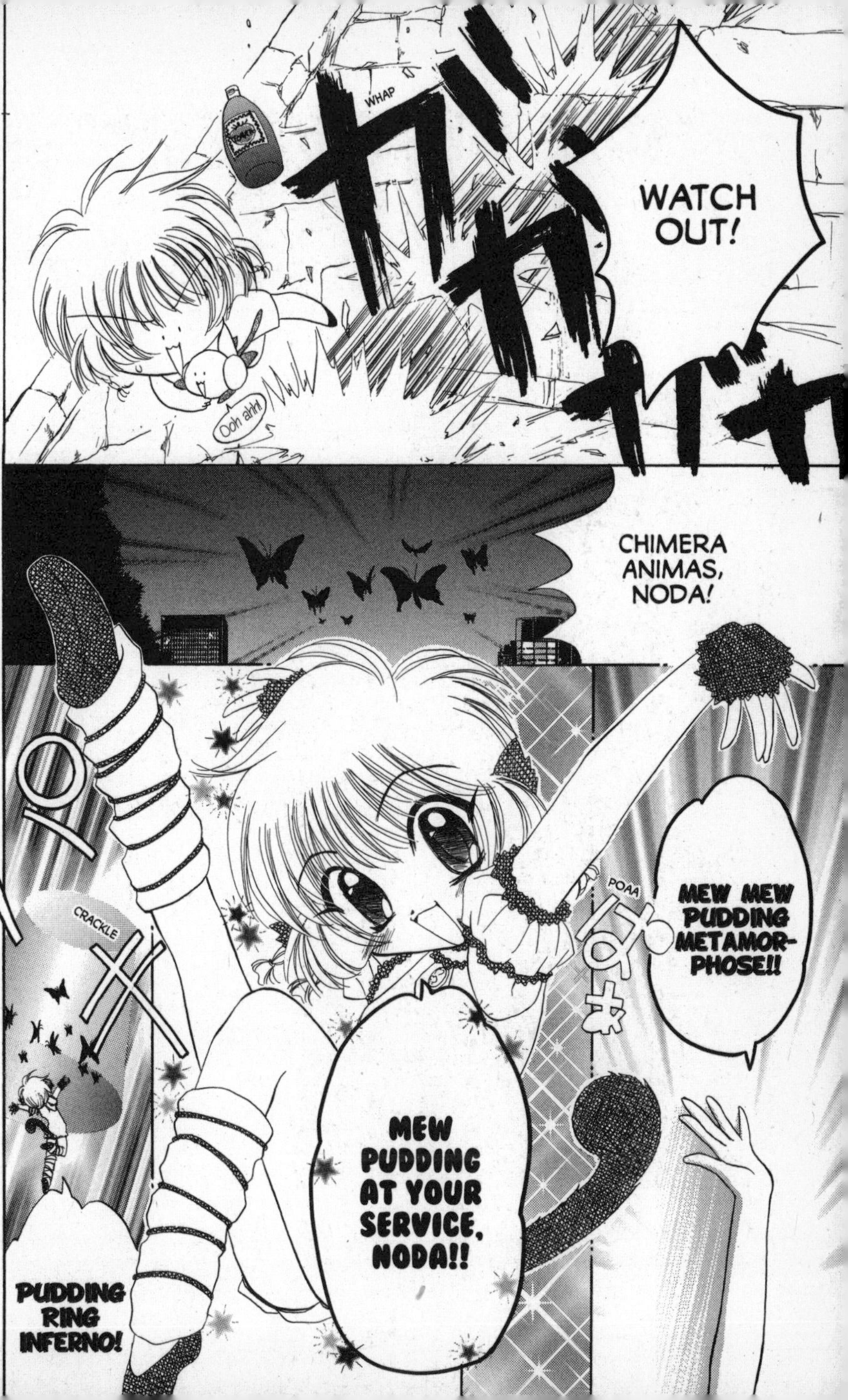
WATCH OUT!
WHAP
Ooh ahh!
CHIMERA ANIMAS, NODA!
POAA
MEW MEW PUDDING METAMOR-PHOSE!!
CRACKLE
MEW PUDDING AT YOUR SERVICE, NODA!!
PUDDING RING INFERNO!

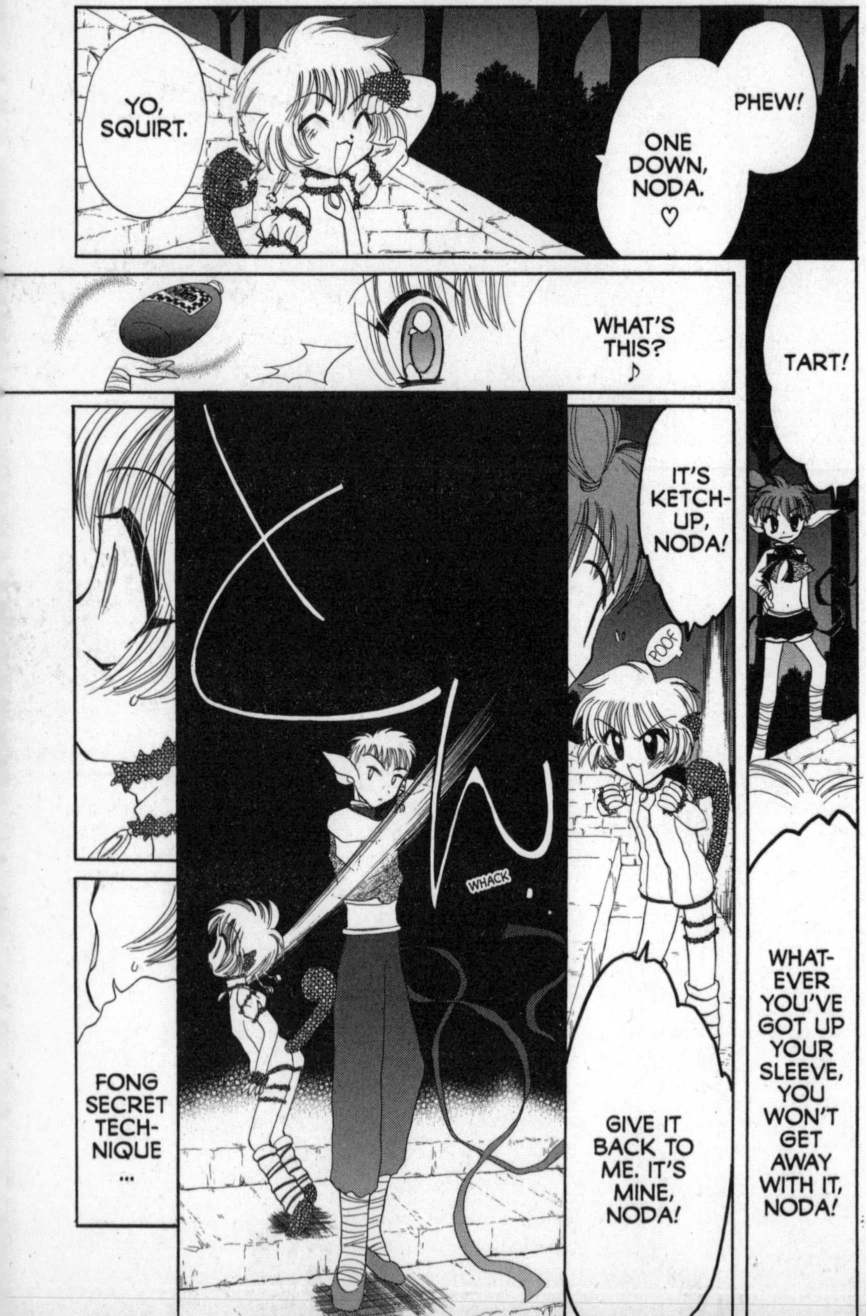
PHEW!
ONE DOWN, NODA. ♡
YO, SQUIRT.
TART!
WHATEVER YOU'VE GOT UP YOUR SLEEVE, YOU WON'T GET AWAY WITH IT, NODA!
WHAT'S THIS? ♪
IT'S KETCHUP, NODA!
POOF
GIVE IT BACK TO ME. IT'S MINE, NODA!
WHACK
FONG SECRET TECHNIQUE ...

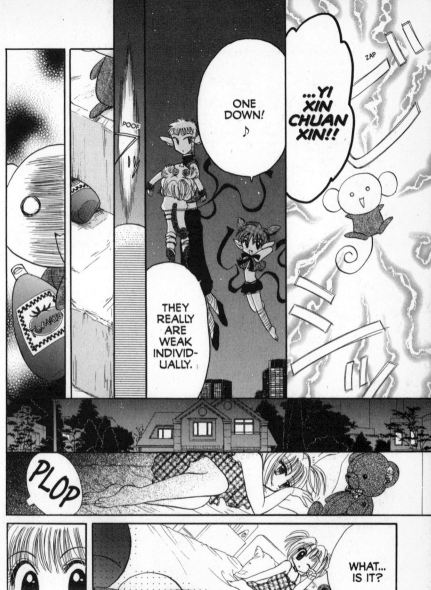

ONE DOWN! ♪

...YI XIN CHUAN XIN!!

ZAP

POOF

THEY REALLY ARE WEAK INDIVIDUALLY.

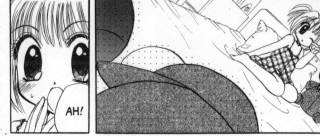

PLOP

AH!

WHAT... IS IT?

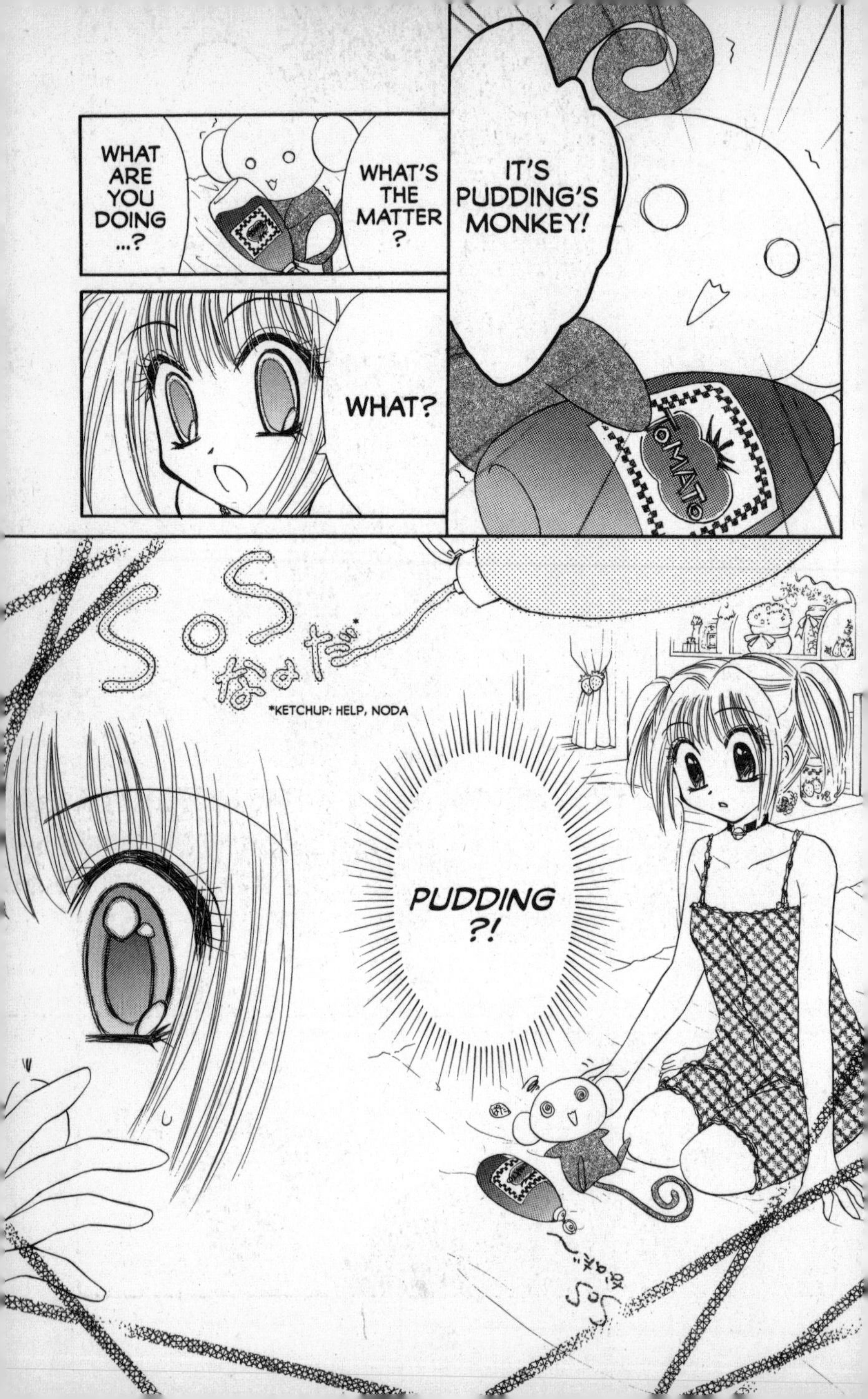

IT'S PUDDING'S MONKEY!
WHAT'S THE MATTER?
WHAT ARE YOU DOING ...?
WHAT?
SOS
*KETCHUP: HELP, NODA
PUDDING ?!

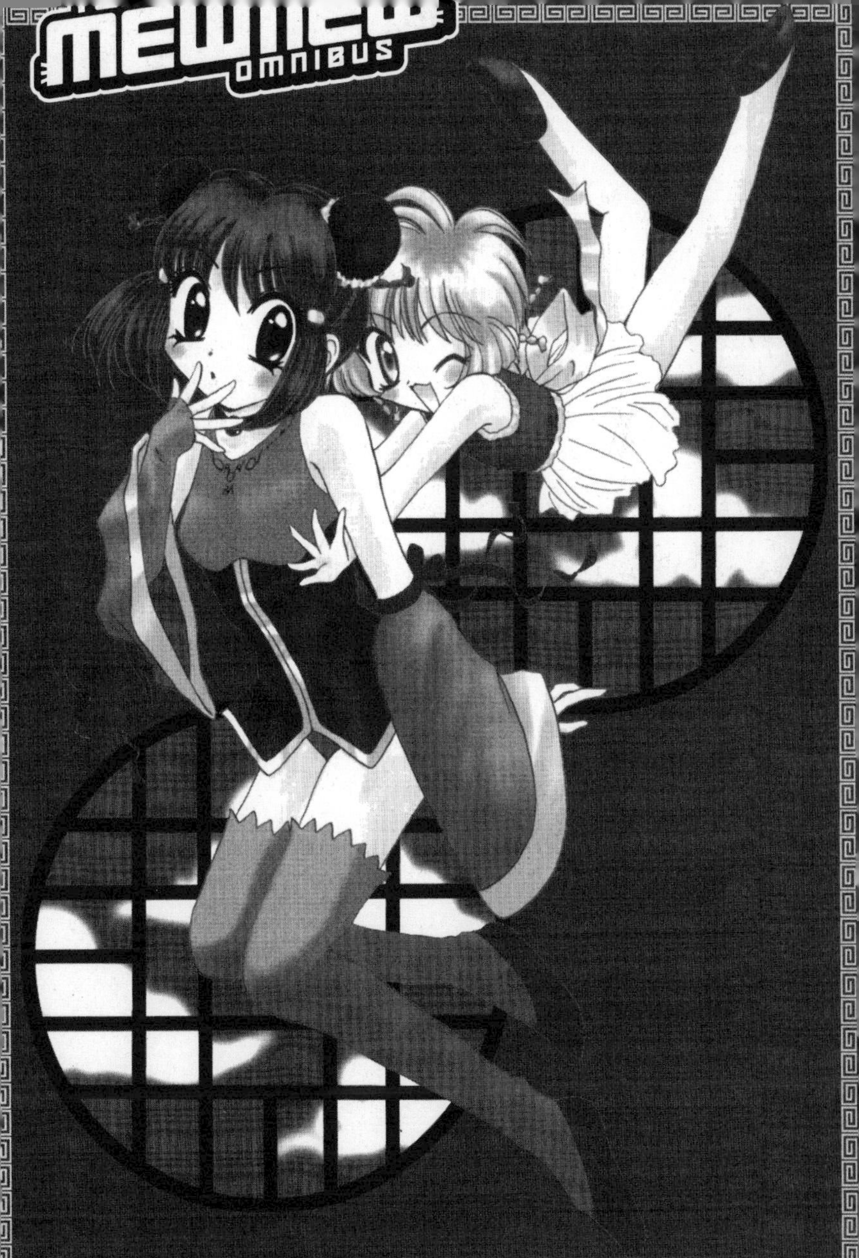
MEWMEW
OMNIBUS

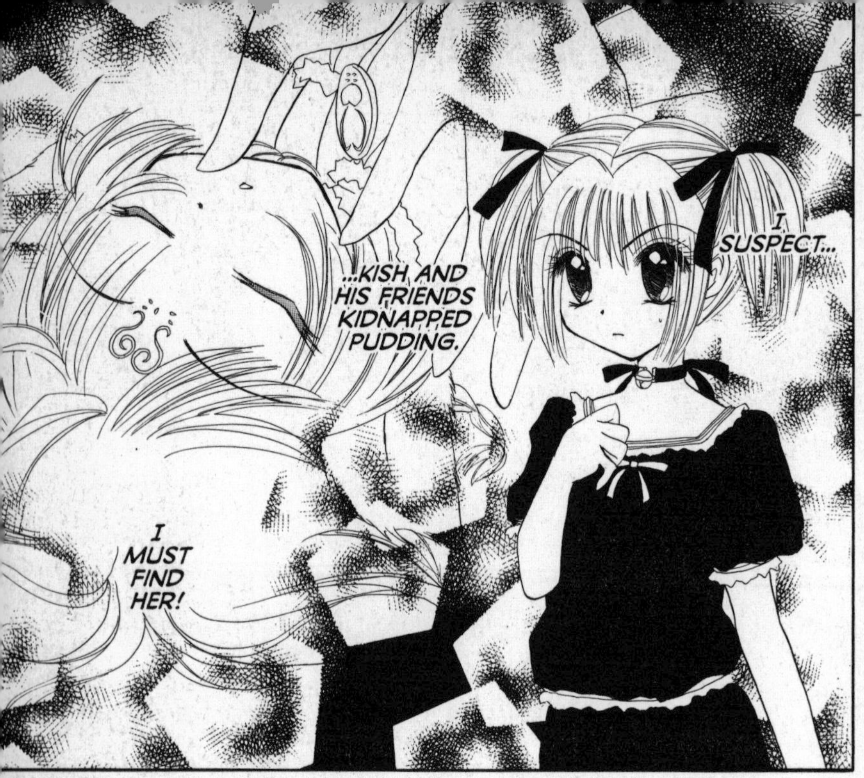
I SUSPECT...
...KISH AND HIS FRIENDS KIDNAPPED PUDDING.
I MUST FIND HER!

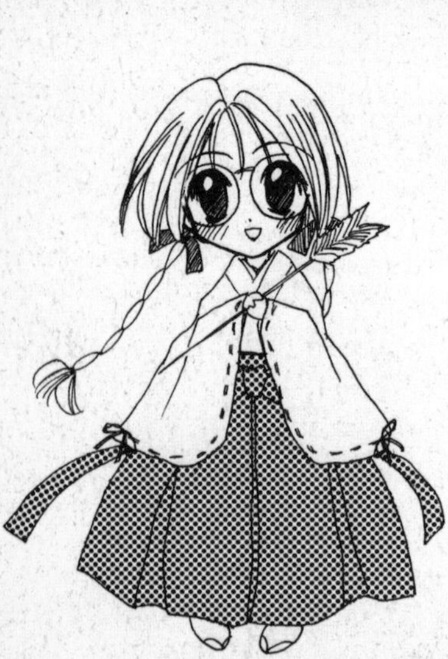

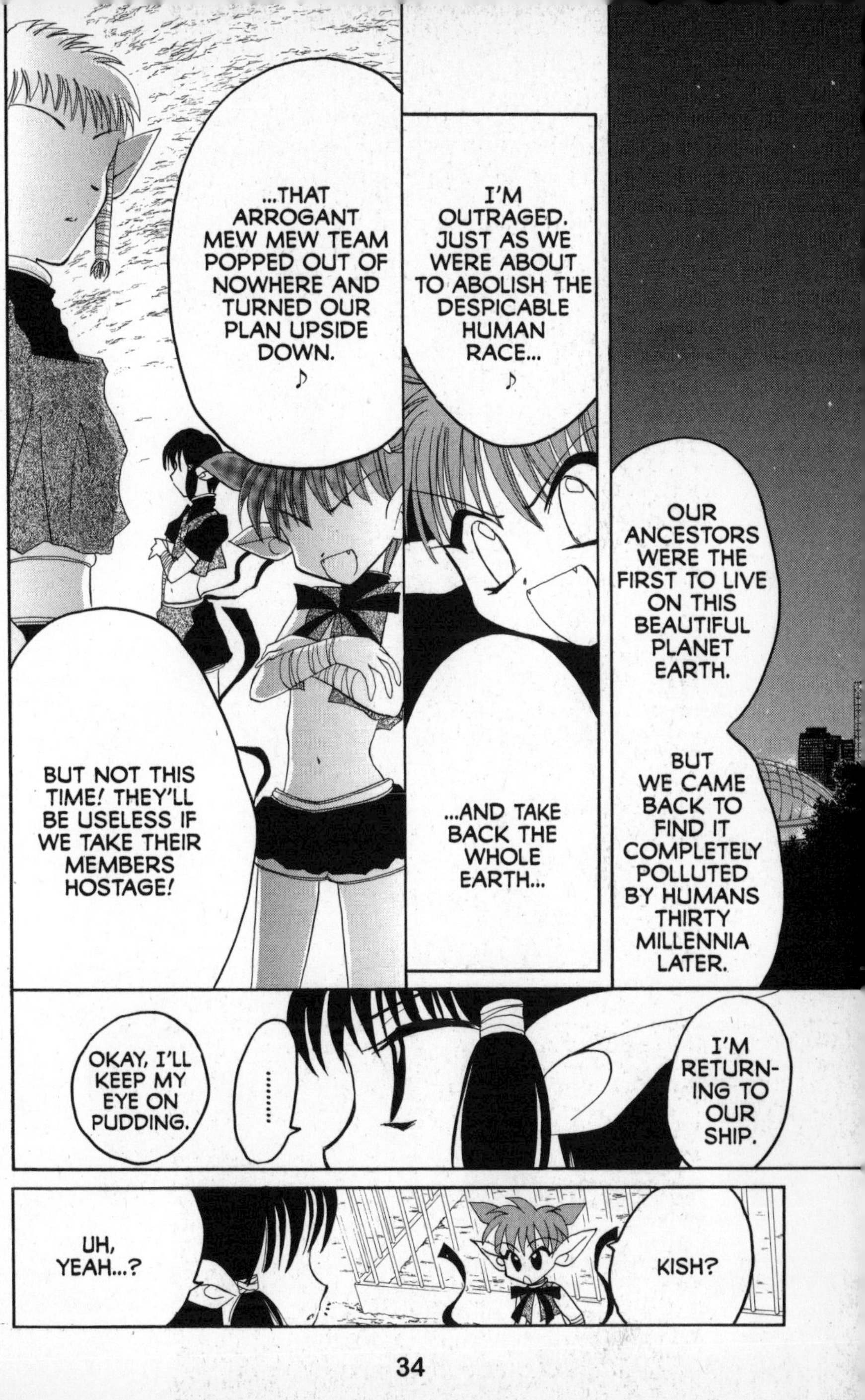
OUR ANCESTORS WERE THE FIRST TO LIVE ON THIS BEAUTIFUL PLANET EARTH.
BUT WE CAME BACK TO FIND IT COMPLETELY POLLUTED BY HUMANS THIRTY MILLENNIA LATER.
I'M OUTRAGED. JUST AS WE WERE ABOUT TO ABOLISH THE DESPICABLE HUMAN RACE... ♪
...AND TAKE BACK THE WHOLE EARTH...
...THAT ARROGANT MEW MEW TEAM POPPED OUT OF NOWHERE AND TURNED OUR PLAN UPSIDE DOWN. ♪
BUT NOT THIS TIME! THEY'LL BE USELESS IF WE TAKE THEIR MEMBERS HOSTAGE!
I'M RETURNING TO OUR SHIP.
....
OKAY, I'LL KEEP MY EYE ON PUDDING.
KISH?
UH, YEAH...?

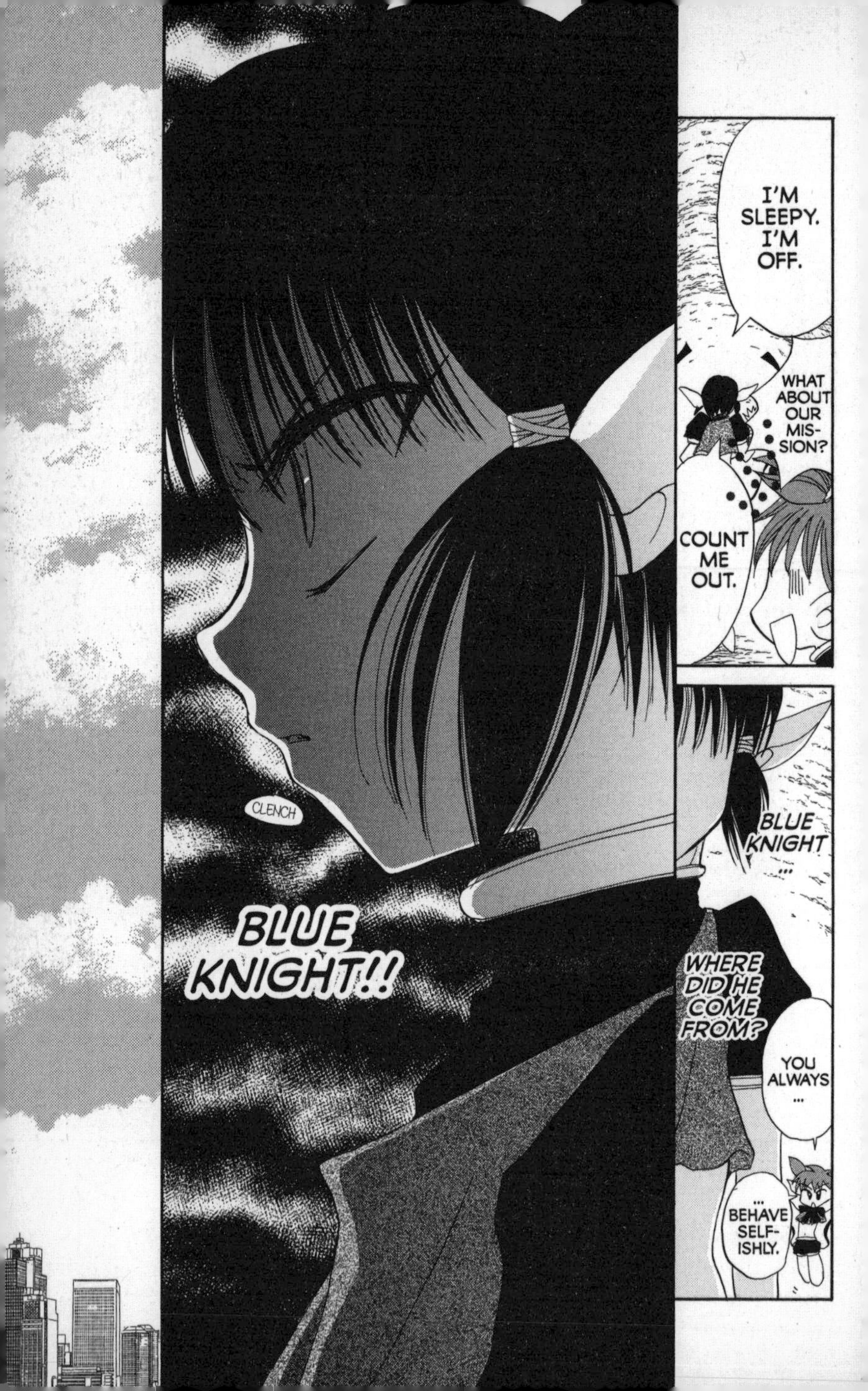
I'M SLEEPY. I'M OFF.
WHAT ABOUT OUR MIS-SION?
COUNT ME OUT.
BLUE KNIGHT ...
WHERE DID HE COME FROM?
YOU ALWAYS ...
... BEHAVE SELF-ISHLY.
CLENCH
BLUE KNIGHT!!

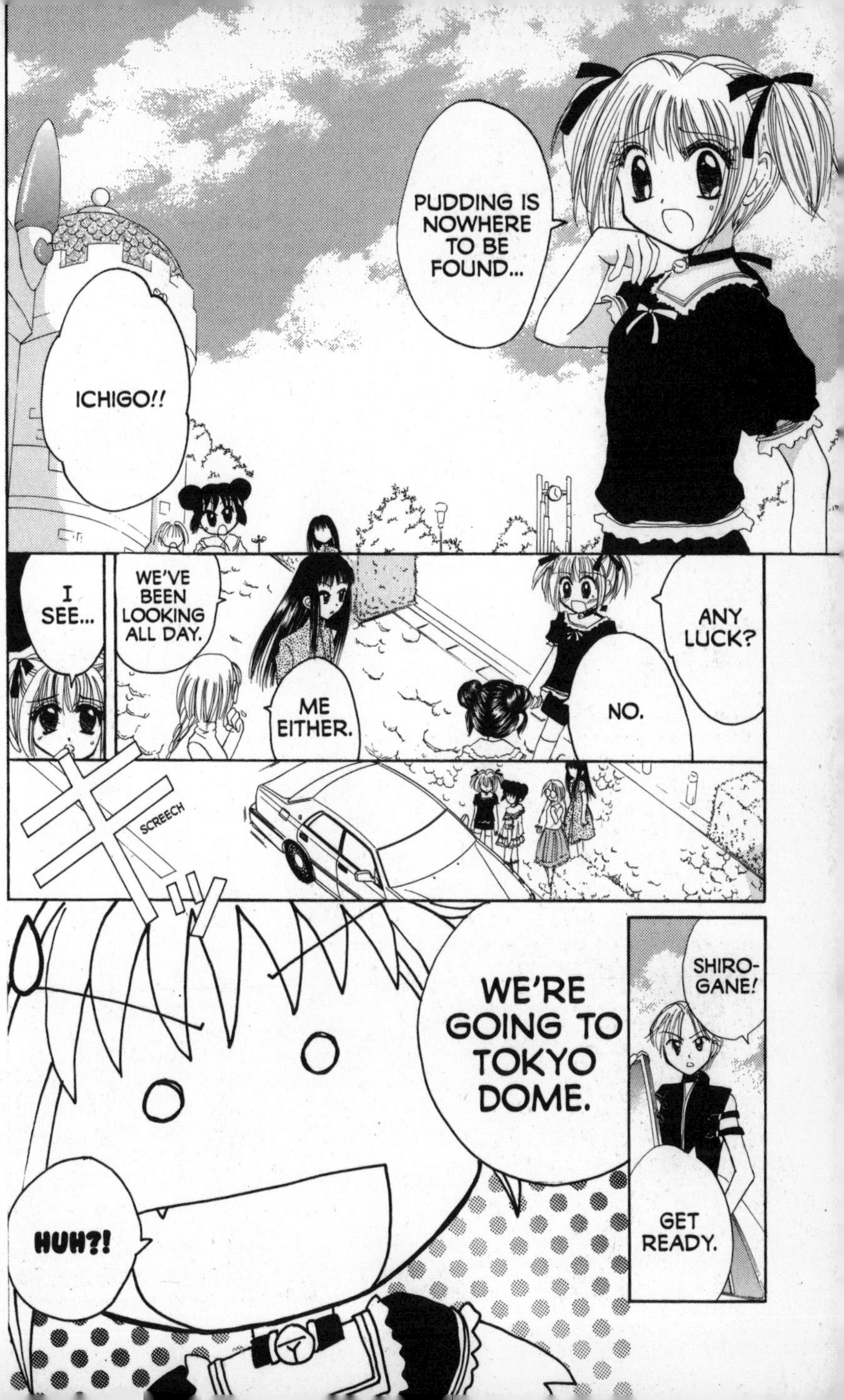
PUDDING IS NOWHERE TO BE FOUND...
ICHIGO!!
ANY LUCK?
NO.
WE'VE BEEN LOOKING ALL DAY.
ME EITHER.
I SEE...
SCREECH
SHIRO-GANE!
GET READY.
WE'RE GOING TO TOKYO DOME.
HUH?!

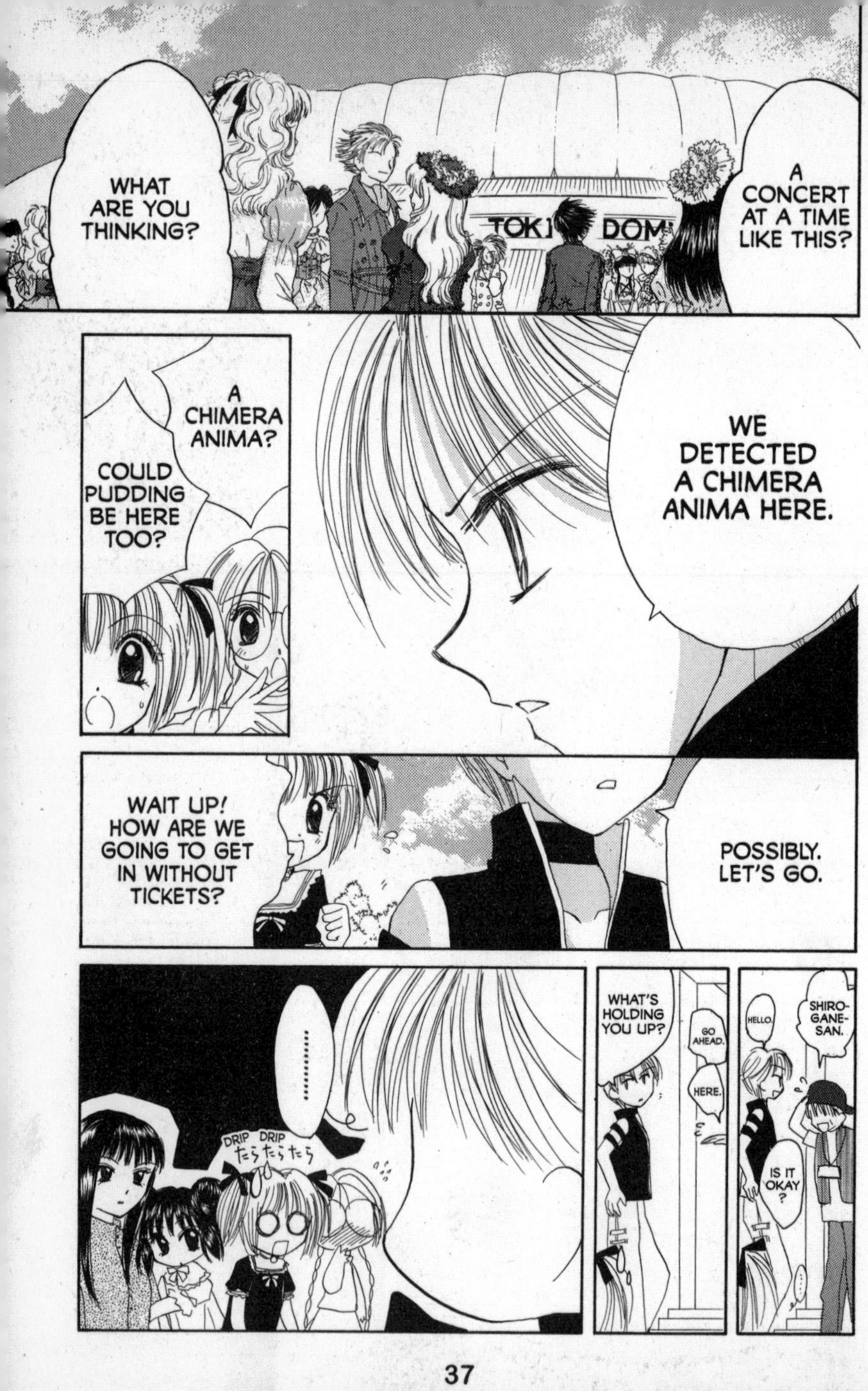
A CONCERT AT A TIME LIKE THIS?
WHAT ARE YOU THINKING?
TOKI DOM
WE DETECTED A CHIMERA ANIMA HERE.
A CHIMERA ANIMA?
COULD PUDDING BE HERE TOO?
POSSIBLY. LET'S GO.
WAIT UP! HOW ARE WE GOING TO GET IN WITHOUT TICKETS?
SHIRO-GANE-SAN.
HELLO.
IS IT OKAY?
...
WHAT'S HOLDING YOU UP?
GO AHEAD.
HERE.
....
DRIP DRIP
たらたらたら

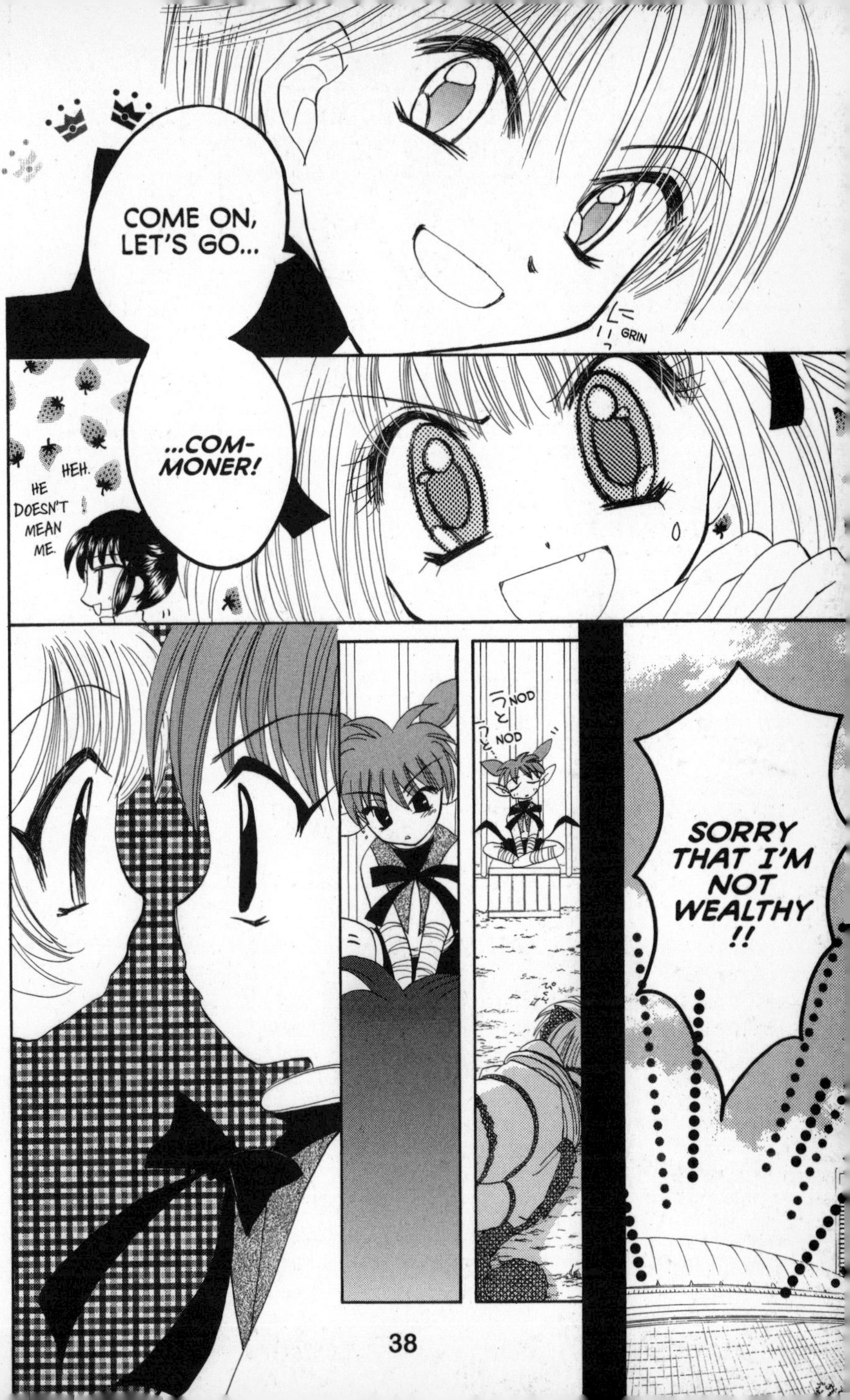
COME ON, LET'S GO...
GRIN
...COM-MONER!
HEH. HE DOESN'T MEAN ME.
SORRY THAT I'M NOT WEALTHY!!
NOD NOD

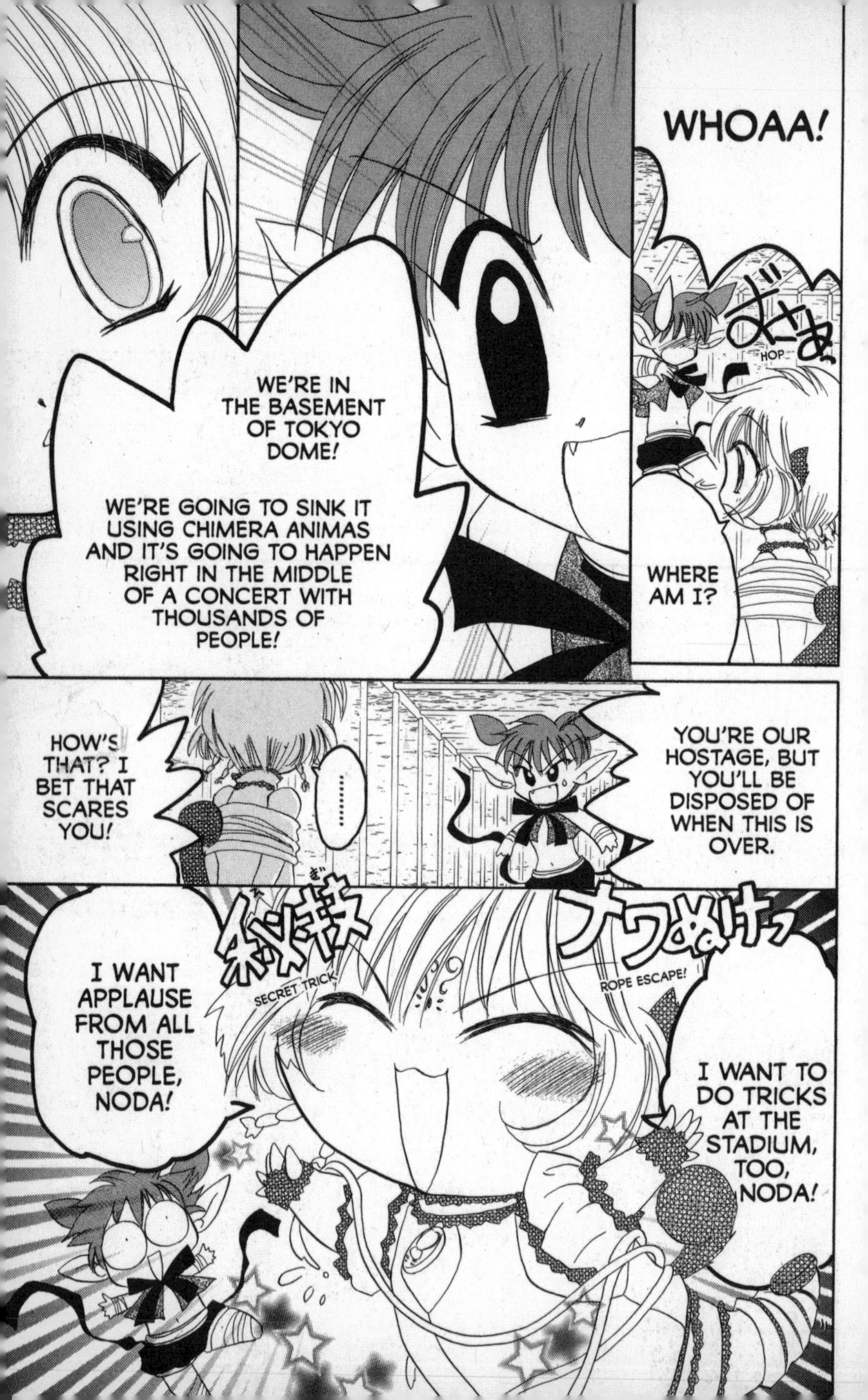
WHOAA!
HOP
WHERE AM I?
WE'RE IN THE BASEMENT OF TOKYO DOME!
WE'RE GOING TO SINK IT USING CHIMERA ANIMAS AND IT'S GOING TO HAPPEN RIGHT IN THE MIDDLE OF A CONCERT WITH THOUSANDS OF PEOPLE!
YOU'RE OUR HOSTAGE, BUT YOU'LL BE DISPOSED OF WHEN THIS IS OVER.
......
HOW'S THAT? I BET THAT SCARES YOU!
ROPE ESCAPE!
SECRET TRICK
I WANT APPLAUSE FROM ALL THOSE PEOPLE, NODA!
I WANT TO DO TRICKS AT THE STADIUM, TOO, NODA!

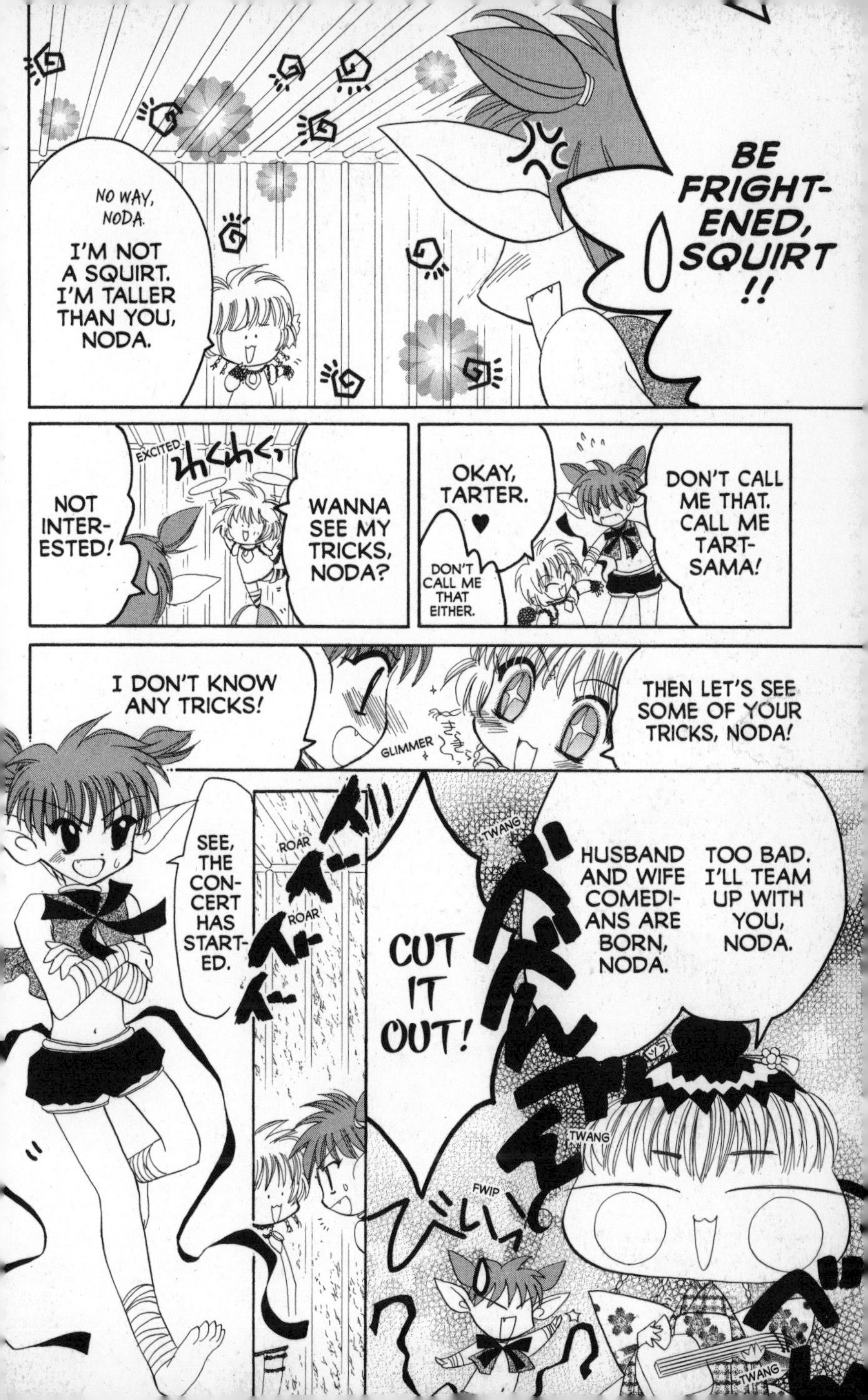
BE FRIGHT-ENED, SQUIRT!!
NO WAY, NODA.
I'M NOT A SQUIRT. I'M TALLER THAN YOU, NODA.
DON'T CALL ME THAT. CALL ME TART-SAMA!
OKAY, TARTER. ♥
DON'T CALL ME THAT EITHER.
WANNA SEE MY TRICKS, NODA?
EXCITED
NOT INTER-ESTED!
THEN LET'S SEE SOME OF YOUR TRICKS, NODA!
GLIMMER
I DON'T KNOW ANY TRICKS!
TOO BAD. I'LL TEAM UP WITH YOU, NODA.
HUSBAND AND WIFE COMEDI-ANS ARE BORN, NODA.
TWANG
TWANG
CUT IT OUT!
FWIP
TWANG
ROAR
ROAR
SEE, THE CON-CERT HAS START-ED.

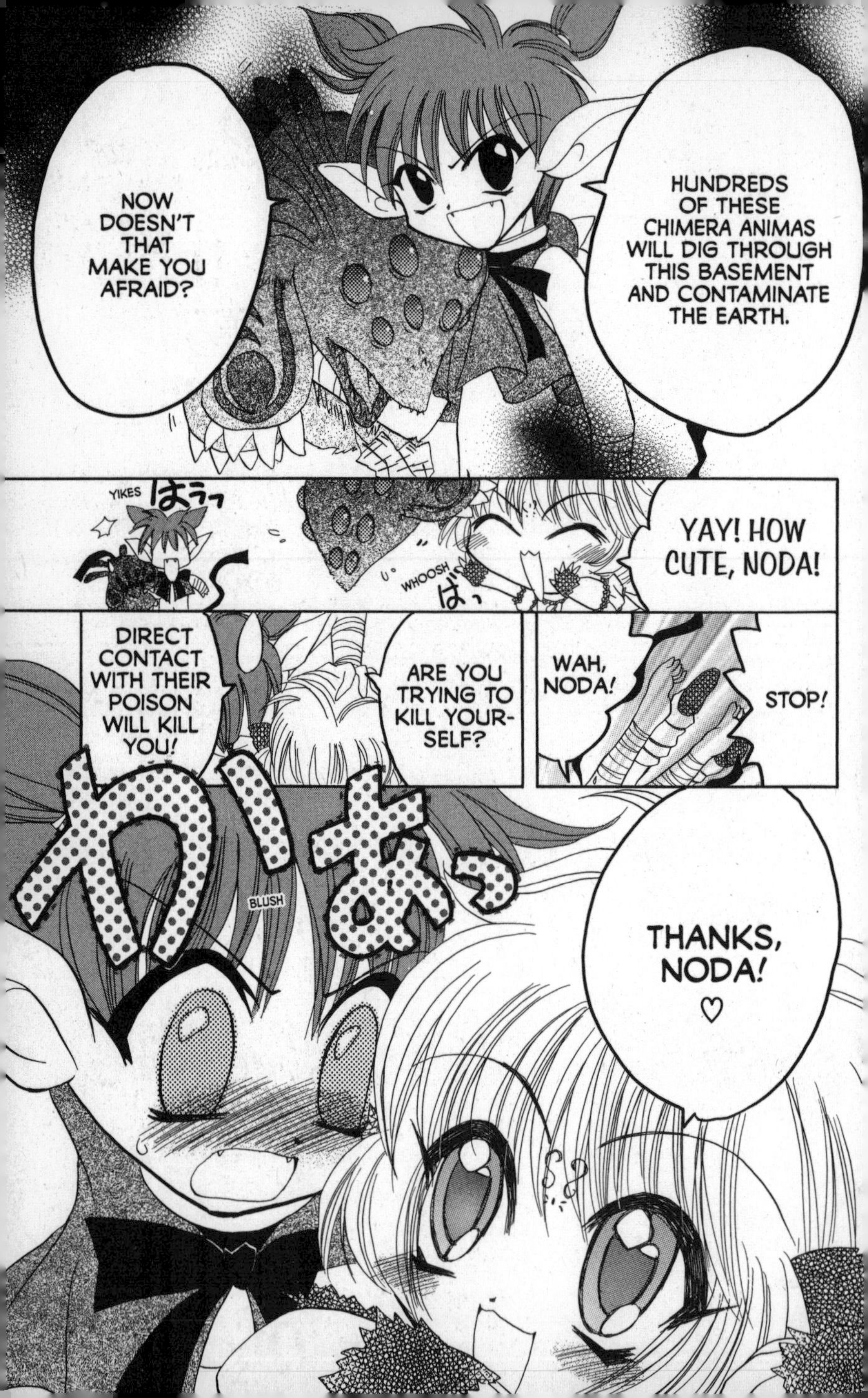
HUNDREDS OF THESE CHIMERA ANIMAS WILL DIG THROUGH THIS BASEMENT AND CONTAMINATE THE EARTH.
NOW DOESN'T THAT MAKE YOU AFRAID?
YAY! HOW CUTE, NODA!
WHOOSH
YIKES
STOP!
WAH, NODA!
ARE YOU TRYING TO KILL YOUR-SELF?
DIRECT CONTACT WITH THEIR POISON WILL KILL YOU!
THANKS, NODA! ♡
BLUSH

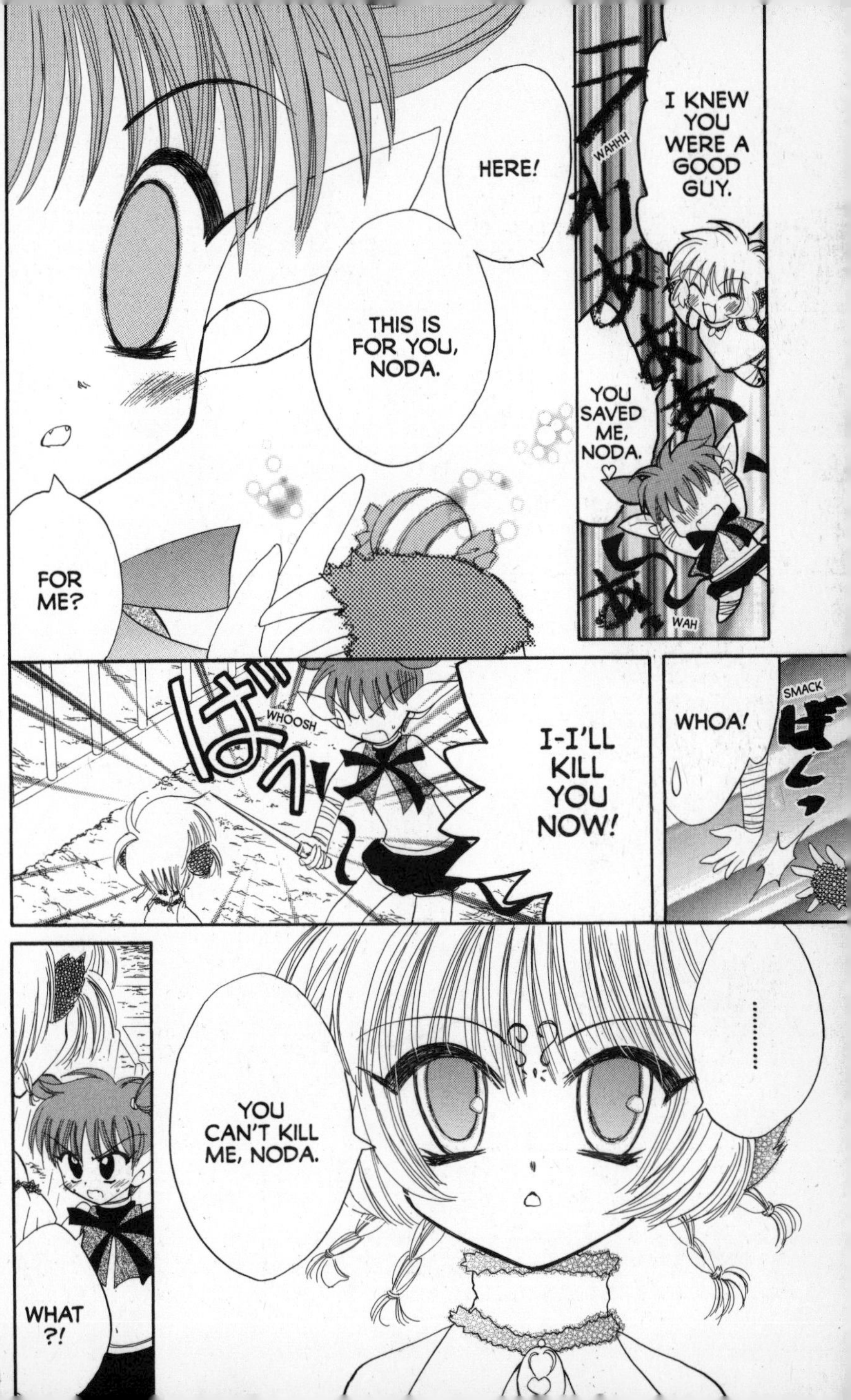
I KNEW YOU WERE A GOOD GUY.
WAHHH
YOU SAVED ME, NODA. ♥
WAH
HERE!
THIS IS FOR YOU, NODA.
FOR ME?
SMACK
WHOA!
WHOOSH
I-I'LL KILL YOU NOW!
......
YOU CAN'T KILL ME, NODA.
WHAT ?!

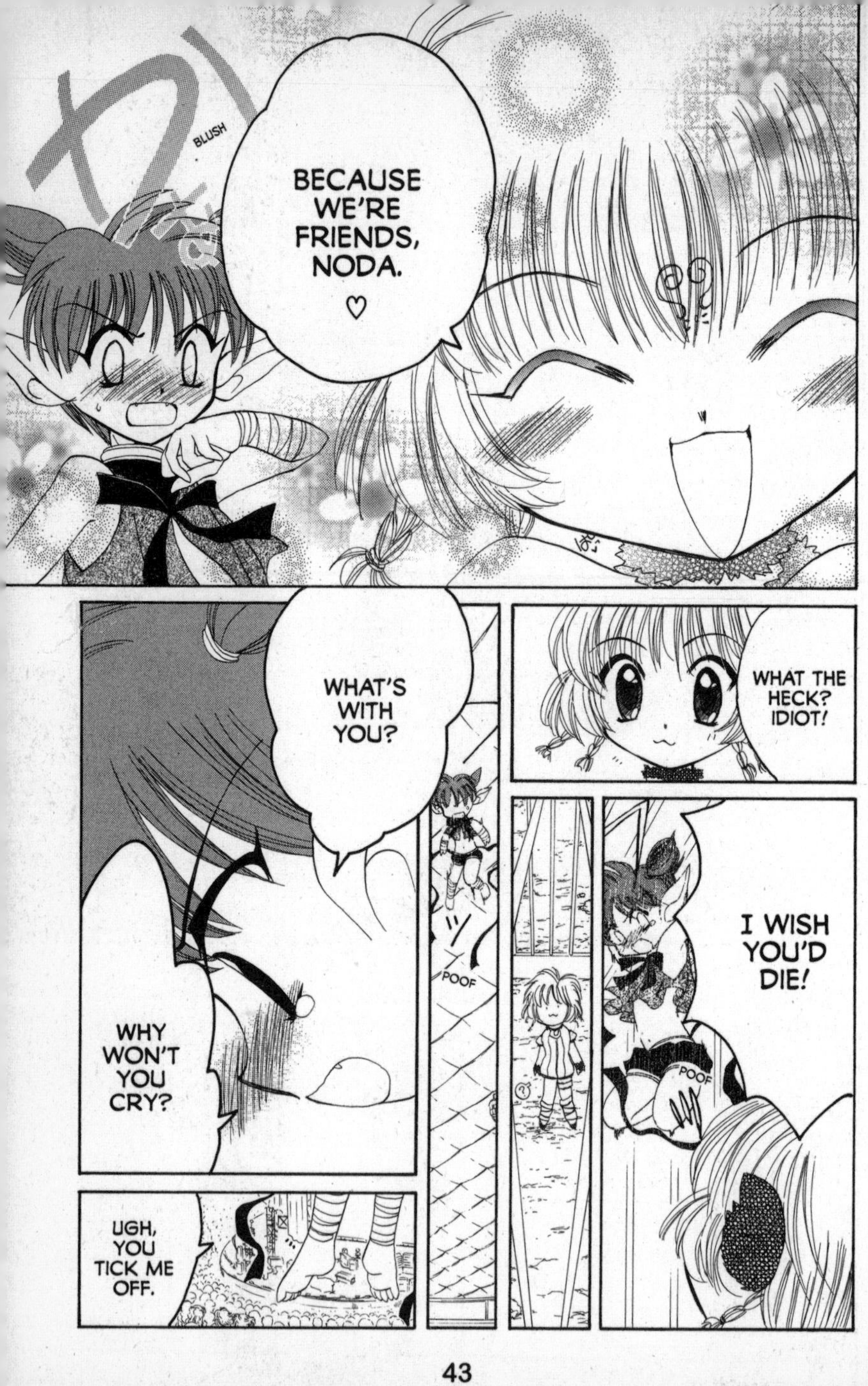
BLUSH
BECAUSE WE'RE FRIENDS, NODA. ♡
WHAT THE HECK? IDIOT!
I WISH YOU'D DIE!
POOF
POOF
WHAT'S WITH YOU?
WHY WON'T YOU CRY?
UGH, YOU TICK ME OFF.

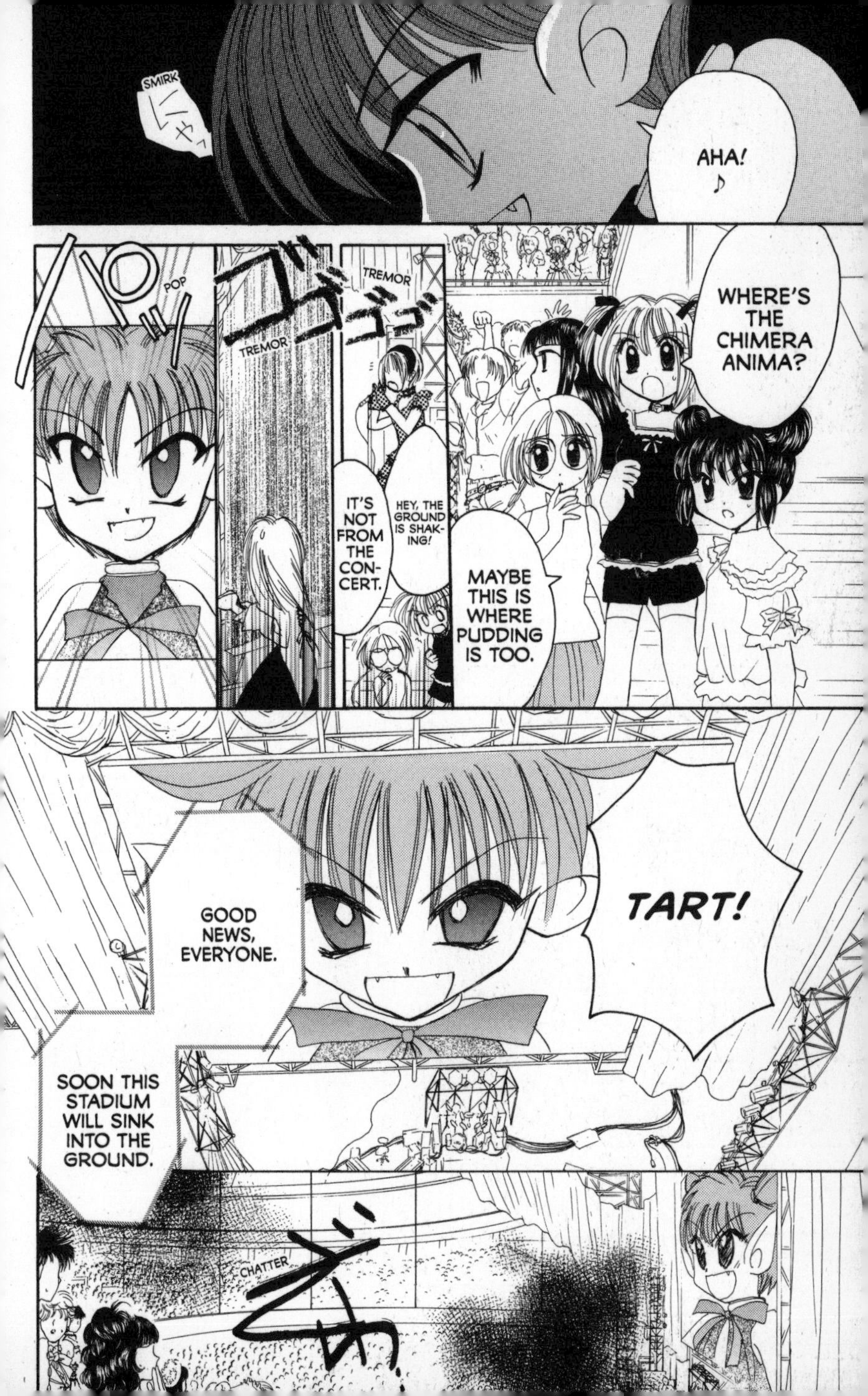
AHA! ♪
SMIRK
WHERE'S THE CHIMERA ANIMA?
MAYBE THIS IS WHERE PUDDING IS TOO.
TREMOR
HEY, THE GROUND IS SHAKING!
IT'S NOT FROM THE CONCERT.
TREMOR
POP
TART!
GOOD NEWS, EVERYONE.
SOON THIS STADIUM WILL SINK INTO THE GROUND.
CHATTER

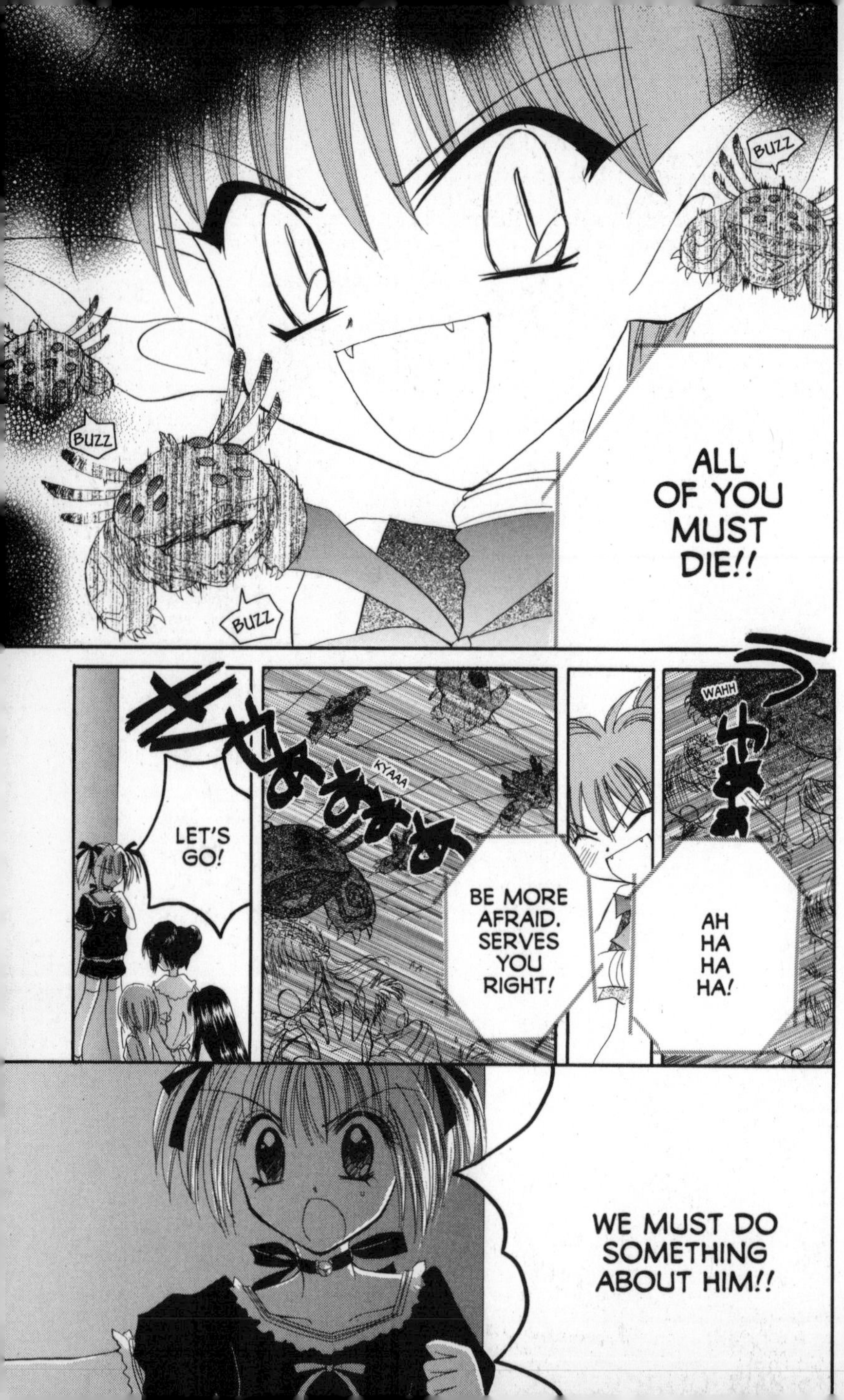
BUZZ
ALL OF YOU MUST DIE!!
BUZZ
BUZZ
WAHH
AH HA HA HA!
BE MORE AFRAID. SERVES YOU RIGHT!
KYAAA
LET'S GO!
WE MUST DO SOMETHING ABOUT HIM!!

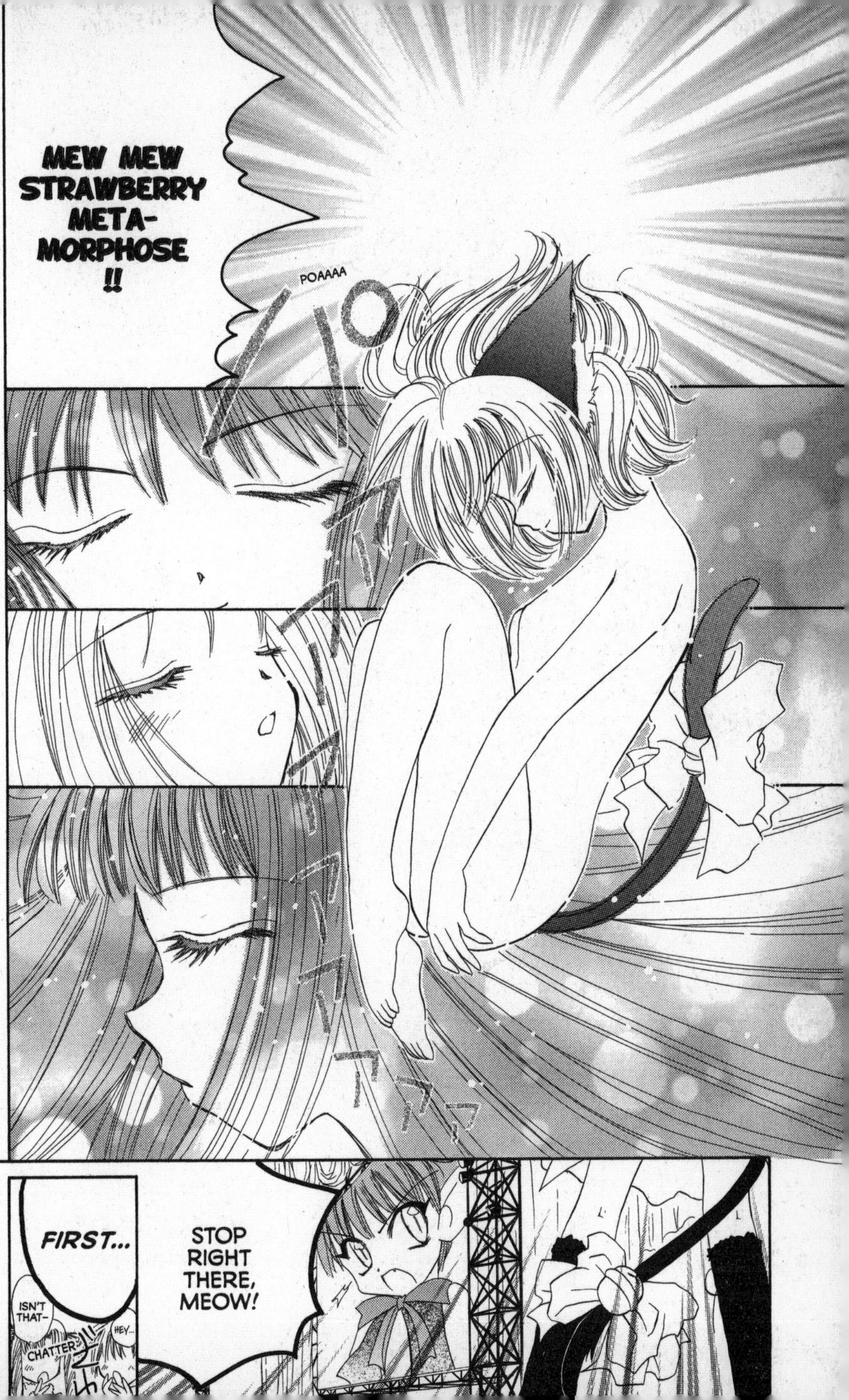
MEW MEW STRAWBERRY META-MORPHOSE !!
POAAAA
STOP RIGHT THERE, MEOW!
FIRST...
HEY...
ISN'T THAT-
CHATTER

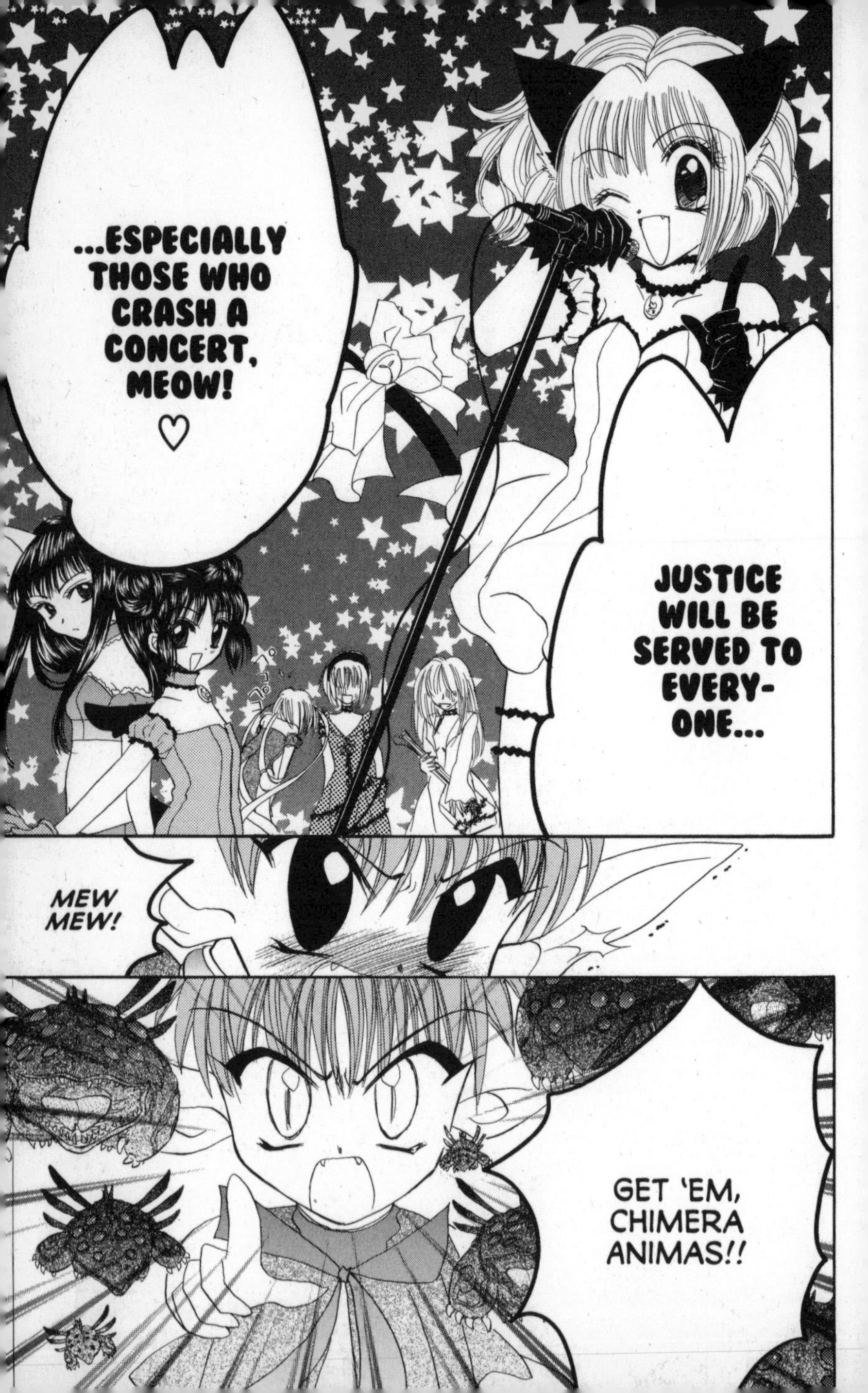
JUSTICE WILL BE SERVED TO EVERY-ONE...
...ESPECIALLY THOSE WHO CRASH A CONCERT, MEOW! ♡
MEW MEW!
GET 'EM, CHIMERA ANIMAS!!

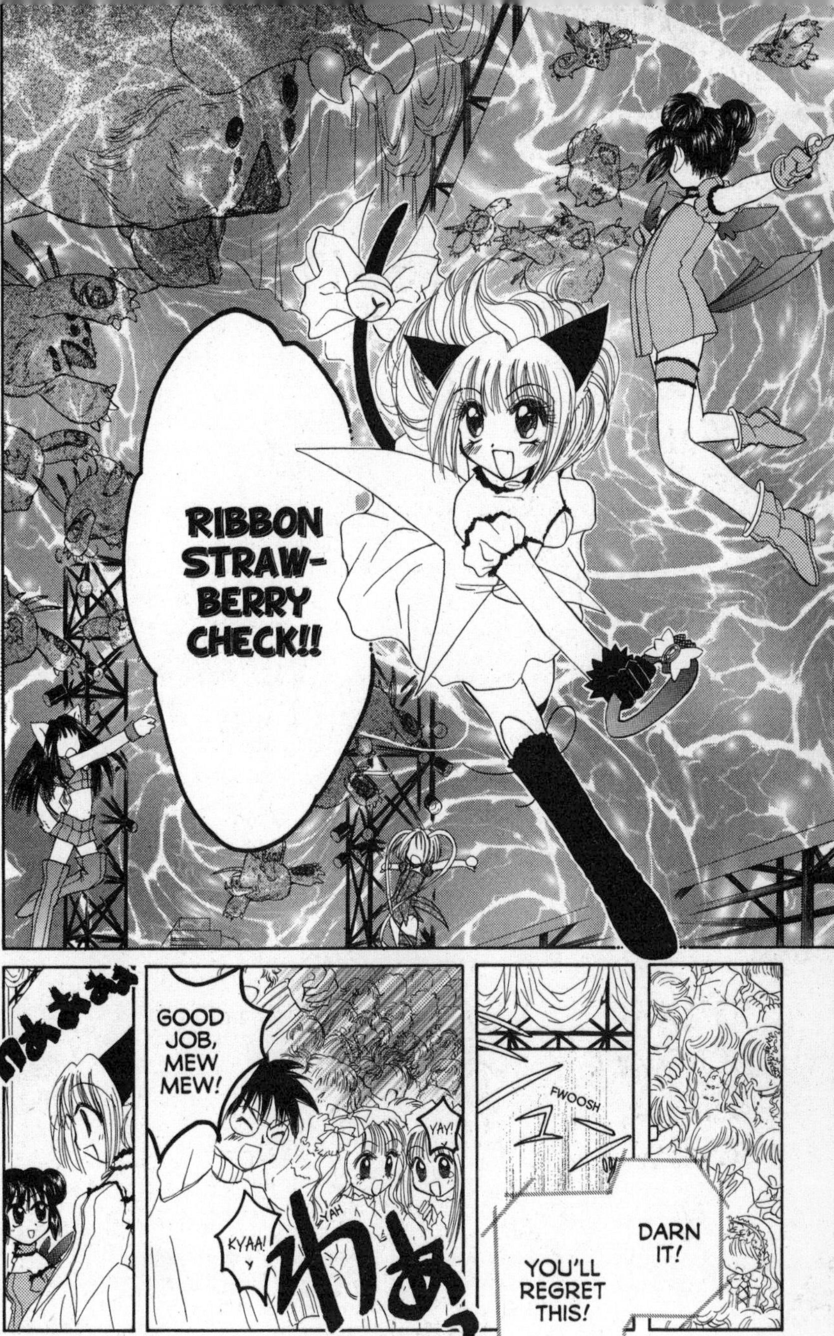
RIBBON STRAWBERRY CHECK!!
FWOOSH
DARN IT!
YOU'LL REGRET THIS!
GOOD JOB, MEW MEW!
YAY!
YAH
KYAA!
わあ

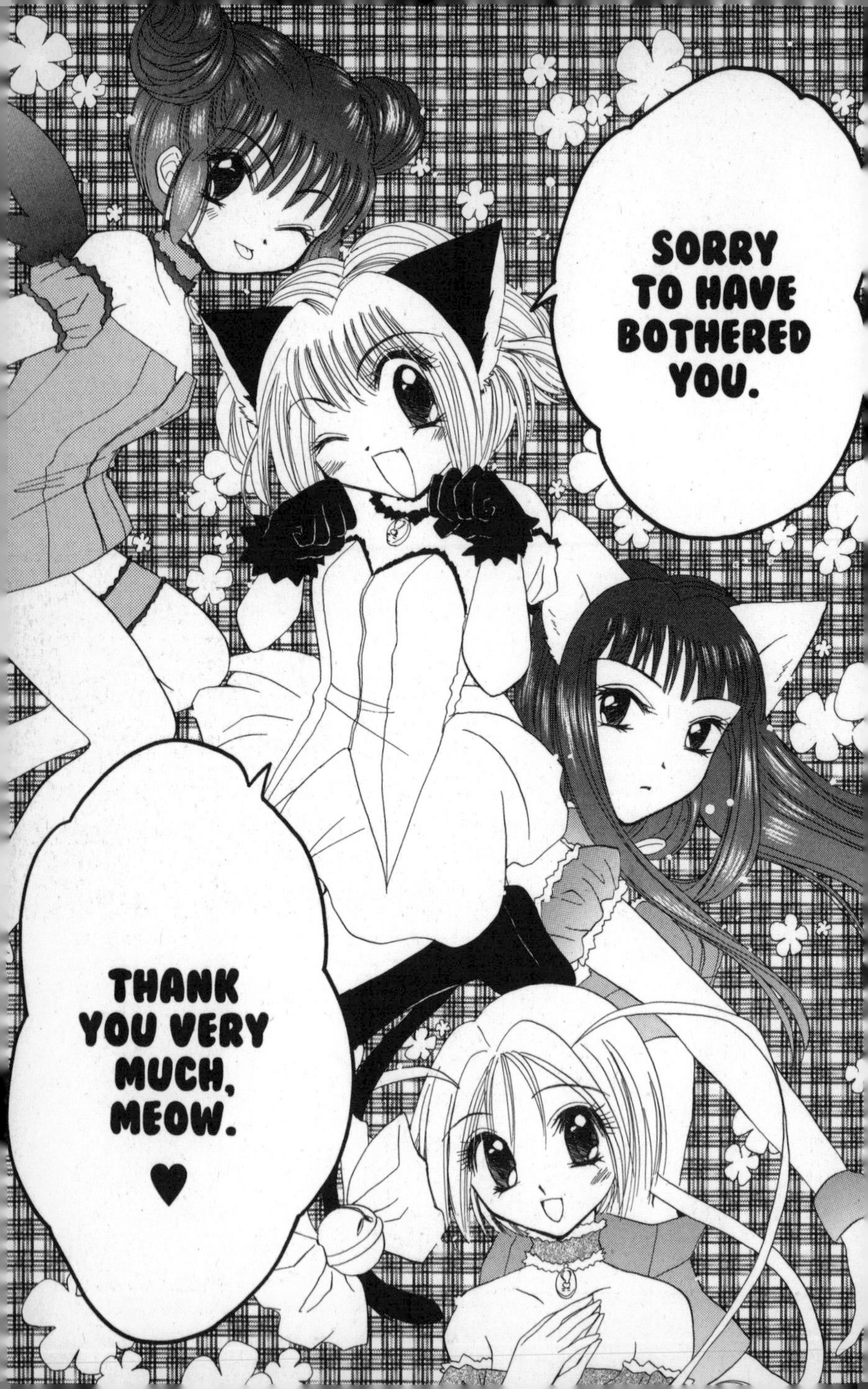
SORRY TO HAVE BOTHERED YOU.
THANK YOU VERY MUCH, MEOW. ♥

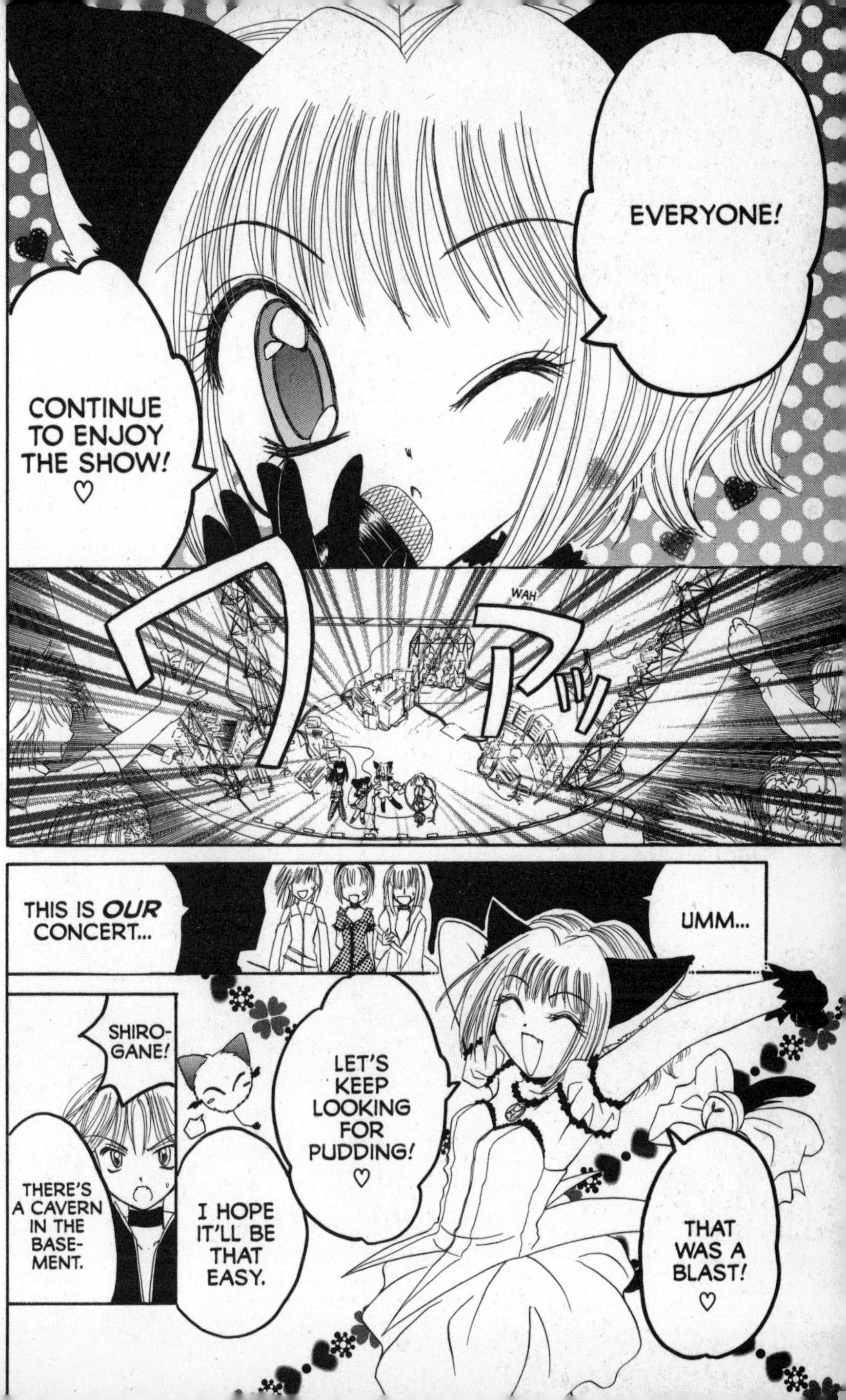
EVERYONE!
CONTINUE TO ENJOY THE SHOW! ♡
WAH
UMM...
THAT WAS A BLAST! ♡
LET'S KEEP LOOKING FOR PUDDING! ♡
THIS IS *OUR* CONCERT...
SHIRO-GANE!
I HOPE IT'LL BE THAT EASY.
THERE'S A CAVERN IN THE BASE-MENT.

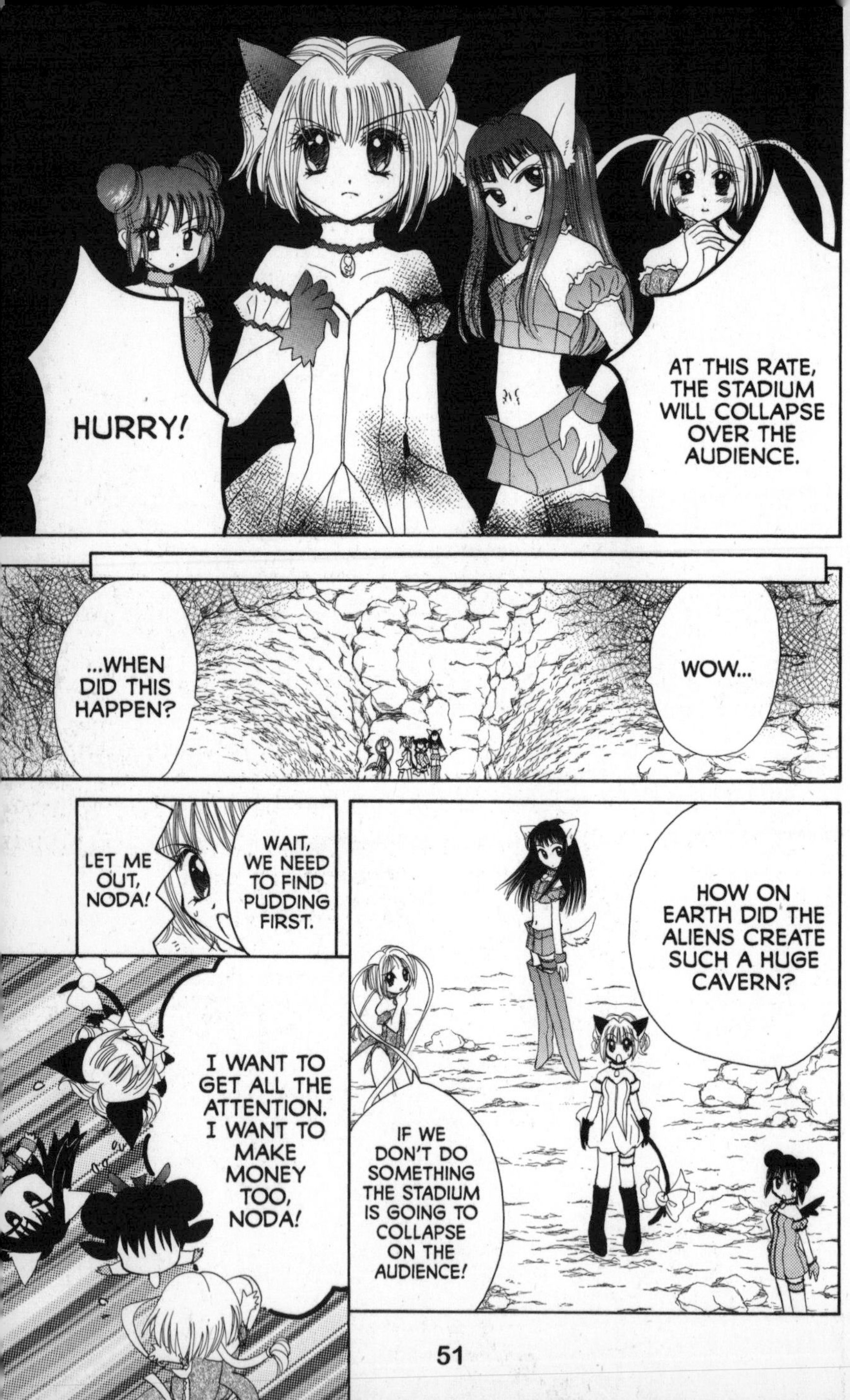
AT THIS RATE, THE STADIUM WILL COLLAPSE OVER THE AUDIENCE.
HURRY!
WOW...
...WHEN DID THIS HAPPEN?
HOW ON EARTH DID THE ALIENS CREATE SUCH A HUGE CAVERN?
IF WE DON'T DO SOMETHING THE STADIUM IS GOING TO COLLAPSE ON THE AUDIENCE!
WAIT, WE NEED TO FIND PUDDING FIRST.
LET ME OUT, NODA!
I WANT TO GET ALL THE ATTENTION. I WANT TO MAKE MONEY TOO, NODA!

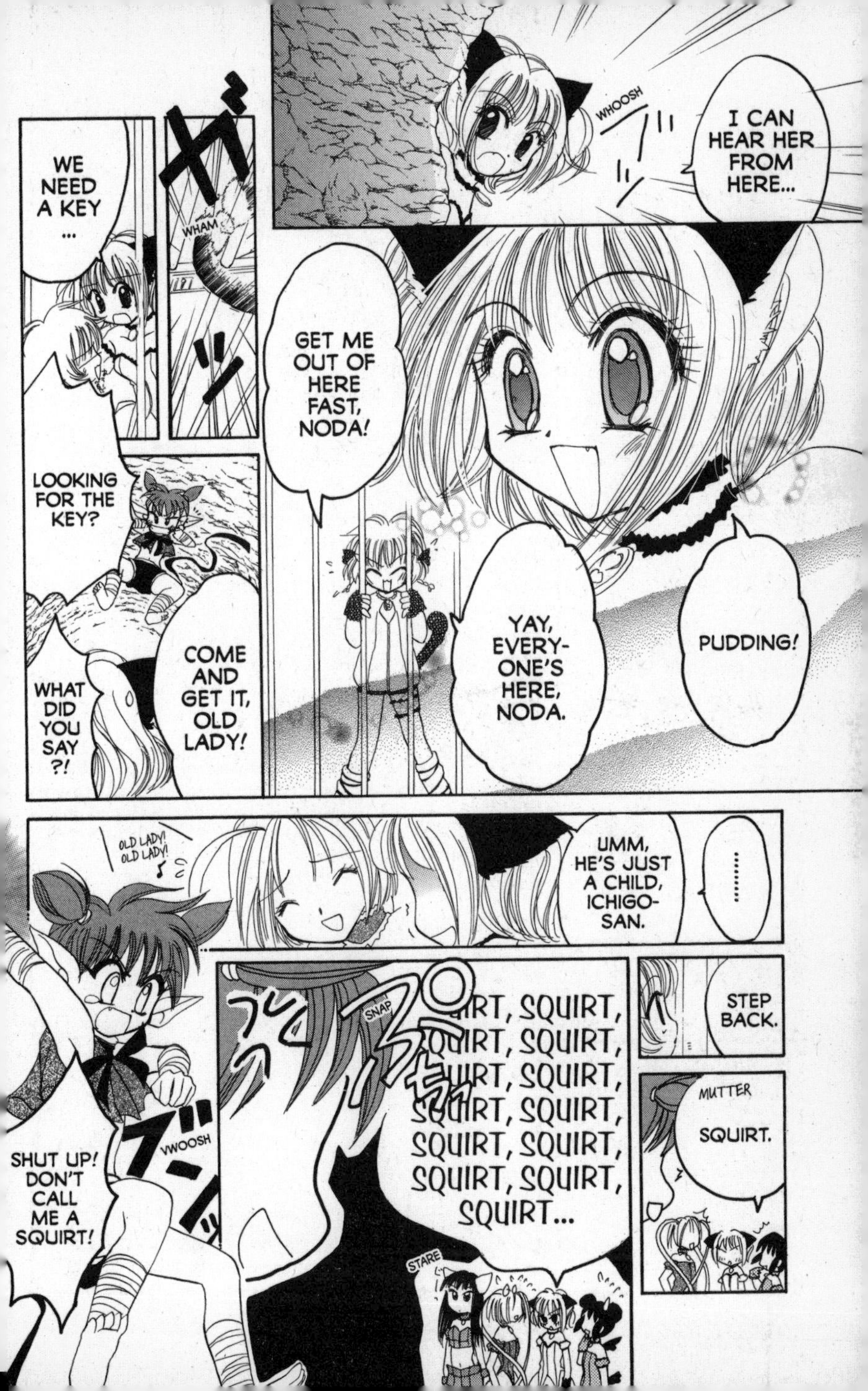
WHOOSH
I CAN HEAR HER FROM HERE...
PUDDING!
YAY, EVERYONE'S HERE, NODA.
GET ME OUT OF HERE FAST, NODA!
WHAM
WE NEED A KEY ...
LOOKING FOR THE KEY?
COME AND GET IT, OLD LADY!
WHAT DID YOU SAY ?!
......
UMM, HE'S JUST A CHILD, ICHIGO-SAN.
OLD LADY! OLD LADY!
STEP BACK.
MUTTER
SQUIRT.
SNAP
SQUIRT, SQUIRT, SQUIRT, SQUIRT, SQUIRT, SQUIRT, SQUIRT, SQUIRT, SQUIRT, SQUIRT, SQUIRT, SQUIRT, SQUIRT...
STARE
VWOOSH
SHUT UP! DON'T CALL ME A SQUIRT!

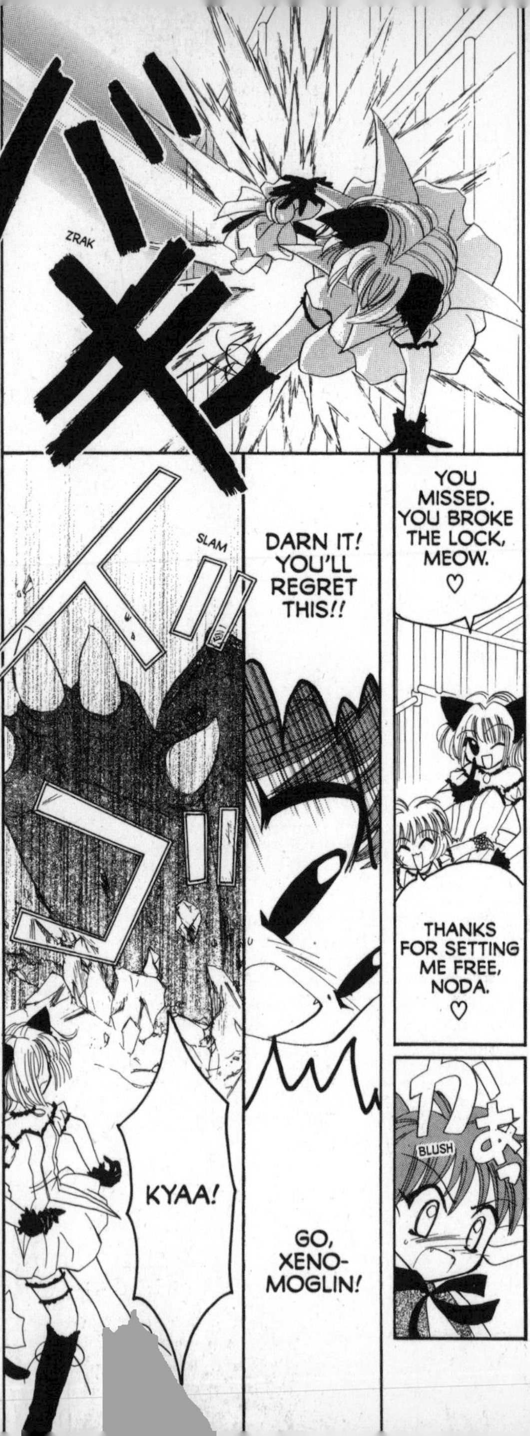
ZRAK
YOU MISSED. YOU BROKE THE LOCK, MEOW. ♡
THANKS FOR SETTING ME FREE, NODA. ♡
BLUSH
DARN IT! YOU'LL REGRET THIS!!
GO, XENO-MOGLIN!
SLAM
KYAA!

Hang On, Masha!

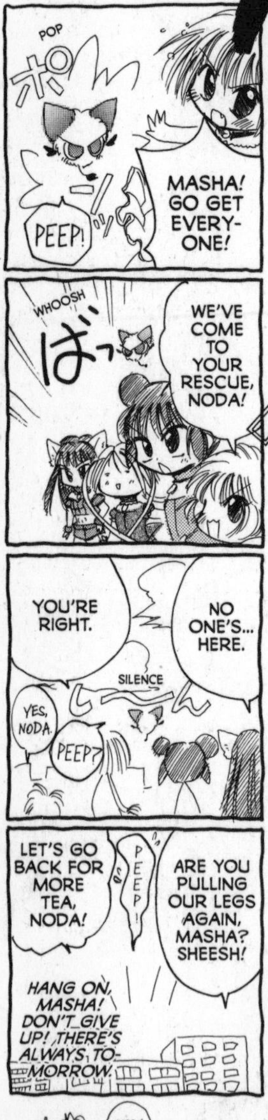
POP
MASHA! GO GET EVERY-ONE!
PEEP!
WHOOSH
WE'VE COME TO YOUR RESCUE, NODA!
NO ONE'S... HERE.
YOU'RE RIGHT.
SILENCE
YES, NODA.
PEEP?
ARE YOU PULLING OUR LEGS AGAIN, MASHA? SHEESH!
PEEP!
LET'S GO BACK FOR MORE TEA, NODA!
HANG ON, MASHA! DON'T GIVE UP! THERE'S ALWAYS TO-MORROW.
SORRY, MASHA.
TEE-HEE
I FORGOT.

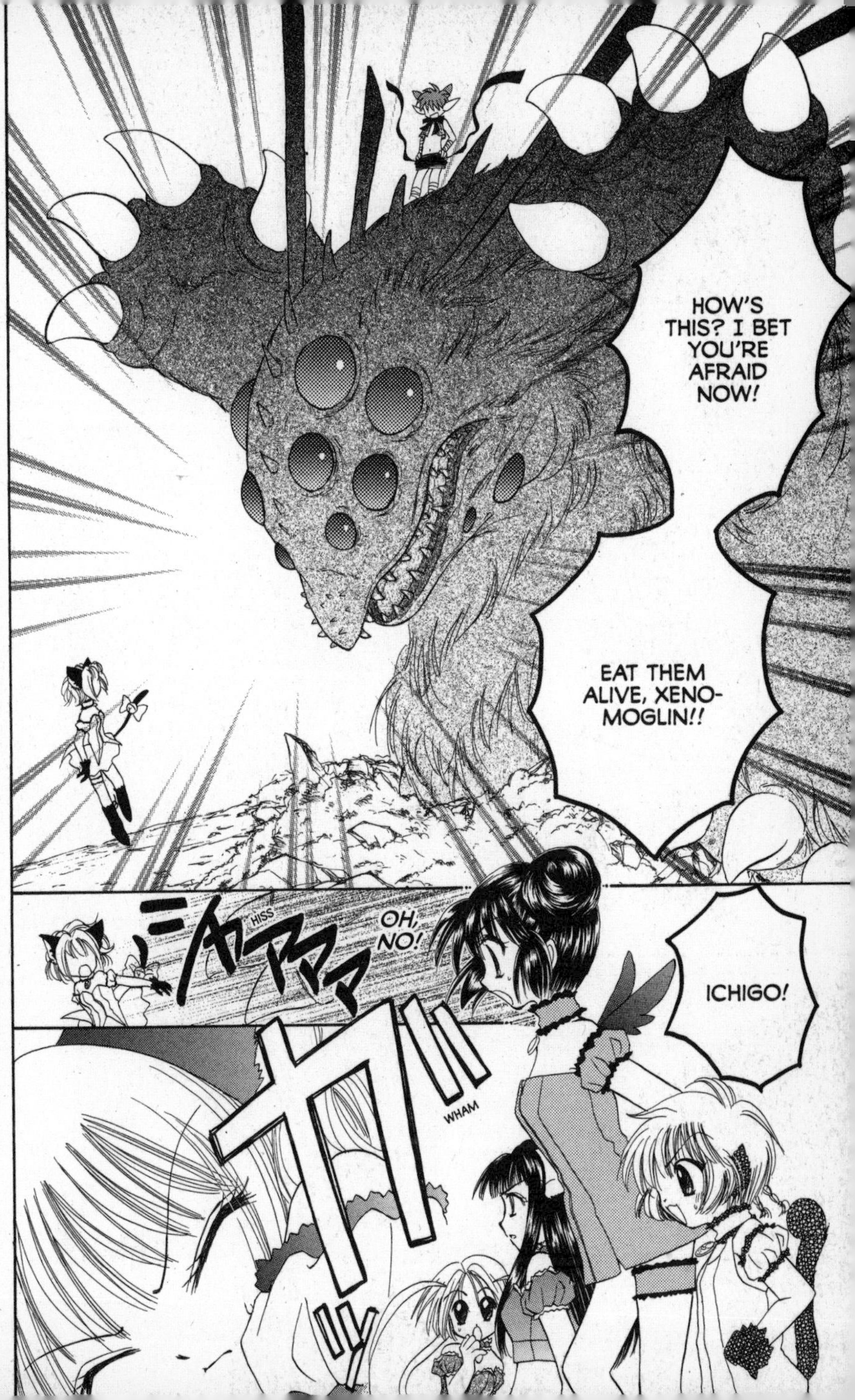
HOW'S THIS? I BET YOU'RE AFRAID NOW!
EAT THEM ALIVE, XENO-MOGLIN!!
ICHIGO!
OH, NO!
HISS
WHAM

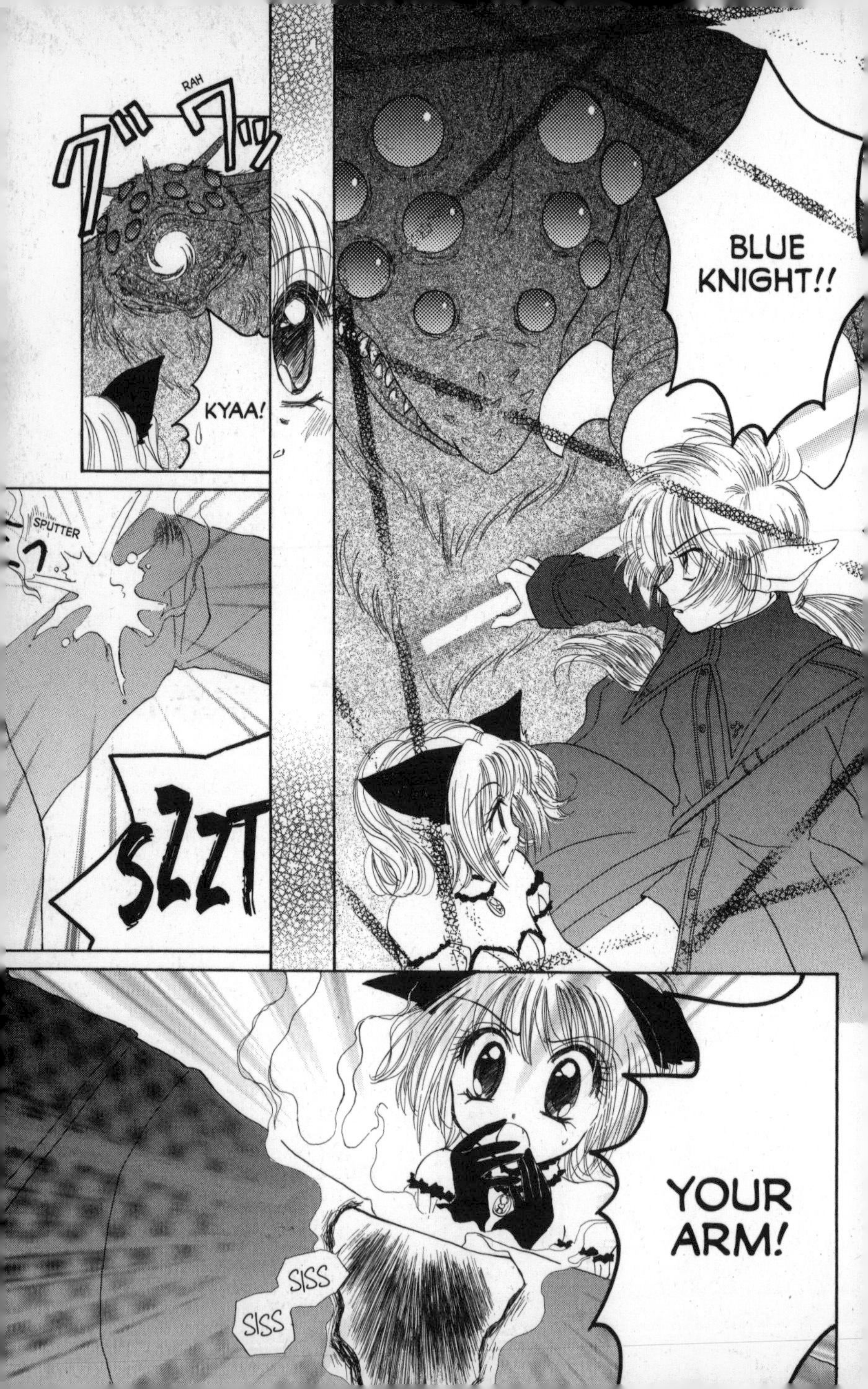
BLUE KNIGHT!!
RAH
KYAA!
SPUTTER
SZZT
YOUR ARM!
SISS
SISS

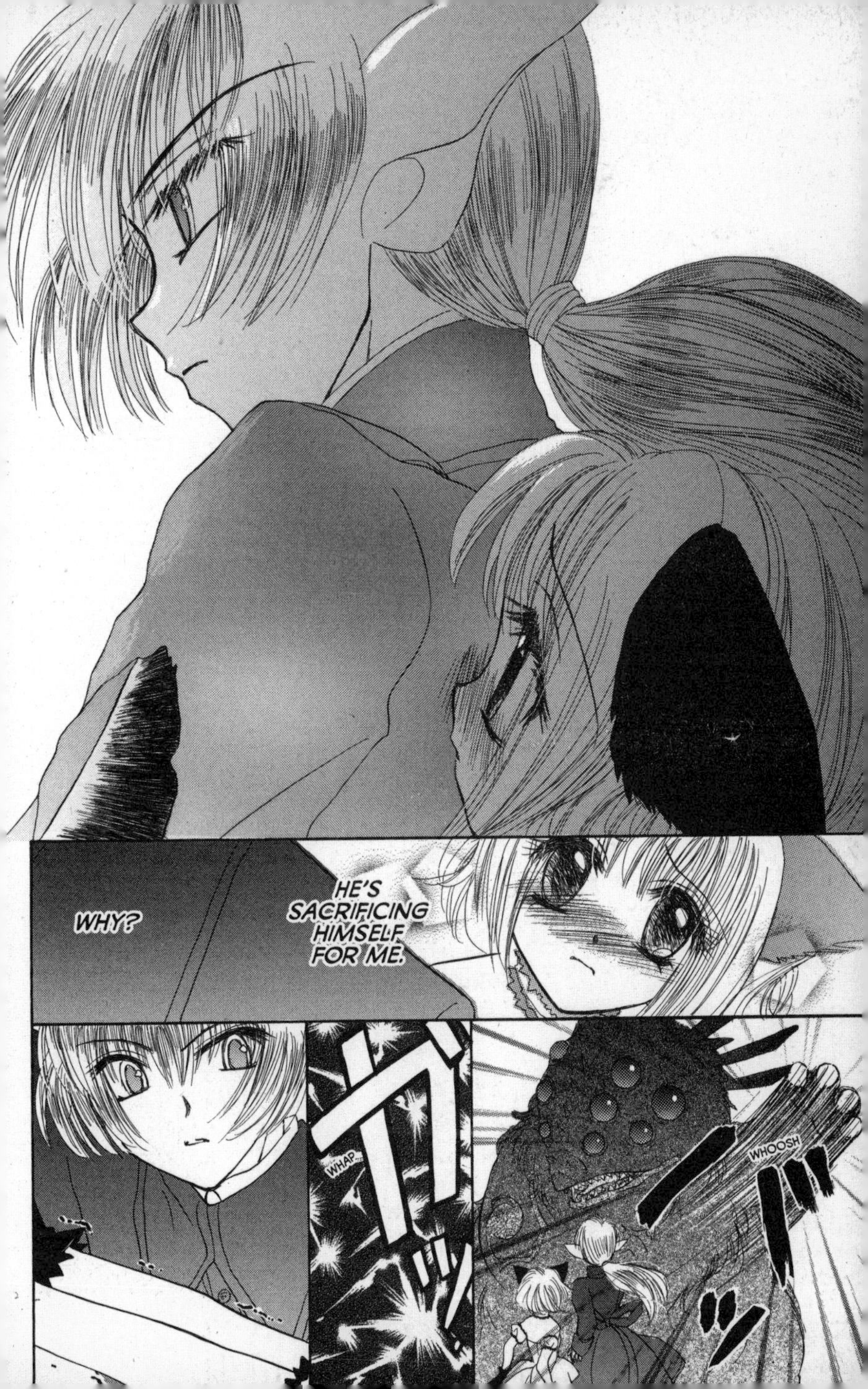
HE'S SACRIFICING HIMSELF FOR ME.
WHY?
WHOOSH
WHAP

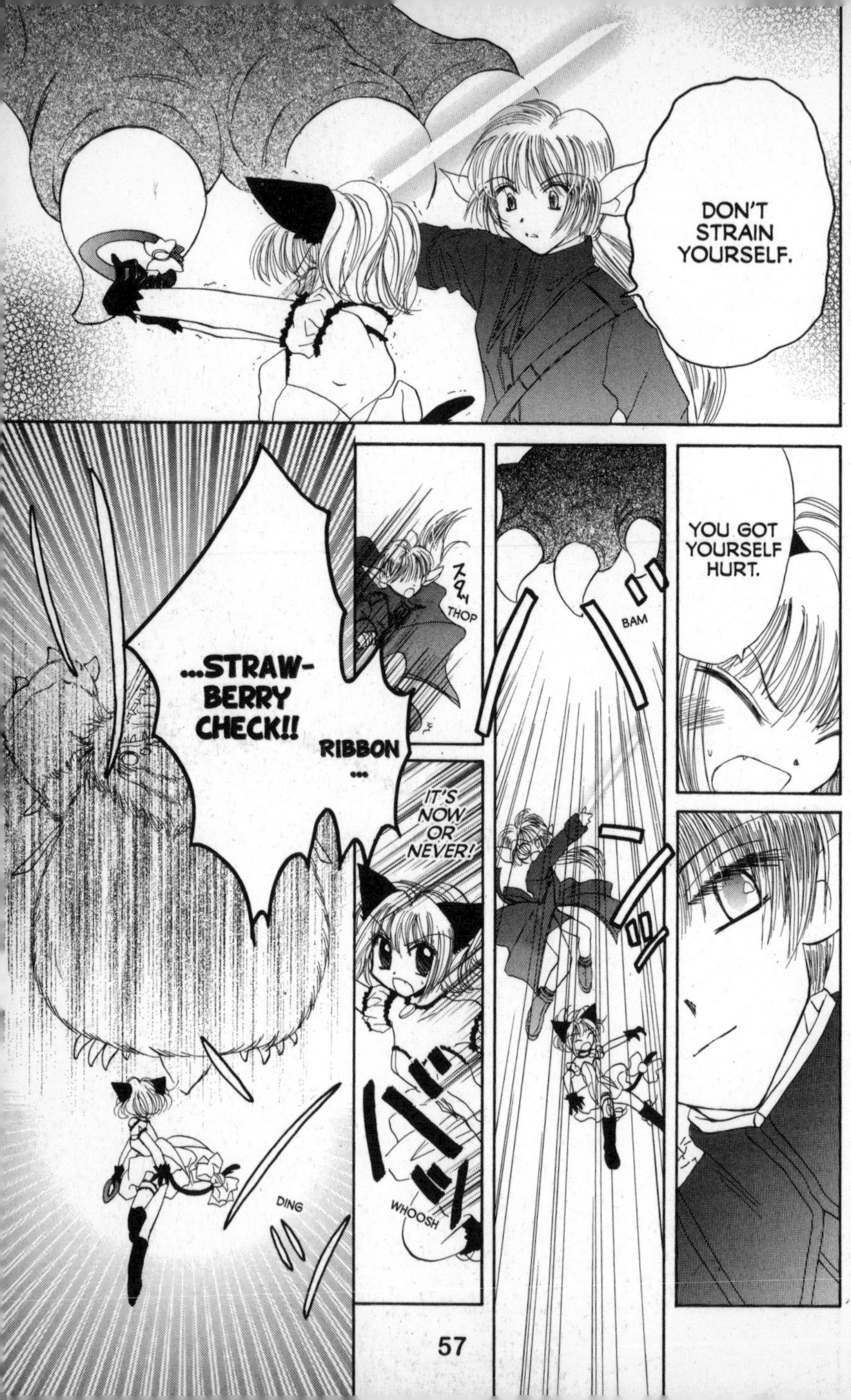
DON'T STRAIN YOURSELF.
YOU GOT YOURSELF HURT.
BAM
THOP
IT'S NOW OR NEVER!
WHOOSH
RIBBON ...
...STRAW-BERRY CHECK!!
DING

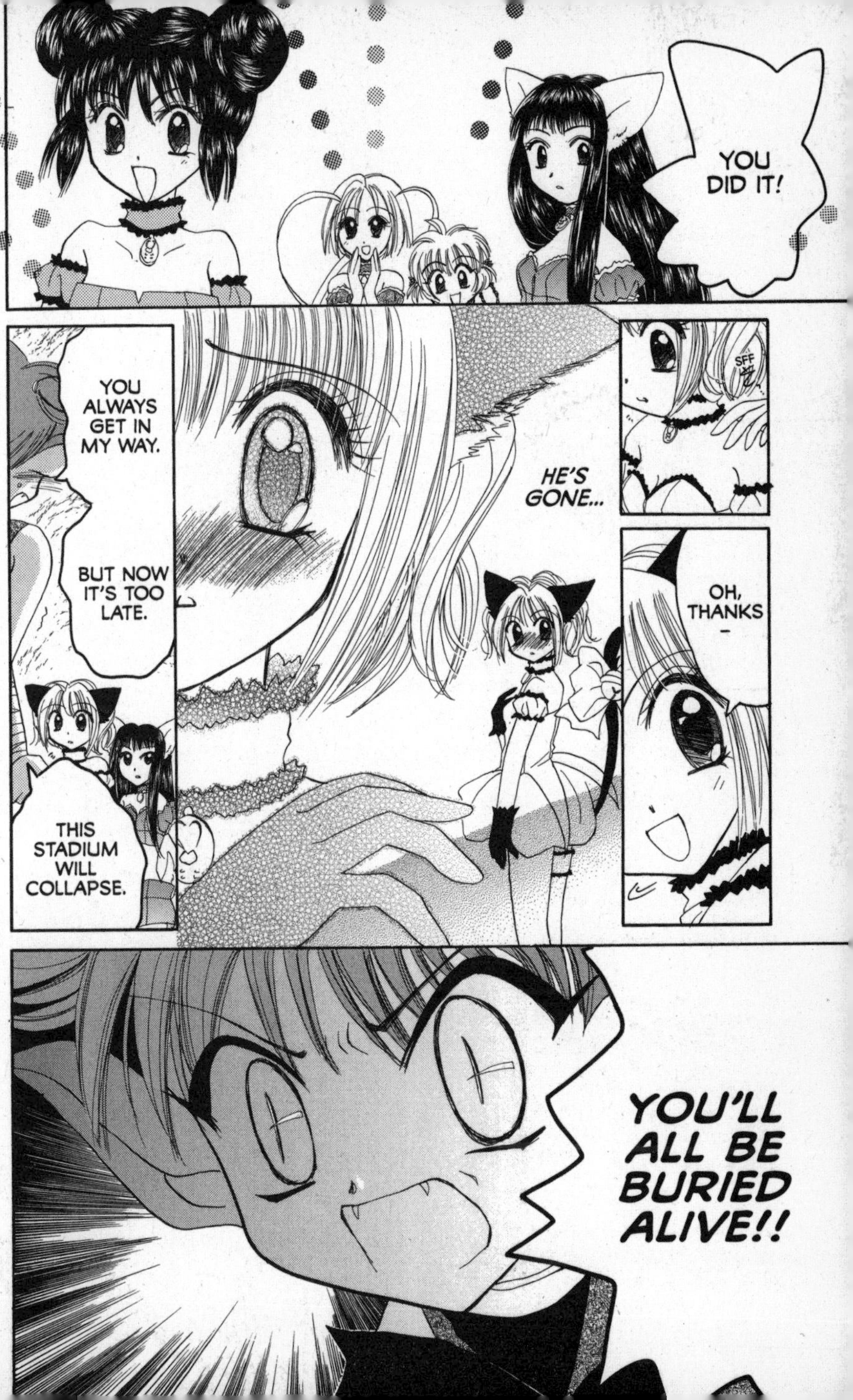
YOU DID IT!
SFF
HE'S GONE...
OH, THANKS –
YOU ALWAYS GET IN MY WAY.
BUT NOW IT'S TOO LATE.
THIS STADIUM WILL COLLAPSE.
YOU'LL ALL BE BURIED ALIVE!!

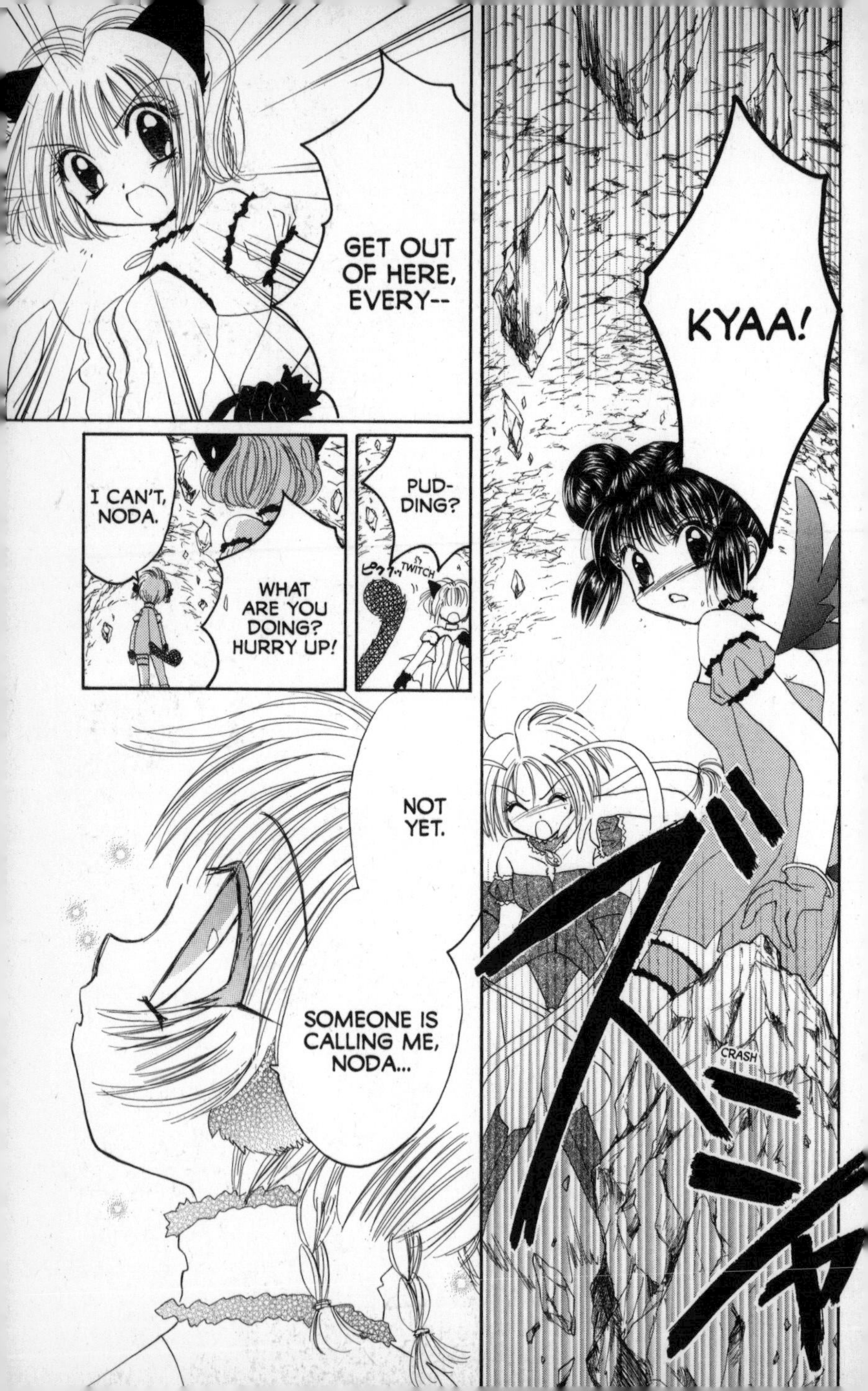
KYAA!
CRASH
GET OUT OF HERE, EVERY--
PUD-DING?
TWITCH
WHAT ARE YOU DOING? HURRY UP!
I CAN'T, NODA.
NOT YET.
SOMEONE IS CALLING ME, NODA...

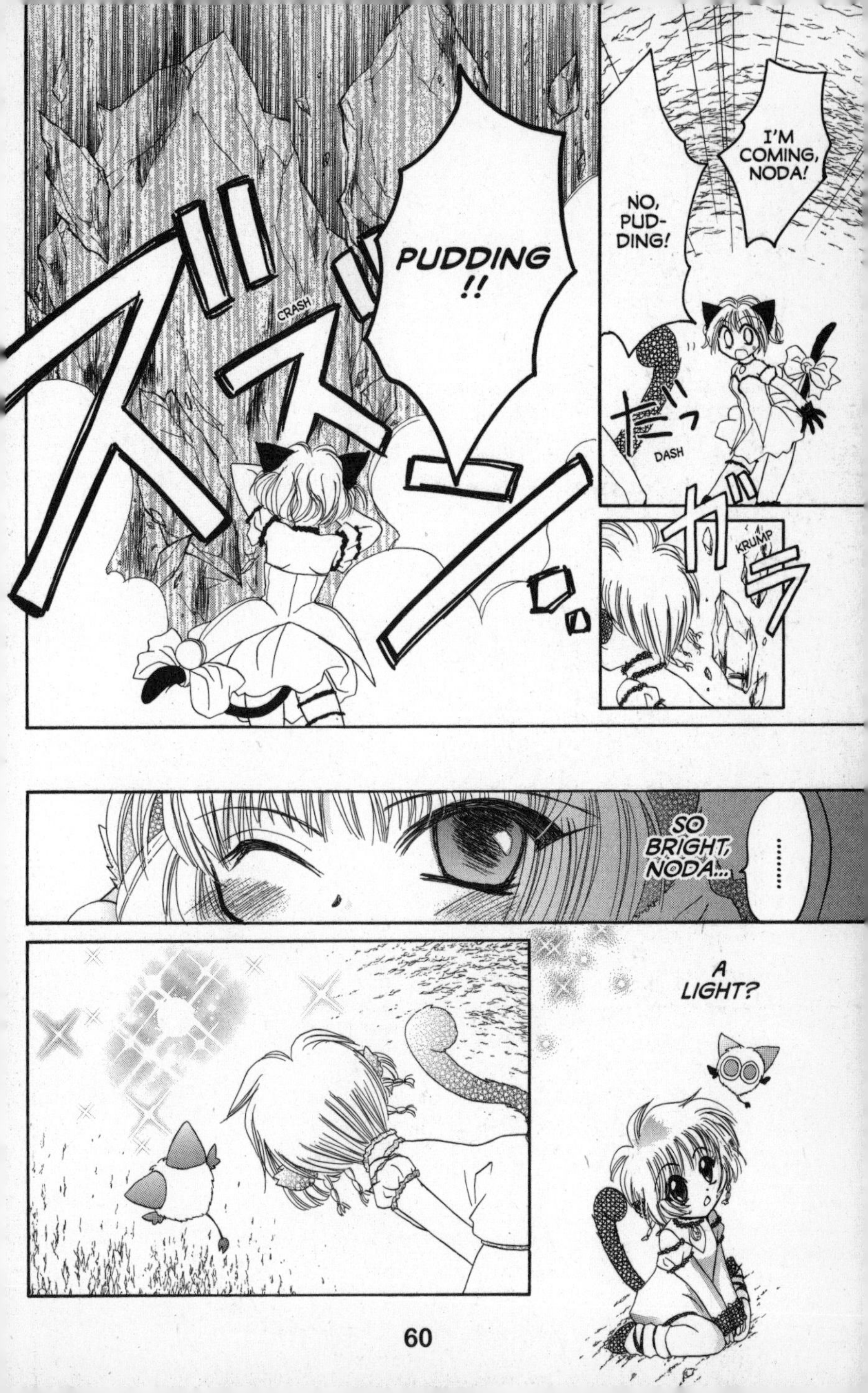
I'M COMING, NODA!
NO, PUD-DING!
DASH
KRUMP
PUDDING !!
CRASH
......
SO BRIGHT, NODA...
A LIGHT?

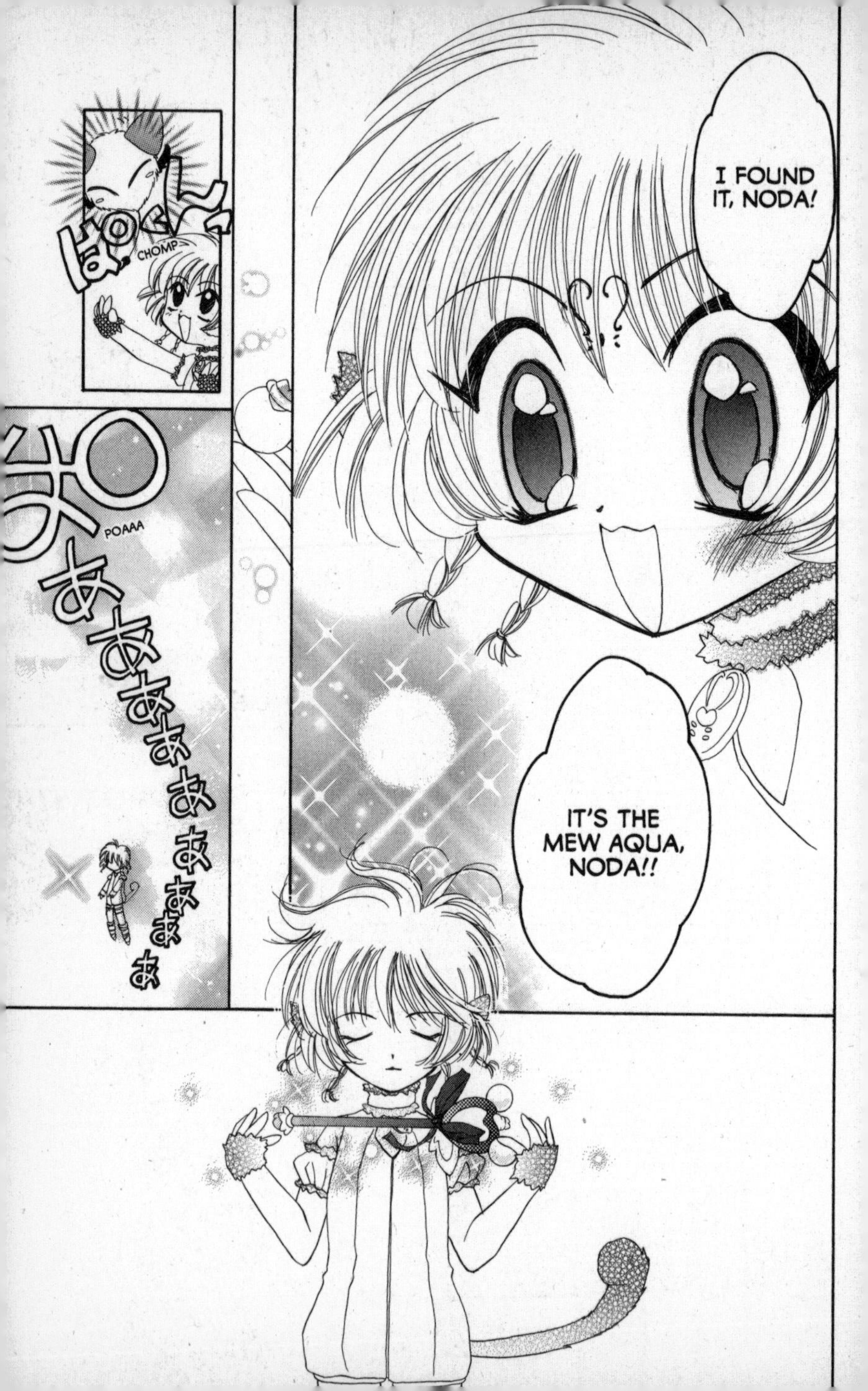
I FOUND IT, NODA!
IT'S THE MEW AQUA, NODA!!
ぱくん～
CHOMP
ぽあああああああああ
POAAA

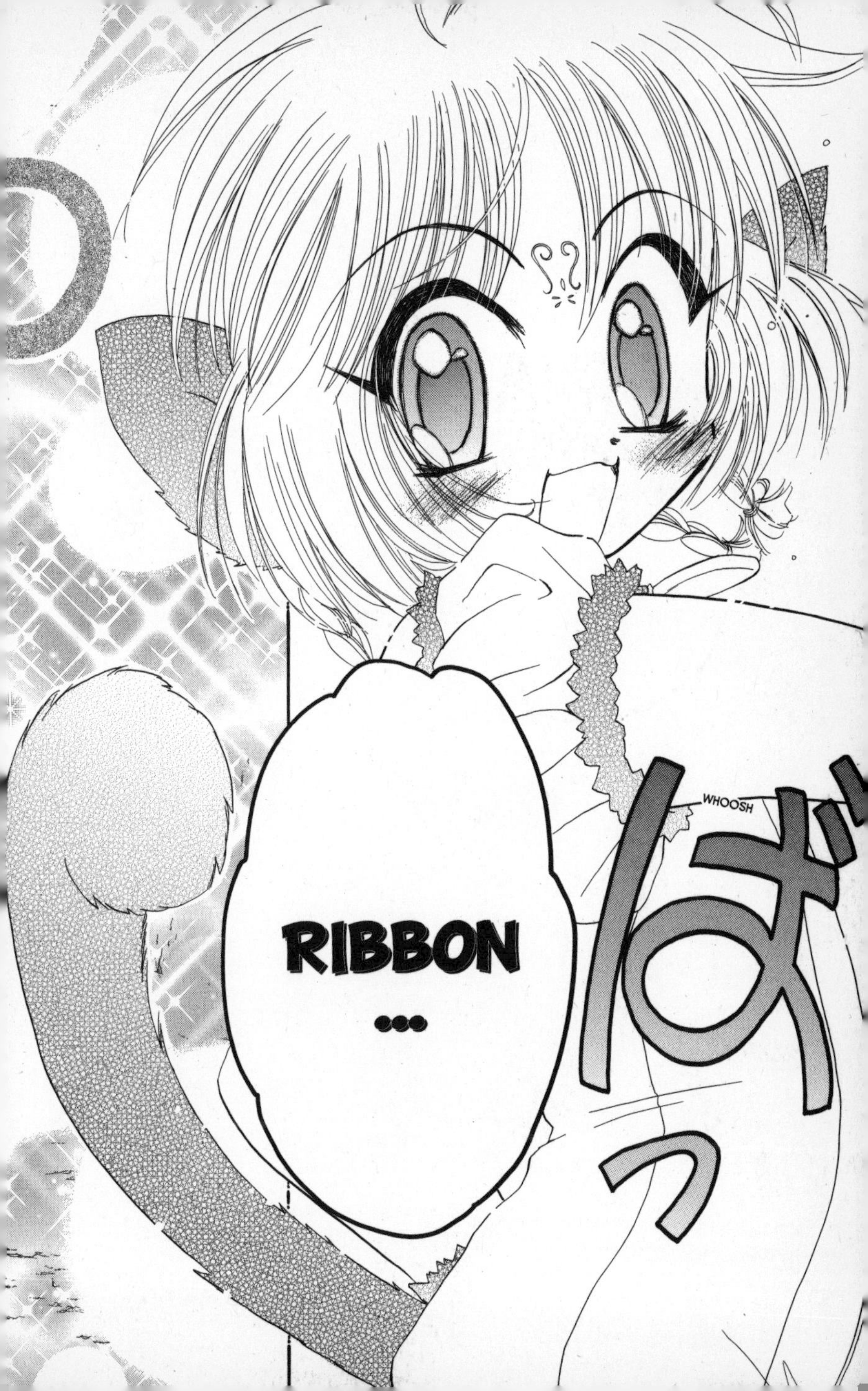
RIBBON
...
WHOOSH
ばっ

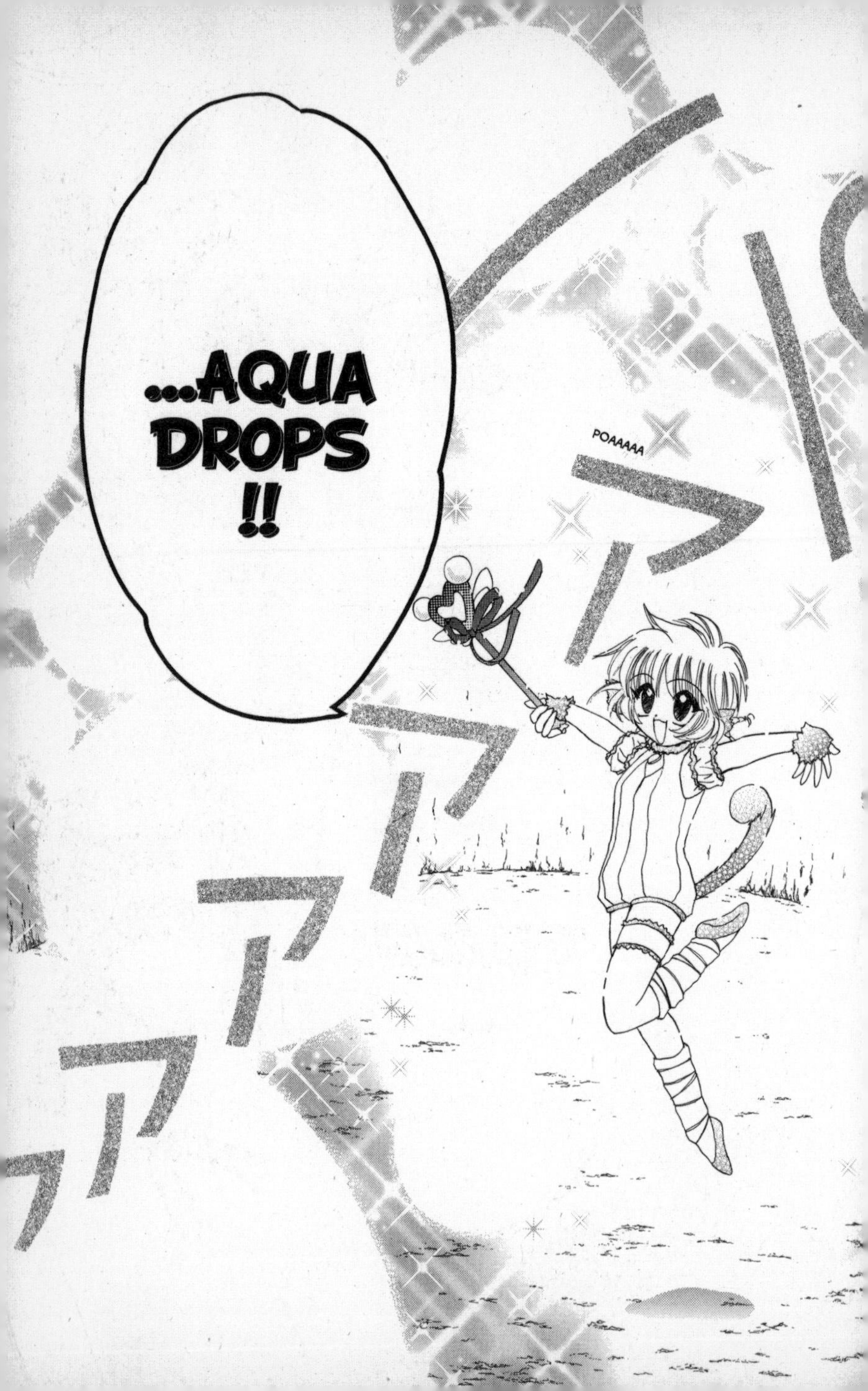
...AQUA DROPS !!
POAAAAA

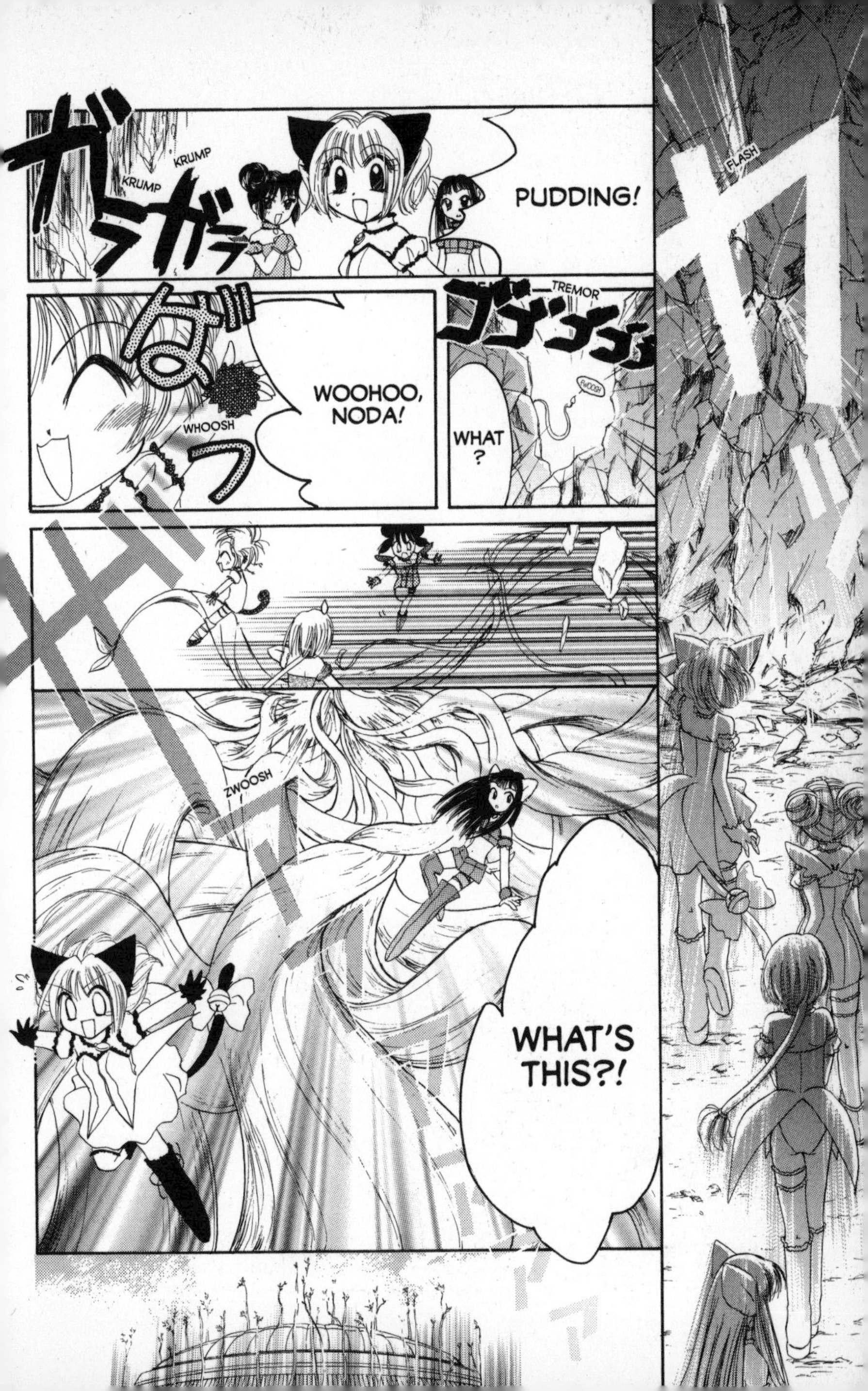
FLASH
PUDDING!
KRUMP
KRUMP
TREMOR
FWOOSH
WHAT?
WOOHOO, NODA!
WHOOSH
ZWOOSH
WHAT'S THIS?!

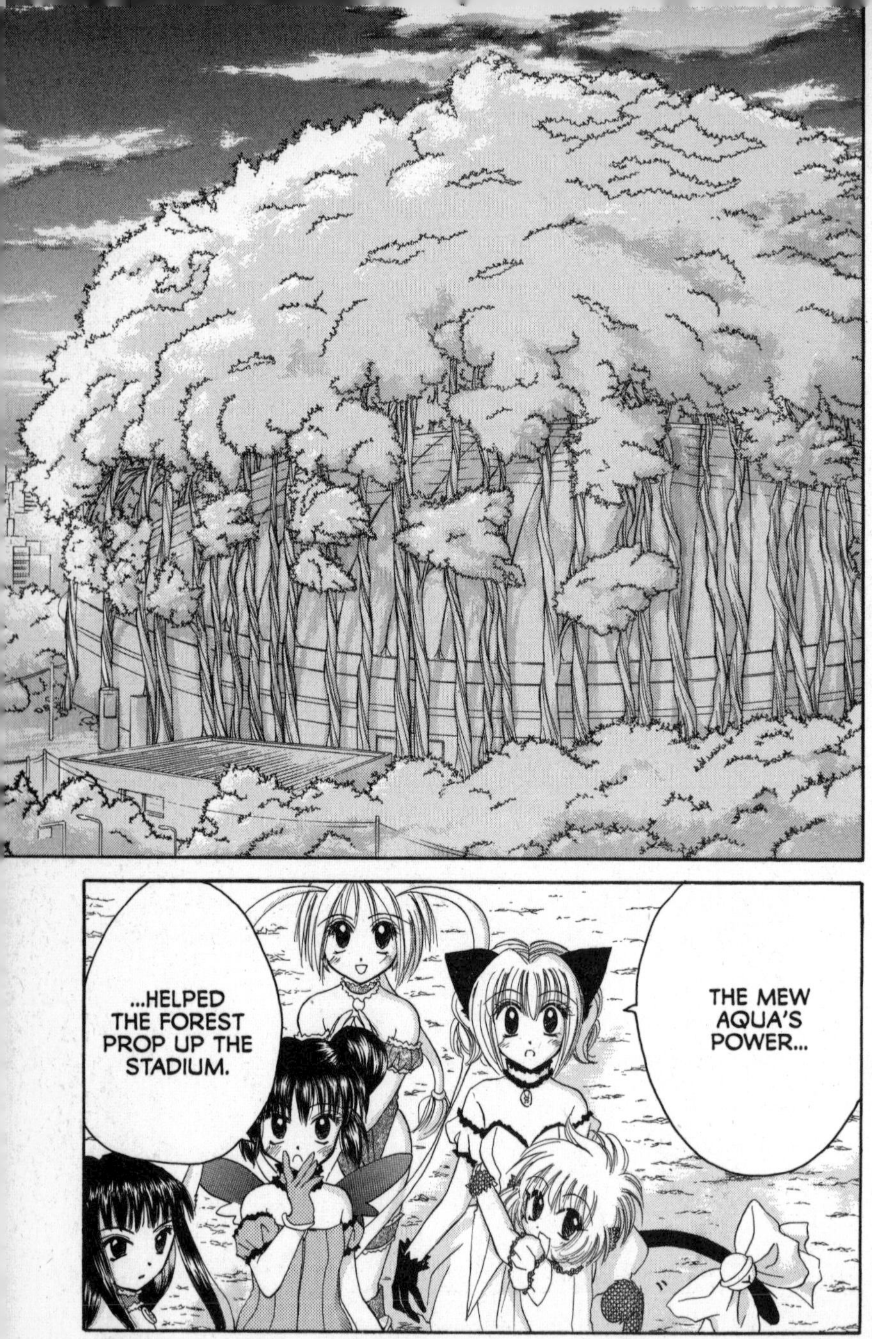
THE MEW AQUA'S POWER...
...HELPED THE FOREST PROP UP THE STADIUM.

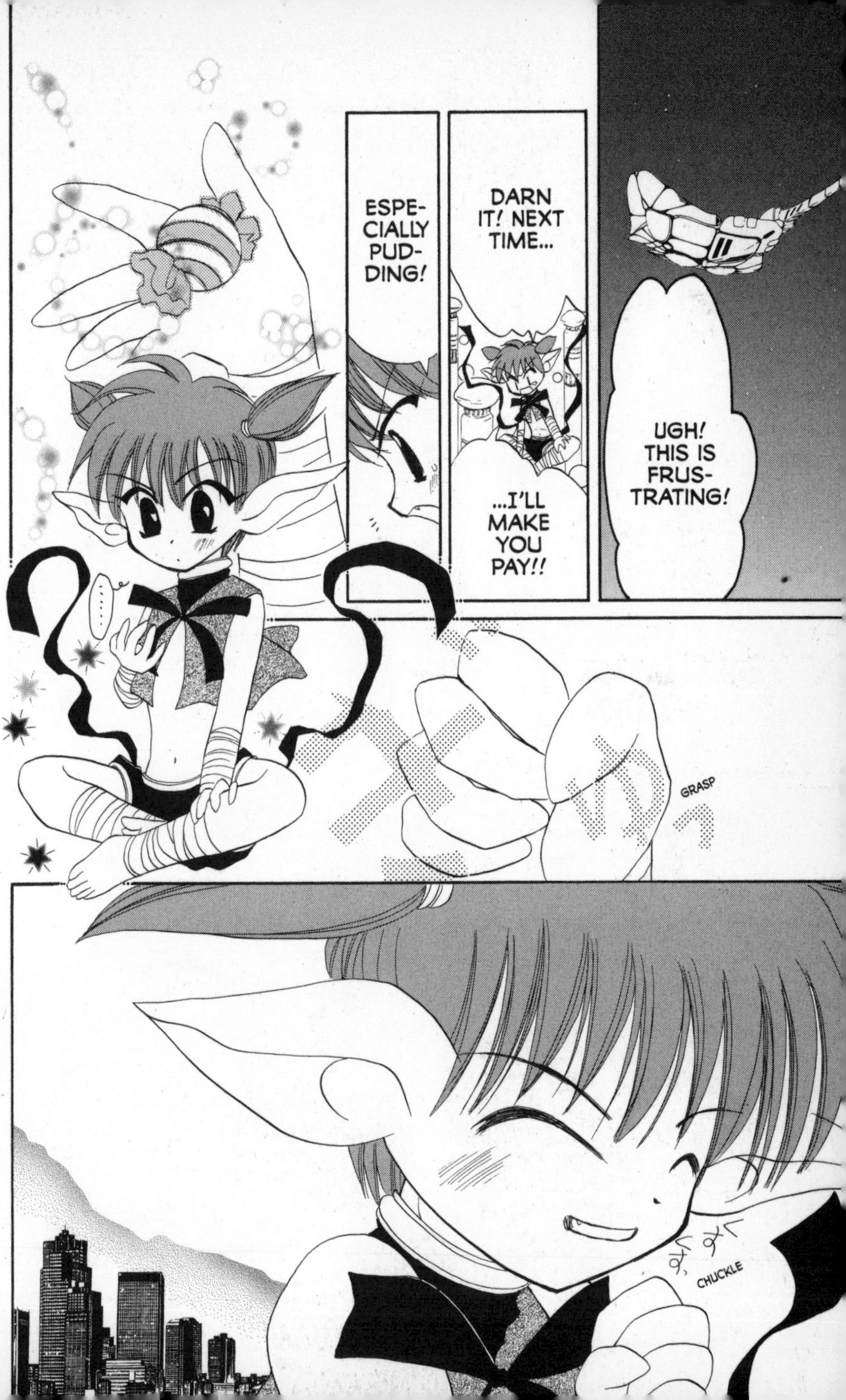
UGH! THIS IS FRUS- TRATING!
DARN IT! NEXT TIME...
...I'LL MAKE YOU PAY!!
ESPE- CIALLY PUD- DING!
GRASP
.....
CHUCKLE

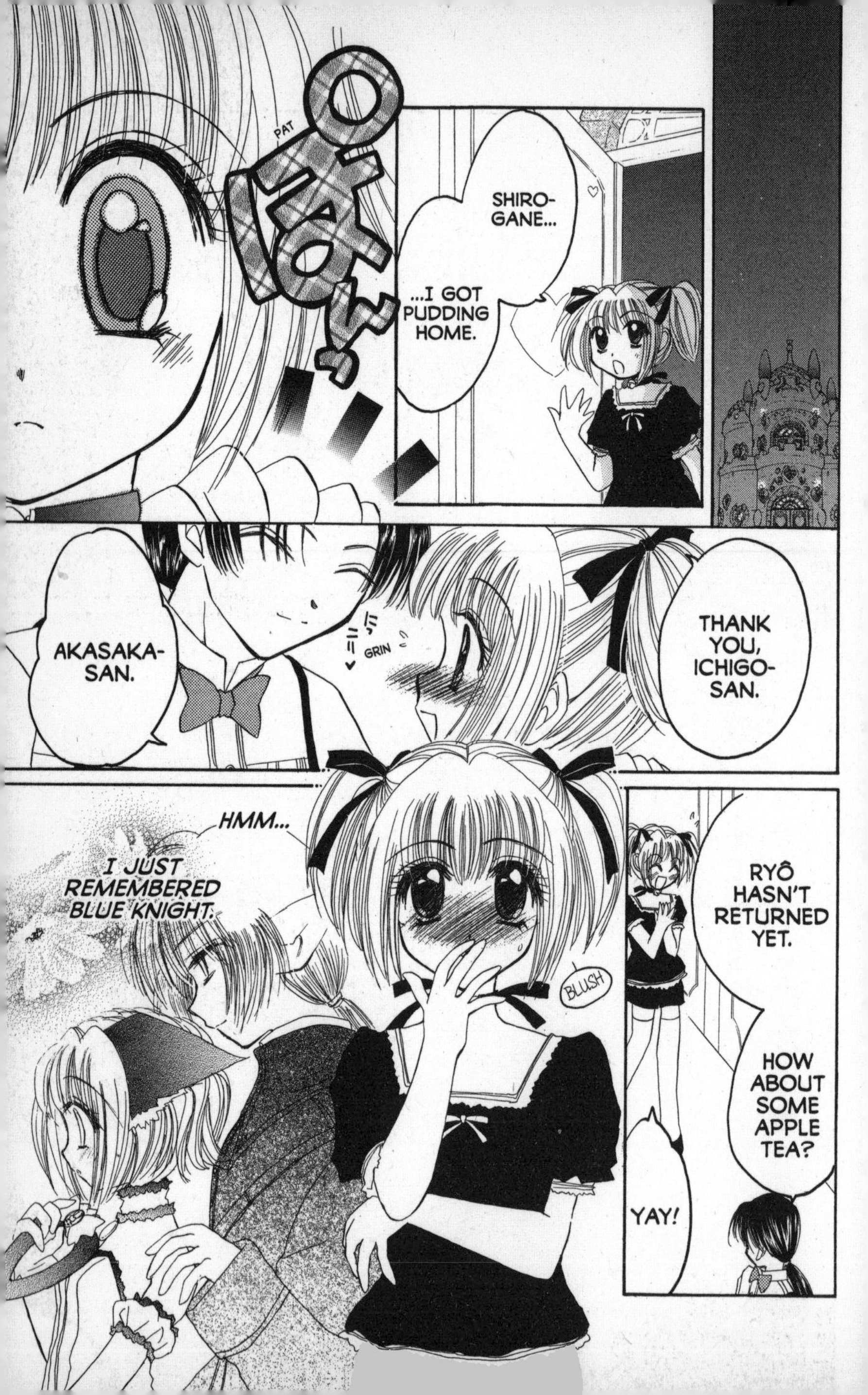
SHIRO-GANE...
...I GOT PUDDING HOME.
PAT
ぽん!
THANK YOU, ICHIGO-SAN.
GRIN
AKASAKA-SAN.
RYÔ HASN'T RETURNED YET.
HOW ABOUT SOME APPLE TEA?
YAY!
BLUSH
HMM...
I JUST REMEMBERED BLUE KNIGHT.

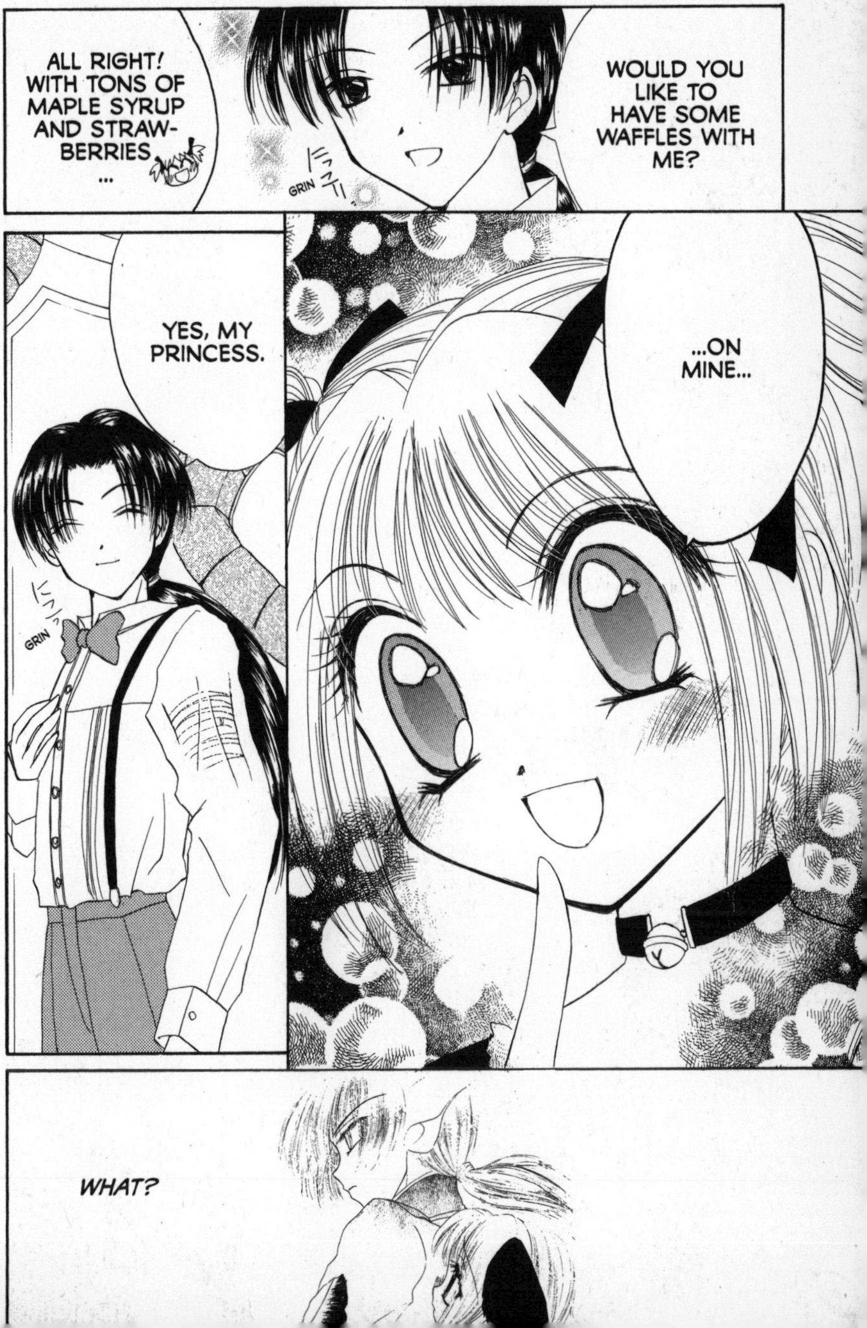
WOULD YOU LIKE TO HAVE SOME WAFFLES WITH ME?
GRIN
ALL RIGHT! WITH TONS OF MAPLE SYRUP AND STRAW-BERRIES ...
...ON MINE...
YES, MY PRINCESS.
GRIN
WHAT?

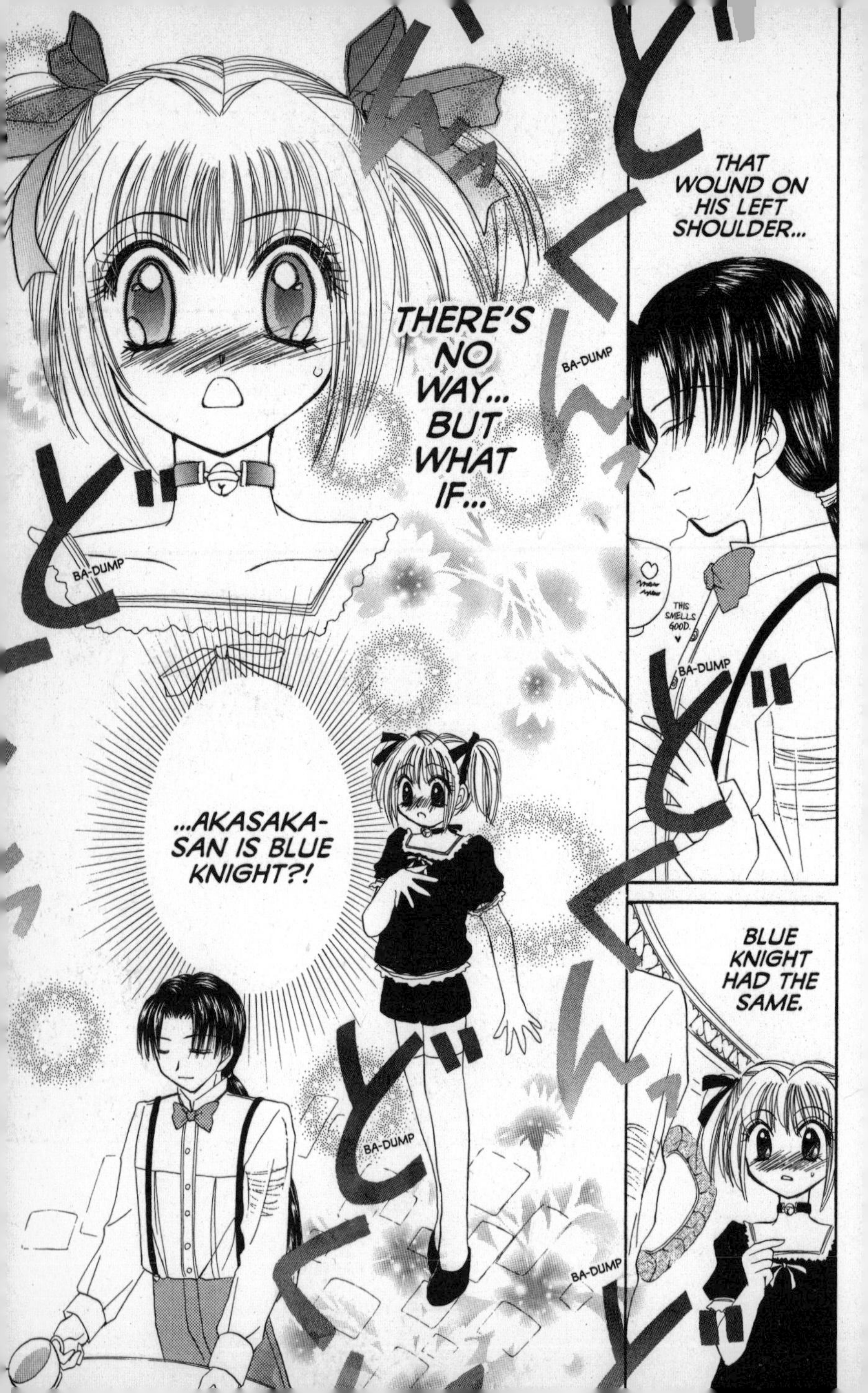
THAT WOUND ON HIS LEFT SHOULDER...
BA-DUMP
THIS SMELLS GOOD.
BA-DUMP
BLUE KNIGHT HAD THE SAME.
BA-DUMP
THERE'S NO WAY... BUT WHAT IF...
BA-DUMP
...AKASAKA-SAN IS BLUE KNIGHT?!
BA-DUMP

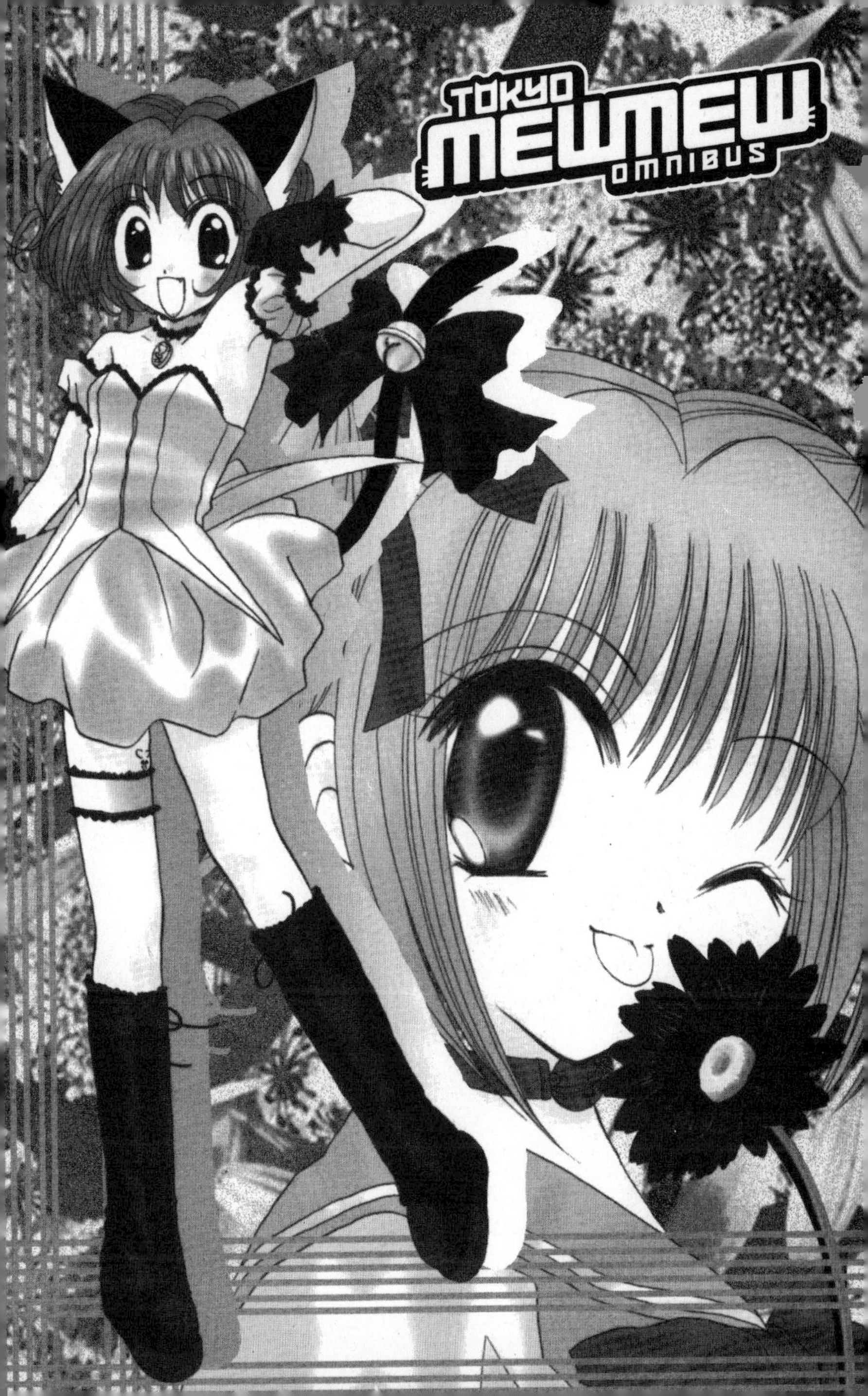
TOKYO MEWMEW OMNIBUS

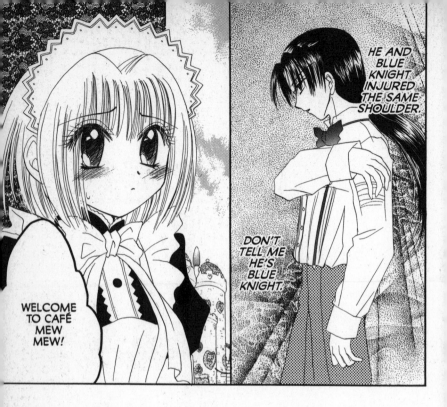

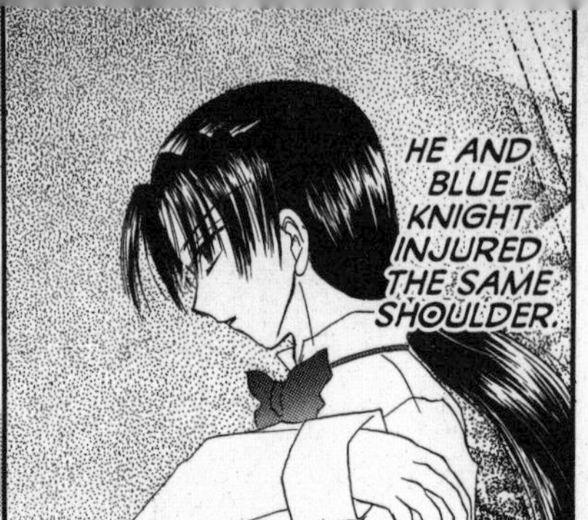
HE AND BLUE KNIGHT INJURED THE SAME SHOULDER.
DON'T TELL ME HE'S BLUE KNIGHT.
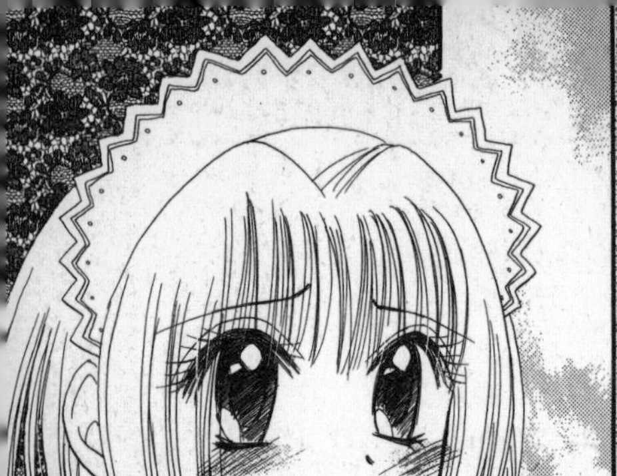
WELCOME TO CAFÉ MEW MEW!
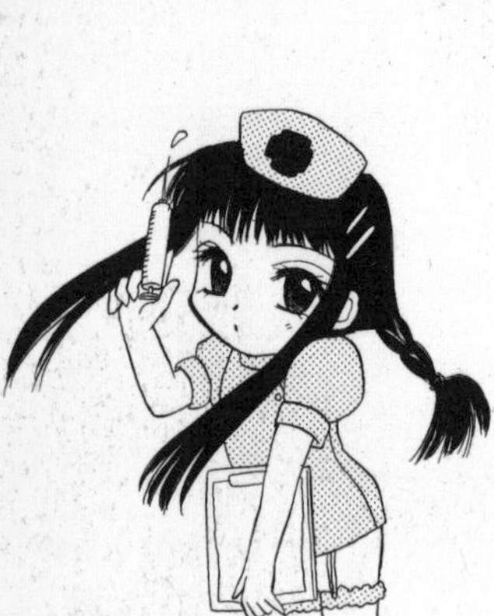

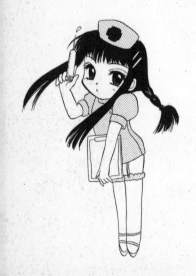

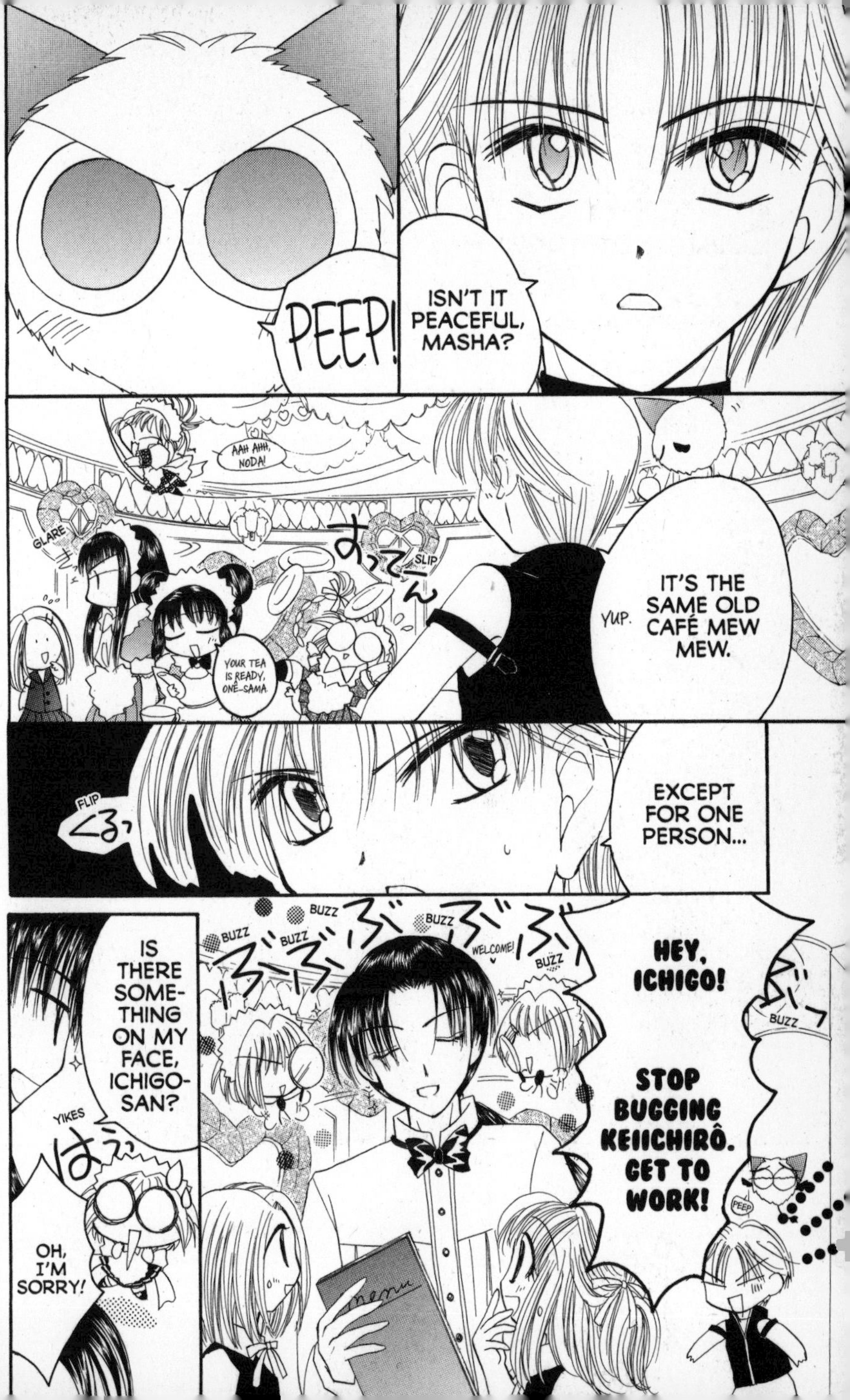

ISN'T IT PEACEFUL, MASHA?
PEEP!
IT'S THE SAME OLD CAFÉ MEW MEW.
YUP.
SLIP
AAH AHH, NODA!
GLARE
YOUR TEA IS READY, ONĒ-SAMA.
EXCEPT FOR ONE PERSON...
FLIP
HEY, ICHIGO!
STOP BUGGING KEIICHIRÔ. GET TO WORK!
BUZZ
PEEP
BUZZ
BUZZ
WELCOME!
BUZZ
BUZZ
BUZZ
IS THERE SOMETHING ON MY FACE, ICHIGO-SAN?
YIKES
OH, I'M SORRY!

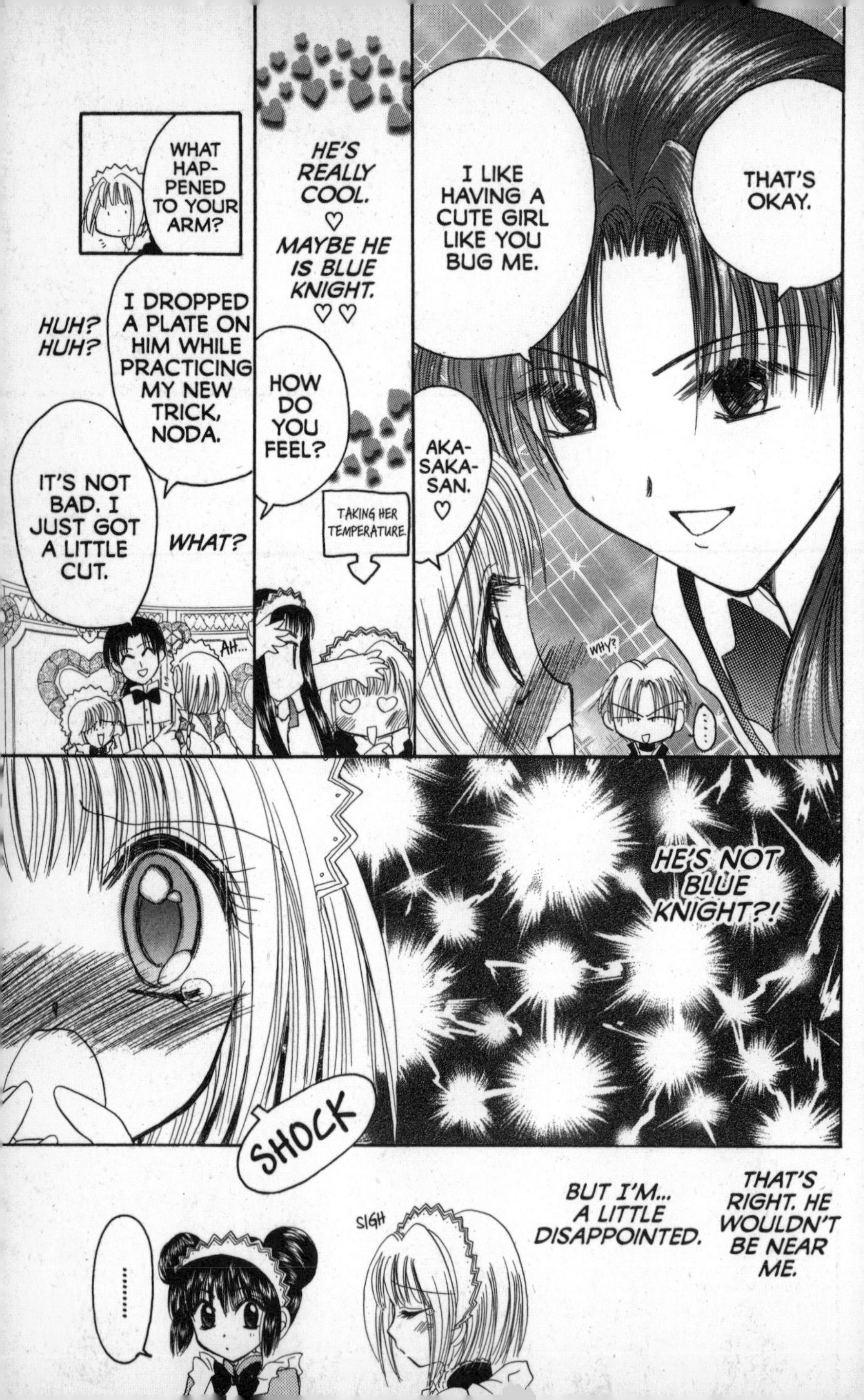
THAT'S OKAY.
I LIKE HAVING A CUTE GIRL LIKE YOU BUG ME.
AKA-SAKA-SAN. ♡
WHY?
...
HE'S REALLY COOL. ♡ MAYBE HE IS BLUE KNIGHT. ♡♡
HOW DO YOU FEEL?
TAKING HER TEMPERATURE.
WHAT HAP-PENED TO YOUR ARM?
I DROPPED A PLATE ON HIM WHILE PRACTICING MY NEW TRICK, NODA.
HUH? HUH?
IT'S NOT BAD. I JUST GOT A LITTLE CUT.
WHAT?
AH...
HE'S NOT BLUE KNIGHT?!
SHOCK
THAT'S RIGHT. HE WOULDN'T BE NEAR ME.
BUT I'M... A LITTLE DISAPPOINTED.
SIGH
....

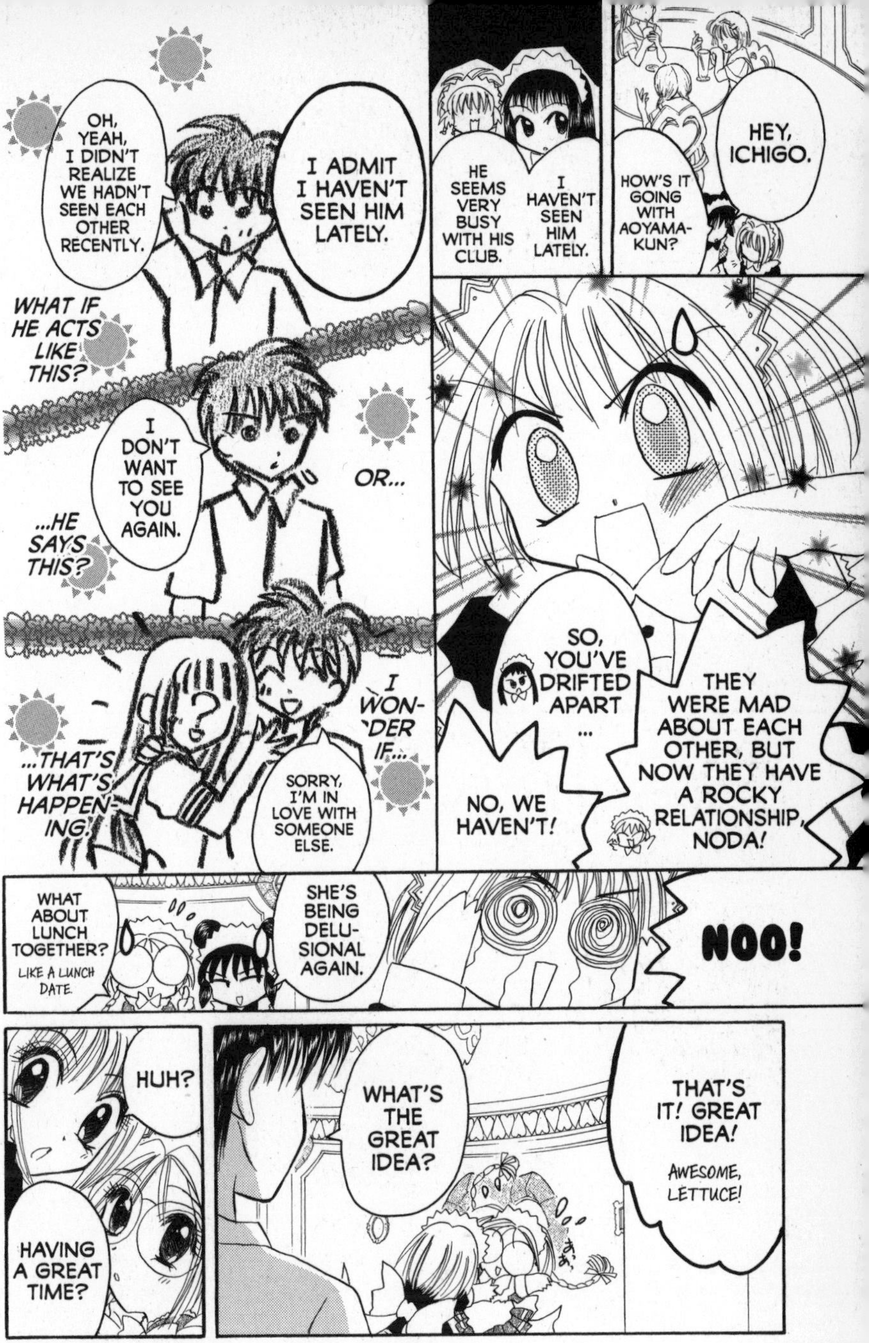
HEY, ICHIGO.
HOW'S IT GOING WITH AOYAMA-KUN?
I HAVEN'T SEEN HIM LATELY.
HE SEEMS VERY BUSY WITH HIS CLUB.
SO, YOU'VE DRIFTED APART ...
THEY WERE MAD ABOUT EACH OTHER, BUT NOW THEY HAVE A ROCKY RELATIONSHIP, NODA!
NO, WE HAVEN'T!
I ADMIT I HAVEN'T SEEN HIM LATELY.
OH, YEAH, I DIDN'T REALIZE WE HADN'T SEEN EACH OTHER RECENTLY.
WHAT IF HE ACTS LIKE THIS?
OR...
I DON'T WANT TO SEE YOU AGAIN.
...HE SAYS THIS?
I WONDER IF...
SORRY, I'M IN LOVE WITH SOMEONE ELSE.
...THAT'S WHAT'S HAPPENING.
NOO!
SHE'S BEING DELUSIONAL AGAIN.
WHAT ABOUT LUNCH TOGETHER?
LIKE A LUNCH DATE.
THAT'S IT! GREAT IDEA!
AWESOME, LETTUCE!
WHAT'S THE GREAT IDEA?
HUH?
HAVING A GREAT TIME?

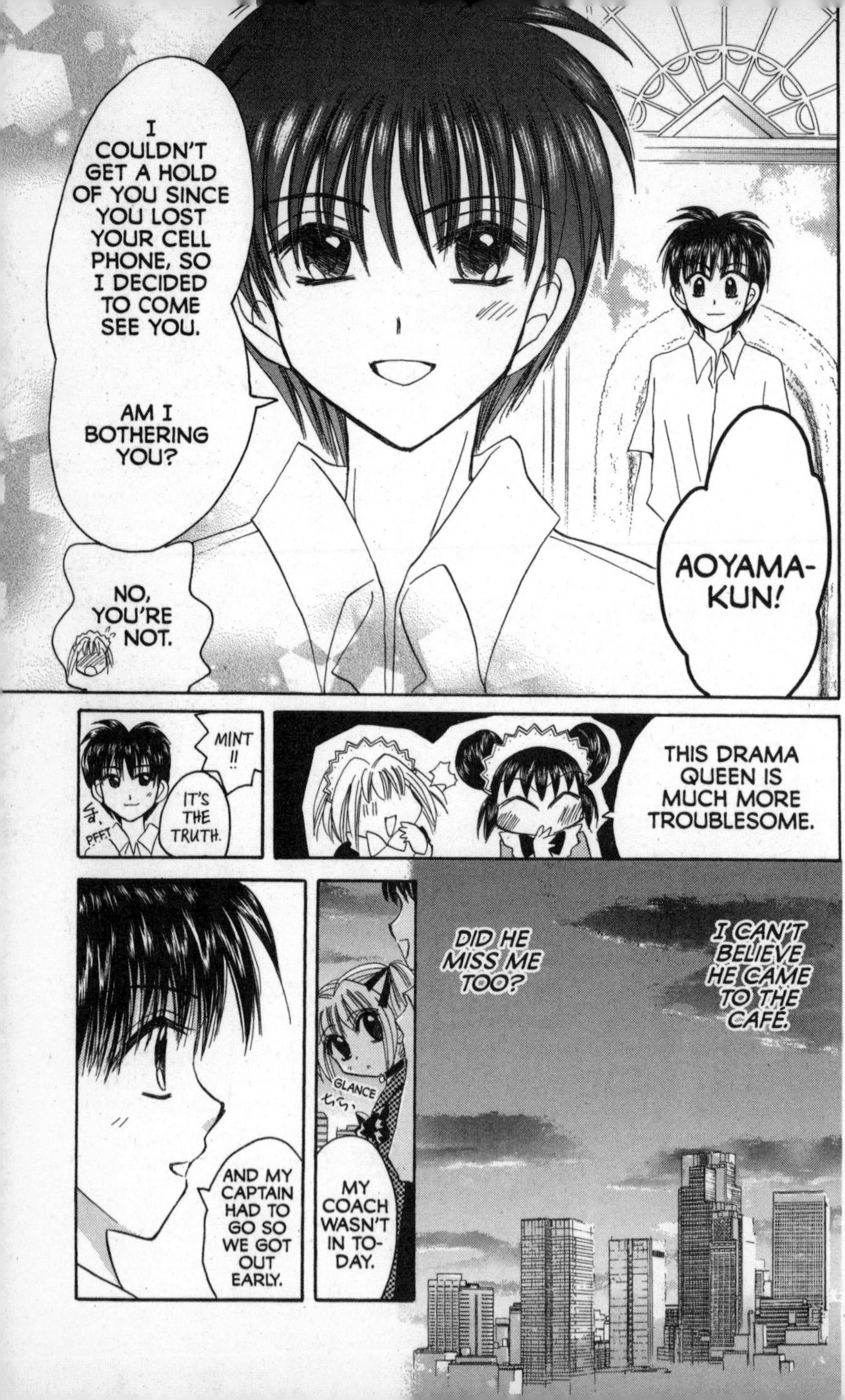
AOYAMA-KUN!
I COULDN'T GET A HOLD OF YOU SINCE YOU LOST YOUR CELL PHONE, SO I DECIDED TO COME SEE YOU.
AM I BOTHERING YOU?
NO, YOU'RE NOT.
THIS DRAMA QUEEN IS MUCH MORE TROUBLESOME.
MINT!!
IT'S THE TRUTH.
PFFT
I CAN'T BELIEVE HE CAME TO THE CAFÉ.
DID HE MISS ME TOO?
GLANCE
MY COACH WASN'T IN TO-DAY.
AND MY CAPTAIN HAD TO GO SO WE GOT OUT EARLY.

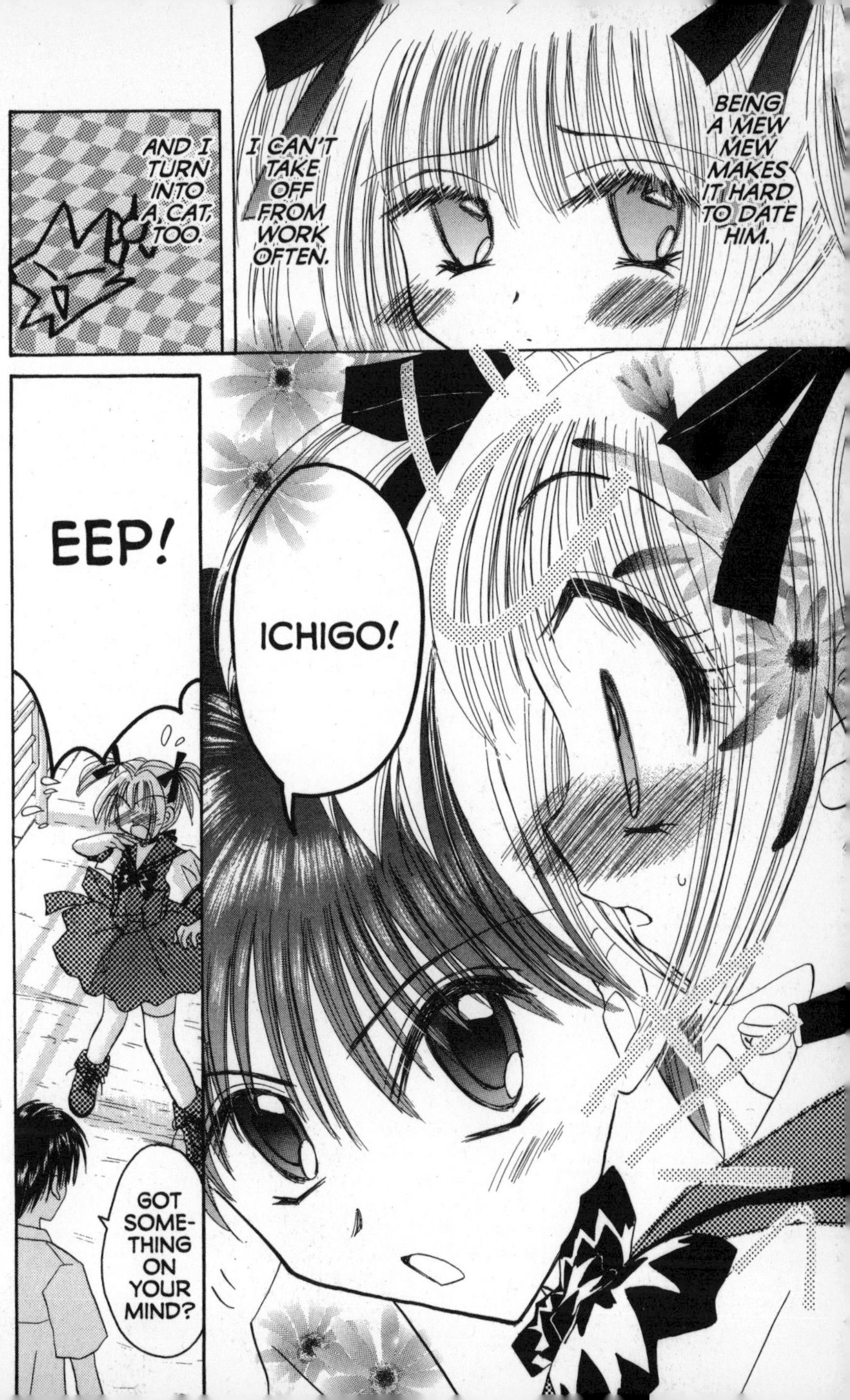
BEING A MEW MEW MAKES IT HARD TO DATE HIM.
I CAN'T TAKE OFF FROM WORK OFTEN.
AND I TURN INTO A CAT, TOO.
ICHIGO!
EEP!
GOT SOME-THING ON YOUR MIND?

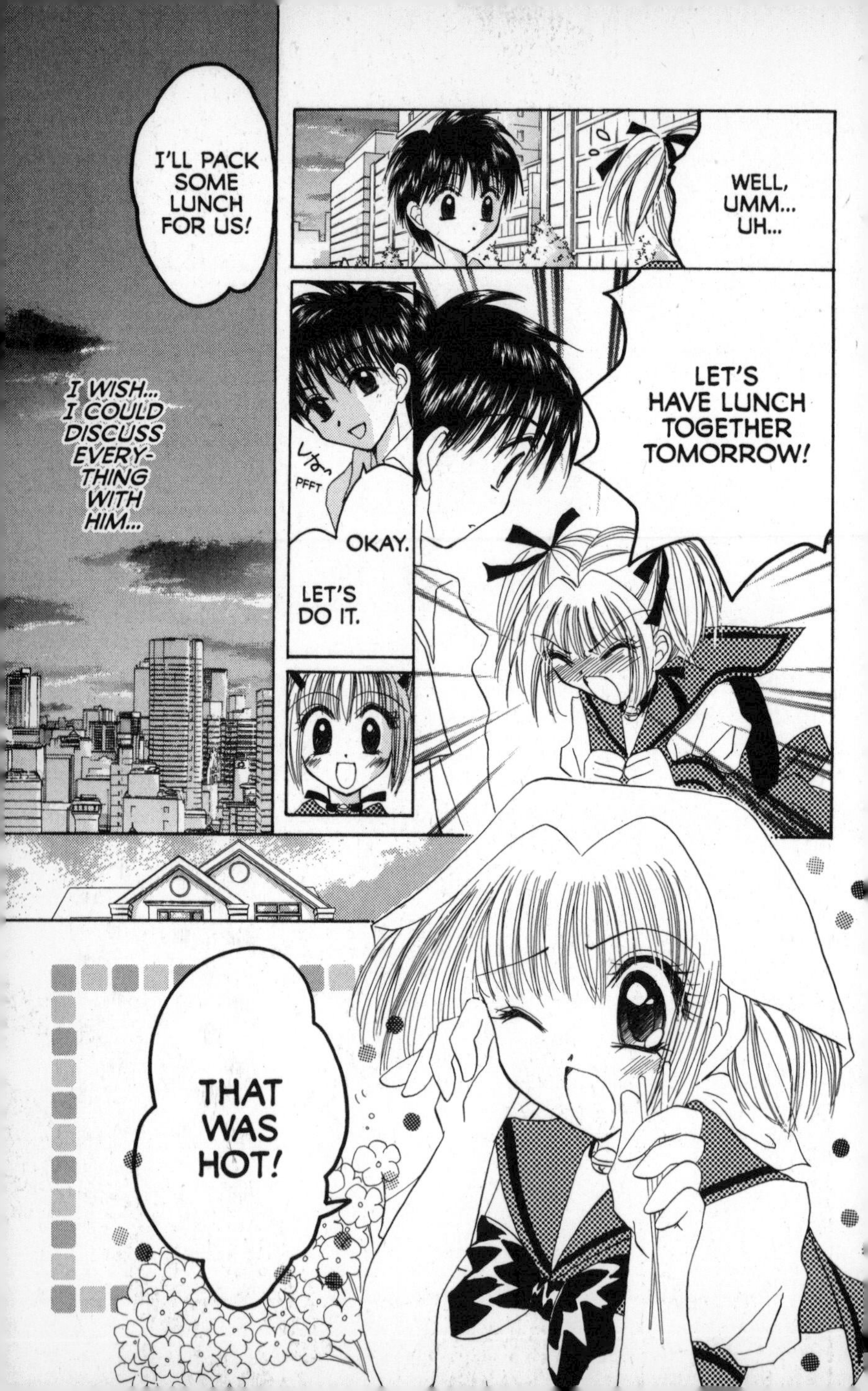
WELL, UMM... UH...
LET'S HAVE LUNCH TOGETHER TOMORROW!
PFFT
OKAY.
LET'S DO IT.
I'LL PACK SOME LUNCH FOR US!
I WISH... I COULD DISCUSS EVERY-THING WITH HIM...
THAT WAS HOT!

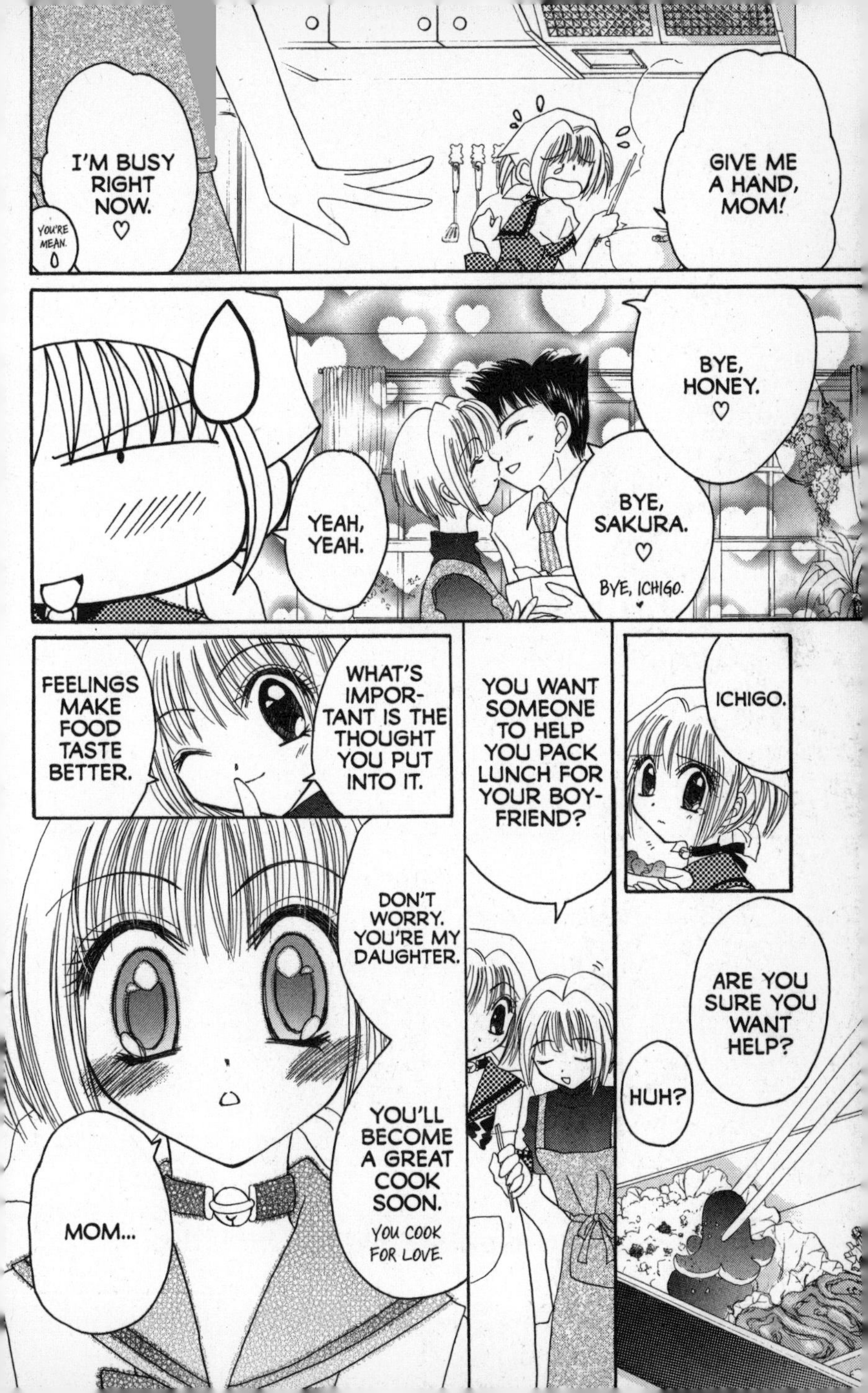
GIVE ME A HAND, MOM!
I'M BUSY RIGHT NOW. ♡
YOU'RE MEAN.
BYE, HONEY. ♡
BYE, SAKURA. ♡
BYE, ICHIGO.
YEAH, YEAH.
ICHIGO.
ARE YOU SURE YOU WANT HELP?
HUH?
YOU WANT SOMEONE TO HELP YOU PACK LUNCH FOR YOUR BOY-FRIEND?
WHAT'S IMPOR-TANT IS THE THOUGHT YOU PUT INTO IT.
FEELINGS MAKE FOOD TASTE BETTER.
DON'T WORRY. YOU'RE MY DAUGHTER.
YOU'LL BECOME A GREAT COOK SOON.
YOU COOK FOR LOVE.
MOM...

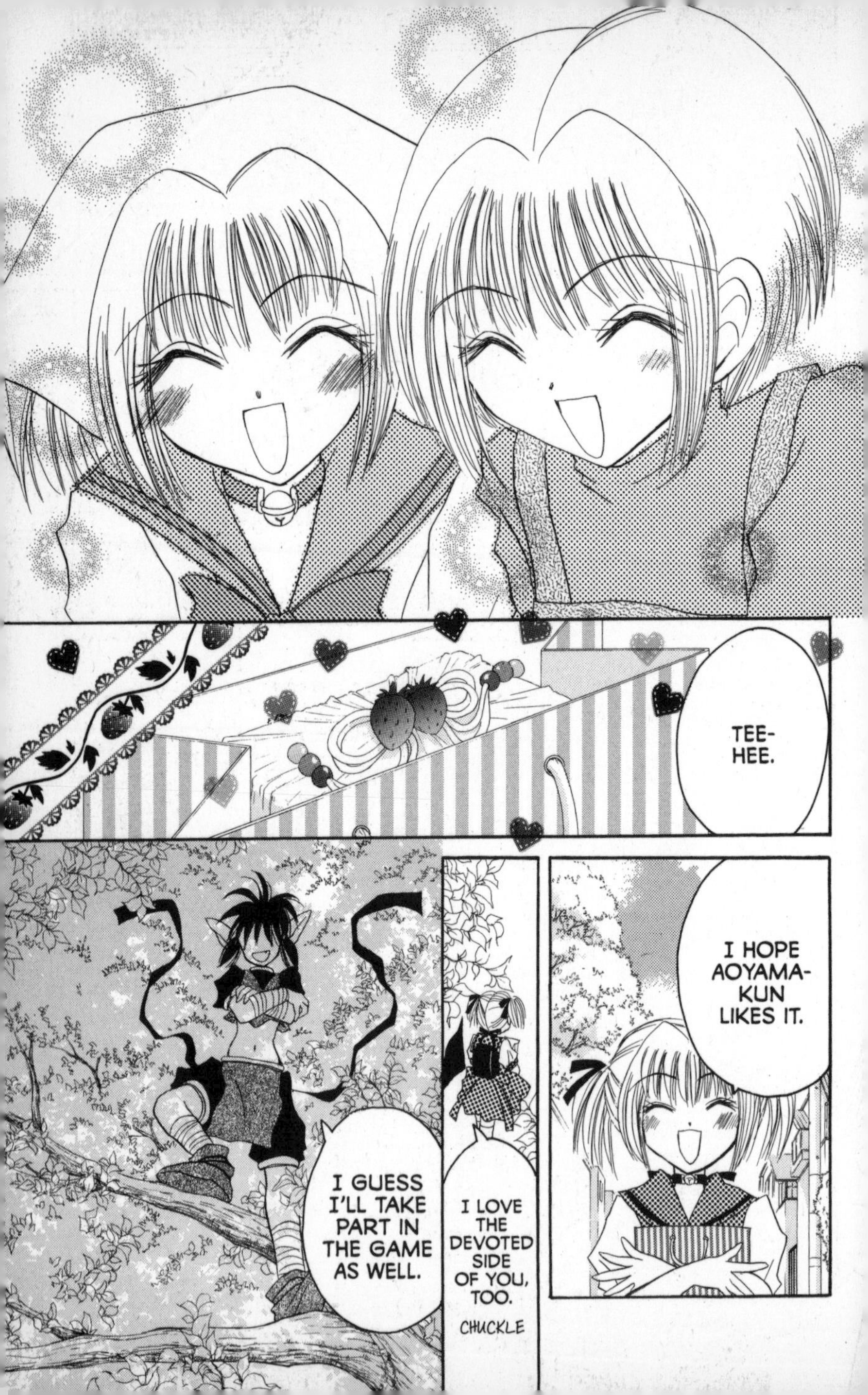
TEE-HEE.
I HOPE AOYAMA-KUN LIKES IT.
I LOVE THE DEVOTED SIDE OF YOU, TOO.
CHUCKLE
I GUESS I'LL TAKE PART IN THE GAME AS WELL.

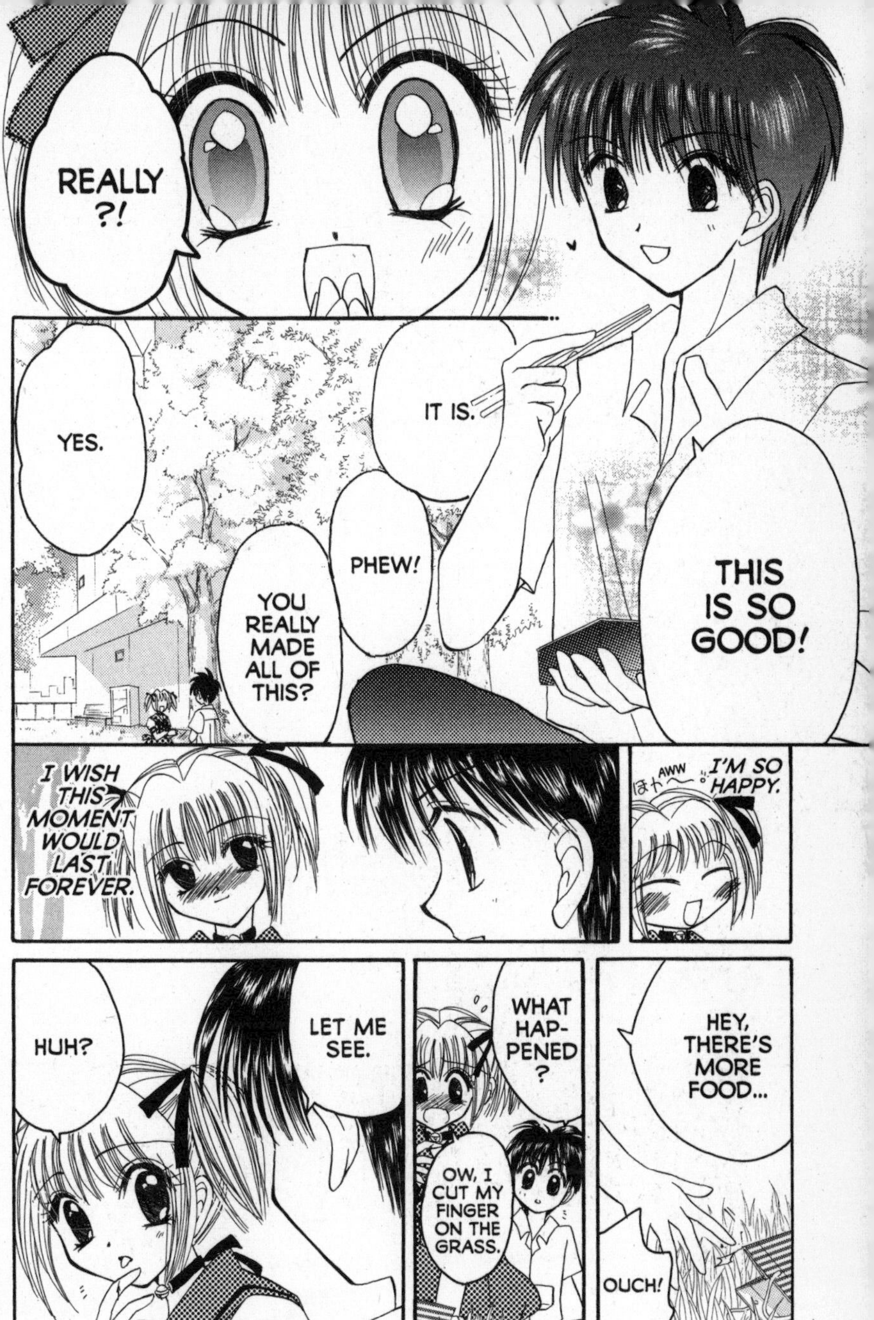
REALLY ?!
THIS IS SO GOOD!
IT IS.
PHEW!
YOU REALLY MADE ALL OF THIS?
YES.
ほわ AWW~
I'M SO HAPPY.
I WISH THIS MOMENT WOULD LAST FOREVER.
HEY, THERE'S MORE FOOD...
OUCH!
WHAT HAP-PENED?
OW, I CUT MY FINGER ON THE GRASS.
LET ME SEE.
HUH?

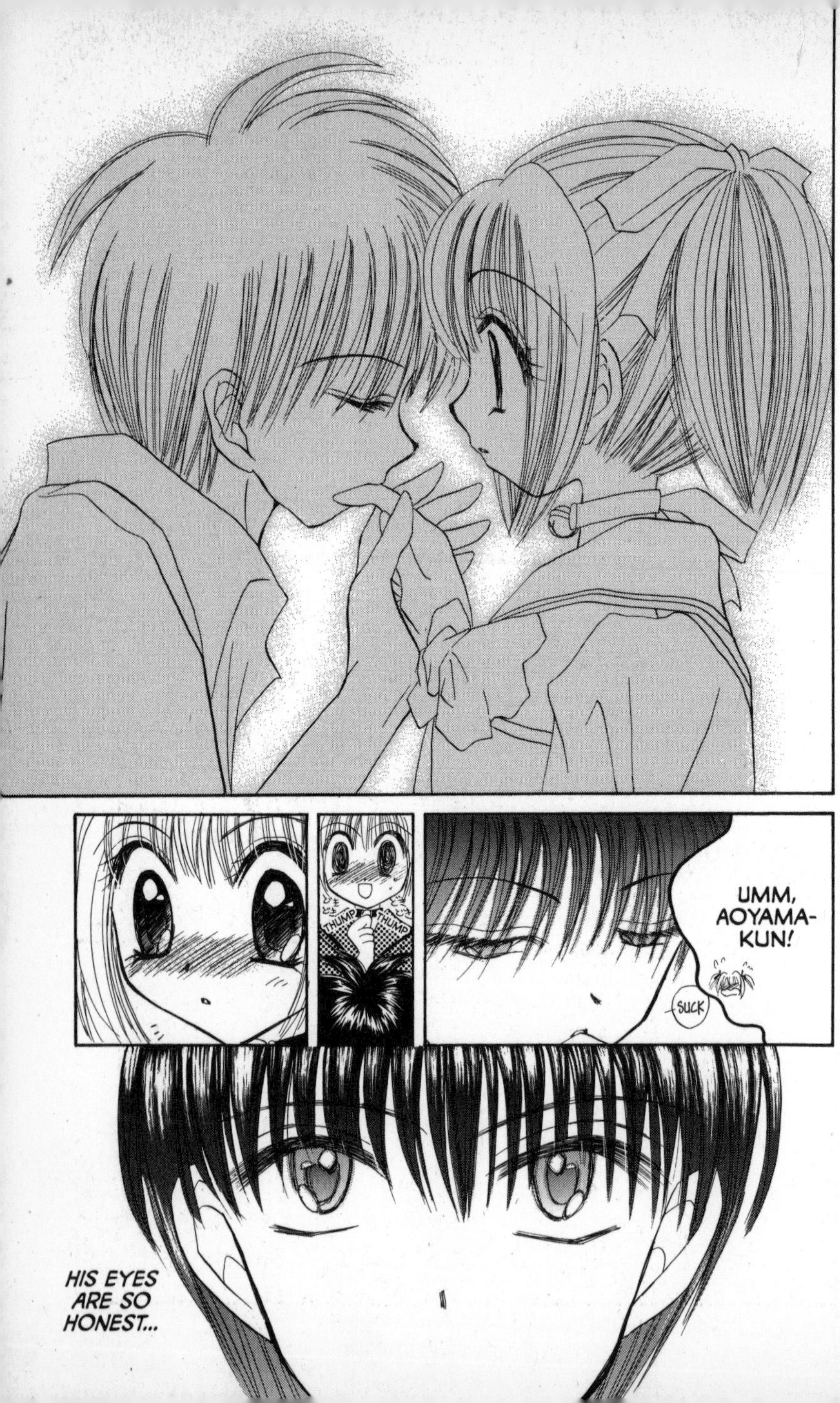
UMM, AOYAMA-KUN!
SUCK
THUMP THUMP
HIS EYES ARE SO HONEST...

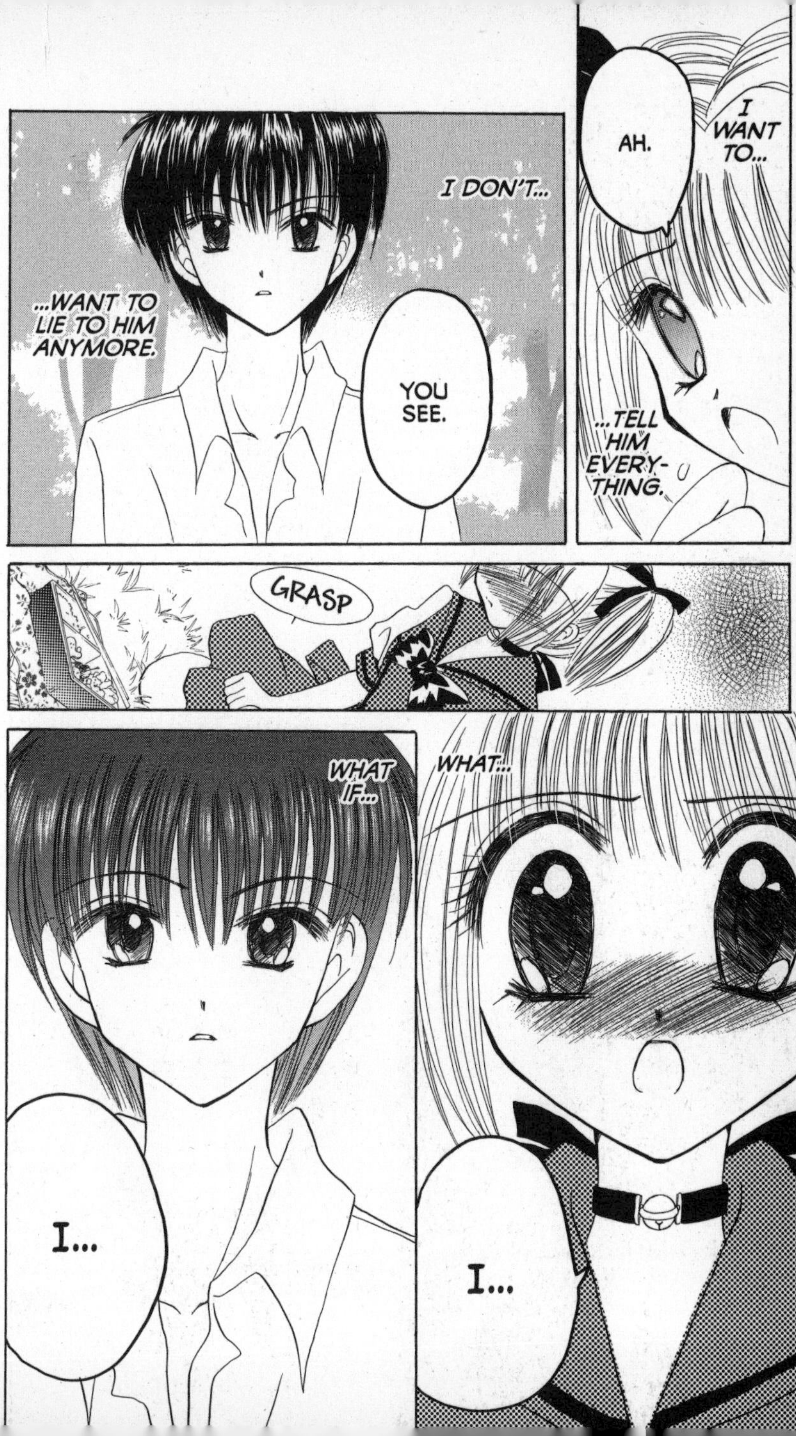
I WANT TO...
AH.
...TELL HIM EVERYTHING.
I DON'T...
YOU SEE.
...WANT TO LIE TO HIM ANYMORE.
GRASP
WHAT...
I...
WHAT IF...
I...

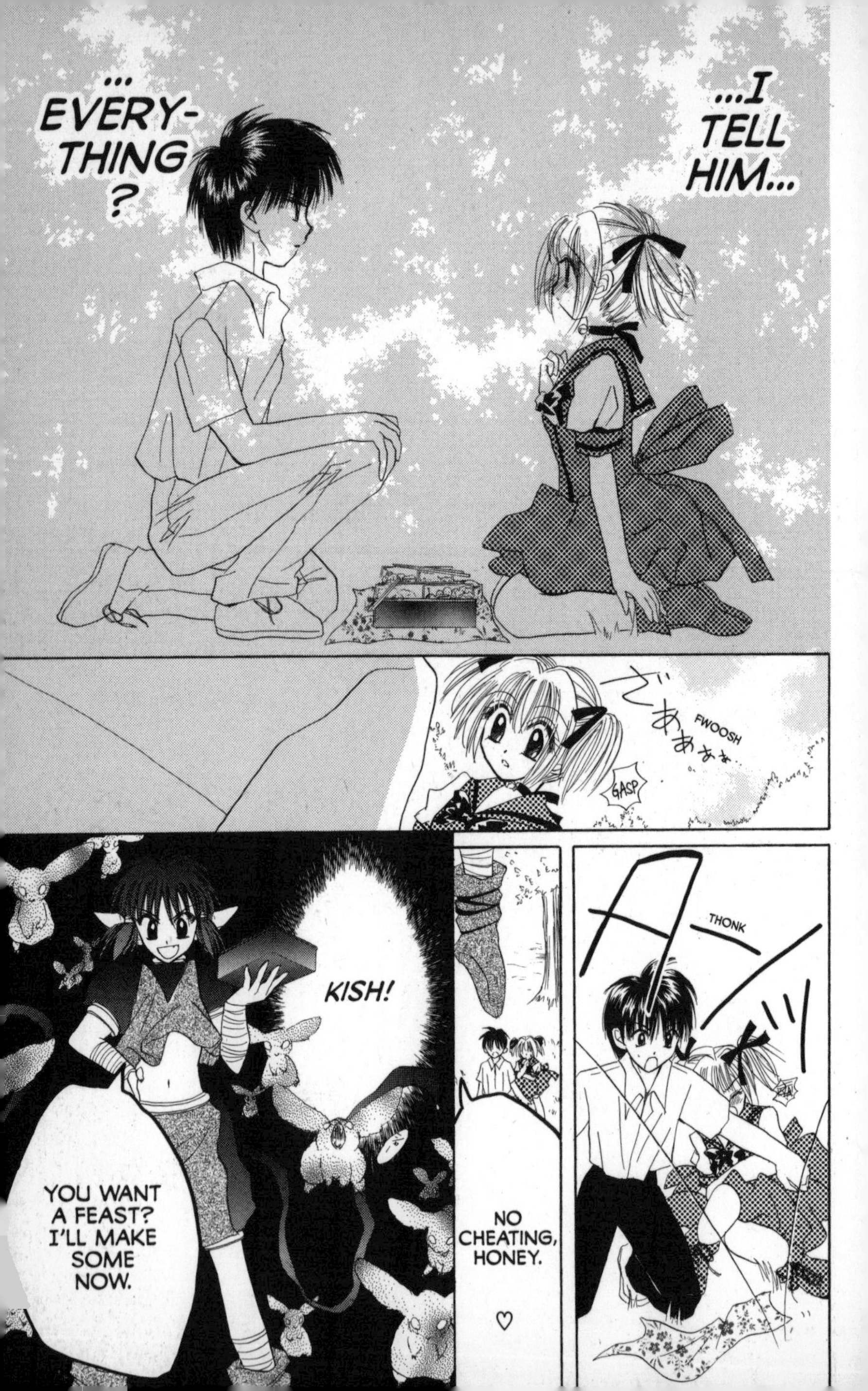

...I TELL HIM...
... EVERY-THING?
ざあああ
FWOOSH
GASP
THONK
NO CHEATING, HONEY. ♡
KISH!
YOU WANT A FEAST? I'LL MAKE SOME NOW.

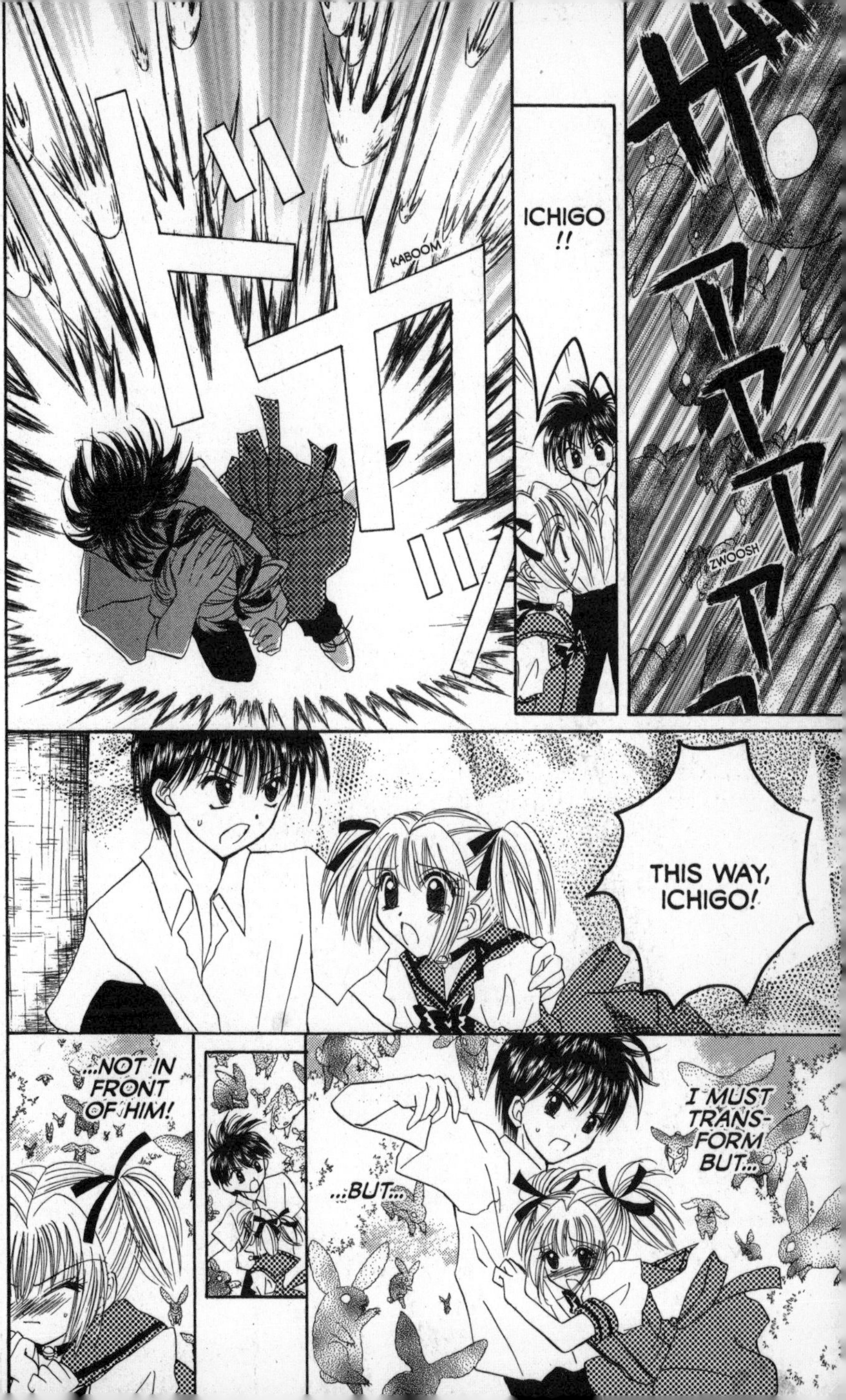
ZWOOSH
ICHIGO !!
KABOOM
THIS WAY, ICHIGO!
I MUST TRANS-FORM BUT...
...BUT...
...NOT IN FRONT OF HIM!

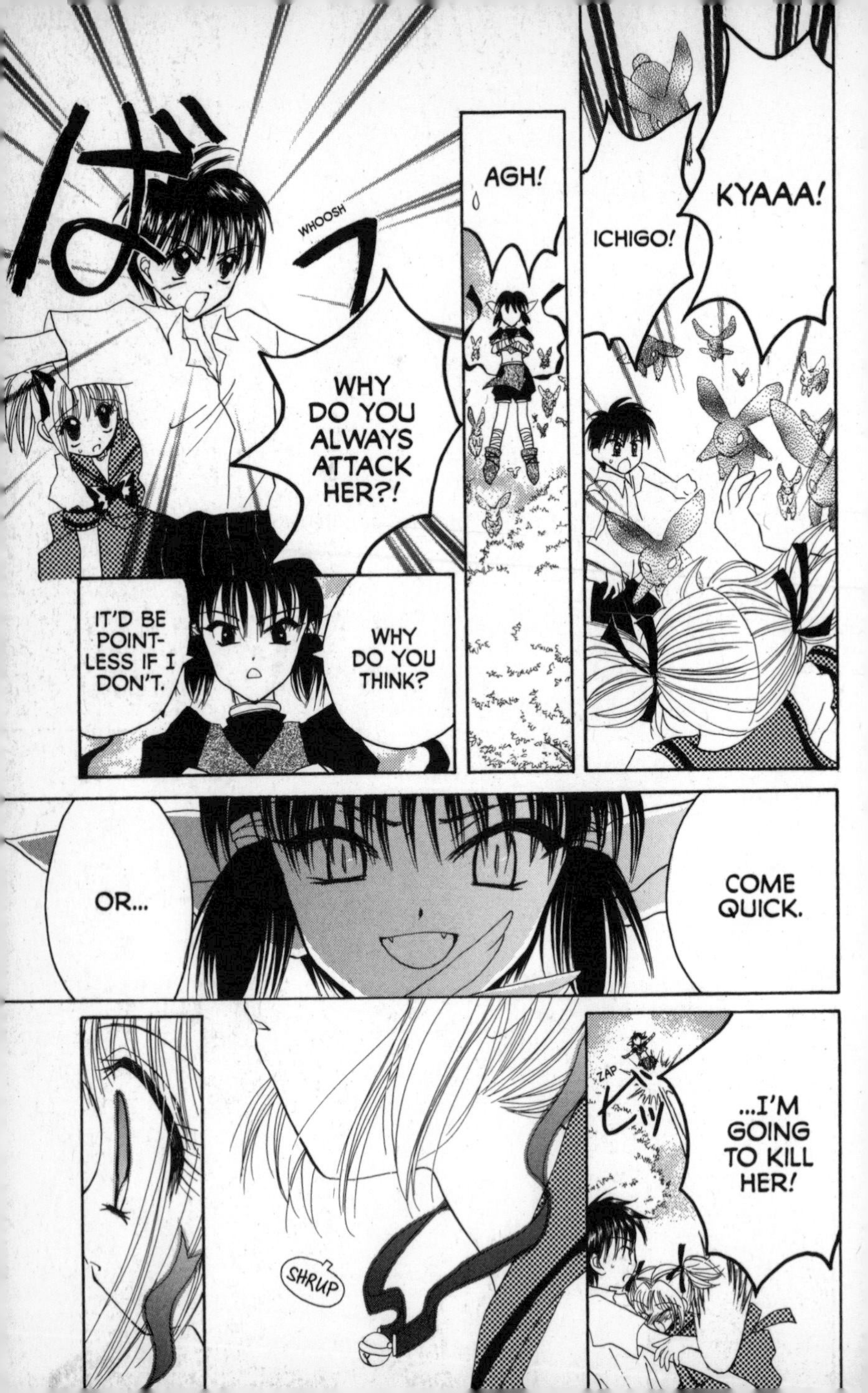
KYAAA!
ICHIGO!
AGH!
ばっ
WHOOSH
WHY DO YOU ALWAYS ATTACK HER?!
WHY DO YOU THINK?
IT'D BE POINT-LESS IF I DON'T.
COME QUICK.
OR...
ZAP
ピッ
...I'M GOING TO KILL HER!
SHRUP

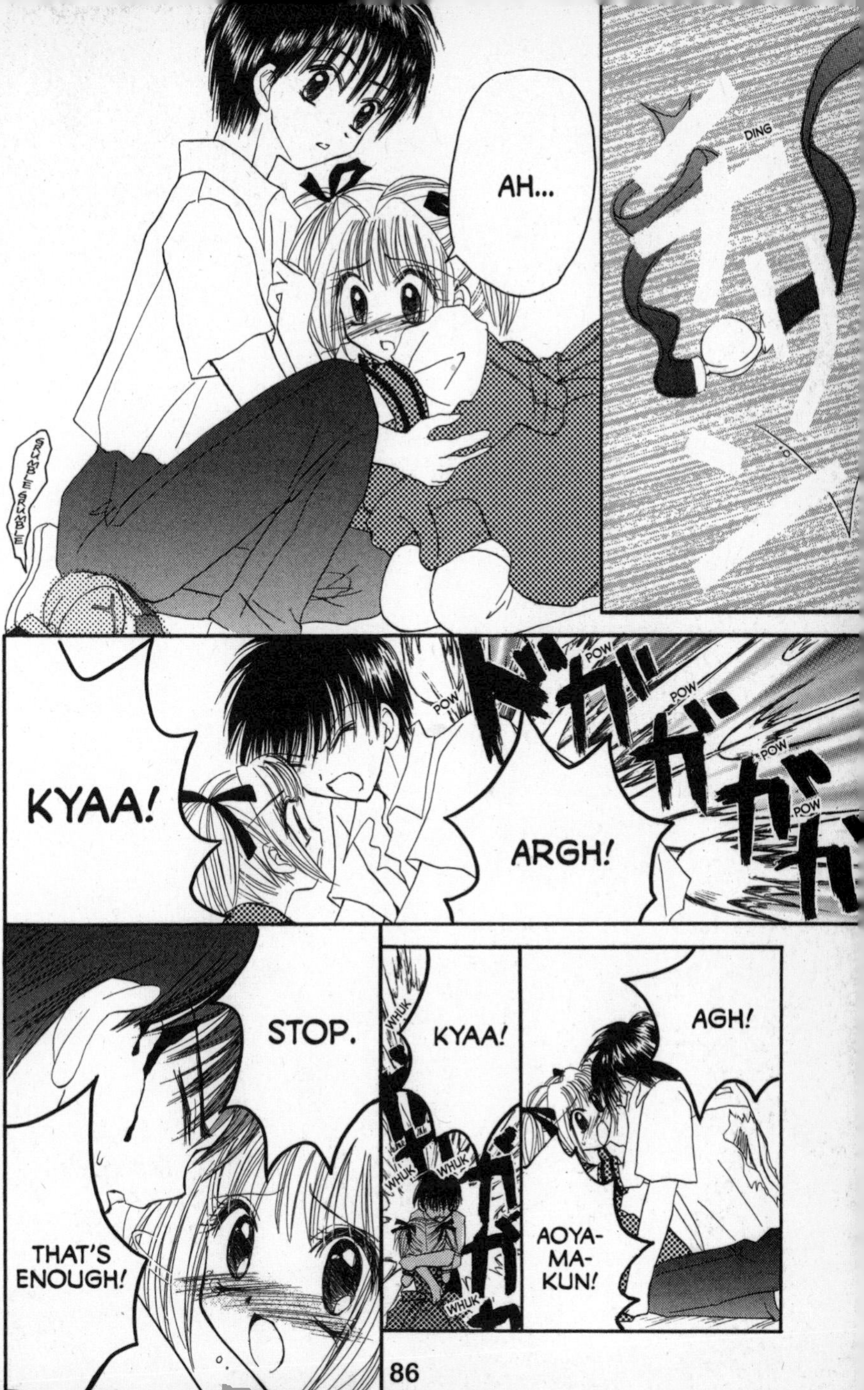
DING
AH...
SCUMBLE SCUMBLE
POW POW POW POW POW
ARGH!
KYAA!
AGH!
AOYA-
MA-
KUN!
KYAA!
WHUK WHUK WHUK WHUK
STOP.
THAT'S
ENOUGH!

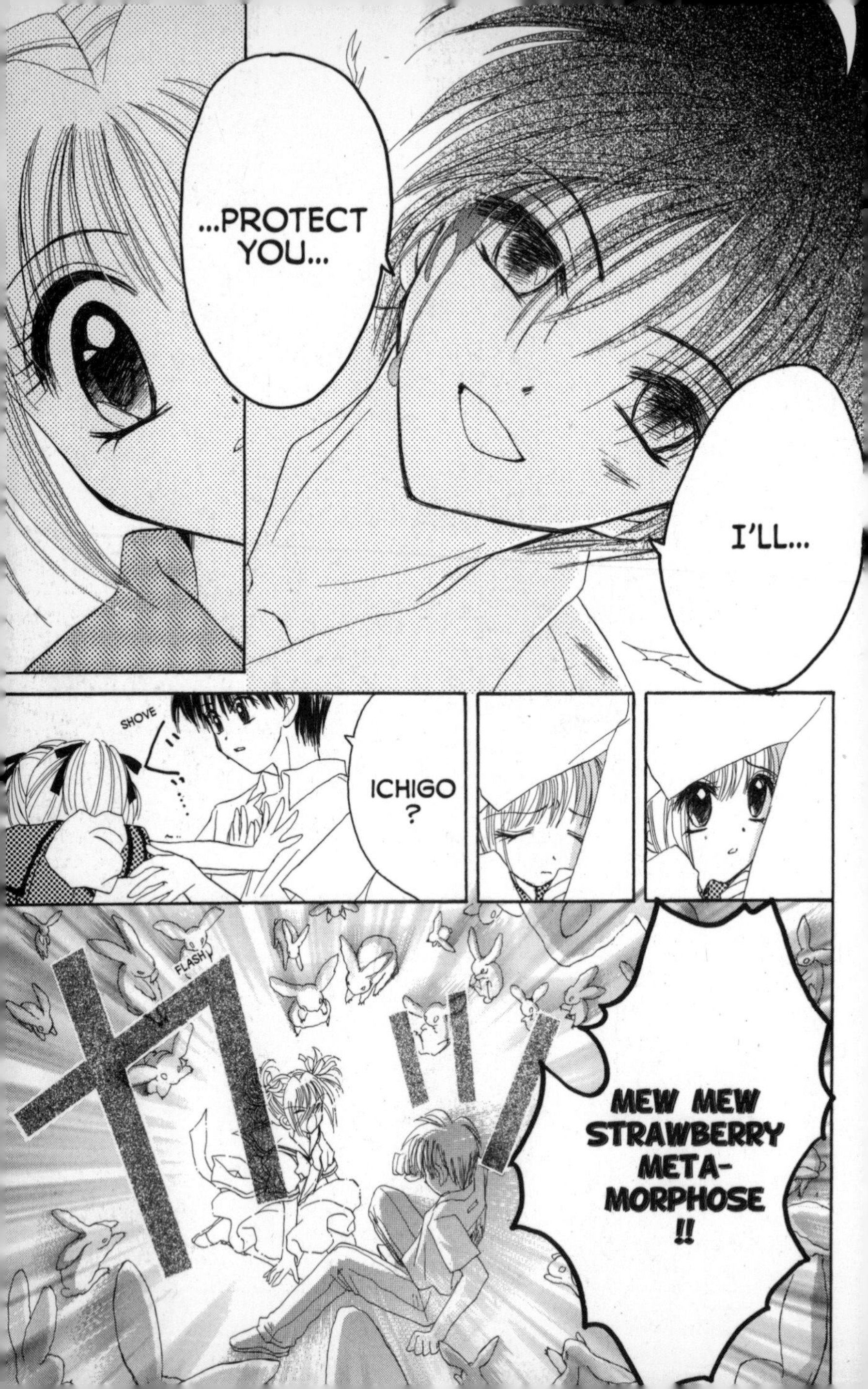
I'LL...
...PROTECT YOU...
ICHIGO?
SHOVE
MEW MEW STRAWBERRY META-MORPHOSE!!
FLASH

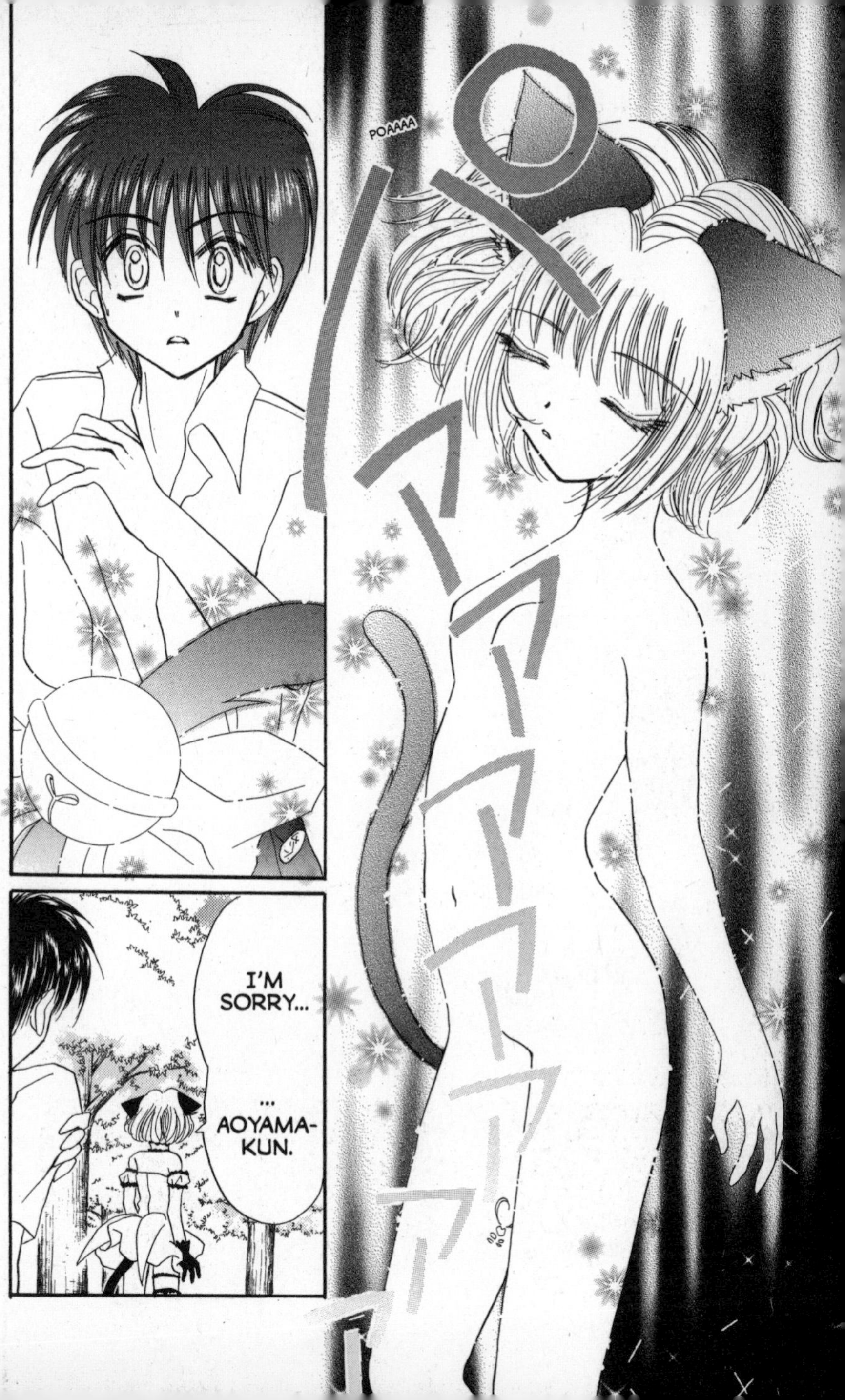
POAAAA
I'M SORRY...
... AOYAMA-KUN.

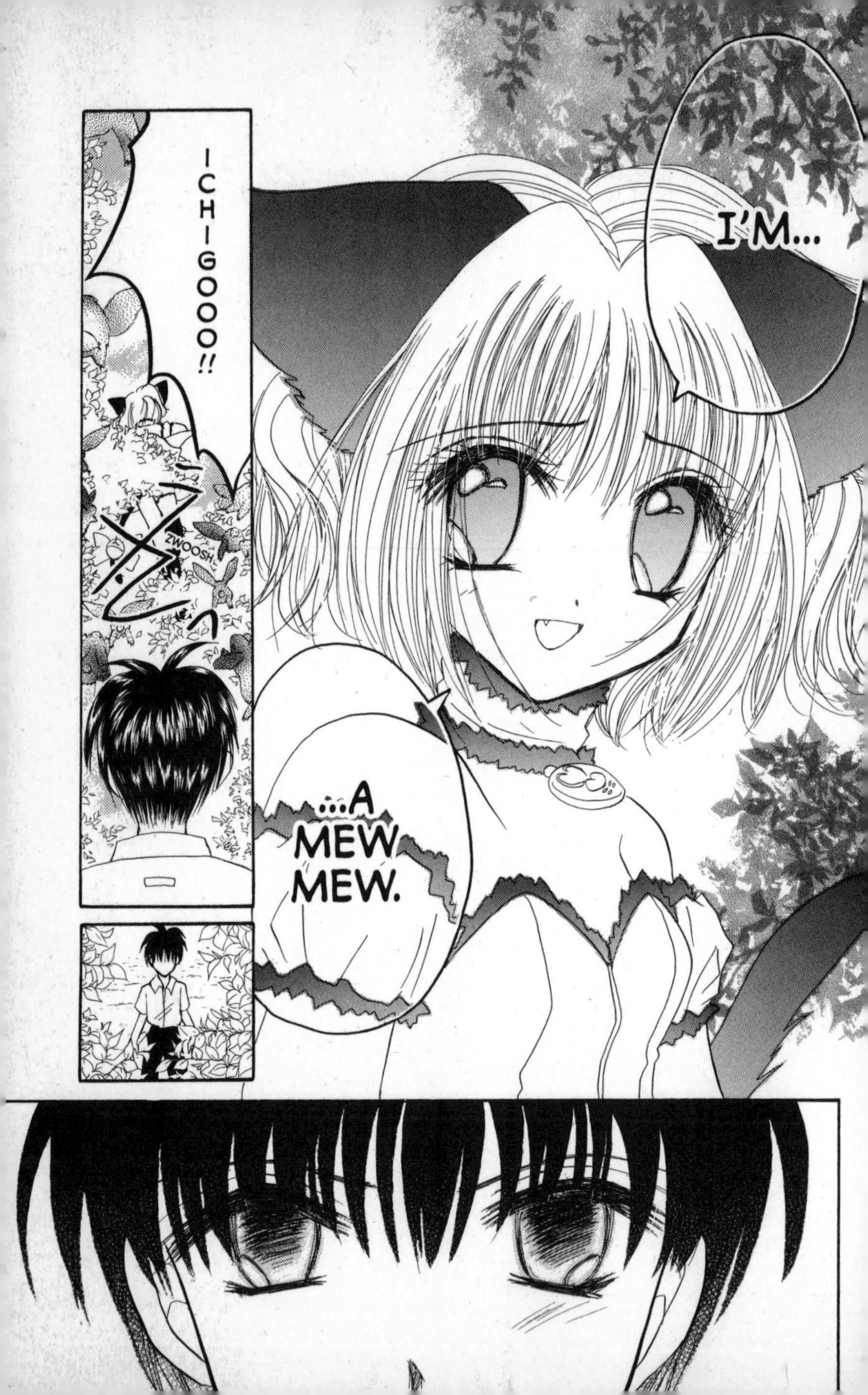
I'M...
...A MEW MEW.
ICHIGOOO!!
ZWOOSH

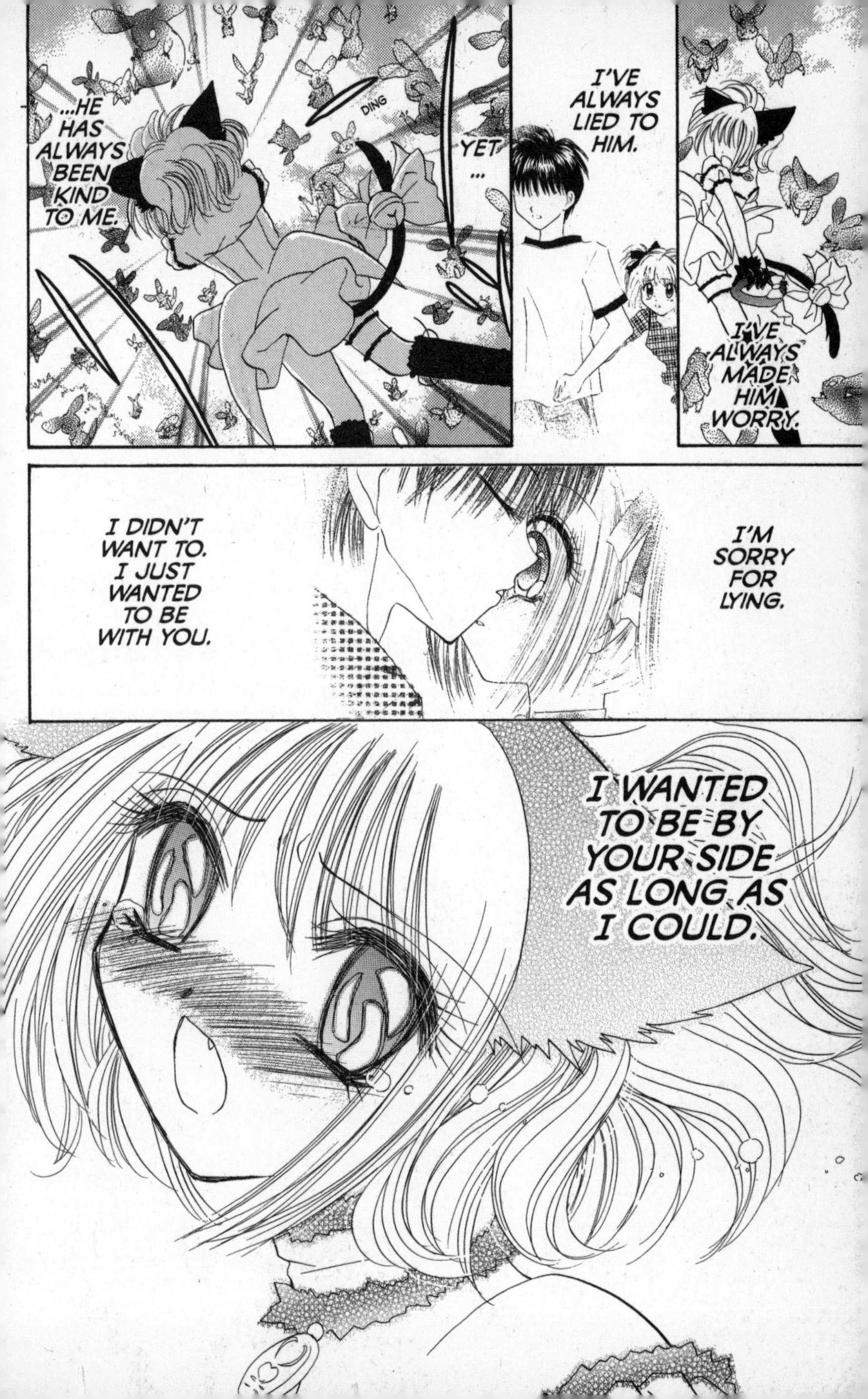
I'VE ALWAYS MADE HIM WORRY.
I'VE ALWAYS LIED TO HIM.
YET ...
DING
...HE HAS ALWAYS BEEN KIND TO ME.
I'M SORRY FOR LYING.
I DIDN'T WANT TO. I JUST WANTED TO BE WITH YOU.
I WANTED TO BE BY YOUR SIDE AS LONG AS I COULD.

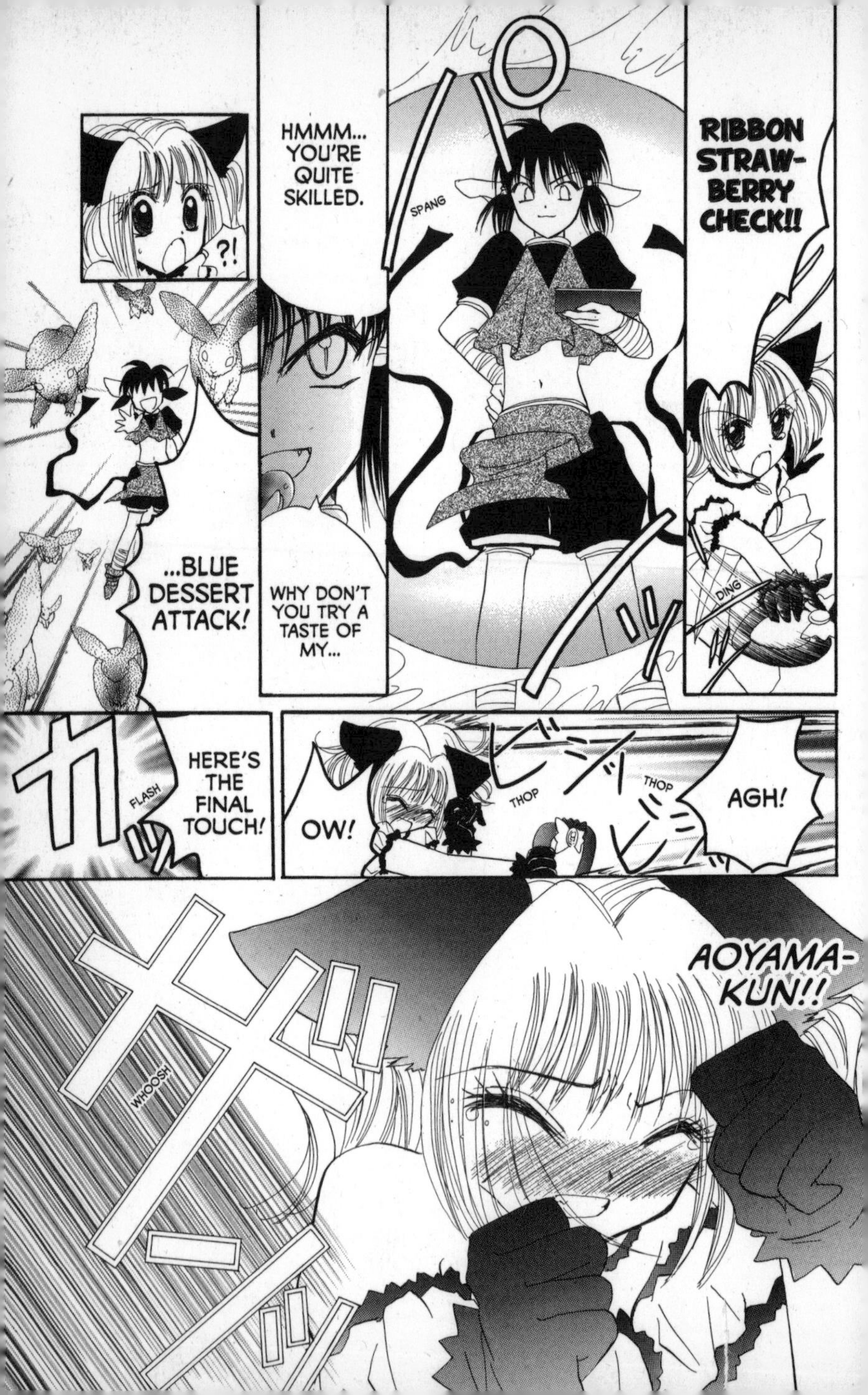

RIBBON STRAW-BERRY CHECK!!
DING
SPANG
HMMM... YOU'RE QUITE SKILLED.
WHY DON'T YOU TRY A TASTE OF MY...
?!
...BLUE DESSERT ATTACK!
AGH!
THOP
THOP
OW!
HERE'S THE FINAL TOUCH!
FLASH
AOYAMA-KUN!!
WHOOSH

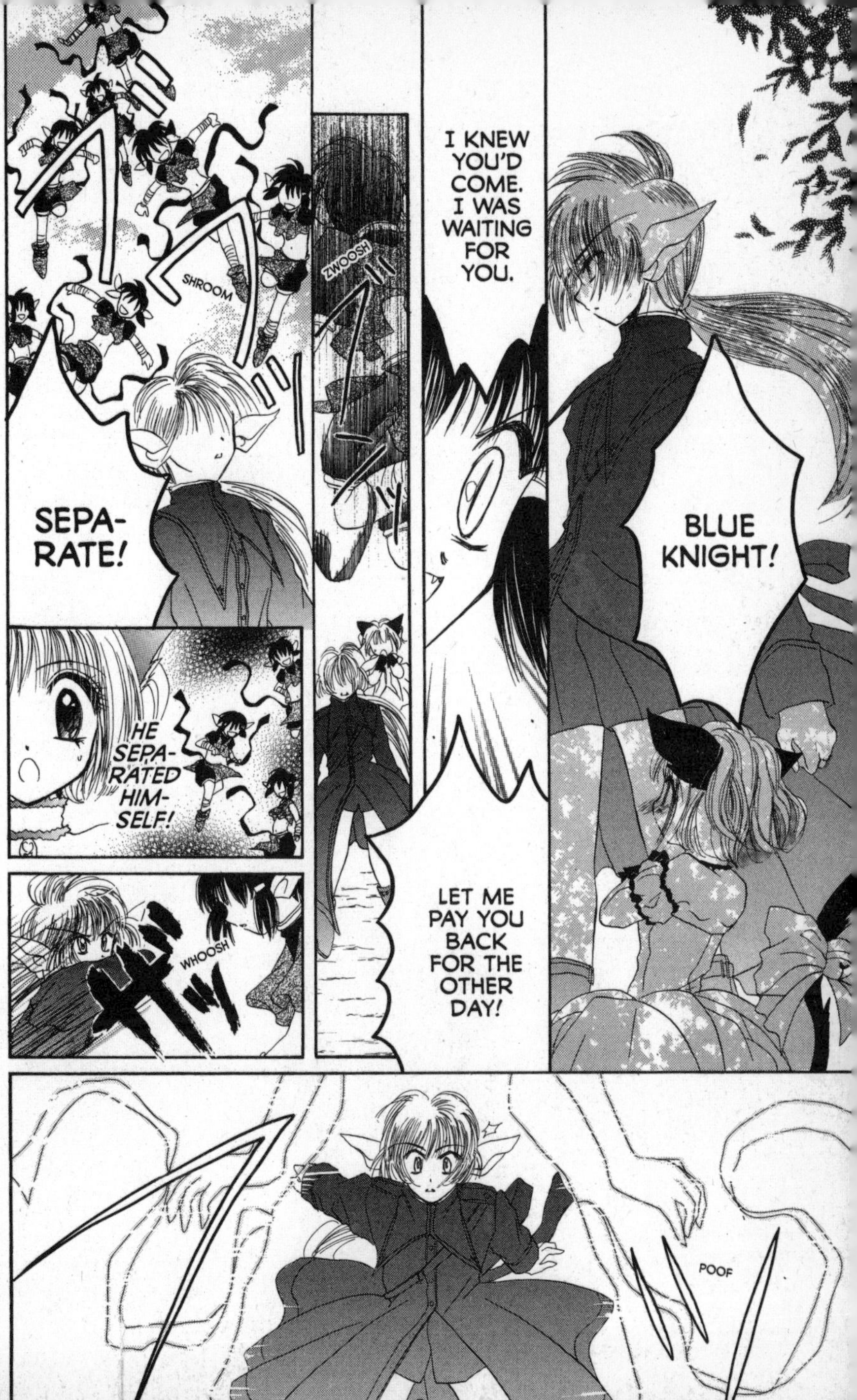
BLUE KNIGHT!
I KNEW YOU'D COME. I WAS WAITING FOR YOU.
LET ME PAY YOU BACK FOR THE OTHER DAY!
ZWOOSH
SHROOM
SEPA-RATE!
HE SEPA-RATED HIM-SELF!
WHOOSH
POOF

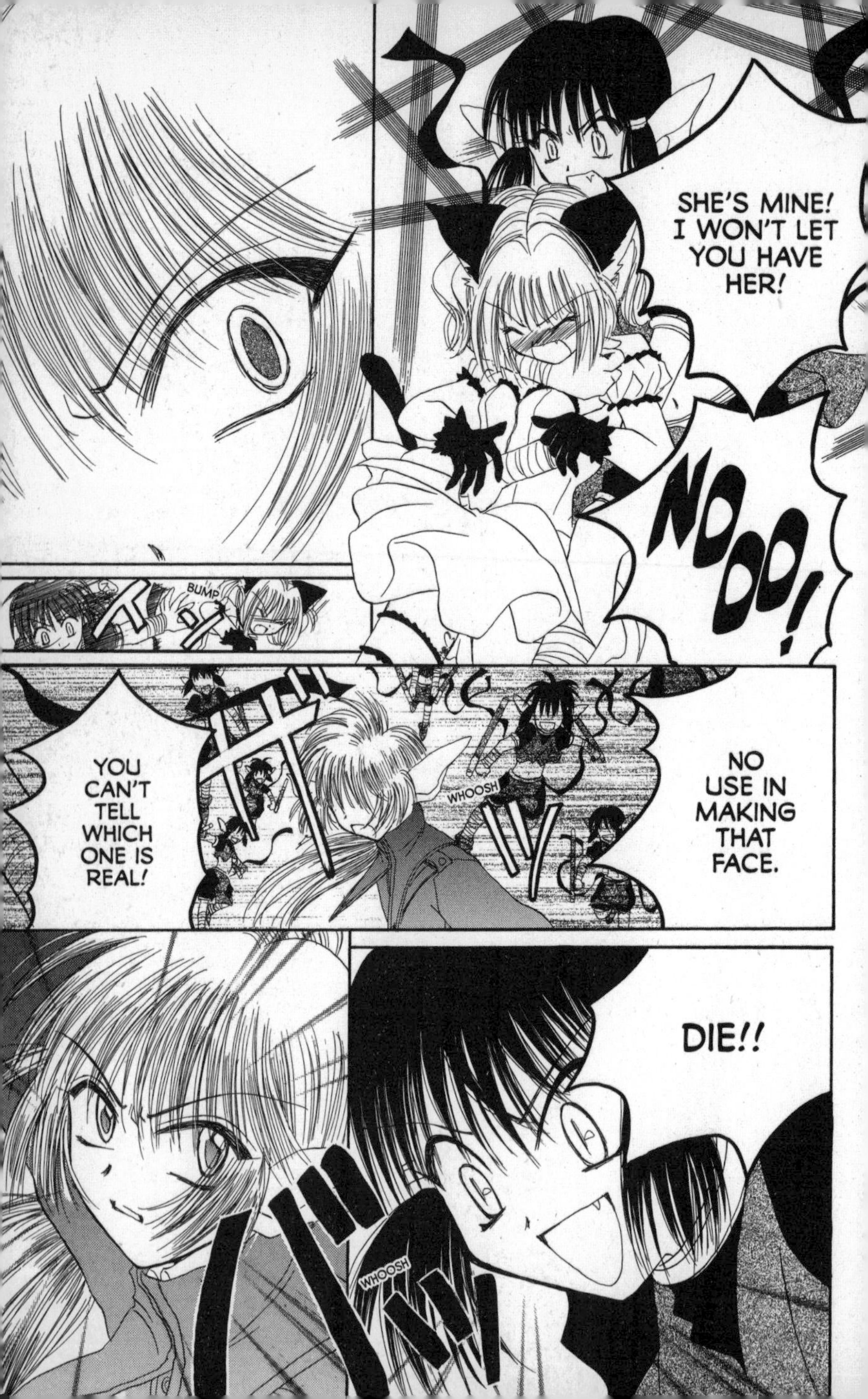
SHE'S MINE! I WON'T LET YOU HAVE HER!
NOOO!
BUMP
NO USE IN MAKING THAT FACE.
WHOOSH
YOU CAN'T TELL WHICH ONE IS REAL!
DIE!!
WHOOSH

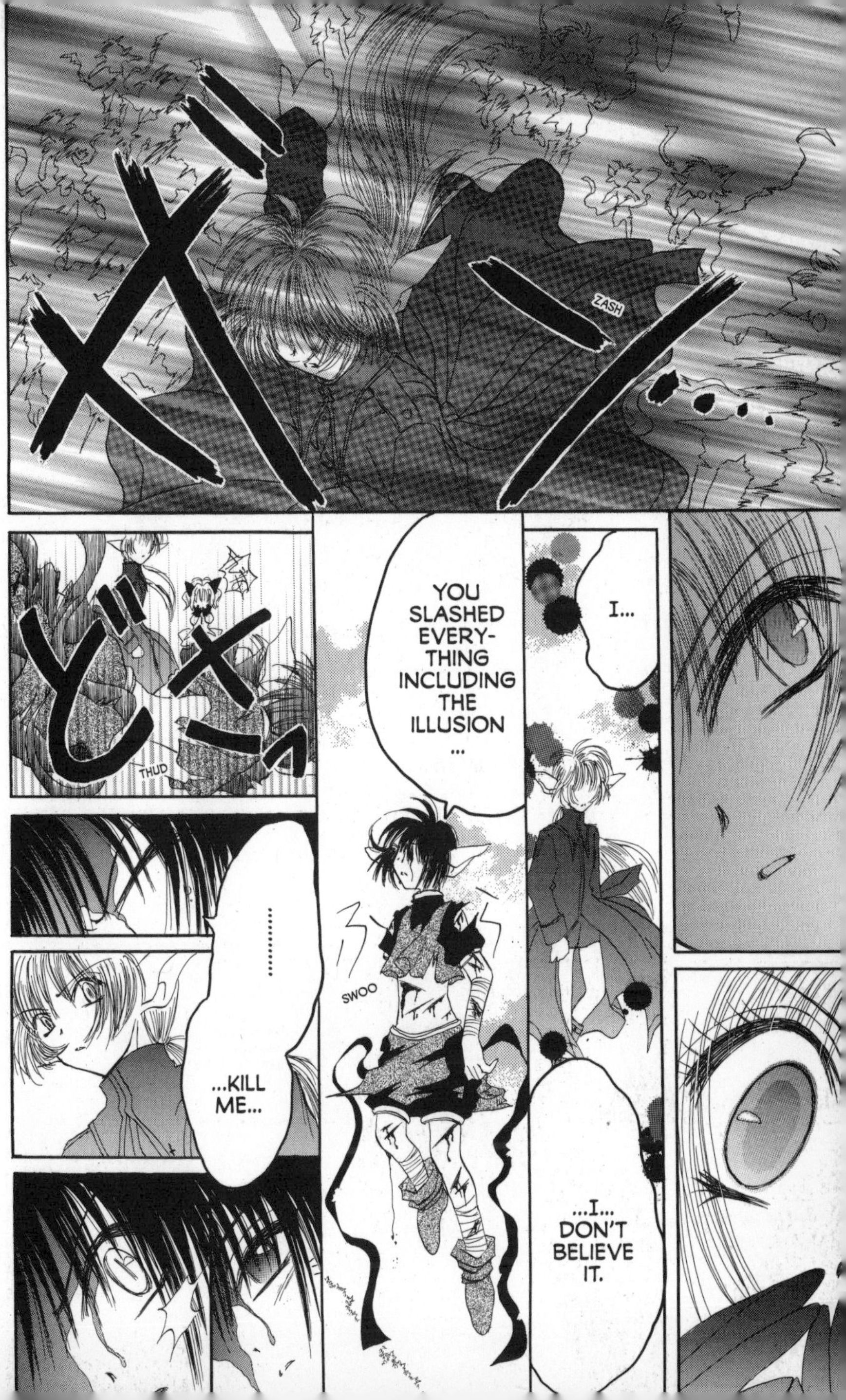
ZASH
I...
...I... DON'T BELIEVE IT.
YOU SLASHED EVERY-THING INCLUDING THE ILLUSION ...
SWOO
THUD
....
...KILL ME...

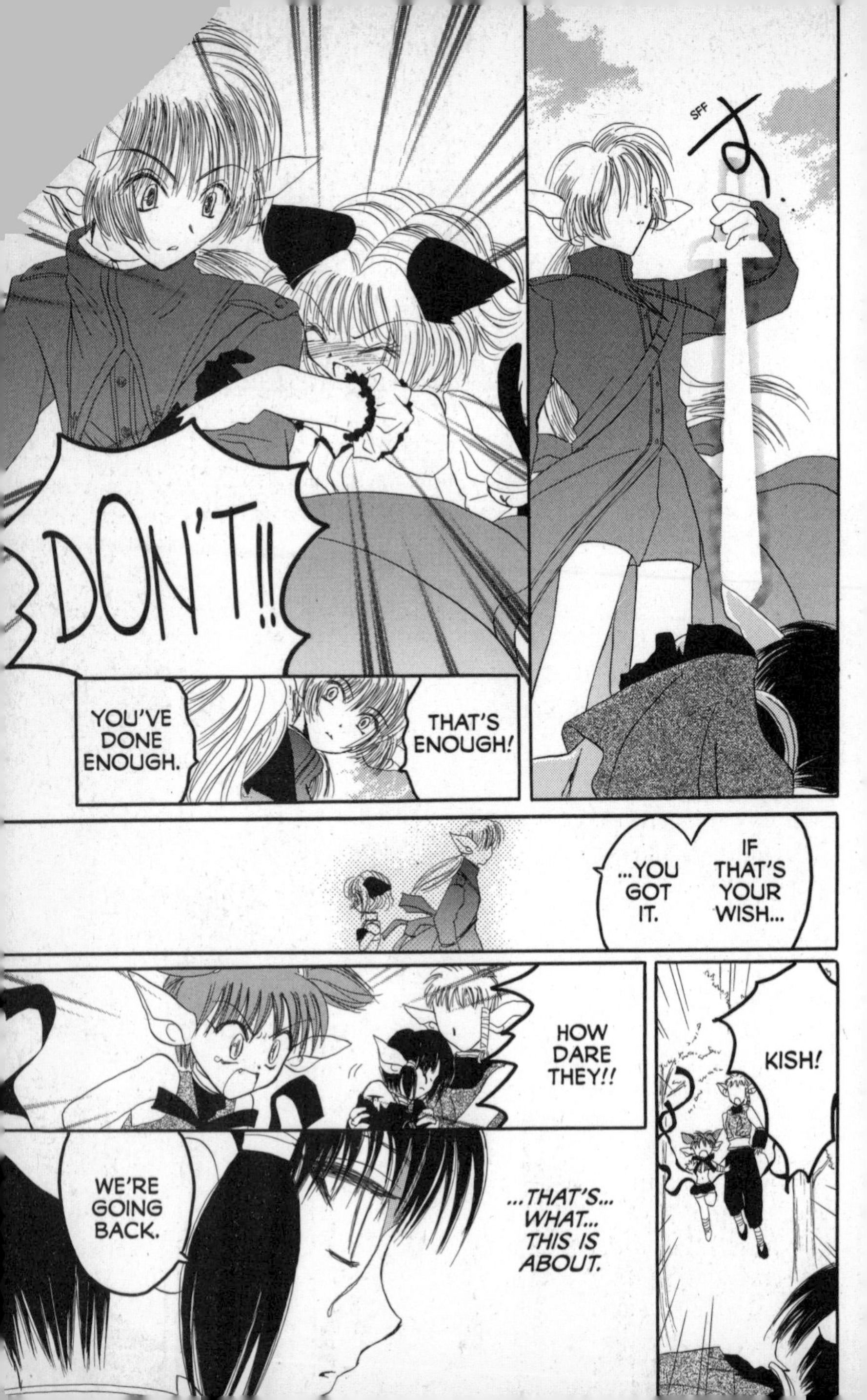
SFF
DON'T!!
THAT'S ENOUGH!
YOU'VE DONE ENOUGH.
IF THAT'S YOUR WISH...
...YOU GOT IT.
KISH!
HOW DARE THEY!!
...THAT'S... WHAT... THIS IS ABOUT.
WE'RE GOING BACK.

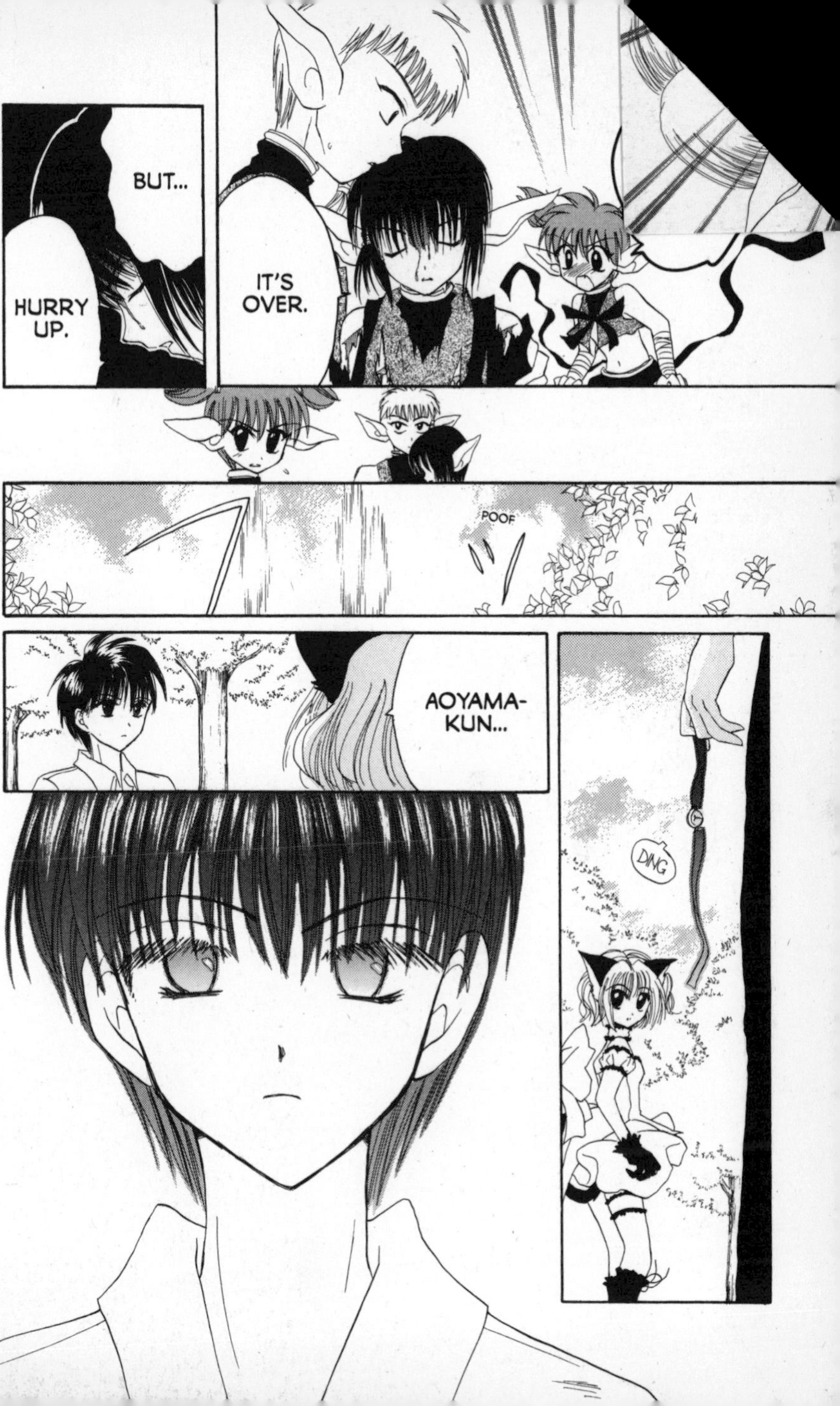

IT'S OVER.
BUT...
HURRY UP.
POOF
DING
AOYAMA-KUN...

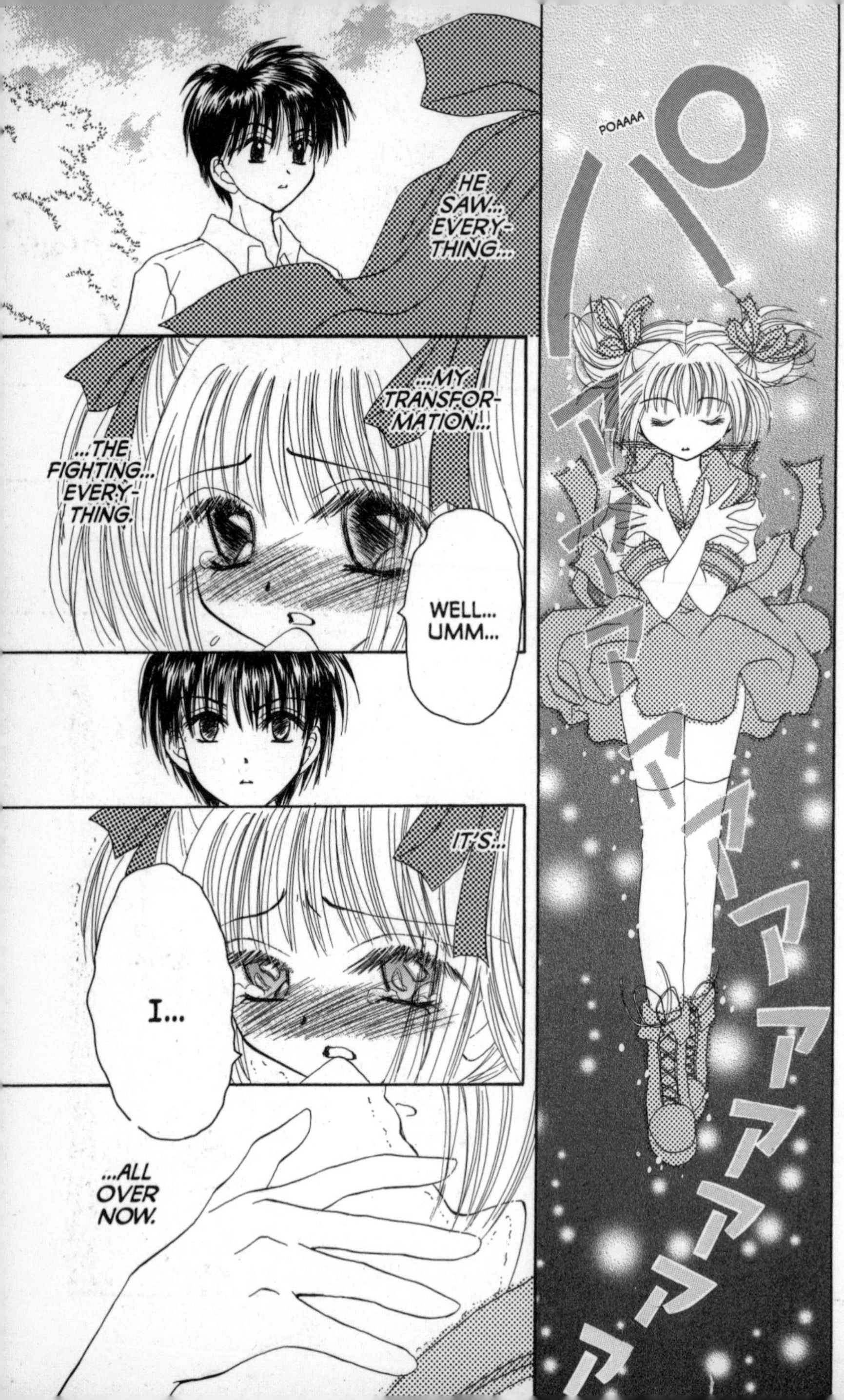
POAAAA
HE SAW... EVERY-THING...
...MY TRANSFOR-MATION...
...THE FIGHTING... EVERY-THING.
WELL... UMM...
IT'S...
I...
...ALL OVER NOW.

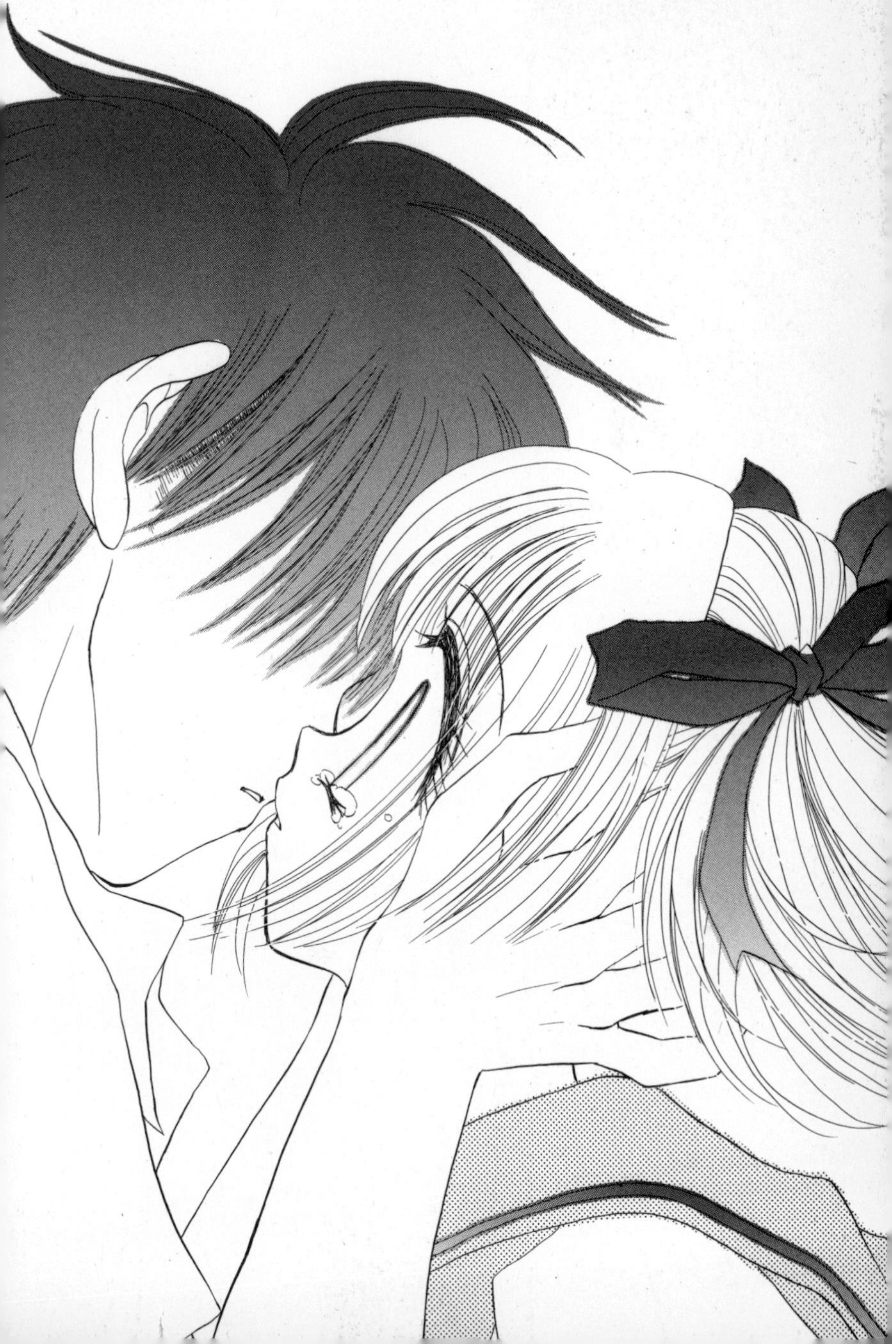

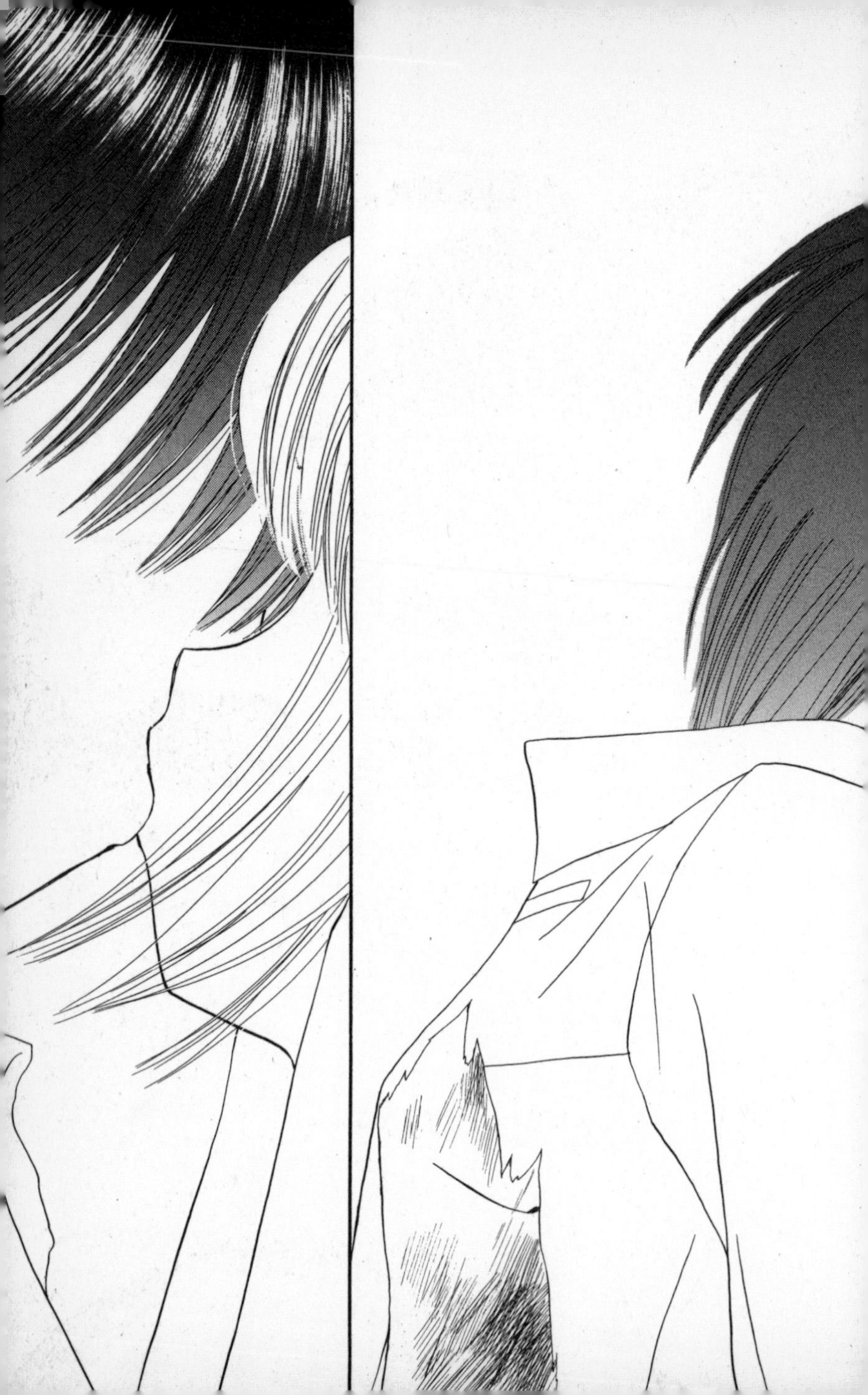

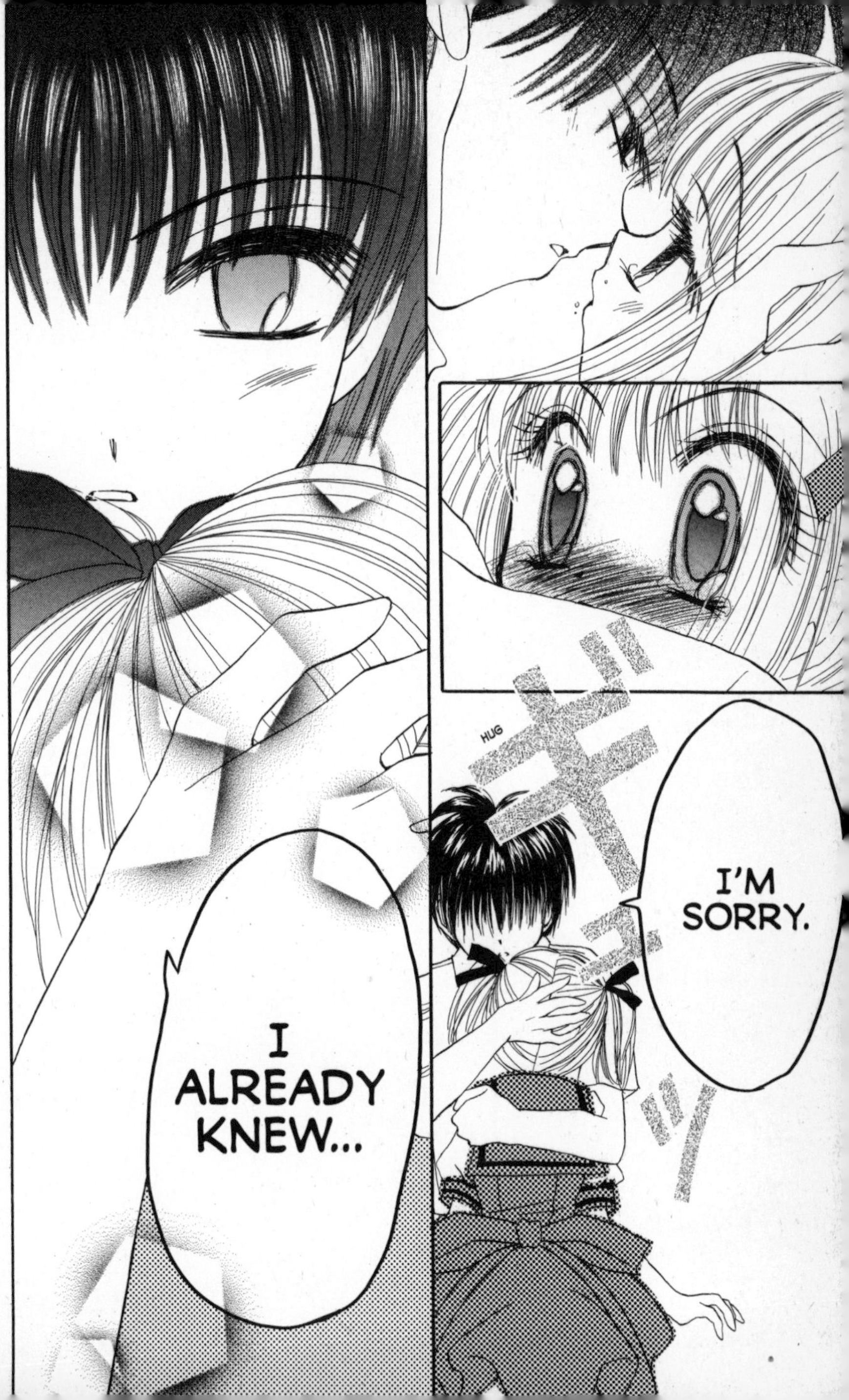
HUG
I'M SORRY.
I ALREADY KNEW...

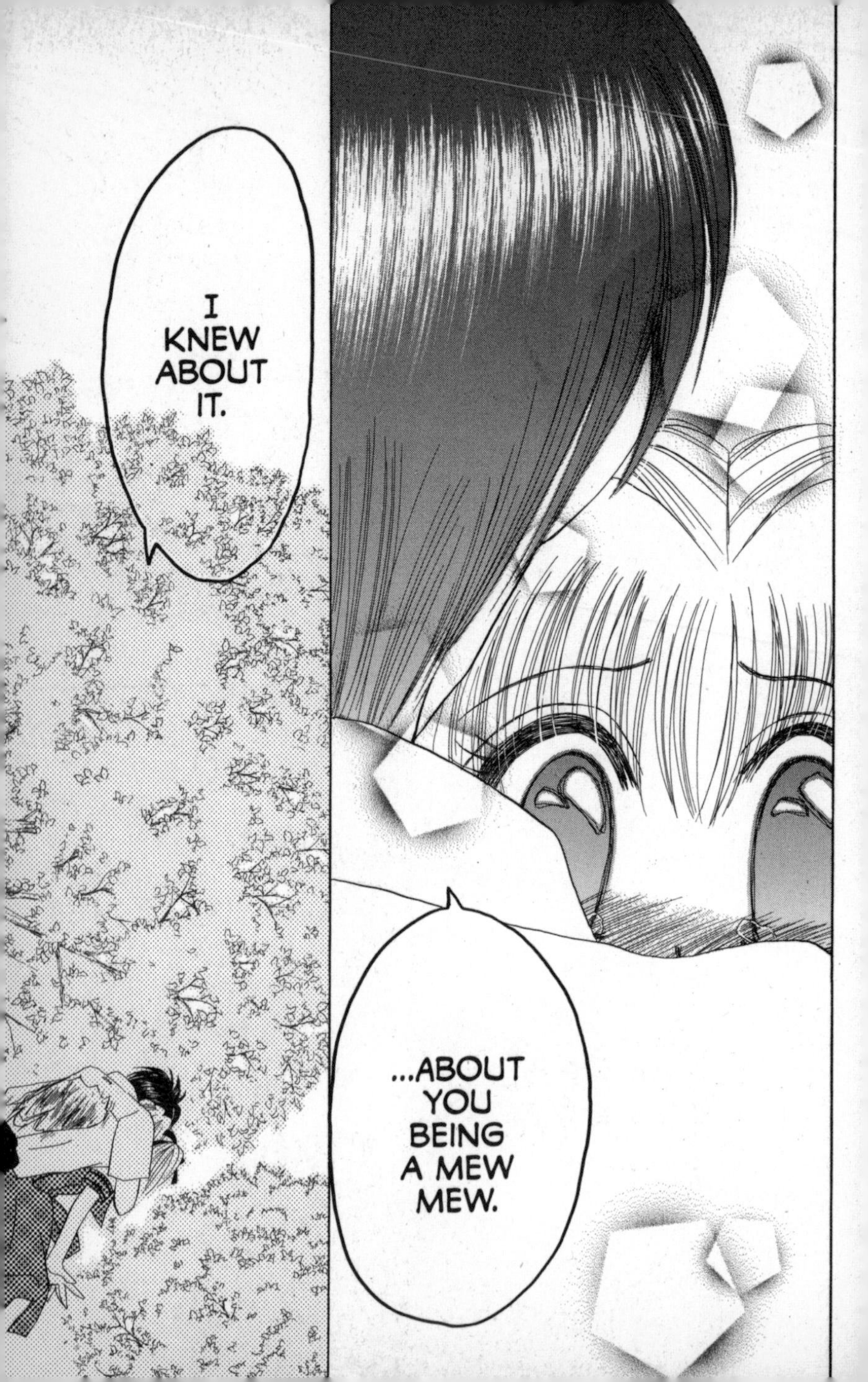
I KNEW ABOUT IT.
...ABOUT YOU BEING A MEW MEW.

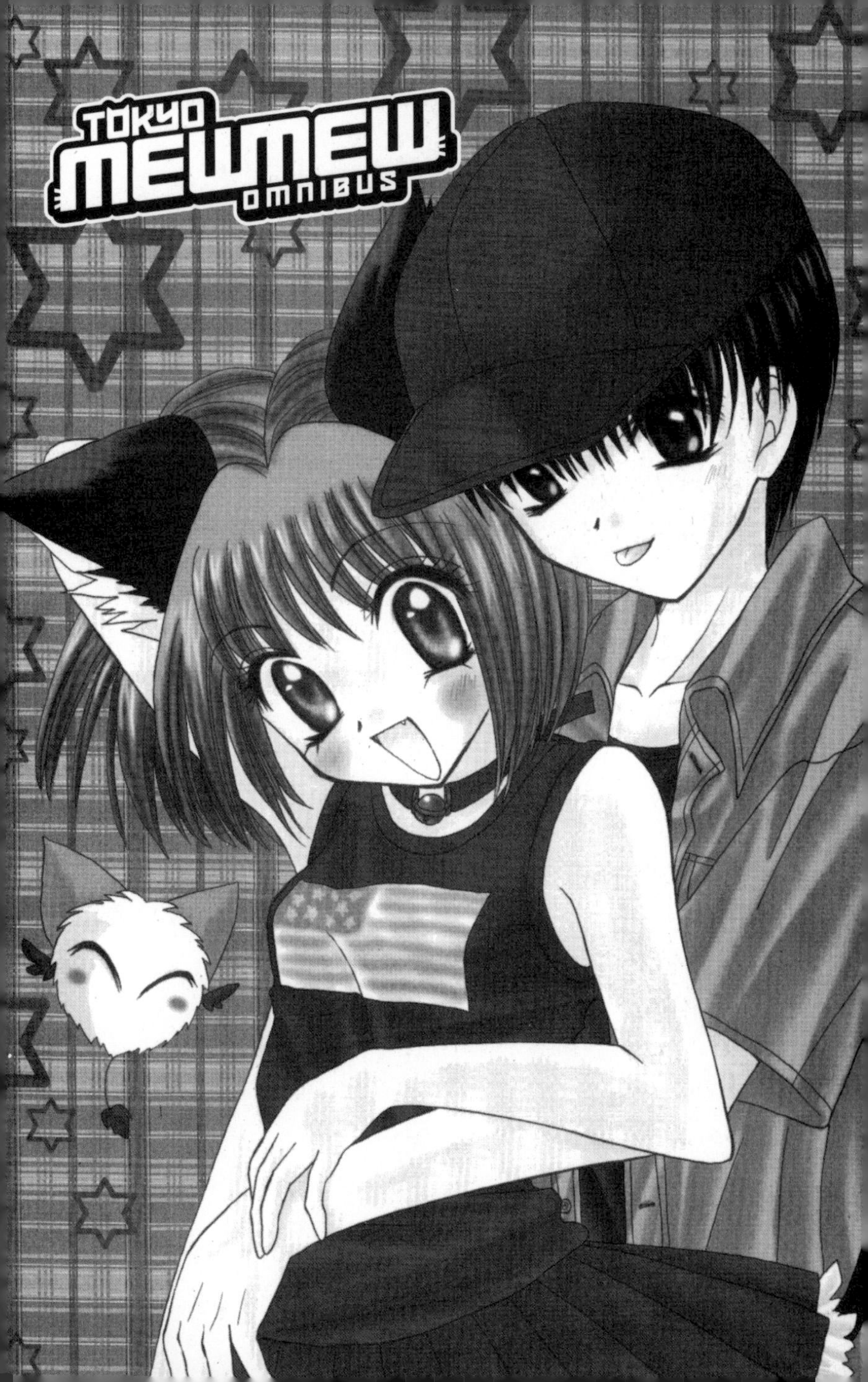
TOKYO
MEWMEW
OMNIBUS

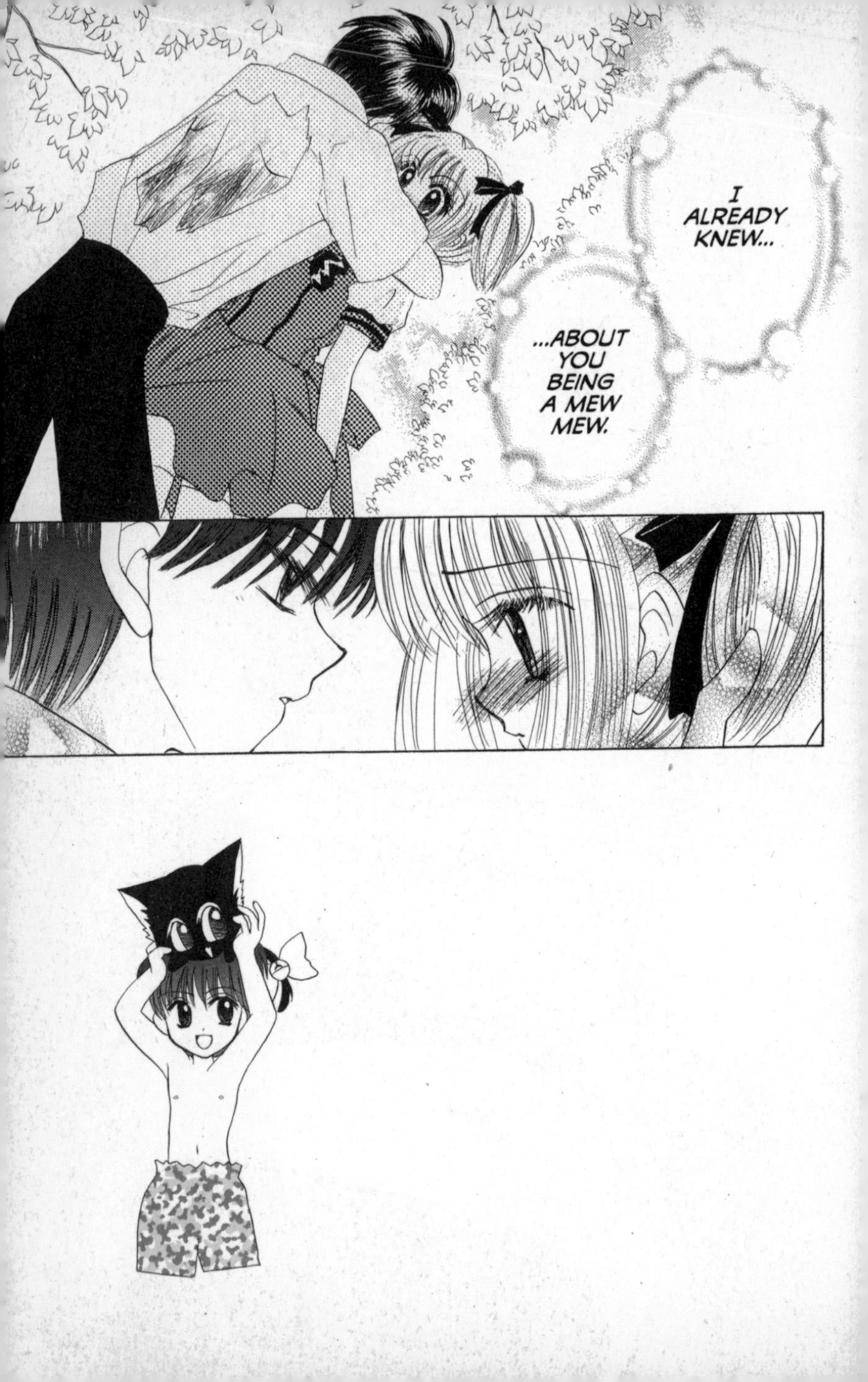
I ALREADY KNEW...
...ABOUT YOU BEING A MEW MEW.

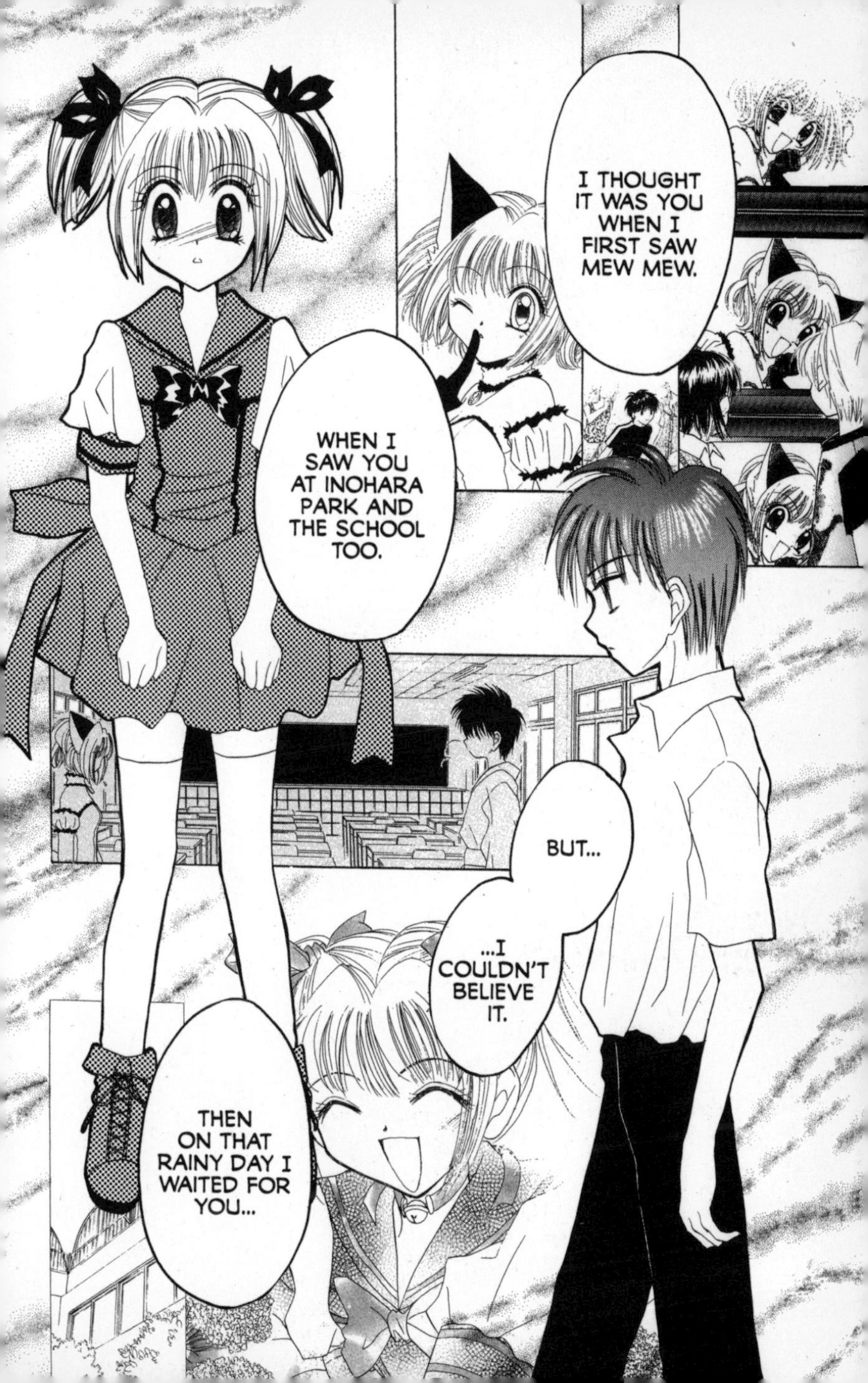
I THOUGHT IT WAS YOU WHEN I FIRST SAW MEW MEW.
WHEN I SAW YOU AT INOHARA PARK AND THE SCHOOL TOO.
BUT...
...I COULDN'T BELIEVE IT.
THEN ON THAT RAINY DAY I WAITED FOR YOU...

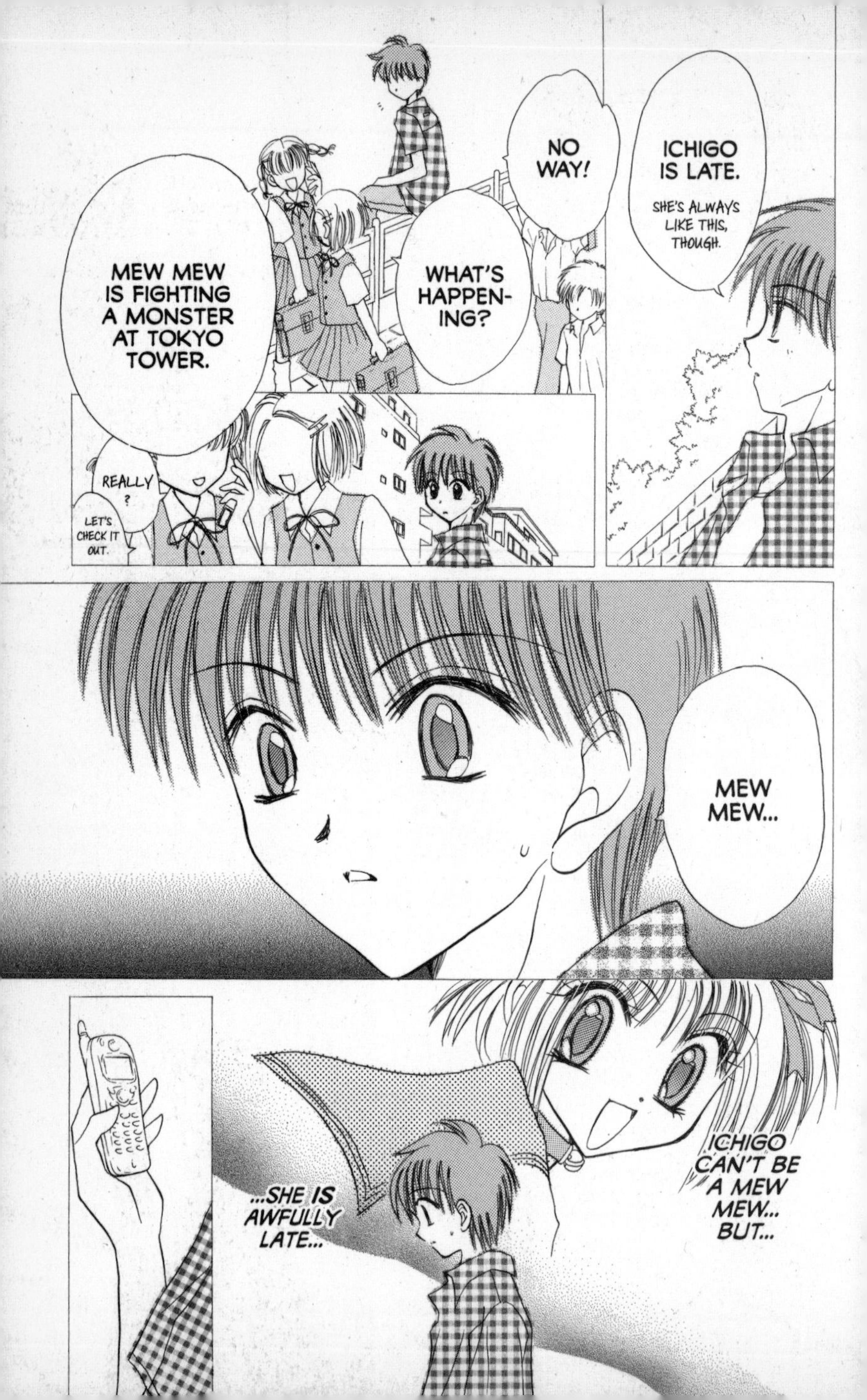
ICHIGO IS LATE.
SHE'S ALWAYS LIKE THIS, THOUGH.
NO WAY!
WHAT'S HAPPEN-ING?
MEW MEW IS FIGHTING A MONSTER AT TOKYO TOWER.
REALLY?
LET'S CHECK IT OUT.
MEW MEW...
ICHIGO CAN'T BE A MEW MEW... BUT...
...SHE IS AWFULLY LATE...

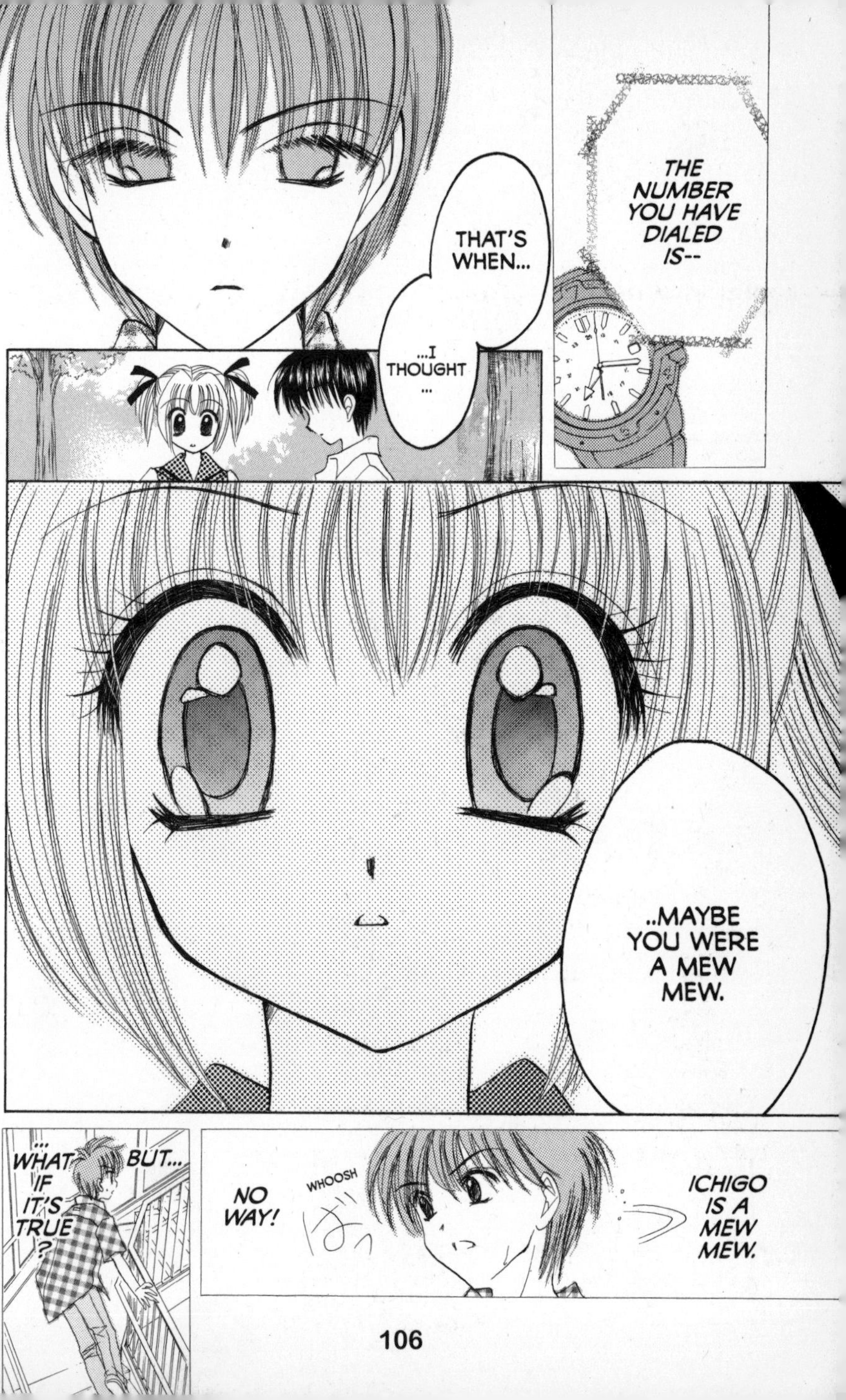
THE NUMBER YOU HAVE DIALED IS--
THAT'S WHEN...
...I THOUGHT ...
..MAYBE YOU WERE A MEW MEW.
ICHIGO IS A MEW MEW.
WHOOSH
NO WAY!
BUT...
...WHAT IF IT'S TRUE?

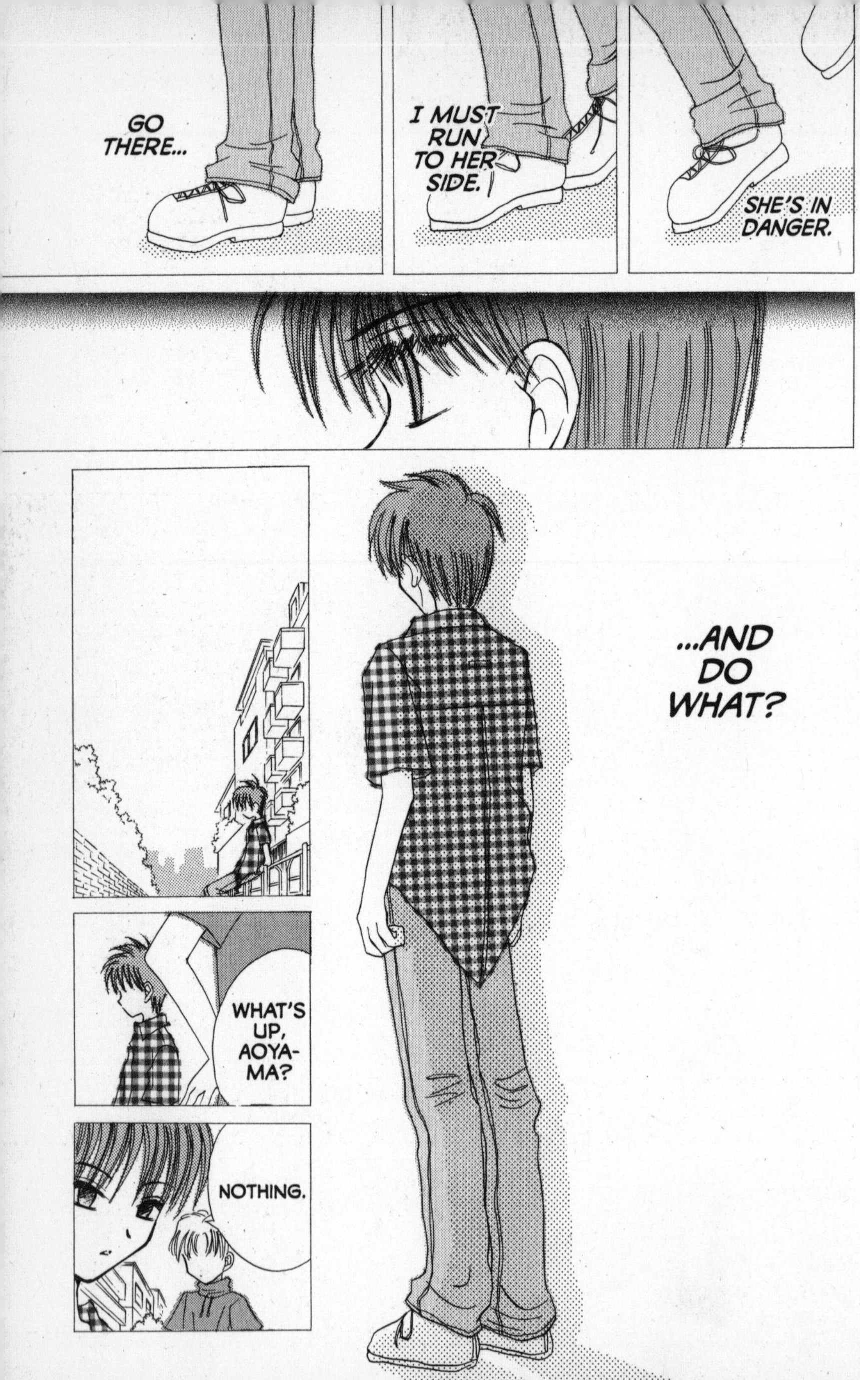
SHE'S IN DANGER.
I MUST RUN TO HER SIDE.
GO THERE...
...AND DO WHAT?
WHAT'S UP, AOYAMA?
NOTHING.

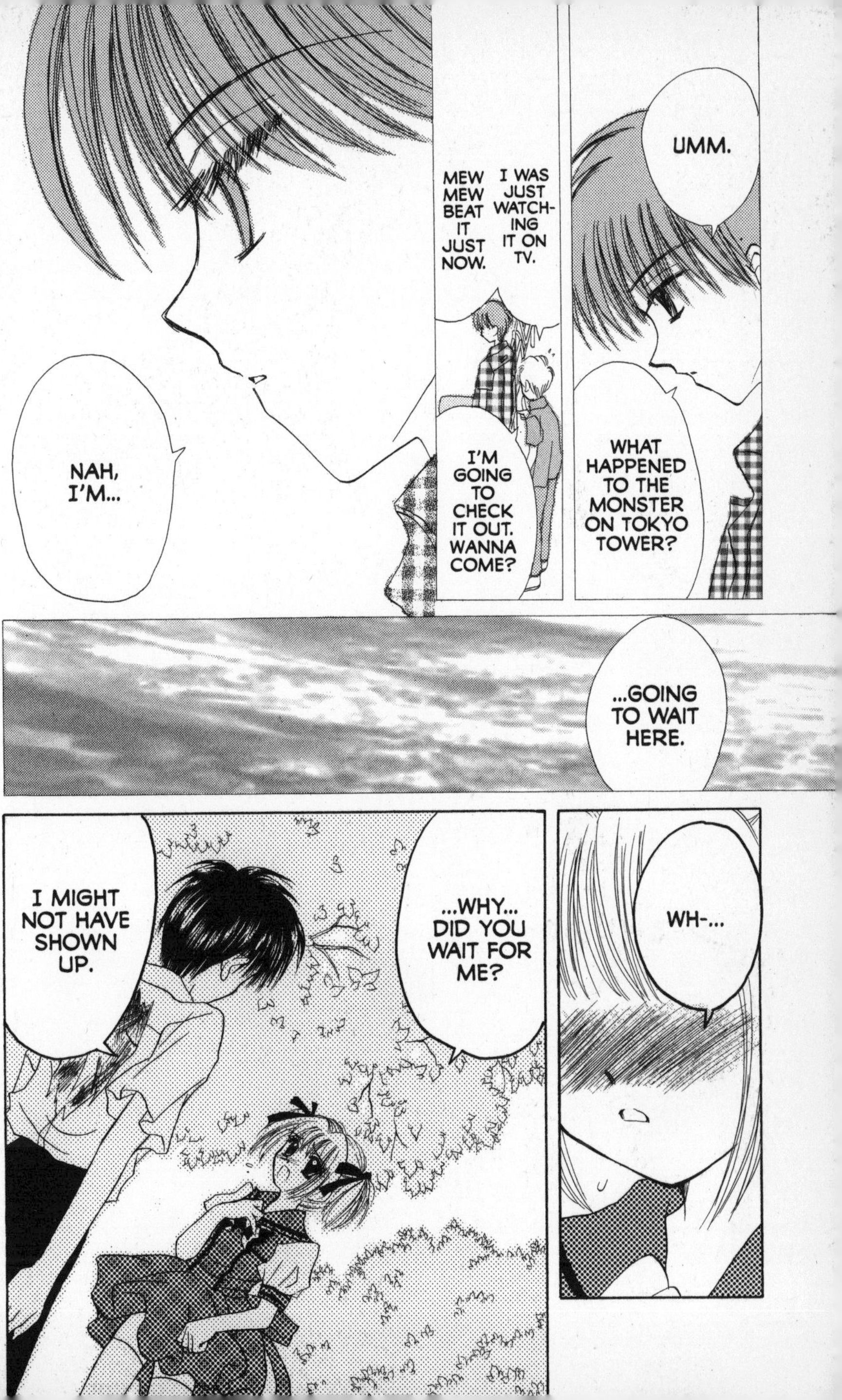
UMM.
WHAT HAPPENED TO THE MONSTER ON TOKYO TOWER?
I WAS JUST WATCHING IT ON TV.
MEW MEW BEAT IT JUST NOW.
I'M GOING TO CHECK IT OUT. WANNA COME?
NAH, I'M...
...GOING TO WAIT HERE.
WH-...
...WHY... DID YOU WAIT FOR ME?
I MIGHT NOT HAVE SHOWN UP.

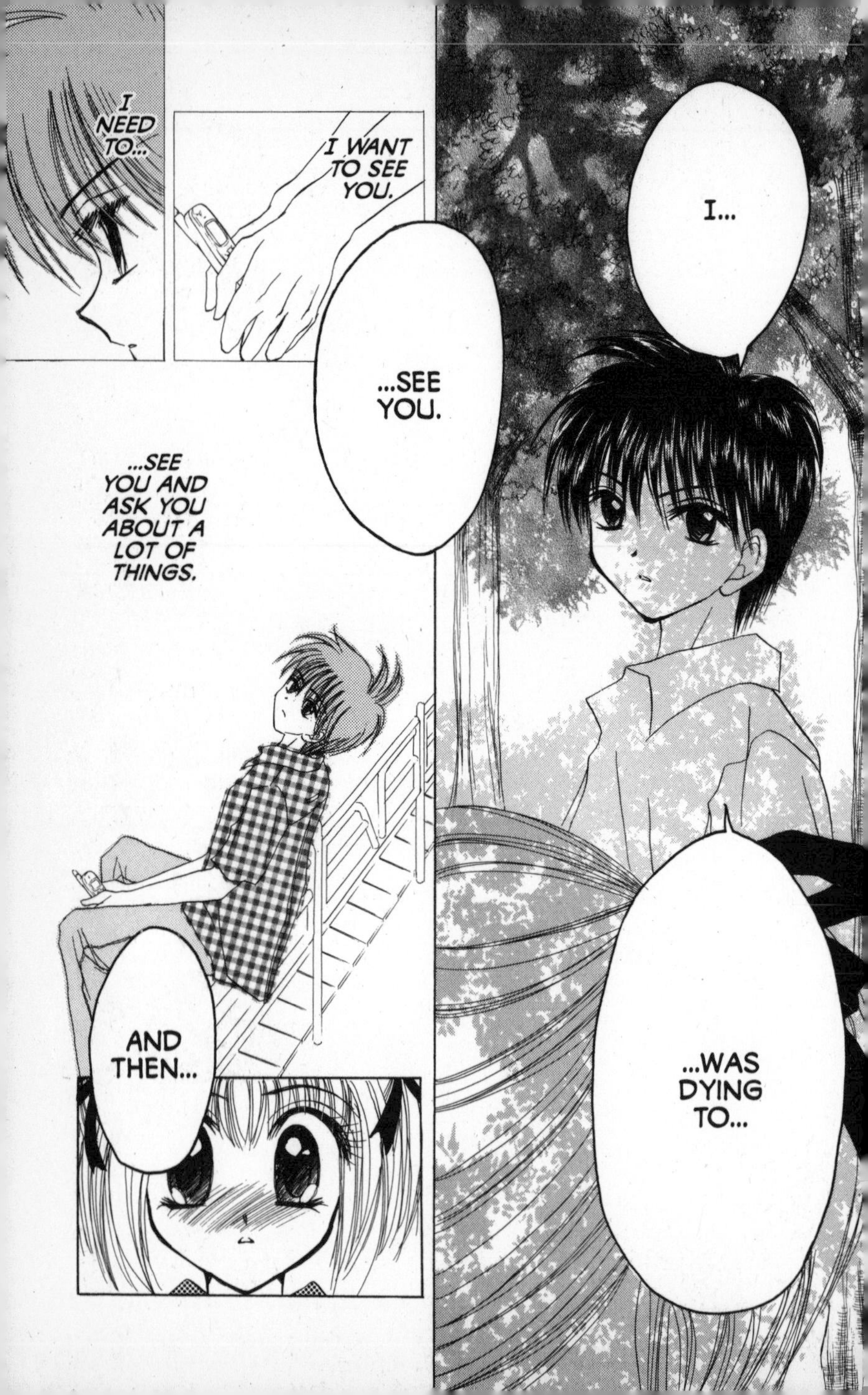
I...
...WAS DYING TO...
I WANT TO SEE YOU.
I NEED TO...
...SEE YOU.
...SEE YOU AND ASK YOU ABOUT A LOT OF THINGS.
AND THEN...

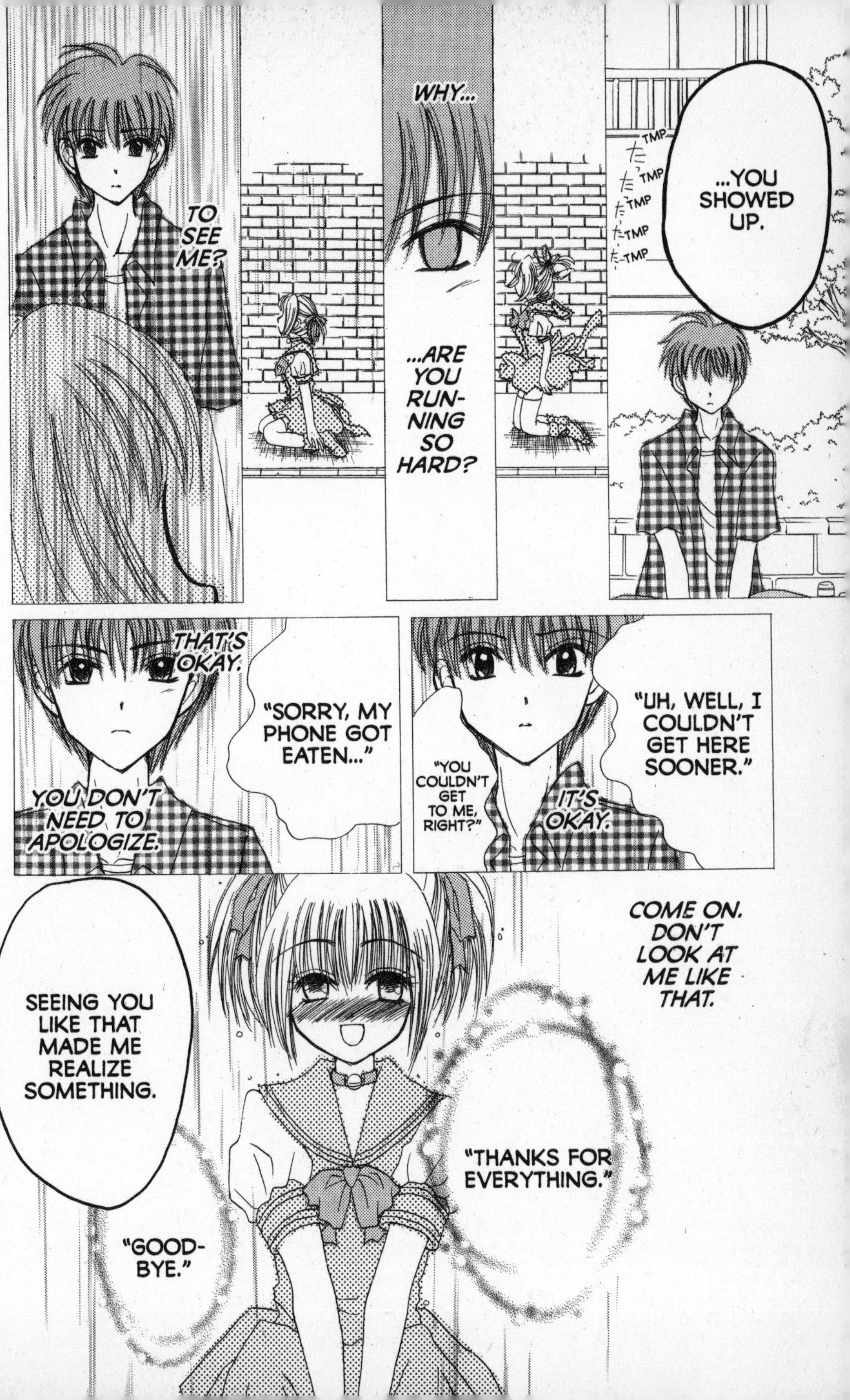
...YOU SHOWED UP.
TMP
TMP
TMP
TMP
TMP
WHY...
...ARE YOU RUN-NING SO HARD?
TO SEE ME?
"UH, WELL, I COULDN'T GET HERE SOONER."
IT'S OKAY.
"YOU COULDN'T GET TO ME, RIGHT?"
"SORRY, MY PHONE GOT EATEN..."
THAT'S OKAY.
YOU DON'T NEED TO APOLOGIZE.
COME ON. DON'T LOOK AT ME LIKE THAT.
"THANKS FOR EVERYTHING."
SEEING YOU LIKE THAT MADE ME REALIZE SOMETHING.
"GOOD-BYE."

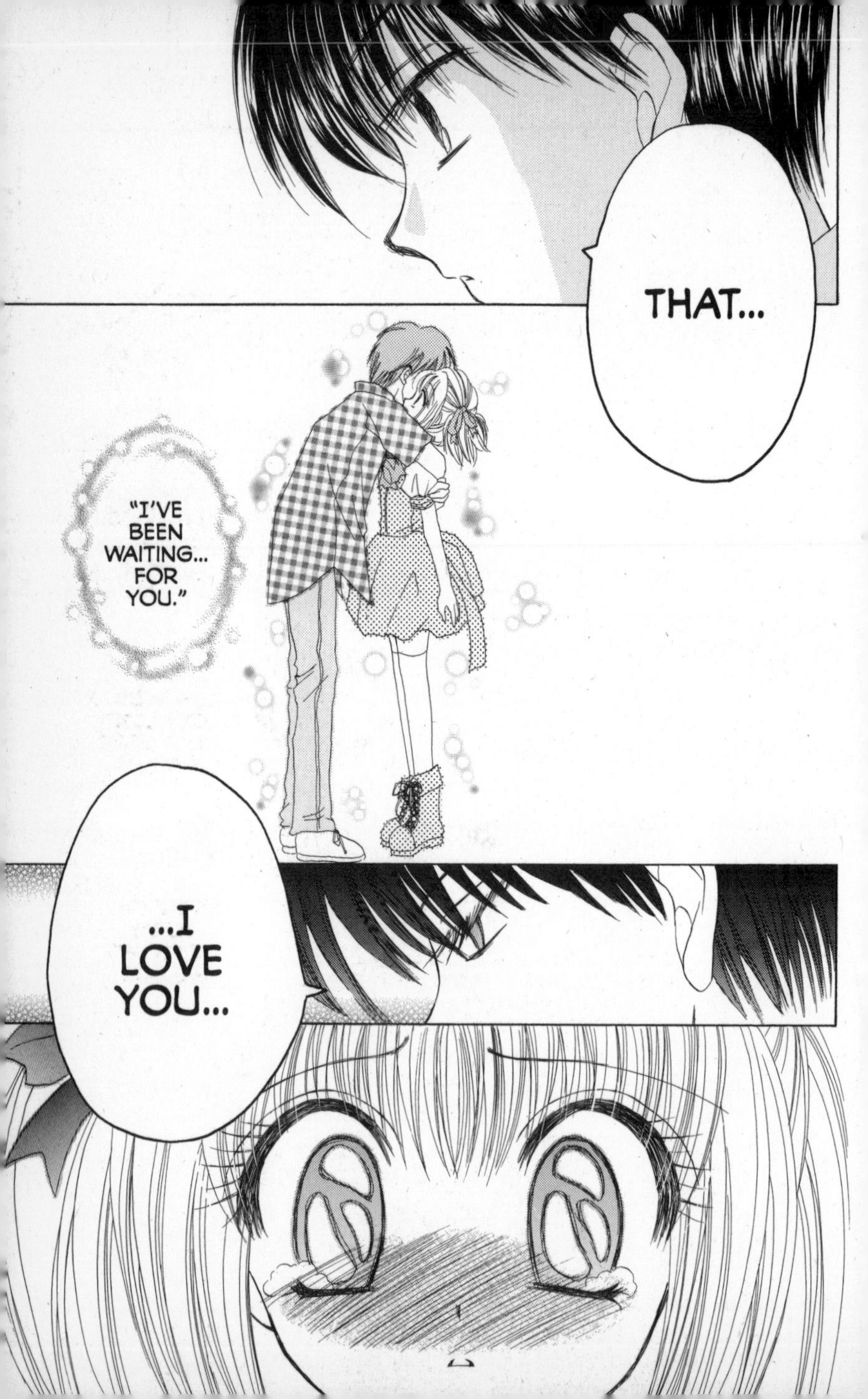
THAT...
"I'VE BEEN WAITING... FOR YOU."
...I LOVE YOU...

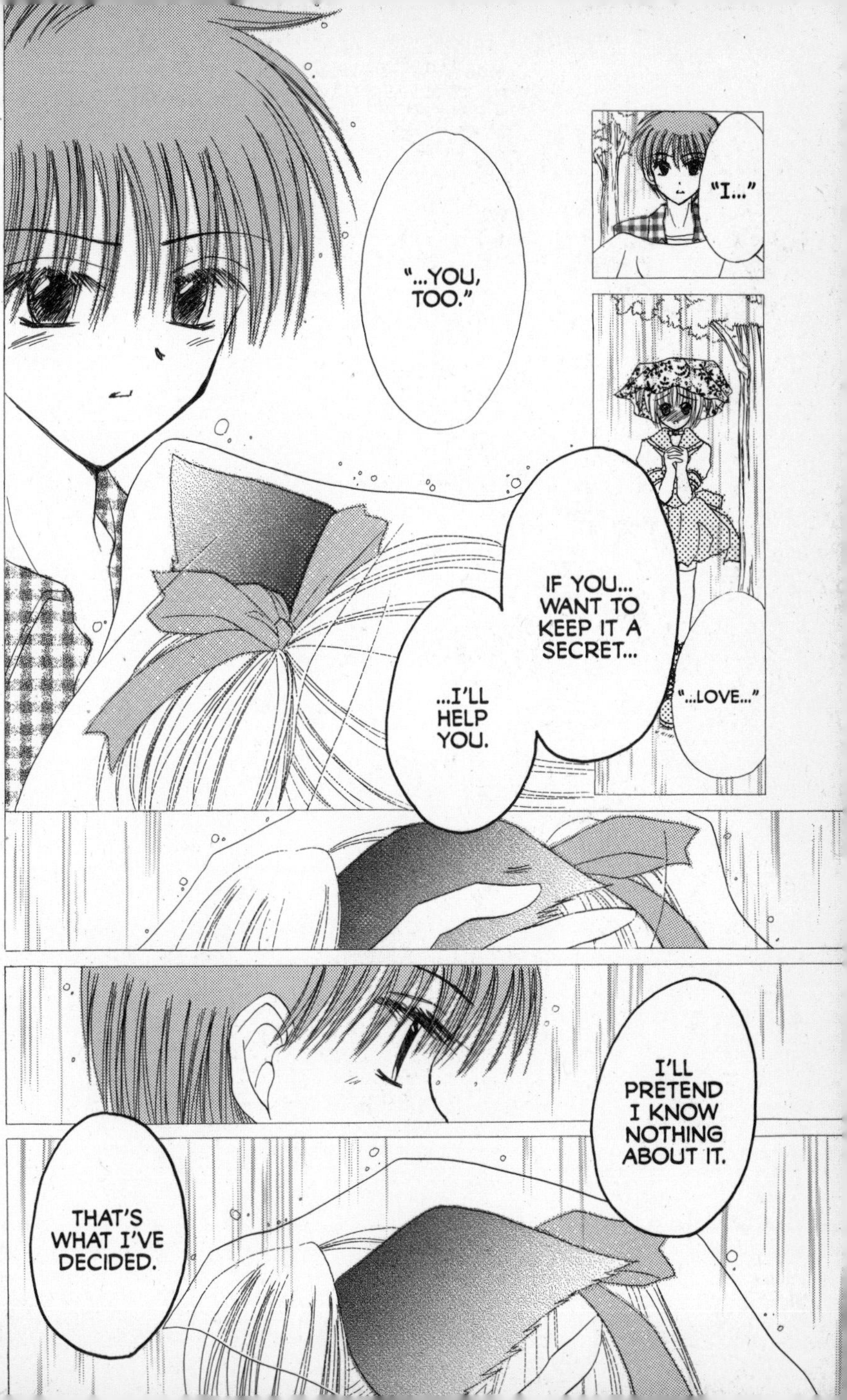
"I..."
"...LOVE..."
"...YOU, TOO."
IF YOU... WANT TO KEEP IT A SECRET...
...I'LL HELP YOU.
I'LL PRETEND I KNOW NOTHING ABOUT IT.
THAT'S WHAT I'VE DECIDED.

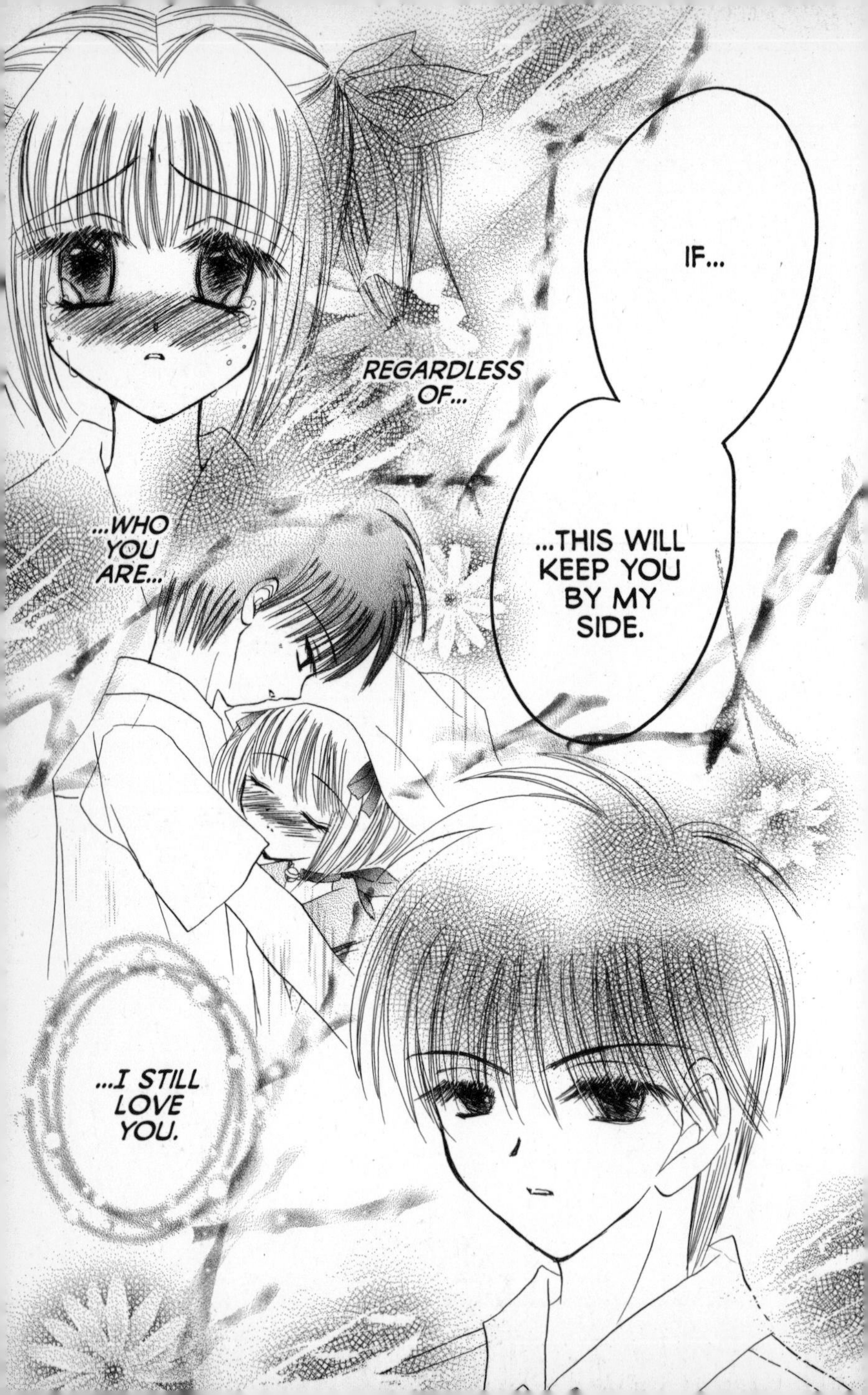
IF...
...THIS WILL KEEP YOU BY MY SIDE.
REGARDLESS OF...
...WHO YOU ARE...
...I STILL LOVE YOU.

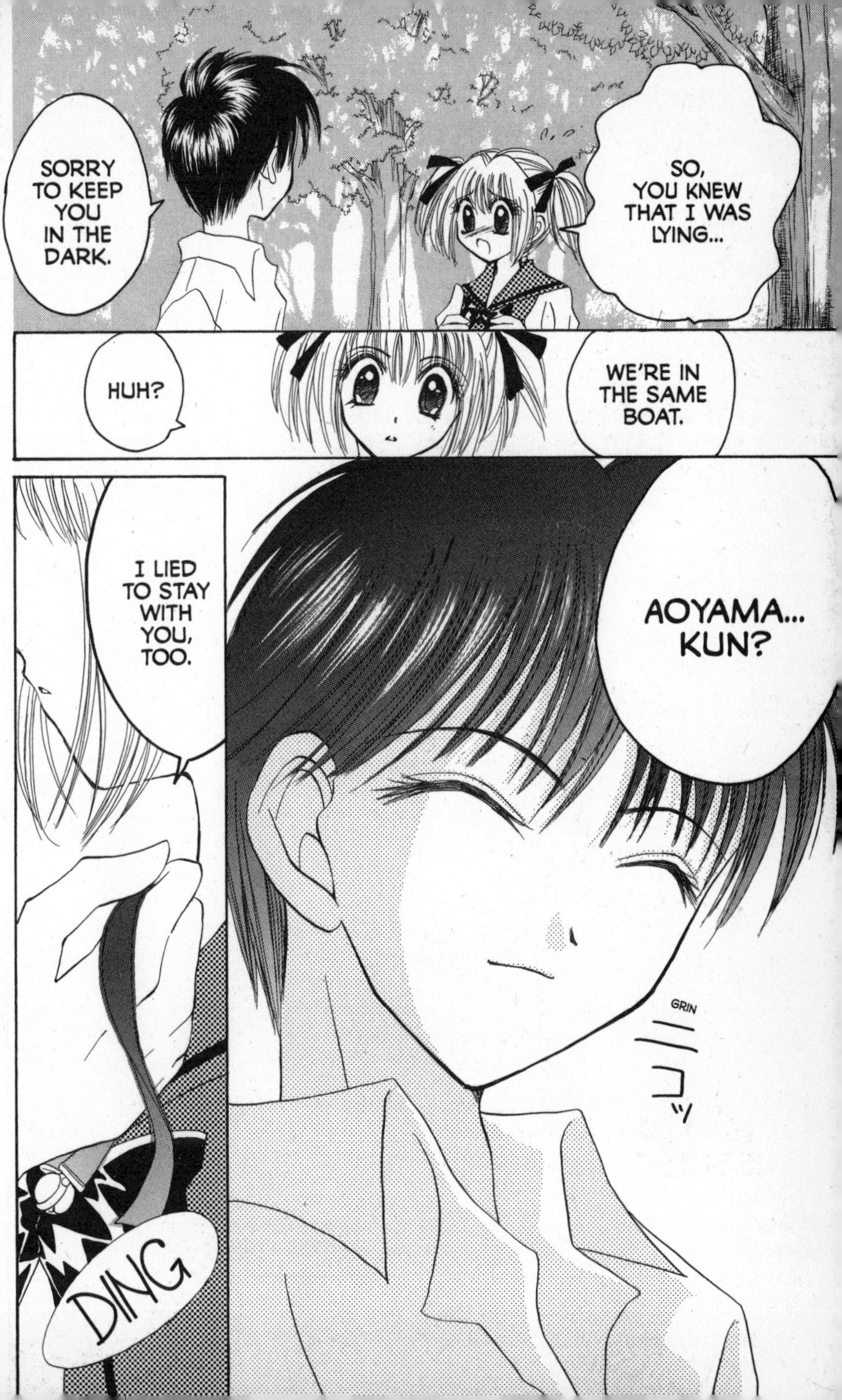
SO, YOU KNEW THAT I WAS LYING...
SORRY TO KEEP YOU IN THE DARK.
WE'RE IN THE SAME BOAT.
HUH?
AOYAMA... KUN?
GRIN
I LIED TO STAY WITH YOU, TOO.
DING

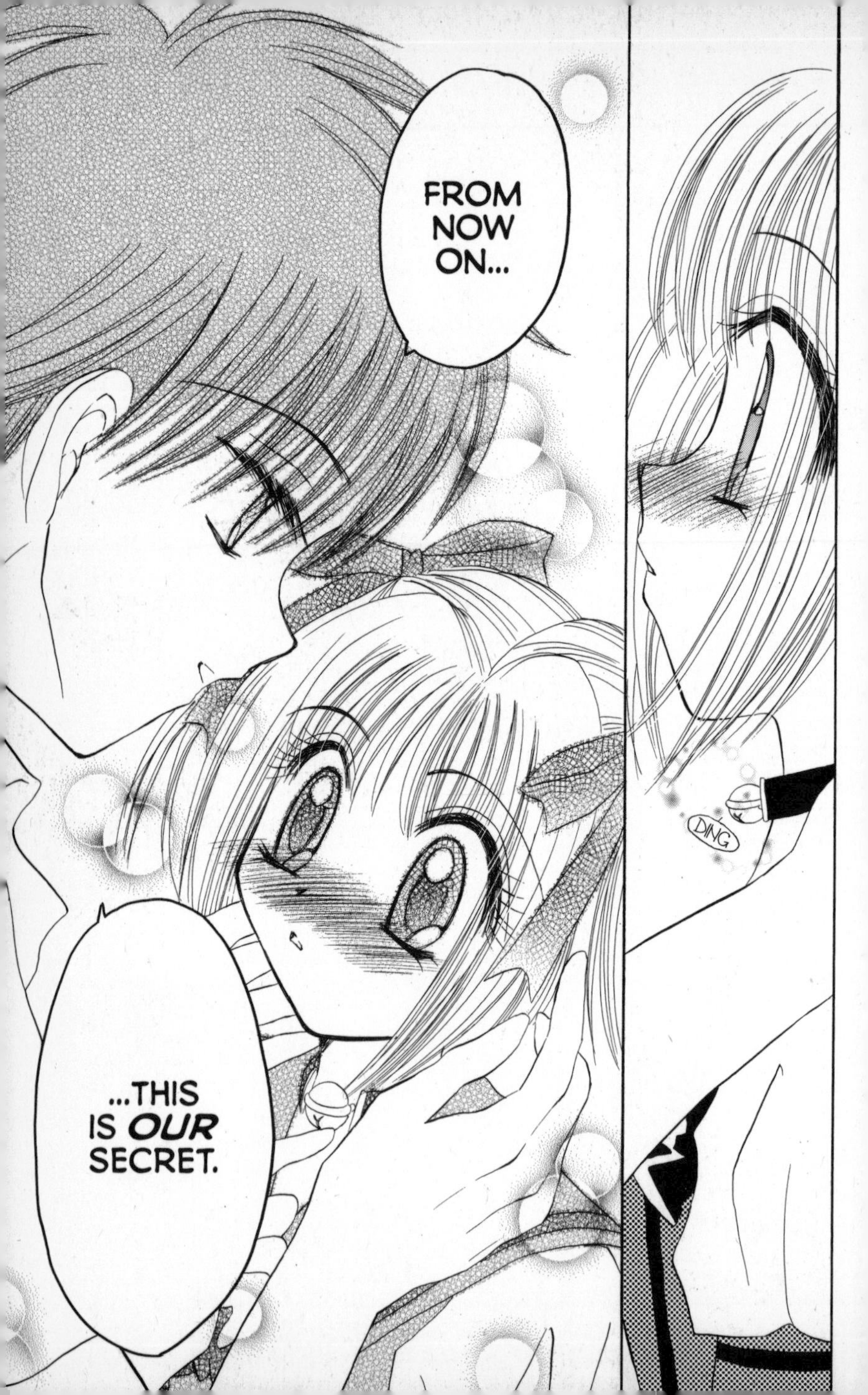
DING
FROM NOW ON...
...THIS IS *OUR* SECRET.

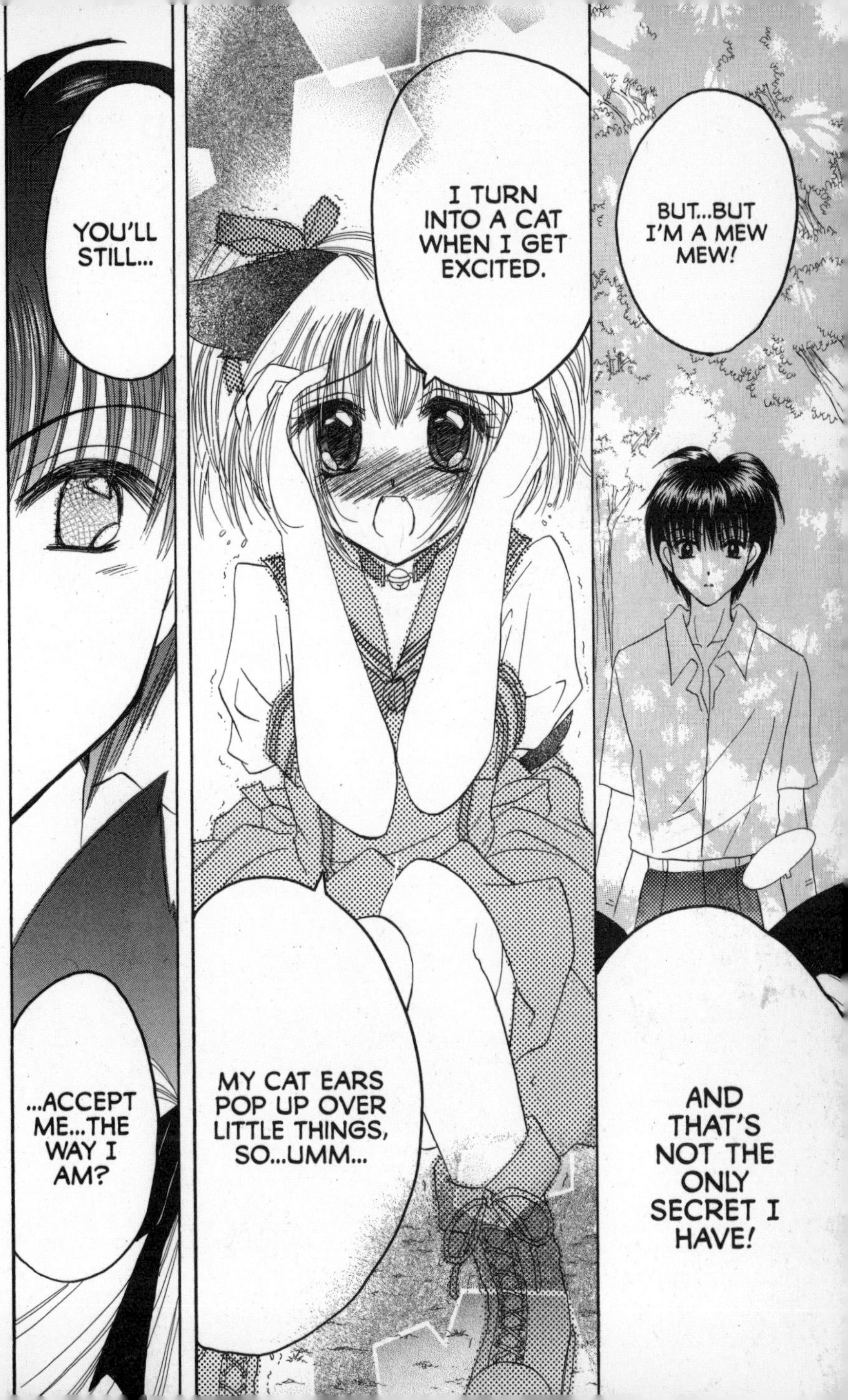
BUT...BUT I'M A MEW MEW!
AND THAT'S NOT THE ONLY SECRET I HAVE!
I TURN INTO A CAT WHEN I GET EXCITED.
MY CAT EARS POP UP OVER LITTLE THINGS, SO...UMM...
YOU'LL STILL...
...ACCEPT ME...THE WAY I AM?

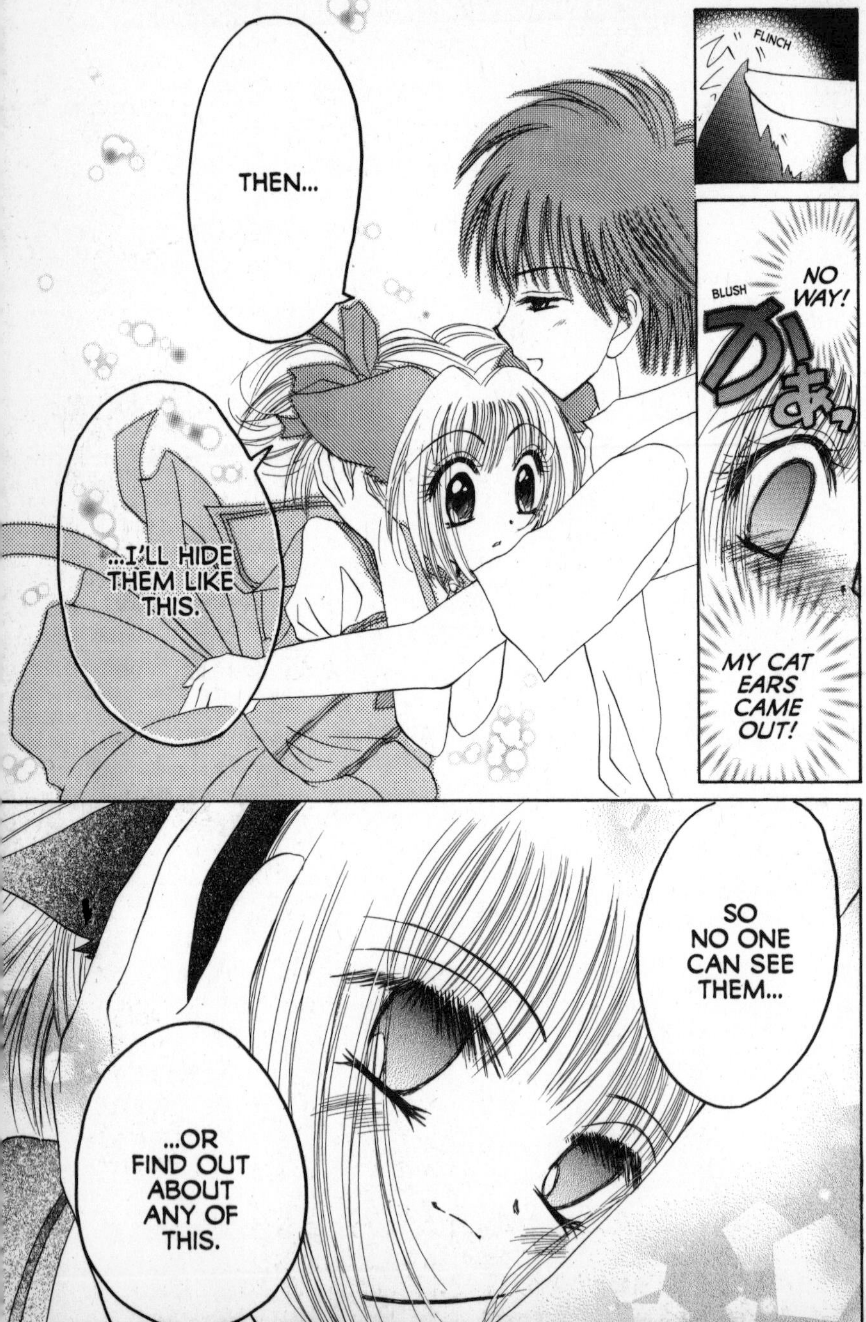
FLINCH
BLUSH
NO WAY!
MY CAT EARS CAME OUT!
THEN...
...I'LL HIDE THEM LIKE THIS.
SO NO ONE CAN SEE THEM...
...OR FIND OUT ABOUT ANY OF THIS.

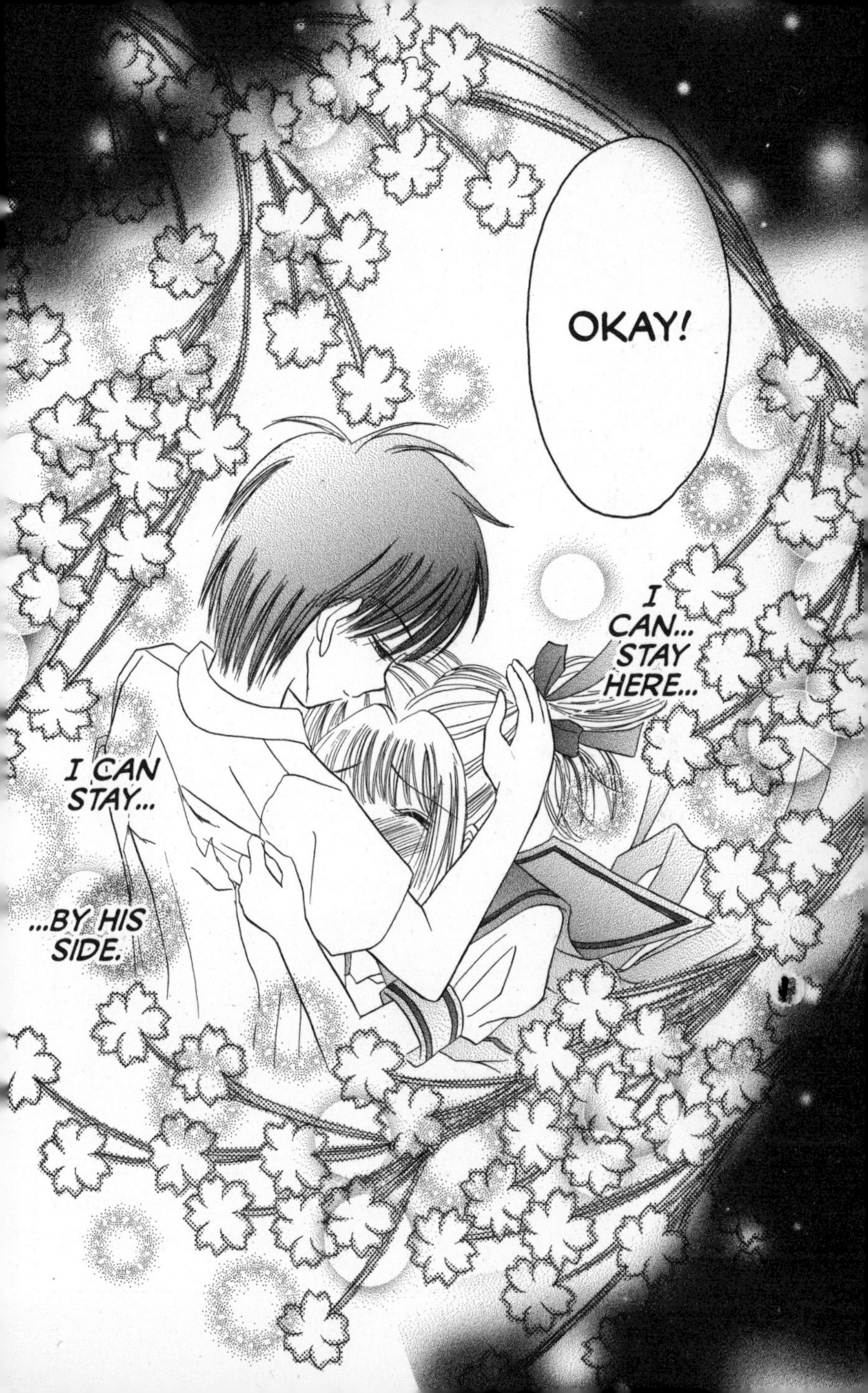
OKAY!
I CAN... STAY HERE...
I CAN STAY...
...BY HIS SIDE.

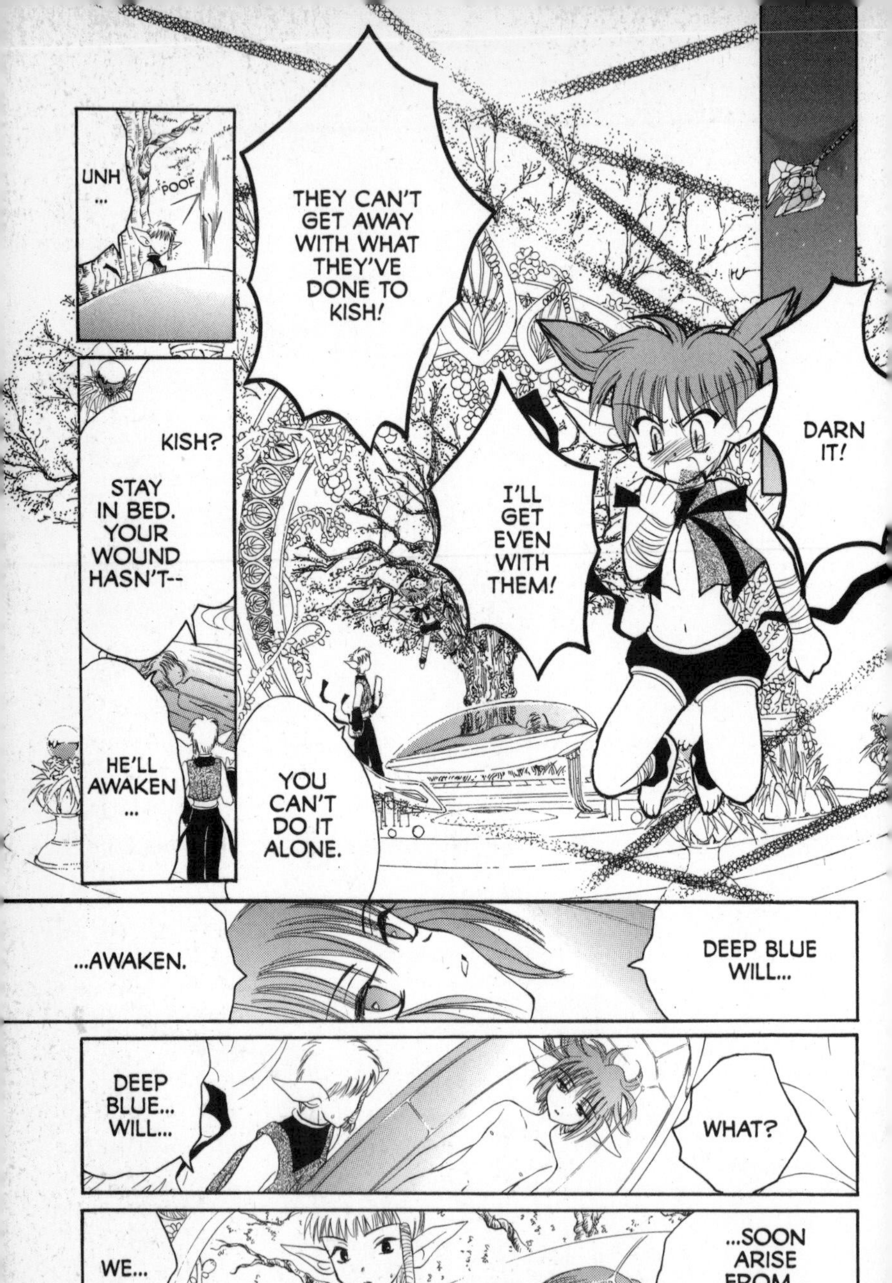
THEY CAN'T GET AWAY WITH WHAT THEY'VE DONE TO KISH!
DARN IT!
I'LL GET EVEN WITH THEM!
YOU CAN'T DO IT ALONE.
UNH ...
POOF
KISH?
STAY IN BED. YOUR WOUND HASN'T--
HE'LL AWAKEN ...
DEEP BLUE WILL...
...AWAKEN.
WHAT?
DEEP BLUE... WILL...
...SOON ARISE FROM... SLEEP.
WE...

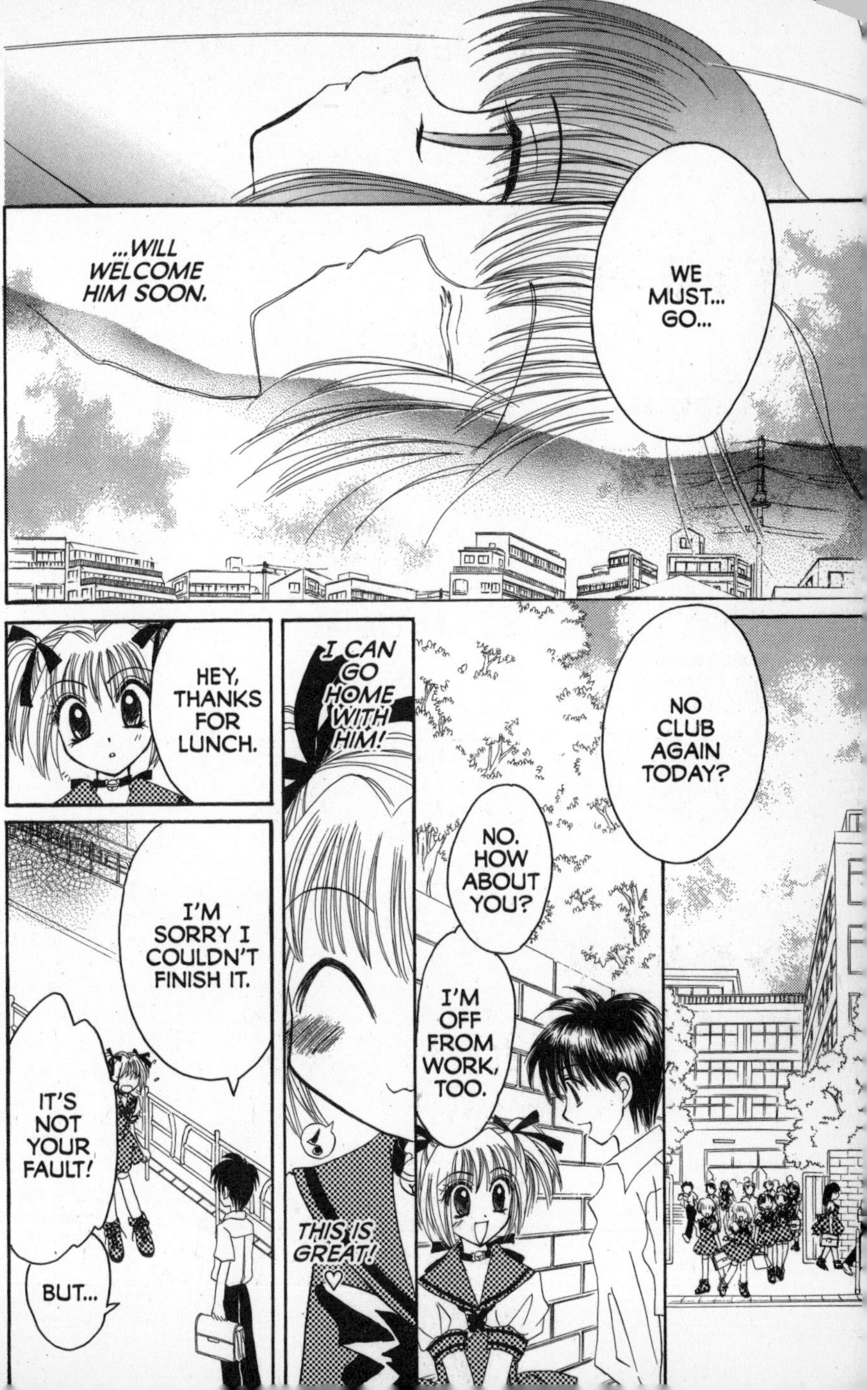
WE MUST... GO...
...WILL WELCOME HIM SOON.
NO CLUB AGAIN TODAY?
NO. HOW ABOUT YOU?
I'M OFF FROM WORK, TOO.
I CAN GO HOME WITH HIM!
THIS IS GREAT! ♡
HEY, THANKS FOR LUNCH.
I'M SORRY I COULDN'T FINISH IT.
IT'S NOT YOUR FAULT!
BUT...

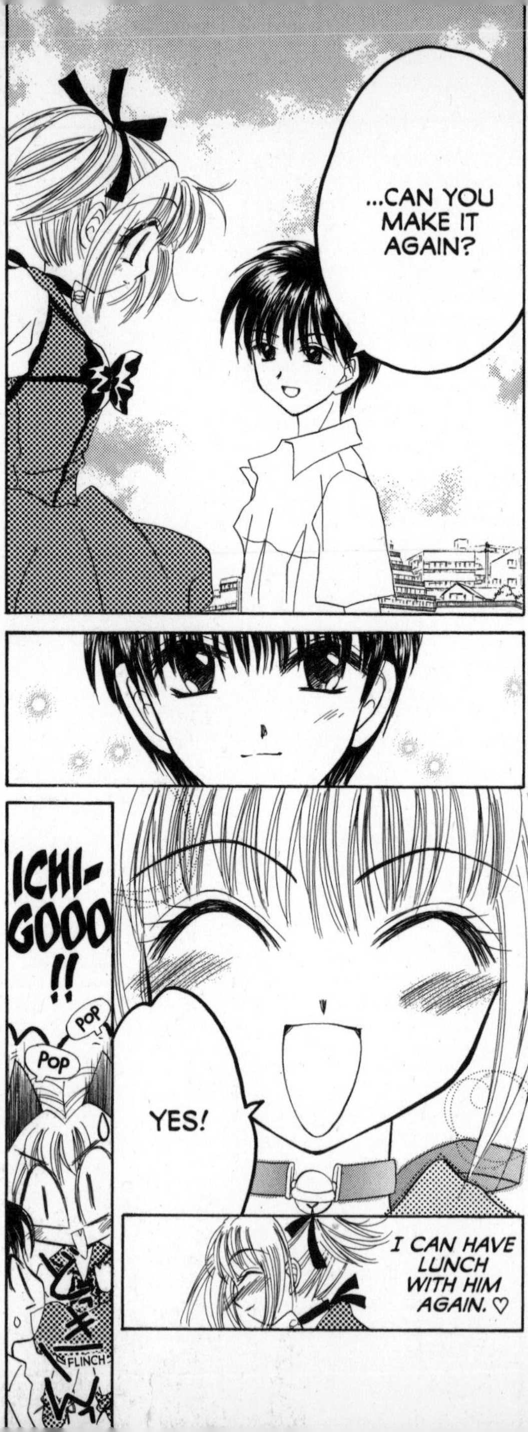
...CAN YOU MAKE IT AGAIN?
YES!
I CAN HAVE LUNCH WITH HIM AGAIN. ♡
ICHI-GOOO!!
POP
POP
FLINCH

SPECIAL THANKS!!

R. YOSHIDA

H. MATSUMOTO
M. OMORI

S. NAOHARA
A. SUZUKI
K. HONDA

H. OIKAWA

M. SEKIYA
S. SUDA

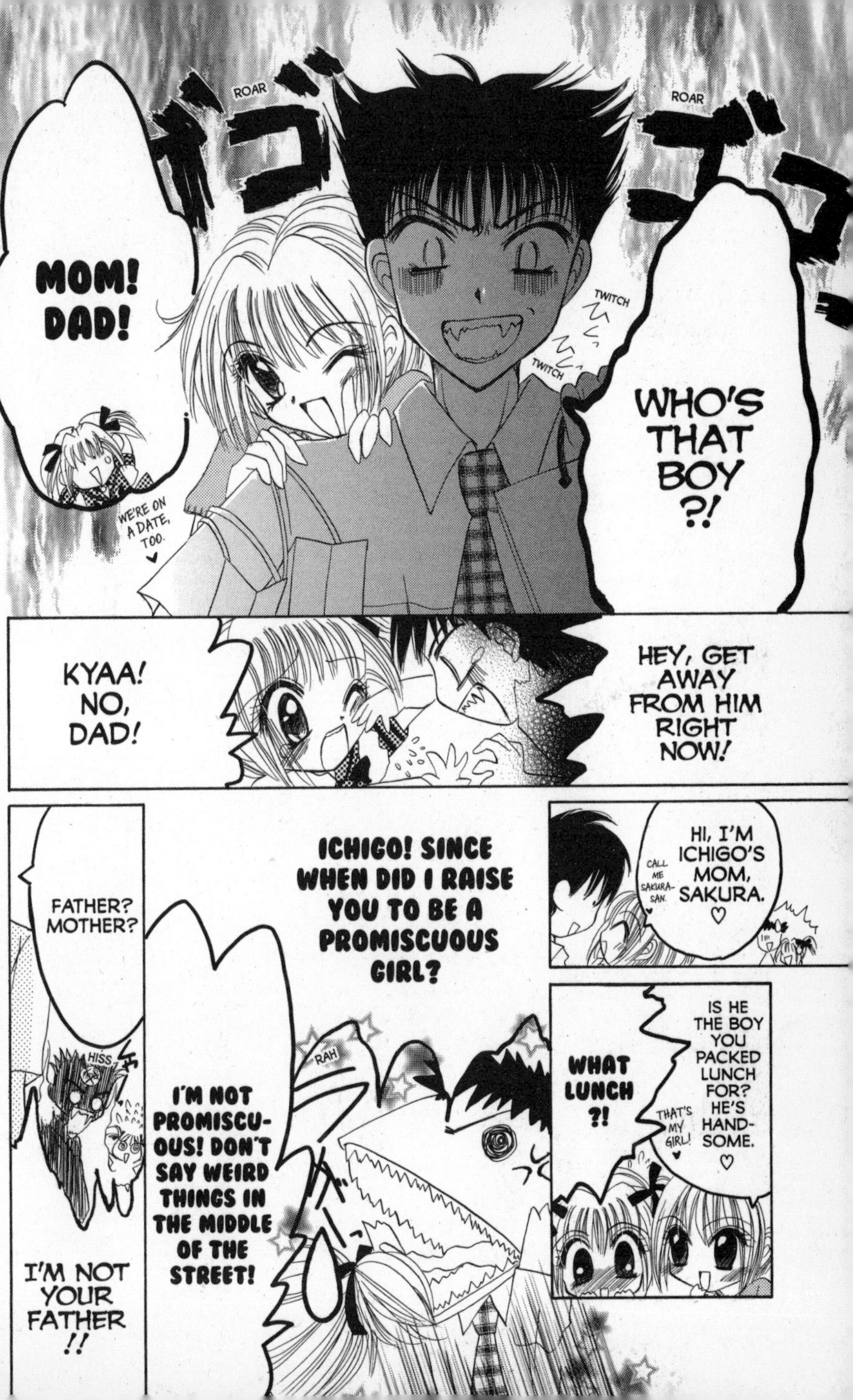
ROAR
WHO'S THAT BOY ?!
TWITCH
TWITCH
ROAR
MOM! DAD!
WE'RE ON A DATE, TOO. ♥
HEY, GET AWAY FROM HIM RIGHT NOW!
KYAA! NO, DAD!
HI, I'M ICHIGO'S MOM, SAKURA. ♡
CALL ME SAKURA-SAN. ♥
IS HE THE BOY YOU PACKED LUNCH FOR? HE'S HANDSOME. ♡
THAT'S MY GIRL! ♥
WHAT LUNCH ?!
ICHIGO! SINCE WHEN DID I RAISE YOU TO BE A PROMISCUOUS GIRL?
RAH
I'M NOT PROMISCU-OUS! DON'T SAY WEIRD THINGS IN THE MIDDLE OF THE STREET!
FATHER? MOTHER?
HISS
I'M NOT YOUR FATHER !!

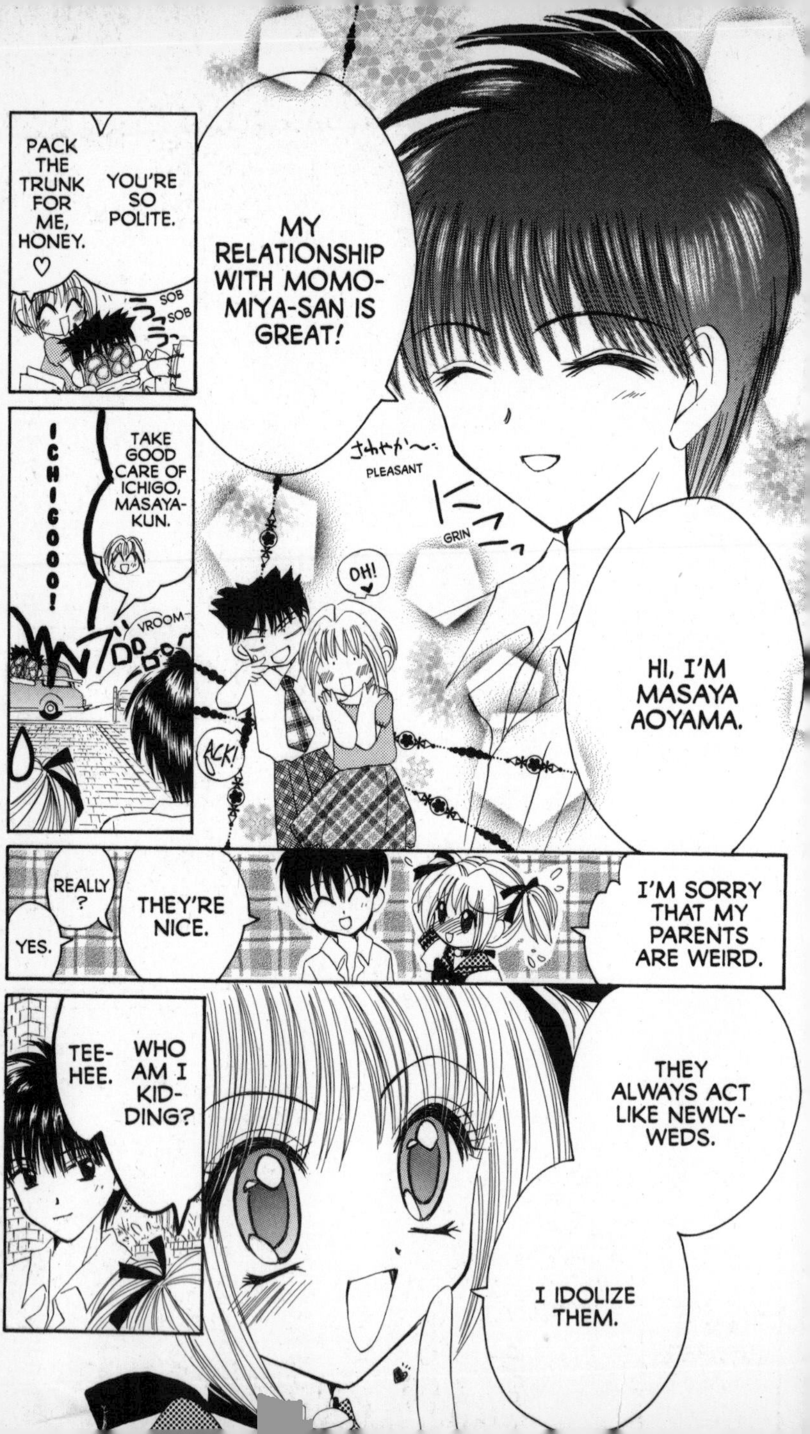
HI, I'M MASAYA AOYAMA.
MY RELATIONSHIP WITH MOMO-MIYA-SAN IS GREAT!
PLEASANT
GRIN
OH!
ACK!
YOU'RE SO POLITE.
PACK THE TRUNK FOR ME, HONEY. ♡
SOB SOB
TAKE GOOD CARE OF ICHIGO, MASAYA-KUN.
ICHIGOOOO!
VROOM
I'M SORRY THAT MY PARENTS ARE WEIRD.
THEY'RE NICE.
REALLY?
YES.
THEY ALWAYS ACT LIKE NEWLY-WEDS.
I IDOLIZE THEM.
WHO AM I KID-DING?
TEE-HEE.

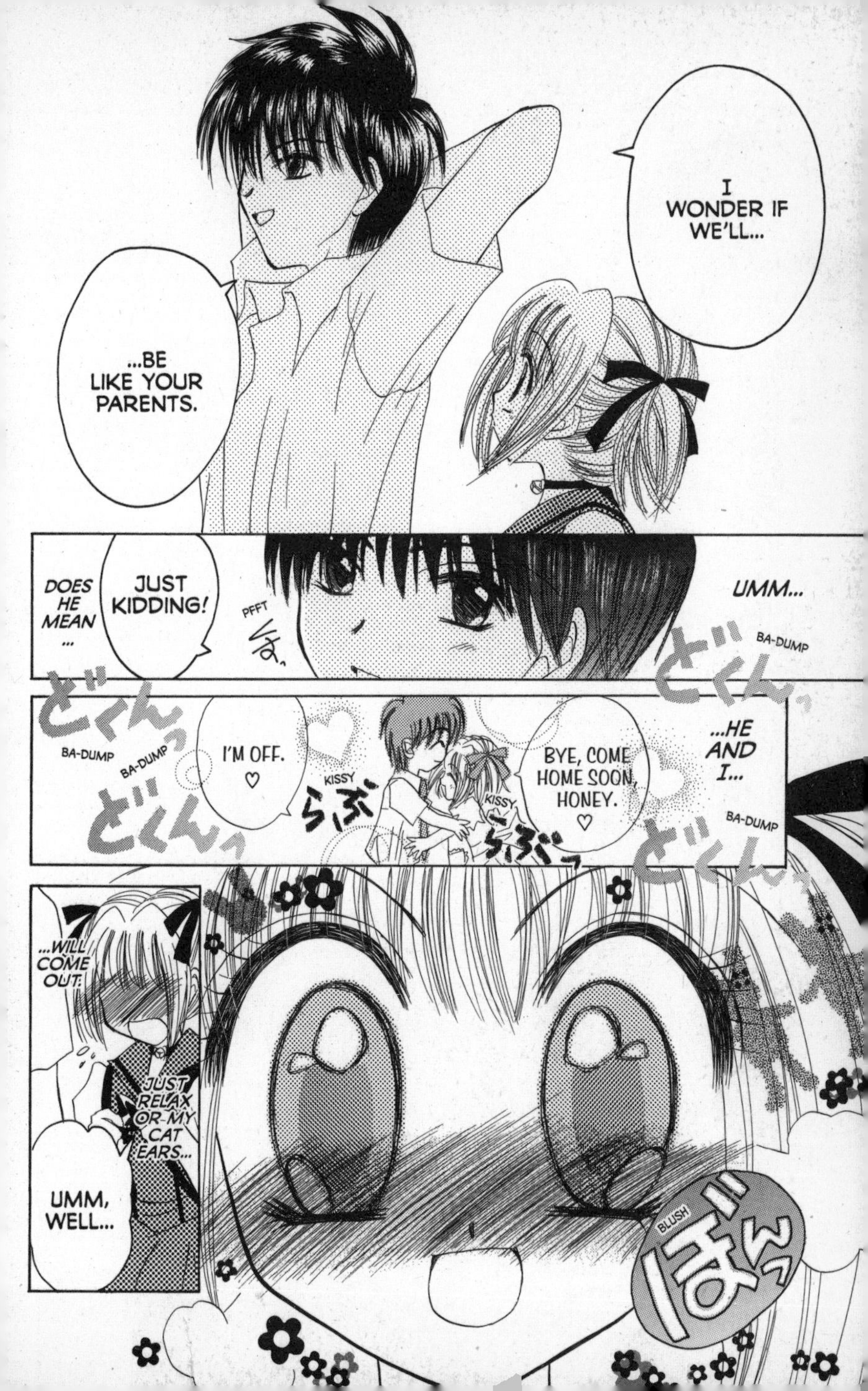
I WONDER IF WE'LL...
...BE LIKE YOUR PARENTS.
UMM...
BA-DUMP
PFFT
JUST KIDDING!
DOES HE MEAN ...
...HE AND I...
BA-DUMP
BYE, COME HOME SOON, HONEY. ♡
KISSY
KISSY
I'M OFF. ♡
BA-DUMP
BA-DUMP
BLUSH
...WILL COME OUT.
JUST RELAX OR MY CAT EARS...
UMM, WELL...

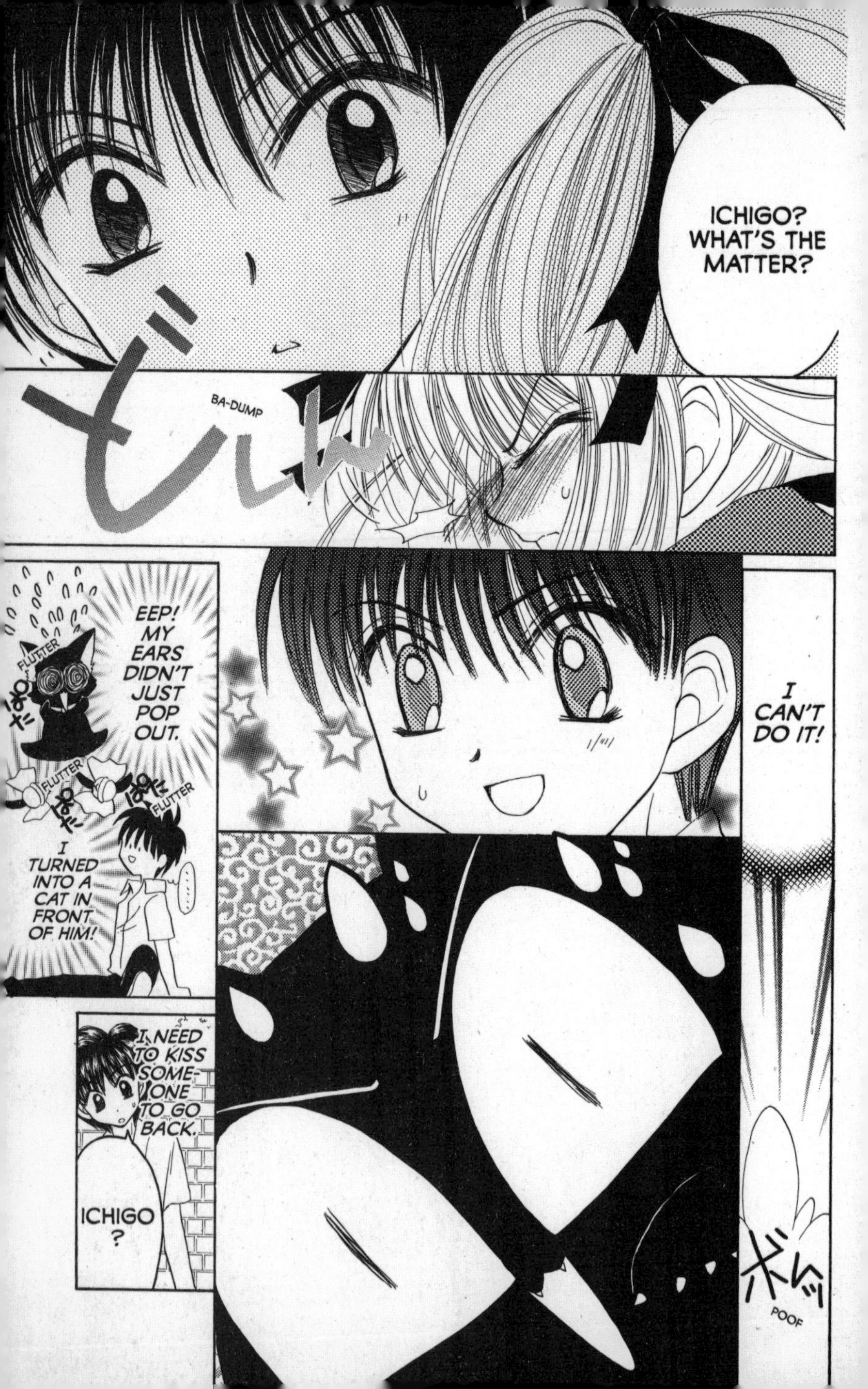
ICHIGO? WHAT'S THE MATTER?
BA-DUMP
I CAN'T DO IT!
POOF
EEP! MY EARS DIDN'T JUST POP OUT.
FLUTTER
FLUTTER
FLUTTER
I TURNED INTO A CAT IN FRONT OF HIM!
......
I NEED TO KISS SOMEONE TO GO BACK.
ICHIGO?

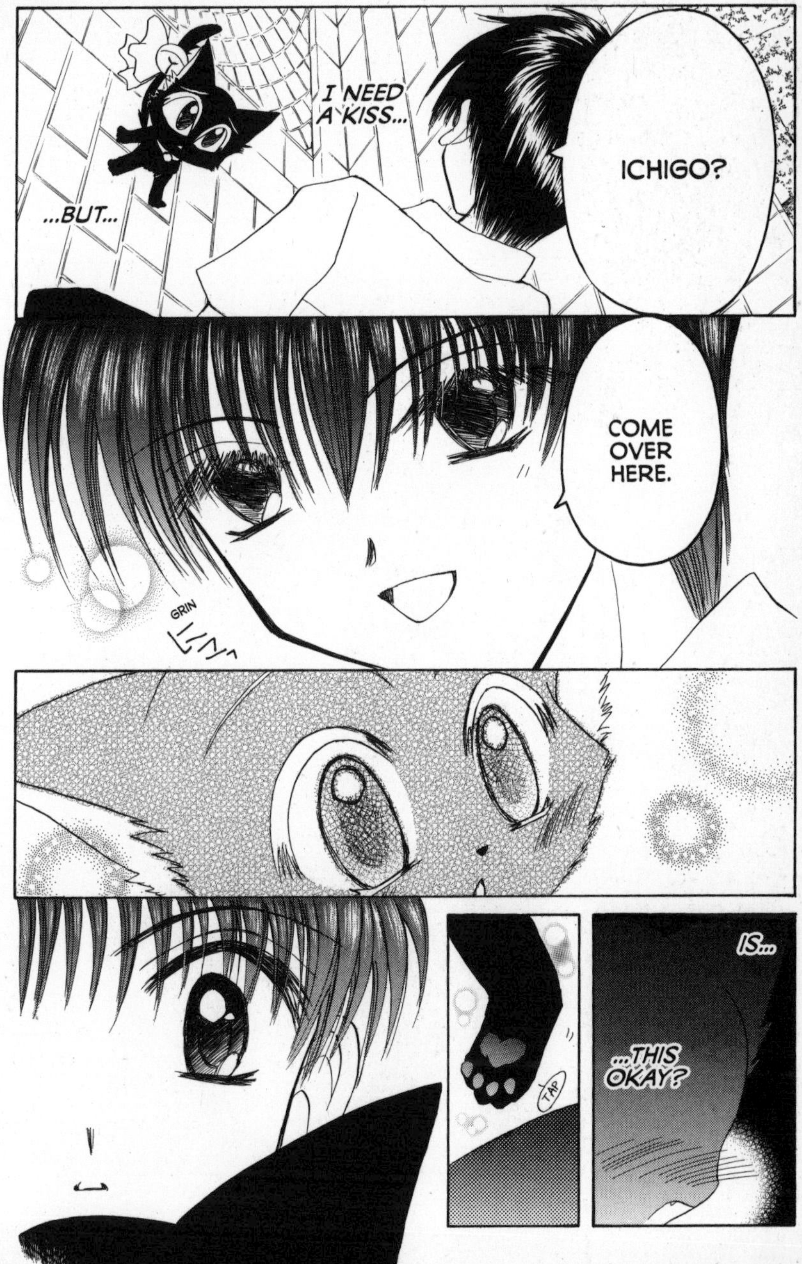
ICHIGO?
I NEED A KISS...
...BUT...
COME OVER HERE.
GRIN
IS...
...THIS OKAY?
TAP

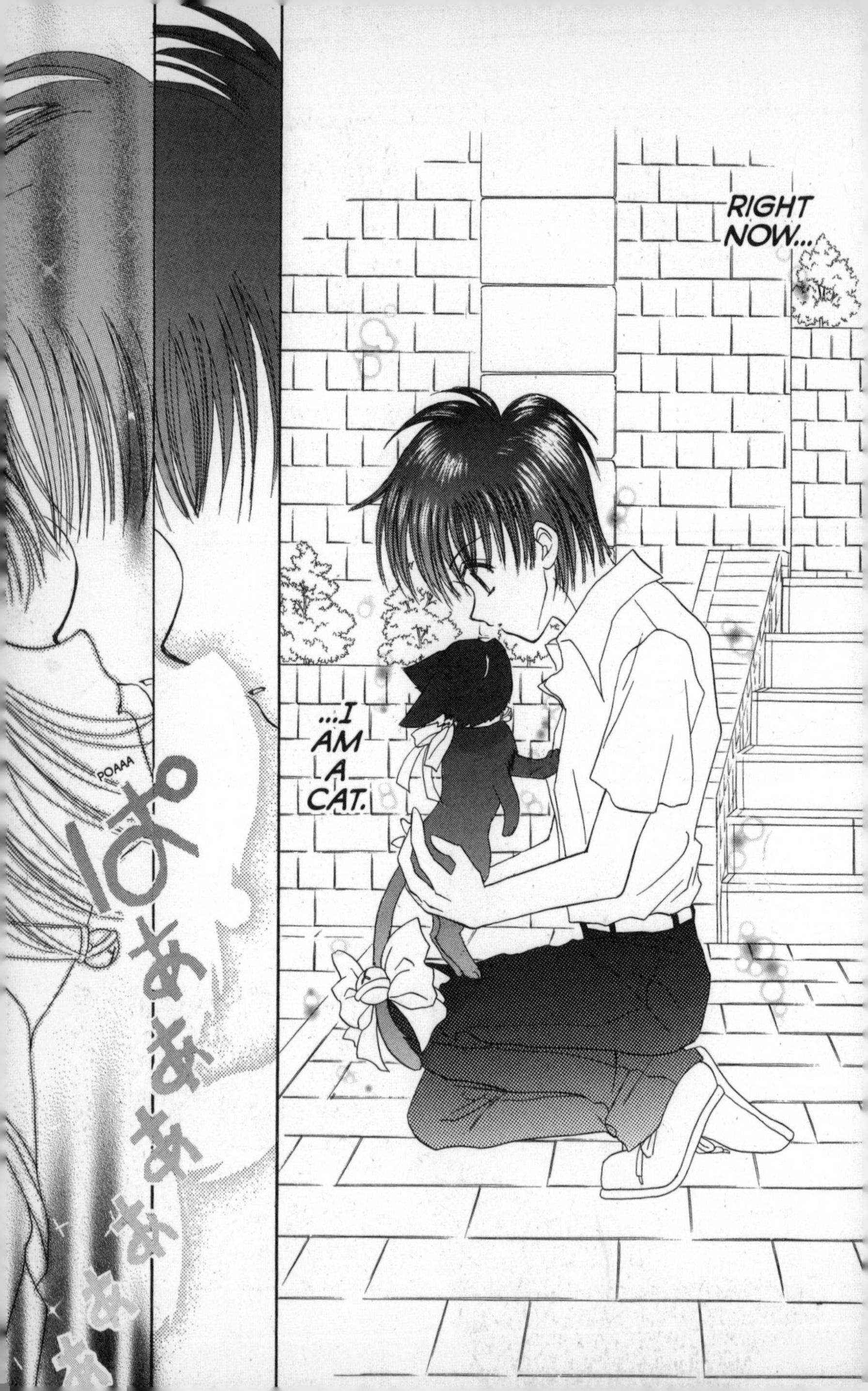
RIGHT NOW...
...I AM A CAT.
POAAA

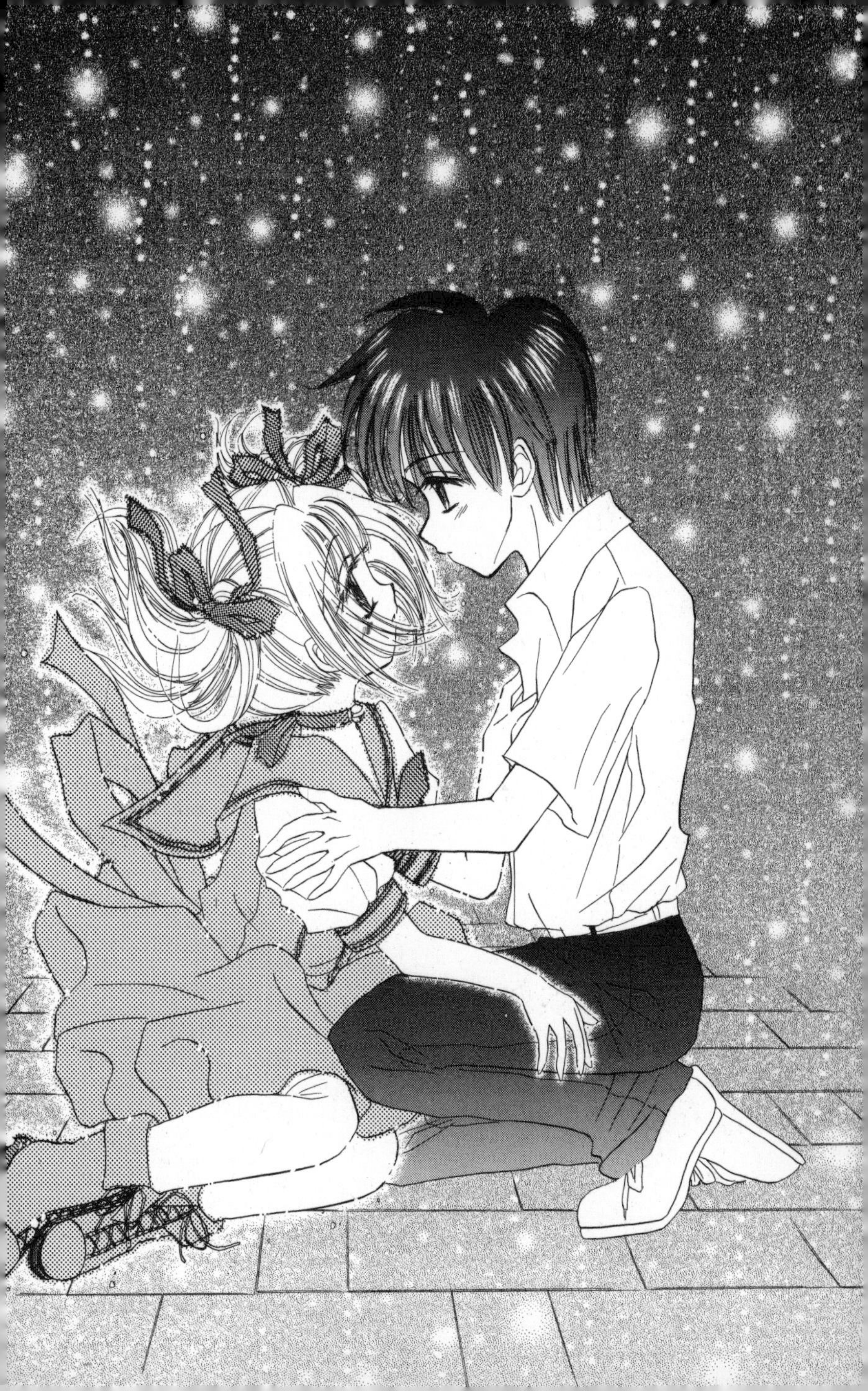

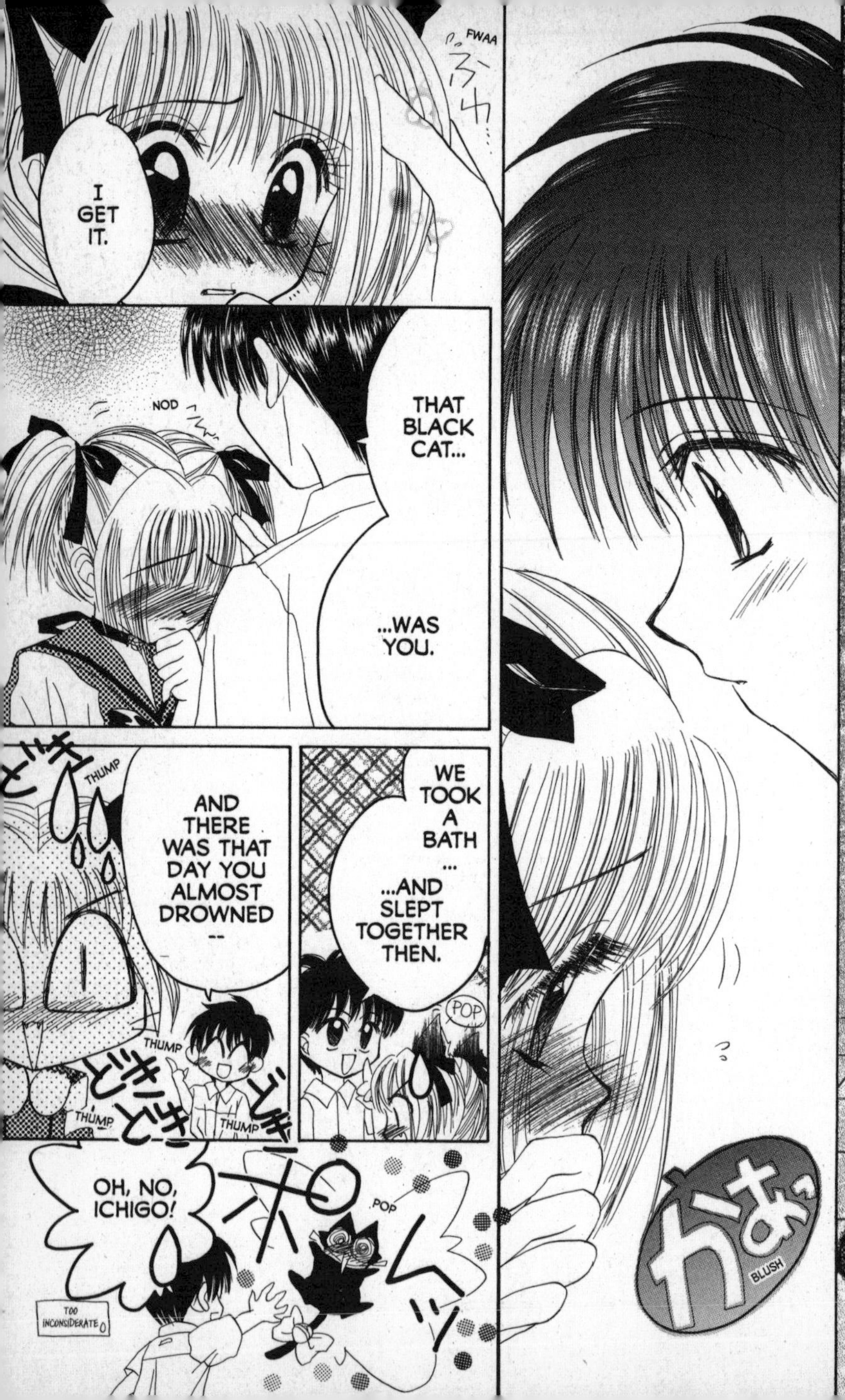
BLUSH
FWAA
I GET IT.
NOD
THAT BLACK CAT...
...WAS YOU.
WE TOOK A BATH ...
...AND SLEPT TOGETHER THEN.
POP
AND THERE WAS THAT DAY YOU ALMOST DROWNED --
THUMP
THUMP
THUMP
THUMP
OH, NO, ICHIGO!
POP
TOO INCONSIDERATE

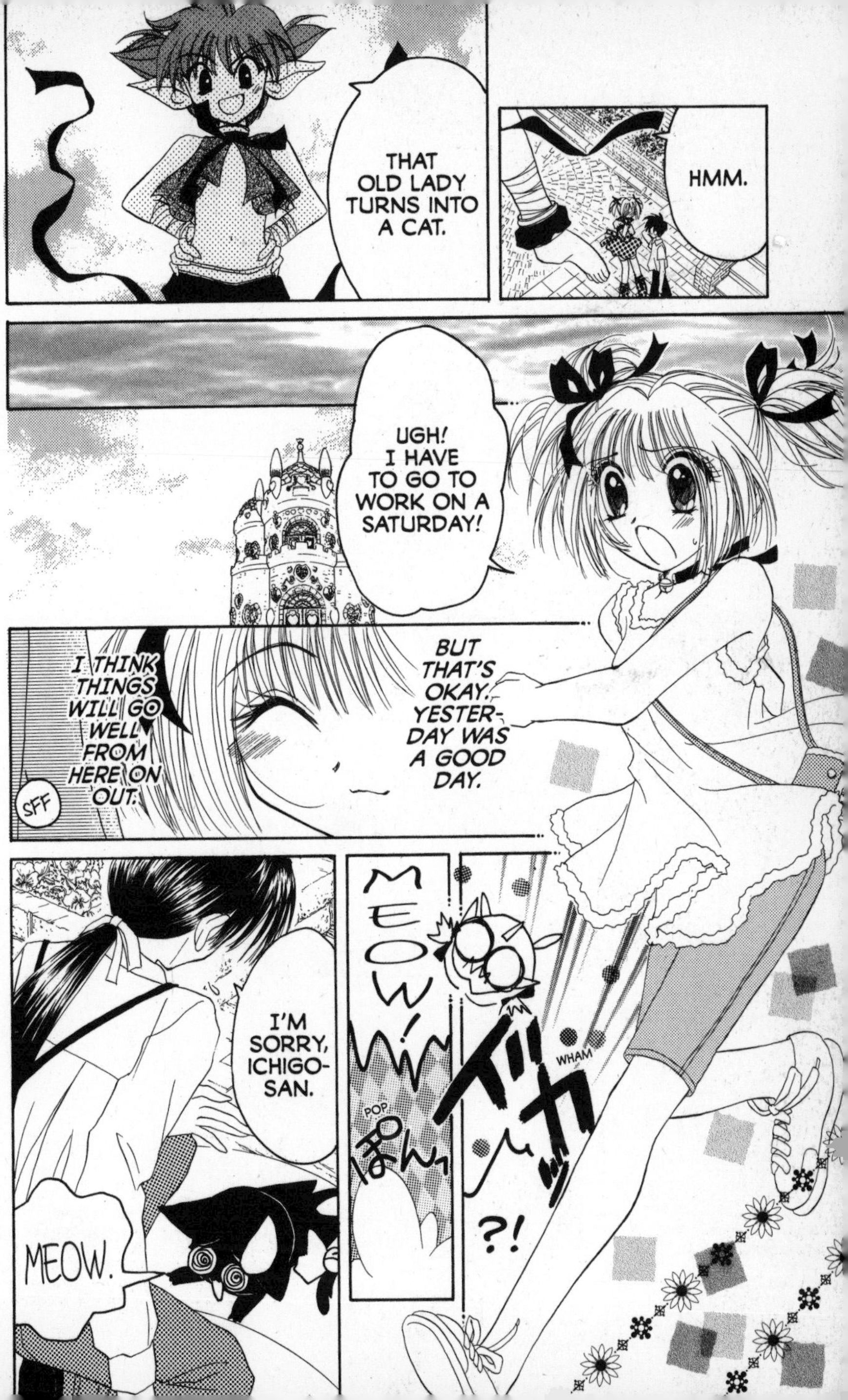
HMM.
THAT OLD LADY TURNS INTO A CAT.
UGH! I HAVE TO GO TO WORK ON A SATURDAY!
BUT THAT'S OKAY. YESTER-DAY WAS A GOOD DAY.
I THINK THINGS WILL GO WELL FROM HERE ON OUT.
SFF
WHAM
?!
MEOW!
POP
ぽん
I'M SORRY, ICHIGO-SAN.
MEOW.

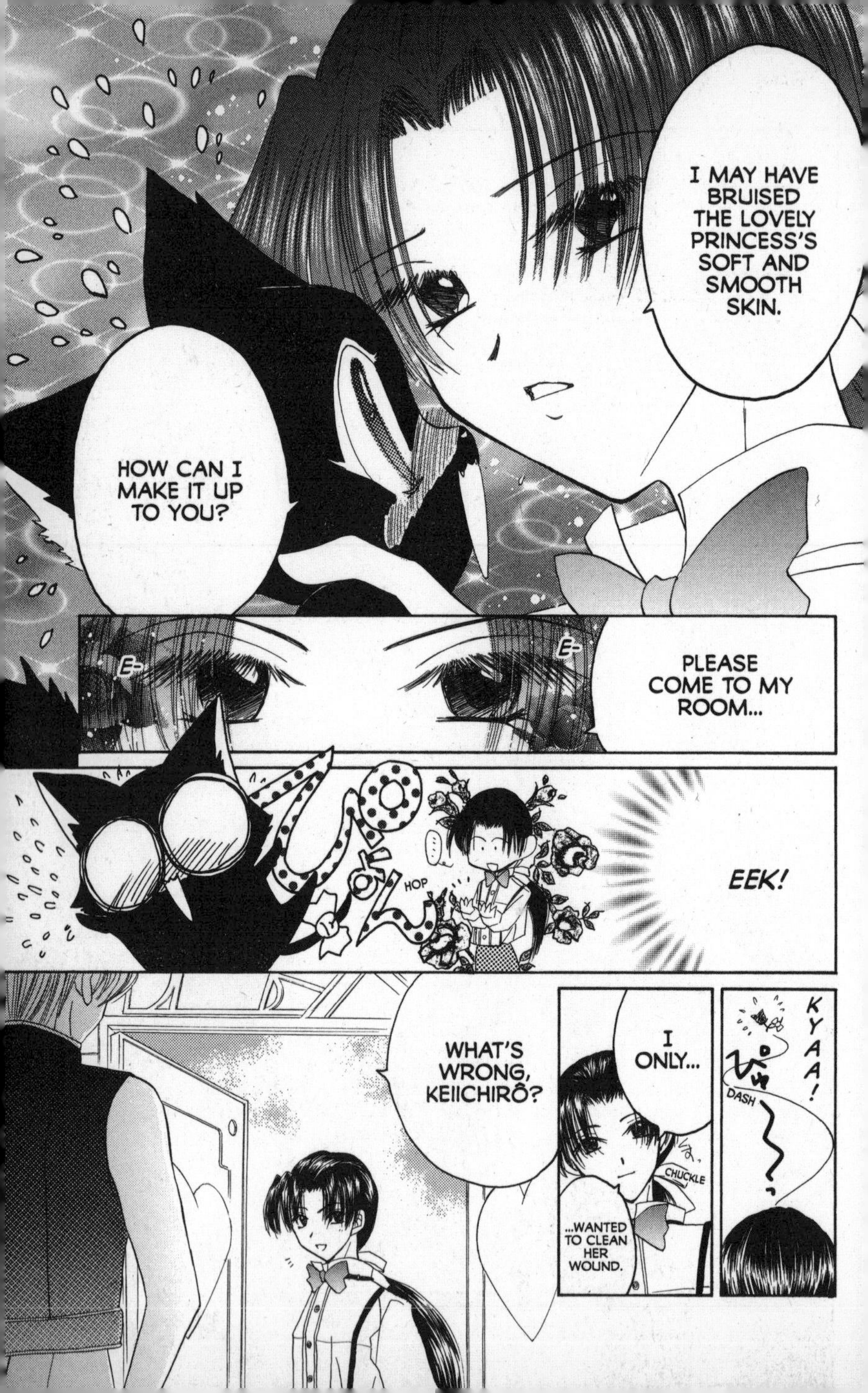
I MAY HAVE BRUISED THE LOVELY PRINCESS'S SOFT AND SMOOTH SKIN.
HOW CAN I MAKE IT UP TO YOU?
PLEASE COME TO MY ROOM...
EEK!
HOP
KYAA!
DASH
I ONLY...
CHUCKLE
...WANTED TO CLEAN HER WOUND.
WHAT'S WRONG, KEIICHIRÔ?

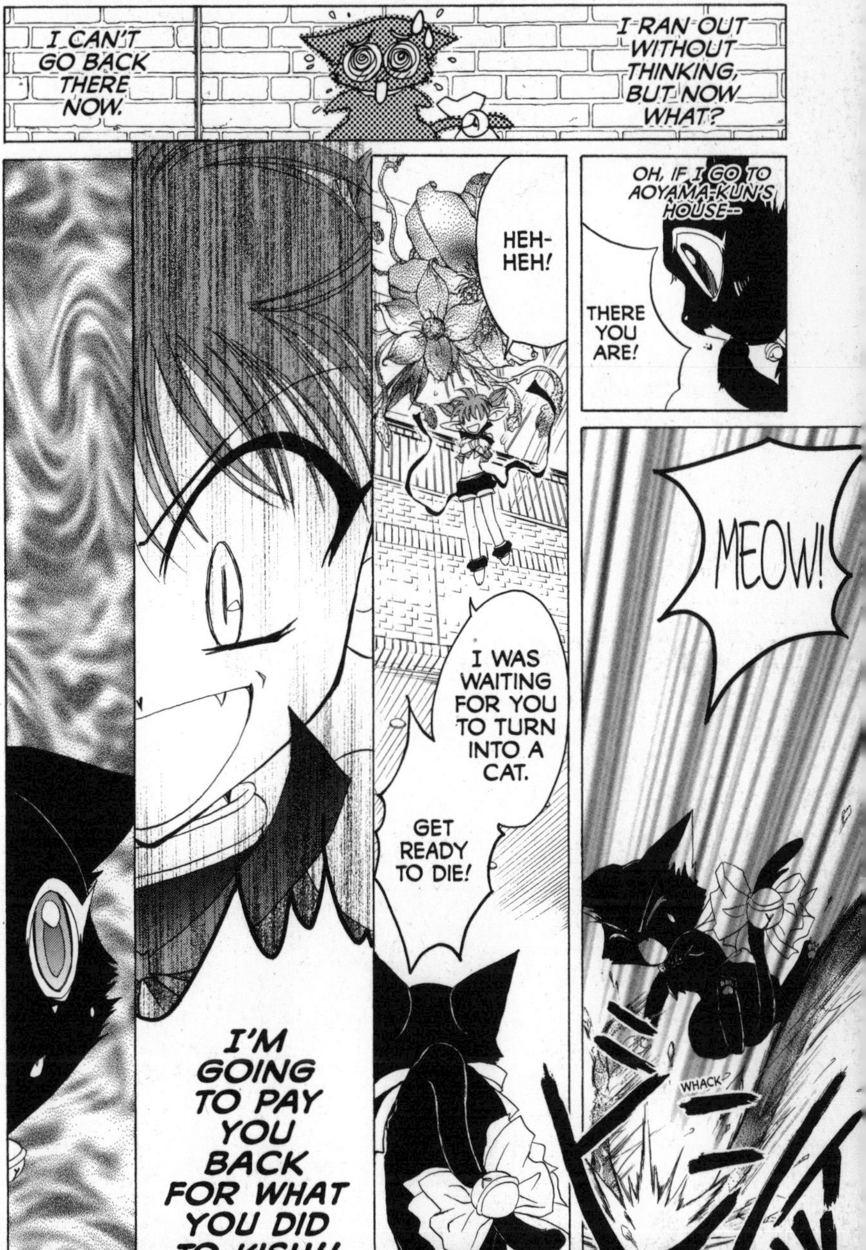
I RAN OUT WITHOUT THINKING, BUT NOW WHAT?
I CAN'T GO BACK THERE NOW.
OH, IF I GO TO AOYAMA-KUN'S HOUSE--
THERE YOU ARE!
MEOW!
WHACK
HEH-HEH!
I WAS WAITING FOR YOU TO TURN INTO A CAT.
GET READY TO DIE!
I'M GOING TO PAY YOU BACK FOR WHAT YOU DID TO KISH!!

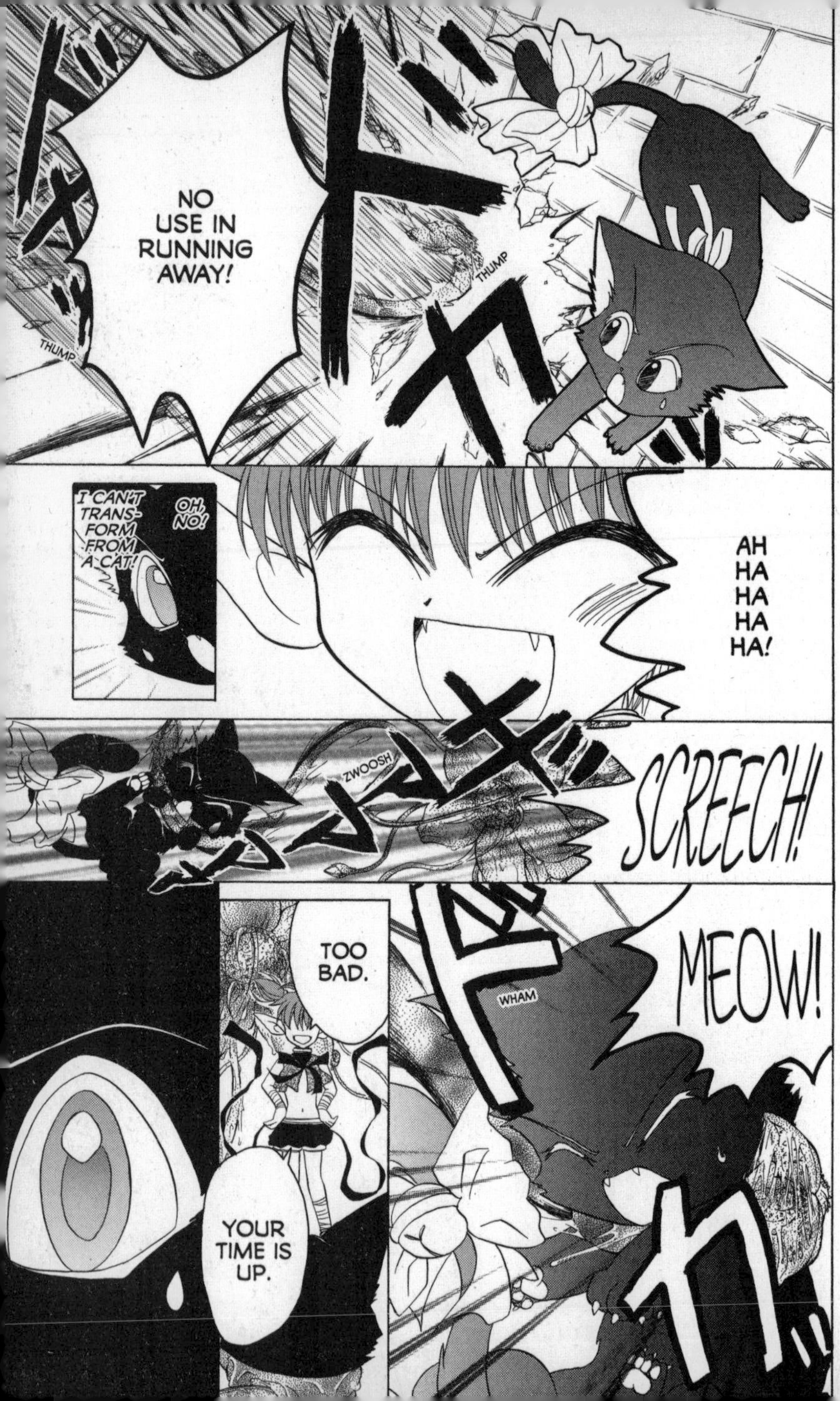
NO USE IN RUNNING AWAY!
THUMP
THUMP
AH HA HA HA HA!
OH, NO!
I CAN'T TRANSFORM FROM A CAT!
SCREECH!
ZWOOSH
MEOW!
WHAM
TOO BAD.
YOUR TIME IS UP.

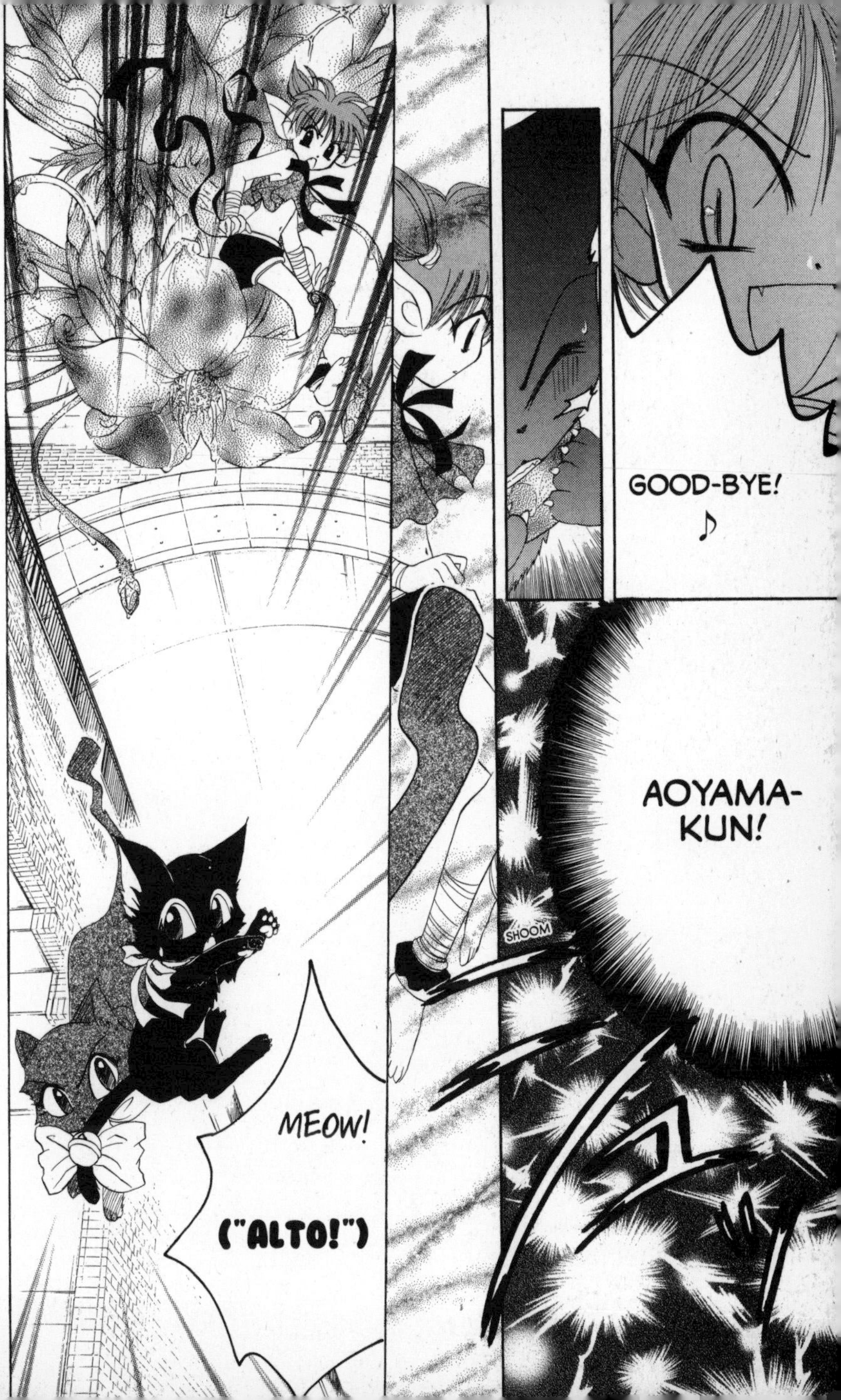
GOOD-BYE! ♪
AOYAMA-KUN!
SHOOM
MEOW!
("ALTO!")

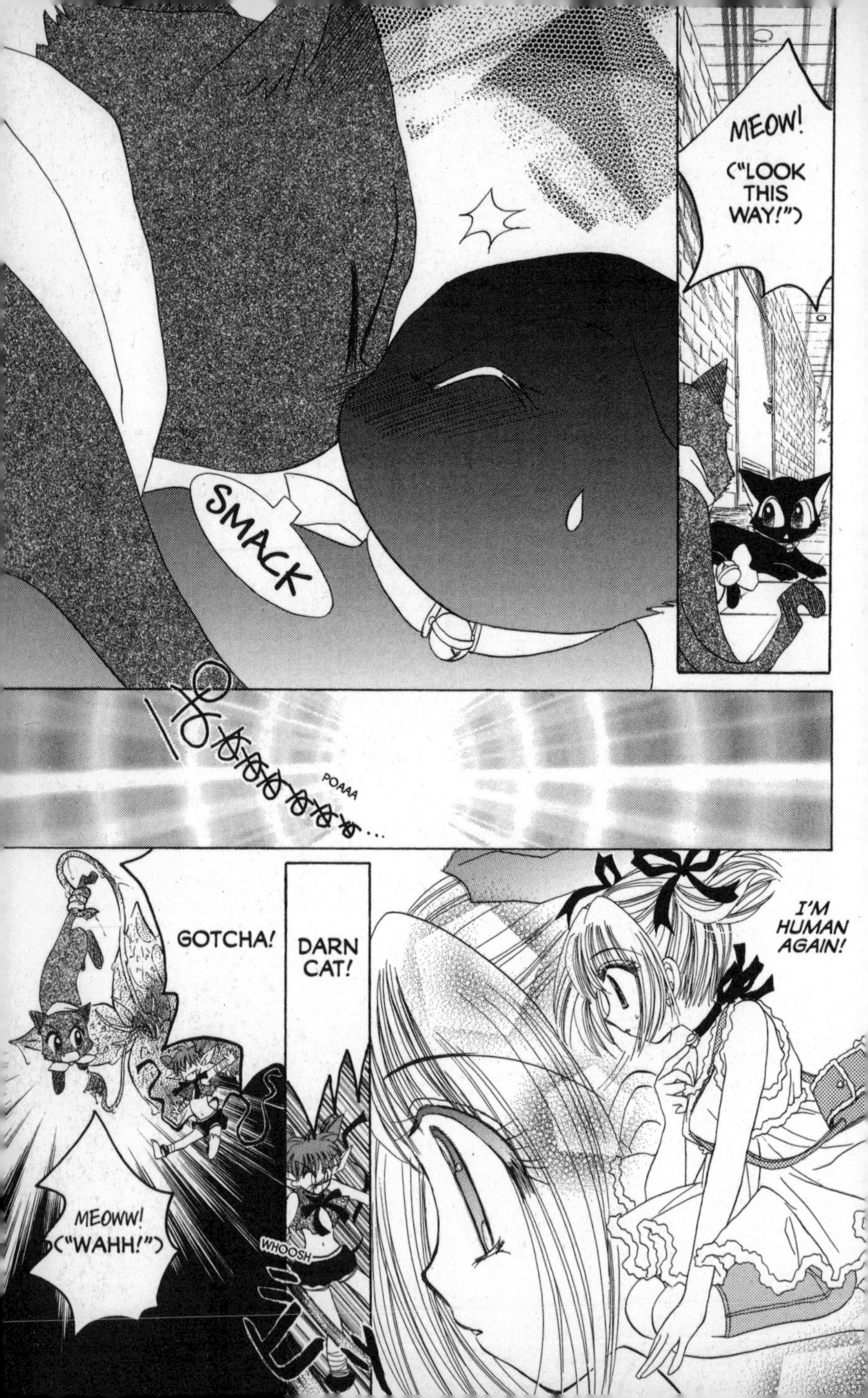
MEOW!
("LOOK THIS WAY!")
SMACK
POAAA
I'M HUMAN AGAIN!
DARN CAT!
GOTCHA!
MEOWW!
("WAHH!")
WHOOSH

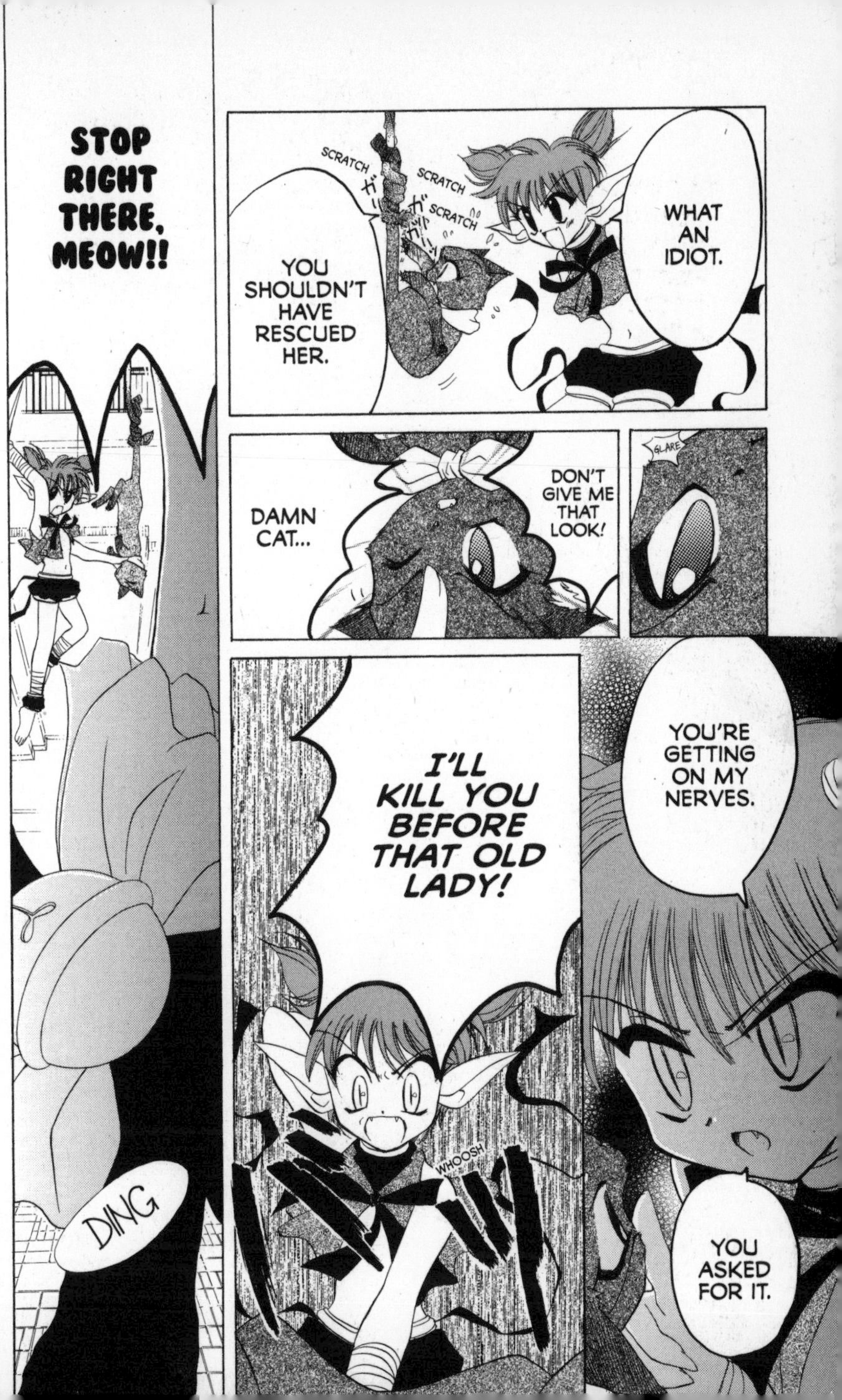
WHAT AN IDIOT.
SCRATCH
SCRATCH
SCRATCH
YOU SHOULDN'T HAVE RESCUED HER.
GLARE
DON'T GIVE ME THAT LOOK!
DAMN CAT...
YOU'RE GETTING ON MY NERVES.
YOU ASKED FOR IT.
I'LL KILL YOU BEFORE THAT OLD LADY!
WHOOSH
STOP RIGHT THERE, MEOW!!
DING

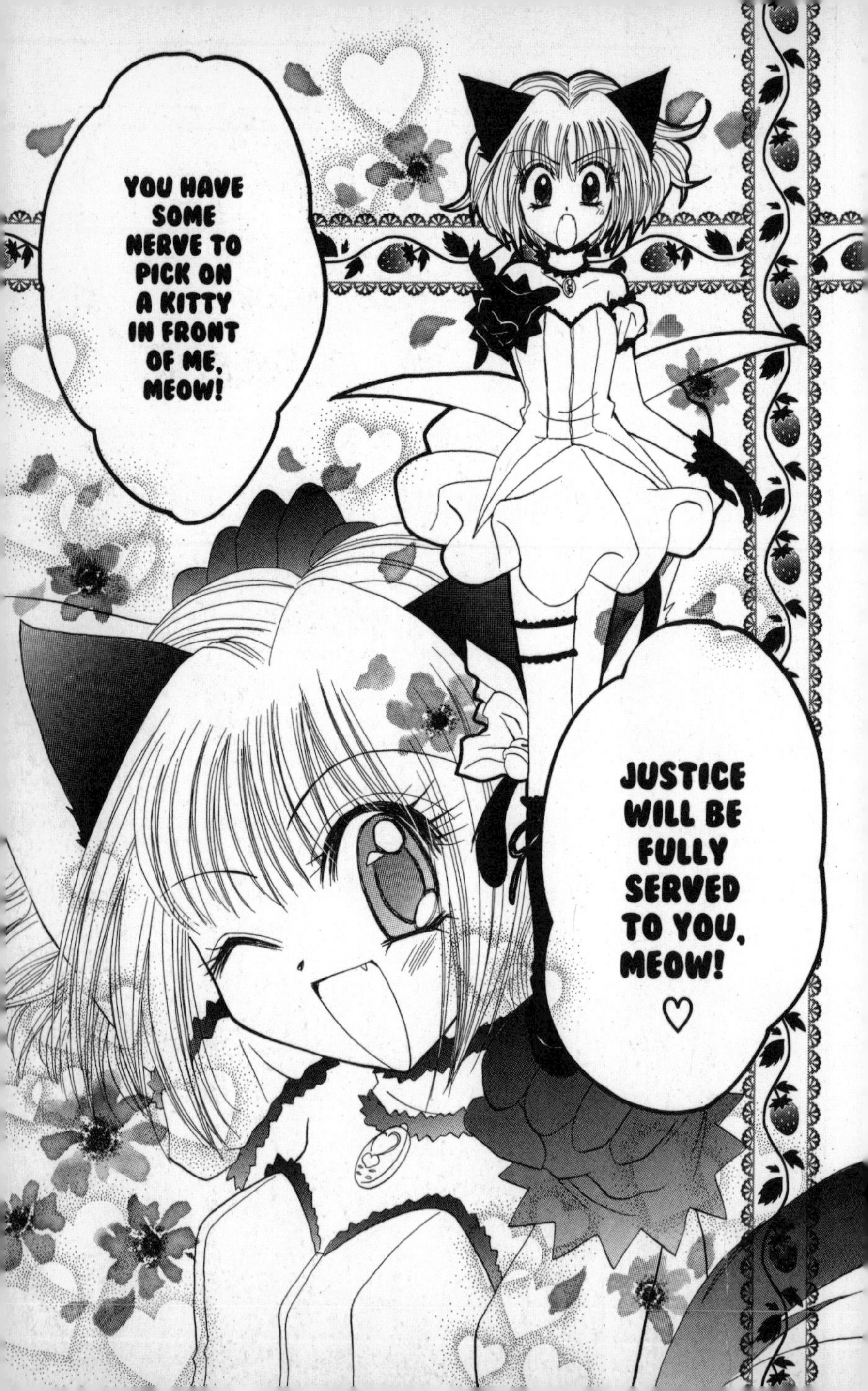
YOU HAVE SOME NERVE TO PICK ON A KITTY IN FRONT OF ME, MEOW!
JUSTICE WILL BE FULLY SERVED TO YOU, MEOW! ♡

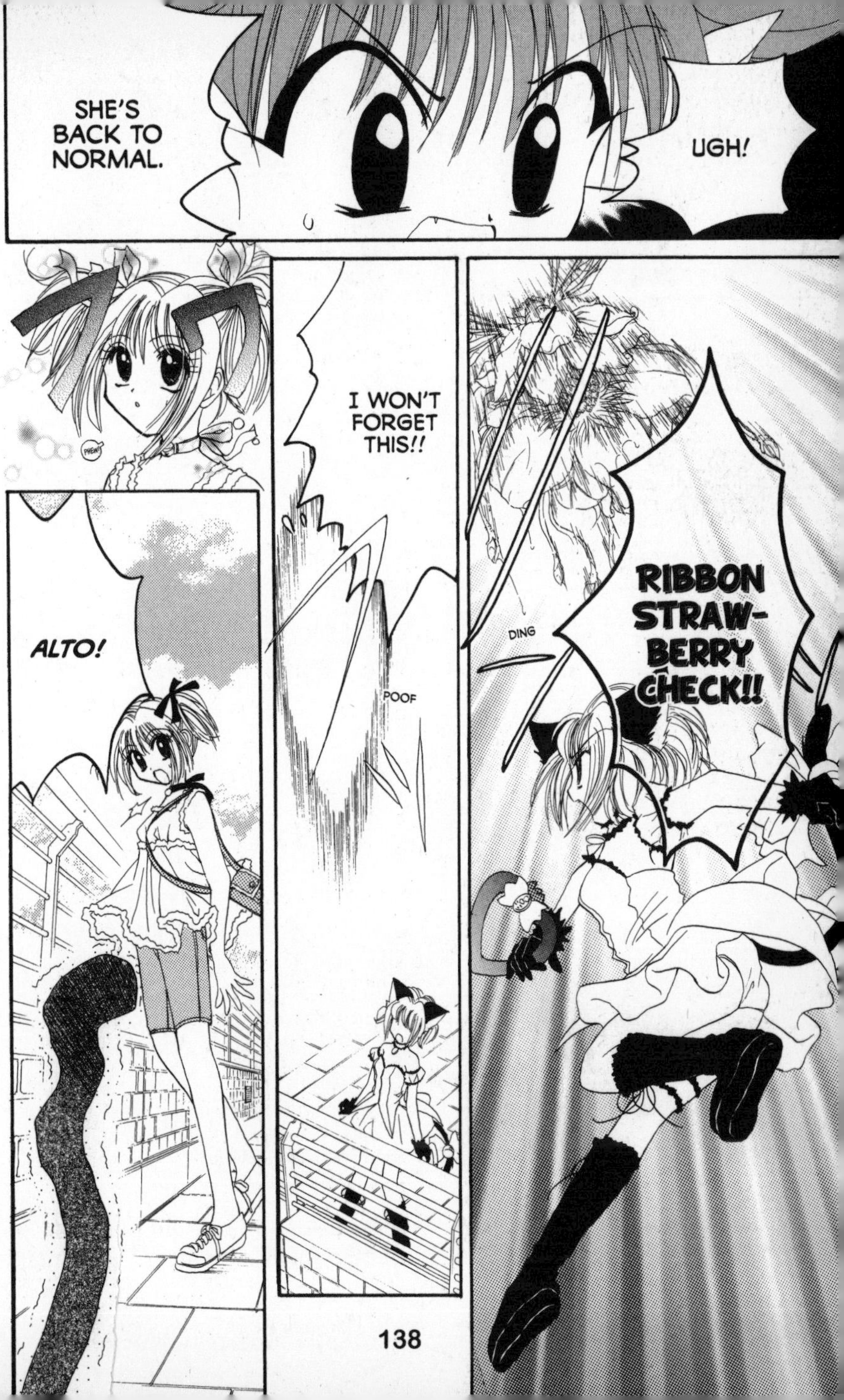

UGH!
SHE'S BACK TO NORMAL.
DING
RIBBON STRAW-BERRY CHECK!!
I WON'T FORGET THIS!!
POOF
PHEW!
ALTO!

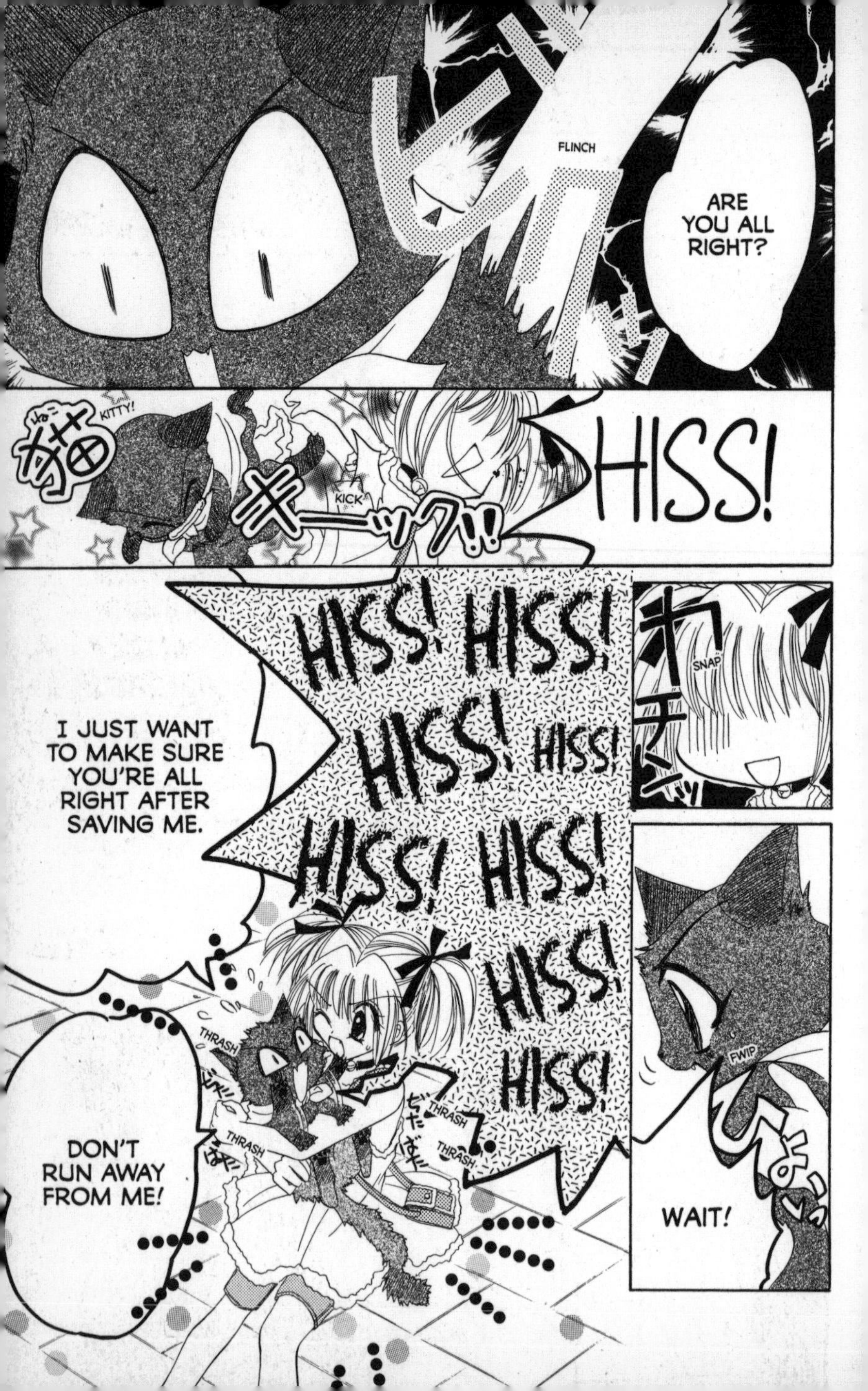
ARE YOU ALL RIGHT?
FLINCH
HISS!
KICK
KITTY!
SNAP
FWIP
WAIT!
HISS! HISS! HISS! HISS! HISS! HISS! HISS! HISS!
I JUST WANT TO MAKE SURE YOU'RE ALL RIGHT AFTER SAVING ME.
THRASH
THRASH
THRASH
THRASH
DON'T RUN AWAY FROM ME!

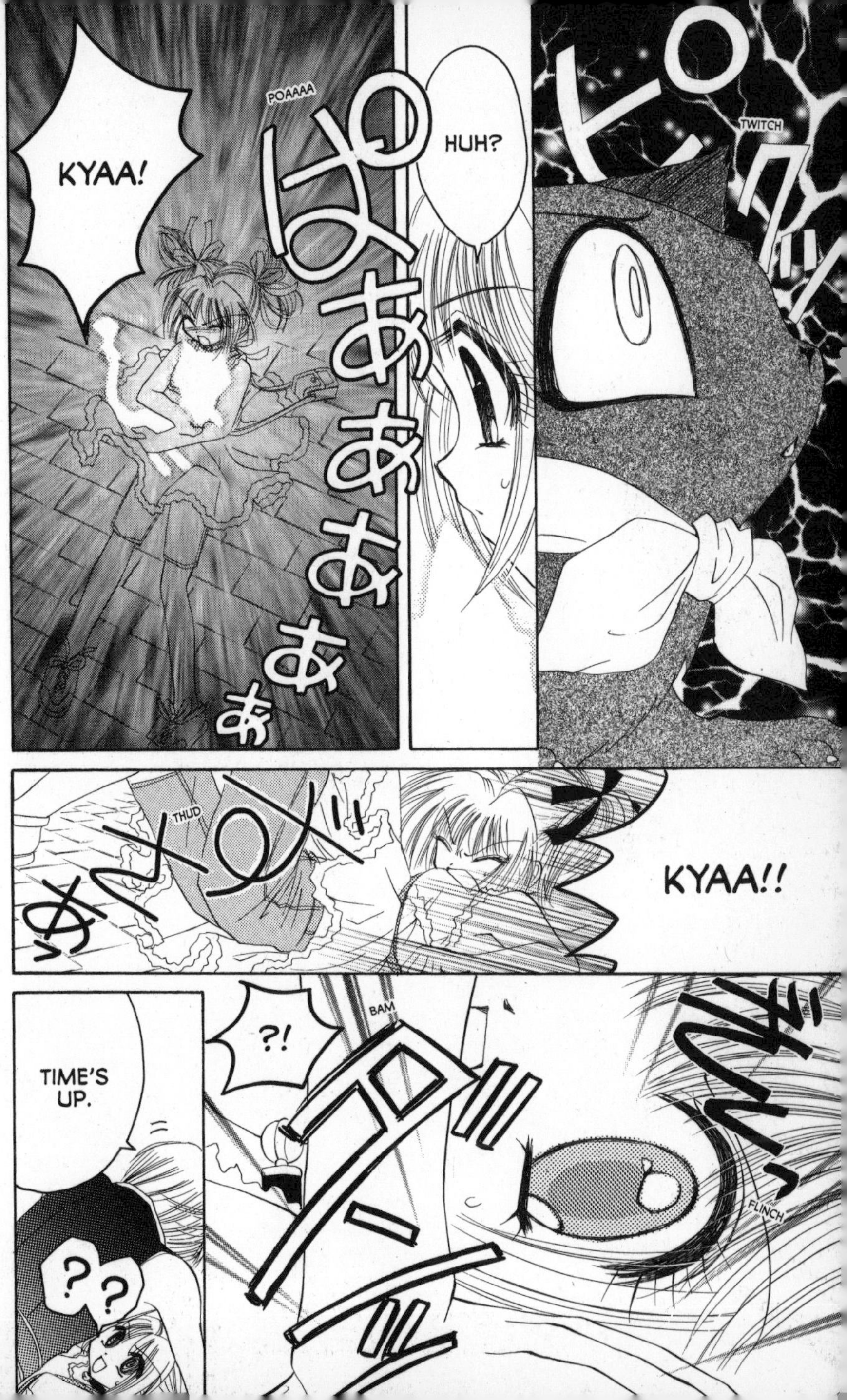

TWITCH
HUH?
POAAAA
KYAA!
KYAA!!
THUD
FLINCH
BAM
?!
TIME'S UP.
??

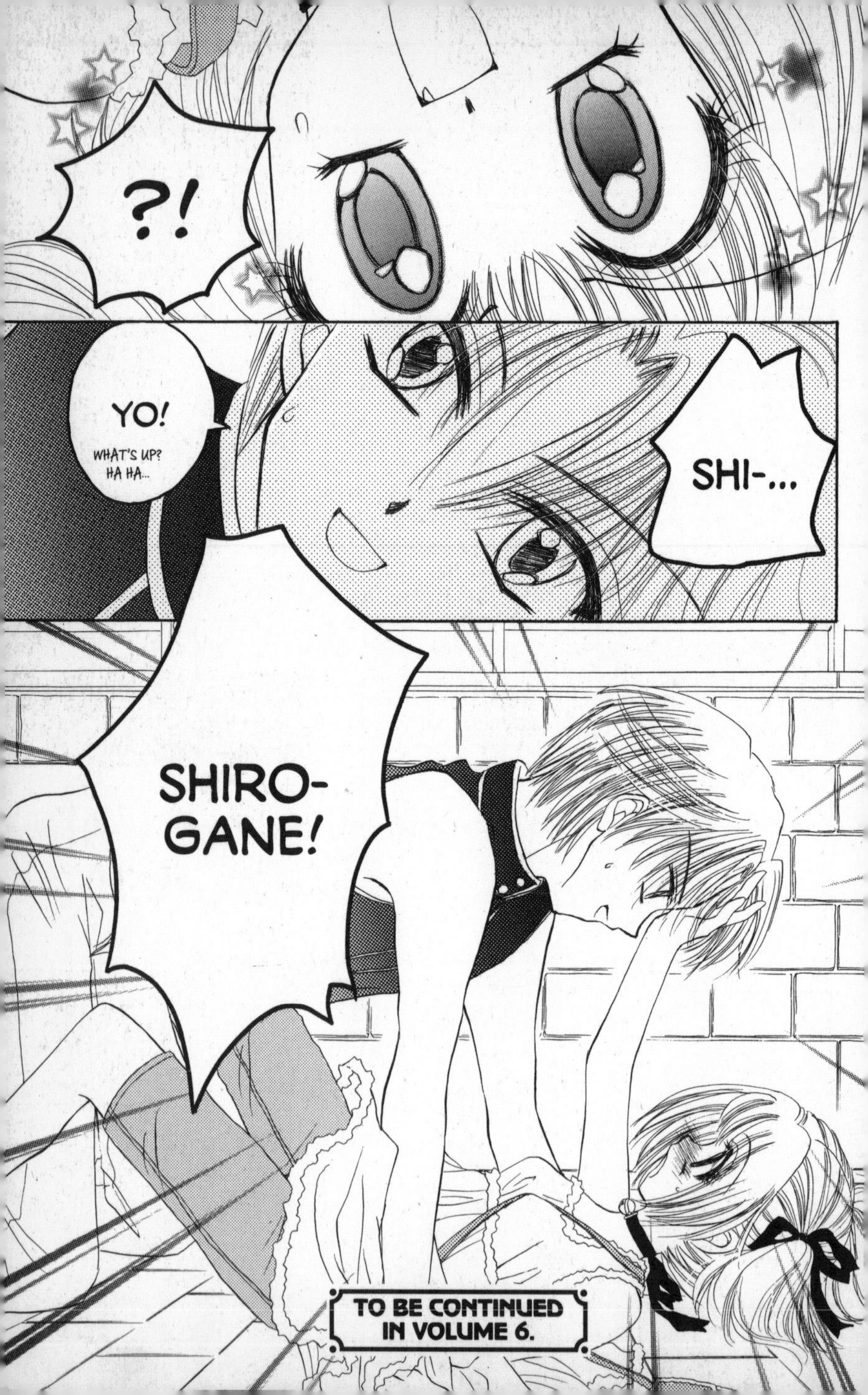
?!
SHI-...
YO!
WHAT'S UP? HA HA...
SHIRO-GANE!
TO BE CONTINUED IN VOLUME 6.

ABOUT VOLUME 5
REIKO YOSHIDA

吉田玲子

MANY BOYS APPEAR IN *MEW MEW:* AOYAMA-KUN, SHIROGANE, AKASAKA-SAN, PIE, KISH AND TART. WHO'S YOUR IDEAL BOY?

IF YOU FEEL YOUR HOBBY OR CAREER IS AS IMPORTANT AS LOVE, I THINK SOMEONE LIKE AOYAMA-KUN IS THE ONE FOR YOU. DON'T GET FRUSTRATED WHEN YOU DON'T KNOW HOW HE FEELS, THOUGH. IF YOU'RE STRONG-WILLED BUT HONEST, YOU MAY GET ALONG WITH SOMEONE LIKE SHIROGANE. IT'S IMPORTANT TO APOLO-GIZE HONESTLY AFTER AN ARGUMENT. SOMEONE WHO IS SELFISH AND WANTS ATTENTION MAY BE A GOOD FIT FOR AKASAKA-SAN. I THINK KISH IS FOR SOMEONE WHO IS PASSIONATE AND PIE IS SURPRISINGLY FOR SOMEONE WHO IS KIND AND QUIET. HE CAN WARM UP YOUR COOL HEART. TART MAY FIT SOMEONE WHO IS FULL OF ENERGY AND LIKE A LITTLE SISTER. HE'LL TAKE GOOD CARE OF YOU, THOUGH YOU MAY BE CHILDISH AND FRIVOLOUS.

AND THERE'S ONE MORE PERSON—OR ANIMAL. A FAT CAT NAMED FRANCOIS IS A BOY TOO, BUT NO ONE LIKES HIM, RIGHT?

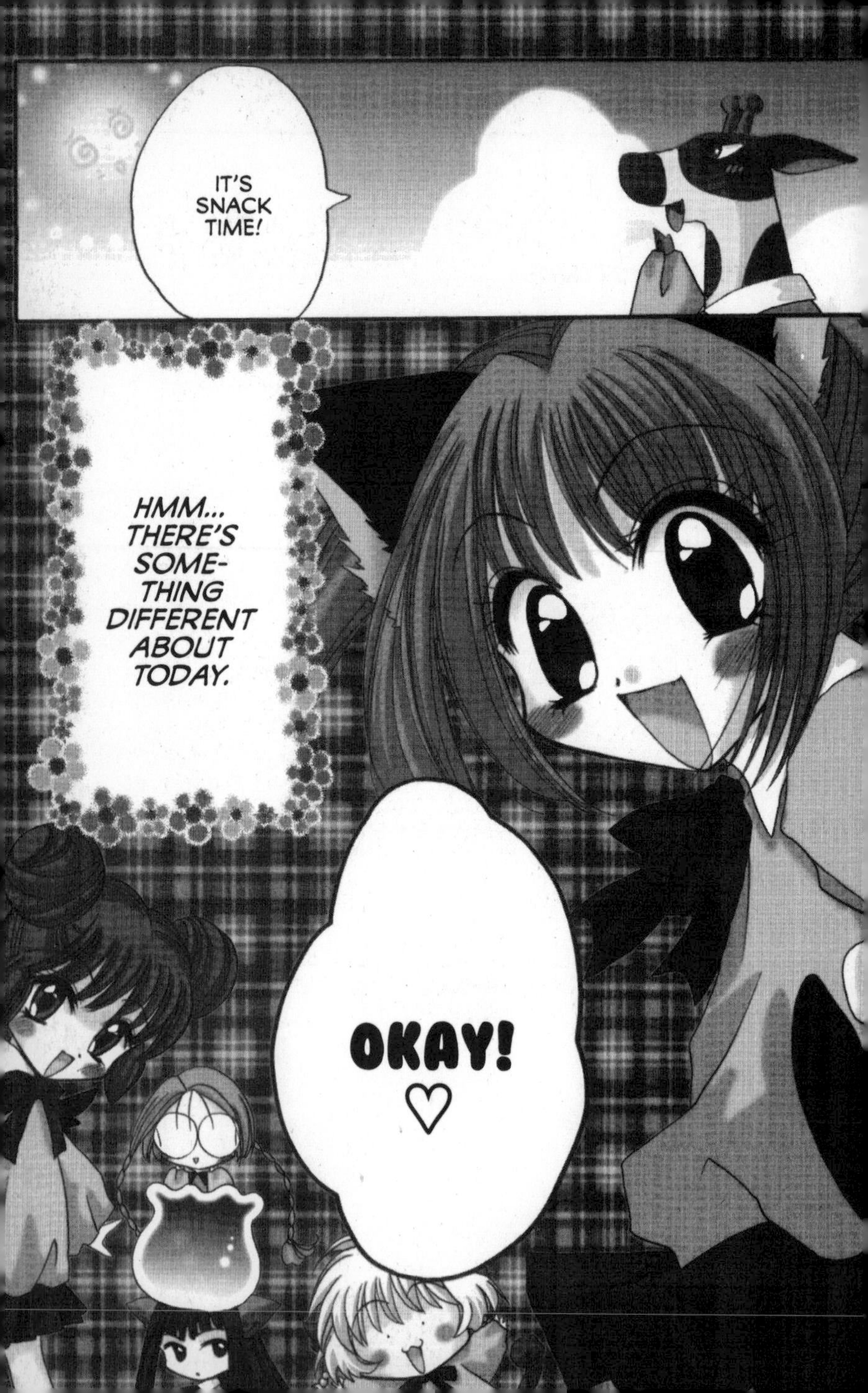
IT'S SNACK TIME!
HMM... THERE'S SOME-THING DIFFERENT ABOUT TODAY.
OKAY! ♡

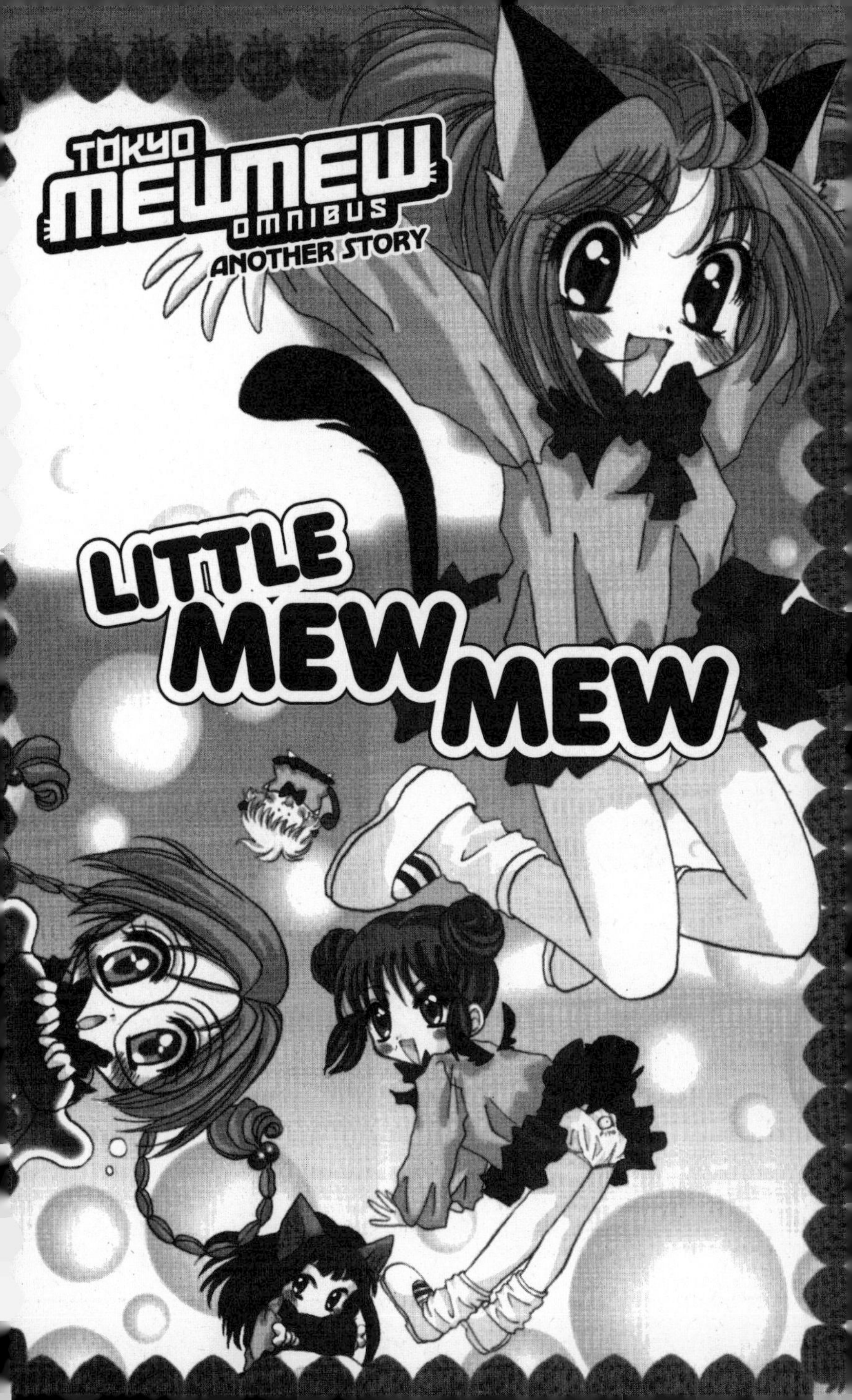
TOKYO MEWMEW OMNIBUS
ANOTHER STORY
LITTLE MEW MEW

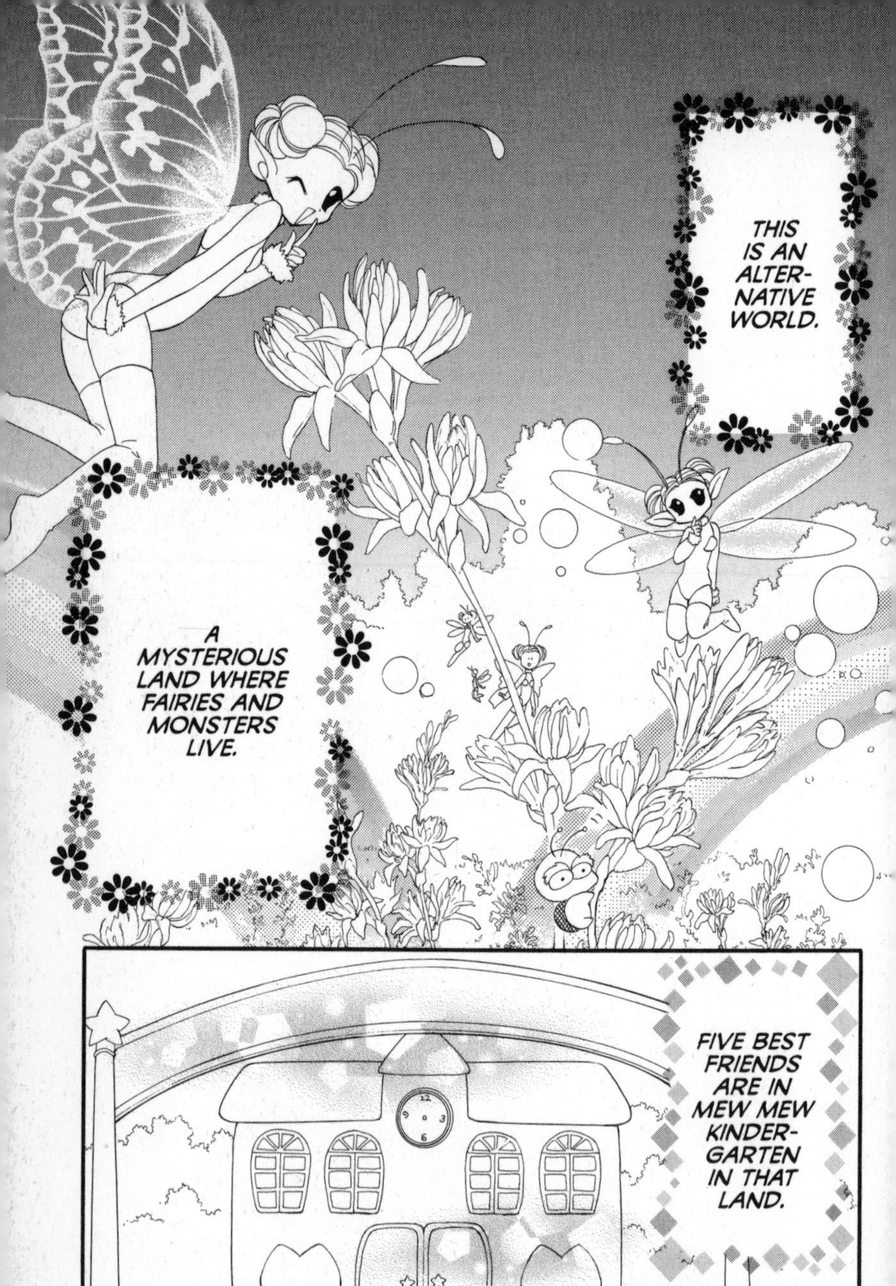
THIS IS AN ALTER-NATIVE WORLD.
A MYSTERIOUS LAND WHERE FAIRIES AND MONSTERS LIVE.
FIVE BEST FRIENDS ARE IN MEW MEW KINDER-GARTEN IN THAT LAND.

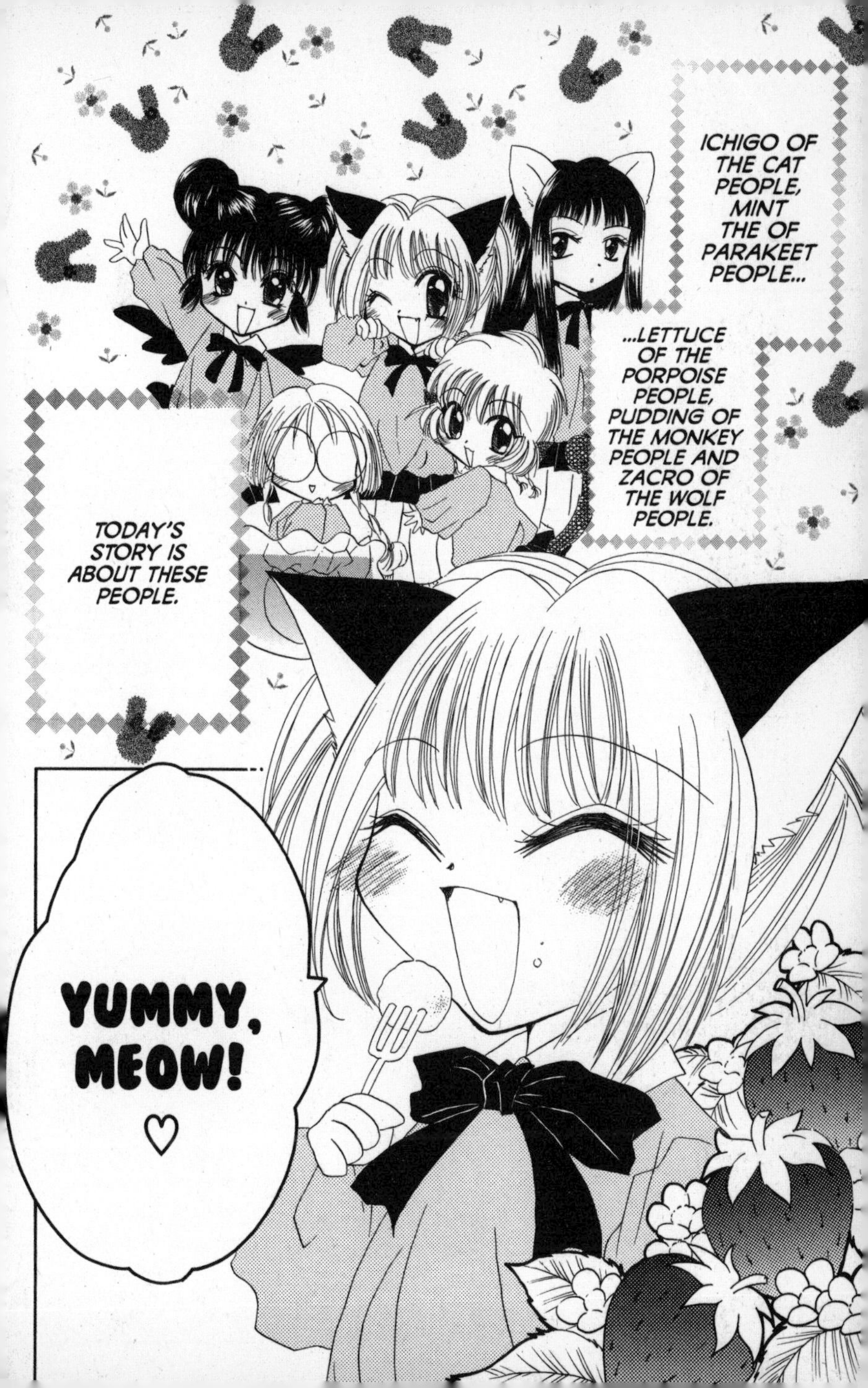
ICHIGO OF THE CAT PEOPLE, MINT THE OF PARAKEET PEOPLE...
...LETTUCE OF THE PORPOISE PEOPLE, PUDDING OF THE MONKEY PEOPLE AND ZACRO OF THE WOLF PEOPLE.
TODAY'S STORY IS ABOUT THESE PEOPLE.
YUMMY, MEOW! ♡

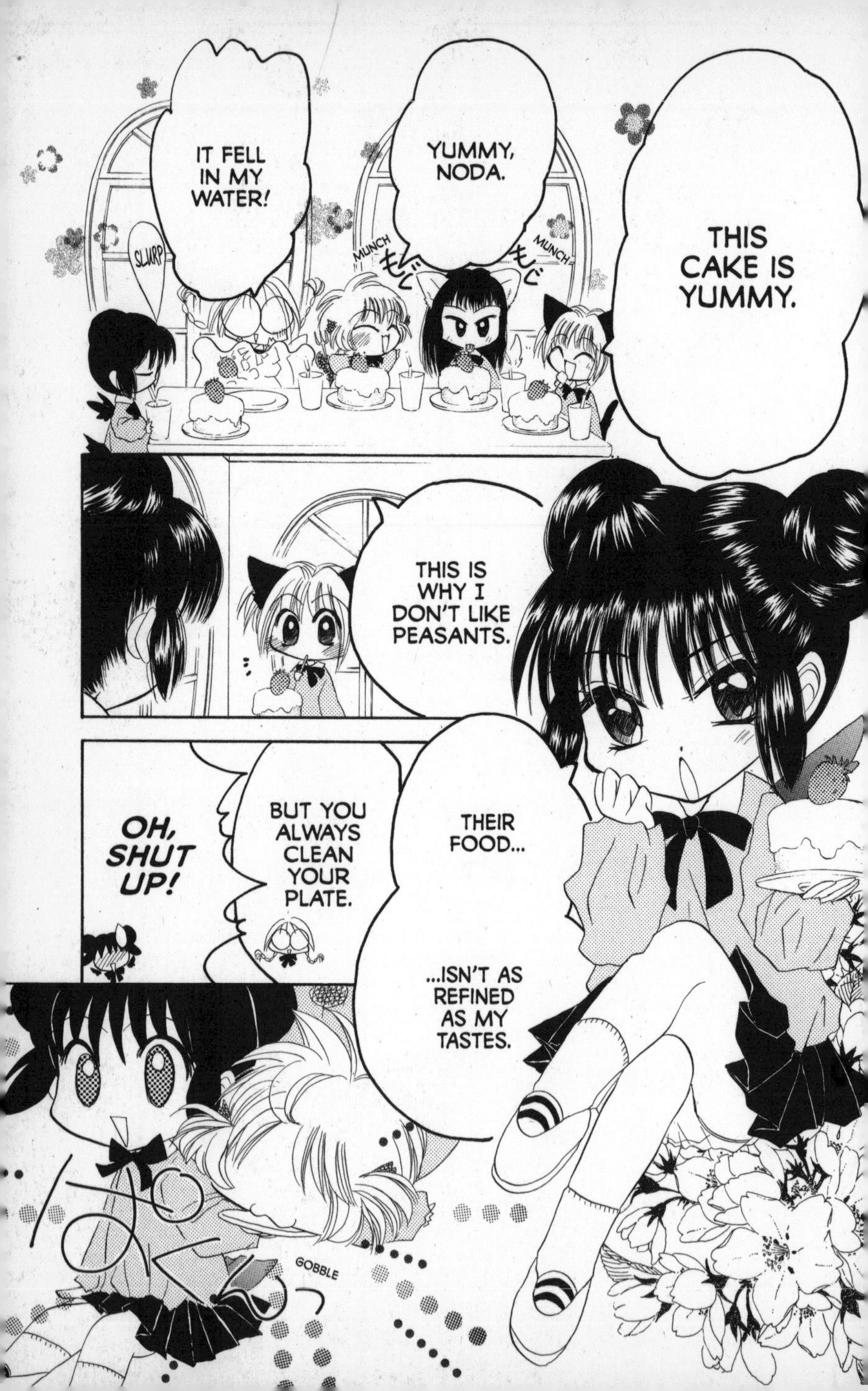
THIS CAKE IS YUMMY.
MUNCH もぐ
YUMMY, NODA.
MUNCH もぐ
IT FELL IN MY WATER!
SLURP
THIS IS WHY I DON'T LIKE PEASANTS.
THEIR FOOD...
...ISN'T AS REFINED AS MY TASTES.
BUT YOU ALWAYS CLEAN YOUR PLATE.
OH, SHUT UP!
GOBBLE

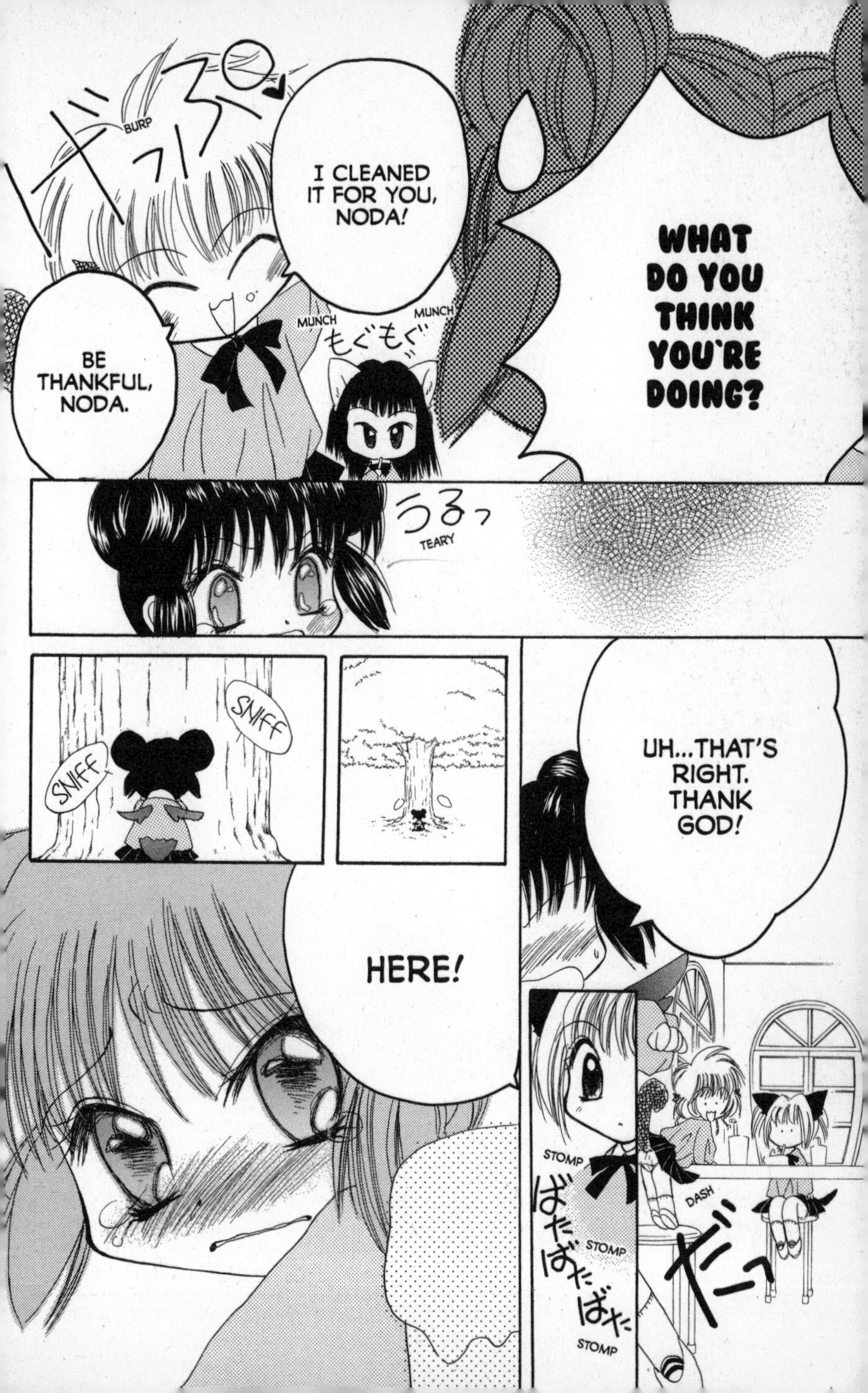
WHAT DO YOU THINK YOU'RE DOING?
I CLEANED IT FOR YOU, NODA!
BURP
ゲフッ
MUNCH MUNCH
もぐもぐ
BE THANKFUL, NODA.
うるっ
TEARY
UH...THAT'S RIGHT. THANK GOD!
STOMP
ばだばだばだ
STOMP
STOMP
DASH
ダーッ
SNIFF
SNIFF
HERE!

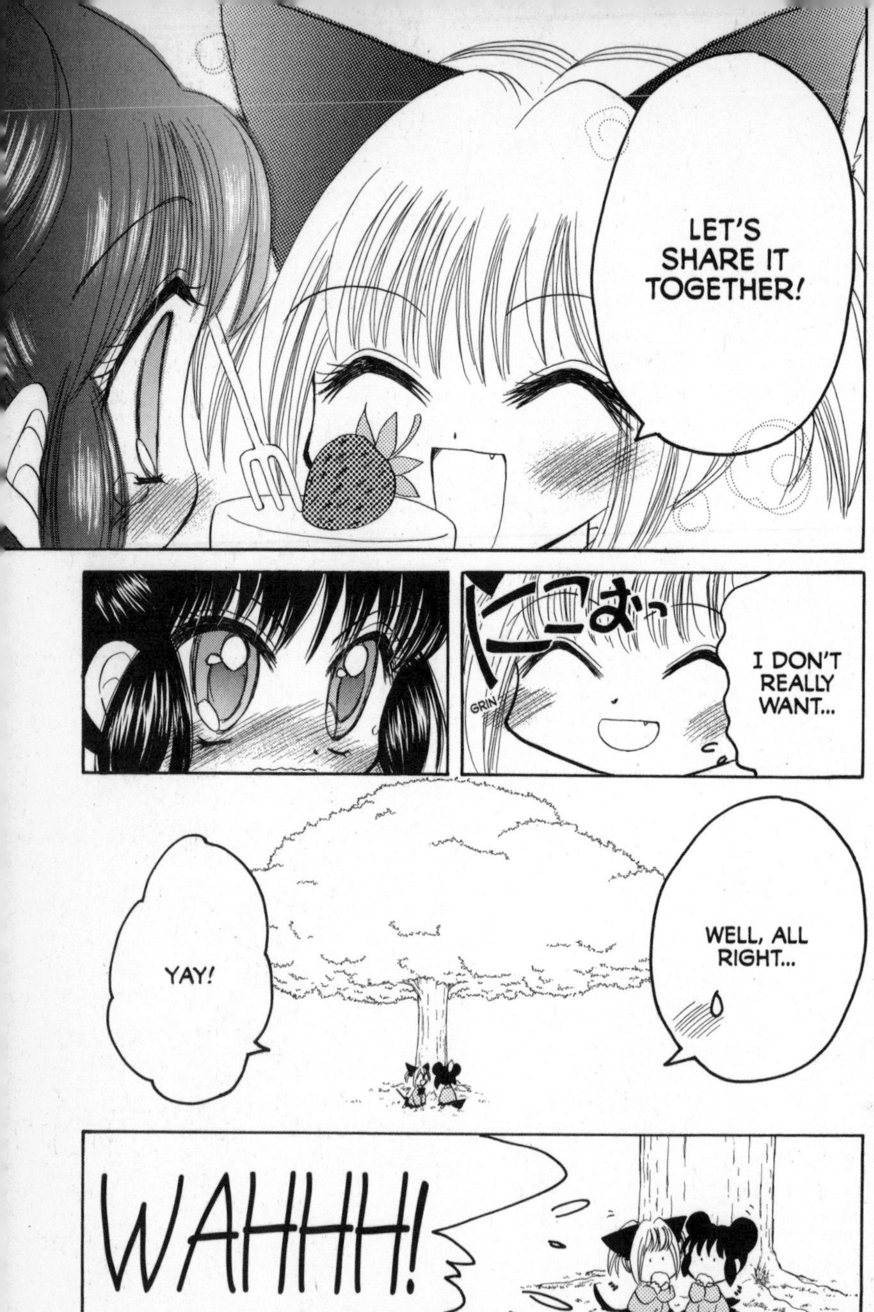

LET'S SHARE IT TOGETHER!
にこぉっ
GRIN
I DON'T REALLY WANT...
WELL, ALL RIGHT...
YAY!
WAHHH!

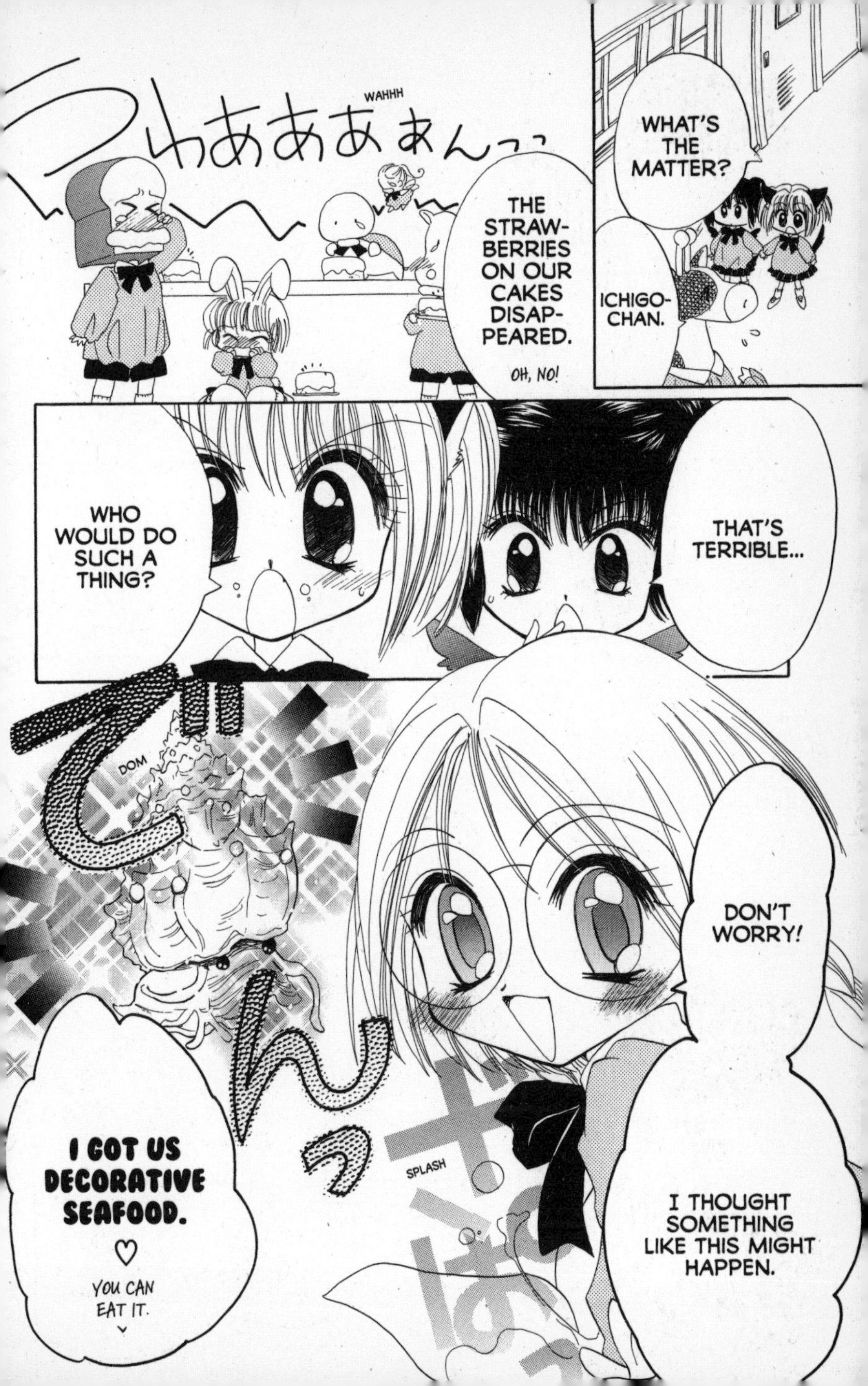
WHAT'S THE MATTER?
ICHIGO-CHAN.
WAHHH
THE STRAW-BERRIES ON OUR CAKES DISAP-PEARED.
OH, NO!
THAT'S TERRIBLE...
WHO WOULD DO SUCH A THING?
DON'T WORRY!
I THOUGHT SOMETHING LIKE THIS MIGHT HAPPEN.
DOM
SPLASH
I GOT US DECORATIVE SEAFOOD. ♡
YOU CAN EAT IT.

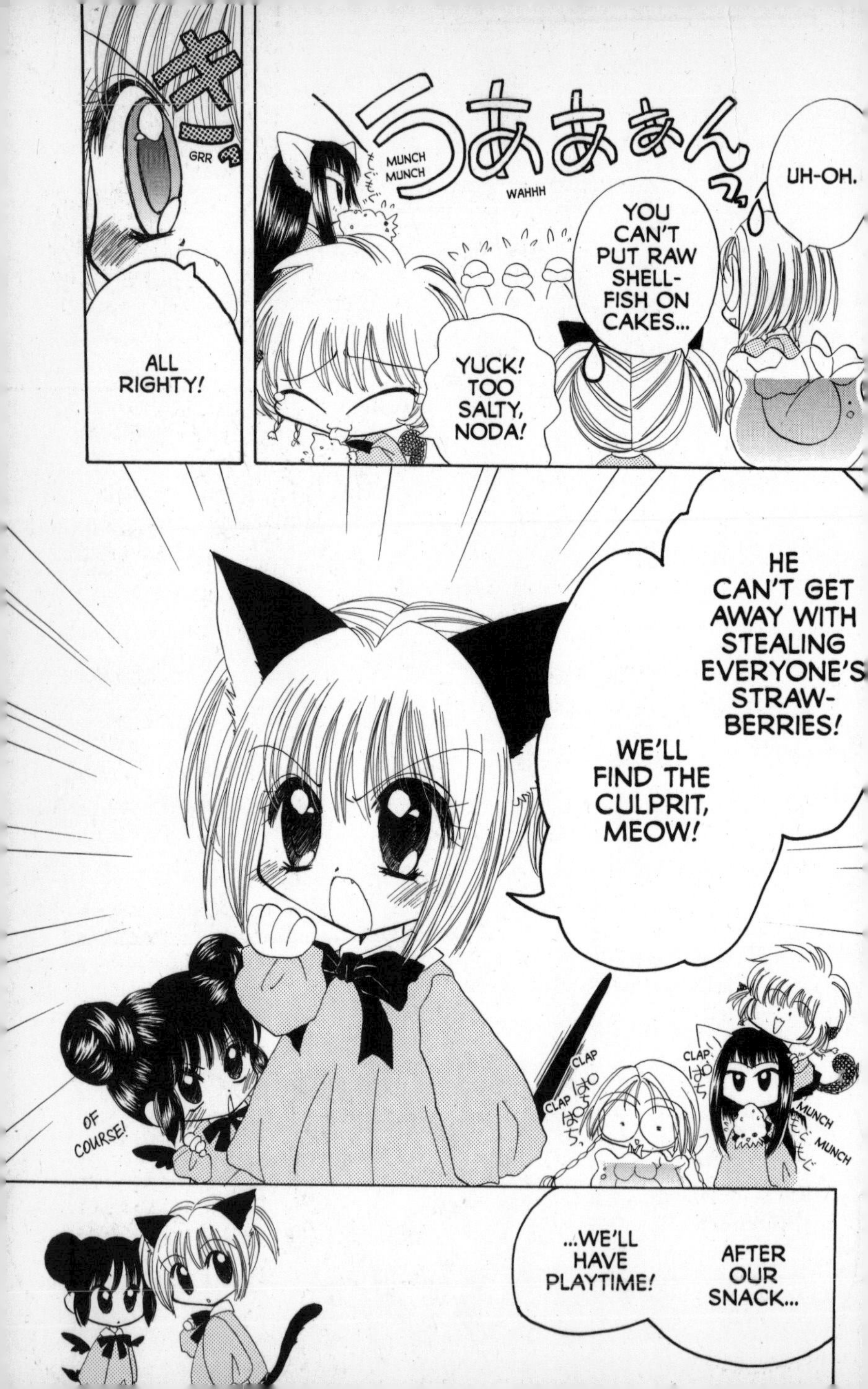
UH-OH.
YOU CAN'T PUT RAW SHELL-FISH ON CAKES...
うあぁぁぁん
WAHHH
MUNCH MUNCH
YUCK! TOO SALTY, NODA!
GRR
ALL RIGHTY!
HE CAN'T GET AWAY WITH STEALING EVERYONE'S STRAW-BERRIES!
WE'LL FIND THE CULPRIT, MEOW!
MUNCH MUNCH
CLAP
CLAP
CLAP
OF COURSE!
AFTER OUR SNACK...
...WE'LL HAVE PLAYTIME!

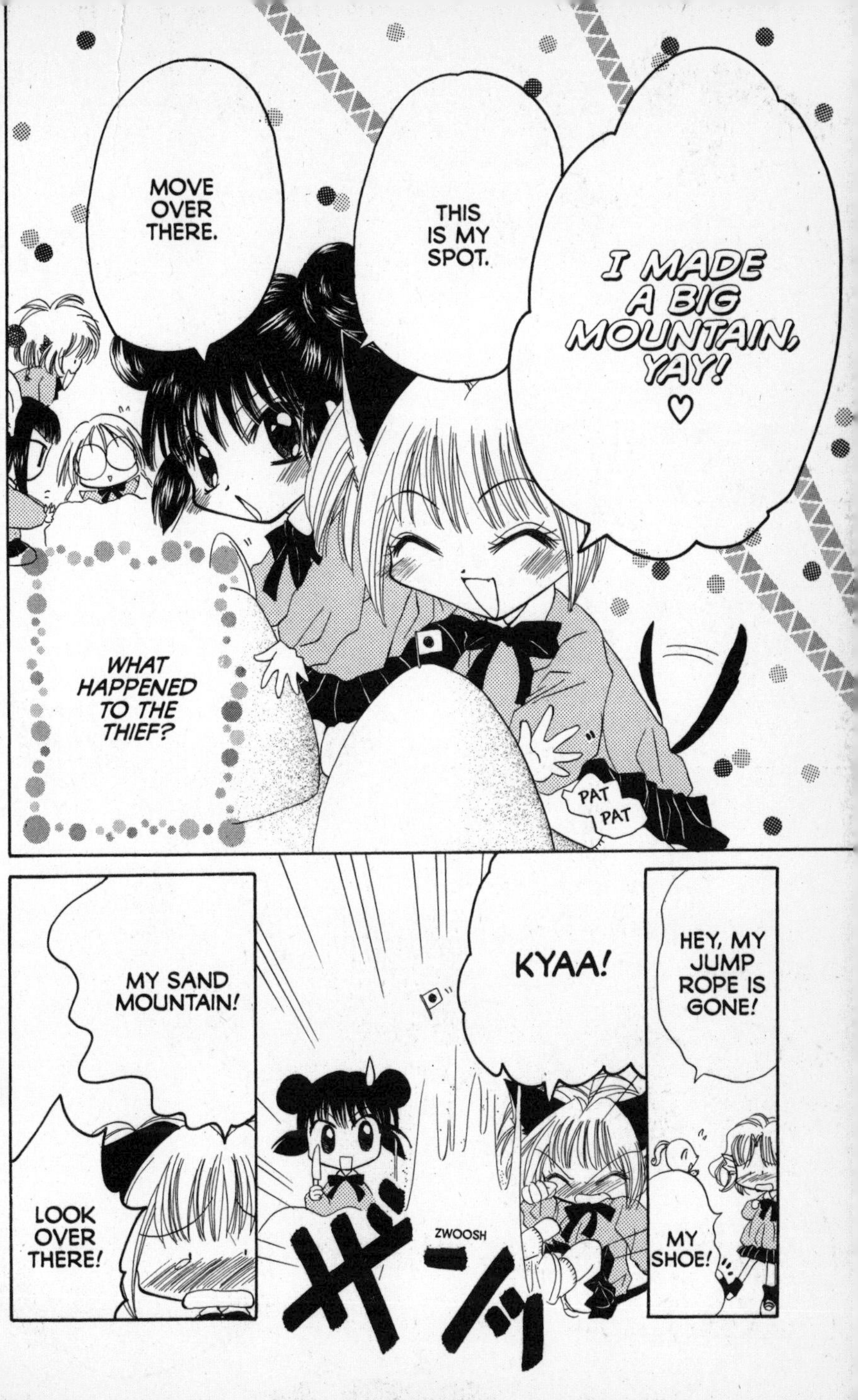
I MADE A BIG MOUNTAIN, YAY! ♥
THIS IS MY SPOT.
MOVE OVER THERE.
WHAT HAPPENED TO THE THIEF?
PAT PAT
HEY, MY JUMP ROPE IS GONE!
MY SHOE!
KYAA!
ZWOOSH
ザーッ
MY SAND MOUNTAIN!
LOOK OVER THERE!

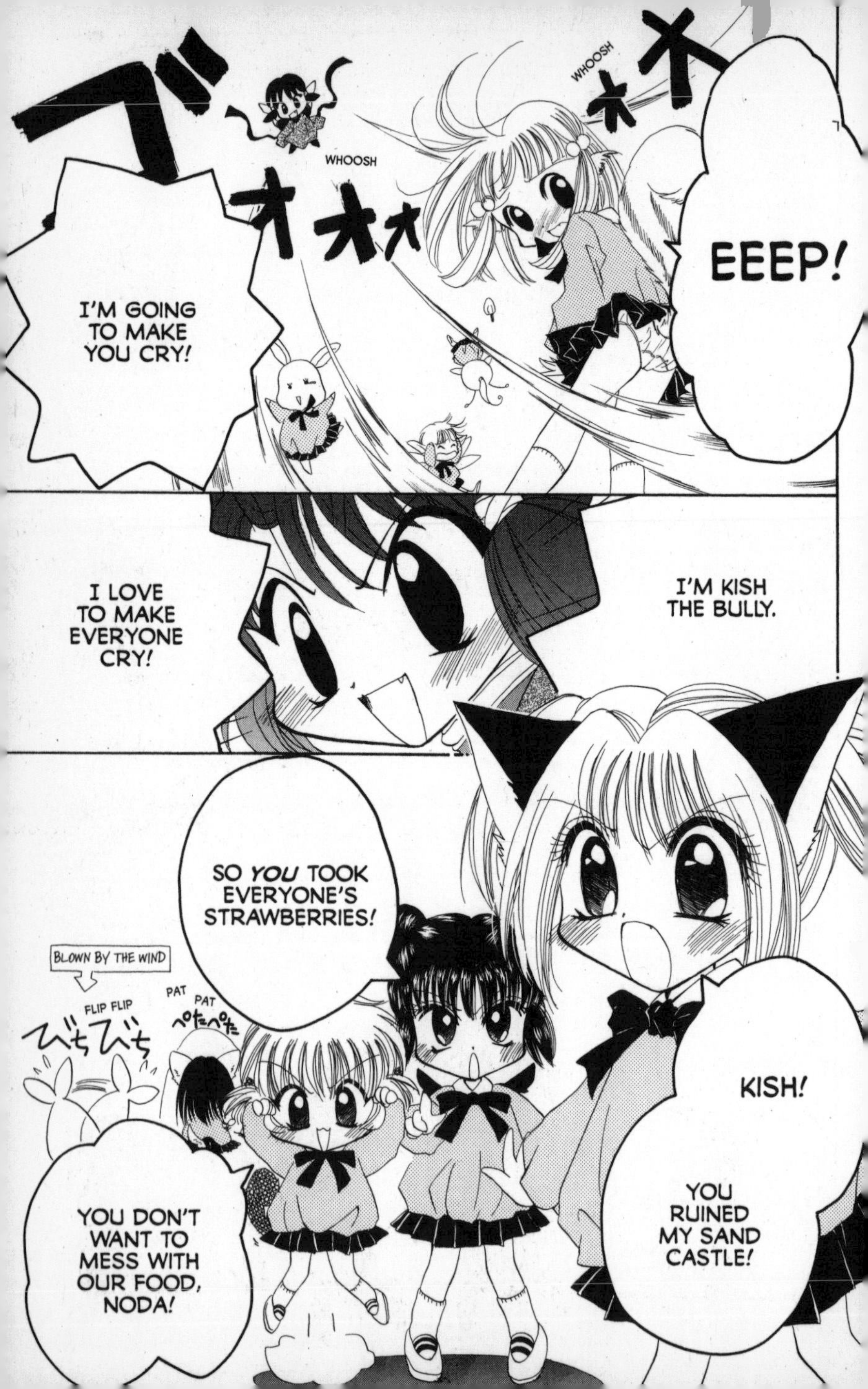
EEEP!
WHOOSH
WHOOSH
ブォォォ
I'M GOING TO MAKE YOU CRY!
I'M KISH THE BULLY.
I LOVE TO MAKE EVERYONE CRY!
KISH!
YOU RUINED MY SAND CASTLE!
SO *YOU* TOOK EVERYONE'S STRAWBERRIES!
PAT PAT
ぺたぺた
FLIP FLIP
ぴちぴち
BLOWN BY THE WIND
YOU DON'T WANT TO MESS WITH OUR FOOD, NODA!

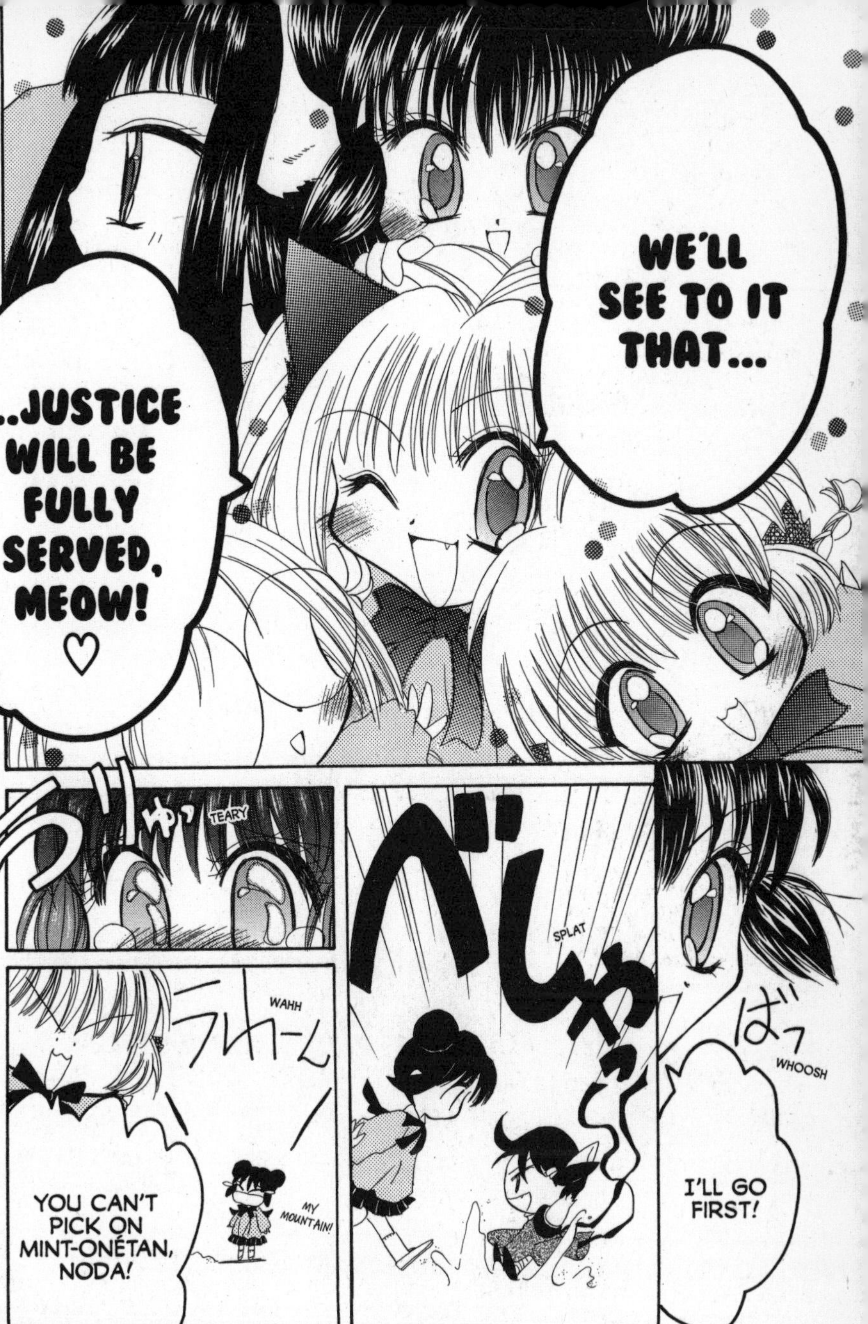
WE'LL SEE TO IT THAT...
...JUSTICE WILL BE FULLY SERVED, MEOW! ♡
ばっ
WHOOSH
I'LL GO FIRST!
べしゃっ
SPLAT
TEARY
WAHH
YOU CAN'T PICK ON MINT-ONÉTAN, NODA!
MY MOUNTAIN!

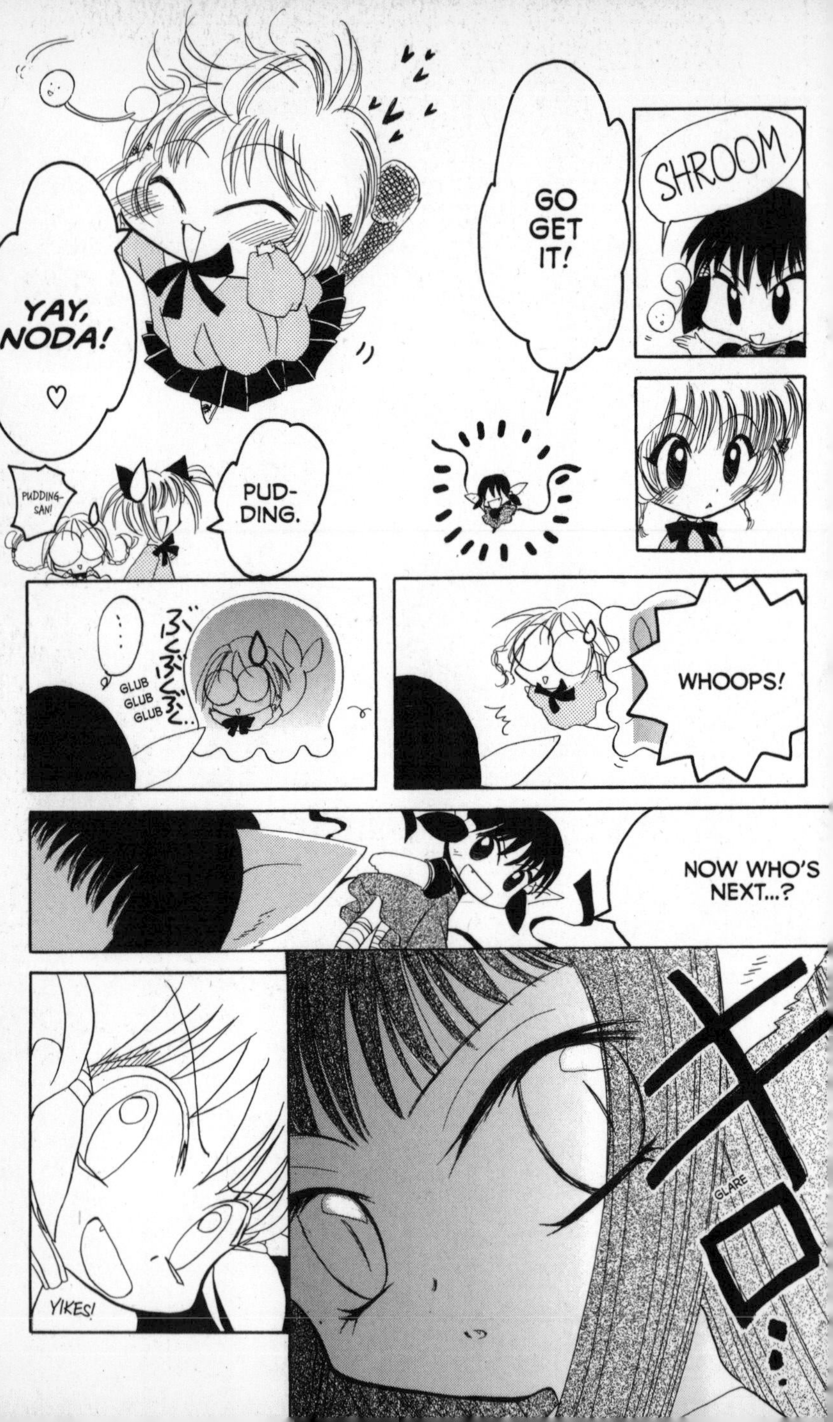
SHROOM
GO GET IT!
YAY, NODA! ♡
PUD-DING.
PUDDING-SAN!
WHOOPS!
...
ぶくぶくぶく
GLUB GLUB GLUB
NOW WHO'S NEXT...?
ギロ
GLARE
YIKES!

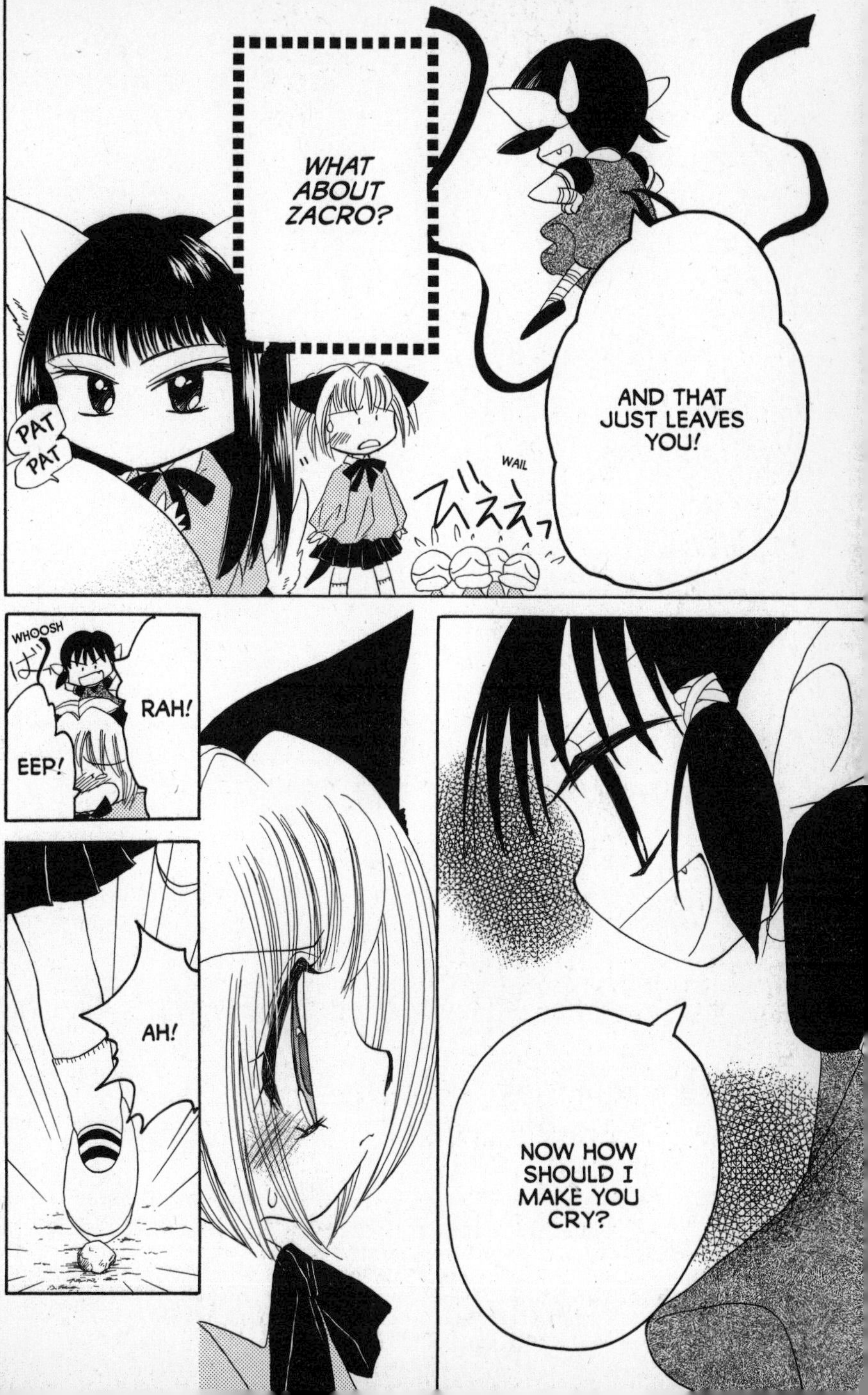
AND THAT JUST LEAVES YOU!
WAIL
ひえええっ
WHAT ABOUT ZACRO?
PAT PAT
NOW HOW SHOULD I MAKE YOU CRY?
WHOOSH
ばっ
RAH!
EEP!
AH!

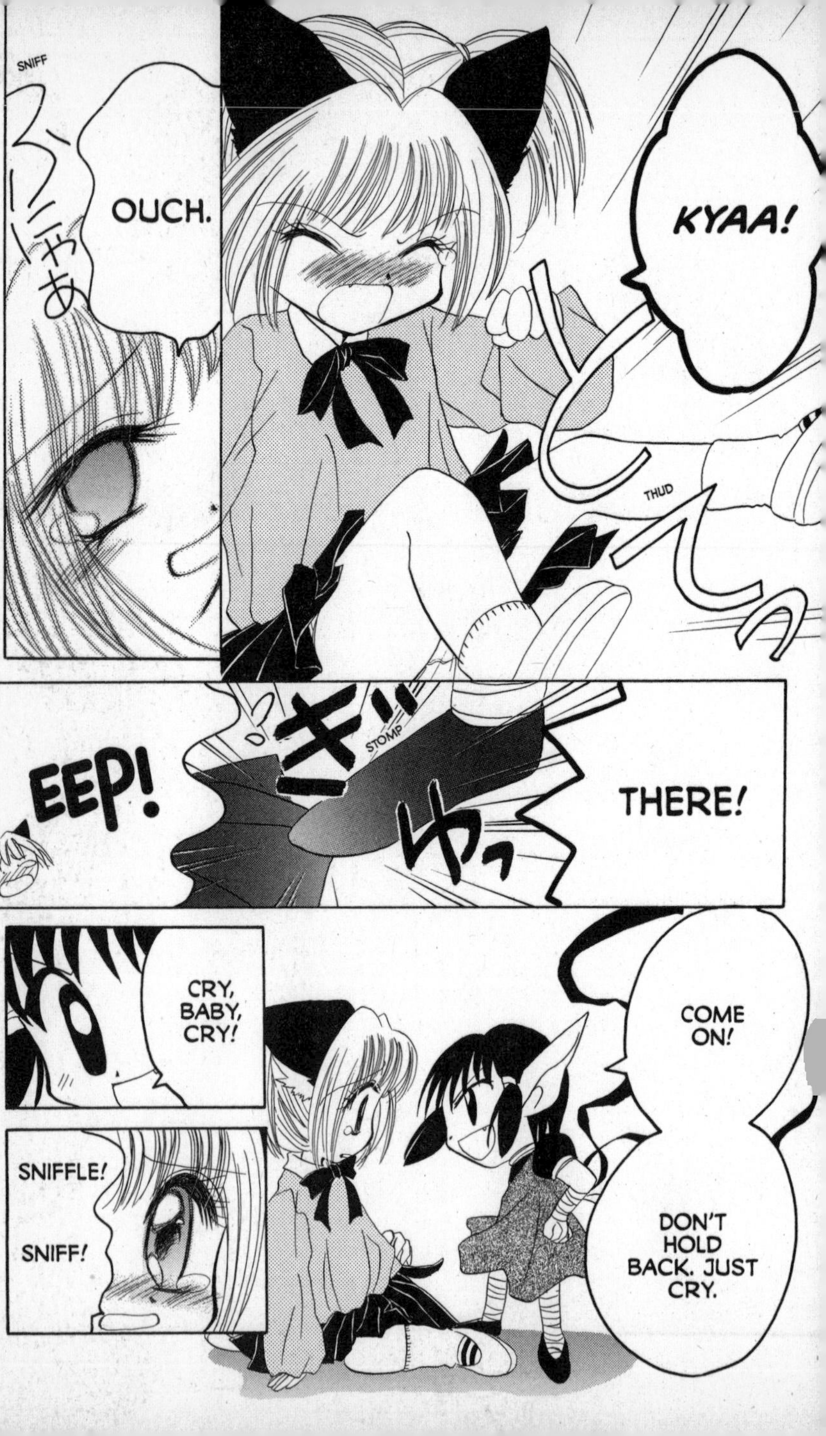
KYAA!
THUD
SNIFF
OUCH.
THERE!
STOMP
EEP!
COME ON!
DON'T HOLD BACK. JUST CRY.
CRY, BABY, CRY!
SNIFFLE!
SNIFF!

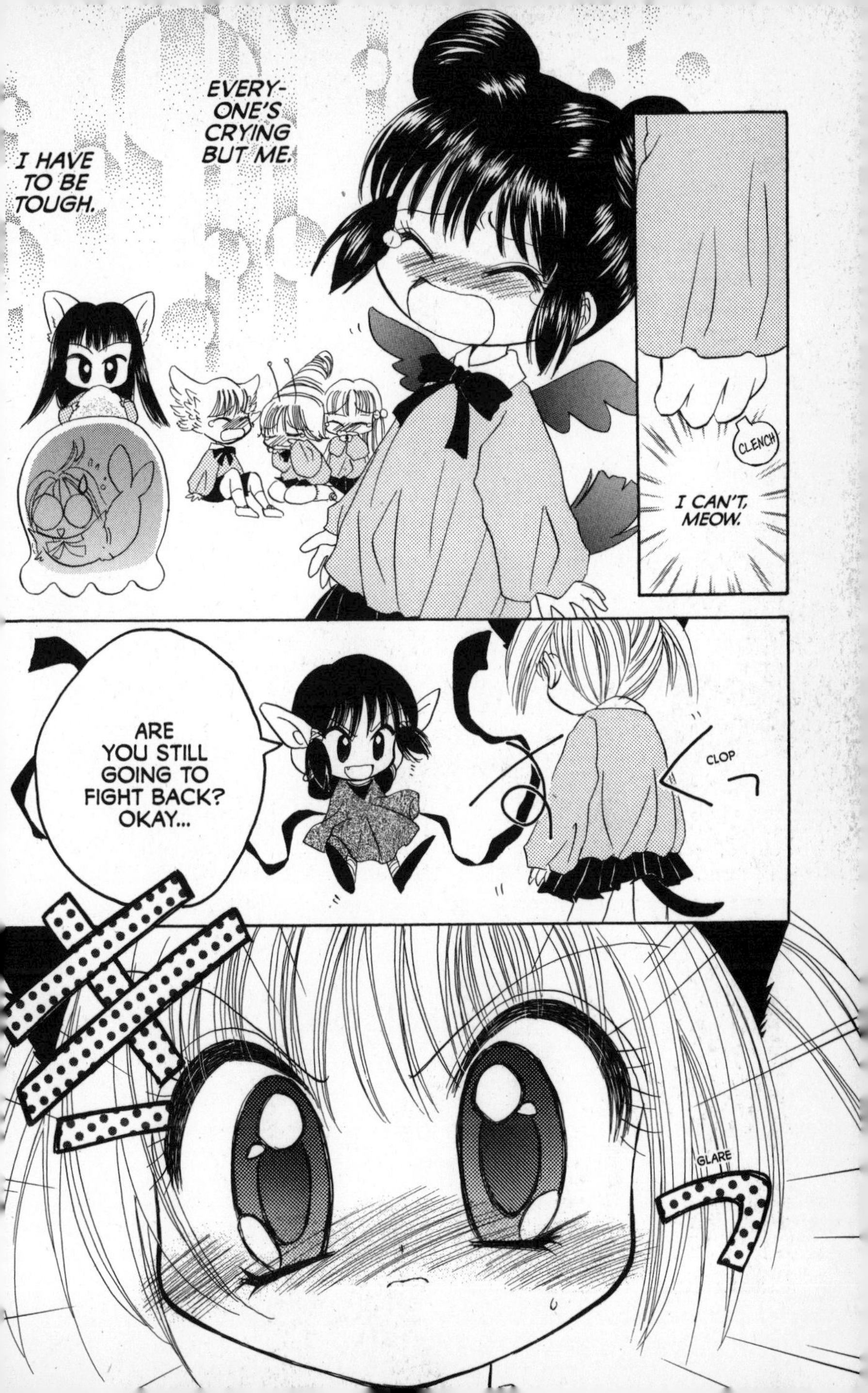
CLENCH
I CAN'T, MEOW.
EVERY-ONE'S CRYING BUT ME.
I HAVE TO BE TOUGH.
CLOP
ARE YOU STILL GOING TO FIGHT BACK? OKAY...
GLARE

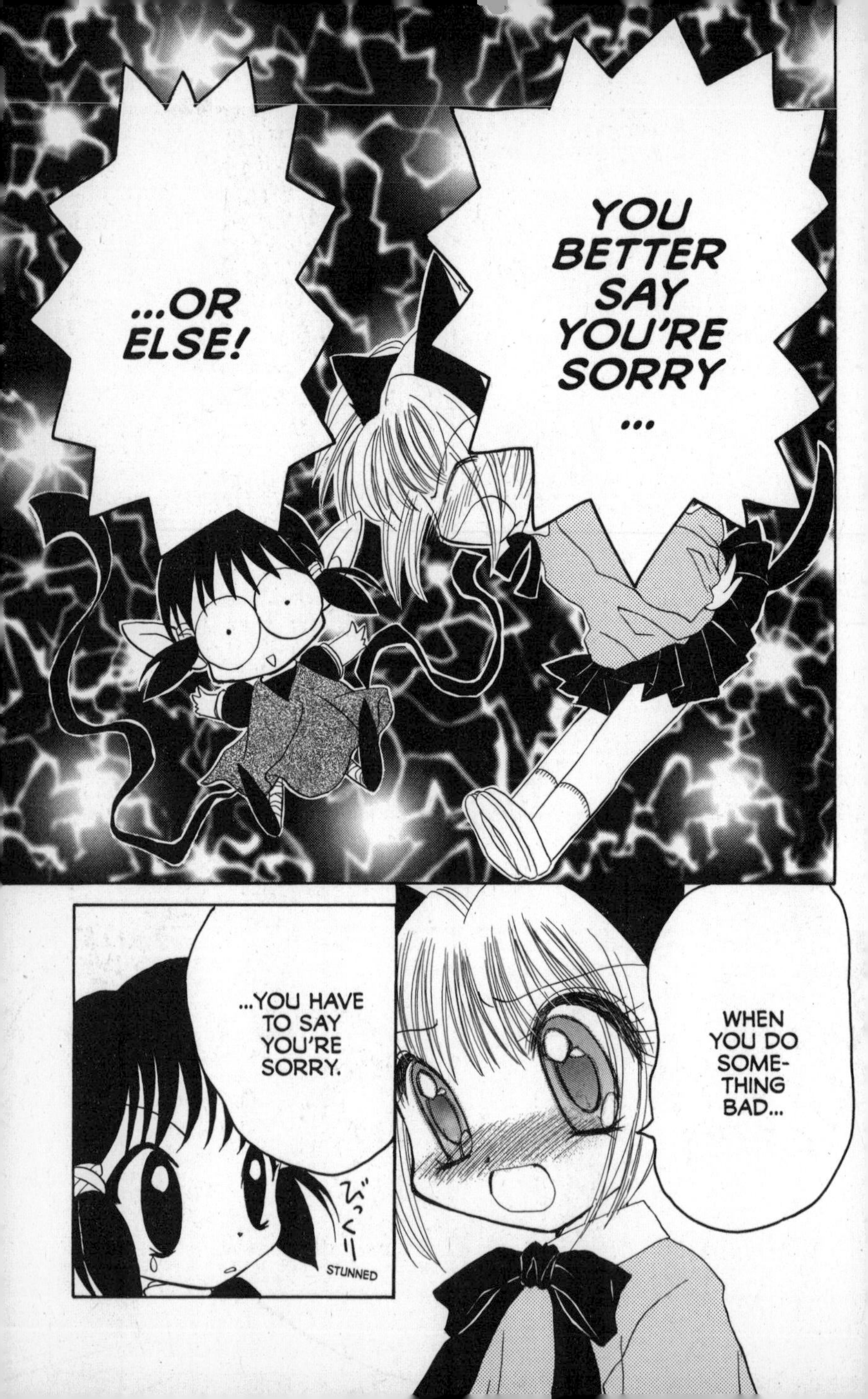
YOU BETTER SAY YOU'RE SORRY ...
...OR ELSE!
WHEN YOU DO SOME-THING BAD...
...YOU HAVE TO SAY YOU'RE SORRY.
びっくり
STUNNED

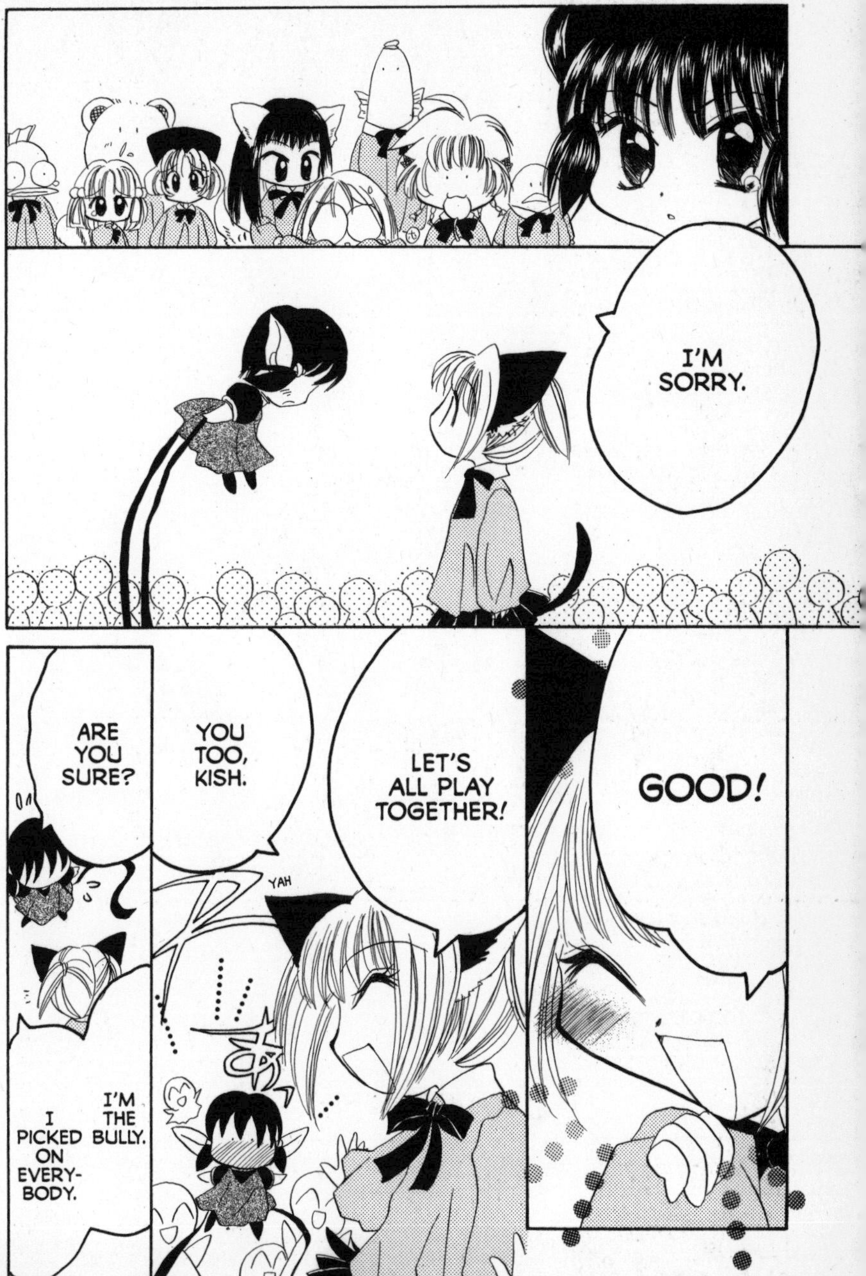
I'M SORRY.
GOOD!
LET'S ALL PLAY TOGETHER!
YOU TOO, KISH.
YAH
ARE YOU SURE?
I'M THE BULLY. I PICKED ON EVERYBODY.

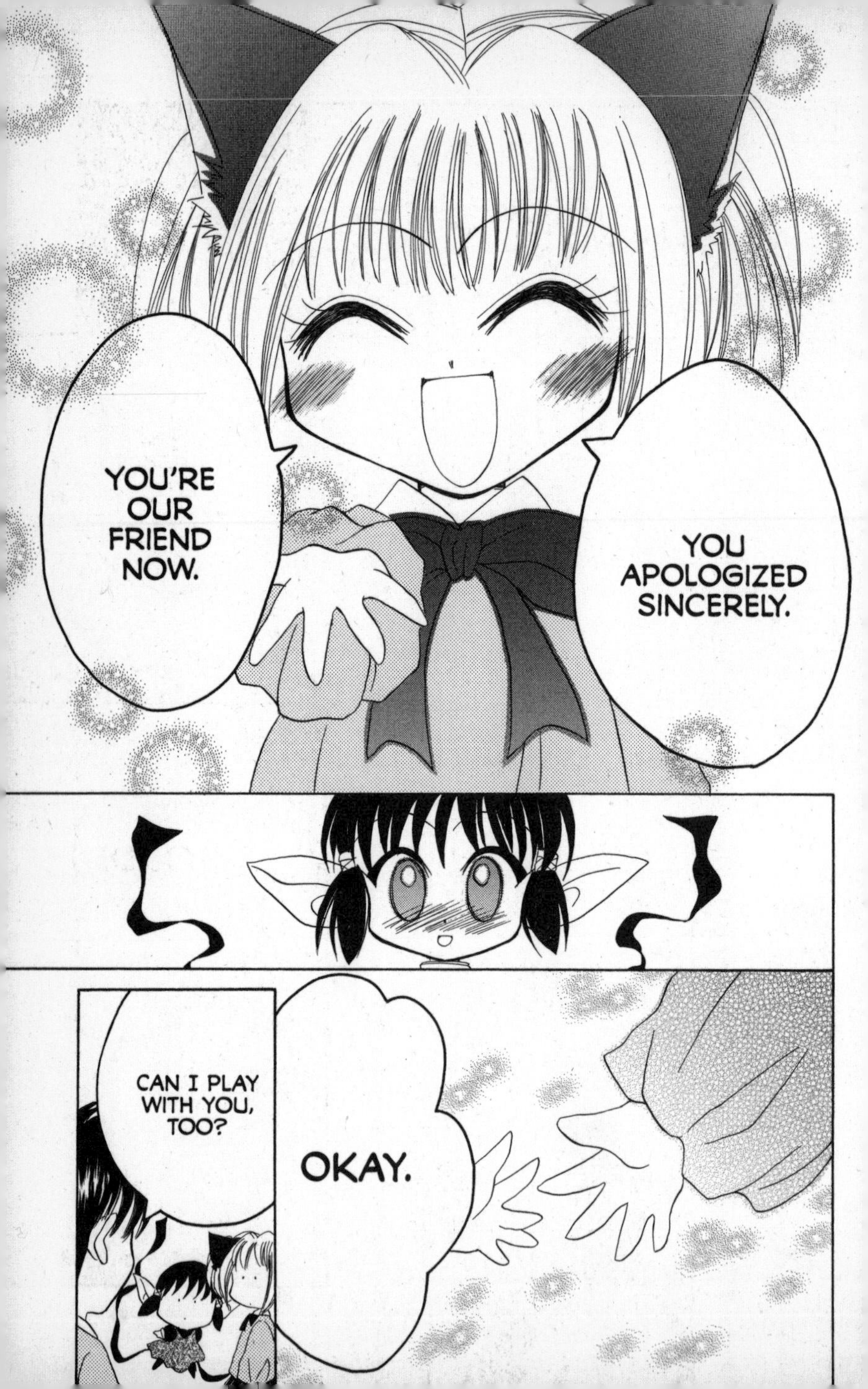
YOU APOLOGIZED SINCERELY.
YOU'RE OUR FRIEND NOW.
CAN I PLAY WITH YOU, TOO?
OKAY.

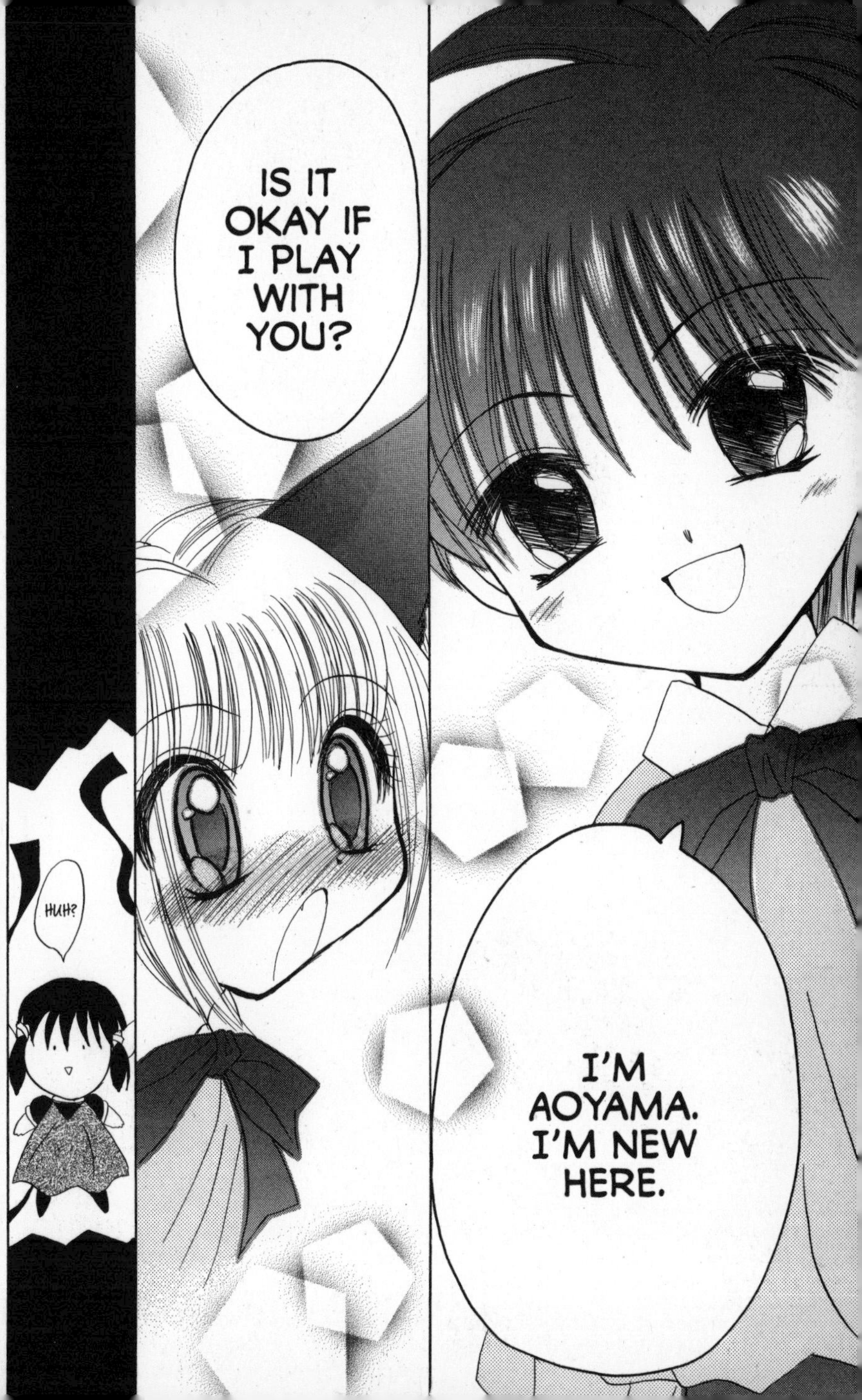
I'M AOYAMA. I'M NEW HERE.
IS IT OKAY IF I PLAY WITH YOU?
HUH?

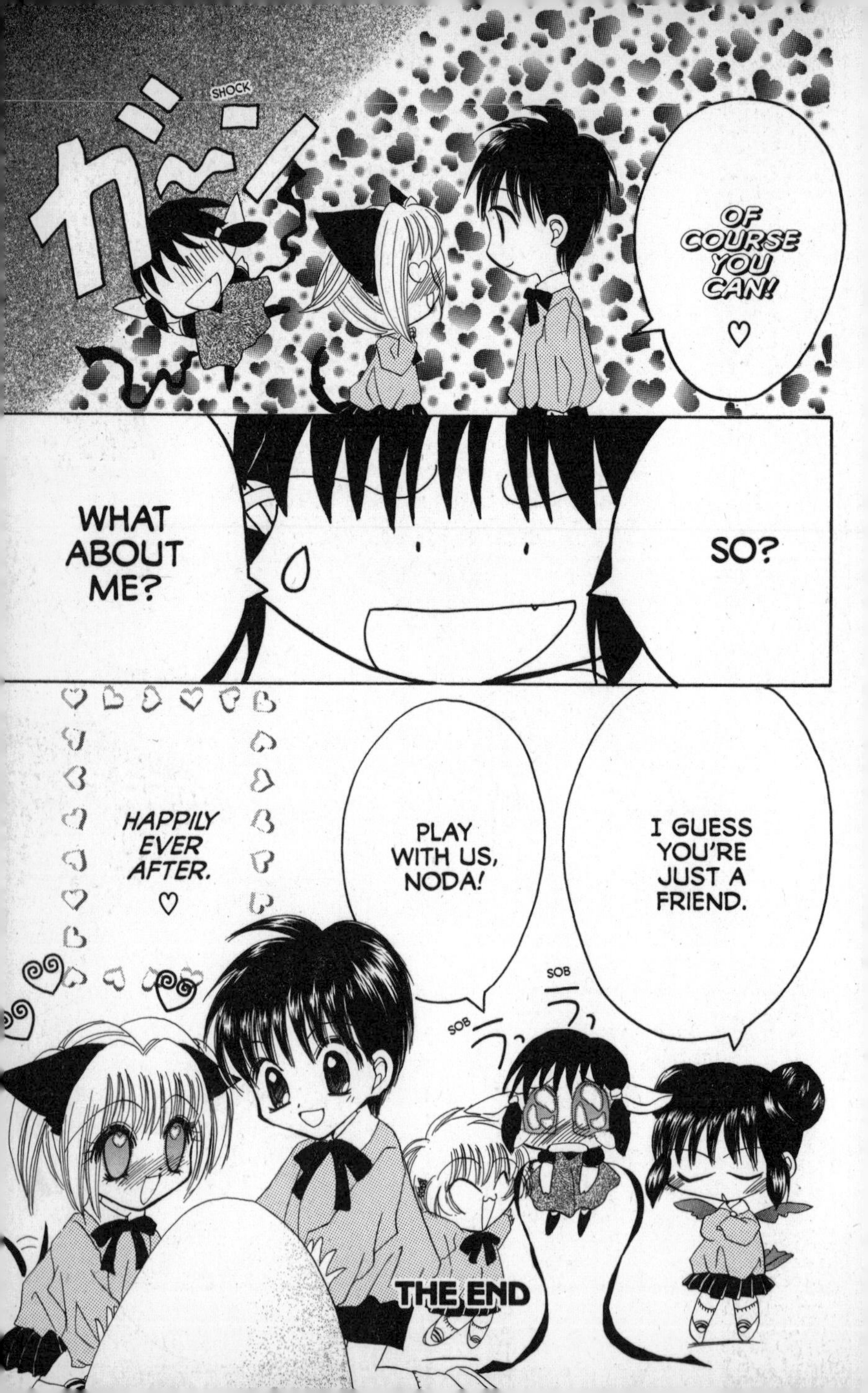
OF COURSE YOU CAN! ♡
SHOCK
SO?
WHAT ABOUT ME?
I GUESS YOU'RE JUST A FRIEND.
PLAY WITH US, NODA!
SOB
SOB
HAPPILY EVER AFTER. ♡
THE END

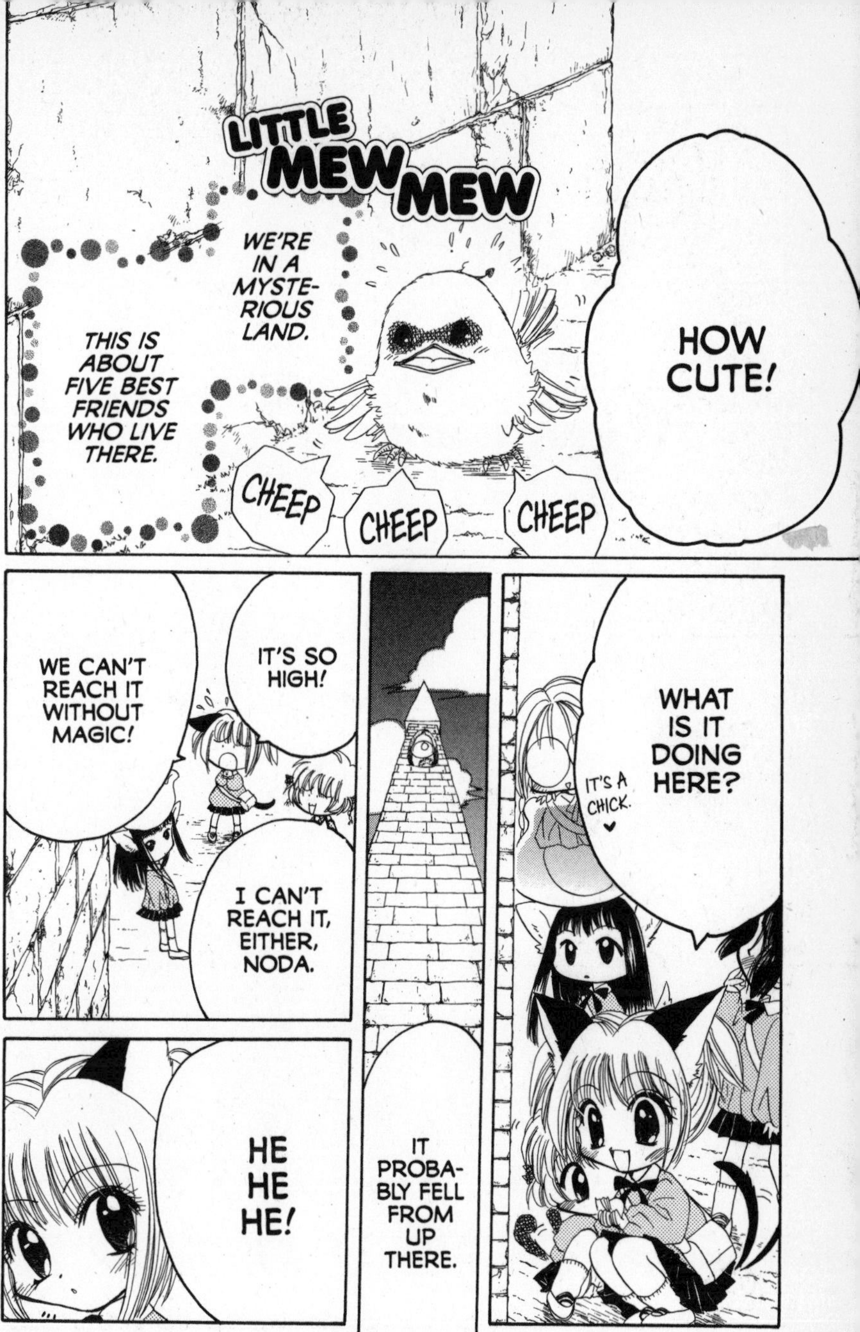
LITTLE MEW MEW
HOW CUTE!
WE'RE IN A MYSTERIOUS LAND.
THIS IS ABOUT FIVE BEST FRIENDS WHO LIVE THERE.
CHEEP
CHEEP
CHEEP
WHAT IS IT DOING HERE?
IT'S A CHICK. ♥
IT PROBABLY FELL FROM UP THERE.
IT'S SO HIGH!
WE CAN'T REACH IT WITHOUT MAGIC!
I CAN'T REACH IT, EITHER, NODA.
HE HE HE!

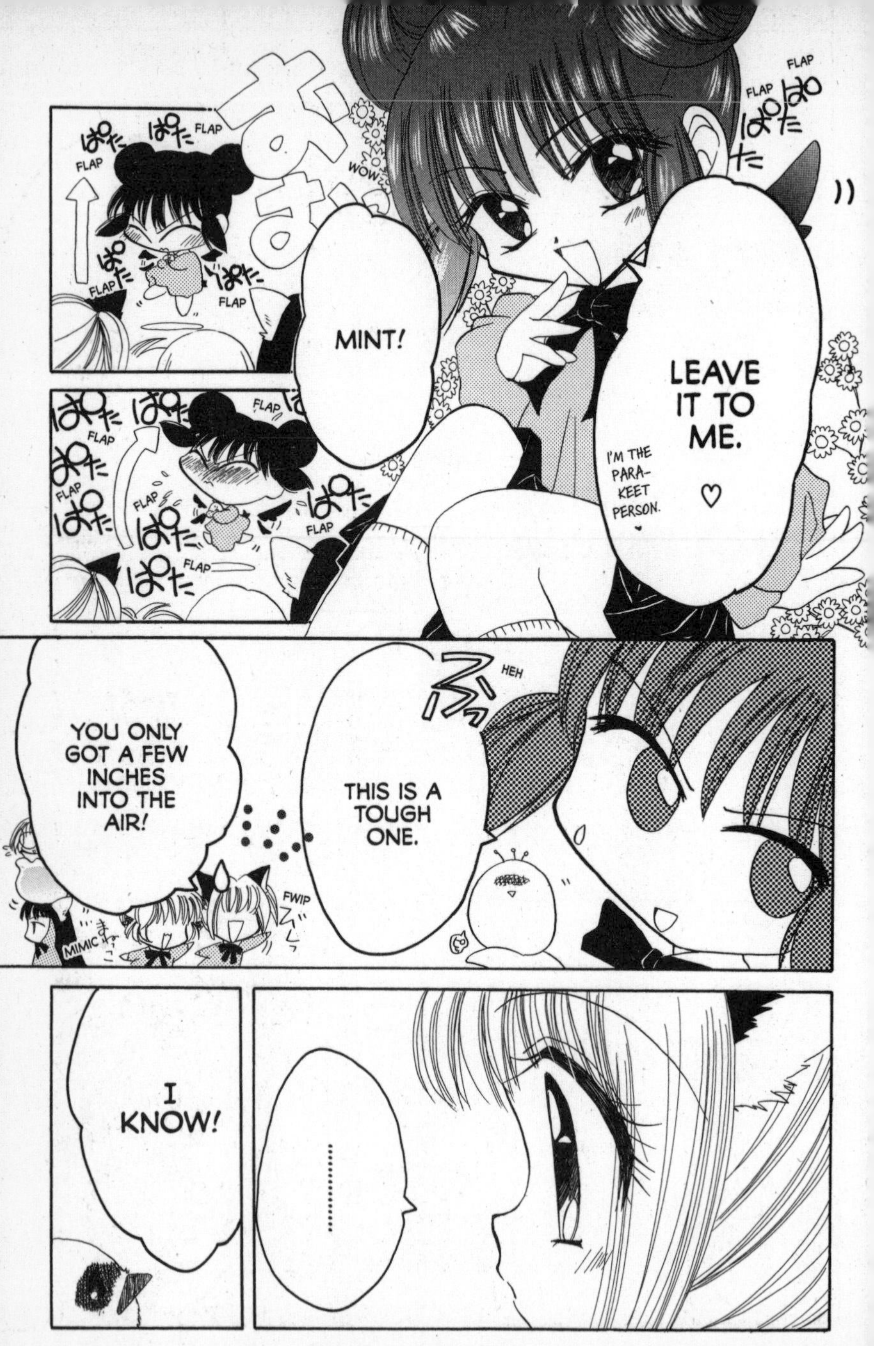
FLAP
FLAP
WOW
LEAVE IT TO ME. ♡
I'M THE PARAKEET PERSON. ♥
MINT!
FLAP
FLAP
FLAP
FLAP
FLAP
FLAP
FLAP
FLAP
FLAP
HEH
THIS IS A TOUGH ONE.
YOU ONLY GOT A FEW INCHES INTO THE AIR!
FWIP
MIMIC
......
I KNOW!

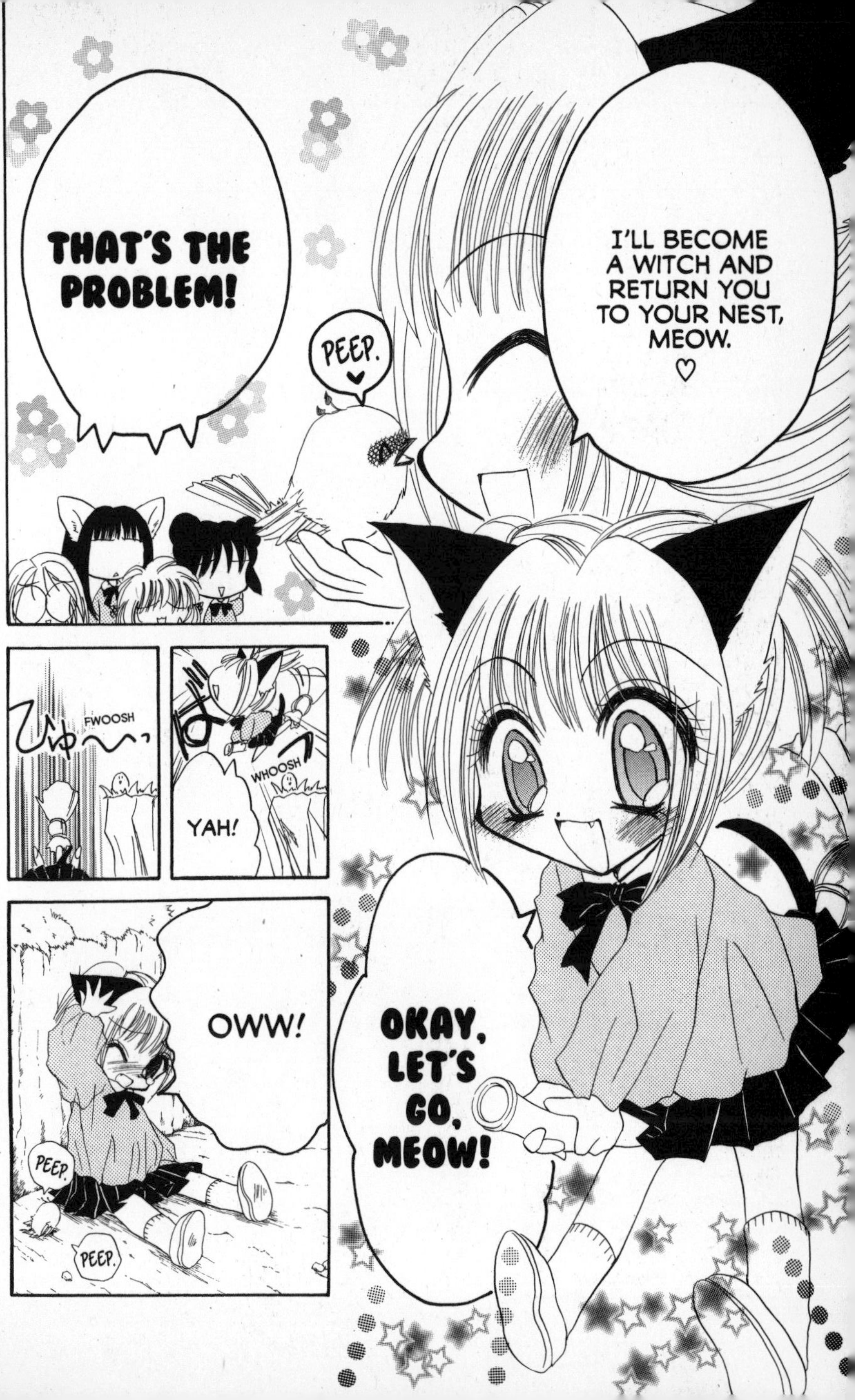

I'LL BECOME A WITCH AND RETURN YOU TO YOUR NEST, MEOW. ♡
PEEP. ♥
THAT'S THE PROBLEM!
OKAY, LET'S GO, MEOW!
WHOOSH
YAH!
FWOOSH
OWW!
PEEP.
PEEP.

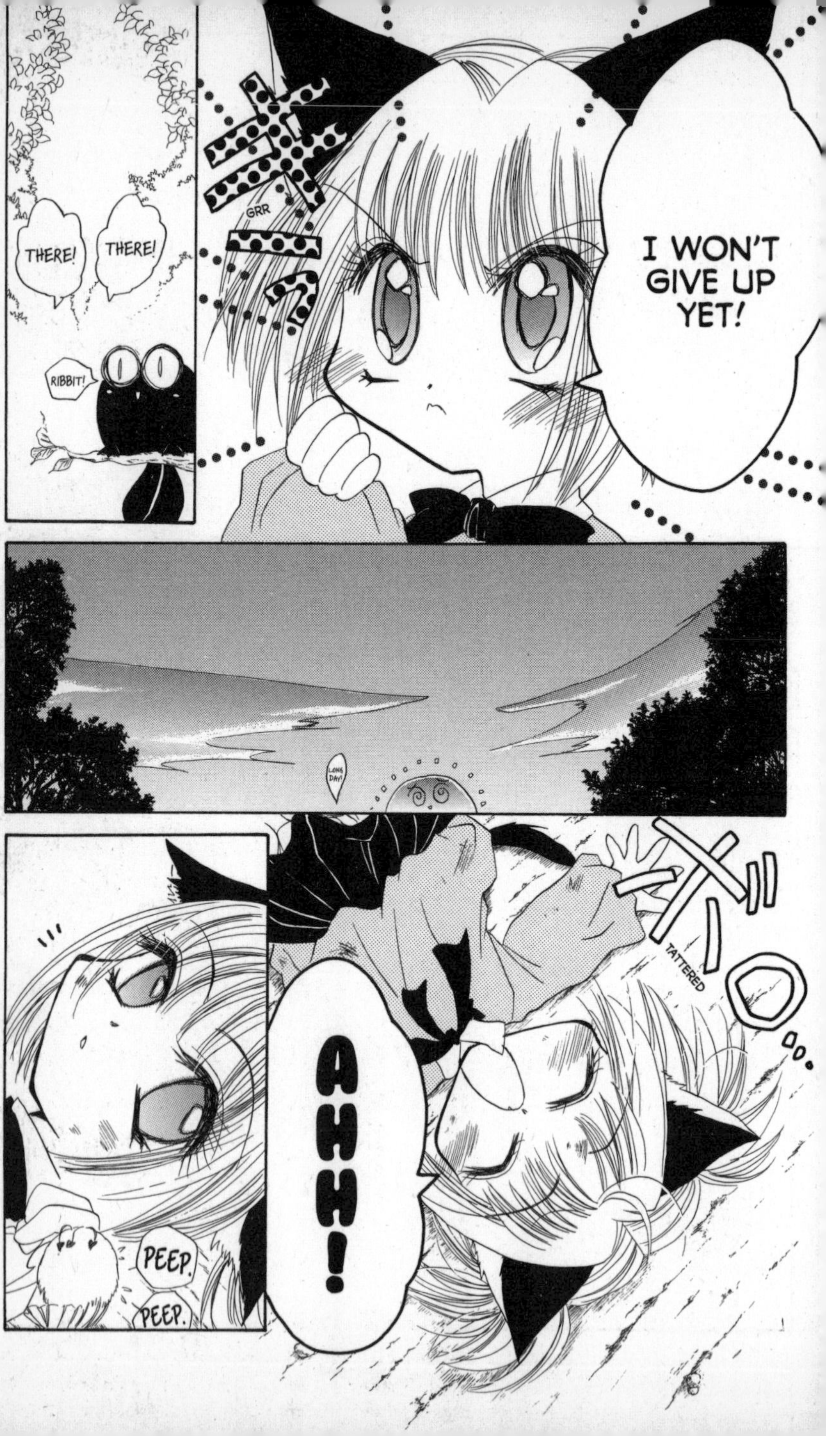
GRR
I WON'T GIVE UP YET!
THERE!
THERE!
RIBBIT!
LONG DAY!
TATTERED
AHHH!
PEEP.
PEEP.

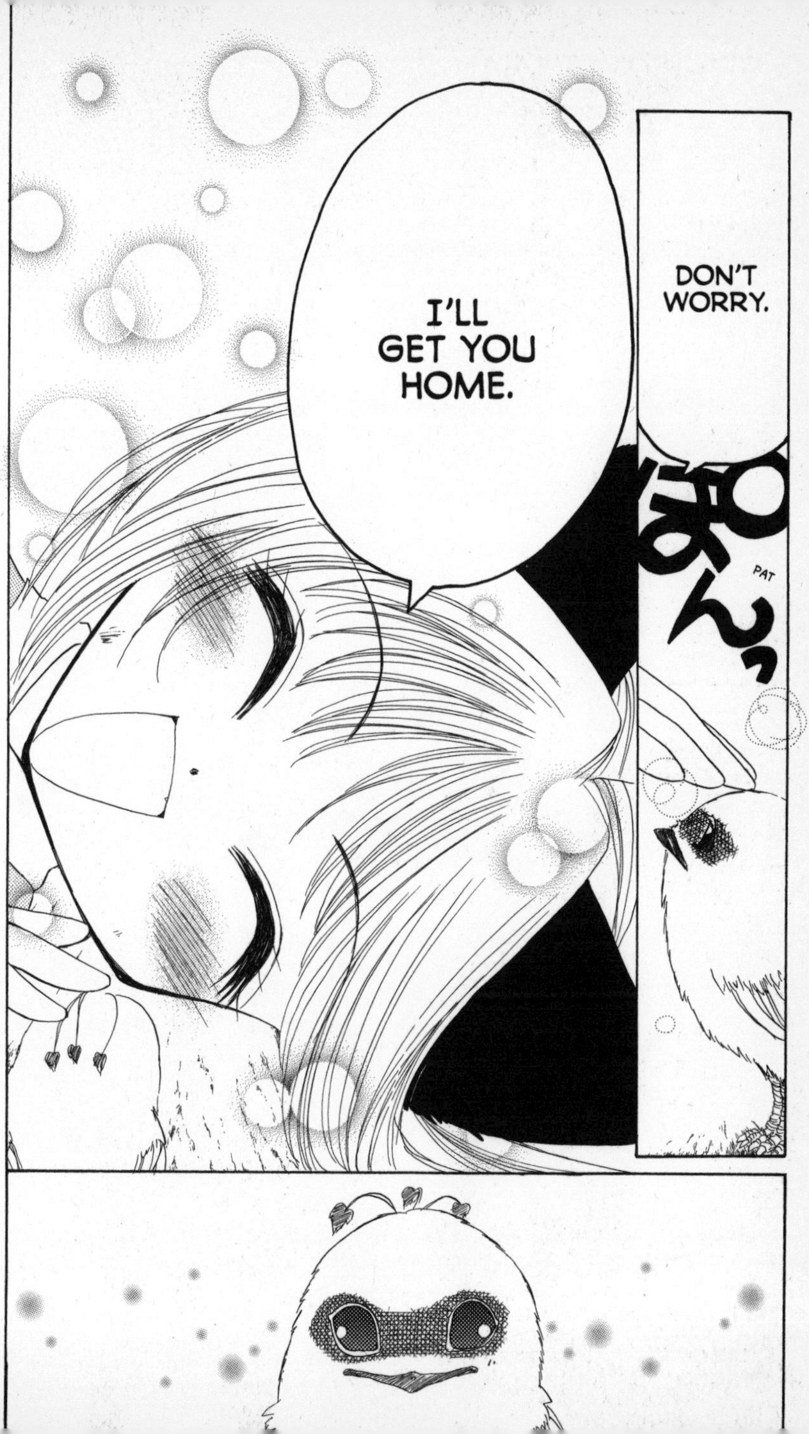
DON'T WORRY.
ぽんっ
PAT
I'LL GET YOU HOME.

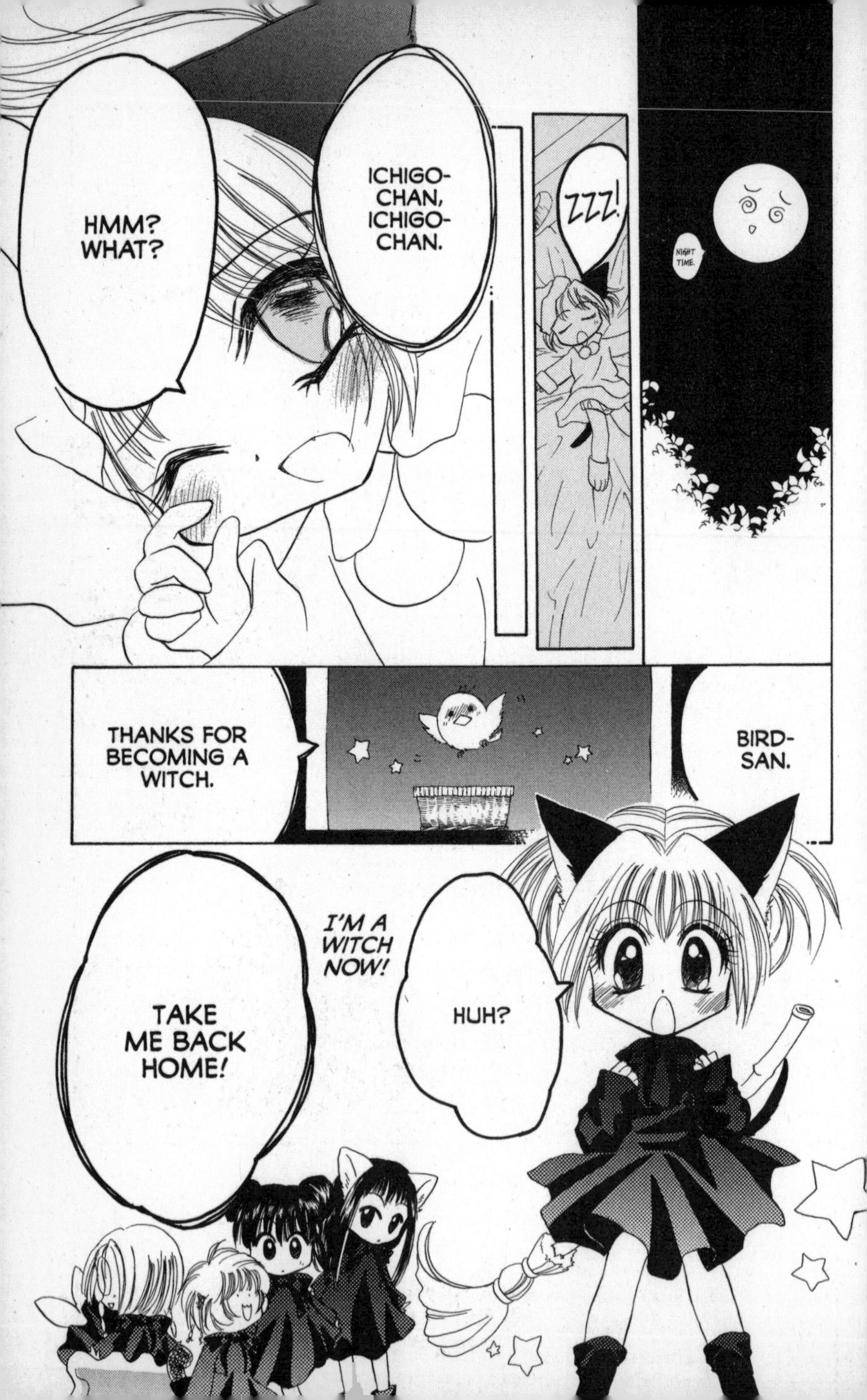
NIGHT TIME.
ZZZ!
ICHIGO-CHAN, ICHIGO-CHAN.
HMM? WHAT?
BIRD-SAN.
THANKS FOR BECOMING A WITCH.
HUH?
I'M A WITCH NOW!
TAKE ME BACK HOME!

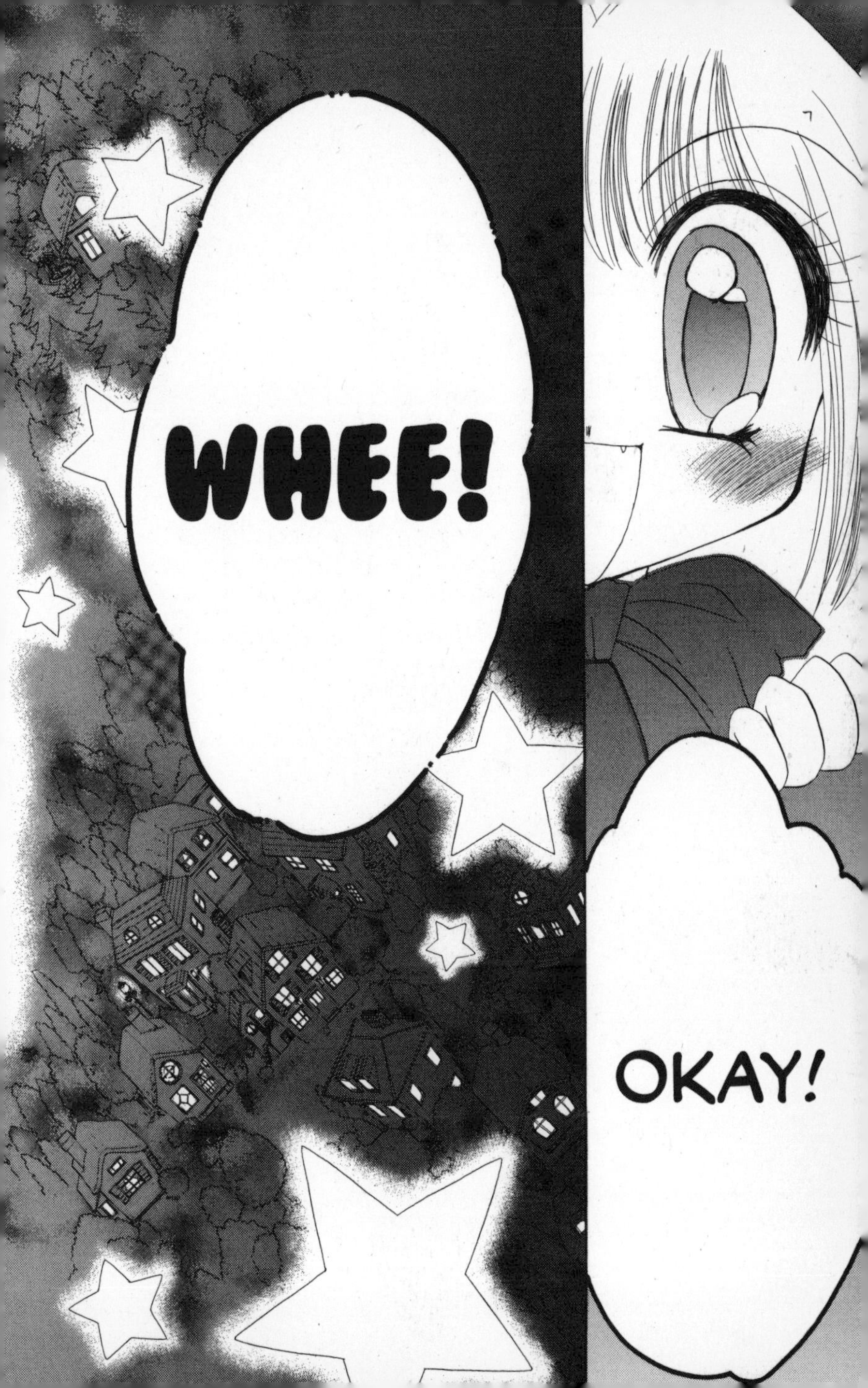
OKAY!
WHEE!

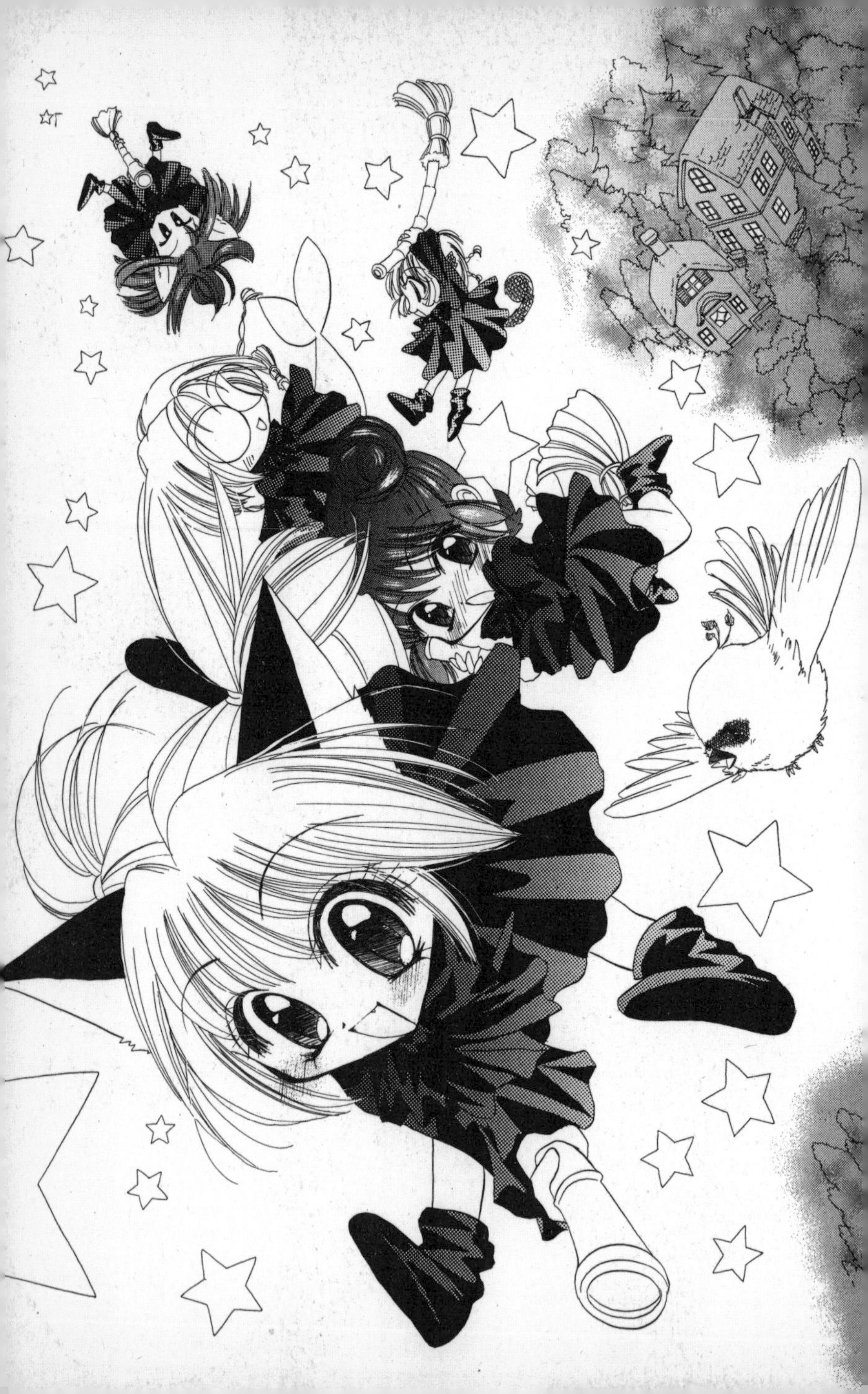

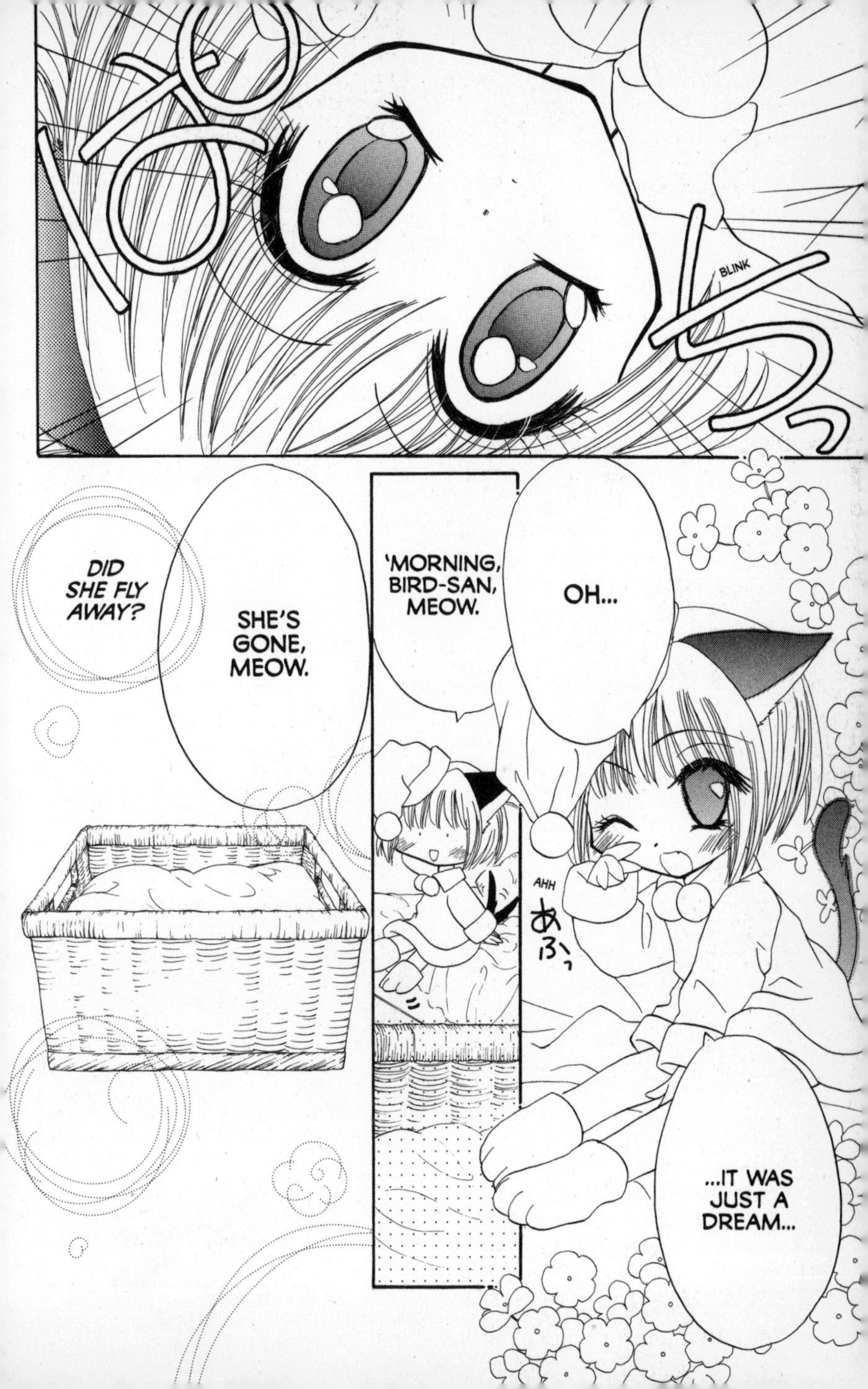
BLINK
OH...
'MORNING, BIRD-SAN, MEOW.
AHH
...IT WAS JUST A DREAM...
SHE'S GONE, MEOW.
DID SHE FLY AWAY?

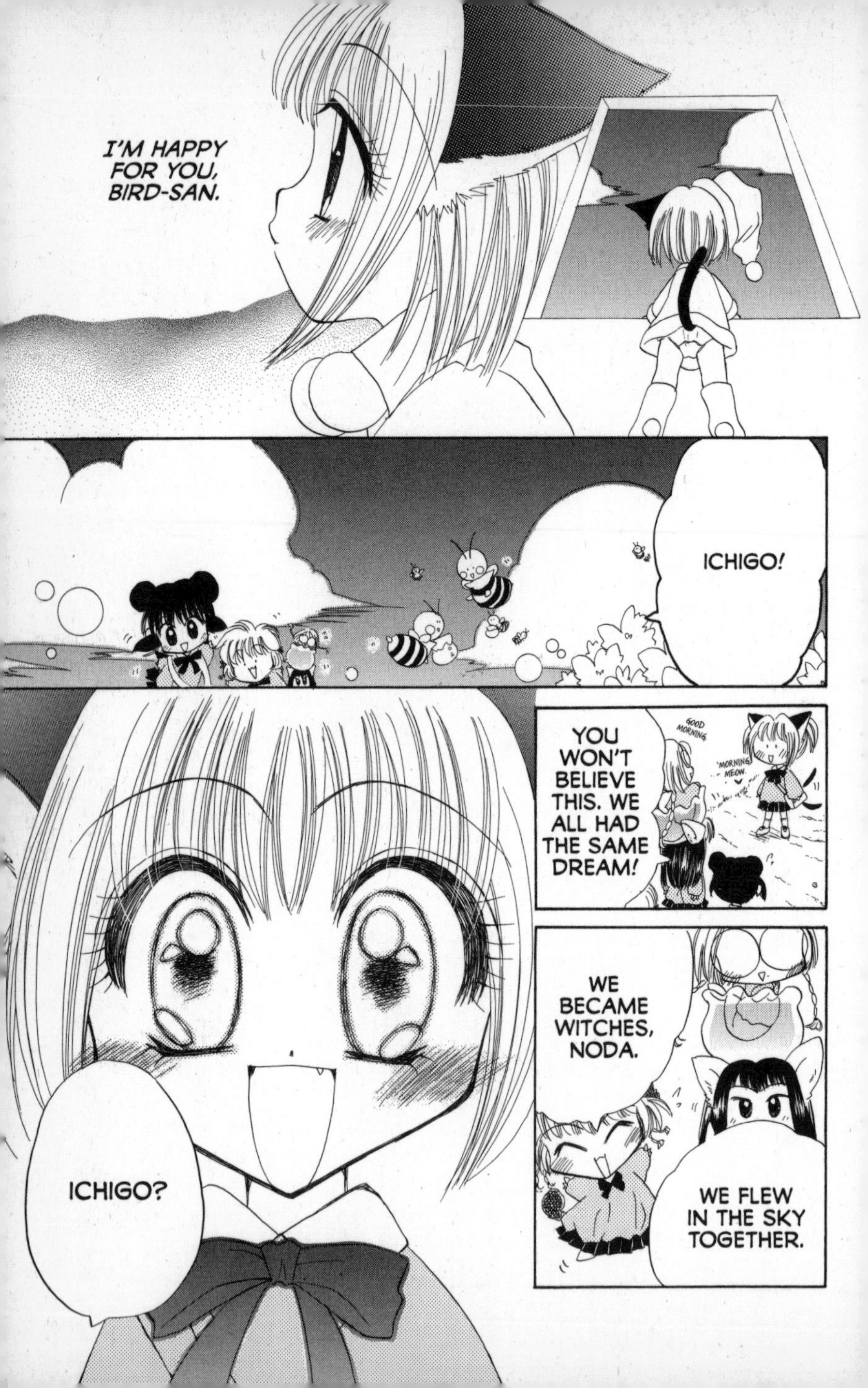

I'M HAPPY FOR YOU, BIRD-SAN.
ICHIGO!
GOOD MORNING.
MORNING MEOW.
YOU WON'T BELIEVE THIS. WE ALL HAD THE SAME DREAM!
WE BECAME WITCHES, NODA.
WE FLEW IN THE SKY TOGETHER.
ICHIGO?

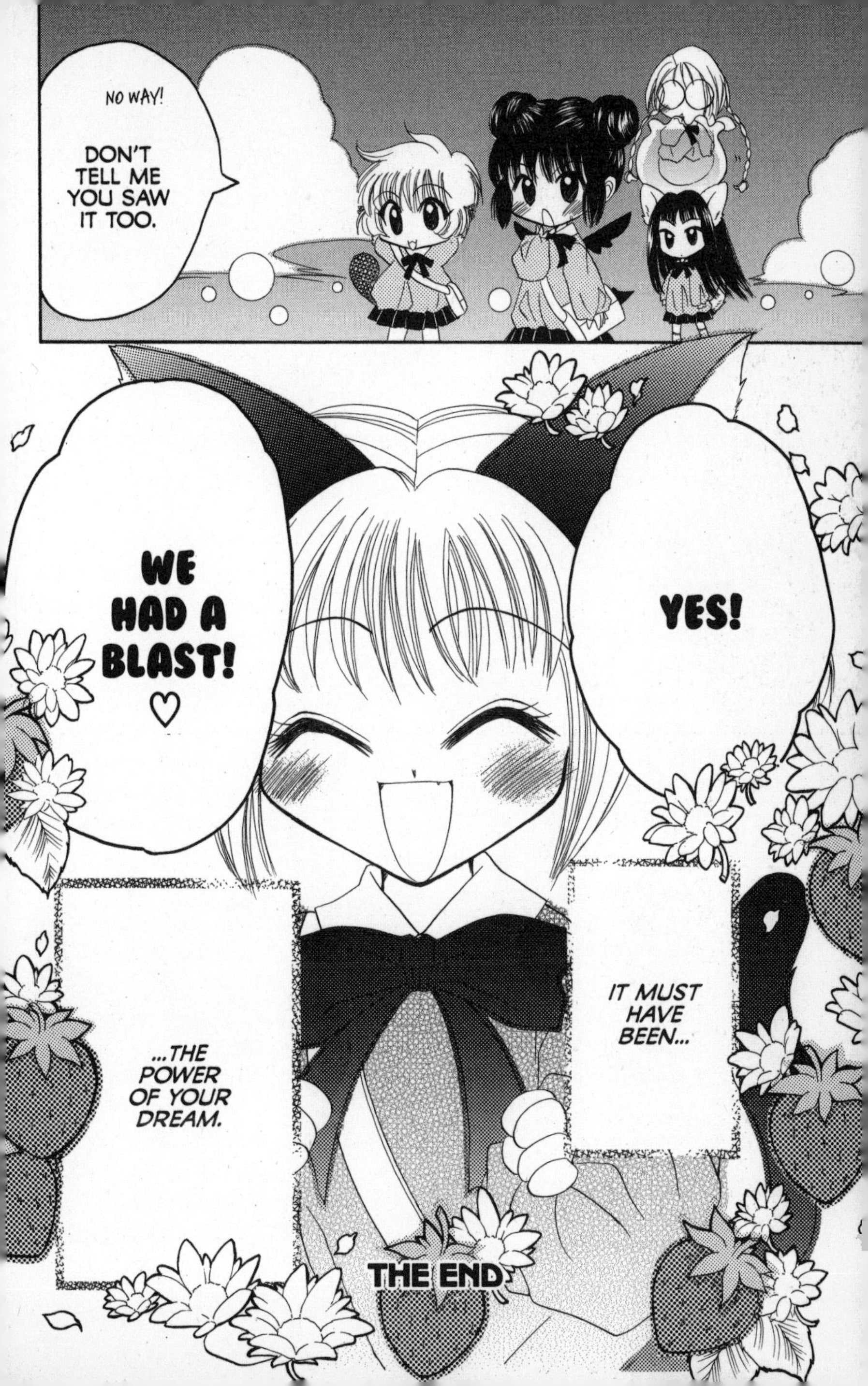
NO WAY! DON'T TELL ME YOU SAW IT TOO.
YES!
WE HAD A BLAST! ♡
IT MUST HAVE BEEN...
...THE POWER OF YOUR DREAM.
THE END

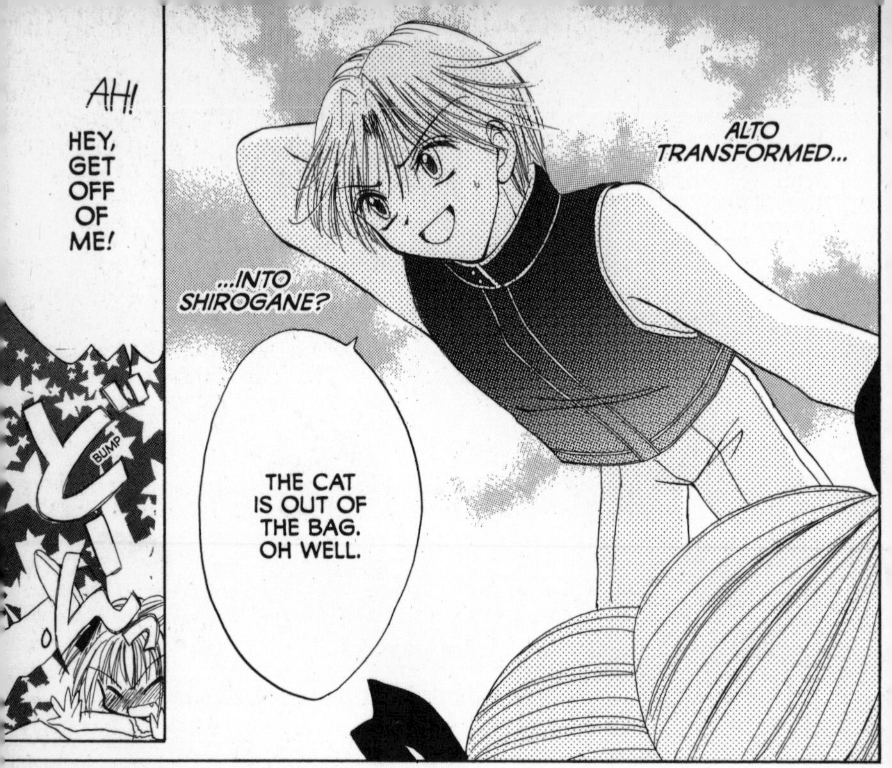
ALTO TRANSFORMED...
...INTO SHIROGANE?
THE CAT IS OUT OF THE BAG. OH WELL.
AH!
HEY, GET OFF OF ME!
BUMP

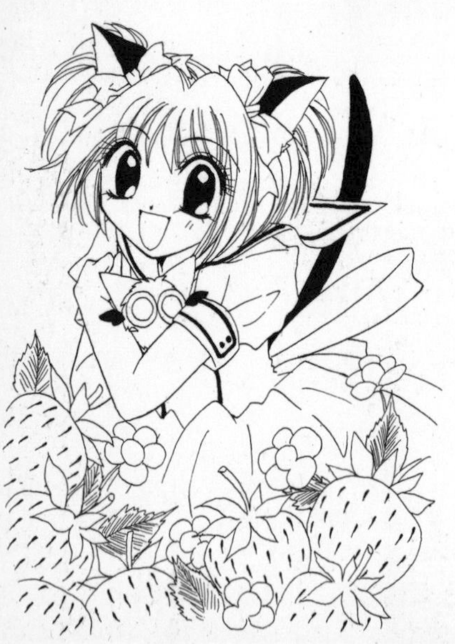

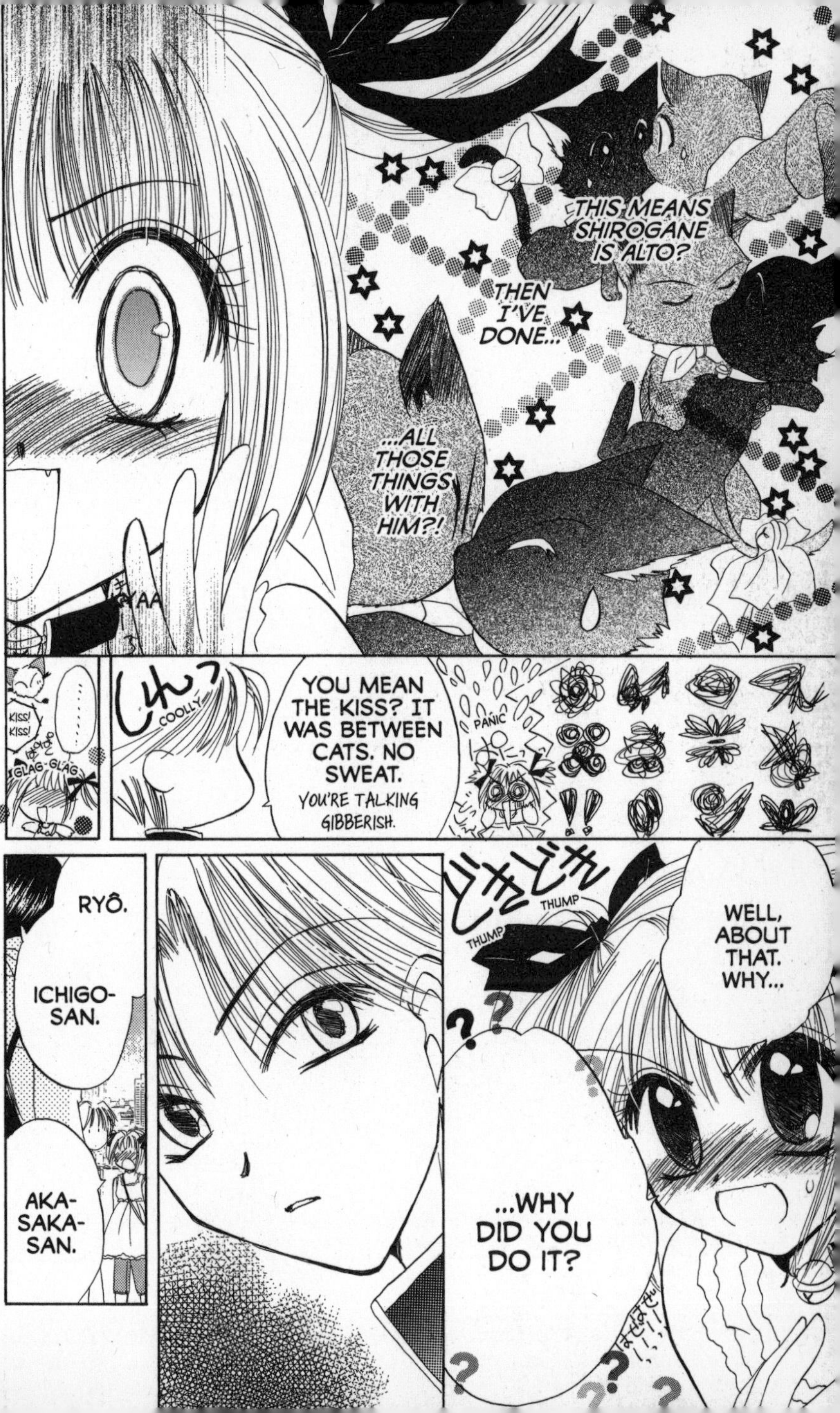
THIS MEANS SHIROGANE IS ALTO?
THEN I'VE DONE...
...ALL THOSE THINGS WITH HIM?!
PANIC
YOU MEAN THE KISS? IT WAS BETWEEN CATS. NO SWEAT.
YOU'RE TALKING GIBBERISH.
COOLLY
KISS! KISS!
GLAG-GLAG
......
THUMP THUMP
WELL, ABOUT THAT. WHY...
...WHY DID YOU DO IT?
RYÔ.
ICHIGO-SAN.
AKA-SAKA-SAN.

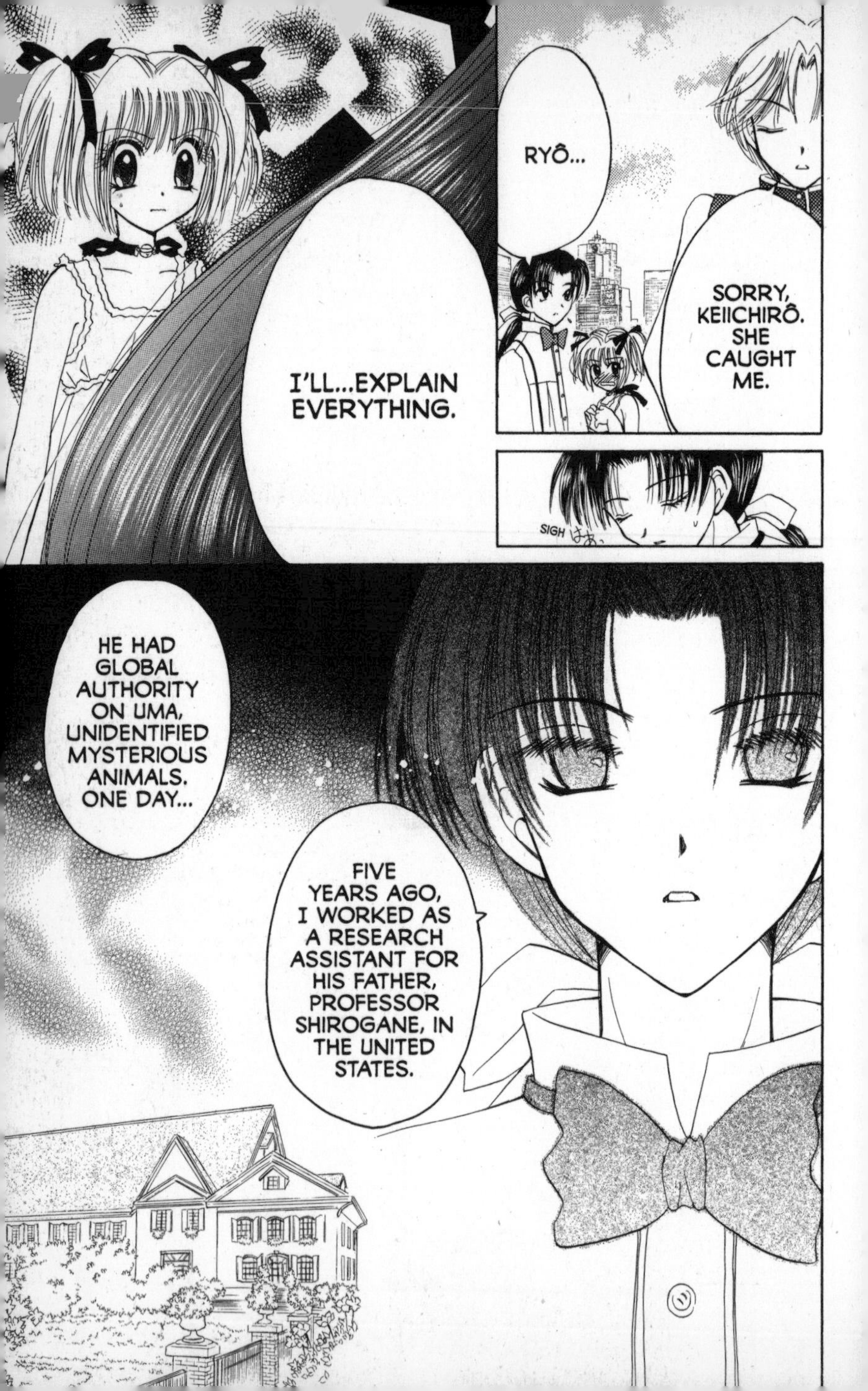
RYÔ...
SORRY, KEIICHIRÔ. SHE CAUGHT ME.
SIGH はあ
I'LL...EXPLAIN EVERYTHING.
FIVE YEARS AGO, I WORKED AS A RESEARCH ASSISTANT FOR HIS FATHER, PROFESSOR SHIROGANE, IN THE UNITED STATES.
HE HAD GLOBAL AUTHORITY ON UMA, UNIDENTIFIED MYSTERIOUS ANIMALS. ONE DAY...

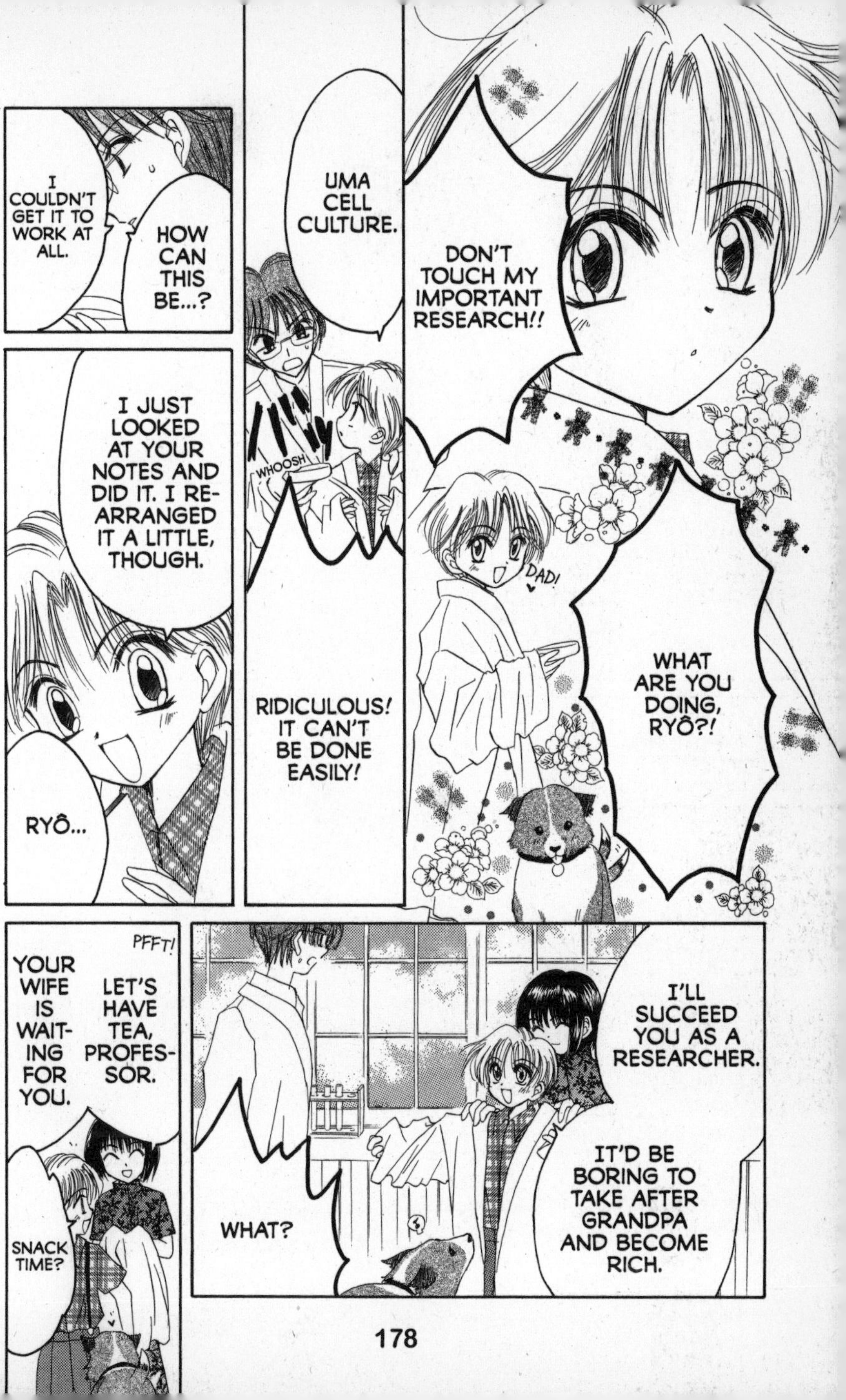

WHAT ARE YOU DOING, RYÔ?!
DON'T TOUCH MY IMPORTANT RESEARCH!!
DAD!
UMA CELL CULTURE.
WHOOSH
RIDICULOUS! IT CAN'T BE DONE EASILY!
HOW CAN THIS BE...?
I COULDN'T GET IT TO WORK AT ALL.
I JUST LOOKED AT YOUR NOTES AND DID IT. I RE-ARRANGED IT A LITTLE, THOUGH.
RYÔ...
I'LL SUCCEED YOU AS A RESEARCHER.
IT'D BE BORING TO TAKE AFTER GRANDPA AND BECOME RICH.
WHAT?
PFFT!
LET'S HAVE TEA, PROFESSOR.
YOUR WIFE IS WAITING FOR YOU.
SNACK TIME?

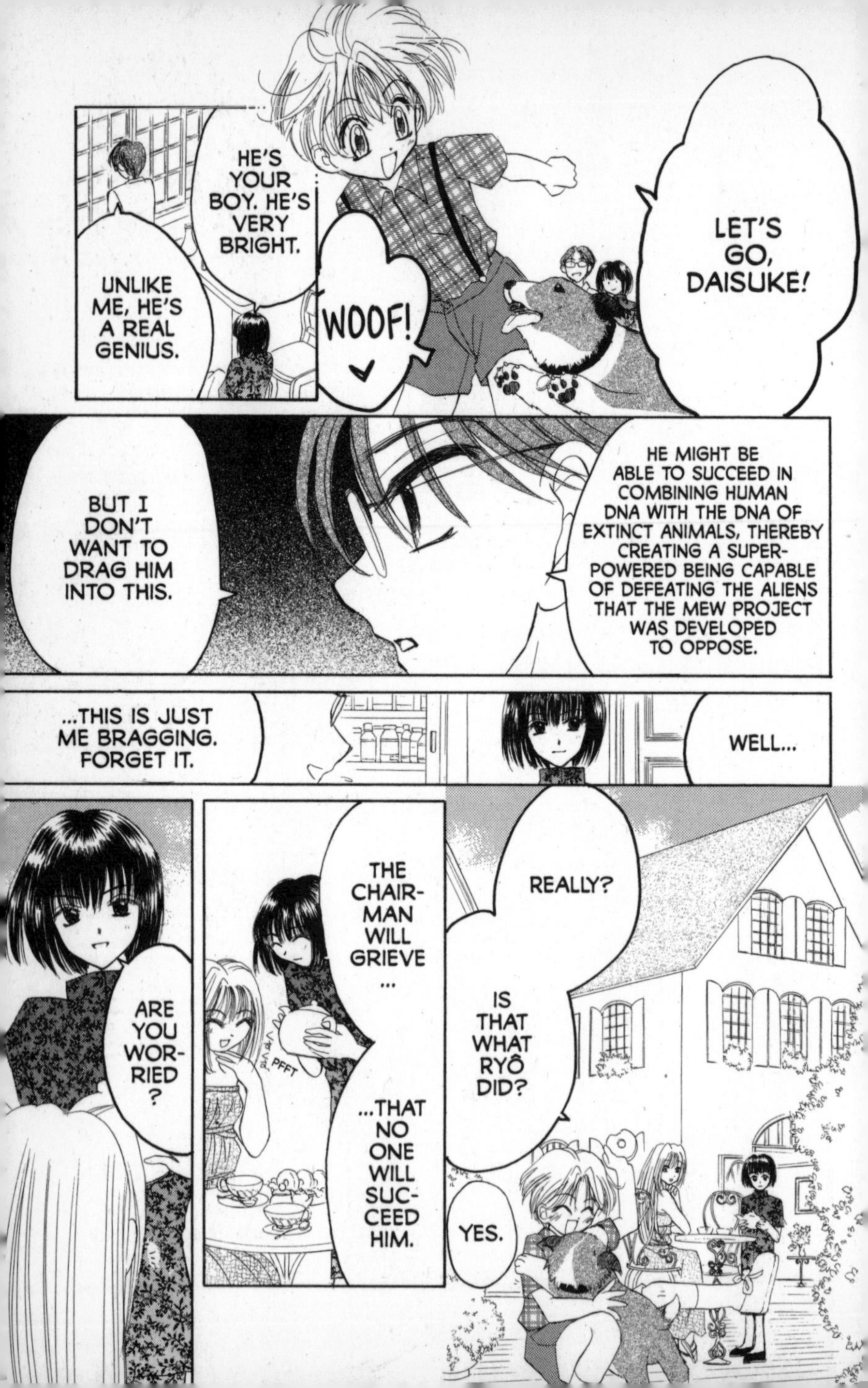
LET'S GO, DAISUKE!
WOOF!
HE'S YOUR BOY. HE'S VERY BRIGHT.
UNLIKE ME, HE'S A REAL GENIUS.
HE MIGHT BE ABLE TO SUCCEED IN COMBINING HUMAN DNA WITH THE DNA OF EXTINCT ANIMALS, THEREBY CREATING A SUPER-POWERED BEING CAPABLE OF DEFEATING THE ALIENS THAT THE MEW PROJECT WAS DEVELOPED TO OPPOSE.
BUT I DON'T WANT TO DRAG HIM INTO THIS.
WELL...
...THIS IS JUST ME BRAGGING. FORGET IT.
REALLY?
IS THAT WHAT RYÔ DID?
YES.
THE CHAIR-MAN WILL GRIEVE ...
...THAT NO ONE WILL SUC-CEED HIM.
PFFT
ARE YOU WOR-RIED ?

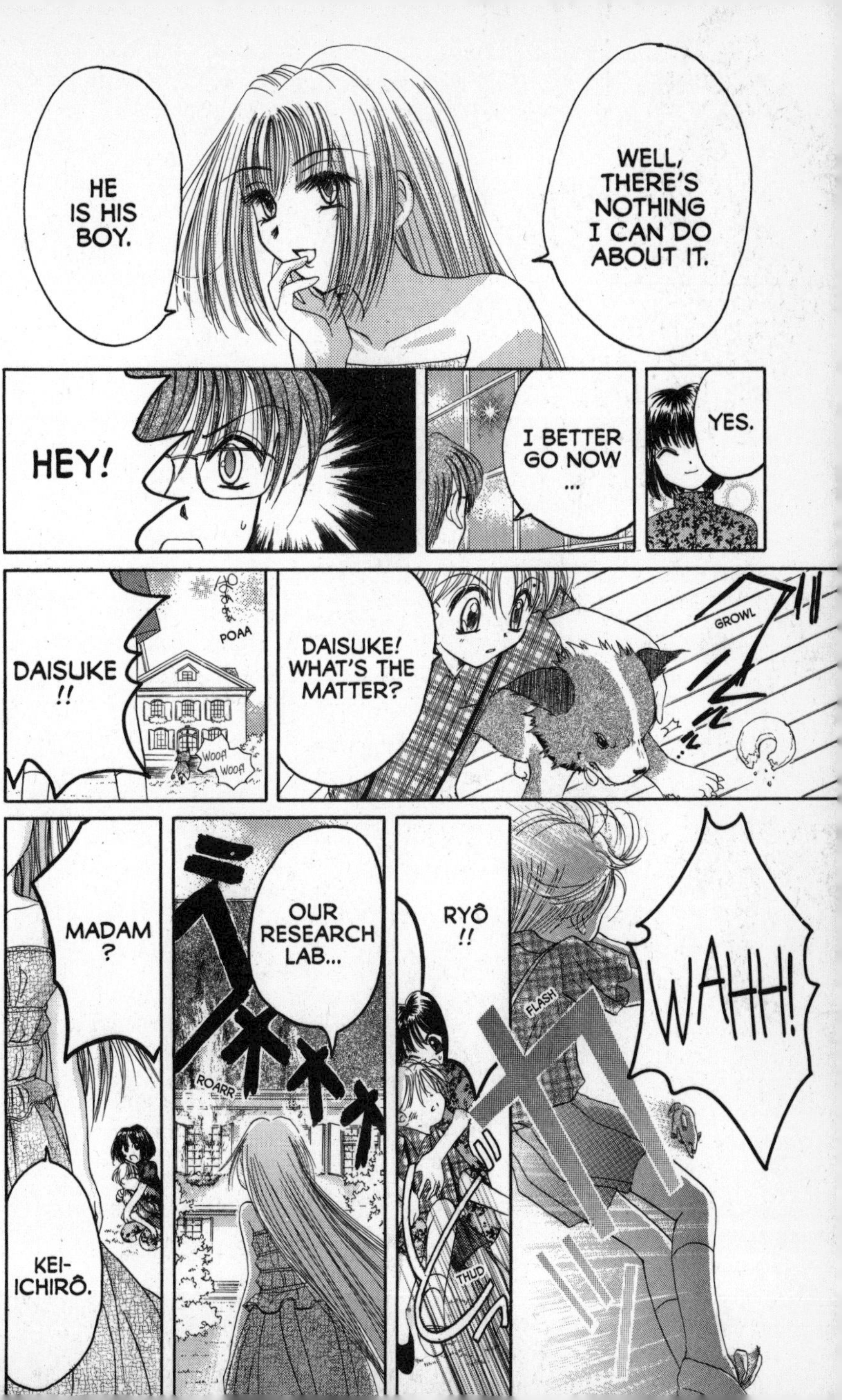
WELL, THERE'S NOTHING I CAN DO ABOUT IT.
HE IS HIS BOY.
YES.
I BETTER GO NOW ...
HEY!
GROWL
DAISUKE! WHAT'S THE MATTER?
POAA
DAISUKE !!
Woof! Woof!
WAHH!
FLASH
THUD
RYÔ !!
OUR RESEARCH LAB...
ROARR
MADAM ?
KEI-ICHIRÔ.

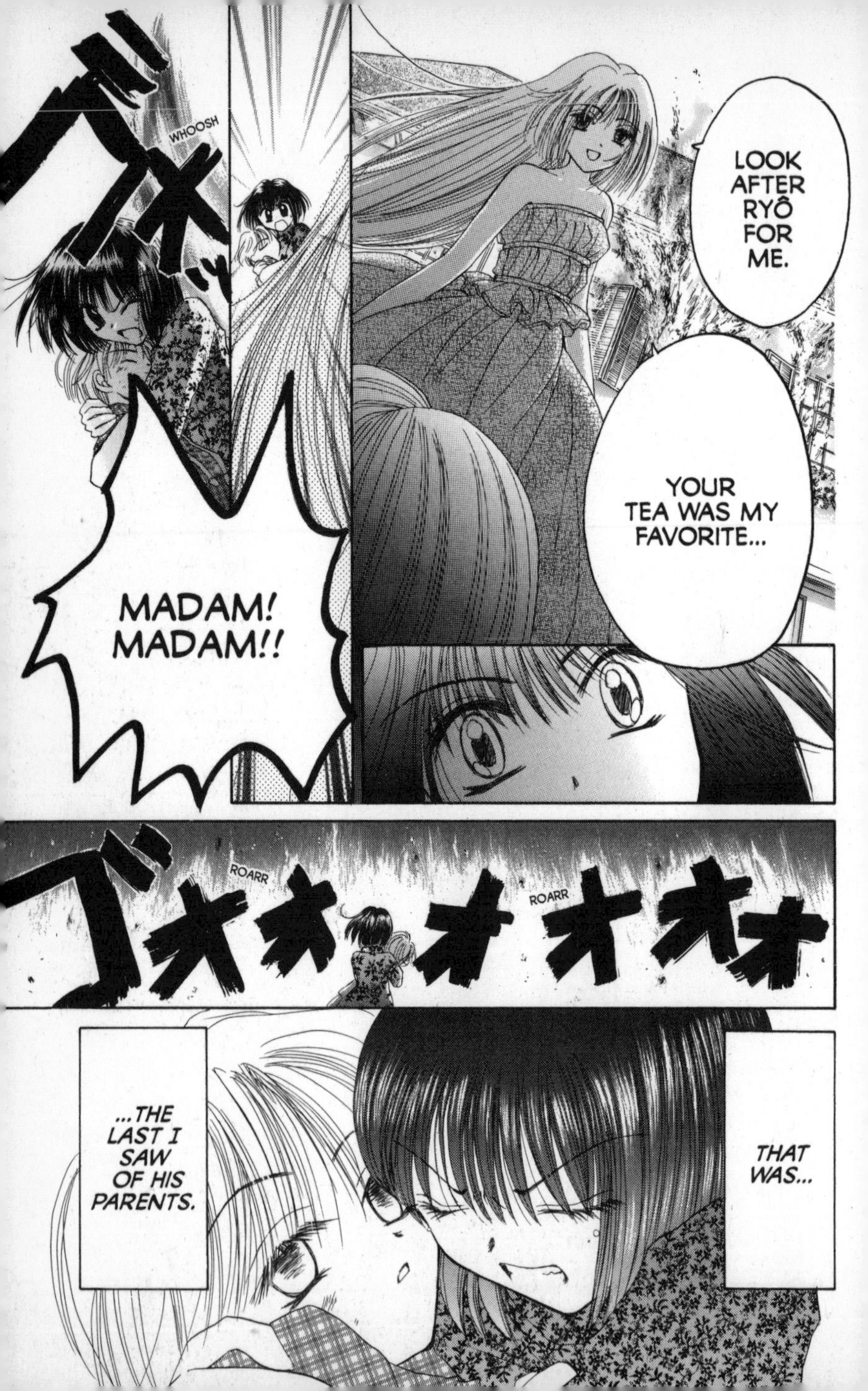
LOOK AFTER RYÔ FOR ME.
YOUR TEA WAS MY FAVORITE...
WHOOSH
MADAM! MADAM!!
ROARR
ROARR
THAT WAS...
...THE LAST I SAW OF HIS PARENTS.

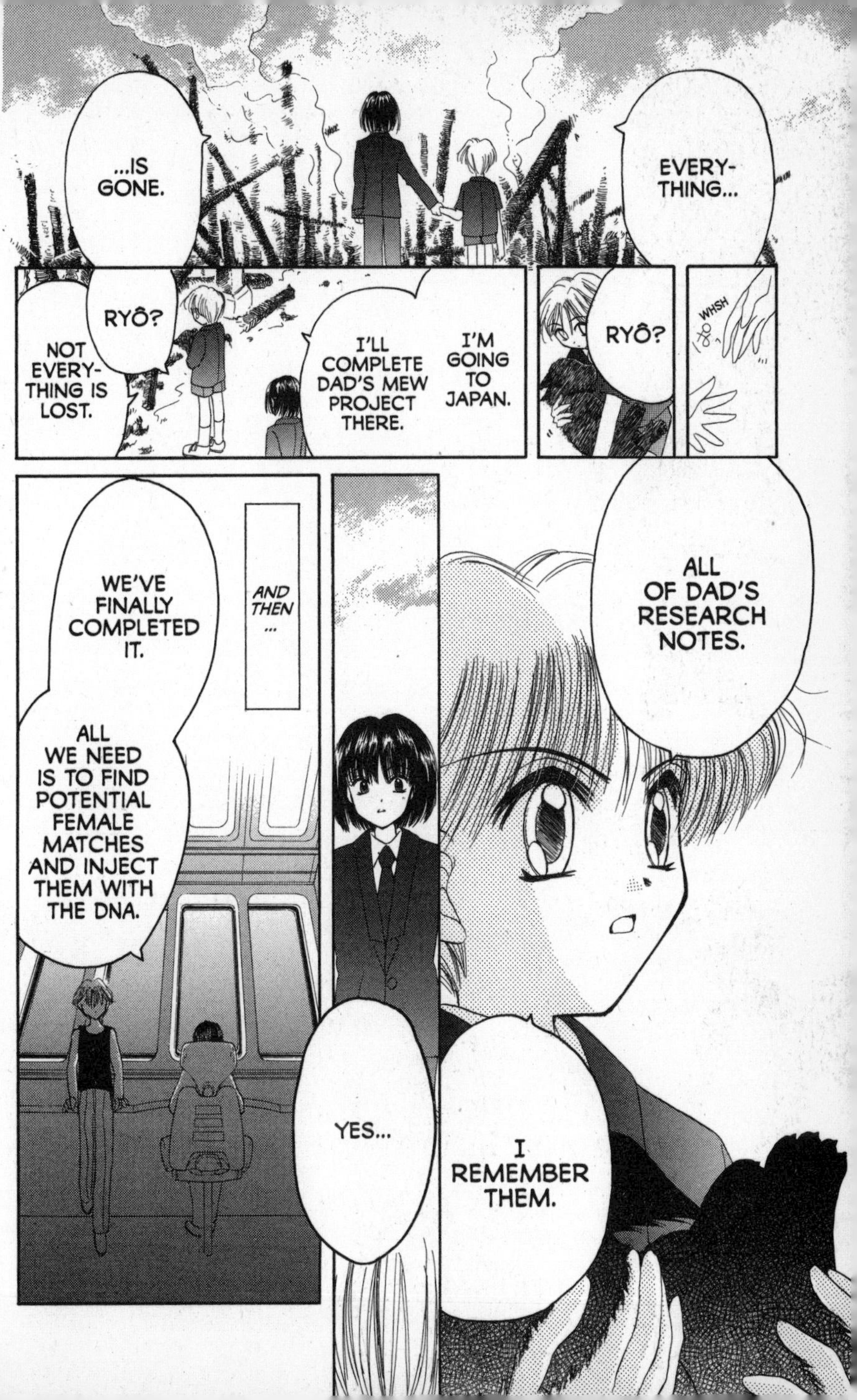
EVERY-THING...
...IS GONE.
WHSH
RYÔ?
I'M GOING TO JAPAN.
I'LL COMPLETE DAD'S MEW PROJECT THERE.
RYÔ?
NOT EVERY-THING IS LOST.
ALL OF DAD'S RESEARCH NOTES.
I REMEMBER THEM.
YES...
AND THEN ...
WE'VE FINALLY COMPLETED IT.
ALL WE NEED IS TO FIND POTENTIAL FEMALE MATCHES AND INJECT THEM WITH THE DNA.

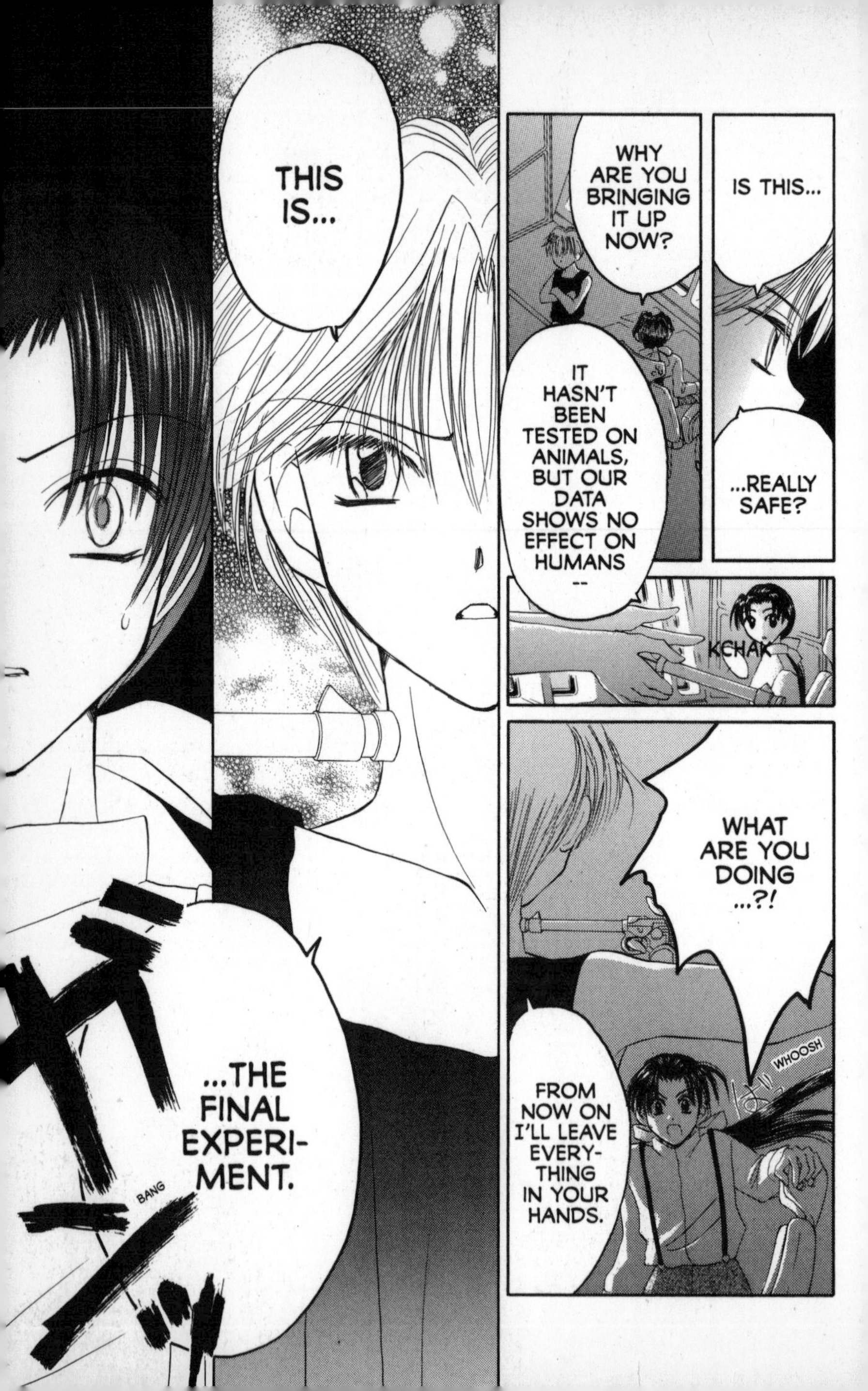
IS THIS...
...REALLY SAFE?
WHY ARE YOU BRINGING IT UP NOW?
IT HASN'T BEEN TESTED ON ANIMALS, BUT OUR DATA SHOWS NO EFFECT ON HUMANS --
KCHAK
WHAT ARE YOU DOING ...?!
WHOOSH
FROM NOW ON I'LL LEAVE EVERY-THING IN YOUR HANDS.
THIS IS...
...THE FINAL EXPERI-MENT.
BANG

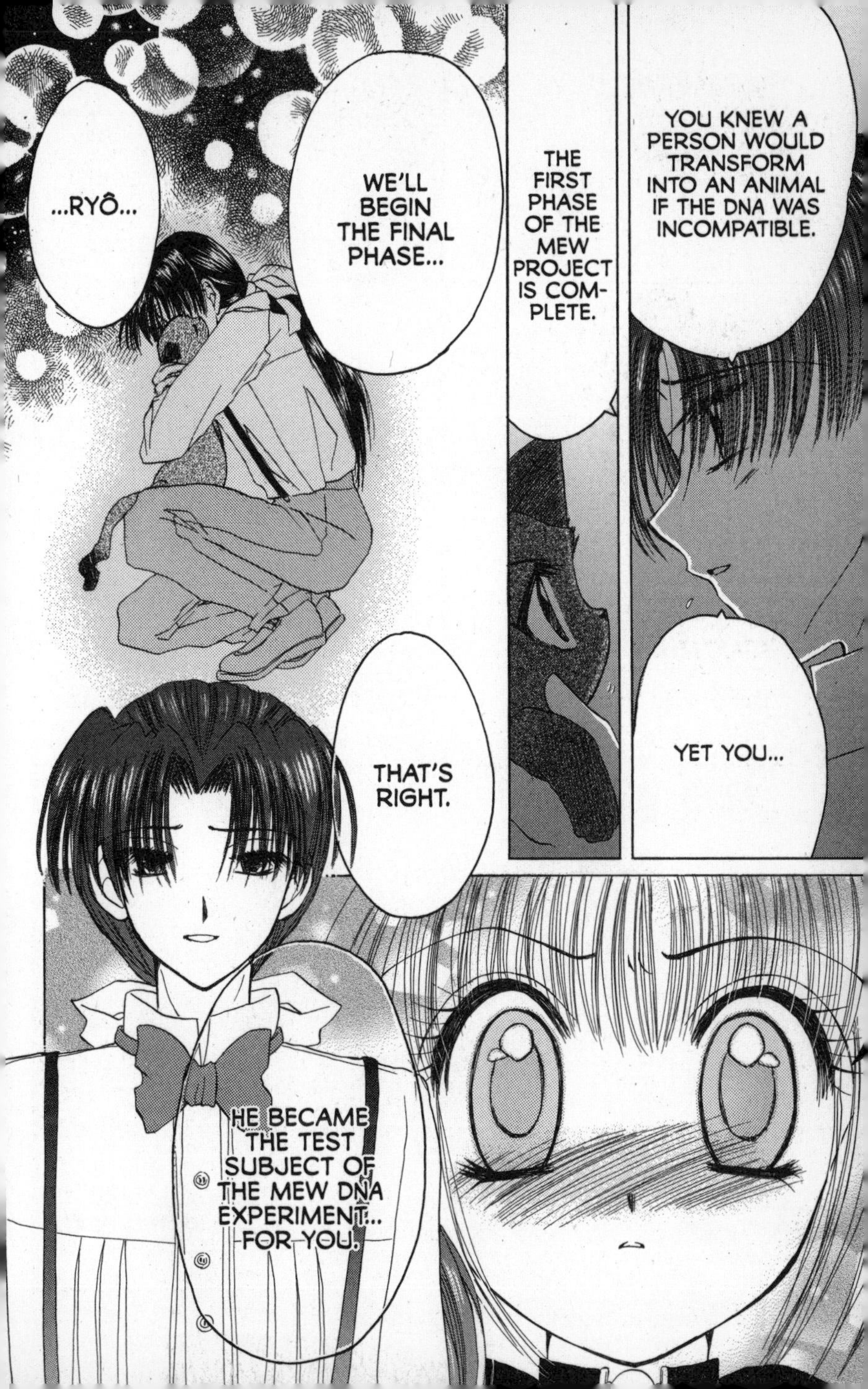
YOU KNEW A PERSON WOULD TRANSFORM INTO AN ANIMAL IF THE DNA WAS INCOMPATIBLE.
YET YOU...
THE FIRST PHASE OF THE MEW PROJECT IS COM-PLETE.
WE'LL BEGIN THE FINAL PHASE...
...RYÔ...
THAT'S RIGHT.
HE BECAME THE TEST SUBJECT OF THE MEW DNA EXPERIMENT... FOR YOU.

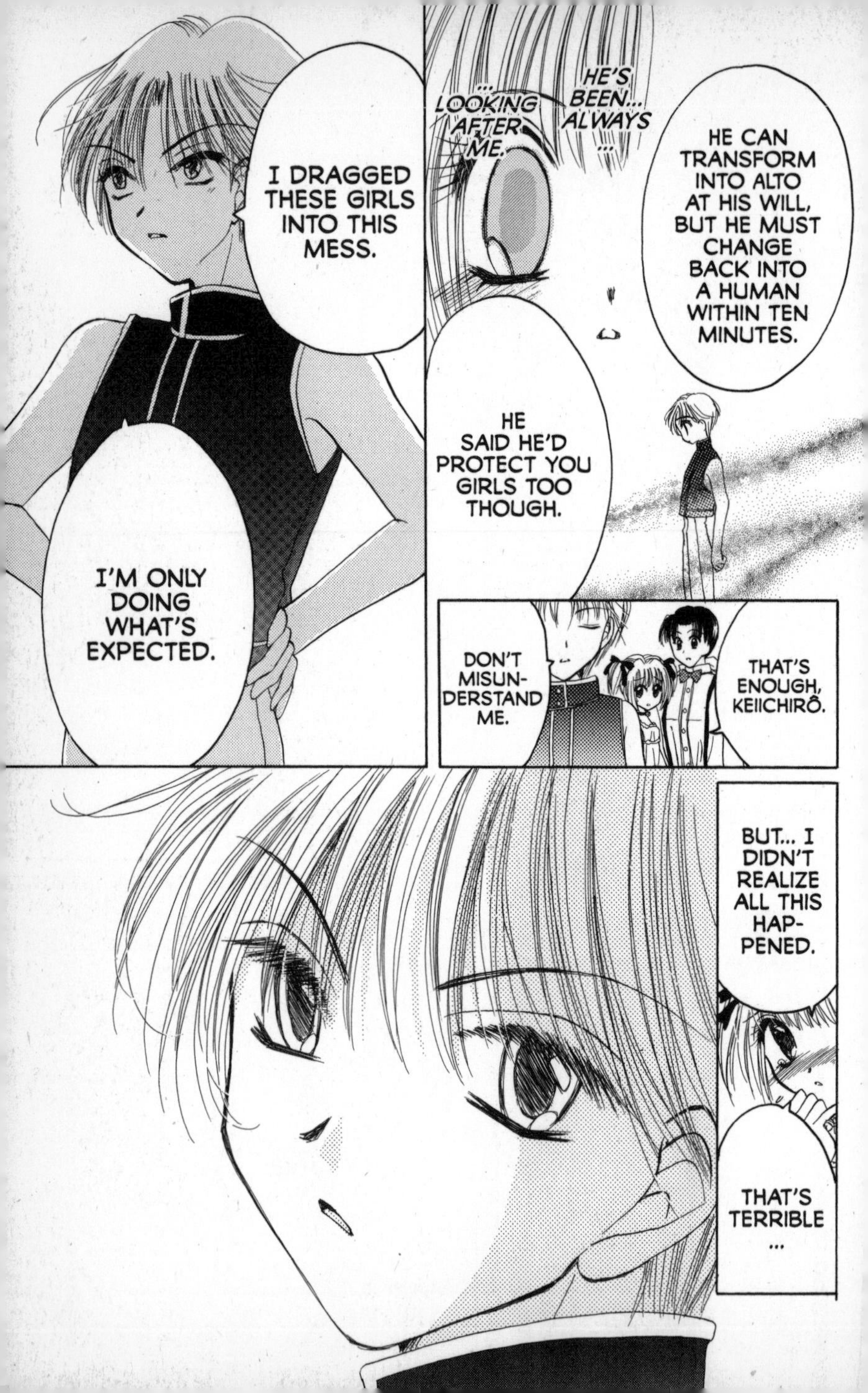

HE CAN TRANSFORM INTO ALTO AT HIS WILL, BUT HE MUST CHANGE BACK INTO A HUMAN WITHIN TEN MINUTES.
HE'S BEEN... ALWAYS ...
...LOOKING AFTER ME.
HE SAID HE'D PROTECT YOU GIRLS TOO THOUGH.
THAT'S ENOUGH, KEIICHIRÔ.
DON'T MISUNDERSTAND ME.
I DRAGGED THESE GIRLS INTO THIS MESS.
I'M ONLY DOING WHAT'S EXPECTED.
BUT... I DIDN'T REALIZE ALL THIS HAPPENED.
THAT'S TERRIBLE ...

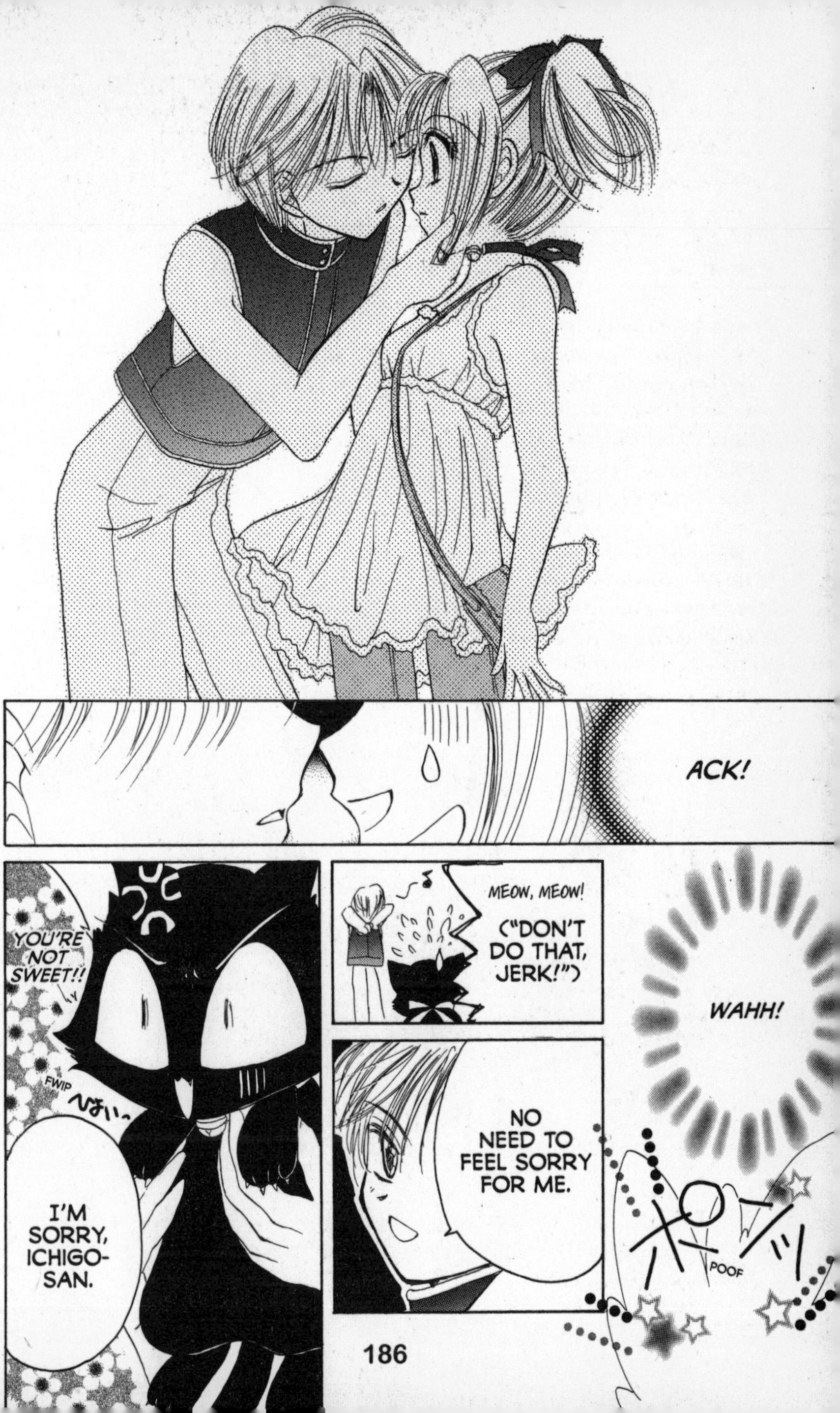
ACK!
WAHH!
POOF
MEOW, MEOW!
("DON'T DO THAT, JERK!")
NO NEED TO FEEL SORRY FOR ME.
YOU'RE NOT SWEET!!
FWIP
I'M SORRY, ICHIGO-SAN.

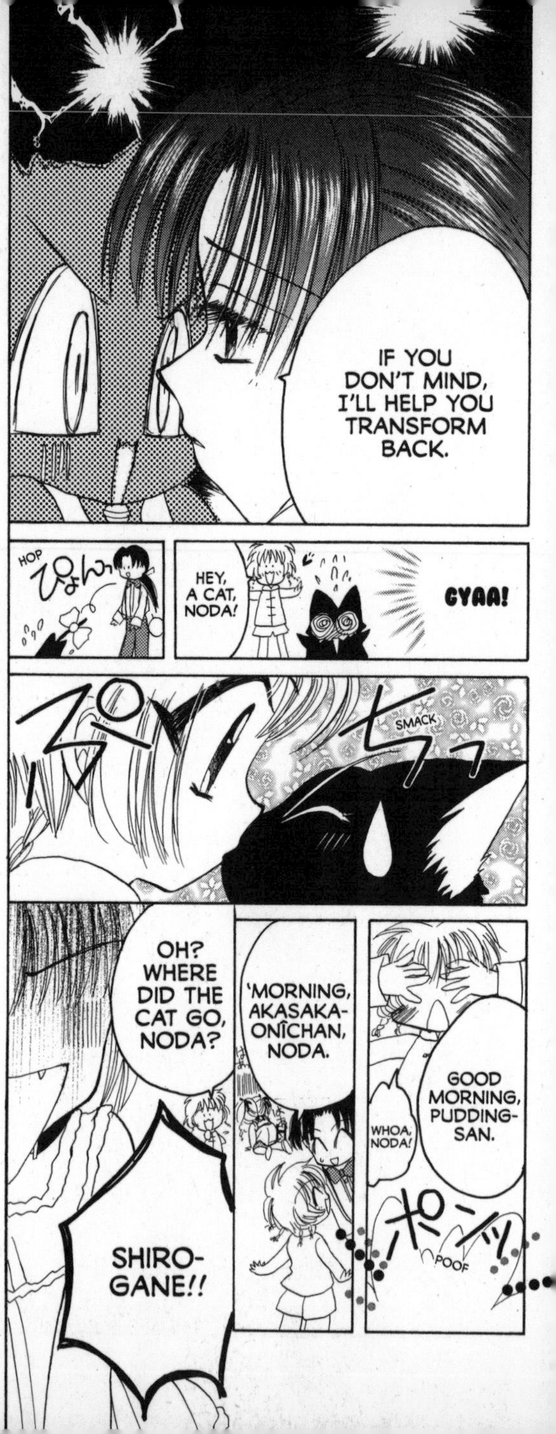
IF YOU DON'T MIND, I'LL HELP YOU TRANSFORM BACK.
GYAA!
HEY, A CAT, NODA!
HOP
SMACK
GOOD MORNING, PUDDING-SAN.
WHOA, NODA!
POOF
'MORNING, AKASAKA-ONÎCHAN, NODA.
OH? WHERE DID THE CAT GO, NODA?
SHIRO-GANE!!

Tokyo Mew Mew: Ichigo's Costume Wanted! Part 1

Tokyo Mew Mew: Ichigo's Costume Wanted! Part 1

Usually I do a four-koma manga here, but I ran a contest to which I got many responses. I drew the Grand Prize winning costume by Kanako Kôzuki-chan on the cover, but I felt it was a shame not to share other submissions. I chose to draw six of the runner-ups. I wanted to share others, but I picked two Semi-Grand winners, two of the five Best ideas winners and two of the five Cute Costumes winners for the limited space. Now let's enjoy Ichigo's fashion show!

This was the Grand Prize costume.

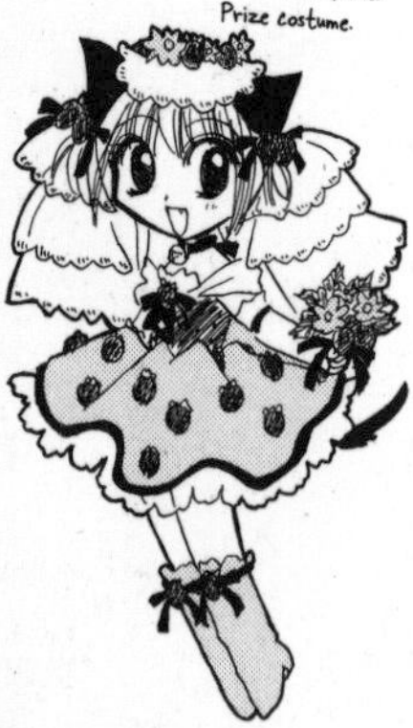

It was a cute, gorgeous dress fit for the Grand Prize, but it was hard to color. o

Unfortunately the contest has already ended.

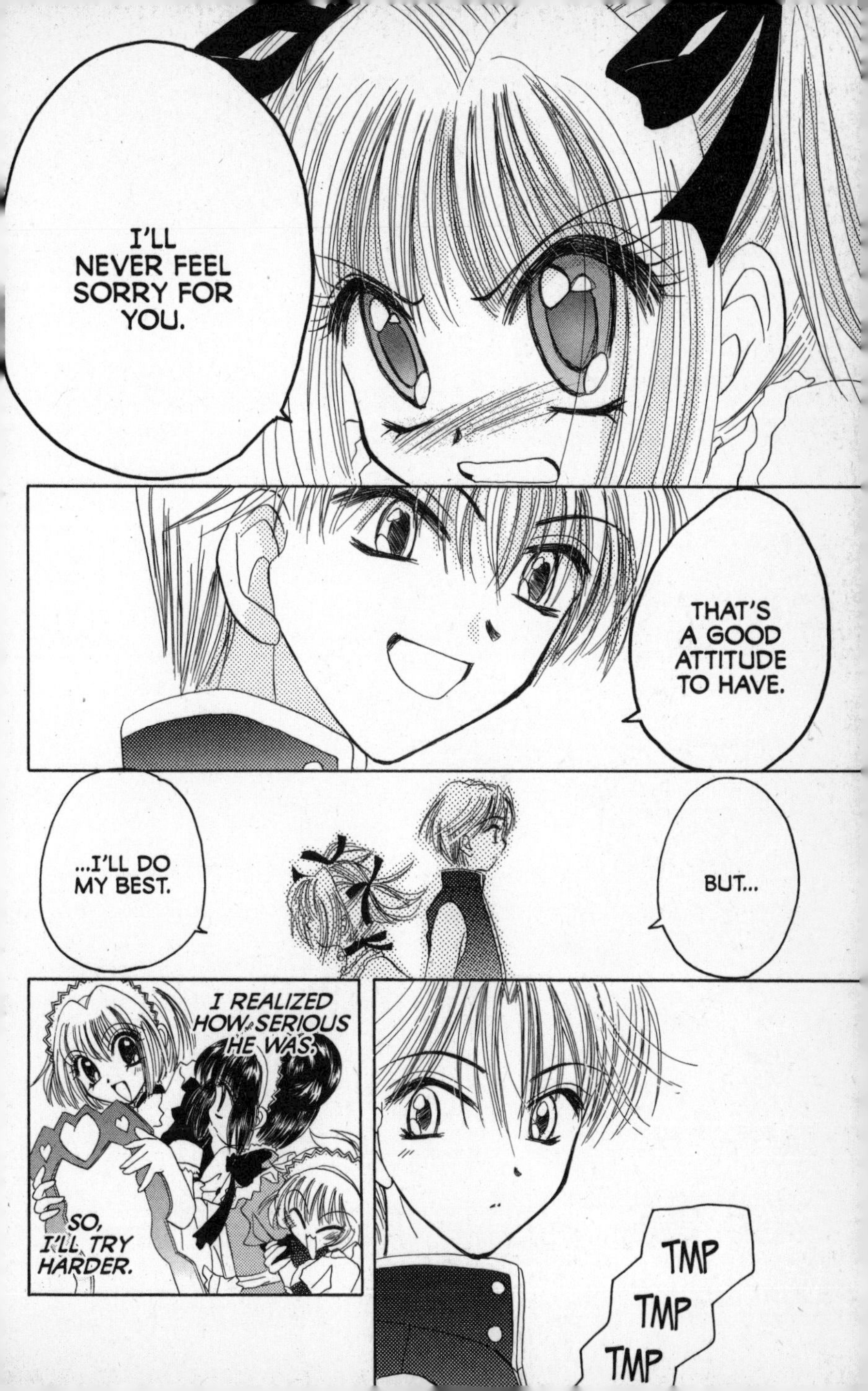
I'LL NEVER FEEL SORRY FOR YOU.
THAT'S A GOOD ATTITUDE TO HAVE.
BUT...
...I'LL DO MY BEST.
TMP TMP TMP
I REALIZED HOW SERIOUS HE WAS.
SO, I'LL TRY HARDER.

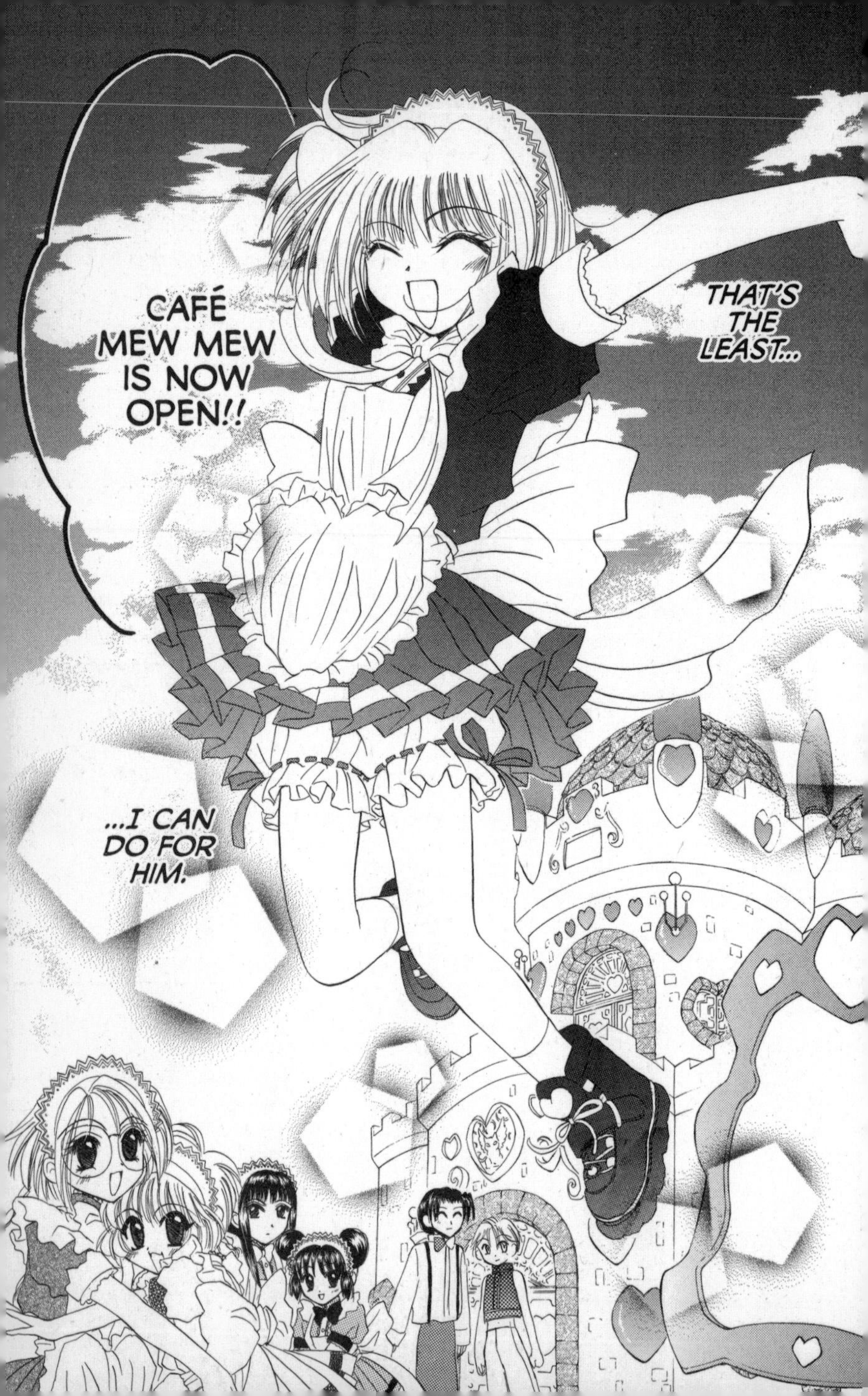
THAT'S THE LEAST...
...I CAN DO FOR HIM.
CAFÉ MEW MEW IS NOW OPEN!!

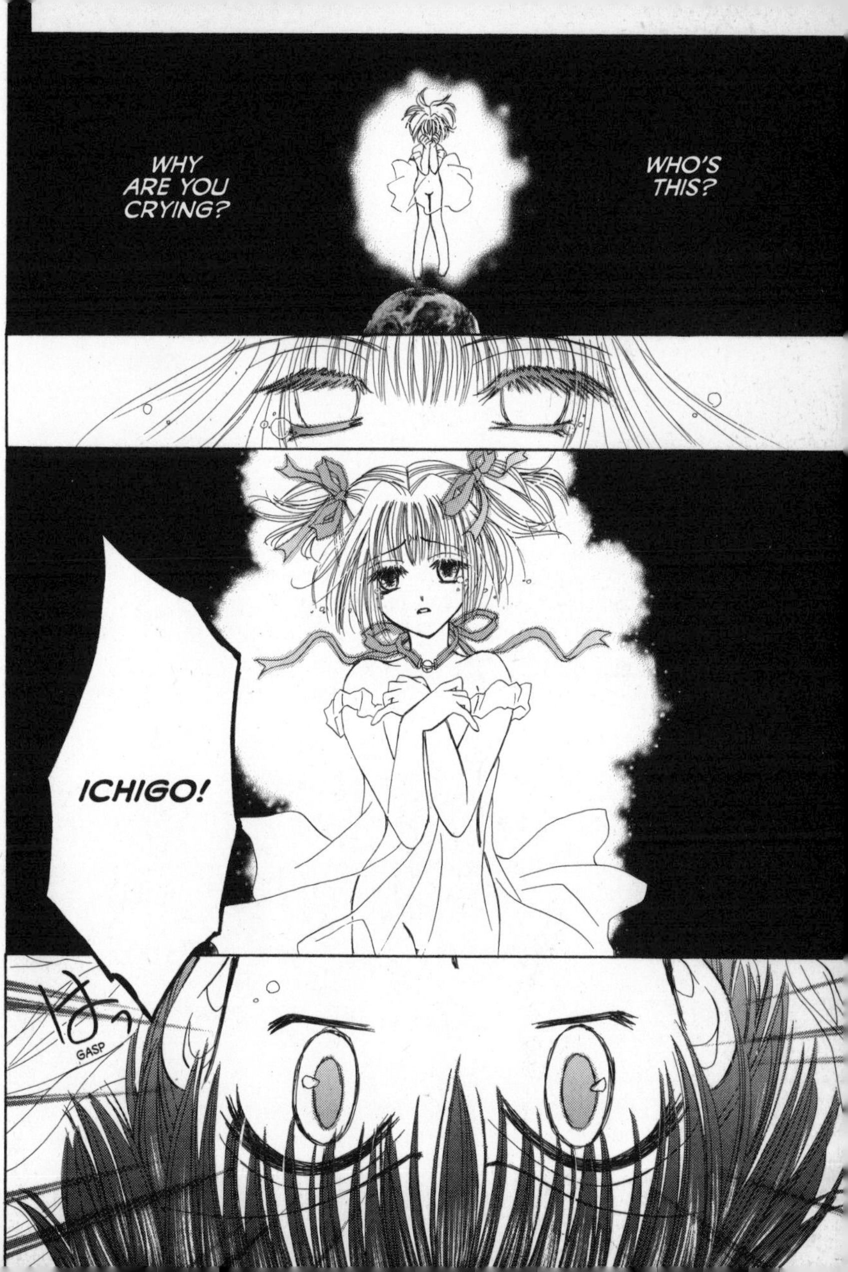

WHO'S THIS?
WHY ARE YOU CRYING?
ICHIGO!
はっ
GASP

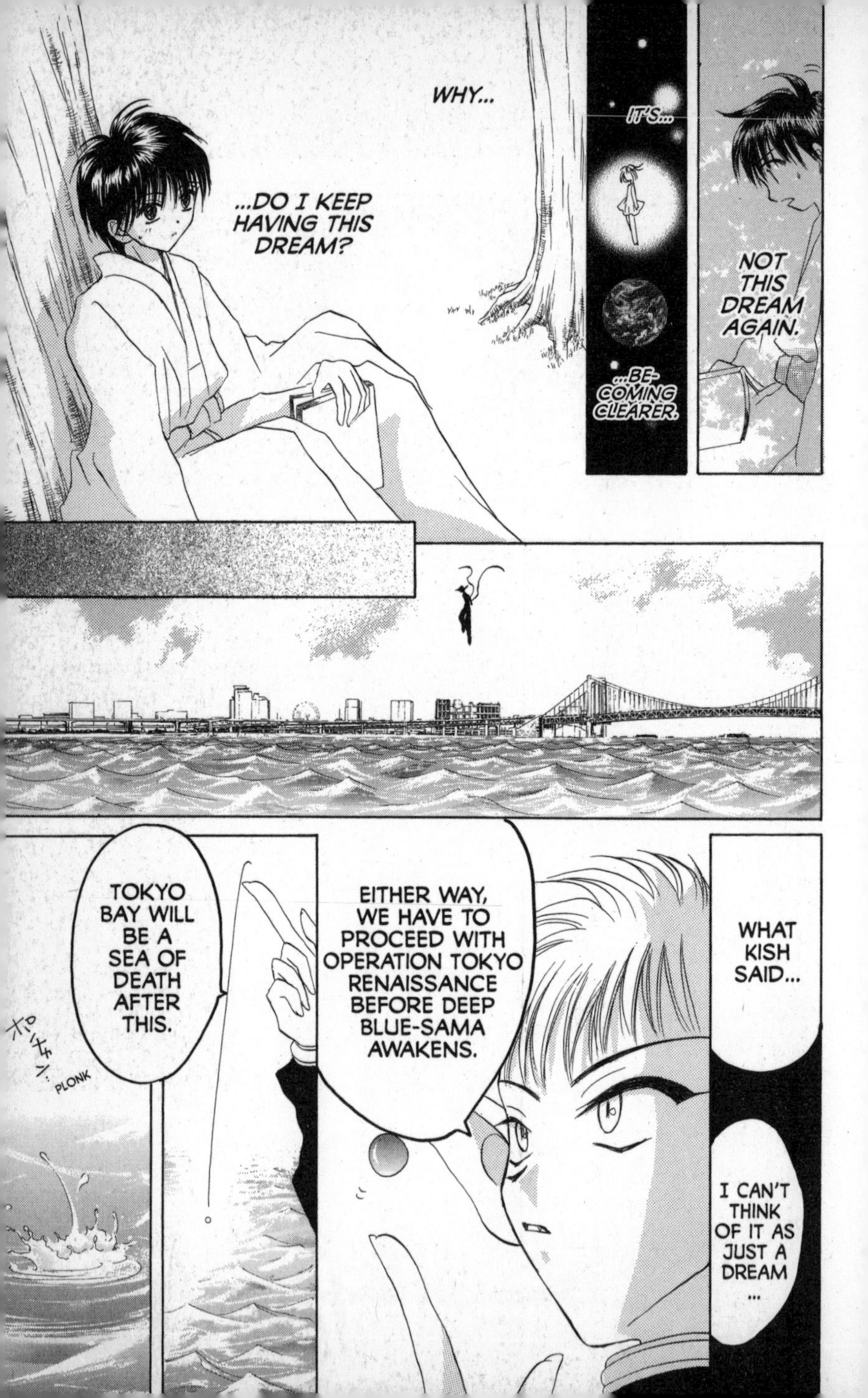
NOT THIS DREAM AGAIN.
IT'S...
...BE-COMING CLEARER.
WHY...
...DO I KEEP HAVING THIS DREAM?
WHAT KISH SAID...
I CAN'T THINK OF IT AS JUST A DREAM...
EITHER WAY, WE HAVE TO PROCEED WITH OPERATION TOKYO RENAISSANCE BEFORE DEEP BLUE-SAMA AWAKENS.
TOKYO BAY WILL BE A SEA OF DEATH AFTER THIS.
ポチャン
PLONK

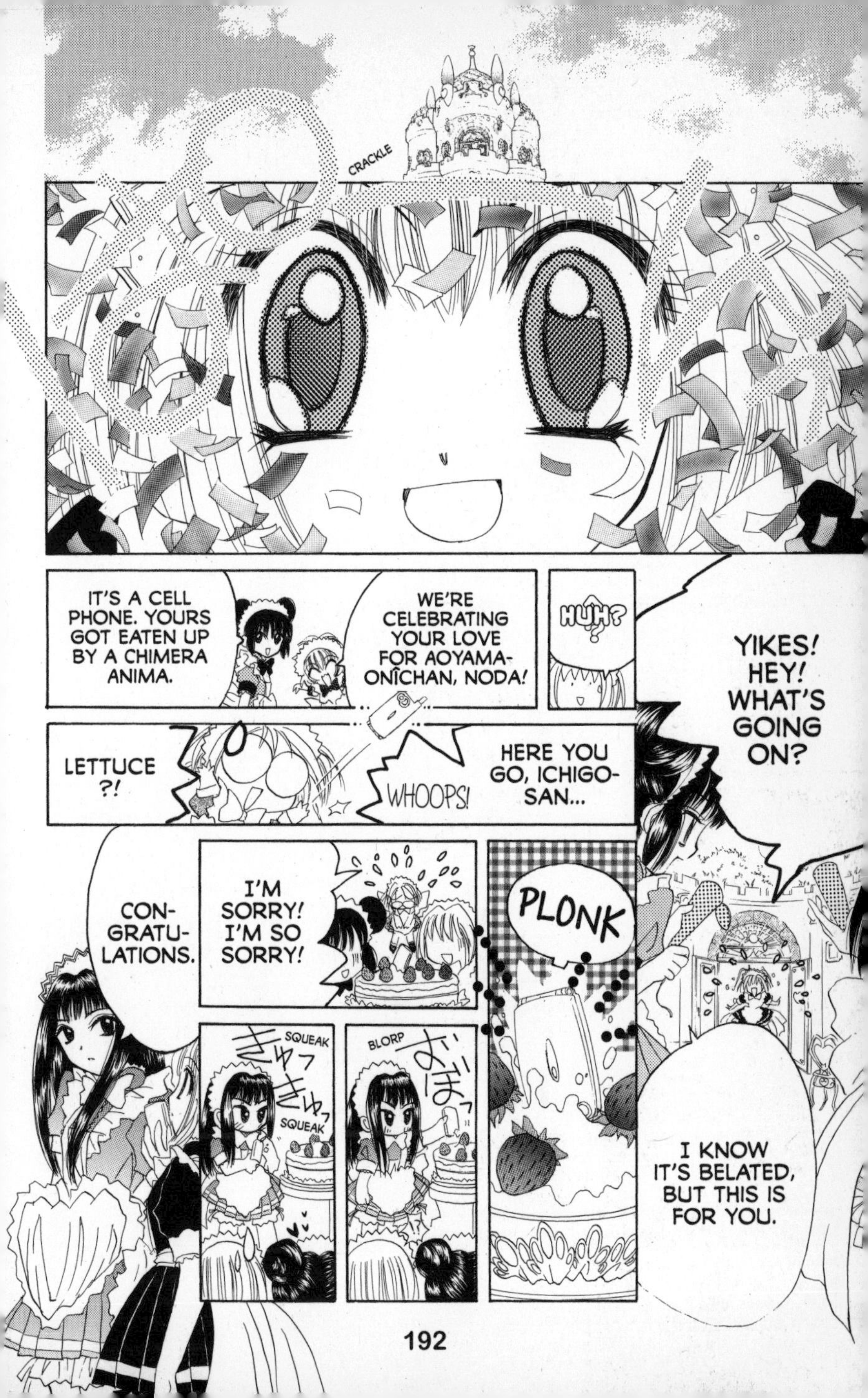
CRACKLE
YIKES! HEY! WHAT'S GOING ON?
I KNOW IT'S BELATED, BUT THIS IS FOR YOU.
HUH?
WE'RE CELEBRATING YOUR LOVE FOR AOYAMA-ONÎCHAN, NODA!
IT'S A CELL PHONE. YOURS GOT EATEN UP BY A CHIMERA ANIMA.
HERE YOU GO, ICHIGO-SAN...
WHOOPS!
LETTUCE ?!
PLONK
I'M SORRY! I'M SO SORRY!
CON-GRATU-LATIONS.
BLORP
SQUEAK
SQUEAK

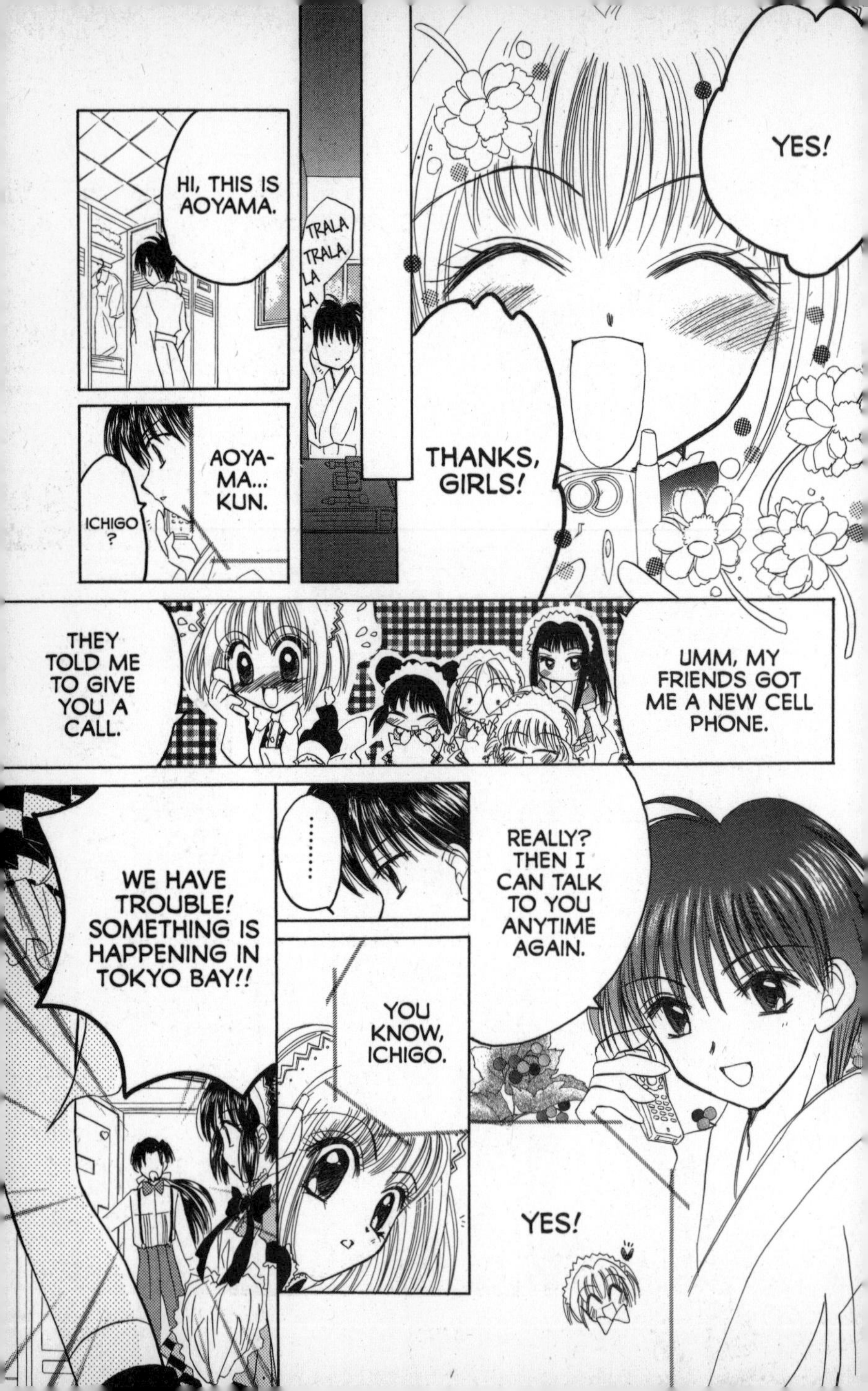
YES!
THANKS, GIRLS!
TRALA TRALA LA LA LA
HI, THIS IS AOYAMA.
AOYAMA... KUN.
ICHIGO?
UMM, MY FRIENDS GOT ME A NEW CELL PHONE.
THEY TOLD ME TO GIVE YOU A CALL.
REALLY? THEN I CAN TALK TO YOU ANYTIME AGAIN.
YES!
....
YOU KNOW, ICHIGO.
WE HAVE TROUBLE! SOMETHING IS HAPPENING IN TOKYO BAY!!

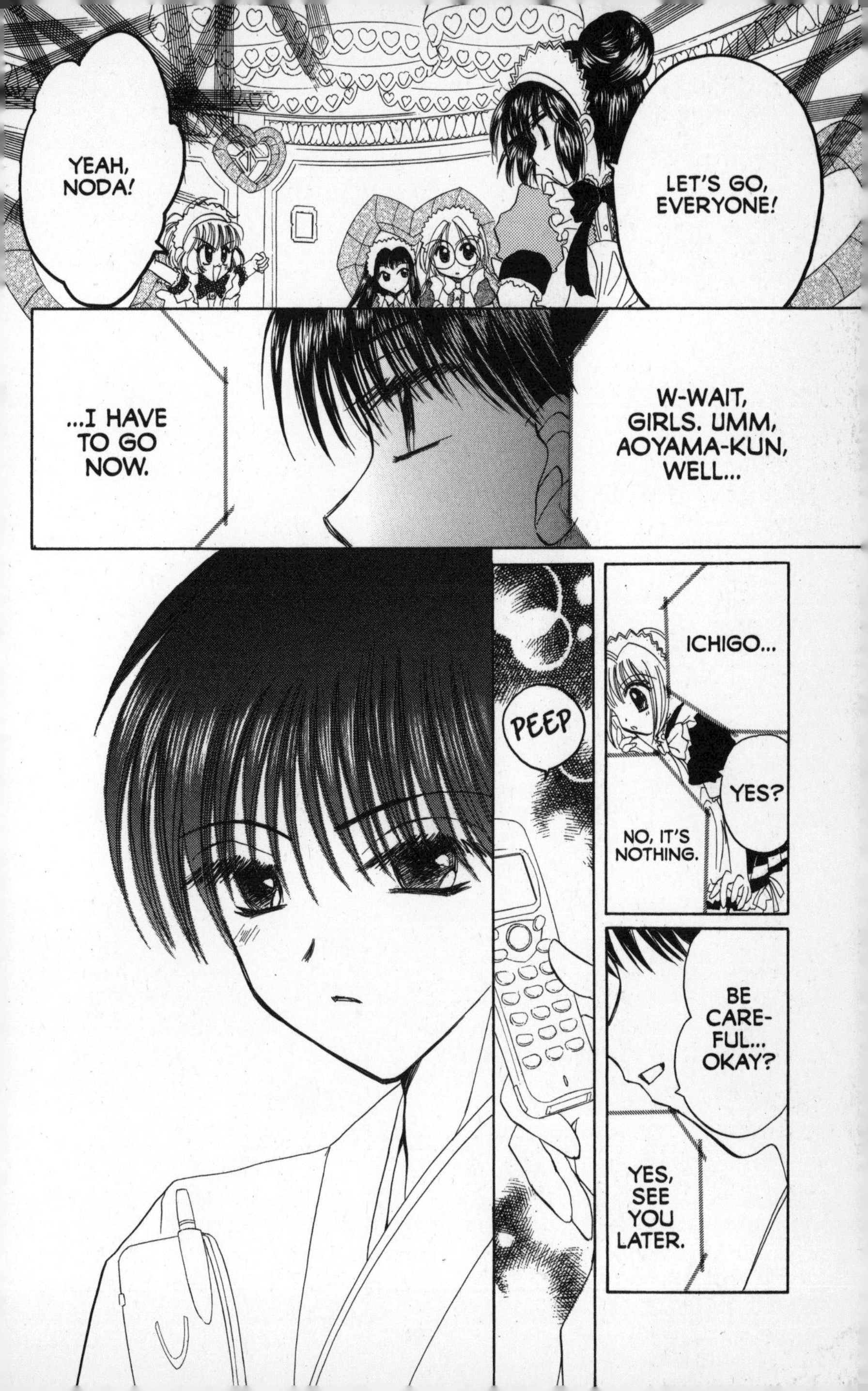
LET'S GO, EVERYONE!
YEAH, NODA!
W-WAIT, GIRLS. UMM, AOYAMA-KUN, WELL...
...I HAVE TO GO NOW.
ICHIGO...
YES?
NO, IT'S NOTHING.
BE CARE-FUL... OKAY?
YES, SEE YOU LATER.
PEEP

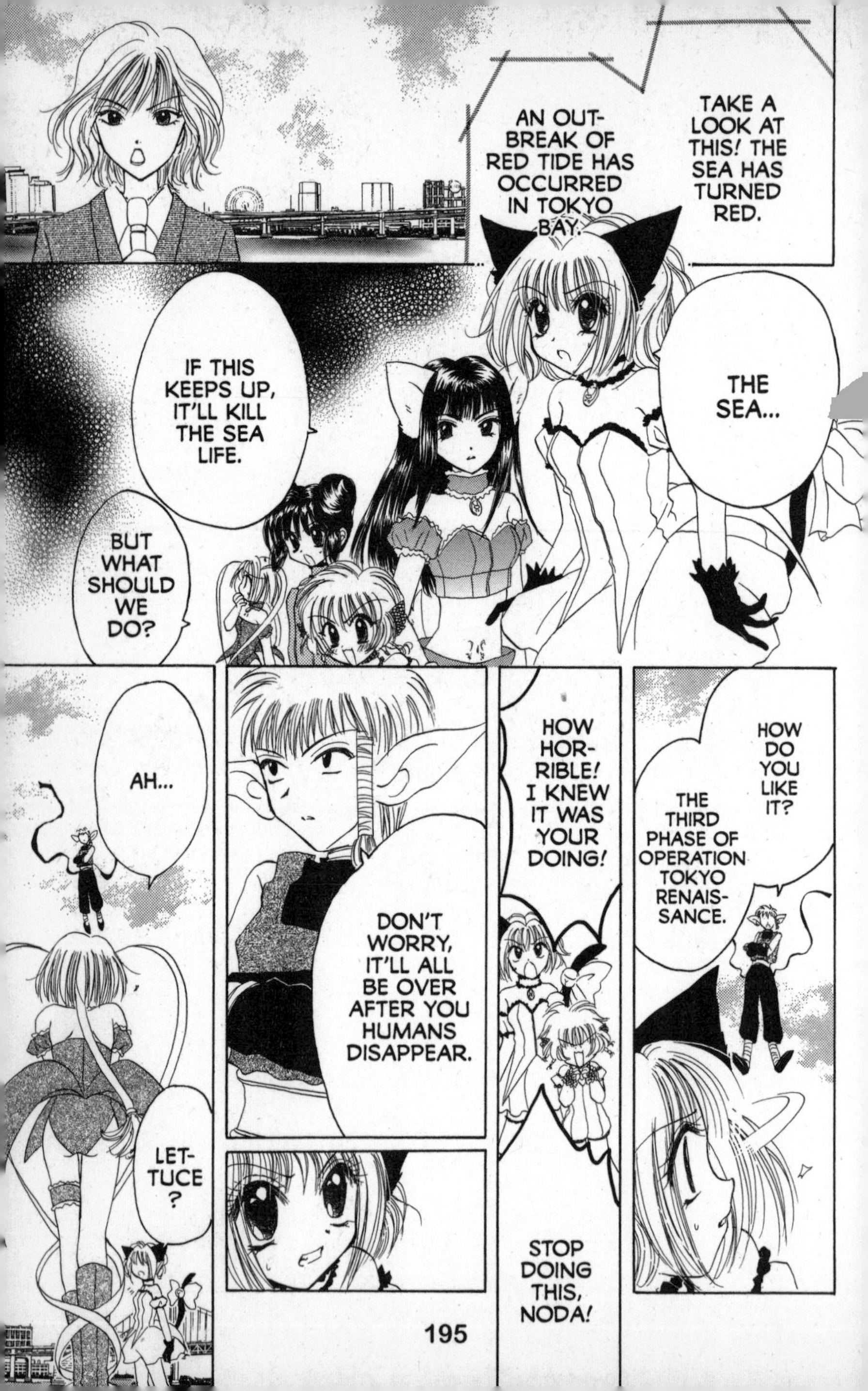
TAKE A LOOK AT THIS! THE SEA HAS TURNED RED.
AN OUT-BREAK OF RED TIDE HAS OCCURRED IN TOKYO BAY.
THE SEA...
IF THIS KEEPS UP, IT'LL KILL THE SEA LIFE.
BUT WHAT SHOULD WE DO?
HOW DO YOU LIKE IT?
THE THIRD PHASE OF OPERATION TOKYO RENAISSANCE.
HOW HORRIBLE! I KNEW IT WAS YOUR DOING!
STOP DOING THIS, NODA!
DON'T WORRY, IT'LL ALL BE OVER AFTER YOU HUMANS DISAPPEAR.
AH...
LET-TUCE?

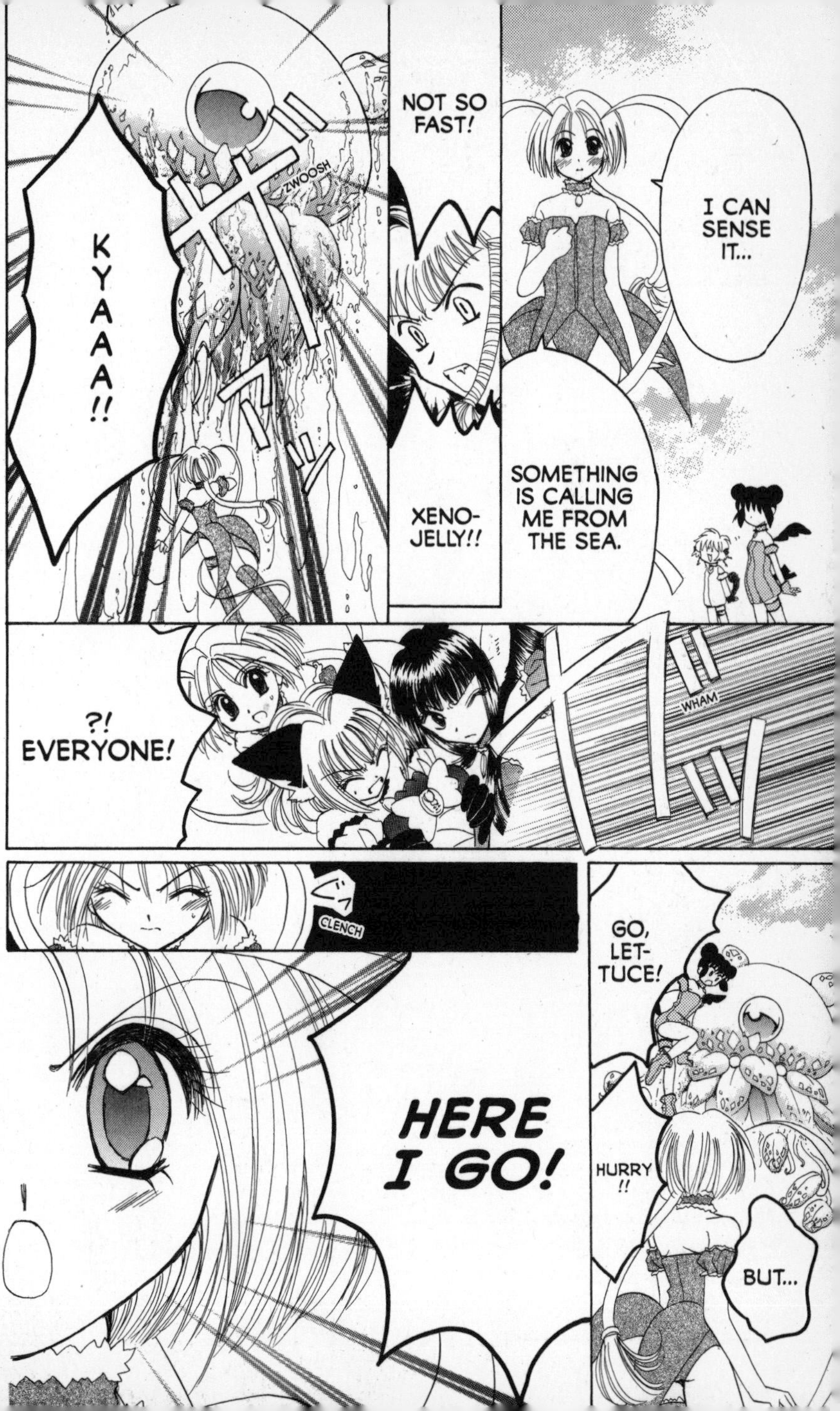
I CAN SENSE IT...
SOMETHING IS CALLING ME FROM THE SEA.
NOT SO FAST!
XENO-JELLY!!
ZWOOSH
KYAAAA!!
WHAM
?! EVERYONE!
GO, LET-TUCE!
HURRY!!
BUT...
CLENCH
HERE I GO!
!

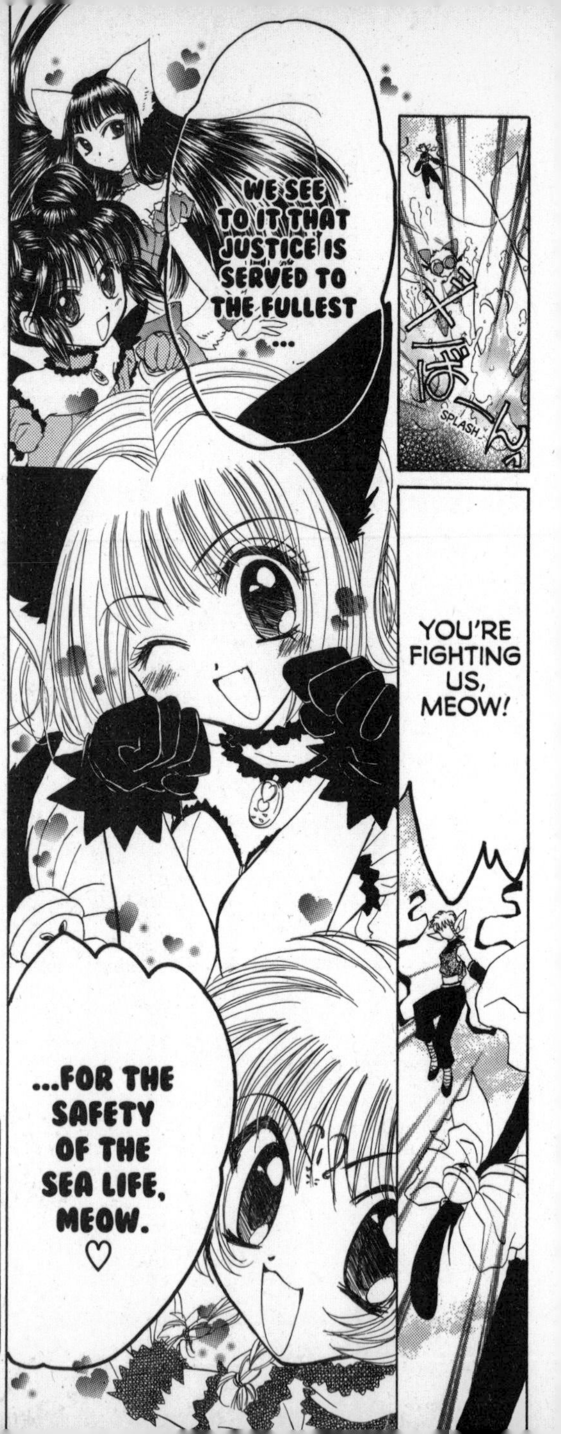
SPLASH
YOU'RE FIGHTING US, MEOW!
WE SEE TO IT THAT JUSTICE IS SERVED TO THE FULLEST...
...FOR THE SAFETY OF THE SEA LIFE, MEOW. ♡

Tokyo Mew Mew:
Ichigo's Costume Wanted! Part 2

SEMI-GRAND PRIZE

AMI HAGANUMA-CHAN,
FUKUSHIMA PREFECTURE,
GRADE 5

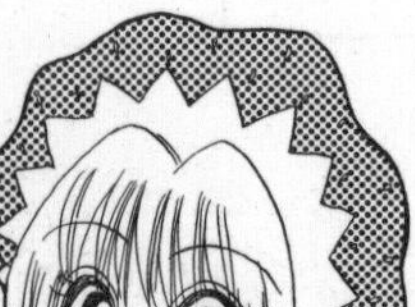

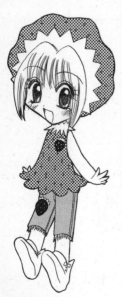

The outfit is casual enough that you can almost go anywhere in it! I wish they'd have it in stores. I think it's a simple yet fashionable outfit that you wouldn't be surprised to find there. it's so cute!

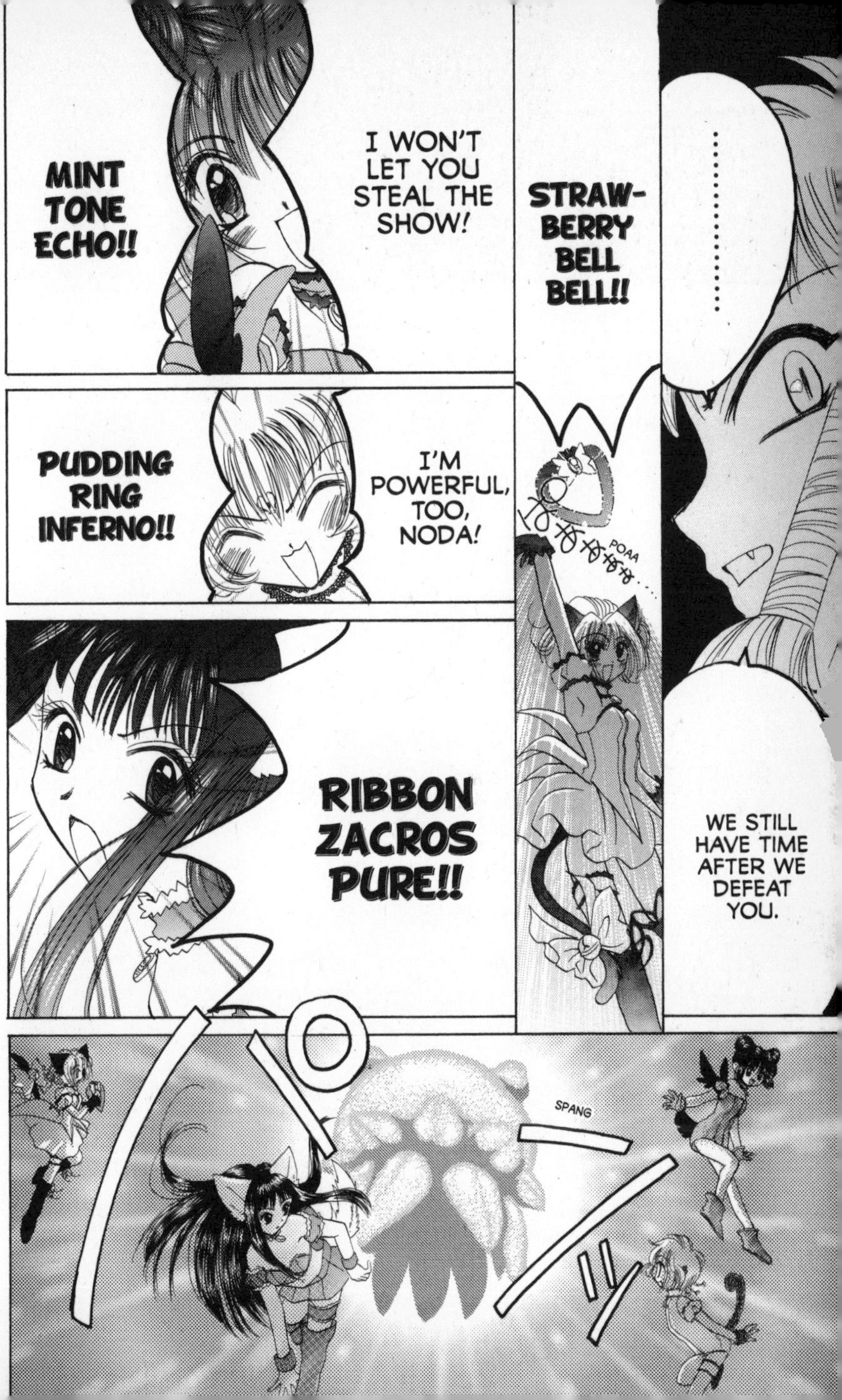
......
WE STILL HAVE TIME AFTER WE DEFEAT YOU.
STRAW-BERRY BELL BELL!!
POAA
I WON'T LET YOU STEAL THE SHOW!
MINT TONE ECHO!!
I'M POWERFUL, TOO, NODA!
PUDDING RING INFERNO!!
RIBBON ZACROS PURE!!
SPANG

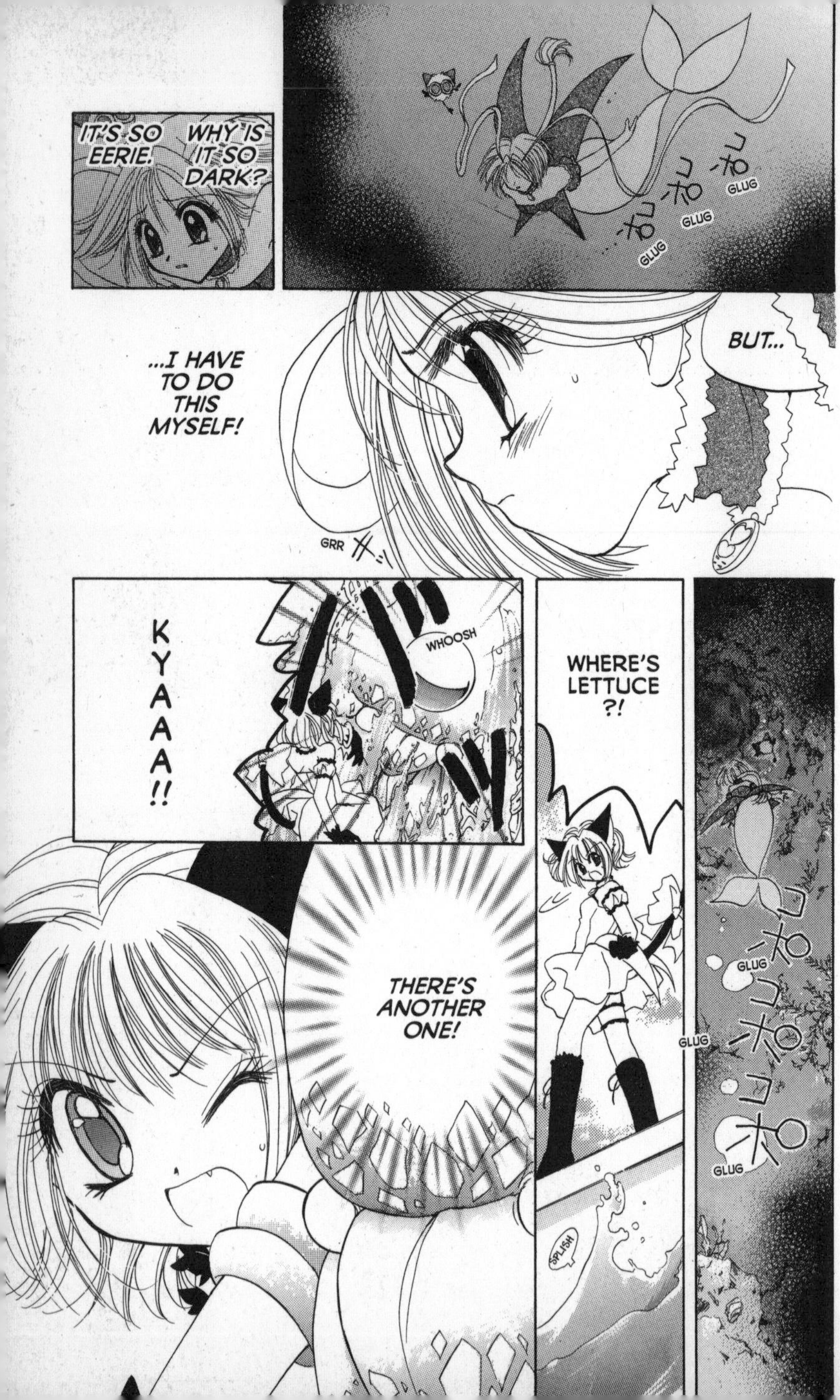
GLUG
GLUG
GLUG
WHY IS IT SO DARK?
IT'S SO EERIE.
BUT...
...I HAVE TO DO THIS MYSELF!
GRR
GLUG
GLUG
GLUG
WHERE'S LETTUCE ?!
SPLISH
WHOOSH
KYAAAA!!
THERE'S ANOTHER ONE!

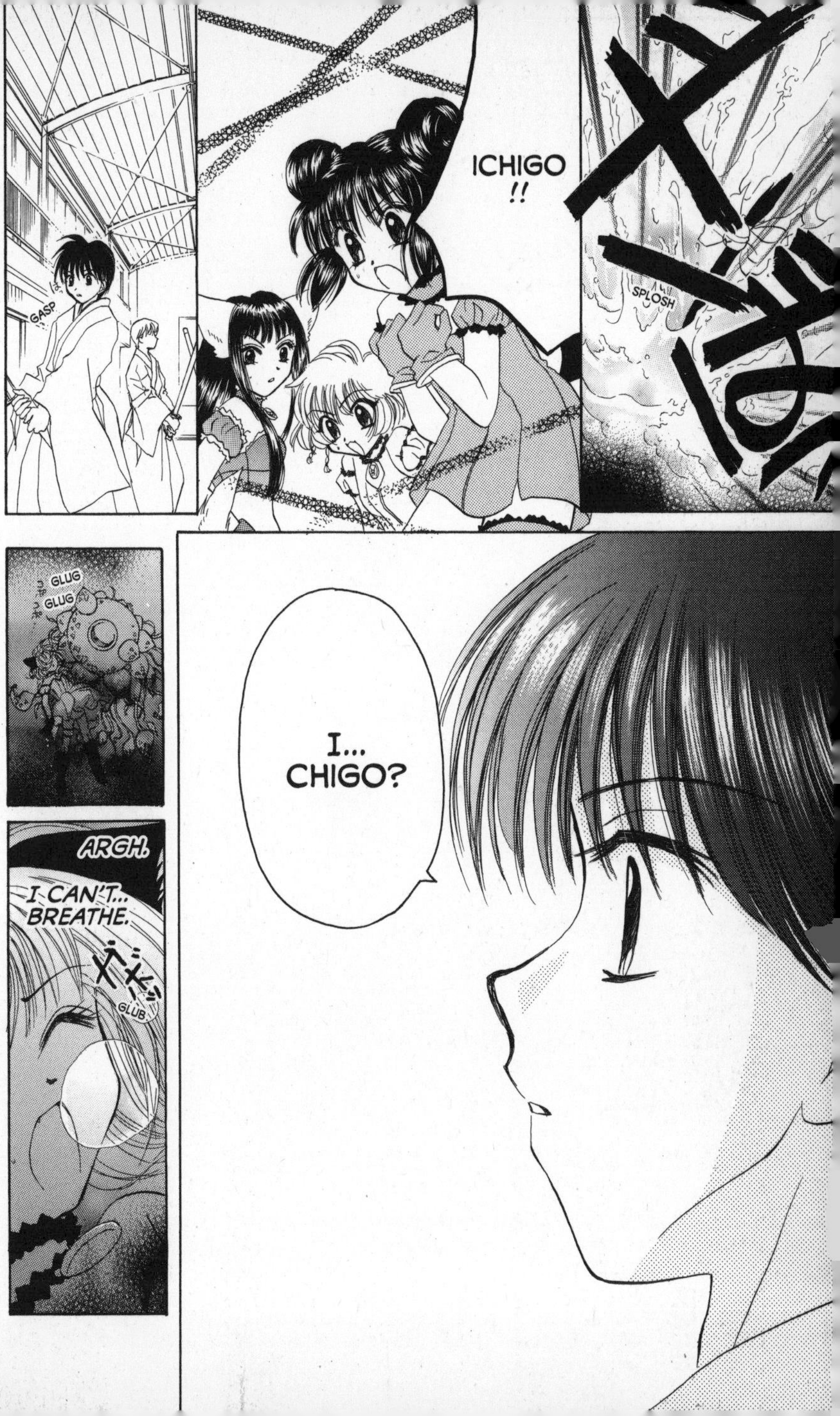
SPLOSH
ICHIGO !!
GASP
I... CHIGO?
GLUG GLUG
ARGH.
I CAN'T... BREATHE.
GLUB

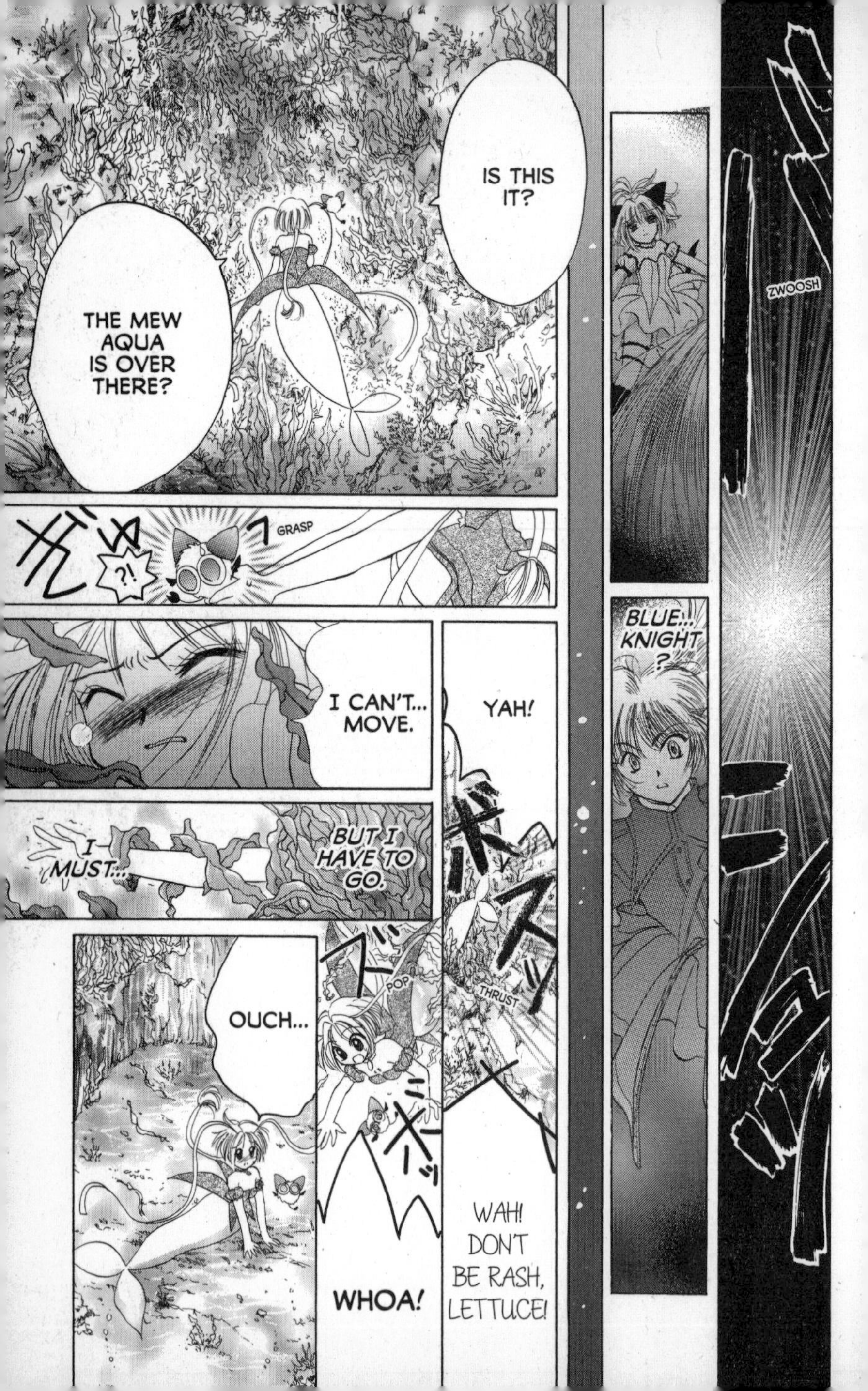
ZWOOSH
BLUE... KNIGHT?
IS THIS IT?
THE MEW AQUA IS OVER THERE?
GRASP
?!
YAH!
THRUST
WAH! DON'T BE RASH, LETTUCE!
I CAN'T... MOVE.
BUT I HAVE TO GO.
I MUST...
POP
WHOA!
OUCH...

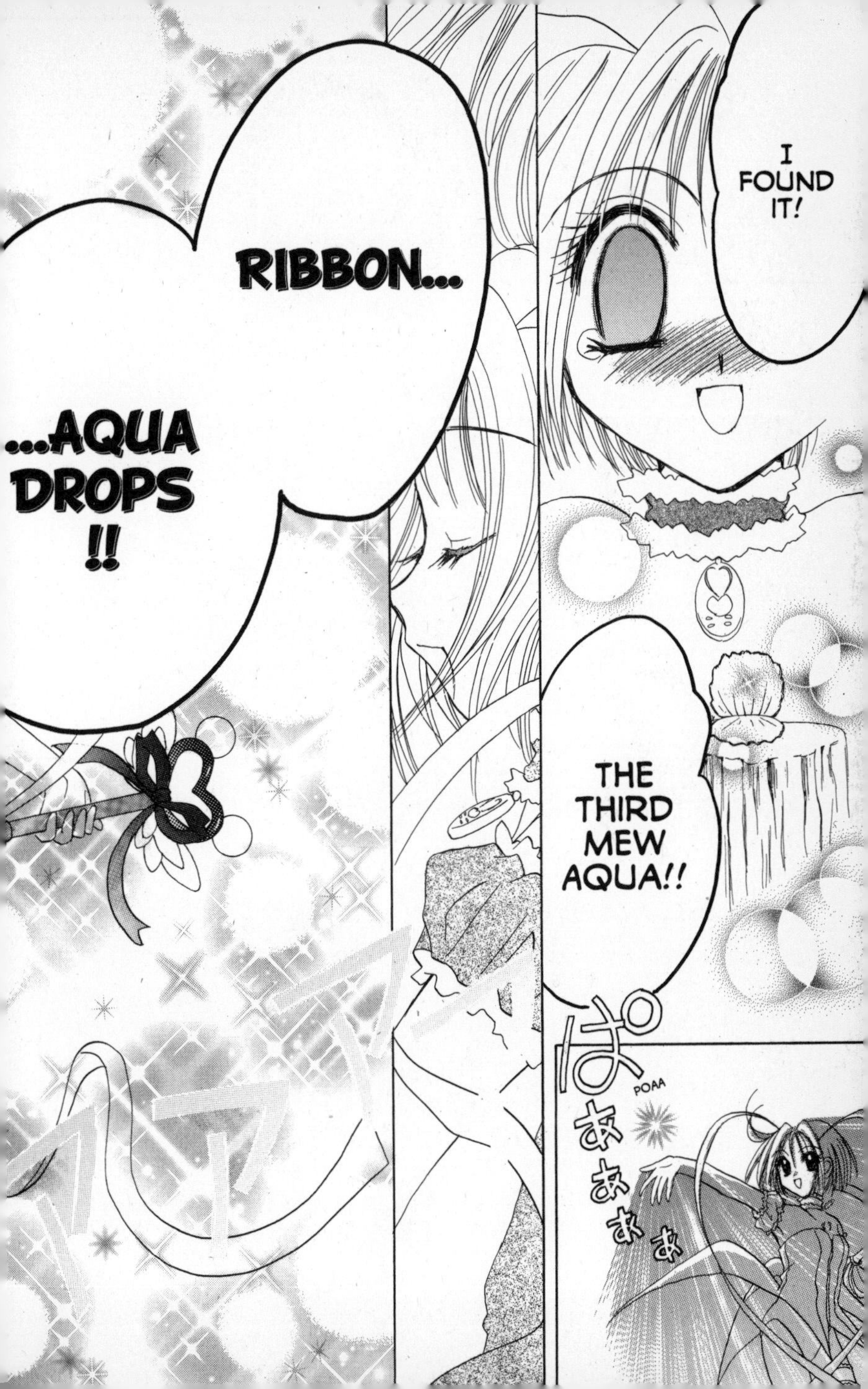
I FOUND IT!
THE THIRD MEW AQUA!!
ぱぁぁぁぁ
POAA
RIBBON...
...AQUA DROPS !!

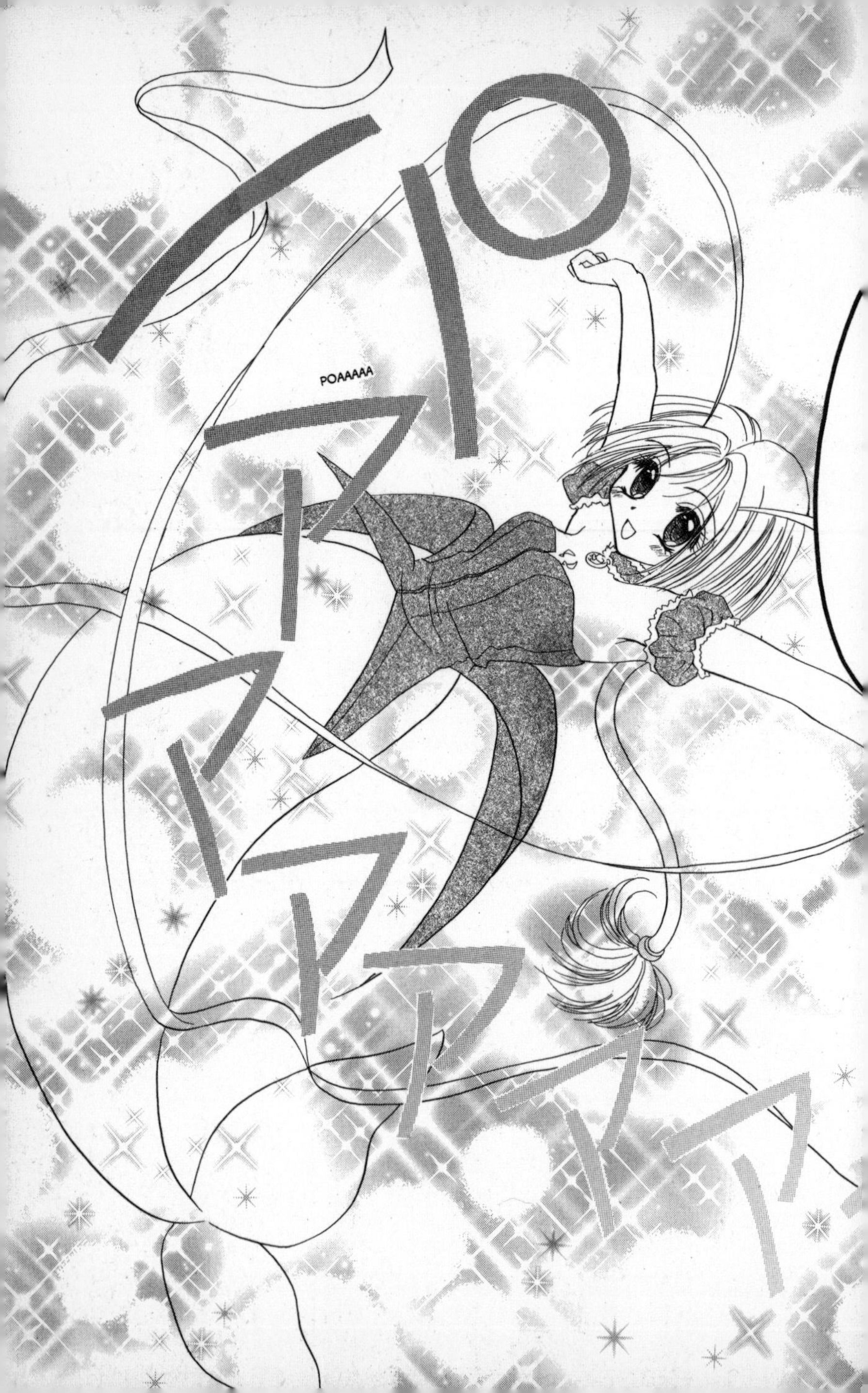
パアアアアアアア
POAAAAA

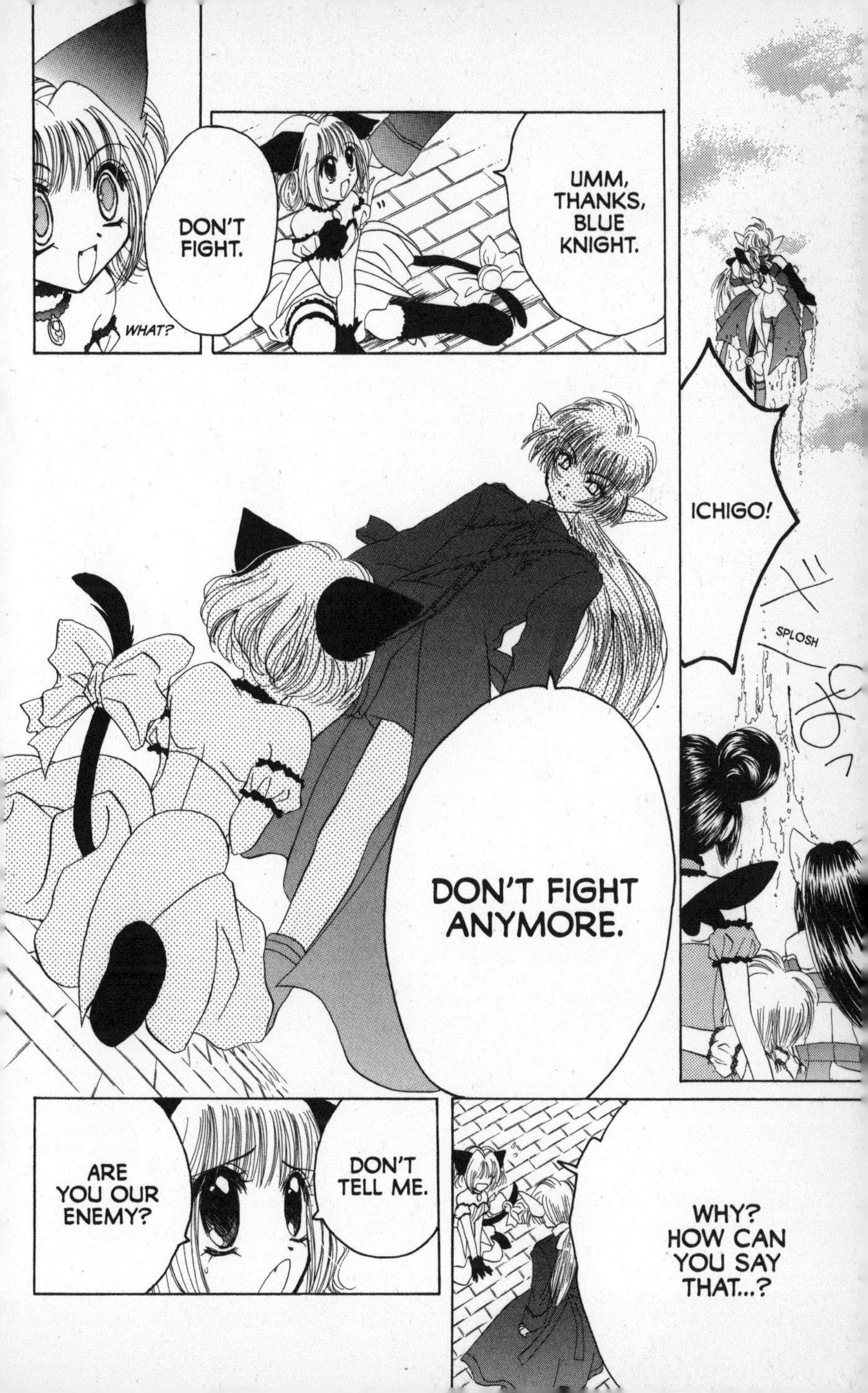
ICHIGO!
SPLOSH
UMM, THANKS, BLUE KNIGHT.
DON'T FIGHT.
WHAT?
DON'T FIGHT ANYMORE.
WHY? HOW CAN YOU SAY THAT...?
DON'T TELL ME.
ARE YOU OUR ENEMY?

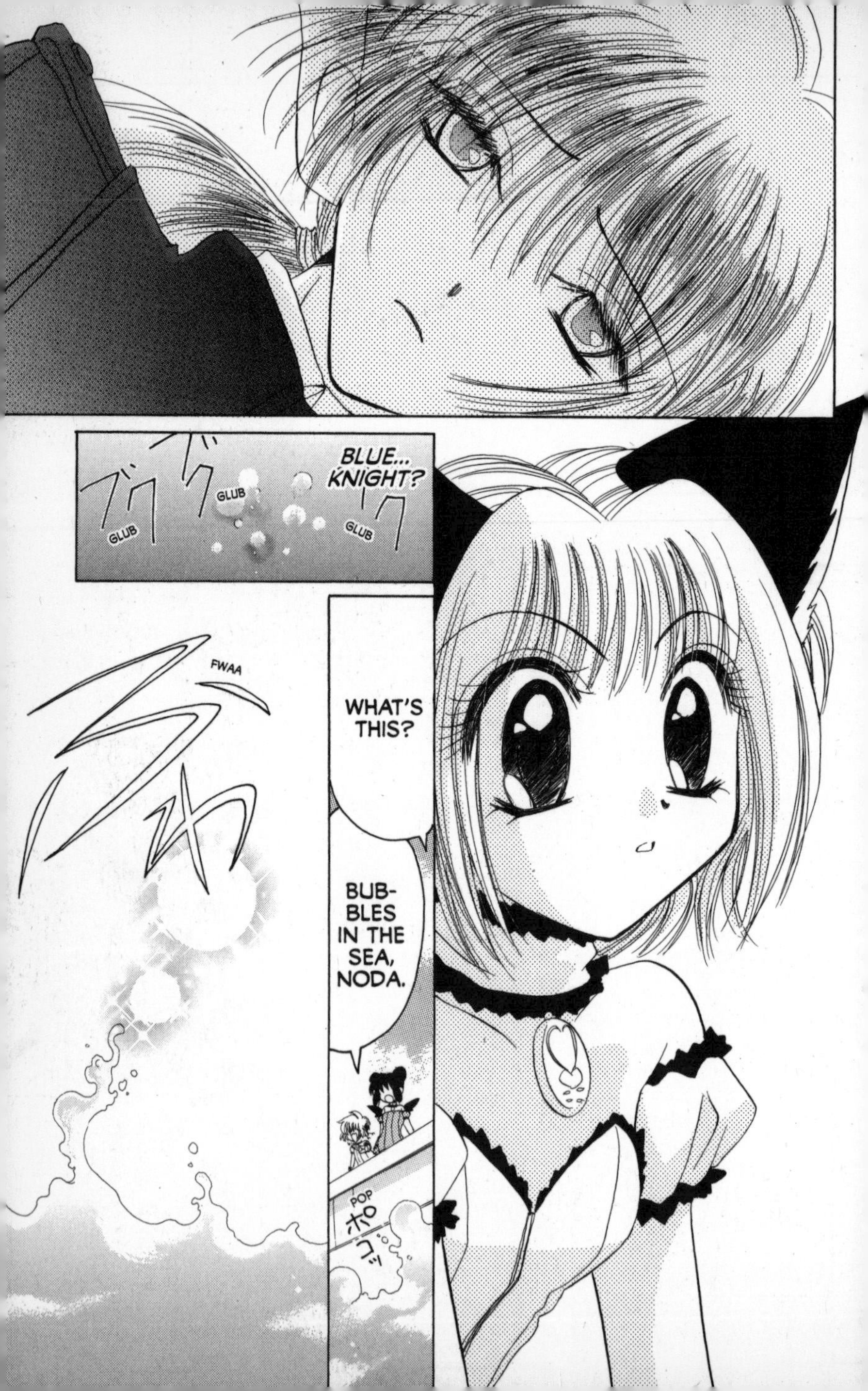
BLUE... KNIGHT?
GLUB
GLUB
GLUB
WHAT'S THIS?
BUB-BLES IN THE SEA, NODA.
POP
FWAA

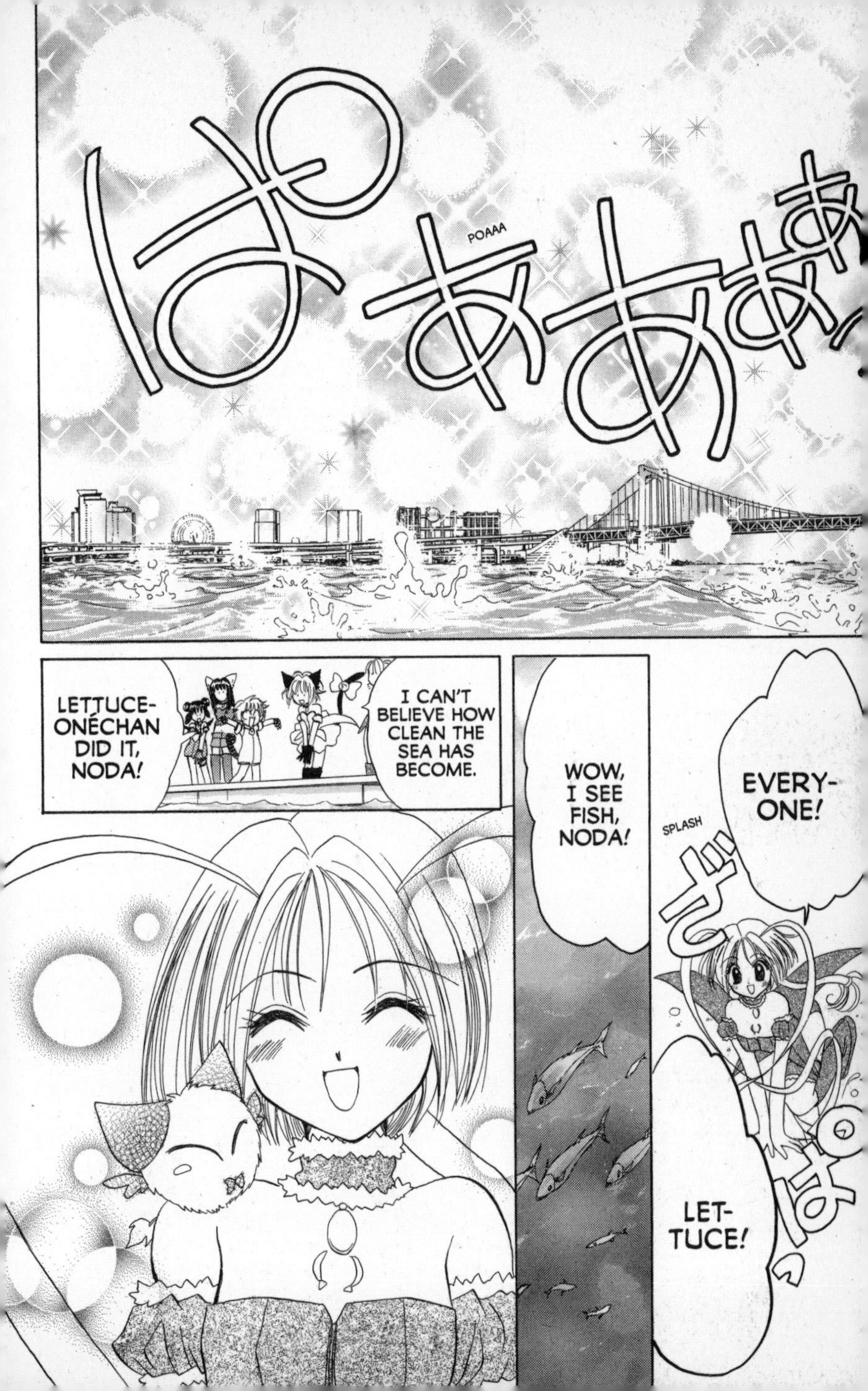
POAAA
EVERY-ONE!
SPLASH
LET-TUCE!
WOW, I SEE FISH, NODA!
I CAN'T BELIEVE HOW CLEAN THE SEA HAS BECOME.
LETTUCE-ONÉCHAN DID IT, NODA!

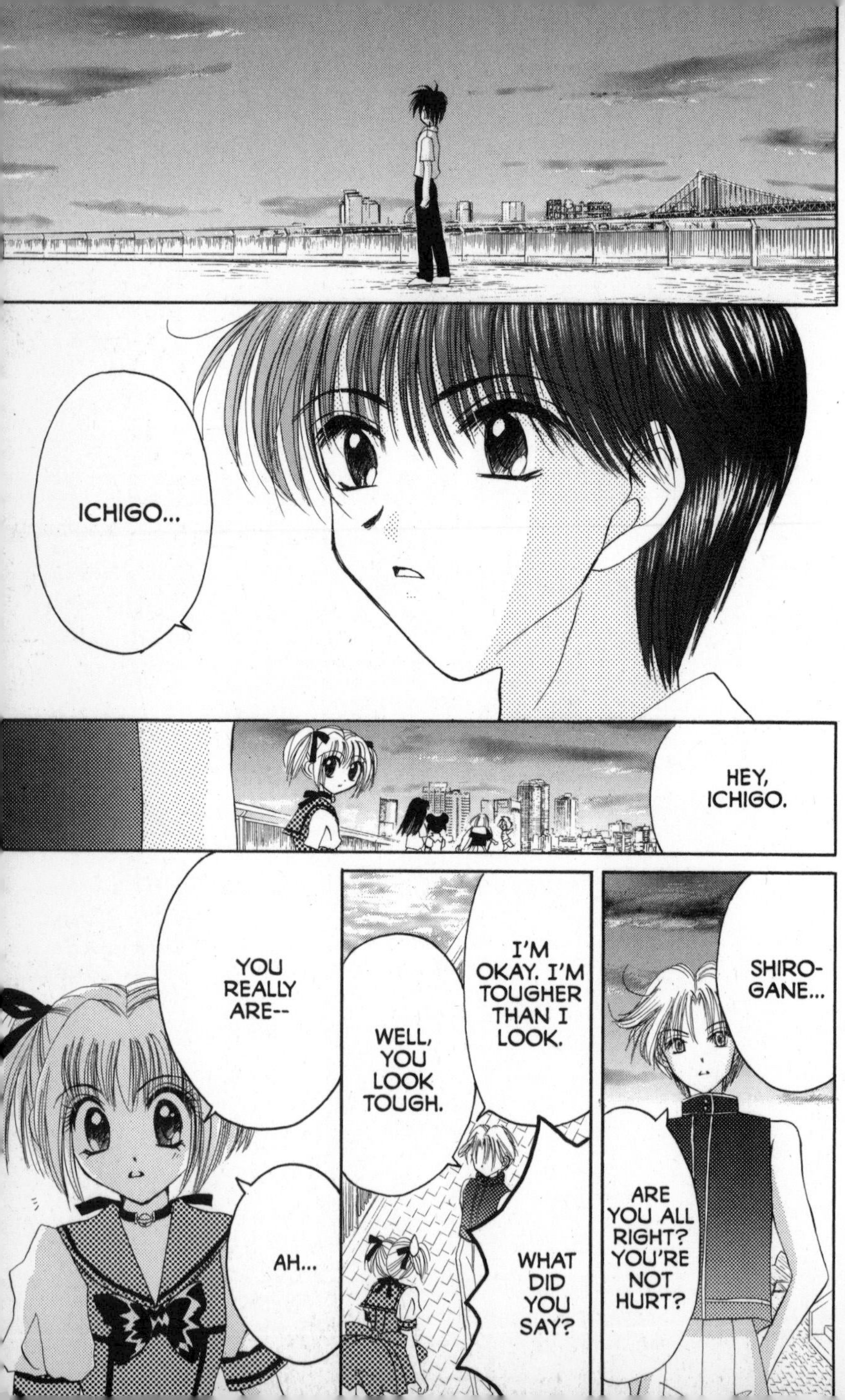
ICHIGO...
HEY, ICHIGO.
SHIRO-GANE...
ARE YOU ALL RIGHT? YOU'RE NOT HURT?
I'M OKAY. I'M TOUGHER THAN I LOOK.
WELL, YOU LOOK TOUGH.
WHAT DID YOU SAY?
YOU REALLY ARE--
AH...

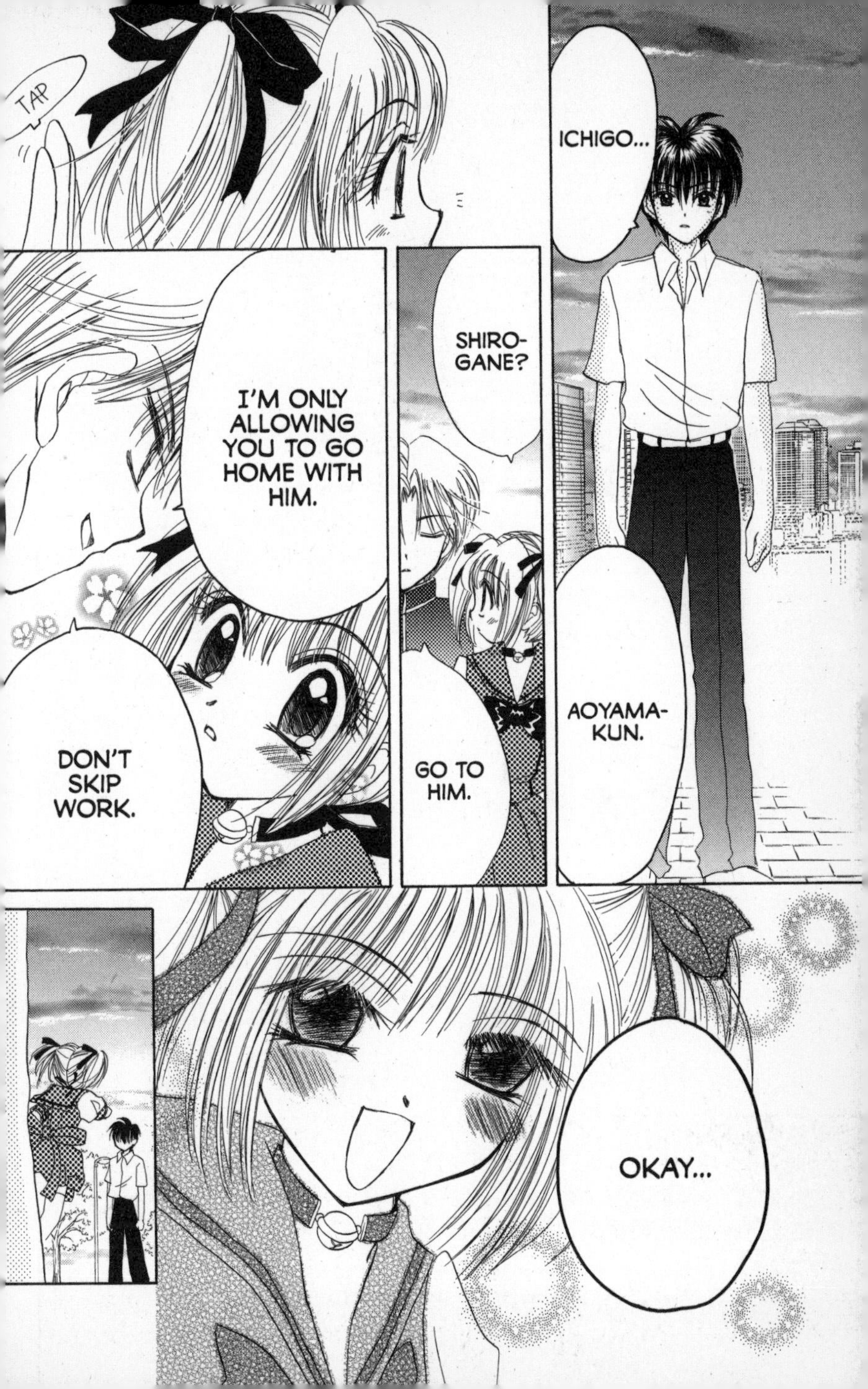
ICHIGO...
AOYAMA-KUN.
TAP
SHIRO-GANE?
GO TO HIM.
I'M ONLY ALLOWING YOU TO GO HOME WITH HIM.
DON'T SKIP WORK.
OKAY...

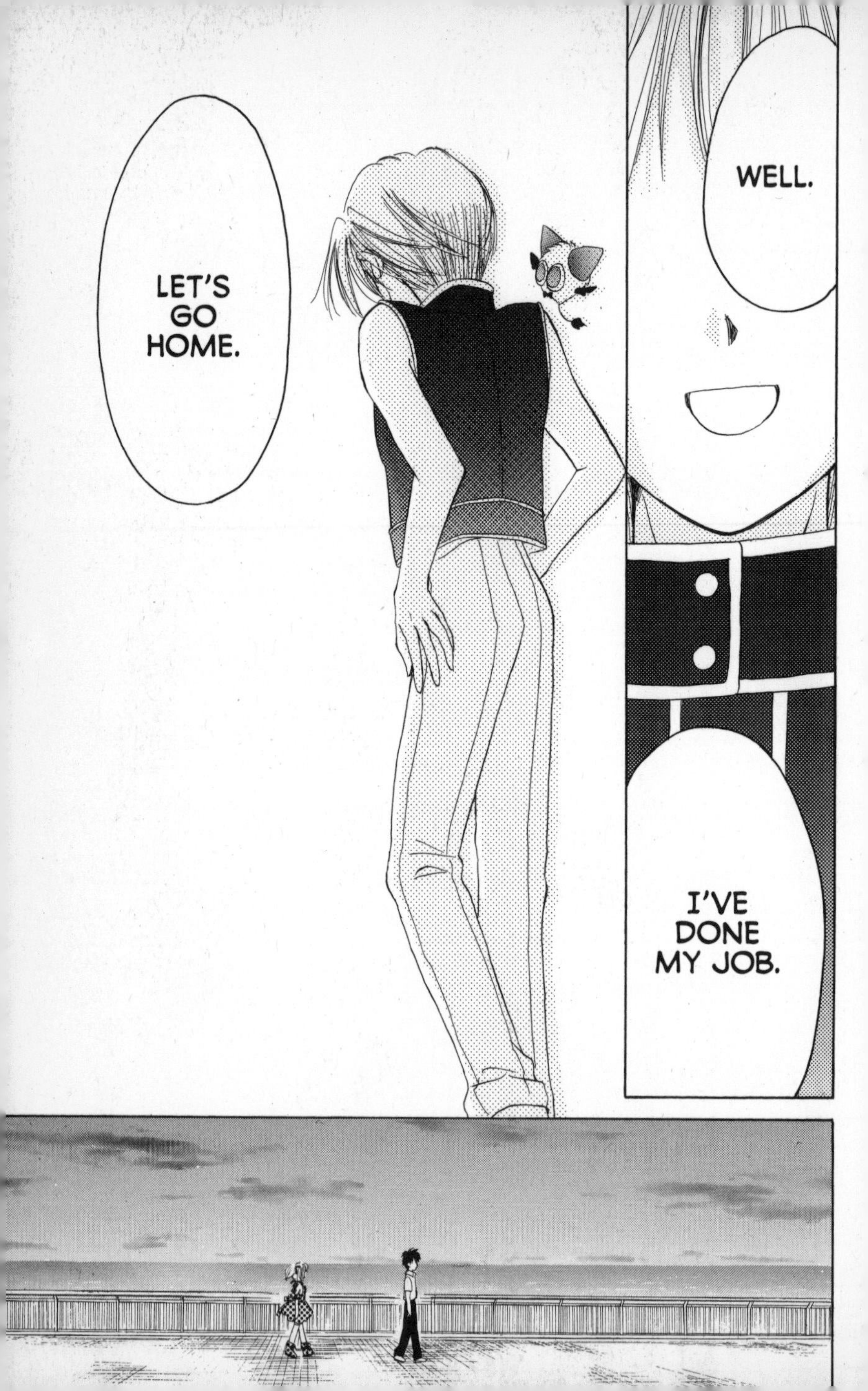
WELL.
I'VE DONE MY JOB.
LET'S GO HOME.

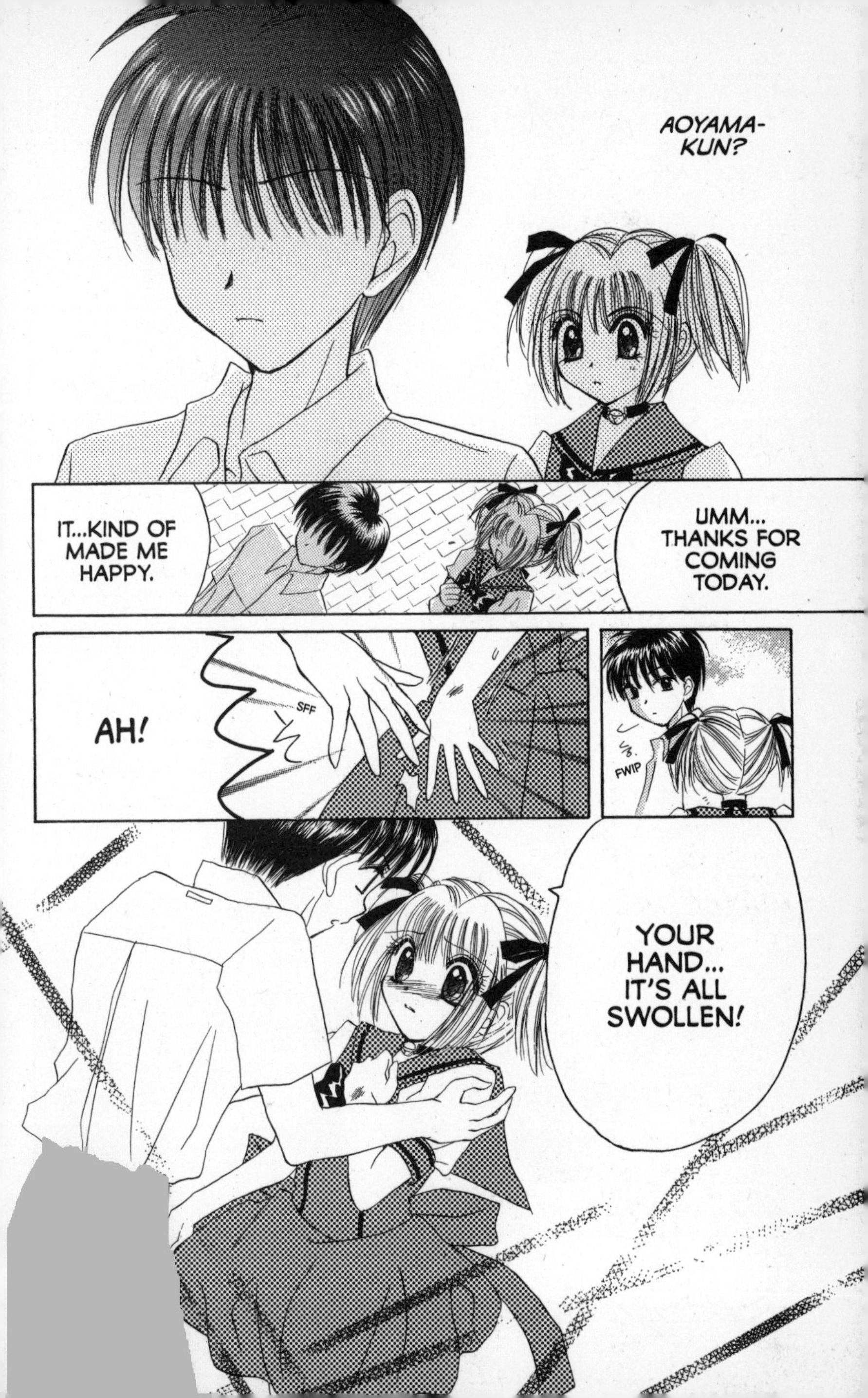
AOYAMA-KUN?
UMM... THANKS FOR COMING TODAY.
IT...KIND OF MADE ME HAPPY.
FWIP
SFF
AH!
YOUR HAND... IT'S ALL SWOLLEN!

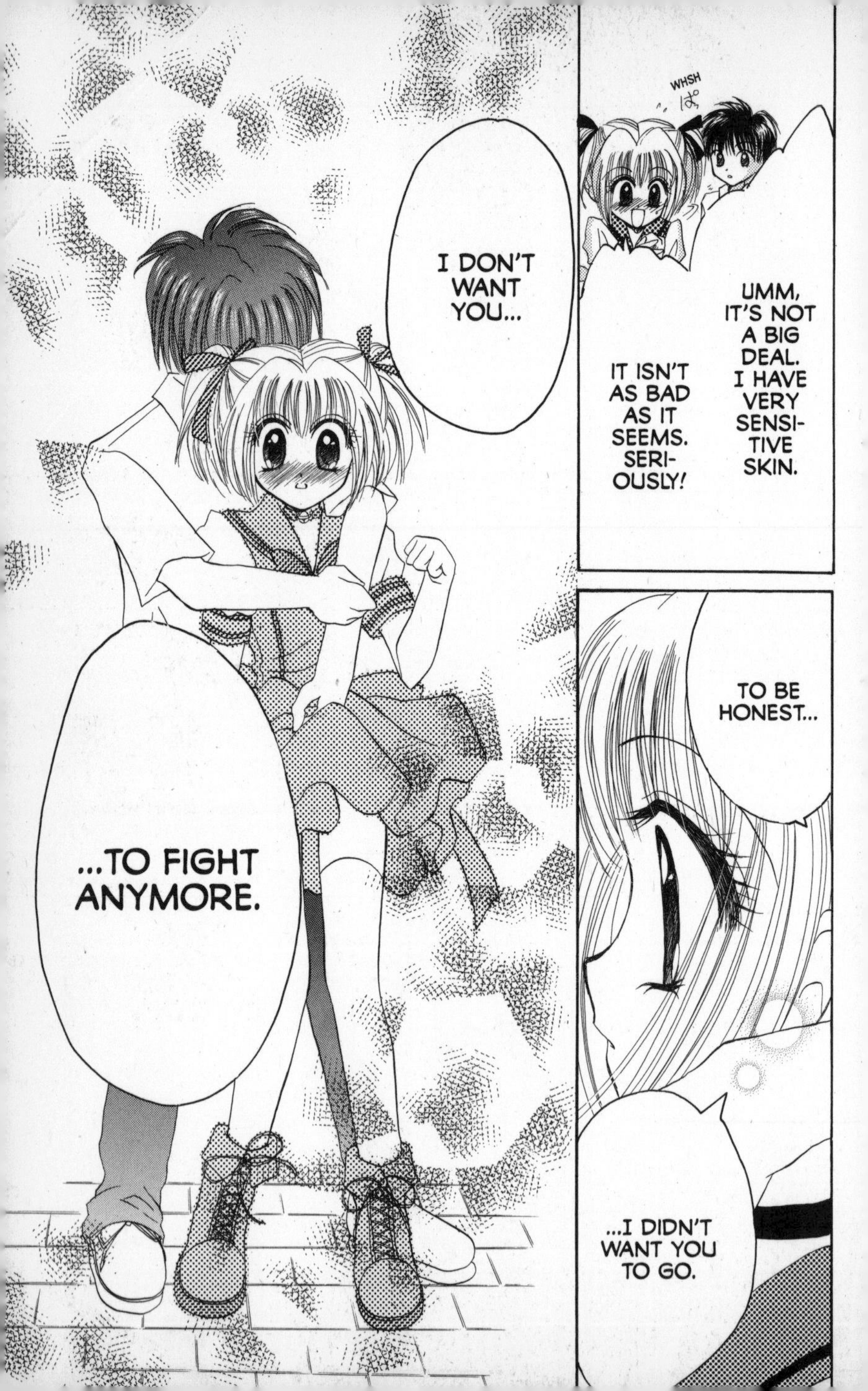
WHSH
ぱ
UMM, IT'S NOT A BIG DEAL. I HAVE VERY SENSI-TIVE SKIN.
IT ISN'T AS BAD AS IT SEEMS. SERI-OUSLY!
TO BE HONEST...
...I DIDN'T WANT YOU TO GO.
I DON'T WANT YOU...
...TO FIGHT ANYMORE.

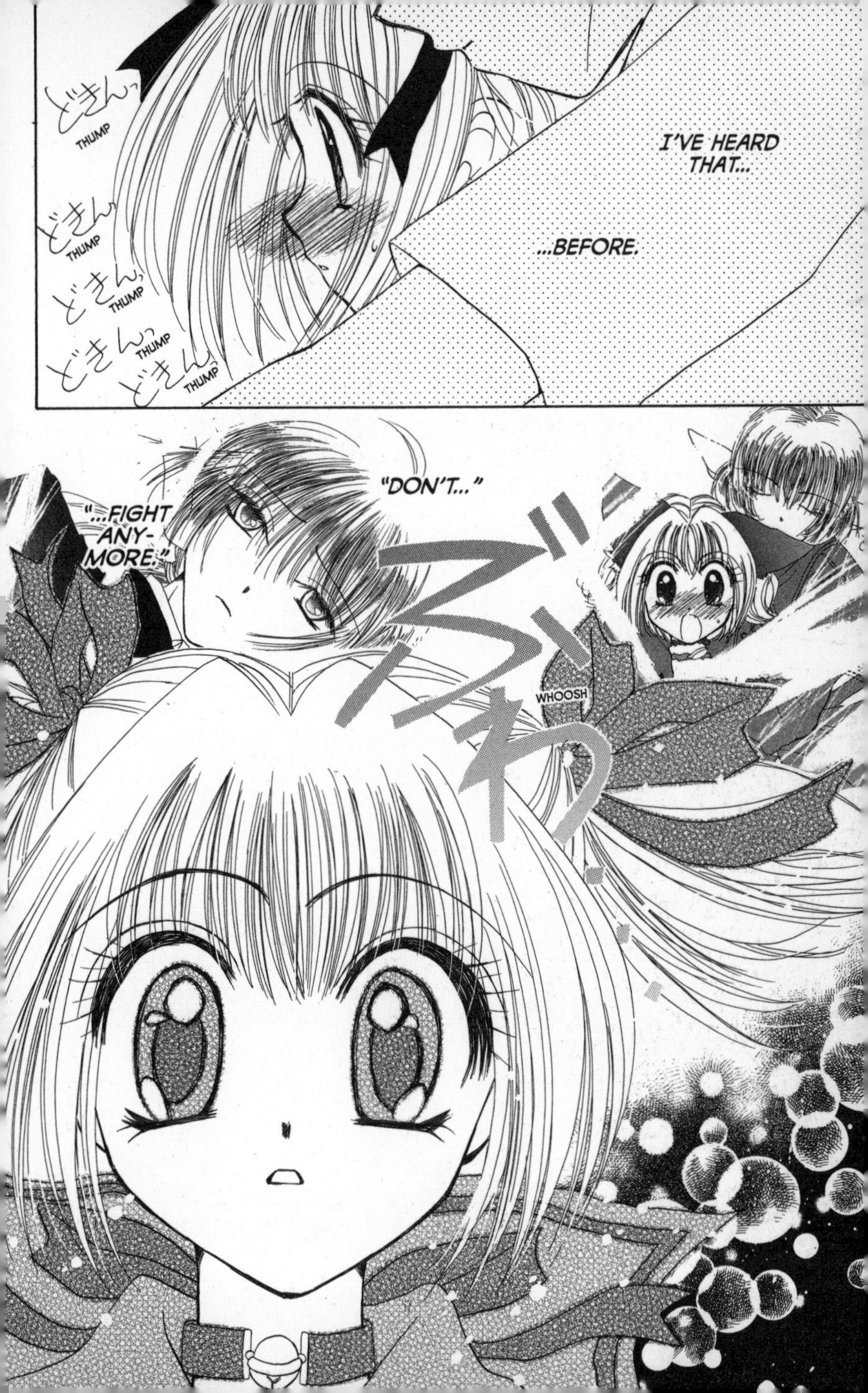
I'VE HEARD THAT...
...BEFORE.
どきんっ THUMP
どきんっ THUMP
どきんっ THUMP
どきんっ THUMP
どきんっ THUMP
"DON'T..."
"...FIGHT ANY-MORE."
ざわっ WHOOSH

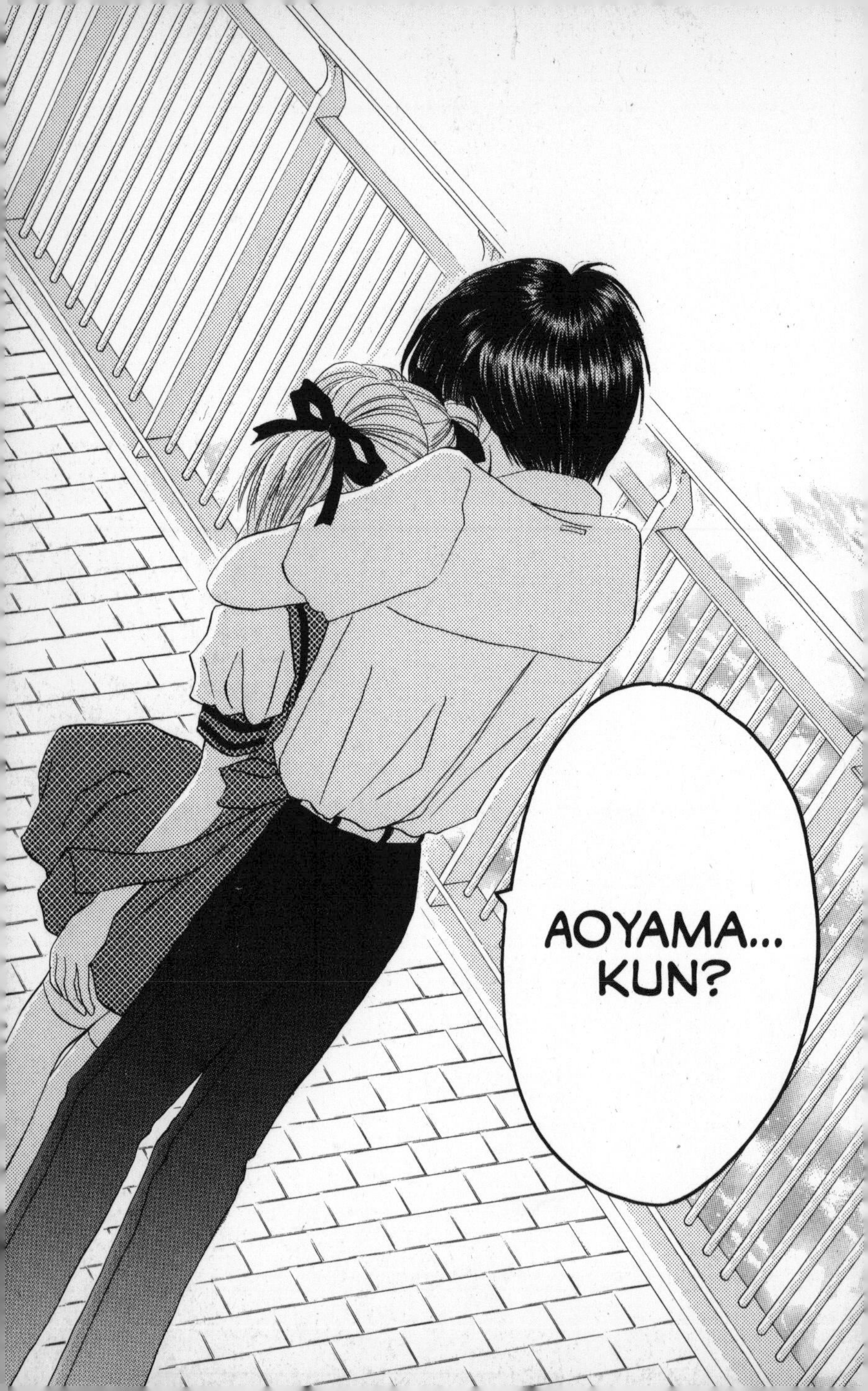
AOYAMA... KUN?

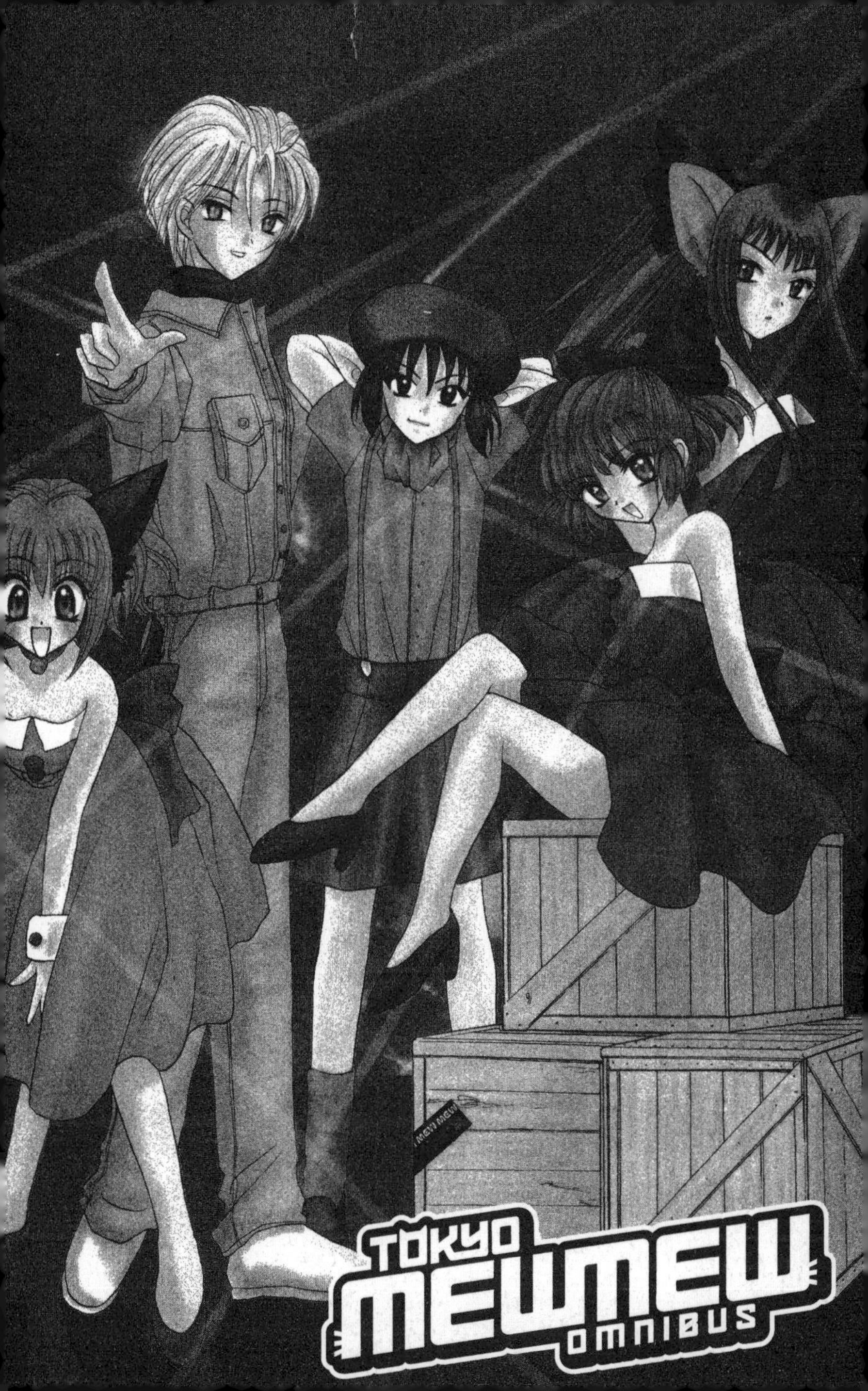
TOKYO
MEWMEW
OMNIBUS

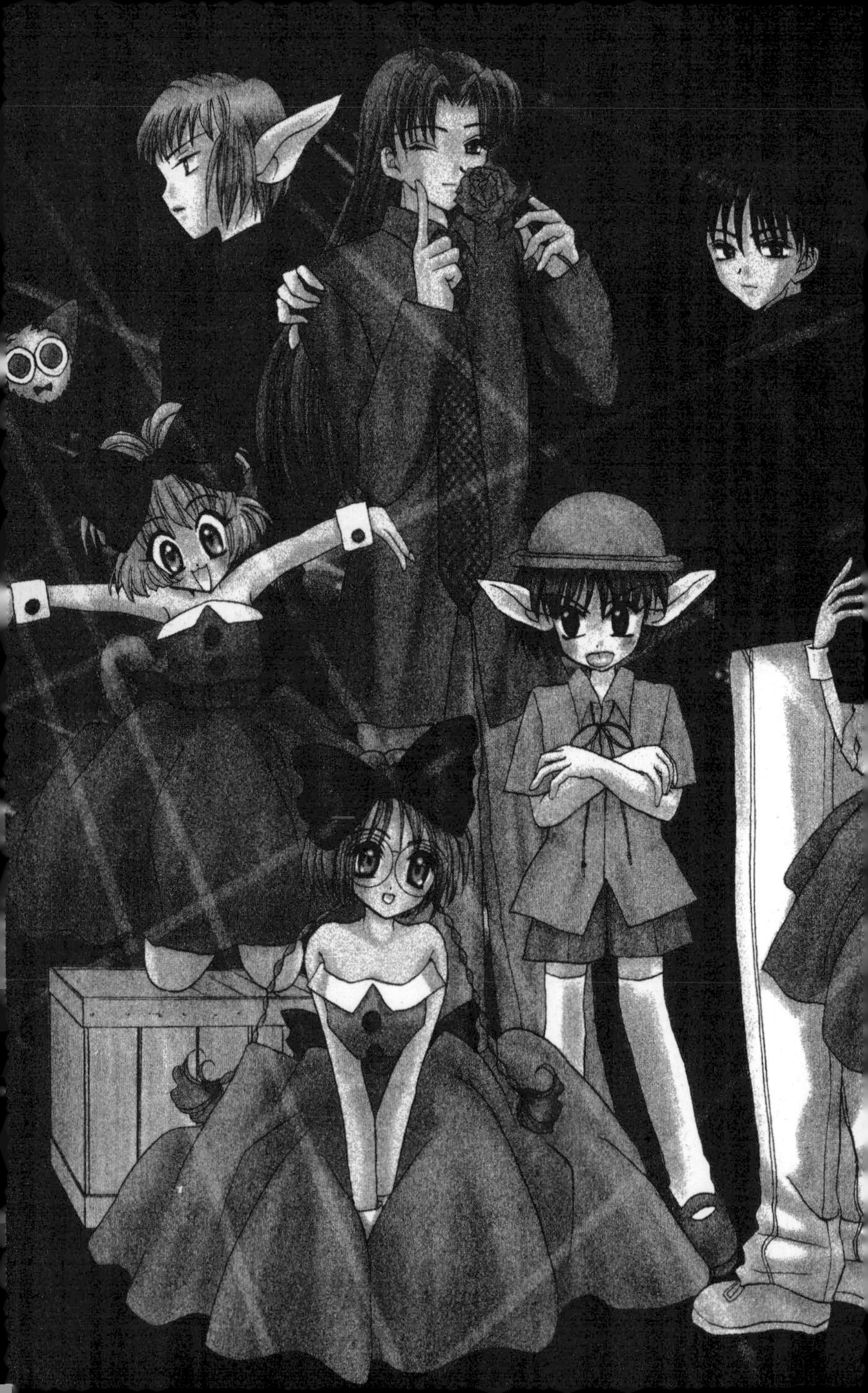

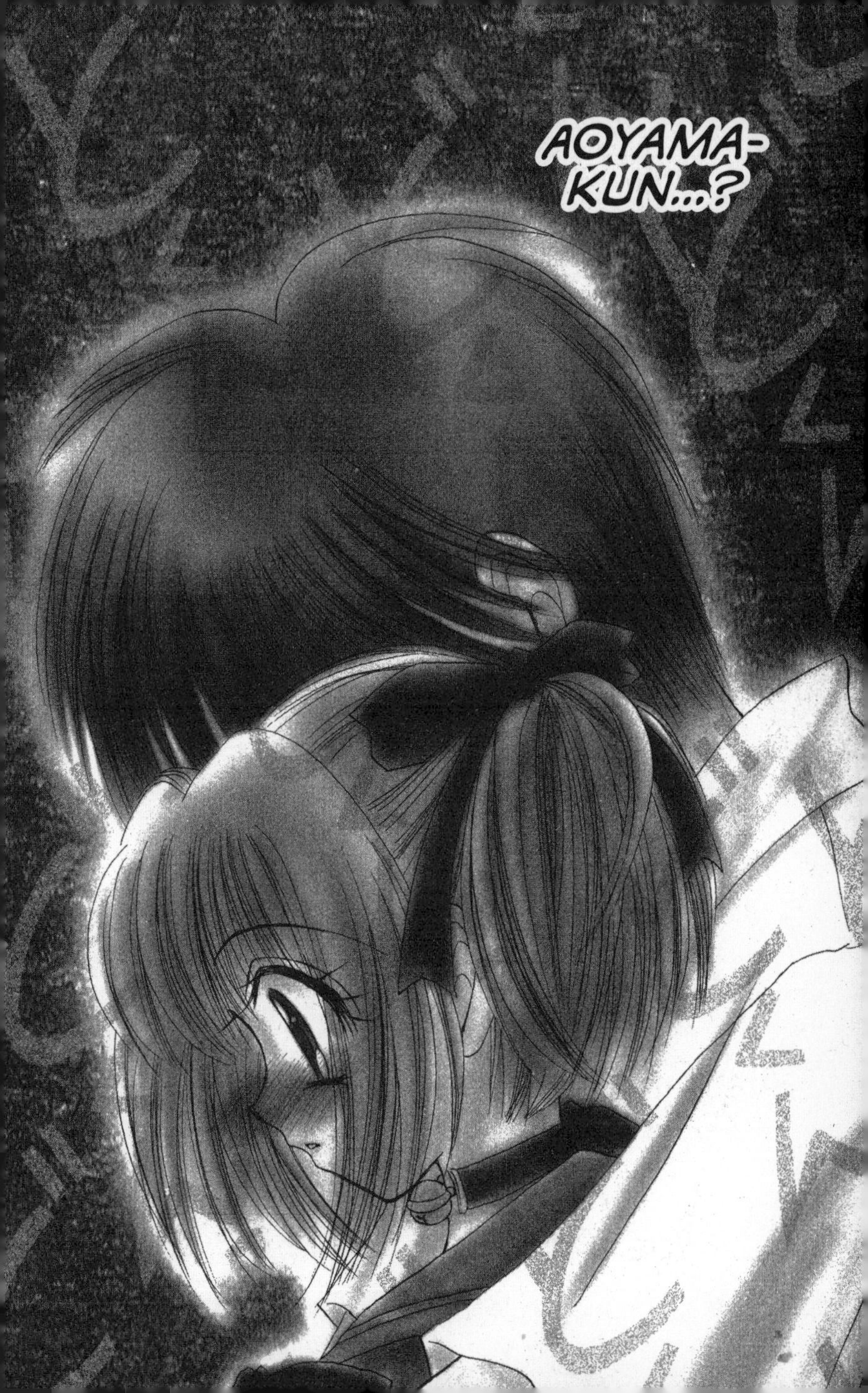
AOYAMA-
KUN...?

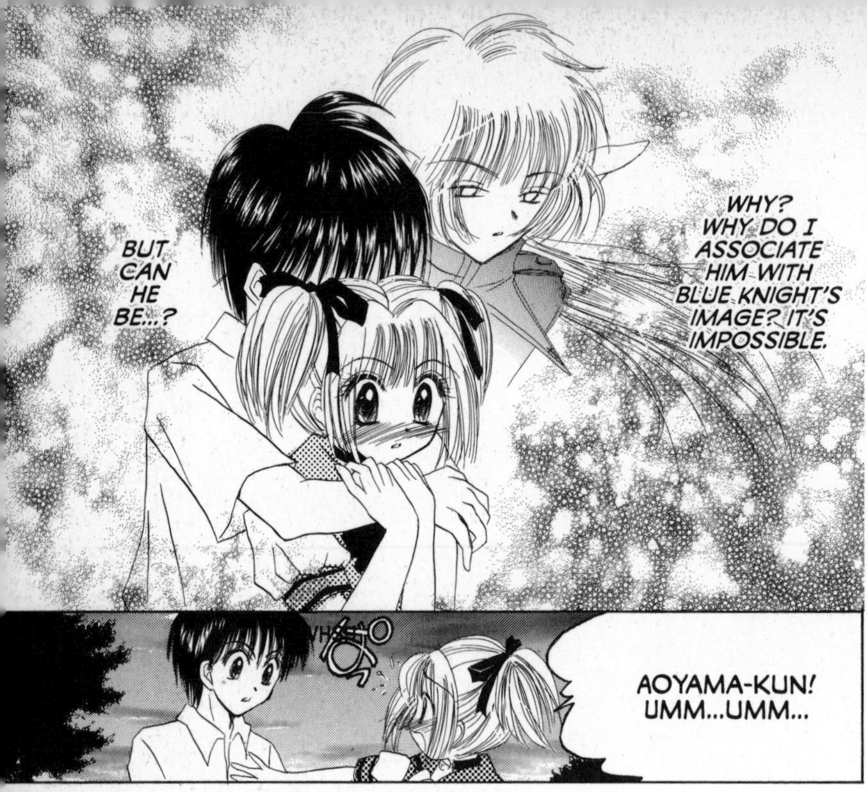
WHY? WHY DO I ASSOCIATE HIM WITH BLUE KNIGHT'S IMAGE? IT'S IMPOSSIBLE.
BUT CAN HE BE...?
AOYAMA-KUN! UMM...UMM...

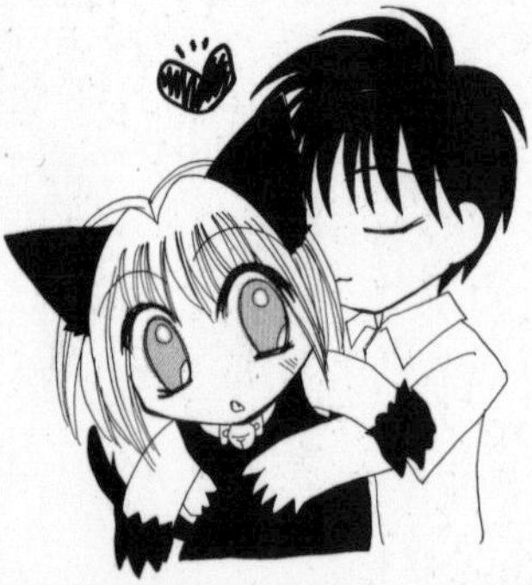

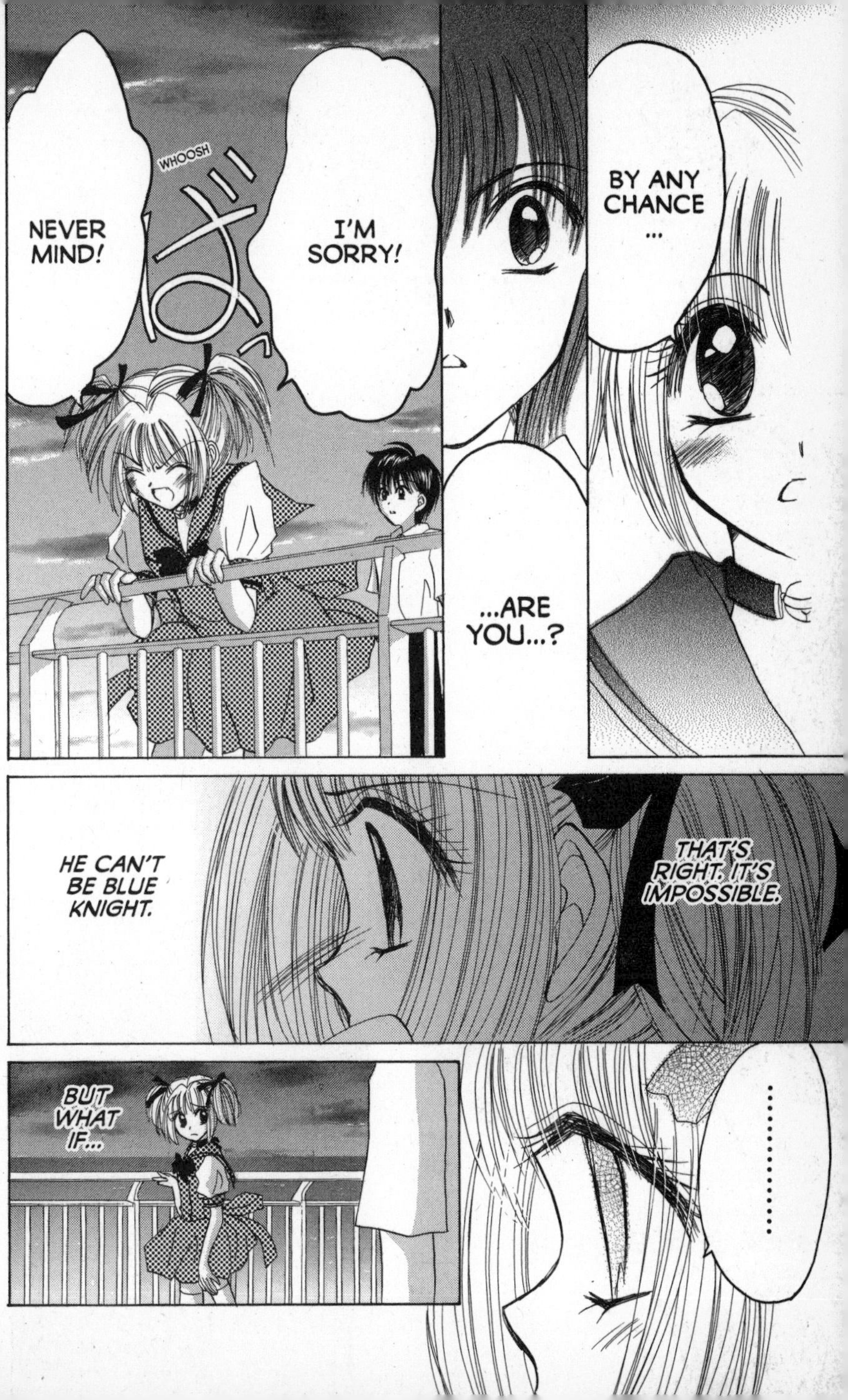
BY ANY CHANCE ...
...ARE YOU...?
I'M SORRY!
WHOOSH
NEVER MIND!
THAT'S RIGHT. IT'S IMPOSSIBLE.
HE CAN'T BE BLUE KNIGHT.
....
BUT WHAT IF...

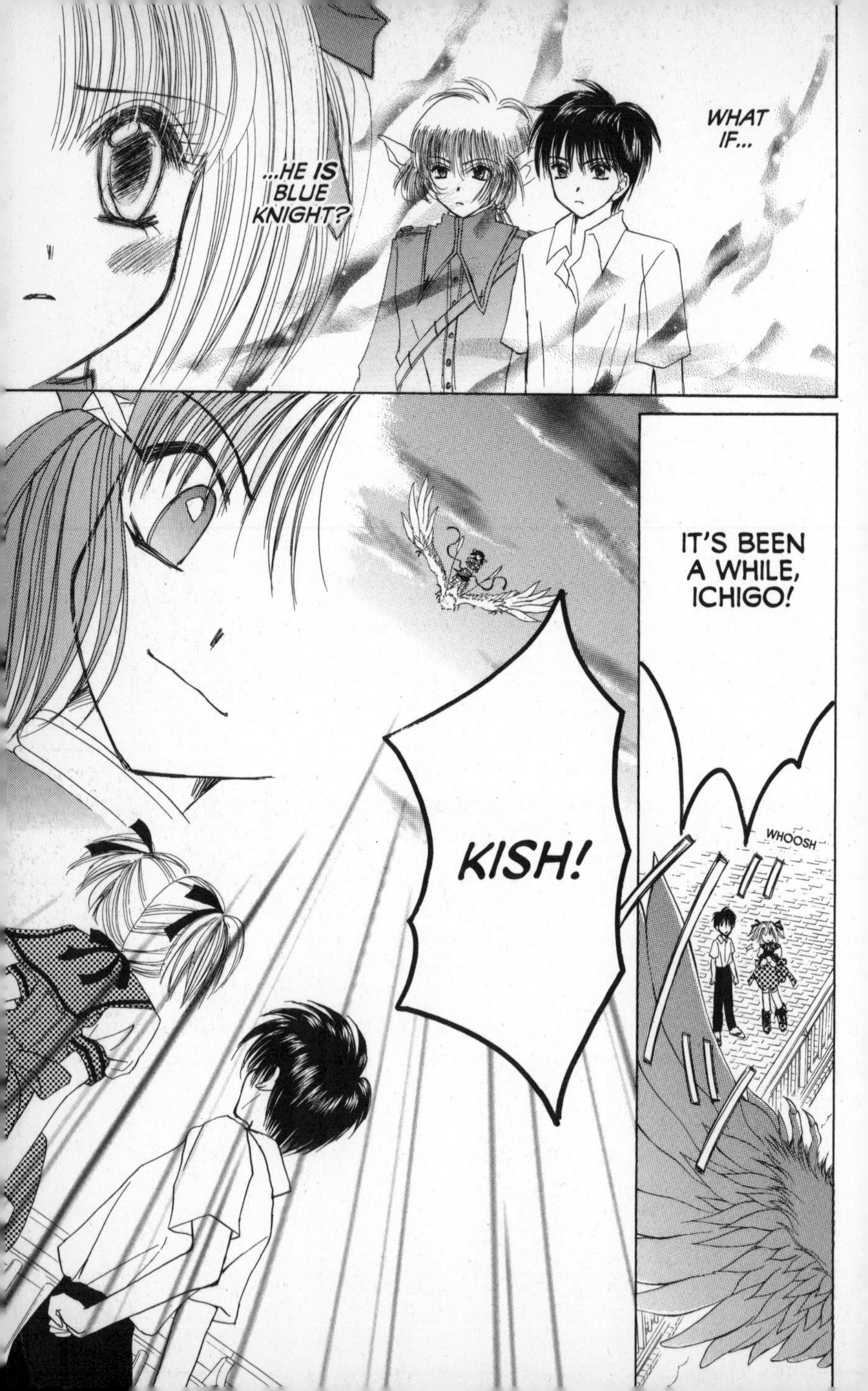
WHAT IF...
...HE IS BLUE KNIGHT?
IT'S BEEN A WHILE, ICHIGO!
WHOOSH
KISH!

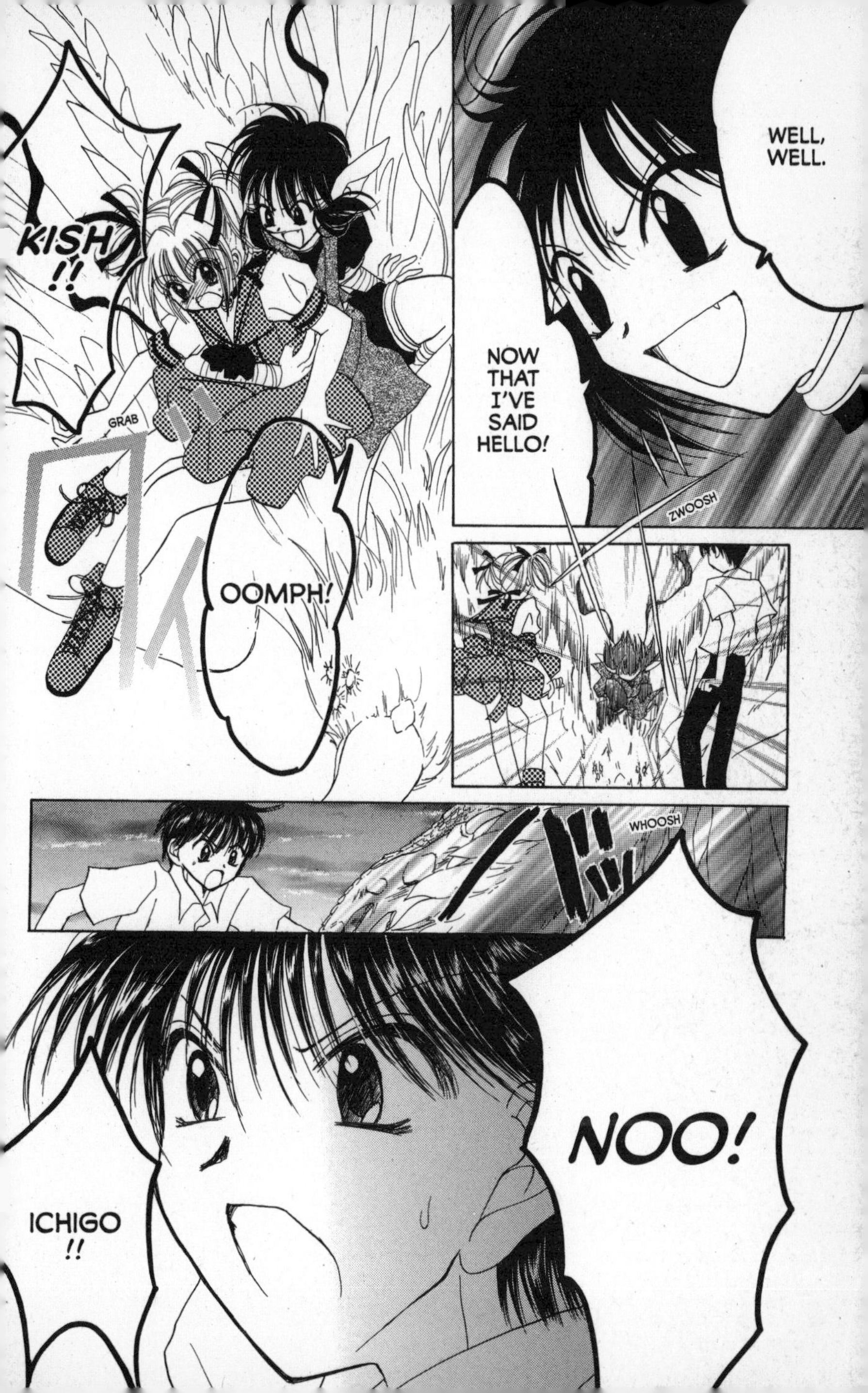
WELL, WELL.
NOW THAT I'VE SAID HELLO!
ZWOOSH
KISH!!
GRAB
OOMPH!
WHOOSH
NOO!
ICHIGO!!

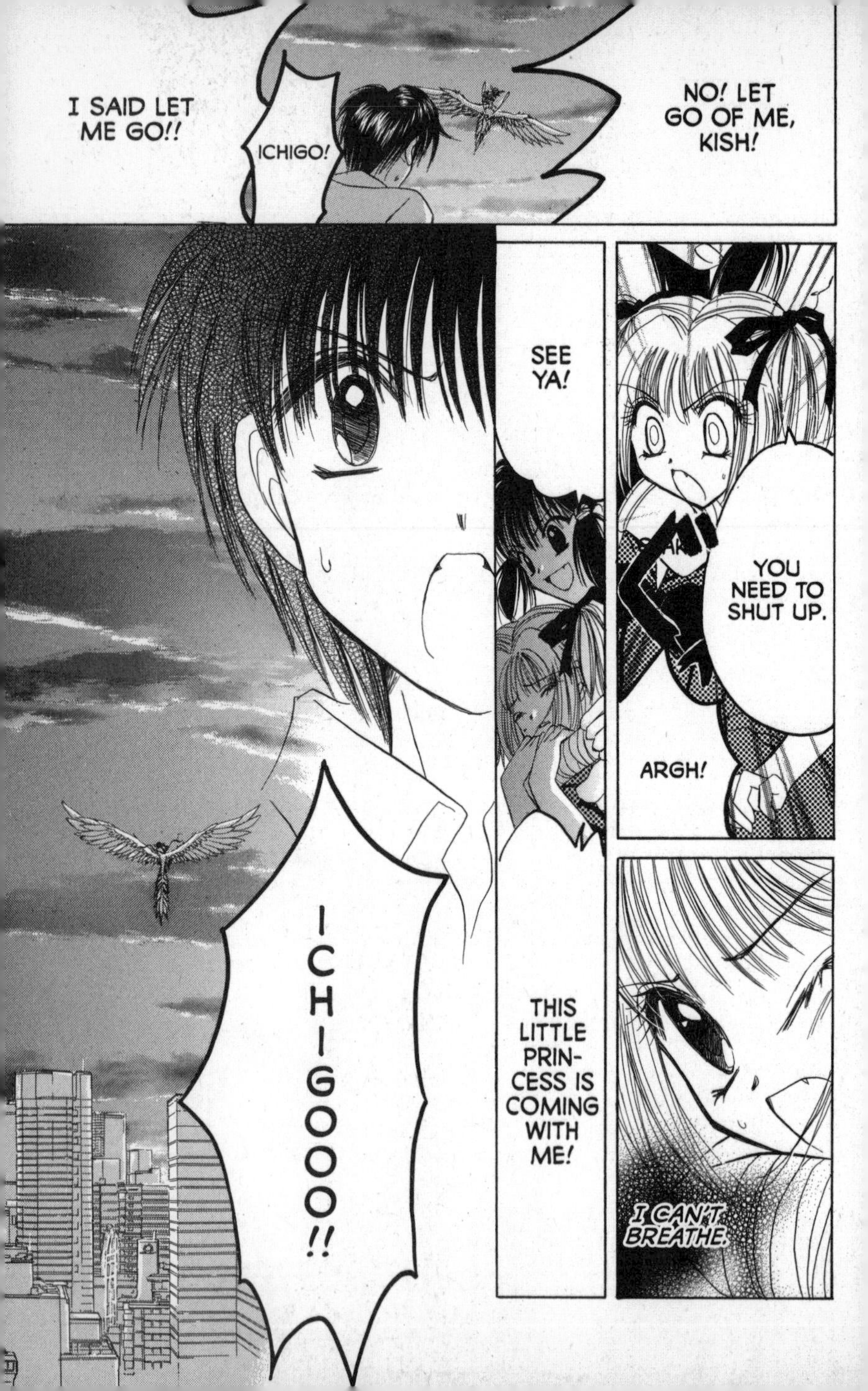

NO! LET GO OF ME, KISH!
ICHIGO!
I SAID LET ME GO!!
YOU NEED TO SHUT UP.
ARGH!
I CAN'T BREATHE.
SEE YA!
THIS LITTLE PRIN-CESS IS COMING WITH ME!
ICHIGOOOO!!

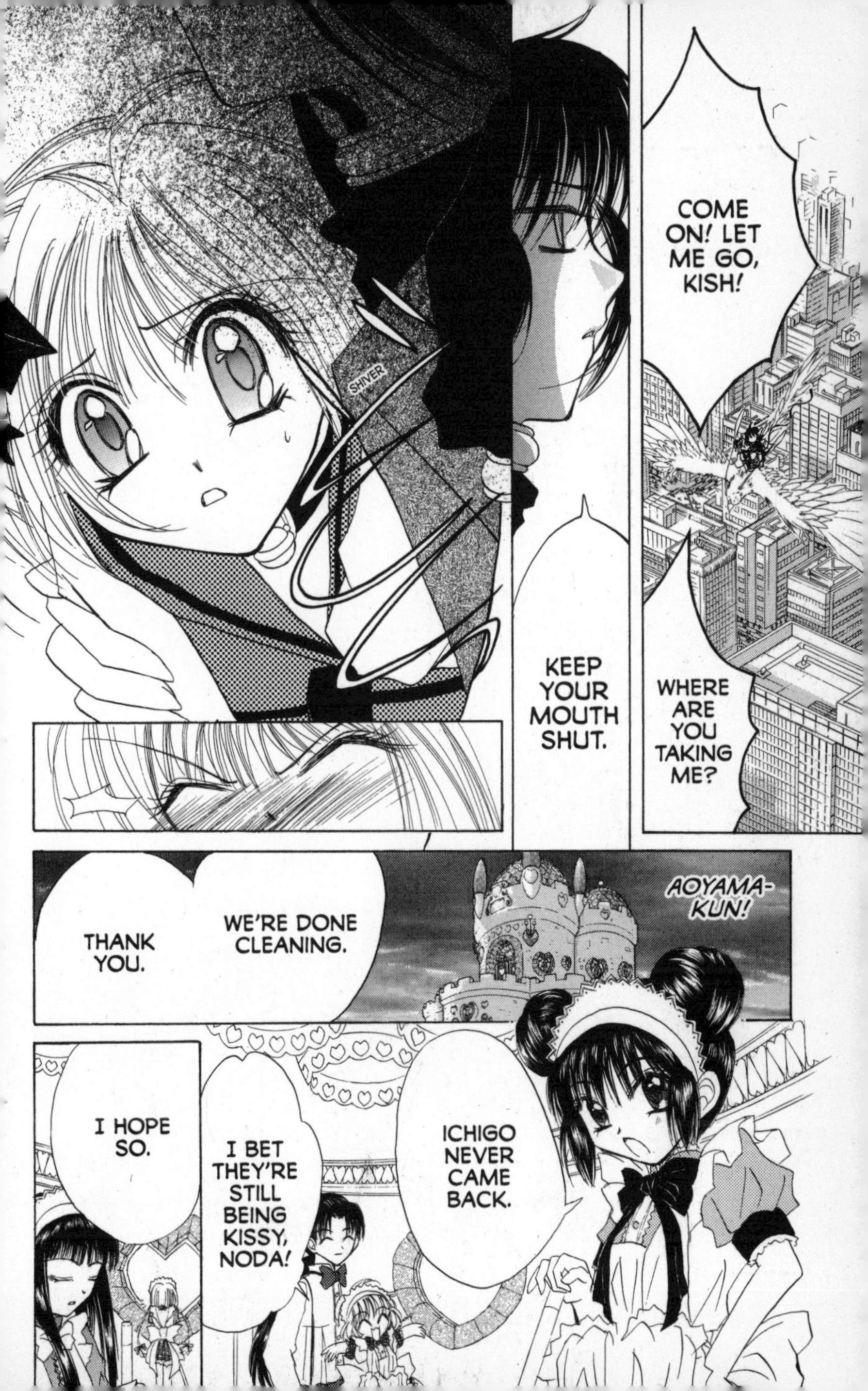
COME ON! LET ME GO, KISH!
WHERE ARE YOU TAKING ME?
KEEP YOUR MOUTH SHUT.
SHIVER
AOYAMA-KUN!
WE'RE DONE CLEANING.
THANK YOU.
ICHIGO NEVER CAME BACK.
I BET THEY'RE STILL BEING KISSY, NODA!
I HOPE SO.

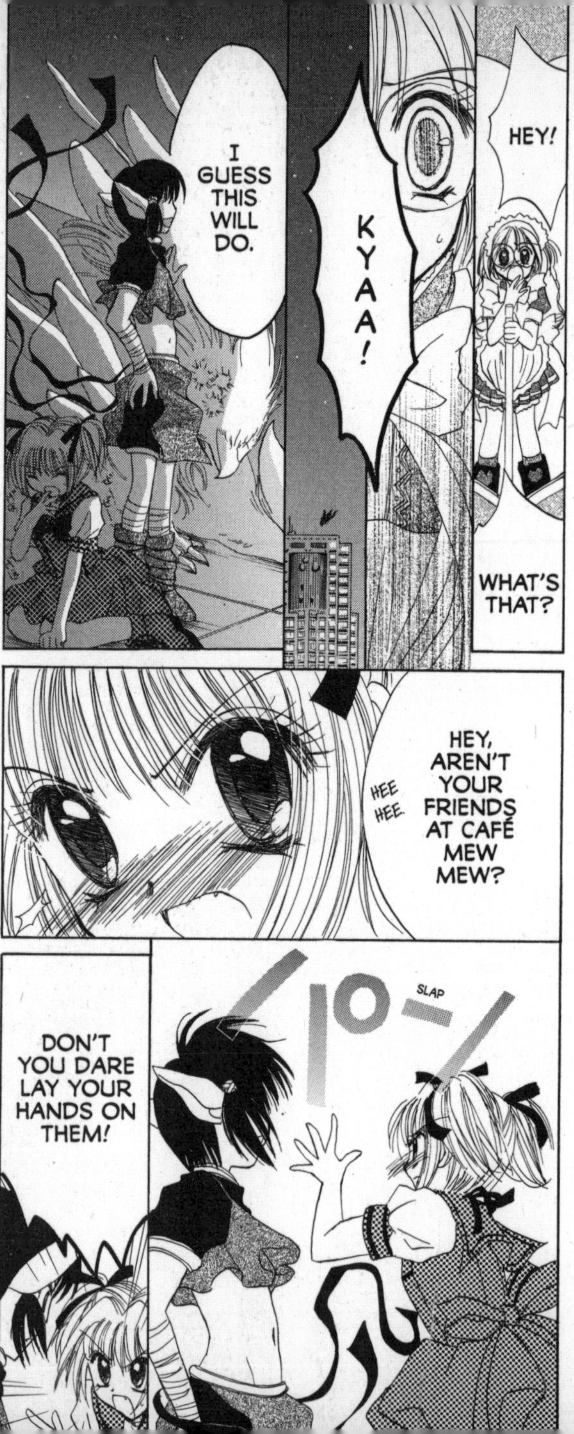
HEY!
WHAT'S THAT?
KYAA!
I GUESS THIS WILL DO.
HEY, AREN'T YOUR FRIENDS AT CAFÉ MEW MEW?
HEE HEE.
SLAP
DON'T YOU DARE LAY YOUR HANDS ON THEM!

Tokyo Mew Mew:
Ichigo's Costume Wanted! Part 3

SEMI-GRAND PRIZE

MARI MURAOKA-CHAN,
TOCHIGI PREFECTURE,
GRADE 6

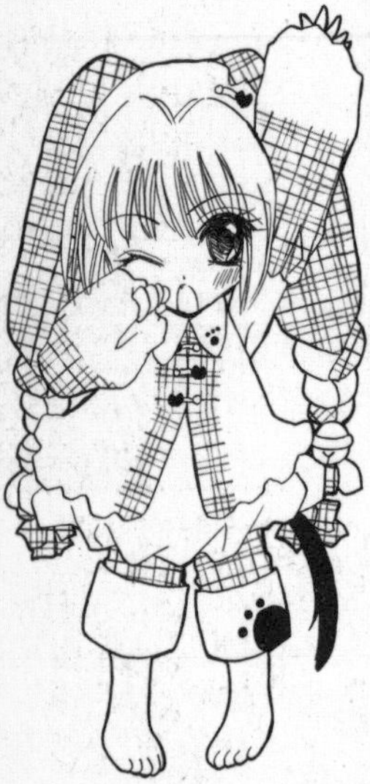

When I mentioned at work that I wanted these pajamas, my assistant offered to sew them for me. She's awesome! By the time this book comes out, I'll be working in these pajamas. Hee hee. it's a very lovely costume.

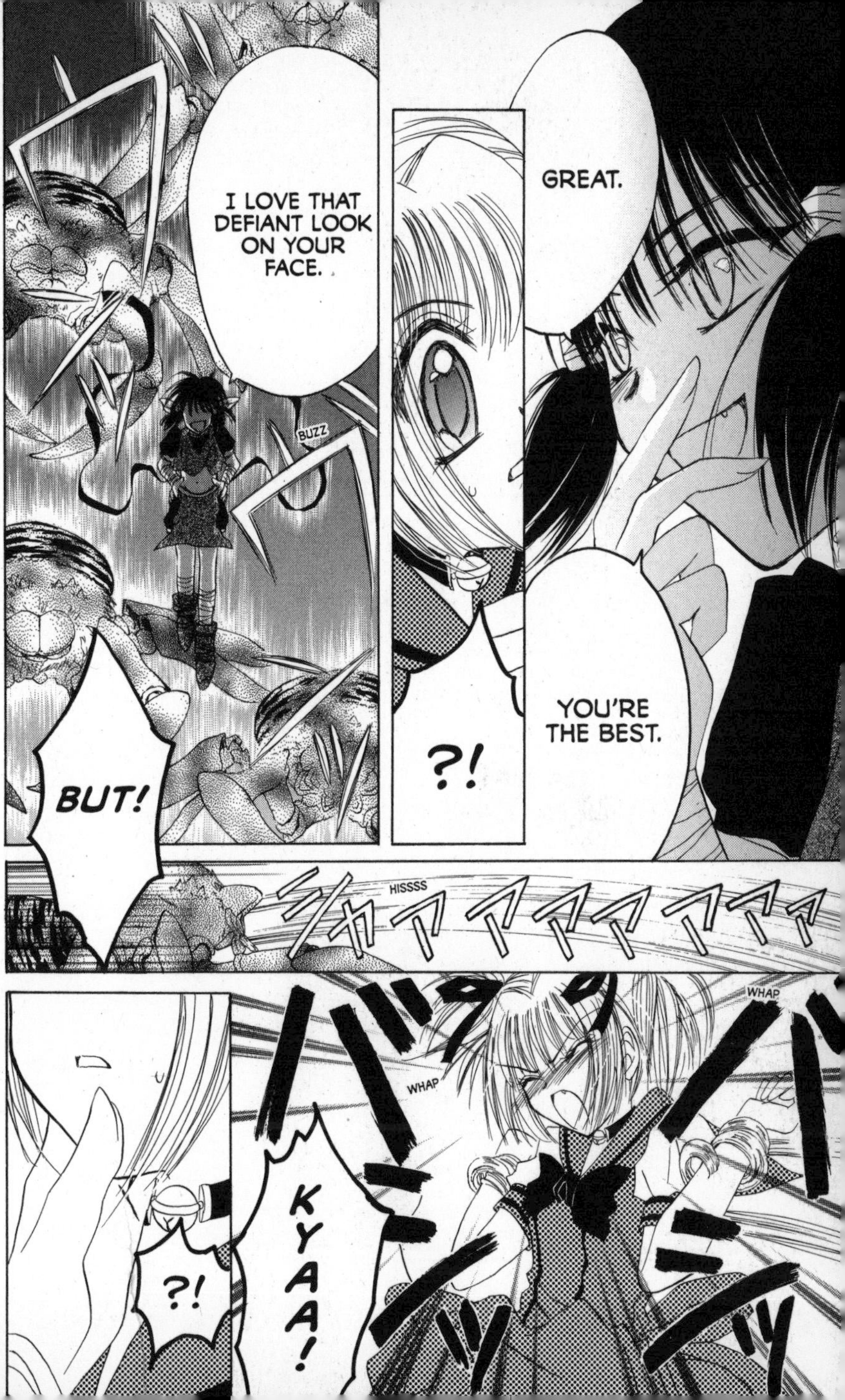
GREAT.
YOU'RE THE BEST.
?!
I LOVE THAT DEFIANT LOOK ON YOUR FACE.
BUZZ
BUT!
HISSSS
WHAP
WHAP
KYAA!
?!

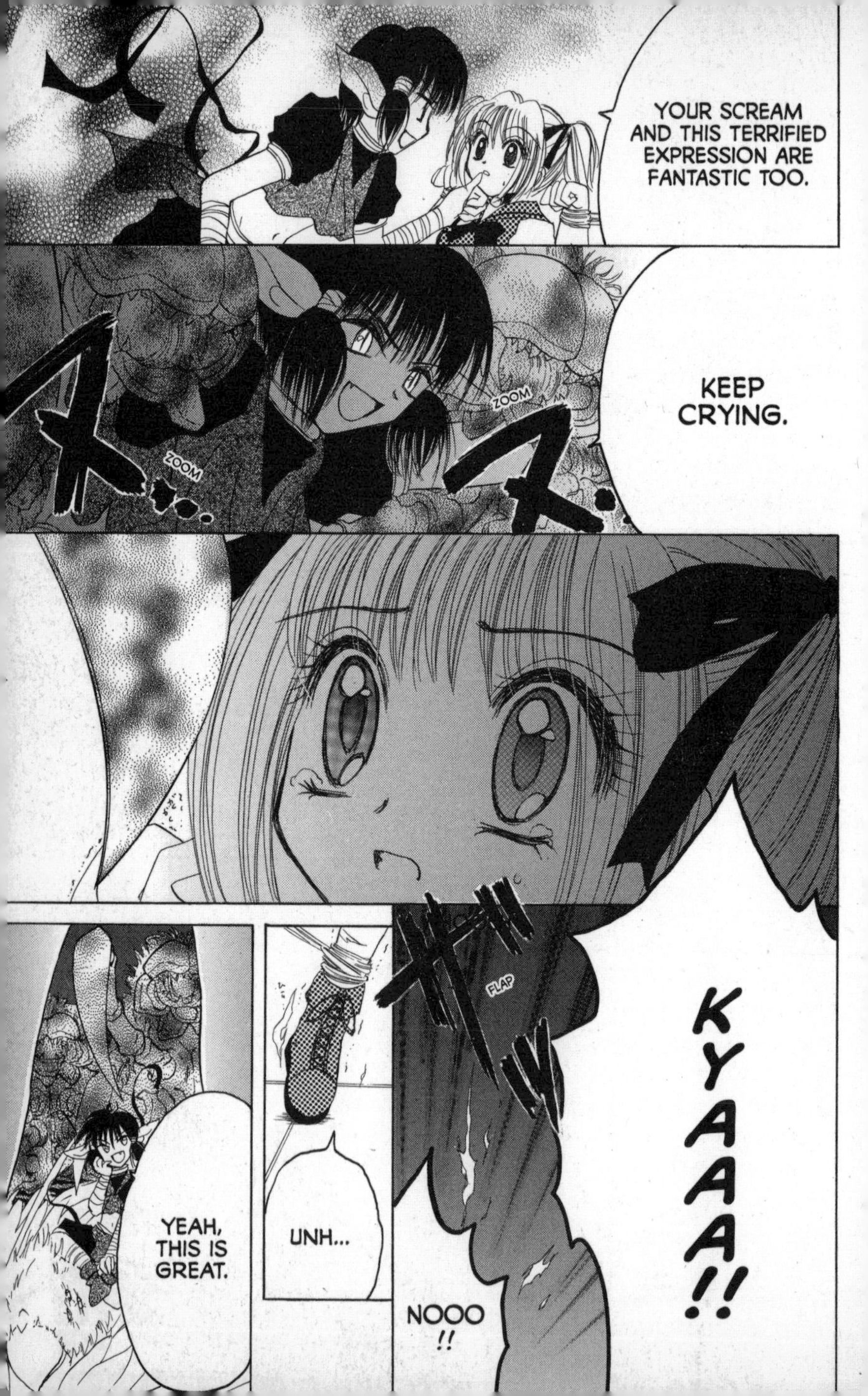
YOUR SCREAM AND THIS TERRIFIED EXPRESSION ARE FANTASTIC TOO.
KEEP CRYING.
ZOOM
ZOOM
FLAP
KYAAAA!!
NOOO !!
UNH...
YEAH, THIS IS GREAT.

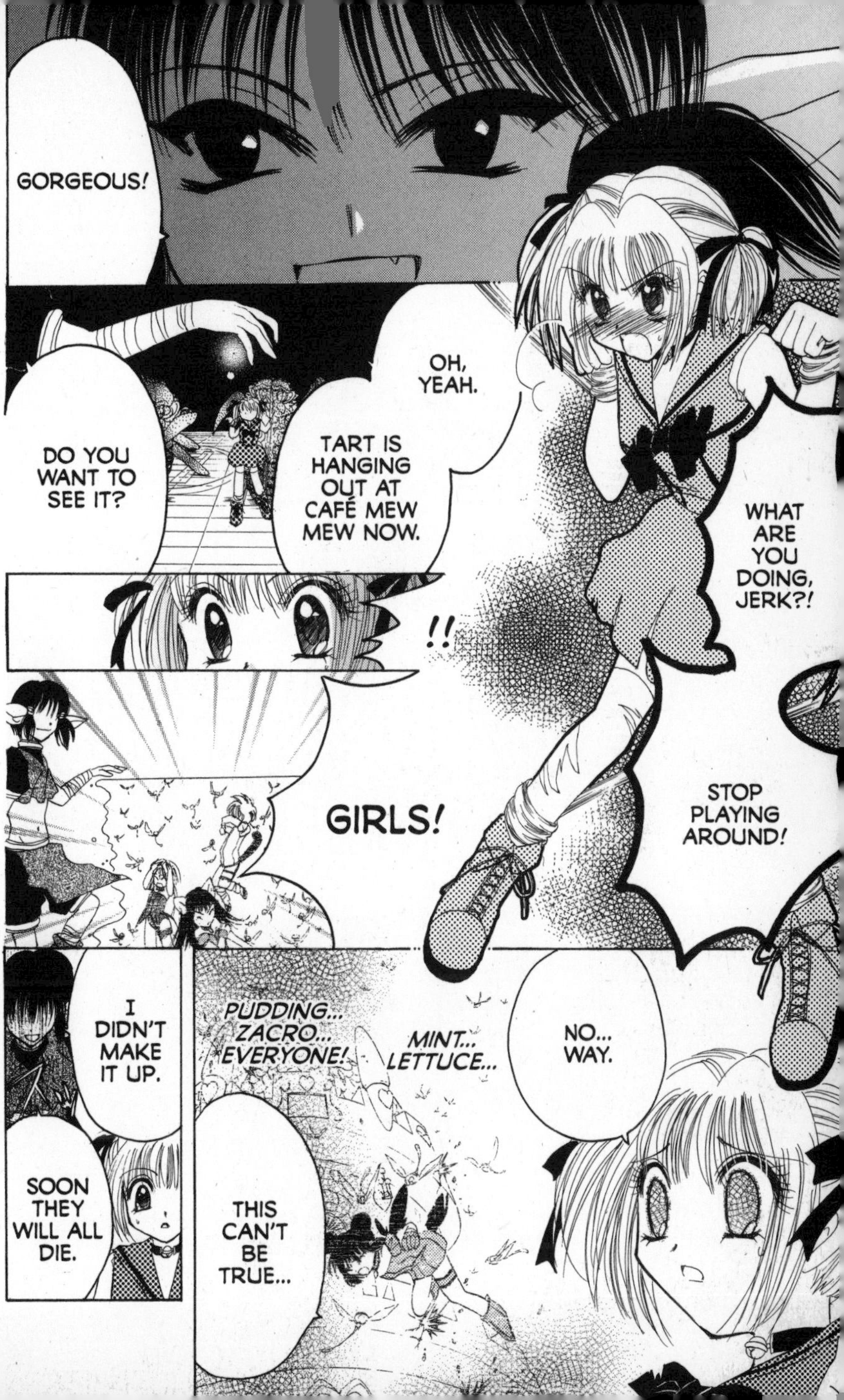
GORGEOUS!
WHAT ARE YOU DOING, JERK?!
STOP PLAYING AROUND!
OH, YEAH.
TART IS HANGING OUT AT CAFÉ MEW MEW NOW.
DO YOU WANT TO SEE IT?
!!
GIRLS!
NO... WAY.
MINT... LETTUCE...
PUDDING... ZACRO... EVERYONE!
THIS CAN'T BE TRUE...
I DIDN'T MAKE IT UP.
SOON THEY WILL ALL DIE.

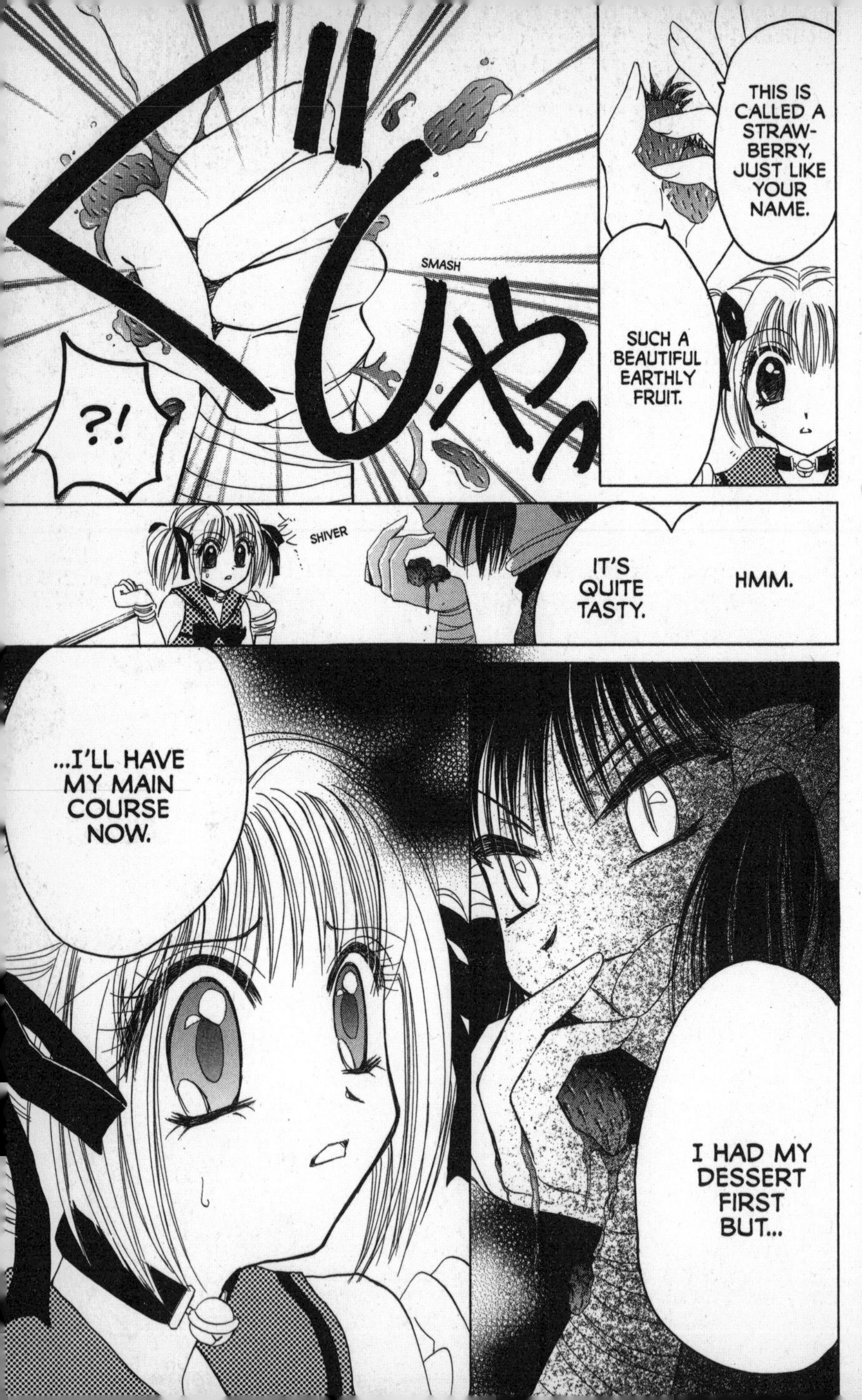
THIS IS CALLED A STRAW-BERRY, JUST LIKE YOUR NAME.
SUCH A BEAUTIFUL EARTHLY FRUIT.
SMASH
?!
HMM.
IT'S QUITE TASTY.
SHIVER
I HAD MY DESSERT FIRST BUT...
...I'LL HAVE MY MAIN COURSE NOW.

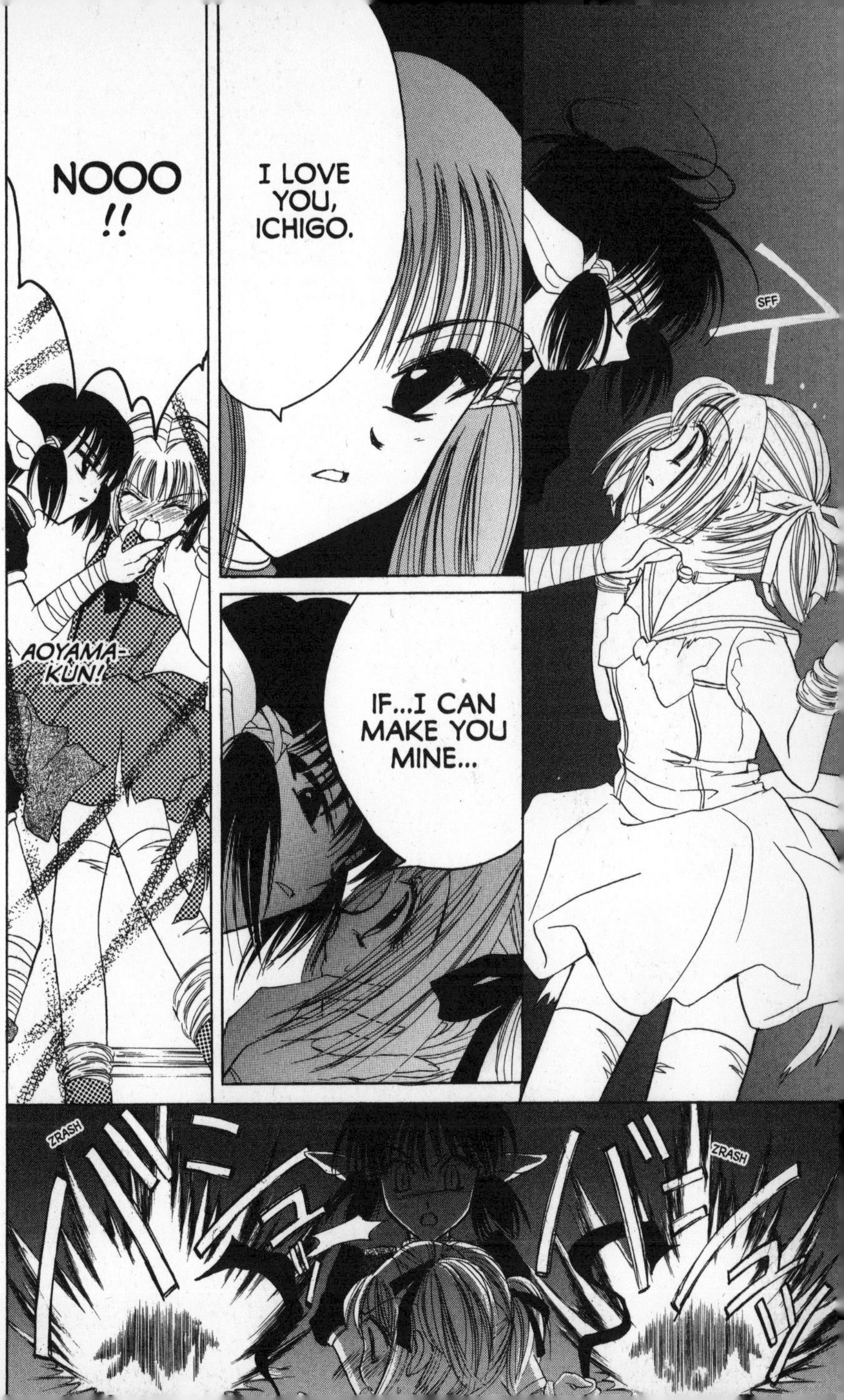
SFF
I LOVE YOU, ICHIGO.
IF...I CAN MAKE YOU MINE...
NOOO !!
AOYAMA-KUN!
ZRASH
ZRASH

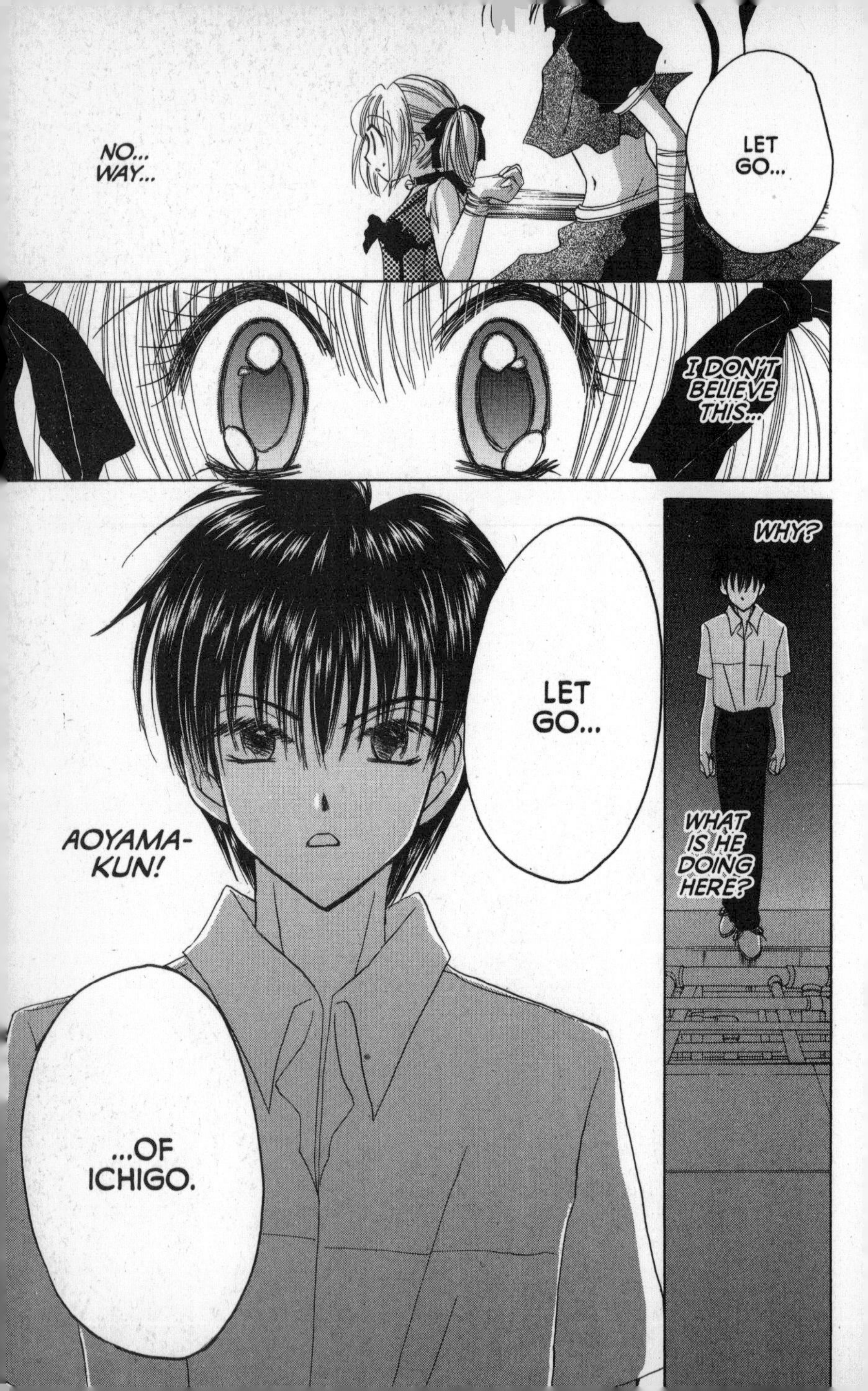
LET GO...
NO... WAY...
I DON'T BELIEVE THIS...
WHY?
WHAT IS HE DOING HERE?
LET GO...
AOYAMA-KUN!
...OF ICHIGO.

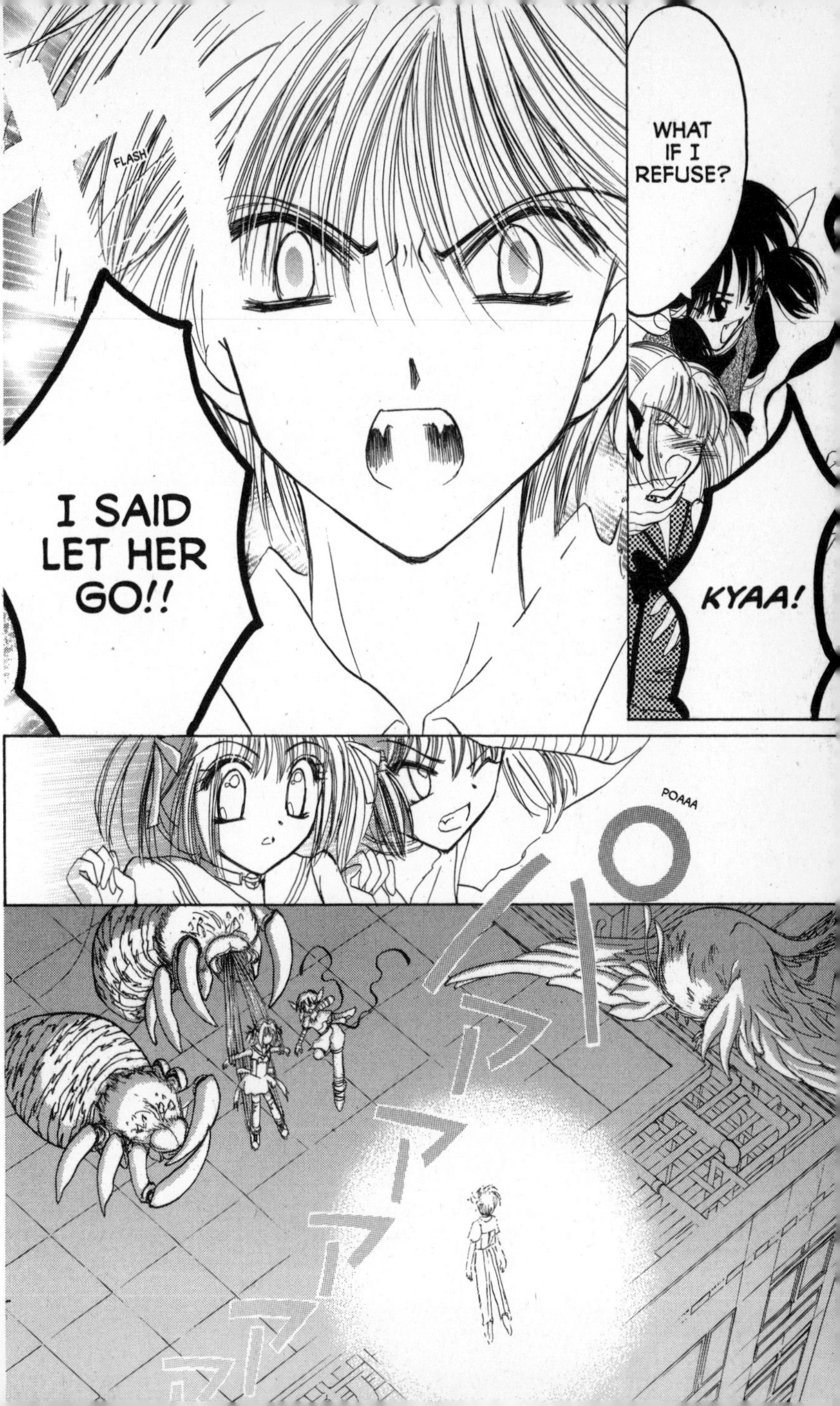
WHAT IF I REFUSE?
KYAA!
FLASH
I SAID LET HER GO!!
POAAA

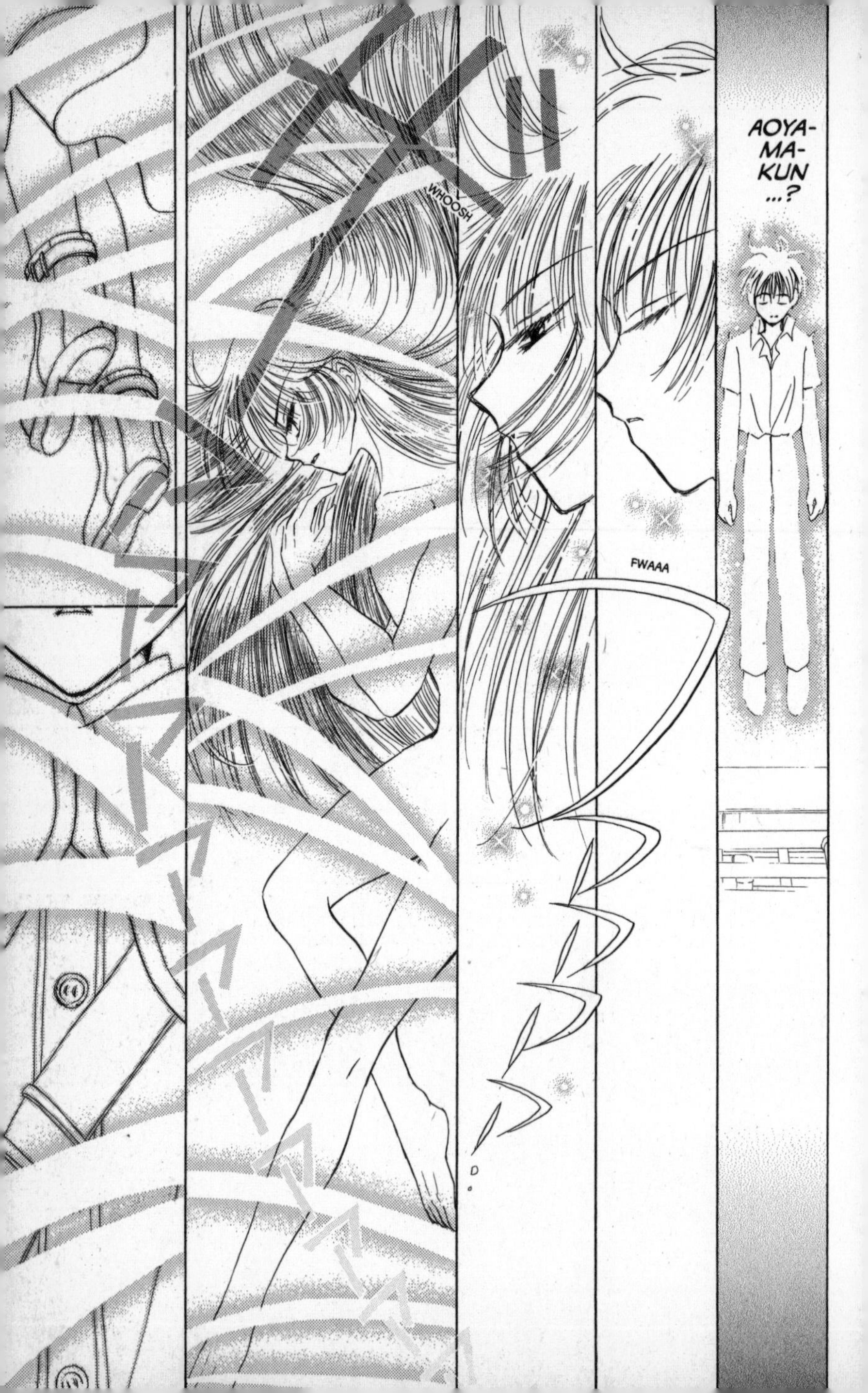
AOYA-
MA-
KUN
...?
FWAAA
WHOOSH

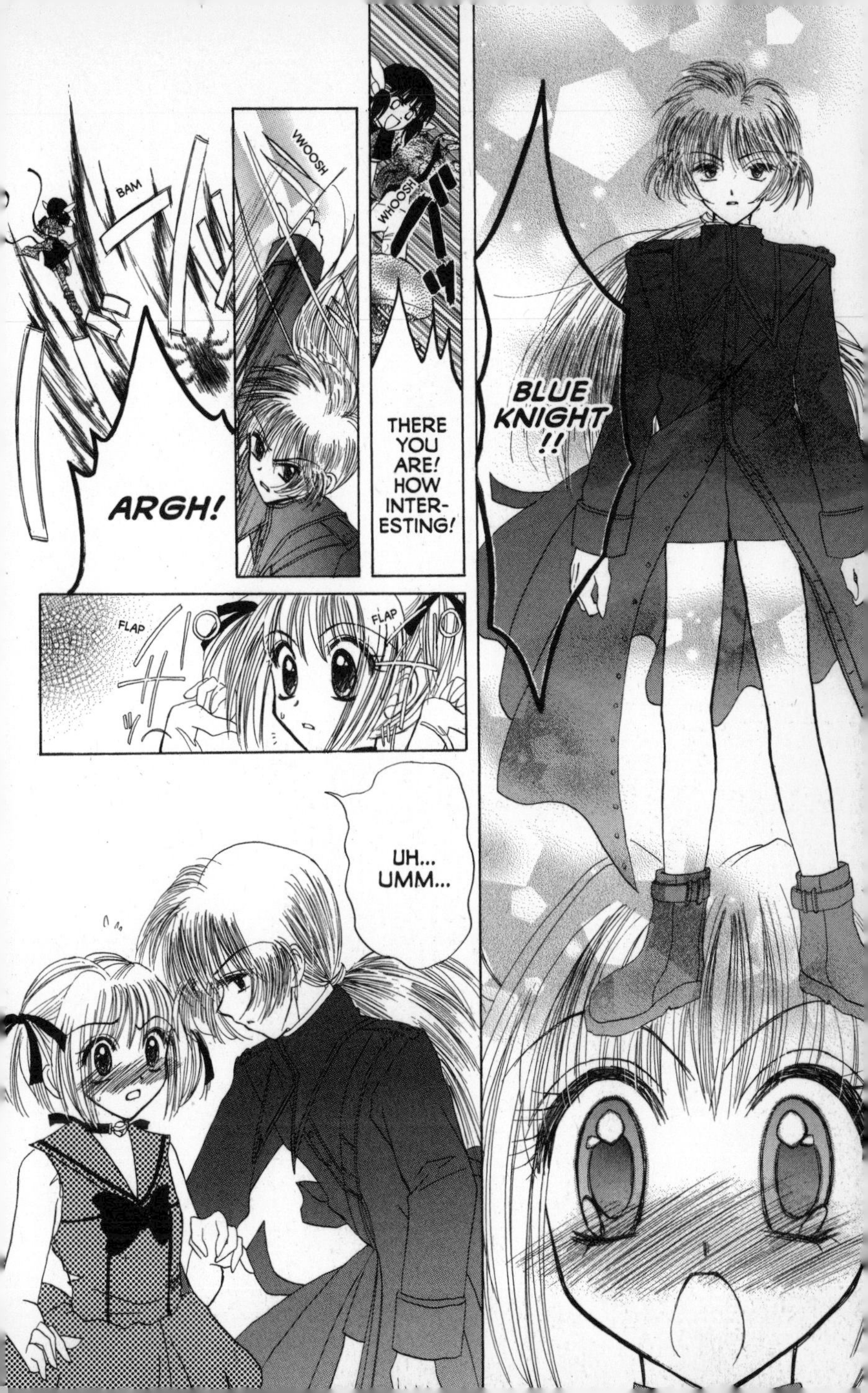
BLUE KNIGHT!!
WHOOSH
THERE YOU ARE! HOW INTERESTING!
VWOOSH
BAM
ARGH!
FLAP
FLAP
UH... UMM...

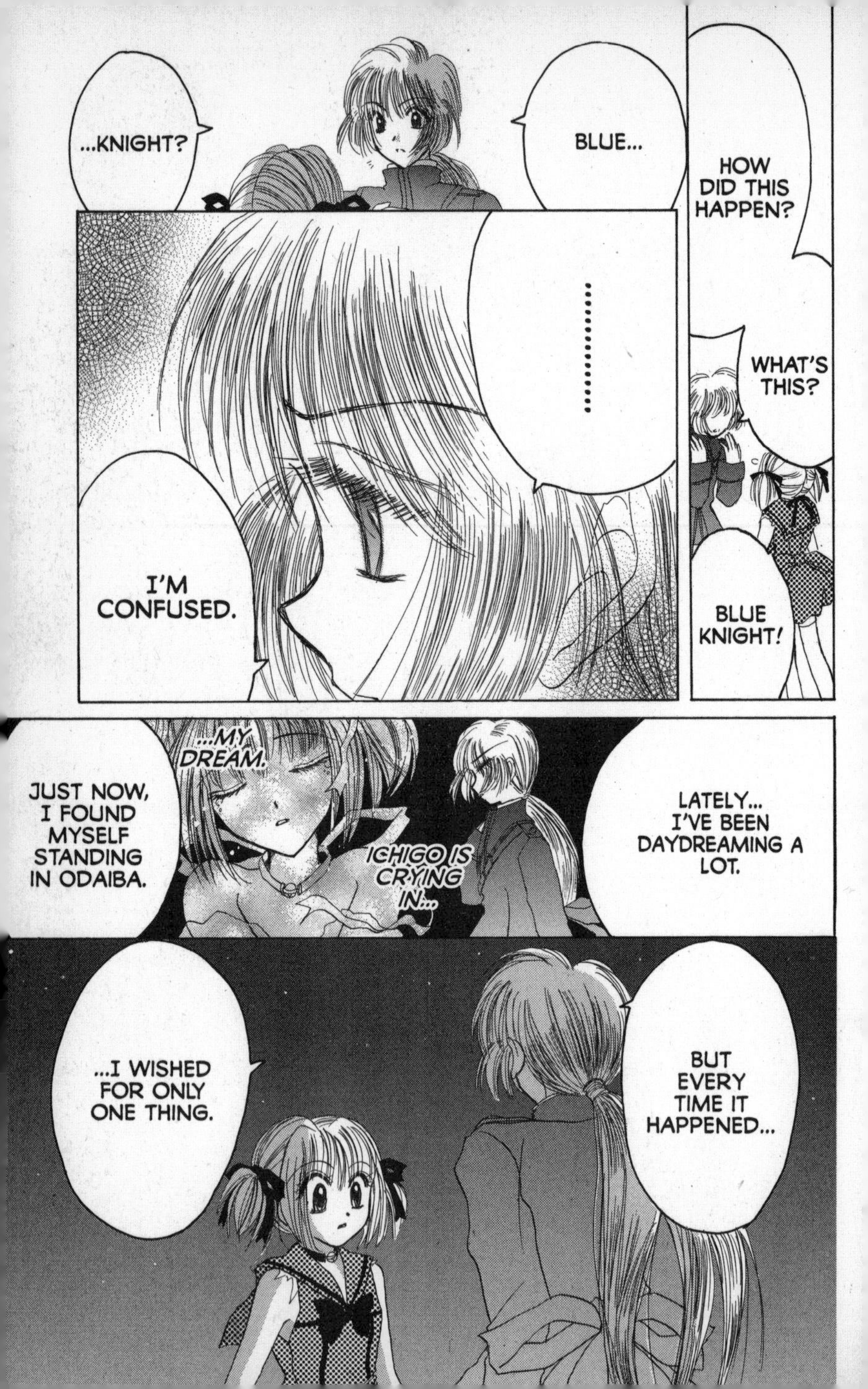
HOW DID THIS HAPPEN?
WHAT'S THIS?
BLUE KNIGHT!
BLUE...
...KNIGHT?
......
I'M CONFUSED.
LATELY... I'VE BEEN DAYDREAMING A LOT.
ICHIGO IS CRYING IN...
...MY DREAM.
JUST NOW, I FOUND MYSELF STANDING IN ODAIBA.
BUT EVERY TIME IT HAPPENED...
...I WISHED FOR ONLY ONE THING.

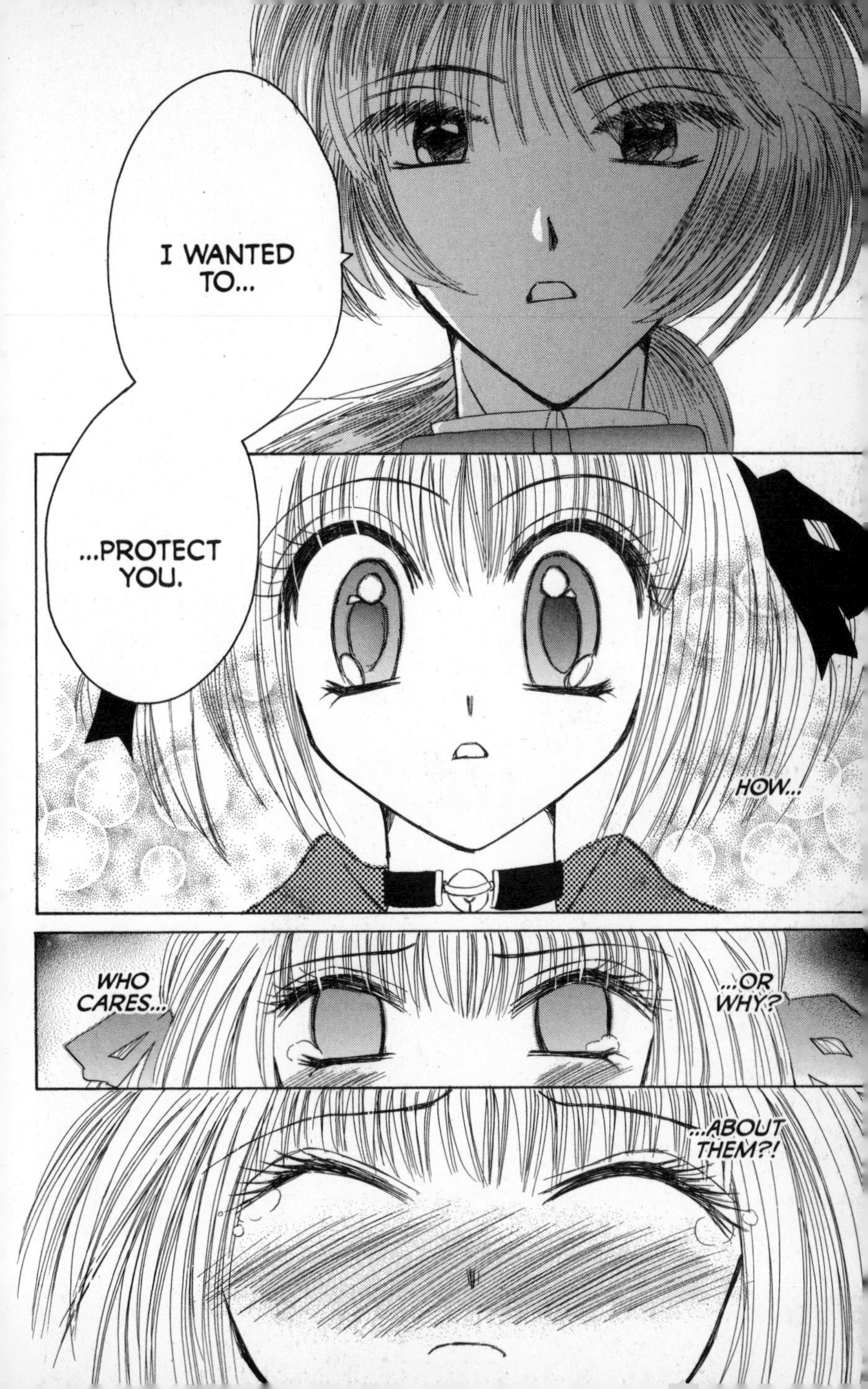
I WANTED TO...
...PROTECT YOU.
HOW...
...OR WHY?
WHO CARES...
...ABOUT THEM?!

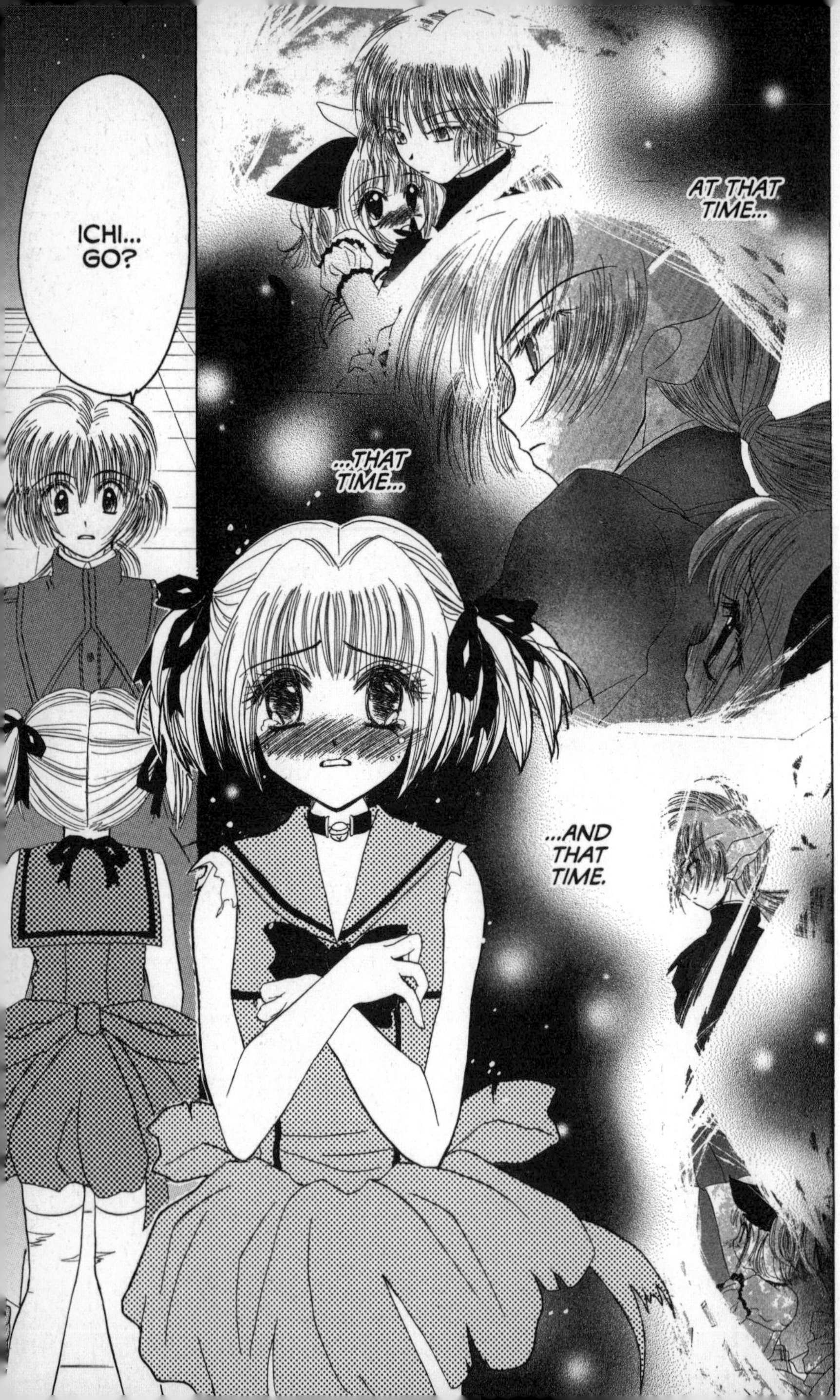
AT THAT TIME...
...THAT TIME...
...AND THAT TIME.
ICHI... GO?

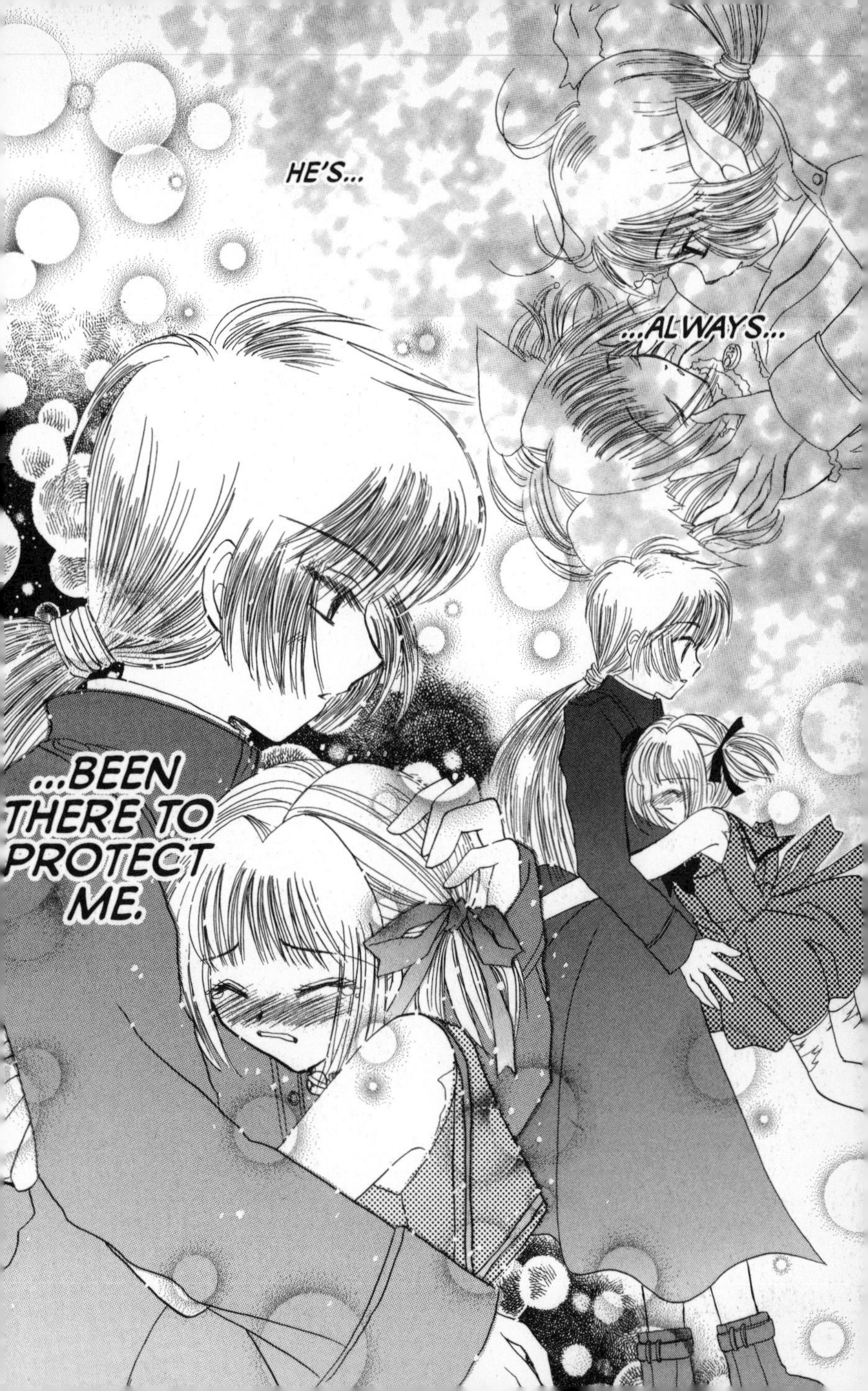
HE'S...
...ALWAYS...
...BEEN THERE TO PROTECT ME.

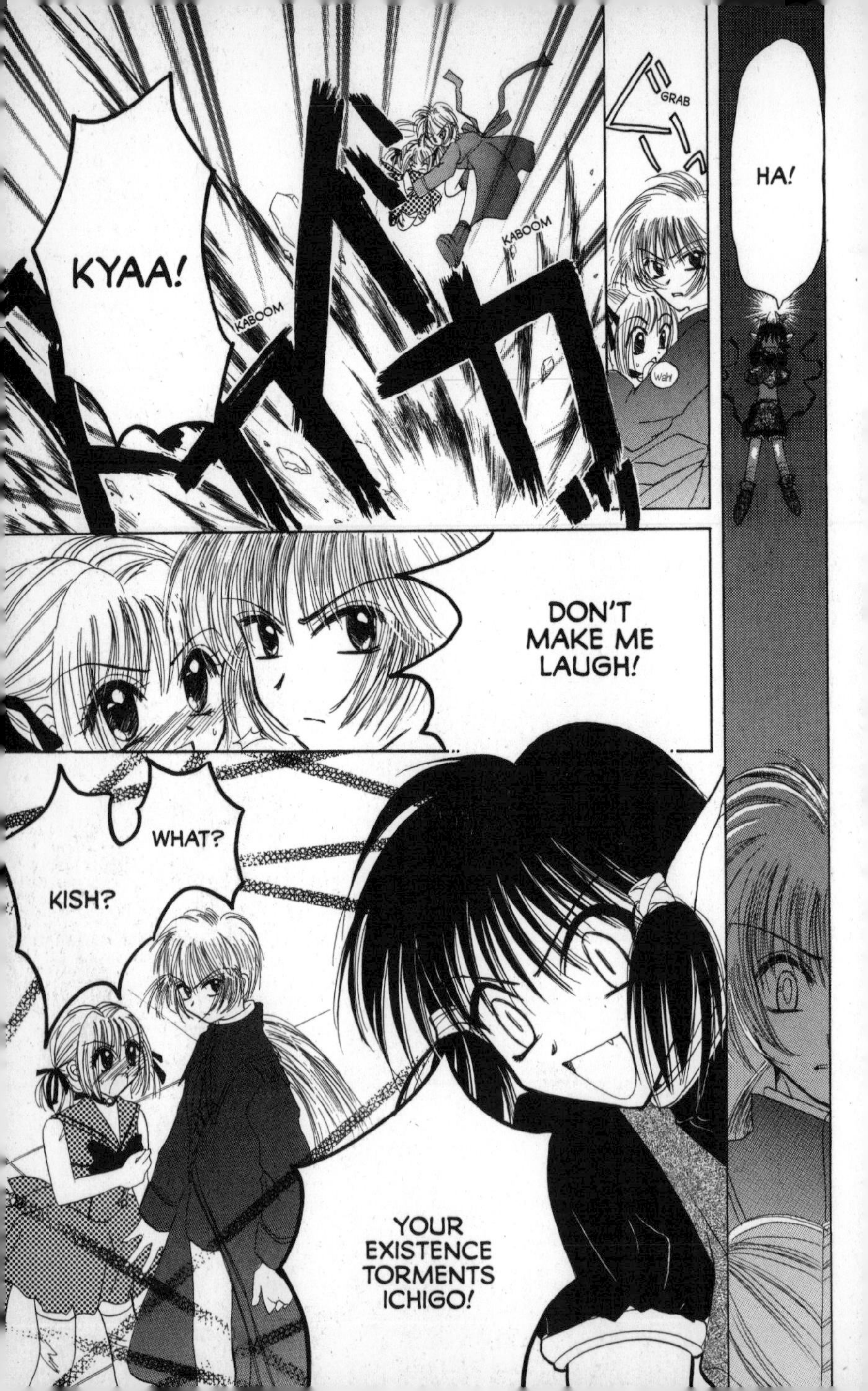
HA!
GRAB
Wah!
KABOOM
KYAA!
KABOOM
DON'T MAKE ME LAUGH!
YOUR EXISTENCE TORMENTS ICHIGO!
WHAT?
KISH?

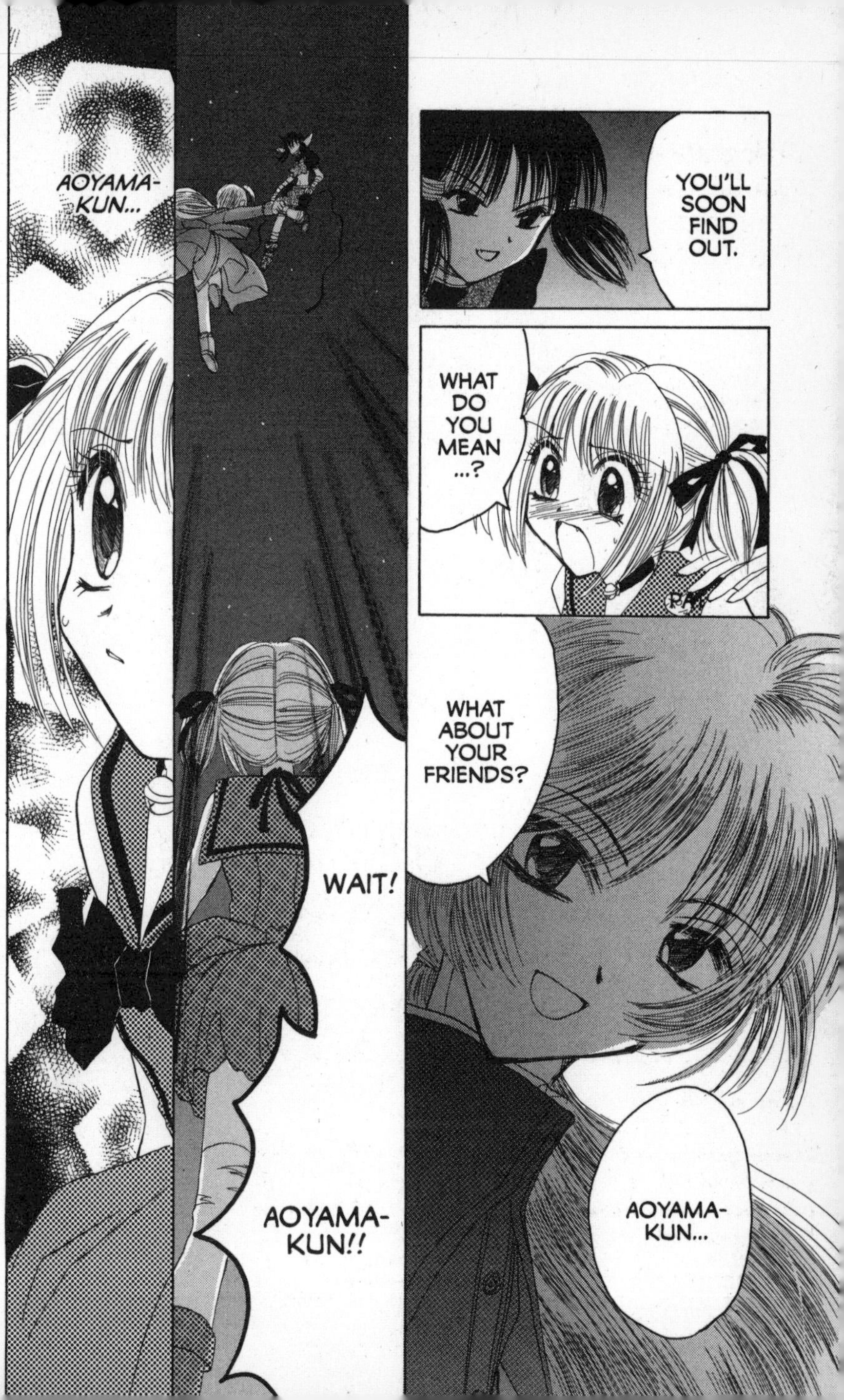
YOU'LL SOON FIND OUT.
WHAT DO YOU MEAN ...?
WHAT ABOUT YOUR FRIENDS?
AOYAMA-KUN...
WAIT!
AOYAMA-KUN!!
AOYAMA-KUN...

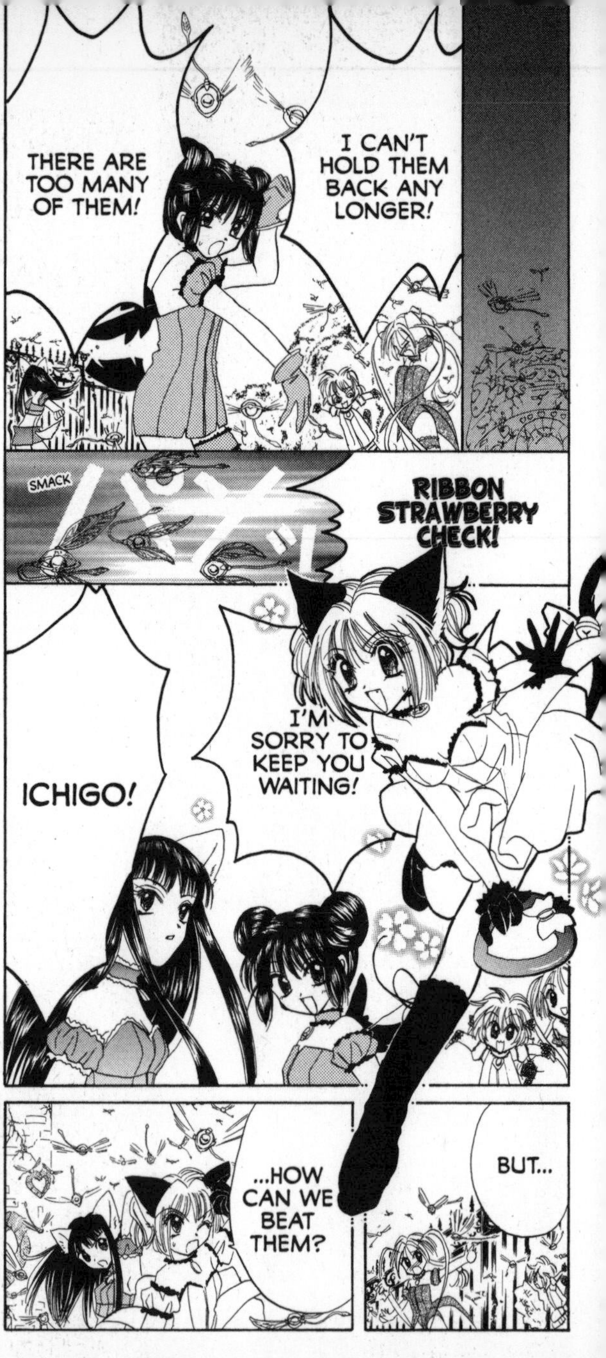
I CAN'T HOLD THEM BACK ANY LONGER!
THERE ARE TOO MANY OF THEM!
RIBBON STRAWBERRY CHECK!
SMACK
I'M SORRY TO KEEP YOU WAITING!
ICHIGO!
BUT...
...HOW CAN WE BEAT THEM?

Tokyo Mew Mew:
Ichigo's Costume Wanted! Part 4

BEST IDEAS AWARD

ATSUKO HISANO-CHAN,
HOKKAIDO PREFECTURE,
JUNIOR HIGH FRESHMAN

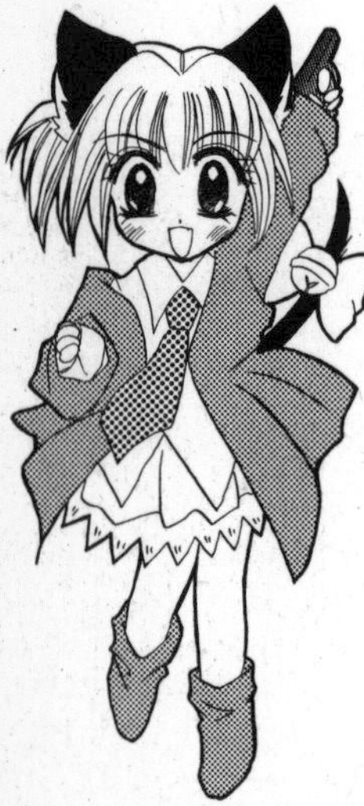

I love baggy clothes and I think wearing men's clothing loosely, especially the coat that hangs over the shoulders, is awesome. The peeking lace was the icing on the cake.

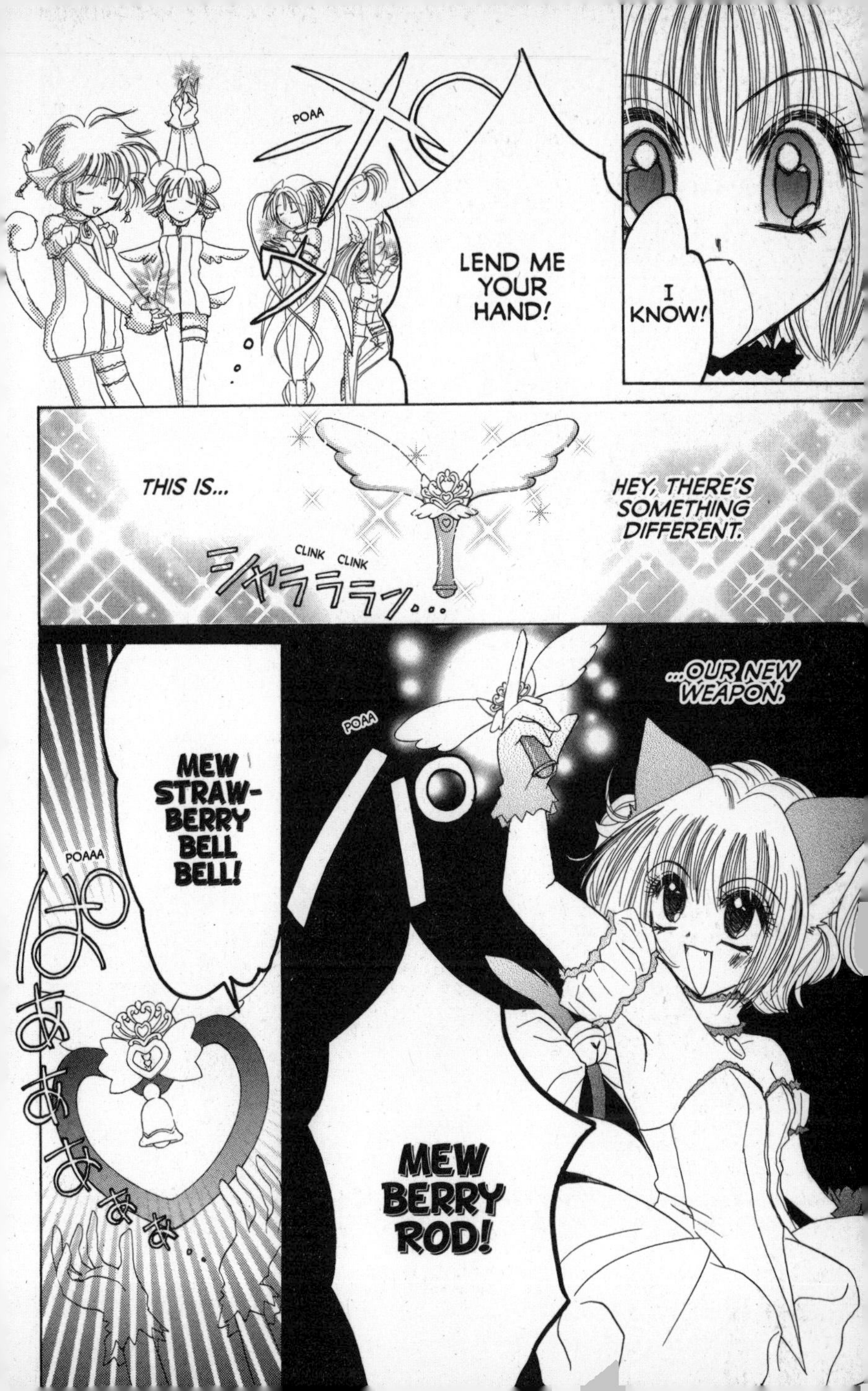
I KNOW!
LEND ME YOUR HAND!
POAA
HEY, THERE'S SOMETHING DIFFERENT.
CLINK CLINK
シャラララン
THIS IS...
...OUR NEW WEAPON.
POAA
MEW BERRY ROD!
MEW STRAW-BERRY BELL BELL!
POAAA

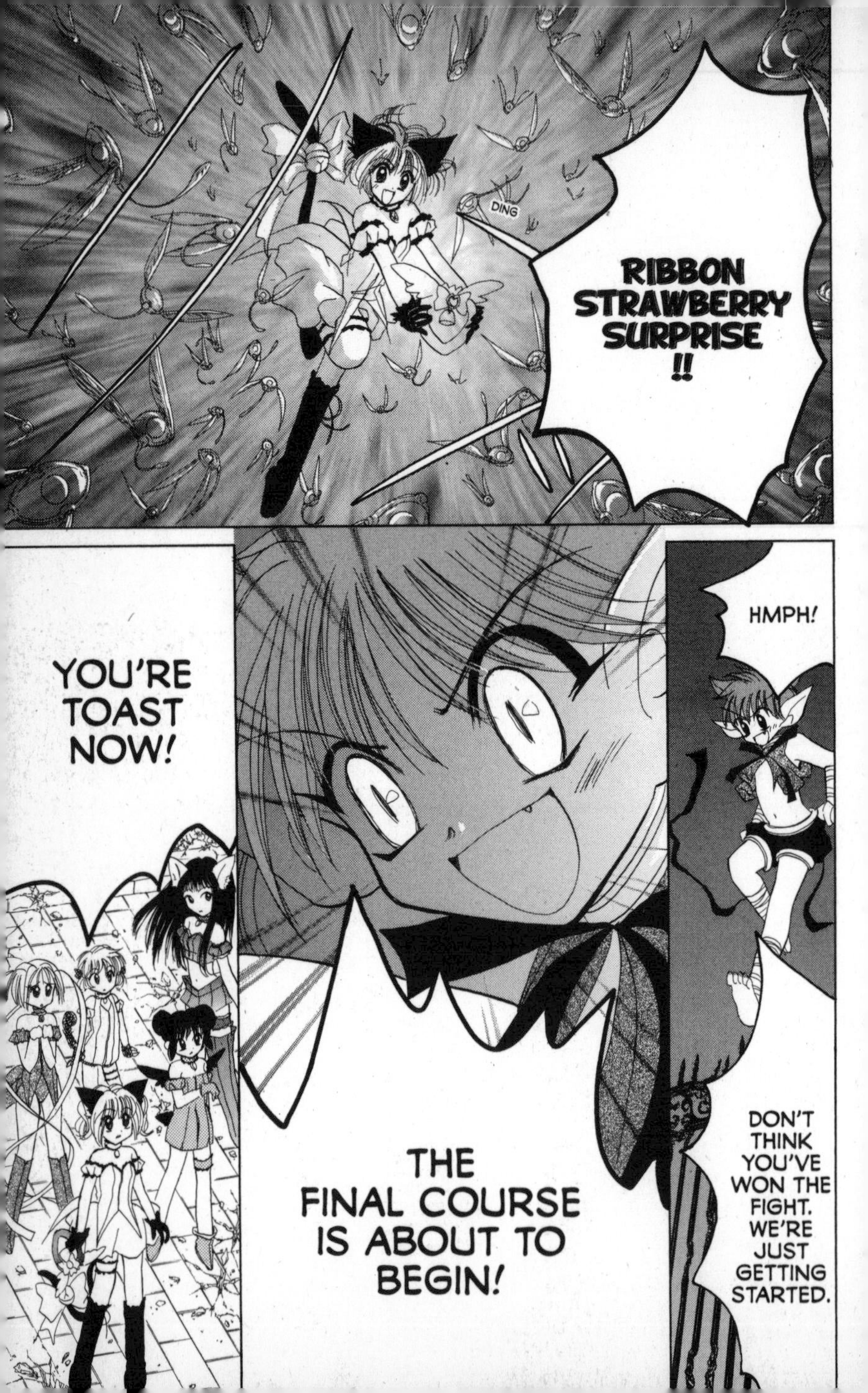
RIBBON STRAWBERRY SURPRISE !!
DING
HMPH!
DON'T THINK YOU'VE WON THE FIGHT. WE'RE JUST GETTING STARTED.
THE FINAL COURSE IS ABOUT TO BEGIN!
YOU'RE TOAST NOW!

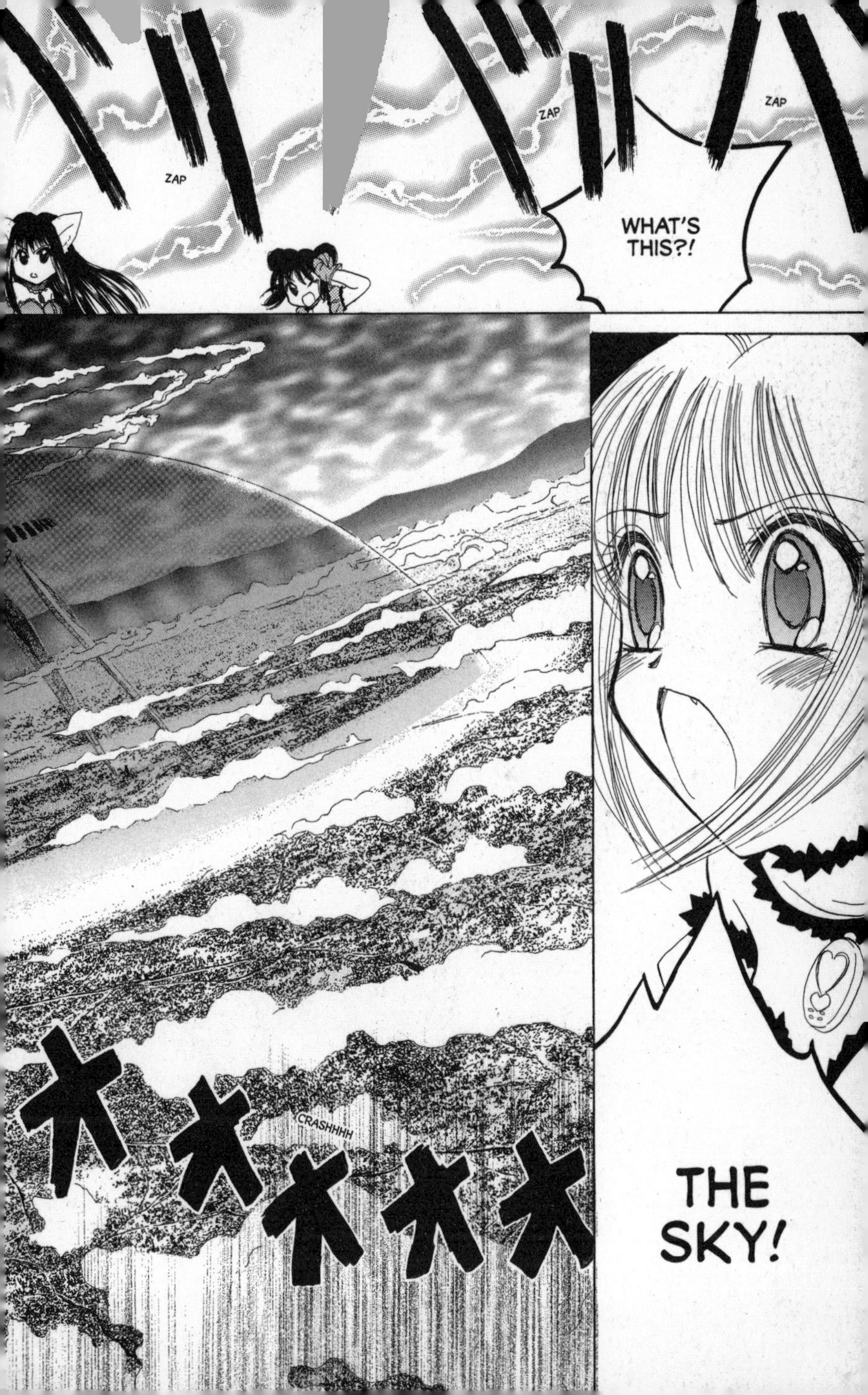
ZAP
WHAT'S THIS?!
ZAP
ZAP
THE SKY!
CRASHHHH

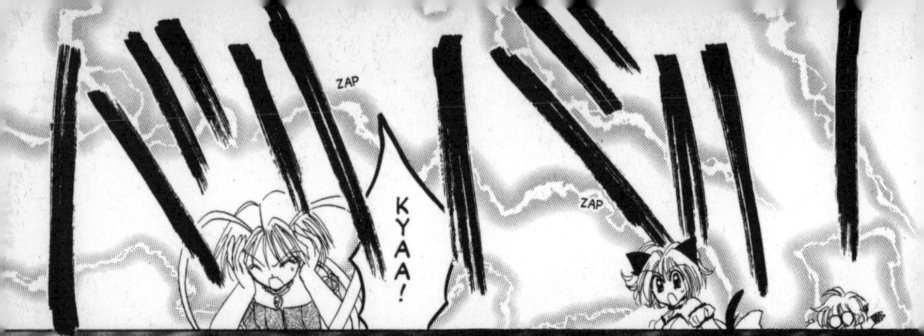
ZAP
KYAA!
ZAP
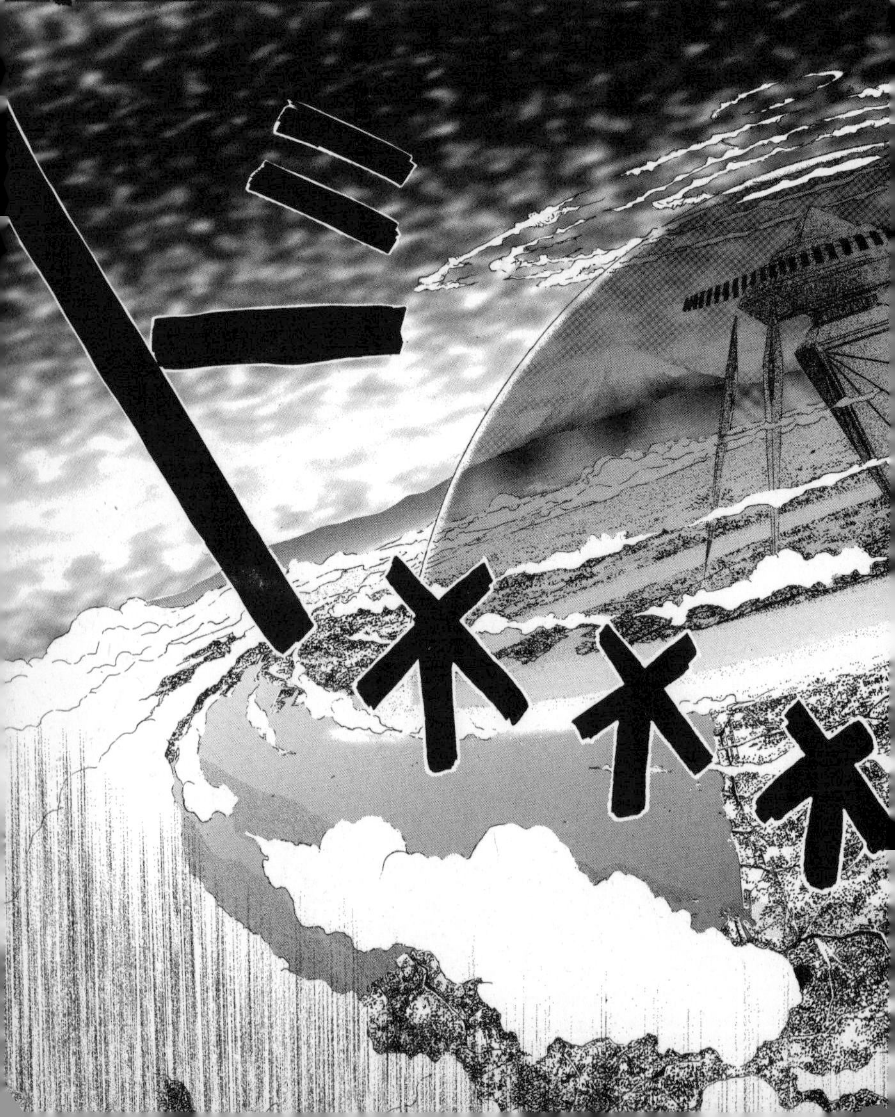

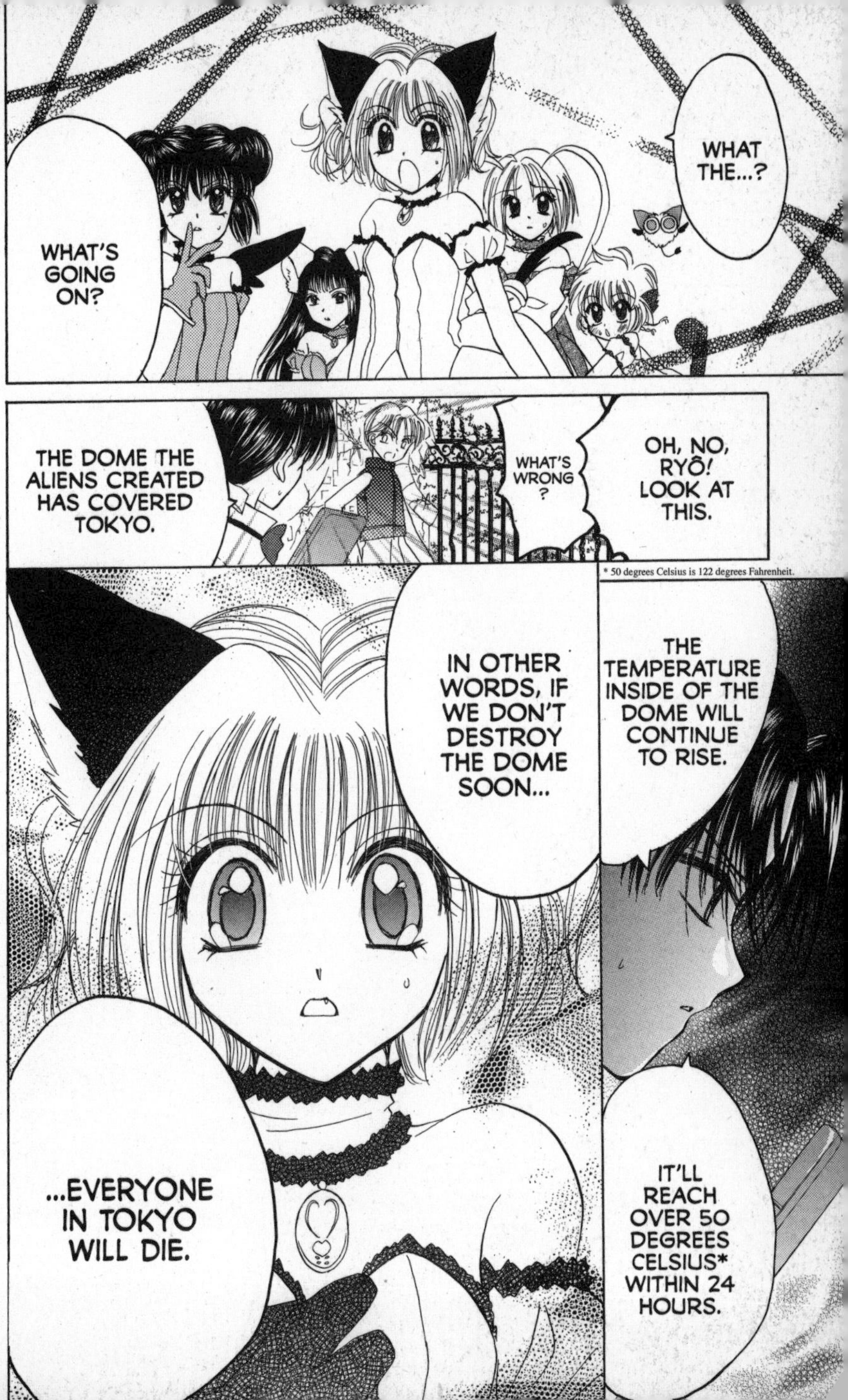
WHAT THE...?
WHAT'S GOING ON?
OH, NO, RYÔ! LOOK AT THIS.
WHAT'S WRONG ?
THE DOME THE ALIENS CREATED HAS COVERED TOKYO.
THE TEMPERATURE INSIDE OF THE DOME WILL CONTINUE TO RISE.
IT'LL REACH OVER 50 DEGREES CELSIUS* WITHIN 24 HOURS.
IN OTHER WORDS, IF WE DON'T DESTROY THE DOME SOON...
...EVERYONE IN TOKYO WILL DIE.

* 50 degrees Celsius is 122 degrees Fahrenheit.

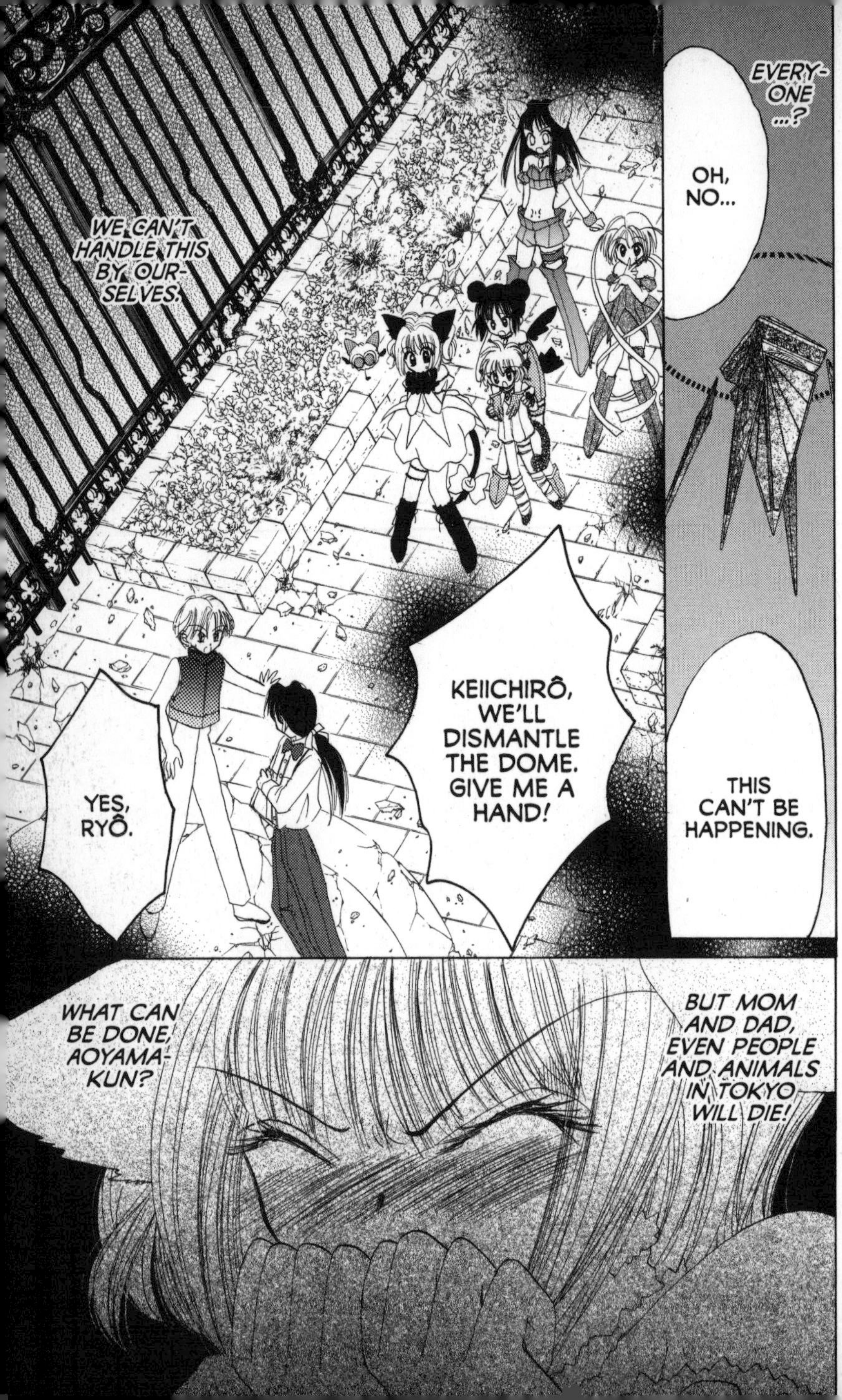
EVERY-ONE ...?
OH, NO...
THIS CAN'T BE HAPPENING.
WE CAN'T HANDLE THIS BY OUR-SELVES.
KEIICHIRÔ, WE'LL DISMANTLE THE DOME. GIVE ME A HAND!
YES, RYÔ.
BUT MOM AND DAD, EVEN PEOPLE AND ANIMALS IN TOKYO WILL DIE!
WHAT CAN BE DONE, AOYAMA-KUN?

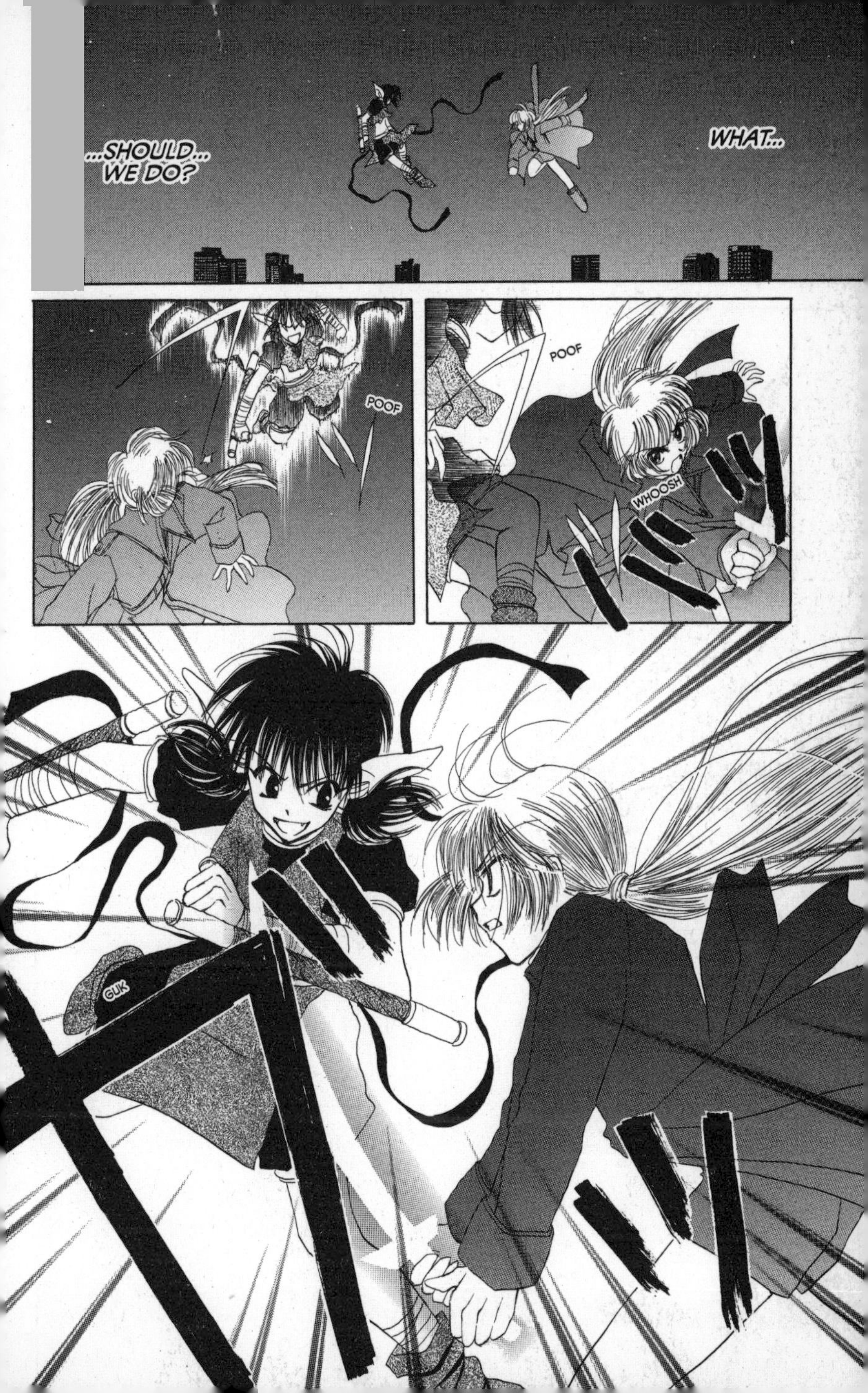
WHAT...
...SHOULD... WE DO?
POOF
WHOOSH
POOF
GUK

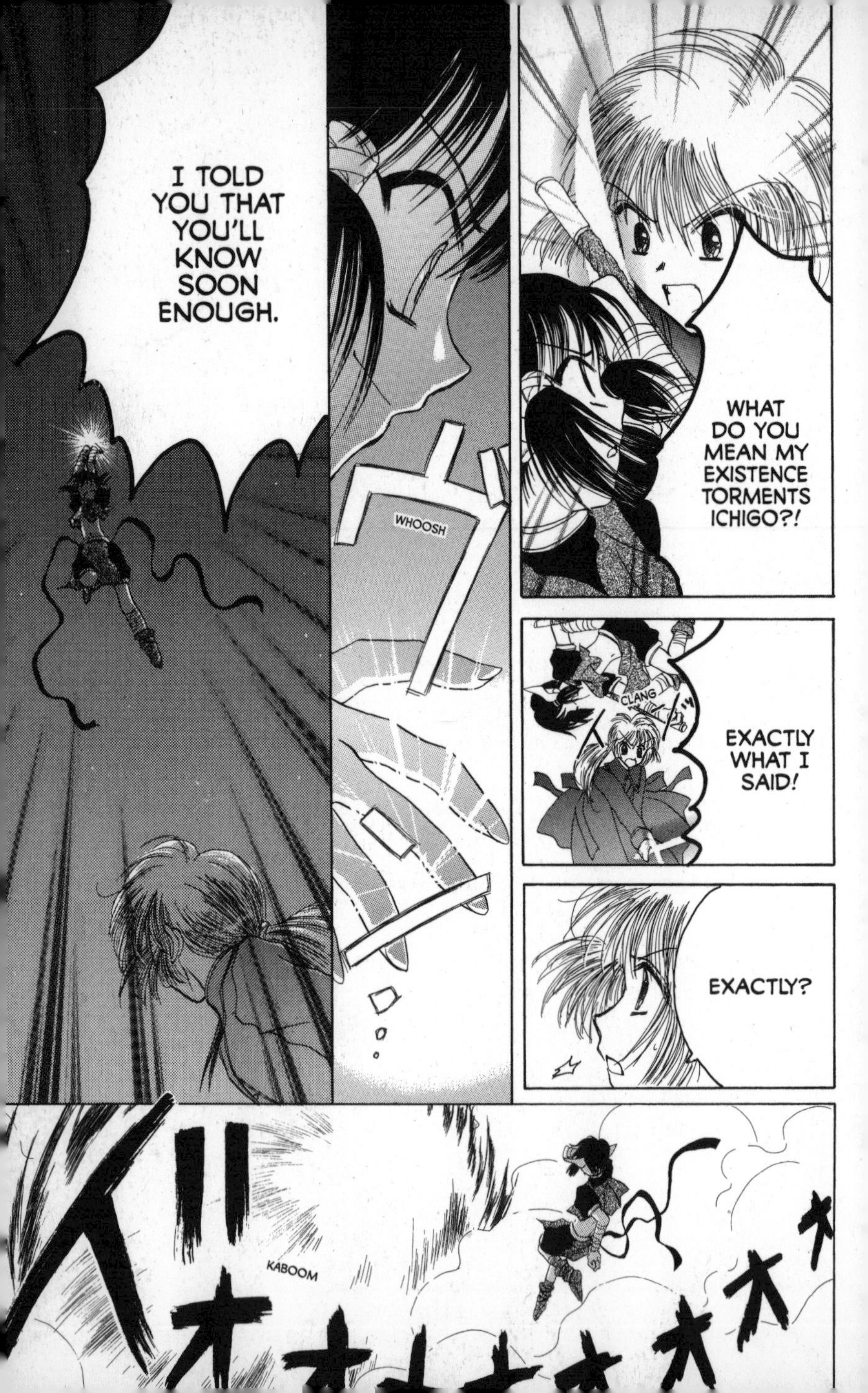
WHAT DO YOU MEAN MY EXISTENCE TORMENTS ICHIGO?!
CLANG
EXACTLY WHAT I SAID!
EXACTLY?
WHOOSH
I TOLD YOU THAT YOU'LL KNOW SOON ENOUGH.
KABOOM

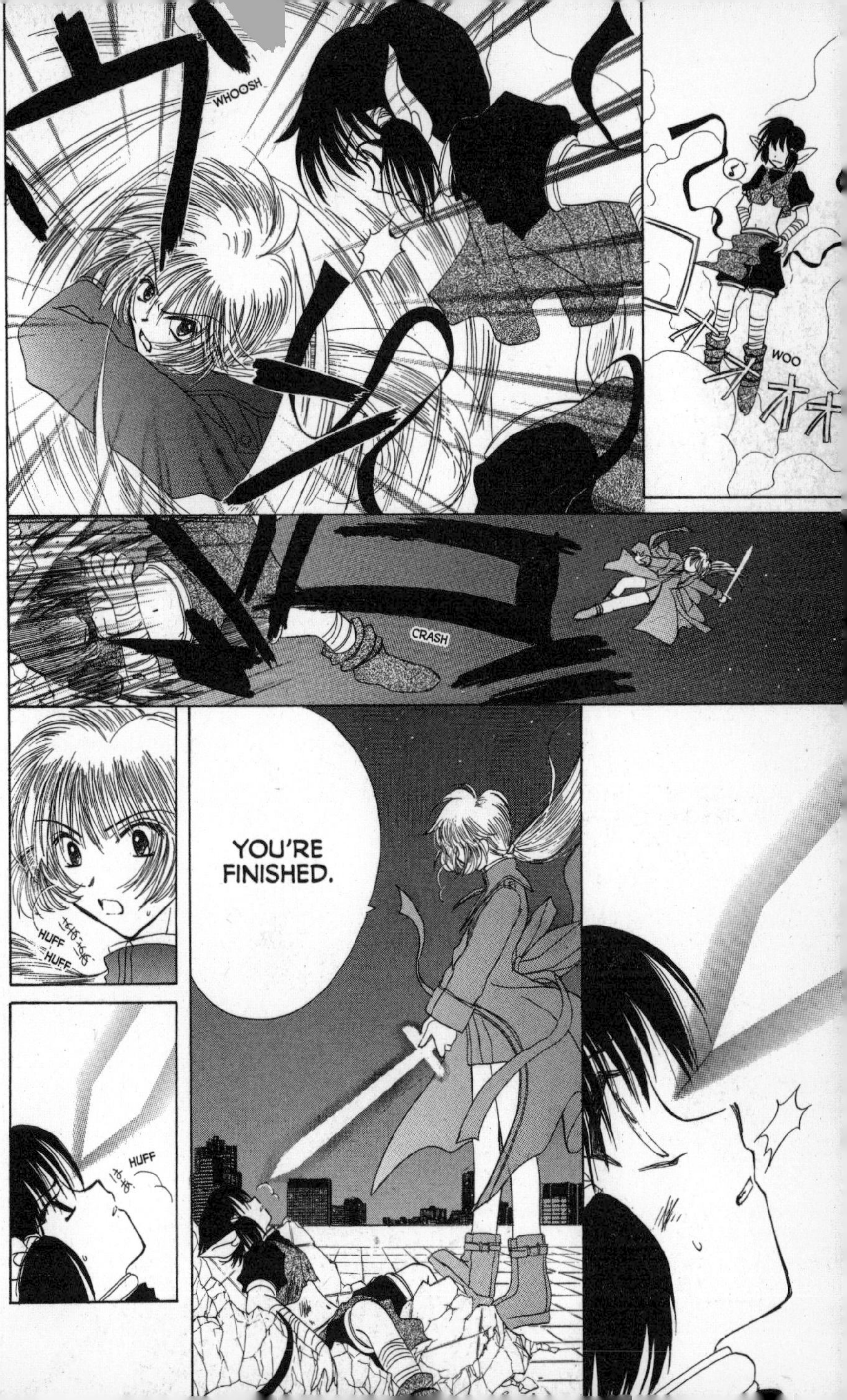
WOO
WHOOSH
CRASH
YOU'RE FINISHED.
HUFF
HUFF
HUFF

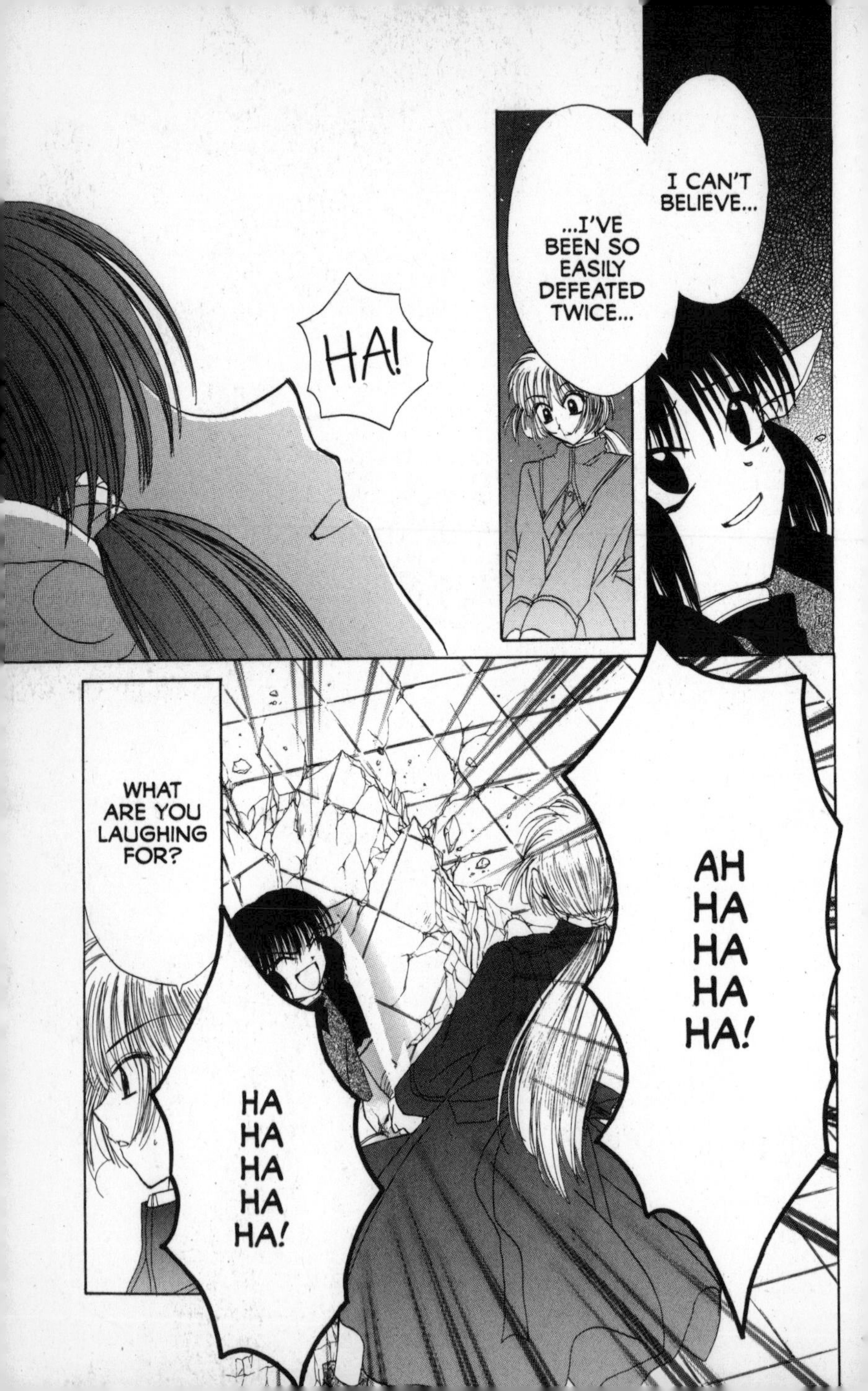

I CAN'T BELIEVE...
...I'VE BEEN SO EASILY DEFEATED TWICE...
HA!
AH HA HA HA HA!
WHAT ARE YOU LAUGHING FOR?
HA HA HA HA HA!

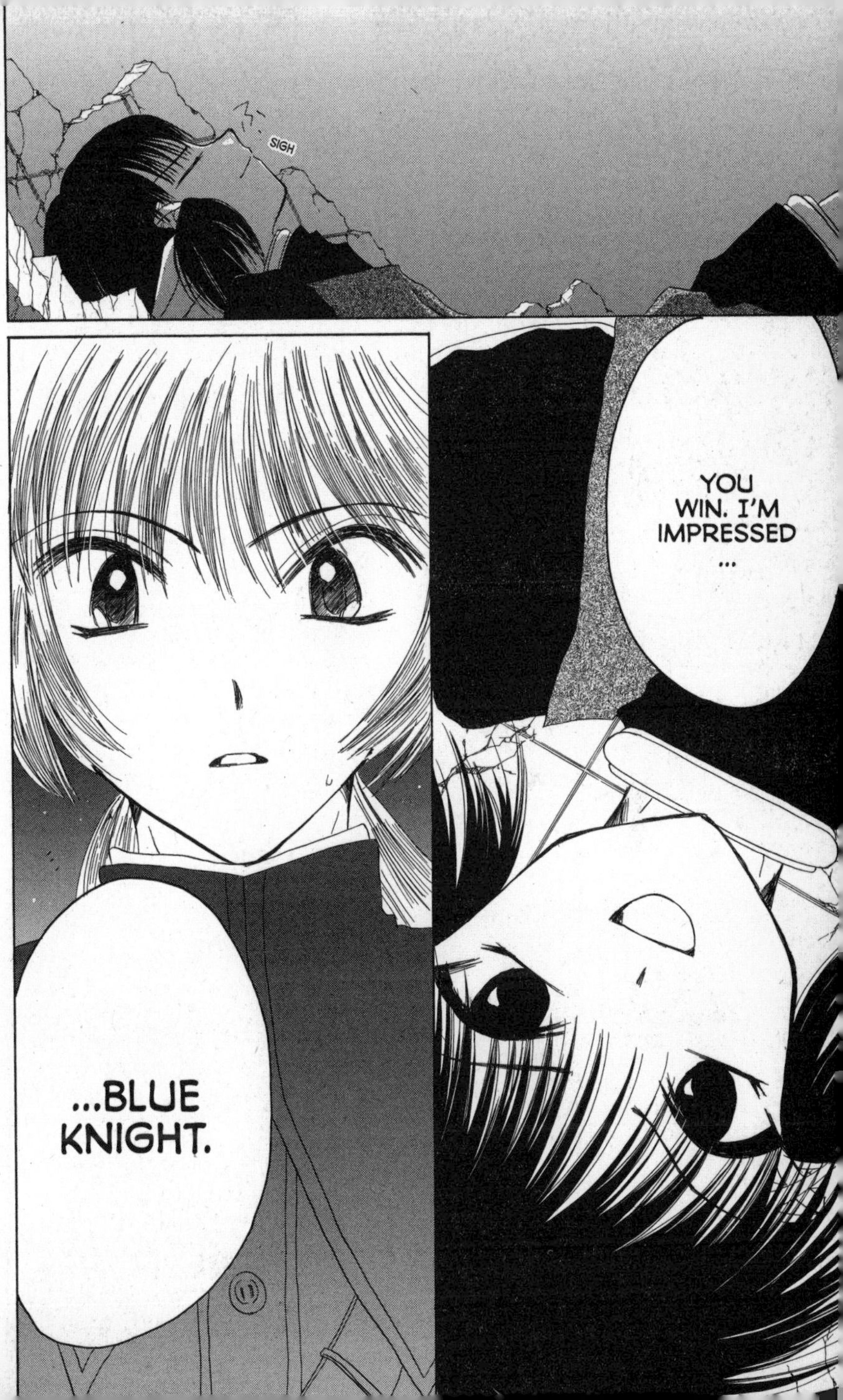
SIGH
YOU WIN. I'M IMPRESSED ...
...BLUE KNIGHT.

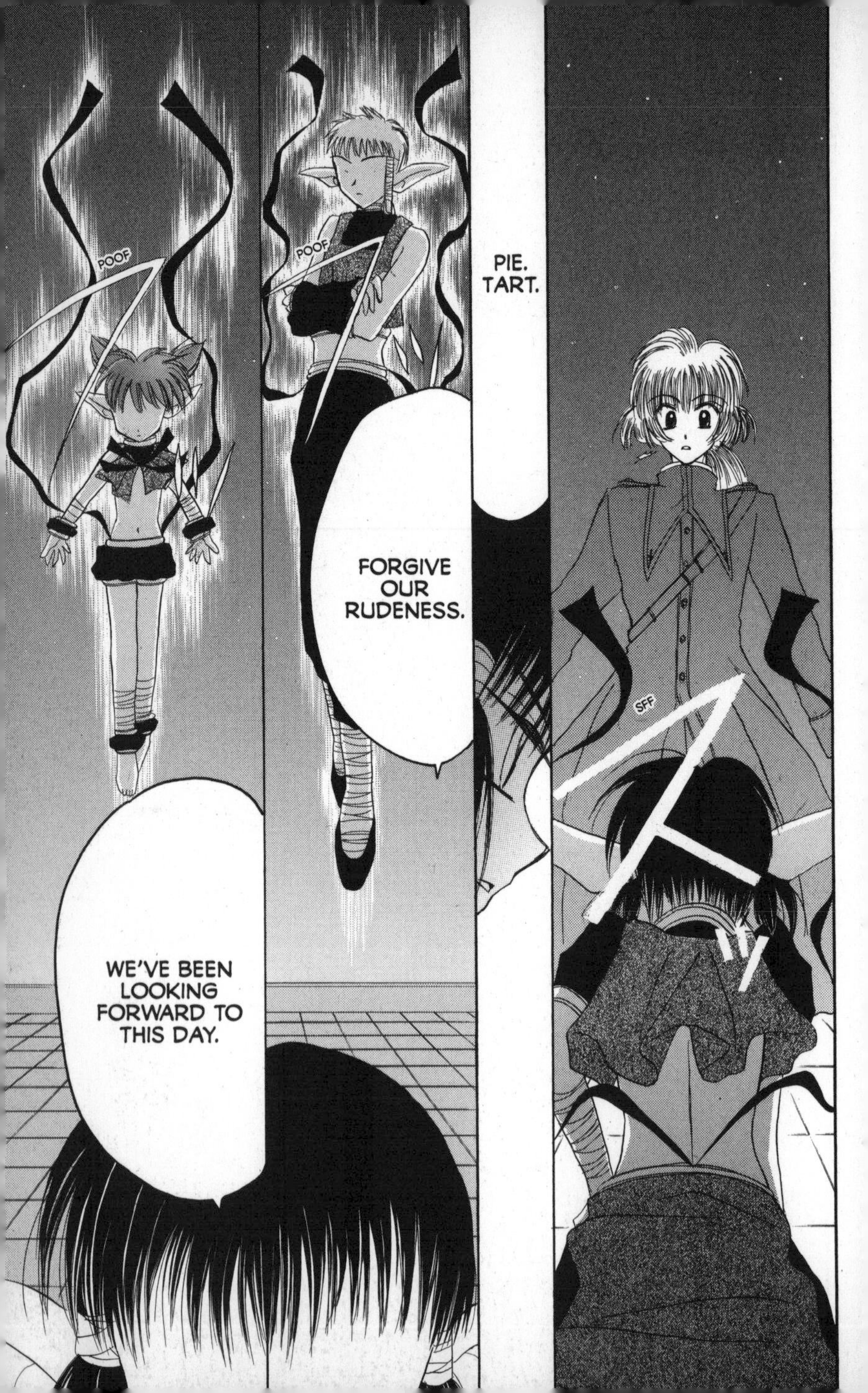
PIE. TART.
SFF
POOF
FORGIVE OUR RUDENESS.
POOF
WE'VE BEEN LOOKING FORWARD TO THIS DAY.

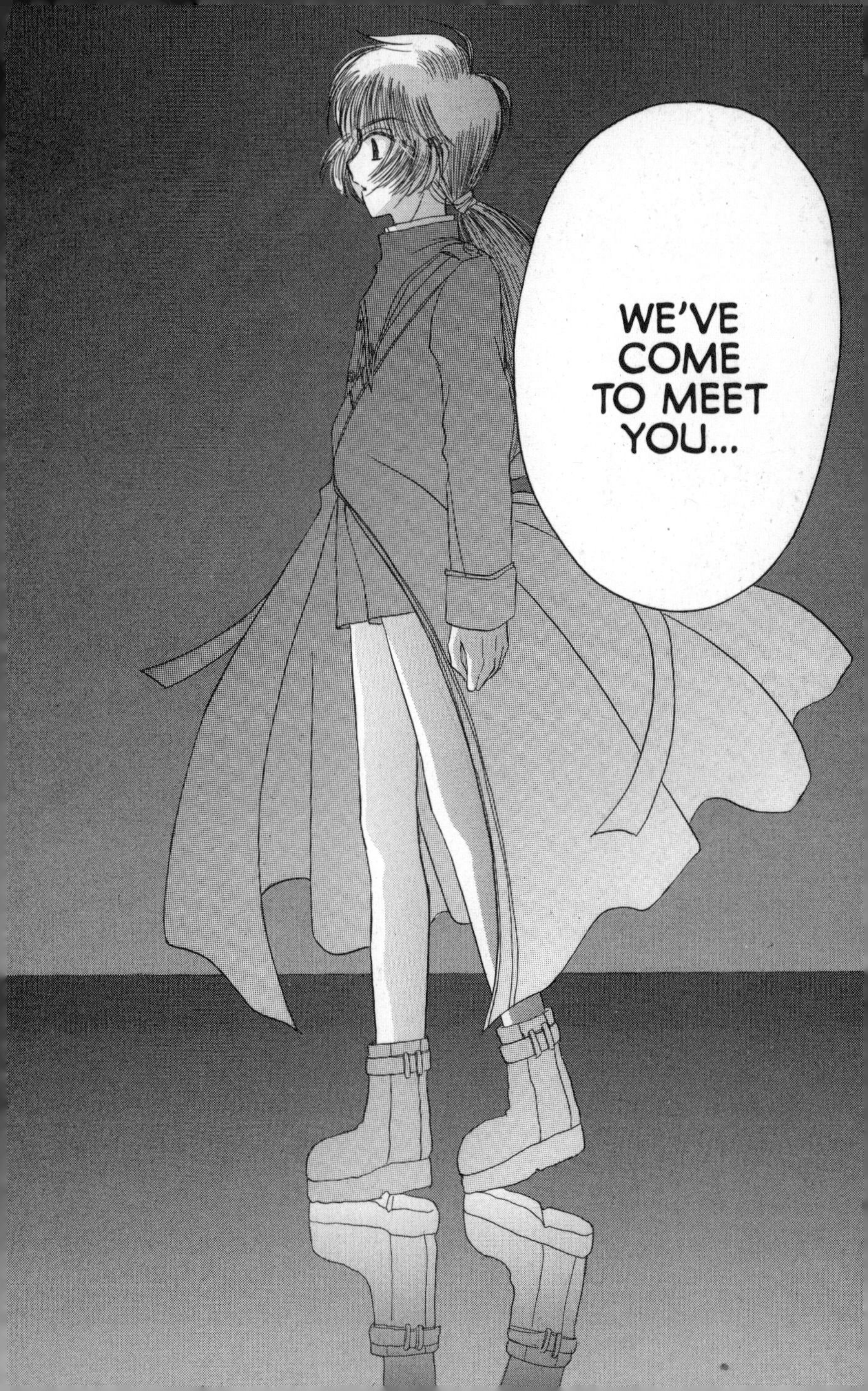
WE'VE COME TO MEET YOU...

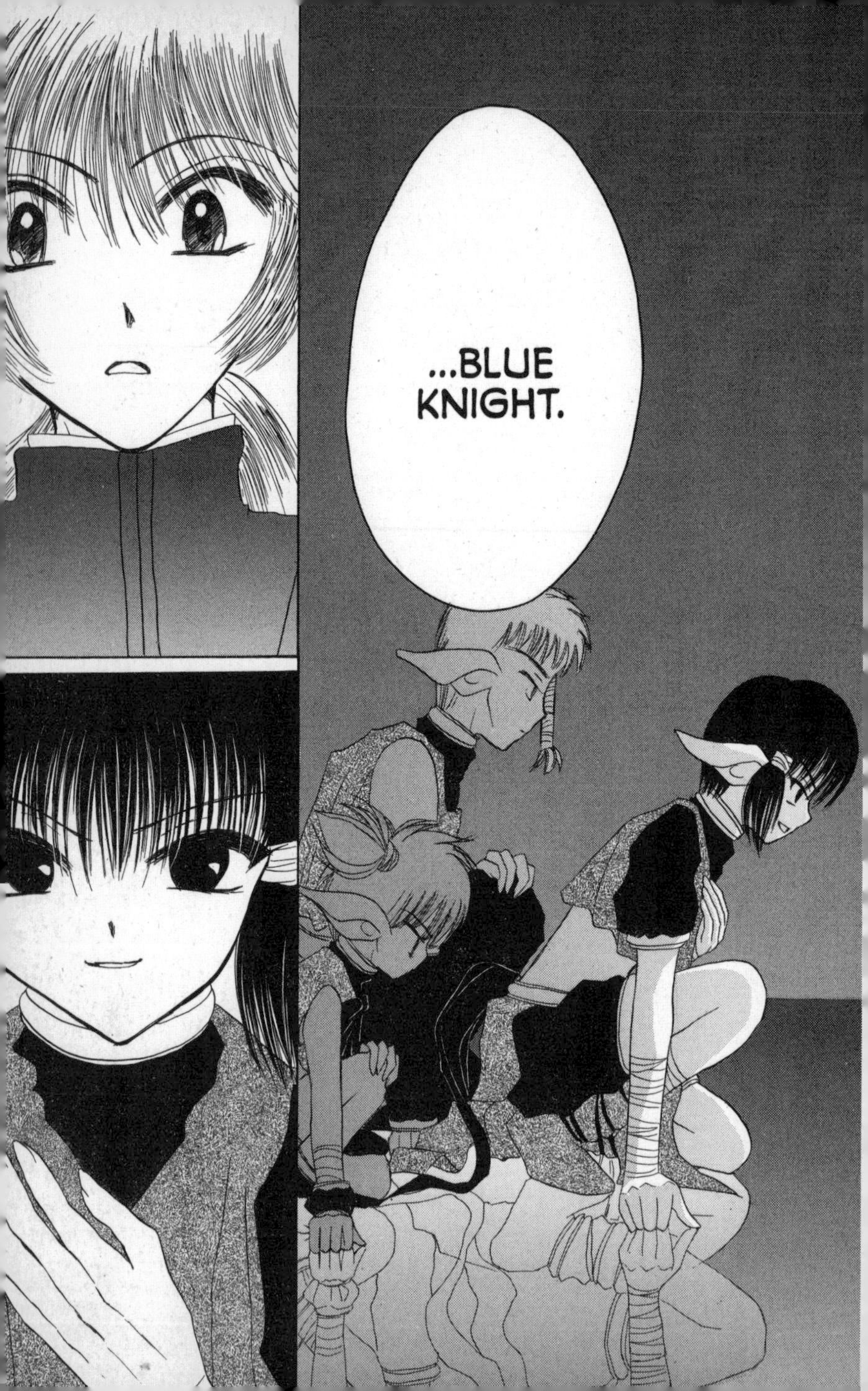
...BLUE
KNIGHT.

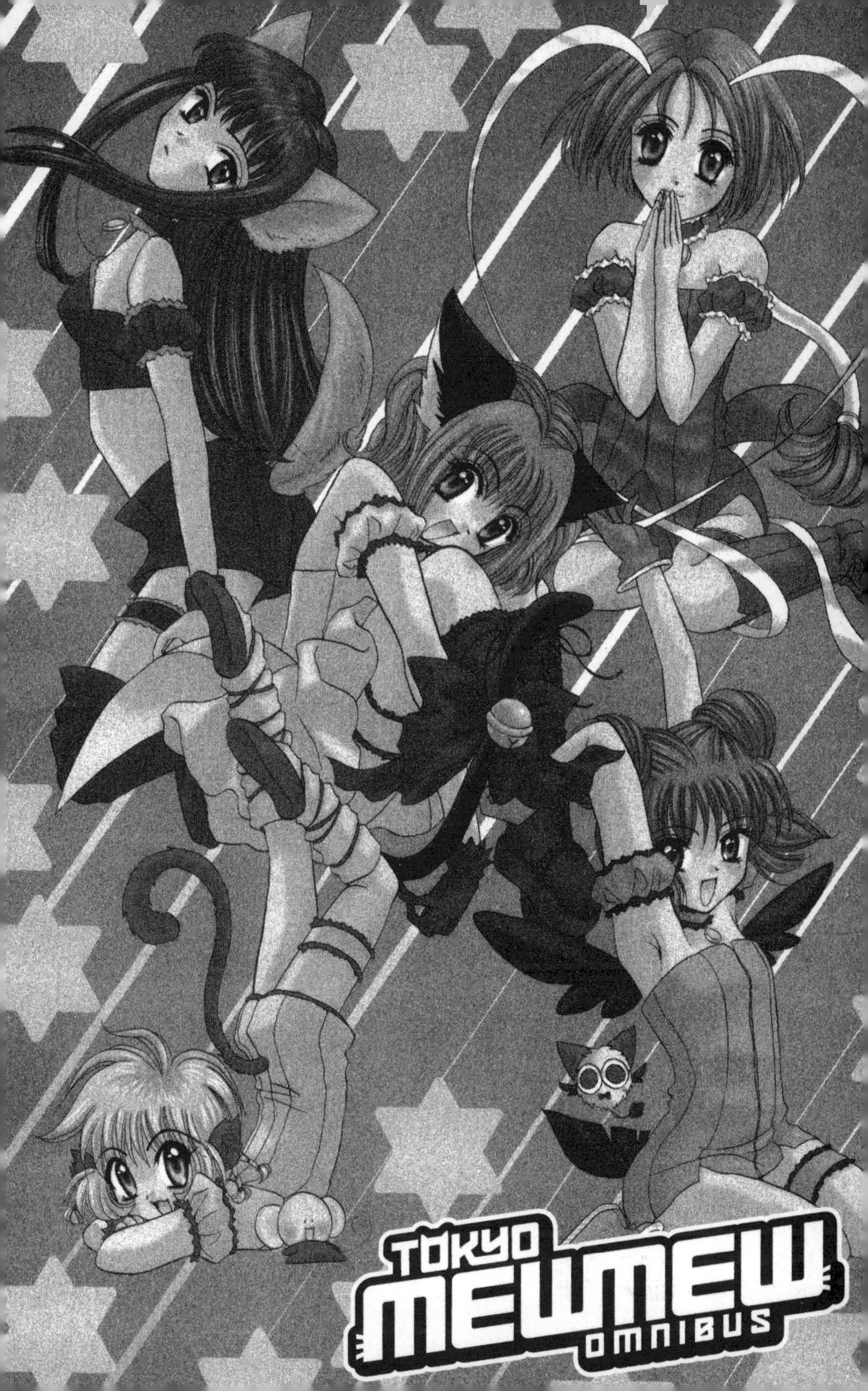
TOKYO
MEWMEW
OMNIBUS

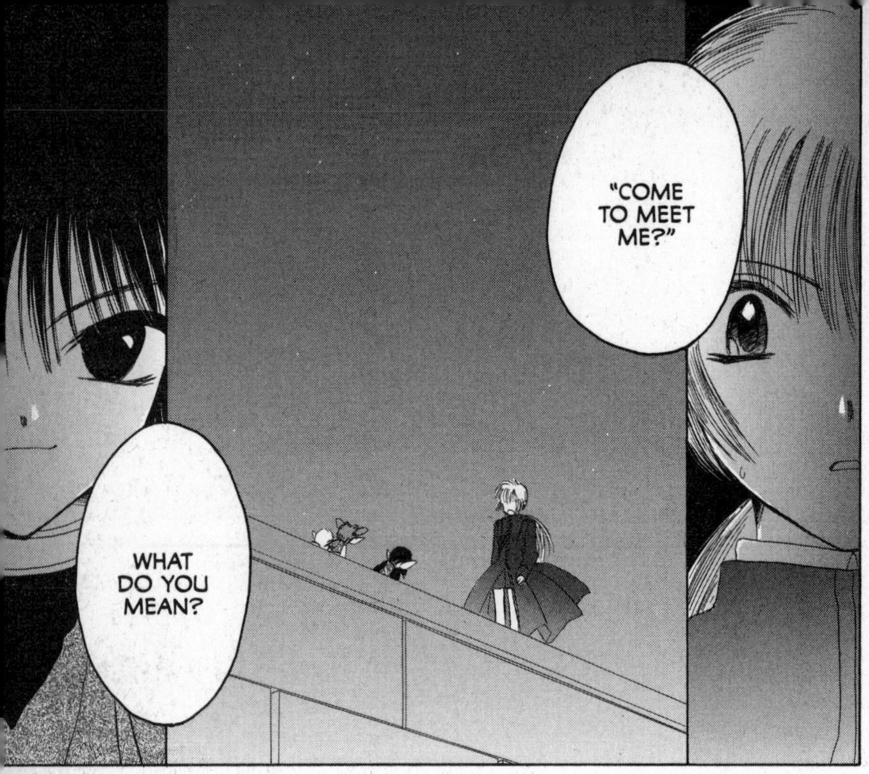
"COME TO MEET ME?"
WHAT DO YOU MEAN?

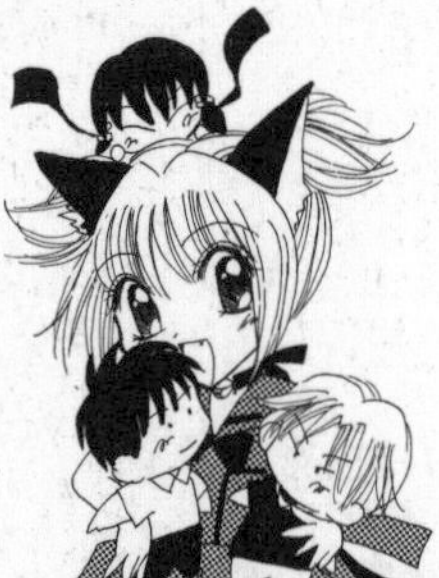

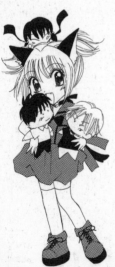

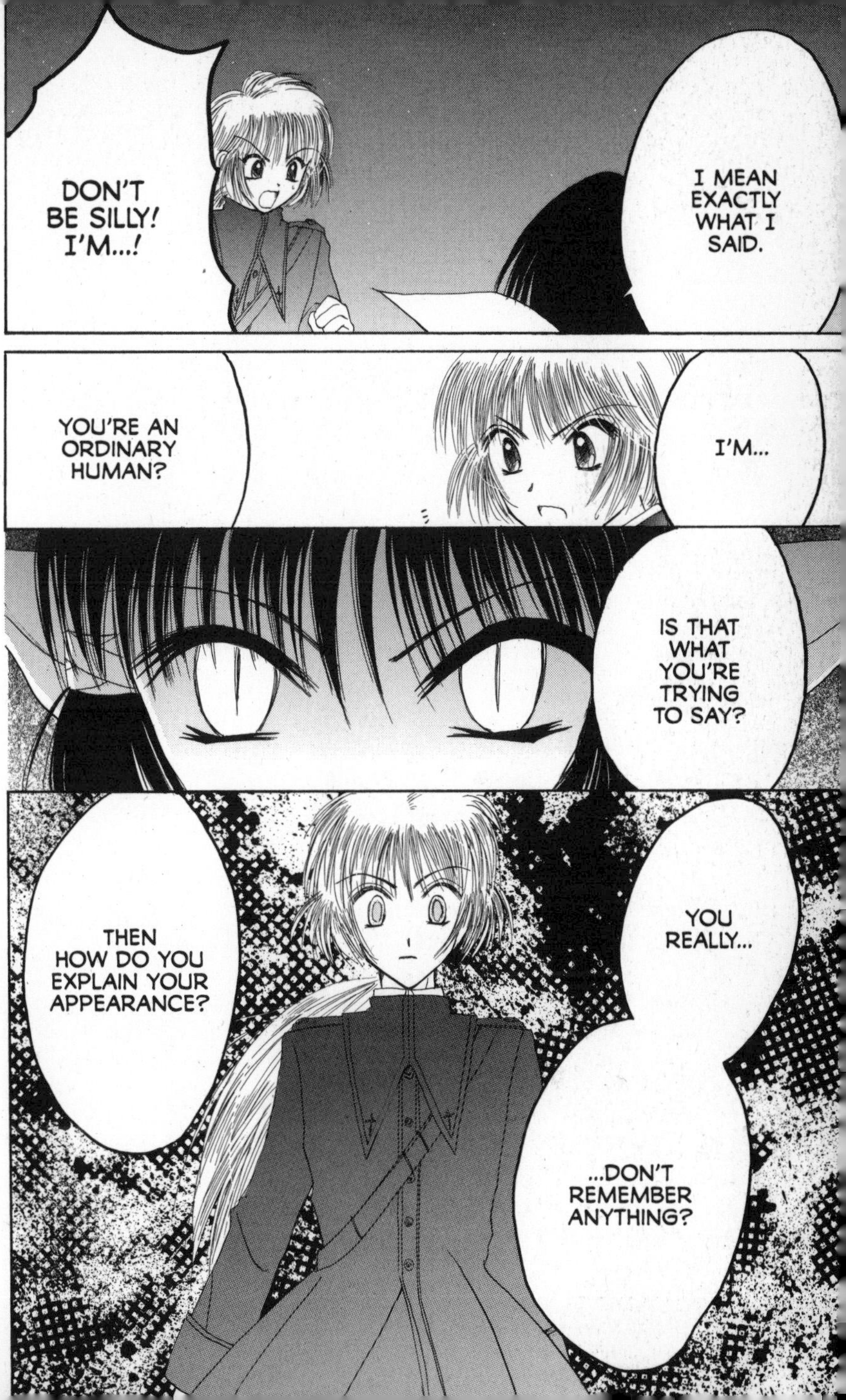
I MEAN EXACTLY WHAT I SAID.
DON'T BE SILLY! I'M...!
I'M...
YOU'RE AN ORDINARY HUMAN?
IS THAT WHAT YOU'RE TRYING TO SAY?
YOU REALLY...
...DON'T REMEMBER ANYTHING?
THEN HOW DO YOU EXPLAIN YOUR APPEARANCE?

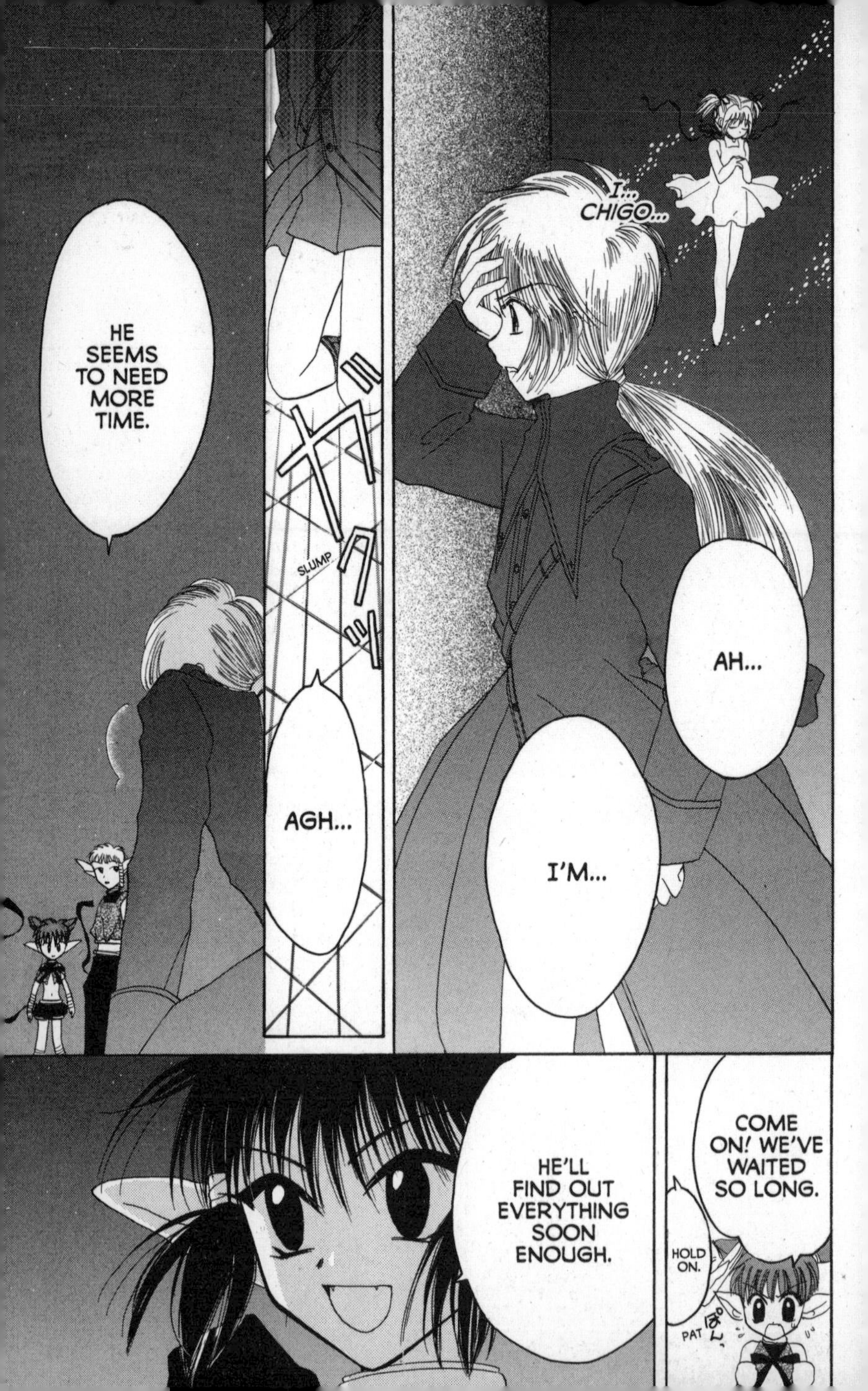
I... CHIGO...
AH...
I'M...
SLUMP
AGH...
HE SEEMS TO NEED MORE TIME.
COME ON! WE'VE WAITED SO LONG.
HOLD ON.
PAT
HE'LL FIND OUT EVERYTHING SOON ENOUGH.

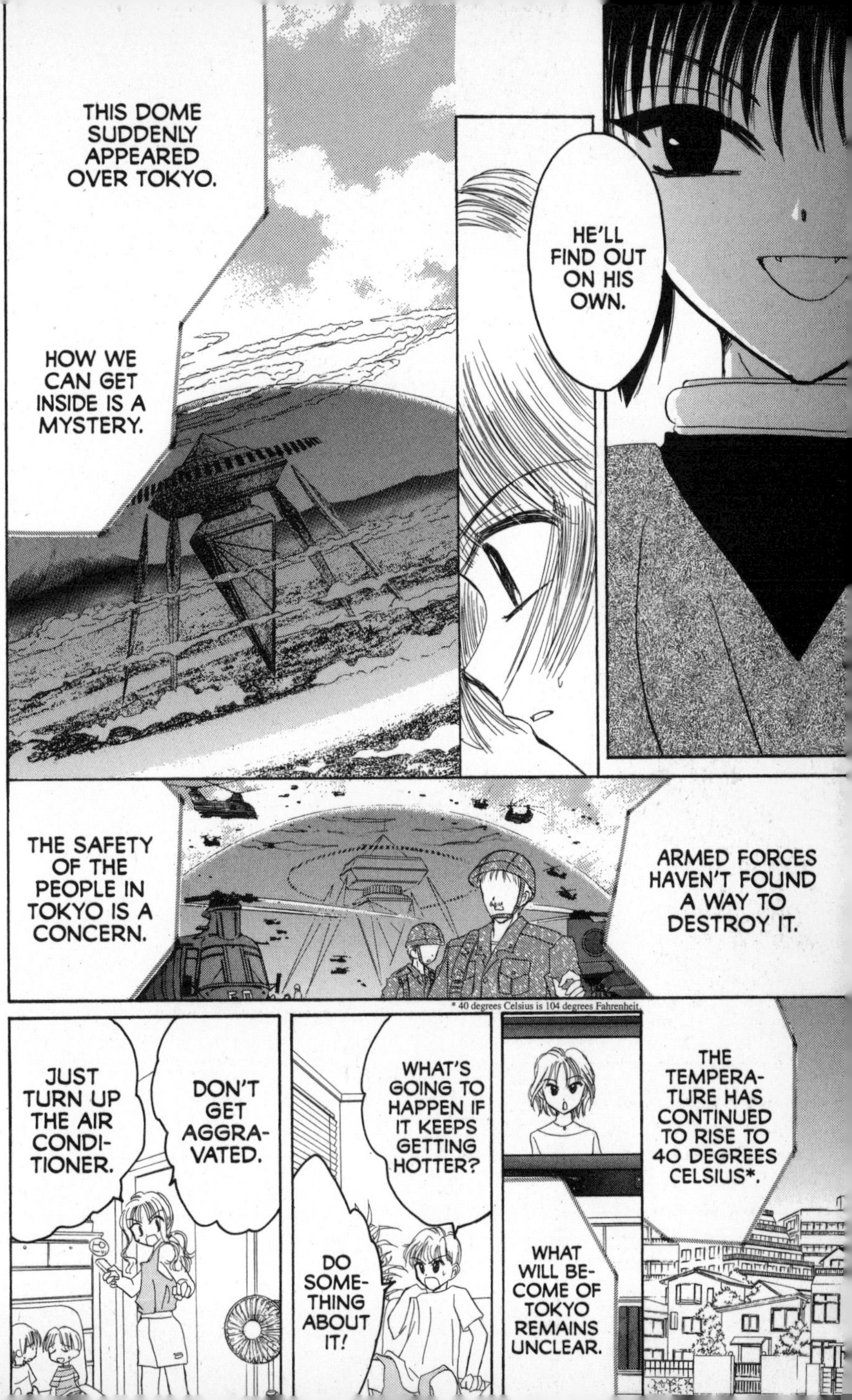
HE'LL FIND OUT ON HIS OWN.
THIS DOME SUDDENLY APPEARED OVER TOKYO.
HOW WE CAN GET INSIDE IS A MYSTERY.
ARMED FORCES HAVEN'T FOUND A WAY TO DESTROY IT.
THE SAFETY OF THE PEOPLE IN TOKYO IS A CONCERN.
THE TEMPERATURE HAS CONTINUED TO RISE TO 40 DEGREES CELSIUS*.
WHAT WILL BECOME OF TOKYO REMAINS UNCLEAR.
WHAT'S GOING TO HAPPEN IF IT KEEPS GETTING HOTTER?
DO SOMETHING ABOUT IT!
DON'T GET AGGRAVATED.
JUST TURN UP THE AIR CONDITIONER.

* 40 degrees Celsius is 104 degrees Fahrenheit.

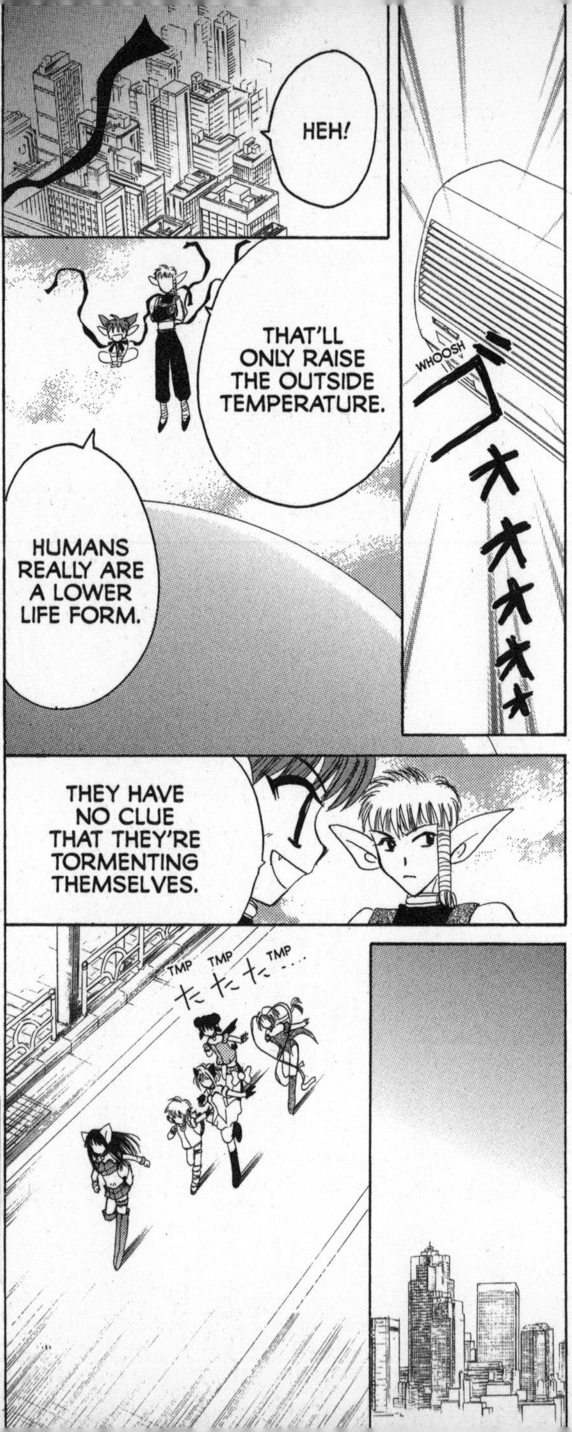
WHOOSH
HEH!
THAT'LL ONLY RAISE THE OUTSIDE TEMPERATURE.
HUMANS REALLY ARE A LOWER LIFE FORM.
THEY HAVE NO CLUE THAT THEY'RE TORMENTING THEMSELVES.
TMP TMP TMP
たたた……

Tokyo Mew Mew:

Ichigo's Costume Wanted! Part 5

BEST IDEAS AWARD

MINAKO TANBA-CHAN,
AICHI PREFECTURE,
HIGH SCHOOL SENIOR

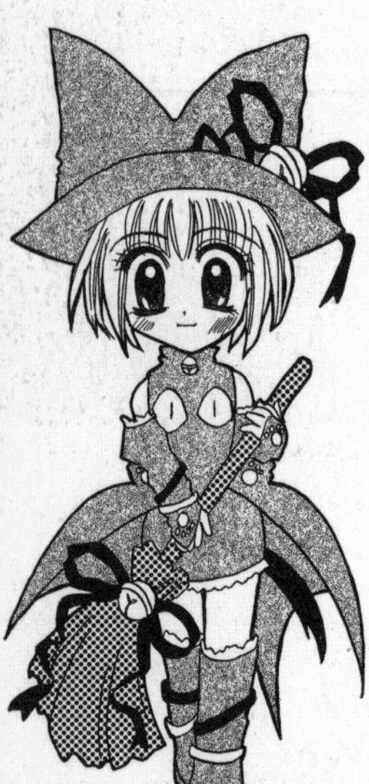

It was the cutest costume for a cosplay I saw in the contest. It's nice that you recognize a cat in its silhouette. The ribbons are arranged nicely too. ♥
I want this broom!

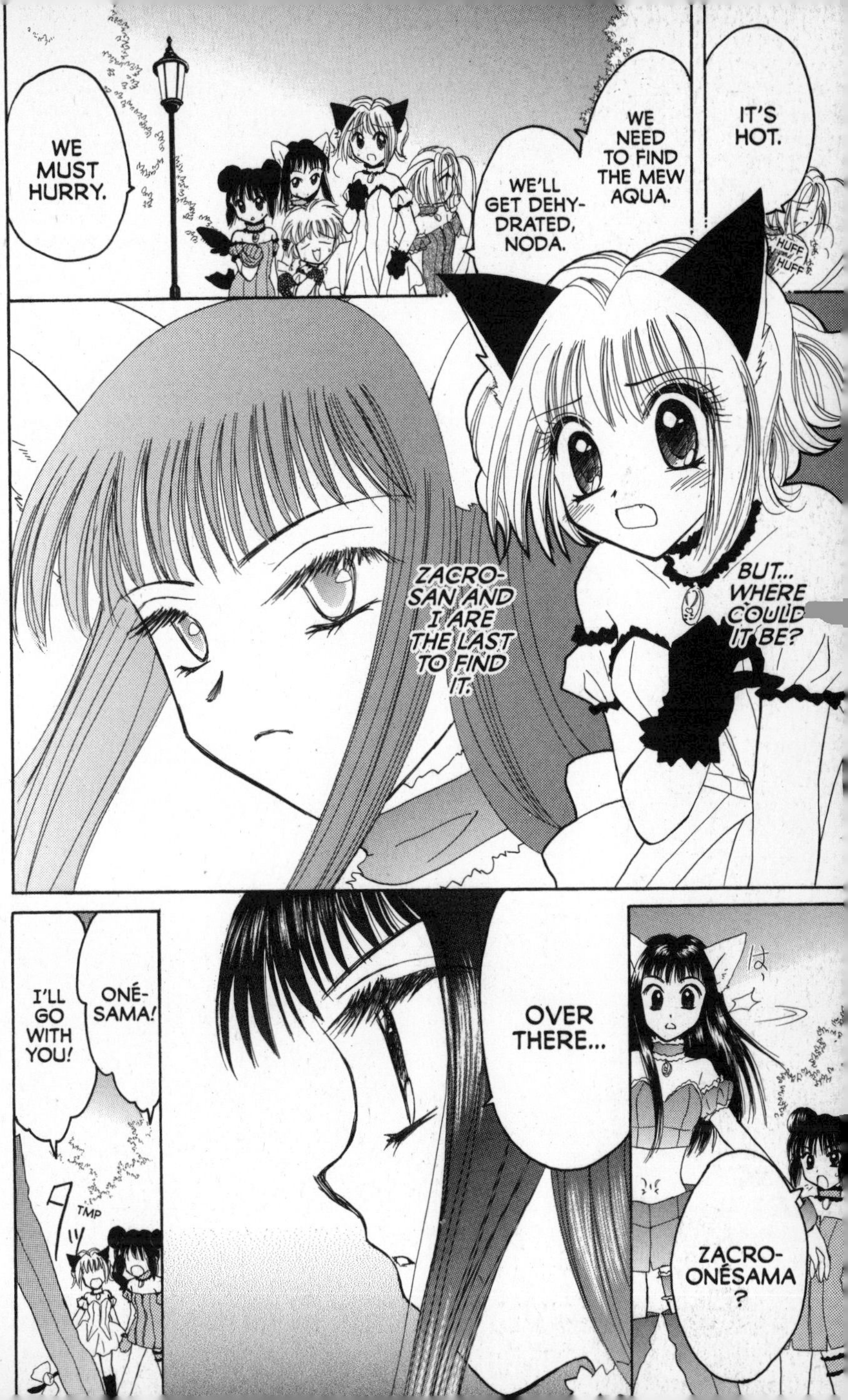
IT'S HOT.
HUFF HUFF
WE NEED TO FIND THE MEW AQUA.
WE'LL GET DEHY-DRATED, NODA.
WE MUST HURRY.
BUT... WHERE COULD IT BE?
ZACRO-SAN AND I ARE THE LAST TO FIND IT.
は
ZACRO-ONÉSAMA?
OVER THERE...
ONÉ-SAMA!
I'LL GO WITH YOU!
TMP

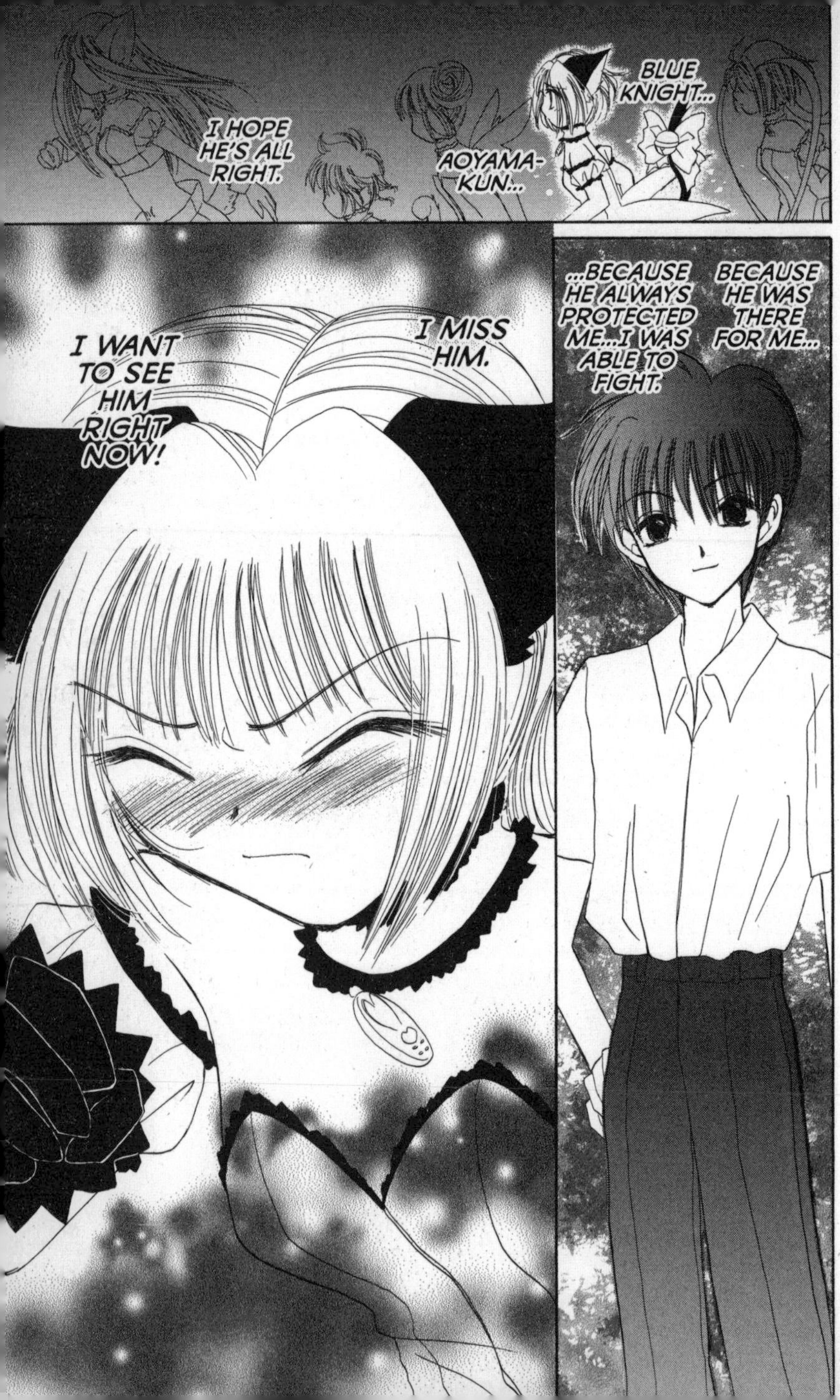
BLUE KNIGHT...
AOYAMA-KUN...
I HOPE HE'S ALL RIGHT.
BECAUSE HE WAS THERE FOR ME...
...BECAUSE HE ALWAYS PROTECTED ME...I WAS ABLE TO FIGHT.
I MISS HIM.
I WANT TO SEE HIM RIGHT NOW!

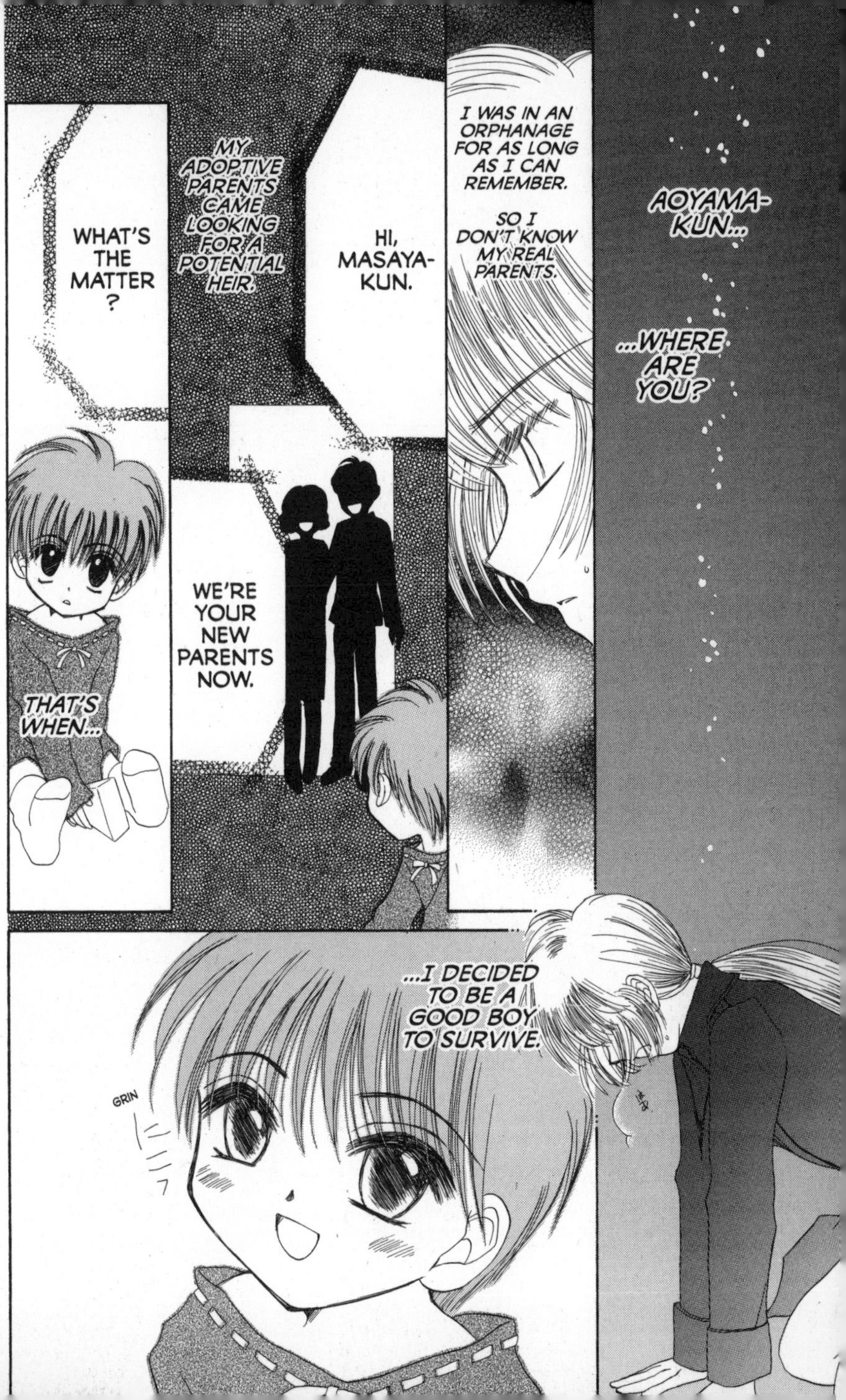
AOYAMA-KUN...
...WHERE ARE YOU?
I WAS IN AN ORPHANAGE FOR AS LONG AS I CAN REMEMBER.
SO I DON'T KNOW MY REAL PARENTS.
MY ADOPTIVE PARENTS CAME LOOKING FOR A POTENTIAL HEIR.
HI, MASAYA-KUN.
WE'RE YOUR NEW PARENTS NOW.
WHAT'S THE MATTER?
THAT'S WHEN...
...I DECIDED TO BE A GOOD BOY TO SURVIVE.
GRIN

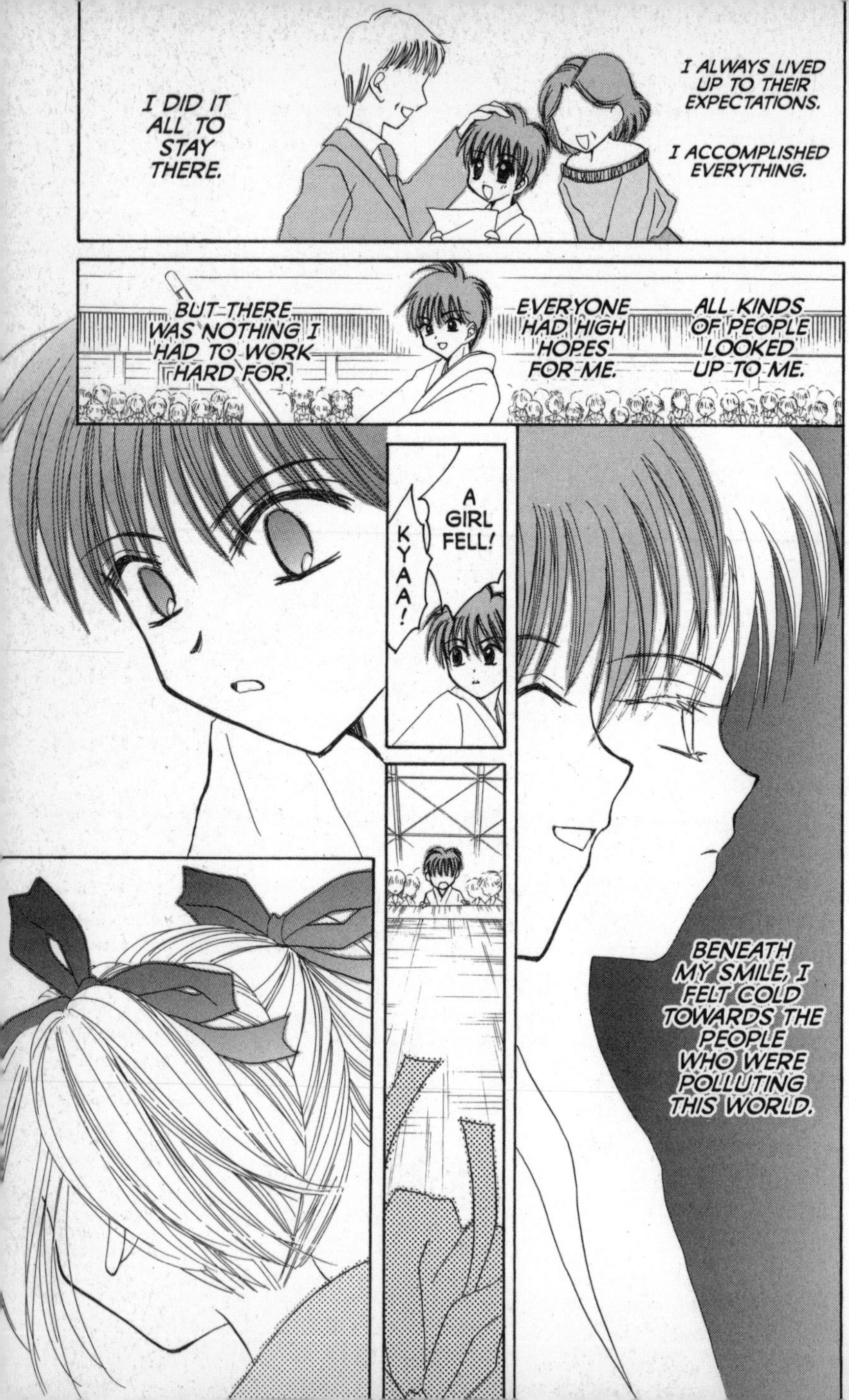
I ALWAYS LIVED UP TO THEIR EXPECTATIONS.
I ACCOMPLISHED EVERYTHING.
I DID IT ALL TO STAY THERE.
ALL KINDS OF PEOPLE LOOKED UP TO ME.
EVERYONE HAD HIGH HOPES FOR ME.
BUT THERE WAS NOTHING I HAD TO WORK HARD FOR.
BENEATH MY SMILE, I FELT COLD TOWARDS THE PEOPLE WHO WERE POLLUTING THIS WORLD.
A GIRL FELL!
KYAA!

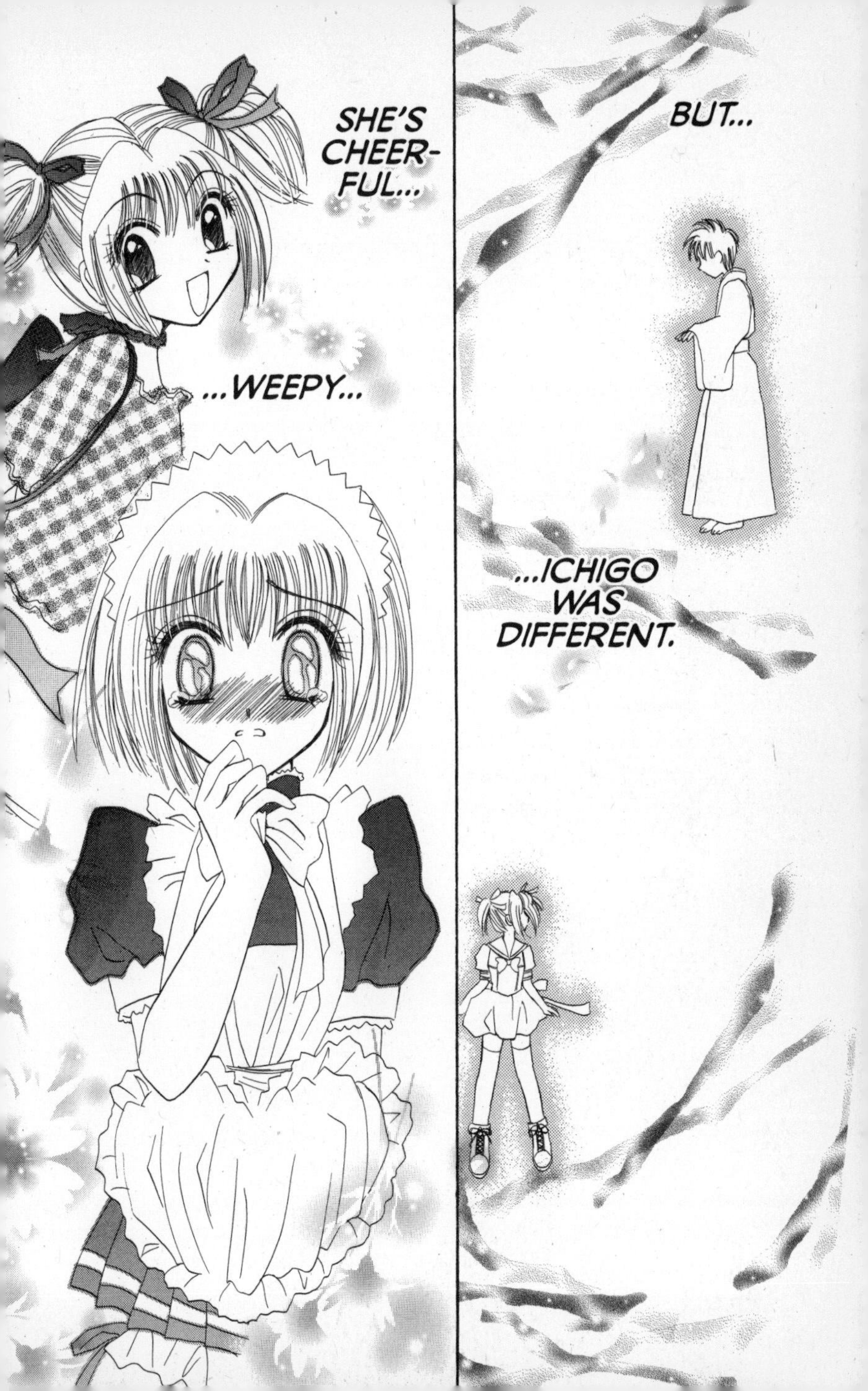
SHE'S CHEERFUL...
...WEEPY...
BUT...
...ICHIGO WAS DIFFERENT.

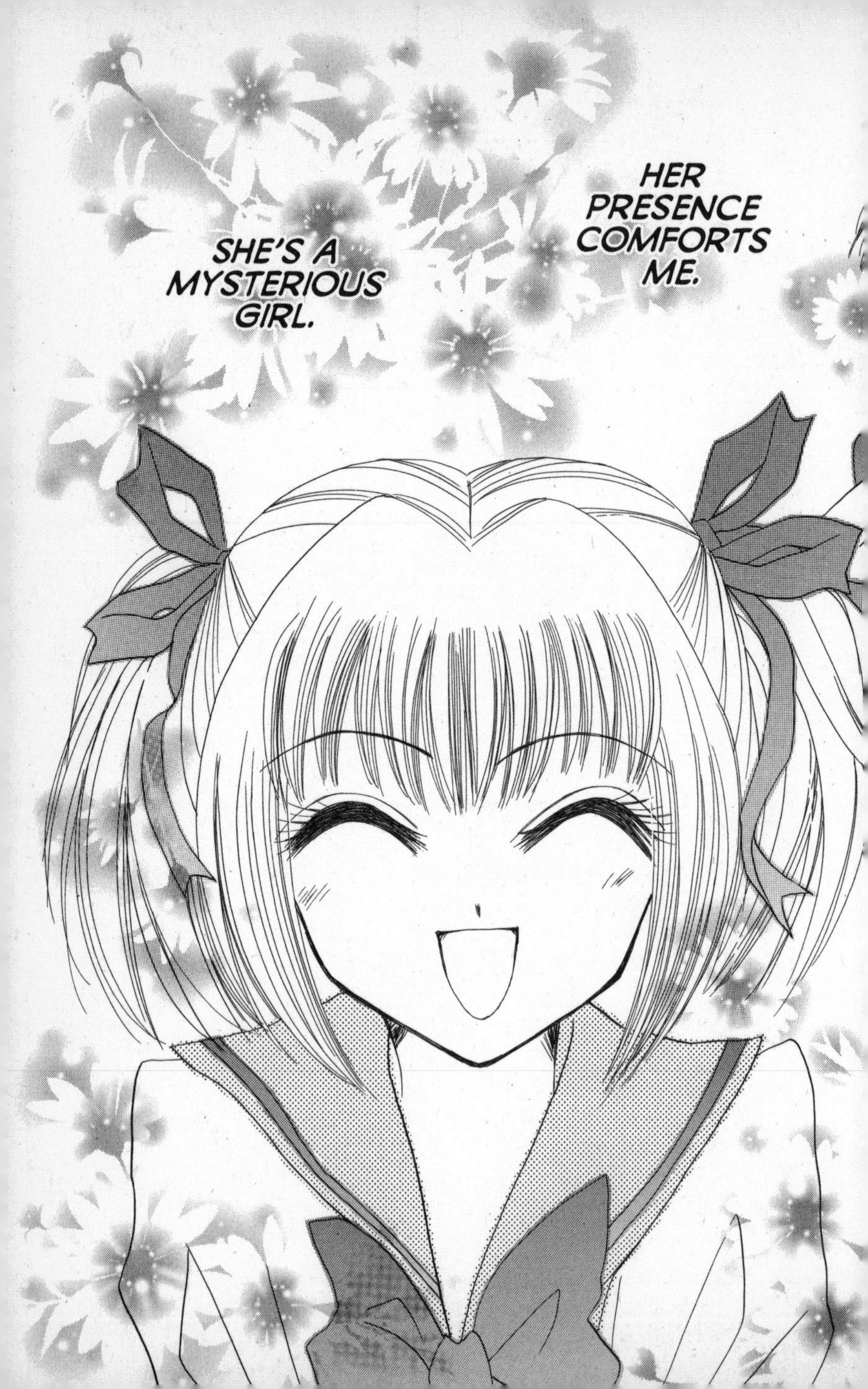
HER PRESENCE COMFORTS ME.
SHE'S A MYSTERIOUS GIRL.

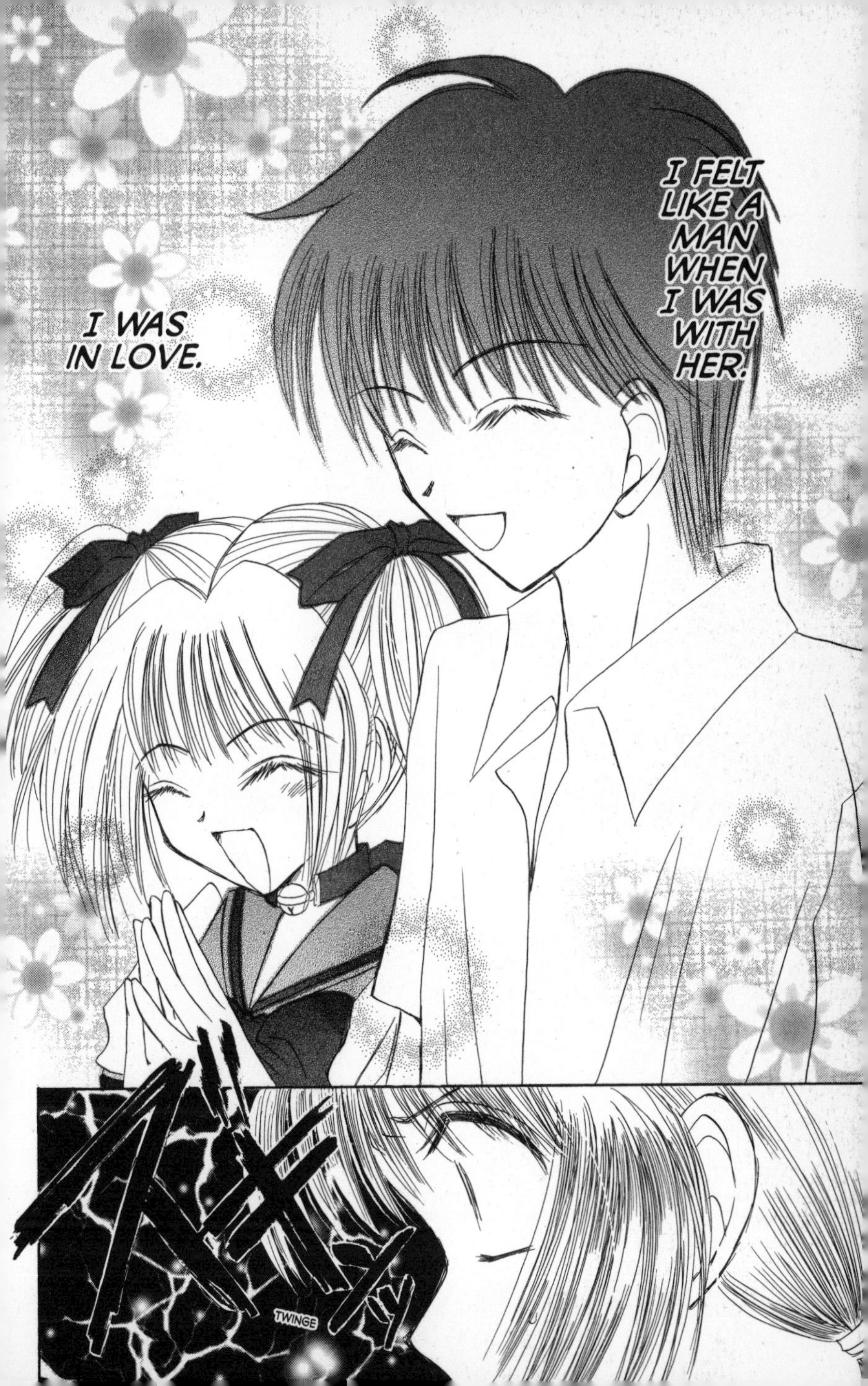
I FELT LIKE A MAN WHEN I WAS WITH HER.
I WAS IN LOVE.
TWINGE

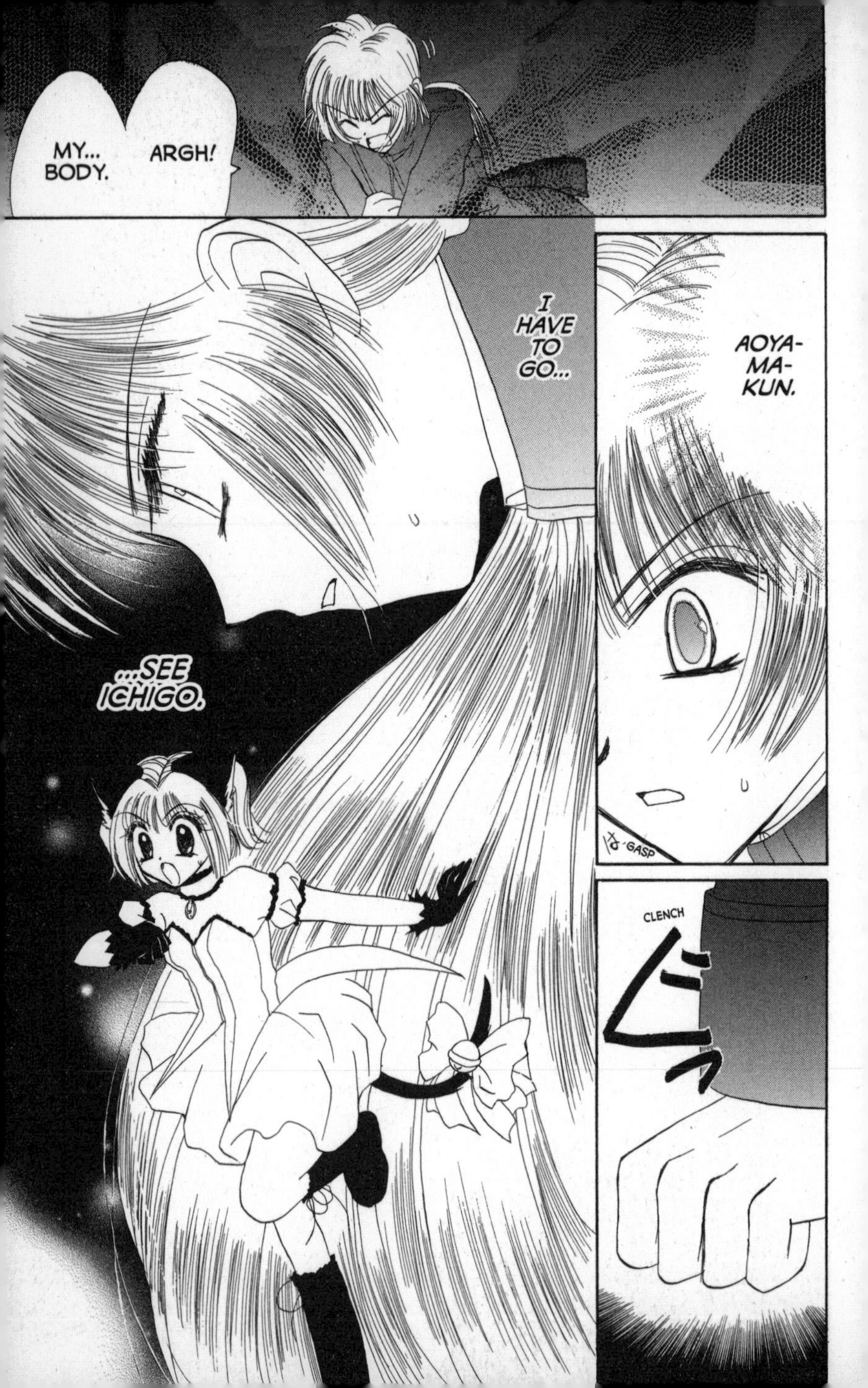
ARGH!
MY... BODY.
AOYA-MA-KUN.
GASP
CLENCH
I HAVE TO GO...
...SEE ICHIGO.

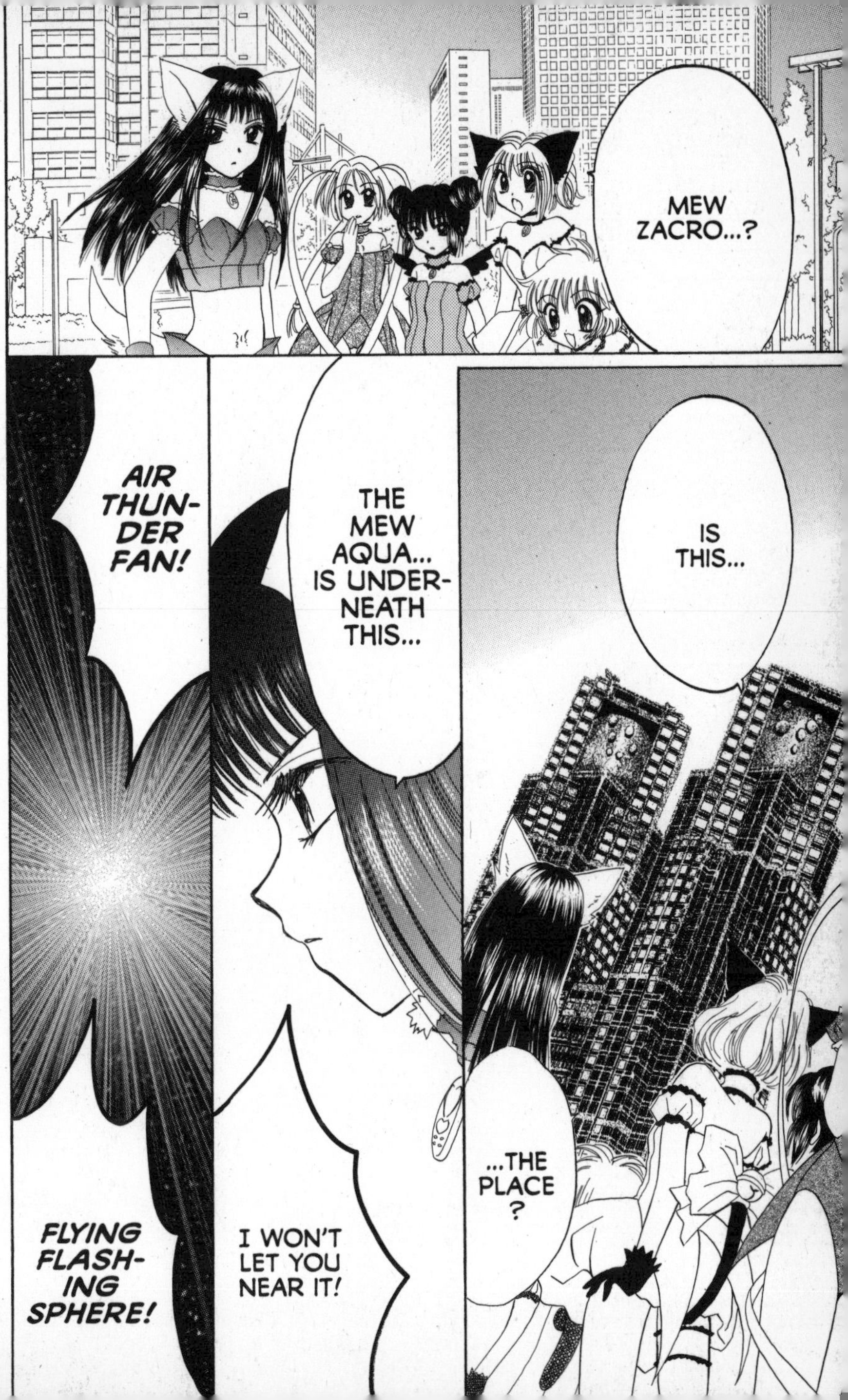
MEW ZACRO...?
IS THIS...
...THE PLACE?
THE MEW AQUA... IS UNDERNEATH THIS...
I WON'T LET YOU NEAR IT!
AIR THUNDER FAN!
FLYING FLASHING SPHERE!

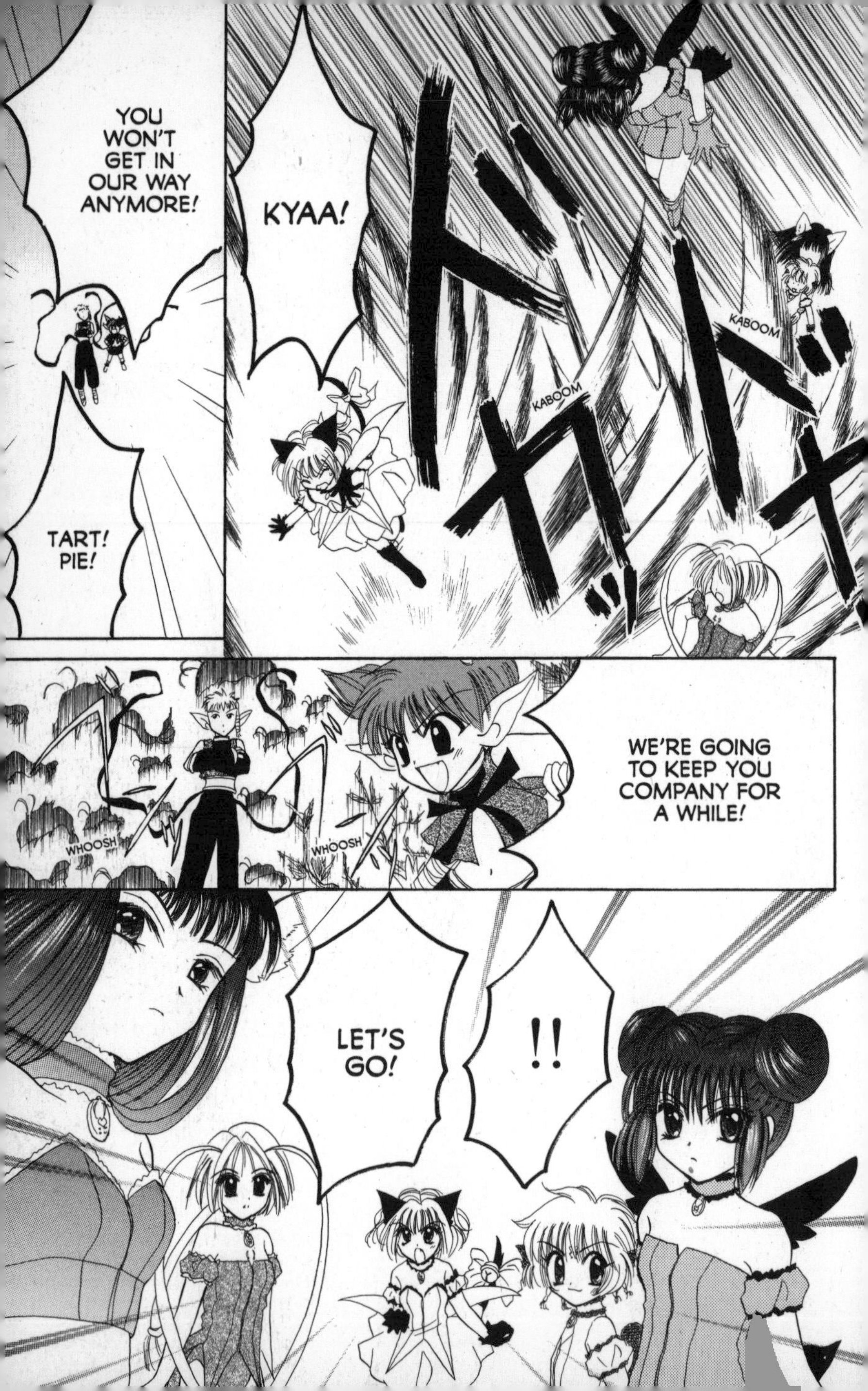
KABOOM
KYAA!
KABOOM
YOU WON'T GET IN OUR WAY ANYMORE!
TART! PIE!
WE'RE GOING TO KEEP YOU COMPANY FOR A WHILE!
WHOOSH
WHOOSH
!!
LET'S GO!

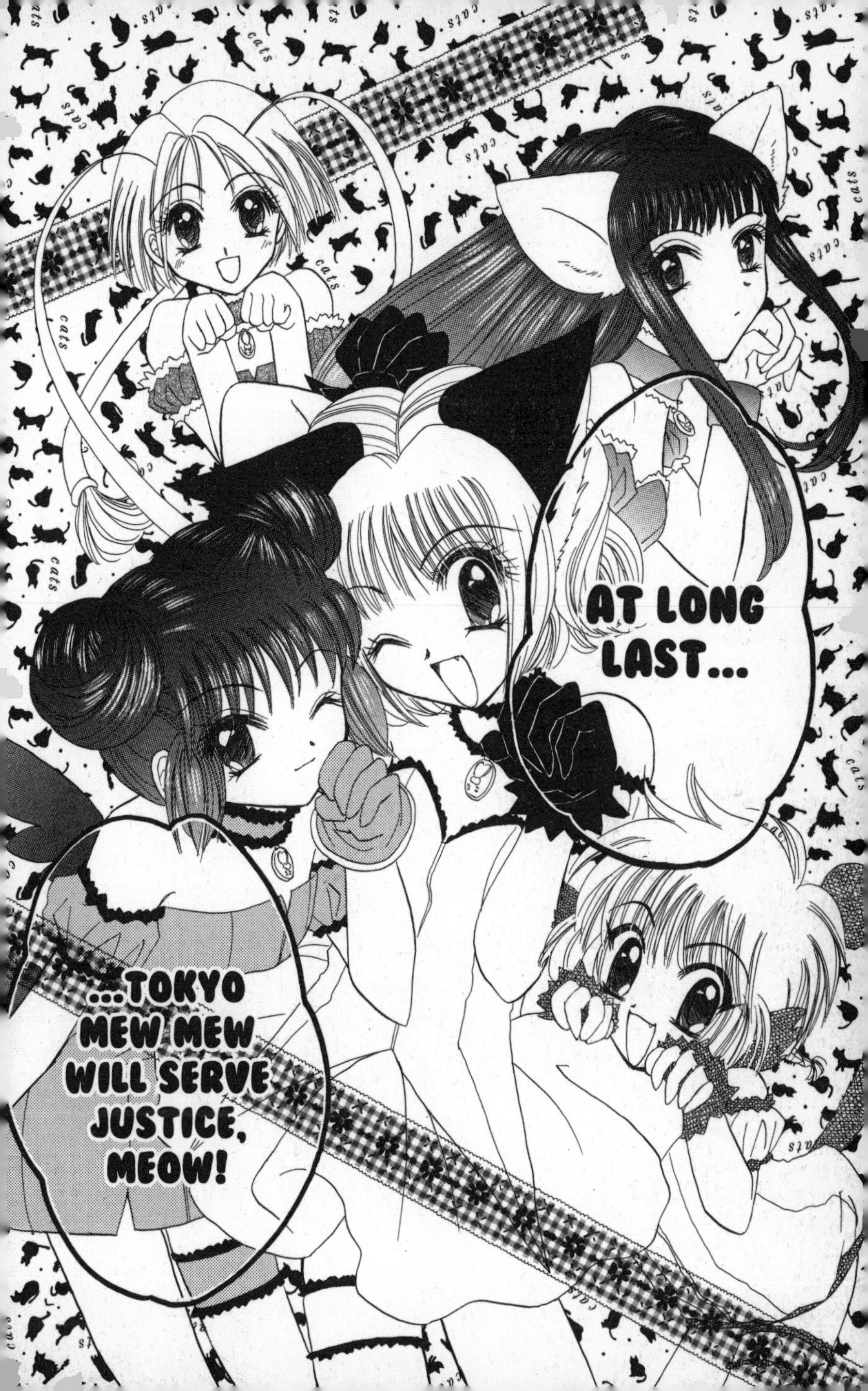
AT LONG LAST...
...TOKYO MEW MEW WILL SERVE JUSTICE, MEOW!
cats

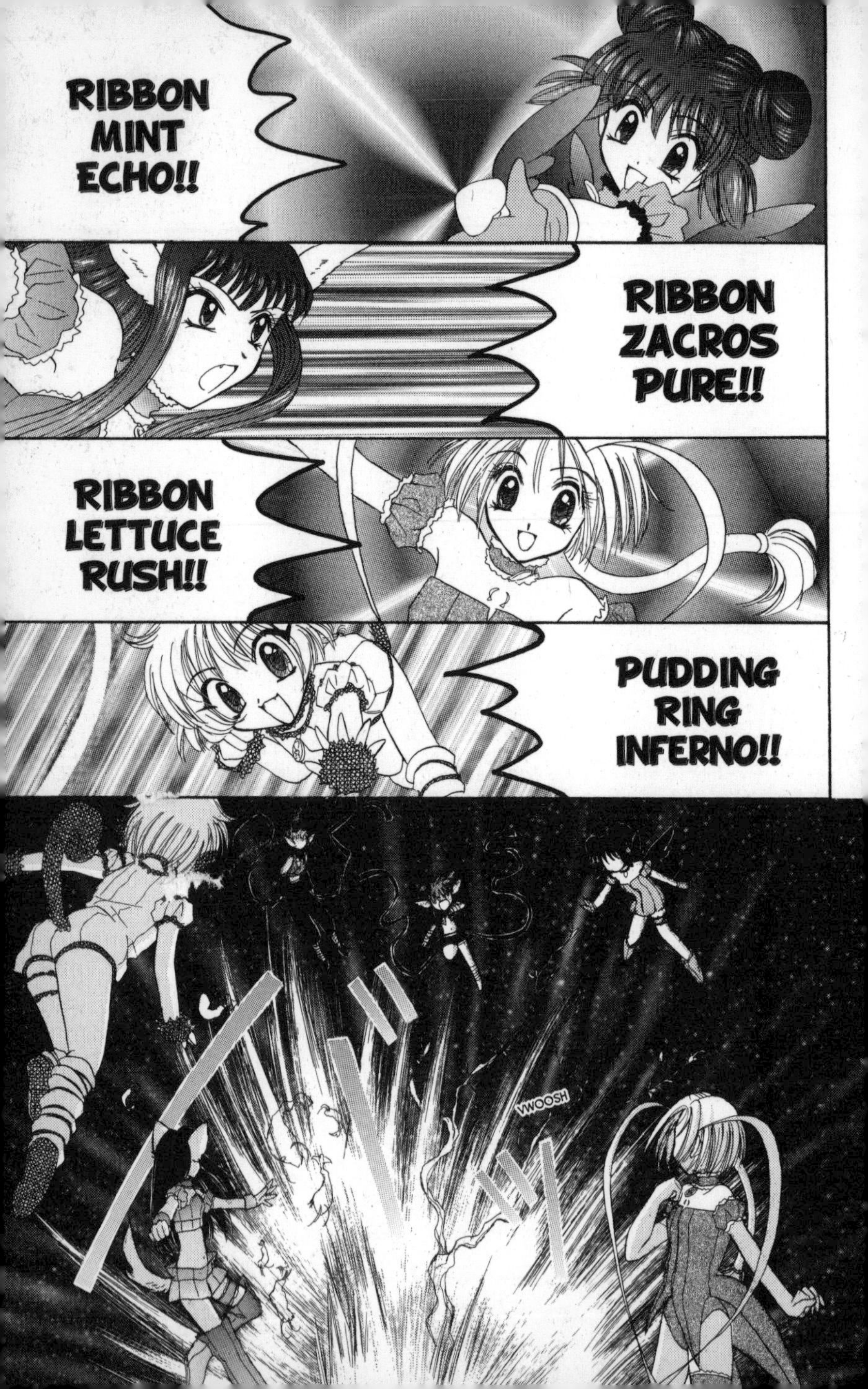
RIBBON MINT ECHO!!
RIBBON ZACROS PURE!!
RIBBON LETTUCE RUSH!!
PUDDING RING INFERNO!!
VWOOSH

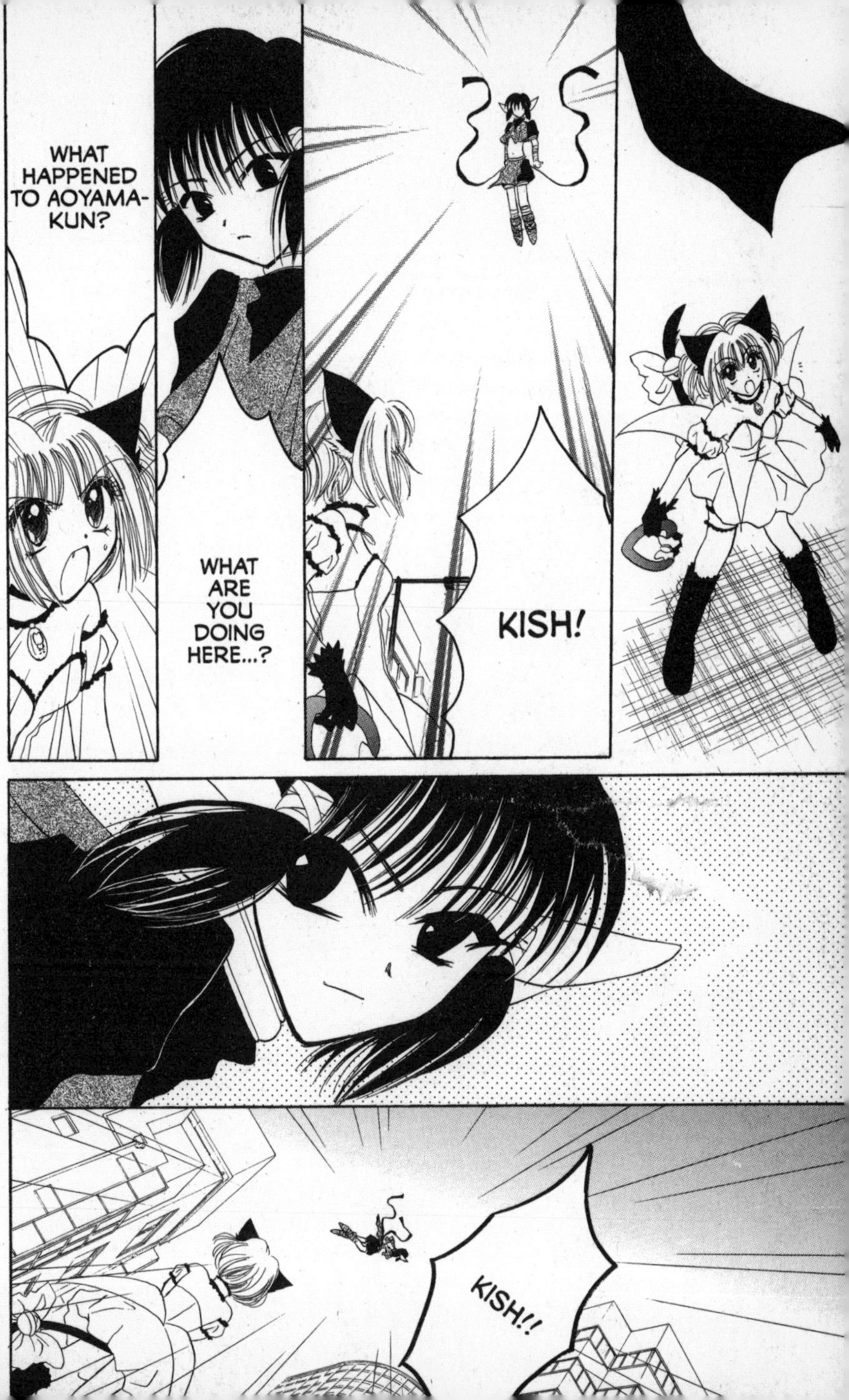

KISH!
WHAT ARE YOU DOING HERE...?
WHAT HAPPENED TO AOYAMA-KUN?
KISH!!

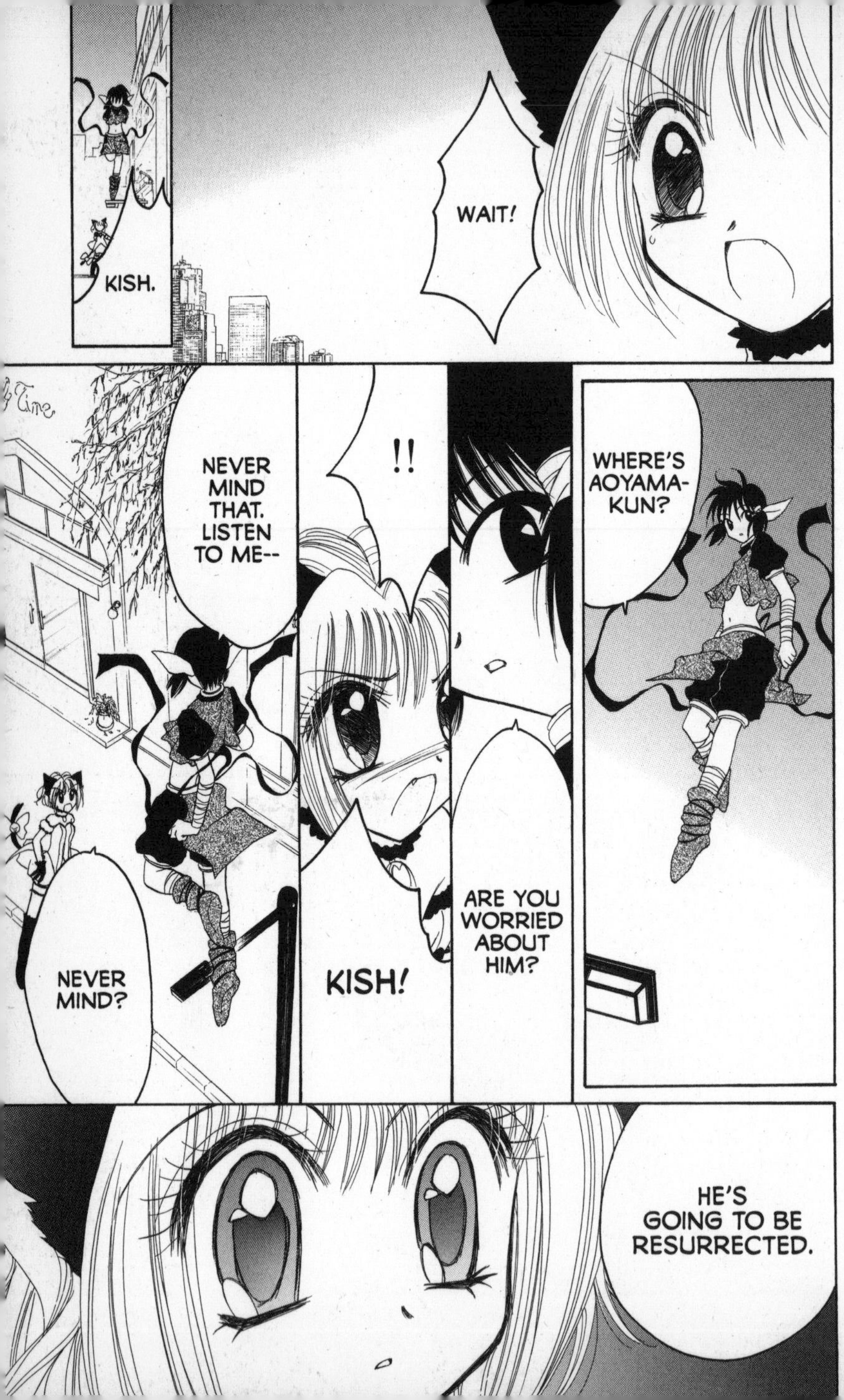
WAIT!
KISH.
WHERE'S AOYAMA-KUN?
ARE YOU WORRIED ABOUT HIM?
!!
KISH!
NEVER MIND THAT. LISTEN TO ME--
NEVER MIND?
HE'S GOING TO BE RESURRECTED.

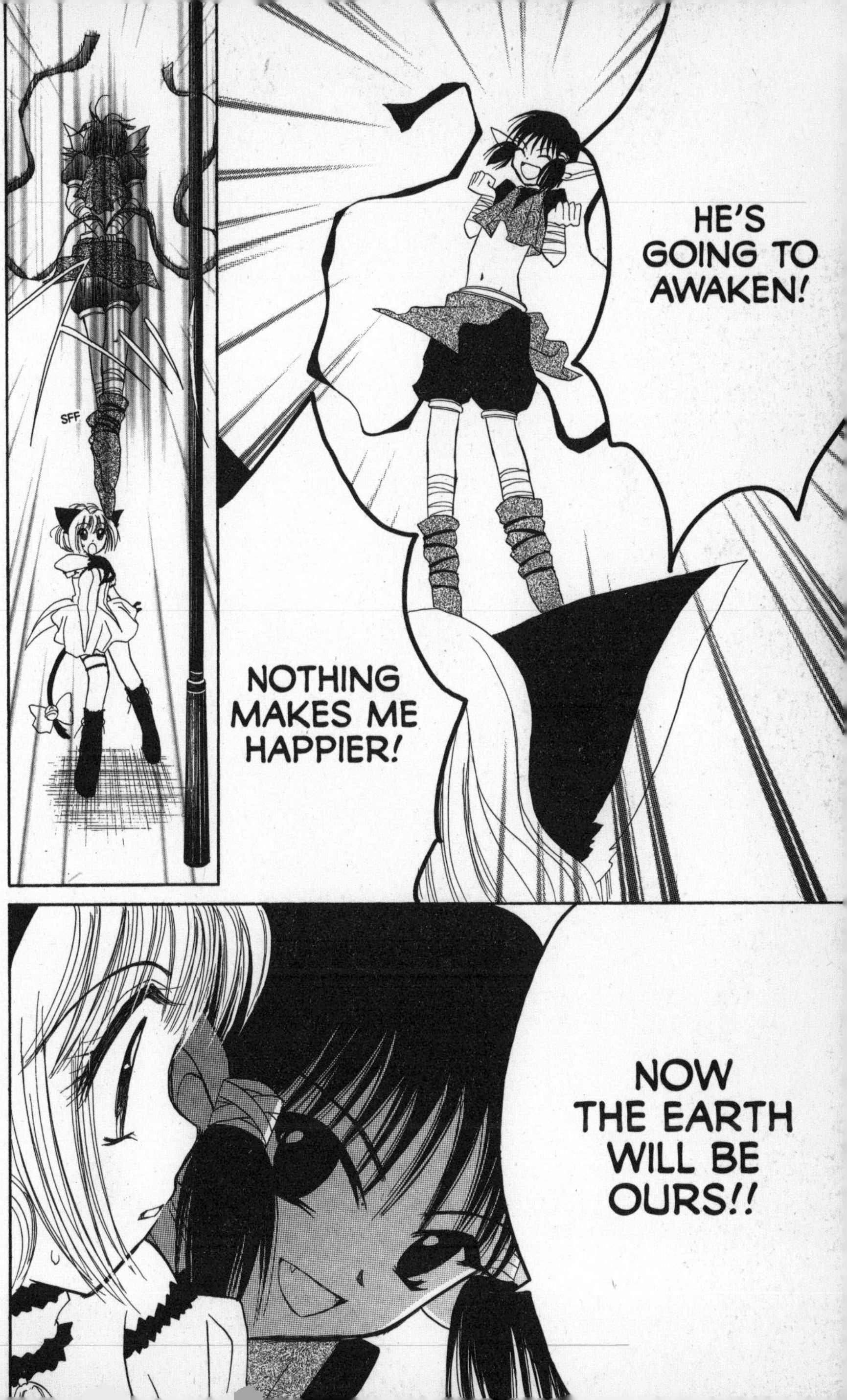
HE'S GOING TO AWAKEN!
NOTHING MAKES ME HAPPIER!
SFF
NOW THE EARTH WILL BE OURS!!

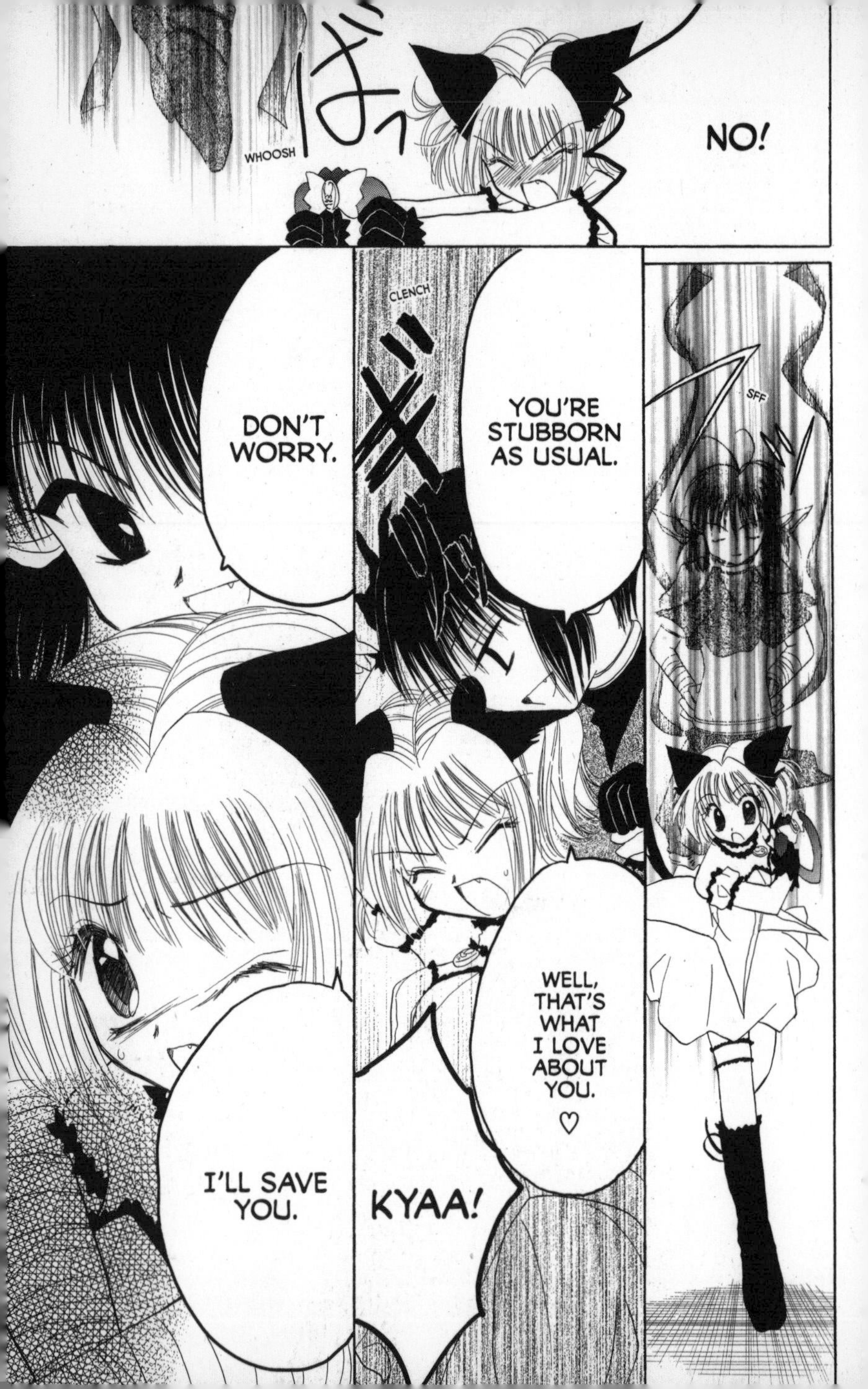
NO!
WHOOSH
SFF
CLENCH
YOU'RE STUBBORN AS USUAL.
WELL, THAT'S WHAT I LOVE ABOUT YOU. ♡
KYAA!
DON'T WORRY.
I'LL SAVE YOU.

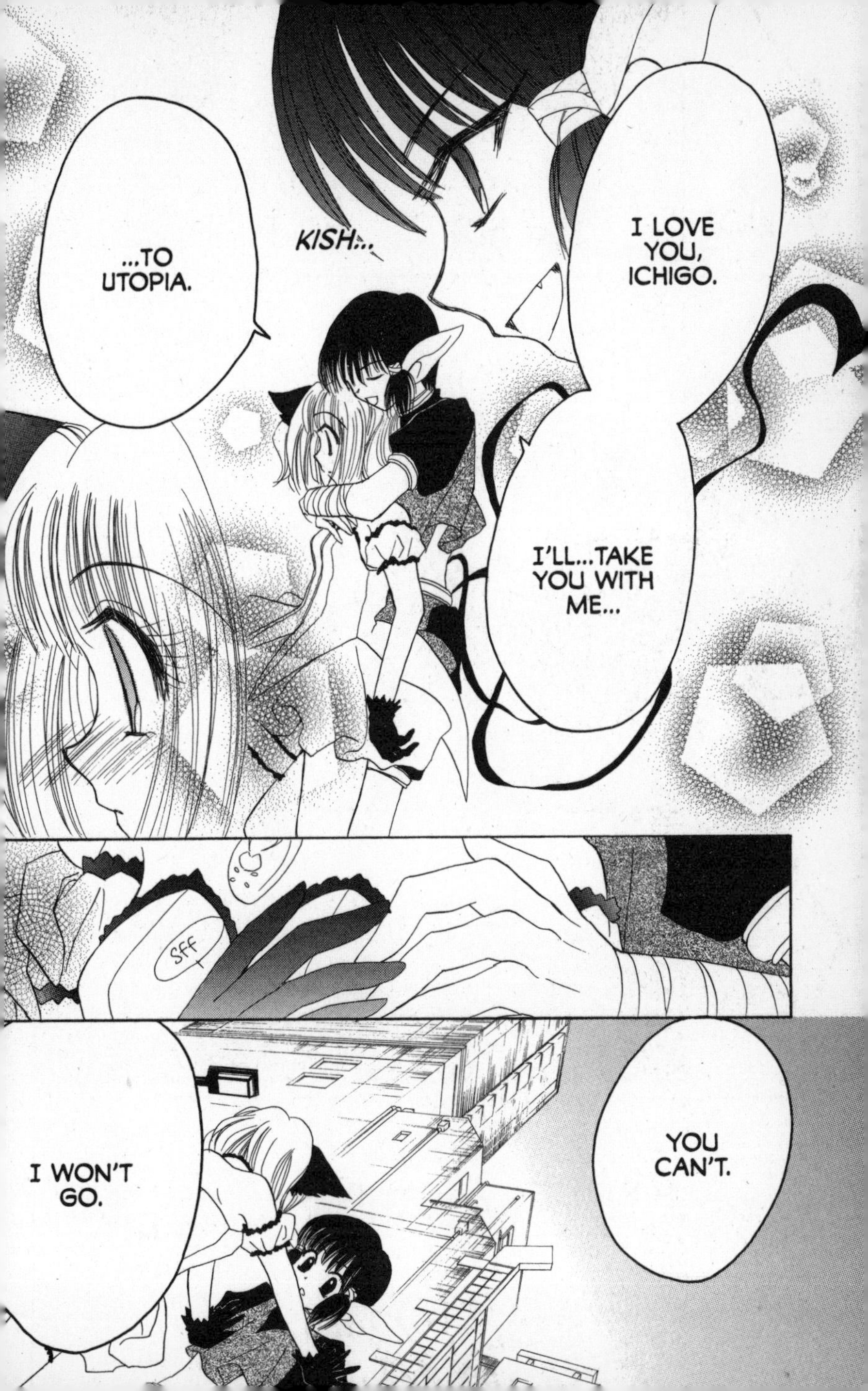
I LOVE YOU, ICHIGO.
KISH...
I'LL...TAKE YOU WITH ME...
...TO UTOPIA.
Sff
YOU CAN'T.
I WON'T GO.

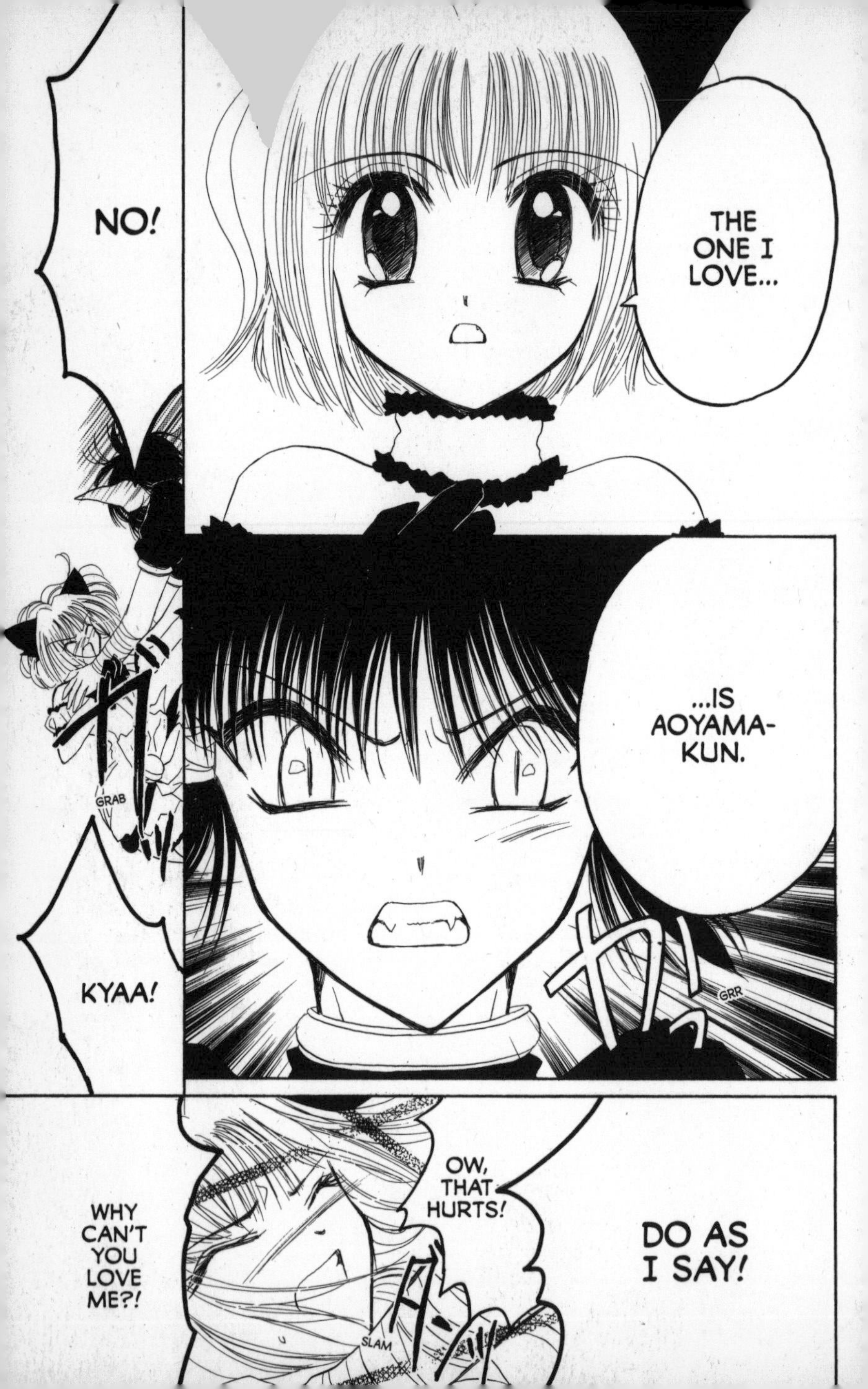
THE ONE I LOVE...
...IS AOYAMA-KUN.
GRR
NO!
GRAB
KYAA!
DO AS I SAY!
OW, THAT HURTS!
WHY CAN'T YOU LOVE ME?!
SLAM

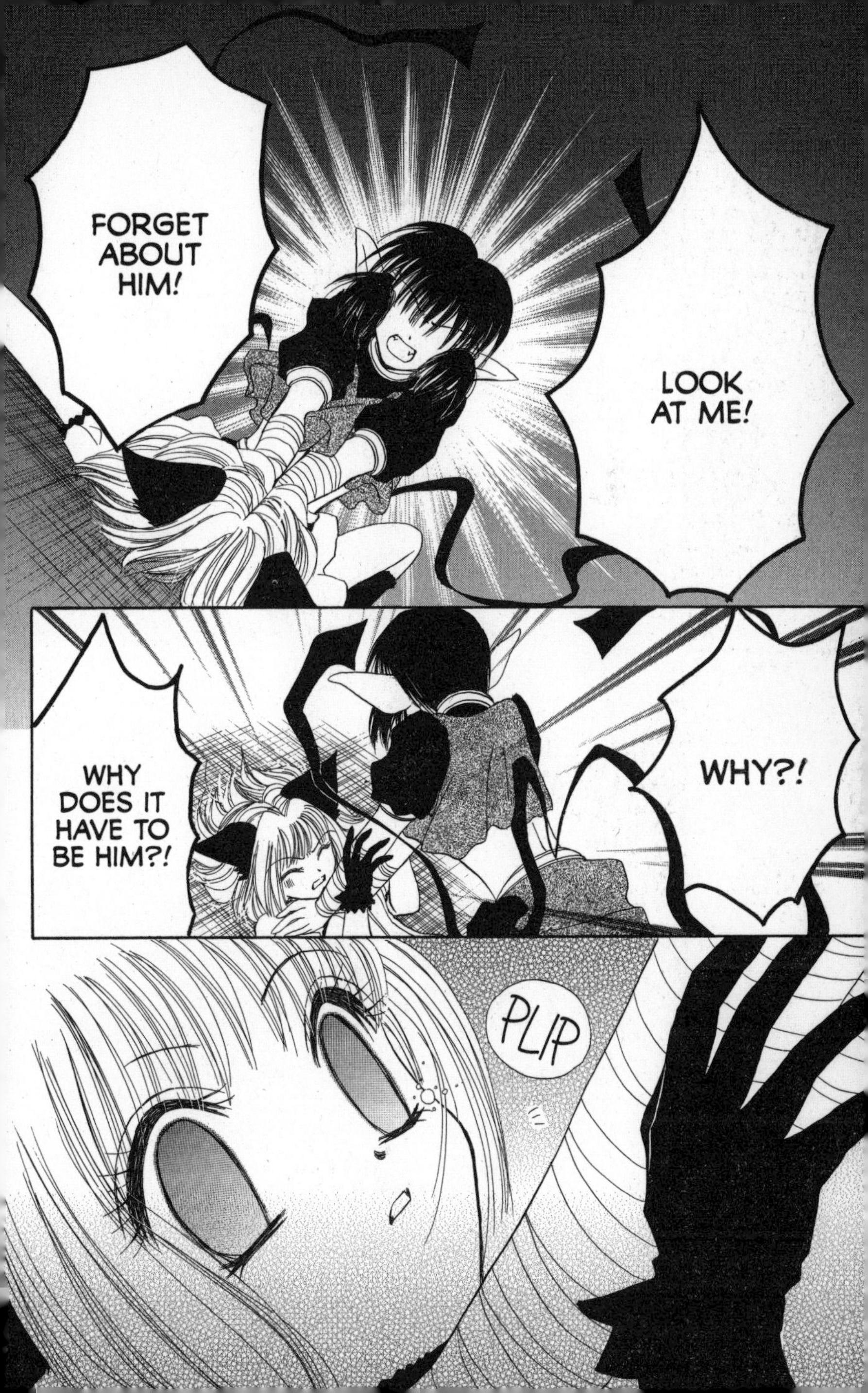
LOOK AT ME!
FORGET ABOUT HIM!
WHY?!
WHY DOES IT HAVE TO BE HIM?!
PLIP

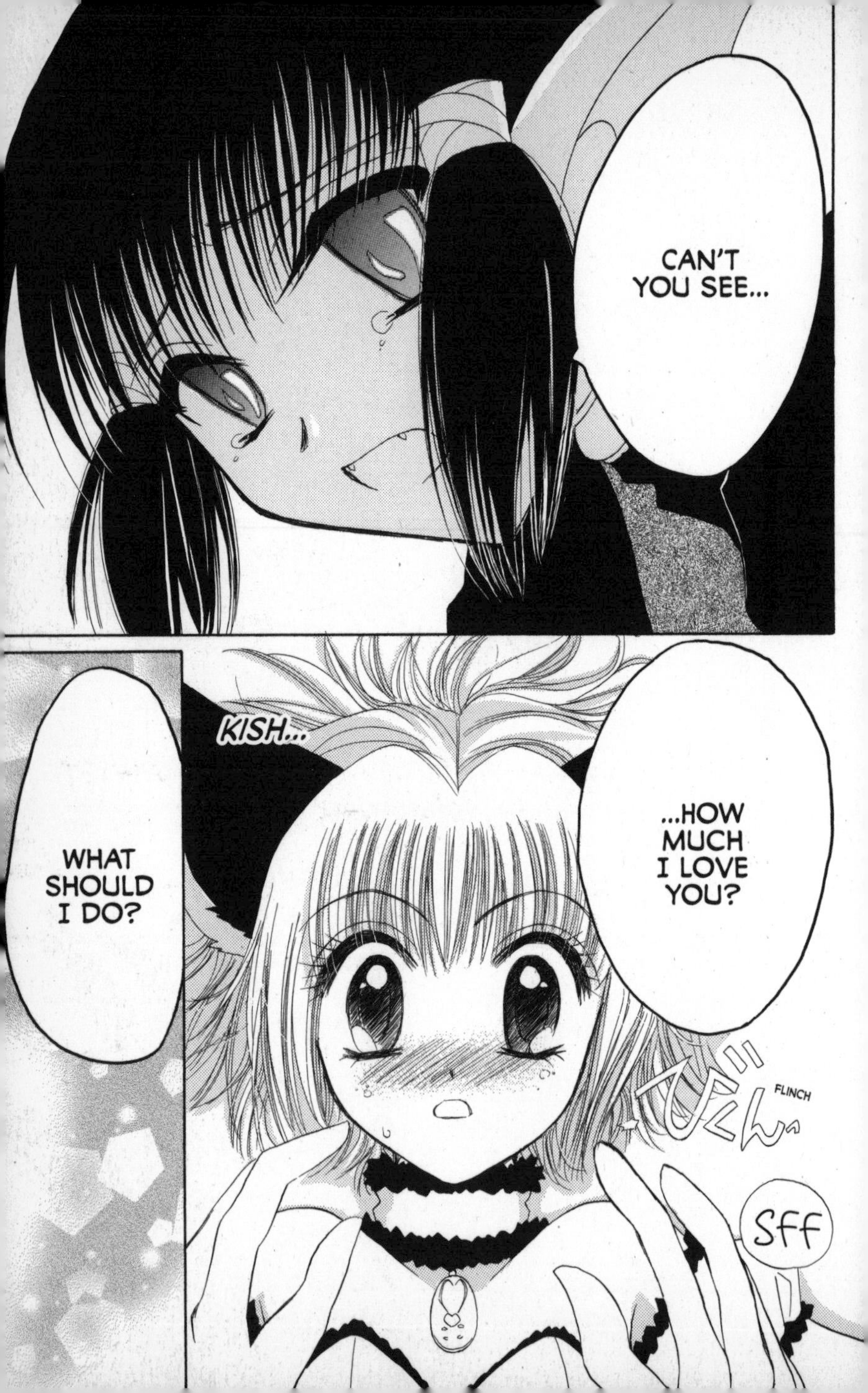
CAN'T YOU SEE...
...HOW MUCH I LOVE YOU?
KISH...
WHAT SHOULD I DO?
FLINCH
SFF

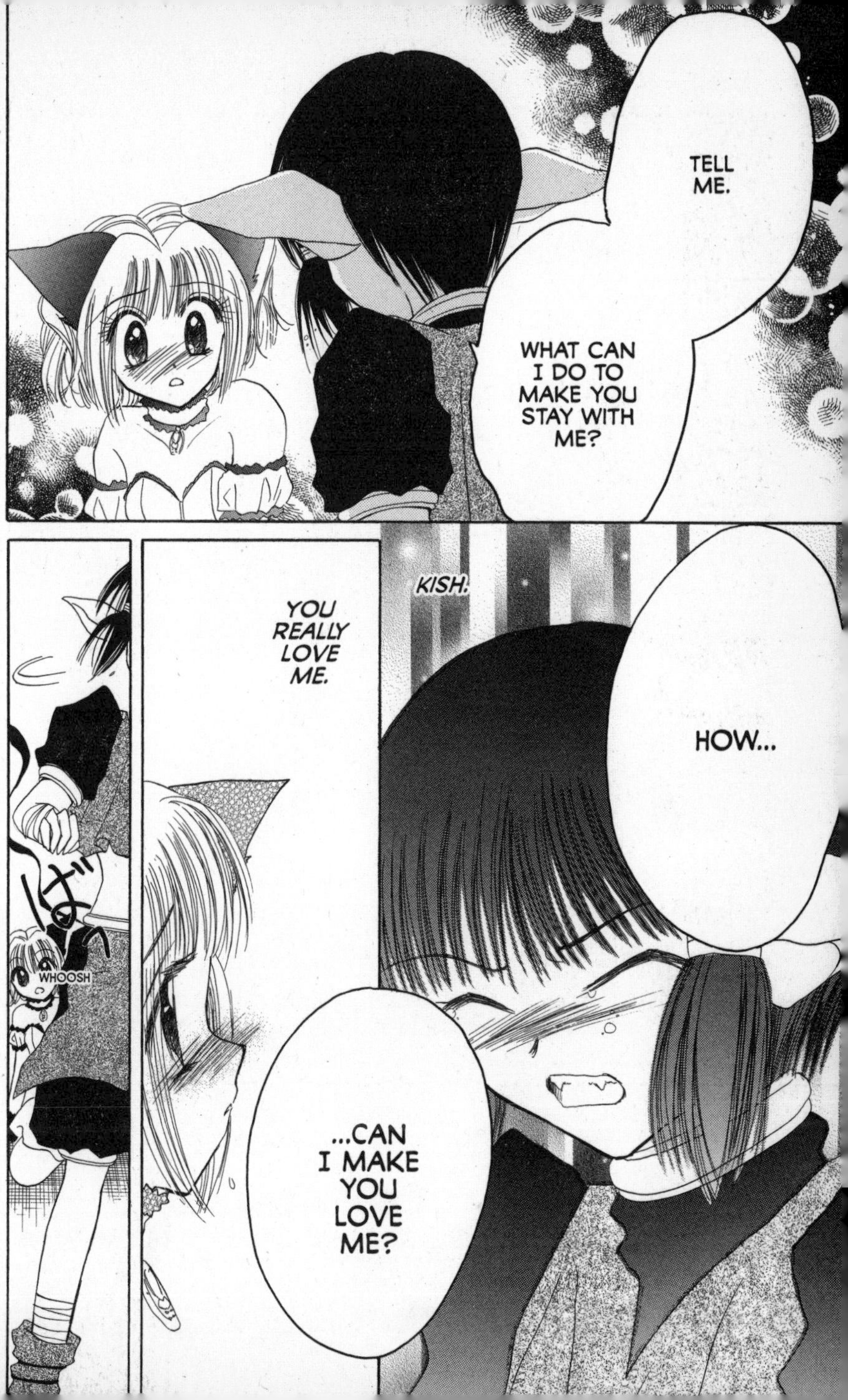
TELL ME.
WHAT CAN I DO TO MAKE YOU STAY WITH ME?
HOW...
...CAN I MAKE YOU LOVE ME?
KISH.
YOU REALLY LOVE ME.
ばっ
WHOOSH

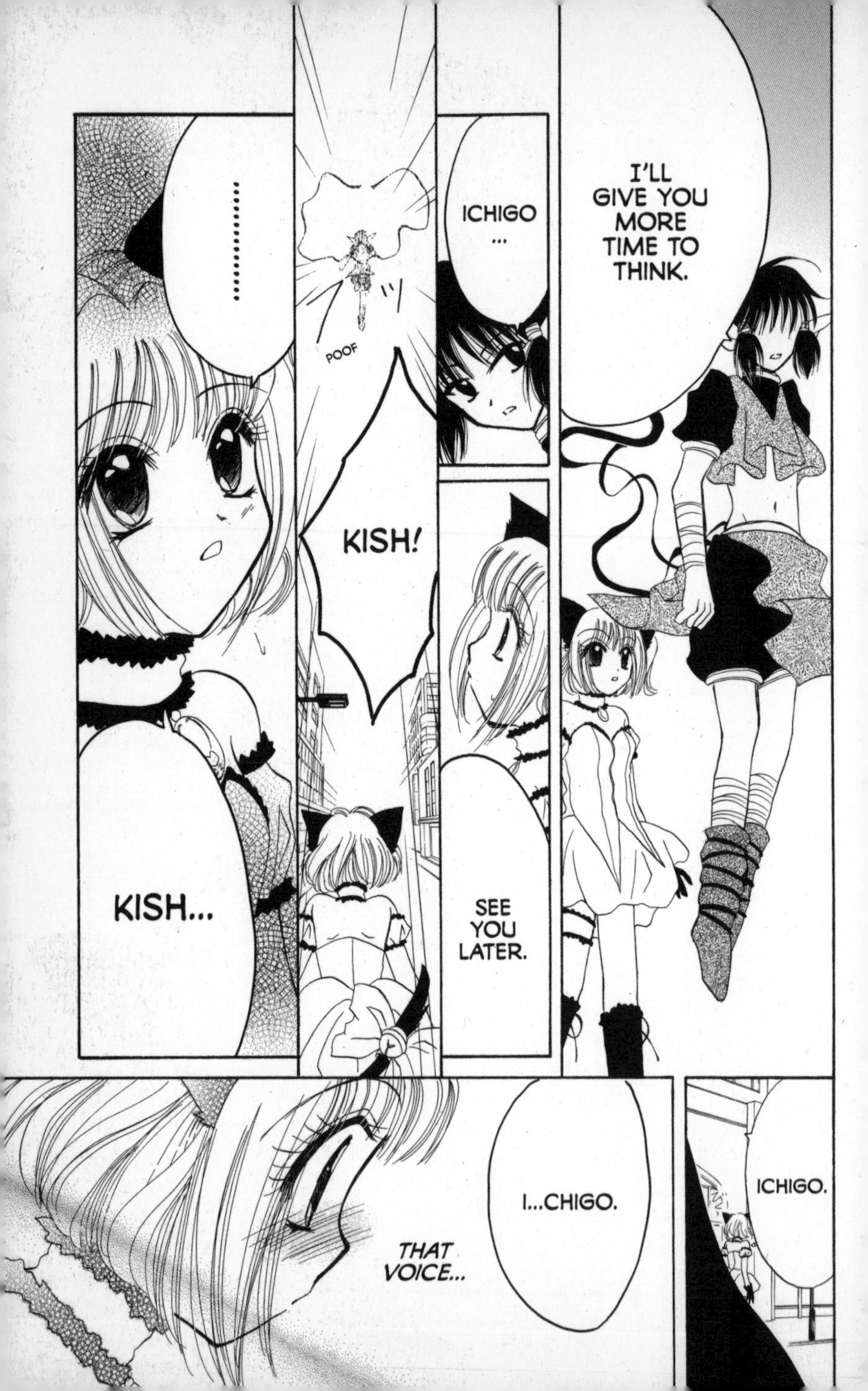
I'LL GIVE YOU MORE TIME TO THINK.
ICHIGO ...
SEE YOU LATER.
POOF
KISH!
....
KISH...
ICHIGO.
I...CHIGO.
THAT VOICE...

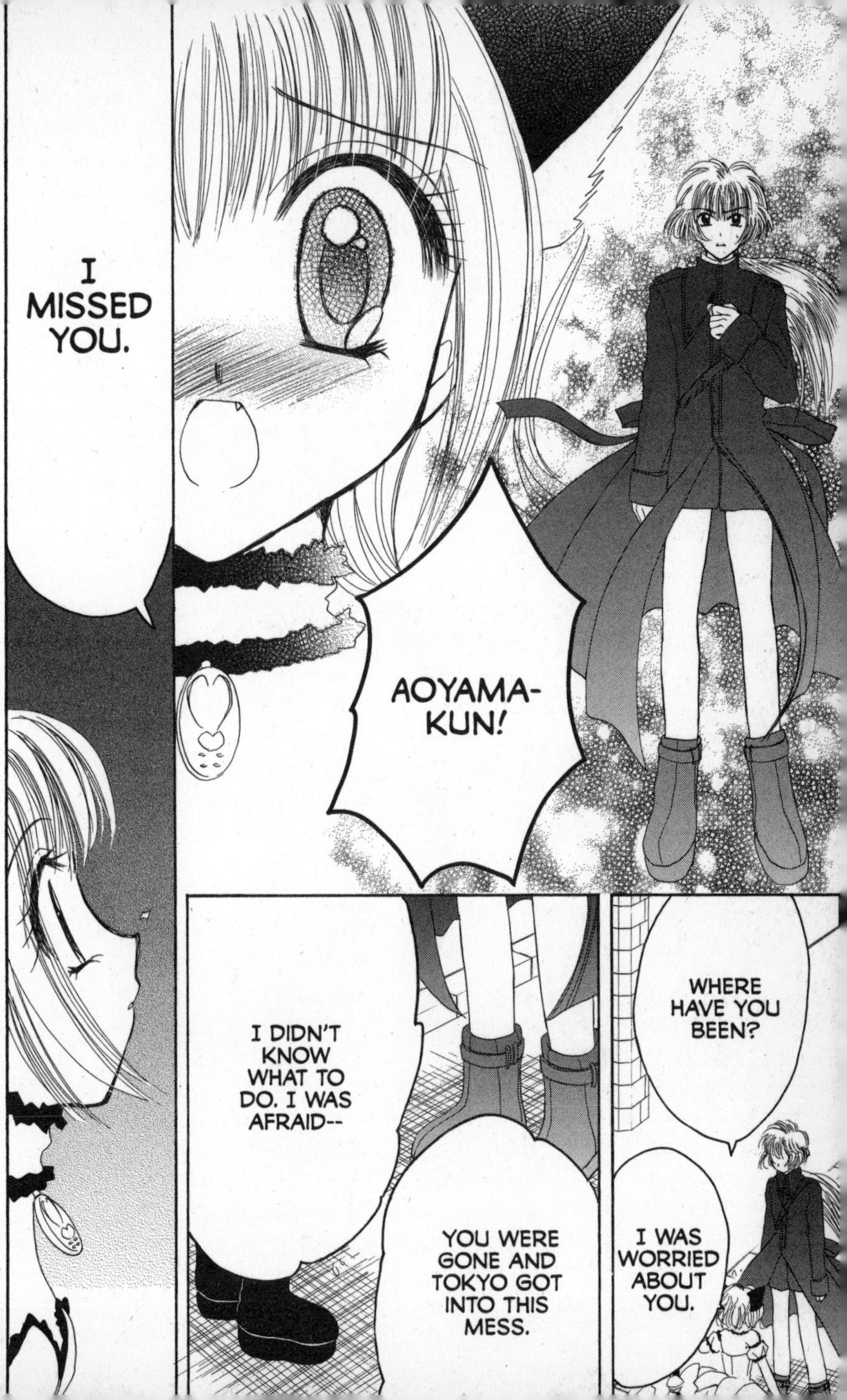
AOYAMA-KUN!
WHERE HAVE YOU BEEN?
I WAS WORRIED ABOUT YOU.
YOU WERE GONE AND TOKYO GOT INTO THIS MESS.
I DIDN'T KNOW WHAT TO DO. I WAS AFRAID--
I MISSED YOU.

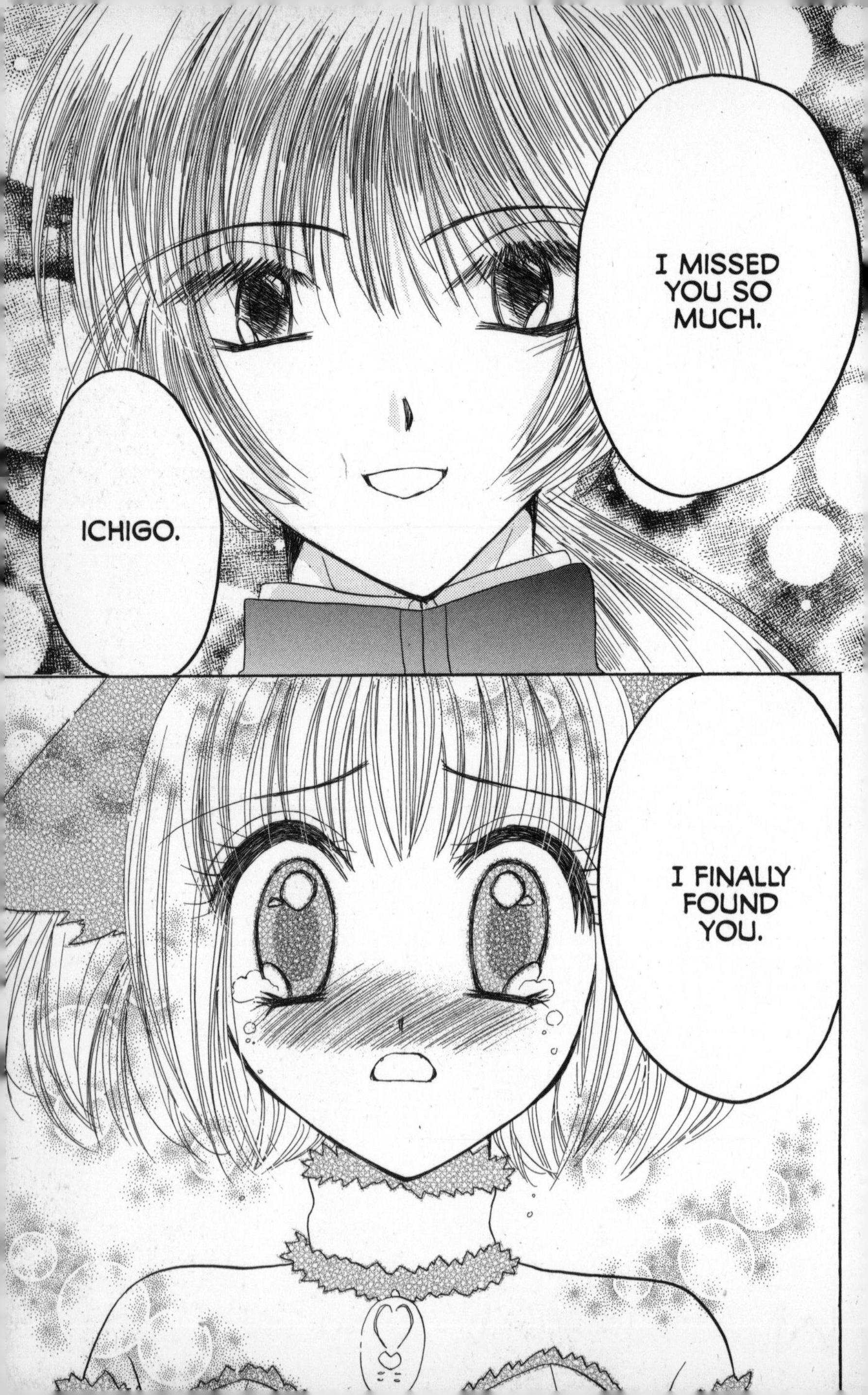
I MISSED YOU SO MUCH.
ICHIGO.
I FINALLY FOUND YOU.

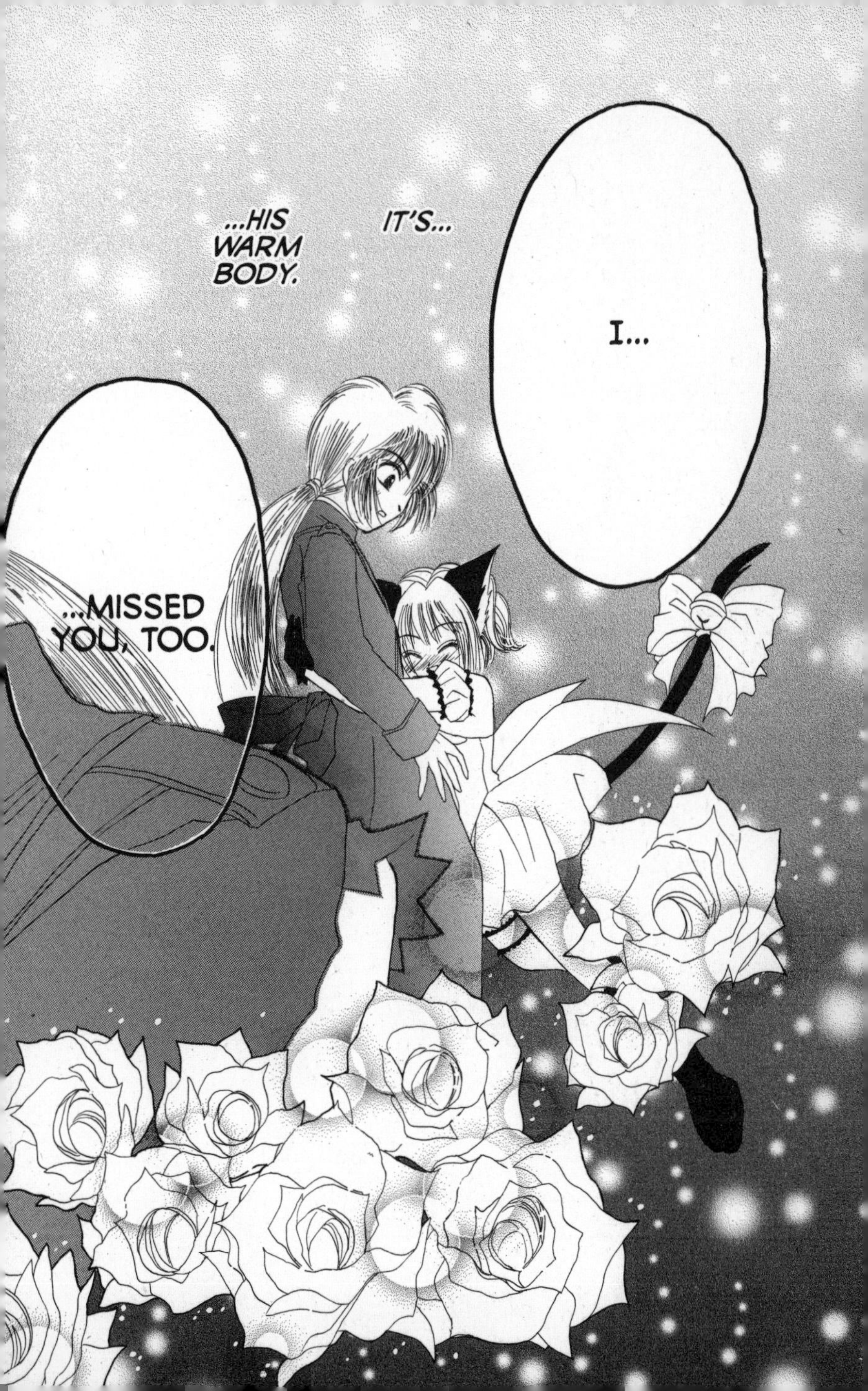
I...
IT'S...
...HIS WARM BODY.
...MISSED YOU, TOO.

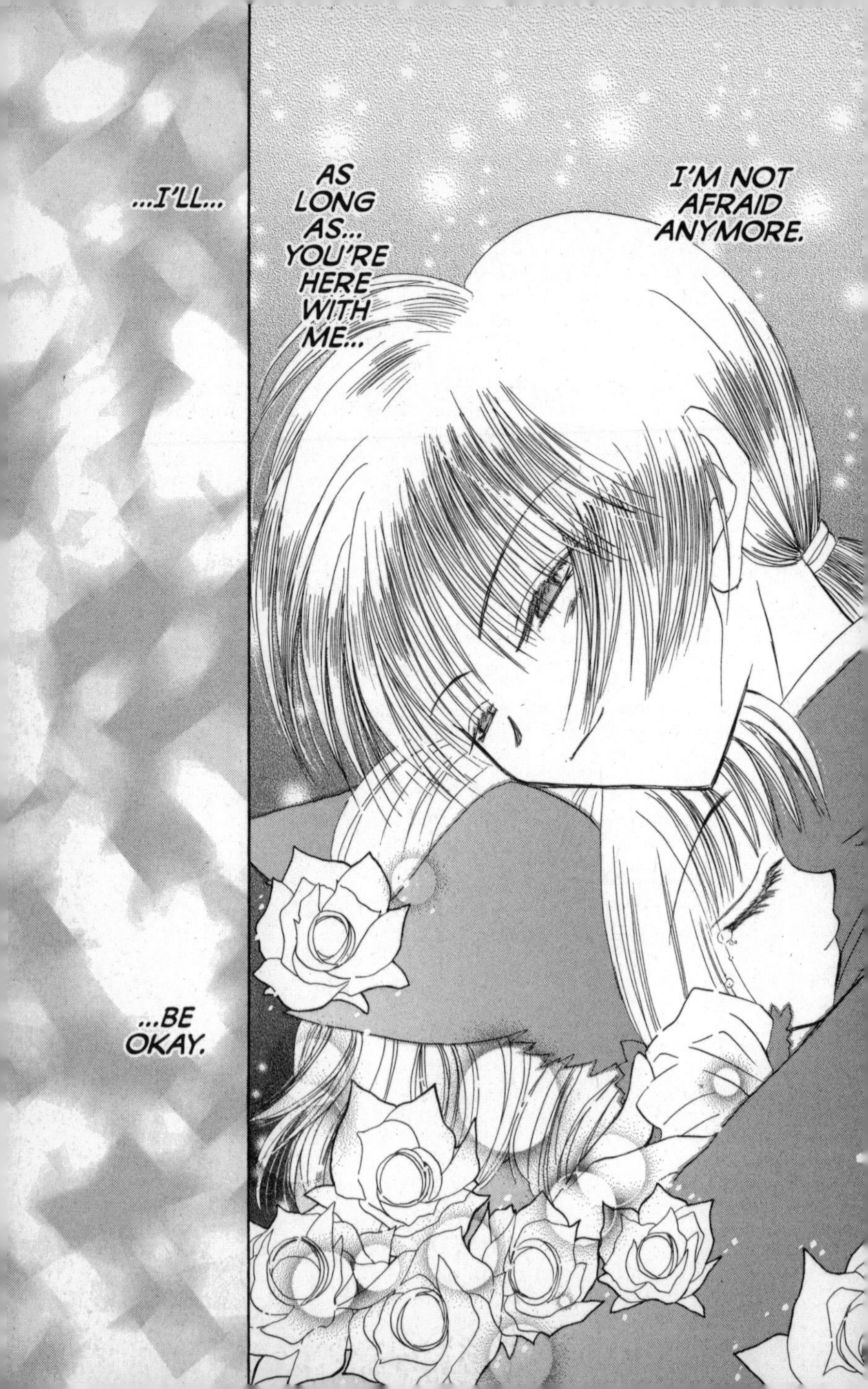
I'M NOT AFRAID ANYMORE.
AS LONG AS... YOU'RE HERE WITH ME...
...I'LL...
...BE OKAY.

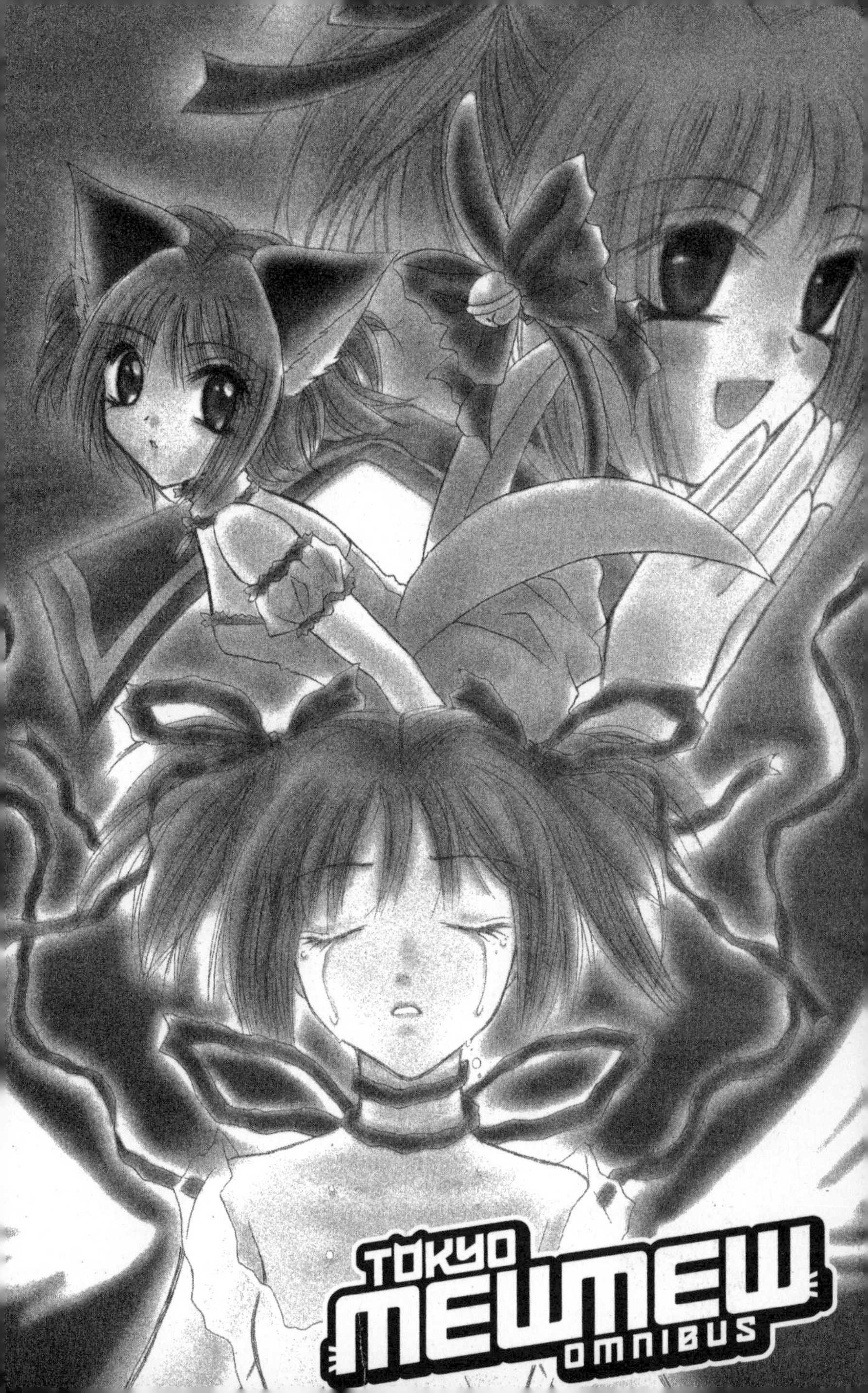
TOKYO
MEWMEW
OMNIBUS

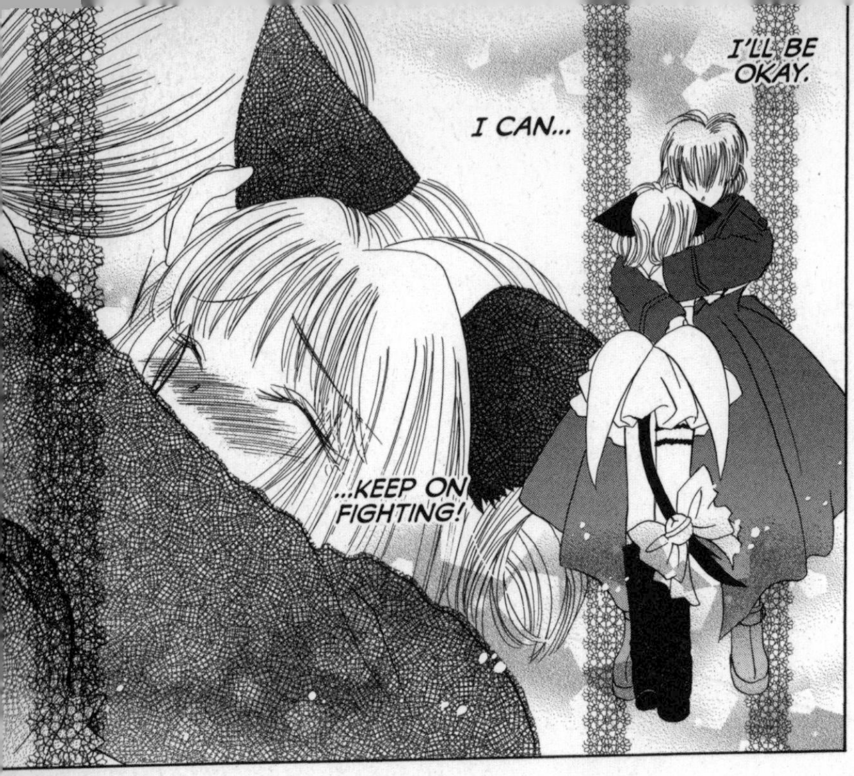
I'LL BE OKAY.
I CAN...
...KEEP ON FIGHTING!

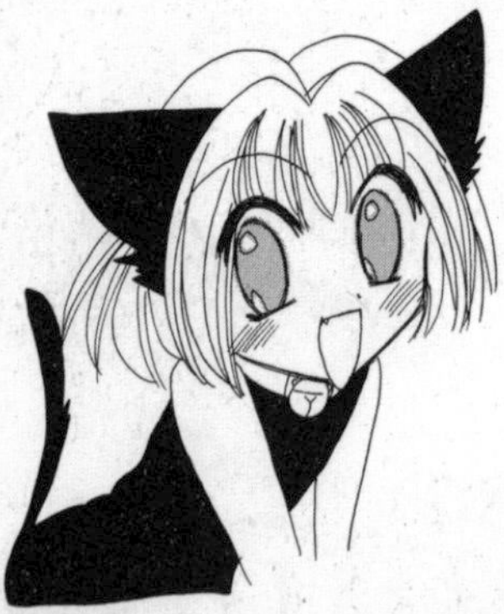

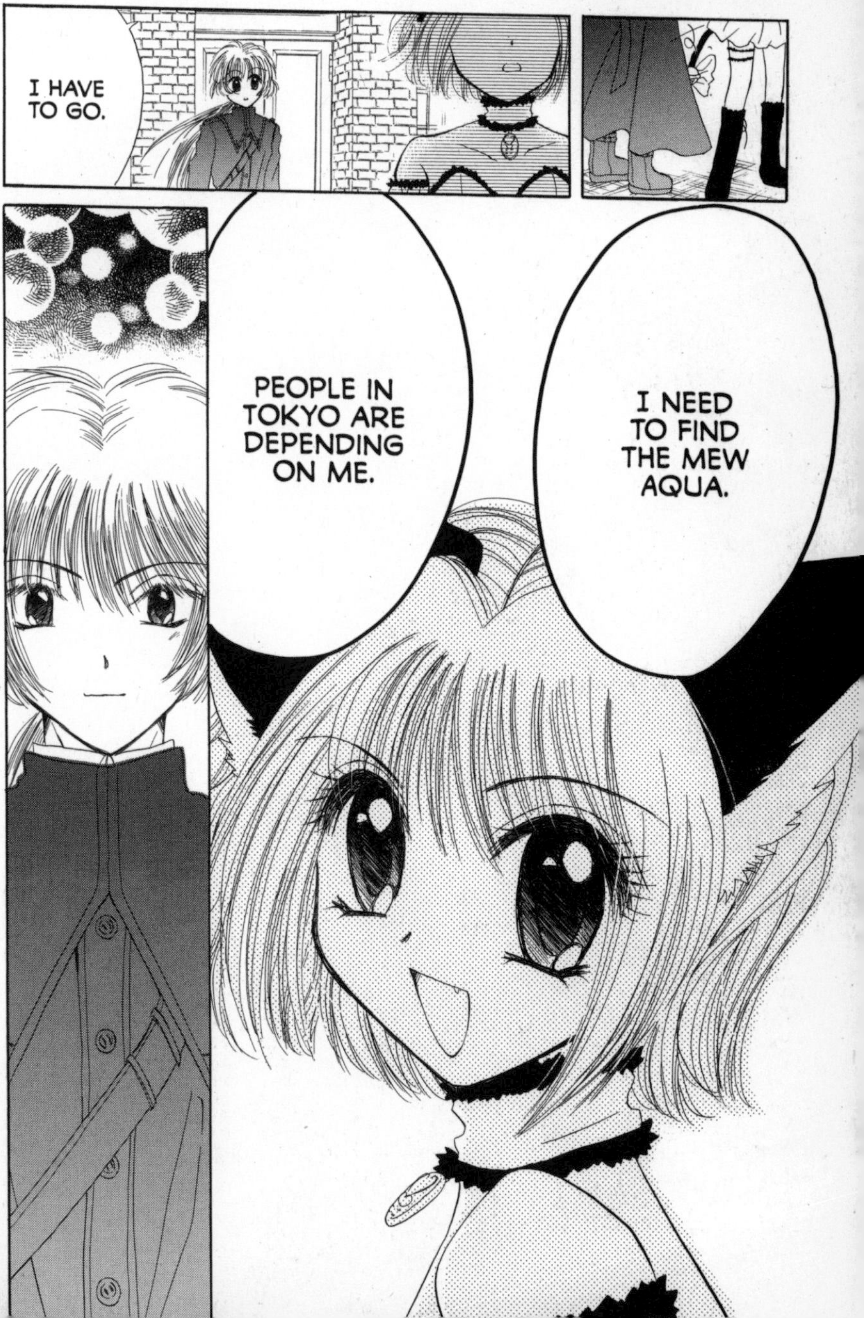
I HAVE TO GO.
I NEED TO FIND THE MEW AQUA.
PEOPLE IN TOKYO ARE DEPENDING ON ME.

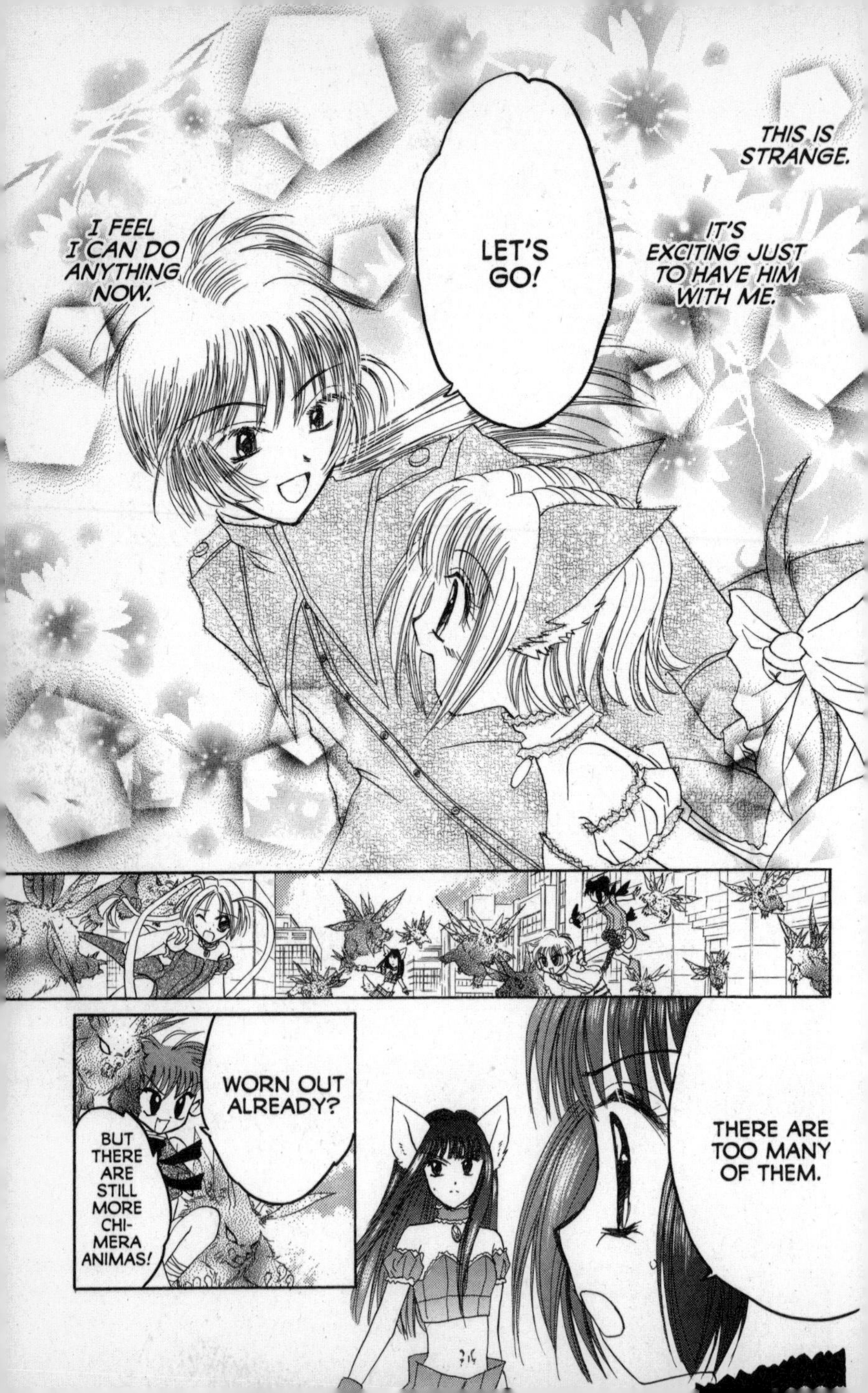
THIS IS STRANGE.
IT'S EXCITING JUST TO HAVE HIM WITH ME.
LET'S GO!
I FEEL I CAN DO ANYTHING NOW.
THERE ARE TOO MANY OF THEM.
WORN OUT ALREADY?
BUT THERE ARE STILL MORE CHI-MERA ANIMAS!

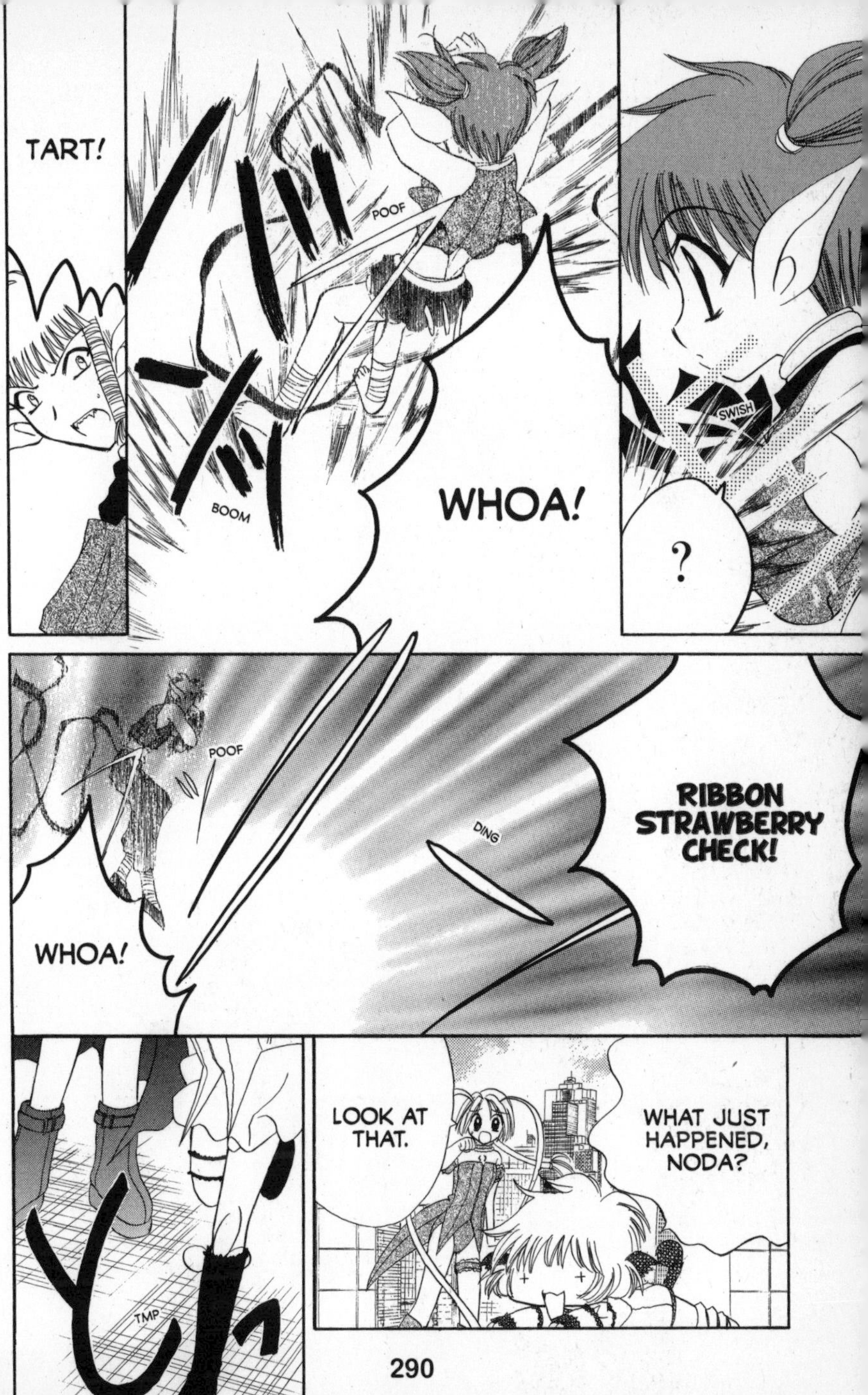
SWISH
?
WHOA!
POOF
BOOM
TART!
RIBBON STRAWBERRY CHECK!
DING
POOF
WHOA!
WHAT JUST HAPPENED, NODA?
LOOK AT THAT.
TMP

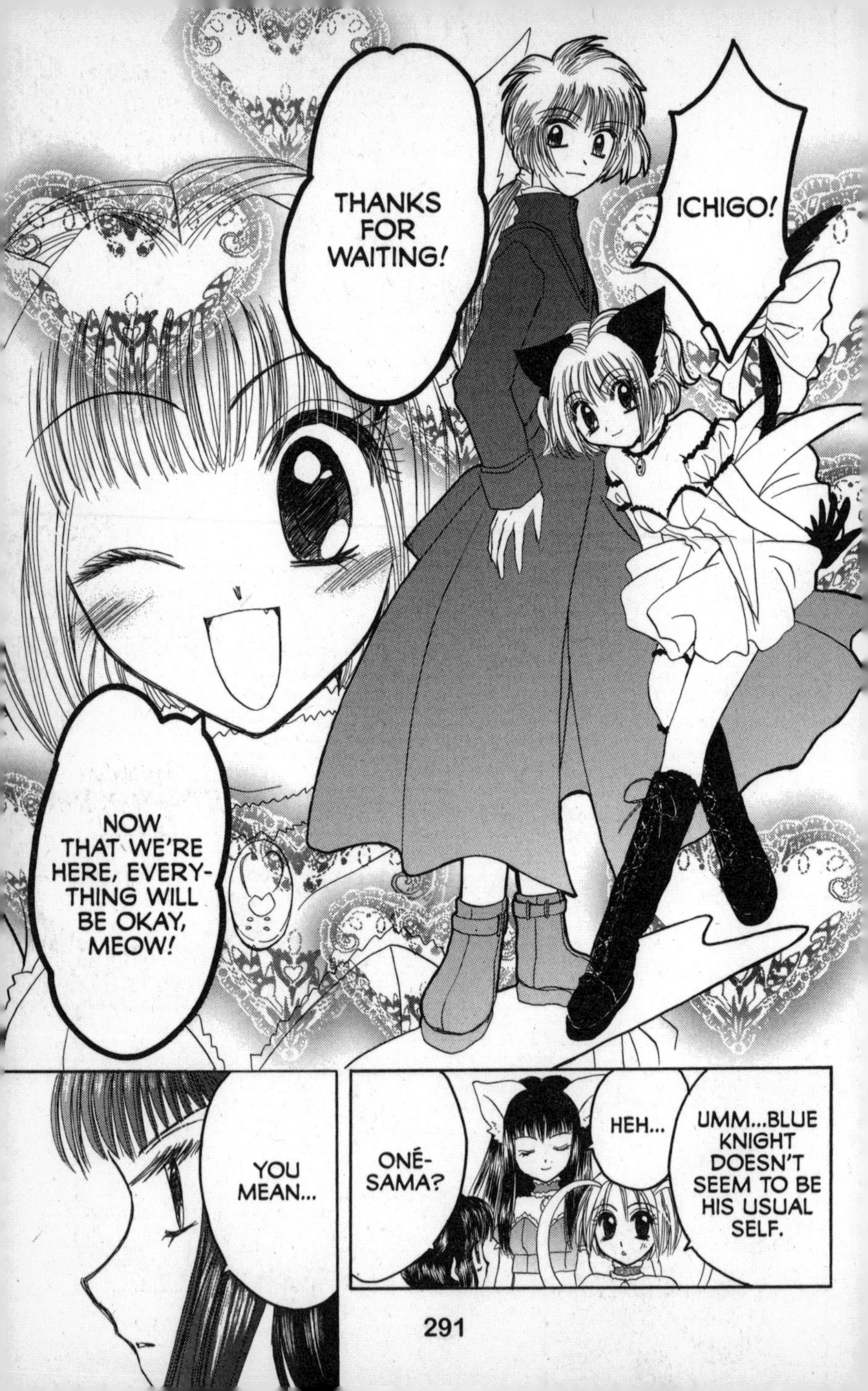
ICHIGO!
THANKS FOR WAITING!
NOW THAT WE'RE HERE, EVERY-THING WILL BE OKAY, MEOW!
UMM...BLUE KNIGHT DOESN'T SEEM TO BE HIS USUAL SELF.
HEH...
ONÉ-SAMA?
YOU MEAN...

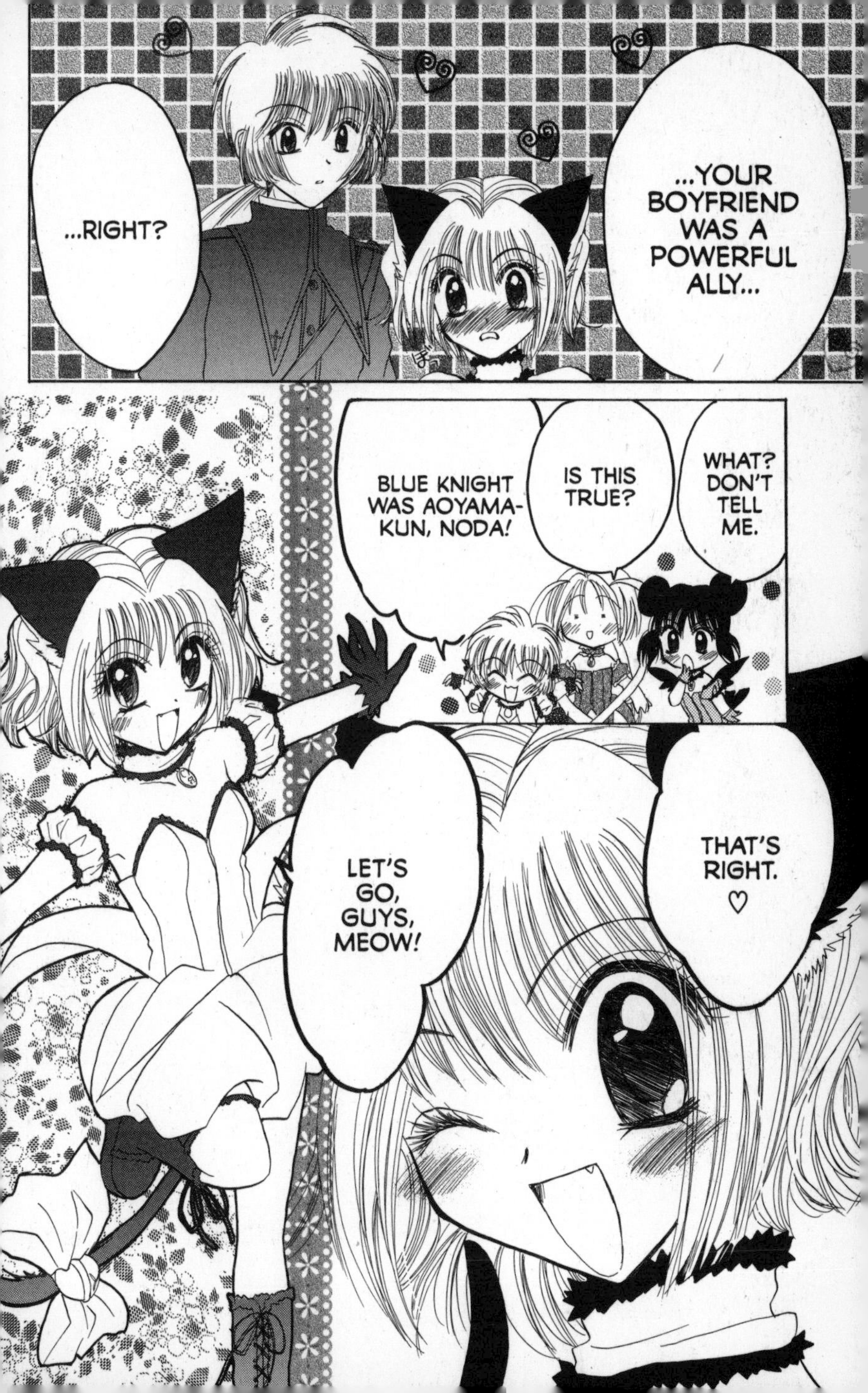
...YOUR BOYFRIEND WAS A POWERFUL ALLY...
...RIGHT?
WHAT? DON'T TELL ME.
IS THIS TRUE?
BLUE KNIGHT WAS AOYAMA-KUN, NODA!
THAT'S RIGHT. ♡
LET'S GO, GUYS, MEOW!

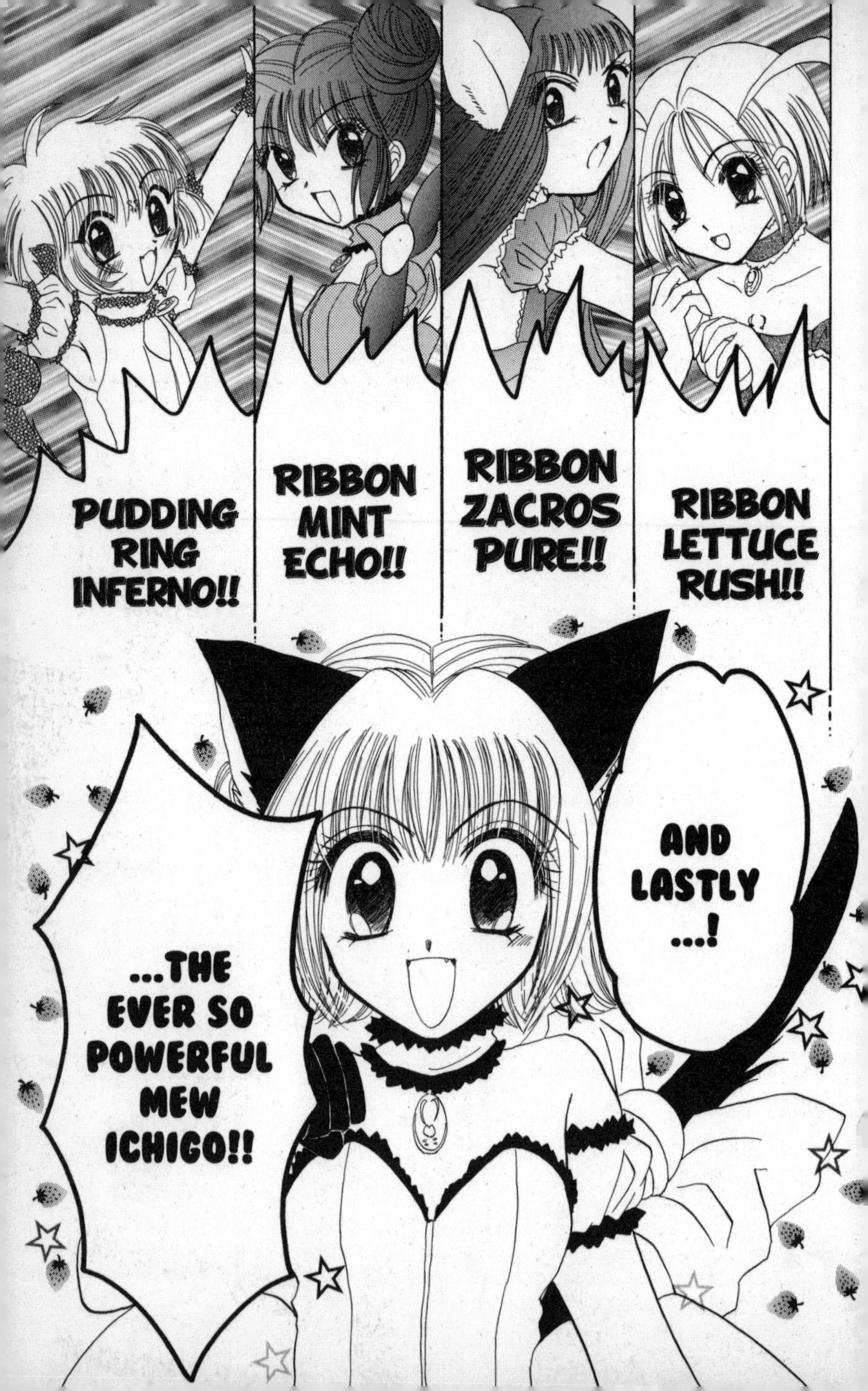
RIBBON LETTUCE RUSH!!
RIBBON ZACROS PURE!!
RIBBON MINT ECHO!!
PUDDING RING INFERNO!!
AND LASTLY ...!
...THE EVER SO POWERFUL MEW ICHIGO!!

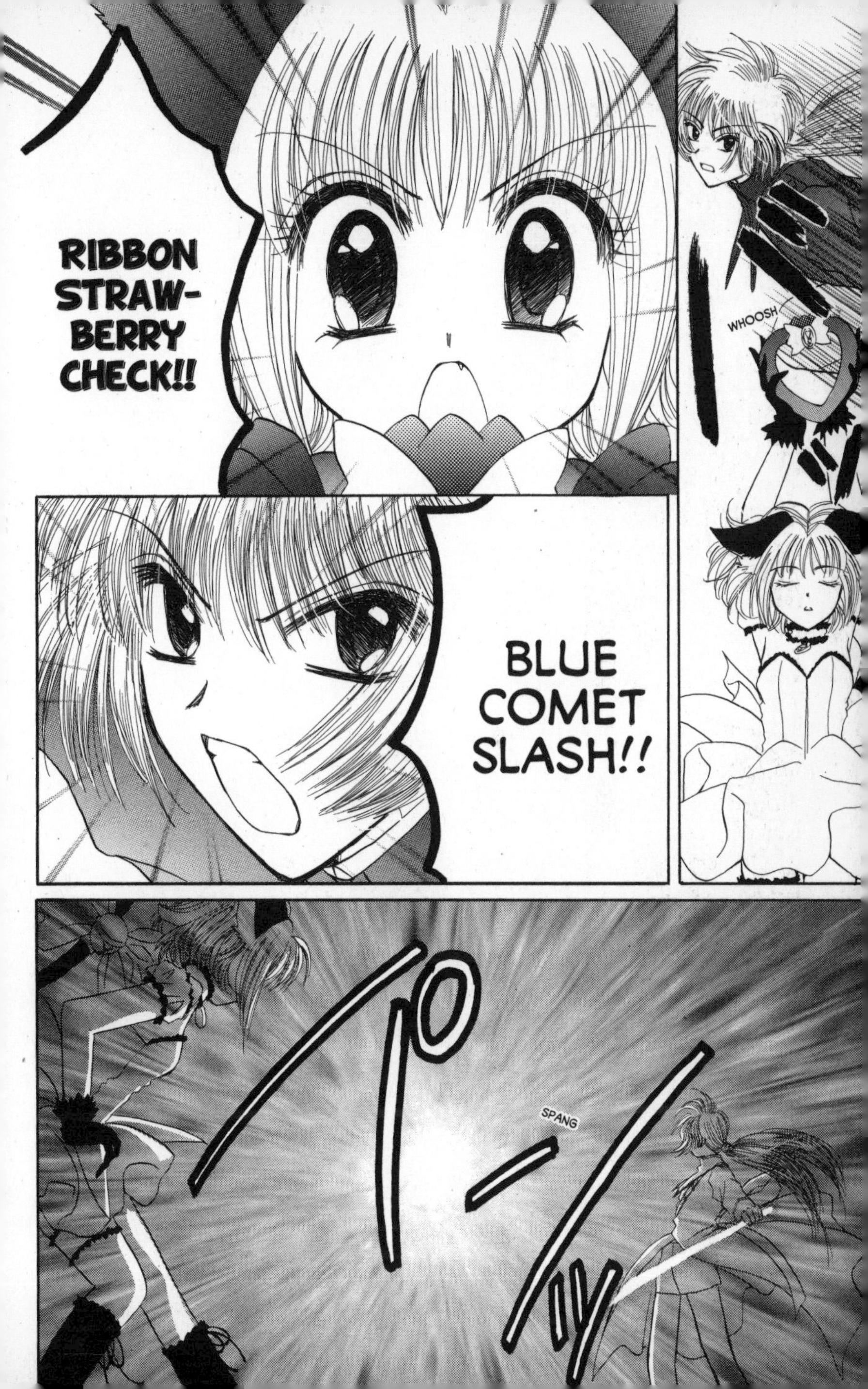

WHOOSH
RIBBON STRAW-BERRY CHECK!!
BLUE COMET SLASH!!
SPANG

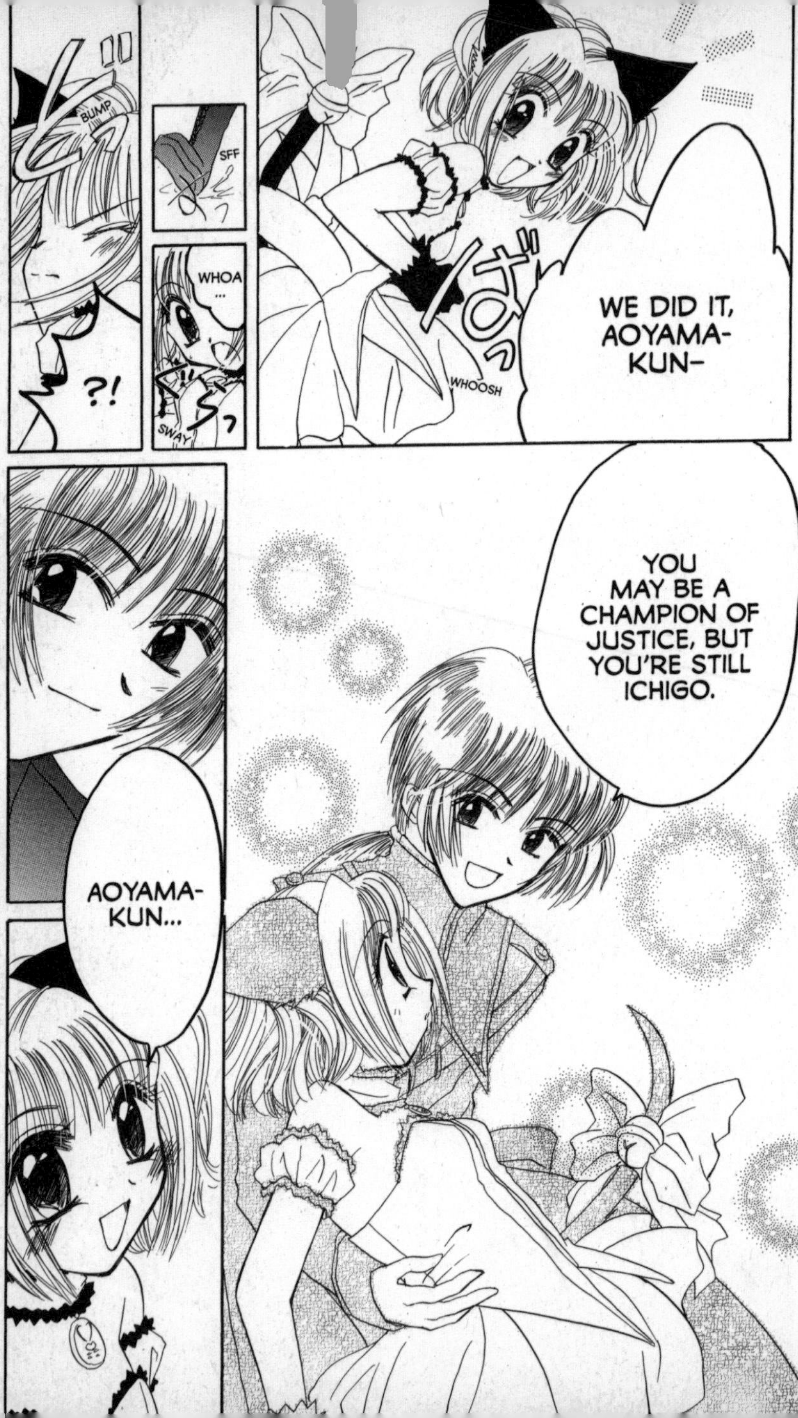

WHOOSH
WE DID IT, AOYAMA-KUN–
SFF
WHOA ...
SWAY
BUMP
?!
YOU MAY BE A CHAMPION OF JUSTICE, BUT YOU'RE STILL ICHIGO.
AOYAMA-KUN...

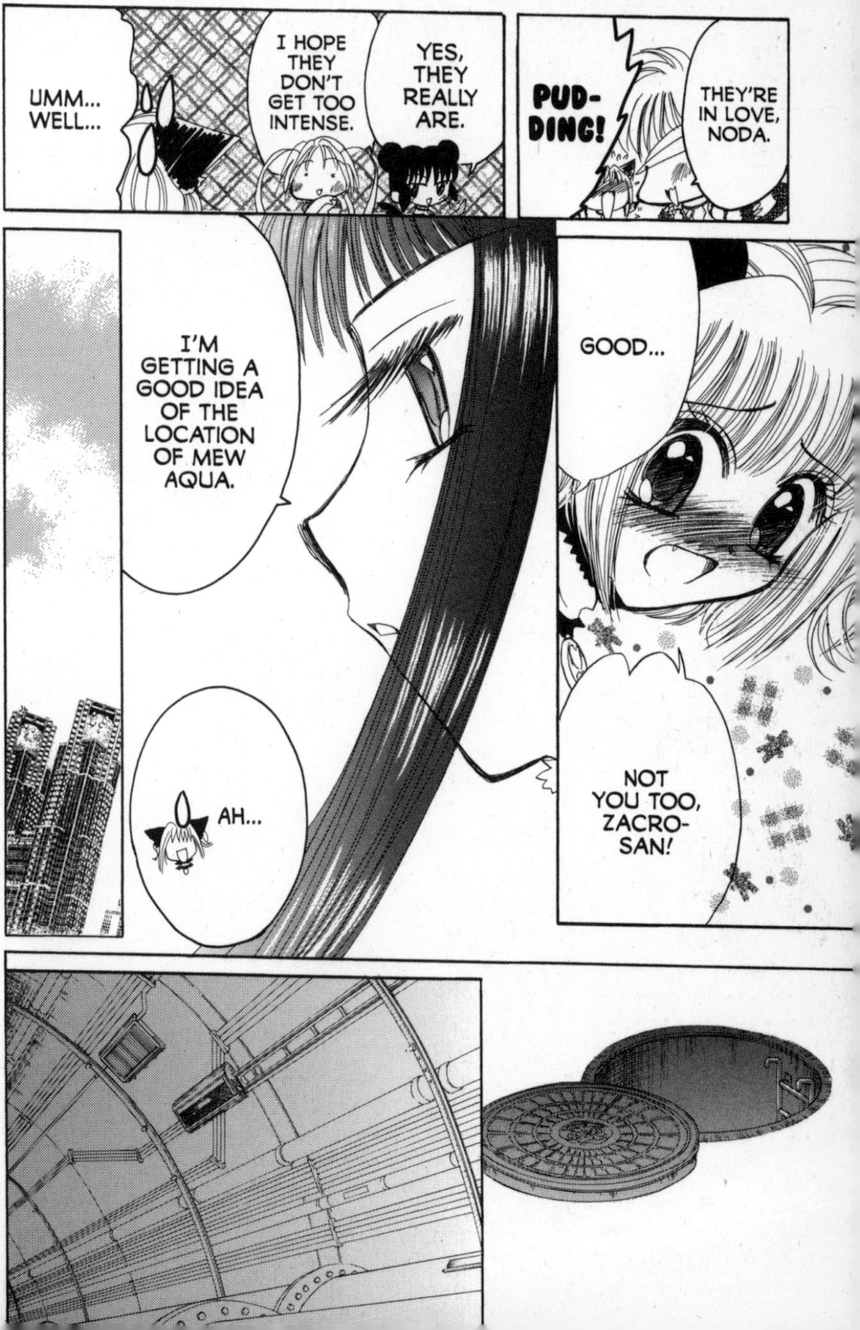
THEY'RE IN LOVE, NODA.
PUD-DING!
YES, THEY REALLY ARE.
I HOPE THEY DON'T GET TOO INTENSE.
UMM... WELL...
GOOD...
NOT YOU TOO, ZACRO-SAN!
I'M GETTING A GOOD IDEA OF THE LOCATION OF MEW AQUA.
AH...

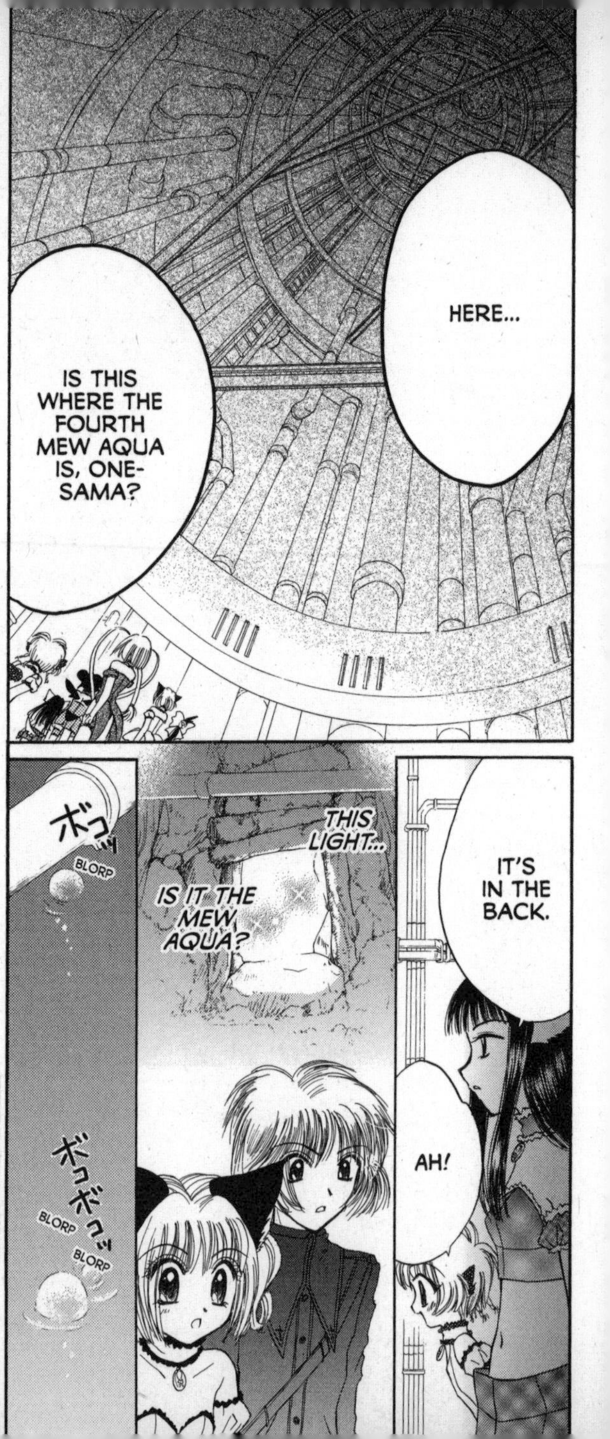
HERE...
IS THIS WHERE THE FOURTH MEW AQUA IS, ONE-SAMA?
IT'S IN THE BACK.
AH!
THIS LIGHT...
IS IT THE MEW AQUA?
ボコッ
BLORP
ボコボコッ
BLORP
BLORP

Tokyo Mew Mew:

Ichigo's Costume Wanted! Part 7

CUTE AWARD

EMI SHIBUYA-CHAN,
KANAGAWA PREFECTURE,
HIGH SCHOOL JUNIOR

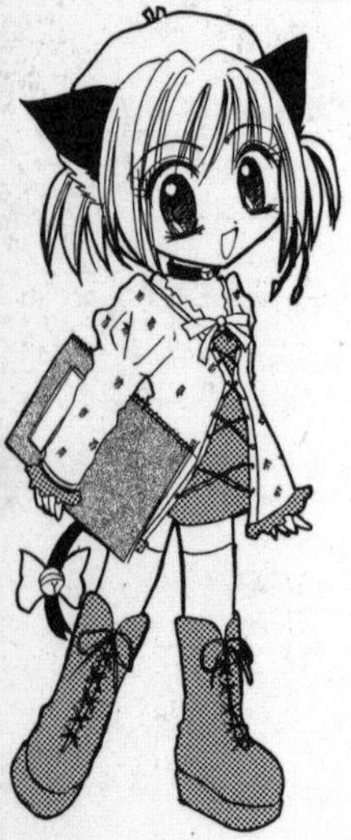

I think the design is unbalanced because of a lack of attention to detail. I'm sorry! It's something we can wear to a library though. I want this jacket for my outing. It was a very cute costume.

Those were the six costumes I wanted to show you. Thanks to everyone for participating in the contest!

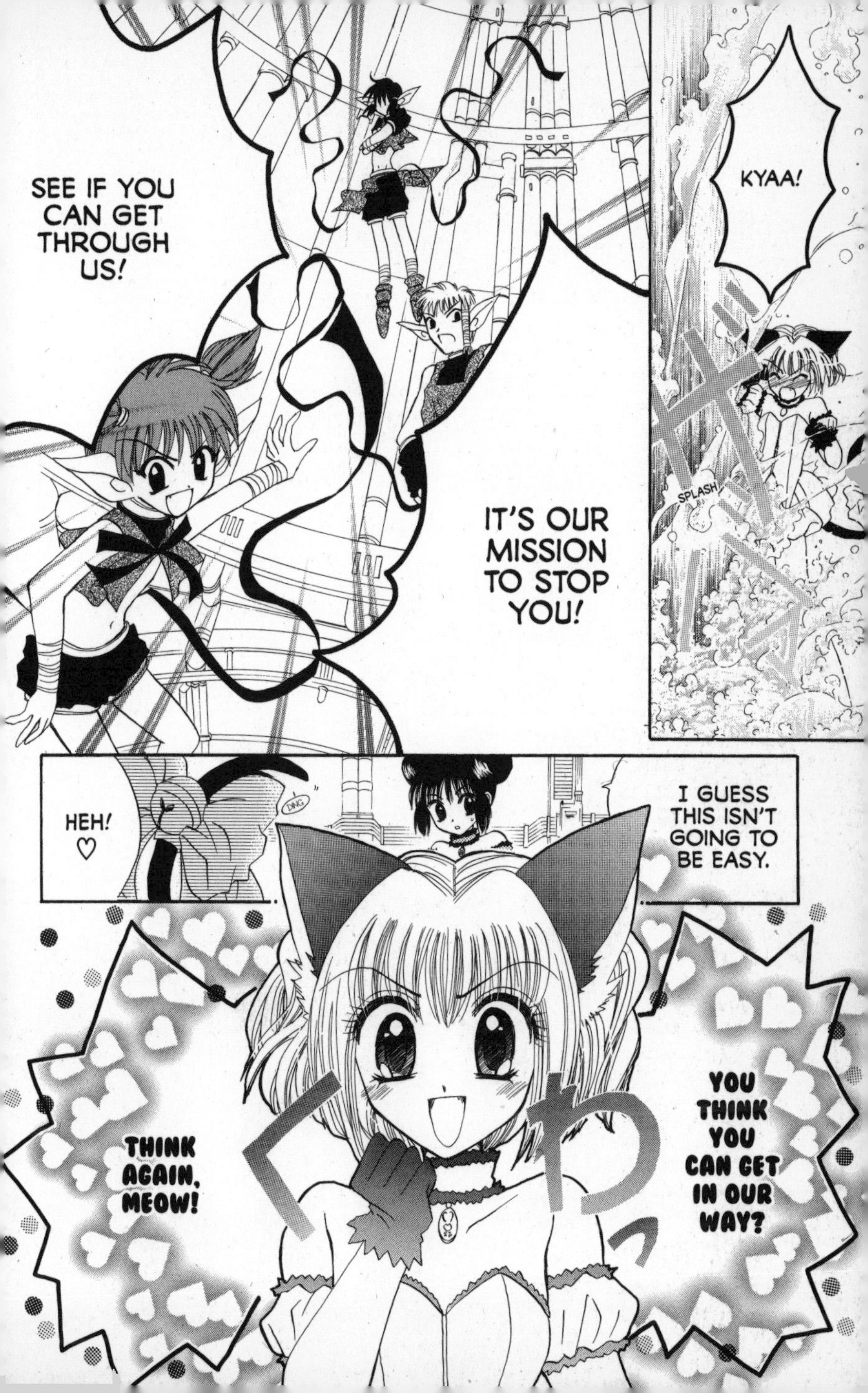
KYAA!
SPLASH
SEE IF YOU CAN GET THROUGH US!
IT'S OUR MISSION TO STOP YOU!
I GUESS THIS ISN'T GOING TO BE EASY.
DING
HEH! ♡
YOU THINK YOU CAN GET IN OUR WAY?
THINK AGAIN, MEOW!

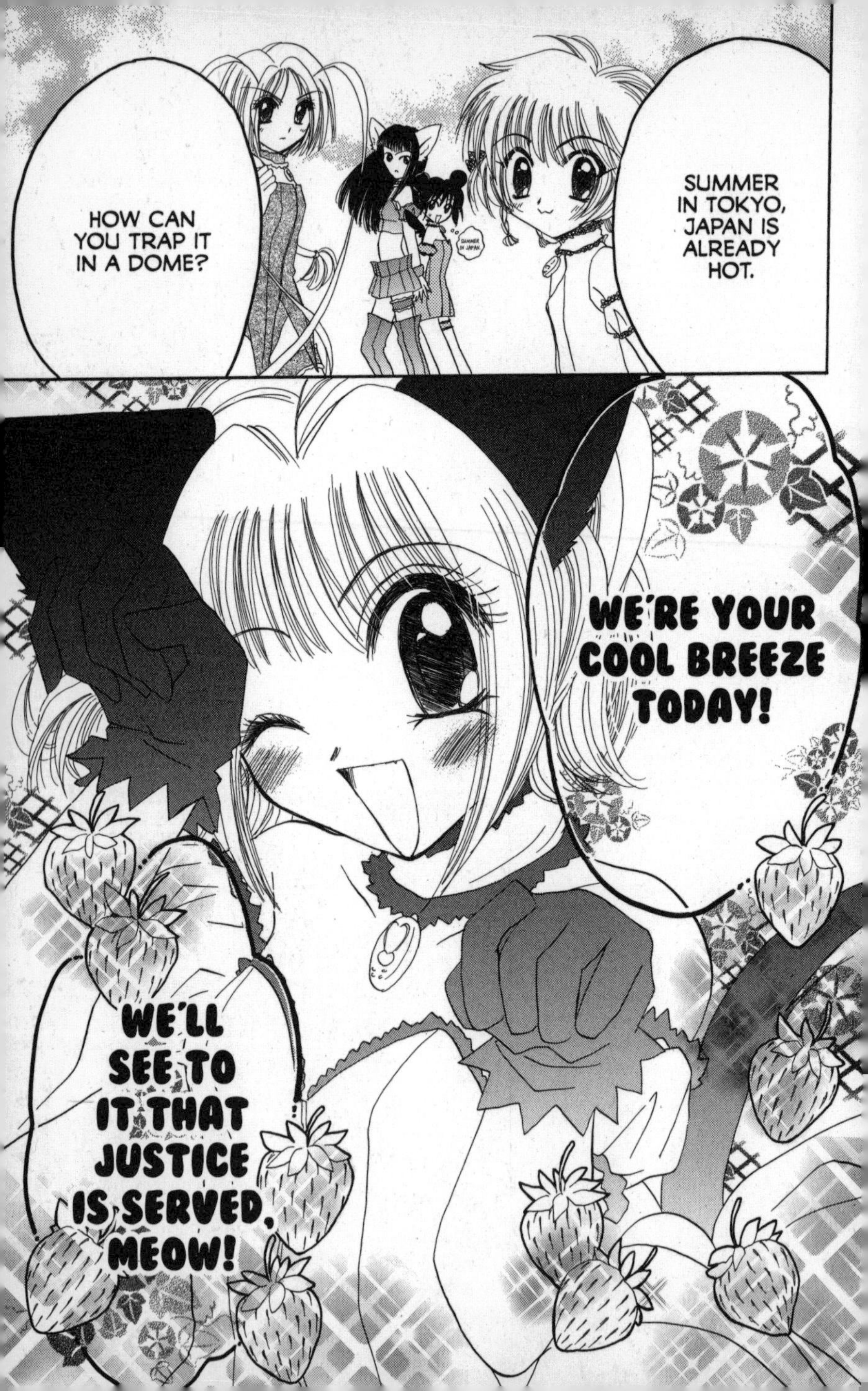
SUMMER IN TOKYO, JAPAN IS ALREADY HOT.
SUMMER IN JAPAN
HOW CAN YOU TRAP IT IN A DOME?
WE'RE YOUR COOL BREEZE TODAY!
WE'LL SEE TO IT THAT JUSTICE IS SERVED, MEOW!

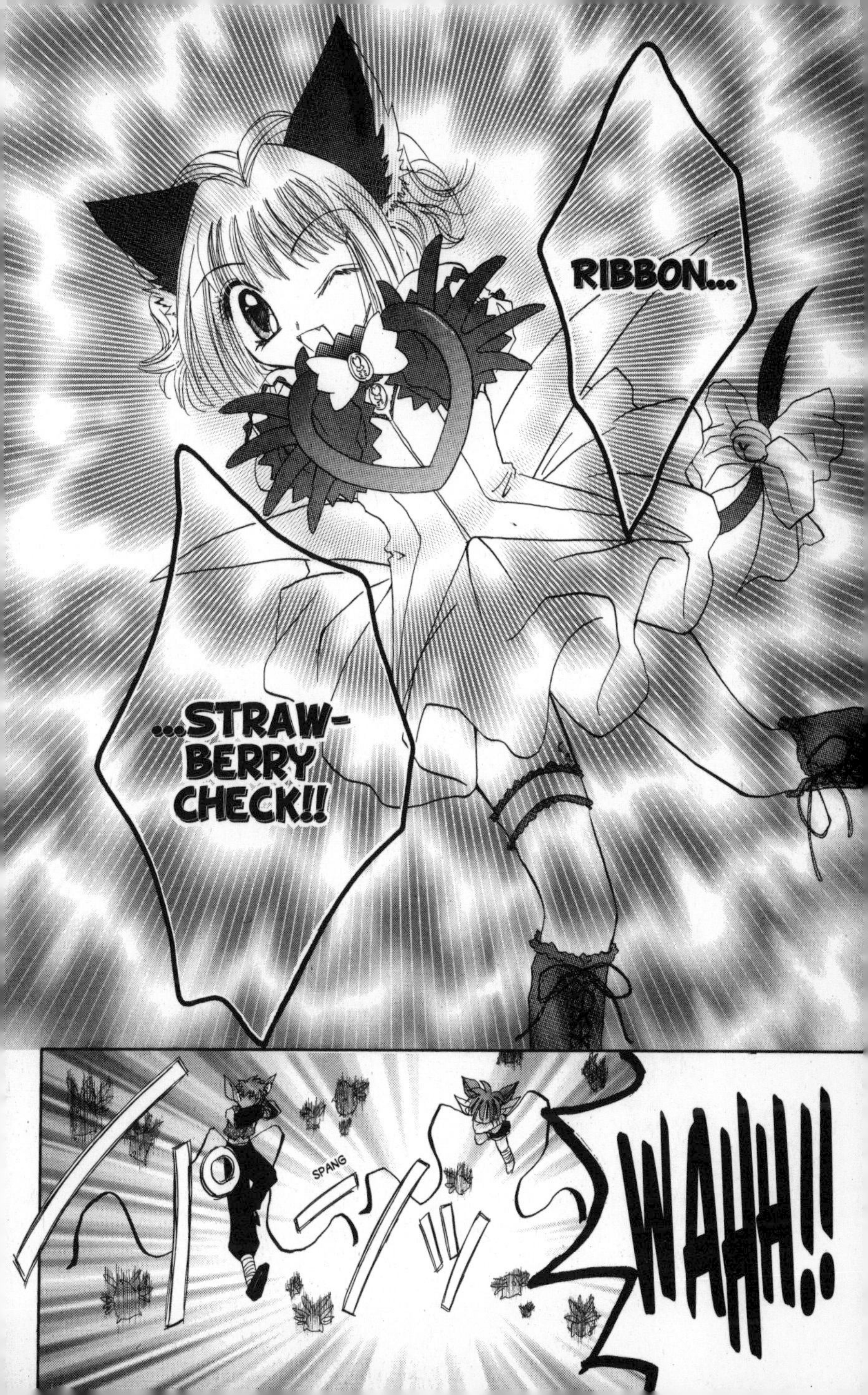
RIBBON...
...STRAW-BERRY CHECK!!
WAHH!!
SPANG

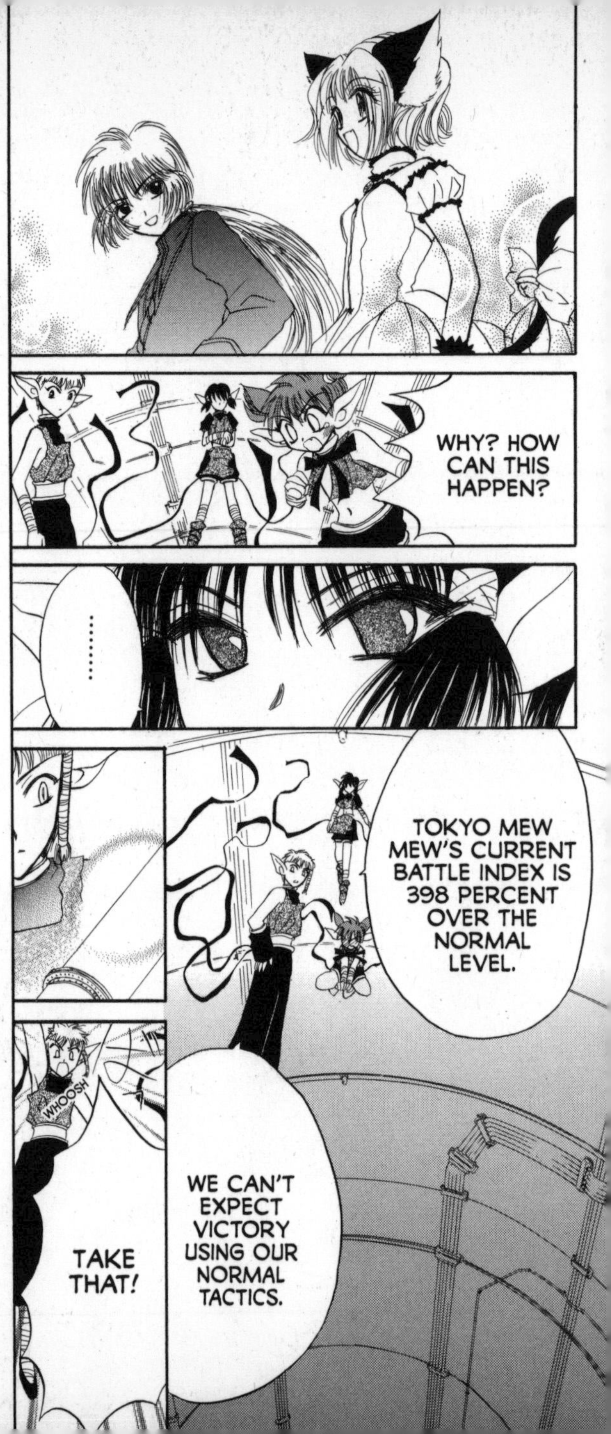
WHY? HOW CAN THIS HAPPEN?
......
TOKYO MEW MEW'S CURRENT BATTLE INDEX IS 398 PERCENT OVER THE NORMAL LEVEL.
WE CAN'T EXPECT VICTORY USING OUR NORMAL TACTICS.
TAKE THAT!
WHOOSH

SPECIAL THANKS!!

R. YOSHIDA

H. MATSUMOTO
M. OMORI

S. NAOHARA
K. HONDA
A. SUZUKI

A. OKAWA
S. NAKAZAWA

H. OIKAWA

M. SEKIYA
S. SUDA

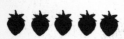

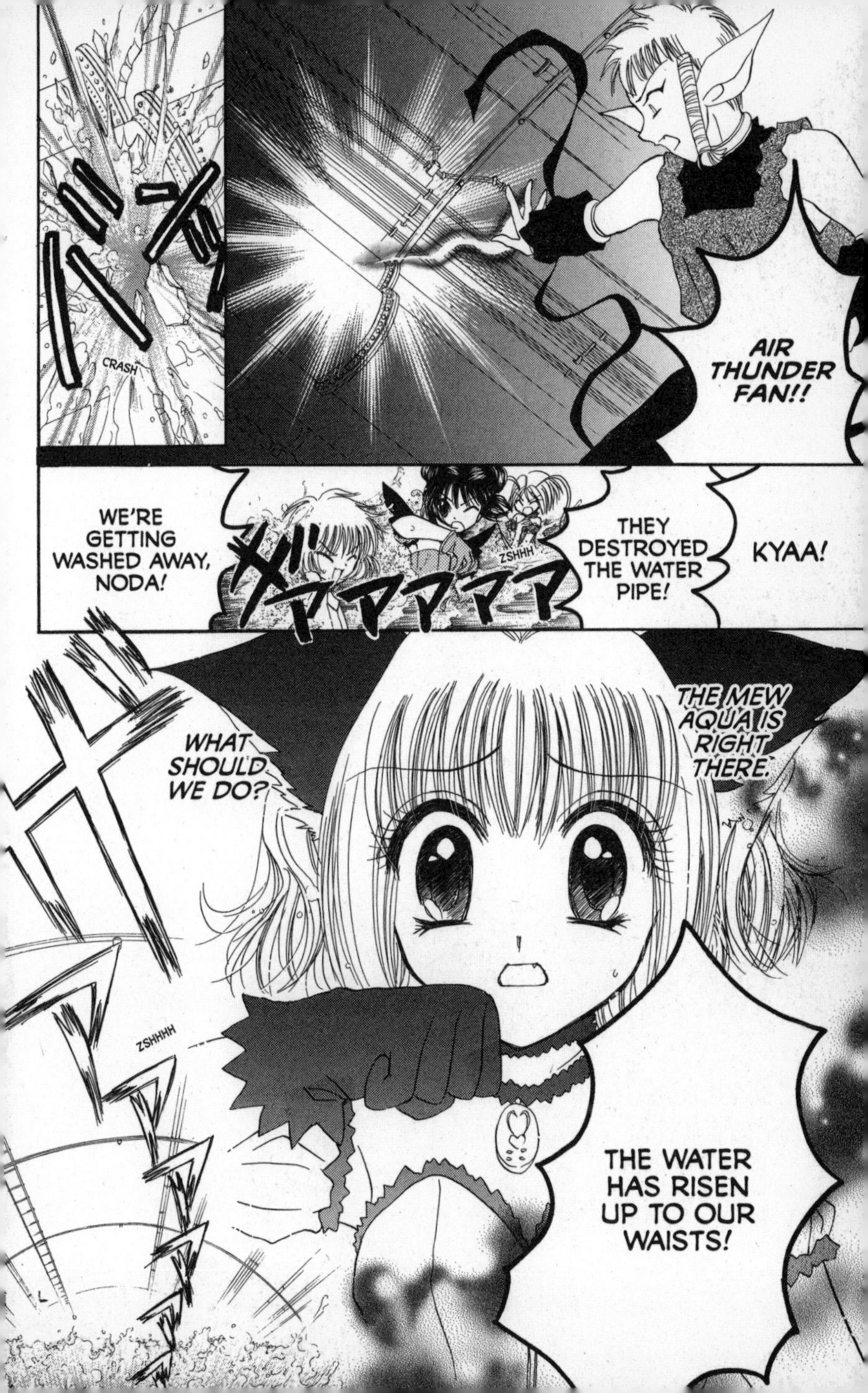
AIR THUNDER FAN!!
CRASH
KYAA!
THEY DESTROYED THE WATER PIPE!
ZSHHH
WE'RE GETTING WASHED AWAY, NODA!
THE MEW AQUA IS RIGHT THERE.
WHAT SHOULD WE DO?
ZSHHHH
THE WATER HAS RISEN UP TO OUR WAISTS!

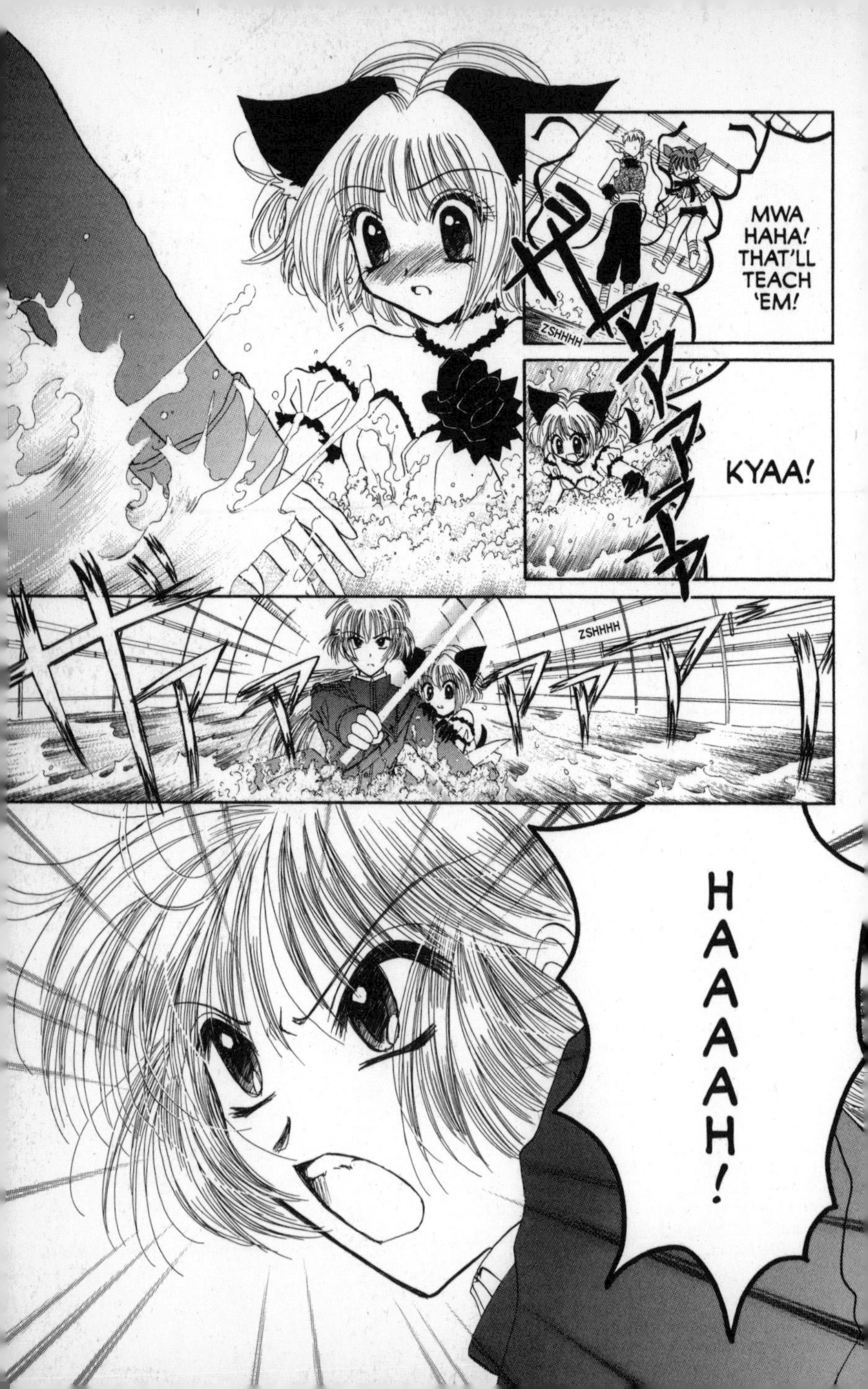
MWA HAHA! THAT'LL TEACH 'EM!
ZSHHHH
KYAA!
ZSHHHH
HAAAAH!

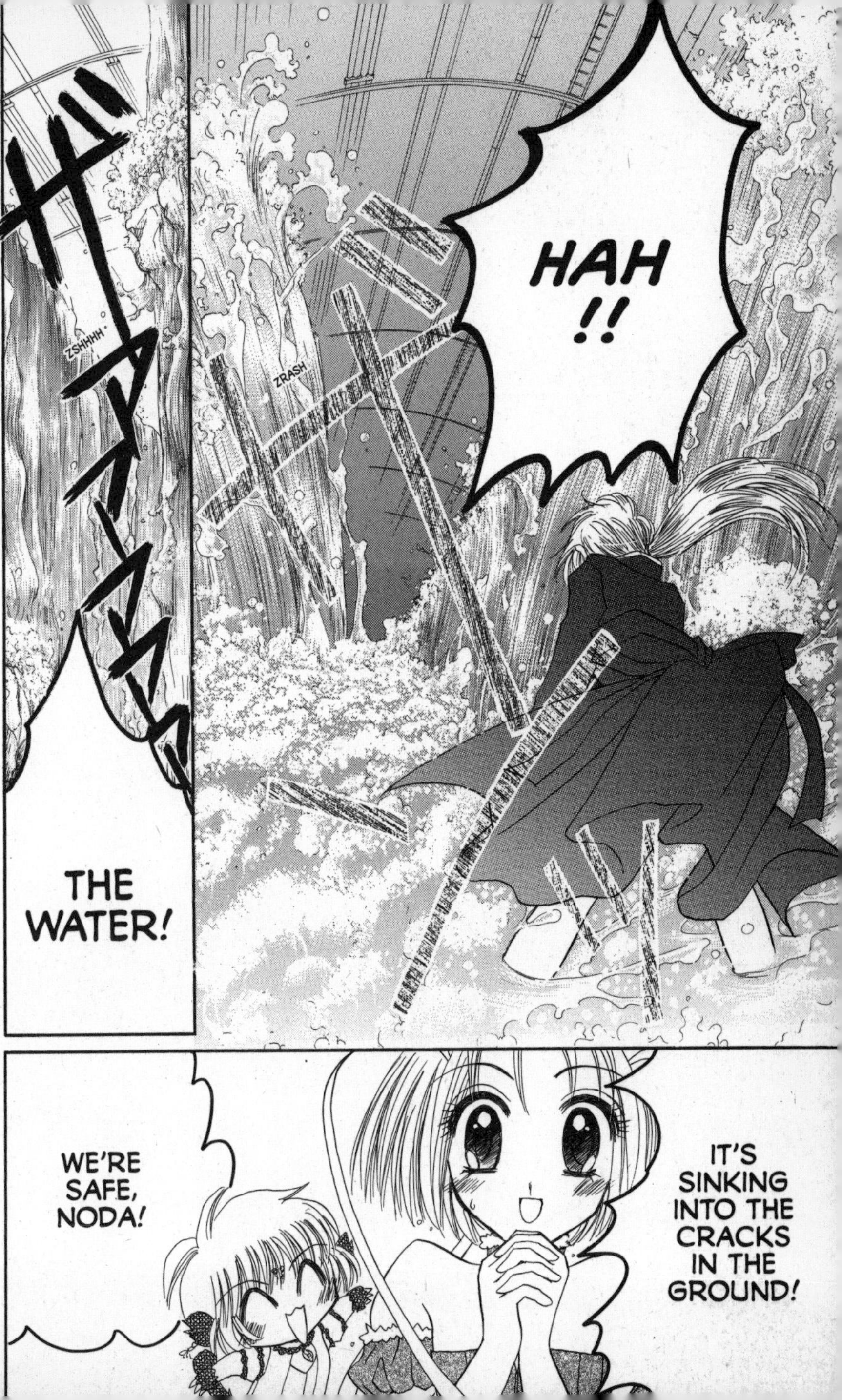
HAH !!
ZRASH
ZSHHHH
THE WATER!
IT'S SINKING INTO THE CRACKS IN THE GROUND!
WE'RE SAFE, NODA!

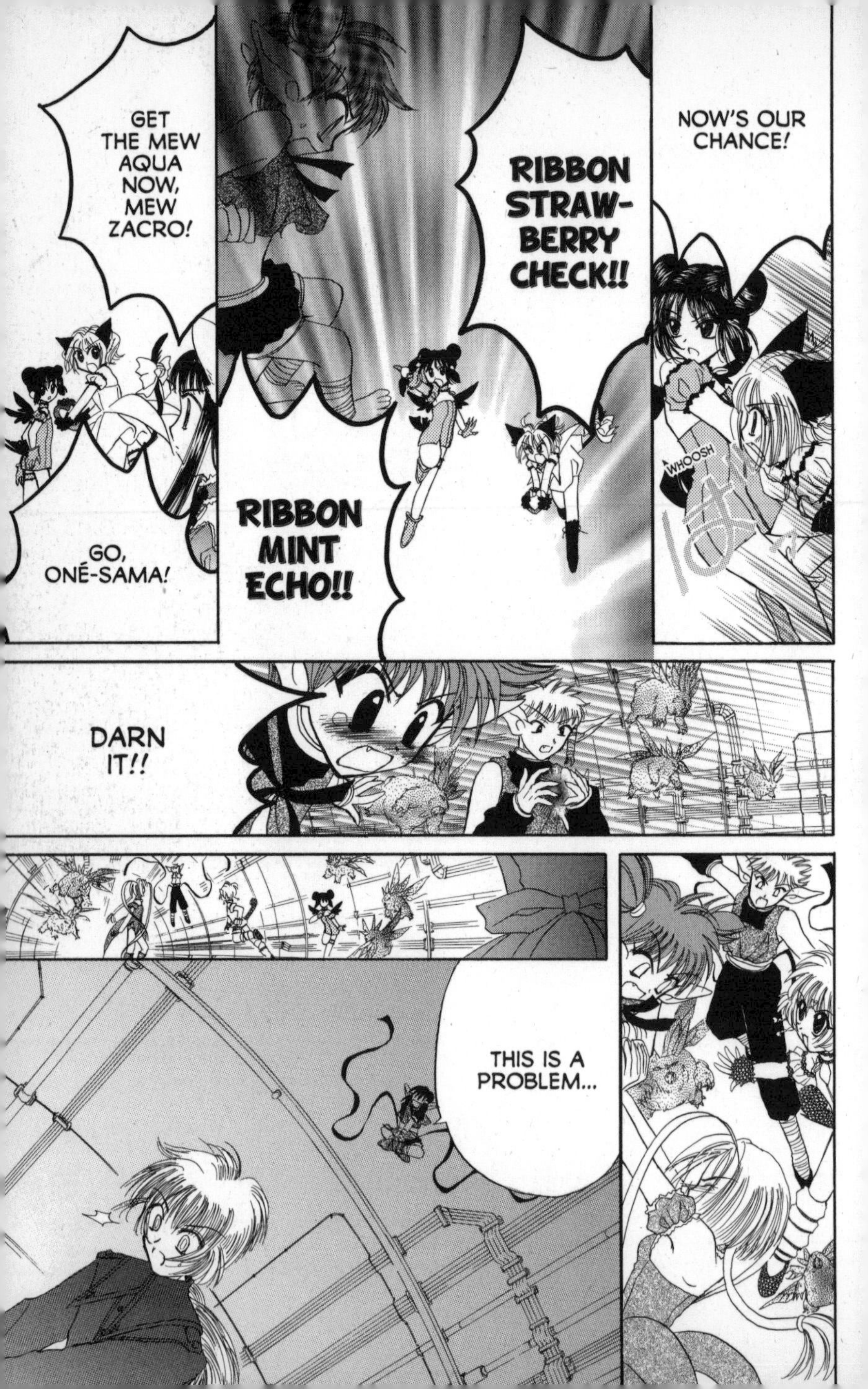
NOW'S OUR CHANCE!
WHOOSH
RIBBON STRAW-BERRY CHECK!!
RIBBON MINT ECHO!!
GET THE MEW AQUA NOW, MEW ZACRO!
GO, ONÉ-SAMA!
DARN IT!!
THIS IS A PROBLEM...

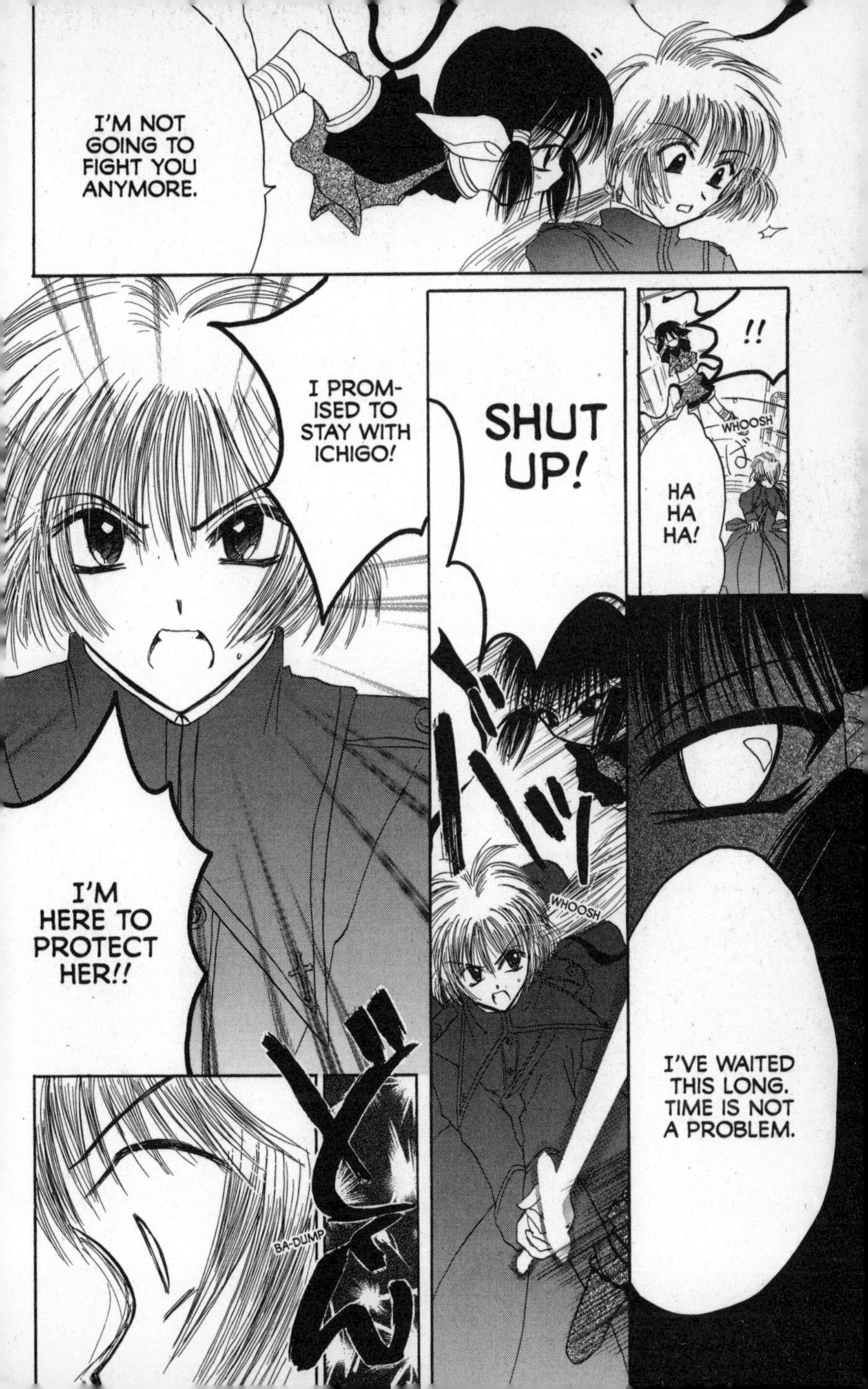
I'M NOT GOING TO FIGHT YOU ANYMORE.
!!
WHOOSH
ば
HA HA HA!
SHUT UP!
I PROMISED TO STAY WITH ICHIGO!
I'M HERE TO PROTECT HER!!
I'VE WAITED THIS LONG. TIME IS NOT A PROBLEM.
WHOOSH
BA-DUMP

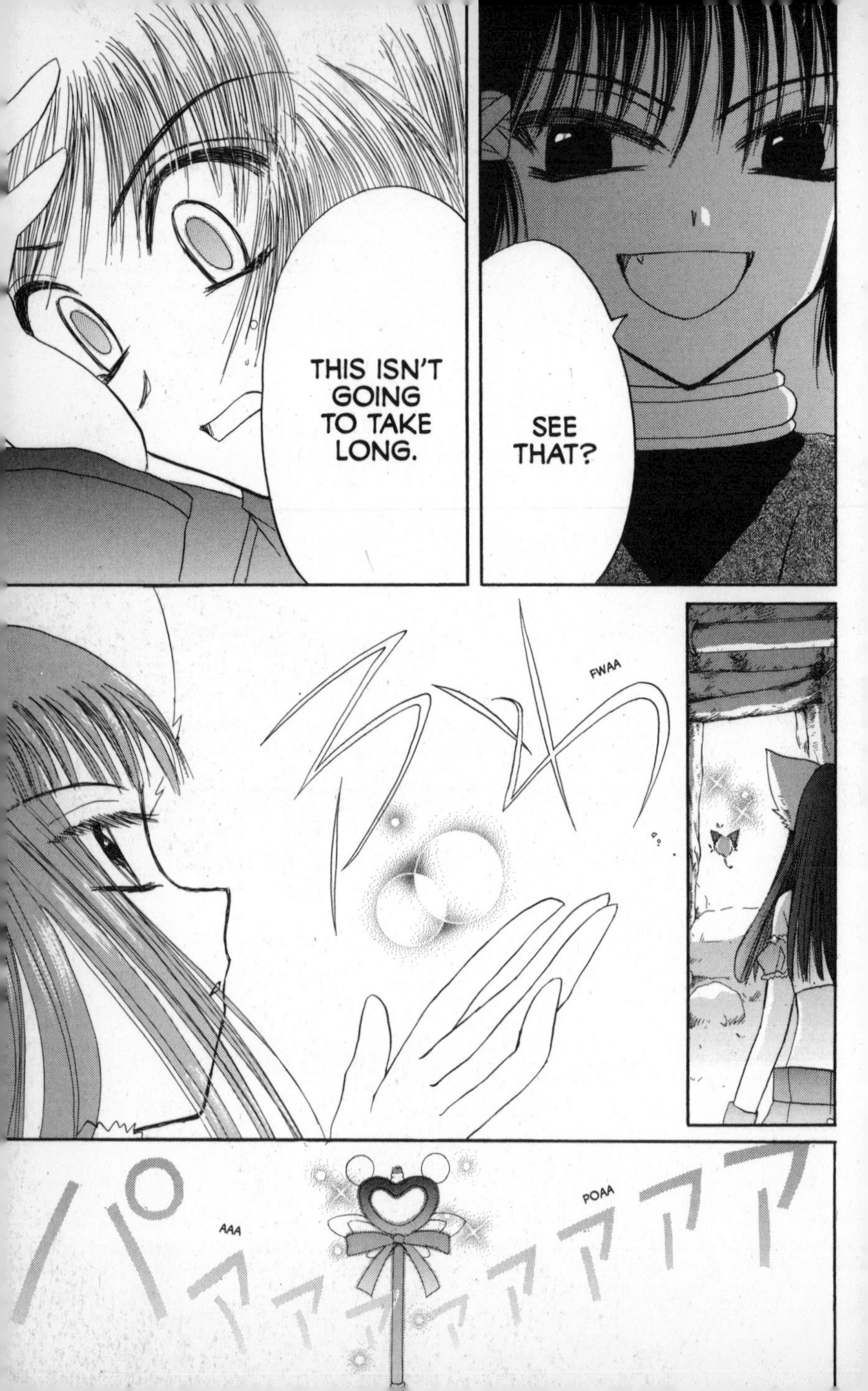
SEE THAT?
THIS ISN'T GOING TO TAKE LONG.
FWAA
POAA
AAA

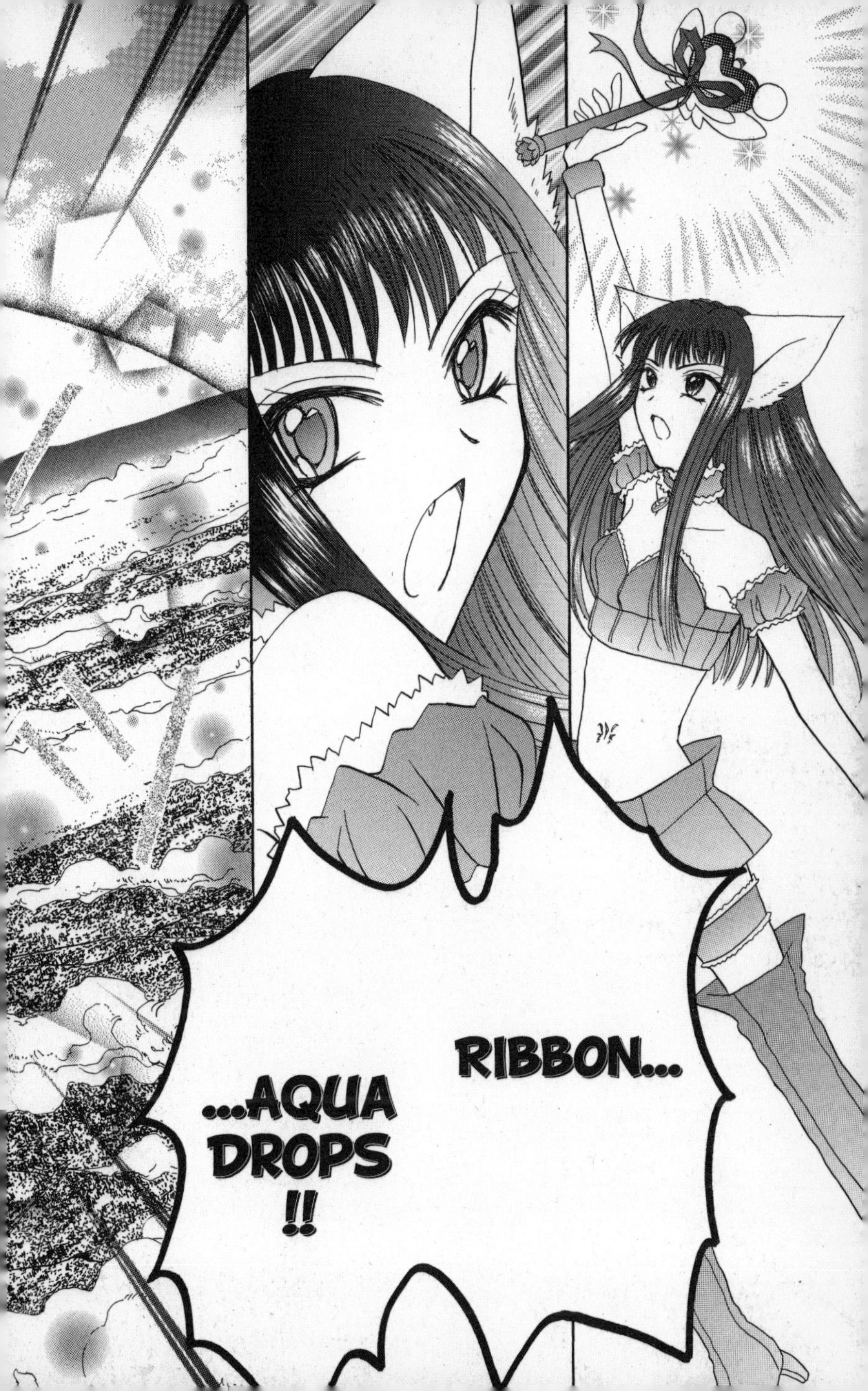
RIBBON...
...AQUA DROPS !!

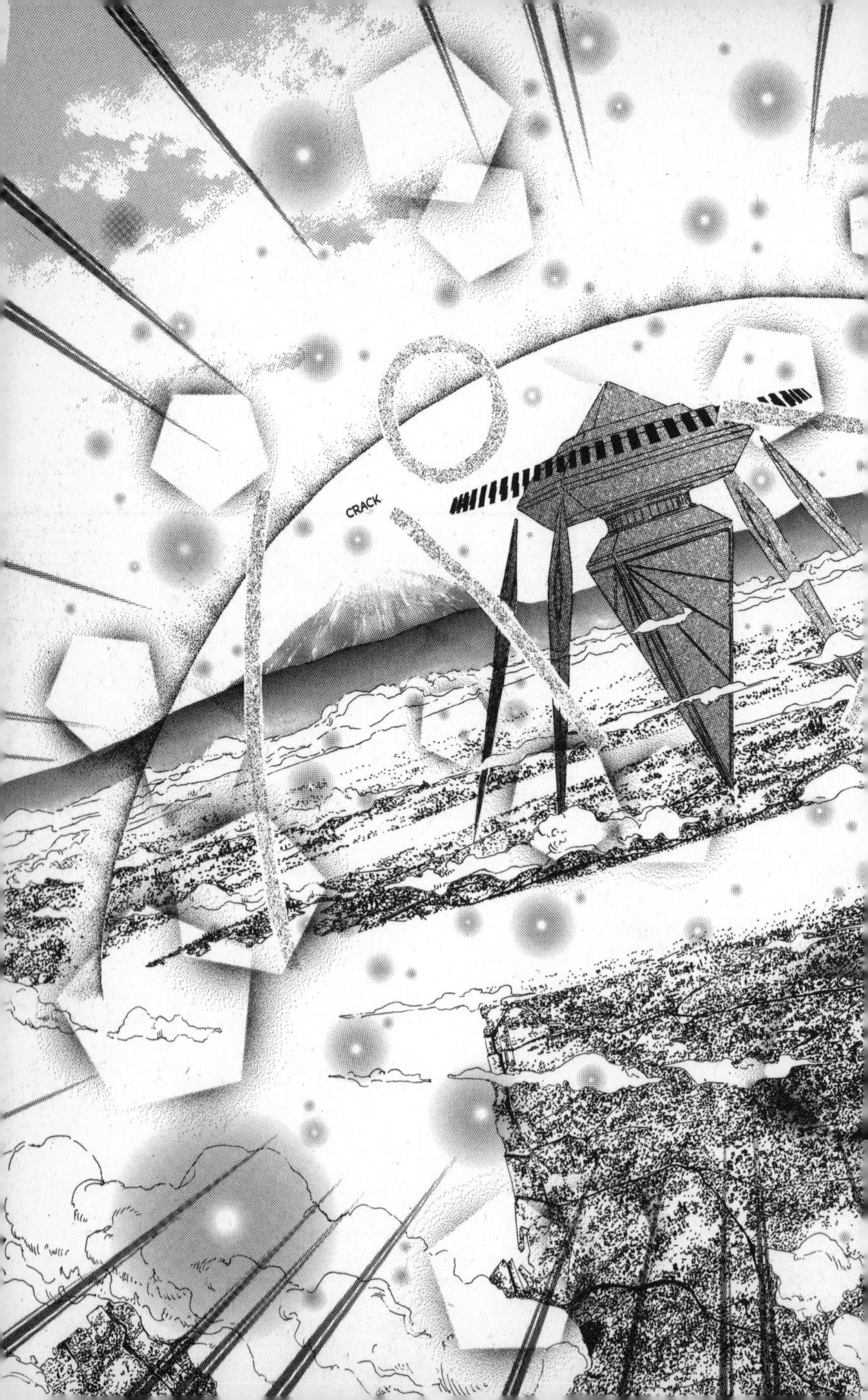
CRACK

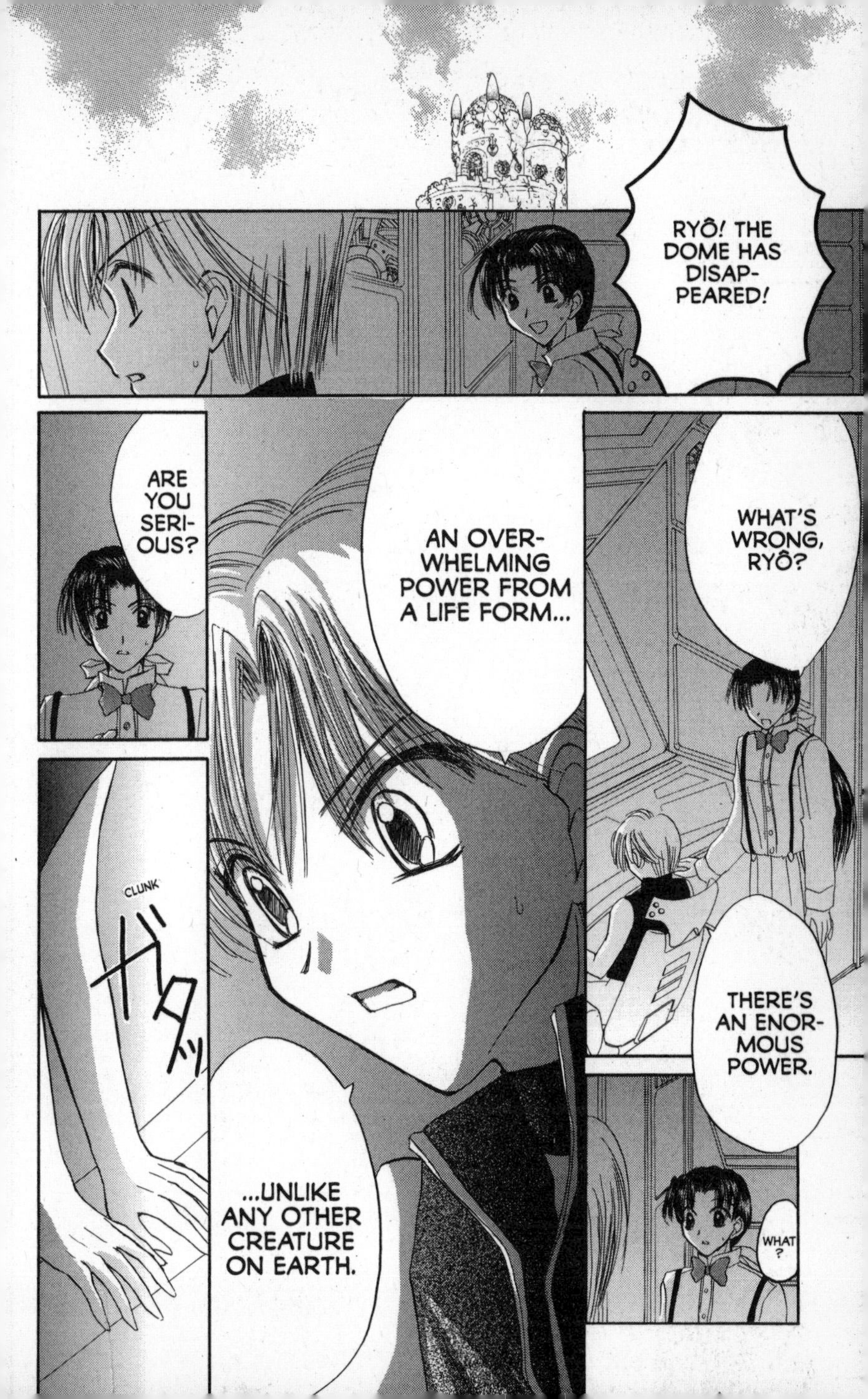
RYÔ! THE DOME HAS DISAPPEARED!
WHAT'S WRONG, RYÔ?
THERE'S AN ENORMOUS POWER.
WHAT?
AN OVERWHELMING POWER FROM A LIFE FORM...
...UNLIKE ANY OTHER CREATURE ON EARTH.
ARE YOU SERIOUS?
CLUNK
ガタッ

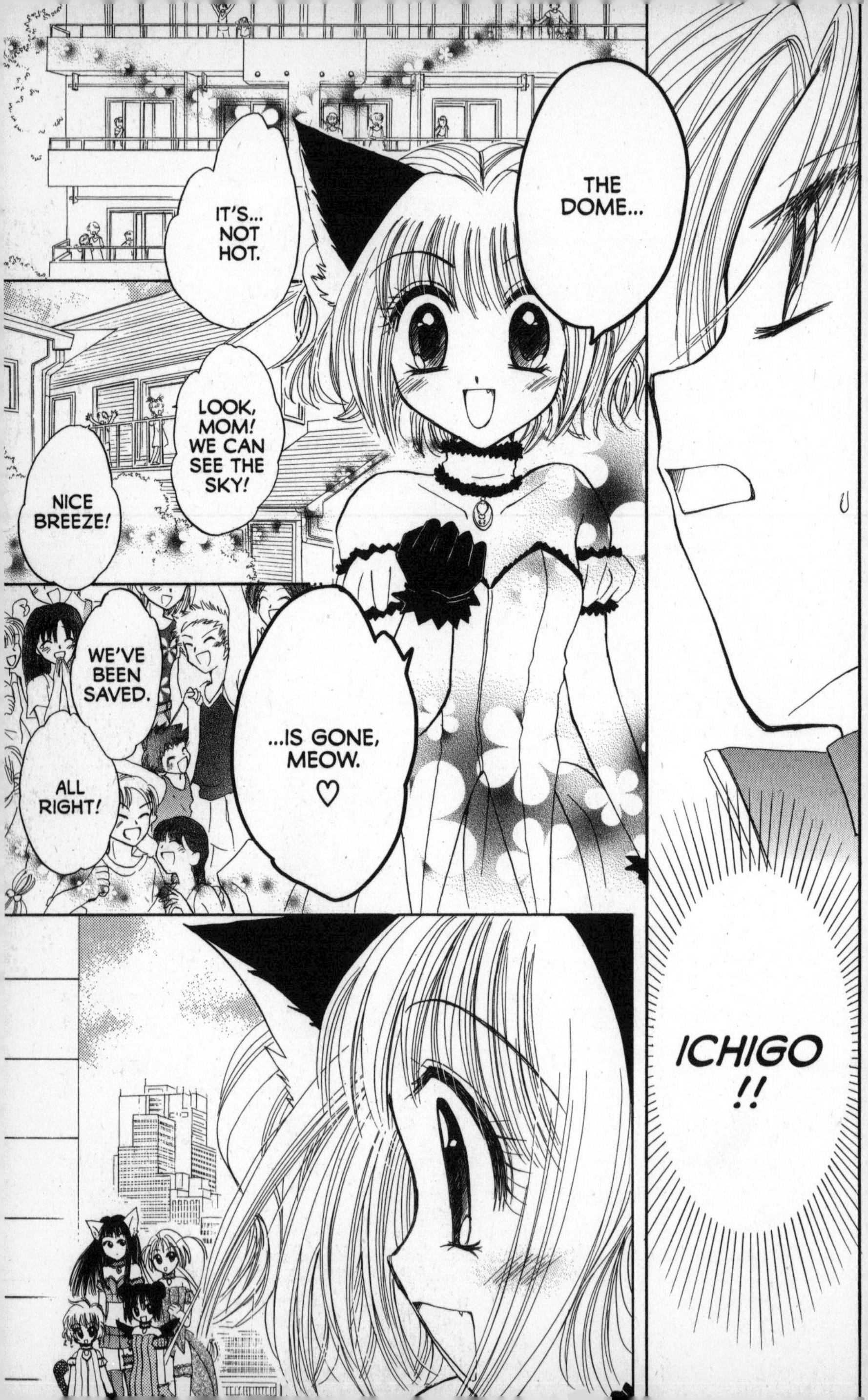
ICHIGO !!
THE DOME...
IT'S... NOT HOT.
LOOK, MOM! WE CAN SEE THE SKY!
NICE BREEZE!
...IS GONE, MEOW. ♡
WE'VE BEEN SAVED.
ALL RIGHT!

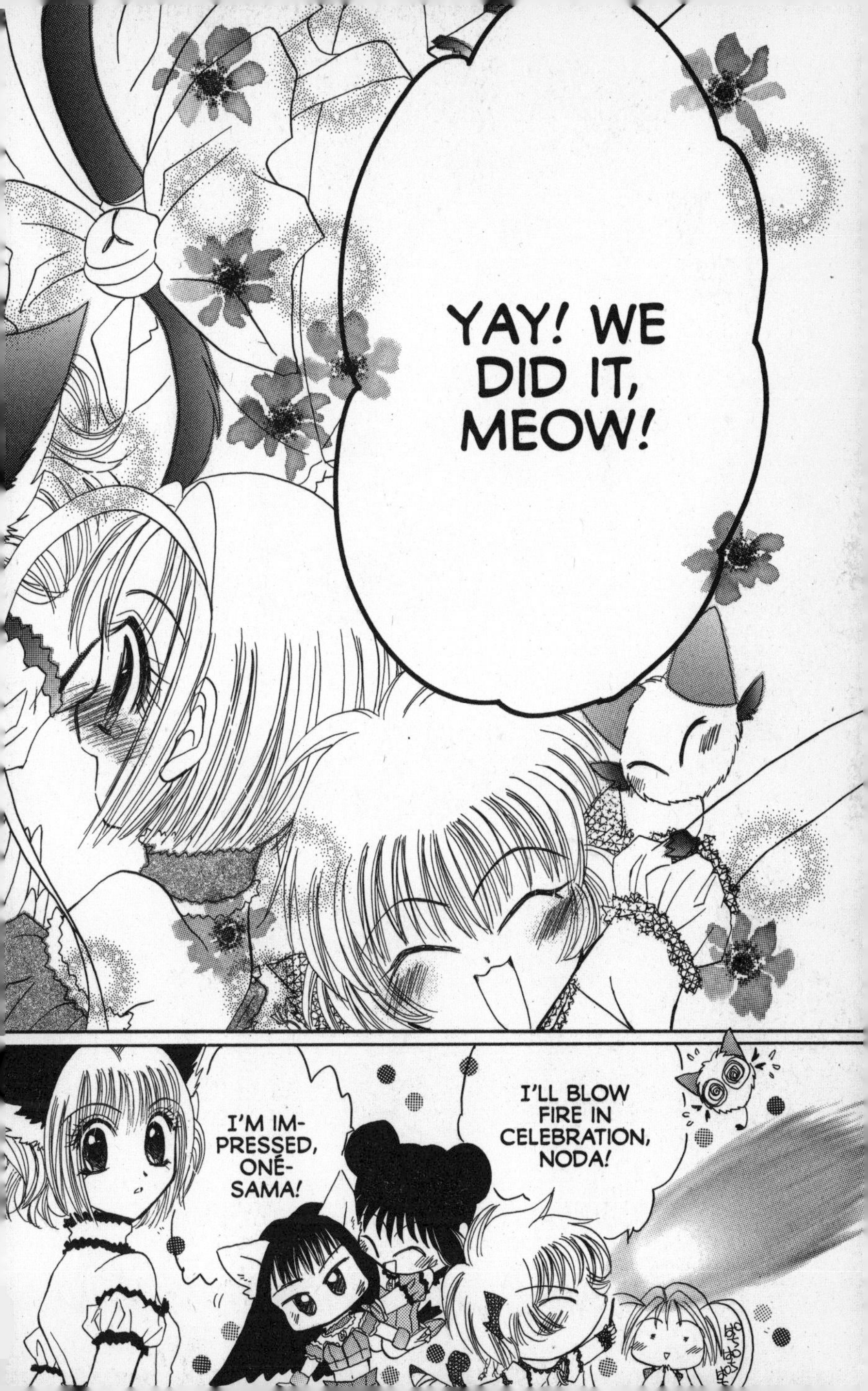
YAY! WE DID IT, MEOW!
I'LL BLOW FIRE IN CELEBRATION, NODA!
I'M IM-PRESSED, ONÉ-SAMA!

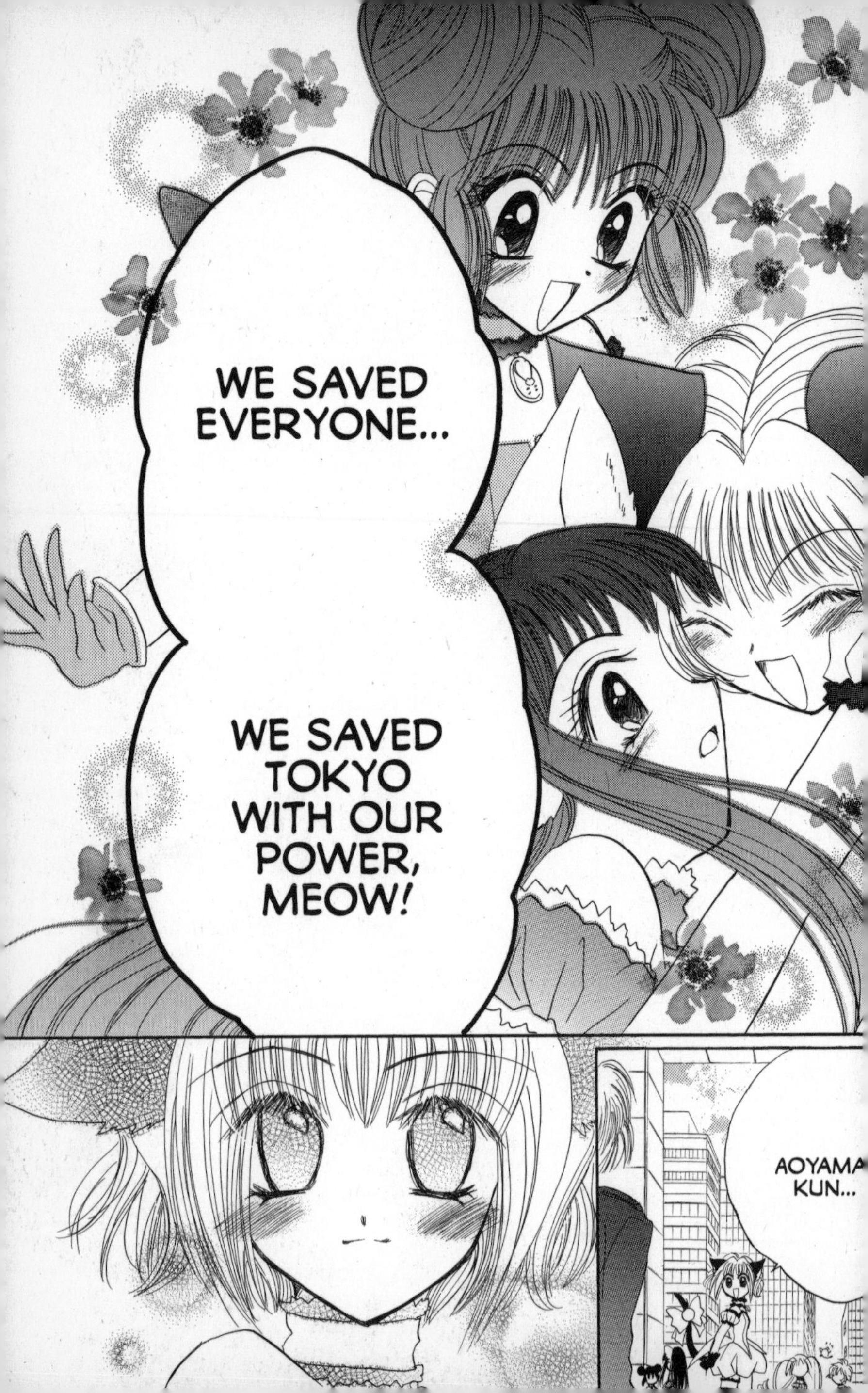
WE SAVED EVERYONE...
WE SAVED TOKYO WITH OUR POWER, MEOW!
AOYAMA KUN...

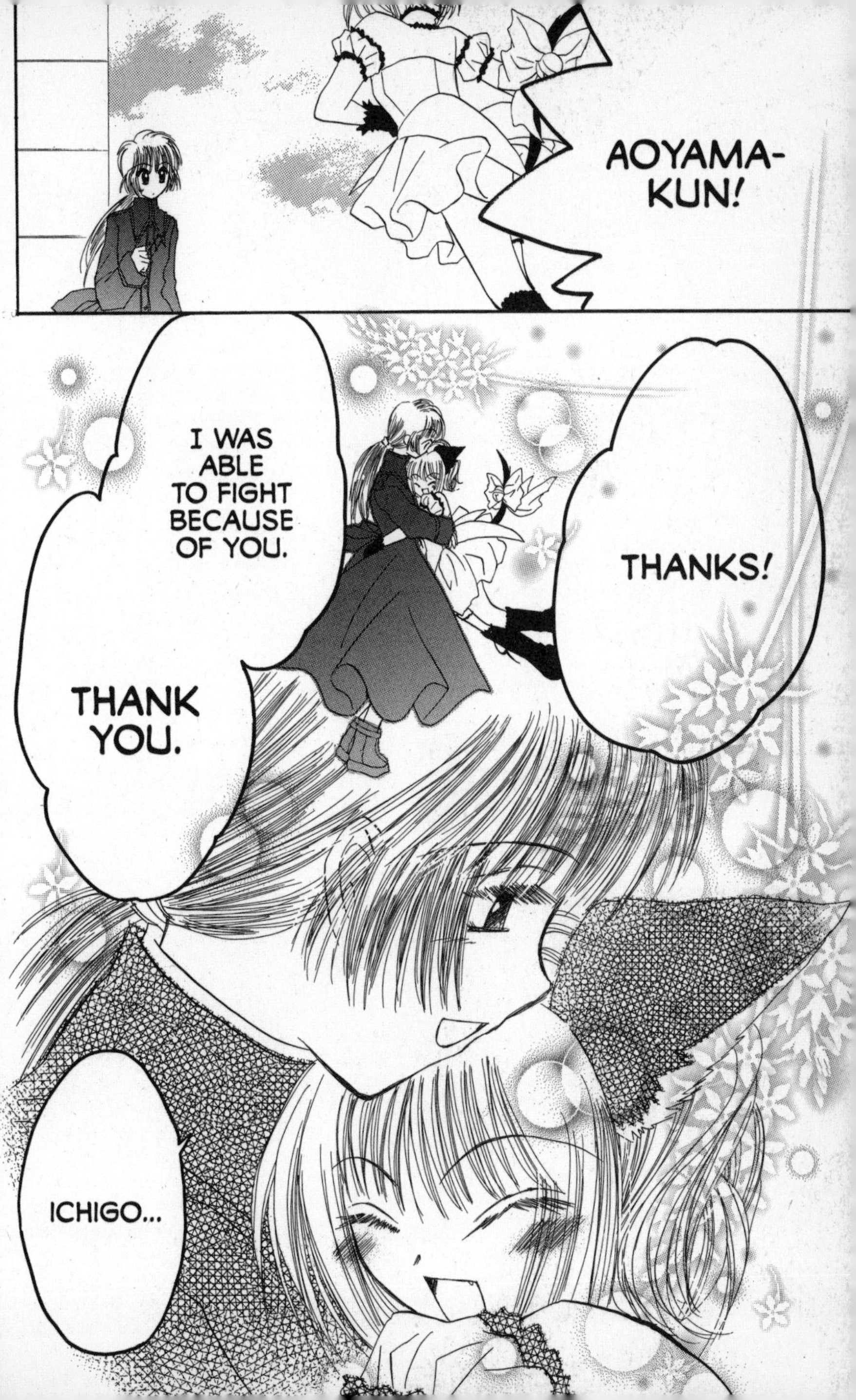
AOYAMA-KUN!
THANKS!
I WAS ABLE TO FIGHT BECAUSE OF YOU.
THANK YOU.
ICHIGO...

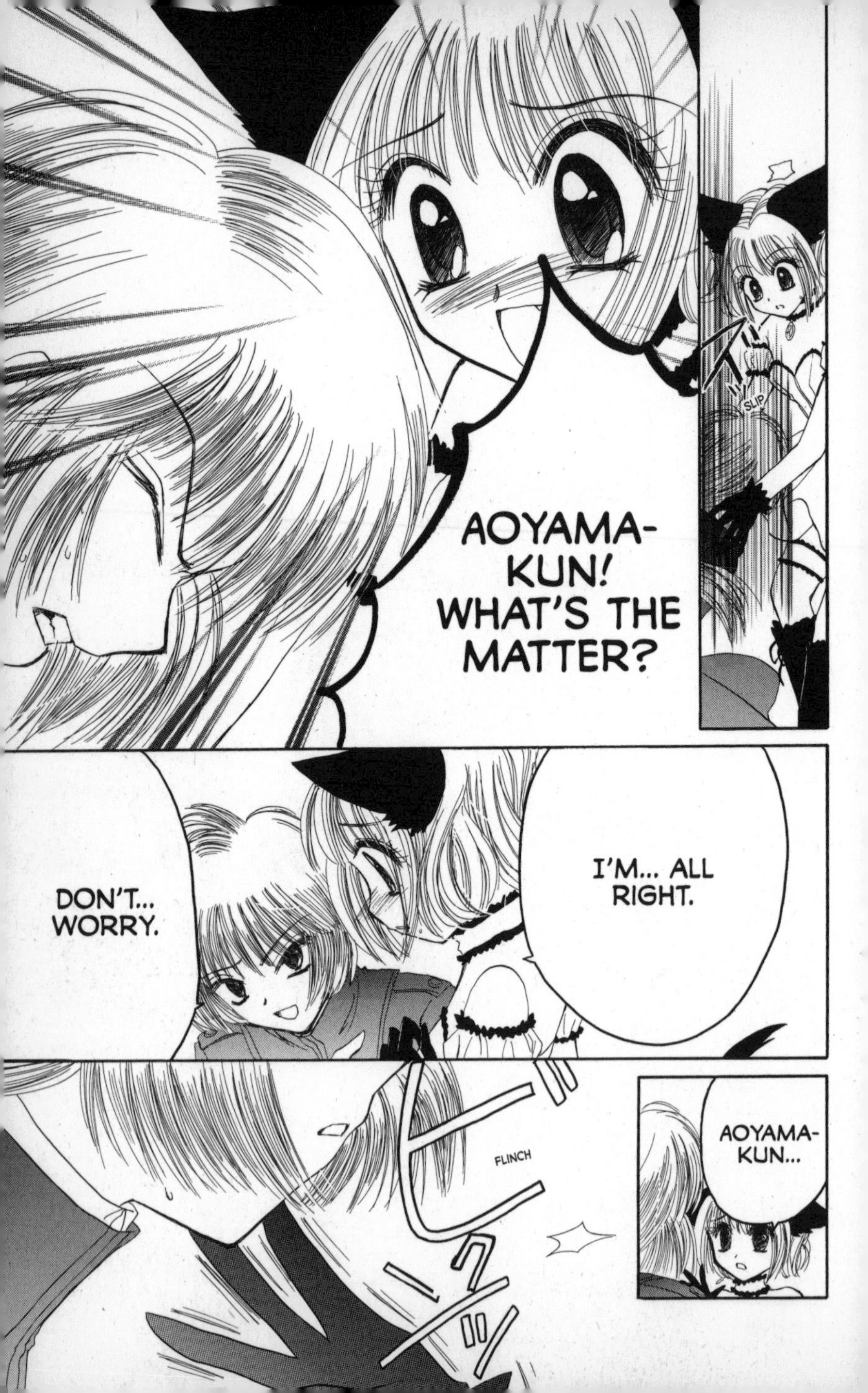
SLIP
AOYAMA-KUN! WHAT'S THE MATTER?
I'M... ALL RIGHT.
DON'T... WORRY.
AOYAMA-KUN...
FLINCH

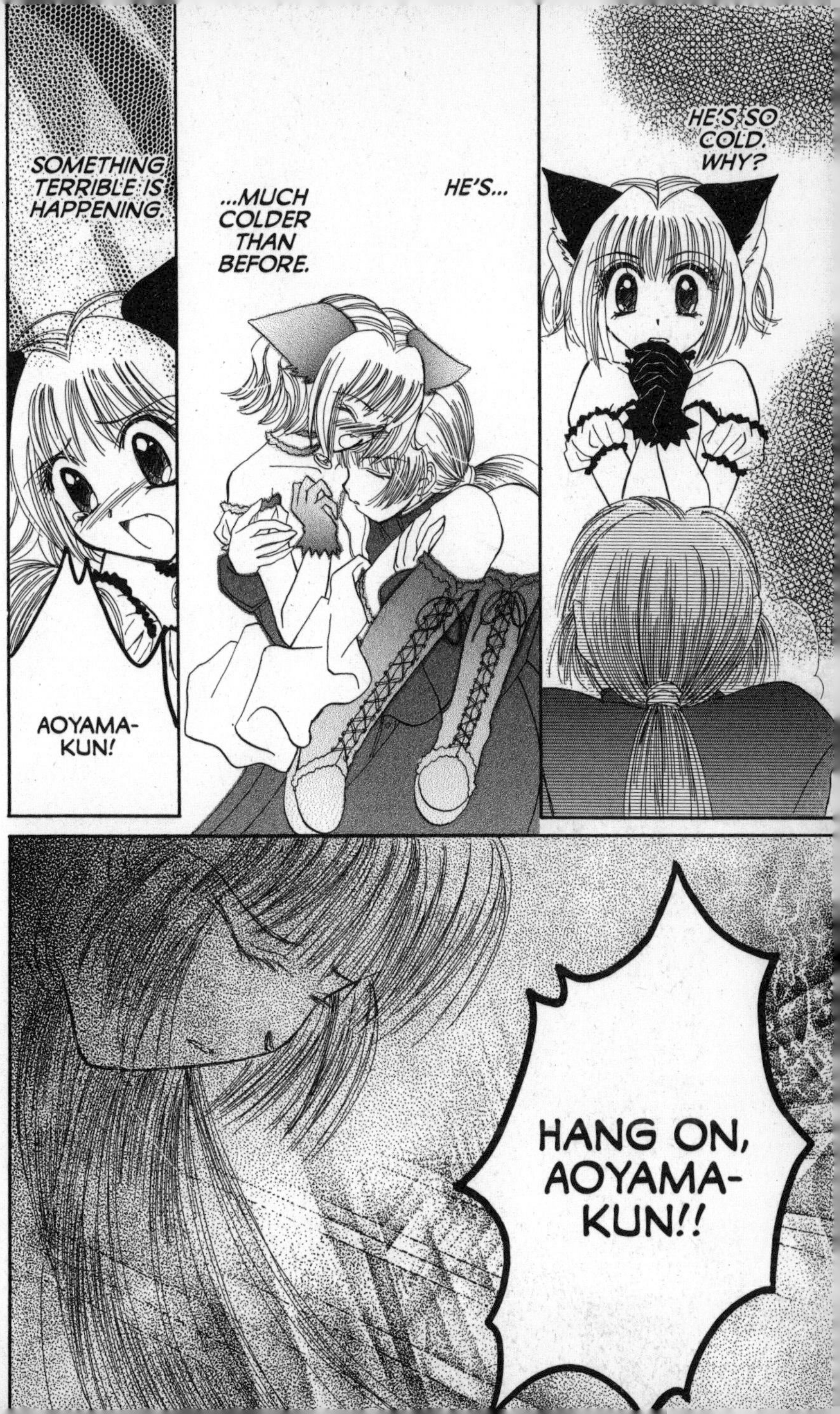
HE'S SO COLD. WHY?
HE'S...
...MUCH COLDER THAN BEFORE.
SOMETHING TERRIBLE IS HAPPENING.
AOYAMA-KUN!
HANG ON, AOYAMA-KUN!!

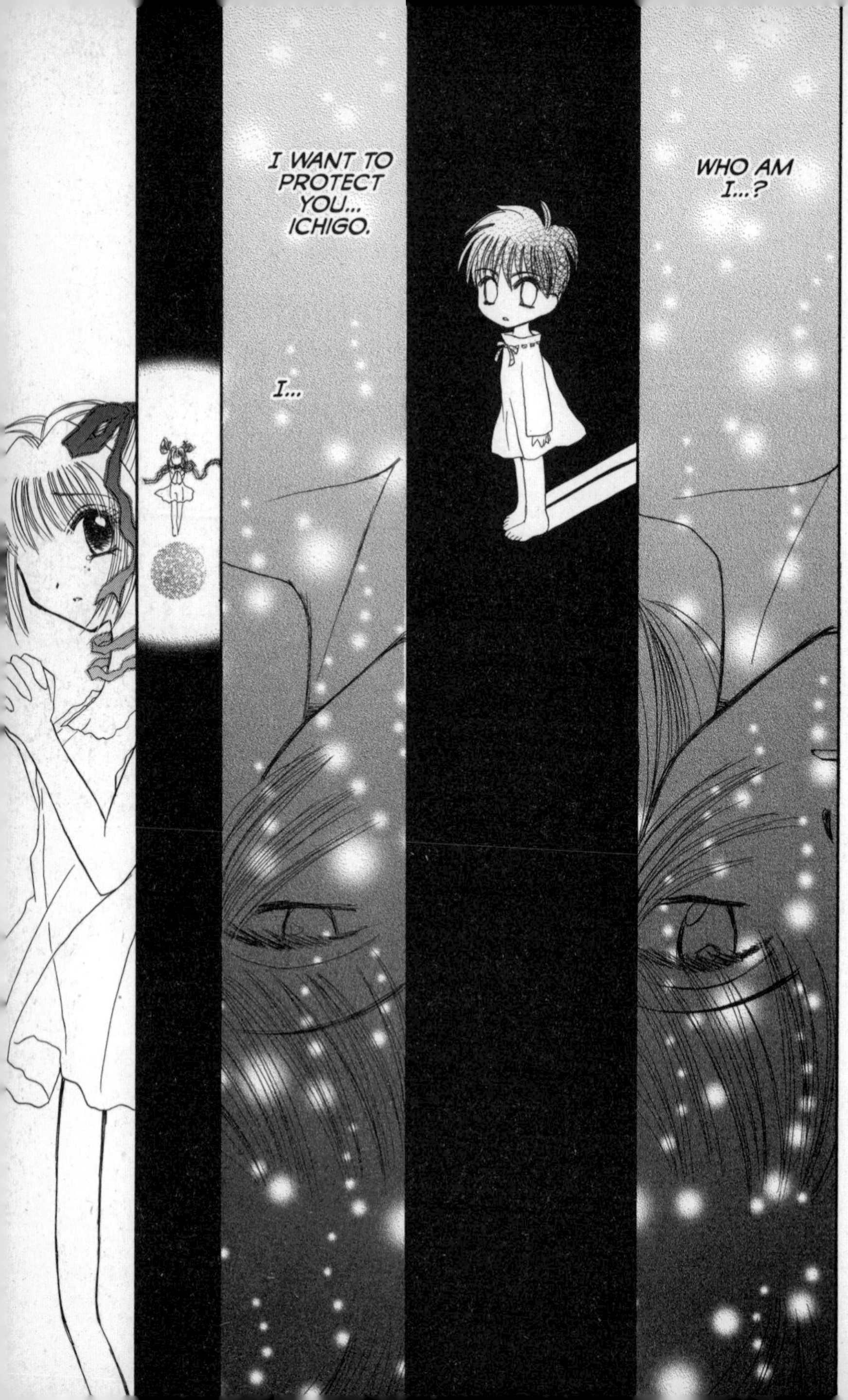
WHO AM I...?
I WANT TO PROTECT YOU... ICHIGO.
I...

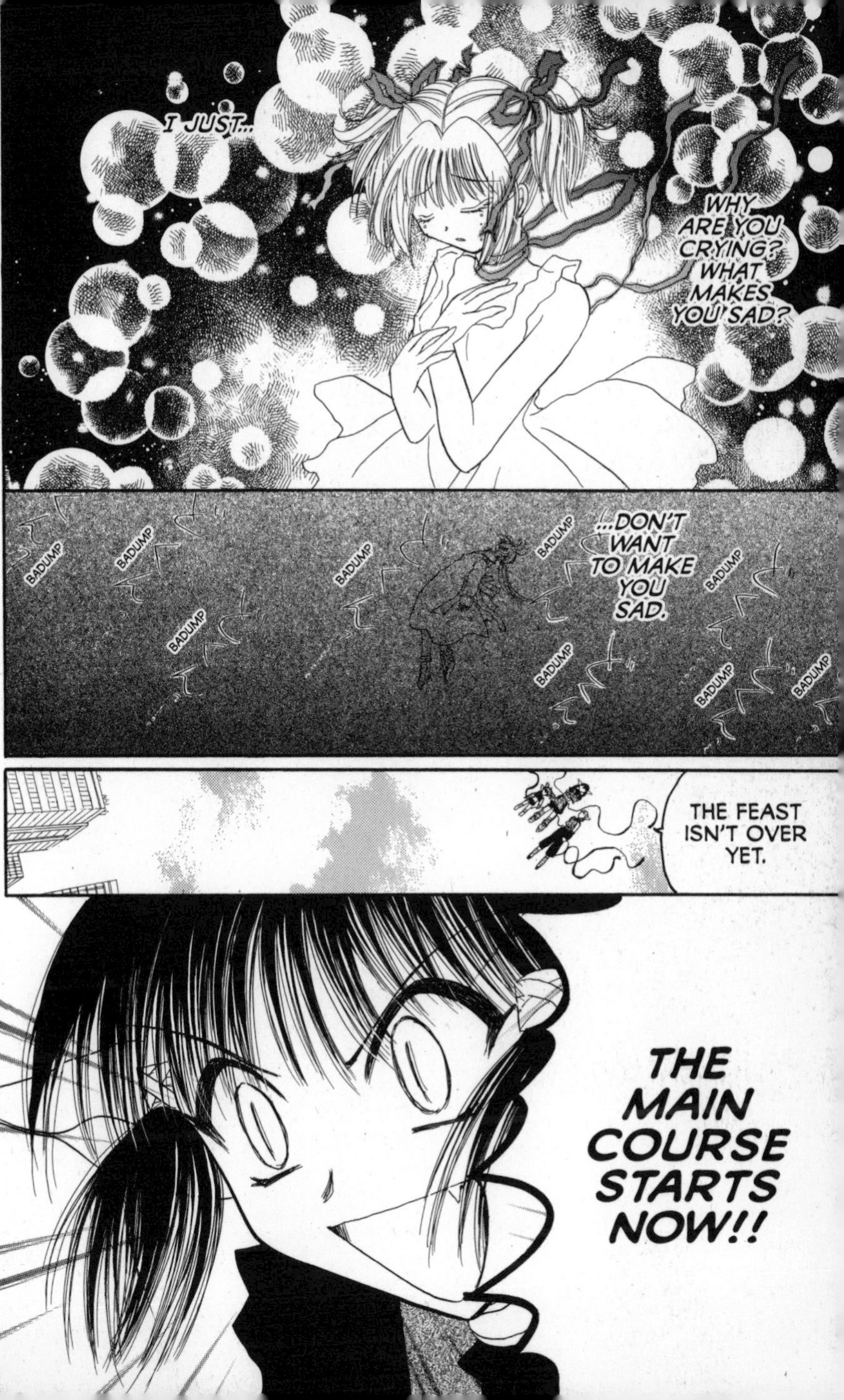
WHY ARE YOU CRYING? WHAT MAKES YOU SAD?
I JUST...
...DON'T WANT TO MAKE YOU SAD.
BADUMP
BADUMP
BADUMP
BADUMP
BADUMP
BADUMP
BADUMP
BADUMP
BADUMP
THE FEAST ISN'T OVER YET.
THE MAIN COURSE STARTS NOW!!

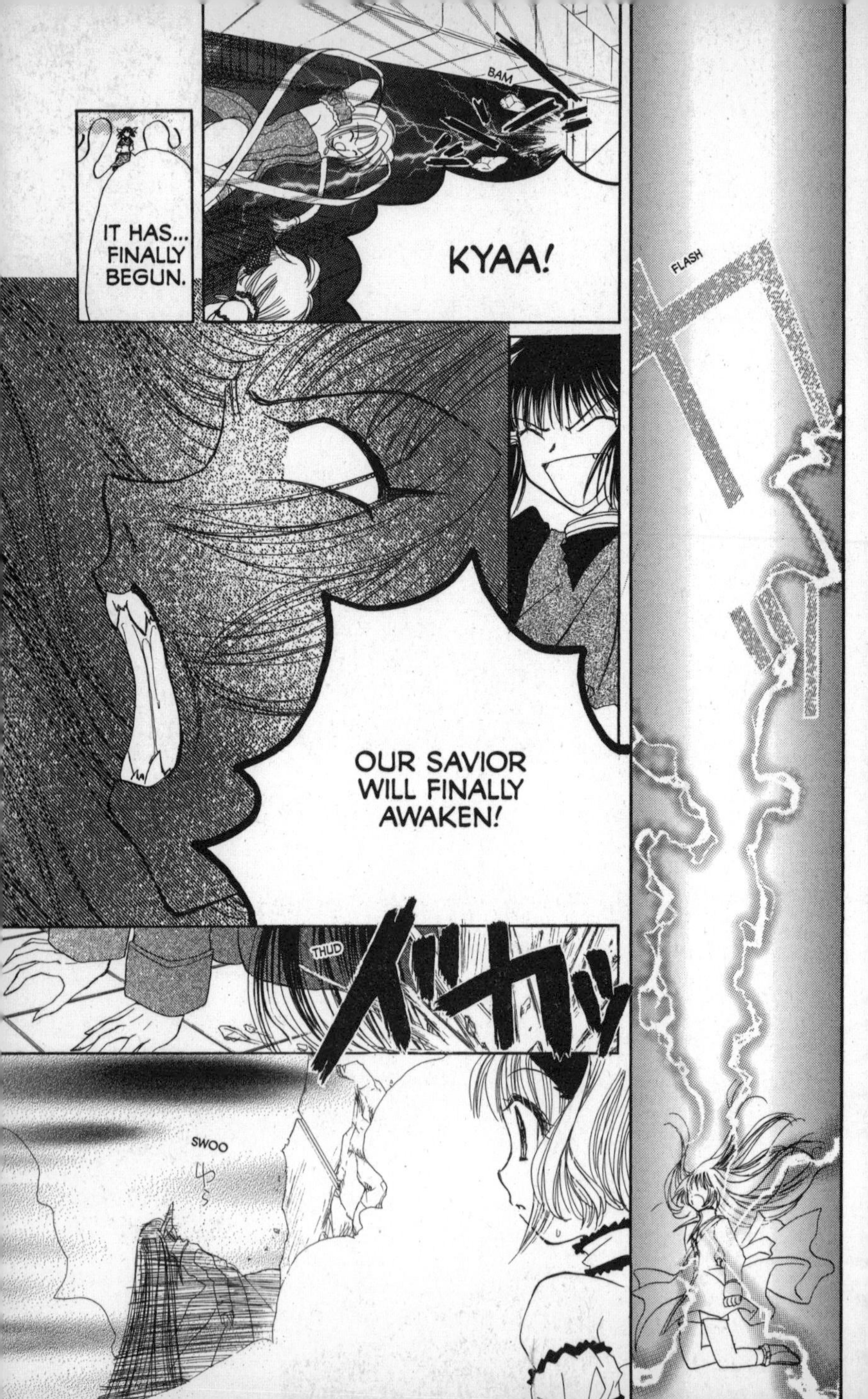
FLASH
BAM
KYAA!
IT HAS... FINALLY BEGUN.
OUR SAVIOR WILL FINALLY AWAKEN!
THUD
SWOO

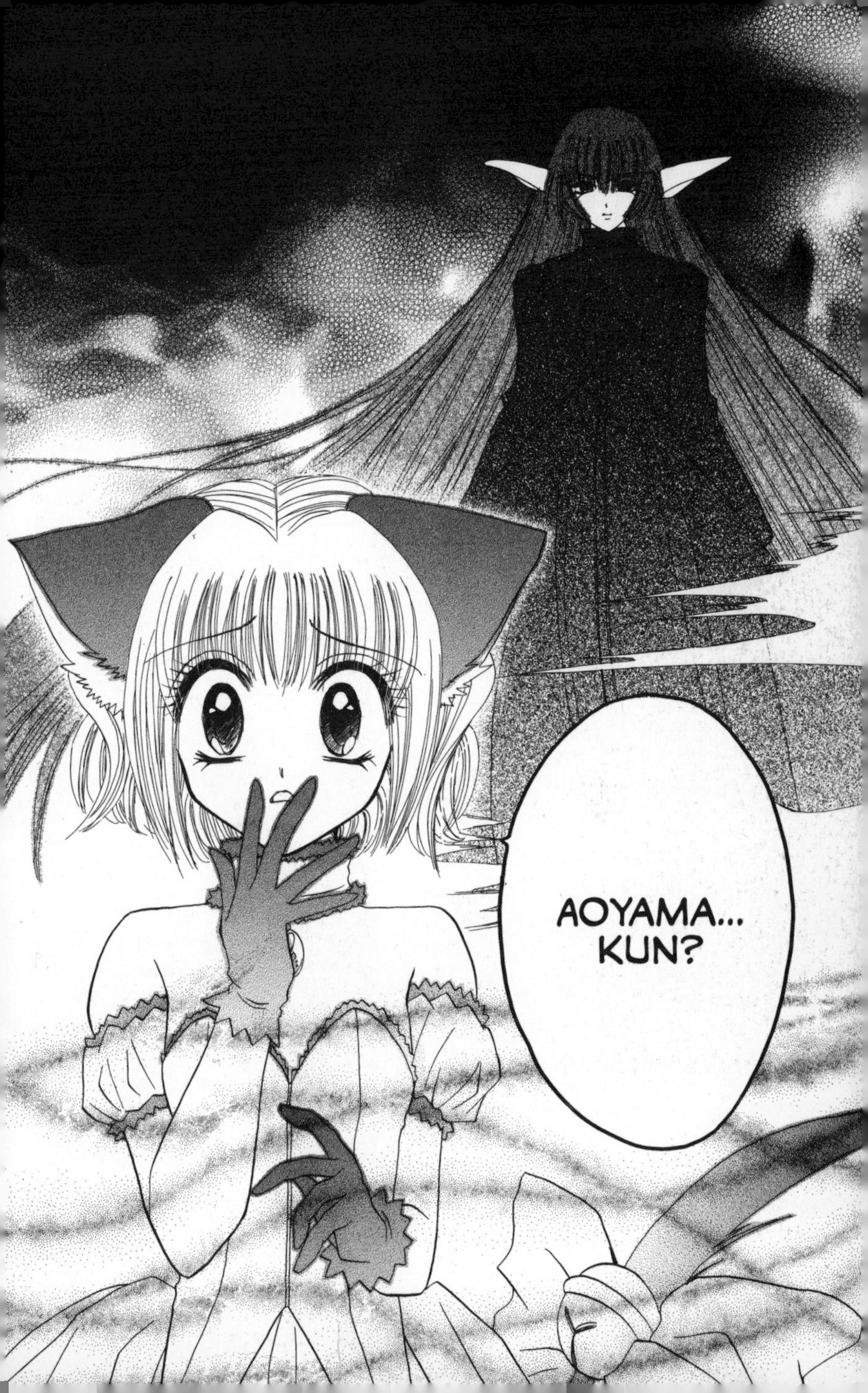
AOYAMA... KUN?

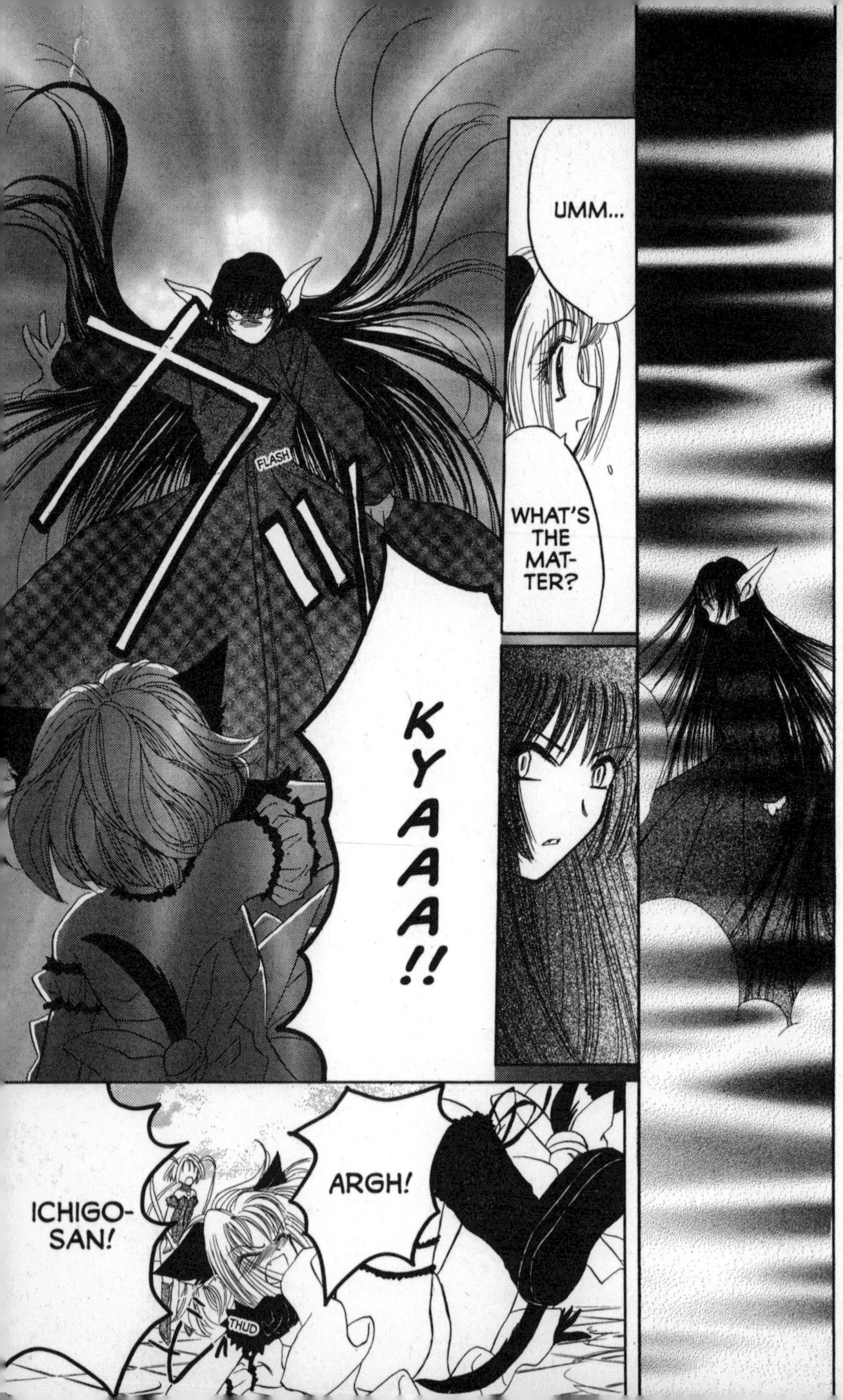
UMM...
WHAT'S THE MATTER?
FLASH
KYAAAA!!
ARGH!
ICHIGO-SAN!
THUD

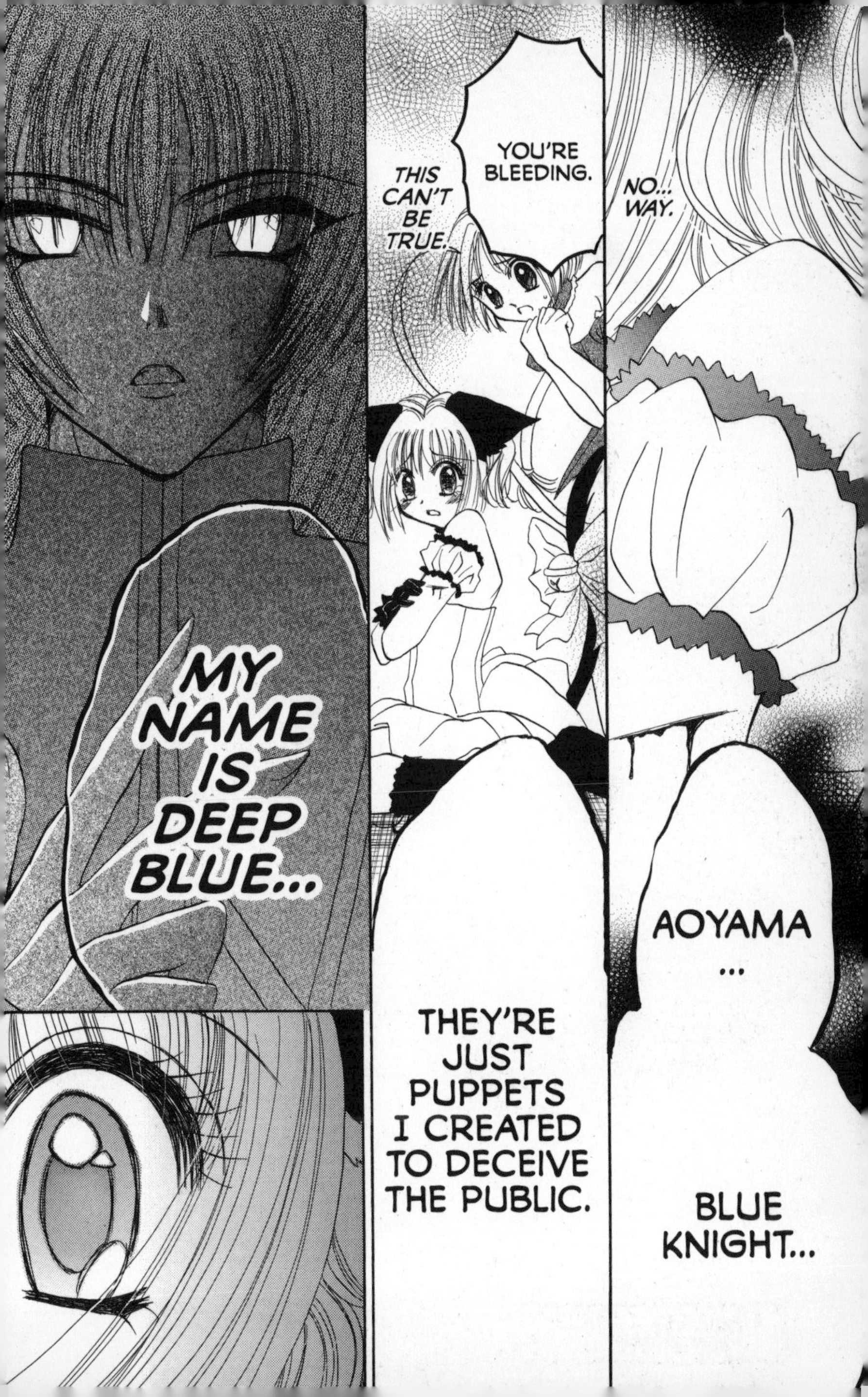
NO... WAY.
AOYAMA ...
BLUE KNIGHT...
YOU'RE BLEEDING.
THIS CAN'T BE TRUE.
THEY'RE JUST PUPPETS I CREATED TO DECEIVE THE PUBLIC.
MY NAME IS DEEP BLUE...

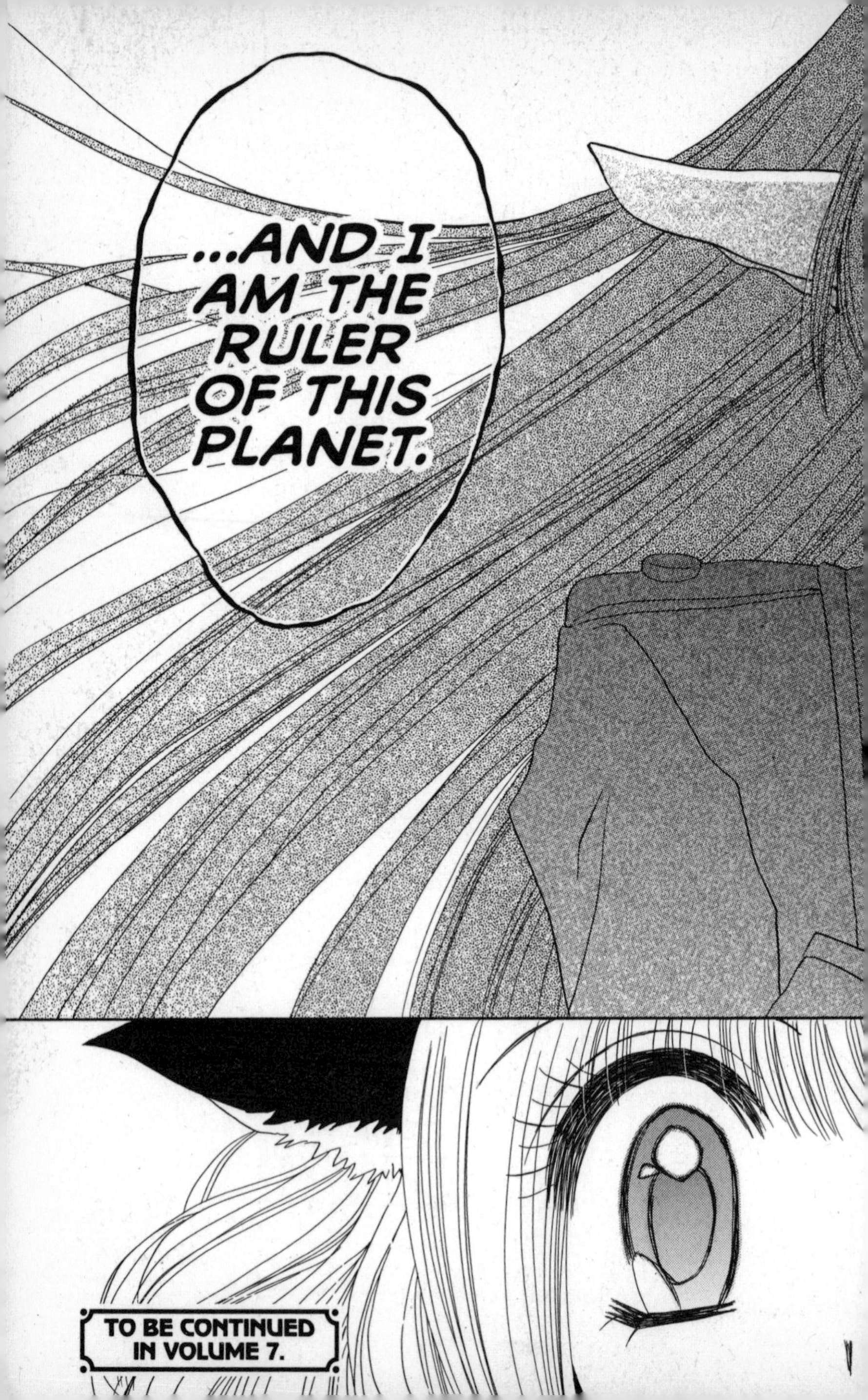
...AND I AM THE RULER OF THIS PLANET.
TO BE CONTINUED IN VOLUME 7.

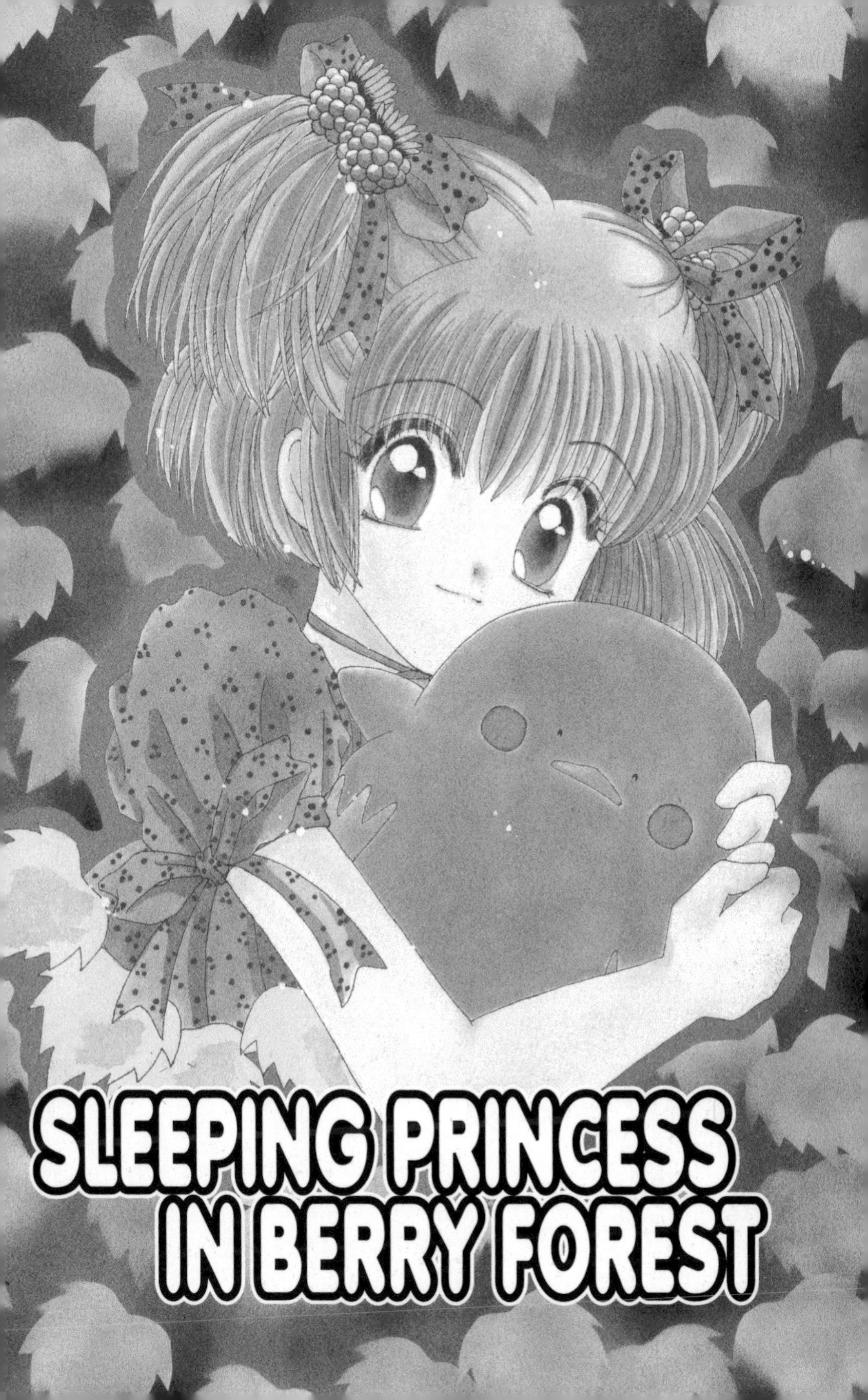
SLEEPING PRINCESS
IN BERRY FOREST

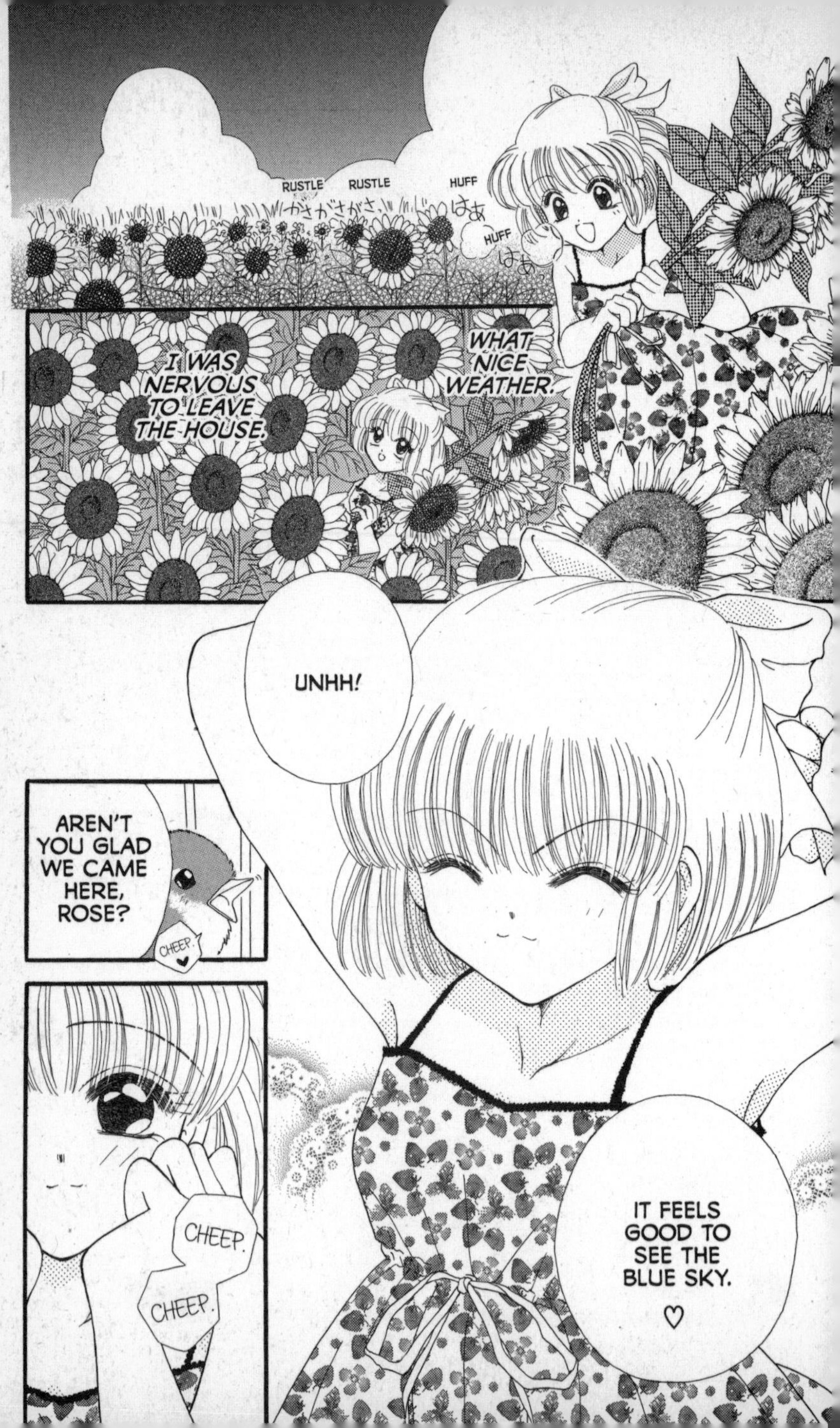
HUFF
はあ
HUFF
はあ
RUSTLE RUSTLE
かさかさかさ
WHAT NICE WEATHER.
I WAS NERVOUS TO LEAVE THE HOUSE.
UNHH!
IT FEELS GOOD TO SEE THE BLUE SKY. ♡
AREN'T YOU GLAD WE CAME HERE, ROSE?
CHEEP. ♥
CHEEP.
CHEEP.

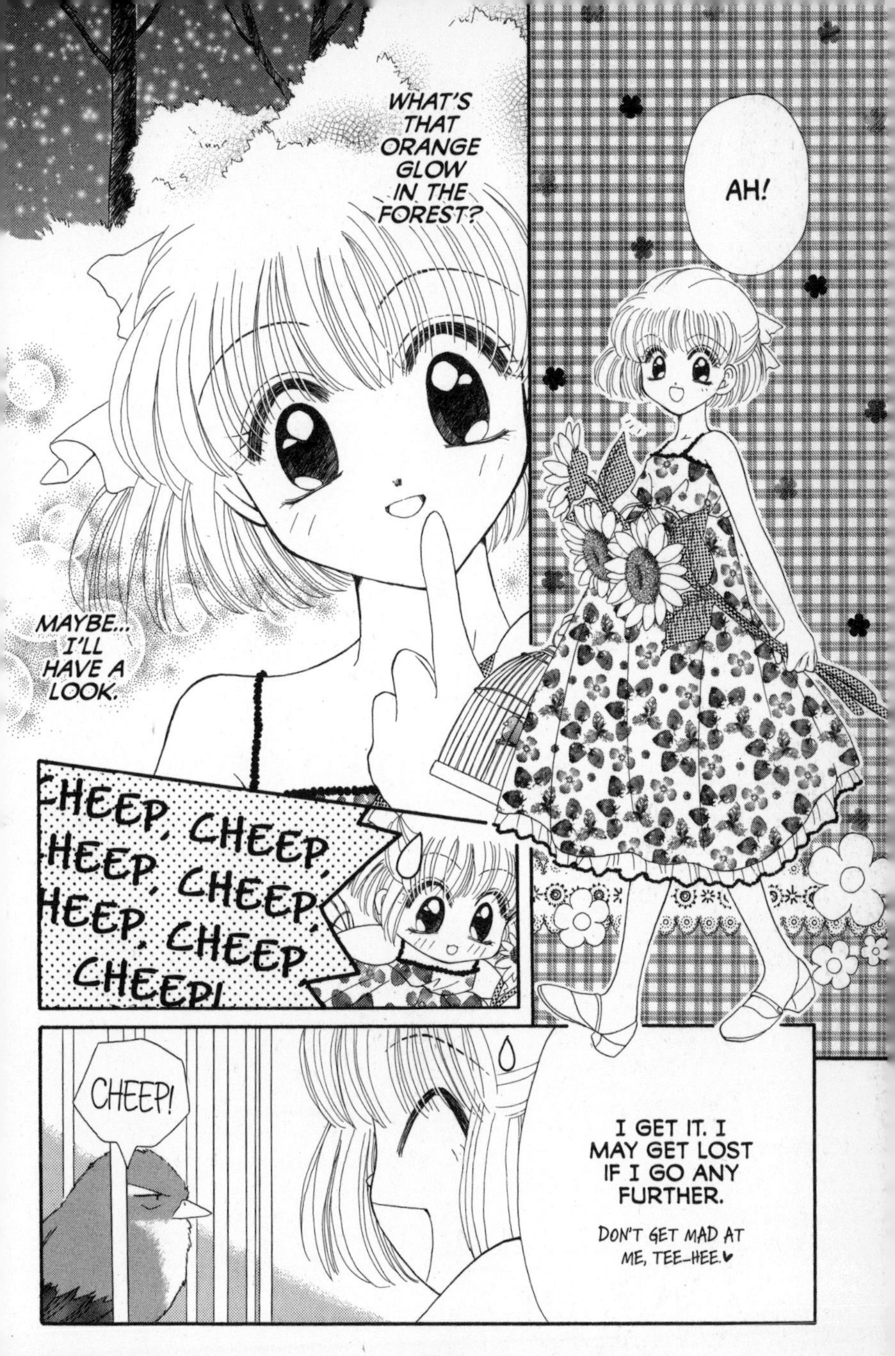
AH!
WHAT'S THAT ORANGE GLOW IN THE FOREST?
MAYBE... I'LL HAVE A LOOK.
CHEEP, CHEEP, HEEP, CHEEP, HEEP, CHEEP CHEEP!
I GET IT. I MAY GET LOST IF I GO ANY FURTHER.
DON'T GET MAD AT ME, TEE-HEE.♥
CHEEP!

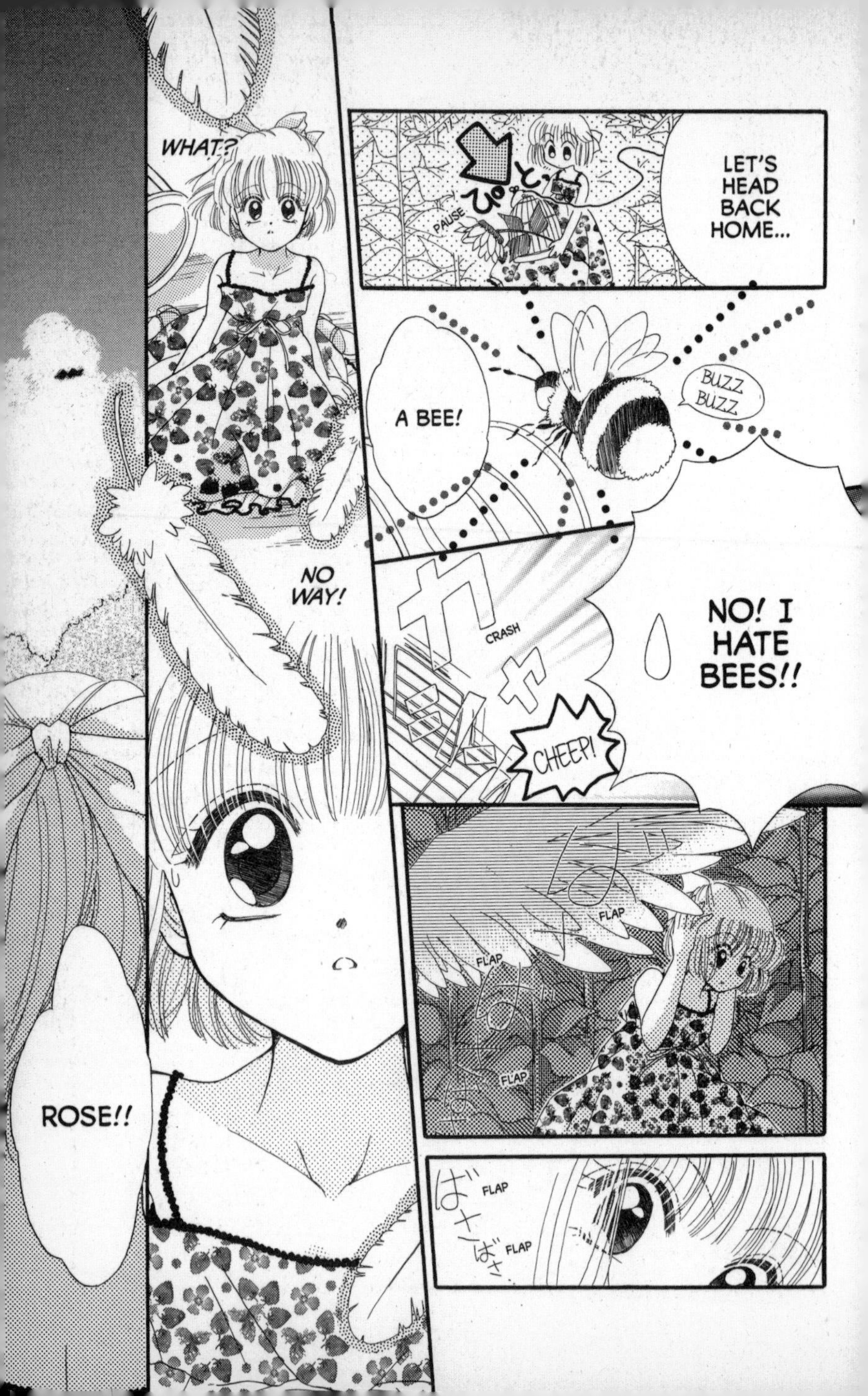
LET'S HEAD BACK HOME...
PAUSE
BUZZ BUZZ
A BEE!
NO! I HATE BEES!!
CRASH
CHEEP!
FLAP
FLAP
FLAP
FLAP
FLAP
WHAT?
NO WAY!
ROSE!!

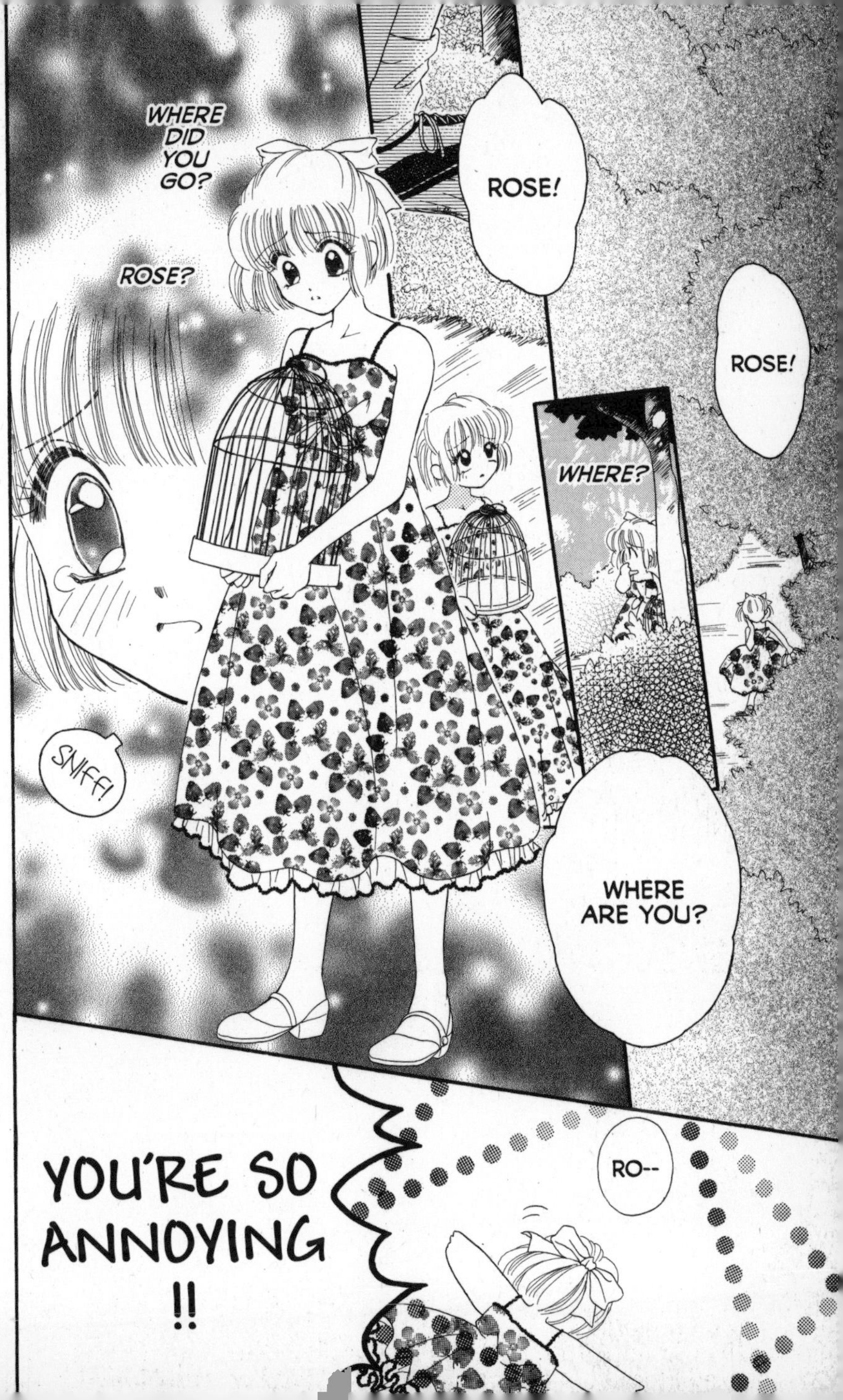
ROSE!
ROSE!
WHERE?
WHERE ARE YOU?
WHERE DID YOU GO?
ROSE?
SNIFF!
RO--
YOU'RE SO ANNOYING!!

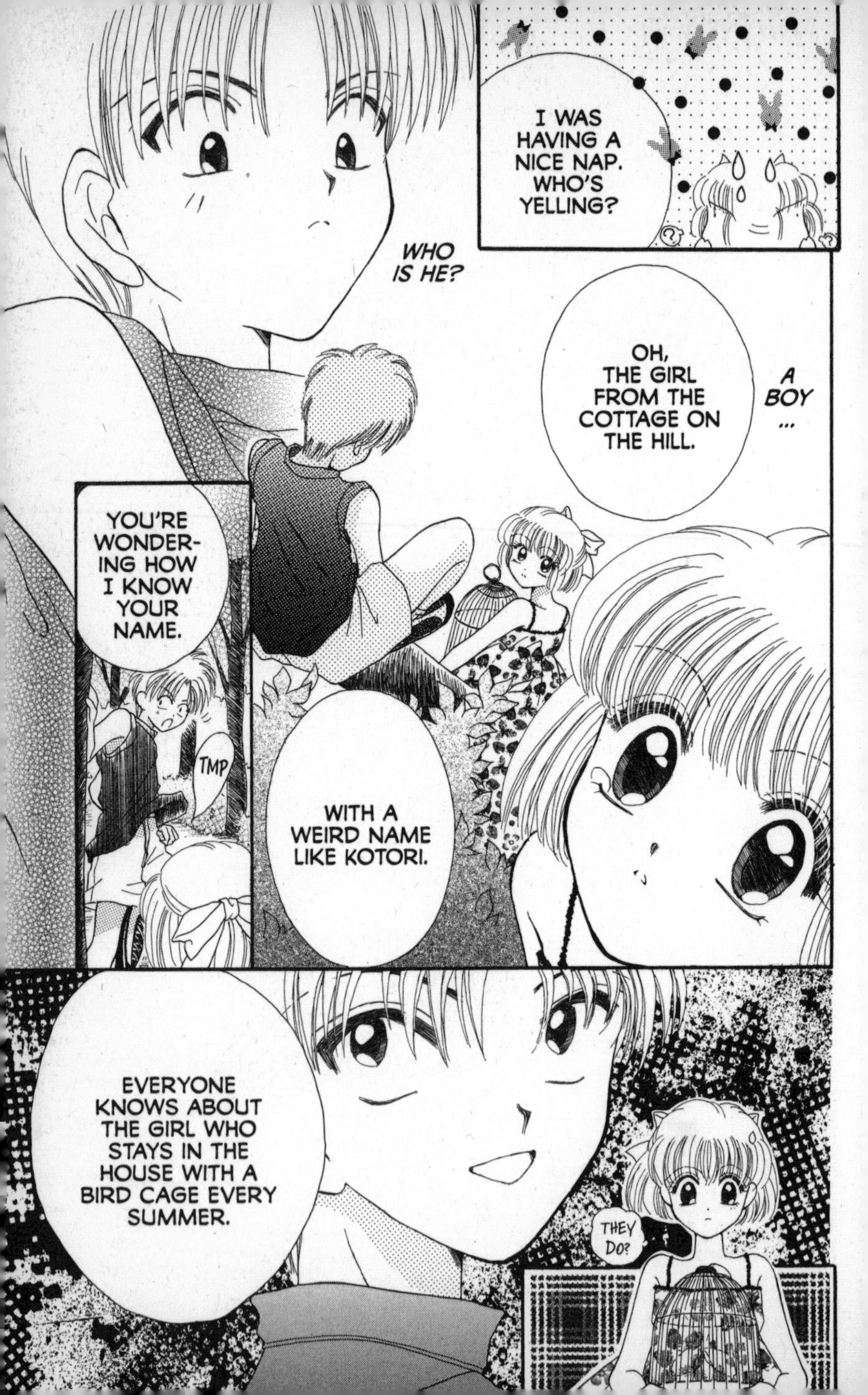
I WAS HAVING A NICE NAP. WHO'S YELLING?
WHO IS HE?
A BOY ...
OH, THE GIRL FROM THE COTTAGE ON THE HILL.
WITH A WEIRD NAME LIKE KOTORI.
YOU'RE WONDERING HOW I KNOW YOUR NAME.
TMP
EVERYONE KNOWS ABOUT THE GIRL WHO STAYS IN THE HOUSE WITH A BIRD CAGE EVERY SUMMER.
THEY DO?

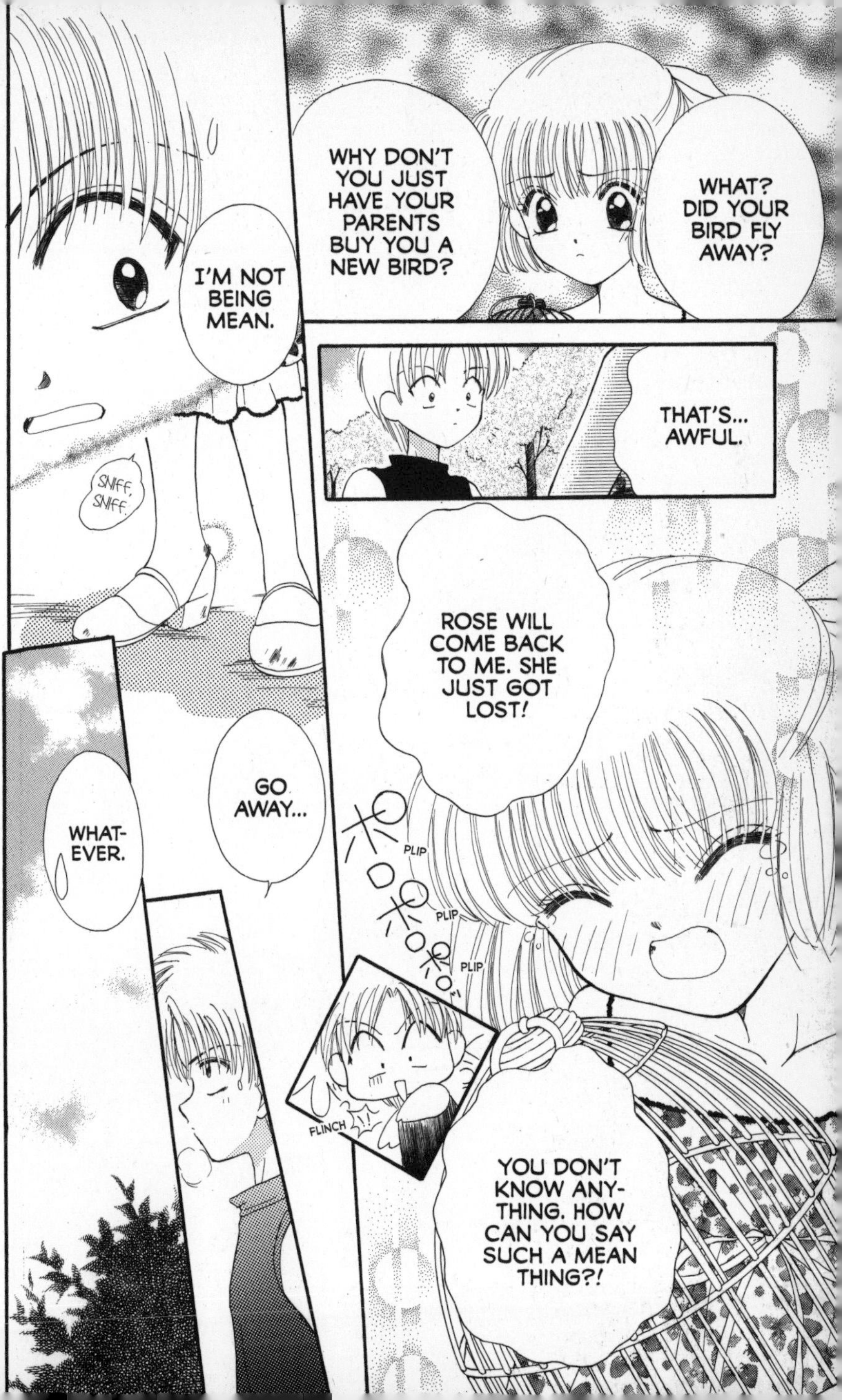
WHAT? DID YOUR BIRD FLY AWAY?
WHY DON'T YOU JUST HAVE YOUR PARENTS BUY YOU A NEW BIRD?
THAT'S... AWFUL.
ROSE WILL COME BACK TO ME. SHE JUST GOT LOST!
PLIP
PLIP
PLIP
YOU DON'T KNOW ANY-THING. HOW CAN YOU SAY SUCH A MEAN THING?!
FLINCH
I'M NOT BEING MEAN.
SNIFF, SNIFF.
GO AWAY...
WHAT-EVER.

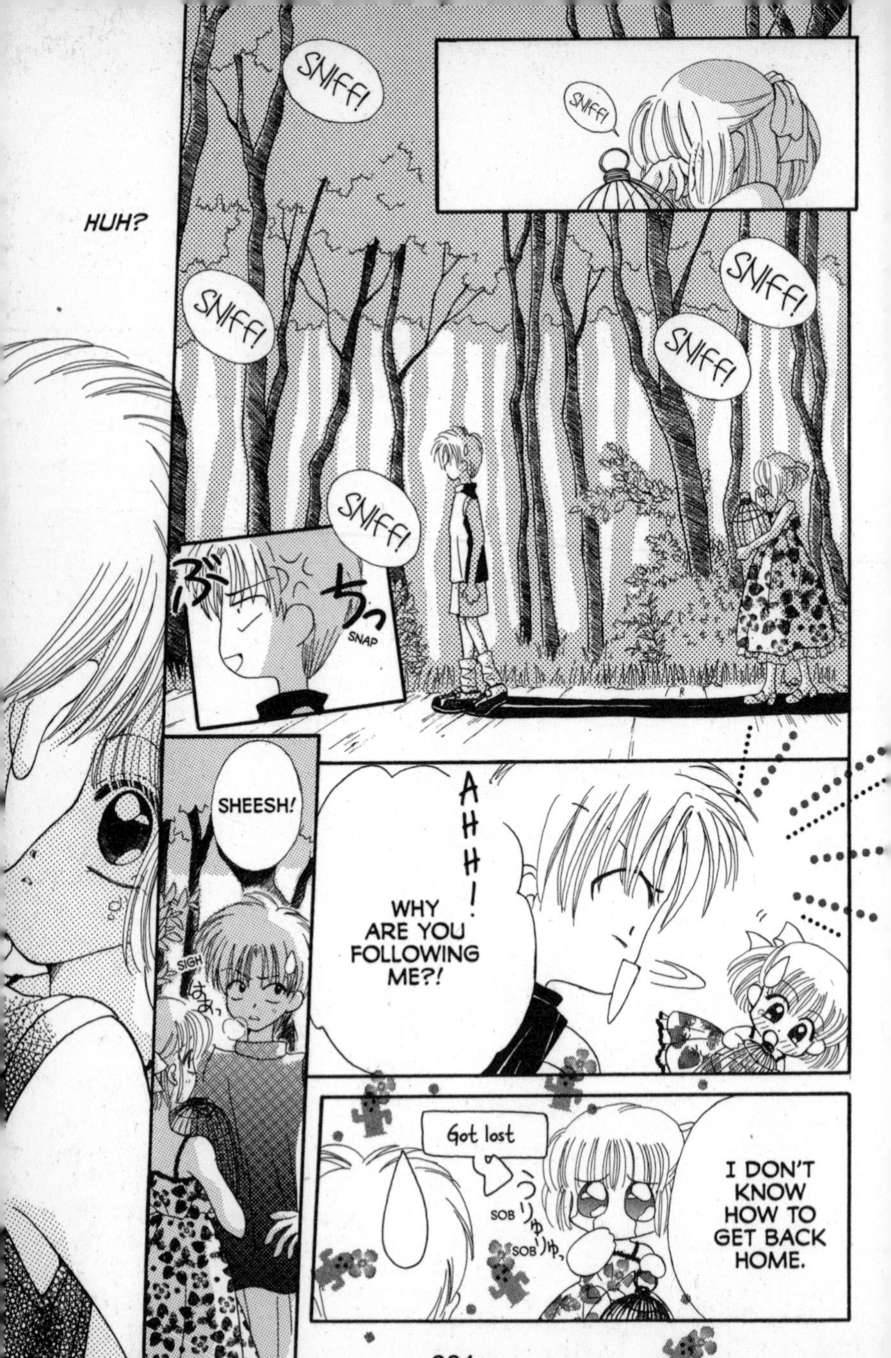
SNIFF!
SNIFF!
SNIFF!
SNIFF!
SNIFF!
SNIFF!
ちっ
SNAP
ぶ
AHH!
WHY ARE YOU FOLLOWING ME?!
I DON'T KNOW HOW TO GET BACK HOME.
うりゅ
SOB
りゅ
SOB
Got lost
SHEESH!
はあっ
SIGH
HUH?

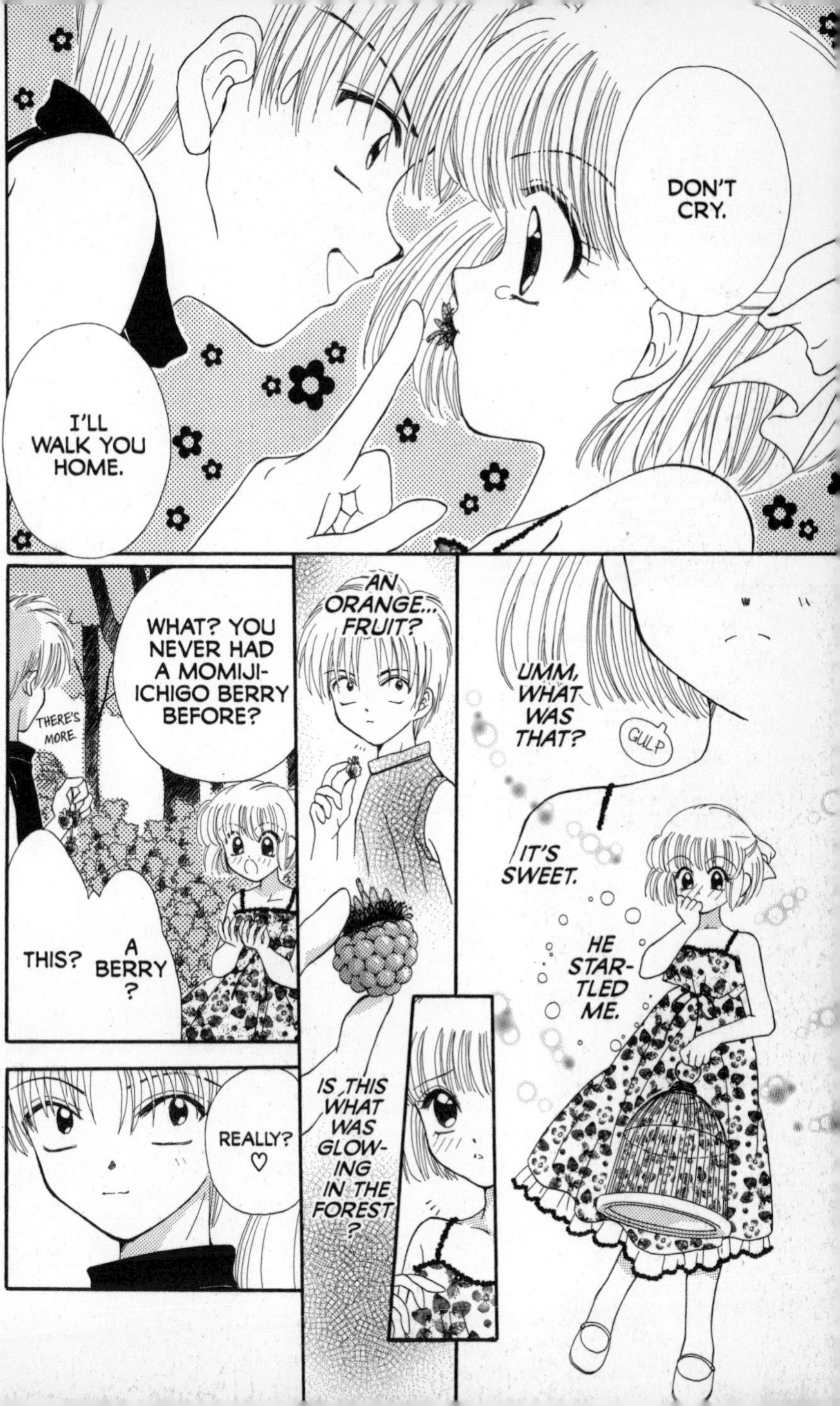
DON'T CRY.
I'LL WALK YOU HOME.
UMM, WHAT WAS THAT?
GULP
IT'S SWEET.
HE STARTLED ME.
AN ORANGE... FRUIT?
WHAT? YOU NEVER HAD A MOMIJI-ICHIGO BERRY BEFORE?
THERE'S MORE.
THIS? A BERRY?
IS THIS WHAT WAS GLOWING IN THE FOREST?
REALLY? ♡

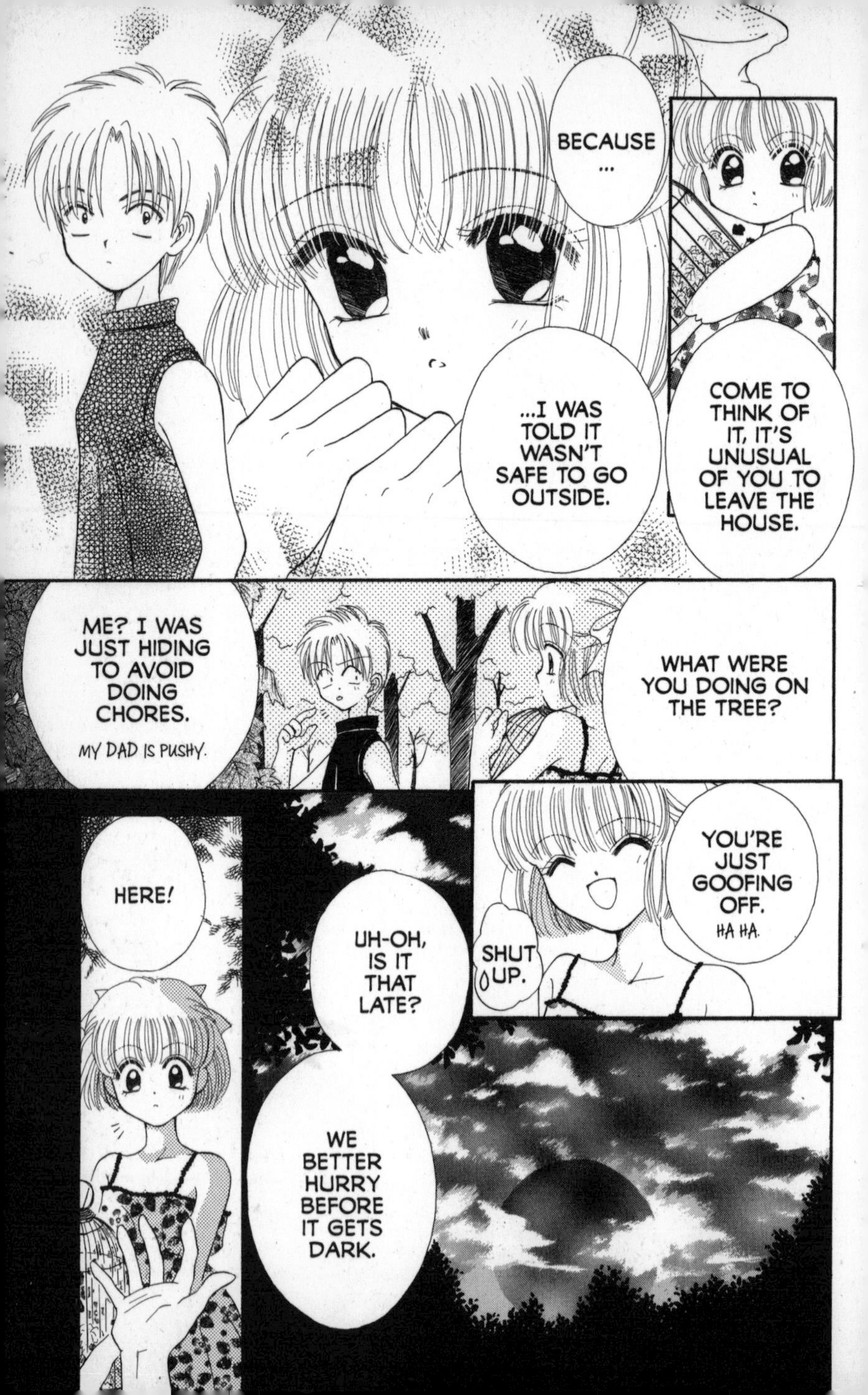
COME TO THINK OF IT, IT'S UNUSUAL OF YOU TO LEAVE THE HOUSE.
BECAUSE ...
...I WAS TOLD IT WASN'T SAFE TO GO OUTSIDE.
WHAT WERE YOU DOING ON THE TREE?
ME? I WAS JUST HIDING TO AVOID DOING CHORES.
MY DAD IS PUSHY.
YOU'RE JUST GOOFING OFF.
HA HA.
SHUT UP.
UH-OH, IS IT THAT LATE?
WE BETTER HURRY BEFORE IT GETS DARK.
HERE!

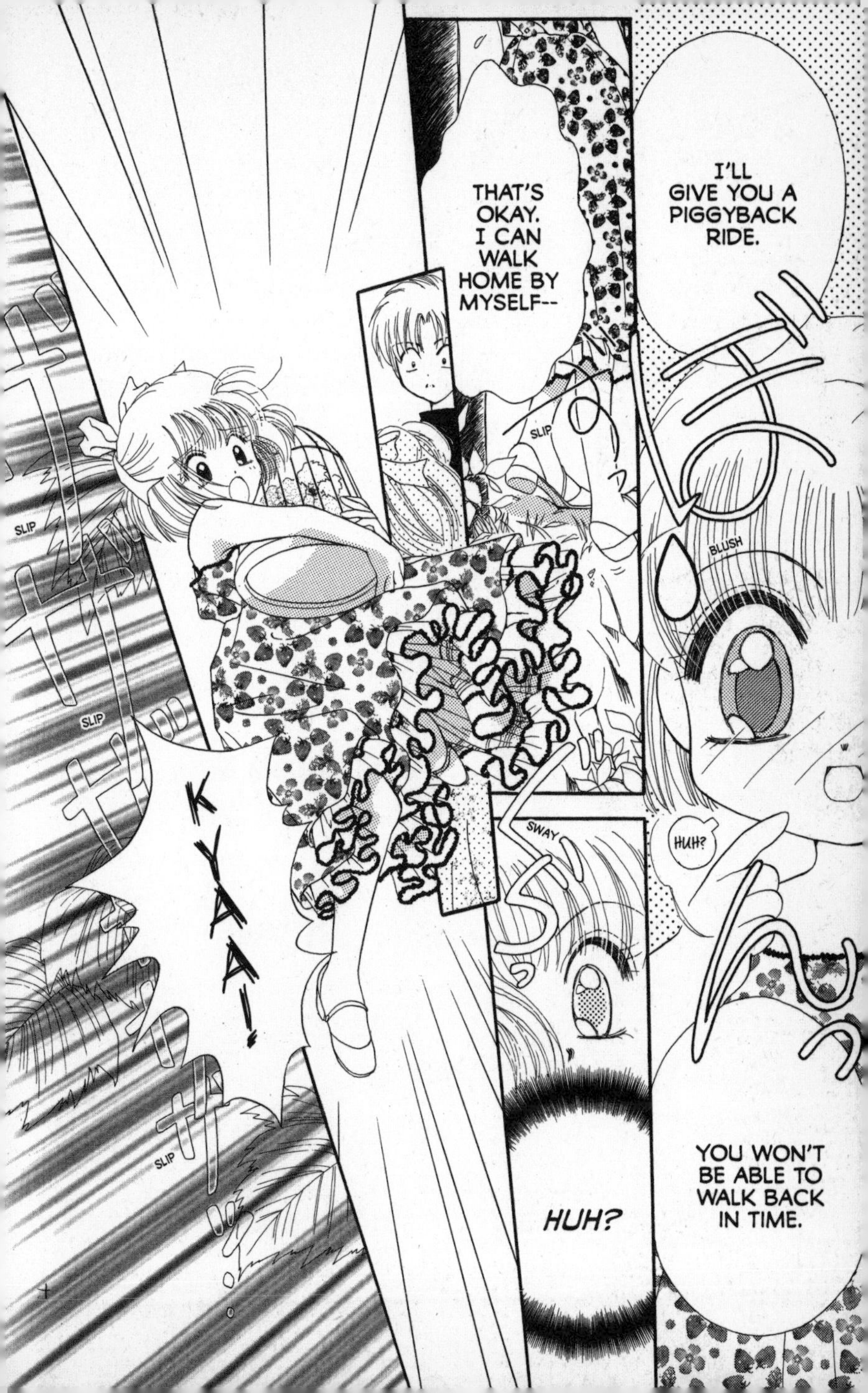
I'LL GIVE YOU A PIGGYBACK RIDE.
BLUSH
HUH?
YOU WON'T BE ABLE TO WALK BACK IN TIME.
THAT'S OKAY. I CAN WALK HOME BY MYSELF--
SLIP
SWAY
HUH?
SLIP
SLIP
KYAA!
SLIP

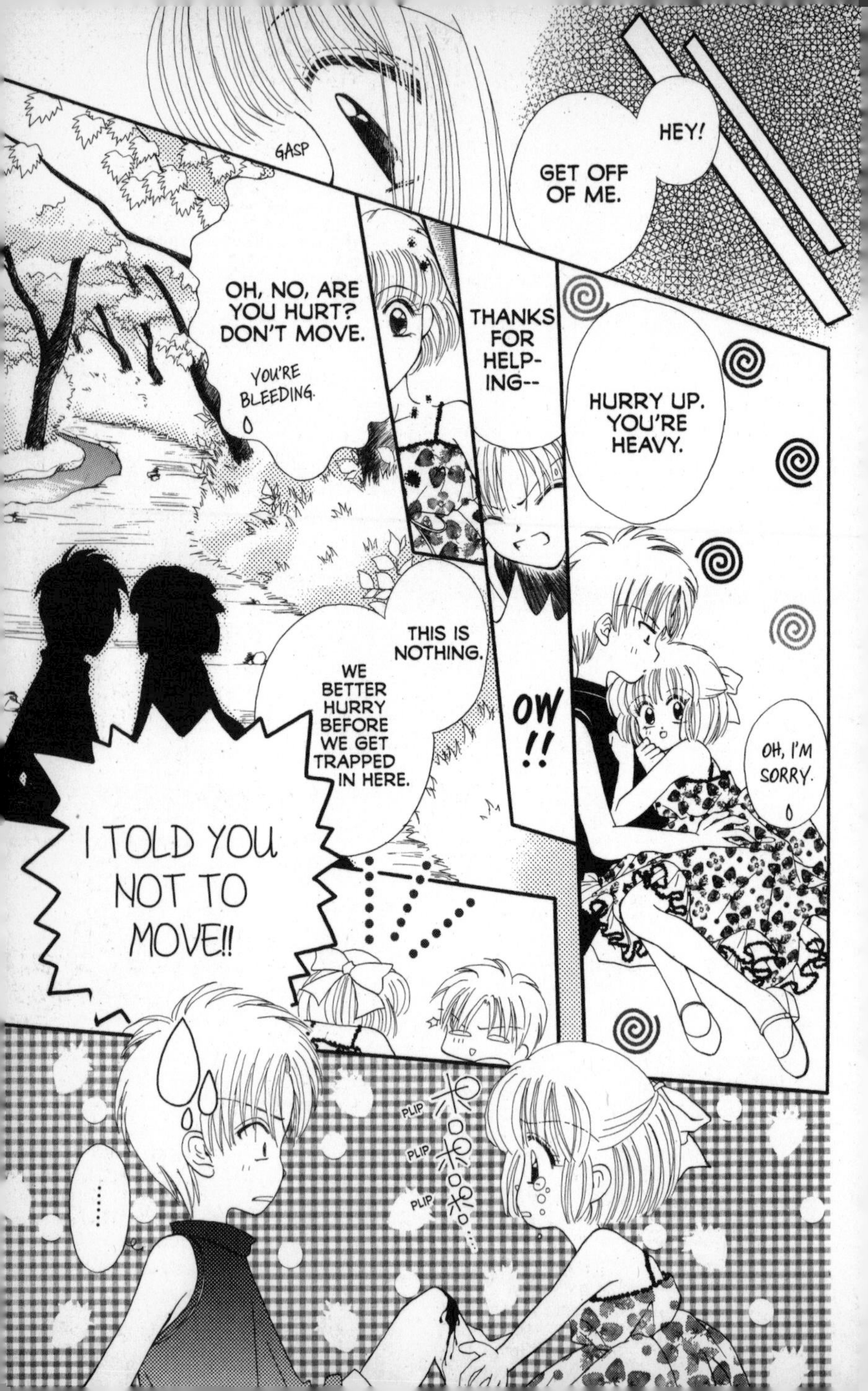
HEY!
GET OFF OF ME.
GASP
HURRY UP. YOU'RE HEAVY.
OH, I'M SORRY.
THANKS FOR HELPING--
OW!!
OH, NO, ARE YOU HURT? DON'T MOVE.
YOU'RE BLEEDING.
THIS IS NOTHING.
WE BETTER HURRY BEFORE WE GET TRAPPED IN HERE.
I TOLD YOU NOT TO MOVE!!
PLIP
PLIP
PLIP
......

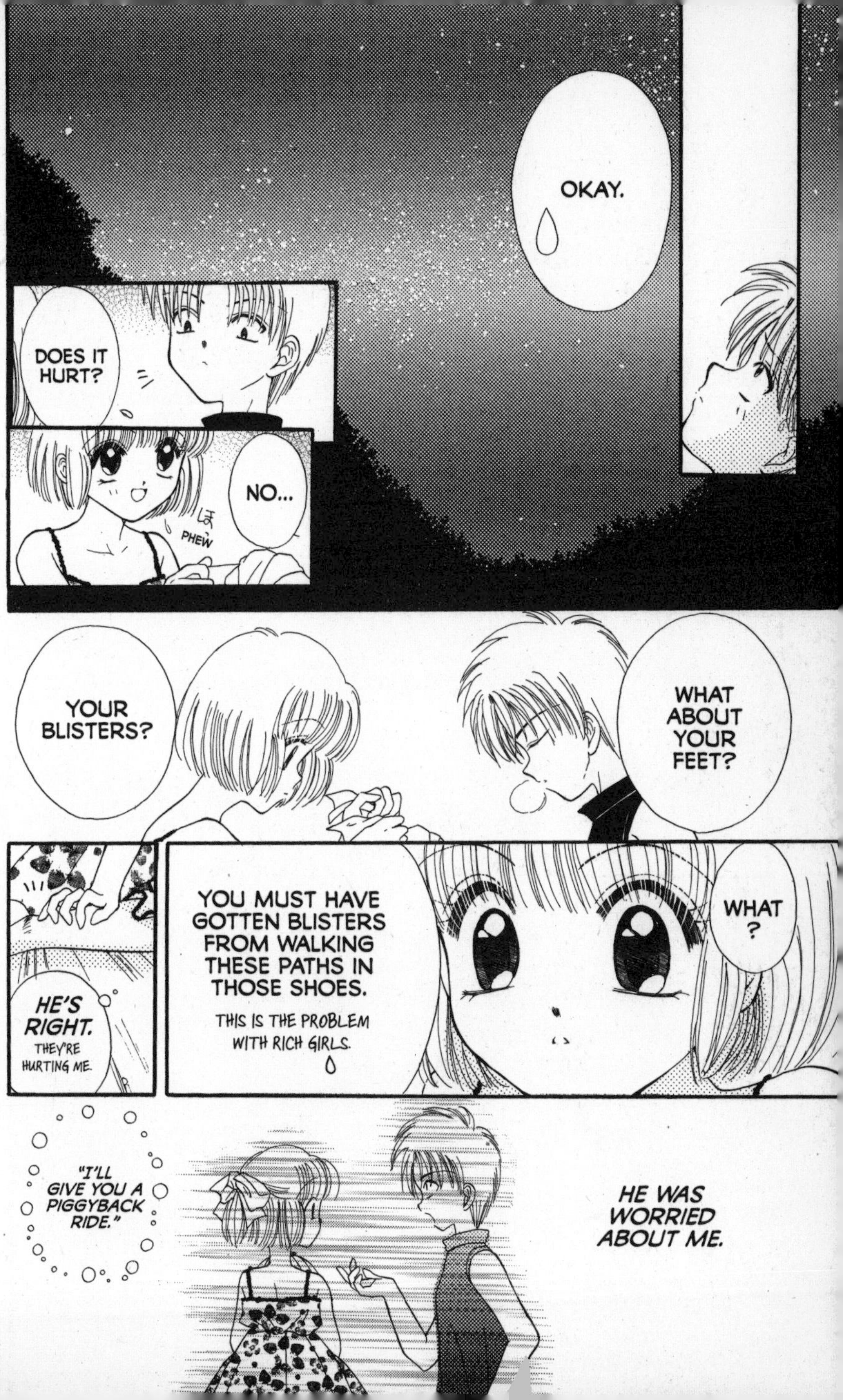
OKAY.
DOES IT HURT?
NO...
ほ PHEW
WHAT ABOUT YOUR FEET?
YOUR BLISTERS?
WHAT?
YOU MUST HAVE GOTTEN BLISTERS FROM WALKING THESE PATHS IN THOSE SHOES.
THIS IS THE PROBLEM WITH RICH GIRLS.
HE'S RIGHT.
THEY'RE HURTING ME.
HE WAS WORRIED ABOUT ME.
"I'LL GIVE YOU A PIGGYBACK RIDE."

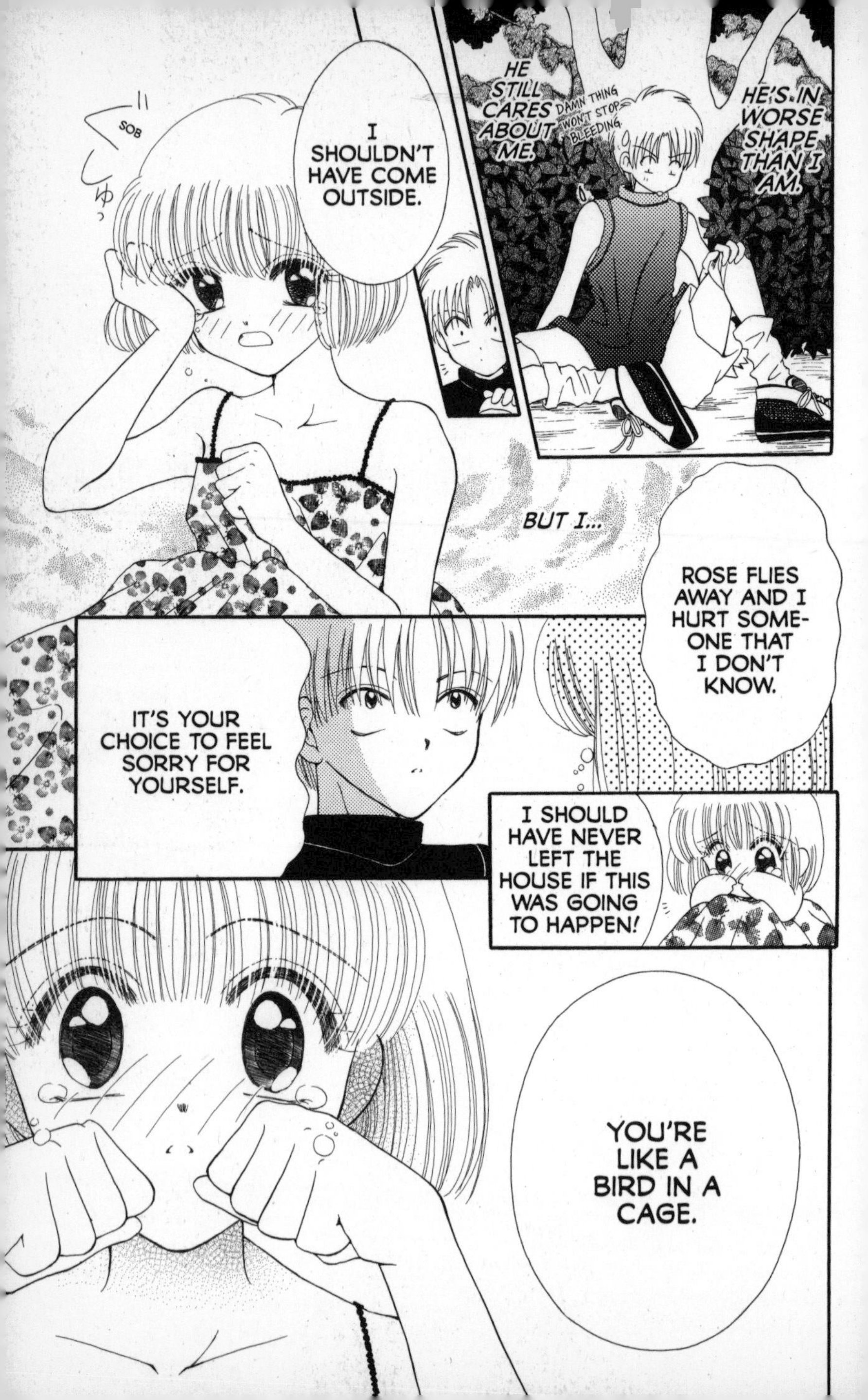
HE'S IN WORSE SHAPE THAN I AM.
DAMN THING WON'T STOP BLEEDING.
HE STILL CARES ABOUT ME.
I SHOULDN'T HAVE COME OUTSIDE.
SOB
BUT I...
ROSE FLIES AWAY AND I HURT SOME-ONE THAT I DON'T KNOW.
I SHOULD HAVE NEVER LEFT THE HOUSE IF THIS WAS GOING TO HAPPEN!
IT'S YOUR CHOICE TO FEEL SORRY FOR YOURSELF.
YOU'RE LIKE A BIRD IN A CAGE.

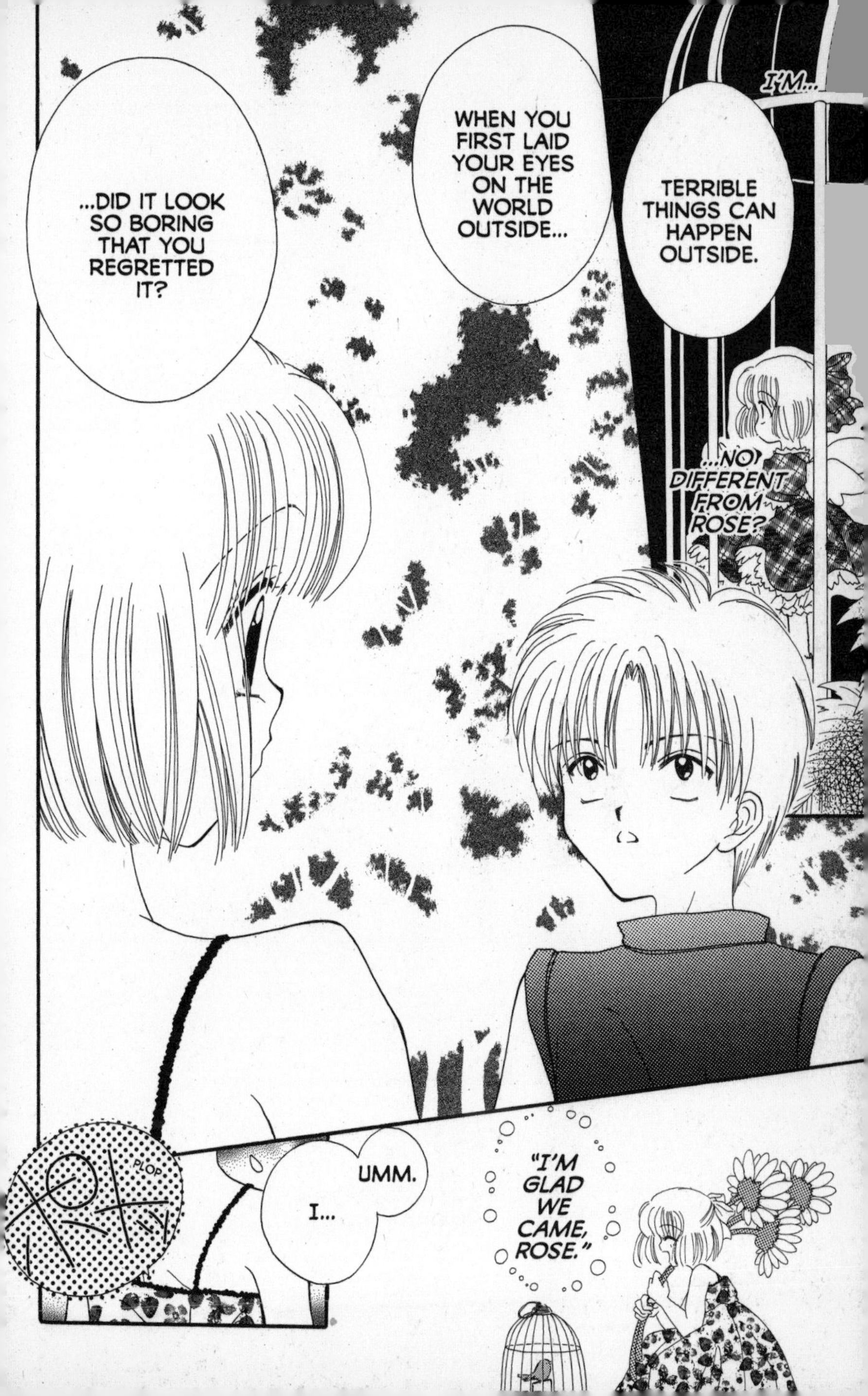
I'M...
TERRIBLE THINGS CAN HAPPEN OUTSIDE.
WHEN YOU FIRST LAID YOUR EYES ON THE WORLD OUTSIDE...
...DID IT LOOK SO BORING THAT YOU REGRETTED IT?
...NO DIFFERENT FROM ROSE?
"I'M GLAD WE CAME, ROSE."
UMM.
I...
PLOP

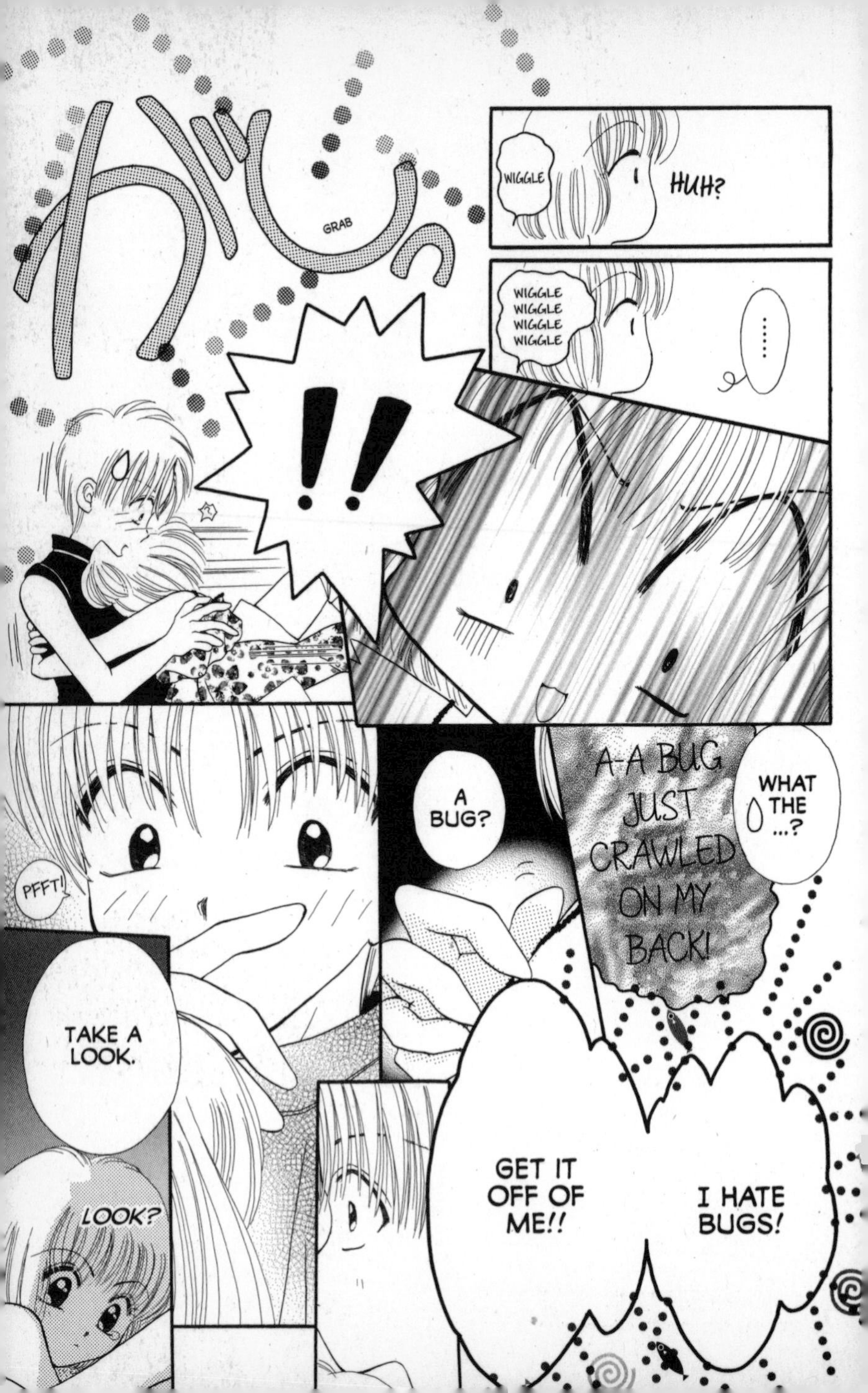
WIGGLE
HUH?
WIGGLE WIGGLE WIGGLE WIGGLE WIGGLE
......
GRAB
!!
WHAT THE ...?
A-A BUG JUST CRAWLED ON MY BACK!
A BUG?
PFFT!
I HATE BUGS!
GET IT OFF OF ME!!
TAKE A LOOK.
LOOK?

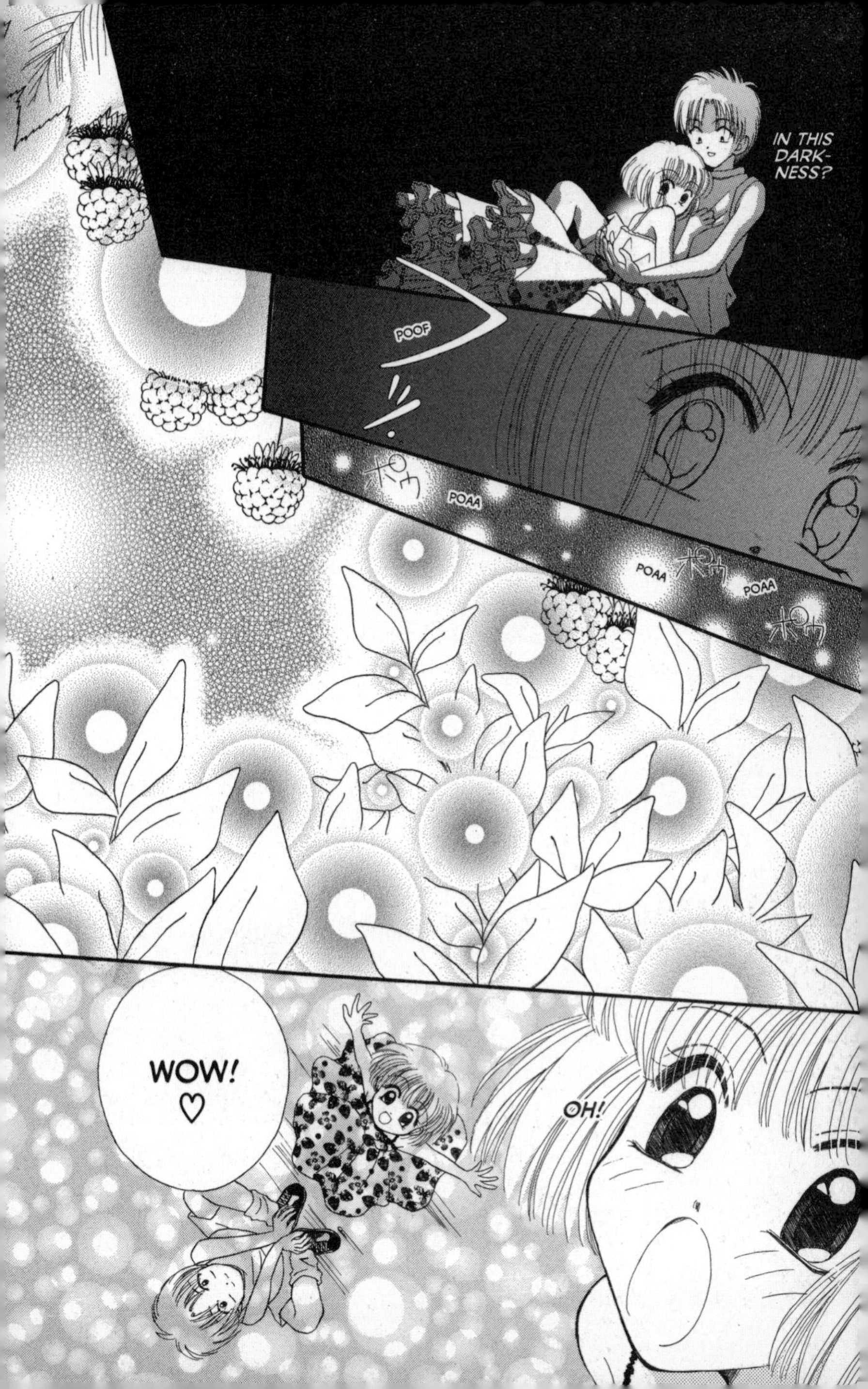
IN THIS DARK- NESS?
POOF
POAA
POAA
POAA
OH!
WOW! ♡

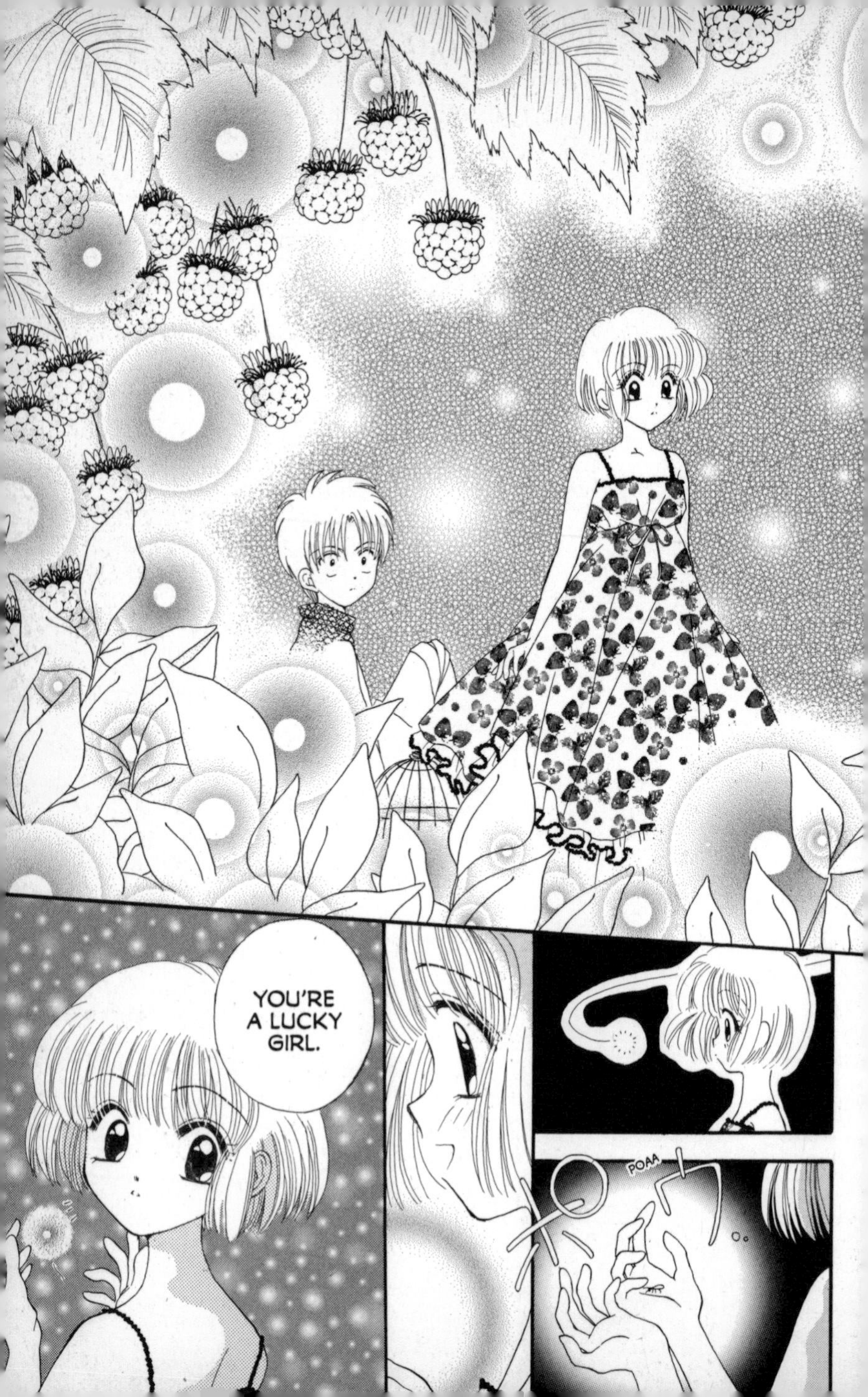
POAA
YOU'RE A LUCKY GIRL.

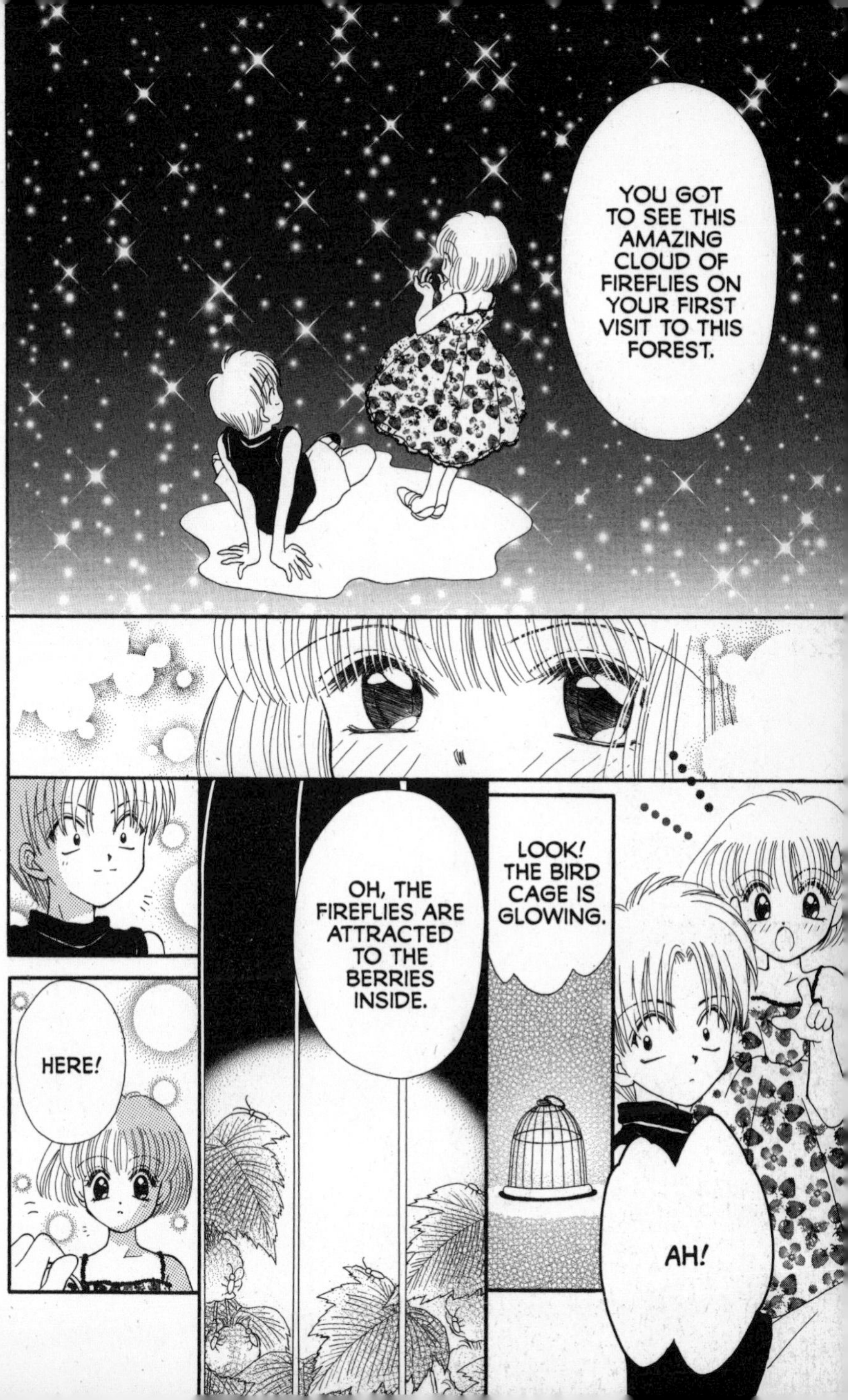
YOU GOT TO SEE THIS AMAZING CLOUD OF FIREFLIES ON YOUR FIRST VISIT TO THIS FOREST.
AH!
LOOK! THE BIRD CAGE IS GLOWING.
OH, THE FIREFLIES ARE ATTRACTED TO THE BERRIES INSIDE.
HERE!

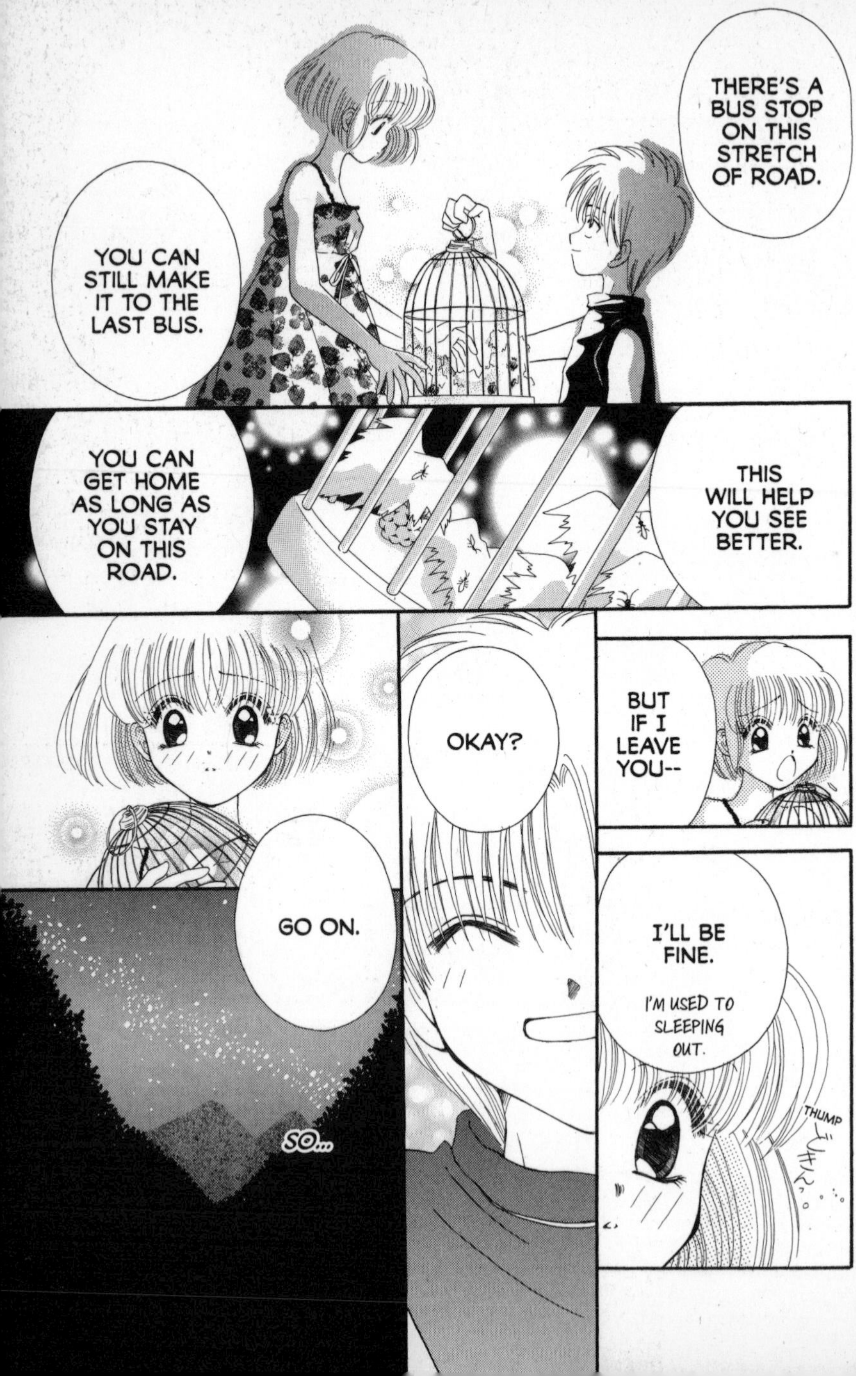
THERE'S A BUS STOP ON THIS STRETCH OF ROAD.
YOU CAN STILL MAKE IT TO THE LAST BUS.
THIS WILL HELP YOU SEE BETTER.
YOU CAN GET HOME AS LONG AS YOU STAY ON THIS ROAD.
BUT IF I LEAVE YOU--
I'LL BE FINE.
I'M USED TO SLEEPING OUT.
THUMP
OKAY?
GO ON.
SO...

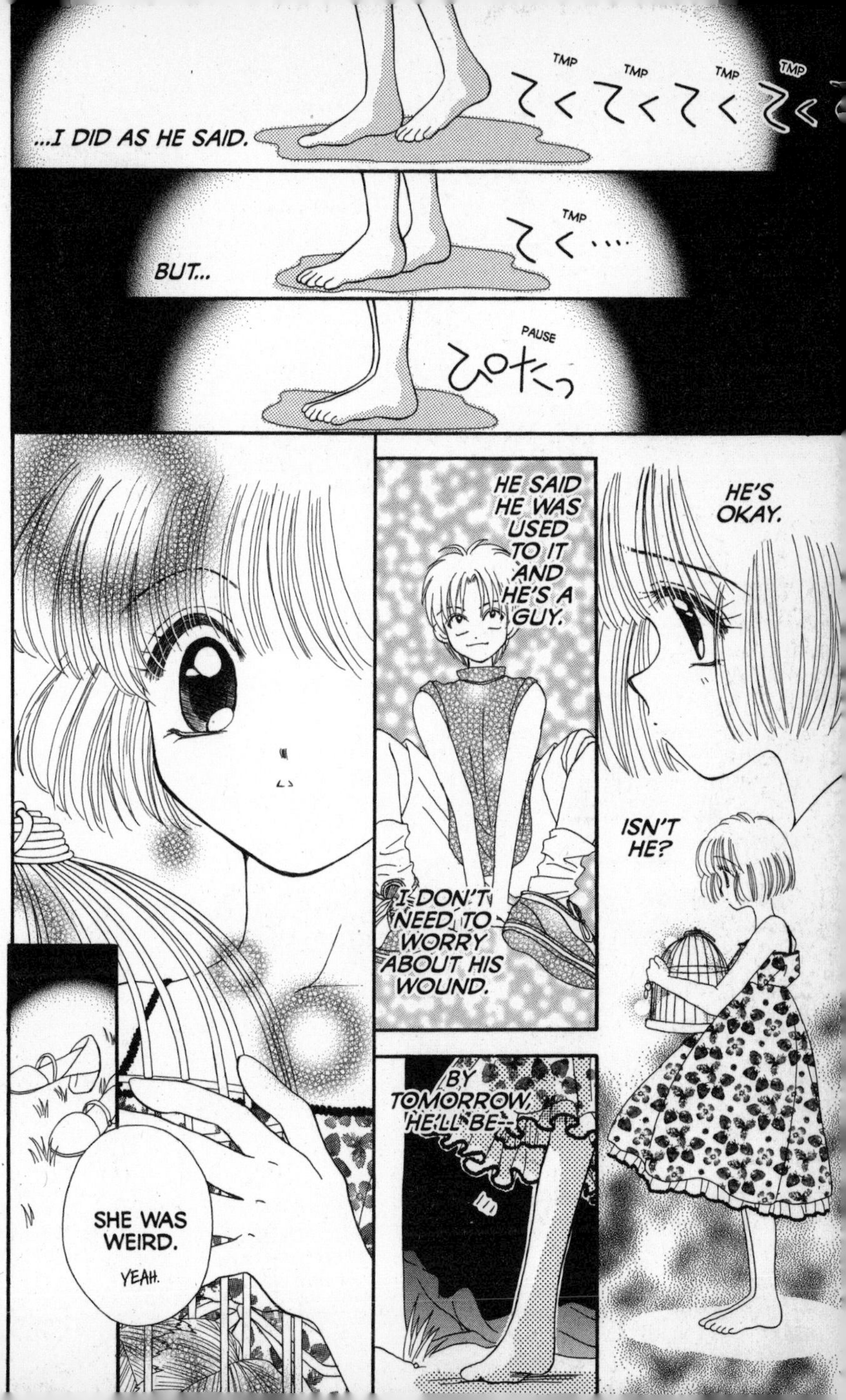

...I DID AS HE SAID.
TMP TMP TMP TMP
てくてくてくてく
BUT...
TMP
てく…
PAUSE
ぴたっ
HE'S OKAY.
ISN'T HE?
HE SAID HE WAS USED TO IT AND HE'S A GUY.
I DON'T NEED TO WORRY ABOUT HIS WOUND.
BY TOMORROW, HE'LL BE--
SHE WAS WEIRD.
YEAH.

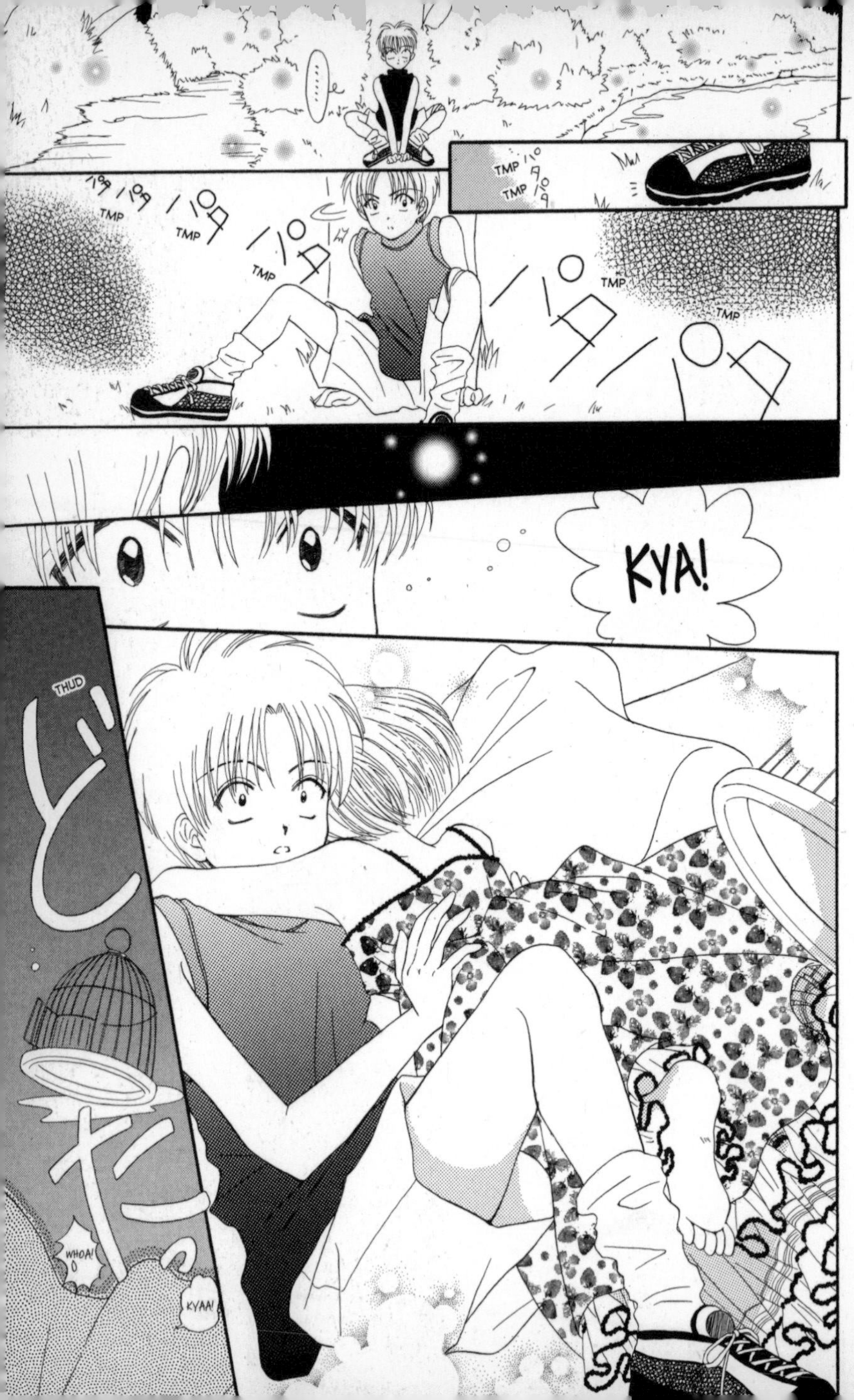
......
TMP パタ
TMP パタ
パタ TMP
パタ TMP
パタ TMP
パタ TMP
パタ TMP
パタパタ TMP
KYA!
THUD
どさーっ
WHOA!
KYAA!

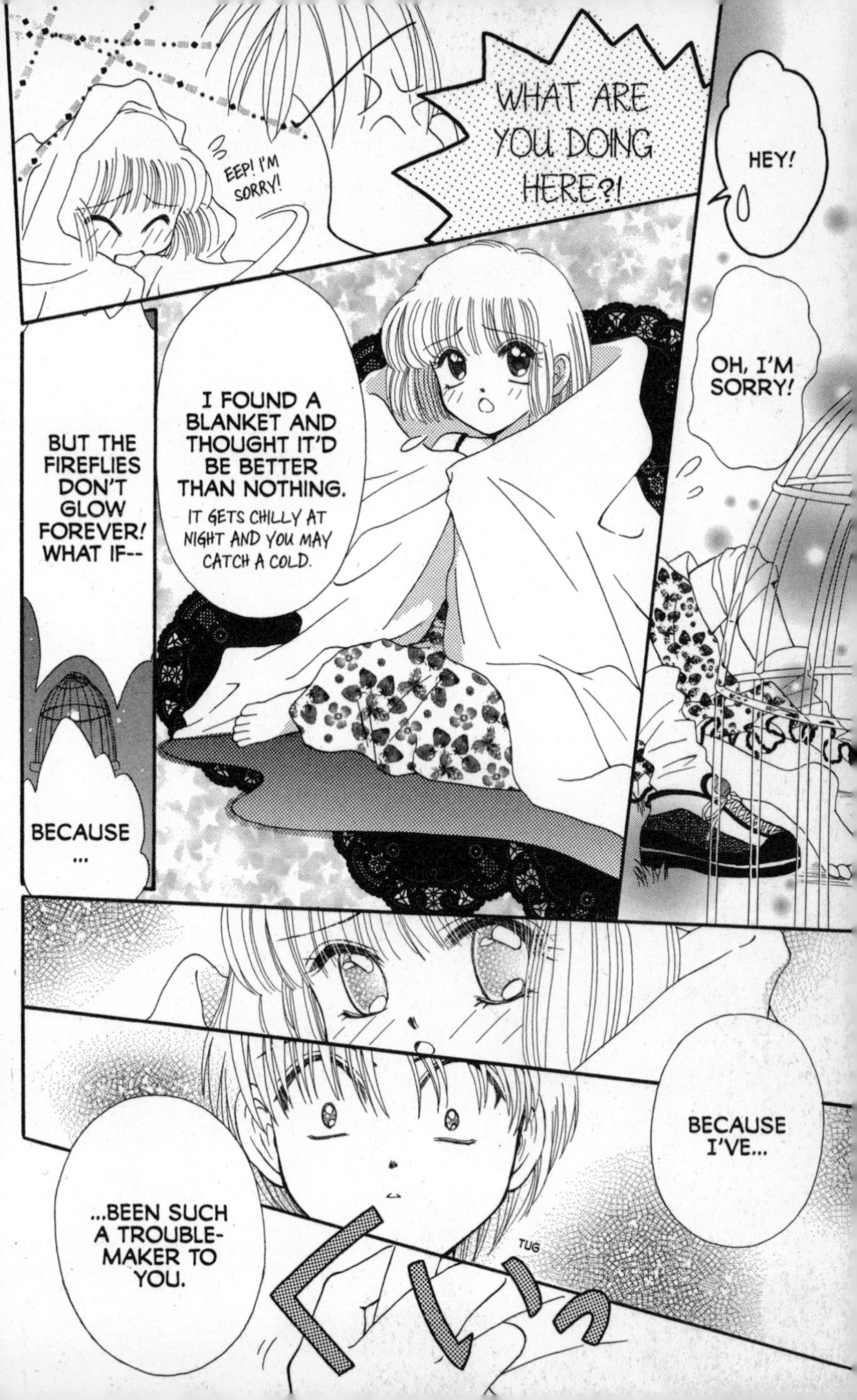
HEY!
OH, I'M SORRY!
WHAT ARE YOU DOING HERE?!
EEP! I'M SORRY!
I FOUND A BLANKET AND THOUGHT IT'D BE BETTER THAN NOTHING.
IT GETS CHILLY AT NIGHT AND YOU MAY CATCH A COLD.
BUT THE FIREFLIES DON'T GLOW FOREVER! WHAT IF--
BECAUSE ...
BECAUSE I'VE...
TUG
...BEEN SUCH A TROUBLE-MAKER TO YOU.

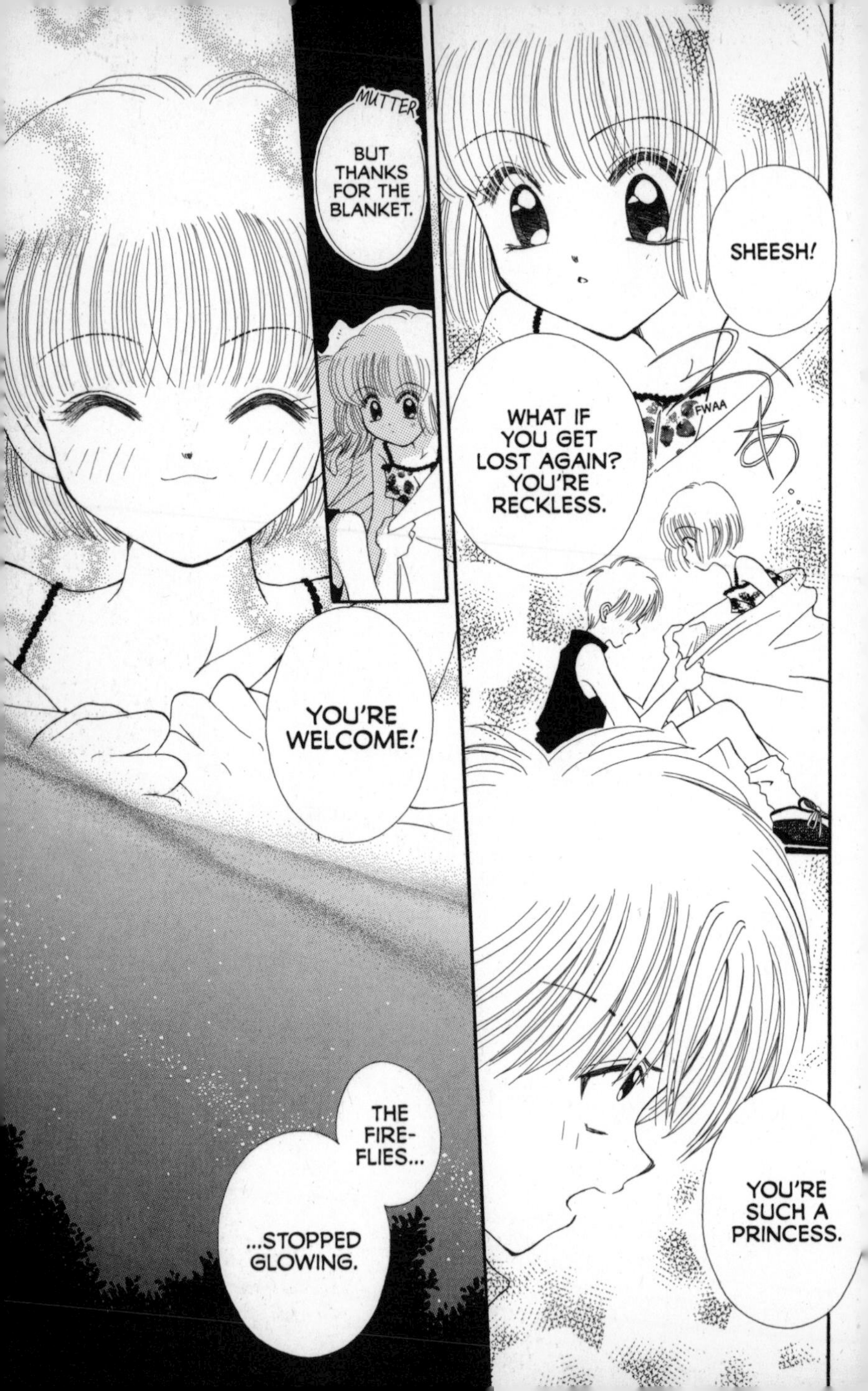
SHEESH!
FWAA
あ
WHAT IF YOU GET LOST AGAIN? YOU'RE RECKLESS.
YOU'RE SUCH A PRINCESS.
MUTTER
BUT THANKS FOR THE BLANKET.
YOU'RE WELCOME!
THE FIRE-FLIES...
...STOPPED GLOWING.

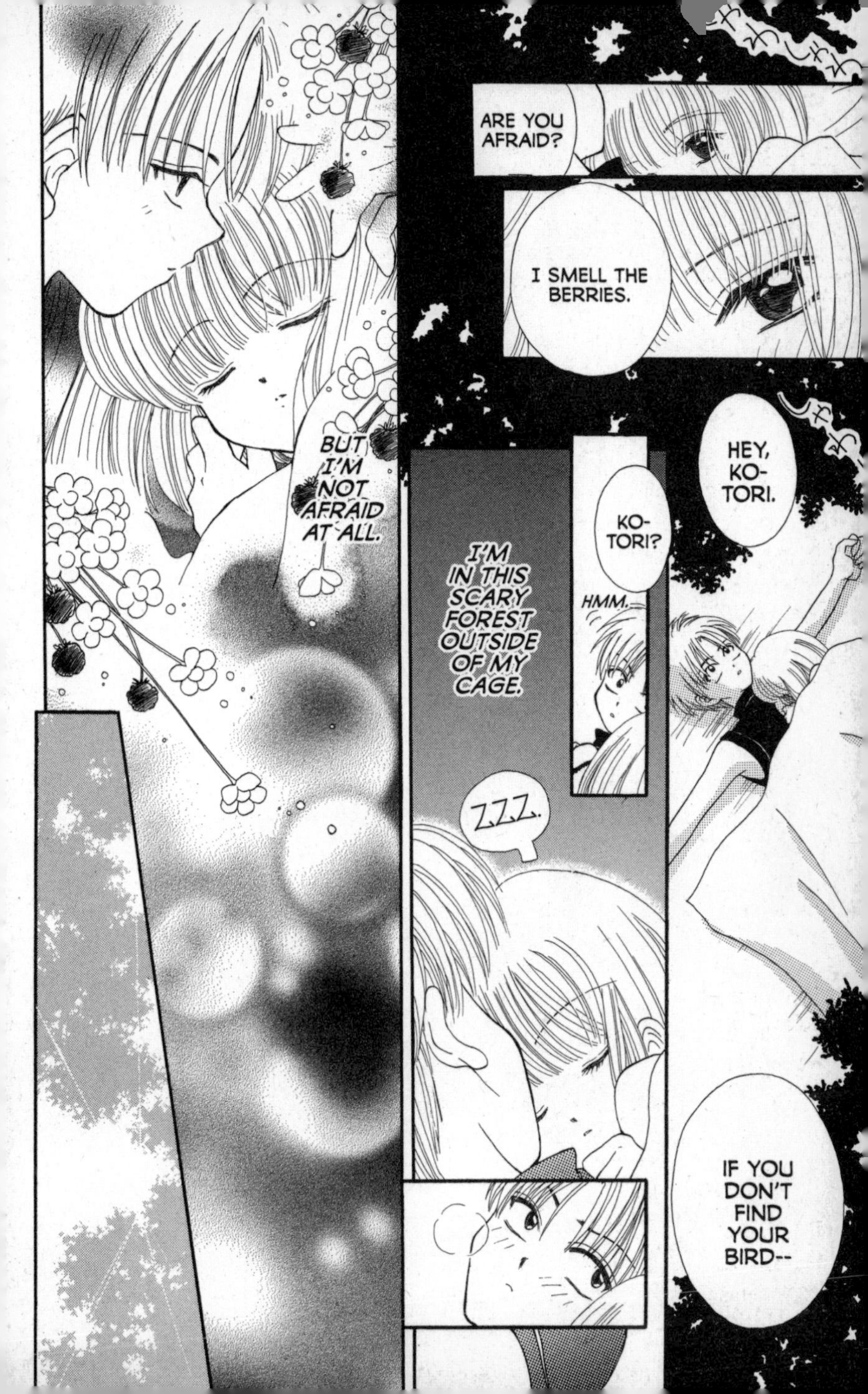
ARE YOU AFRAID?
I SMELL THE BERRIES.
HEY, KO-TORI.
KO-TORI?
HMM.
I'M IN THIS SCARY FOREST OUTSIDE OF MY CAGE.
Z.Z.Z.
IF YOU DON'T FIND YOUR BIRD--
BUT I'M NOT AFRAID AT ALL.

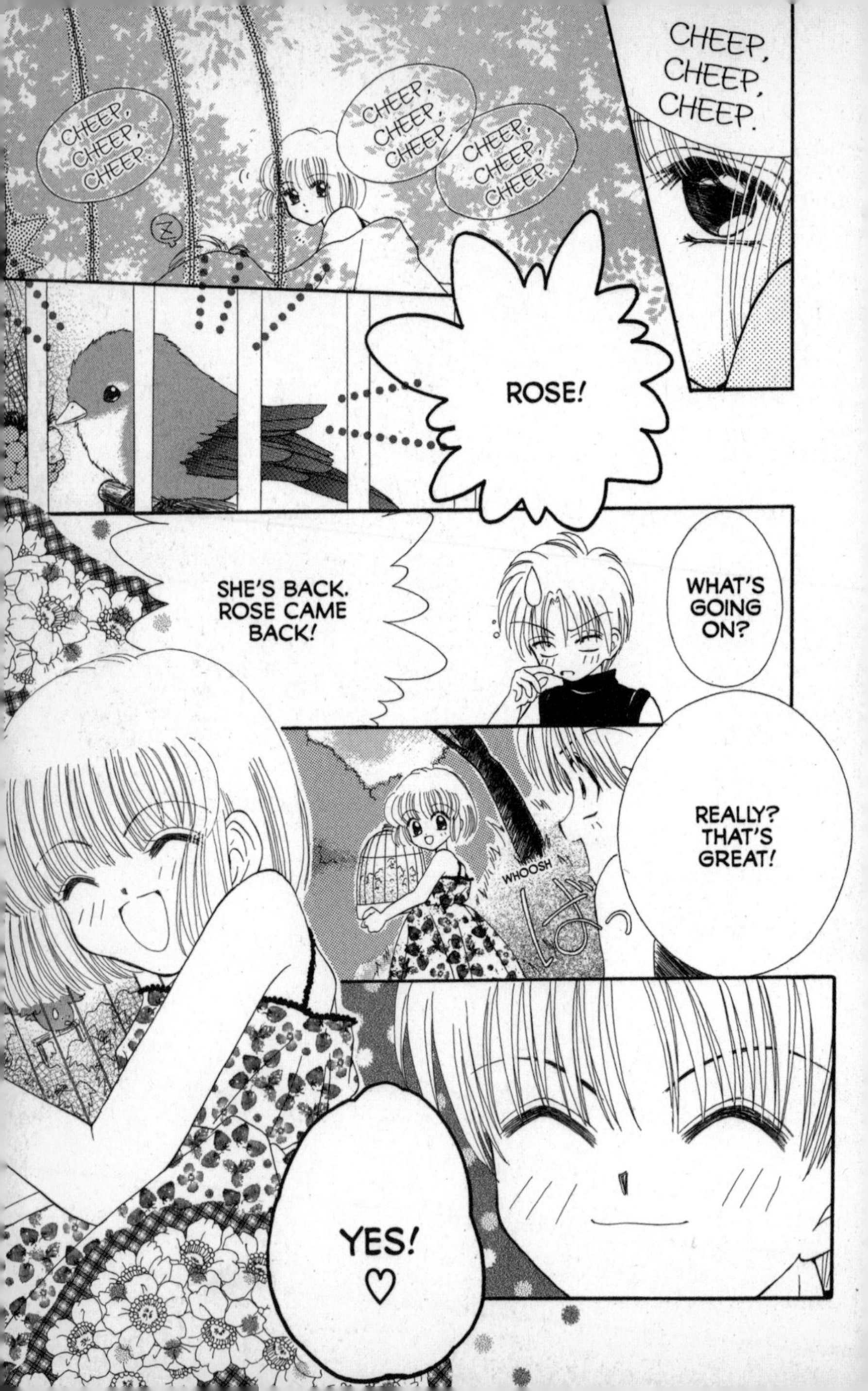
CHEEP, CHEEP, CHEEP.
CHEEP, CHEEP, CHEEP.
CHEEP, CHEEP, CHEEP.
CHEEP, CHEEP, CHEEP.
ROSE!
WHAT'S GOING ON?
SHE'S BACK. ROSE CAME BACK!
REALLY? THAT'S GREAT!
WHOOSH
YES! ♡

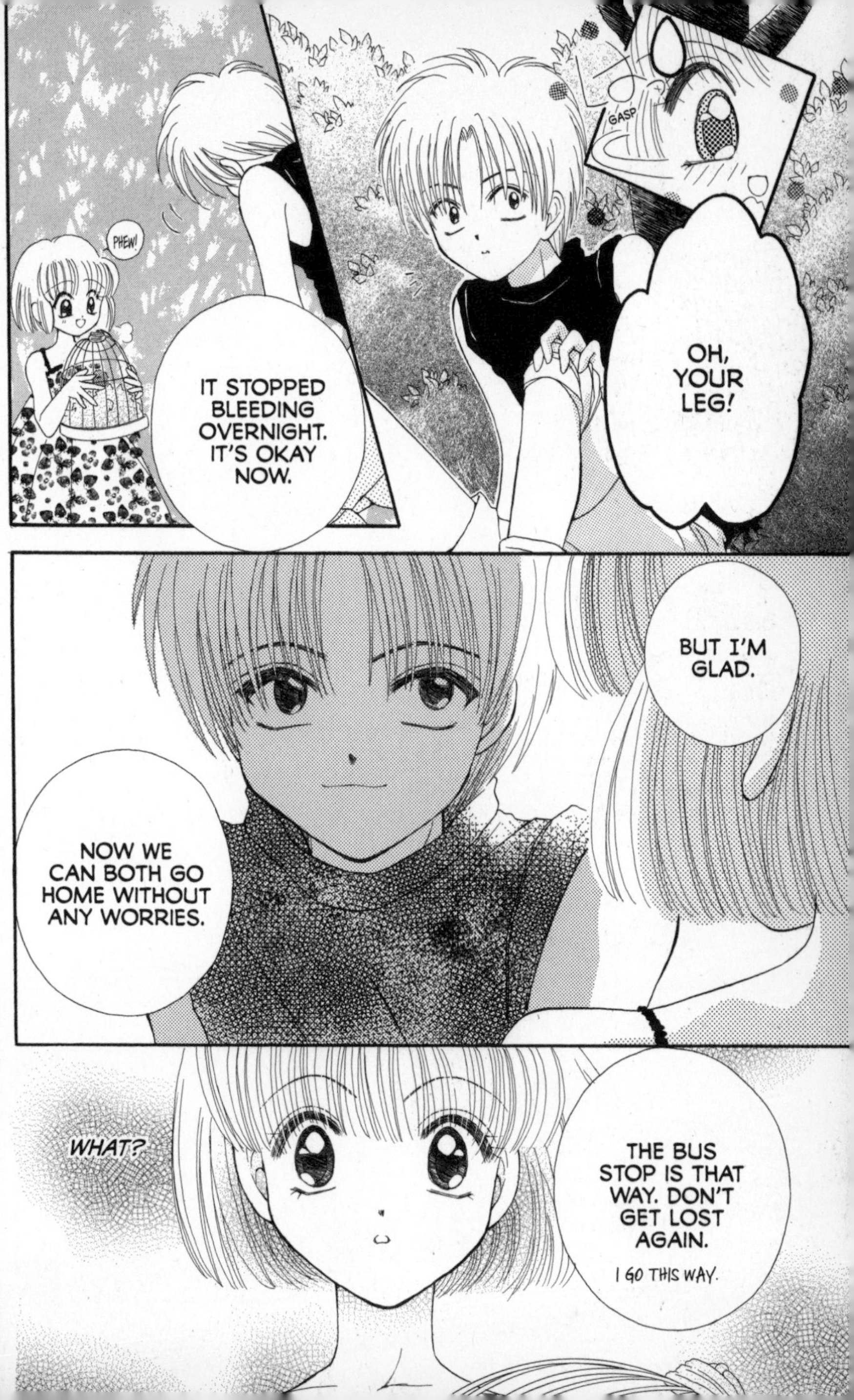
GASP
OH, YOUR LEG!
IT STOPPED BLEEDING OVERNIGHT. IT'S OKAY NOW.
PHEW!
BUT I'M GLAD.
NOW WE CAN BOTH GO HOME WITHOUT ANY WORRIES.
THE BUS STOP IS THAT WAY. DON'T GET LOST AGAIN.
I GO THIS WAY.
WHAT?

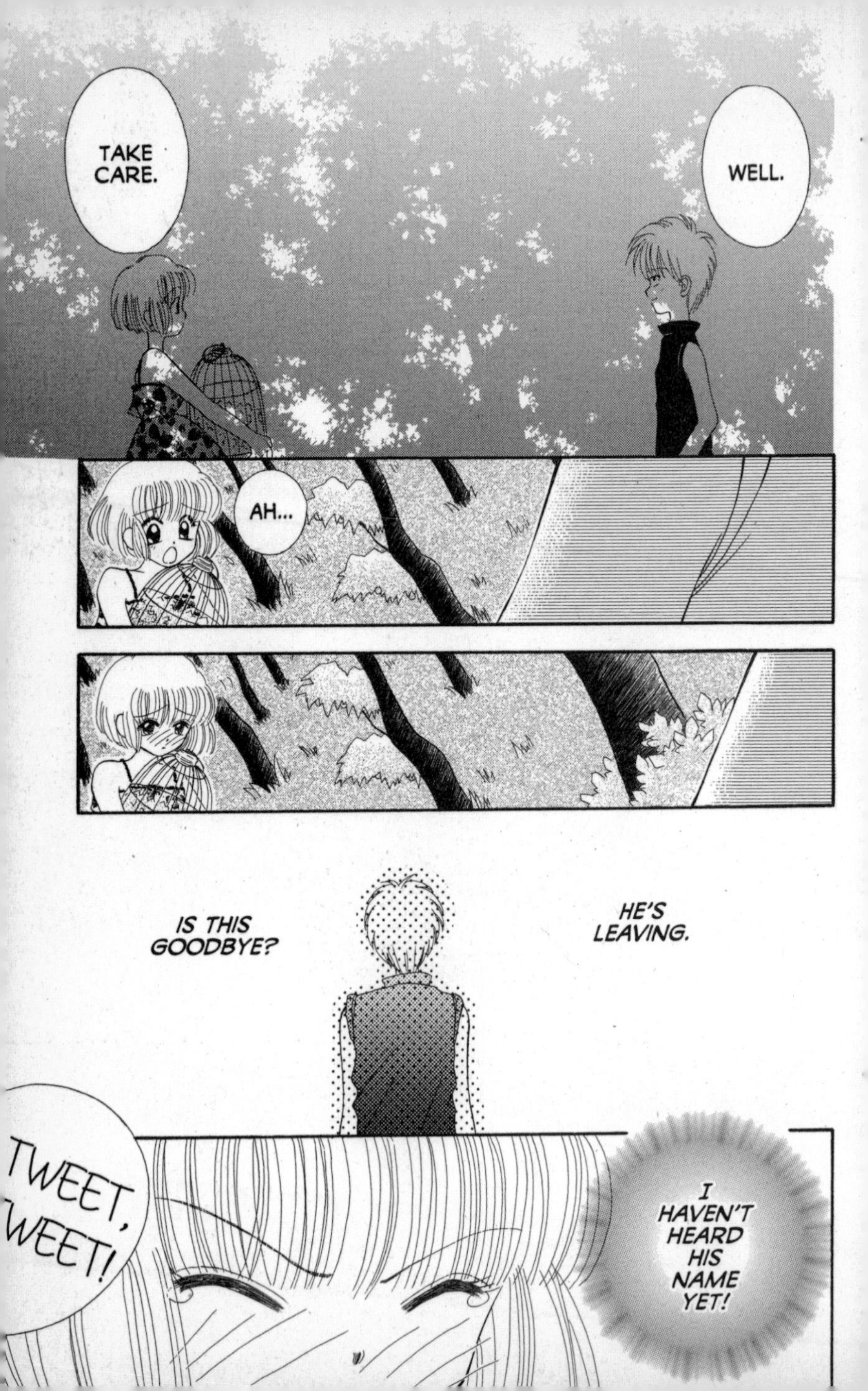
WELL.
TAKE CARE.
AH...
HE'S LEAVING.
IS THIS GOODBYE?
I HAVEN'T HEARD HIS NAME YET!
TWEET, WEET, WEET!

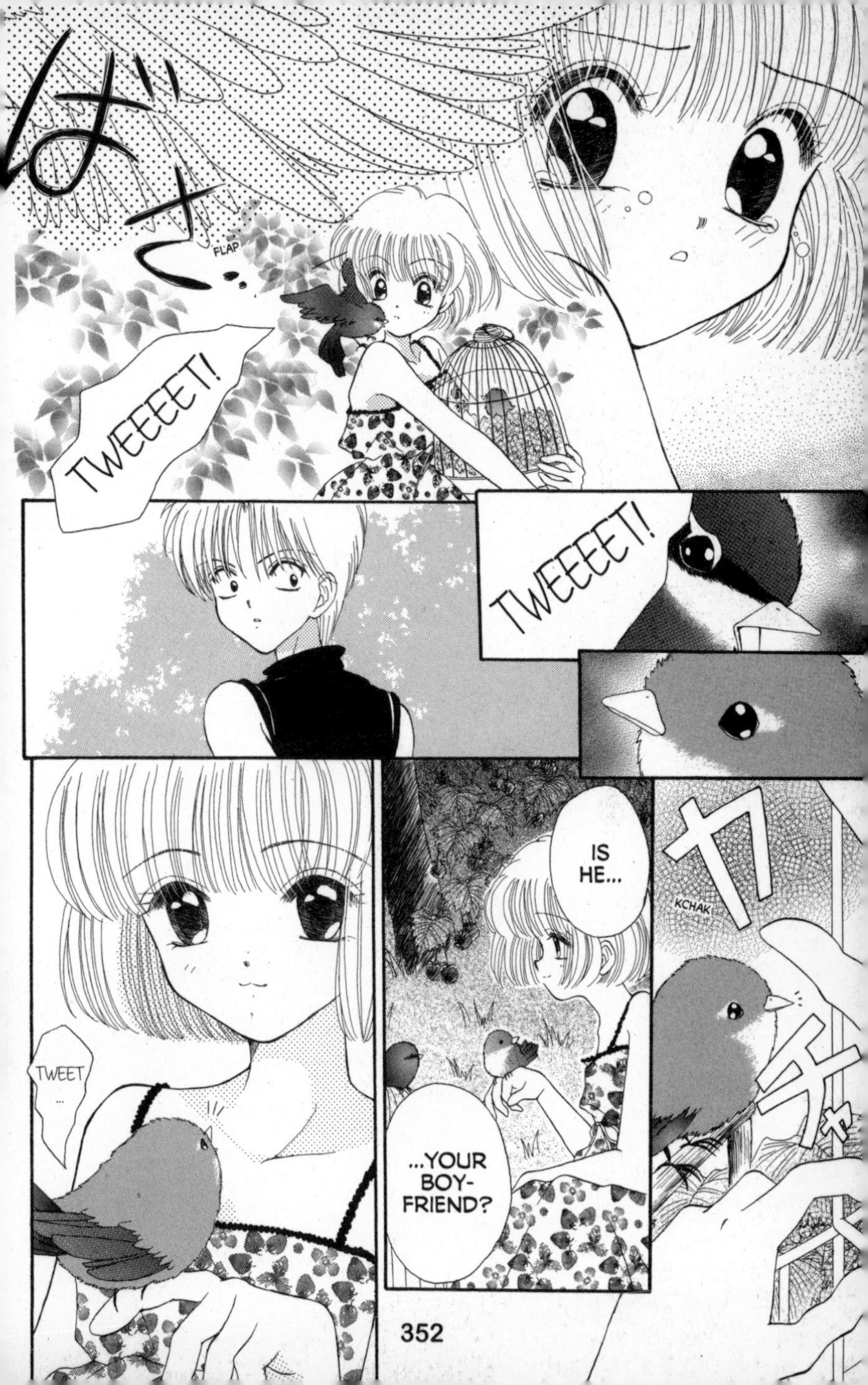
FLAP
TWEEEEET!
TWEEEEET!
KCHAK
IS HE...
...YOUR BOY-FRIEND?
TWEET ...

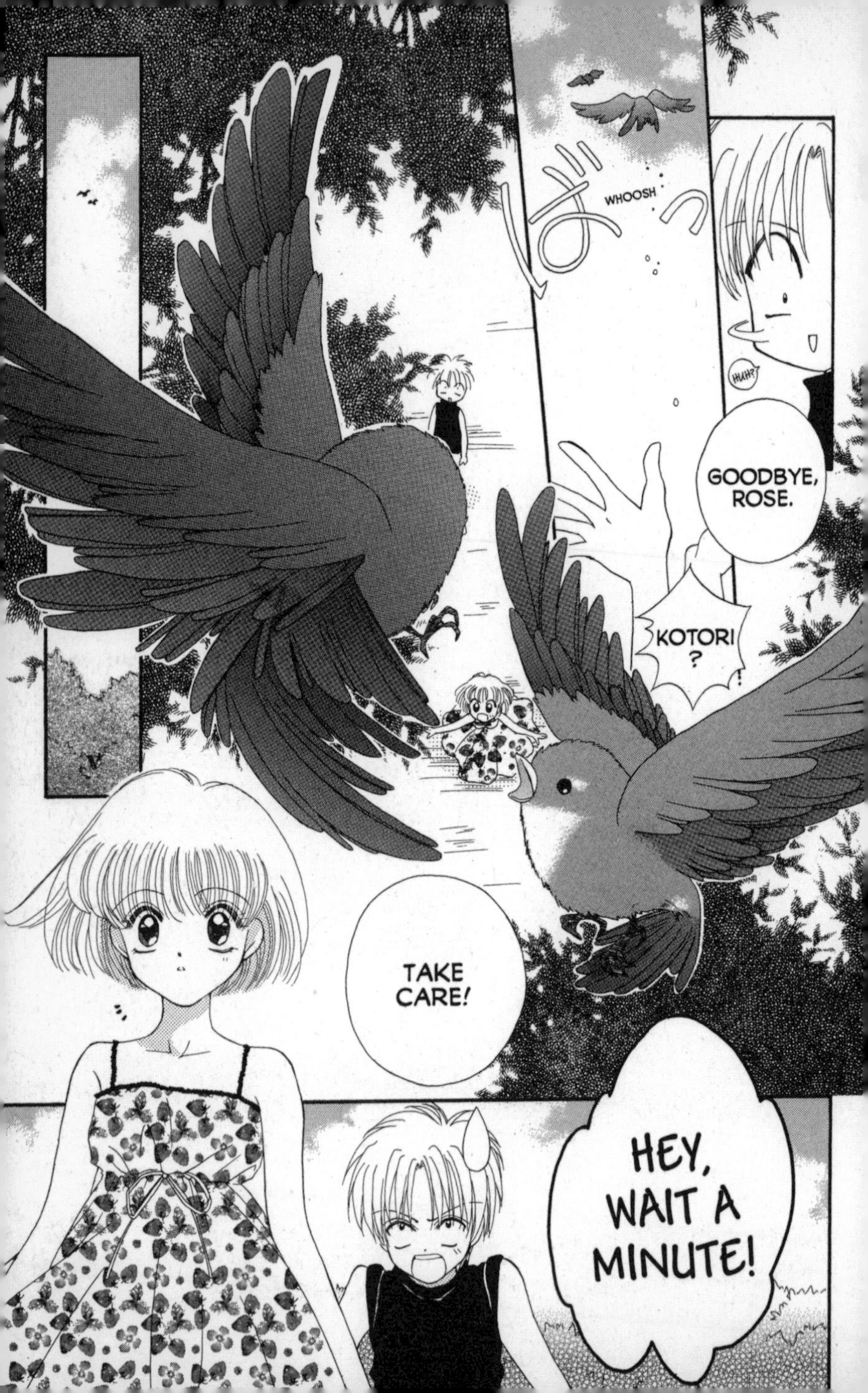
WHOOSH
HUH?
GOODBYE, ROSE.
KOTORI?
TAKE CARE!
HEY, WAIT A MINUTE!

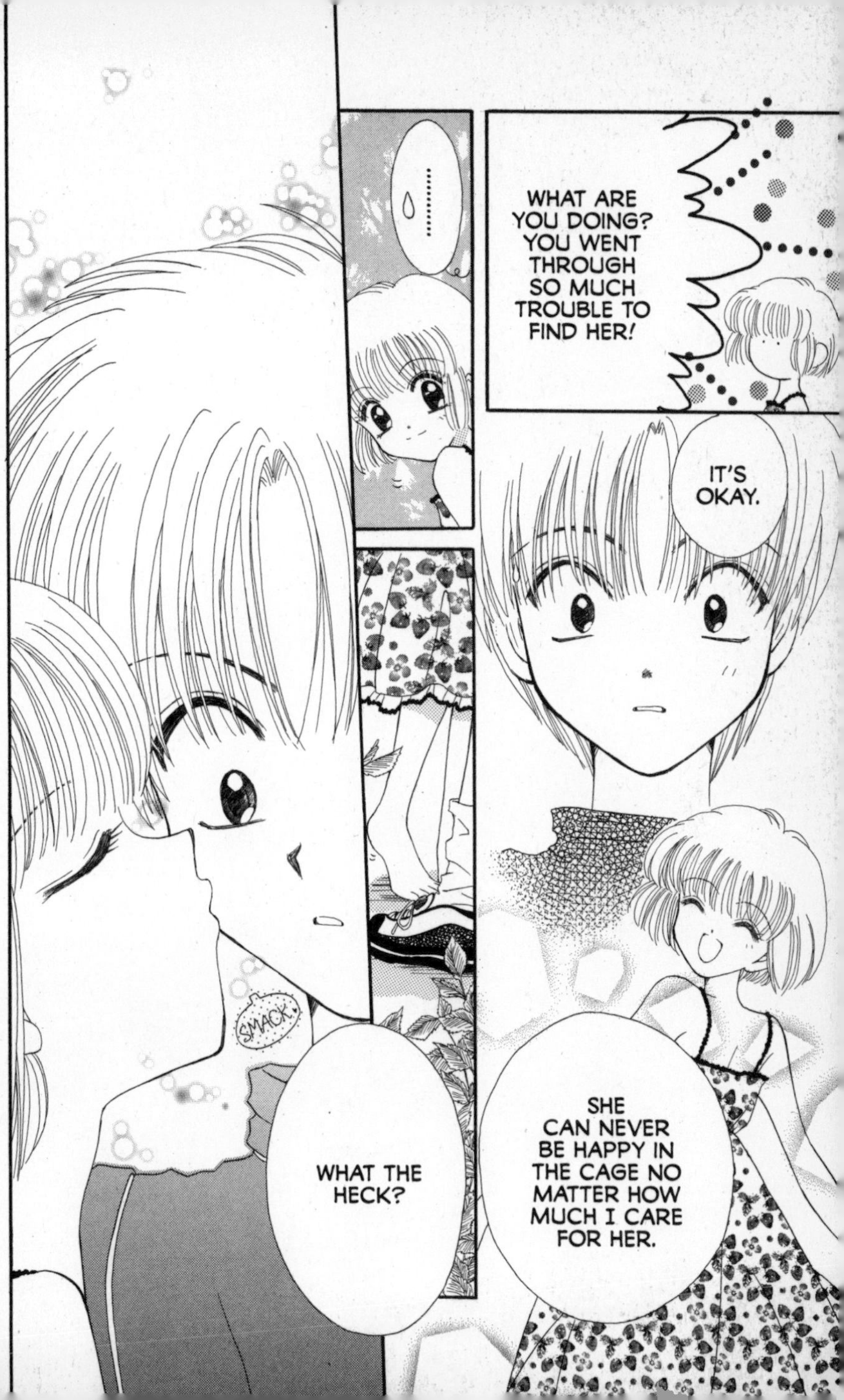
WHAT ARE YOU DOING? YOU WENT THROUGH SO MUCH TROUBLE TO FIND HER!
....
IT'S OKAY.
SHE CAN NEVER BE HAPPY IN THE CAGE NO MATTER HOW MUCH I CARE FOR HER.
SMACK
WHAT THE HECK?

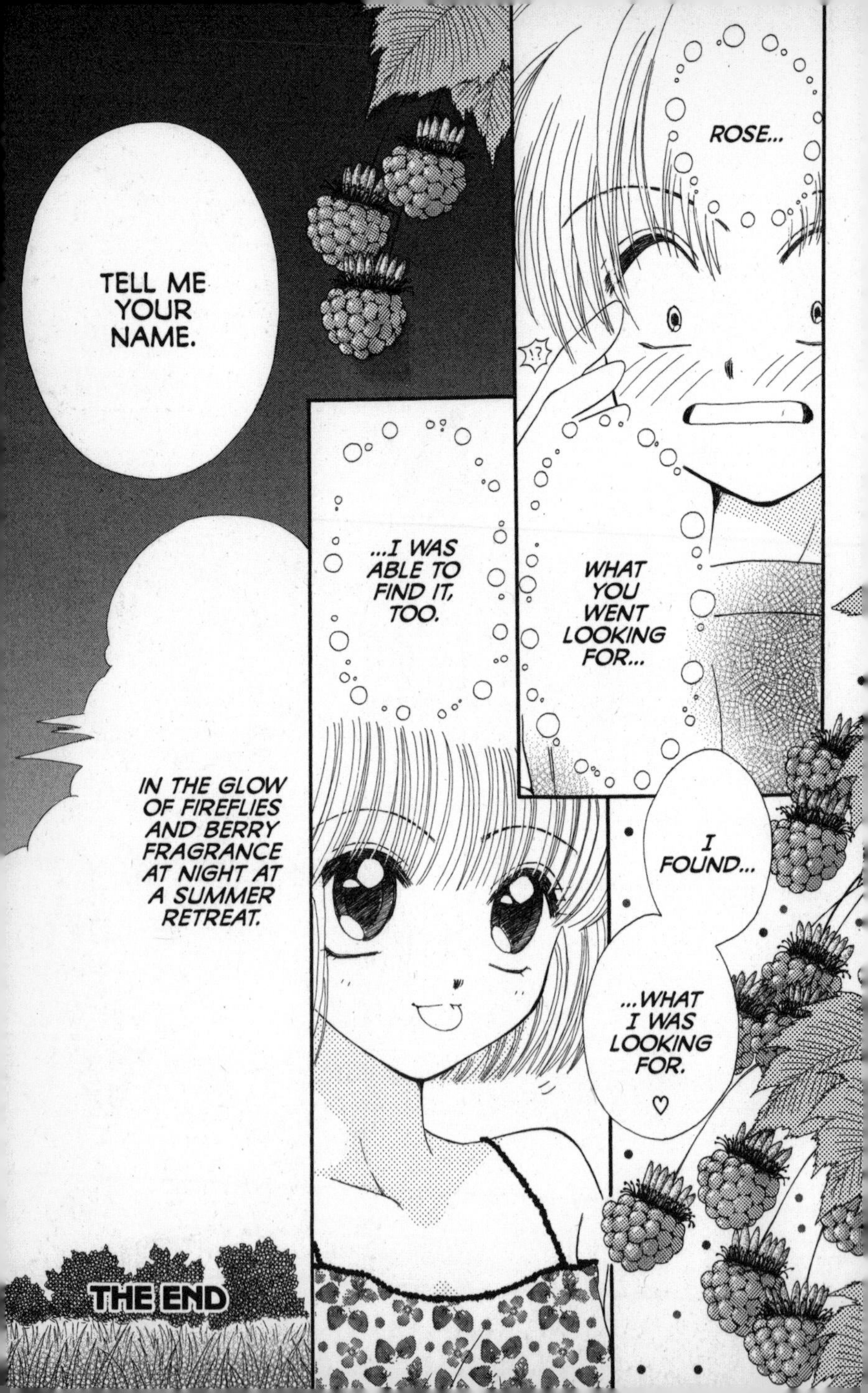
ROSE...
!?
WHAT YOU WENT LOOKING FOR...
...I WAS ABLE TO FIND IT, TOO.
I FOUND...
...WHAT I WAS LOOKING FOR. ♡
TELL ME YOUR NAME.
IN THE GLOW OF FIREFLIES AND BERRY FRAGRANCE AT NIGHT AT A SUMMER RETREAT.
THE END

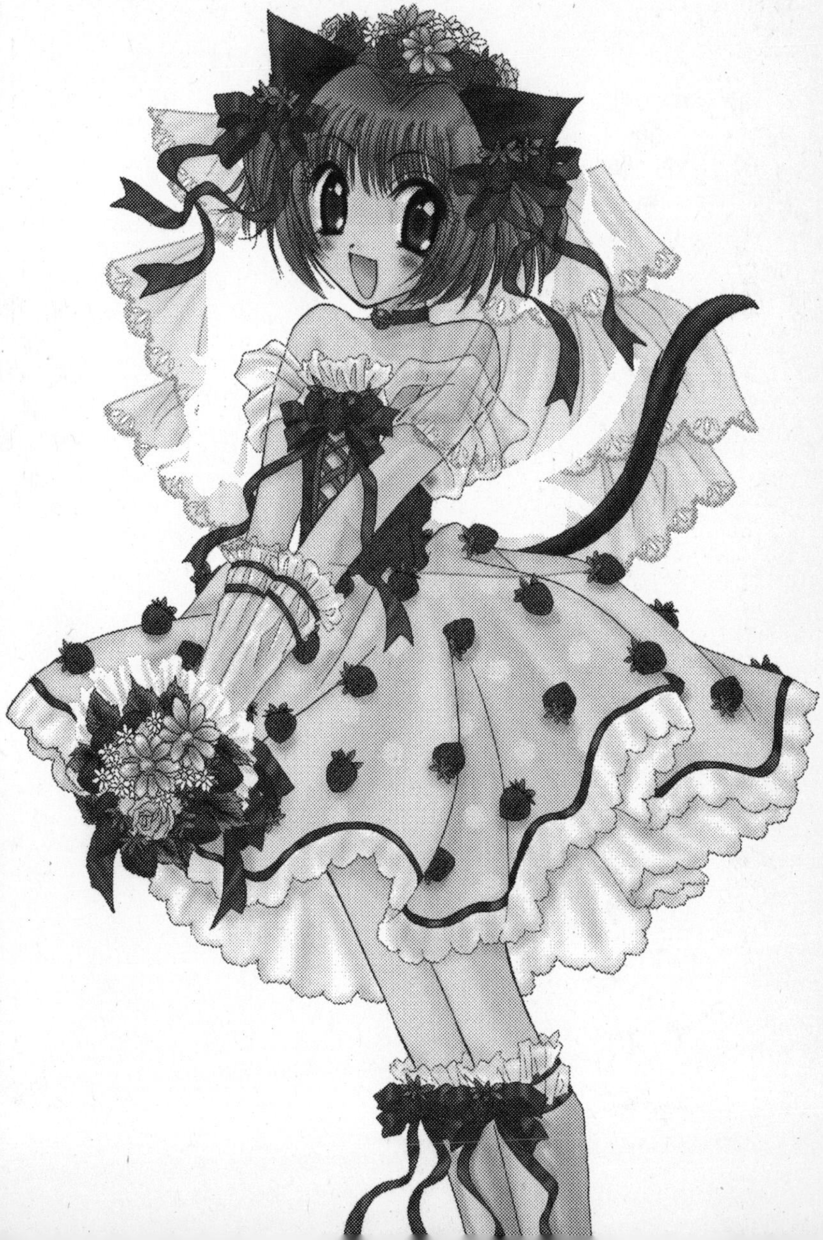

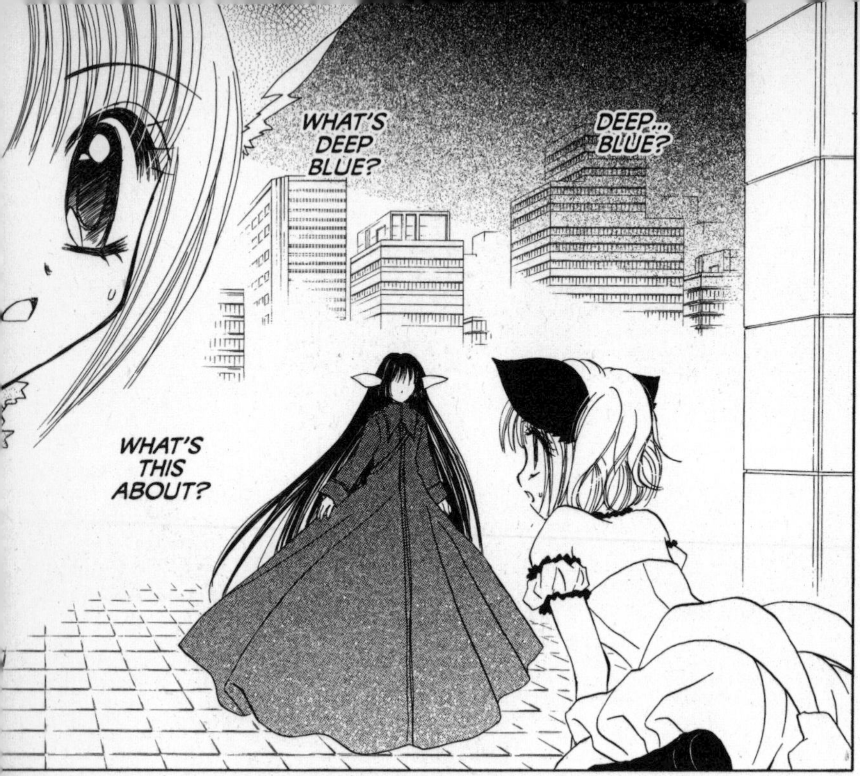
DEEP... BLUE?
WHAT'S DEEP BLUE?
WHAT'S THIS ABOUT?

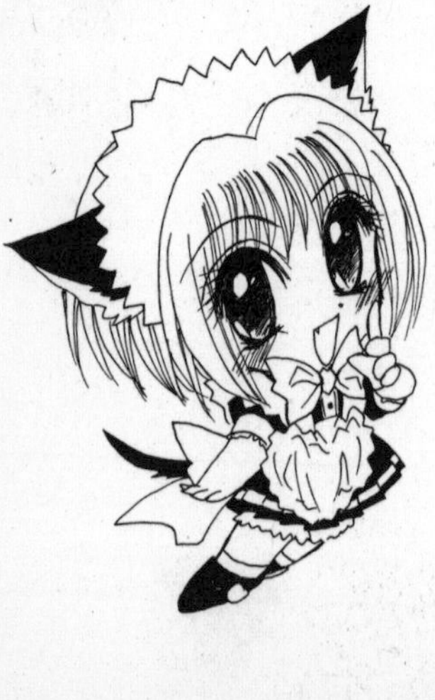

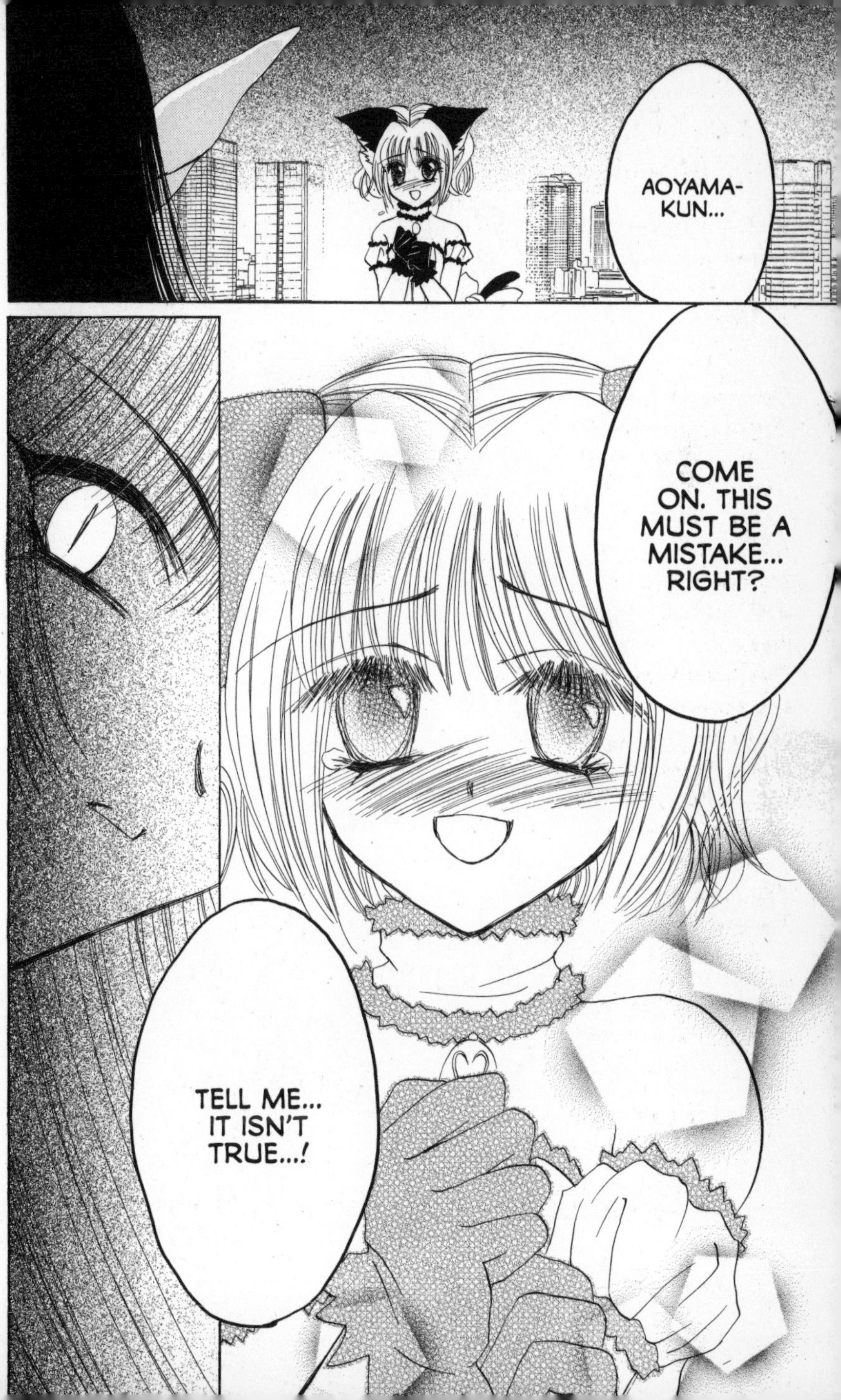
AOYAMA-KUN...
COME ON. THIS MUST BE A MISTAKE... RIGHT?
TELL ME... IT ISN'T TRUE...!

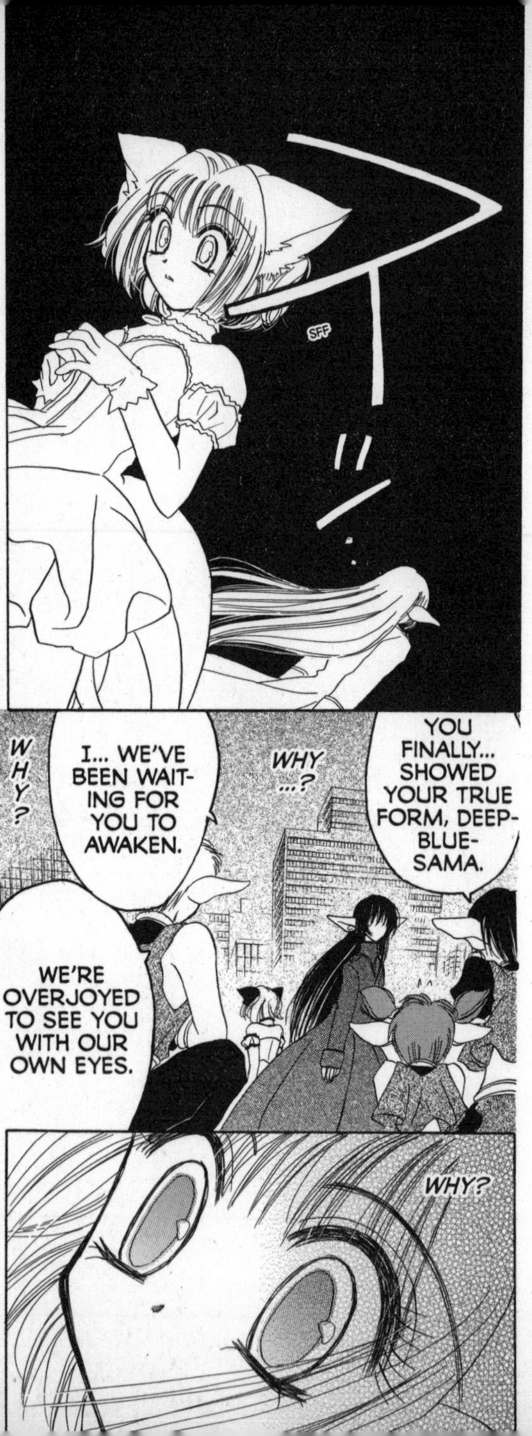
SFF
YOU FINALLY... SHOWED YOUR TRUE FORM, DEEP-BLUE-SAMA.
WHY ...?
I... WE'VE BEEN WAIT-ING FOR YOU TO AWAKEN.
WHY?
WE'RE OVERJOYED TO SEE YOU WITH OUR OWN EYES.
WHY?

Yo, This Is Ikumi!

It's been a while so welcome new readers. It's Ikumi. Here's the final volume of Tokyo Mew Mew. ♥

I know it's abrupt but I decided to draw my staff as hamsters for a change. There's someone in my staff who can draw cute hamsters well, so I had her do our portraits. It came out so good that I asked her to draw a four-koma manga. Since it may be hard to recognize each staff member as a hamster, I recommend reading the introduction on page 191 first. I hope you can see how friendly our workplace is. ☆
This explains our four-koma manga.

I hope you enjoy the final volume of Tokyo Mew Mew!

♥♥

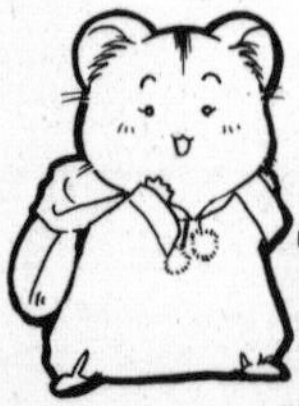

THIS IS ME. I WAS SERIOUSLY WORKING IN A BUNNY COSTUME. I'M NOT KIDDING!

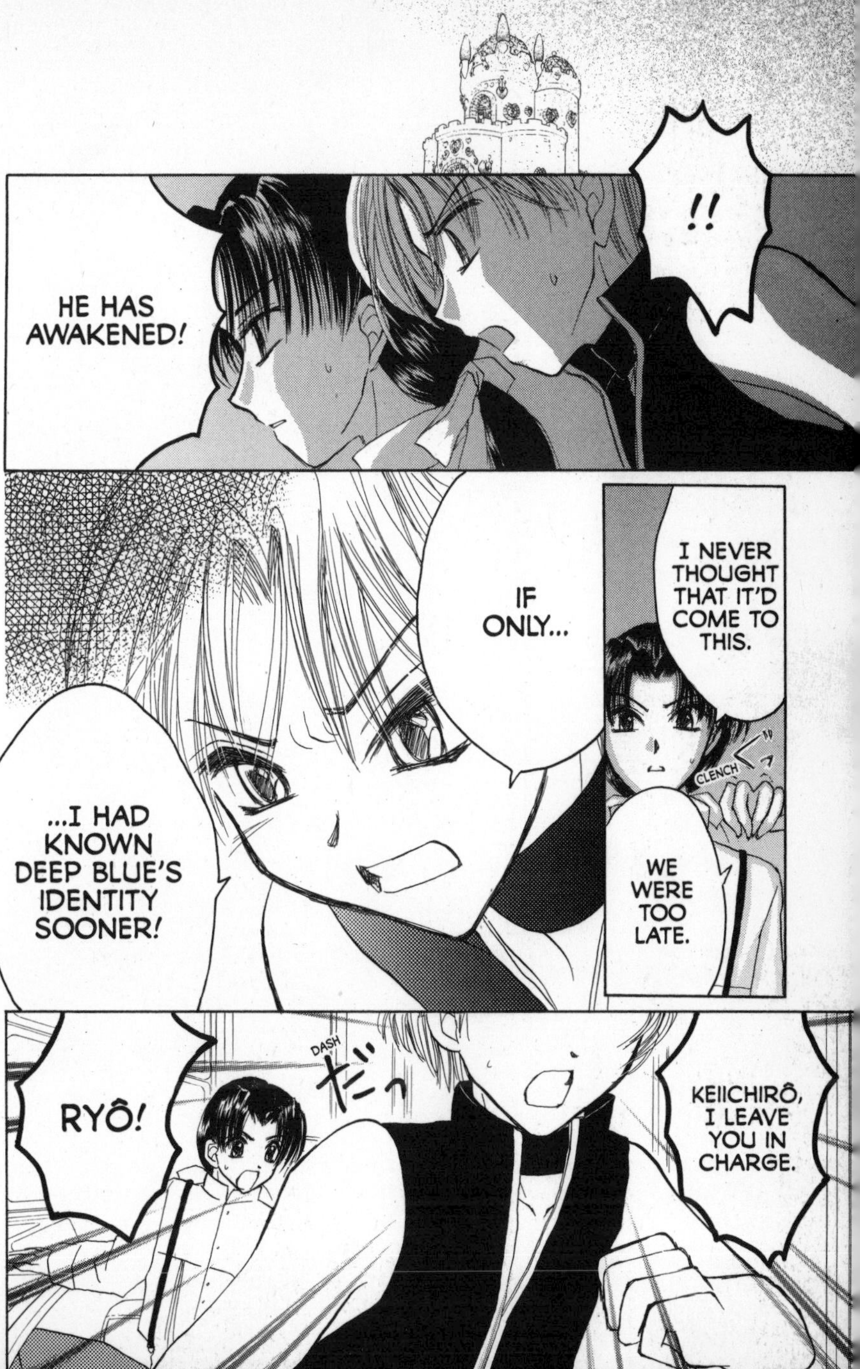
!!
HE HAS AWAKENED!
I NEVER THOUGHT THAT IT'D COME TO THIS.
CLENCH
WE WERE TOO LATE.
IF ONLY...
...I HAD KNOWN DEEP BLUE'S IDENTITY SOONER!
KEIICHIRÔ, I LEAVE YOU IN CHARGE.
DASH
RYÔ!

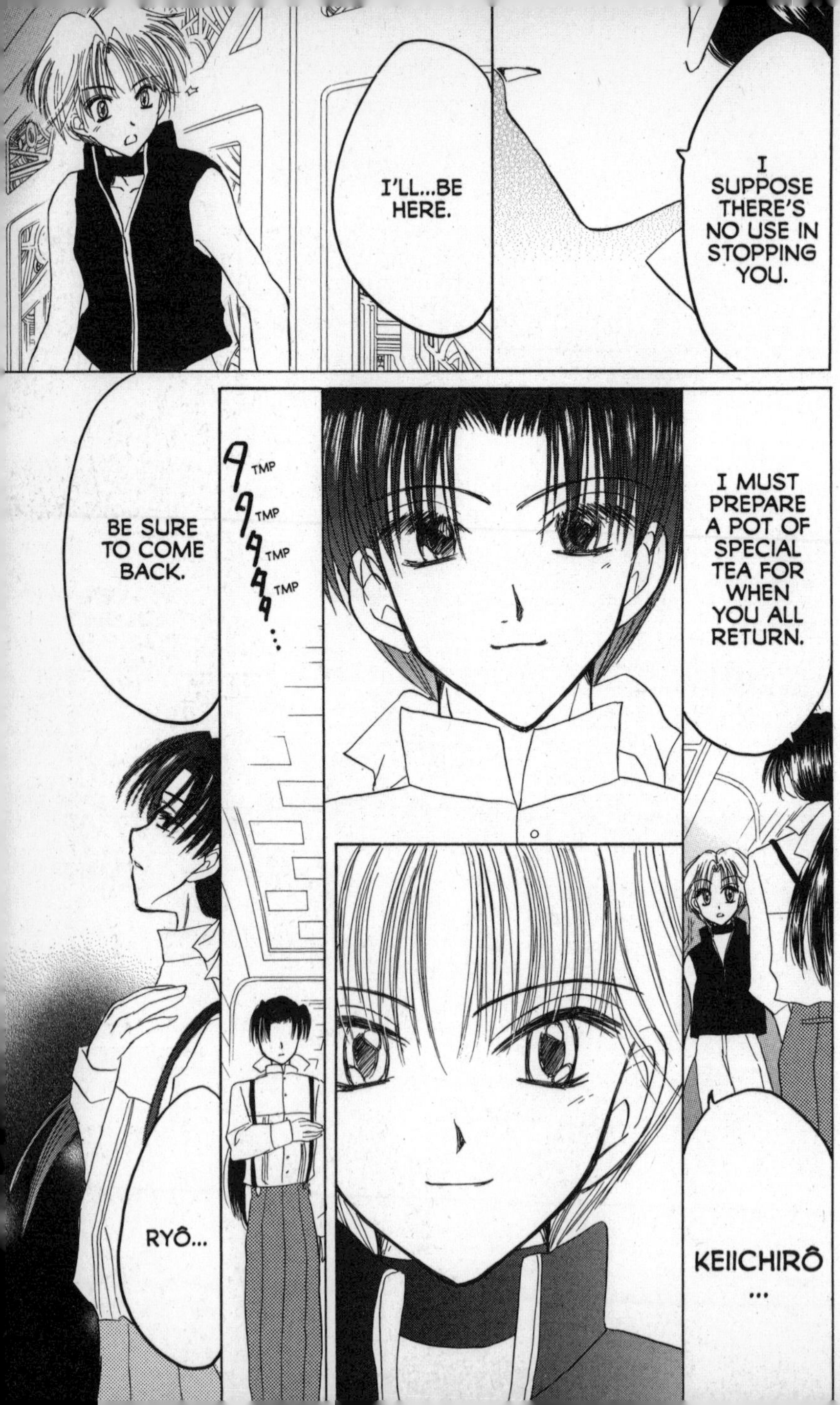
I SUPPOSE THERE'S NO USE IN STOPPING YOU.
I'LL...BE HERE.
I MUST PREPARE A POT OF SPECIAL TEA FOR WHEN YOU ALL RETURN.
KEIICHIRÔ...
TMP TMP TMP TMP...
BE SURE TO COME BACK.
RYÔ...

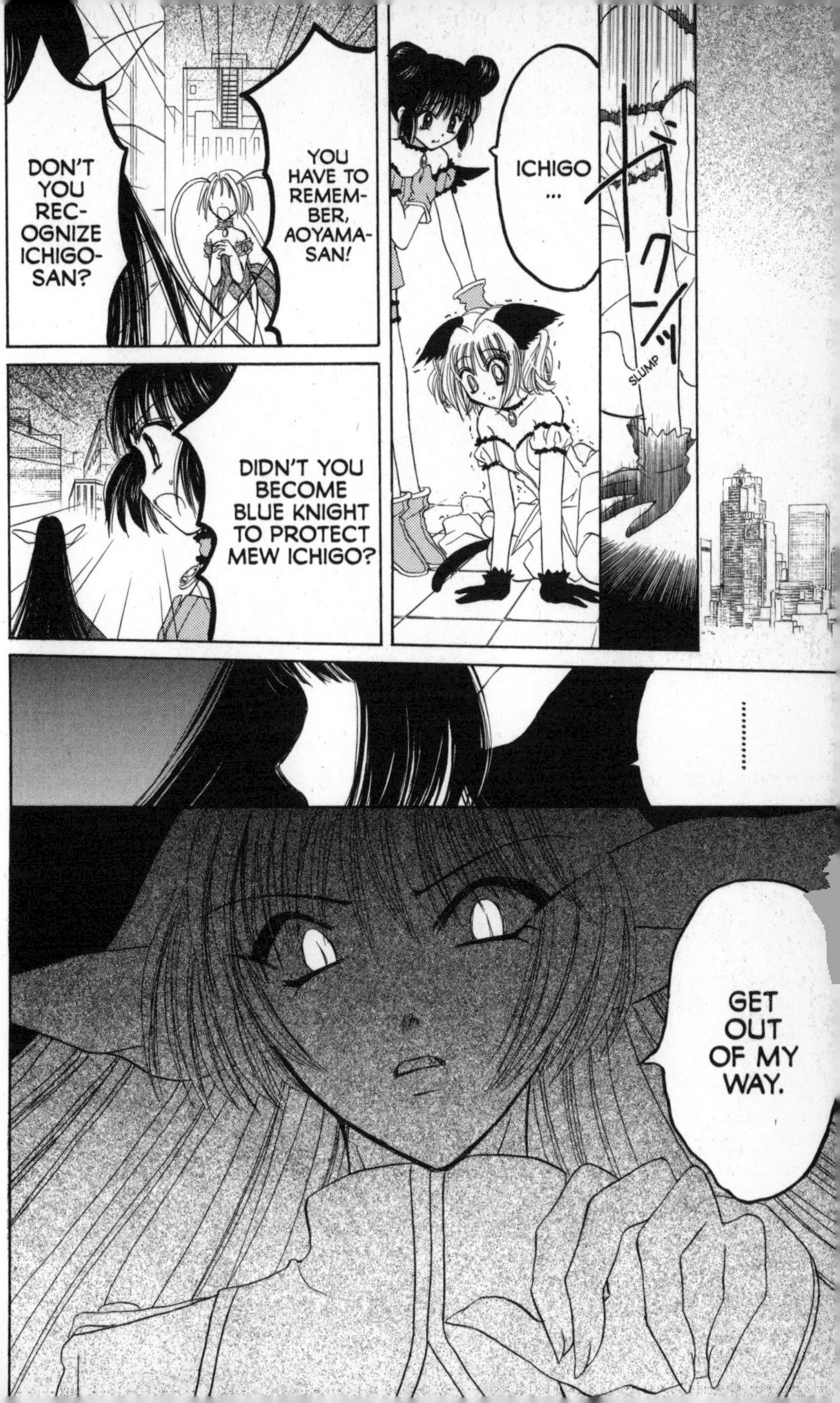
ガクーンッ
SLUMP
ICHIGO ...
YOU HAVE TO REMEMBER, AOYAMA-SAN!
DON'T YOU RECOGNIZE ICHIGO-SAN?
DIDN'T YOU BECOME BLUE KNIGHT TO PROTECT MEW ICHIGO?
....
GET OUT OF MY WAY.

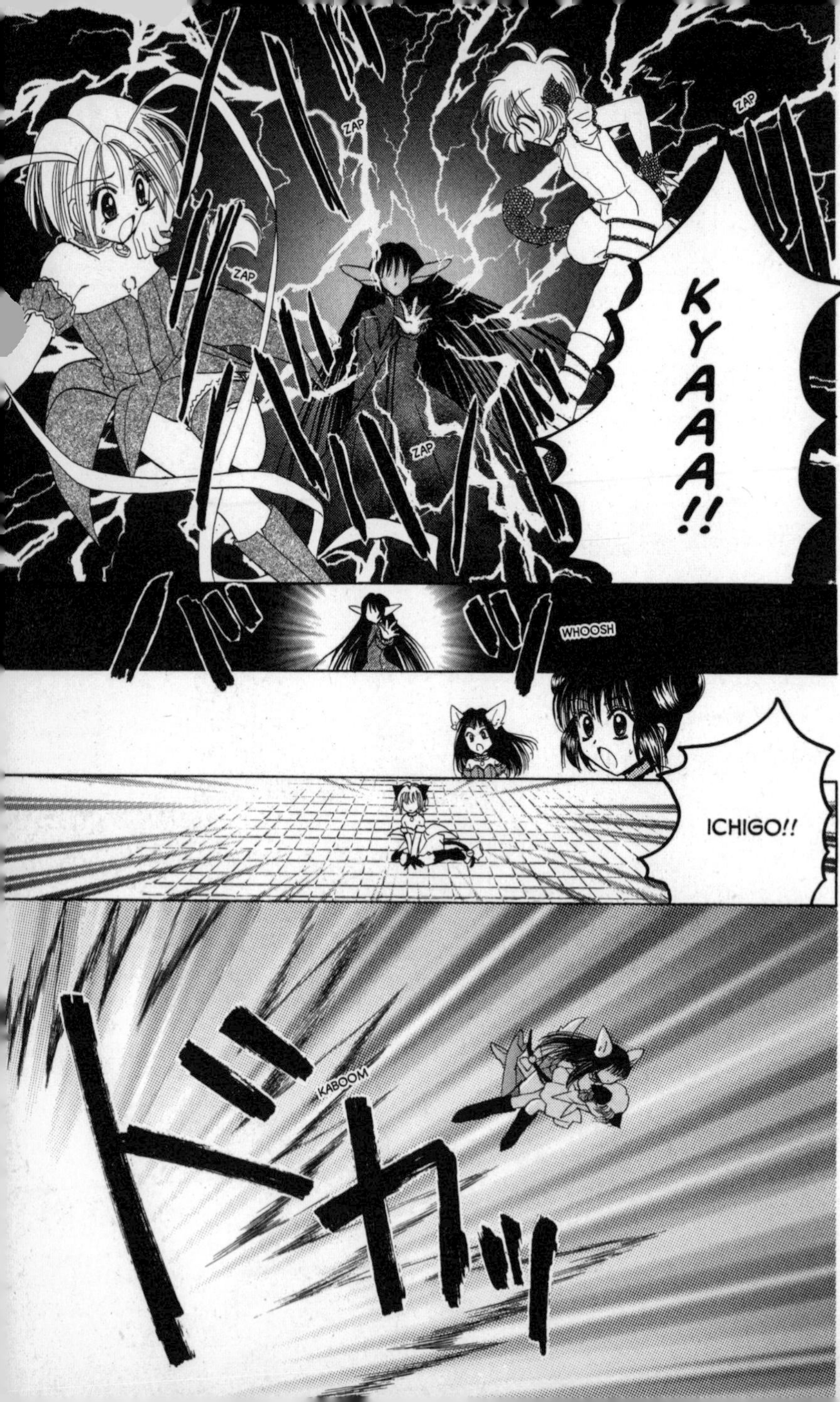
KYAAAA!!
ZAP
ZAP
ZAP
ZAP
WHOOSH
ICHIGO!!
KABOOM

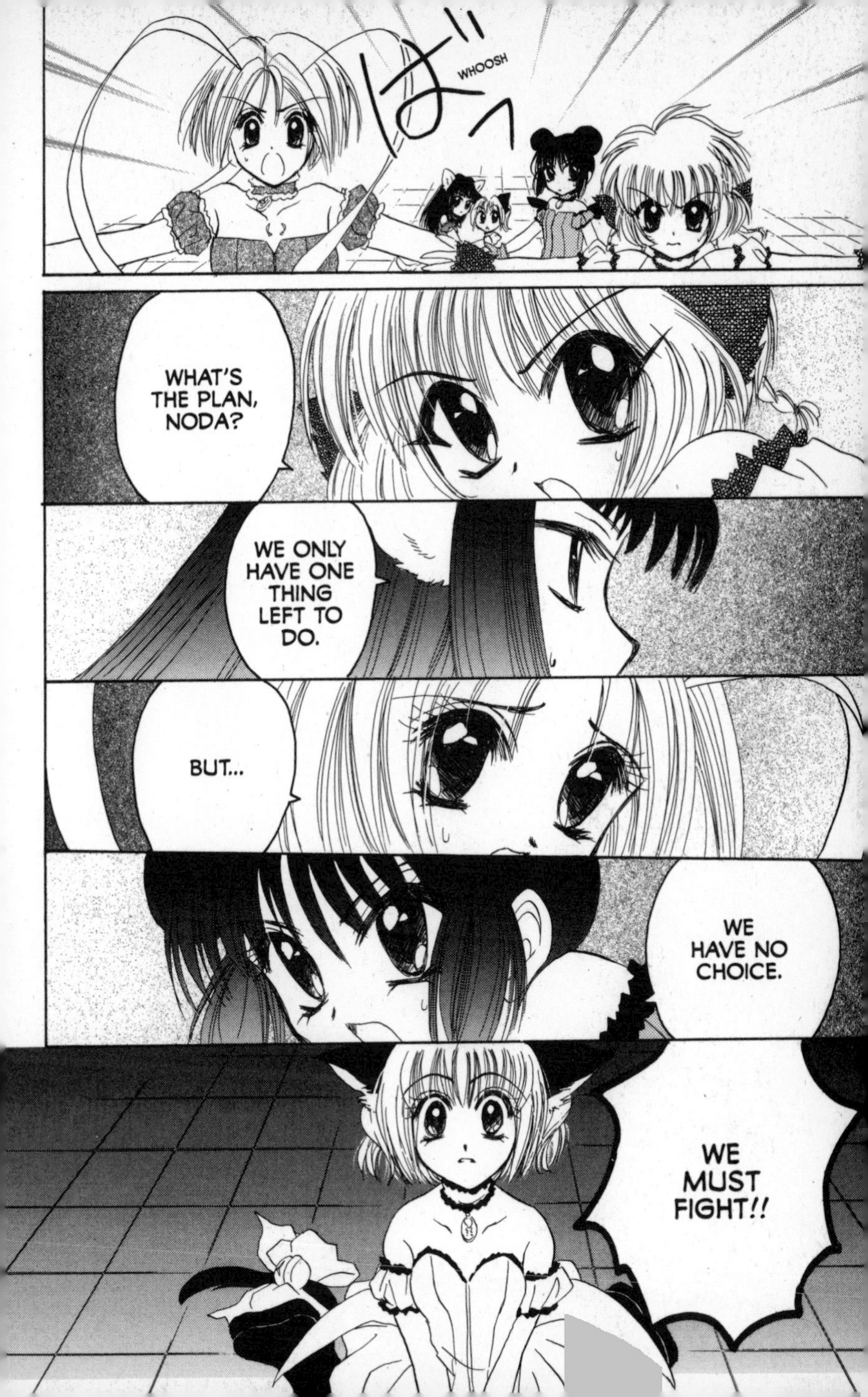
ぱっ
WHOOSH
WHAT'S THE PLAN, NODA?
WE ONLY HAVE ONE THING LEFT TO DO.
BUT...
WE HAVE NO CHOICE.
WE MUST FIGHT!!

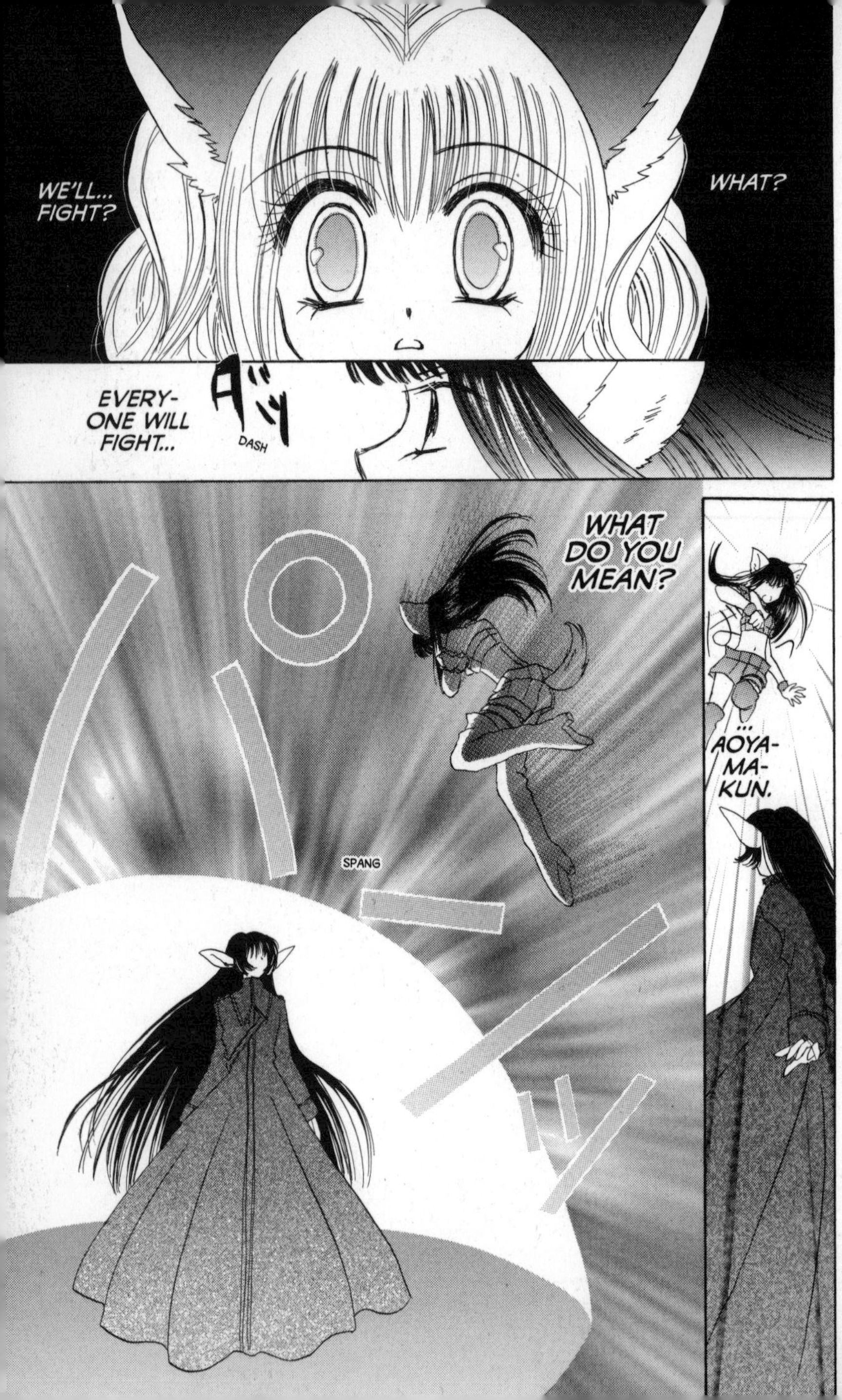
WHAT?
WE'LL... FIGHT?
ダッ
DASH
EVERY-ONE WILL FIGHT...
... AOYAMA-KUN.
WHAT DO YOU MEAN?
SPANG

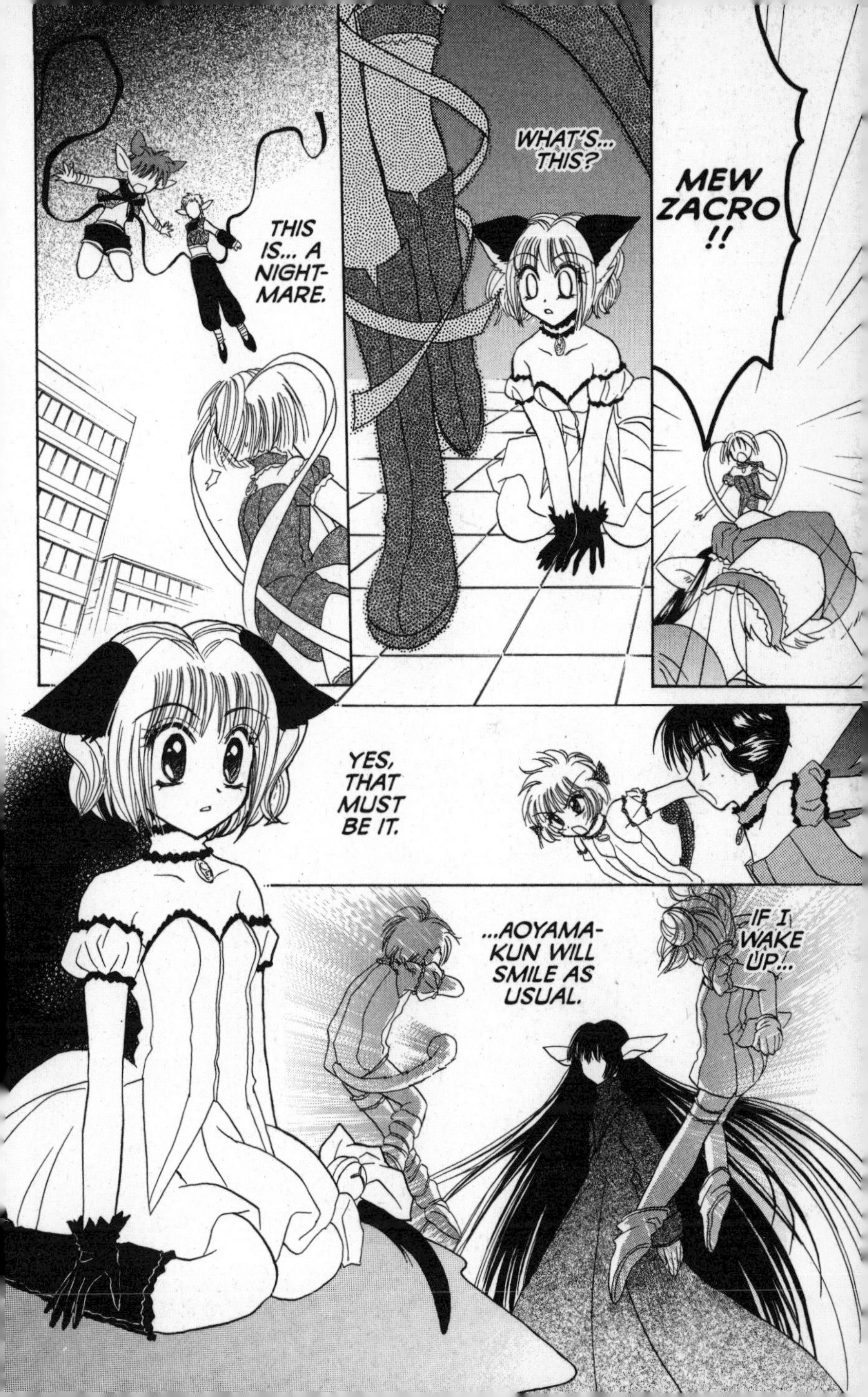
MEW ZACRO!!
WHAT'S... THIS?
THIS IS... A NIGHTMARE.
YES, THAT MUST BE IT.
IF I WAKE UP...
...AOYAMA-KUN WILL SMILE AS USUAL.

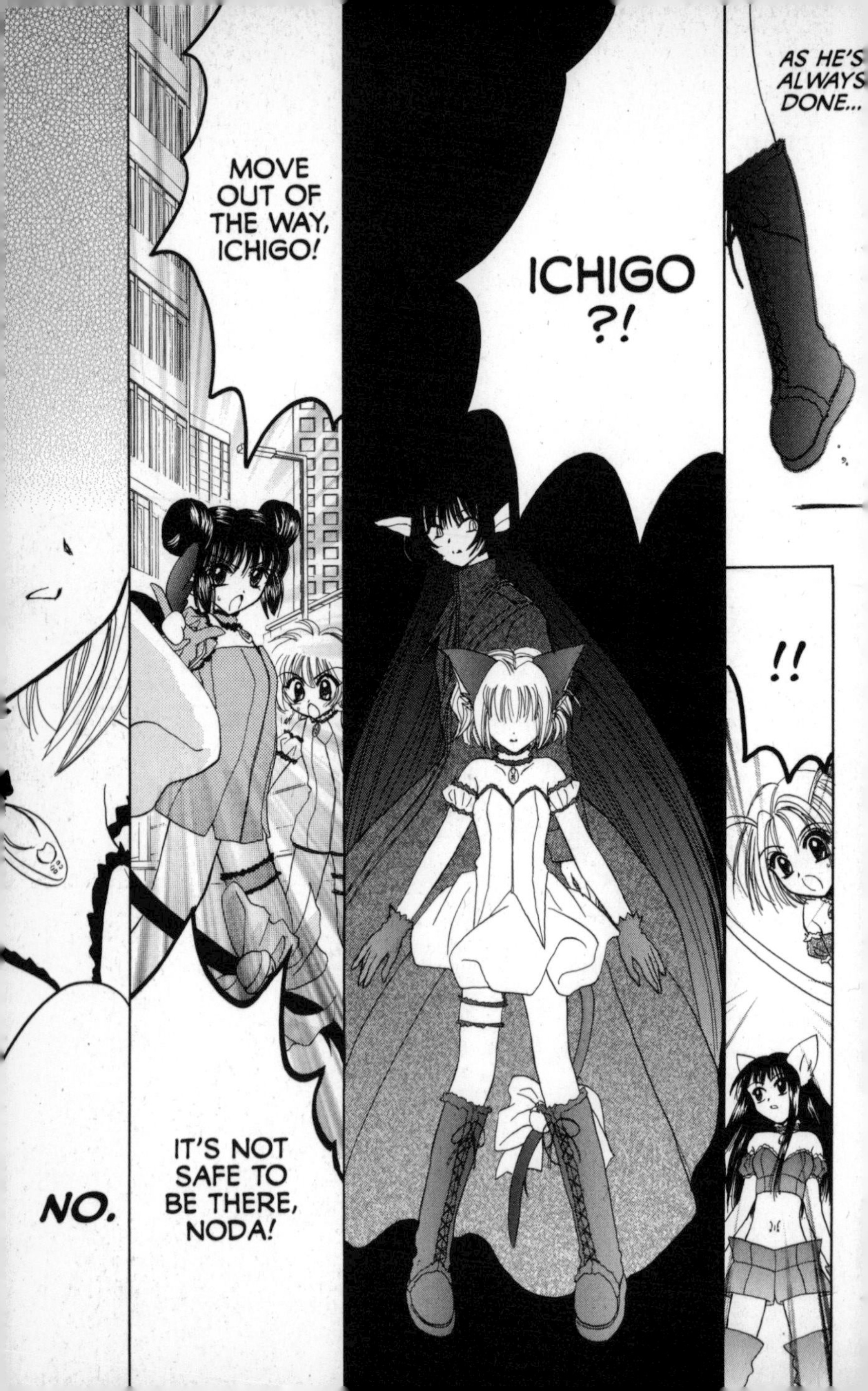
AS HE'S ALWAYS DONE...
!!
ICHIGO ?!
MOVE OUT OF THE WAY, ICHIGO!
IT'S NOT SAFE TO BE THERE, NODA!
NO.

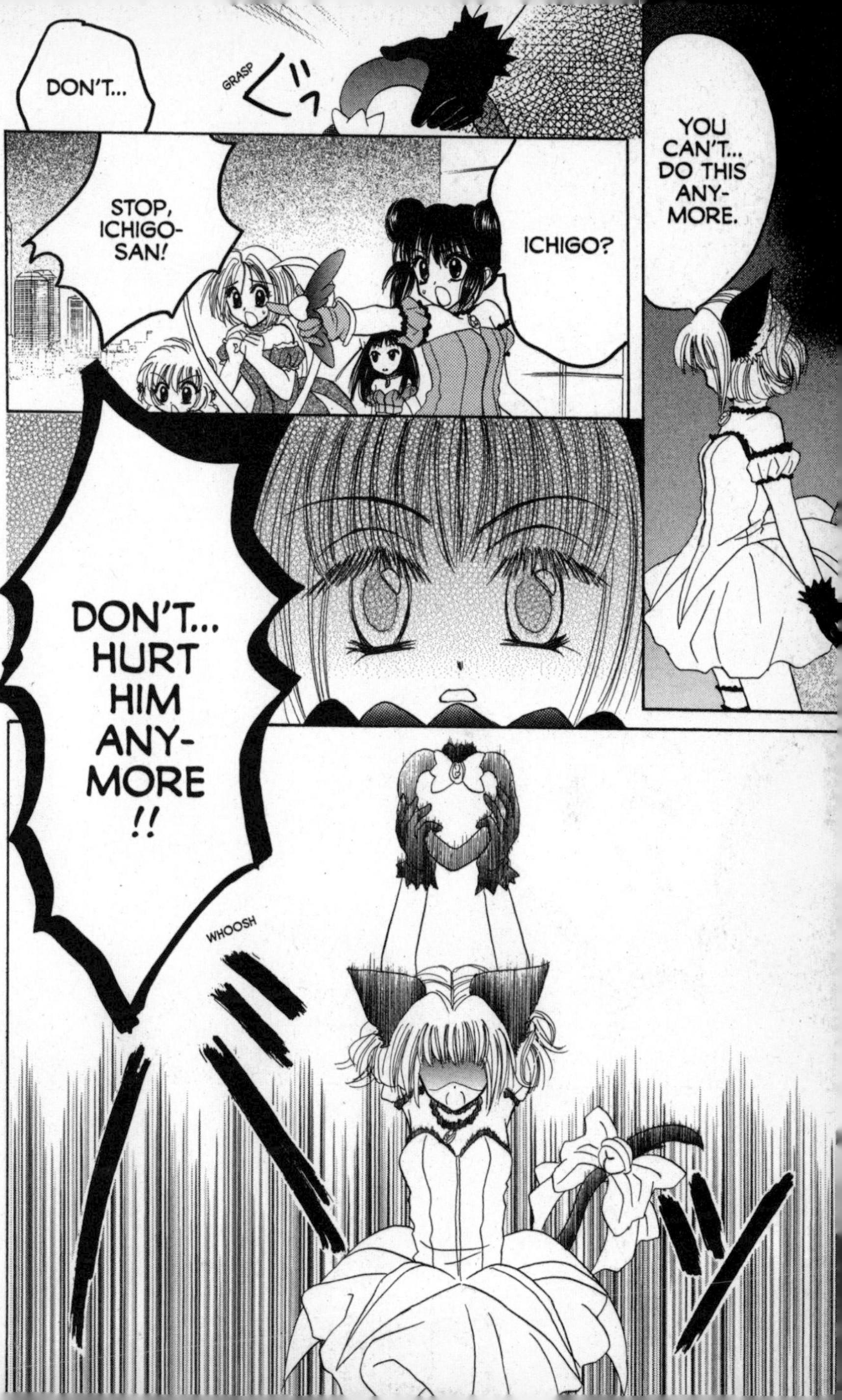
YOU CAN'T... DO THIS ANY-MORE.
DON'T...
GRASP
ICHIGO?
STOP, ICHIGO-SAN!
DON'T... HURT HIM ANY-MORE !!
WHOOSH

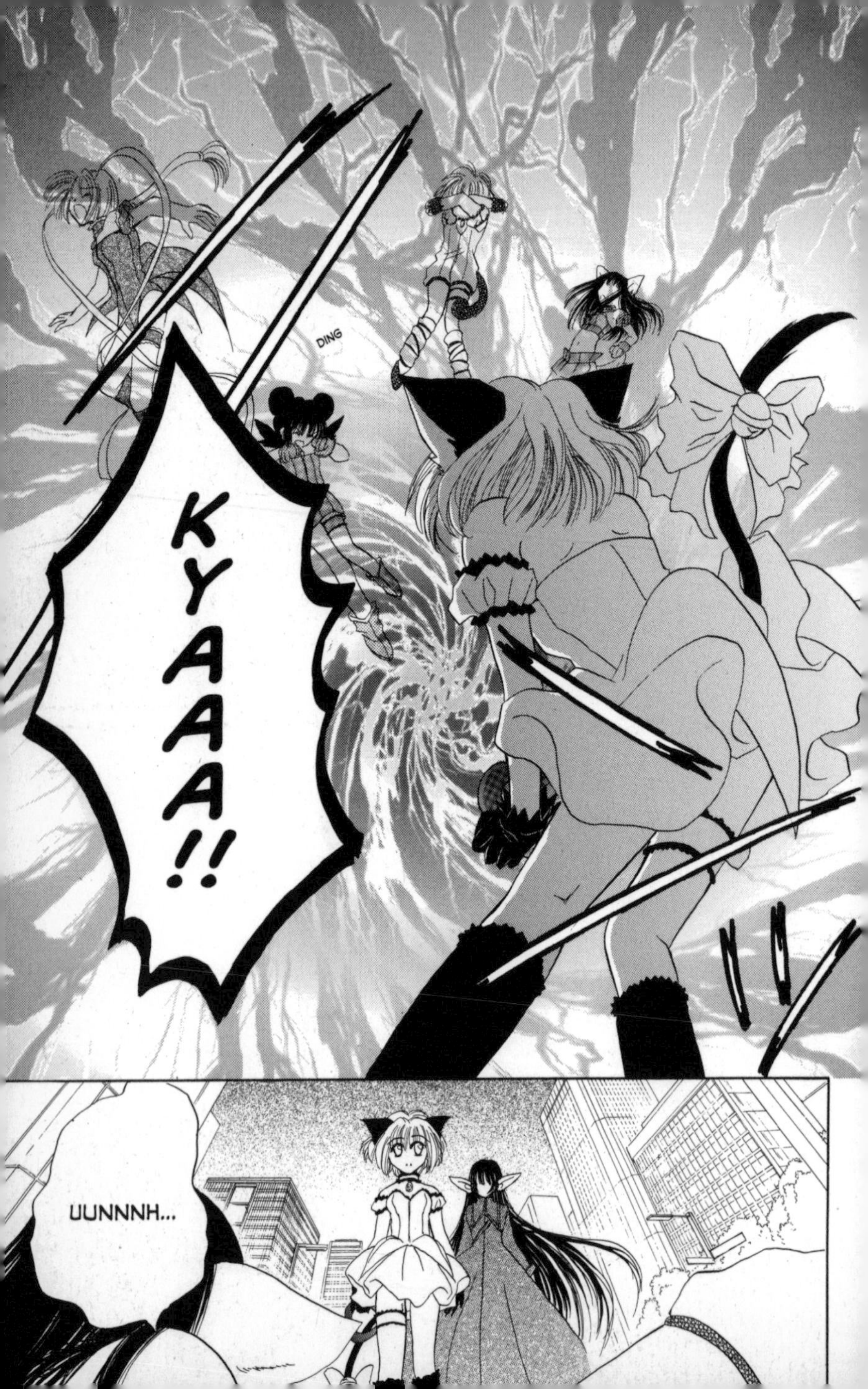
DING
KYAAAA!!
UUNNNH...

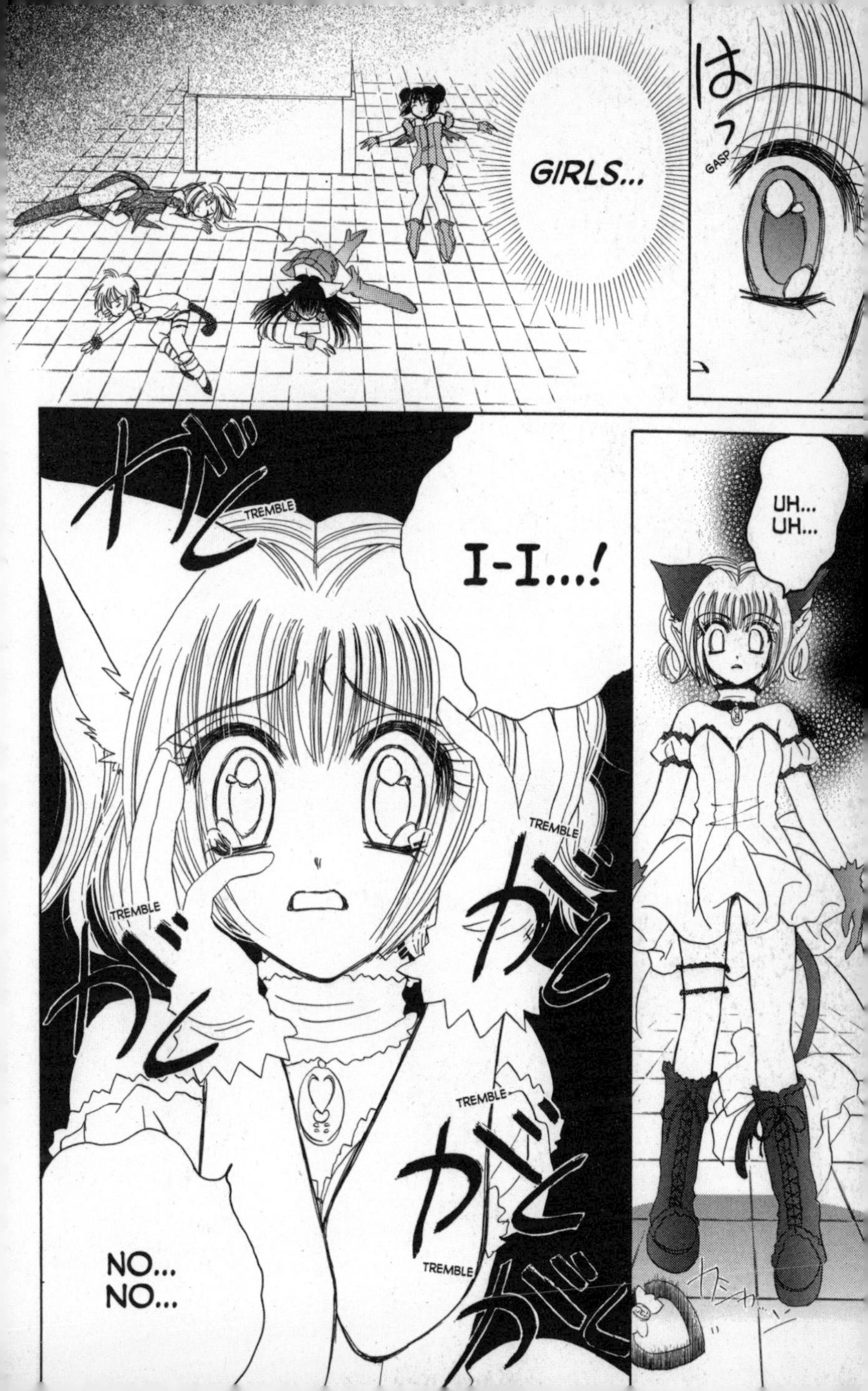
はっ
GASP
GIRLS...
UH... UH...
TREMBLE
I-I...!
TREMBLE
TREMBLE
TREMBLE
TREMBLE
NO... NO...

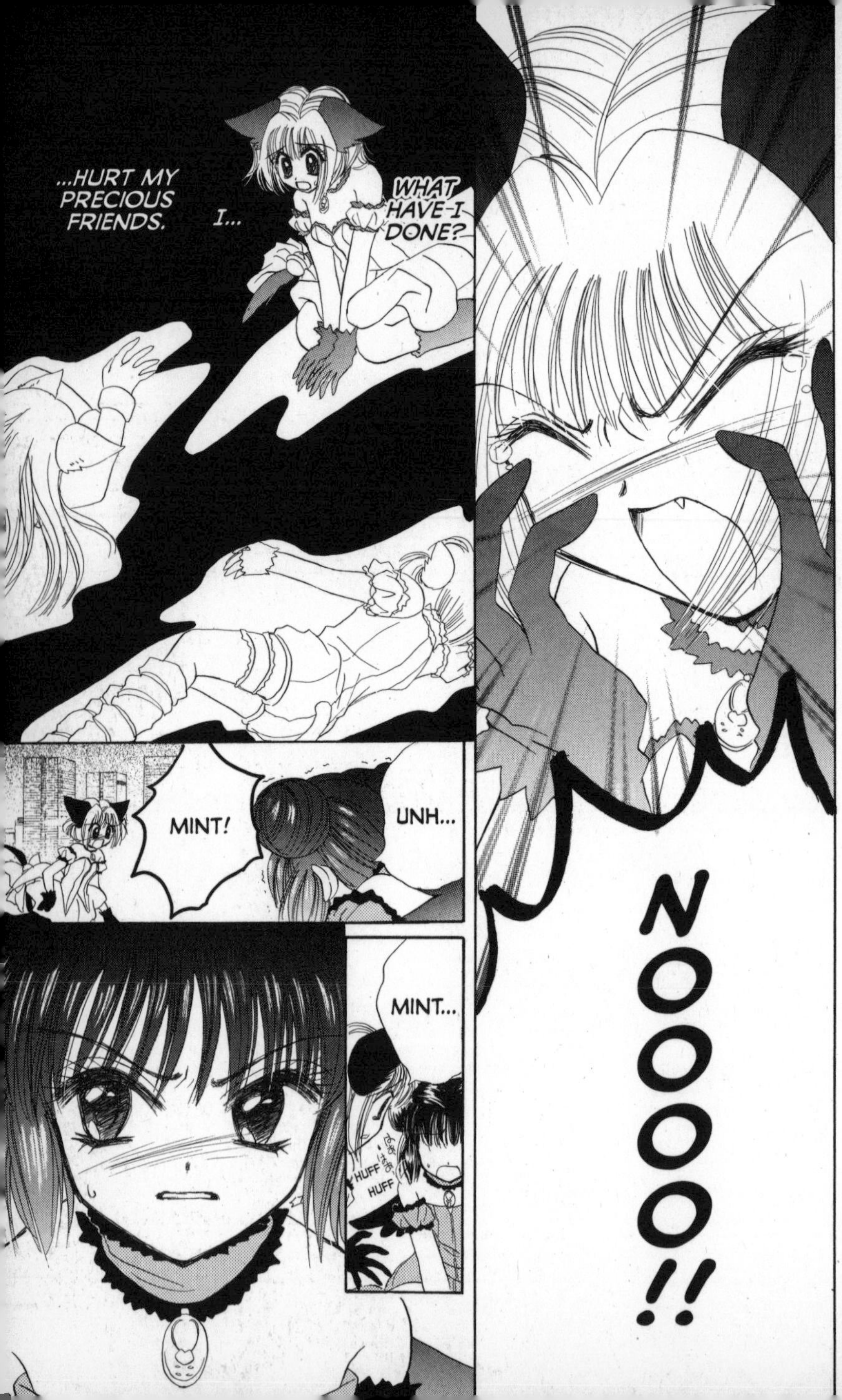
NOOOO!!
WHAT HAVE-I DONE?
I...
...HURT MY PRECIOUS FRIENDS.
UNH...
MINT!
MINT...
HUFF HUFF

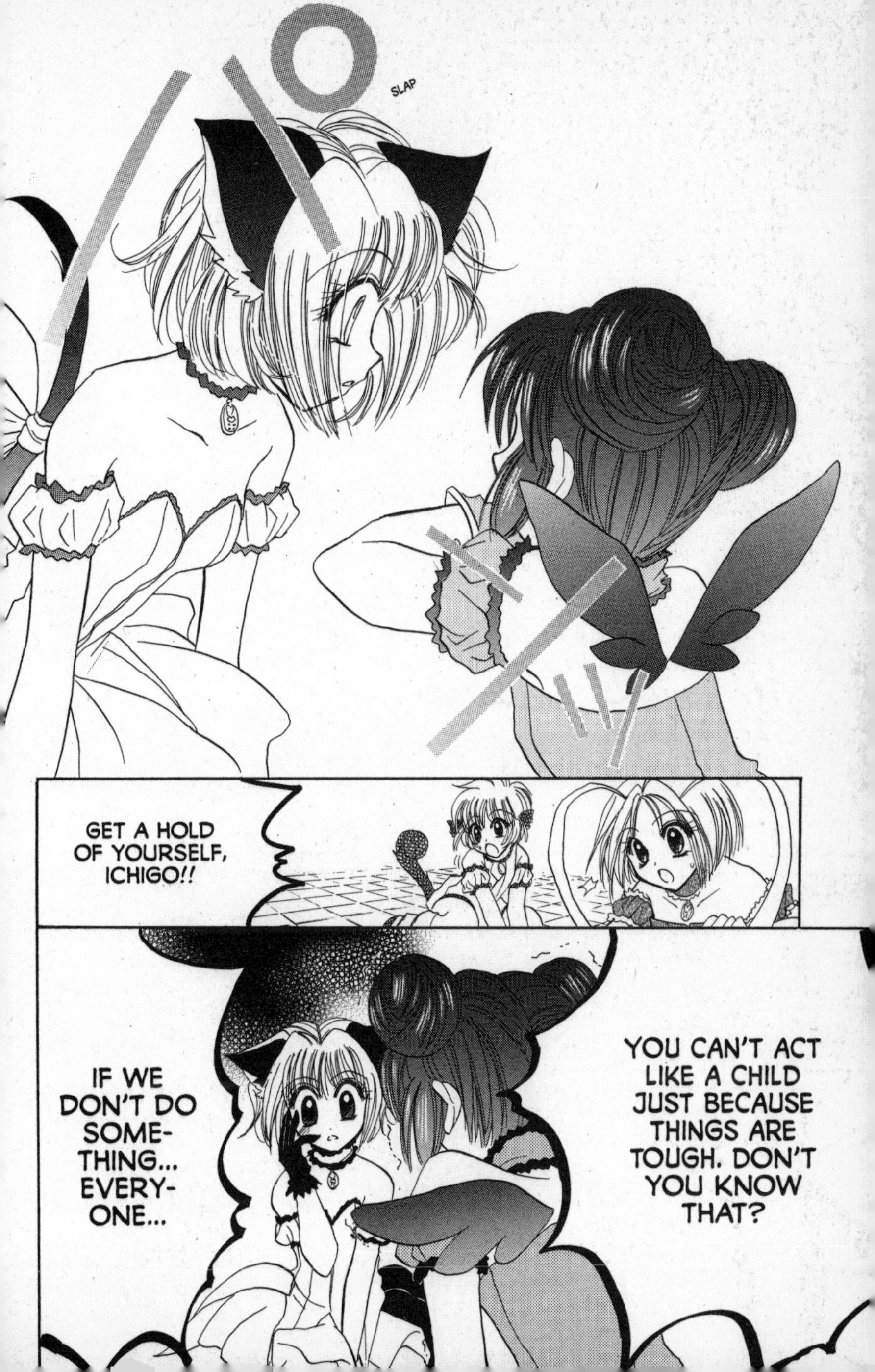
SLAP
GET A HOLD OF YOURSELF, ICHIGO!!
YOU CAN'T ACT LIKE A CHILD JUST BECAUSE THINGS ARE TOUGH. DON'T YOU KNOW THAT?
IF WE DON'T DO SOME-THING... EVERY-ONE...

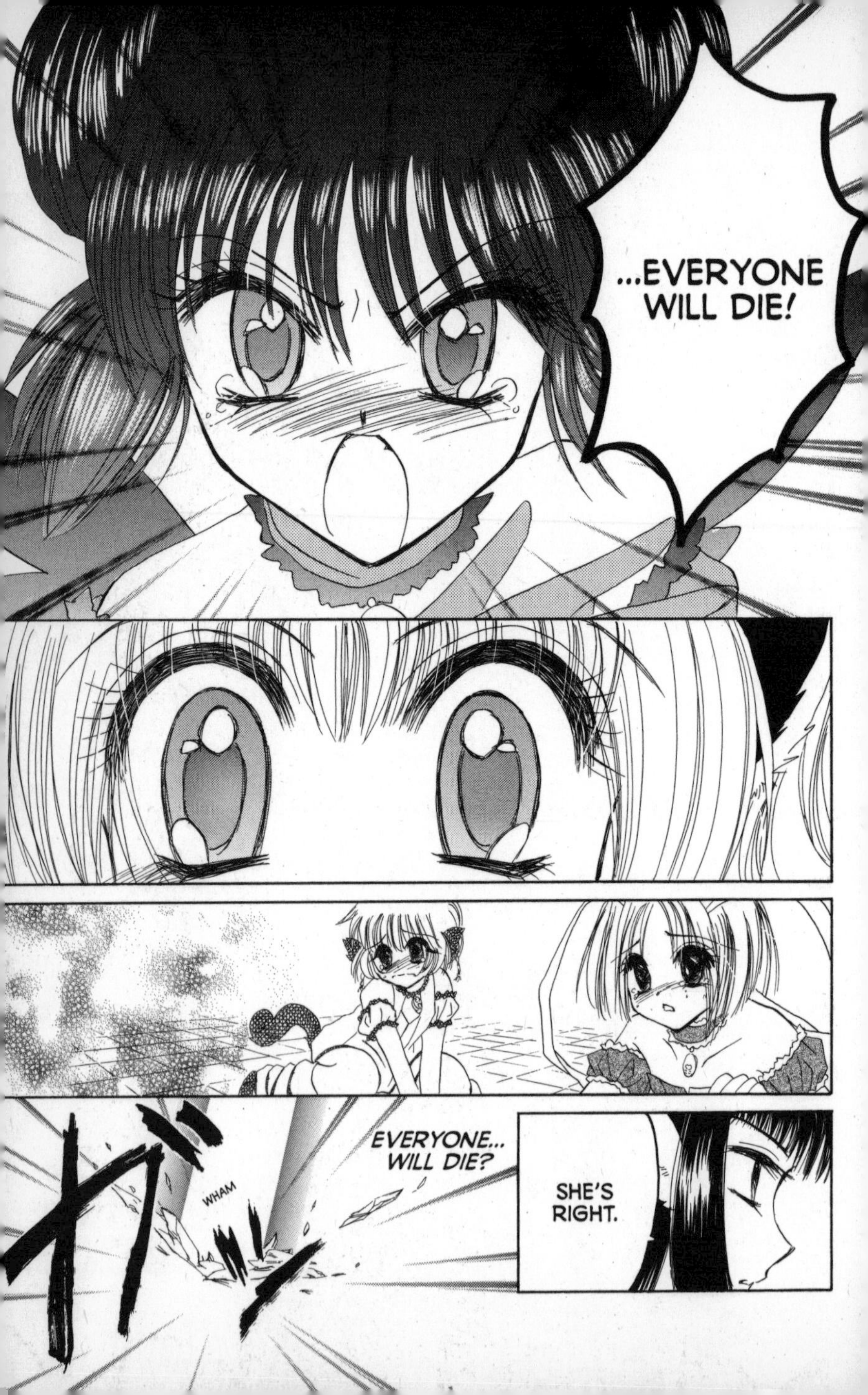
...EVERYONE WILL DIE!
SHE'S RIGHT.
EVERYONE... WILL DIE?
WHAM

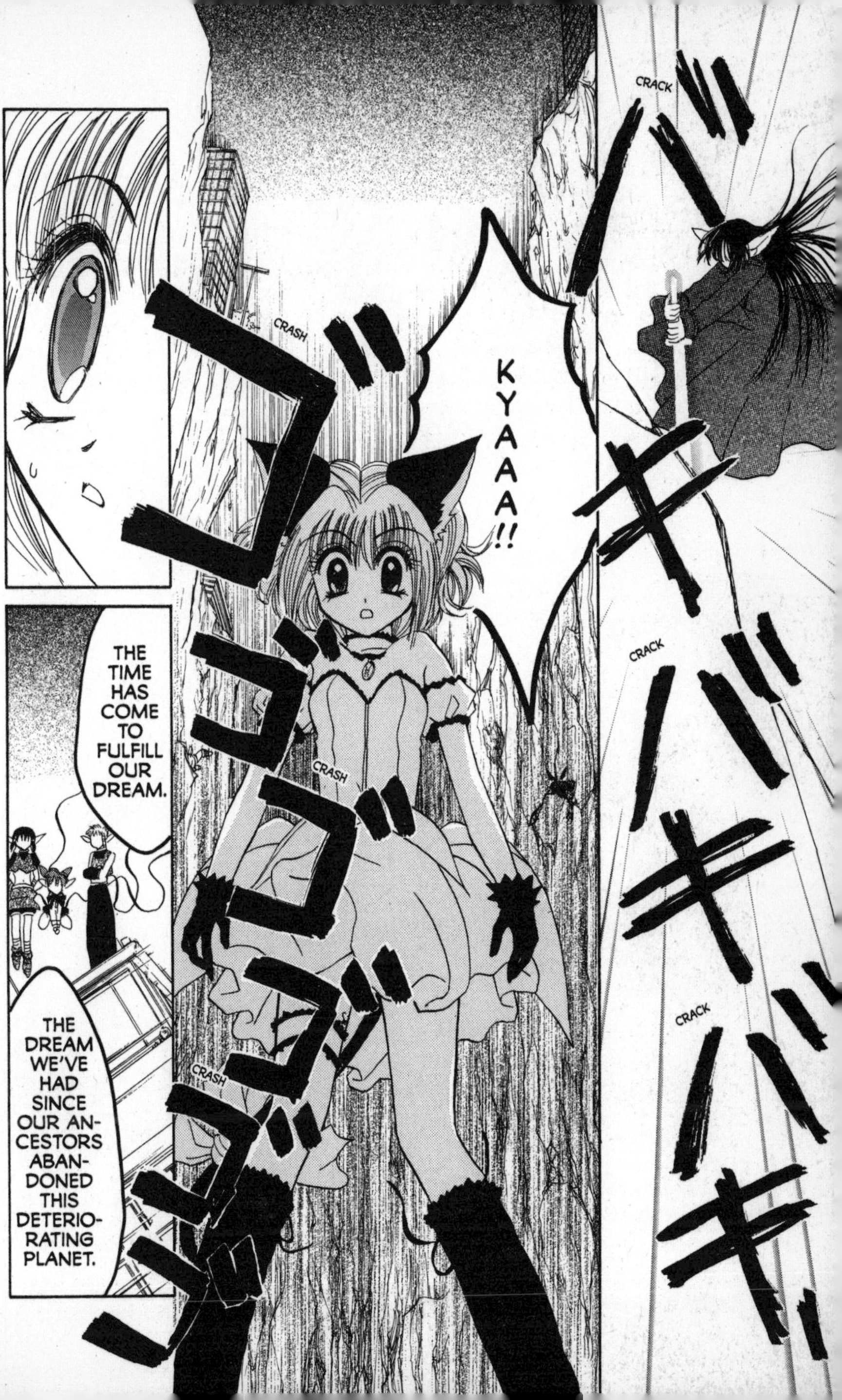
CRACK
CRACK
CRACK
KYAAA!!
CRASH
CRASH
CRASH
THE TIME HAS COME TO FULFILL OUR DREAM.
THE DREAM WE'VE HAD SINCE OUR ANCESTORS ABANDONED THIS DETERIORATING PLANET.

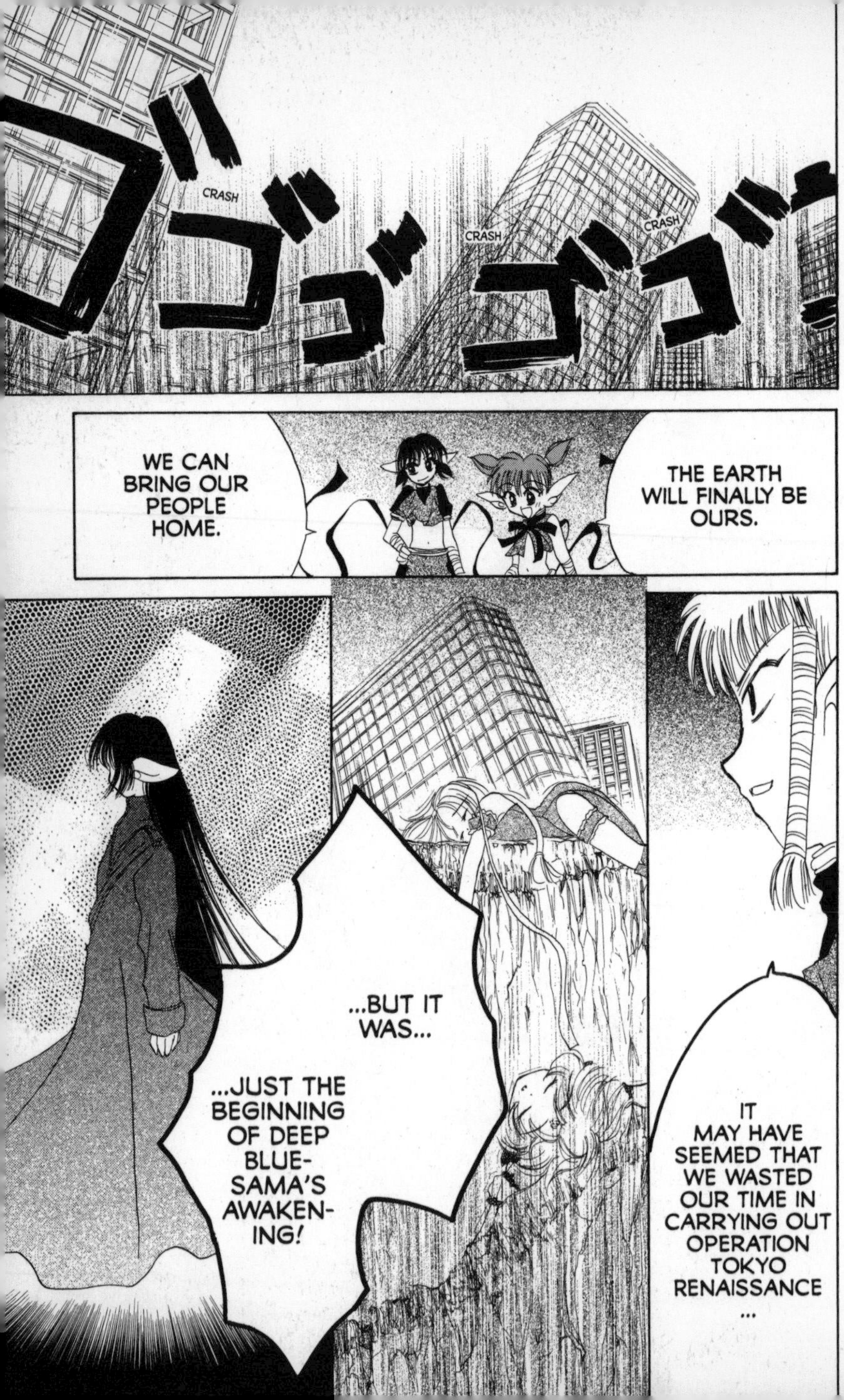
CRASH
CRASH
CRASH
THE EARTH WILL FINALLY BE OURS.
WE CAN BRING OUR PEOPLE HOME.
IT MAY HAVE SEEMED THAT WE WASTED OUR TIME IN CARRYING OUT OPERATION TOKYO RENAISSANCE...
...BUT IT WAS...
...JUST THE BEGINNING OF DEEP BLUE-SAMA'S AWAKENING!

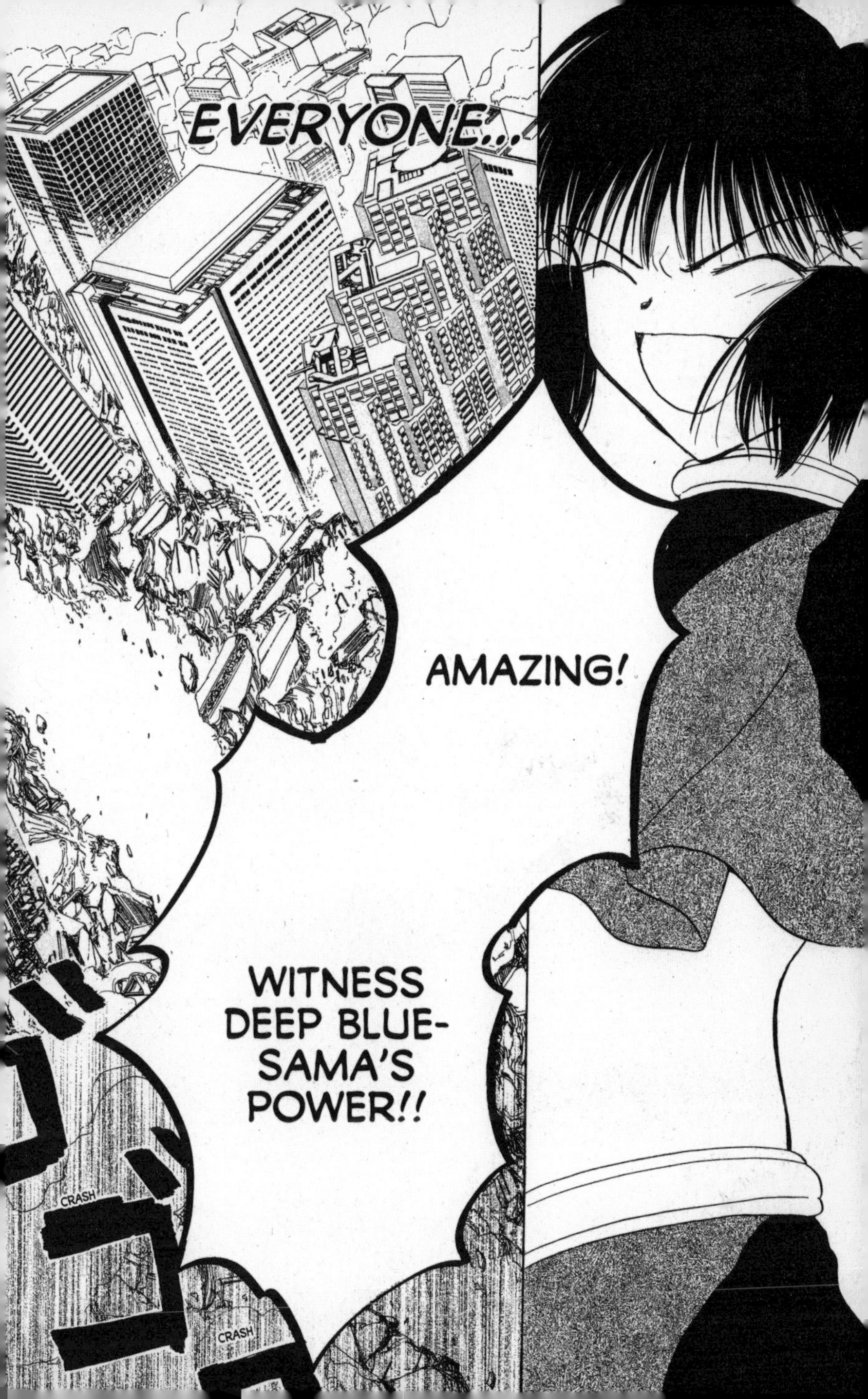
EVERYONE...
AMAZING!
WITNESS DEEP BLUE-SAMA'S POWER!!
CRASH
CRASH

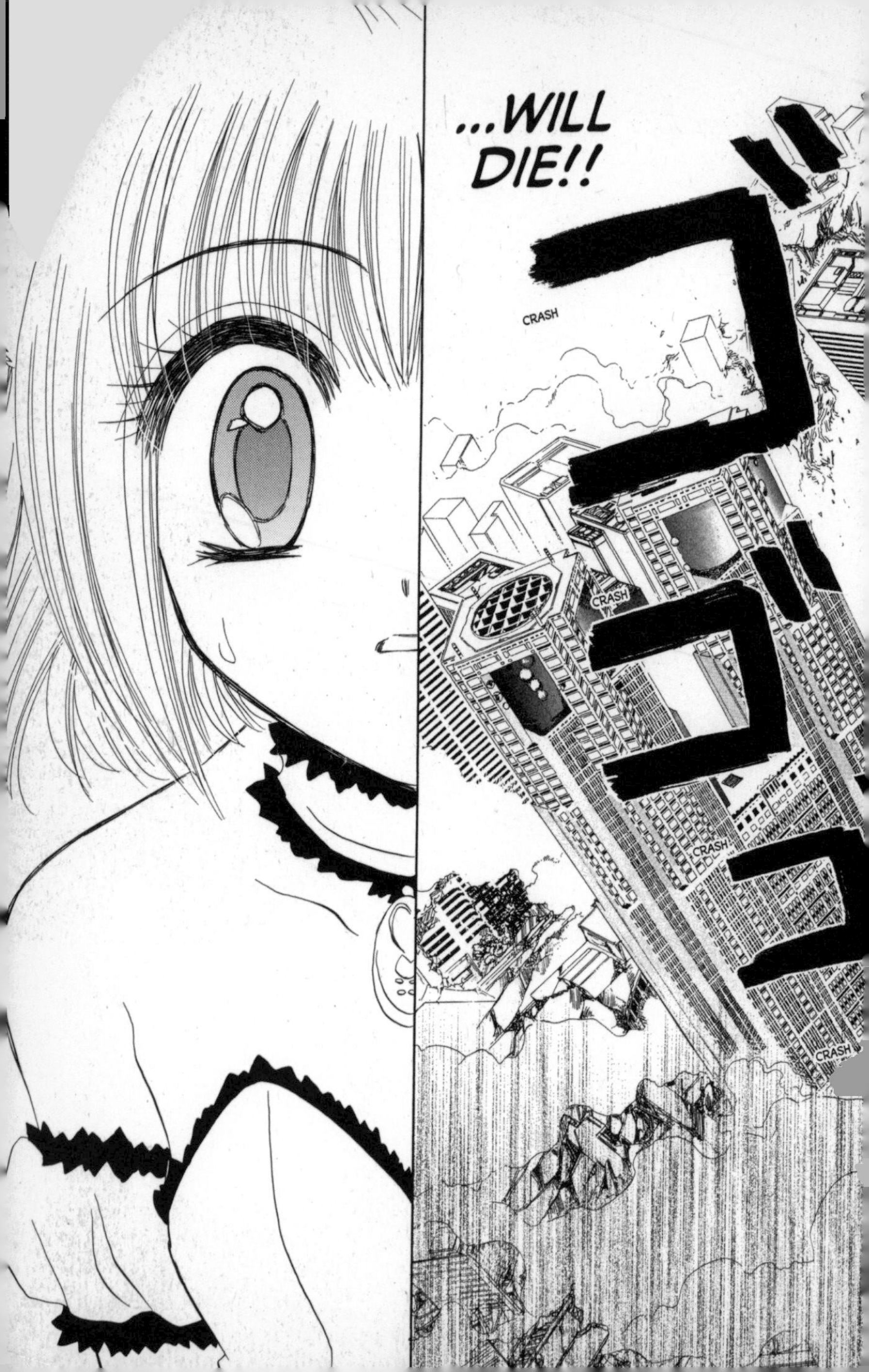

...WILL DIE!!
CRASH
CRASH
CRASH
CRASH

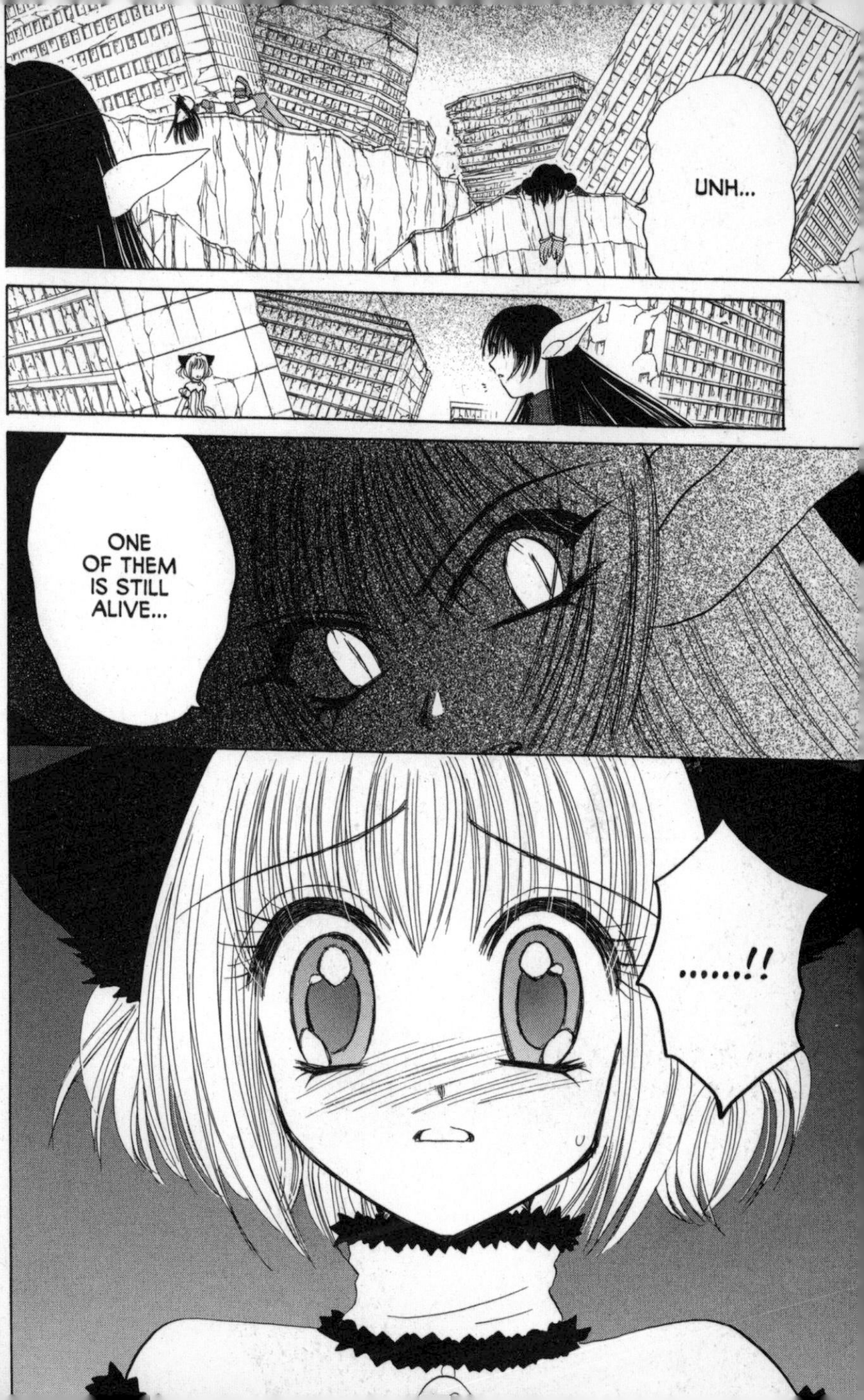
UNH...
ONE OF THEM IS STILL ALIVE...
......!!

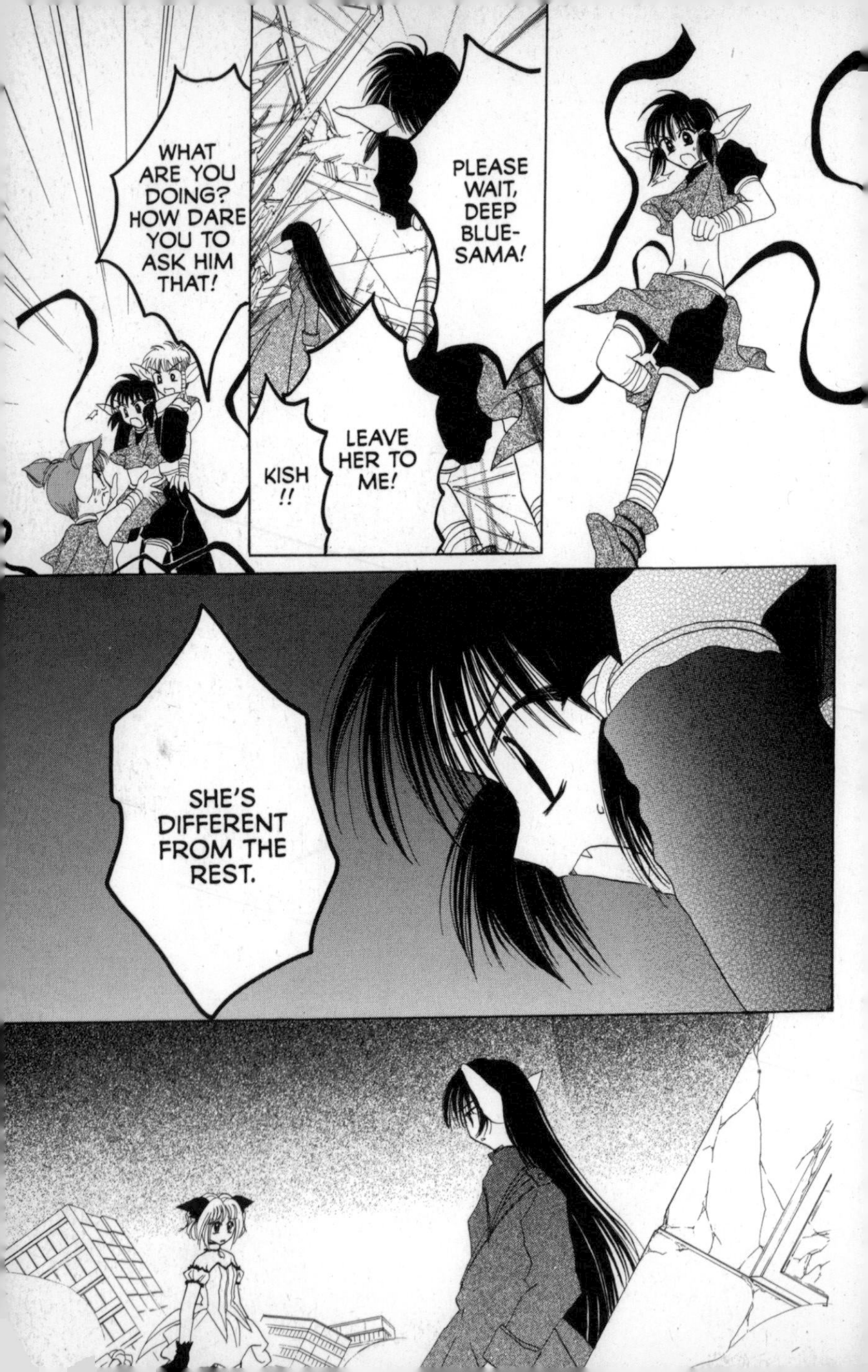
PLEASE WAIT, DEEP BLUE-SAMA!
LEAVE HER TO ME!
KISH !!
WHAT ARE YOU DOING? HOW DARE YOU TO ASK HIM THAT!
SHE'S DIFFERENT FROM THE REST.

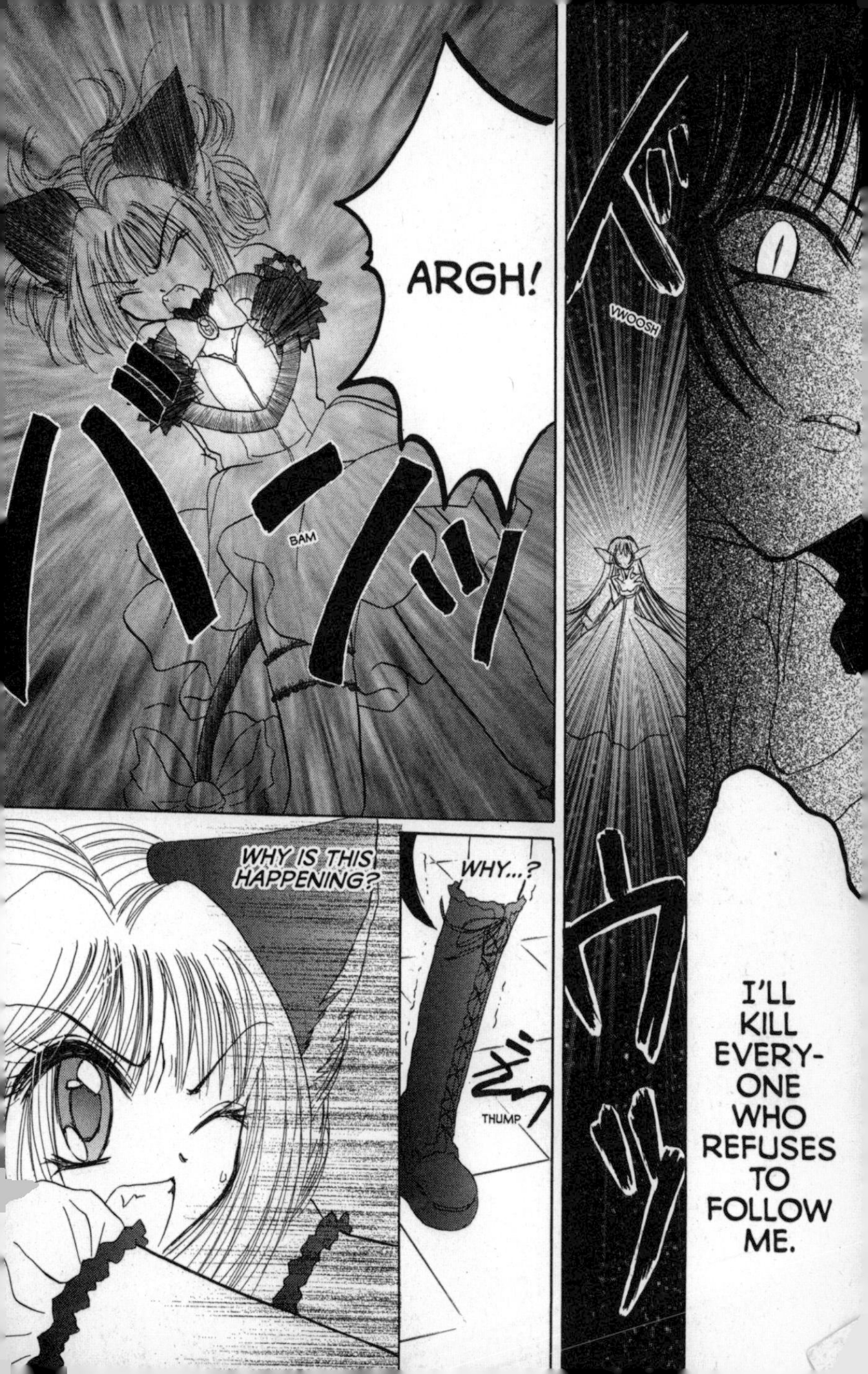
VWOOSH
I'LL KILL EVERY-ONE WHO REFUSES TO FOLLOW ME.
ARGH!
BAM
WHY...?
THUMP
WHY IS THIS HAPPENING?

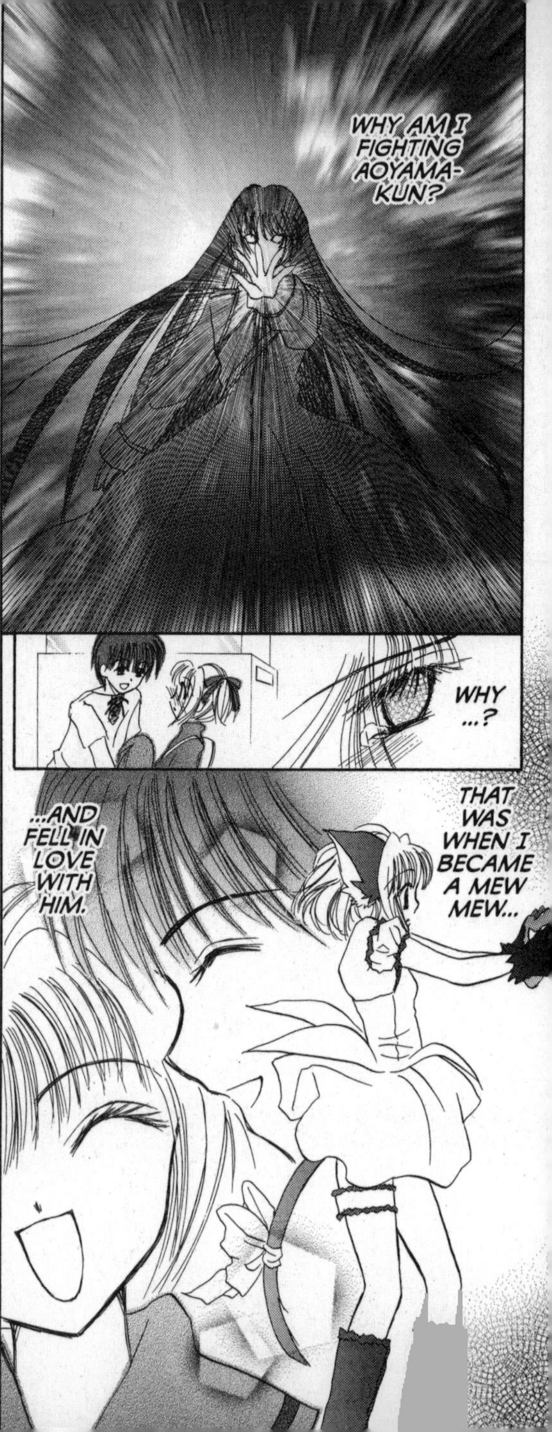
WHY AM I FIGHTING AOYAMA-KUN?
WHY ...?
THAT WAS WHEN I BECAME A MEW MEW...
...AND FELL IN LOVE WITH HIM.

TOKYO HAM HAM

ART BY CHIEF MATSUMOTO, ARRANGED BY MIA IKUMI

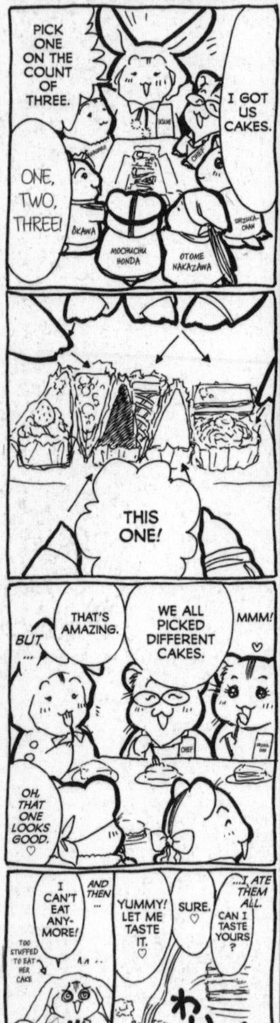
I GOT US CAKES.
PICK ONE ON THE COUNT OF THREE.
ONE, TWO, THREE!
SHIZUKA-CHAN
OTOME NAKAZAWA
MOCHUCHU HONDA
OKAWA
THIS ONE!
MMM!
WE ALL PICKED DIFFERENT CAKES.
THAT'S AMAZING.
BUT ...
OH, THAT ONE LOOKS GOOD. ♡
...I ATE THEM ALL.
CAN I TASTE YOURS?
SURE. ♡
YUMMY! LET ME TASTE IT. ♡
AND THEN ...
I CAN'T EAT ANYMORE!
TOO STUFFED TO EAT HER CAKE
わい CHATTER
わい CHATTER
MMM! ♡
I'LL HAVE IT!
FWIP
EATS LEFTOVERS

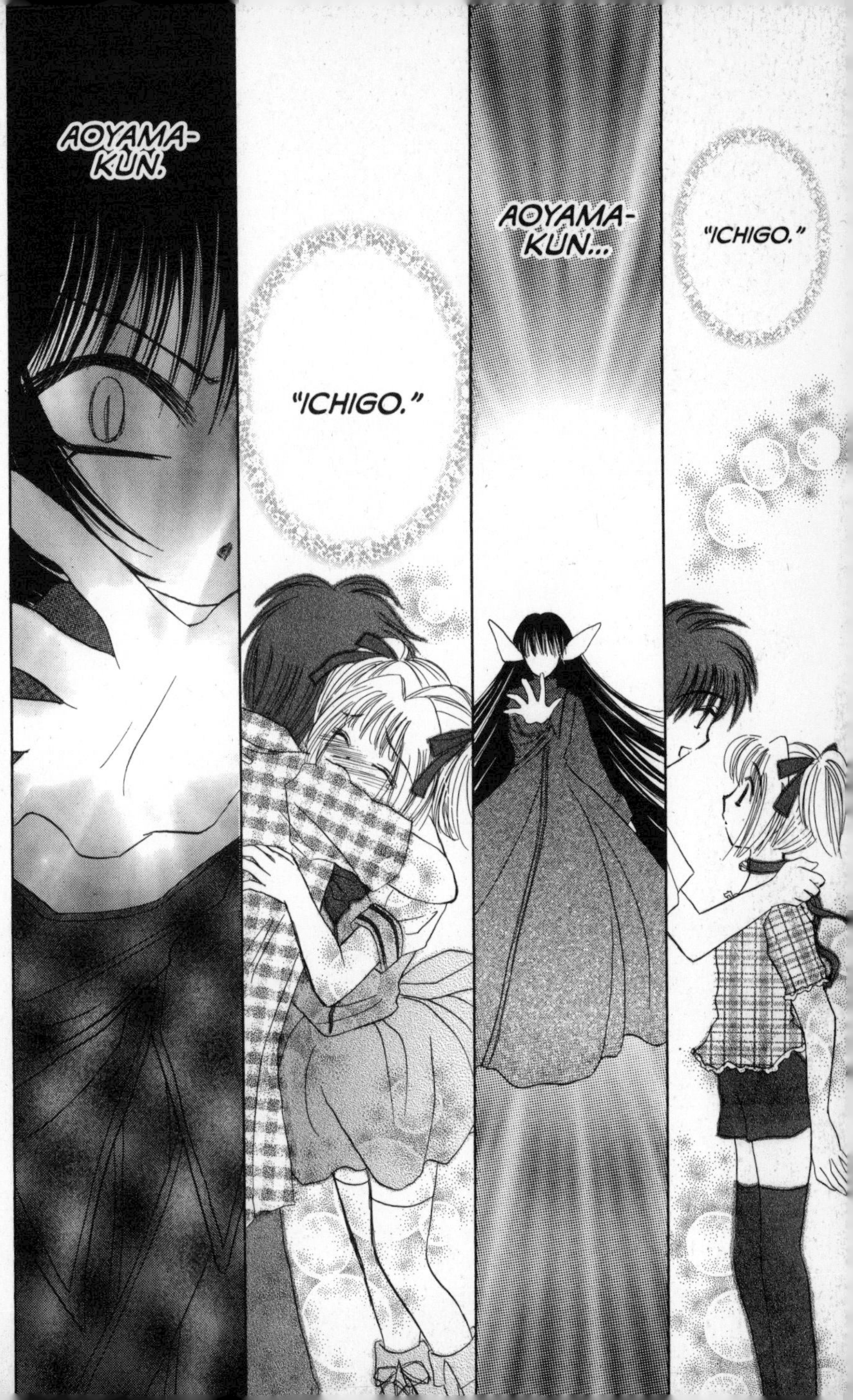
"ICHIGO."
AOYAMA-KUN...
"ICHIGO."
AOYAMA-KUN.

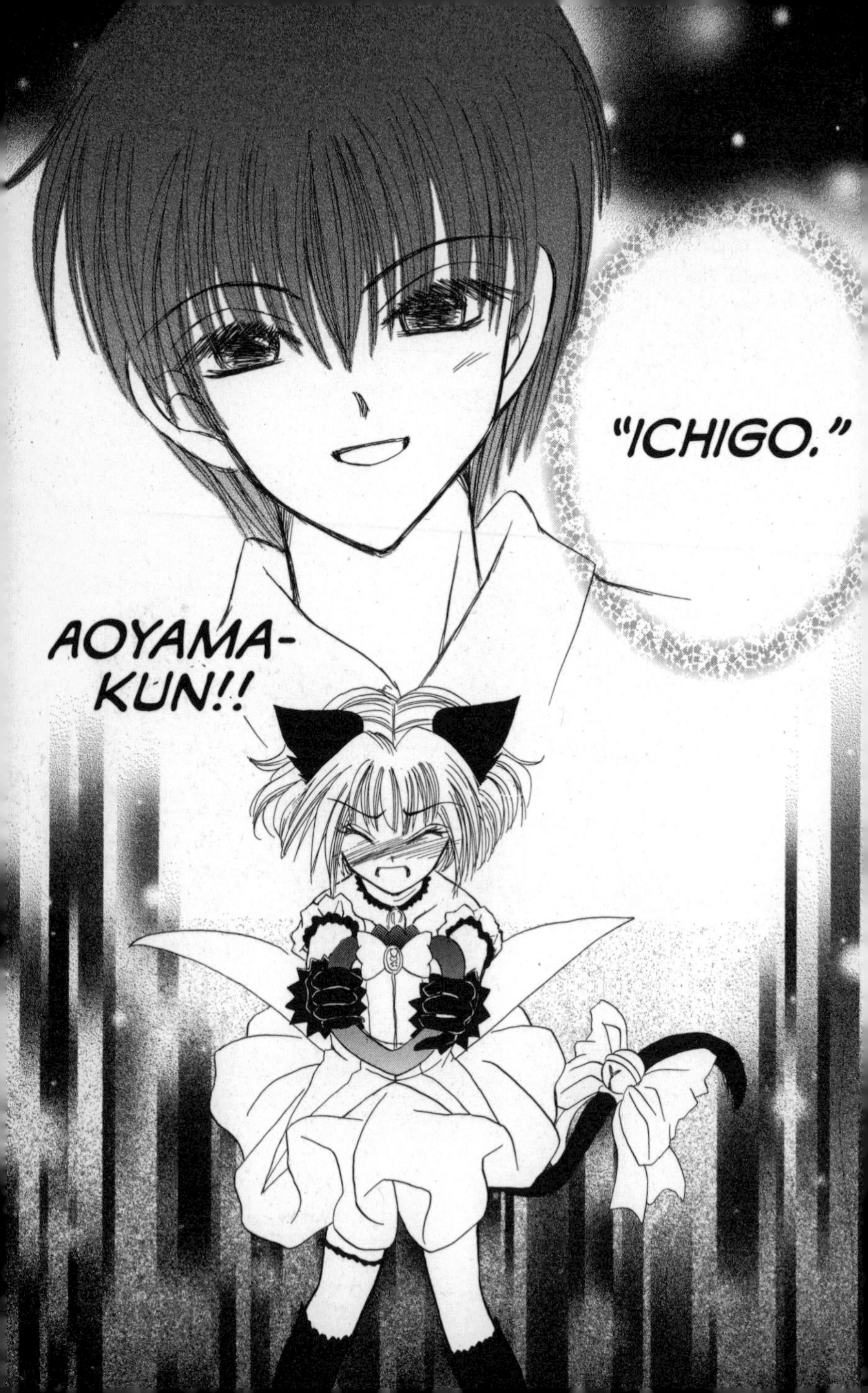
"ICHIGO."
AOYAMA-KUN!!

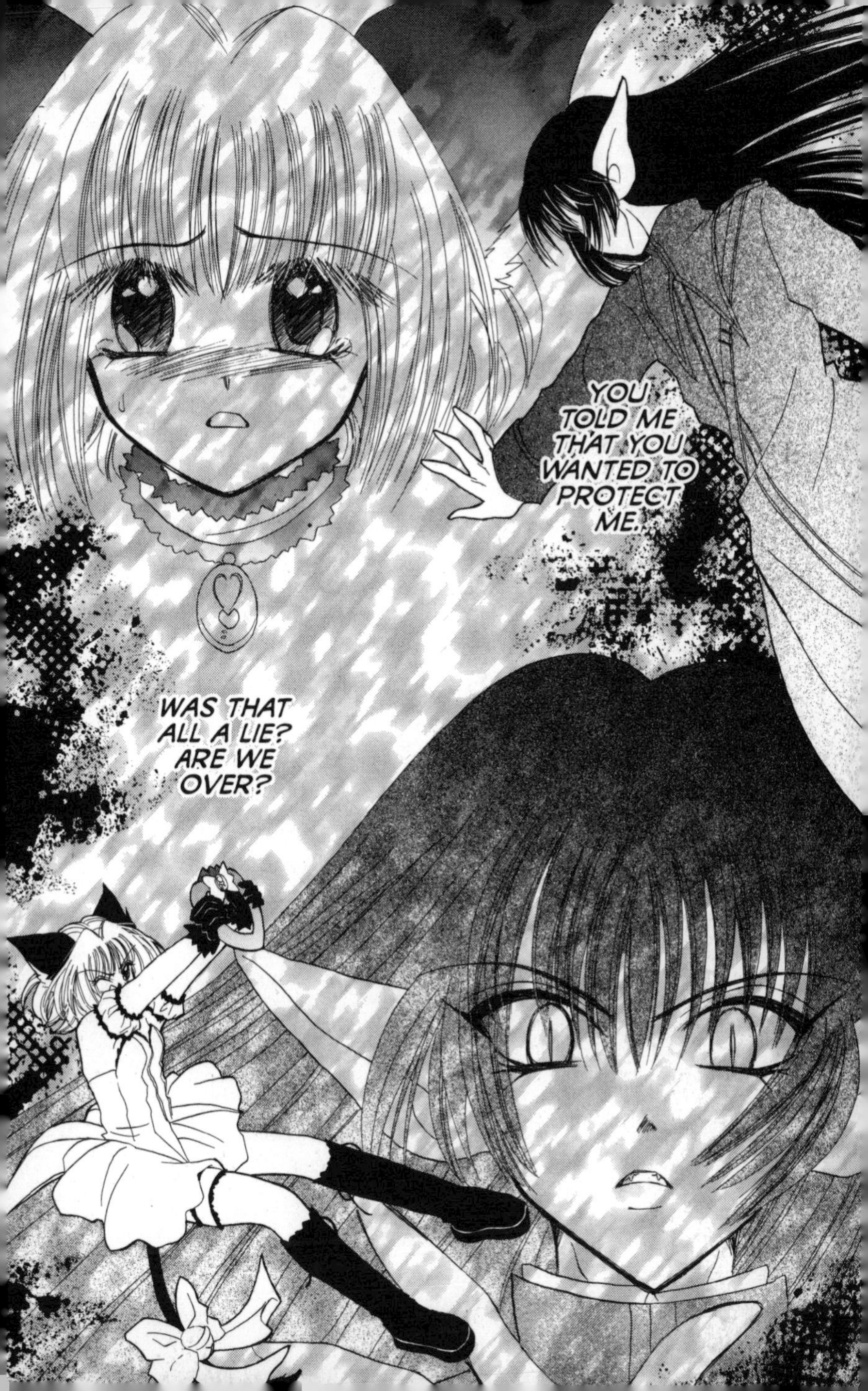
YOU TOLD ME THAT YOU WANTED TO PROTECT ME.
WAS THAT ALL A LIE? ARE WE OVER?

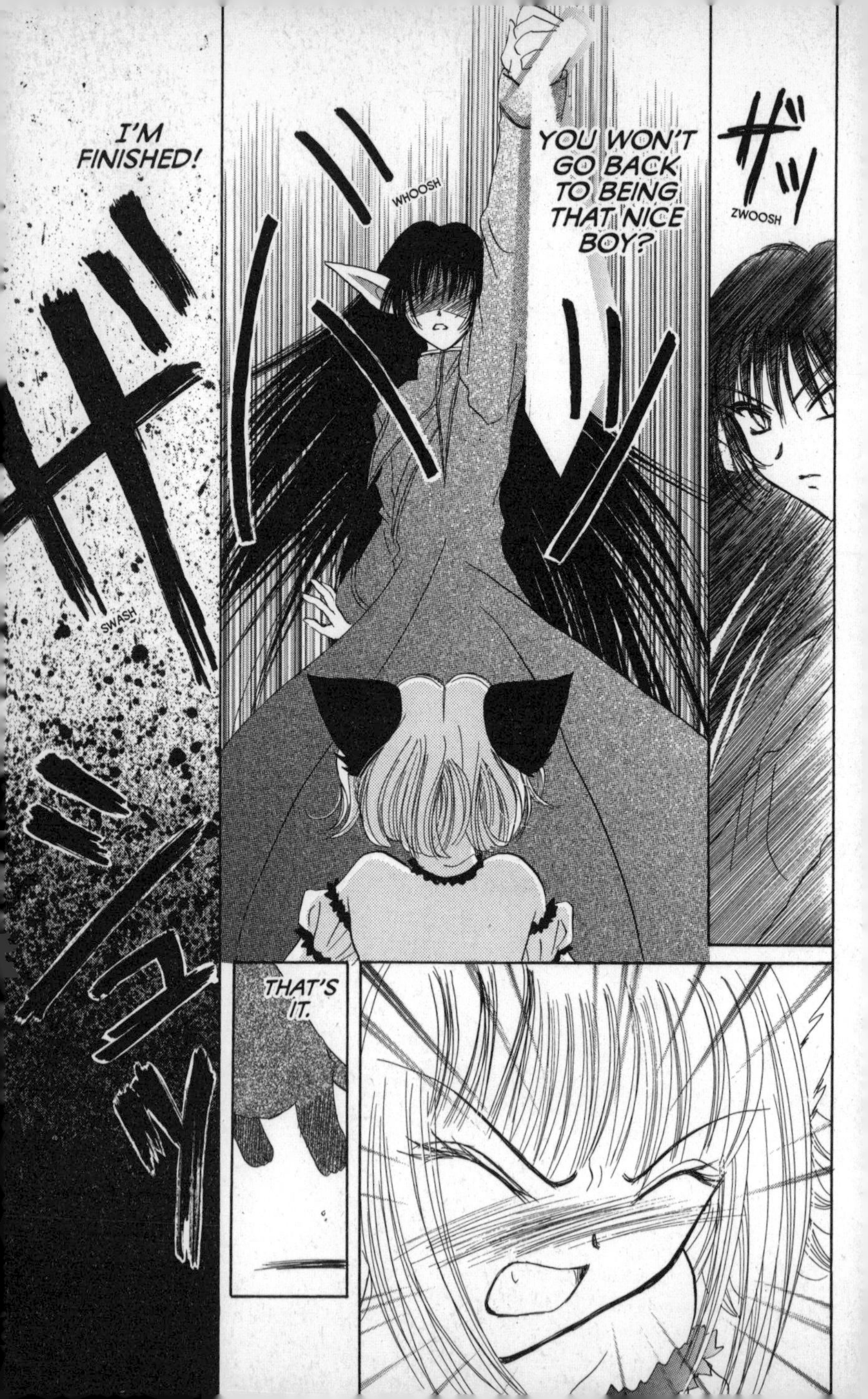
ザッ
ZWOOSH
YOU WON'T GO BACK TO BEING THAT NICE BOY?
WHOOSH
THAT'S IT.
I'M FINISHED!
SWASH

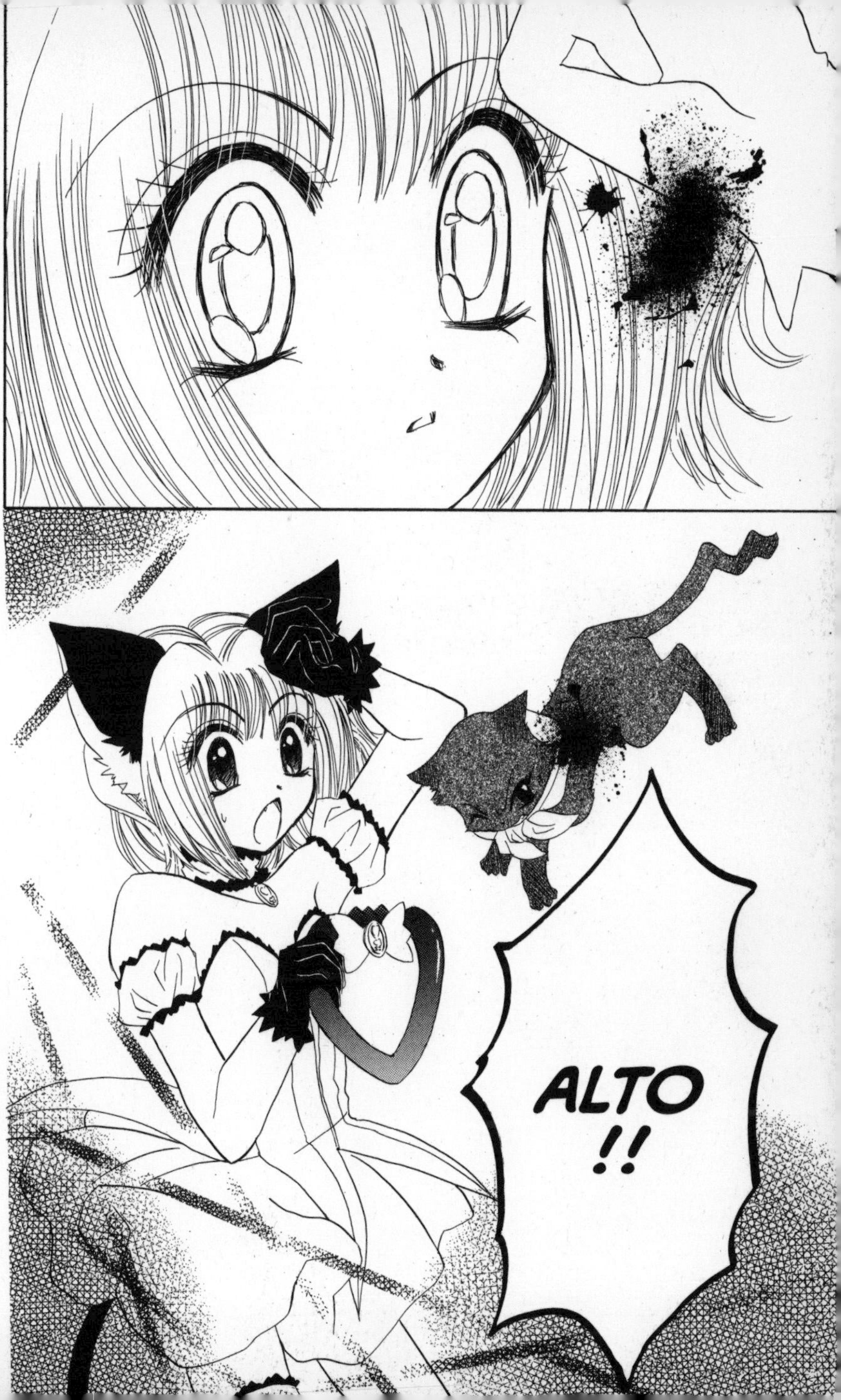
ALTO !!

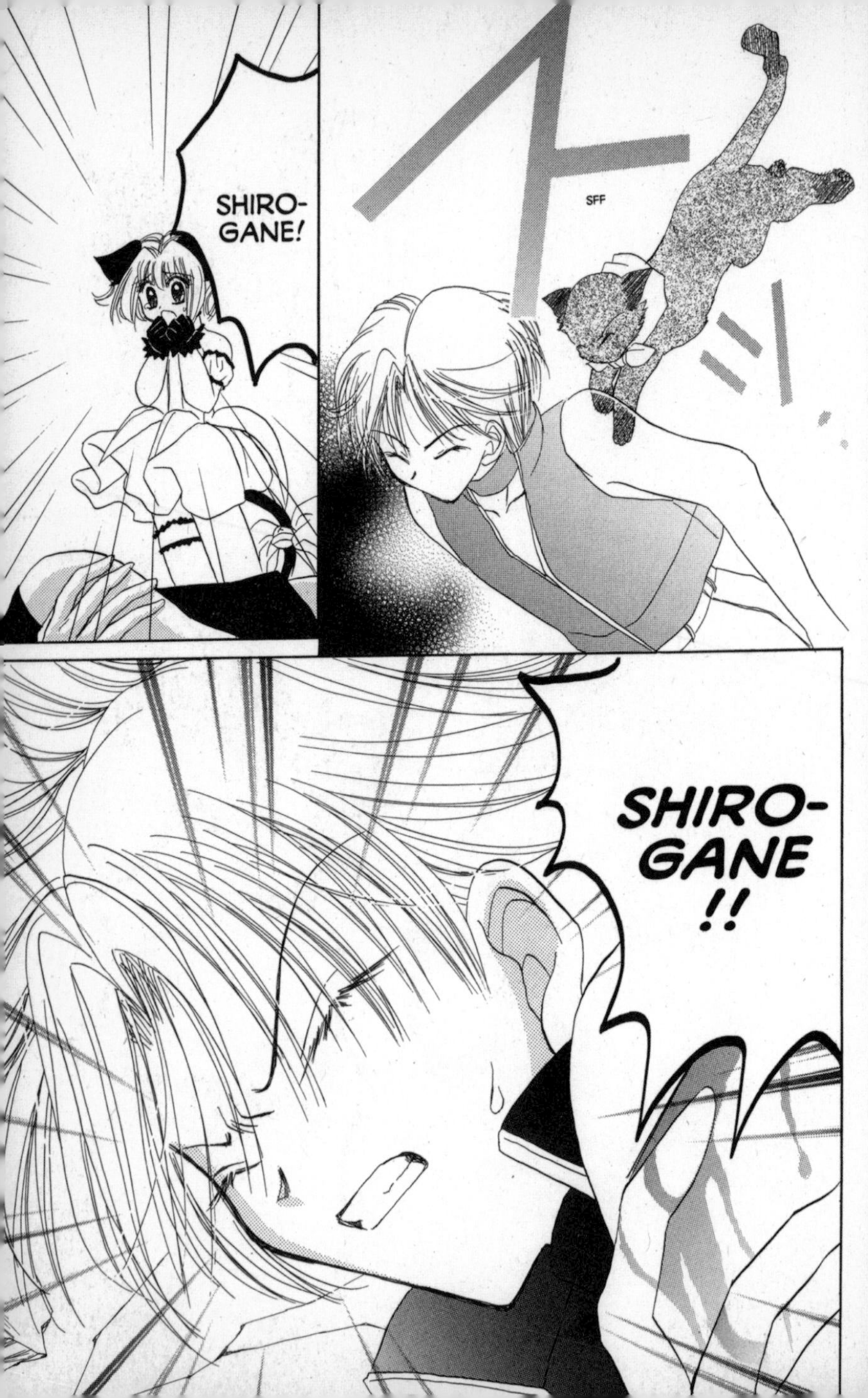
SFF
SHIRO-GANE!
SHIRO-GANE !!

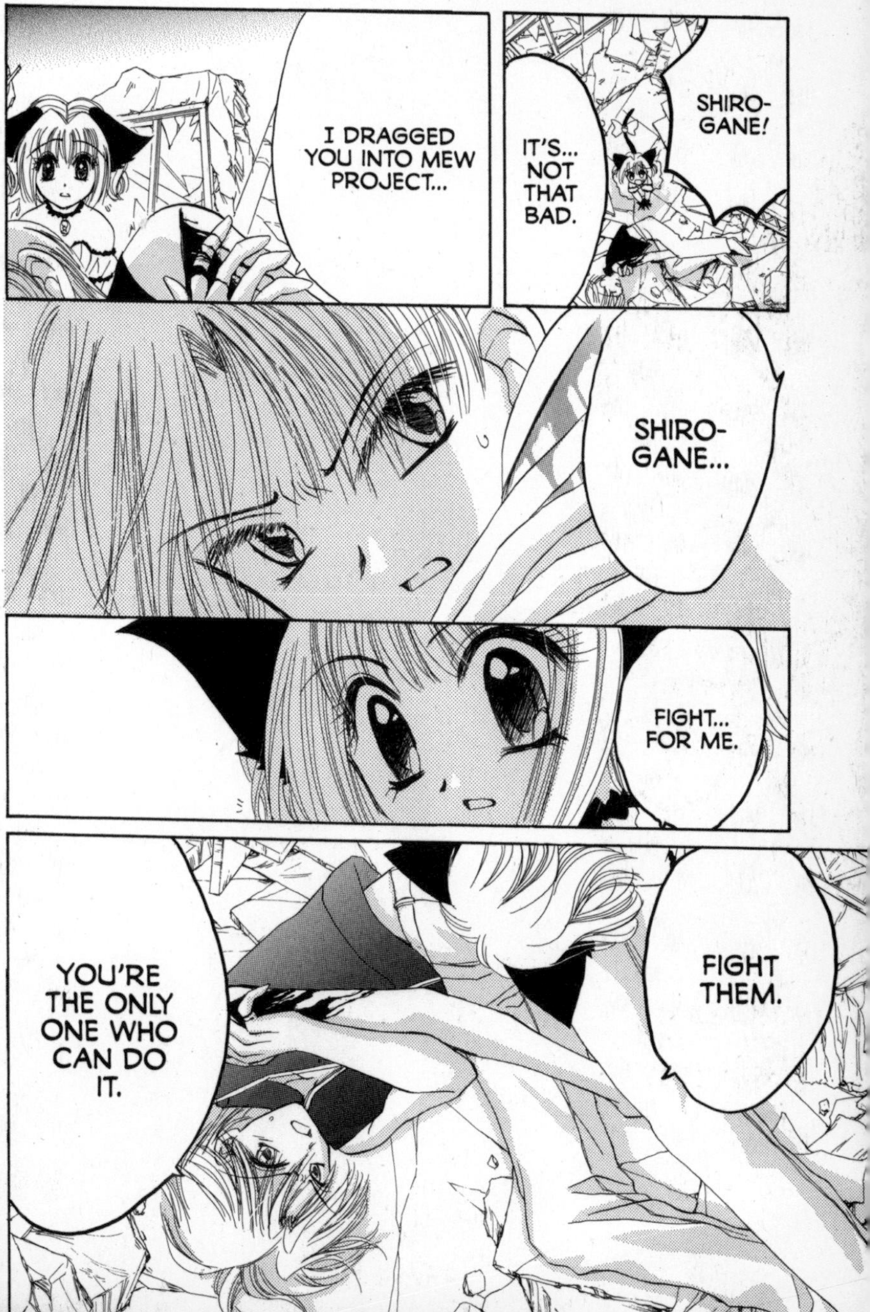
SHIRO-GANE!
IT'S... NOT THAT BAD.
I DRAGGED YOU INTO MEW PROJECT...
SHIRO-GANE...
FIGHT... FOR ME.
FIGHT THEM.
YOU'RE THE ONLY ONE WHO CAN DO IT.

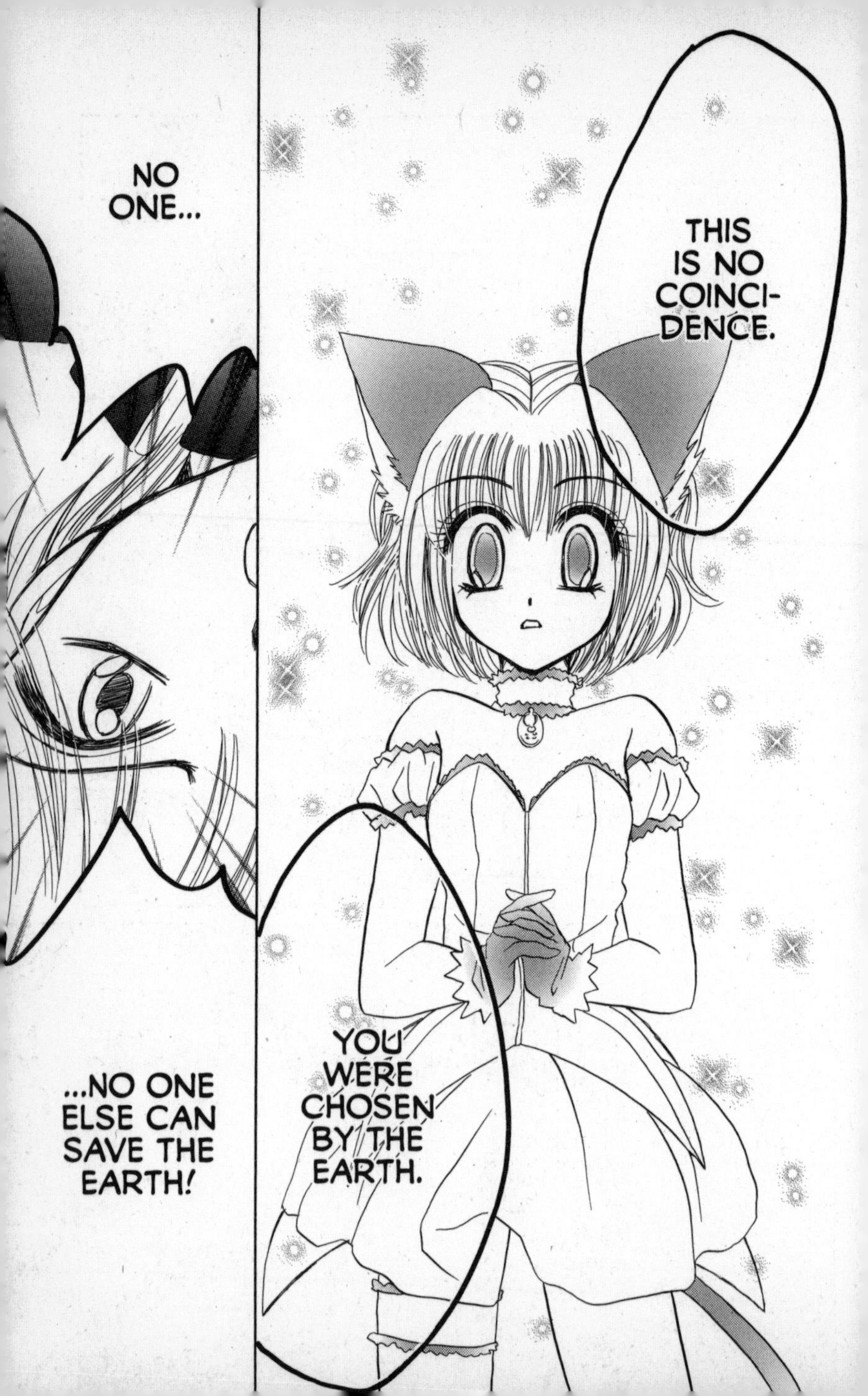
THIS IS NO COINCIDENCE.
YOU WERE CHOSEN BY THE EARTH.
NO ONE...
...NO ONE ELSE CAN SAVE THE EARTH!

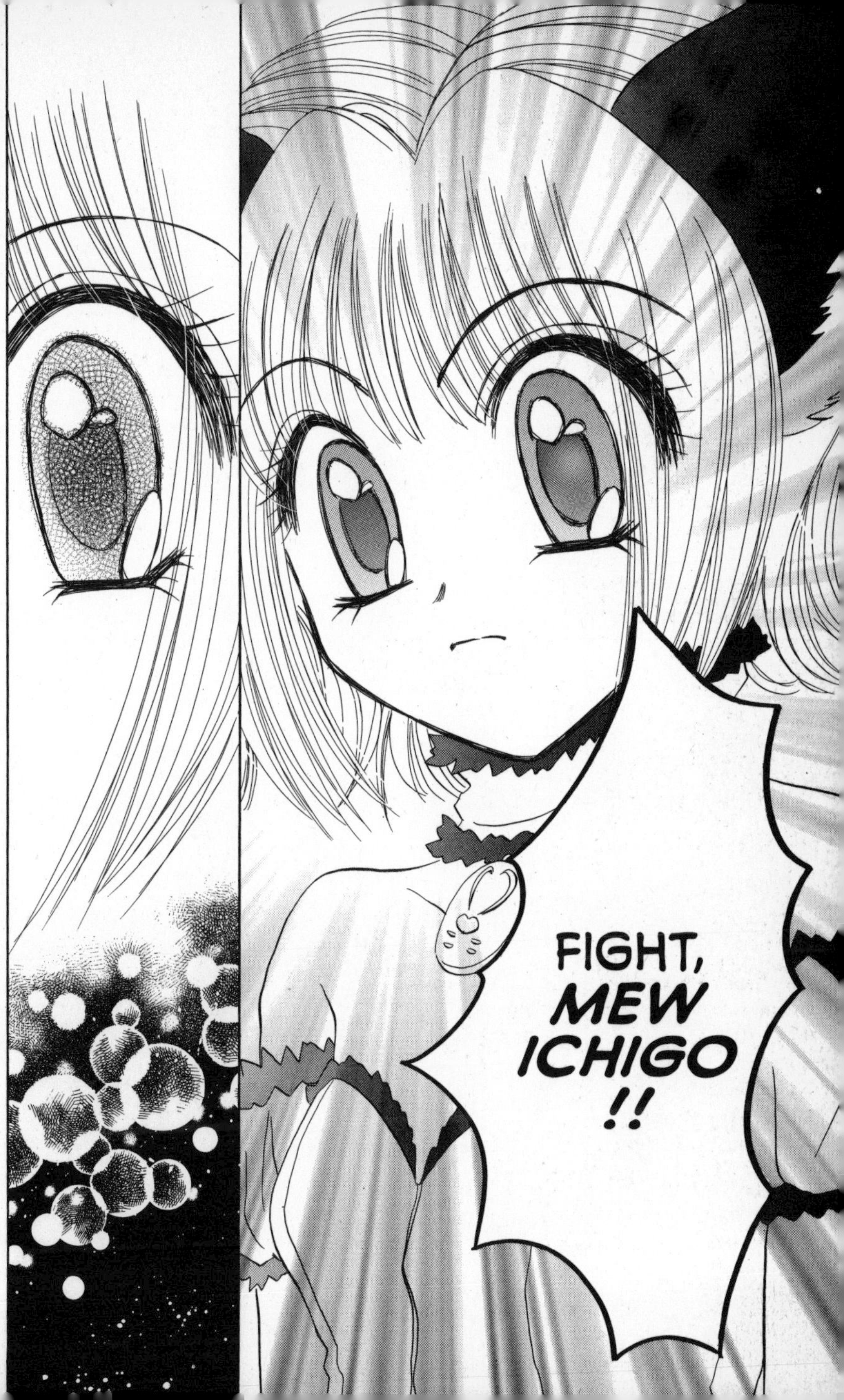
FIGHT, MEW ICHIGO !!

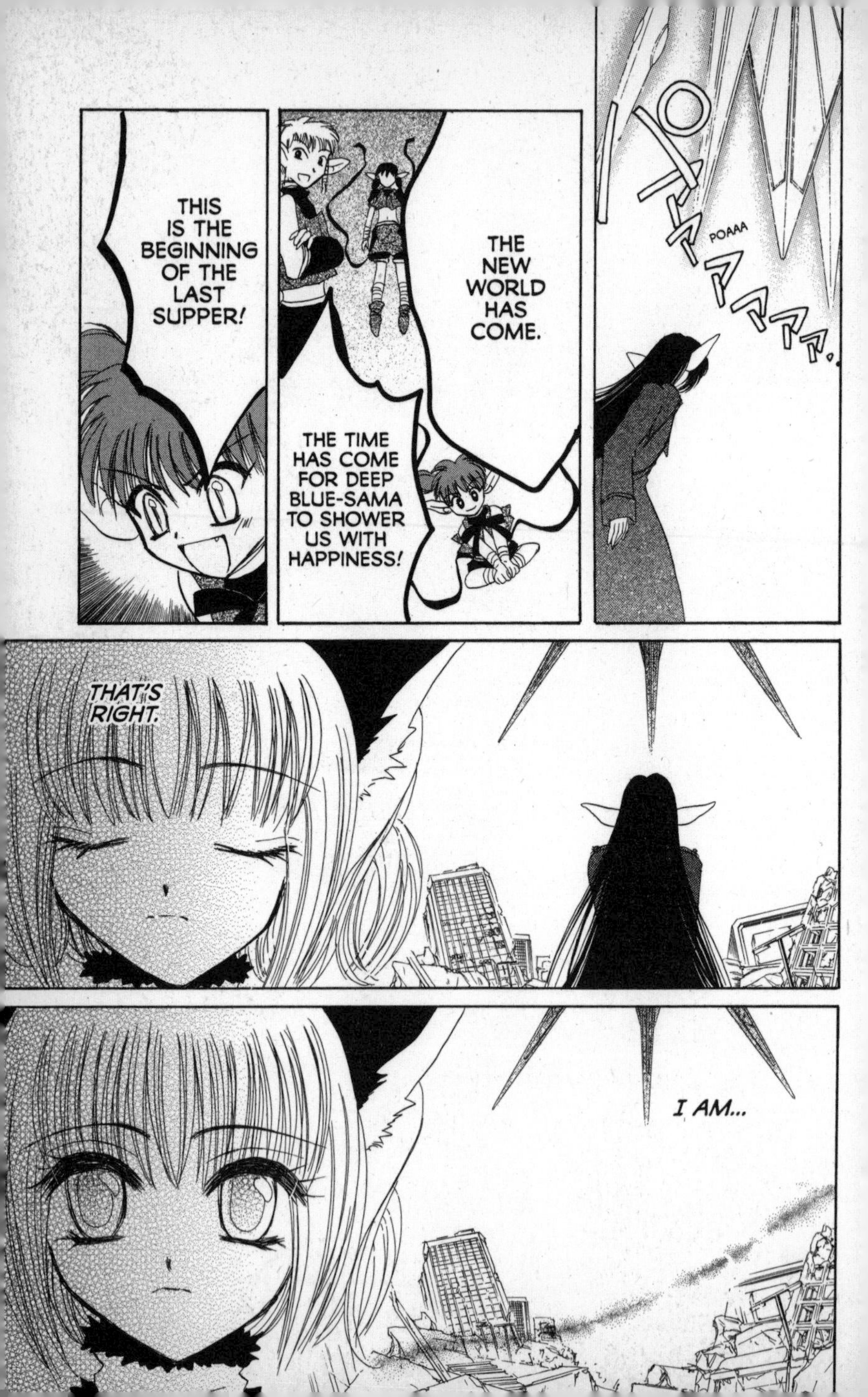
POAAA
THE NEW WORLD HAS COME.
THE TIME HAS COME FOR DEEP BLUE-SAMA TO SHOWER US WITH HAPPINESS!
THIS IS THE BEGINNING OF THE LAST SUPPER!
THAT'S RIGHT.
I AM...

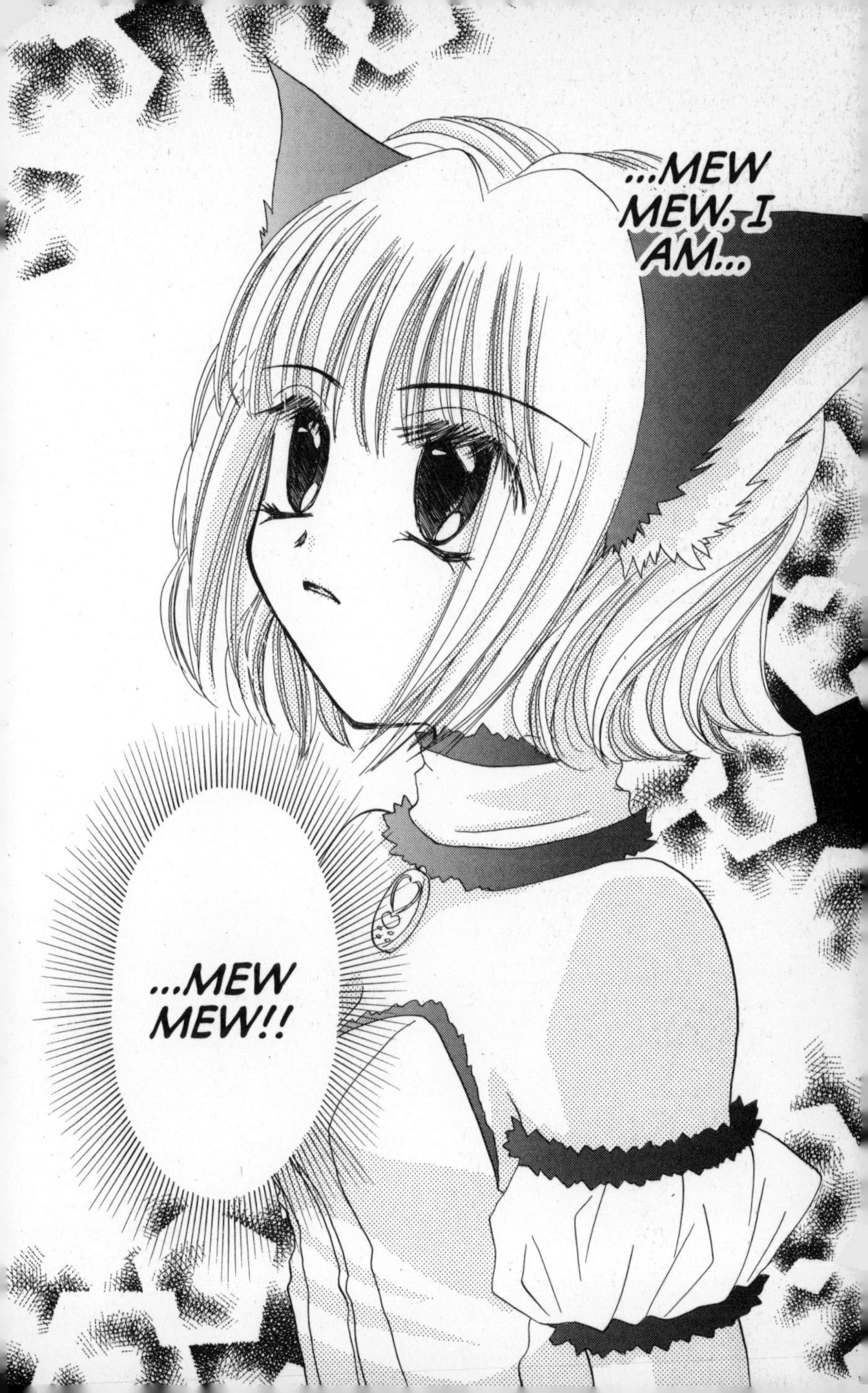
...MEW MEW. I AM...
...MEW MEW!!

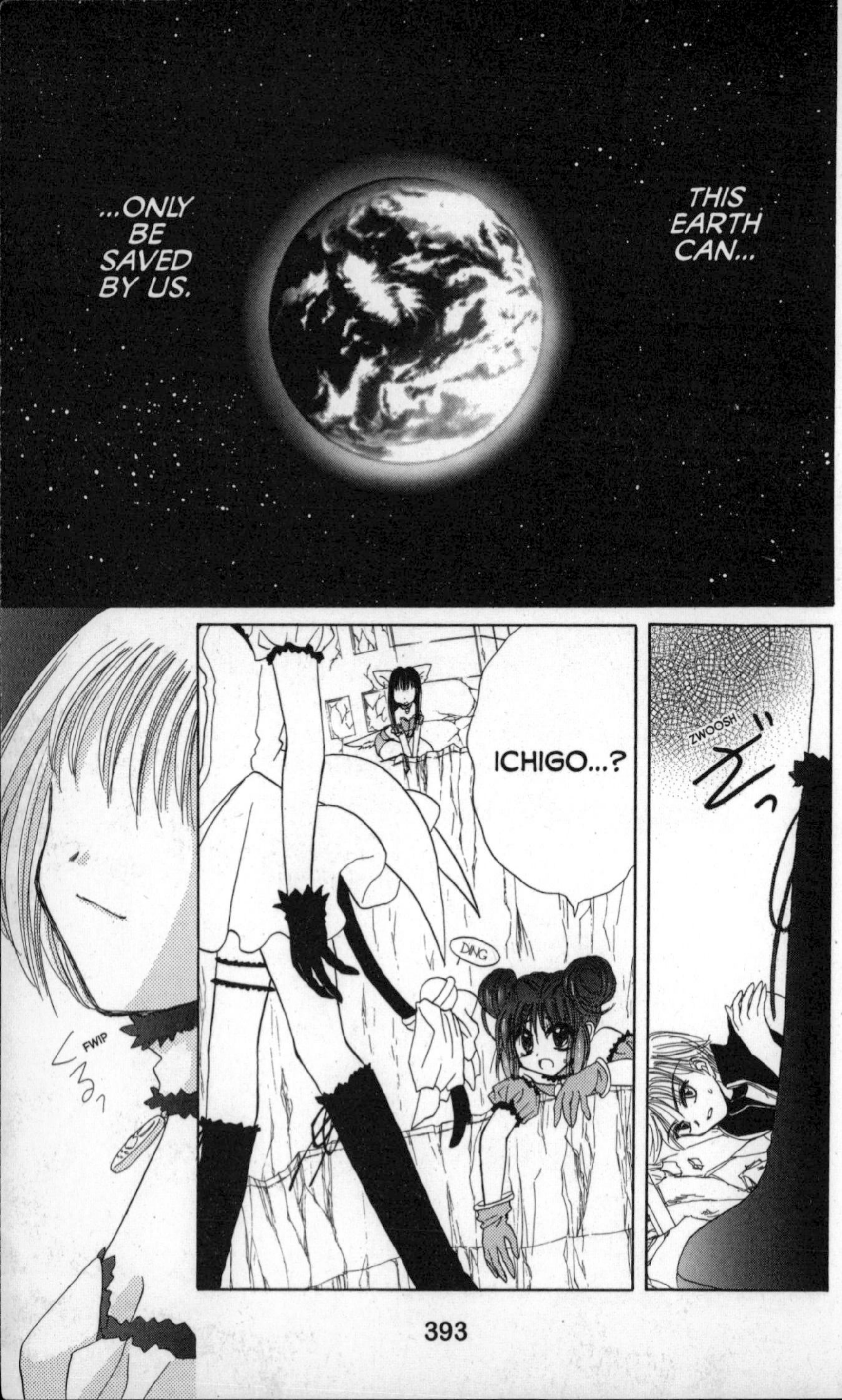
THIS EARTH CAN...
...ONLY BE SAVED BY US.
ZWOOSH
ICHIGO...?
DING
FWIP

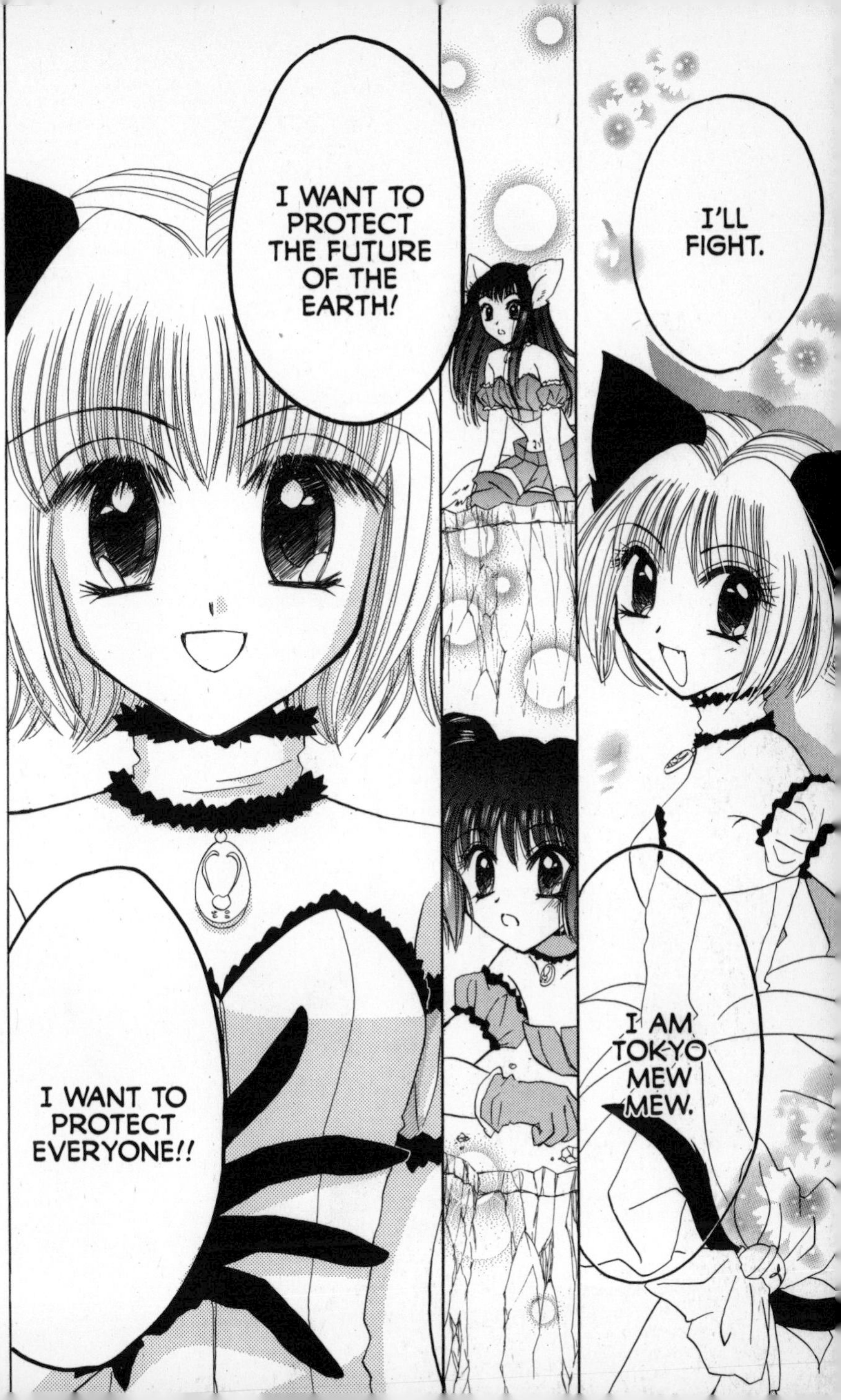
I'LL FIGHT.
I AM TOKYO MEW MEW.
I WANT TO PROTECT THE FUTURE OF THE EARTH!
I WANT TO PROTECT EVERYONE!!

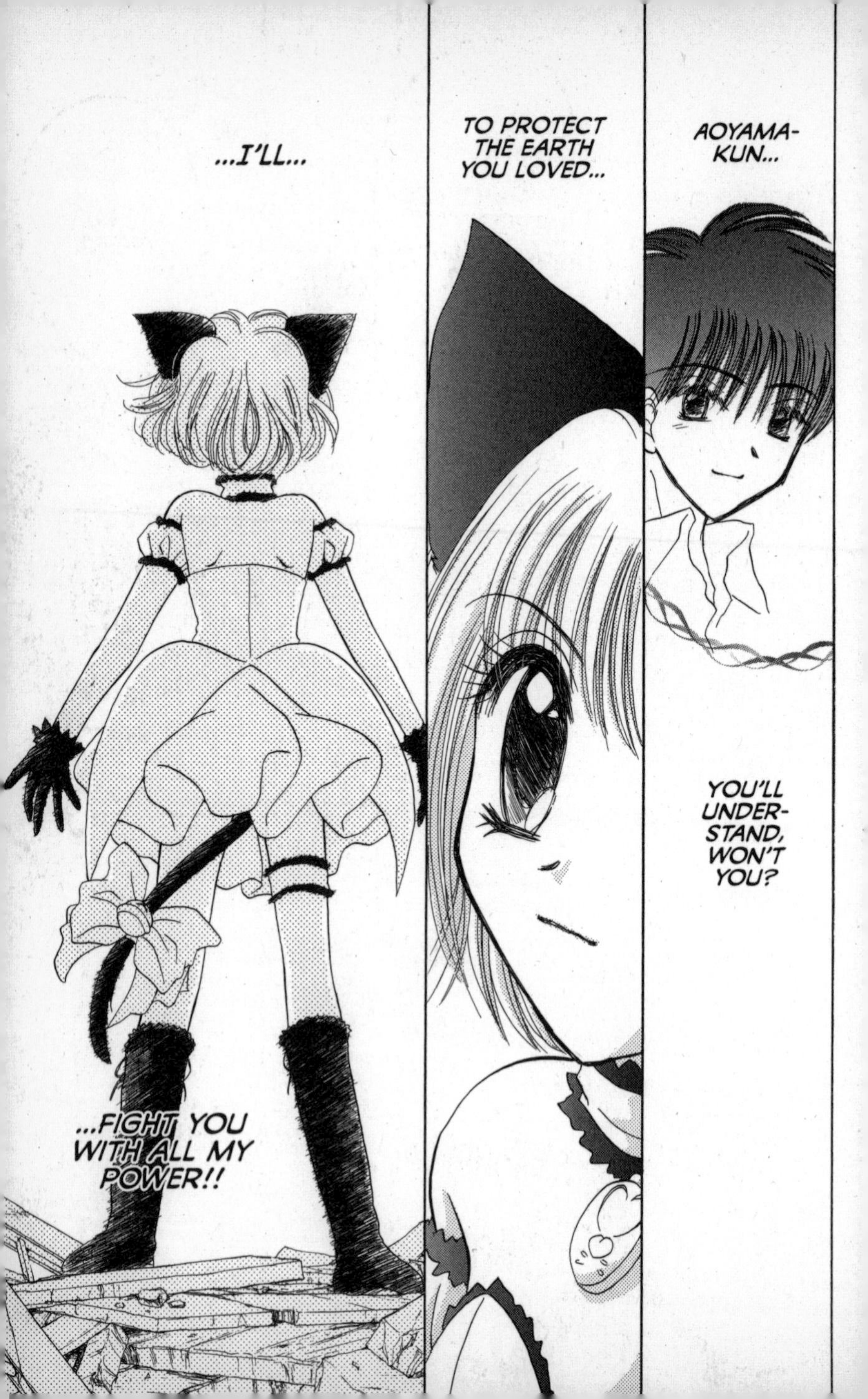
AOYAMA-KUN...
YOU'LL UNDER-STAND, WON'T YOU?
TO PROTECT THE EARTH YOU LOVED...
...I'LL...
...FIGHT YOU WITH ALL MY POWER!!

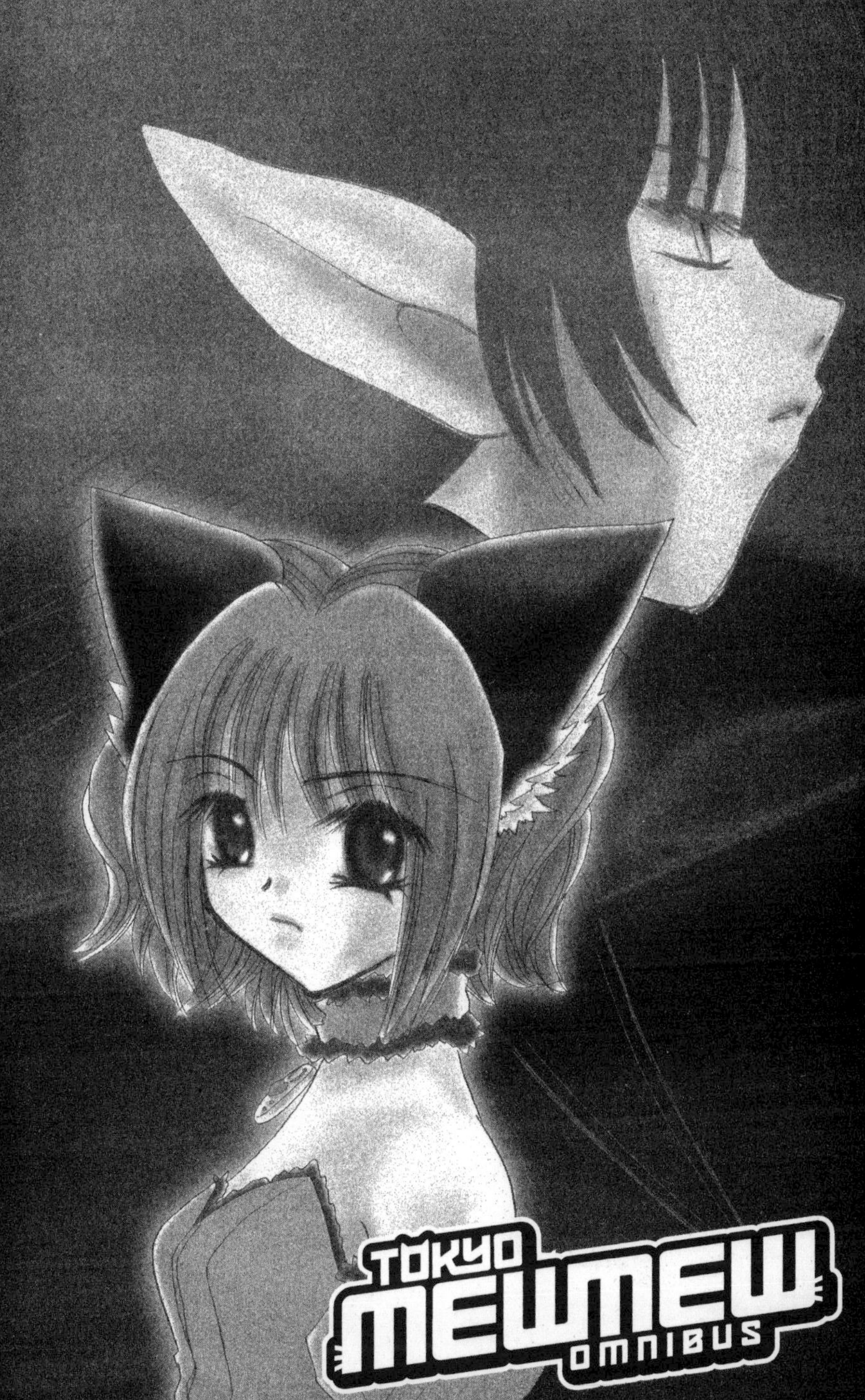
TOKYO
MEWMEW
OMNIBUS

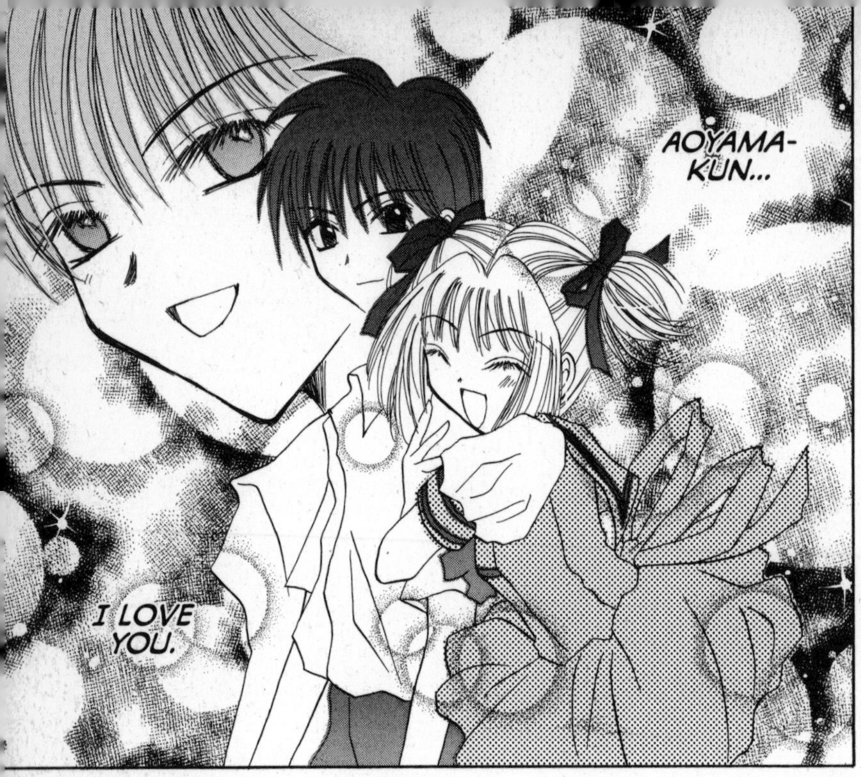
AOYAMA-KUN...
I LOVE YOU.

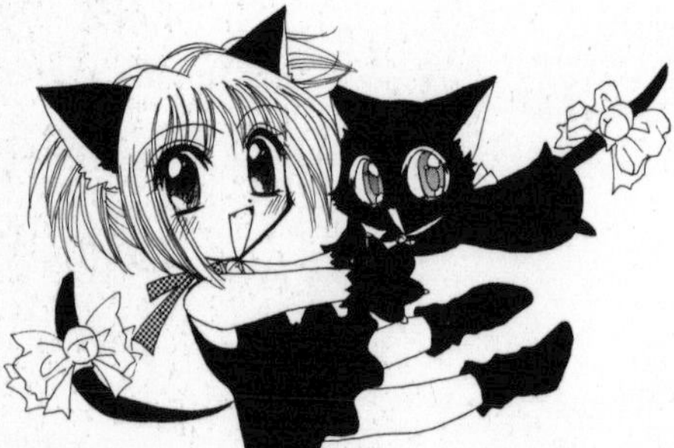

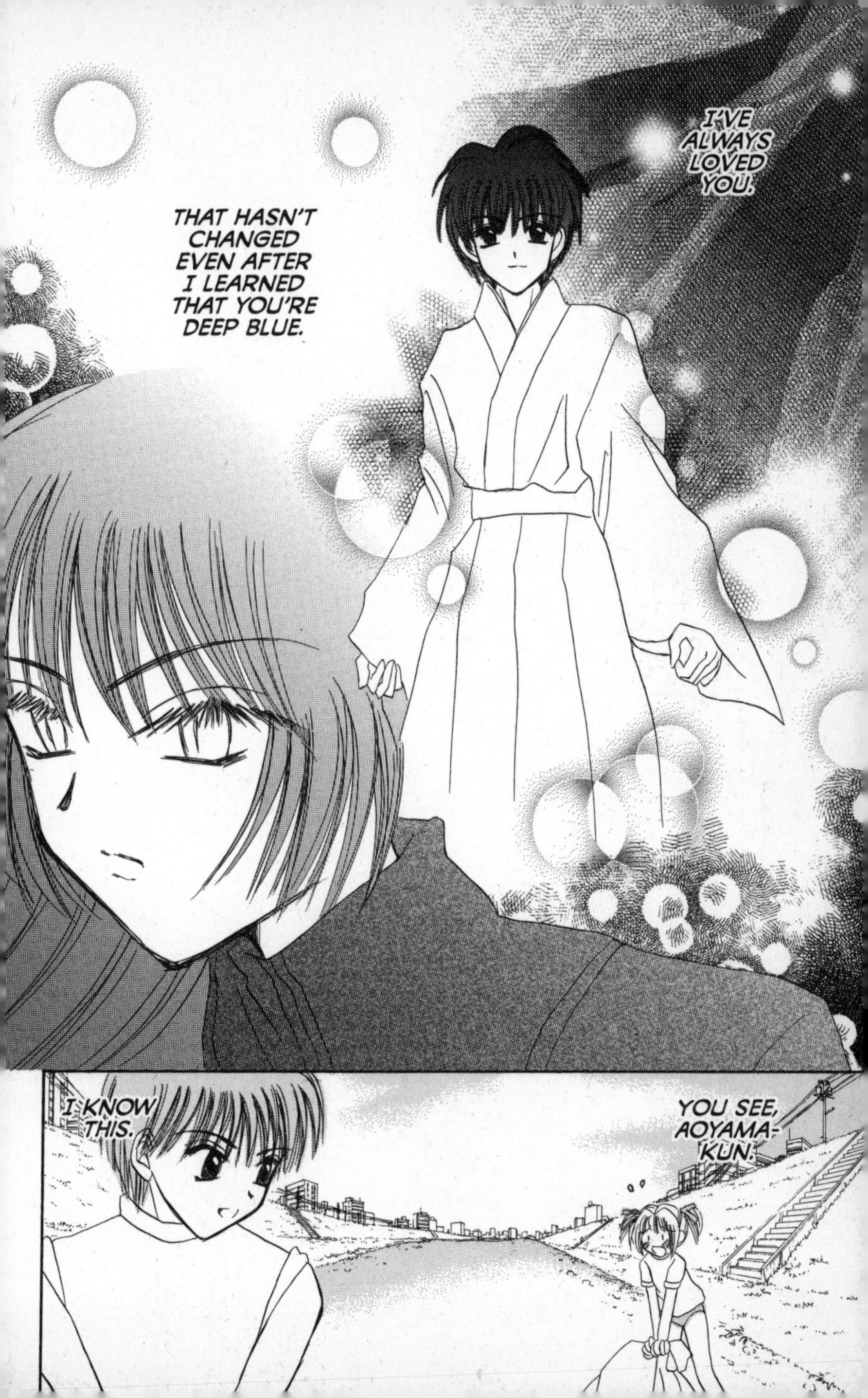
I'VE ALWAYS LOVED YOU.
THAT HASN'T CHANGED EVEN AFTER I LEARNED THAT YOU'RE DEEP BLUE.
YOU SEE, AOYAMA-KUN.
I KNOW THIS.

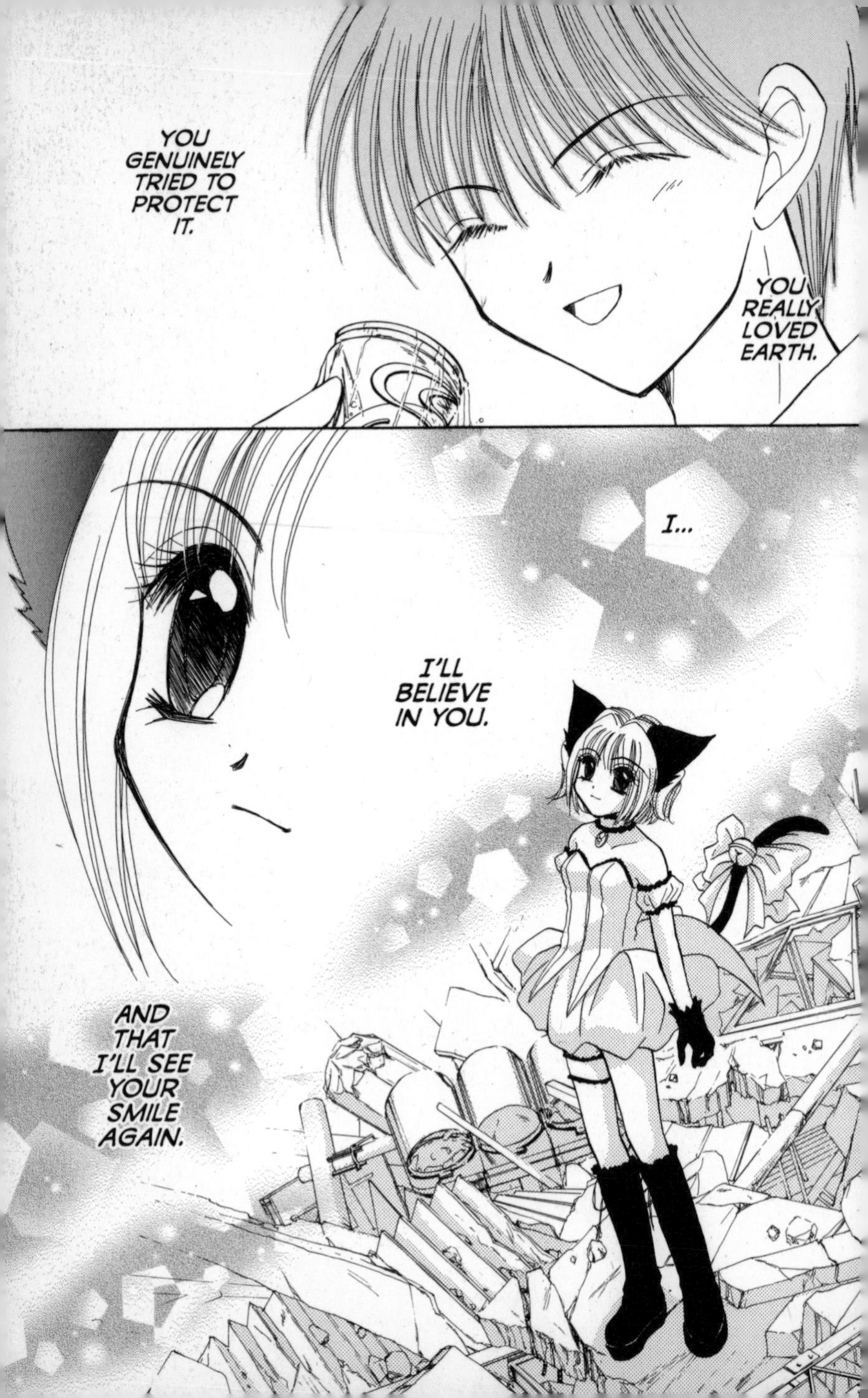
YOU REALLY LOVED EARTH.
YOU GENUINELY TRIED TO PROTECT IT.
I...
I'LL BELIEVE IN YOU.
AND THAT I'LL SEE YOUR SMILE AGAIN.

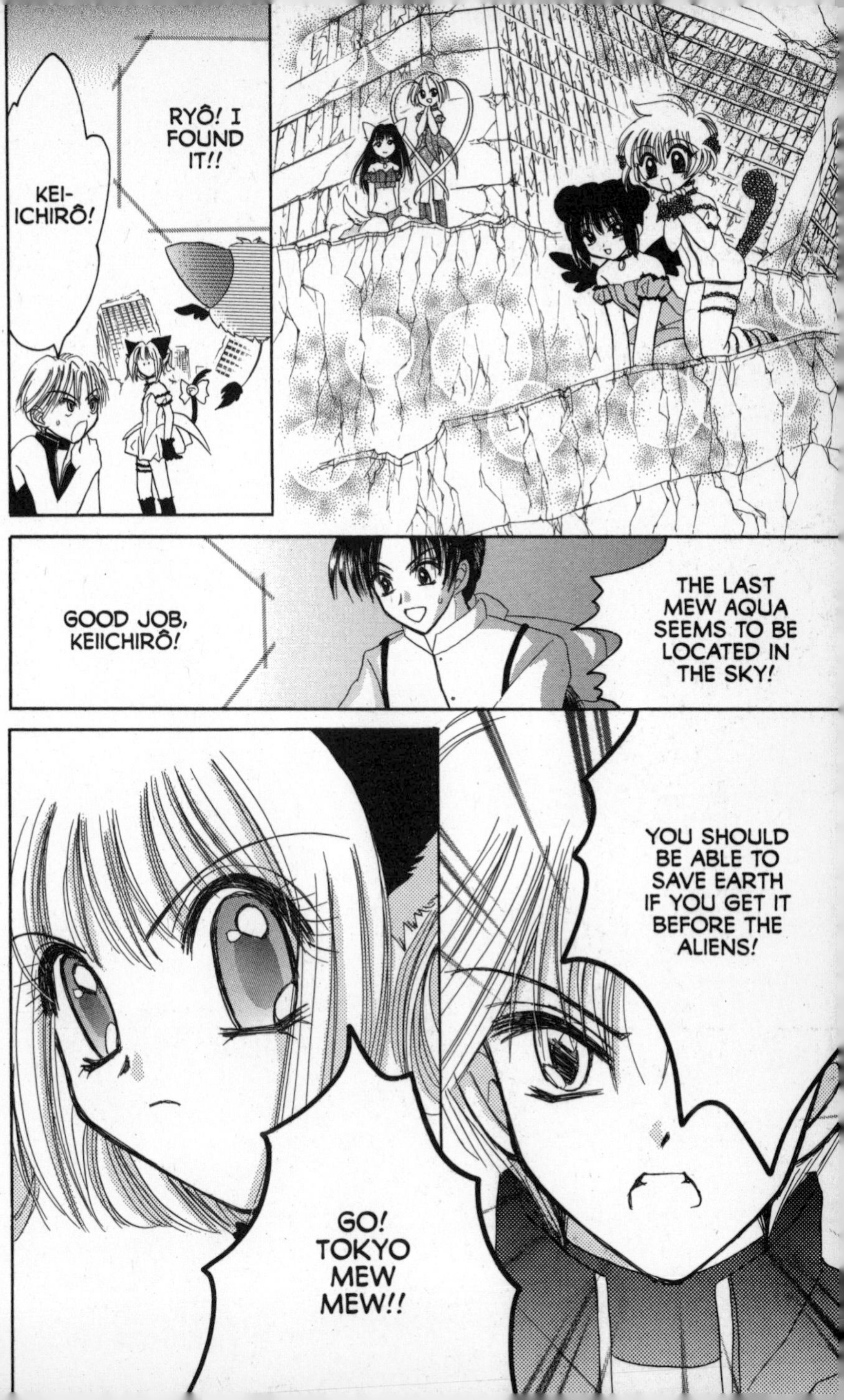
RYÔ! I FOUND IT!!
KEI-ICHIRÔ!
THE LAST MEW AQUA SEEMS TO BE LOCATED IN THE SKY!
GOOD JOB, KEIICHIRÔ!
YOU SHOULD BE ABLE TO SAVE EARTH IF YOU GET IT BEFORE THE ALIENS!
GO! TOKYO MEW MEW!!

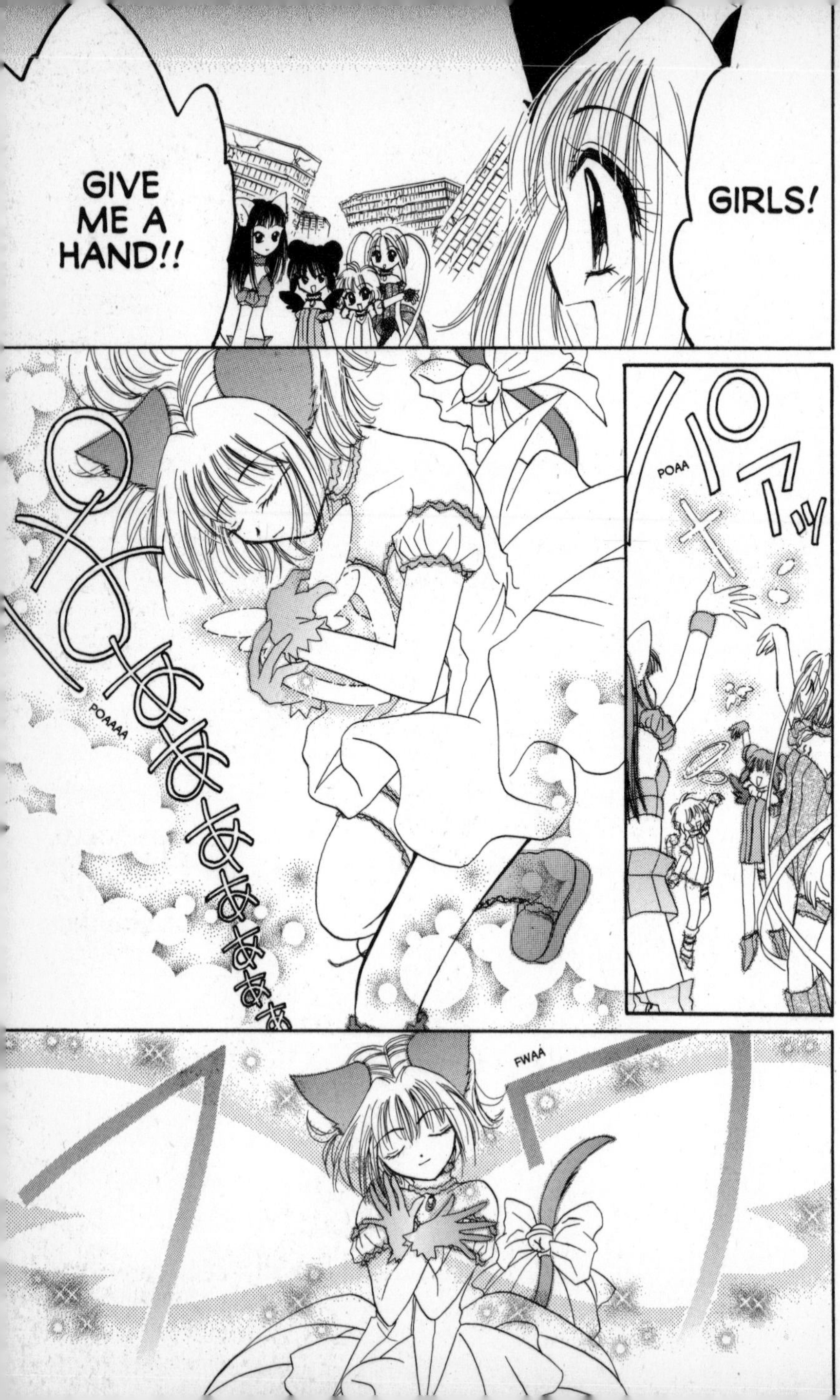

GIRLS!
GIVE ME A HAND!!
POAA
POAAAA
FWAA

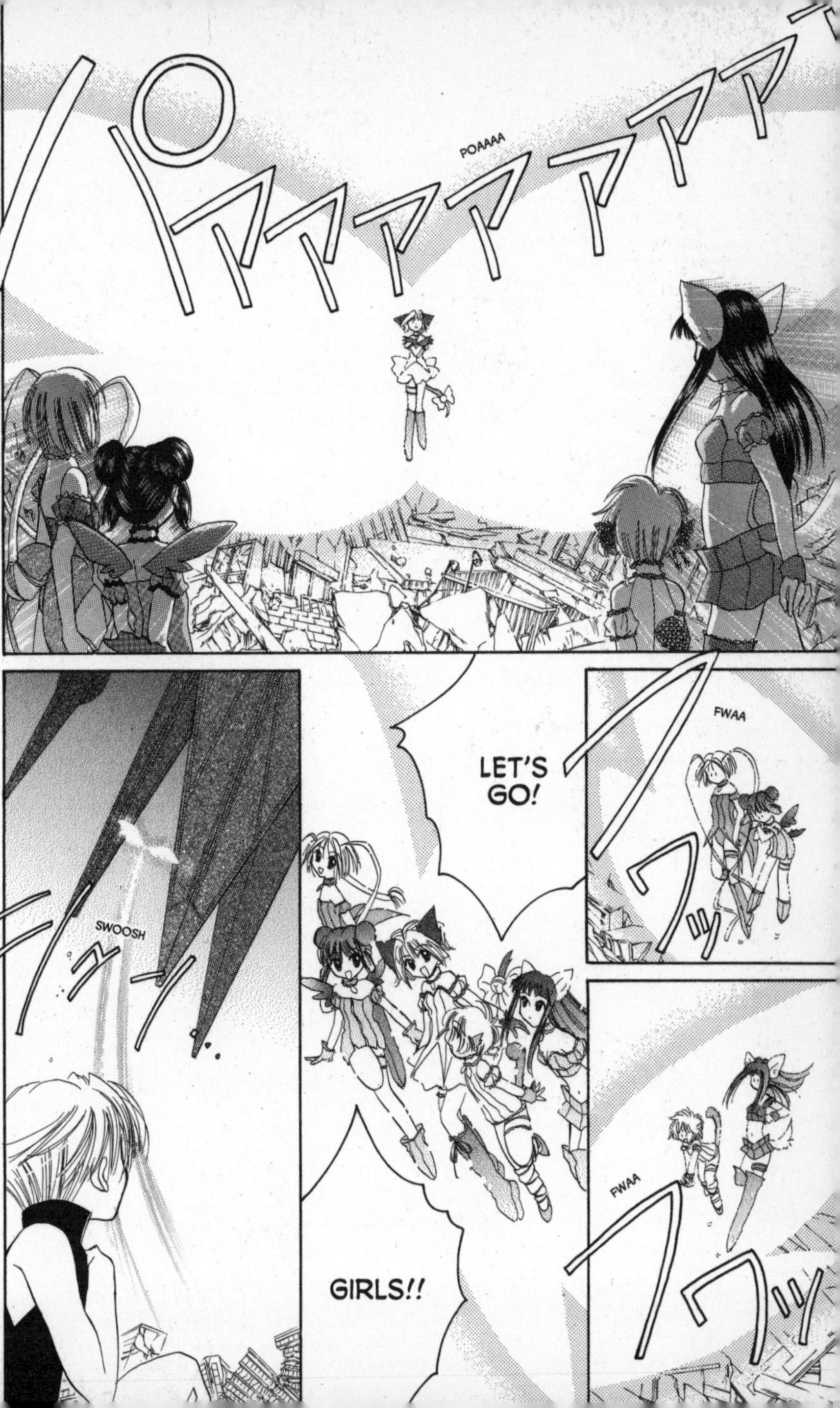
POAAAA
FWAA
FWAA
LET'S GO!
GIRLS!!
SWOOSH

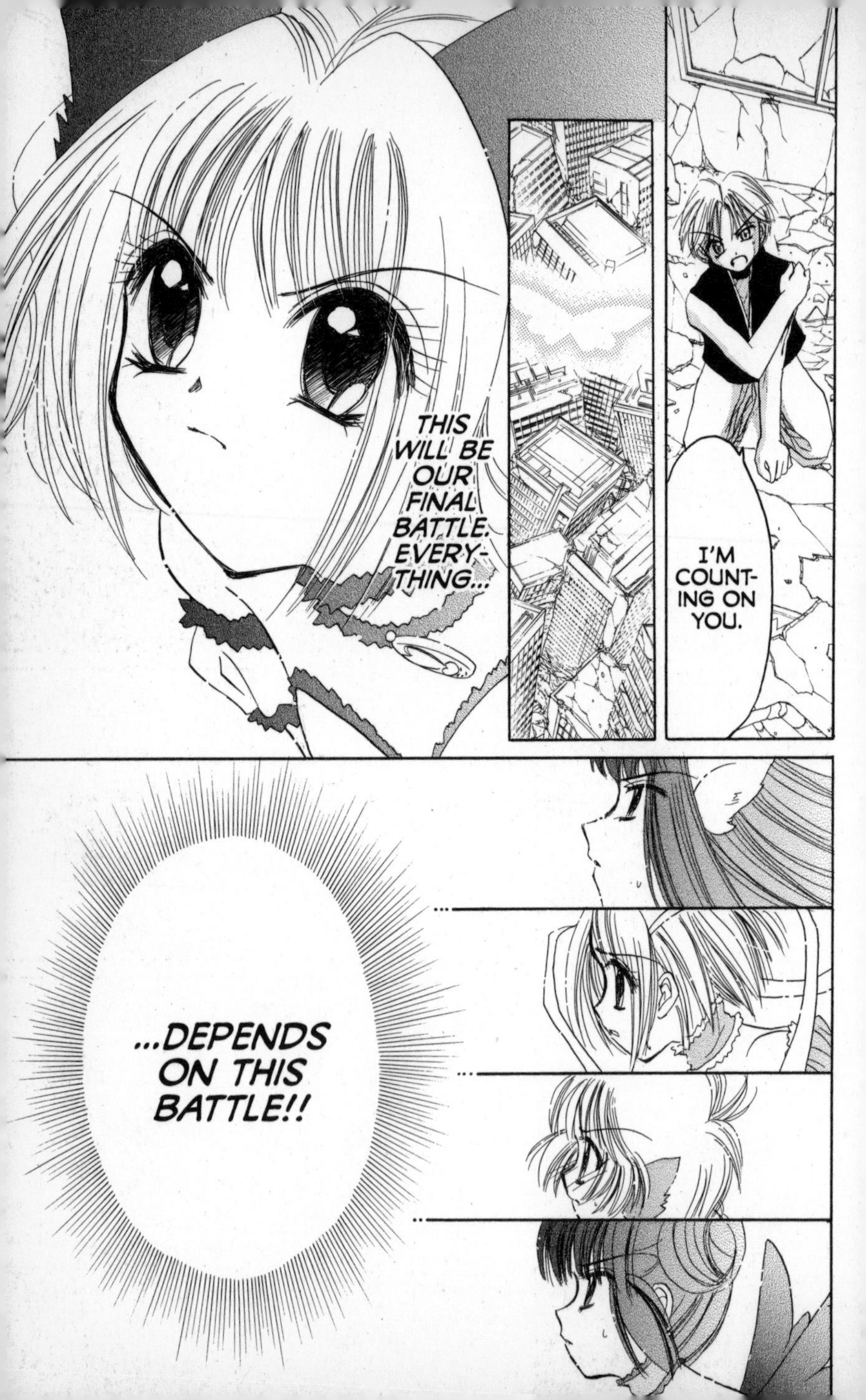
I'M COUNTING ON YOU.
THIS WILL BE OUR FINAL BATTLE. EVERYTHING...
...
...
...
...DEPENDS ON THIS BATTLE!!

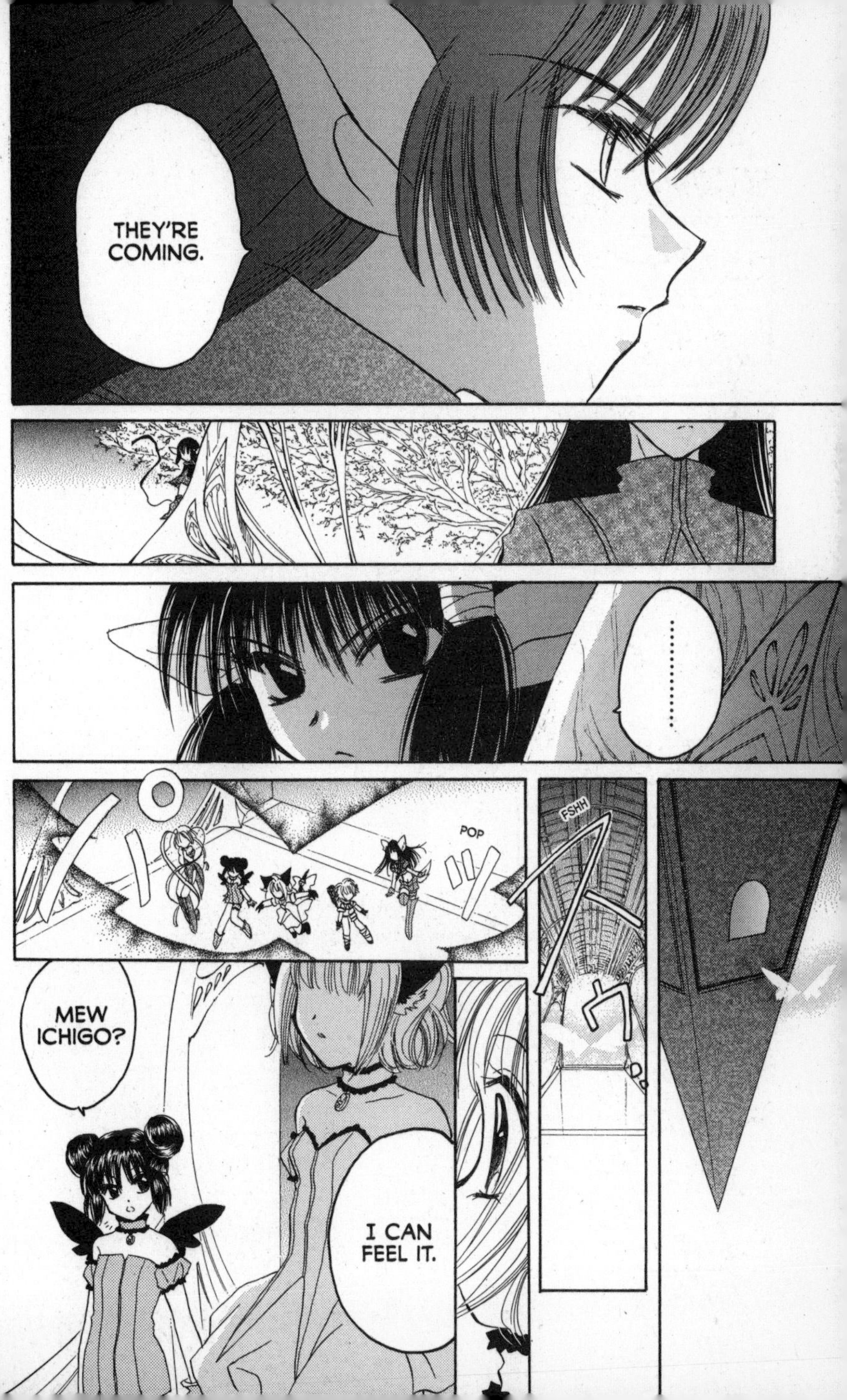
THEY'RE COMING.
......
FSHH
POP
MEW ICHIGO?
I CAN FEEL IT.

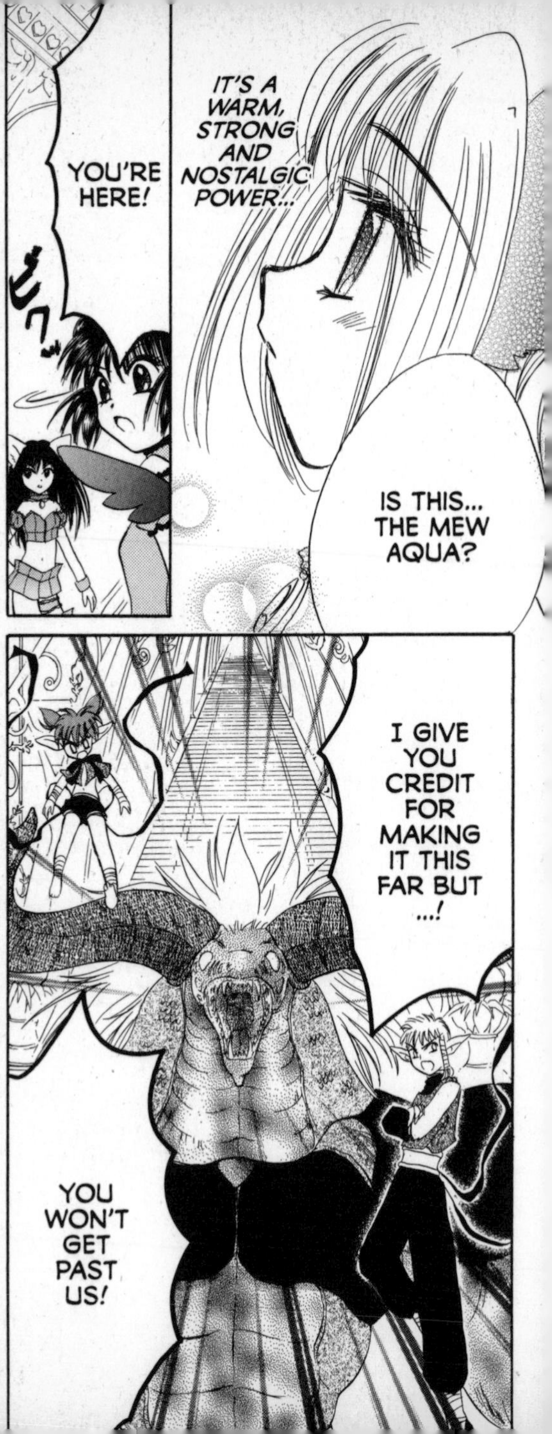
IT'S A WARM, STRONG AND NOSTALGIC POWER...
IS THIS... THE MEW AQUA?
YOU'RE HERE!
I GIVE YOU CREDIT FOR MAKING IT THIS FAR BUT ...!
YOU WON'T GET PAST US!

TOKYO HAM HAM

ART BY CHIEF MATSUMOTO, ARRANGED BY MIA IKUMI

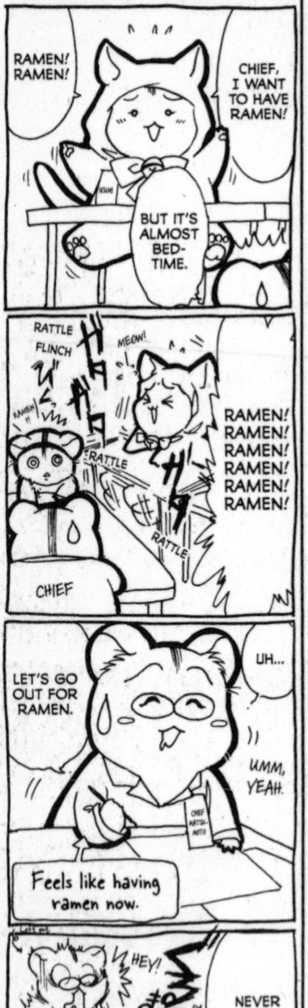
RAMEN! RAMEN!
CHIEF, I WANT TO HAVE RAMEN!
BUT IT'S ALMOST BED-TIME.
RATTLE
FLINCH
MEOW!
RAMEN! RAMEN! RAMEN! RAMEN! RAMEN! RAMEN!
RATTLE
RATTLE
CHIEF
UH...
LET'S GO OUT FOR RAMEN.
UMM, YEAH.
Feels like having ramen now.
HEY!
GROWL
GROWL
NEVER MIND.
I JUST WANTED TO SAY IT.
PFFT!

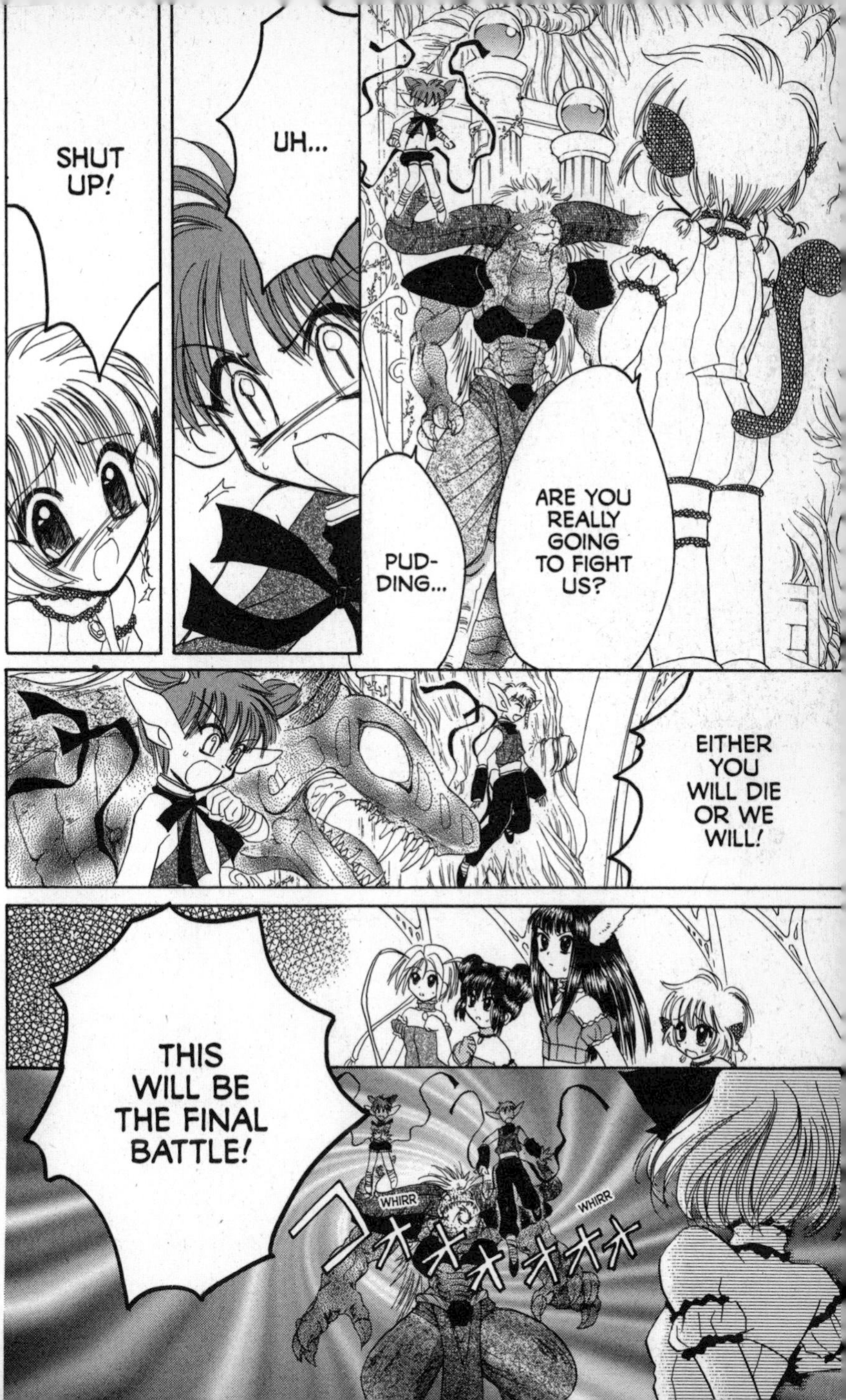
ARE YOU REALLY GOING TO FIGHT US?
PUD-DING...
UH...
SHUT UP!
EITHER YOU WILL DIE OR WE WILL!
THIS WILL BE THE FINAL BATTLE!
WHIRR
WHIRR

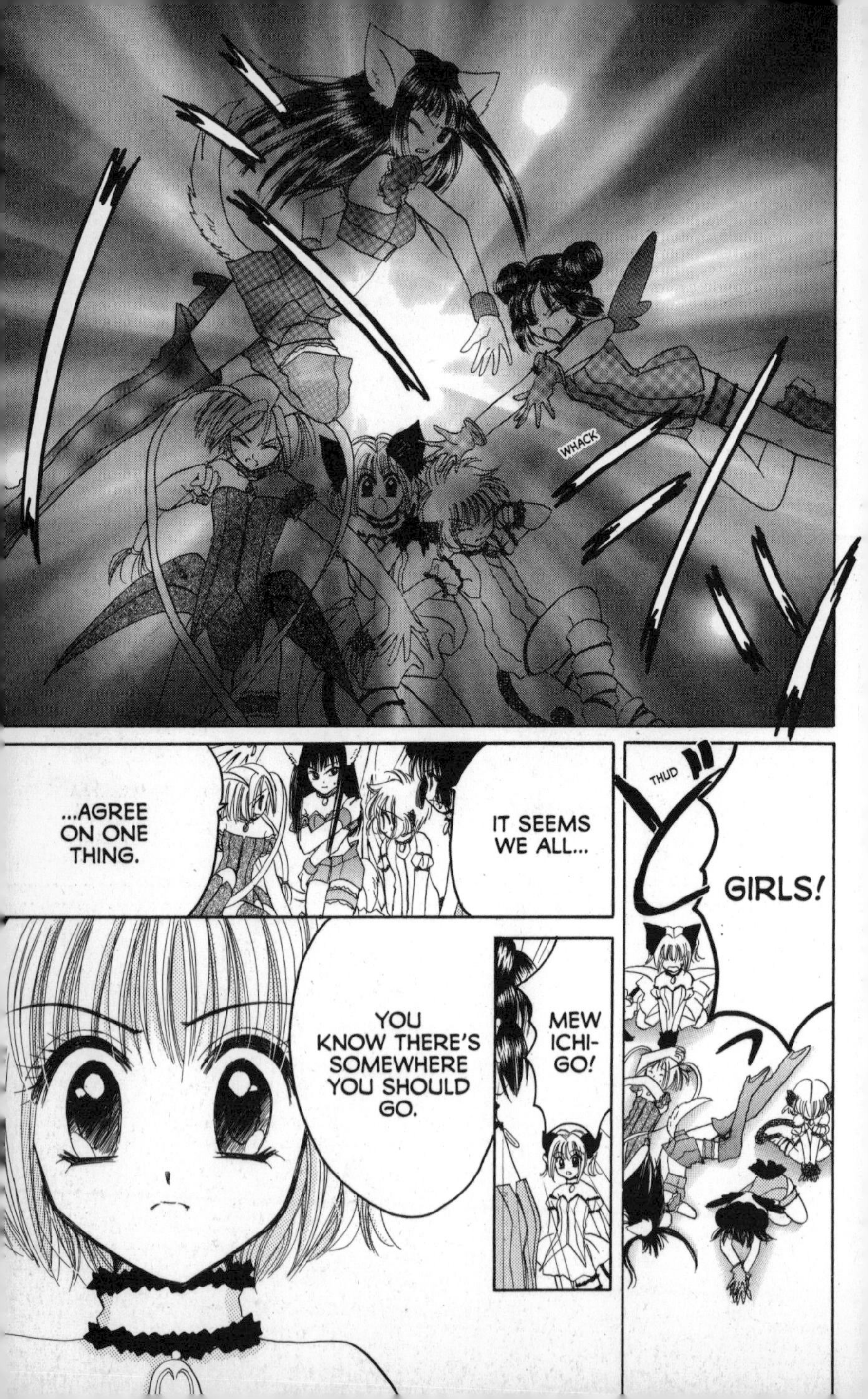
WHACK
THUD
GIRLS!
IT SEEMS WE ALL...
...AGREE ON ONE THING.
MEW ICHIGO!
YOU KNOW THERE'S SOMEWHERE YOU SHOULD GO.

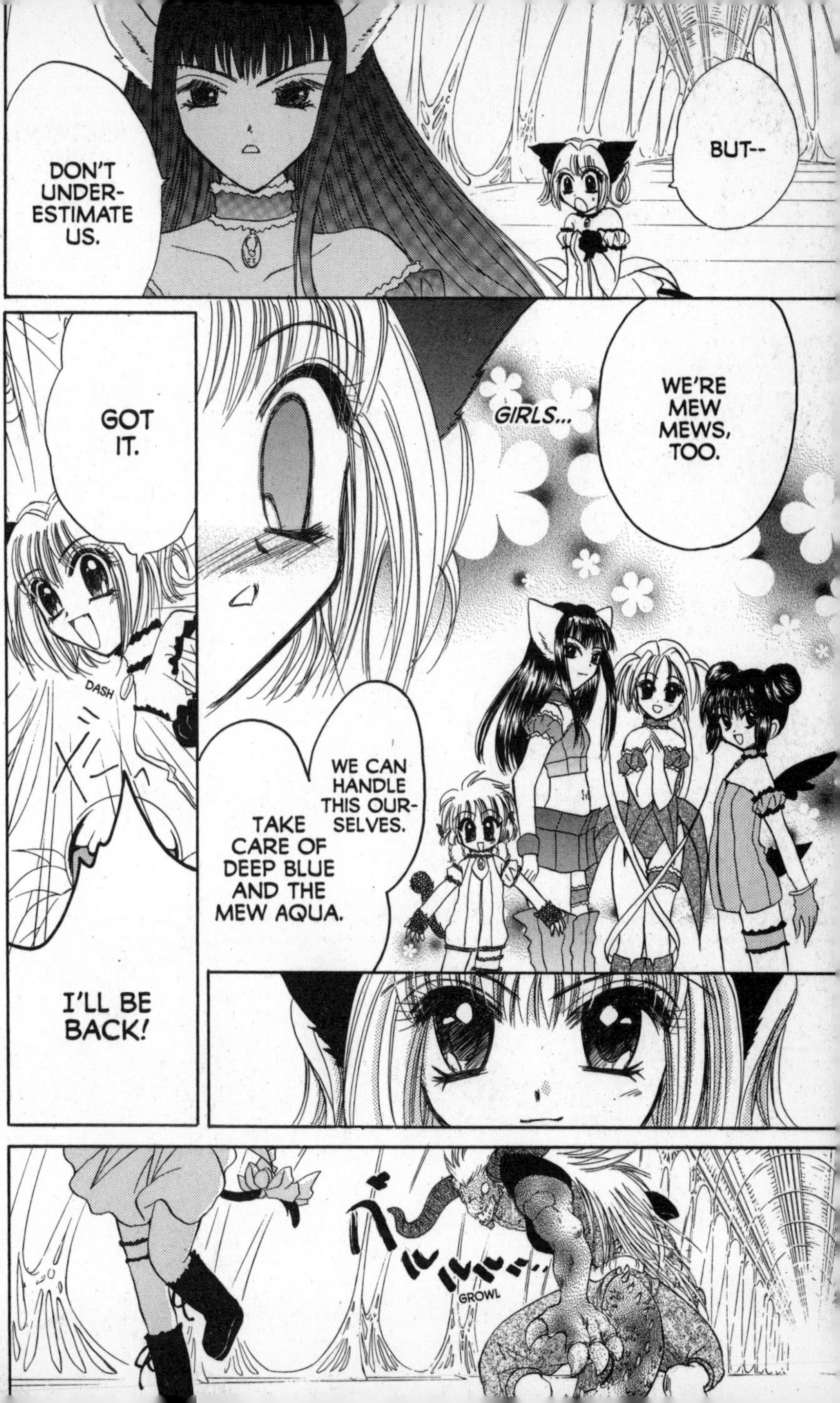
BUT--
DON'T UNDER-ESTIMATE US.
WE'RE MEW MEWS, TOO.
GIRLS...
WE CAN HANDLE THIS OUR-SELVES.
TAKE CARE OF DEEP BLUE AND THE MEW AQUA.
GOT IT.
DASH
I'LL BE BACK!
GROWL

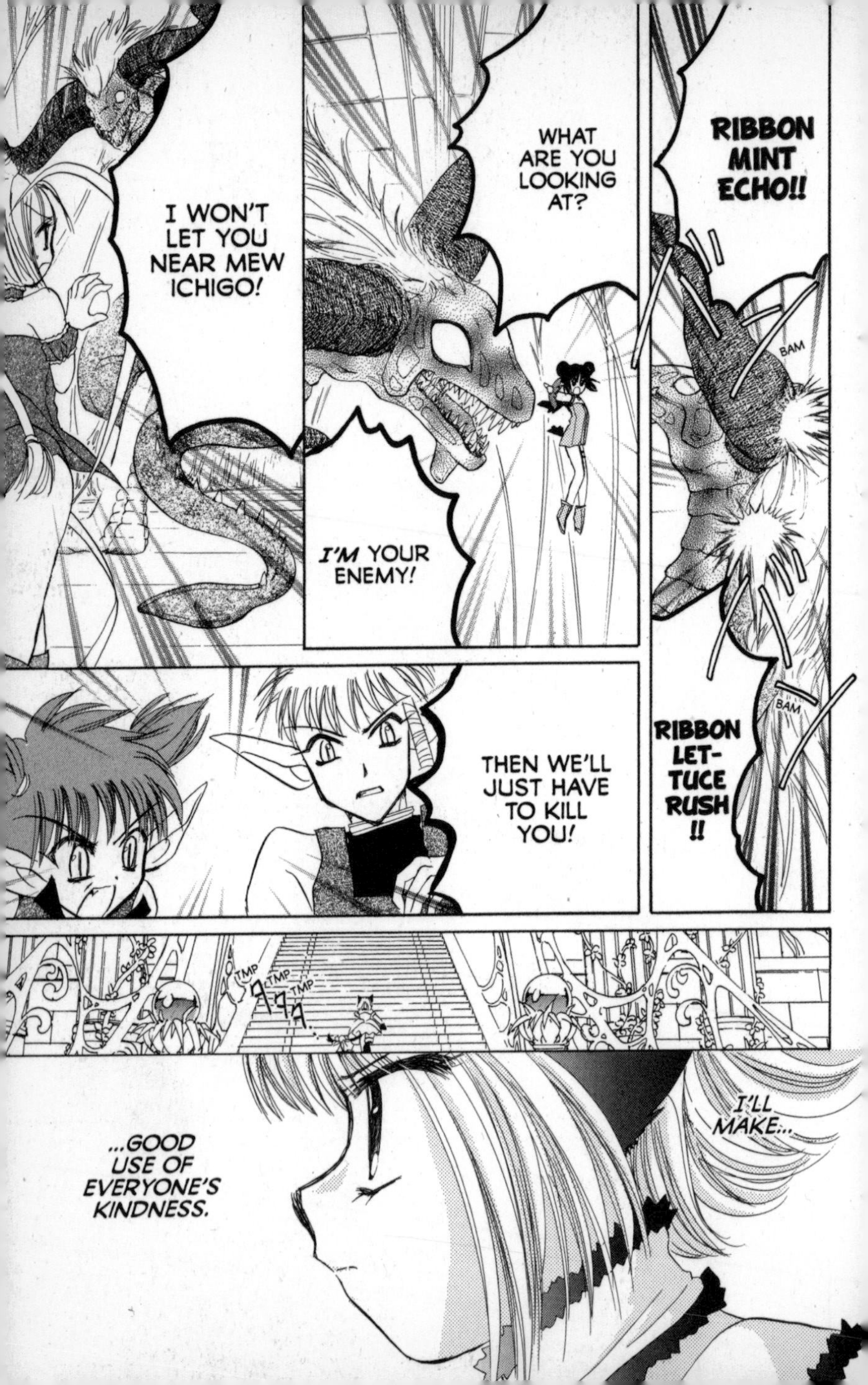
RIBBON MINT ECHO!!
BAM
BAM
RIBBON LET-TUCE RUSH!!
WHAT ARE YOU LOOKING AT?
I'M YOUR ENEMY!
I WON'T LET YOU NEAR MEW ICHIGO!
THEN WE'LL JUST HAVE TO KILL YOU!
TMP TMP TMP
I'LL MAKE...
...GOOD USE OF EVERYONE'S KINDNESS.

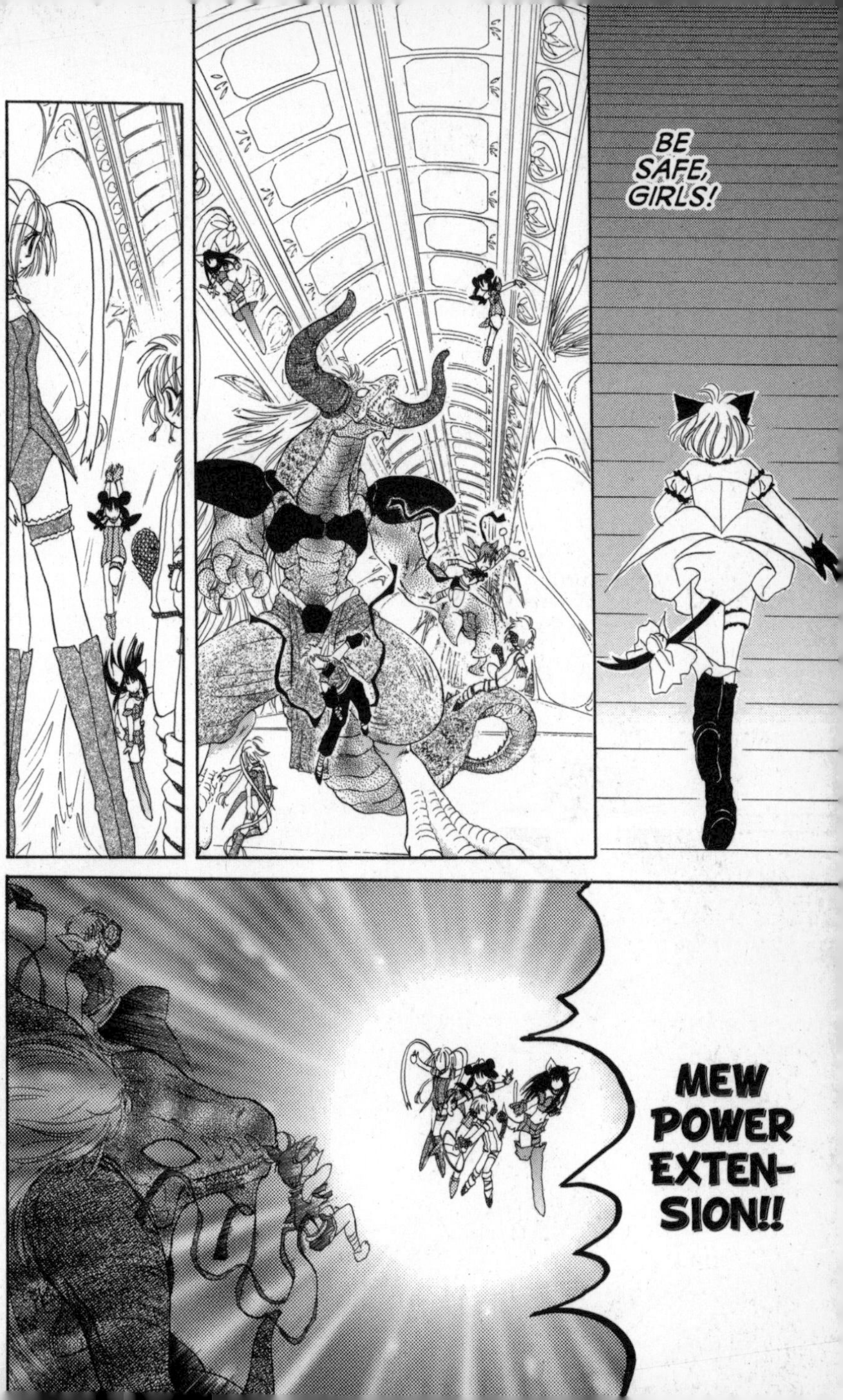
BE SAFE, GIRLS!
MEW POWER EXTENSION!!

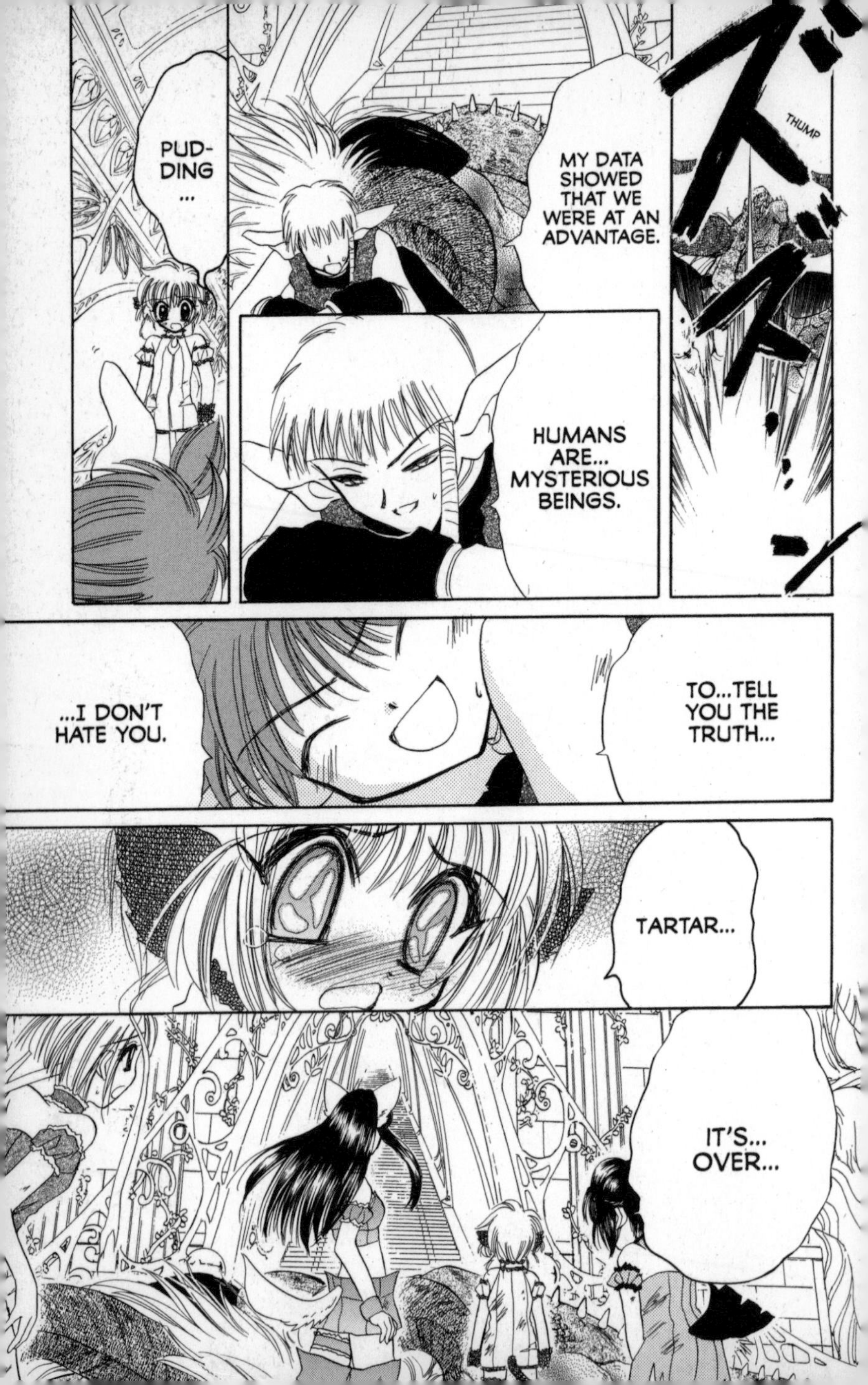
THUMP
MY DATA SHOWED THAT WE WERE AT AN ADVANTAGE.
HUMANS ARE... MYSTERIOUS BEINGS.
PUD-DING ...
TO...TELL YOU THE TRUTH...
...I DON'T HATE YOU.
TARTAR...
IT'S... OVER...

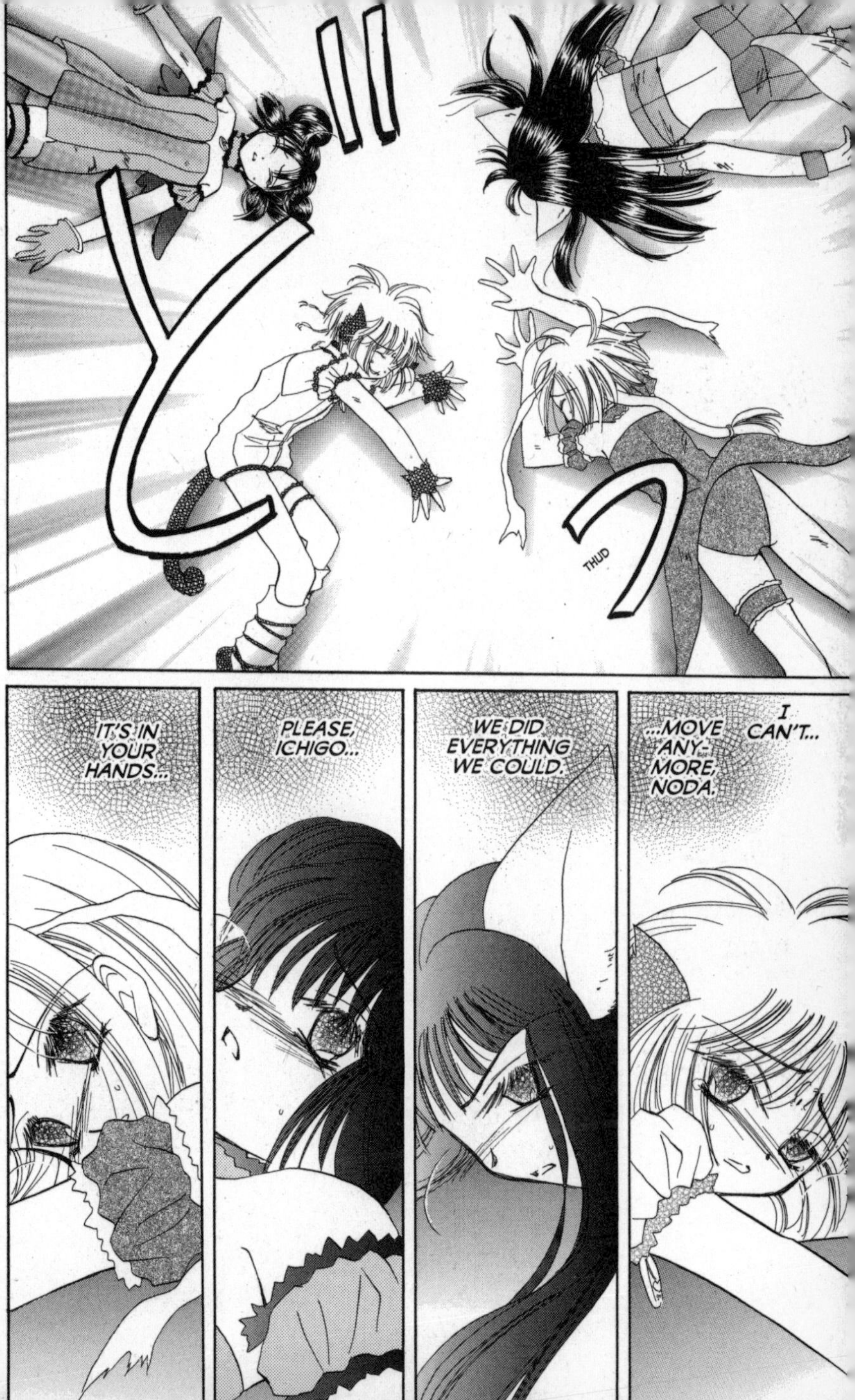
THUD
I CAN'T...
...MOVE ANY-MORE, NODA.
WE DID EVERYTHING WE COULD.
PLEASE, ICHIGO...
IT'S IN YOUR HANDS...

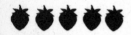

SPECIAL THANKS!!

R. YOSHIDA

H. MATSUMOTO
M. OMORI

S. NAOHARA
K. HONDA

A. OKAWA
S. NAKAZAWA

H. OIKAWA

M. SEKIYA
K. NAKAMA

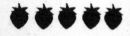

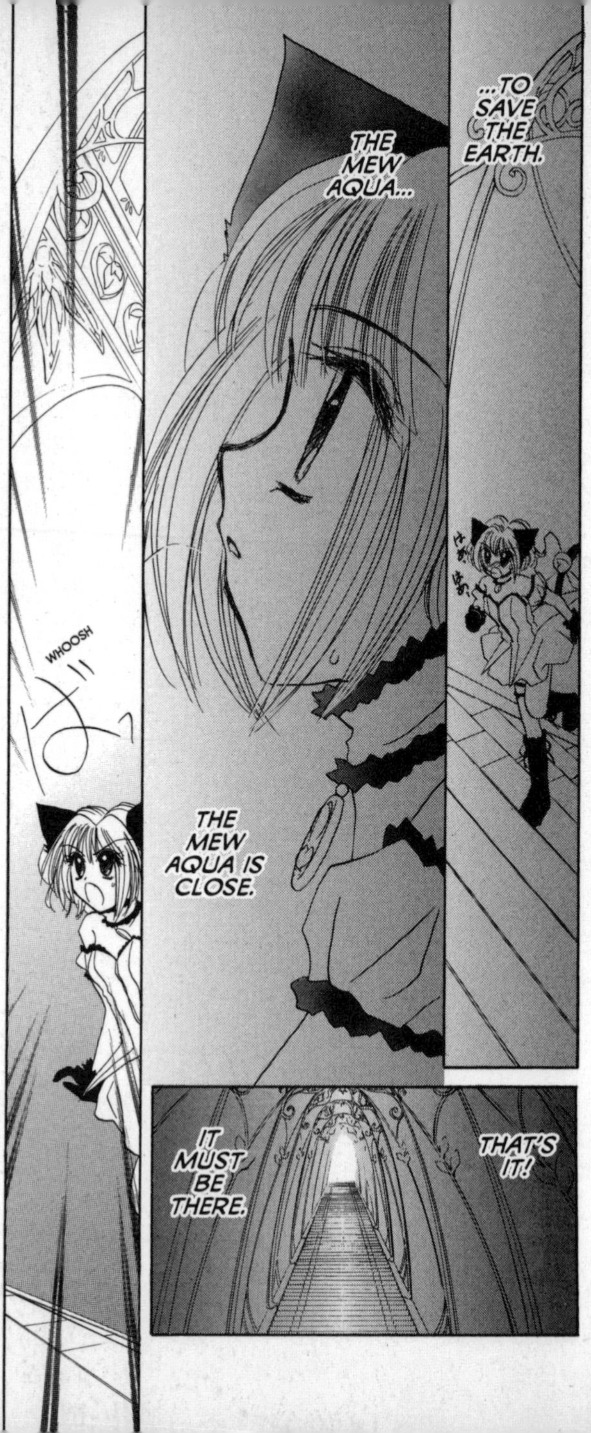
...TO SAVE THE EARTH.
THE MEW AQUA...
THE MEW AQUA IS CLOSE.
THAT'S IT!
IT MUST BE THERE.
WHOOSH

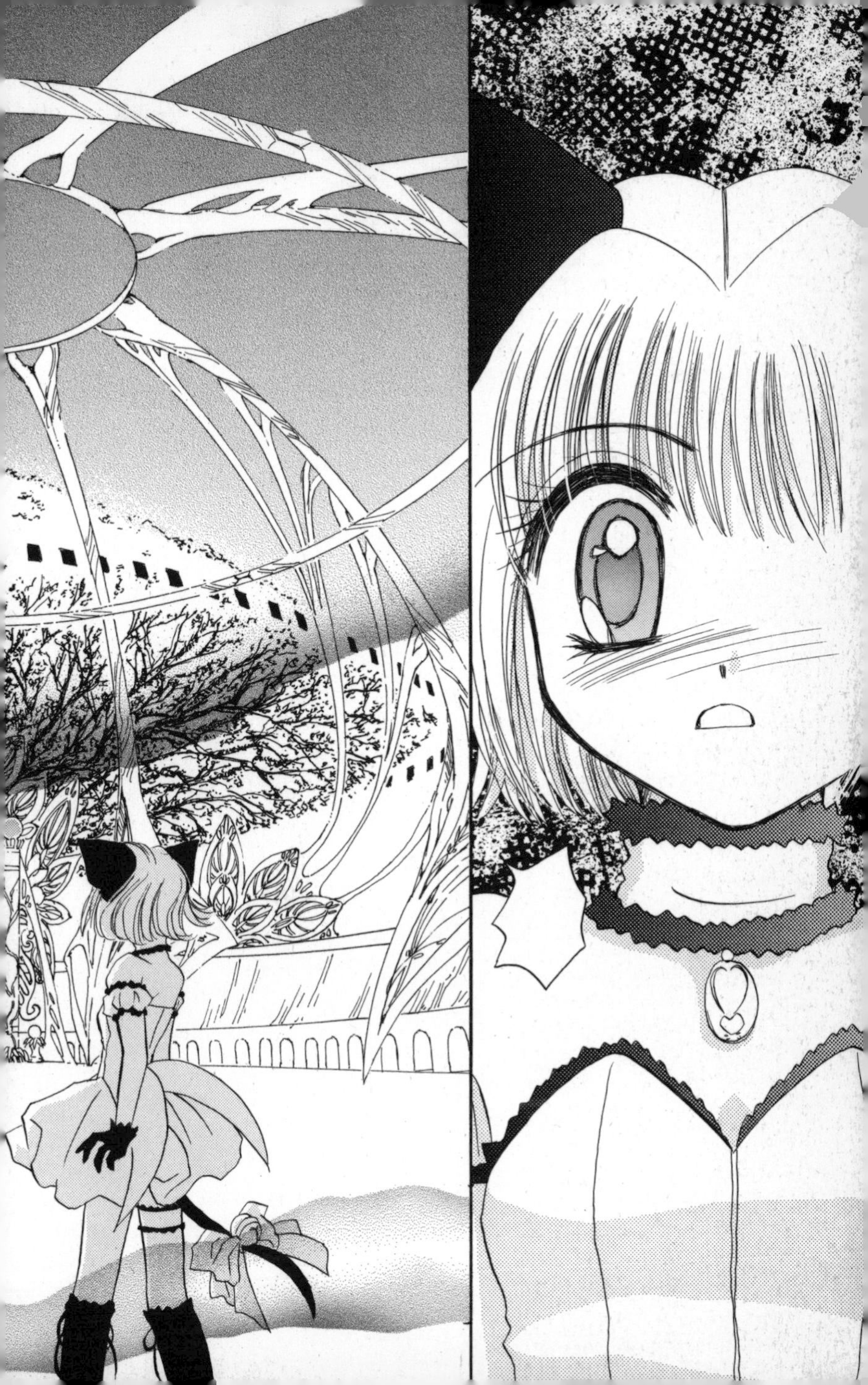

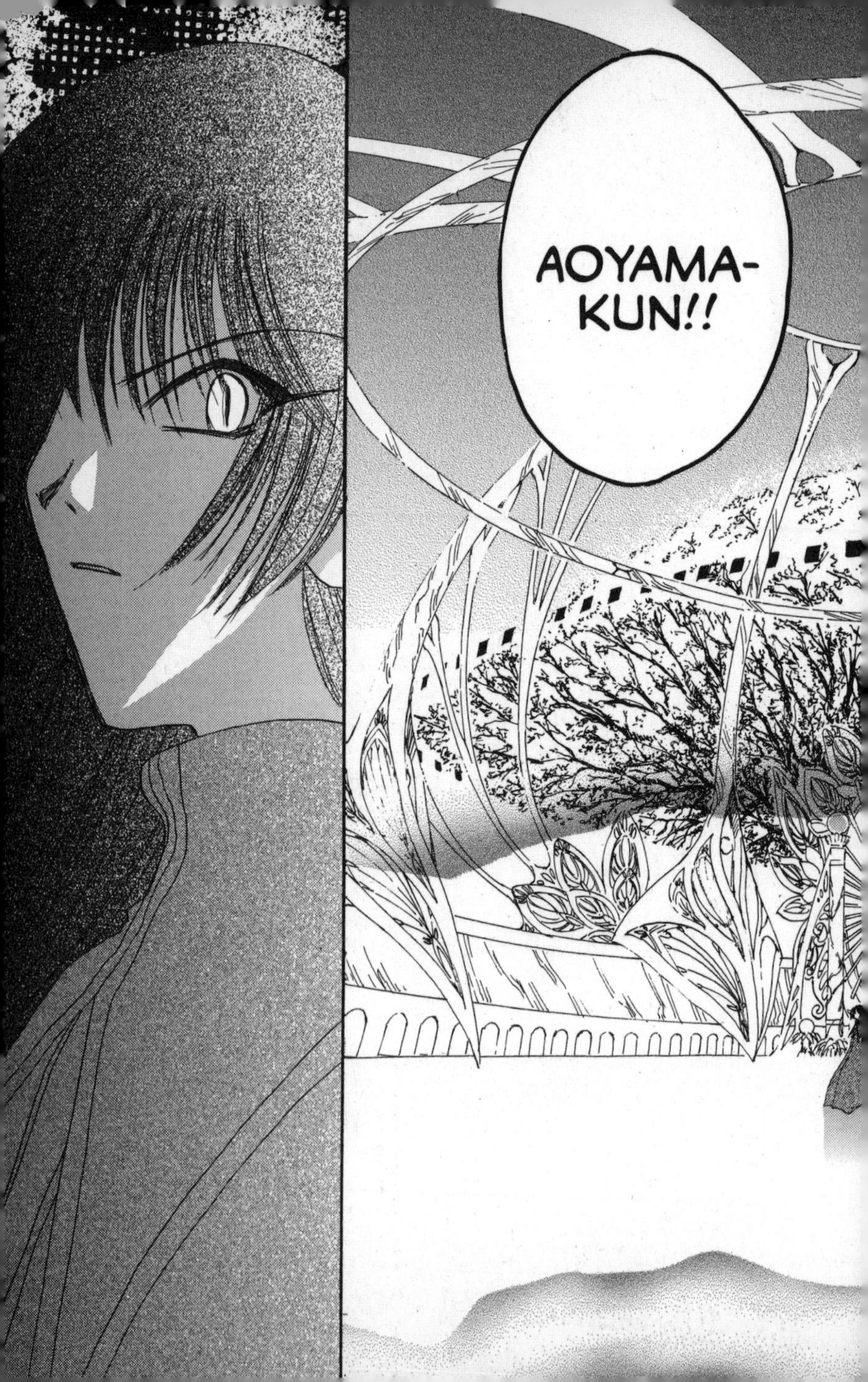
AOYAMA-KUN!!

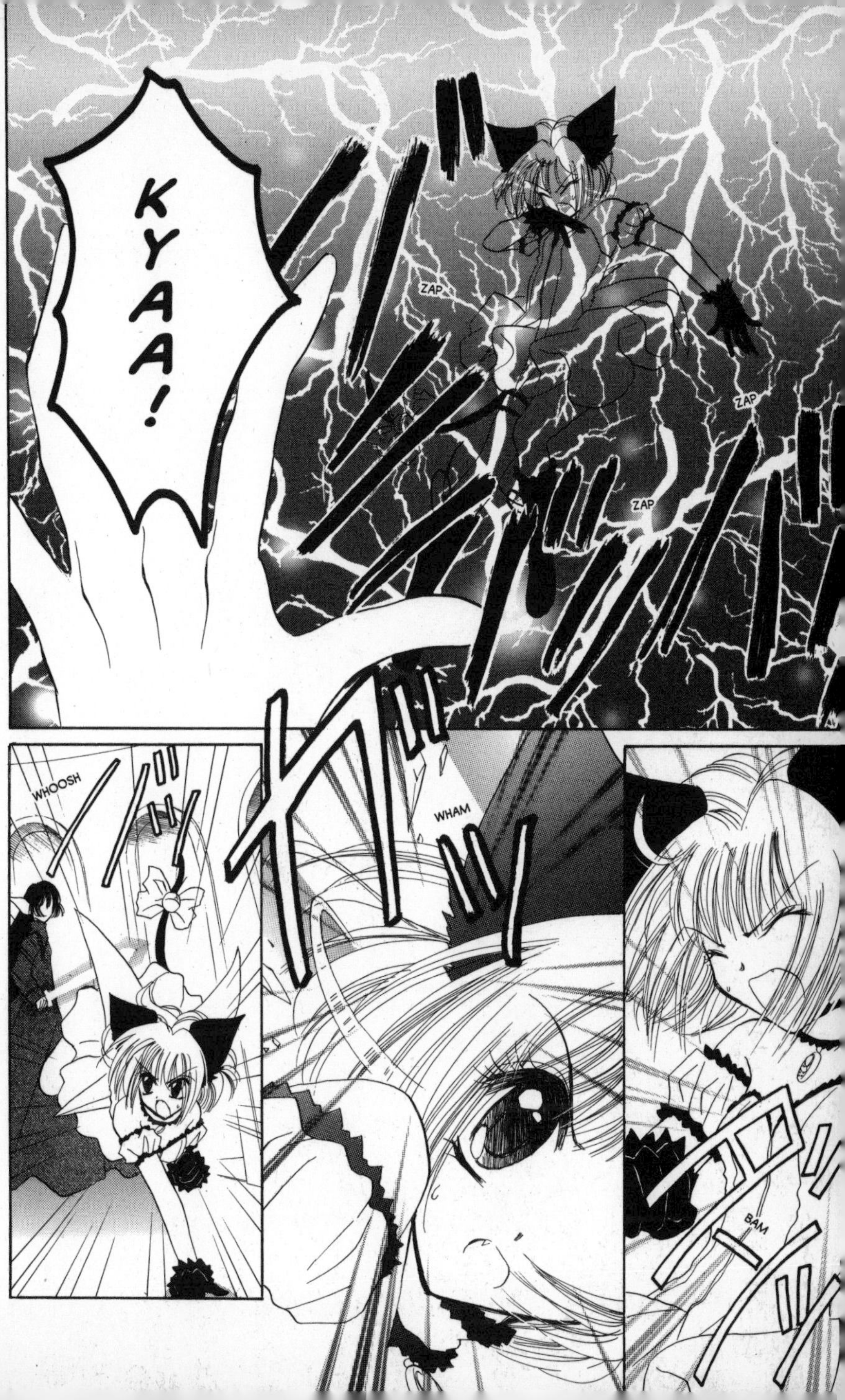
KYAA!
ZAP
ZAP
ZAP
BAM
WHAM
WHOOSH

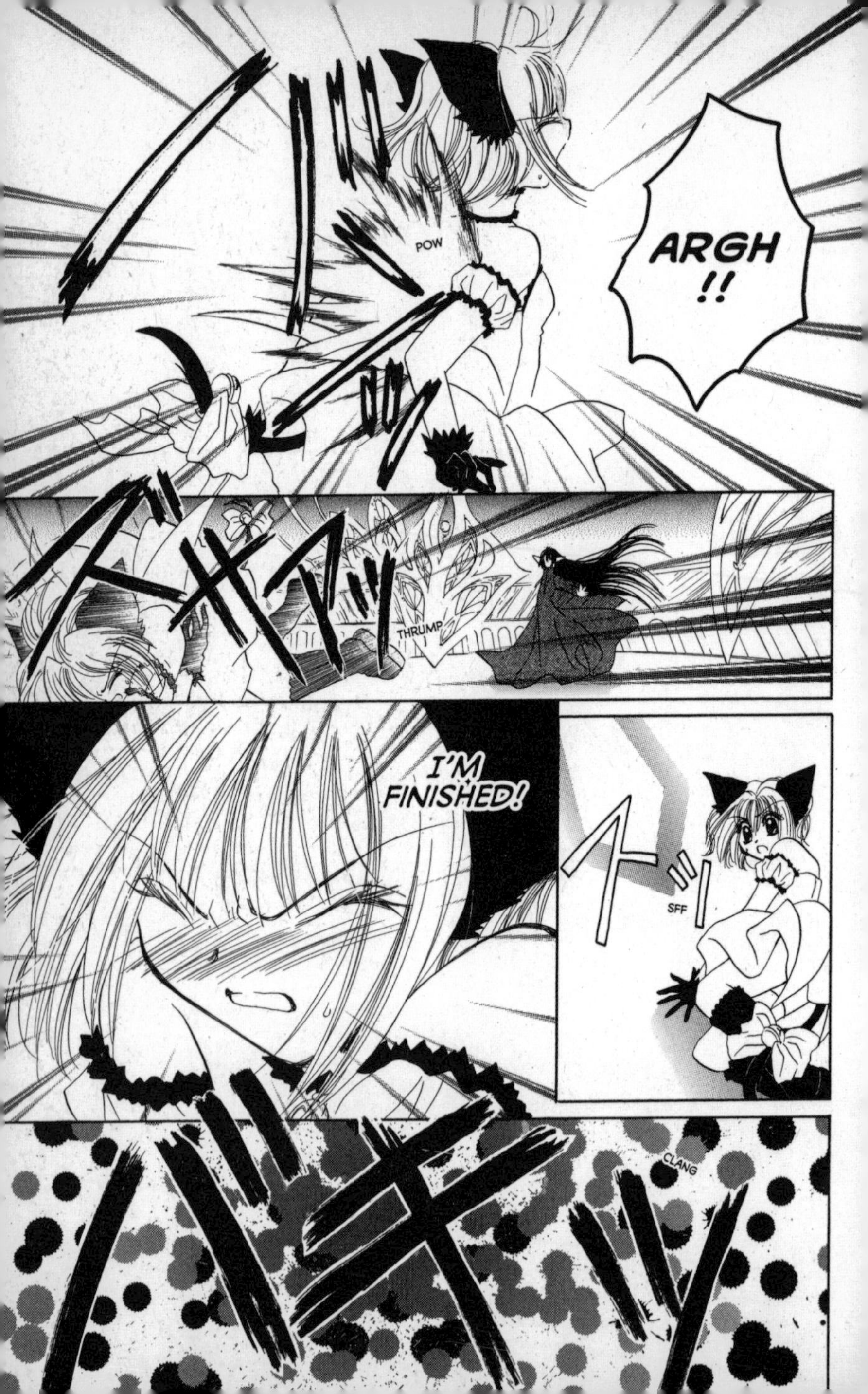
ARGH!!
POW
THRUMP
SFF
I'M FINISHED!
CLANG

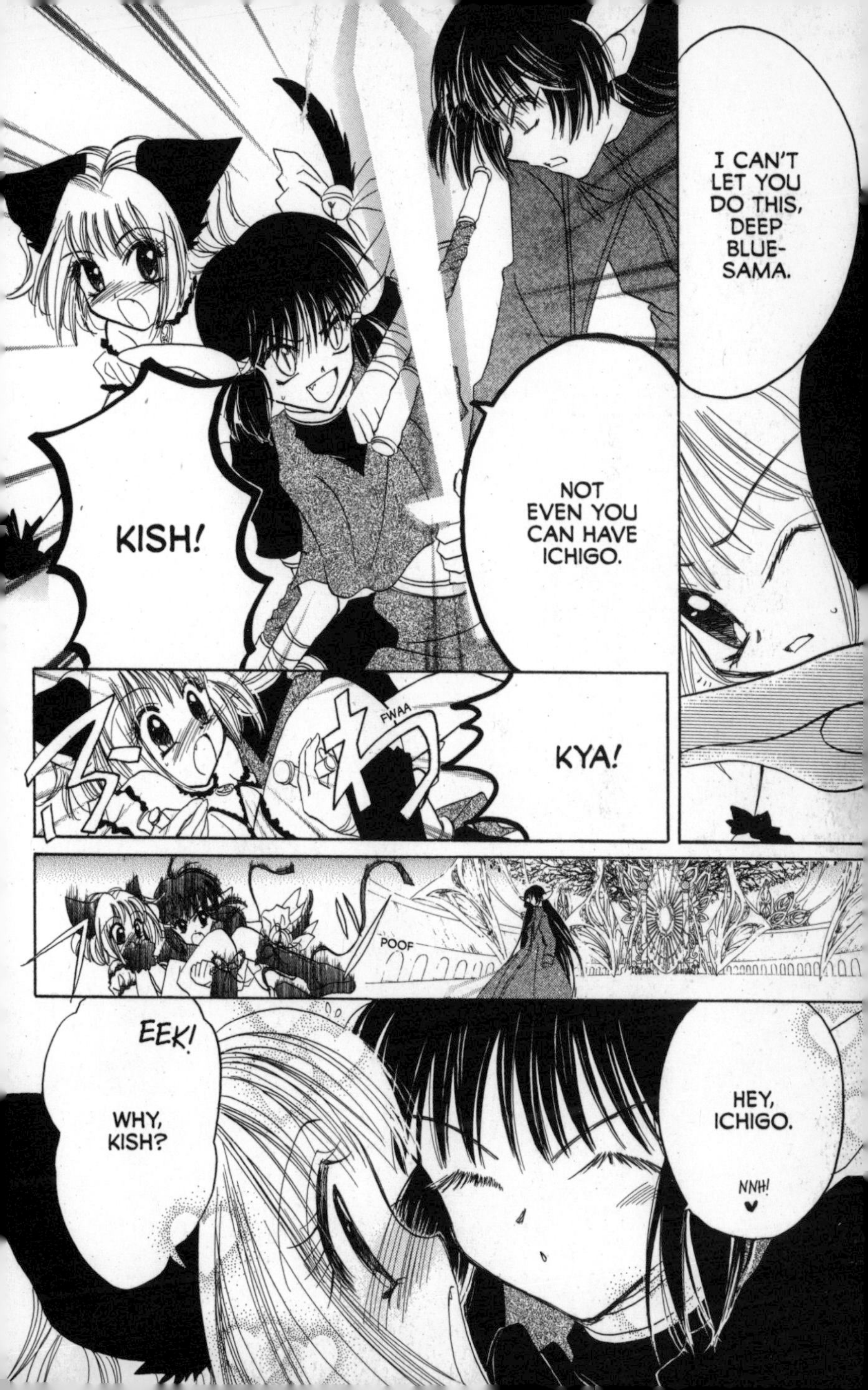
I CAN'T LET YOU DO THIS, DEEP BLUE-SAMA.
NOT EVEN YOU CAN HAVE ICHIGO.
KISH!
KYA!
FWAA
POOF
HEY, ICHIGO.
NNH!
EEK!
WHY, KISH?

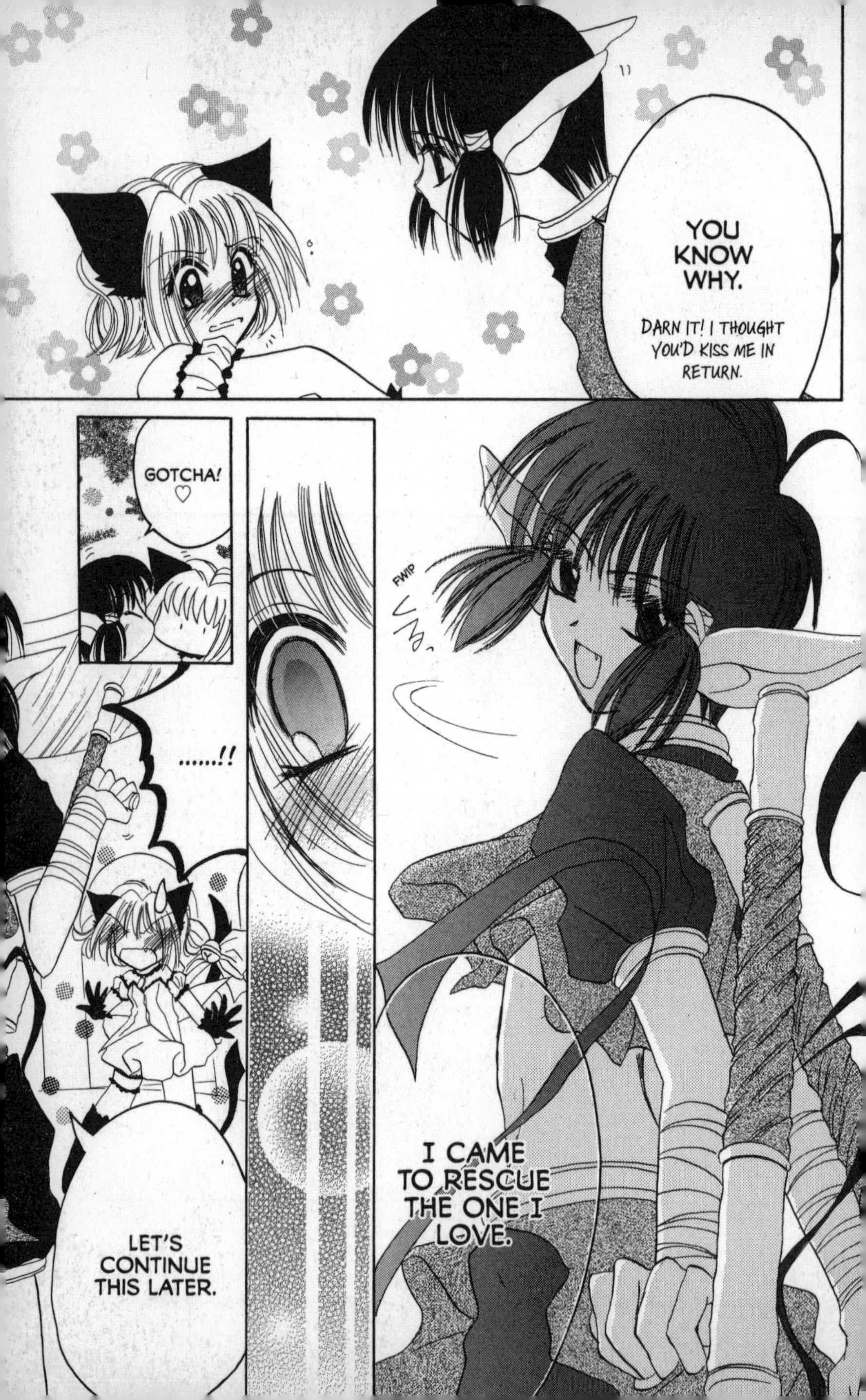
YOU KNOW WHY.
DARN IT! I THOUGHT YOU'D KISS ME IN RETURN.
FWIP
I CAME TO RESCUE THE ONE I LOVE.
GOTCHA! ♡
......!!
LET'S CONTINUE THIS LATER.

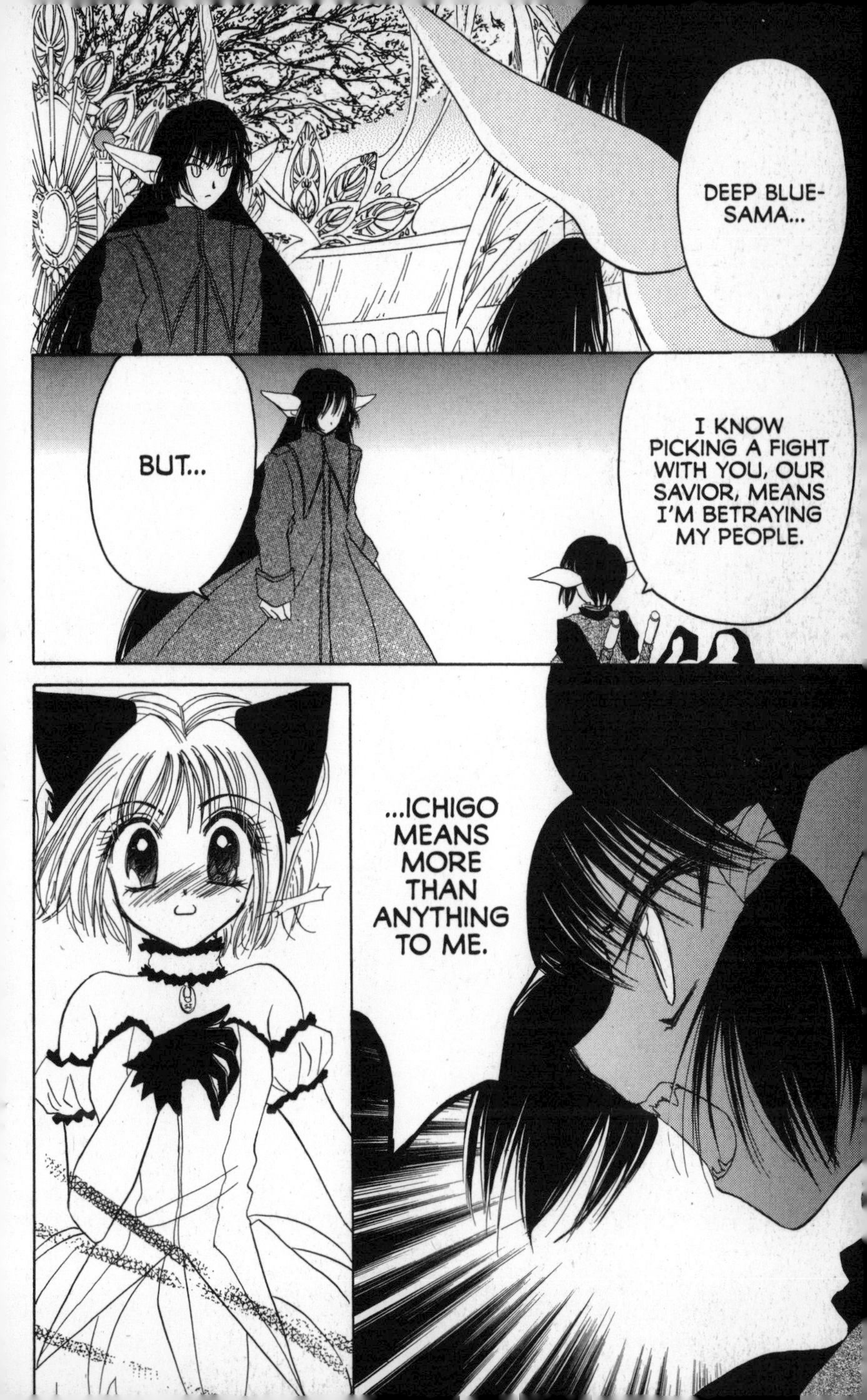
DEEP BLUE-SAMA...
I KNOW PICKING A FIGHT WITH YOU, OUR SAVIOR, MEANS I'M BETRAYING MY PEOPLE.
BUT...
...ICHIGO MEANS MORE THAN ANYTHING TO ME.

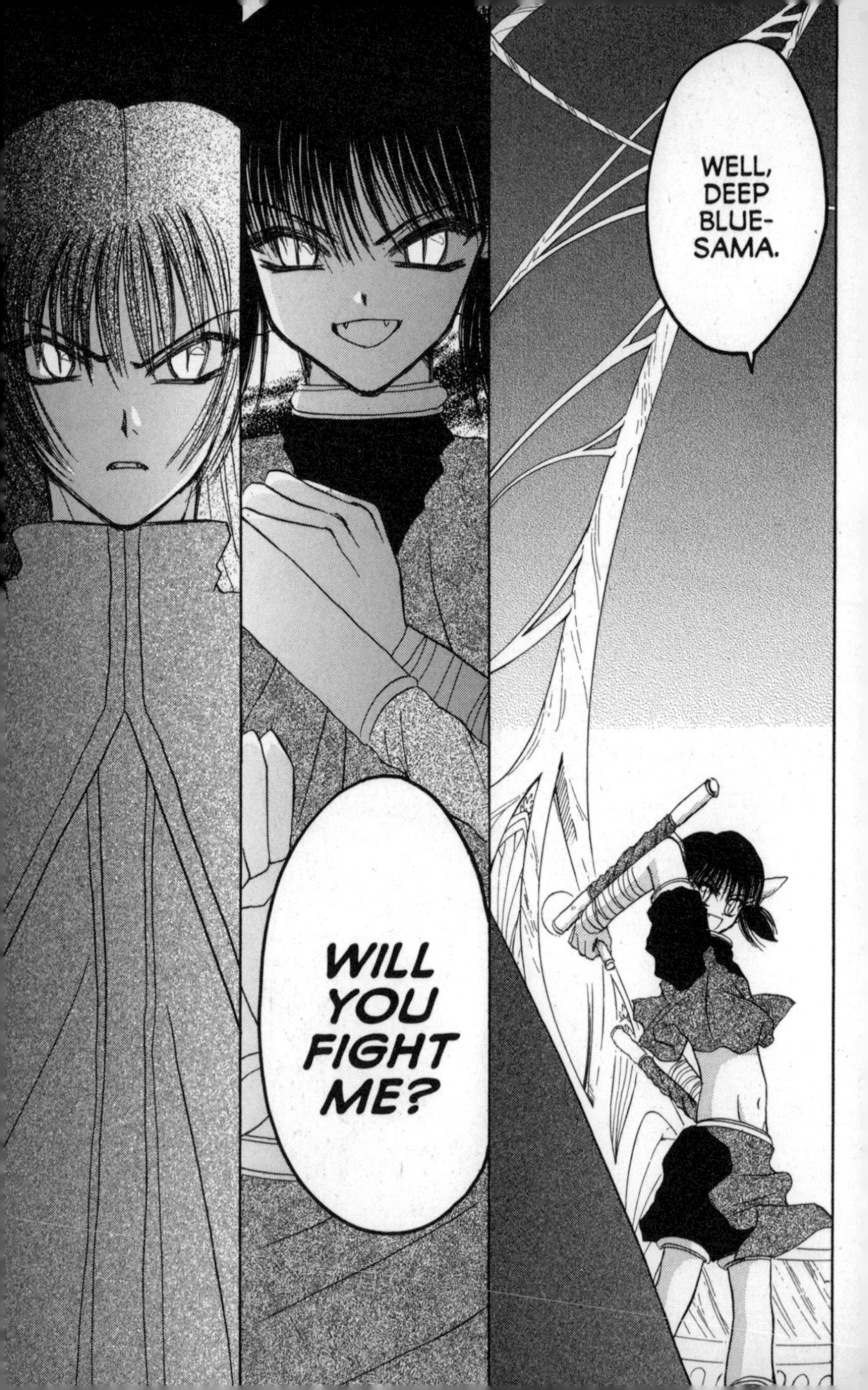
WELL, DEEP BLUE-SAMA.
WILL YOU FIGHT ME?

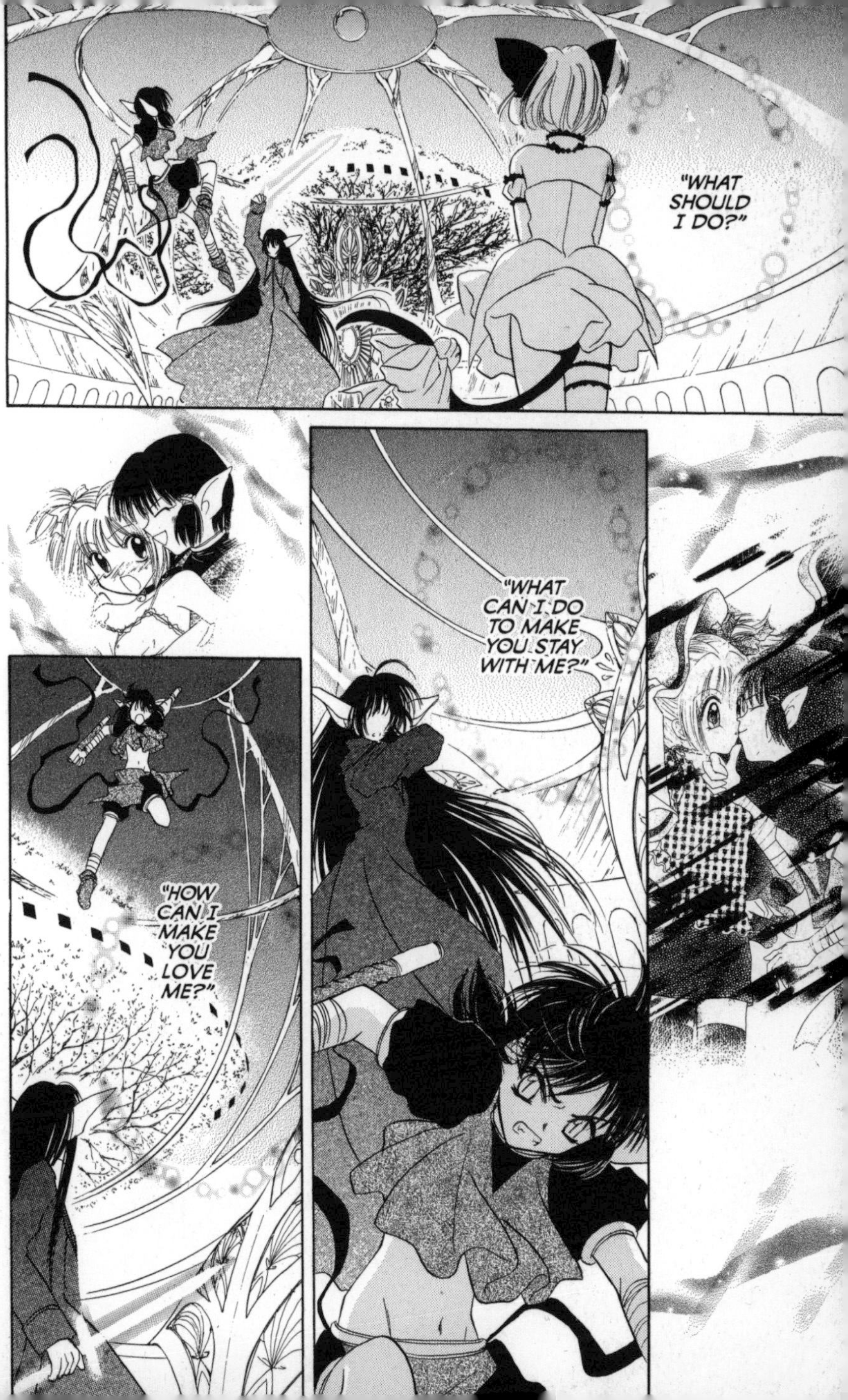
"WHAT SHOULD I DO?"
"WHAT CAN I DO TO MAKE YOU STAY WITH ME?"
"HOW CAN I MAKE YOU LOVE ME?"

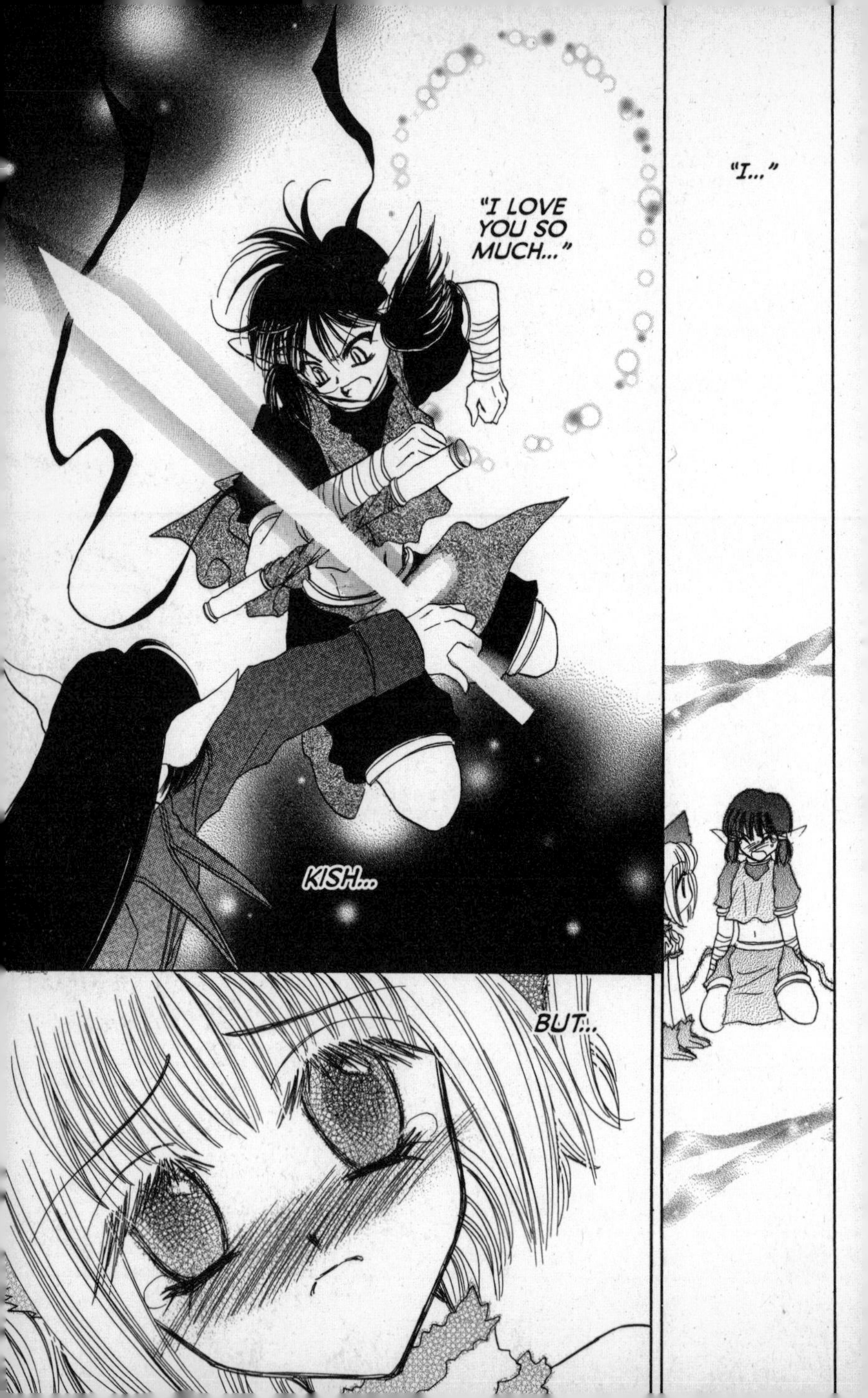
"I..."
"I LOVE YOU SO MUCH..."
KISH...
BUT...

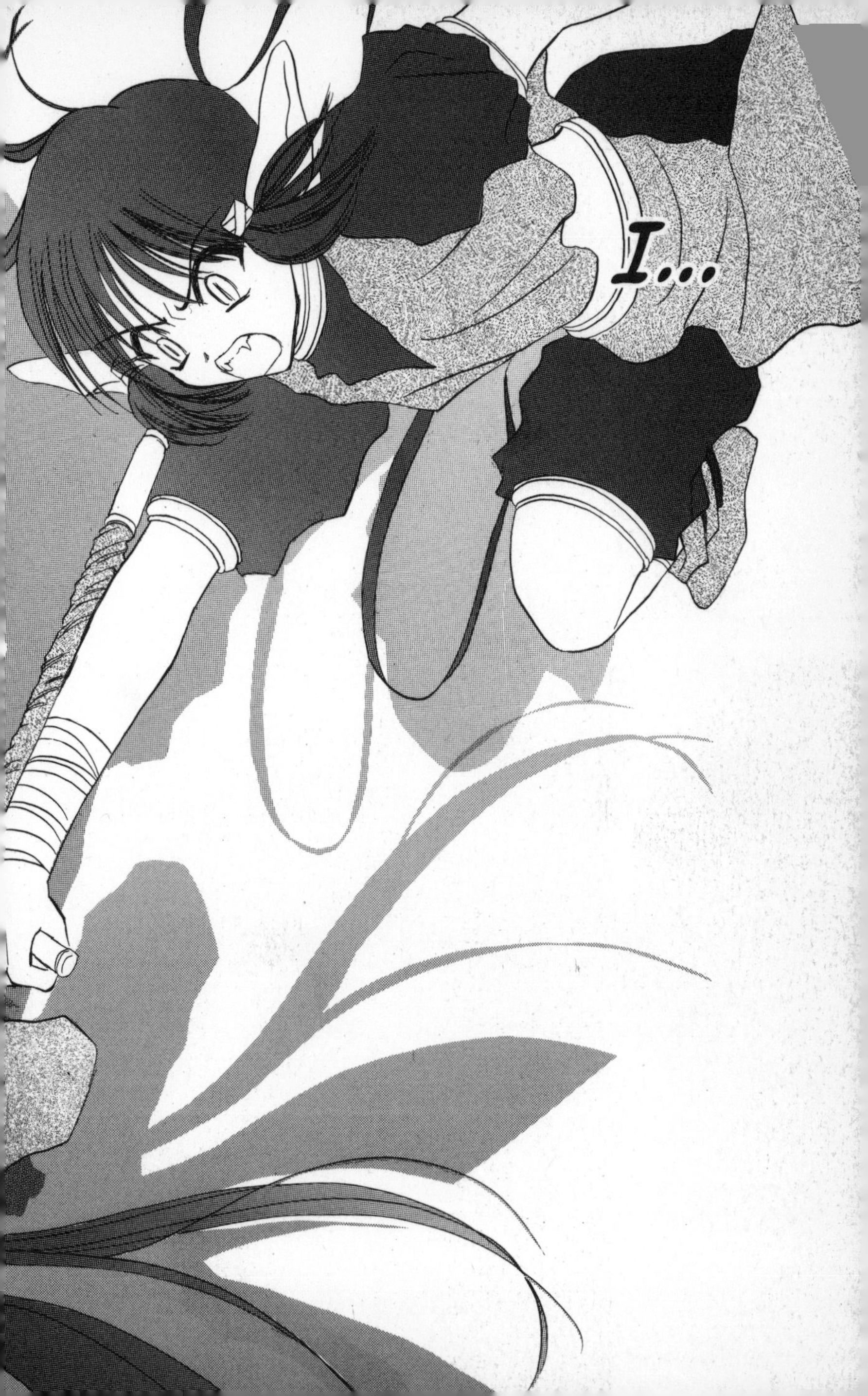
I...

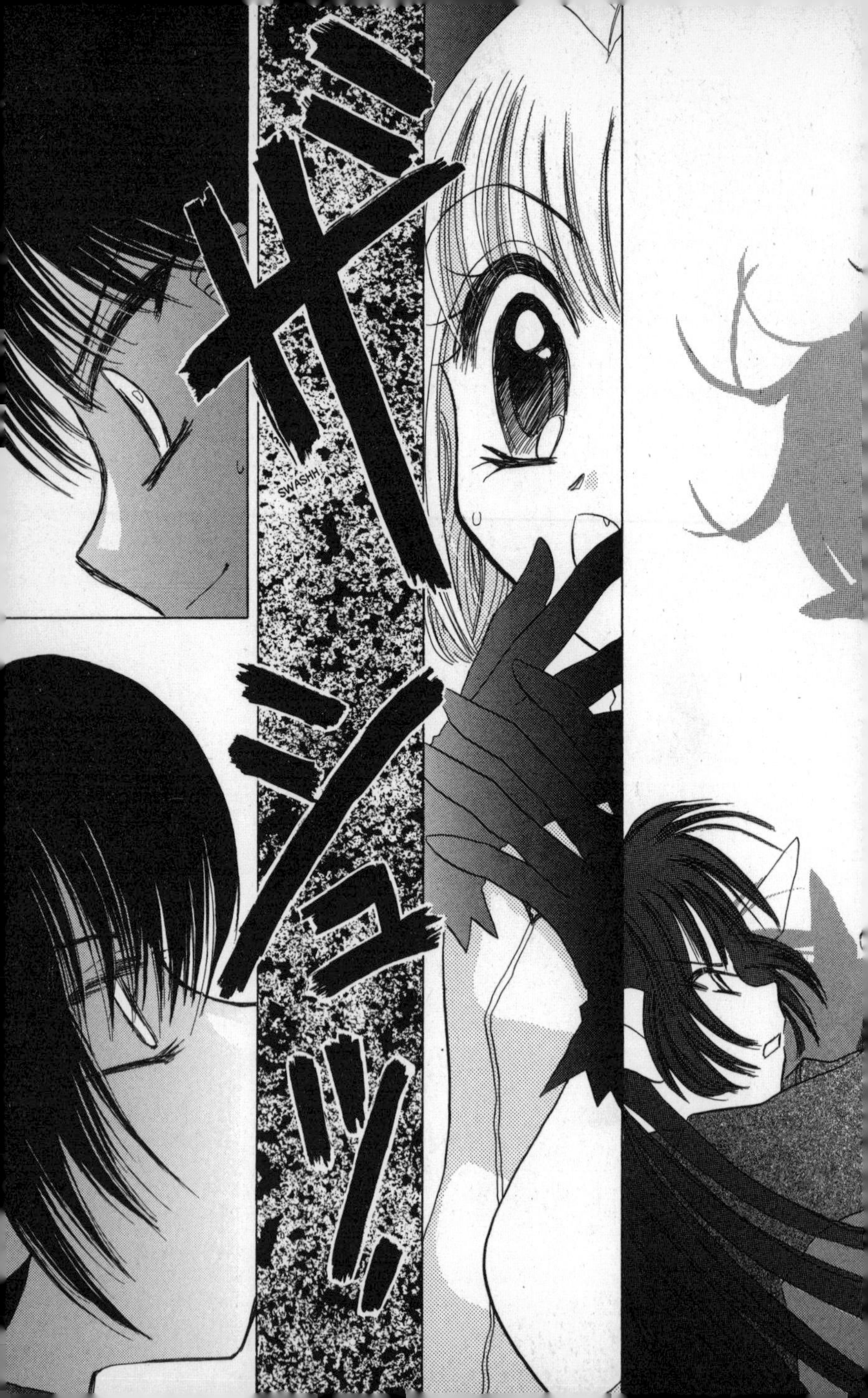
SWASHH

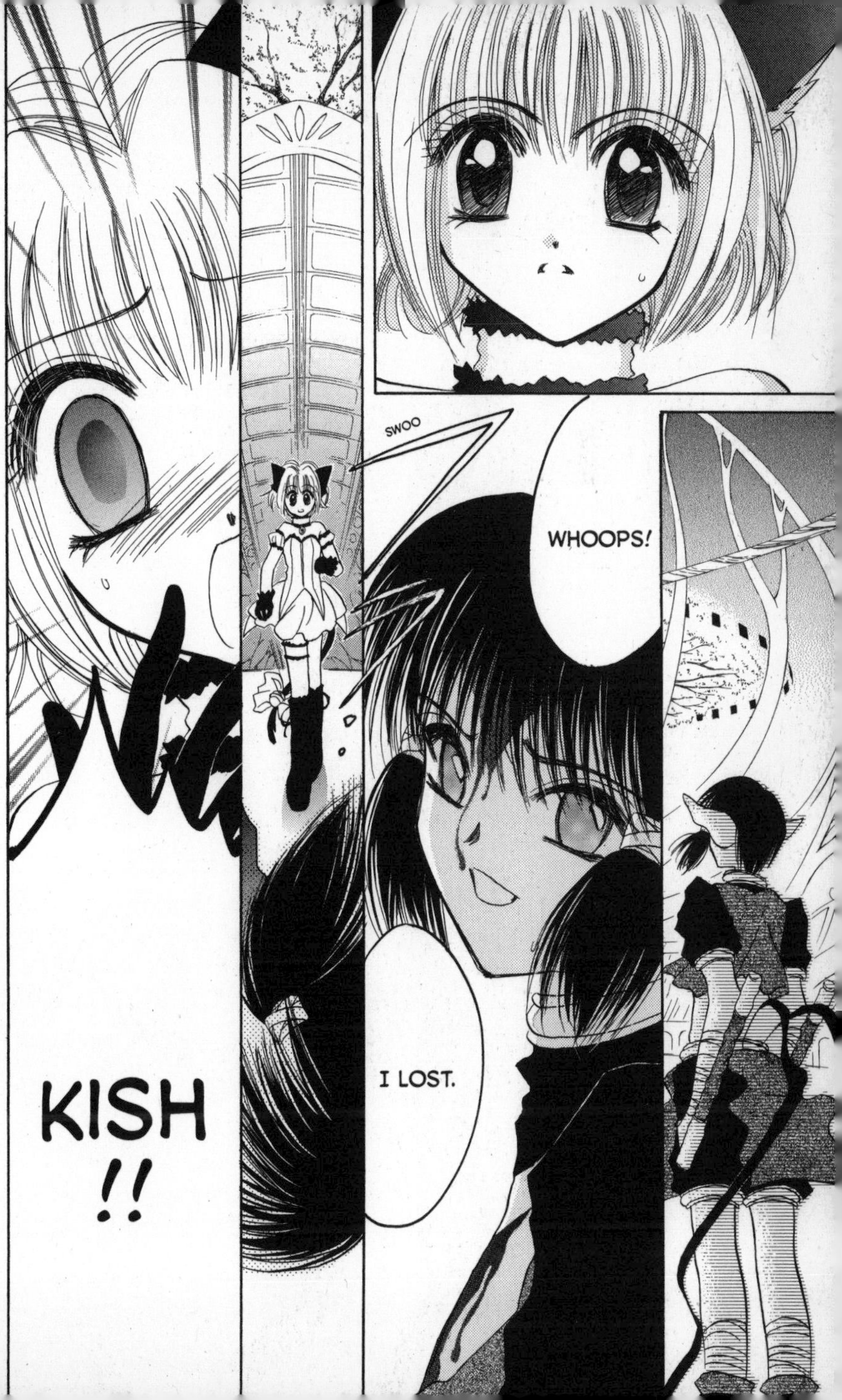
WHOOPS!
SWOO
I LOST.
KISH !!

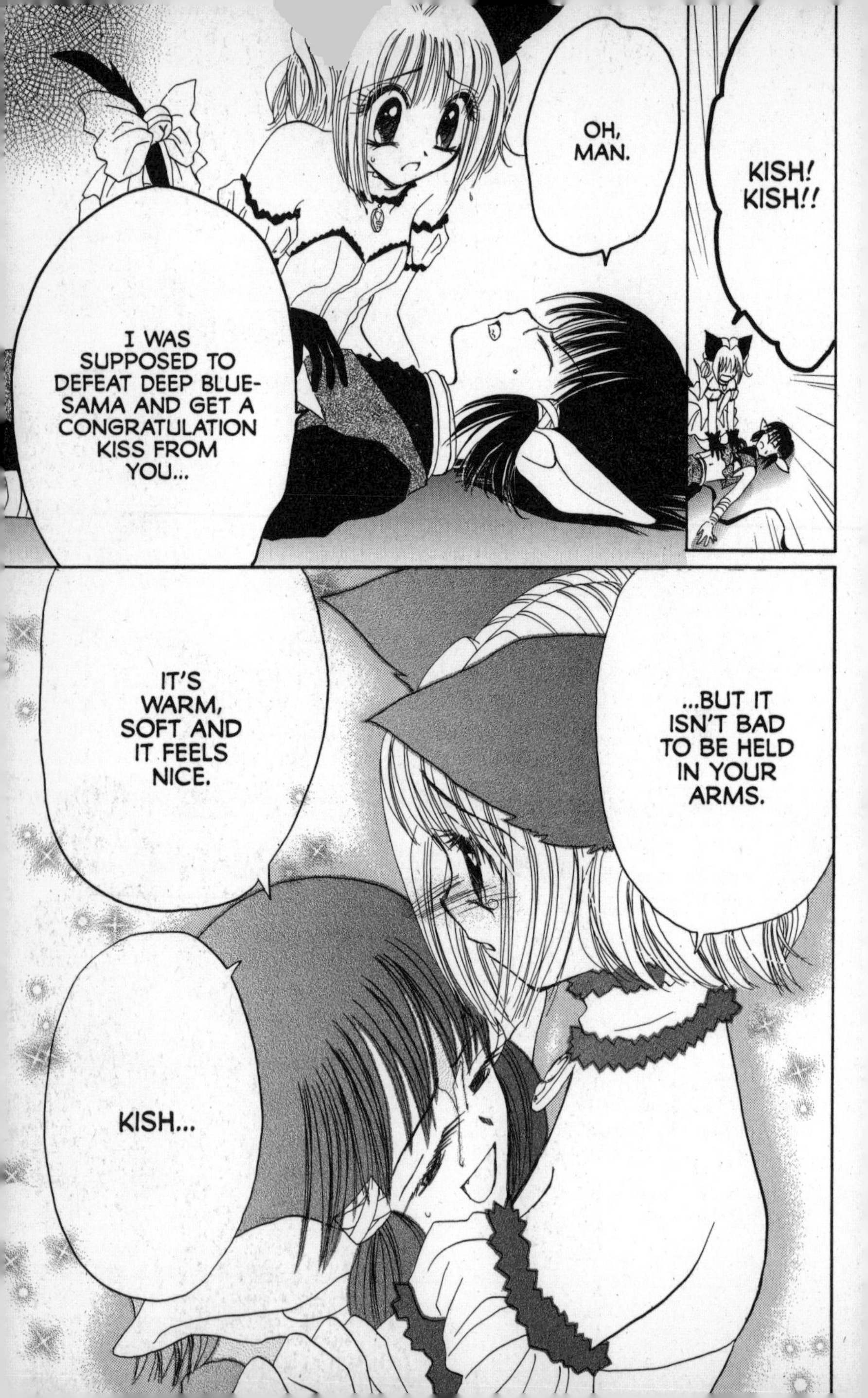
KISH! KISH!!
OH, MAN.
I WAS SUPPOSED TO DEFEAT DEEP BLUE-SAMA AND GET A CONGRATULATION KISS FROM YOU...
...BUT IT ISN'T BAD TO BE HELD IN YOUR ARMS.
IT'S WARM, SOFT AND IT FEELS NICE.
KISH...

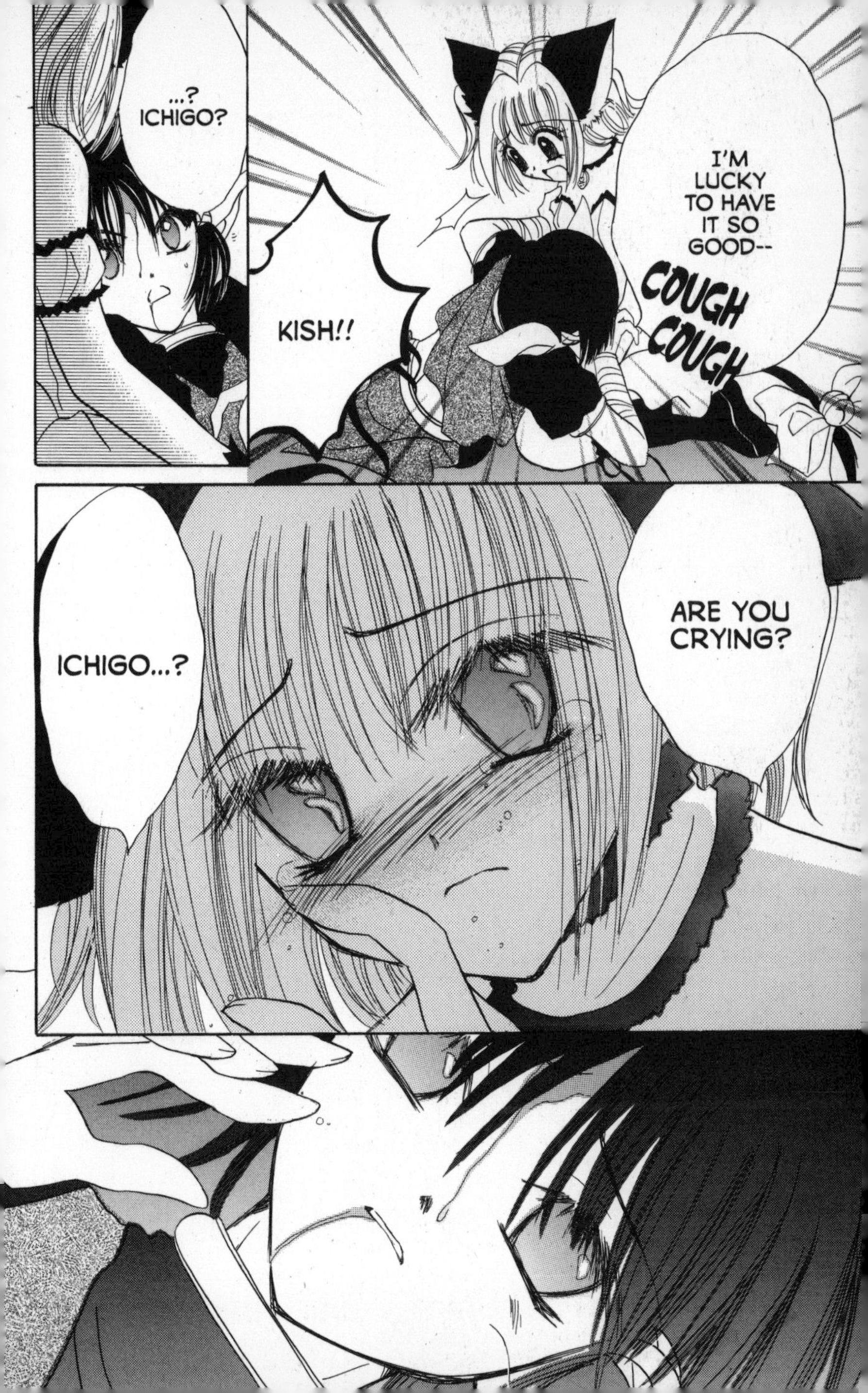
I'M LUCKY TO HAVE IT SO GOOD--
COUGH COUGH
KISH!!
...? ICHIGO?
ARE YOU CRYING?
ICHIGO...?

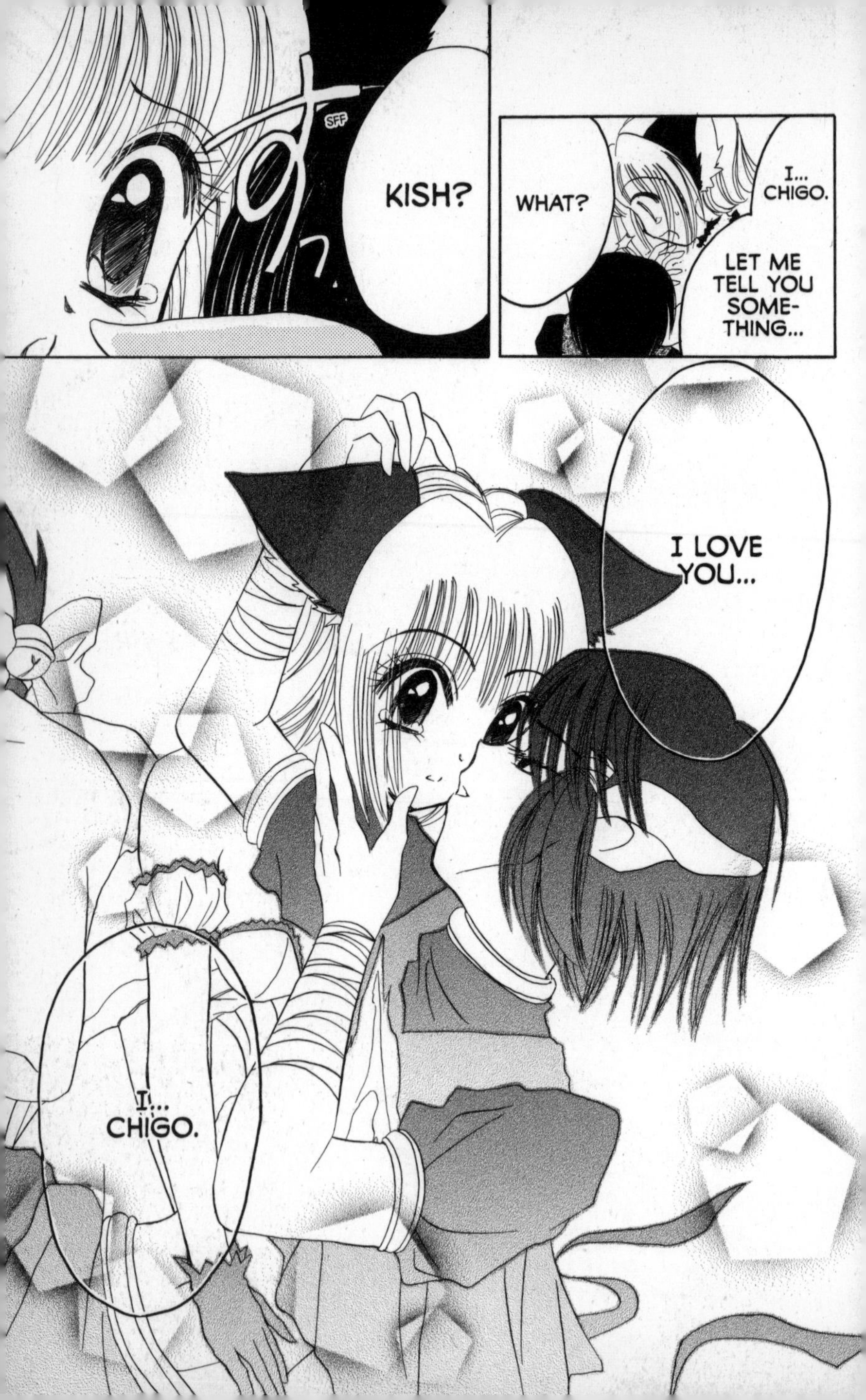
I... CHIGO.
LET ME TELL YOU SOME-THING...
WHAT?
SFF
KISH?
I LOVE YOU...
I... CHIGO.

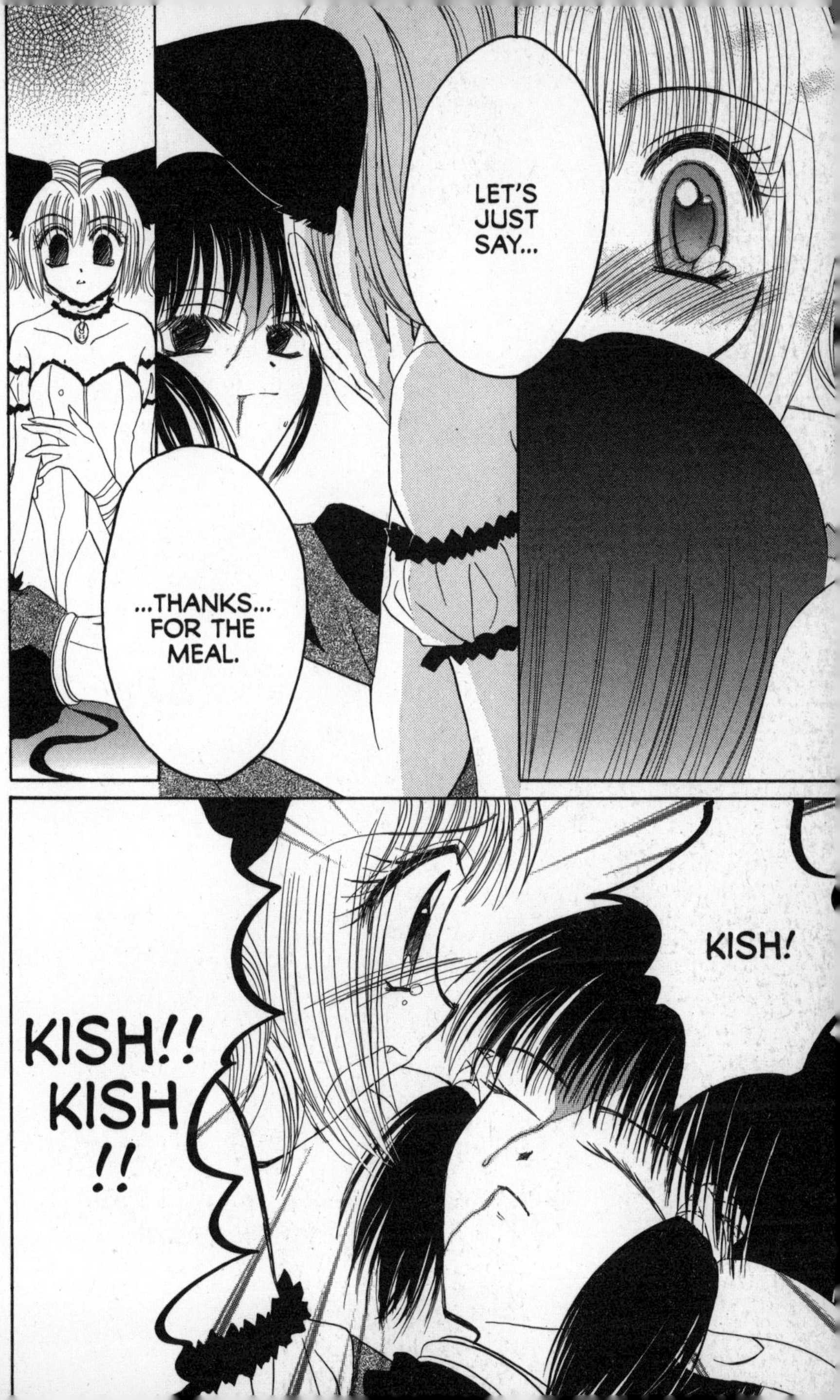
LET'S JUST SAY...
...THANKS... FOR THE MEAL.
KISH!
KISH!! KISH !!

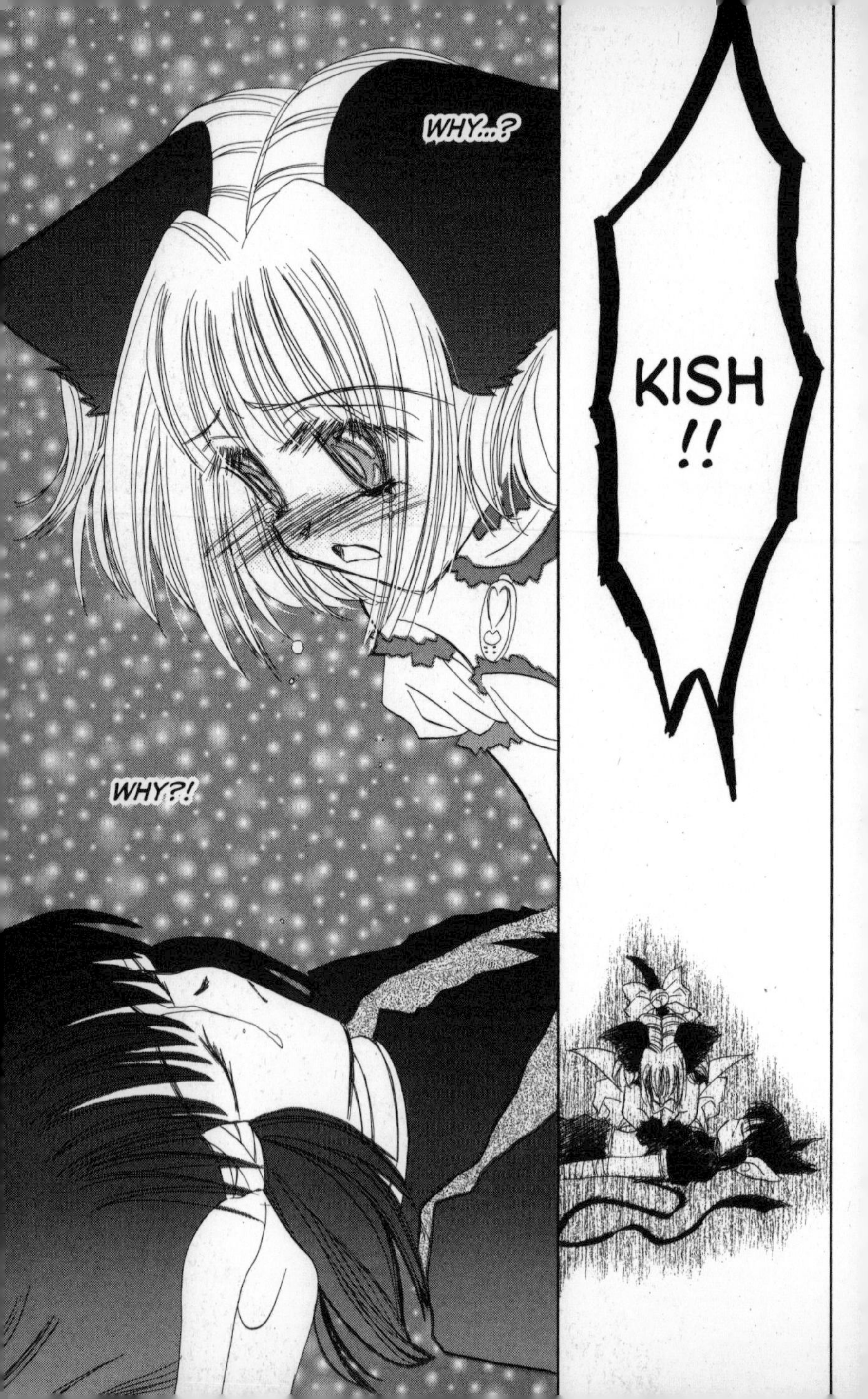
KISH!!
WHY...?
WHY?!

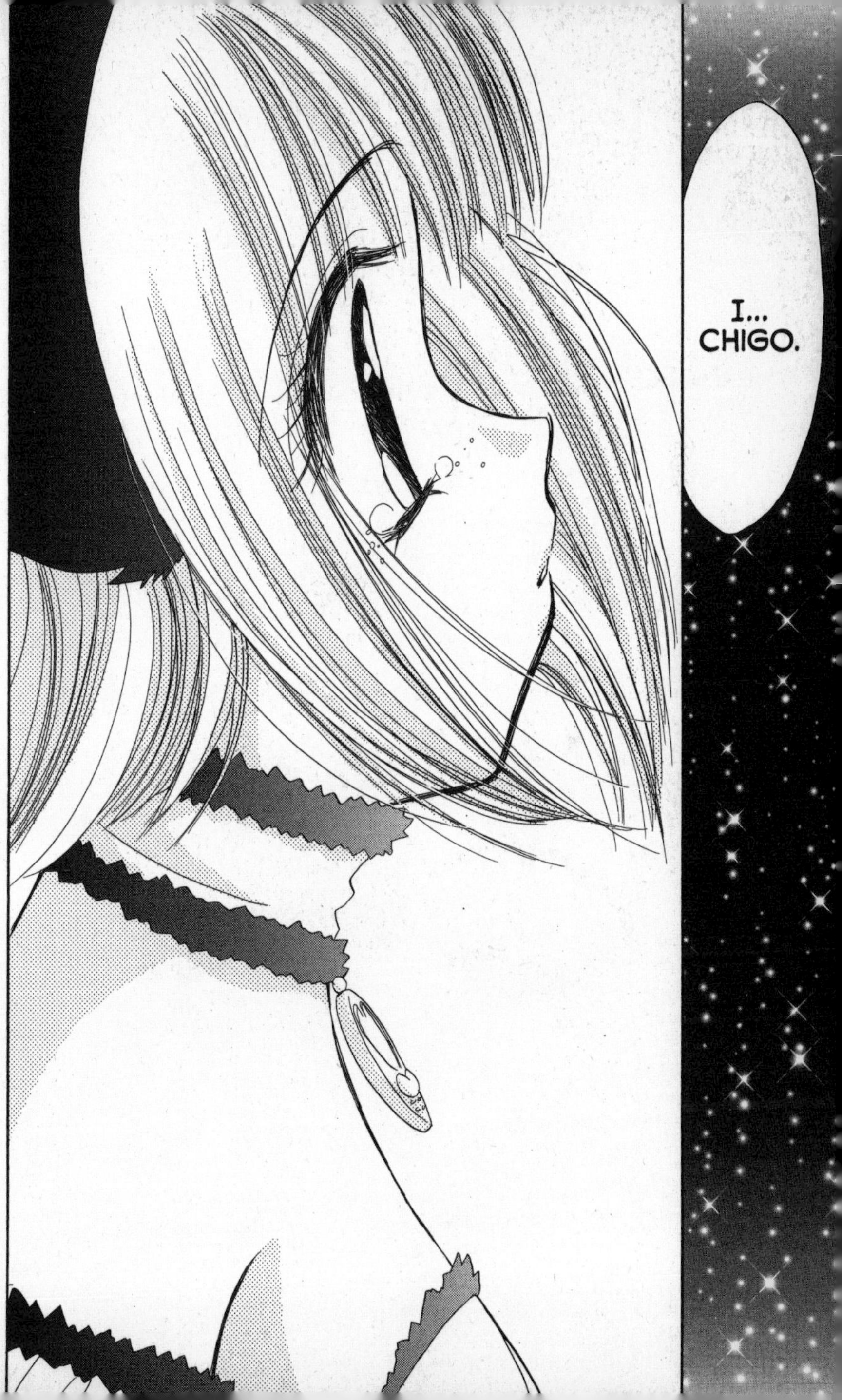
I... CHIGO.

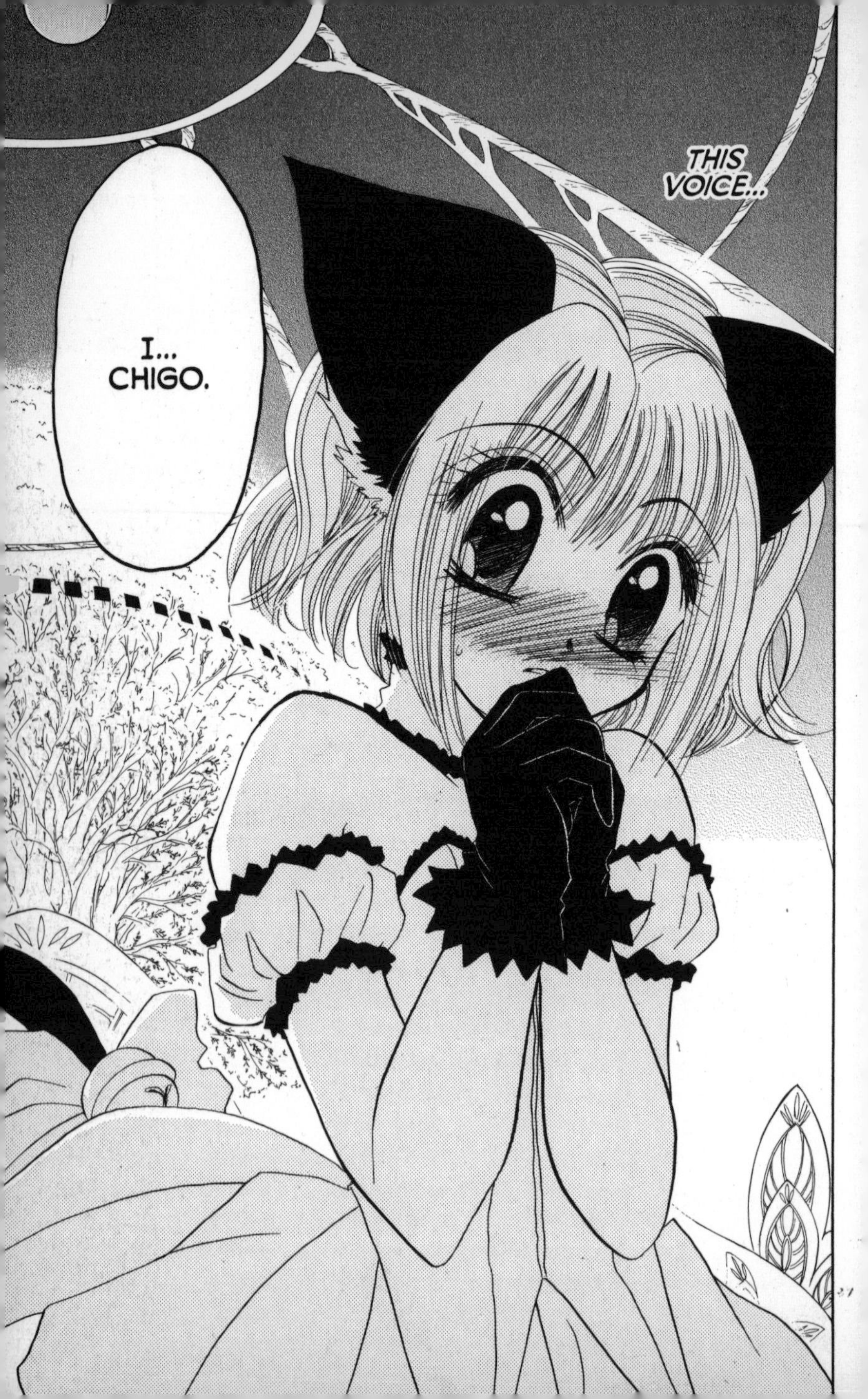
THIS VOICE...
I... CHIGO.

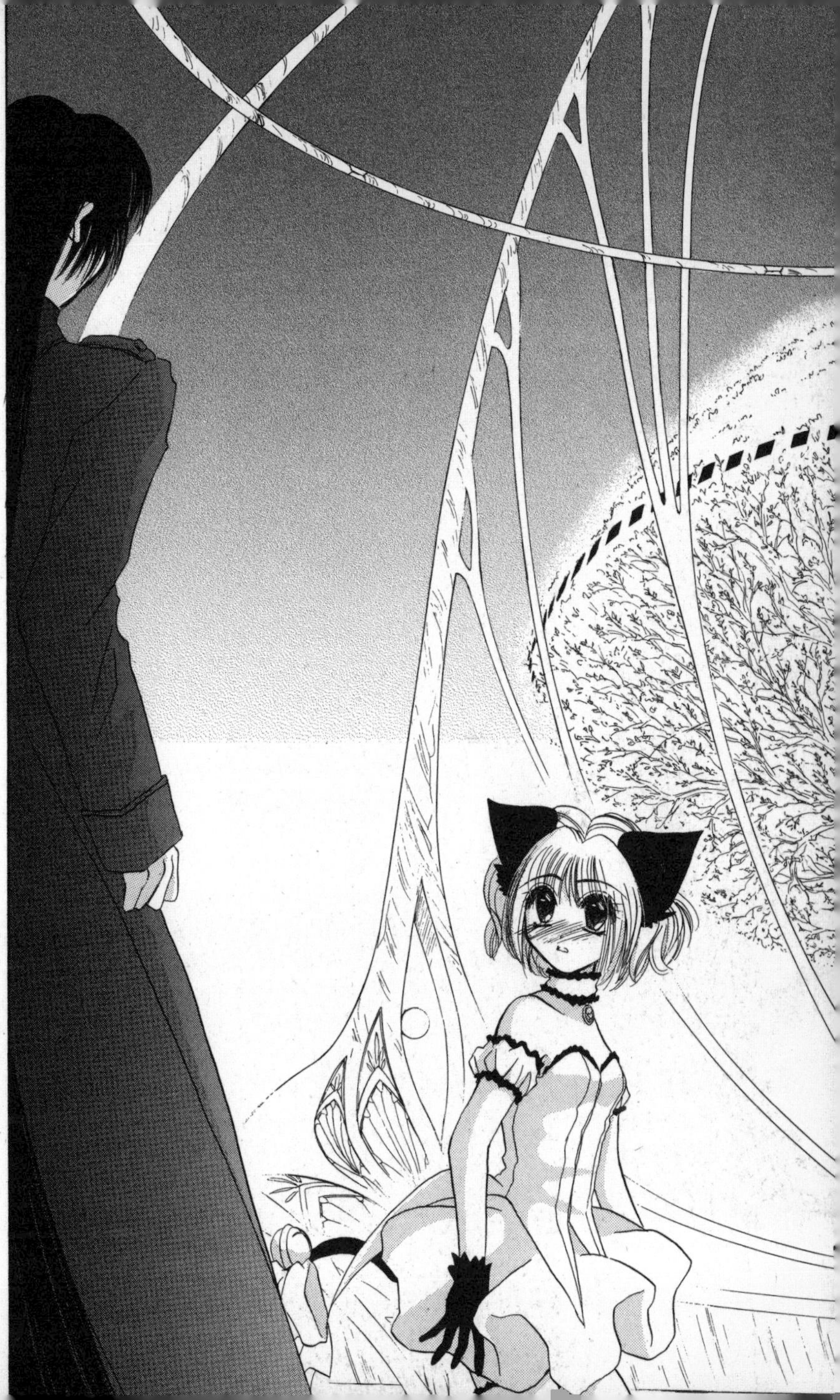

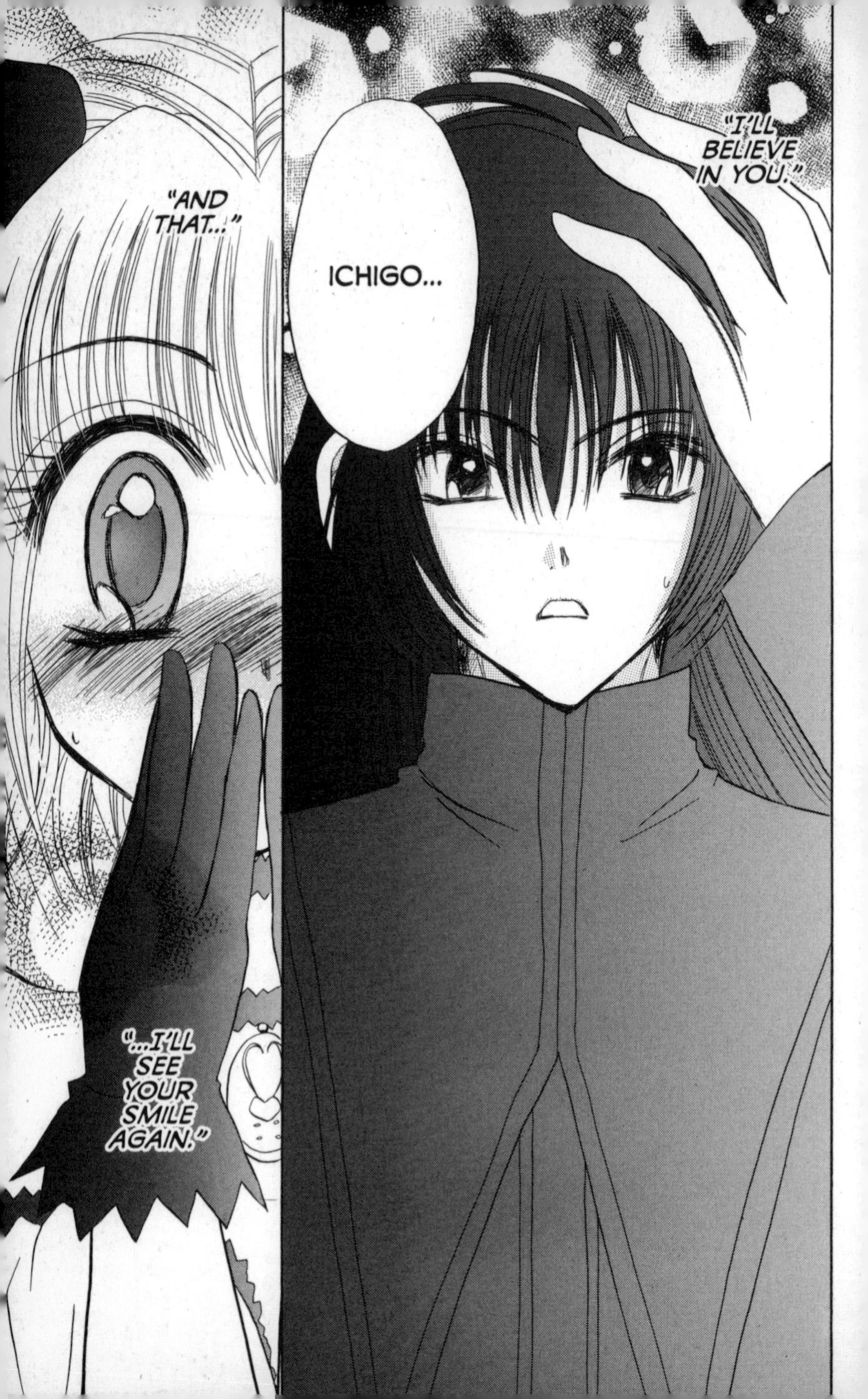
"I'LL BELIEVE IN YOU."
ICHIGO...
"AND THAT..."
"...I'LL SEE YOUR SMILE AGAIN."

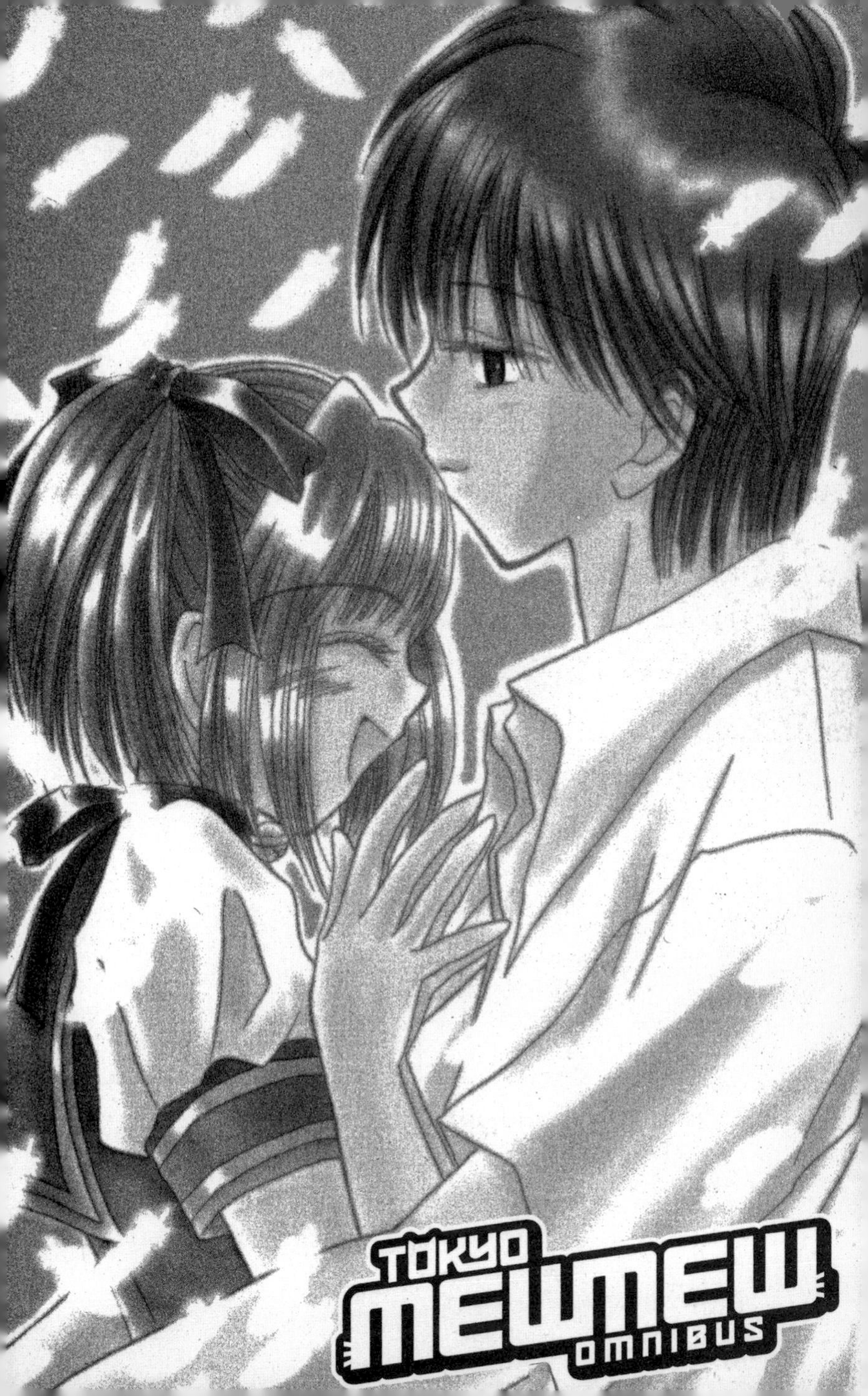
TOKYO
MEWMEW
OMNIBUS

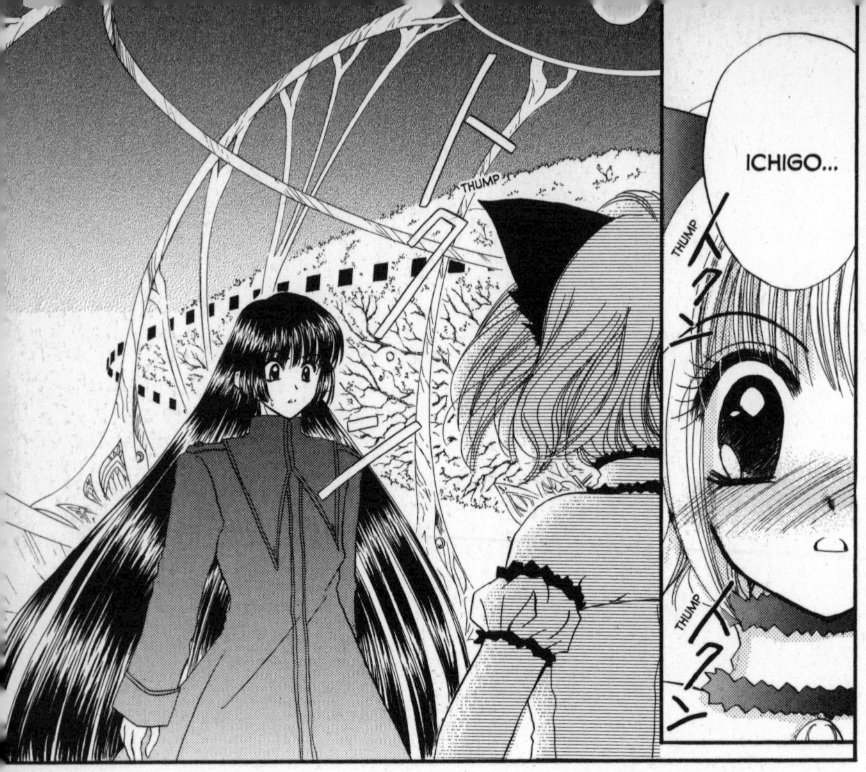
ICHIGO...
THUMP
THUMP
THUMP

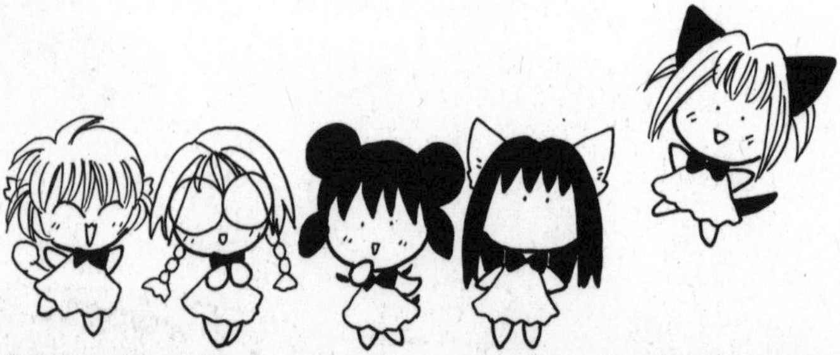

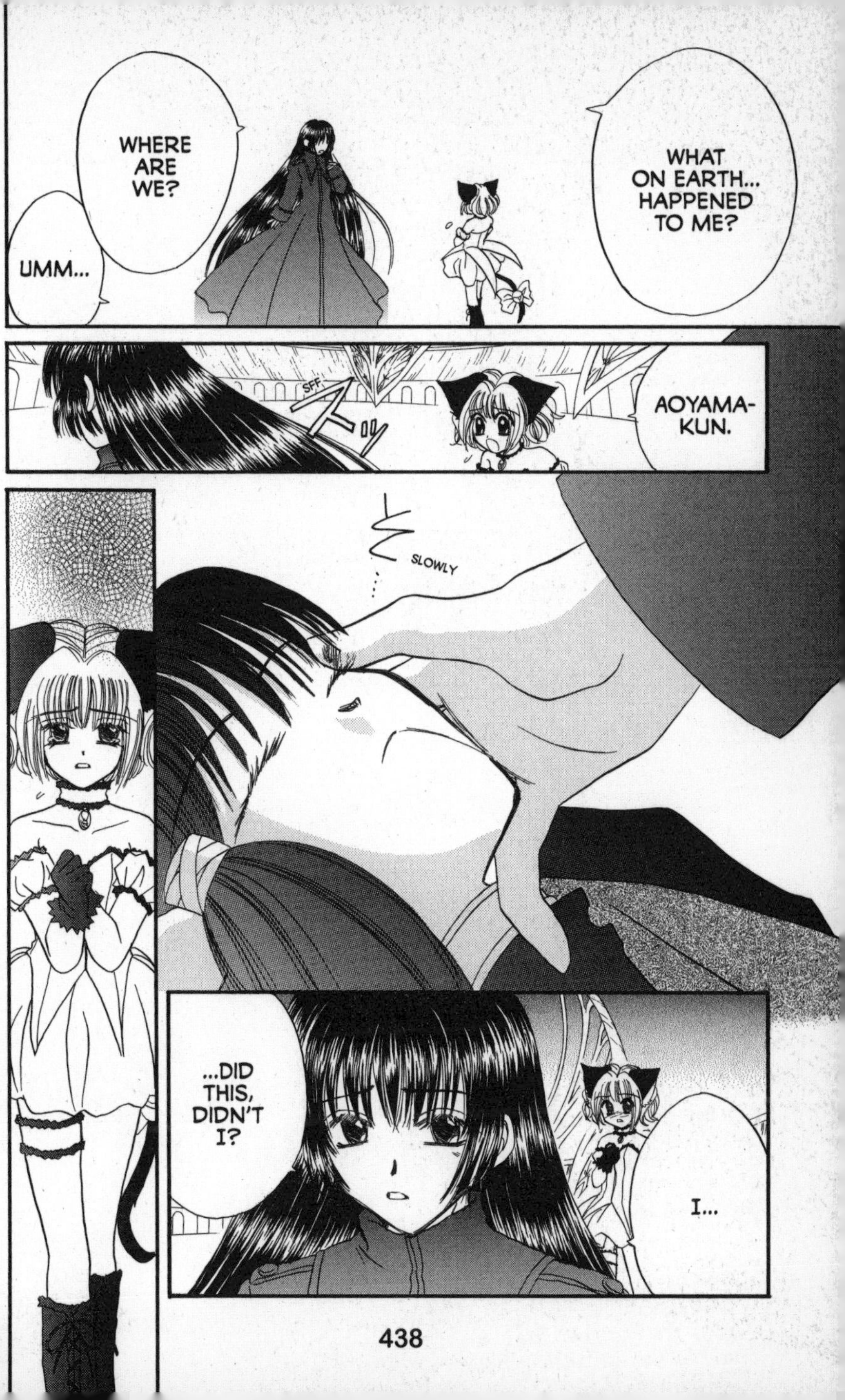
WHAT ON EARTH... HAPPENED TO ME?
WHERE ARE WE?
UMM...
AOYAMA-KUN.
SFF
SLOWLY
I...
...DID THIS, DIDN'T I?

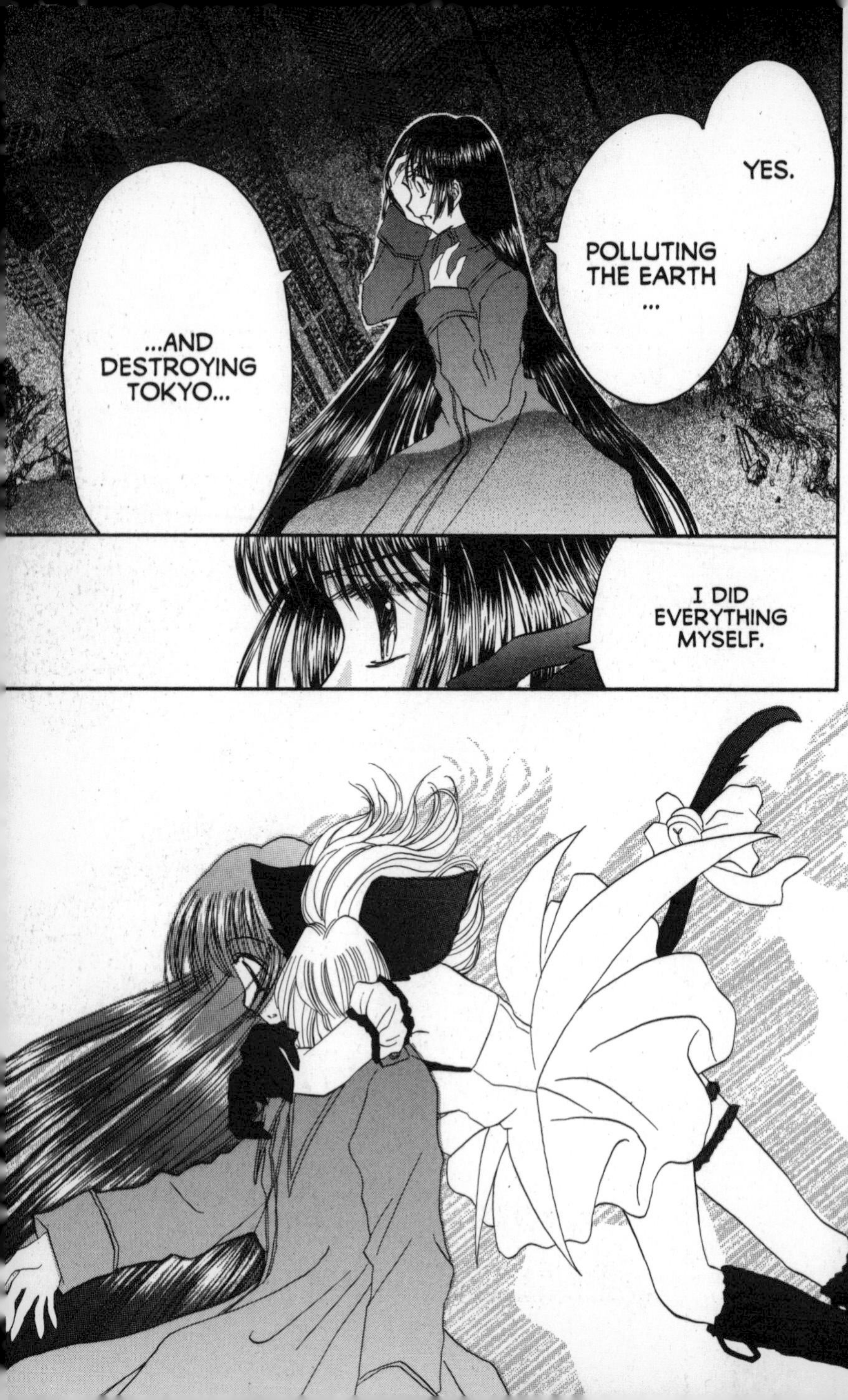
YES.
POLLUTING THE EARTH ...
...AND DESTROYING TOKYO...
I DID EVERYTHING MYSELF.

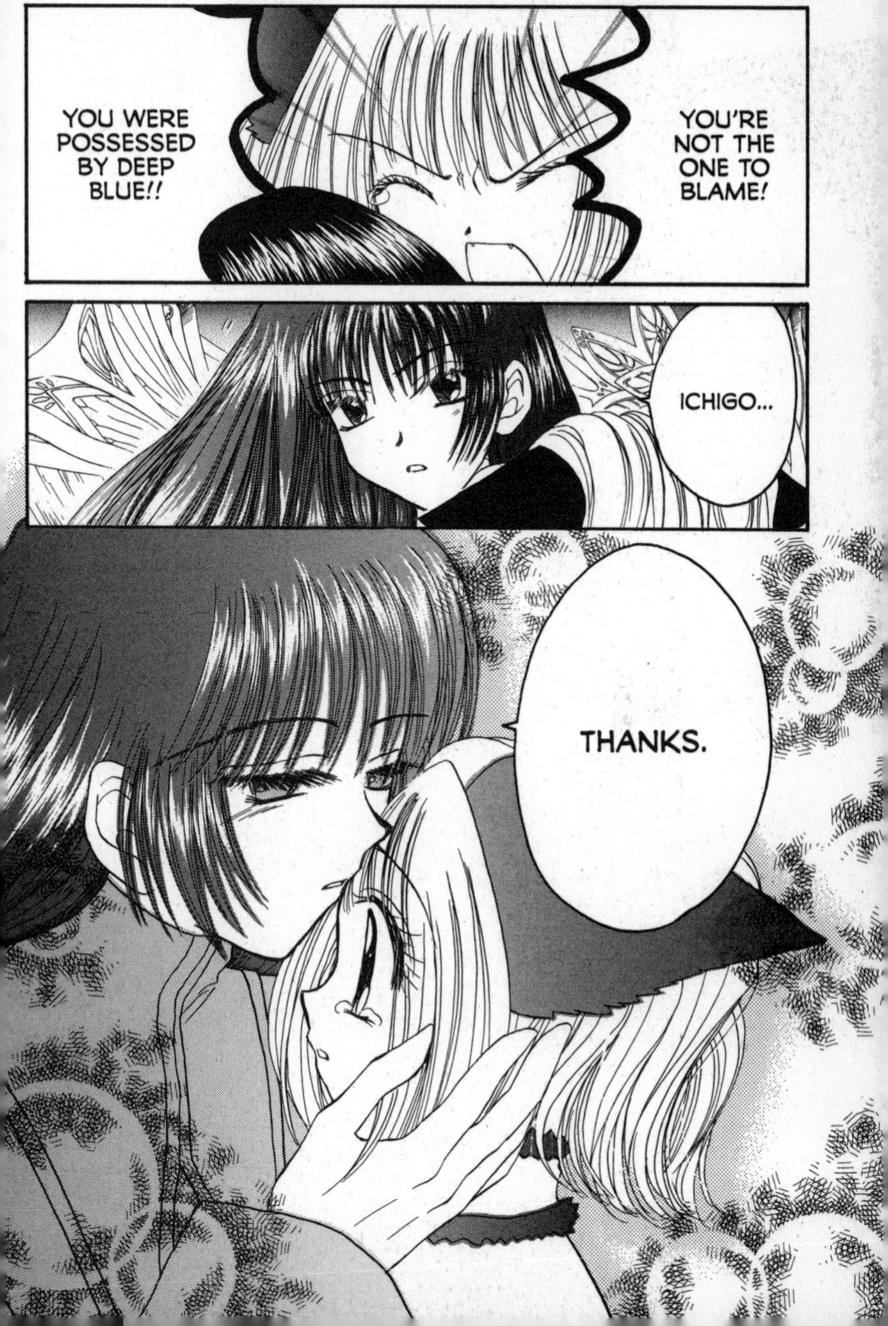
YOU'RE NOT THE ONE TO BLAME!
YOU WERE POSSESSED BY DEEP BLUE!!
ICHIGO...
THANKS.

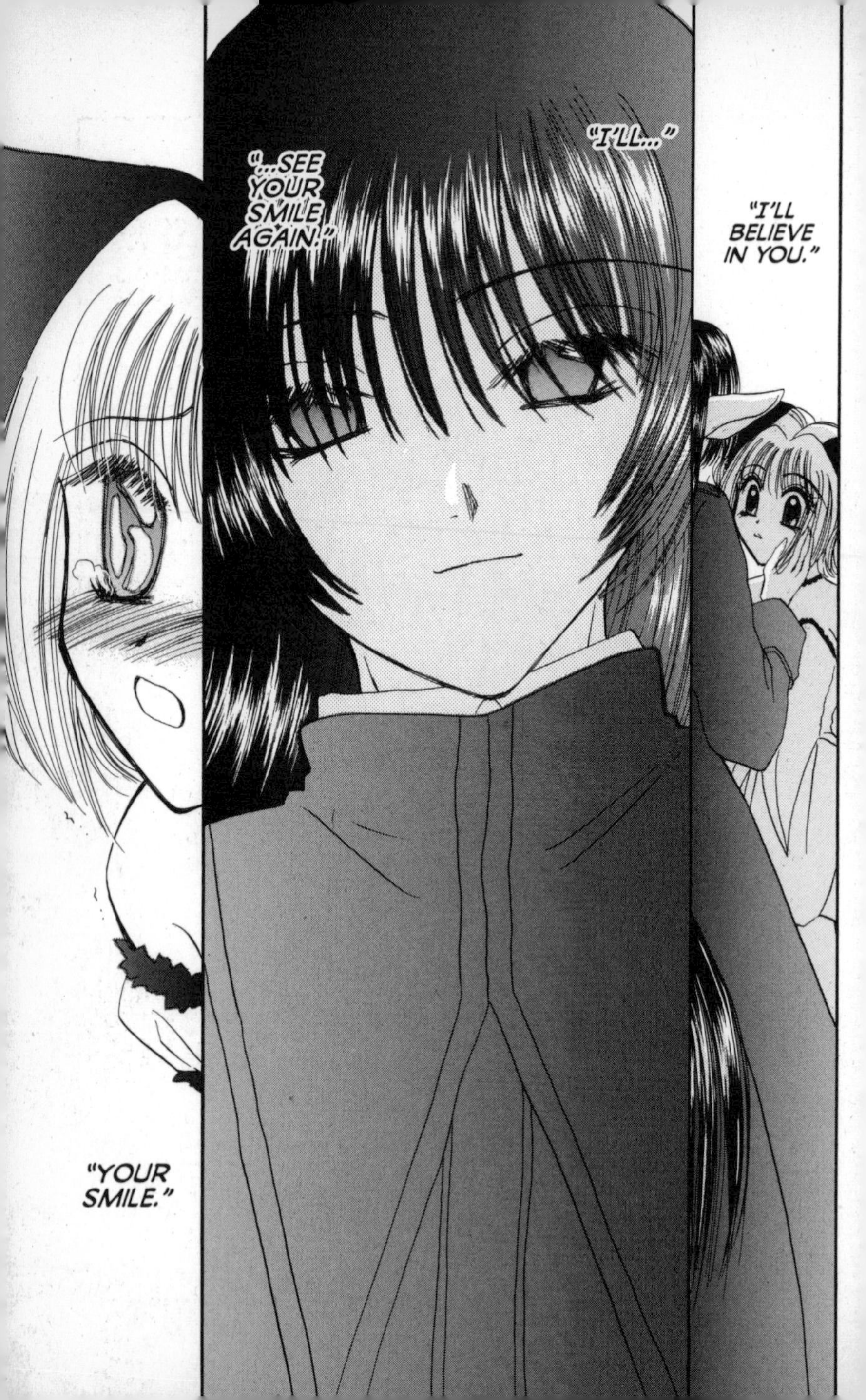
"I'LL BELIEVE IN YOU."
"I'LL..."
"...SEE YOUR SMILE AGAIN."
"YOUR SMILE."

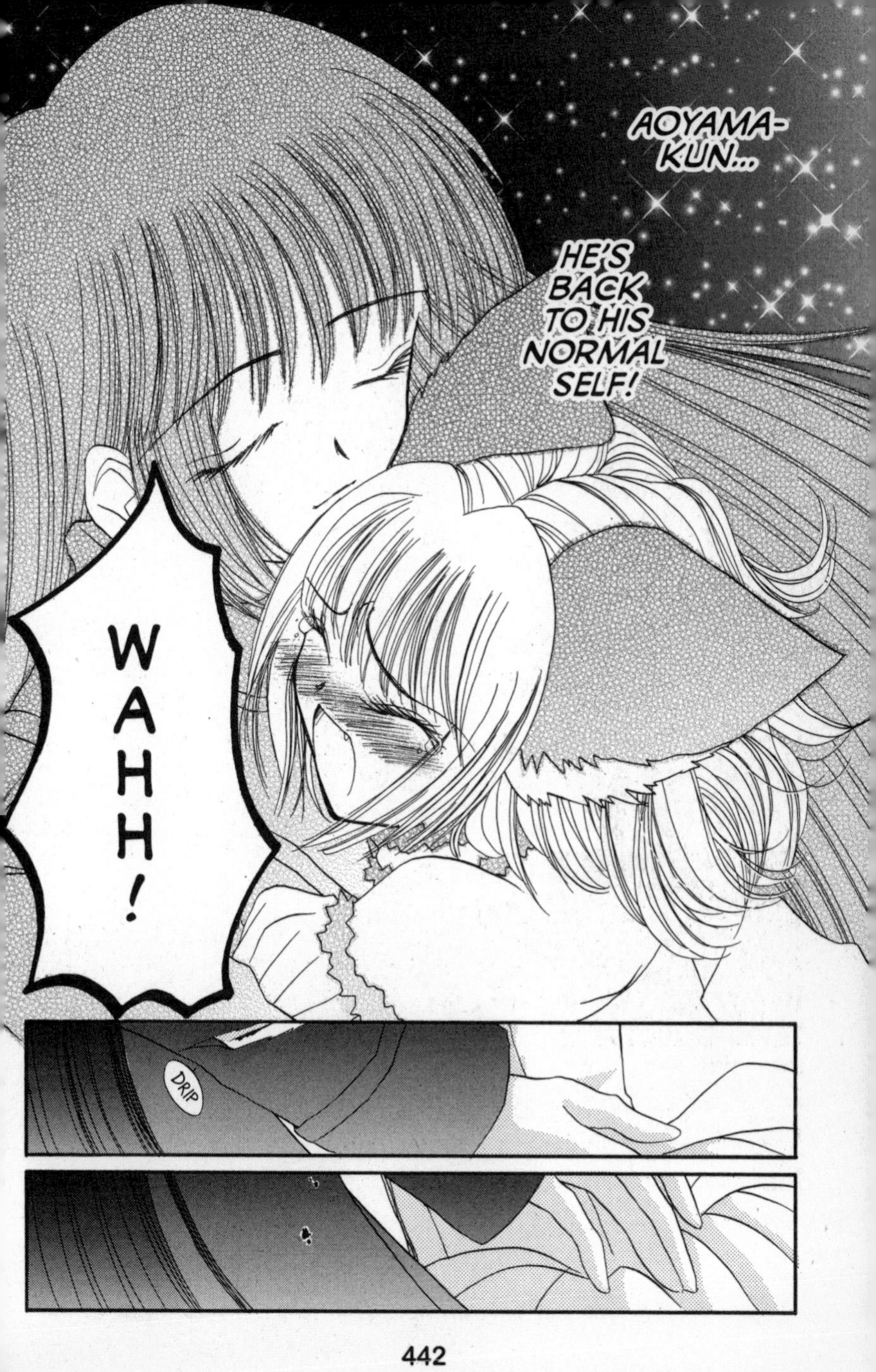
AOYAMA-KUN...
HE'S BACK TO HIS NORMAL SELF!
WAHH!
DRIP

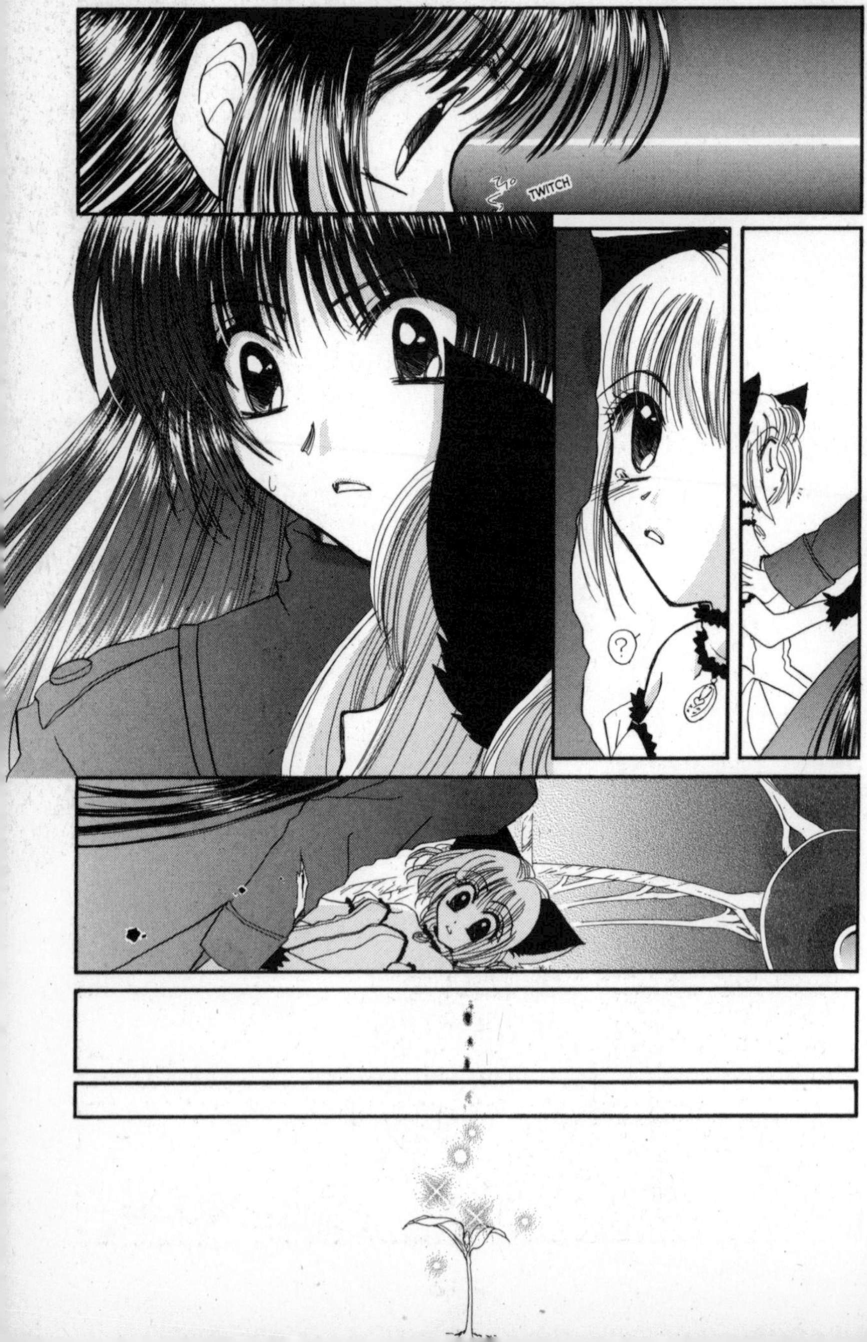
TWITCH
?

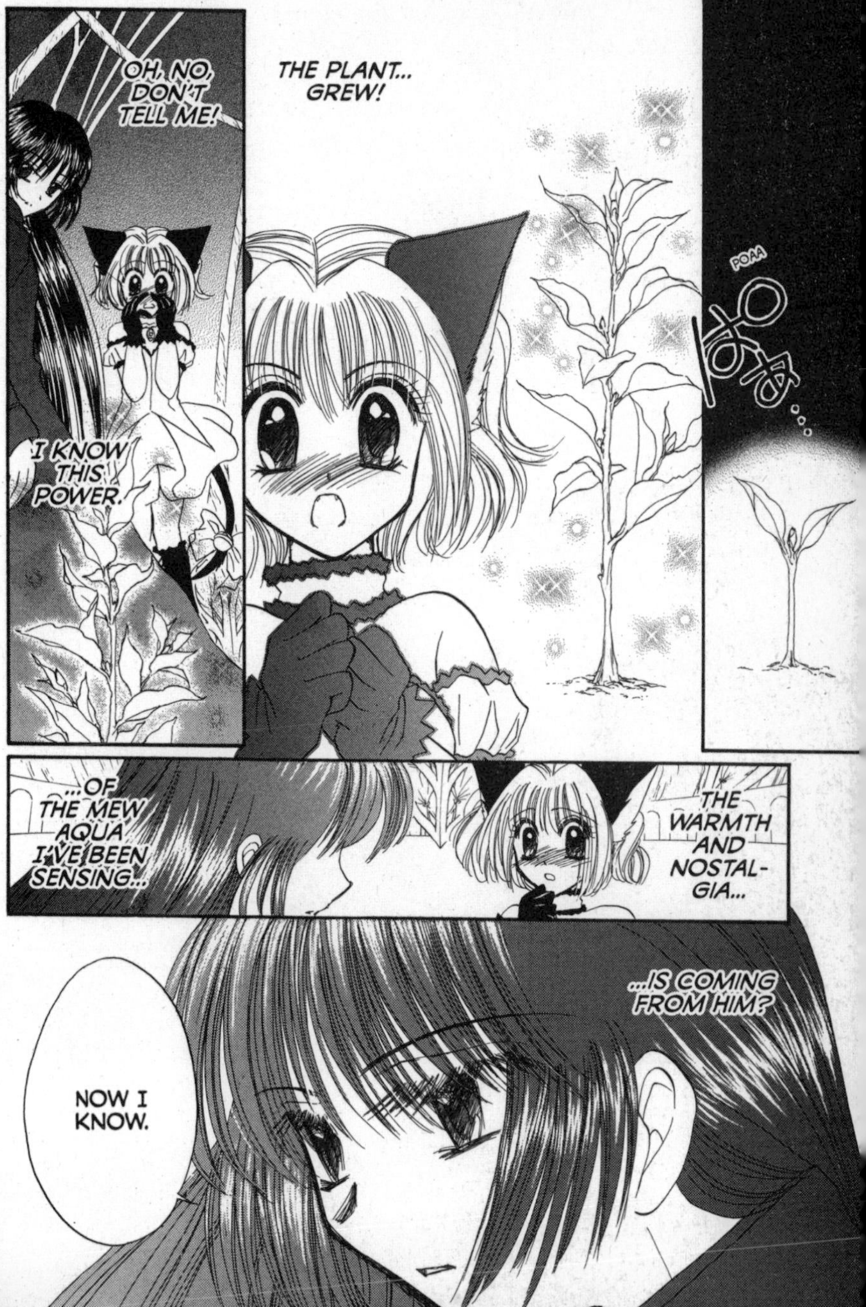
POAA
THE PLANT... GREW!
OH, NO, DON'T TELL ME!
I KNOW THIS POWER.
THE WARMTH AND NOSTAL-GIA...
...OF THE MEW AQUA I'VE BEEN SENSING...
...IS COMING FROM HIM?
NOW I KNOW.

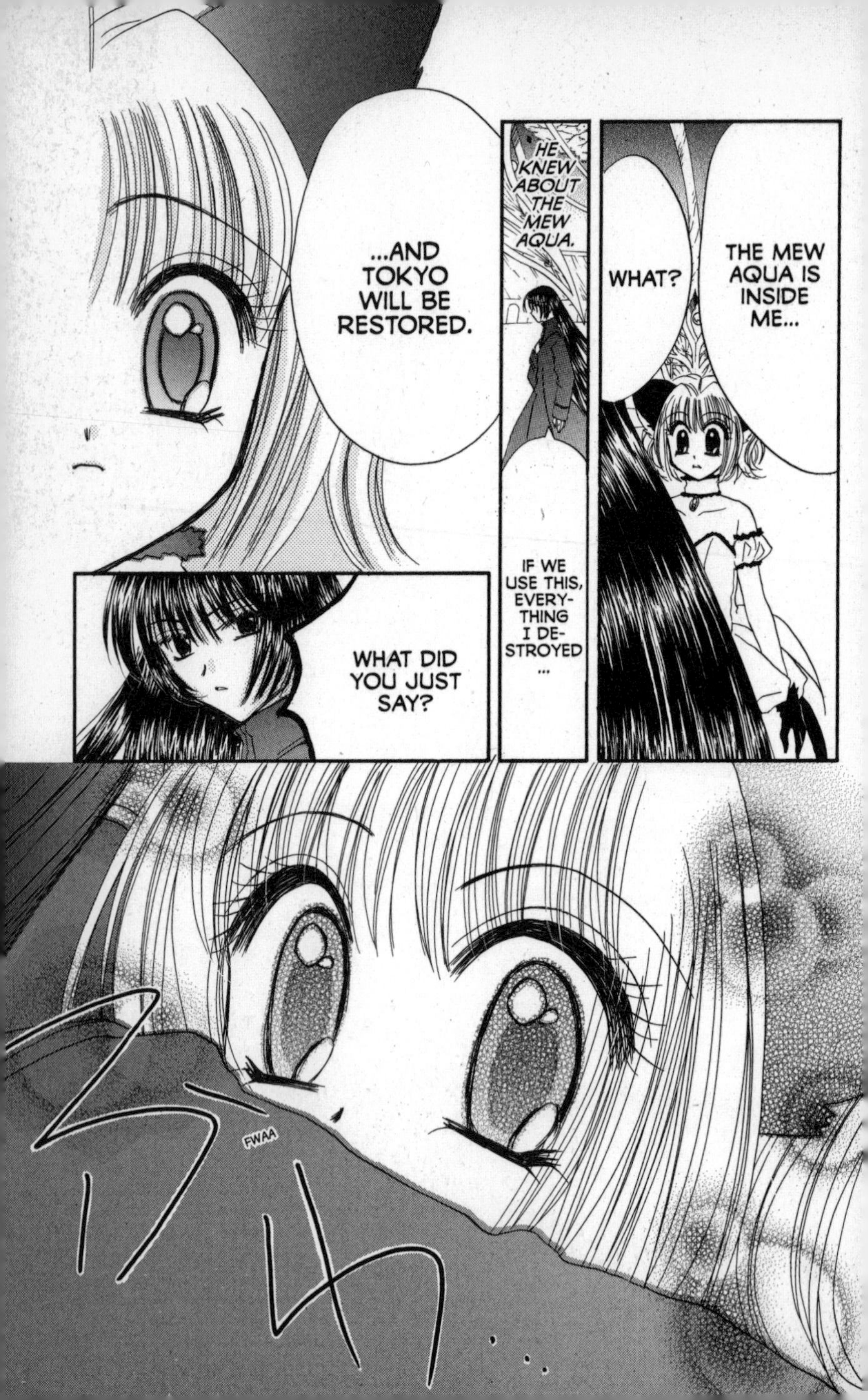
THE MEW AQUA IS INSIDE ME...
WHAT?
HE KNEW ABOUT THE MEW AQUA.
IF WE USE THIS, EVERY-THING I DE-STROYED ...
...AND TOKYO WILL BE RESTORED.
WHAT DID YOU JUST SAY?
FWAA

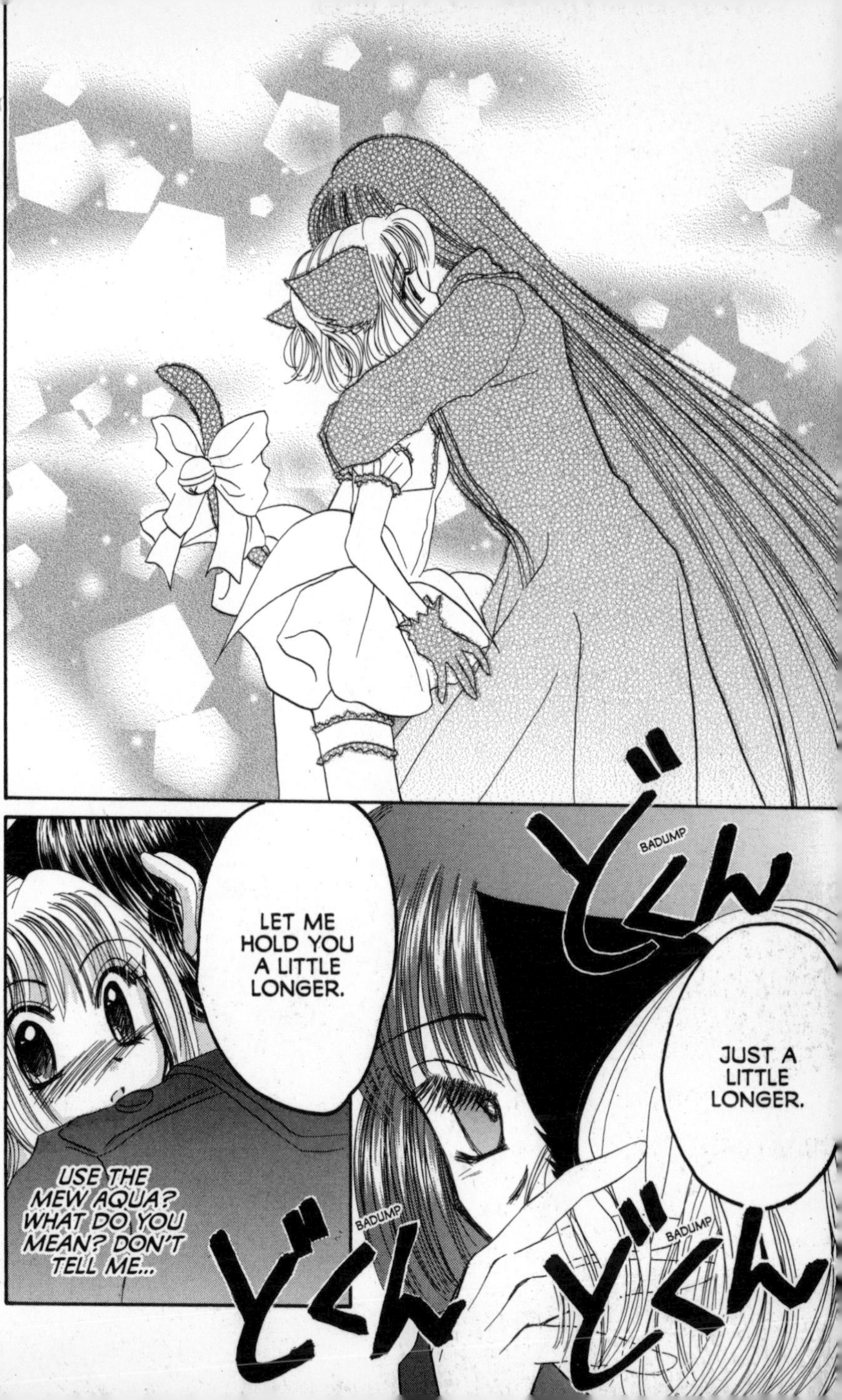

どくん
BADUMP
LET ME HOLD YOU A LITTLE LONGER.
JUST A LITTLE LONGER.
どくん
BADUMP
どくん
BADUMP
USE THE MEW AQUA? WHAT DO YOU MEAN? DON'T TELL ME...

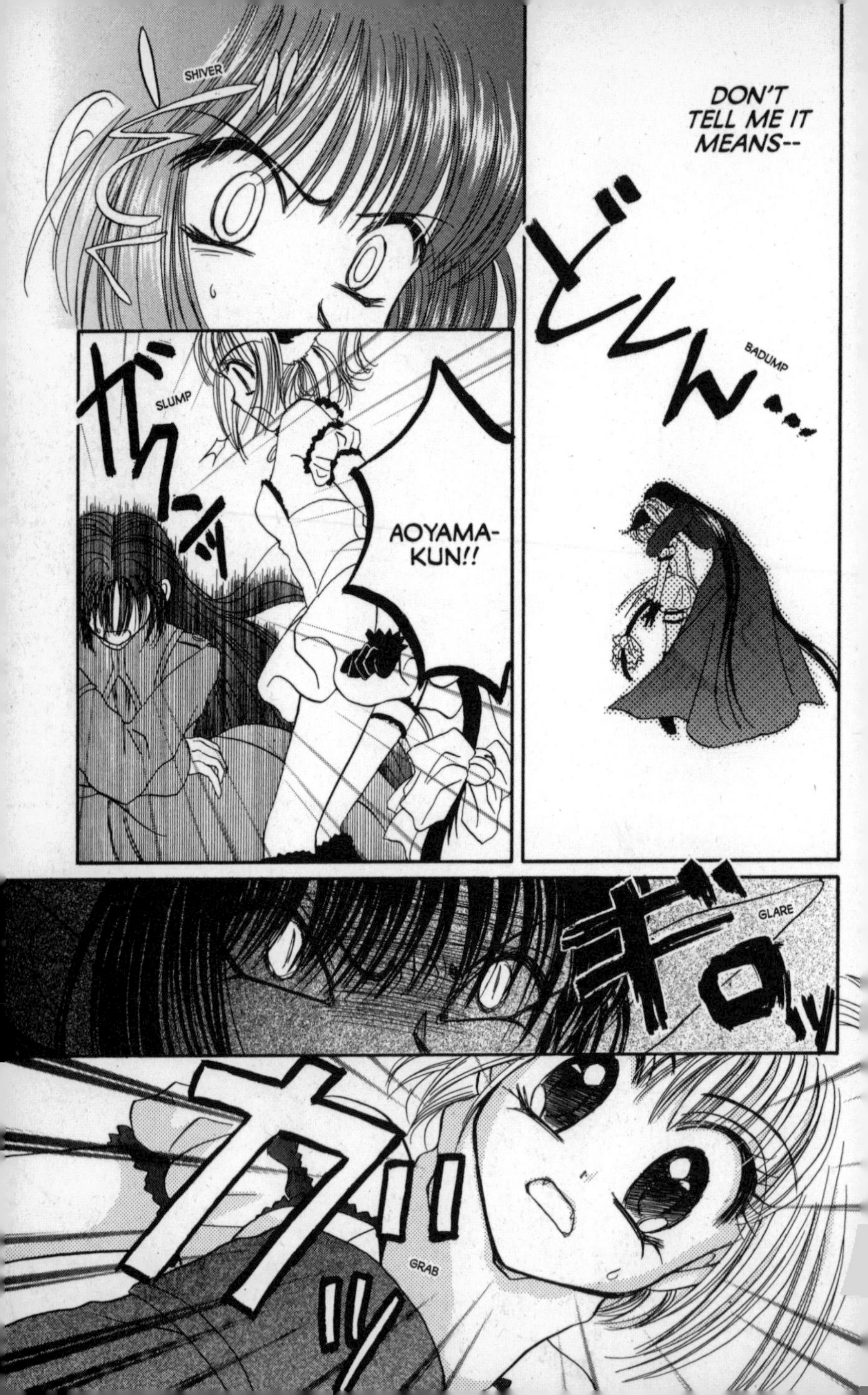
DON'T TELL ME IT MEANS--
どくん…
BADUMP
SHIVER
SLUMP
AOYAMA-KUN!!
GLARE
GRAB

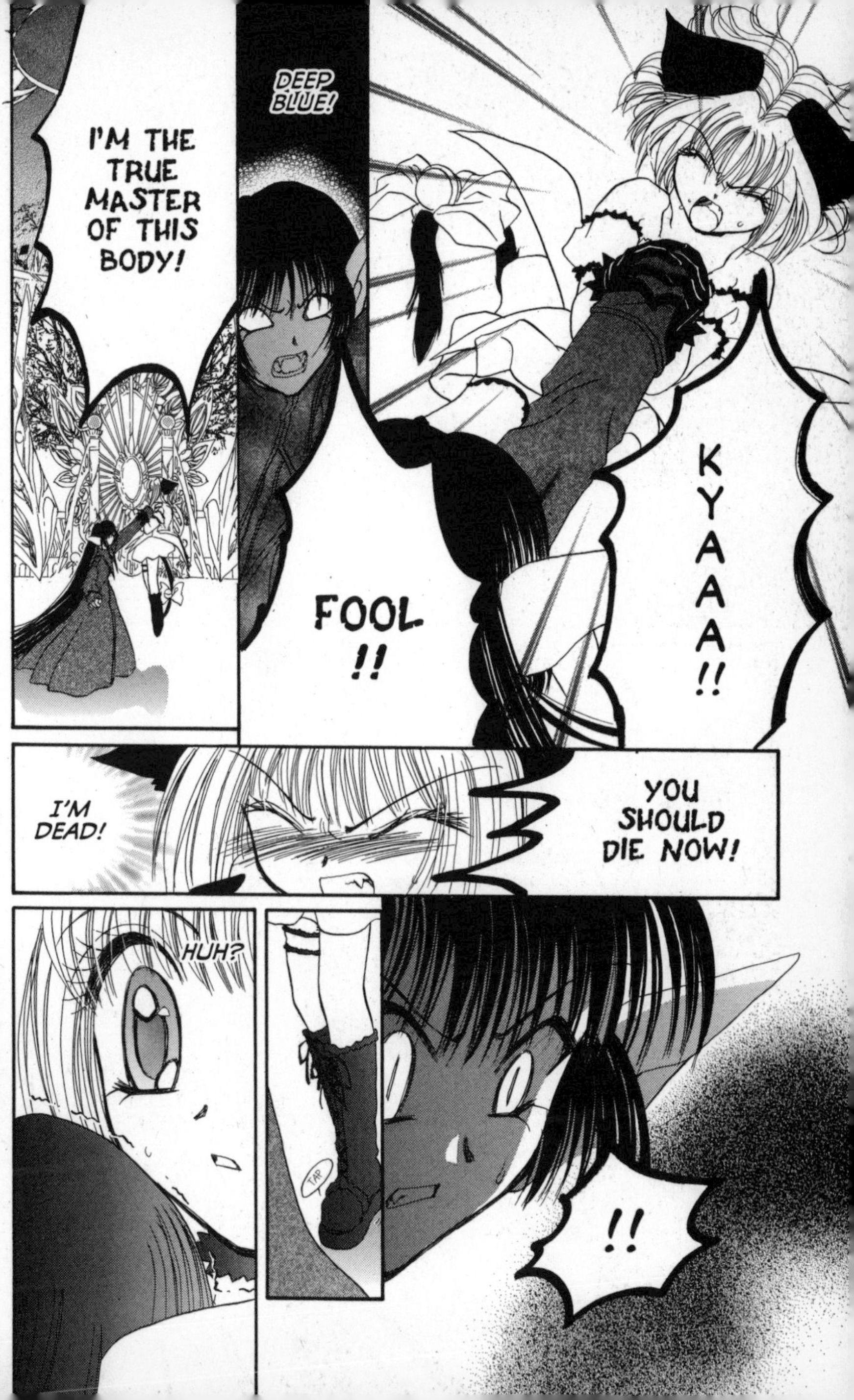
KYAAA!!
FOOL!!
DEEP BLUE!
I'M THE TRUE MASTER OF THIS BODY!
YOU SHOULD DIE NOW!
I'M DEAD!
!!
TAP
HUH?

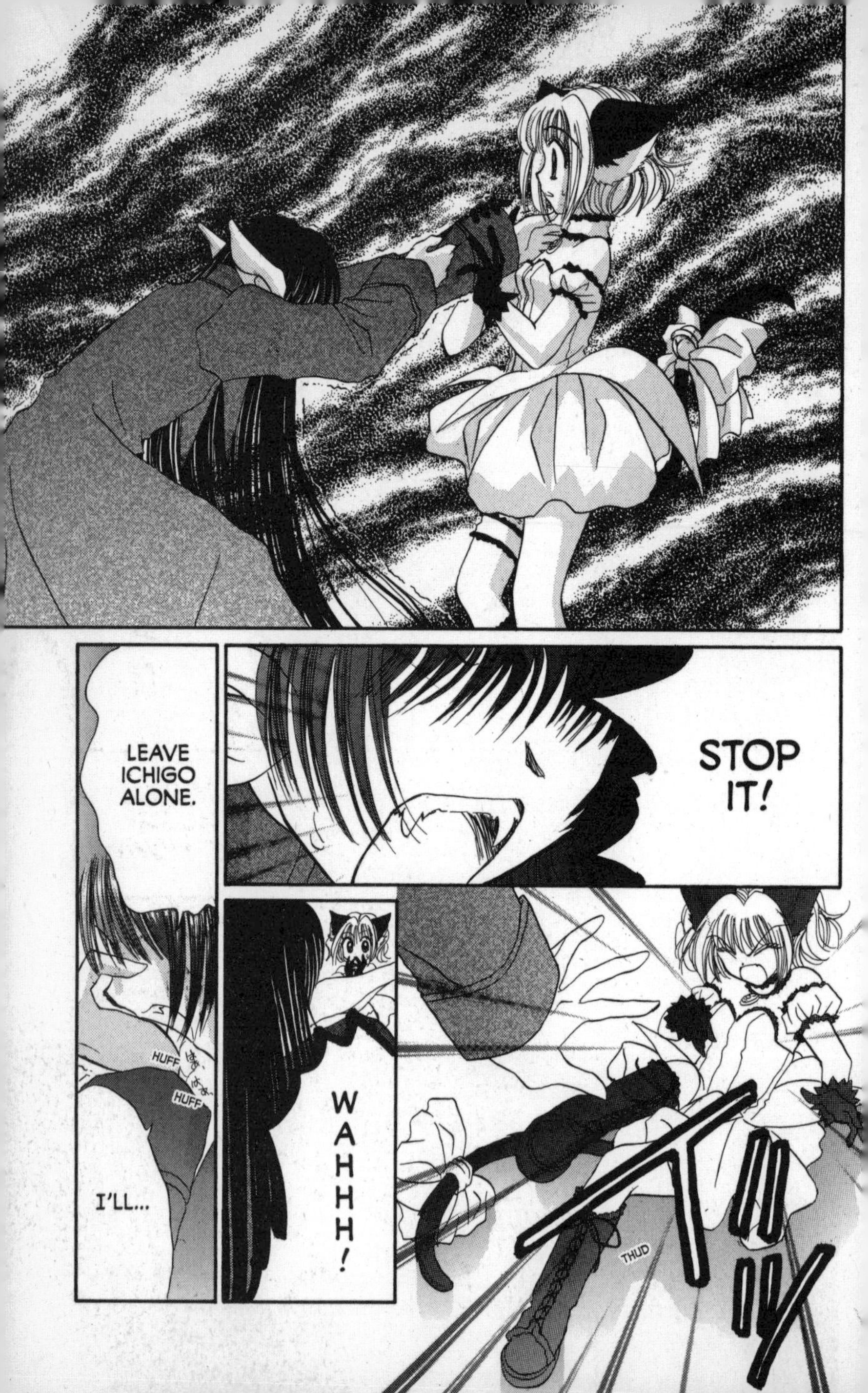
STOP IT!
THUD
WAHHH!
LEAVE ICHIGO ALONE.
HUFF
HUFF
I'LL...

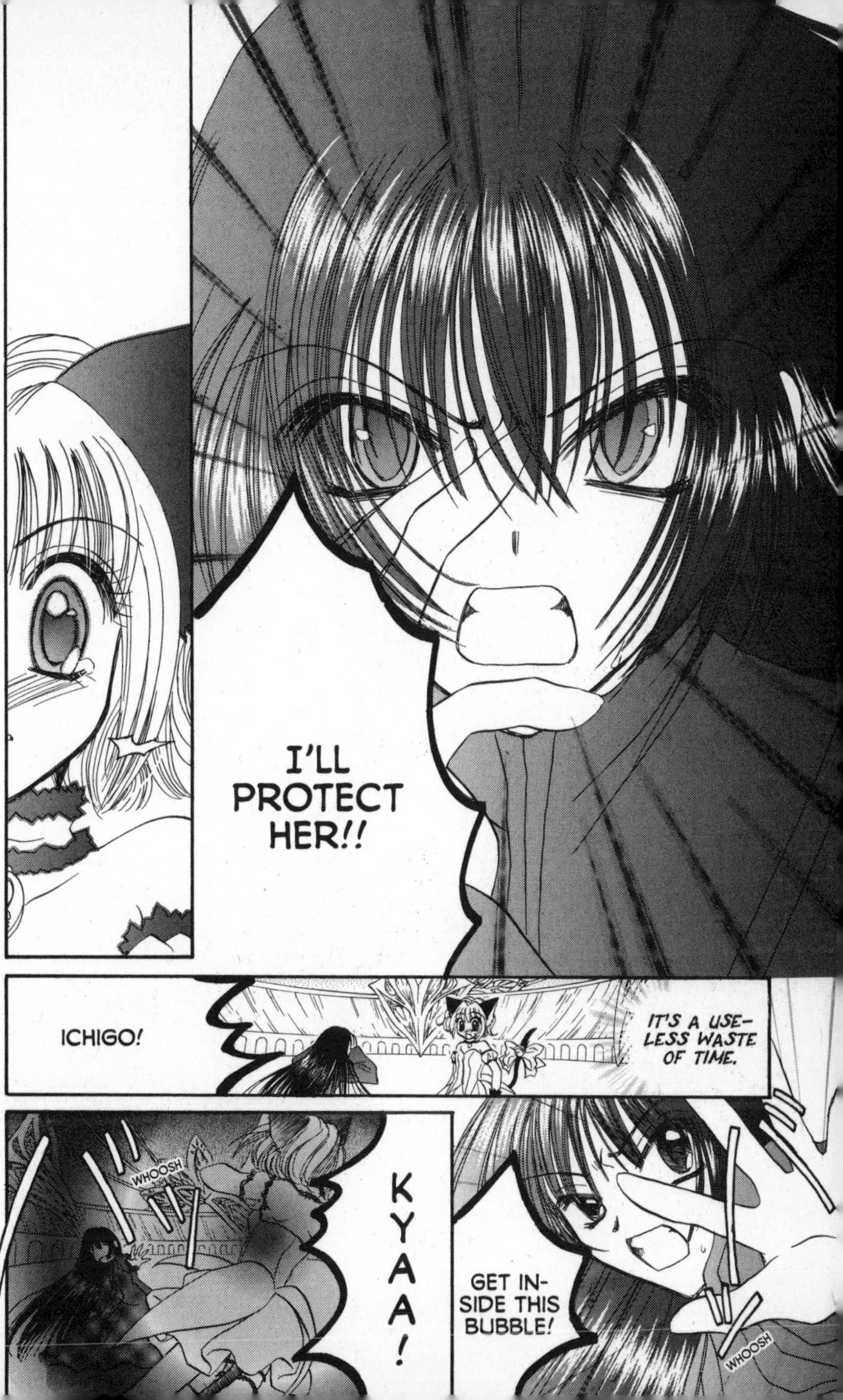
I'LL PROTECT HER!!
IT'S A USE-LESS WASTE OF TIME.
ICHIGO!
GET IN-SIDE THIS BUBBLE!
WHOOSH
KYAA!
WHOOSH

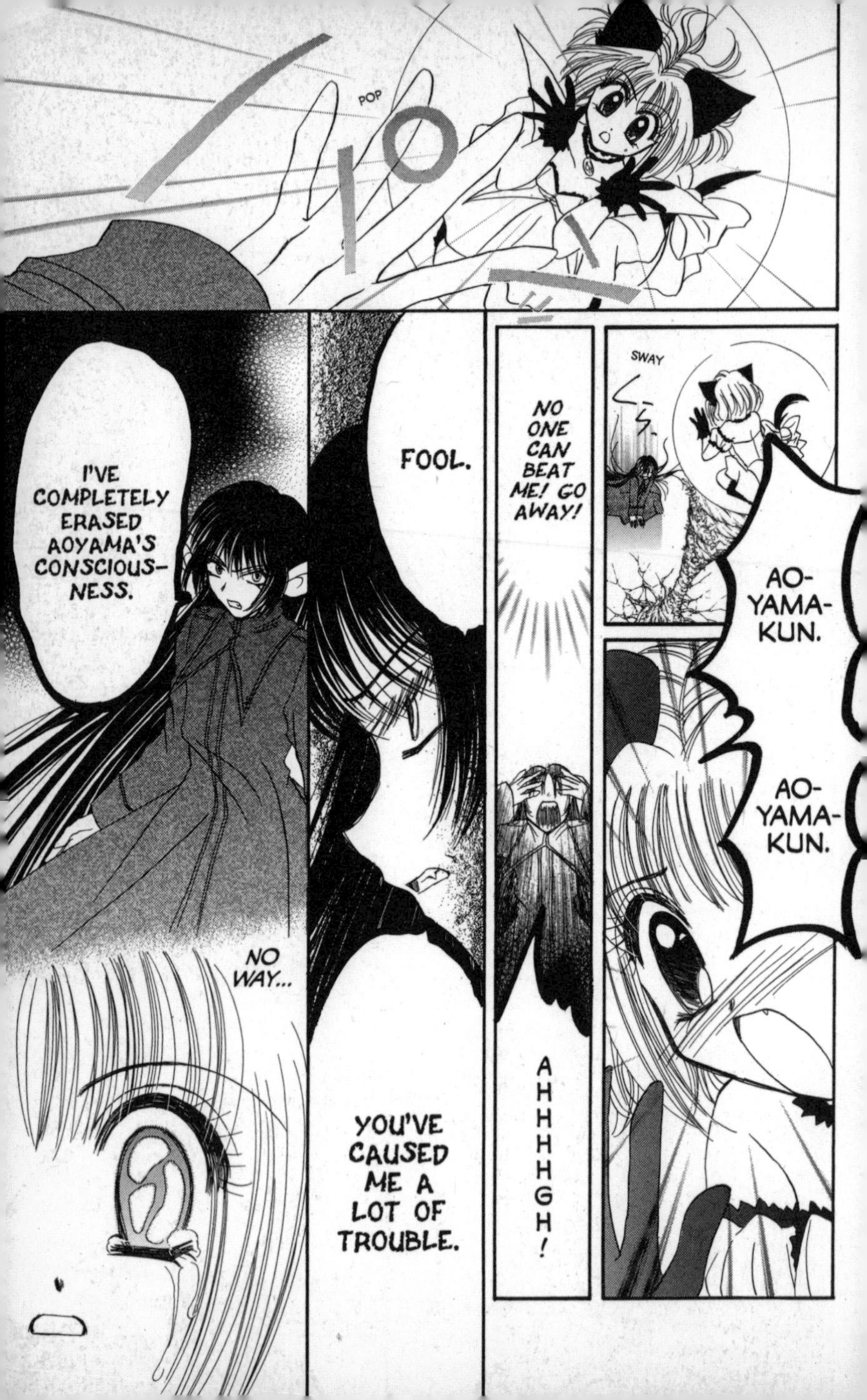
POP
SWAY
AO-YAMA-KUN.
AO-YAMA-KUN.
NO ONE CAN BEAT ME! GO AWAY!
AHHHHGH!
FOOL.
YOU'VE CAUSED ME A LOT OF TROUBLE.
I'VE COMPLETELY ERASED AOYAMA'S CONSCIOUSNESS.
NO WAY...

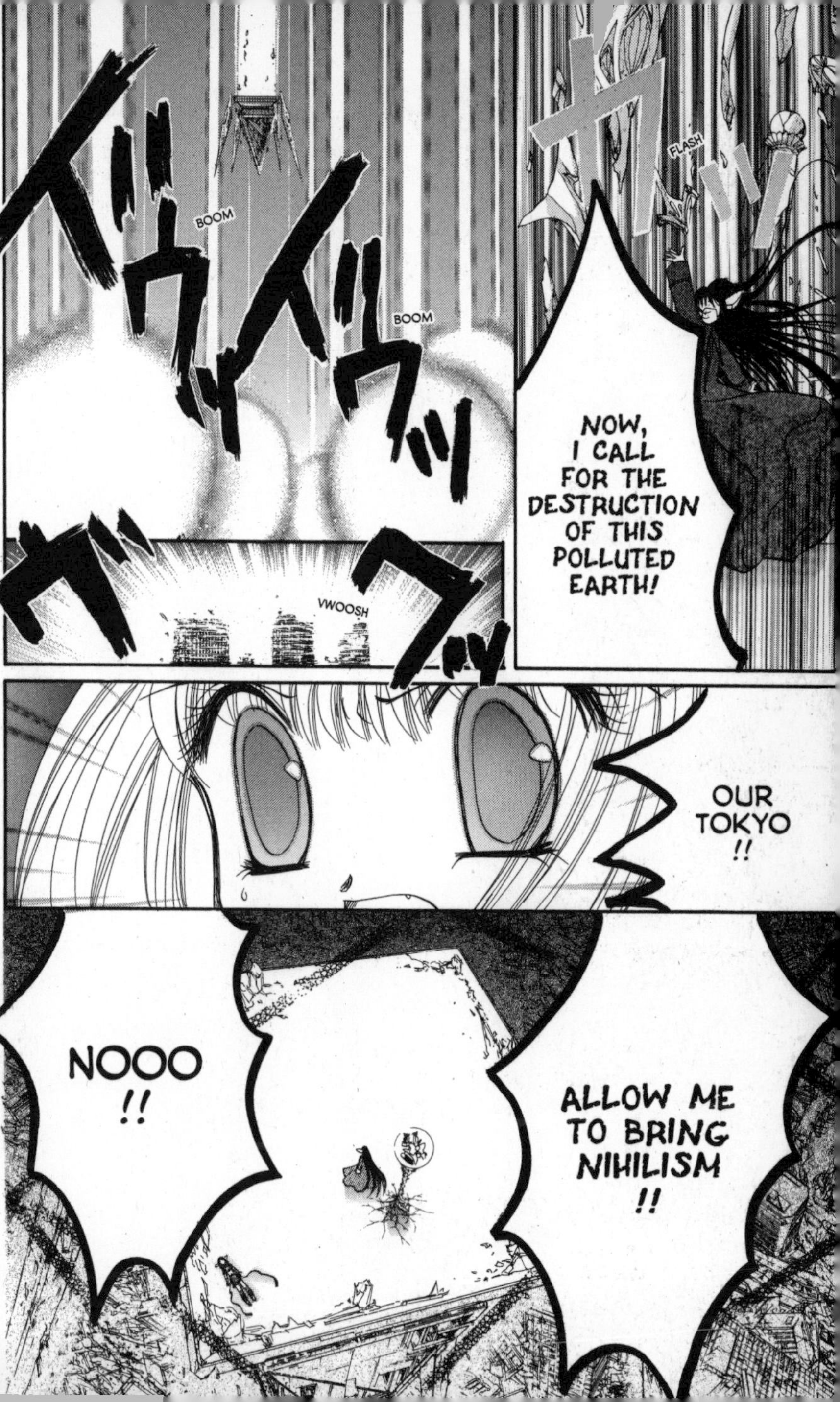
FLASH
NOW, I CALL FOR THE DESTRUCTION OF THIS POLLUTED EARTH!
BOOM
BOOM
VWOOSH
OUR TOKYO !!
ALLOW ME TO BRING NIHILISM !!
NOOO !!

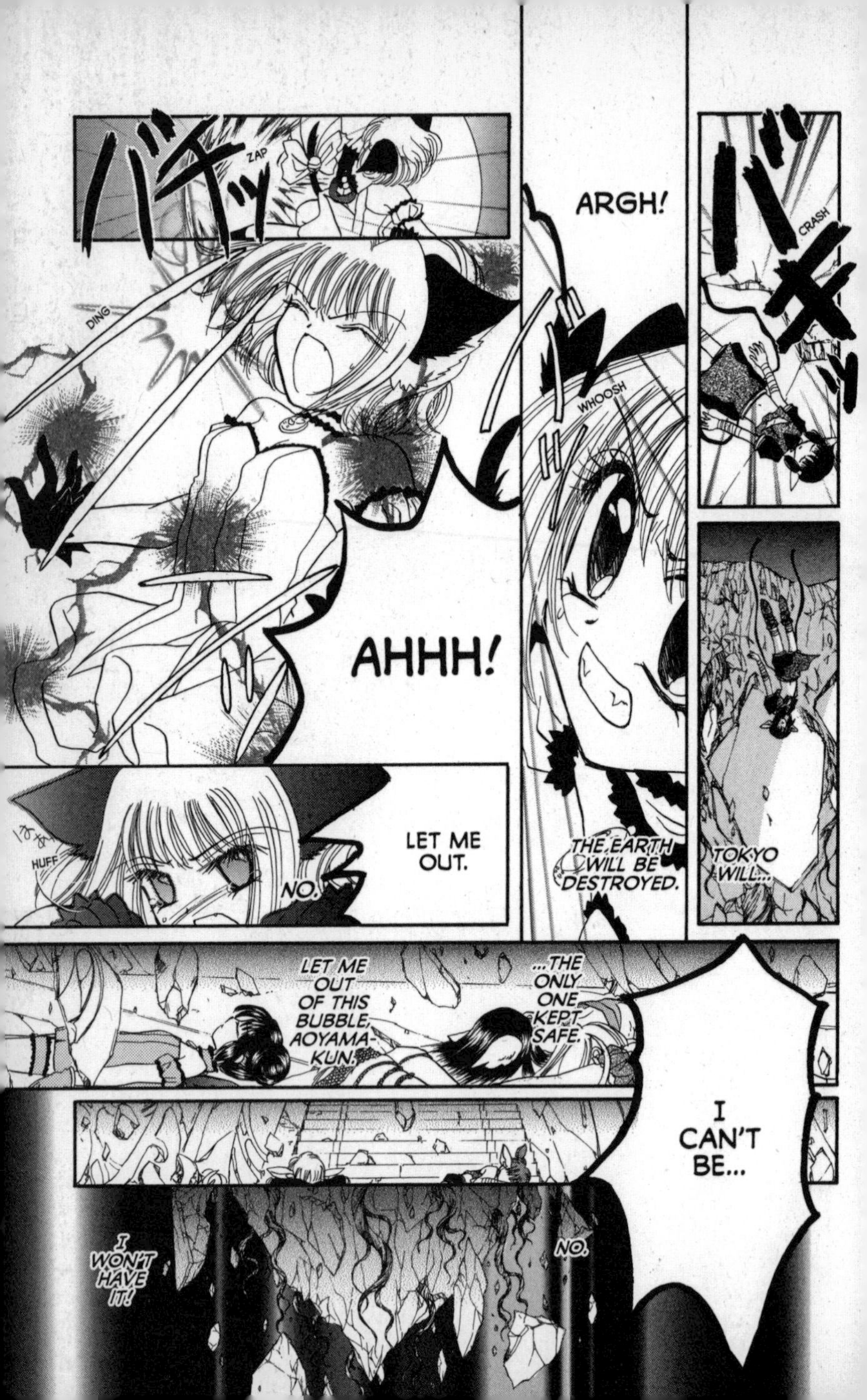

CRASH
TOKYO WILL...
ARGH!
WHOOSH
THE EARTH WILL BE DESTROYED.
ZAP
DING
AHHH!
LET ME OUT.
NO.
HUFF
I CAN'T BE...
...THE ONLY ONE KEPT SAFE.
LET ME OUT OF THIS BUBBLE, AOYAMA-KUN.
NO.
I WON'T HAVE IT!

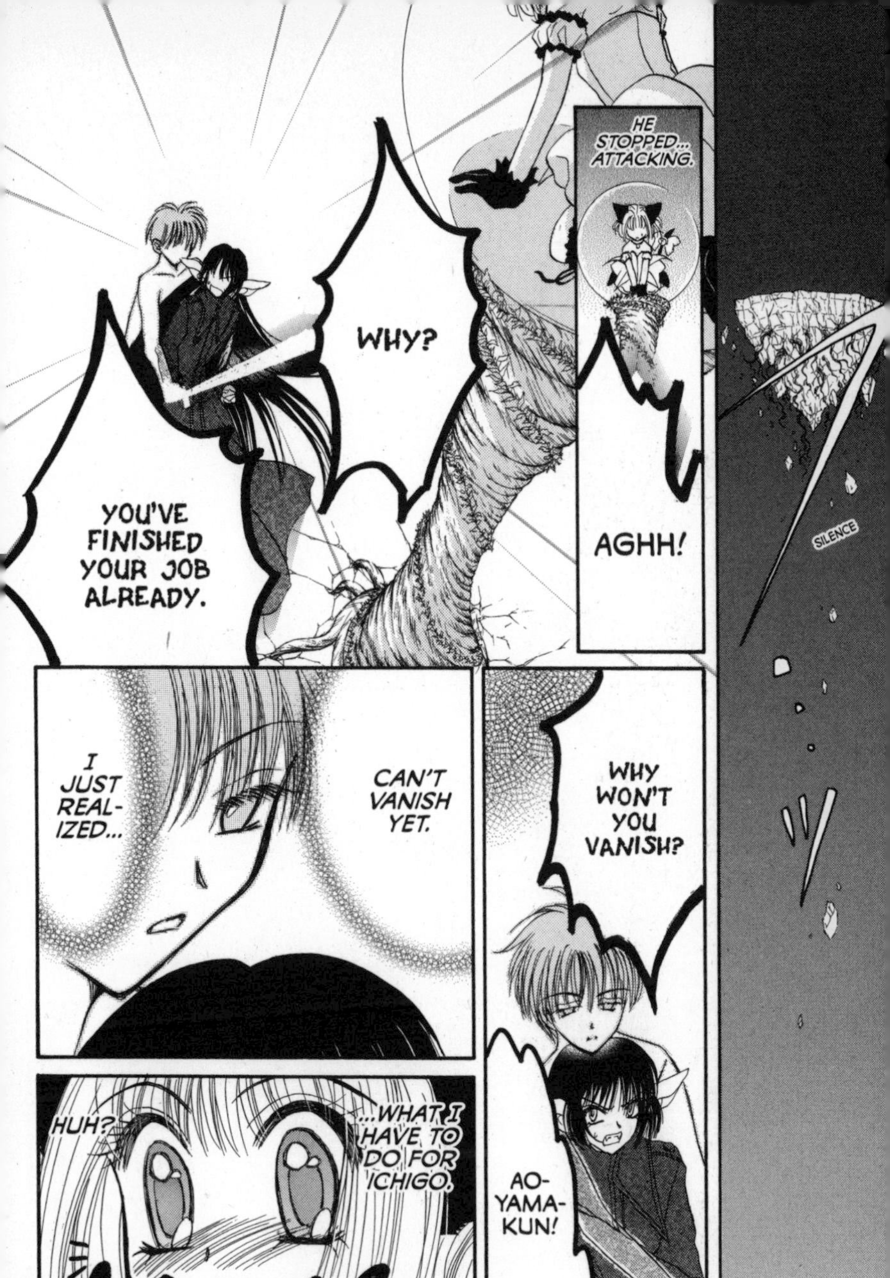
SILENCE
HE STOPPED... ATTACKING.
AGHH!
WHY?
YOU'VE FINISHED YOUR JOB ALREADY.
WHY WON'T YOU VANISH?
AO-YAMA-KUN!
CAN'T VANISH YET.
I JUST REALIZED...
...WHAT I HAVE TO DO FOR ICHIGO.
HUH?

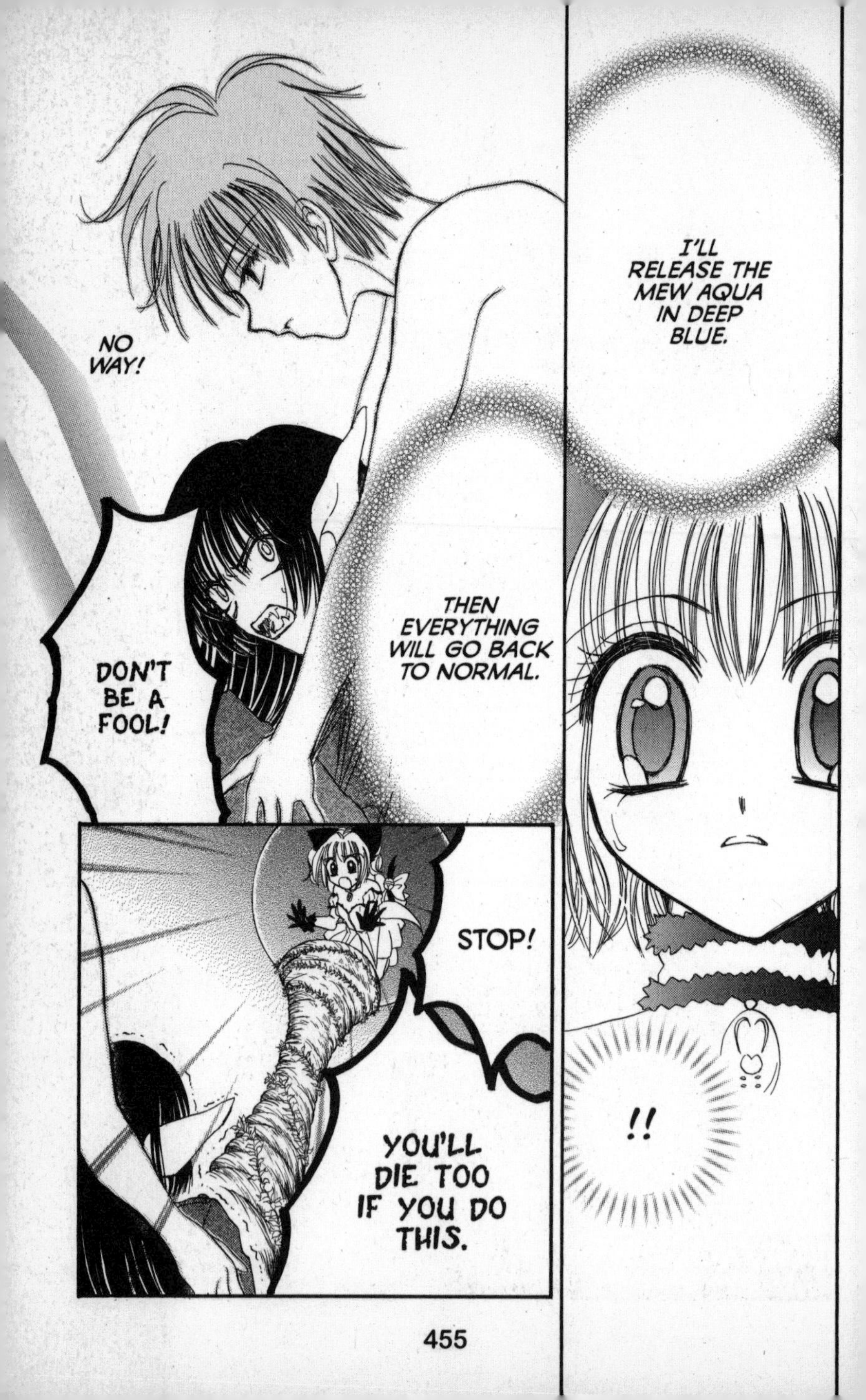
I'LL RELEASE THE MEW AQUA IN DEEP BLUE.
!!
THEN EVERYTHING WILL GO BACK TO NORMAL.
NO WAY!
DON'T BE A FOOL!
STOP!
YOU'LL DIE TOO IF YOU DO THIS.

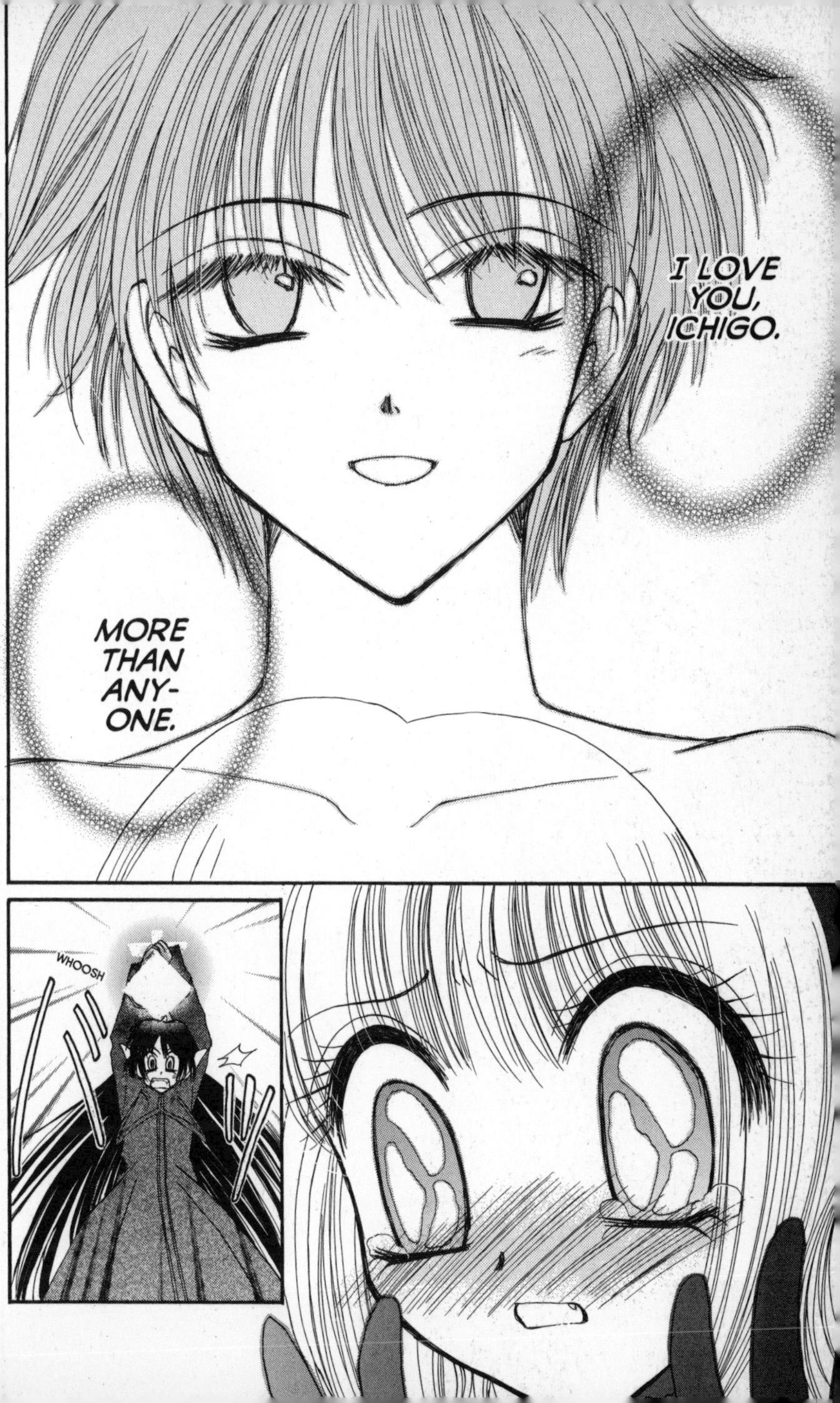
I LOVE YOU, ICHIGO.
MORE THAN ANY-ONE.
WHOOSH

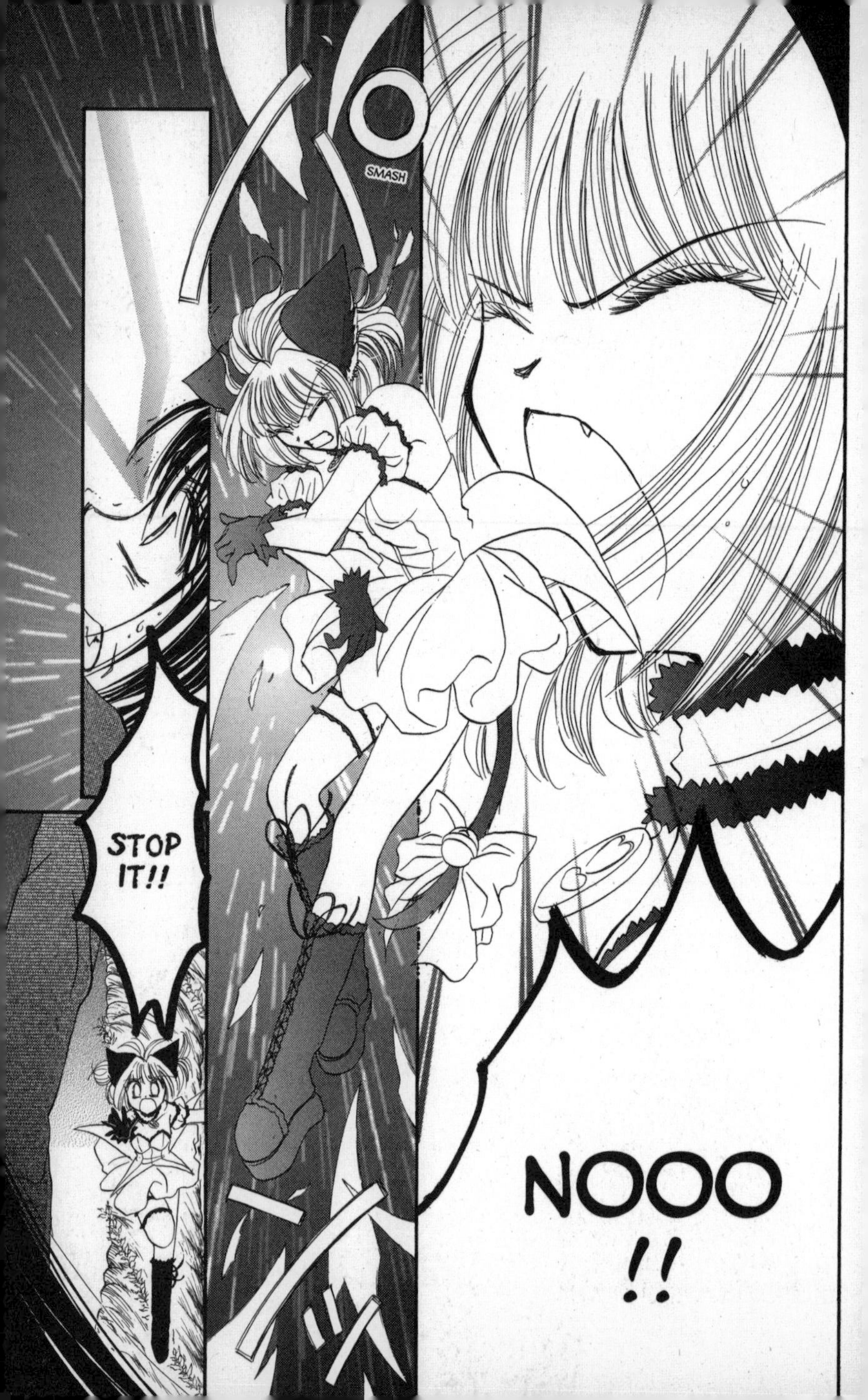
NOOO !!
SMASH
STOP IT!!

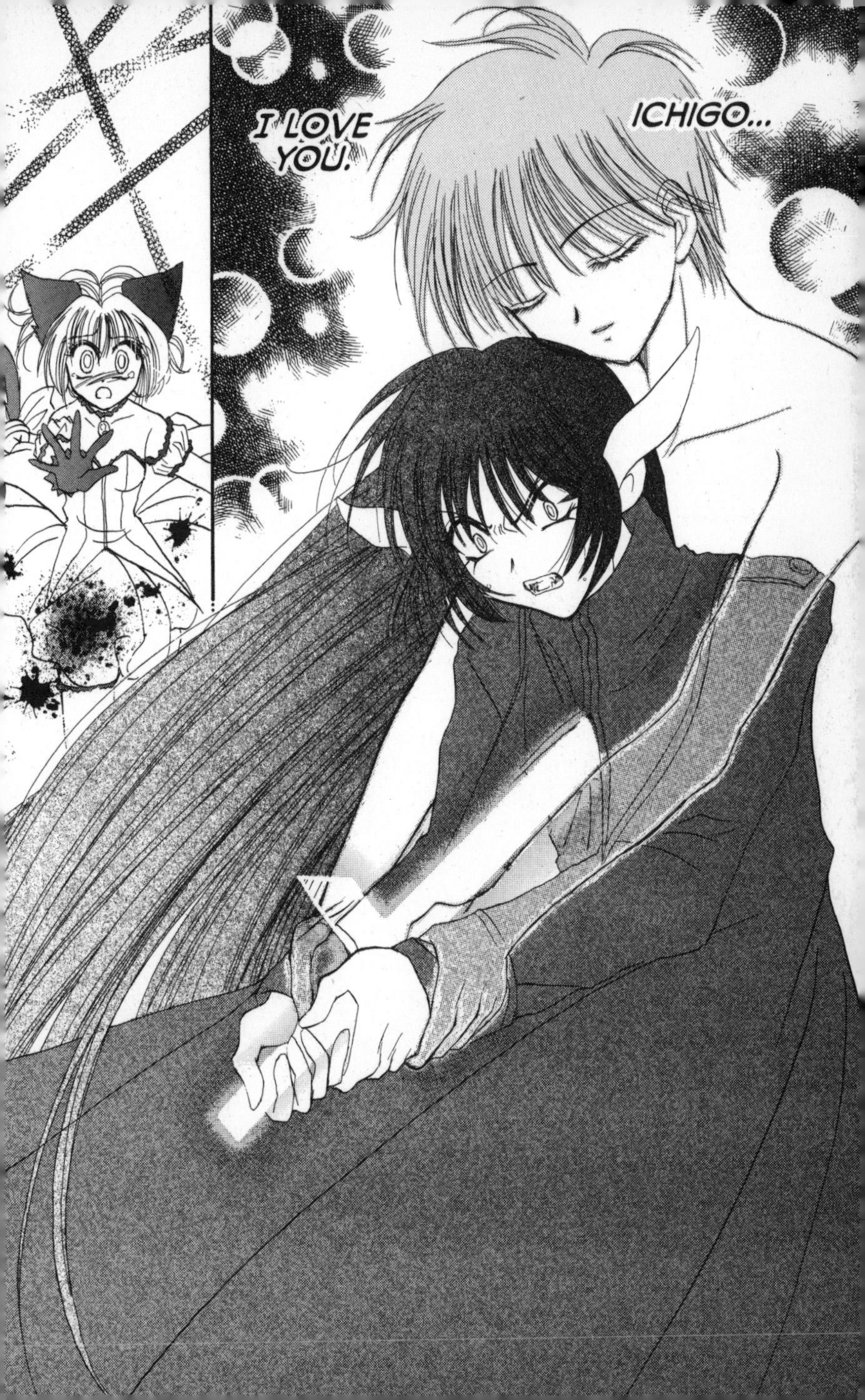
ICHIGO...
I LOVE YOU.

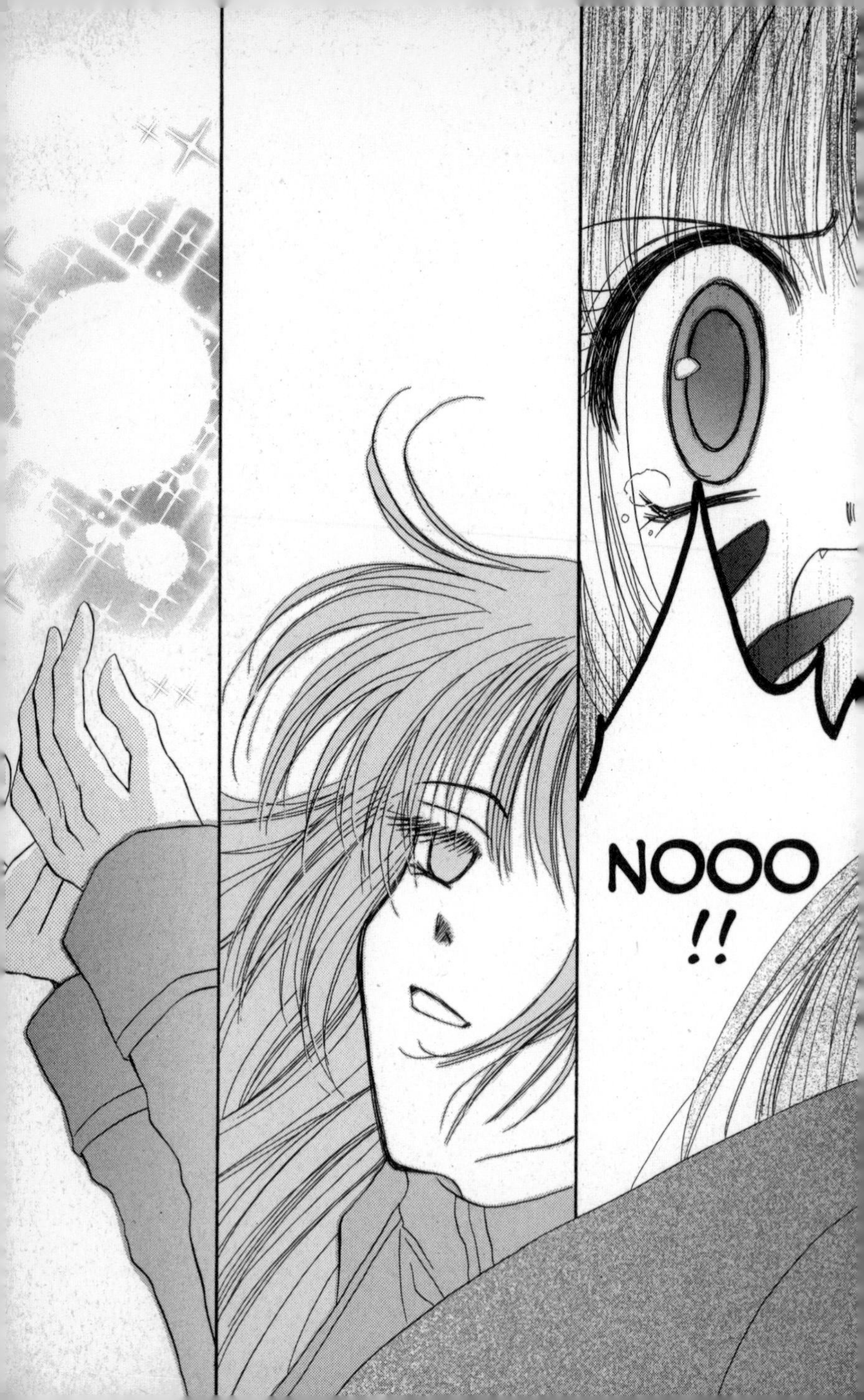
NOOO
!!

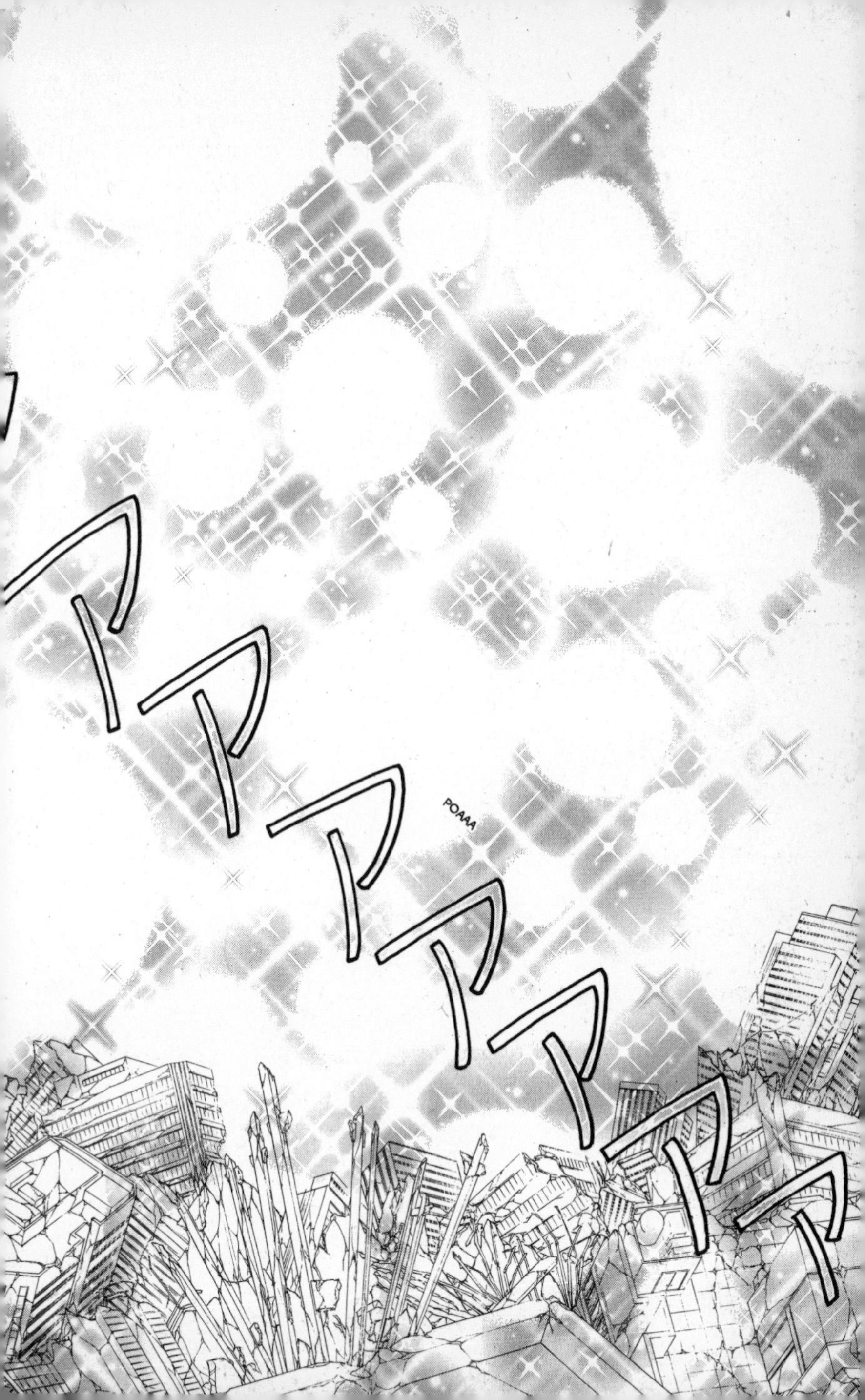
アアアアアアアア
POAAA

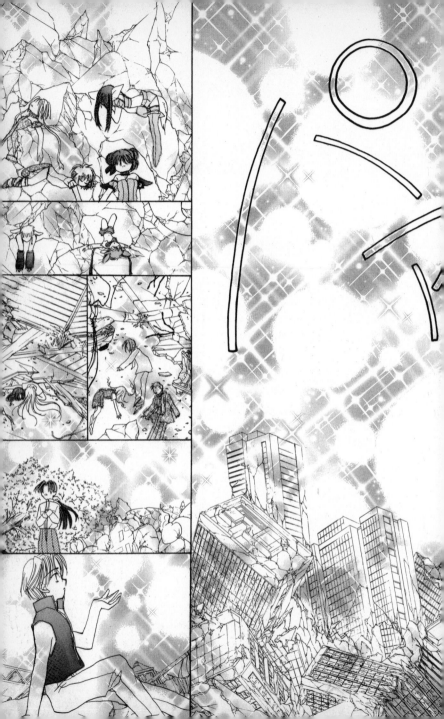

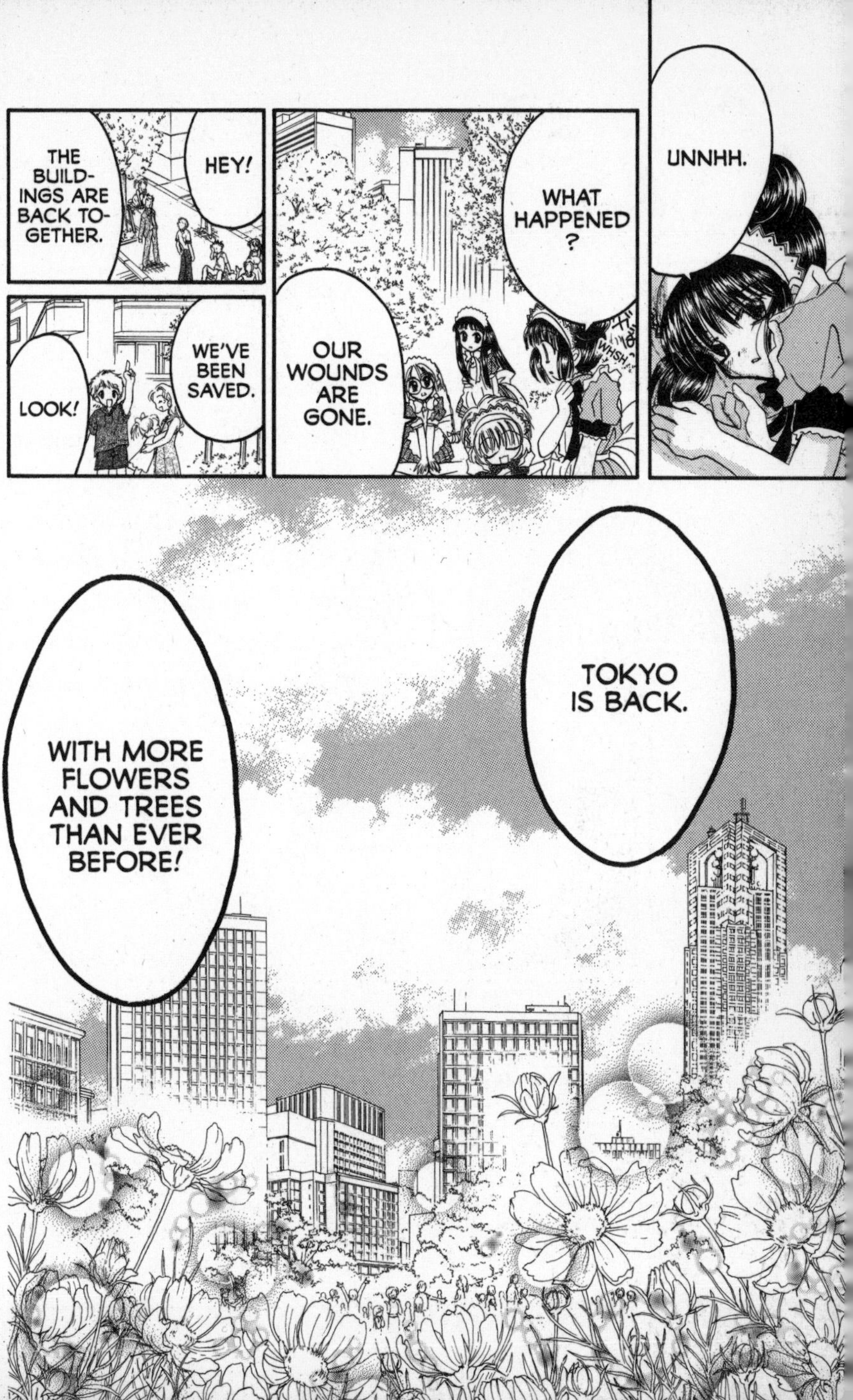
UNNHH.
WHAT HAPPENED?
WHSH
OUR WOUNDS ARE GONE.
HEY!
THE BUILD-INGS ARE BACK TO-GETHER.
WE'VE BEEN SAVED.
LOOK!
TOKYO IS BACK.
WITH MORE FLOWERS AND TREES THAN EVER BEFORE!

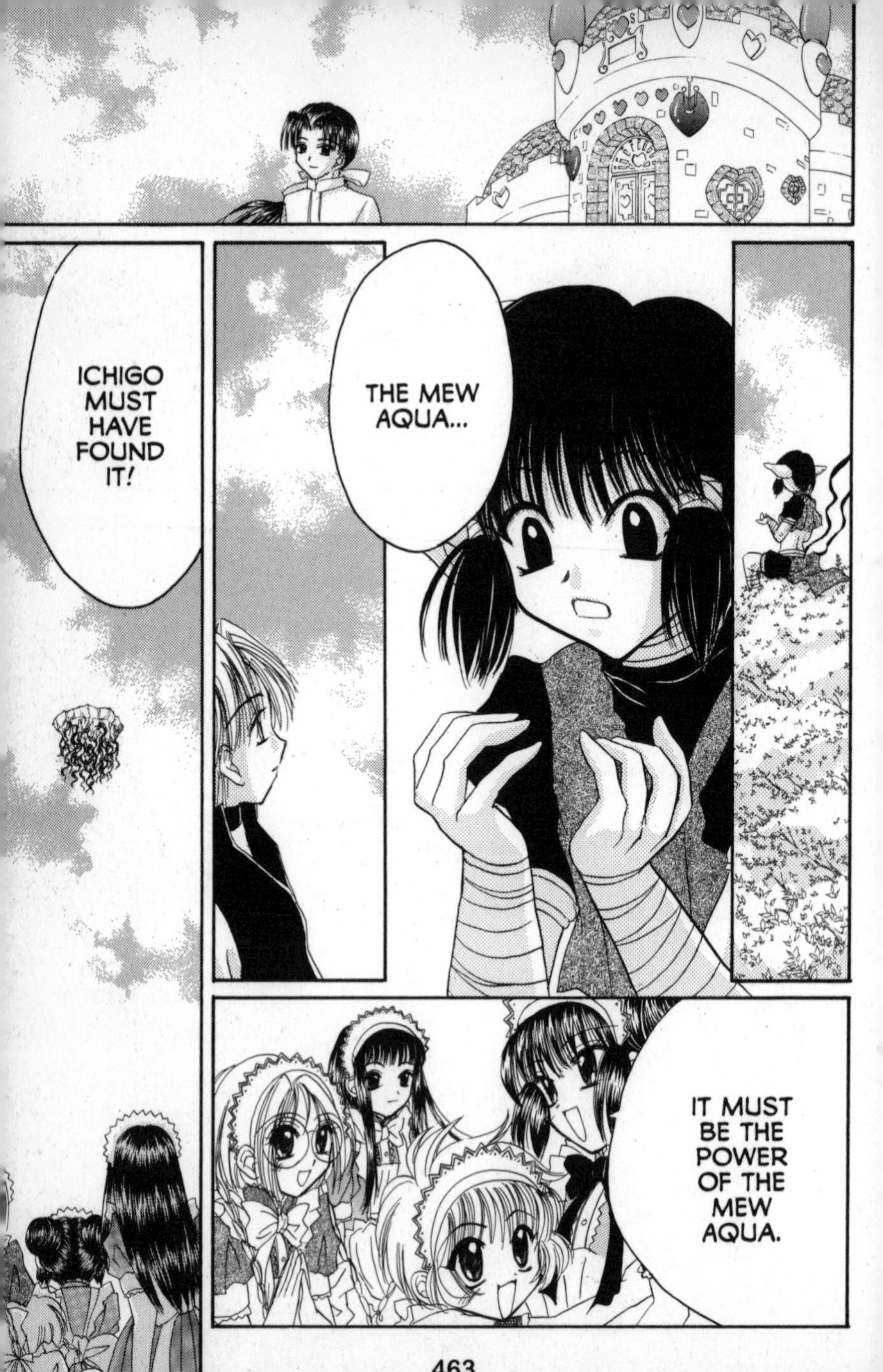
THE MEW AQUA...
ICHIGO MUST HAVE FOUND IT!
IT MUST BE THE POWER OF THE MEW AQUA.

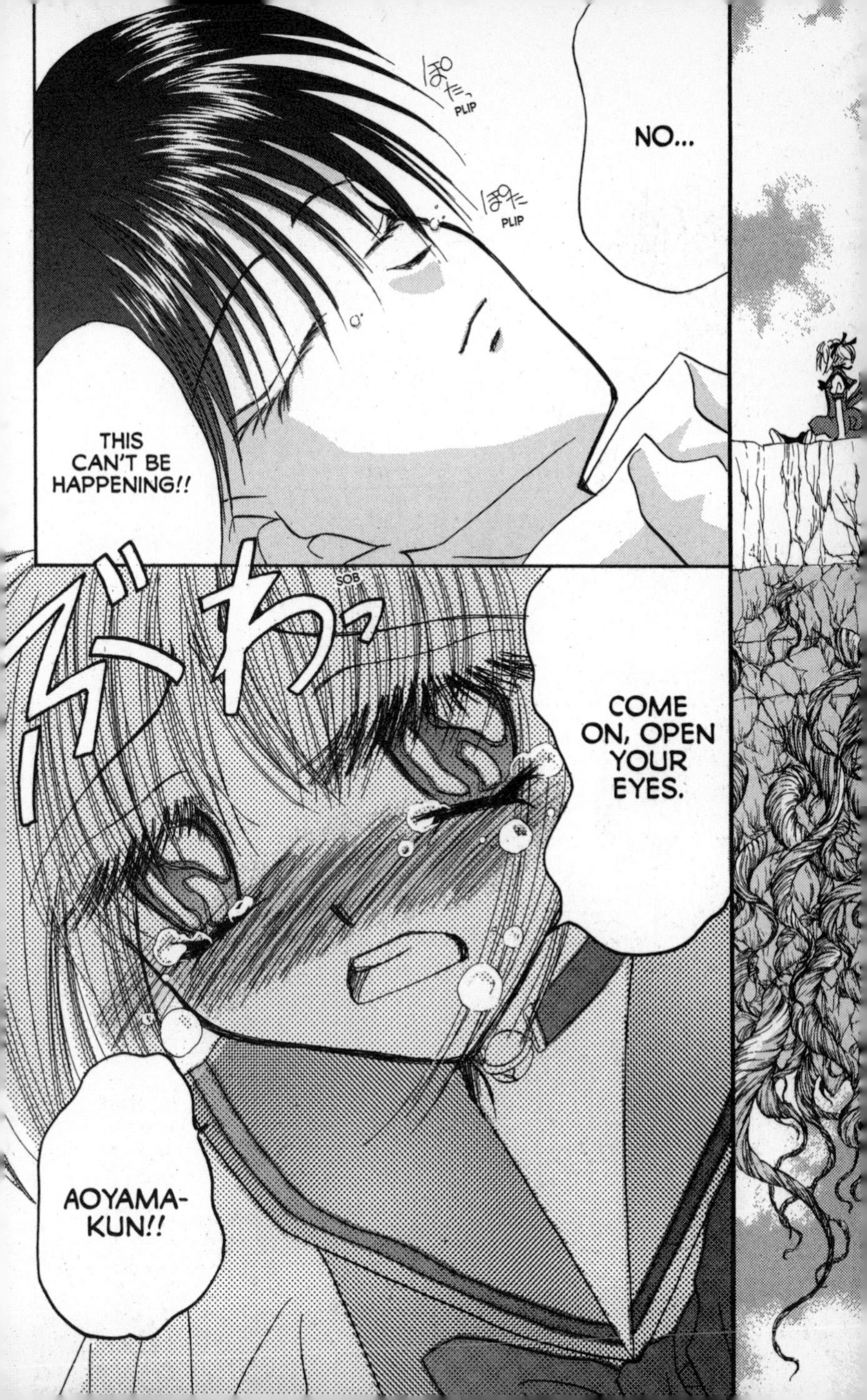
NO...
ぽたっ
PLIP
ぽた
PLIP
THIS CAN'T BE HAPPENING!!
ゔわっ
SOB
COME ON, OPEN YOUR EYES.
AOYAMA-KUN!!

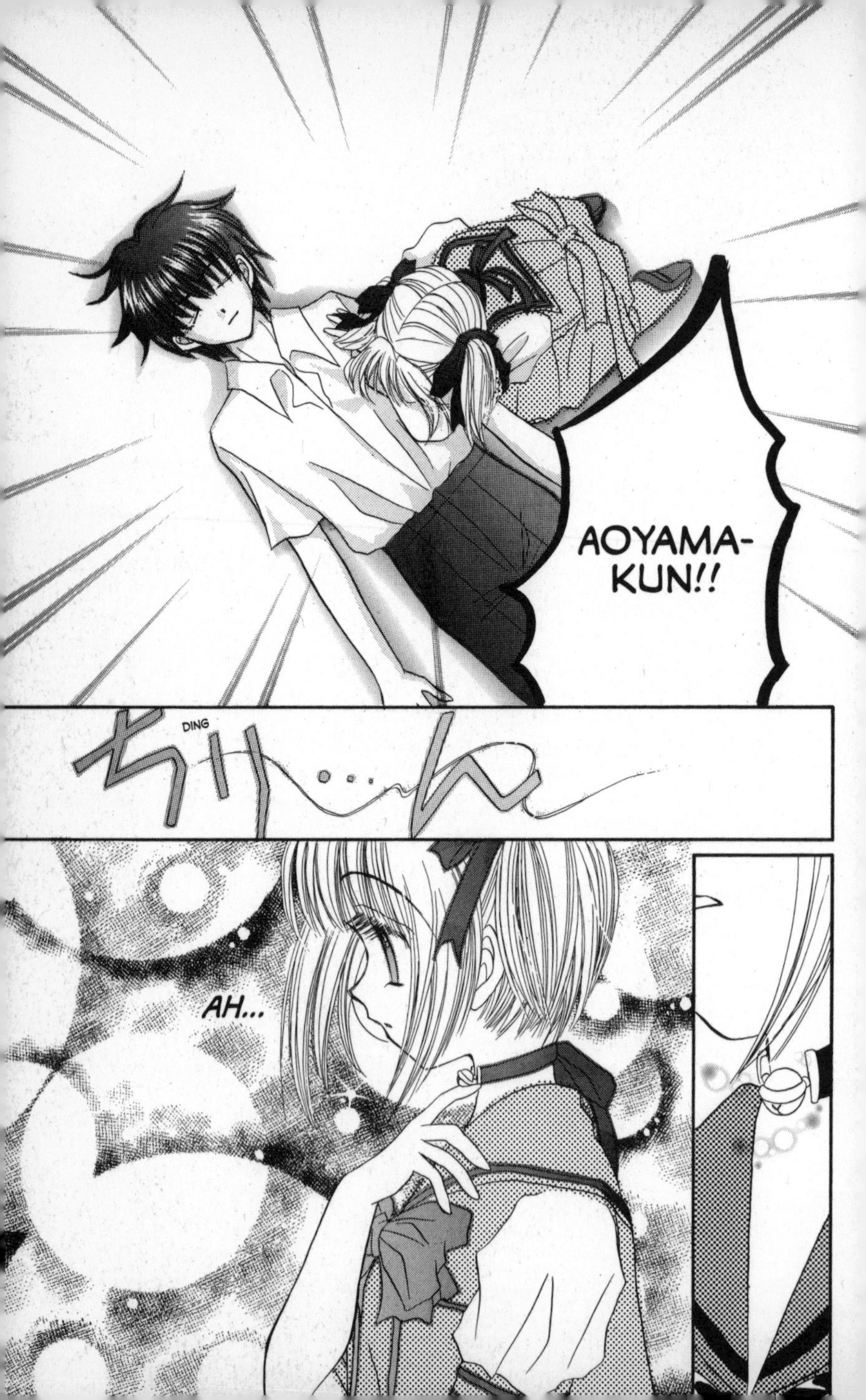
AOYAMA-KUN!!
ちりーん...
DING
AH...

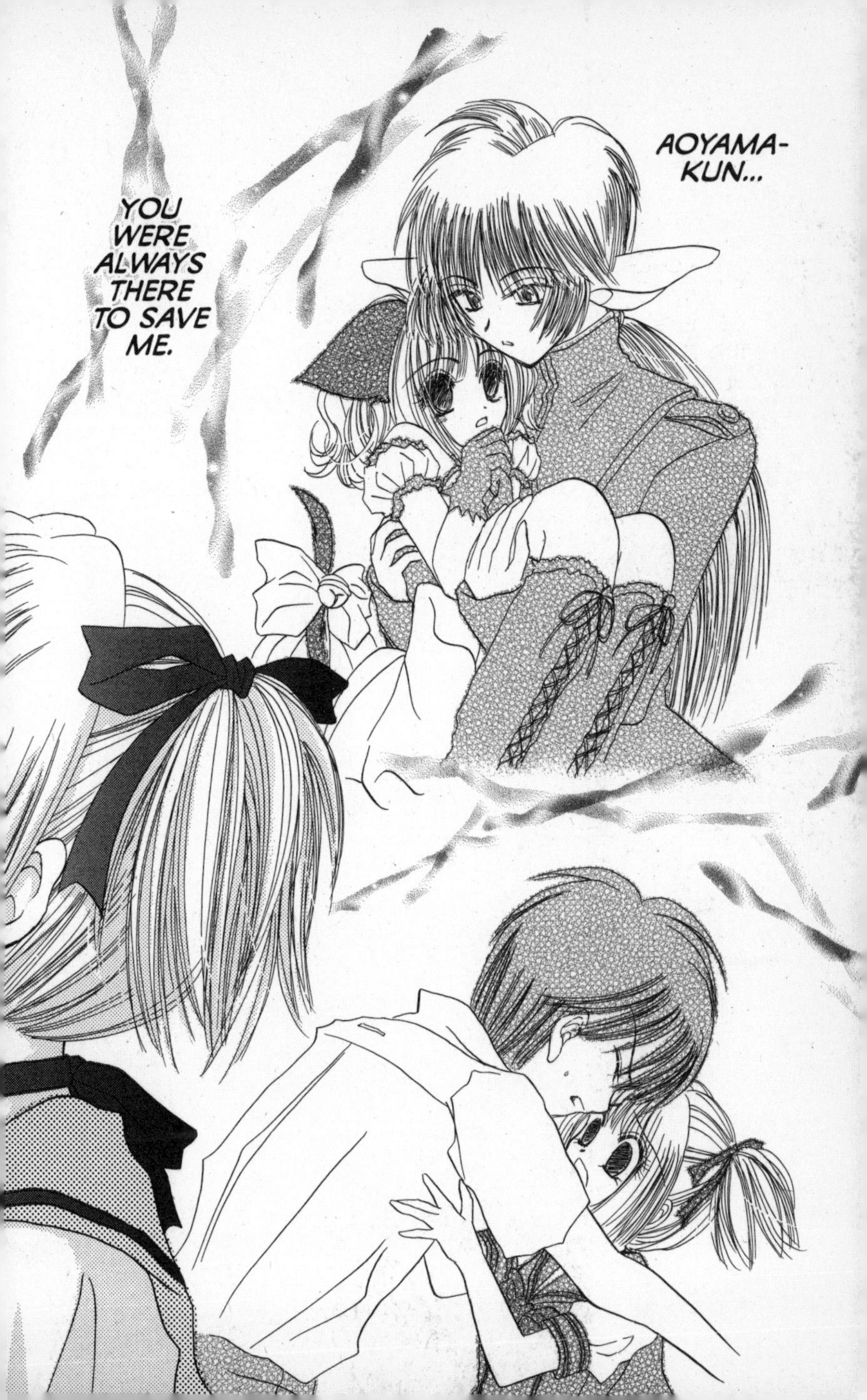
AOYAMA-
KUN...
YOU
WERE
ALWAYS
THERE
TO SAVE
ME.

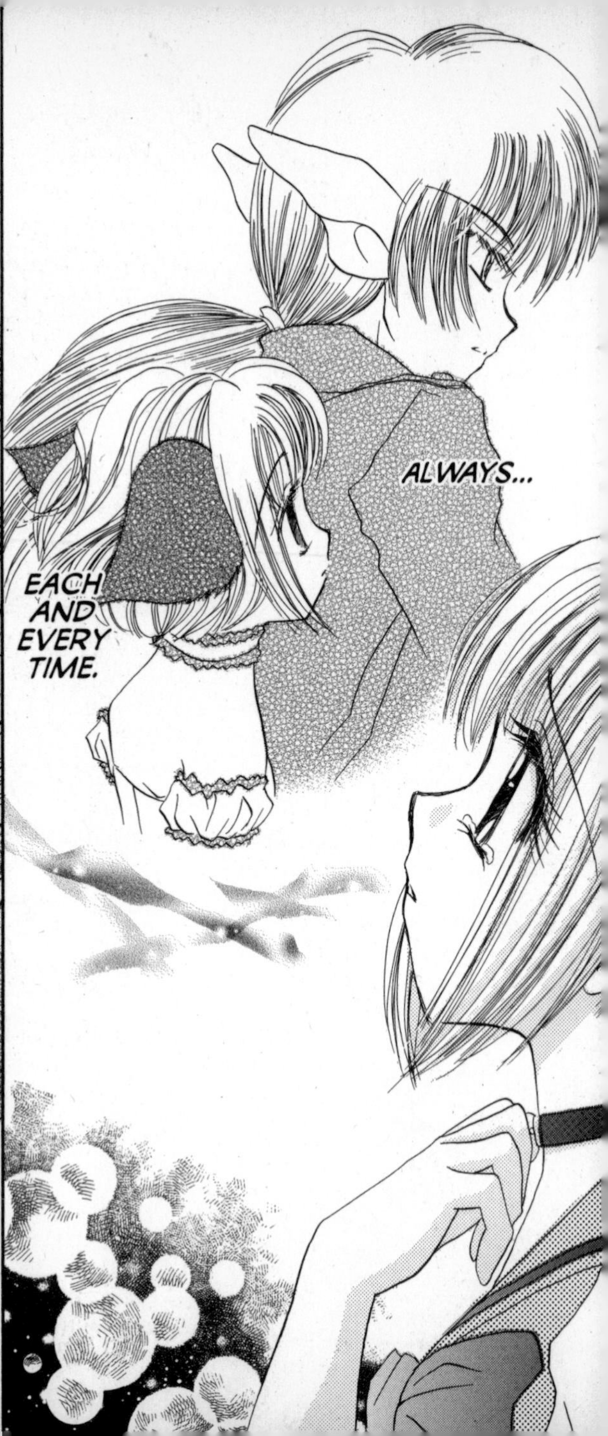
ALWAYS...
EACH AND EVERY TIME.
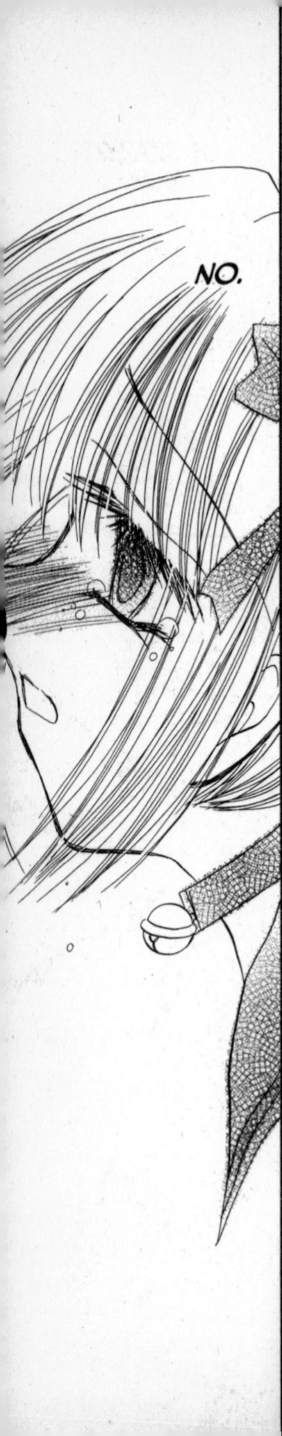
NO.

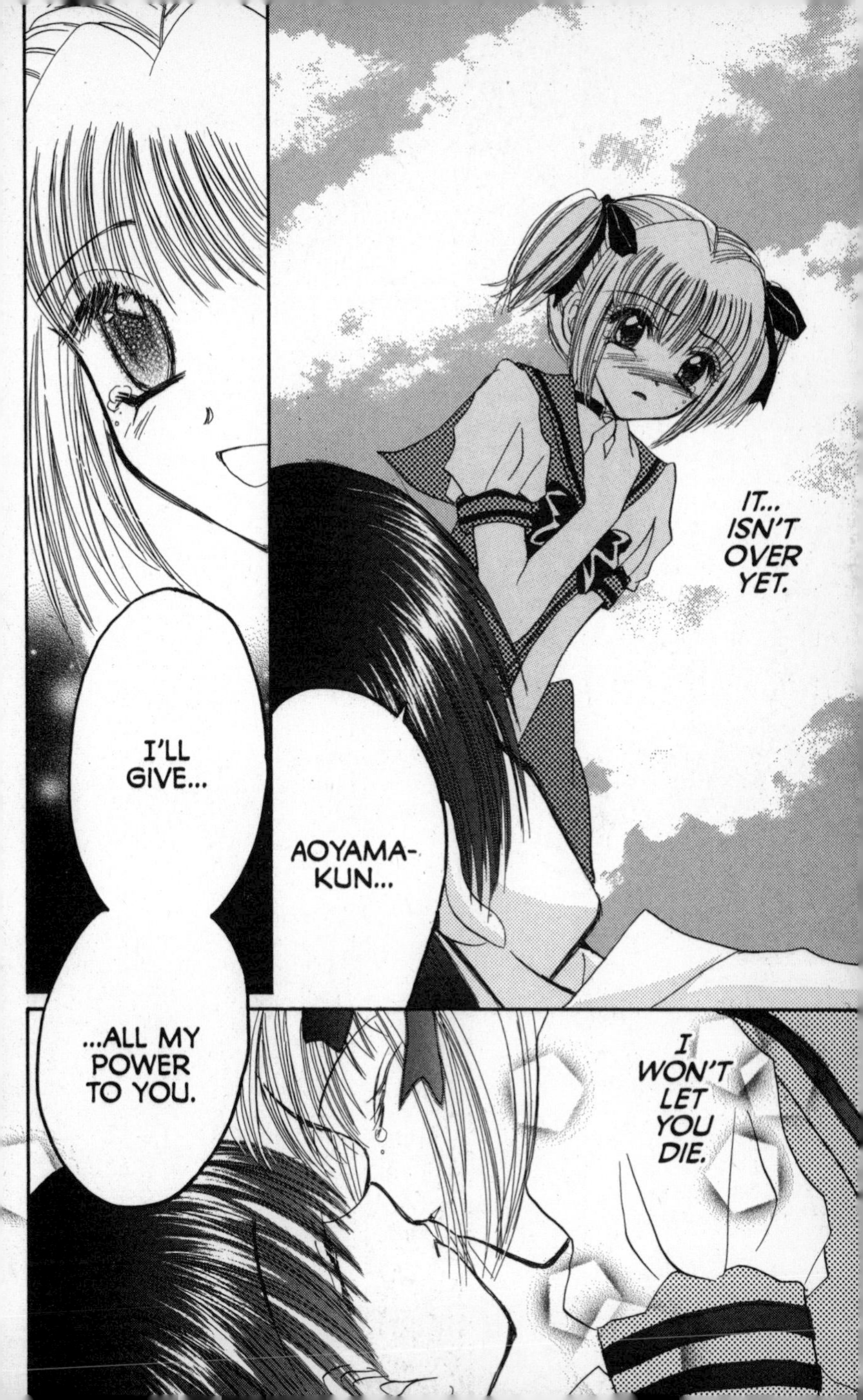
IT... ISN'T OVER YET.
AOYAMA-KUN...
I'LL GIVE...
...ALL MY POWER TO YOU.
I WON'T LET YOU DIE.

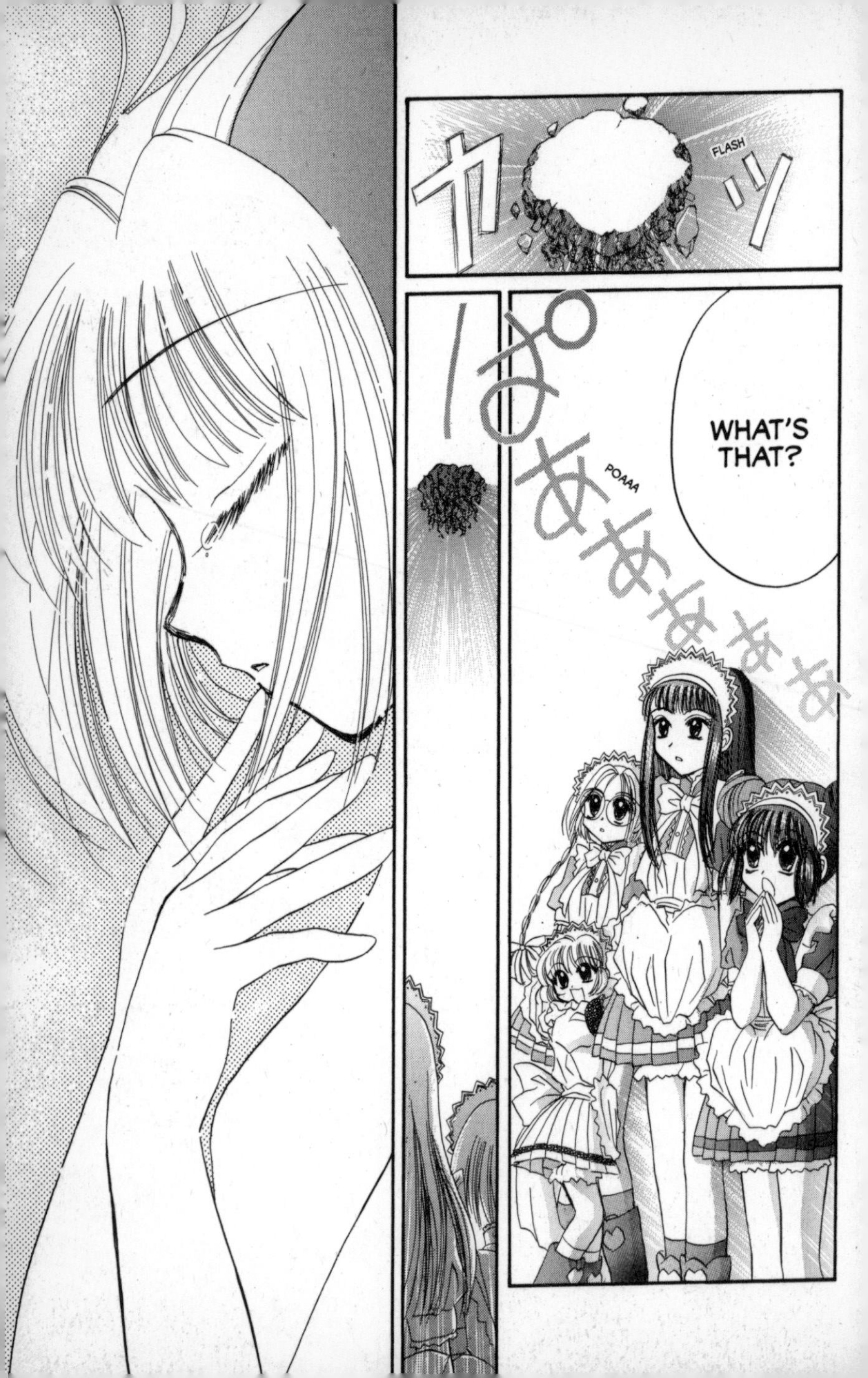
カッ
FLASH
WHAT'S THAT?
ぱあああああ
POAAA

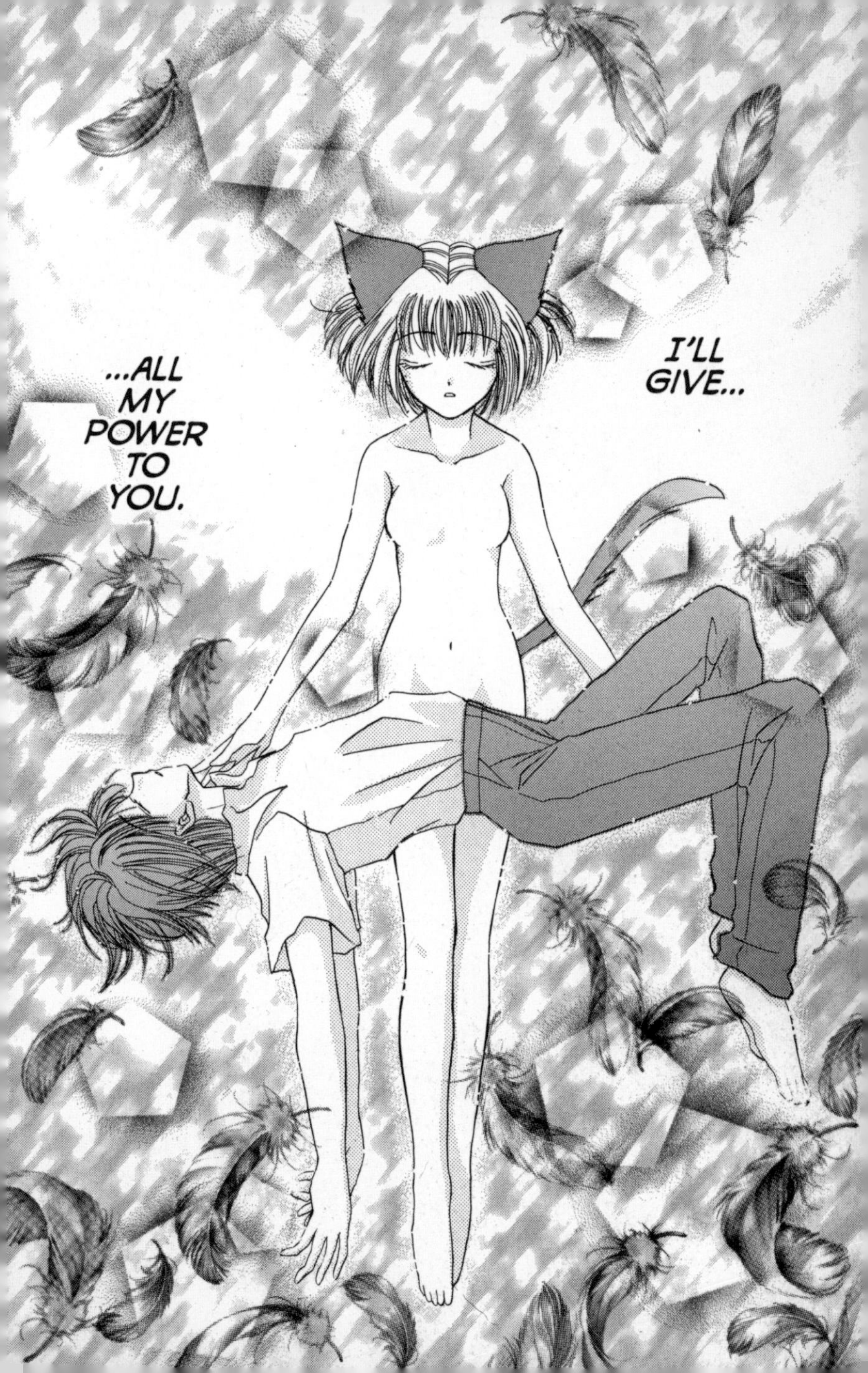
I'LL GIVE...
...ALL MY POWER TO YOU.

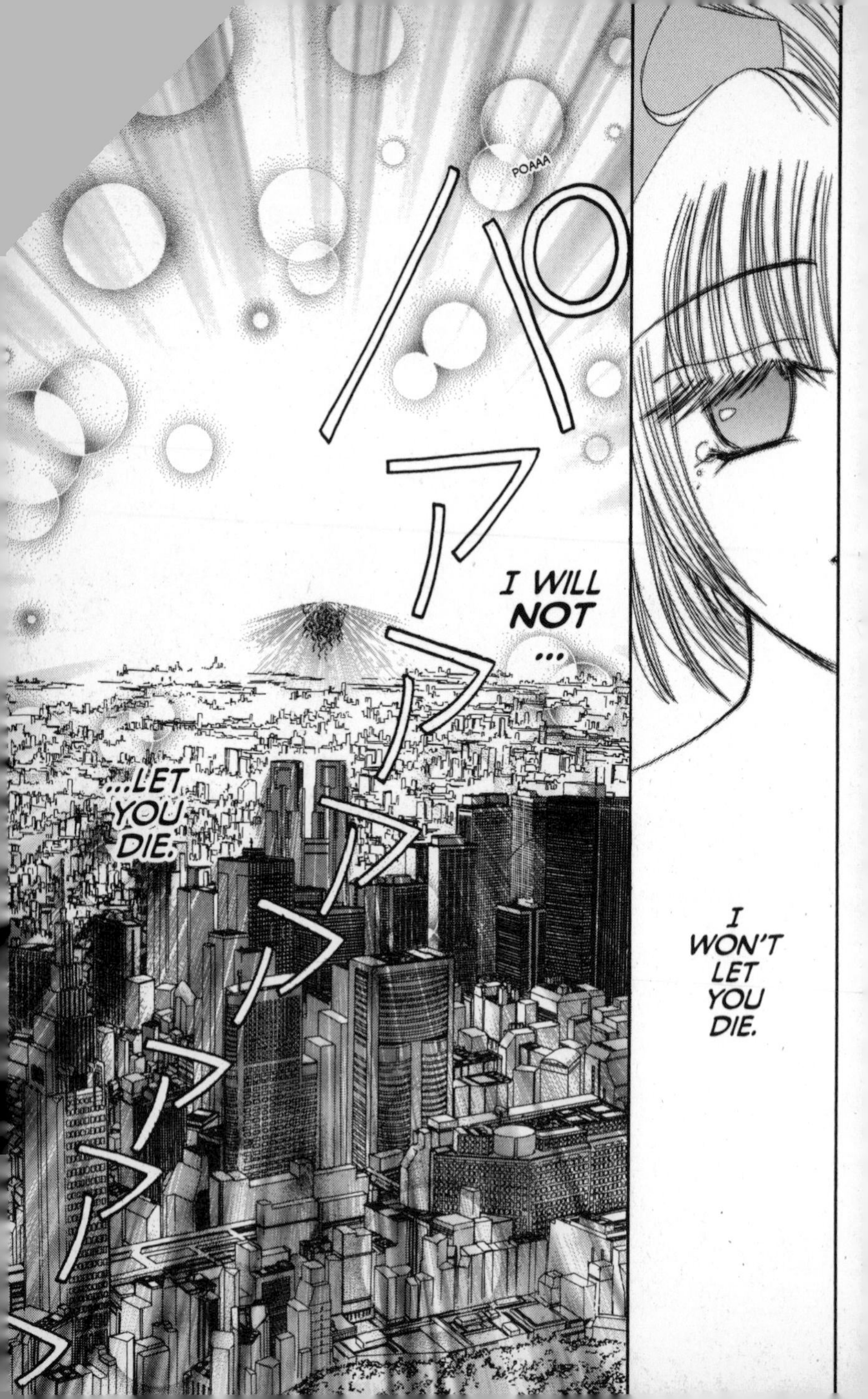
I WON'T LET YOU DIE.
POAAA
I WILL NOT ...
...LET YOU DIE.

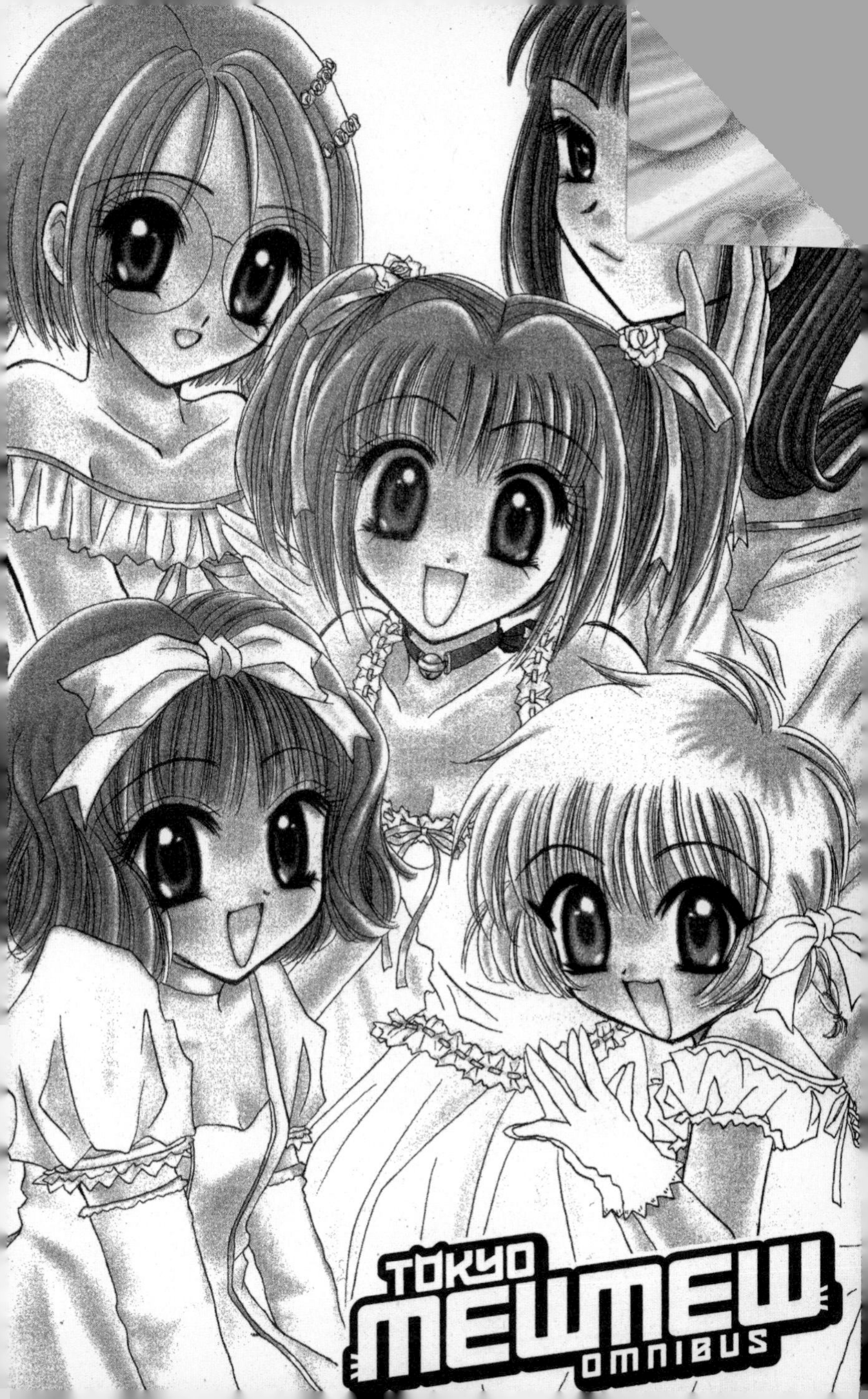
TOKYO
MEWMEW
OMNIBUS

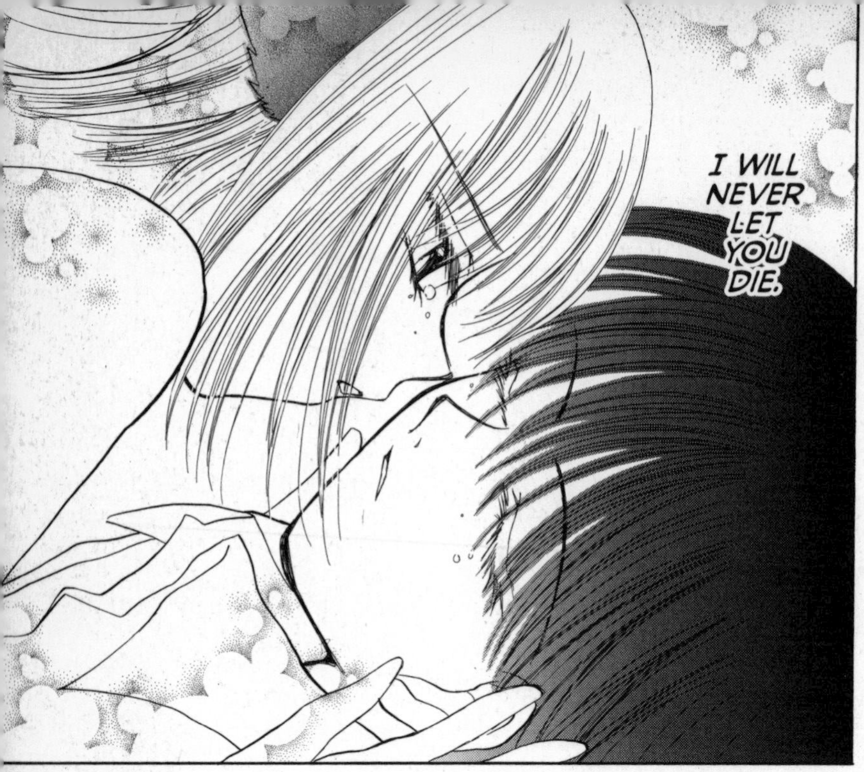
I WILL NEVER LET YOU DIE.

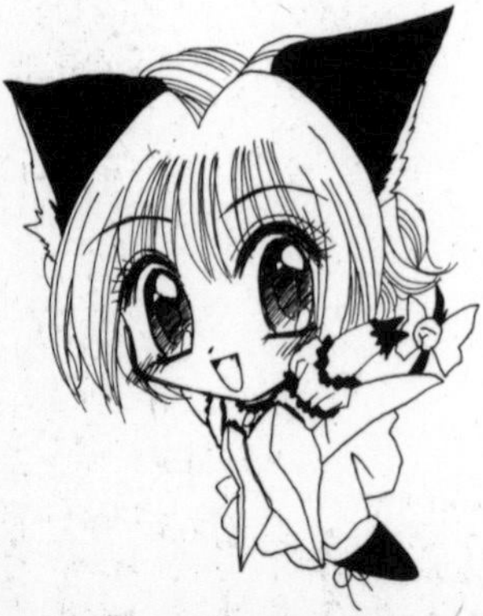

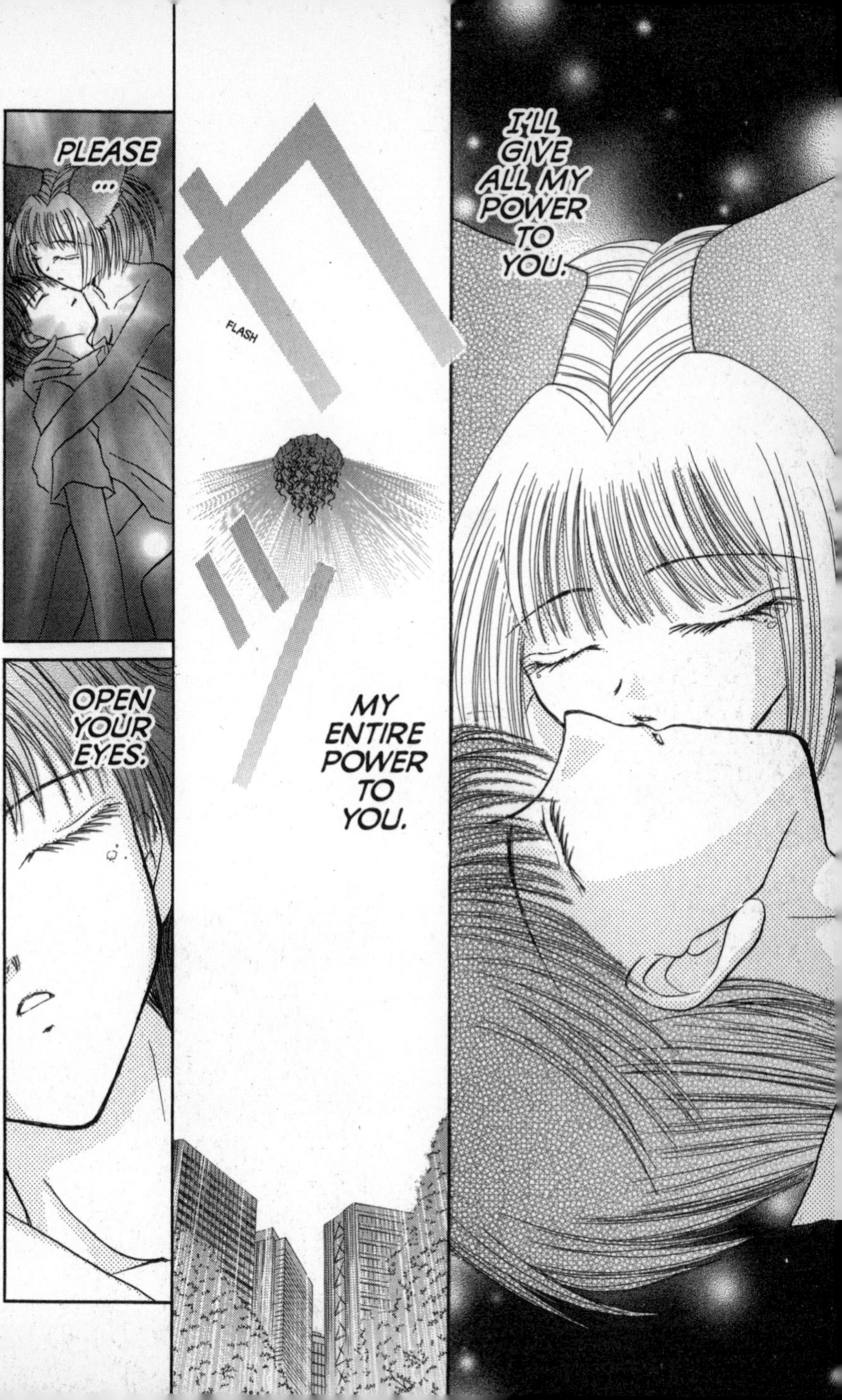
I'LL GIVE ALL MY POWER TO YOU.
FLASH
MY ENTIRE POWER TO YOU.
PLEASE ...
OPEN YOUR EYES.

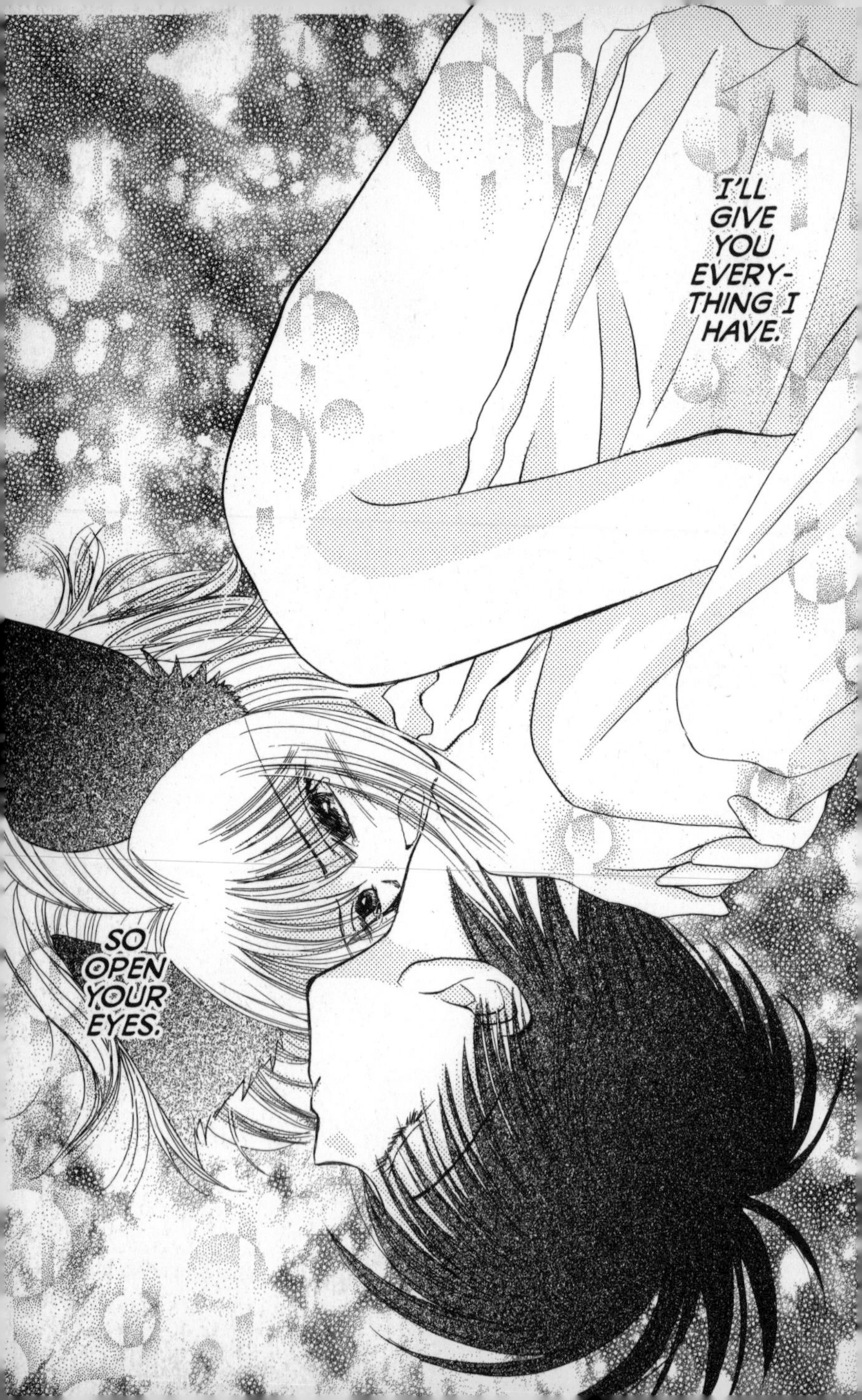
I'LL GIVE YOU EVERY-THING I HAVE.
SO OPEN YOUR EYES.

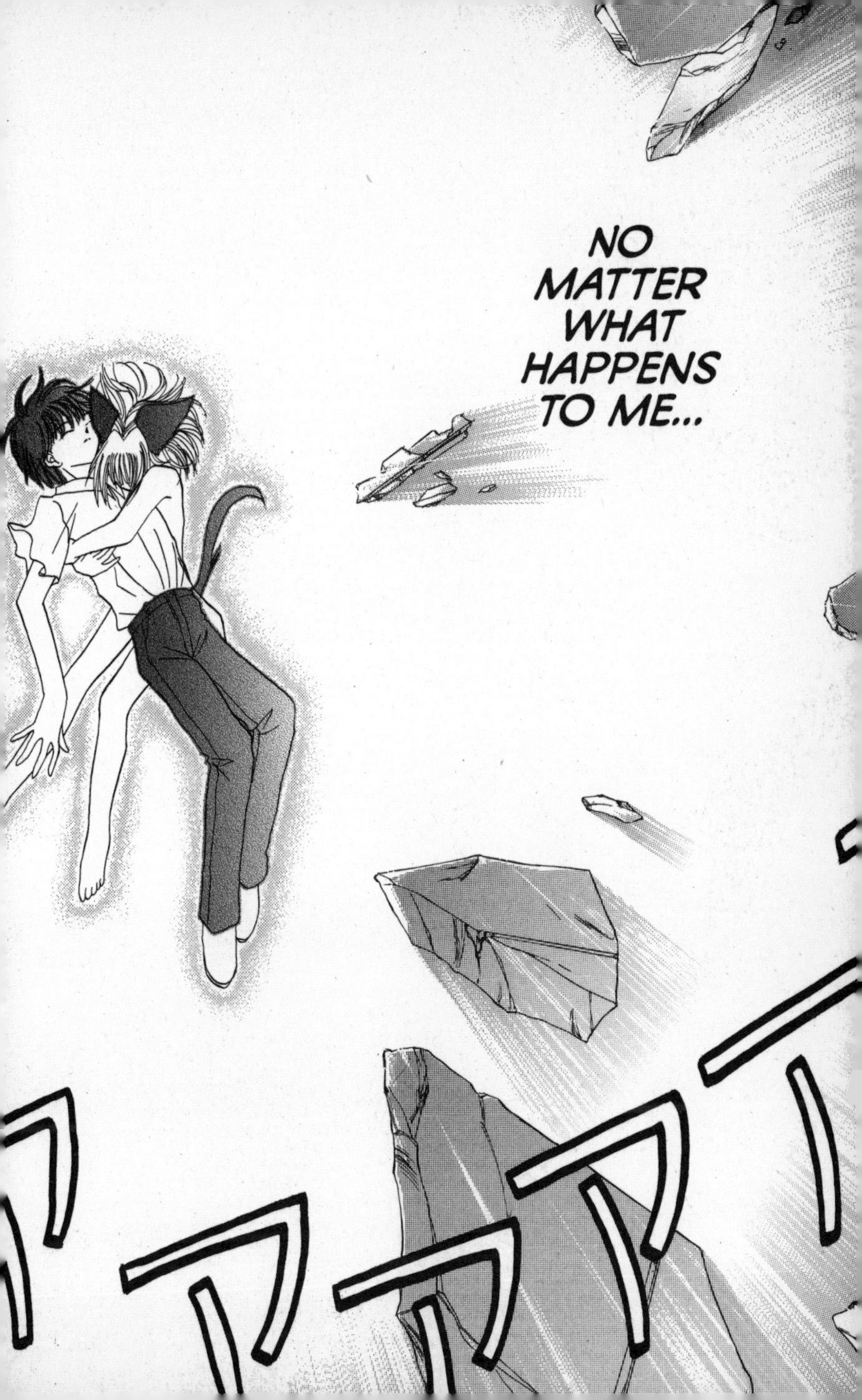
NO MATTER WHAT HAPPENS TO ME...
アアアアア

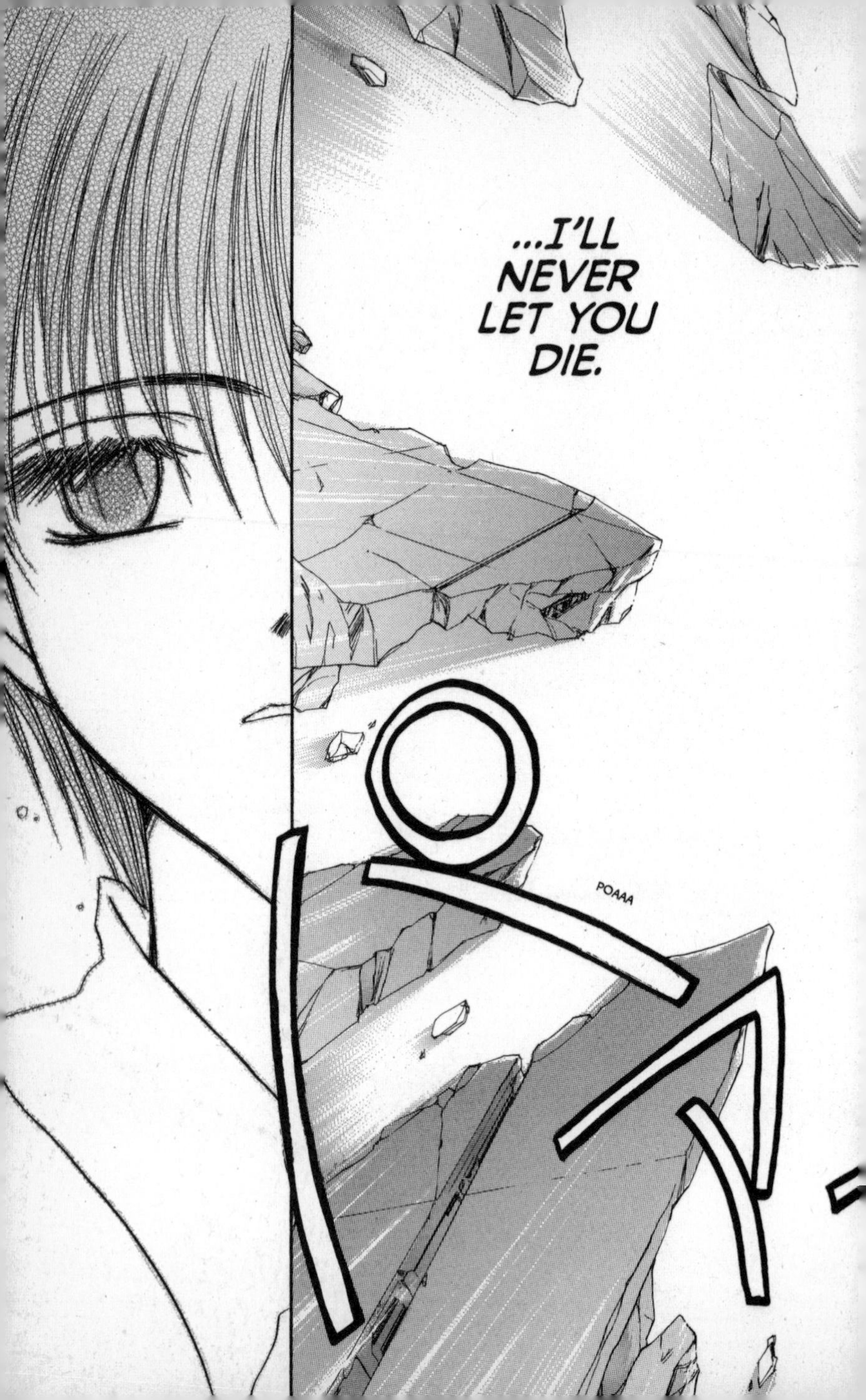
...I'LL NEVER LET YOU DIE.
POAAA

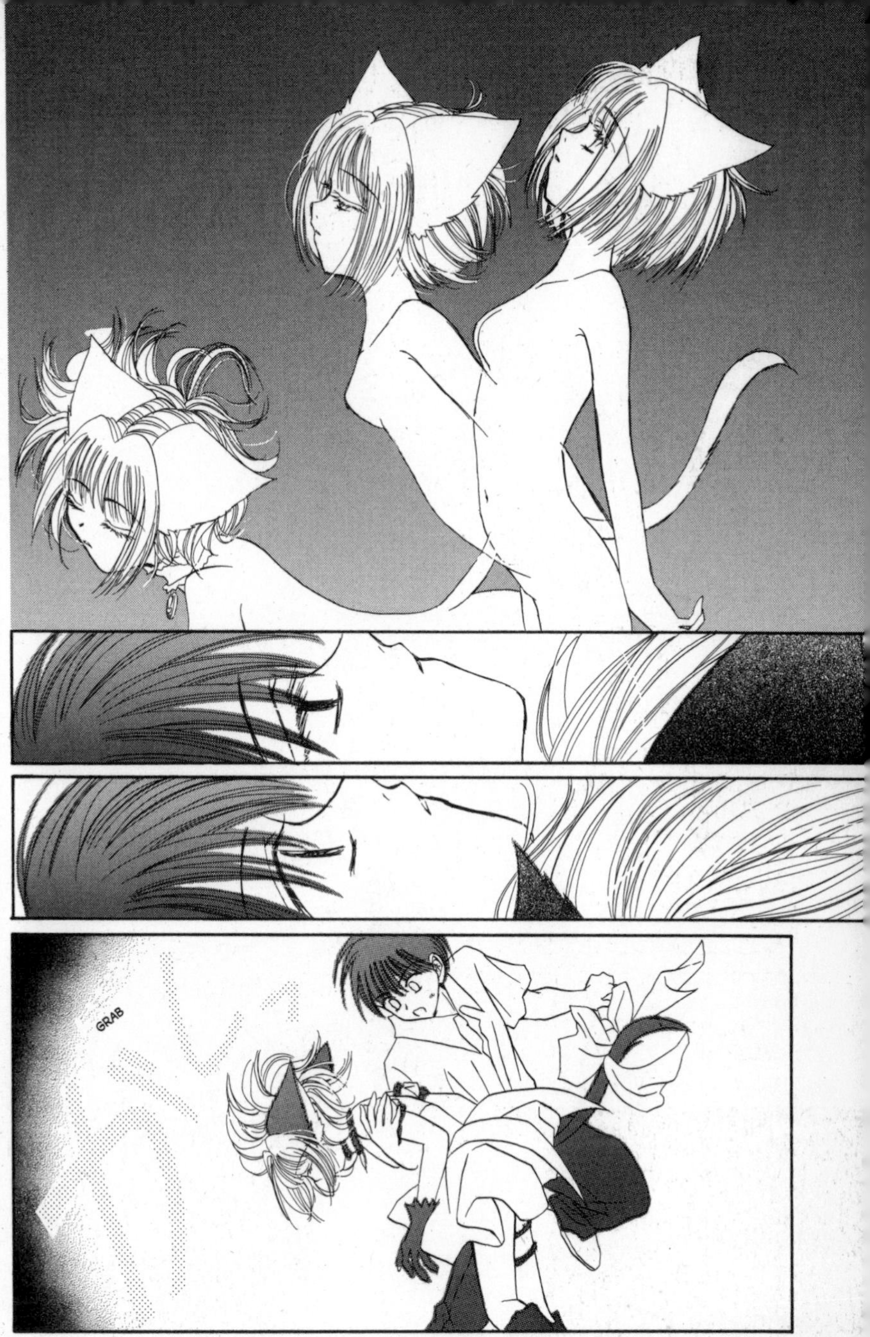
GRAB

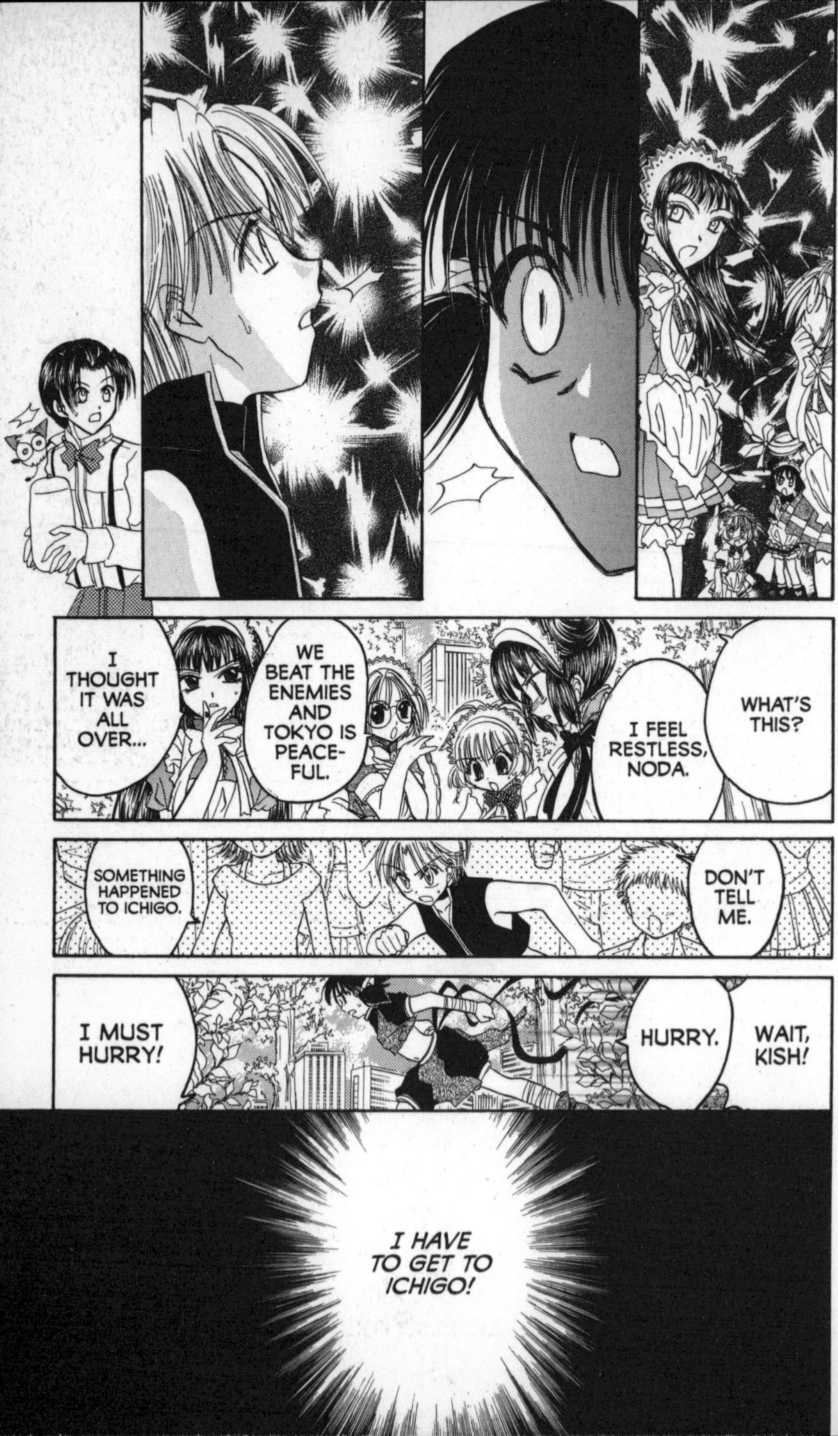
WHAT'S THIS?
I FEEL RESTLESS, NODA.
WE BEAT THE ENEMIES AND TOKYO IS PEACE-FUL.
I THOUGHT IT WAS ALL OVER...
DON'T TELL ME.
SOMETHING HAPPENED TO ICHIGO.
WAIT, KISH!
HURRY.
I MUST HURRY!
I HAVE TO GET TO ICHIGO!

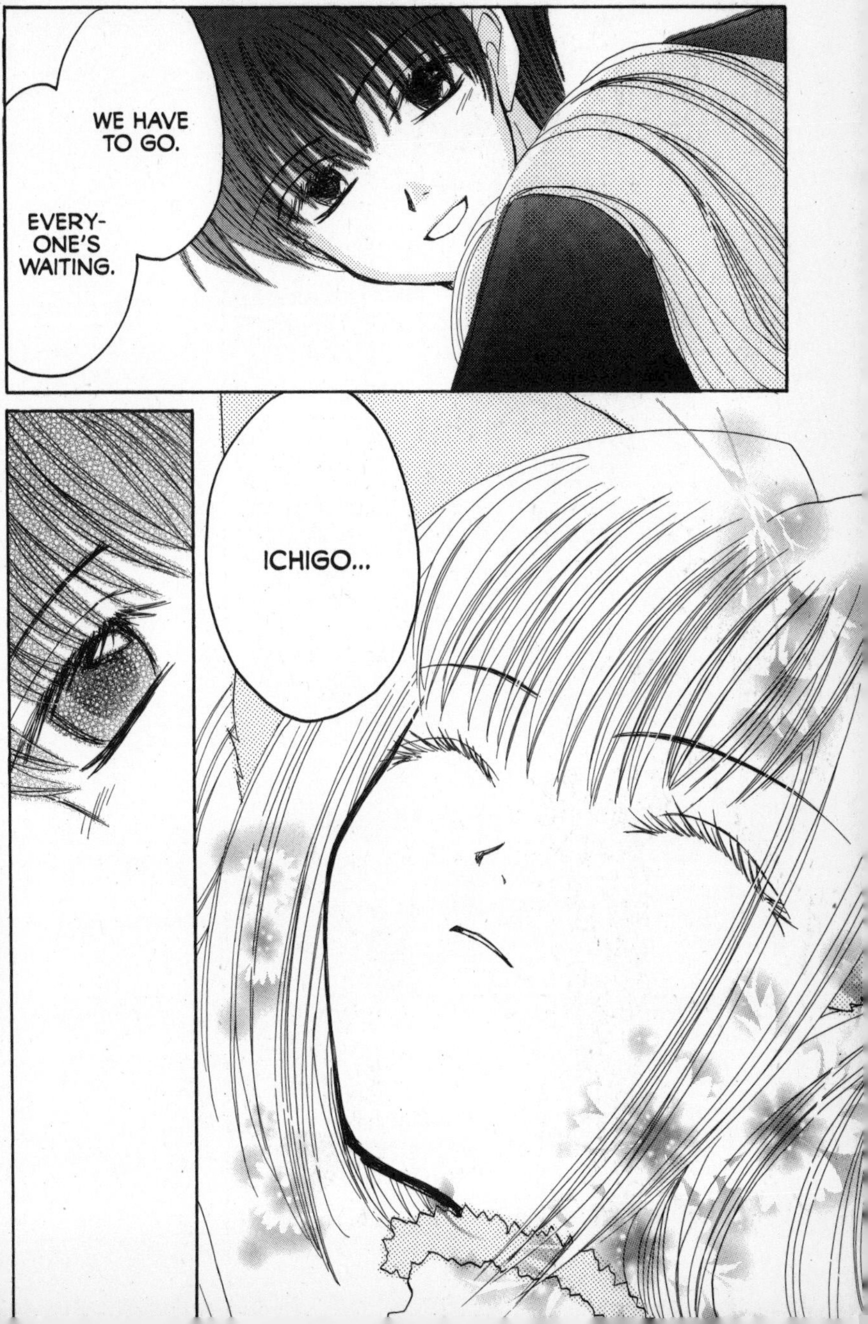
WE HAVE TO GO.
EVERY-ONE'S WAITING.
ICHIGO...

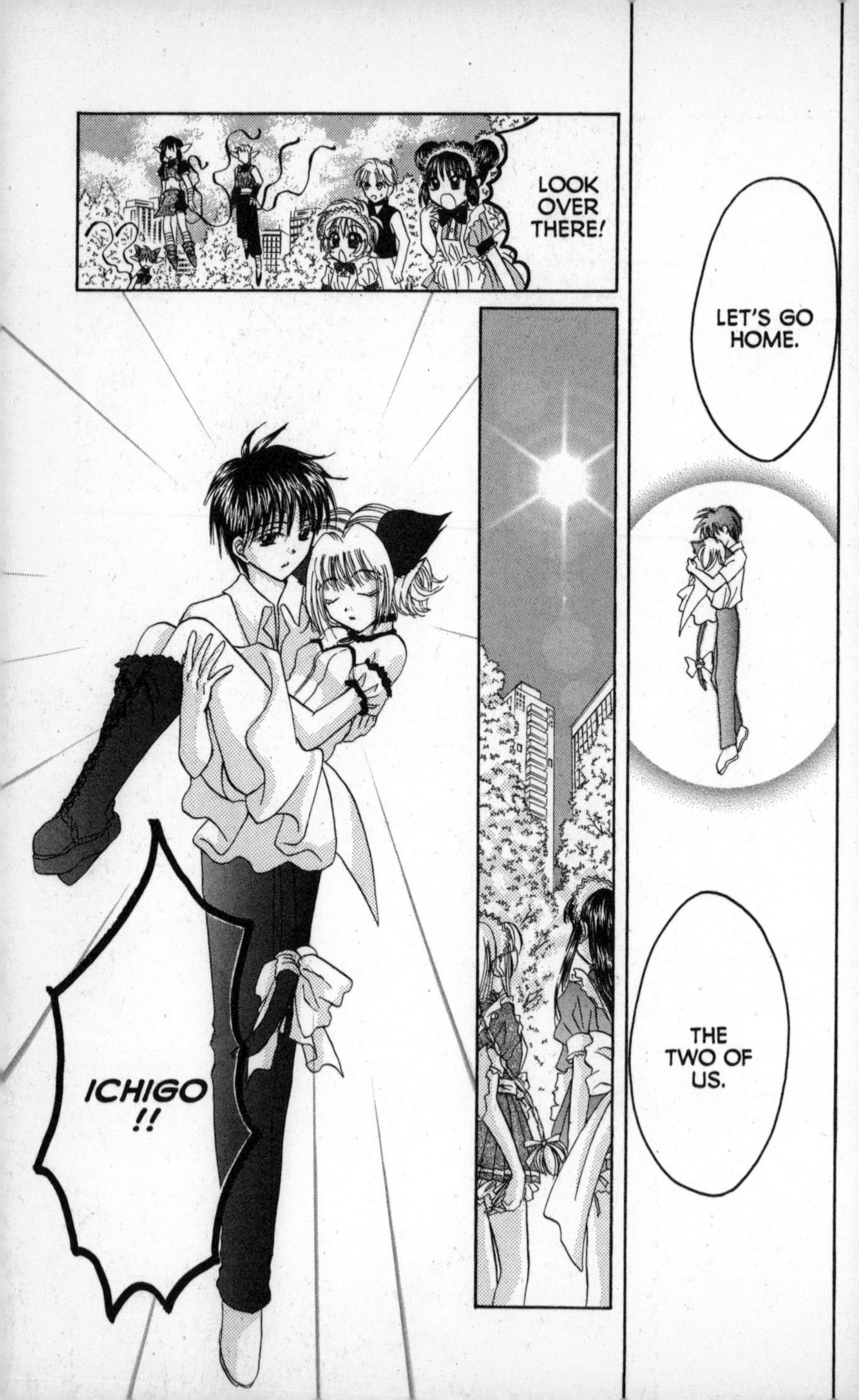
LET'S GO HOME.
THE TWO OF US.
LOOK OVER THERE!
ICHIGO !!

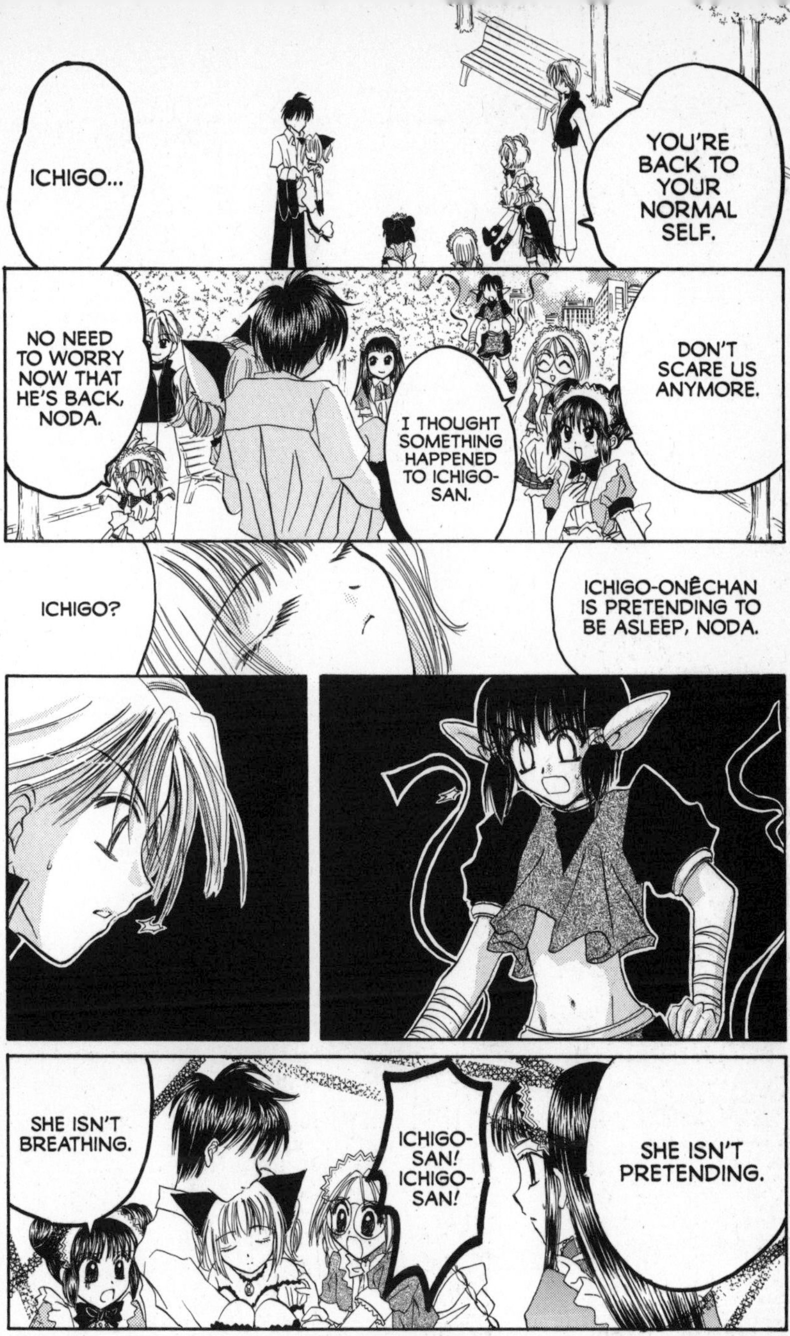
YOU'RE BACK TO YOUR NORMAL SELF.
ICHIGO...
DON'T SCARE US ANYMORE.
I THOUGHT SOMETHING HAPPENED TO ICHIGO-SAN.
NO NEED TO WORRY NOW THAT HE'S BACK, NODA.
ICHIGO-ONÊCHAN IS PRETENDING TO BE ASLEEP, NODA.
ICHIGO?
SHE ISN'T PRETENDING.
ICHIGO-SAN! ICHIGO-SAN!
SHE ISN'T BREATHING.

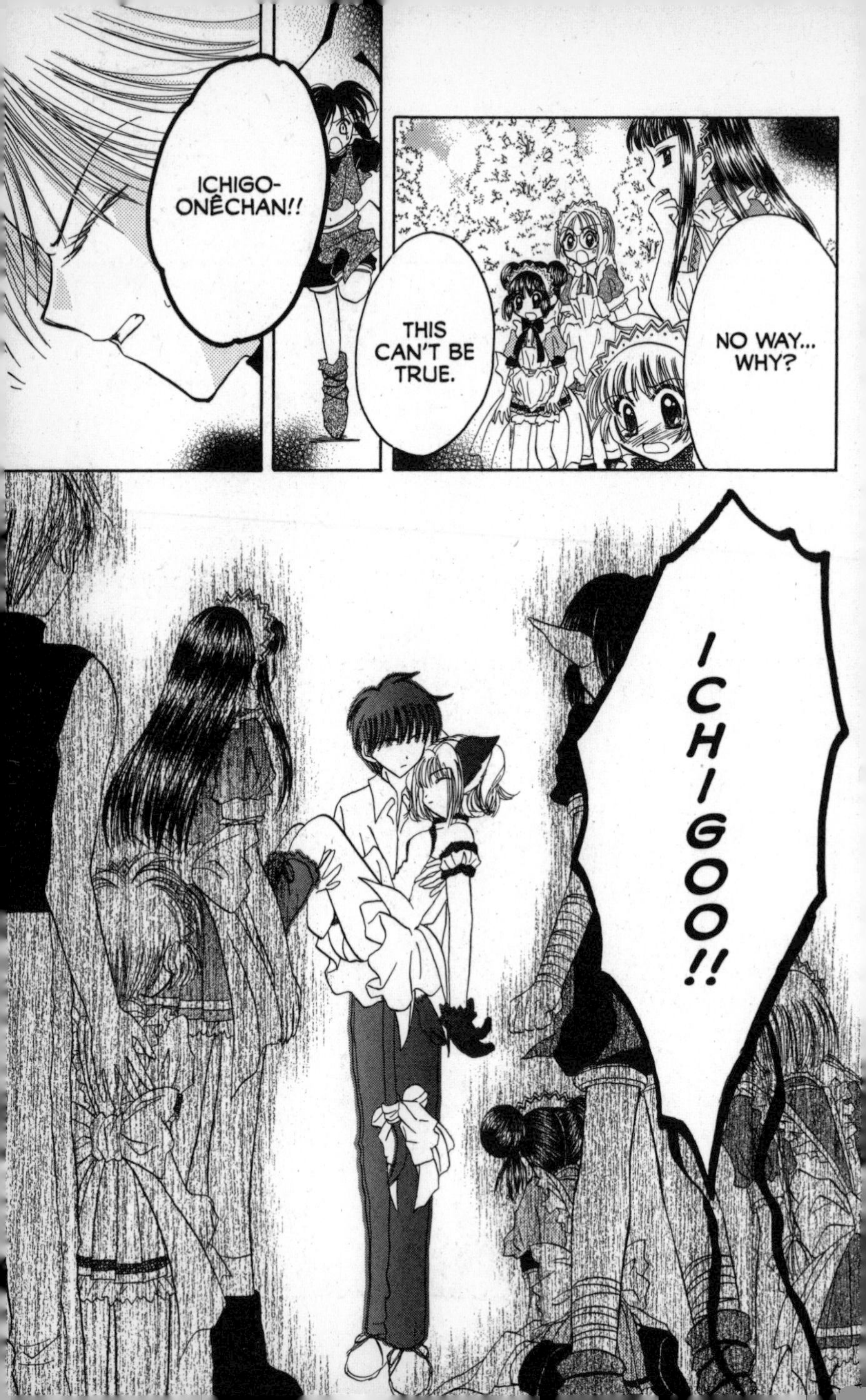
NO WAY... WHY?
THIS CAN'T BE TRUE.
ICHIGO-ONÊCHAN!!
ICHIGOOO!!

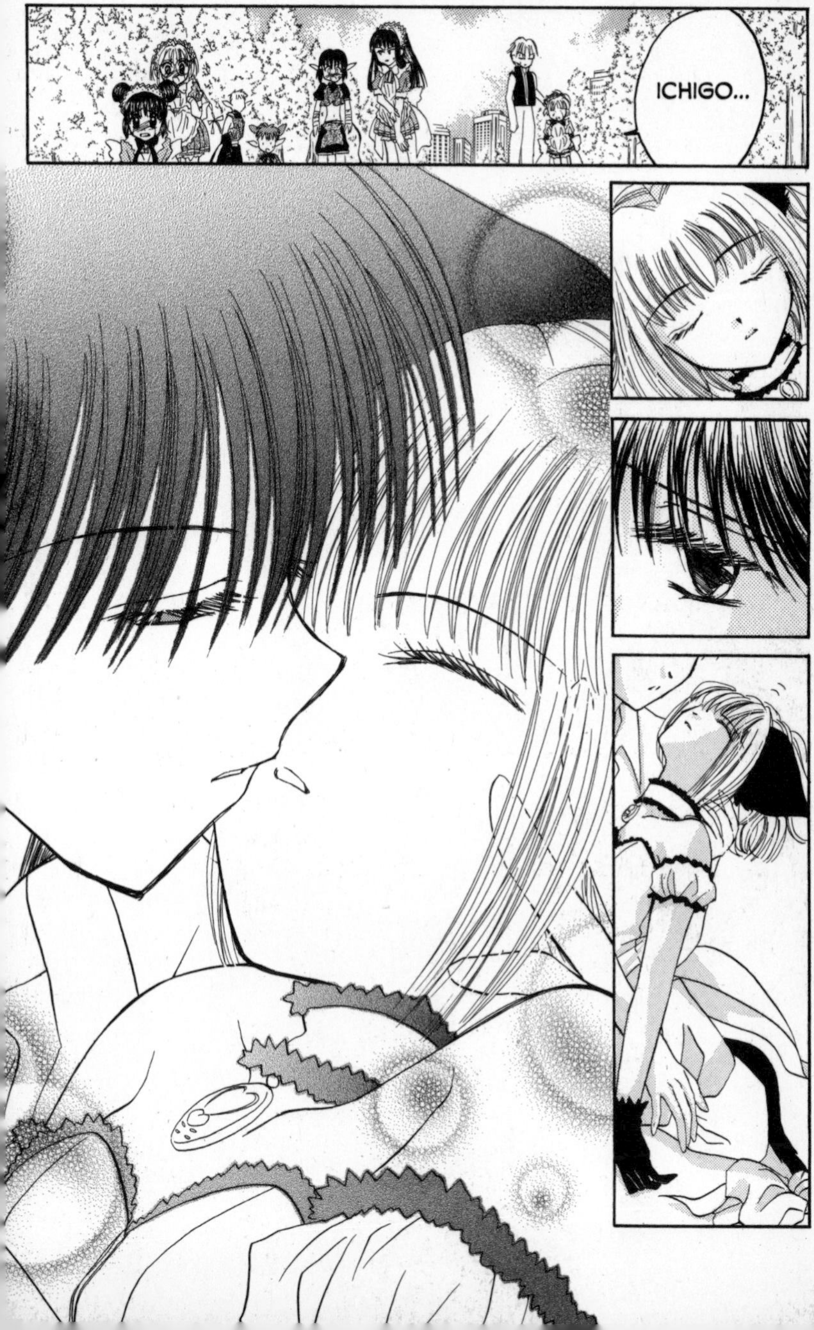
ICHIGO...

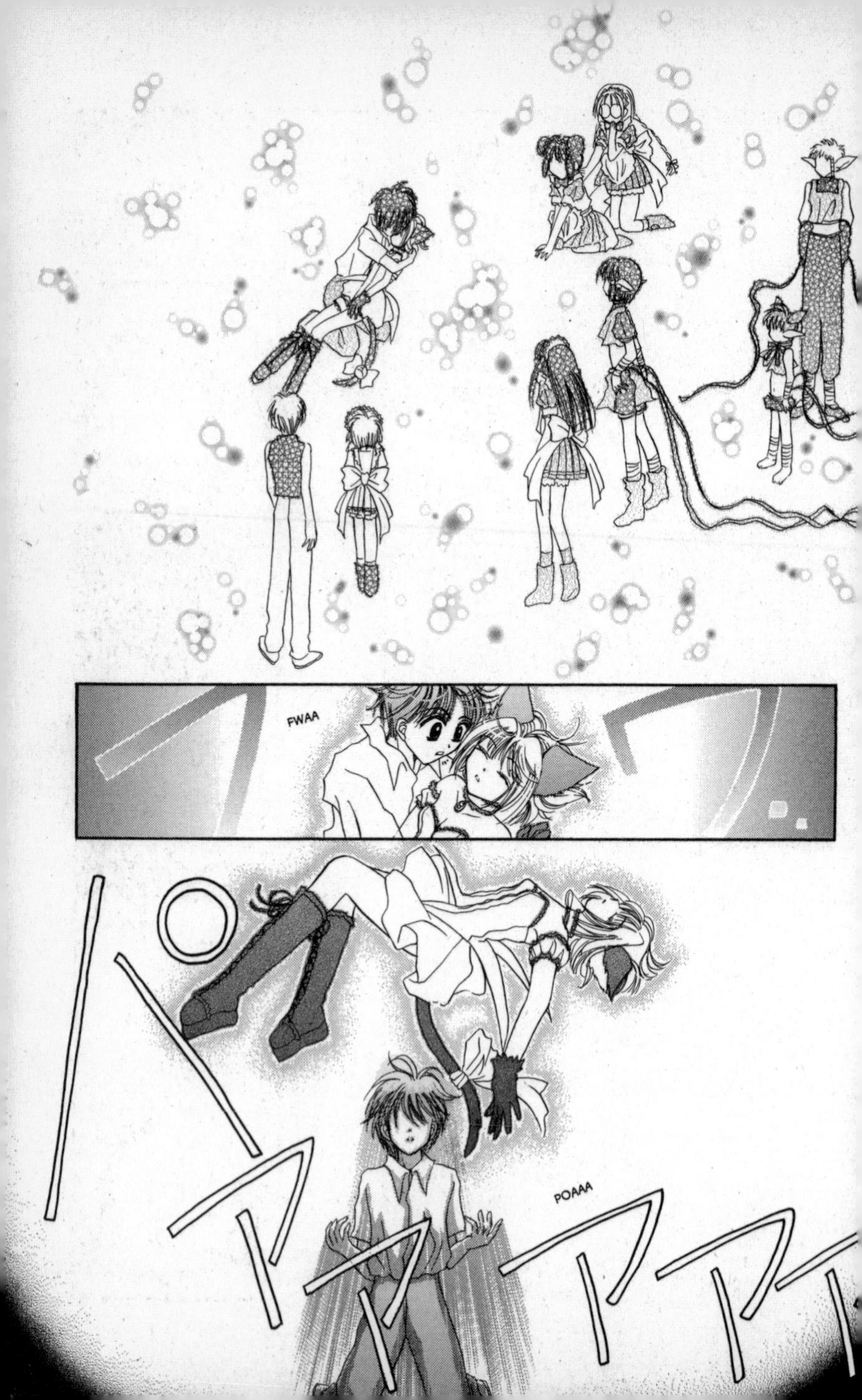
FWAA
POAAA

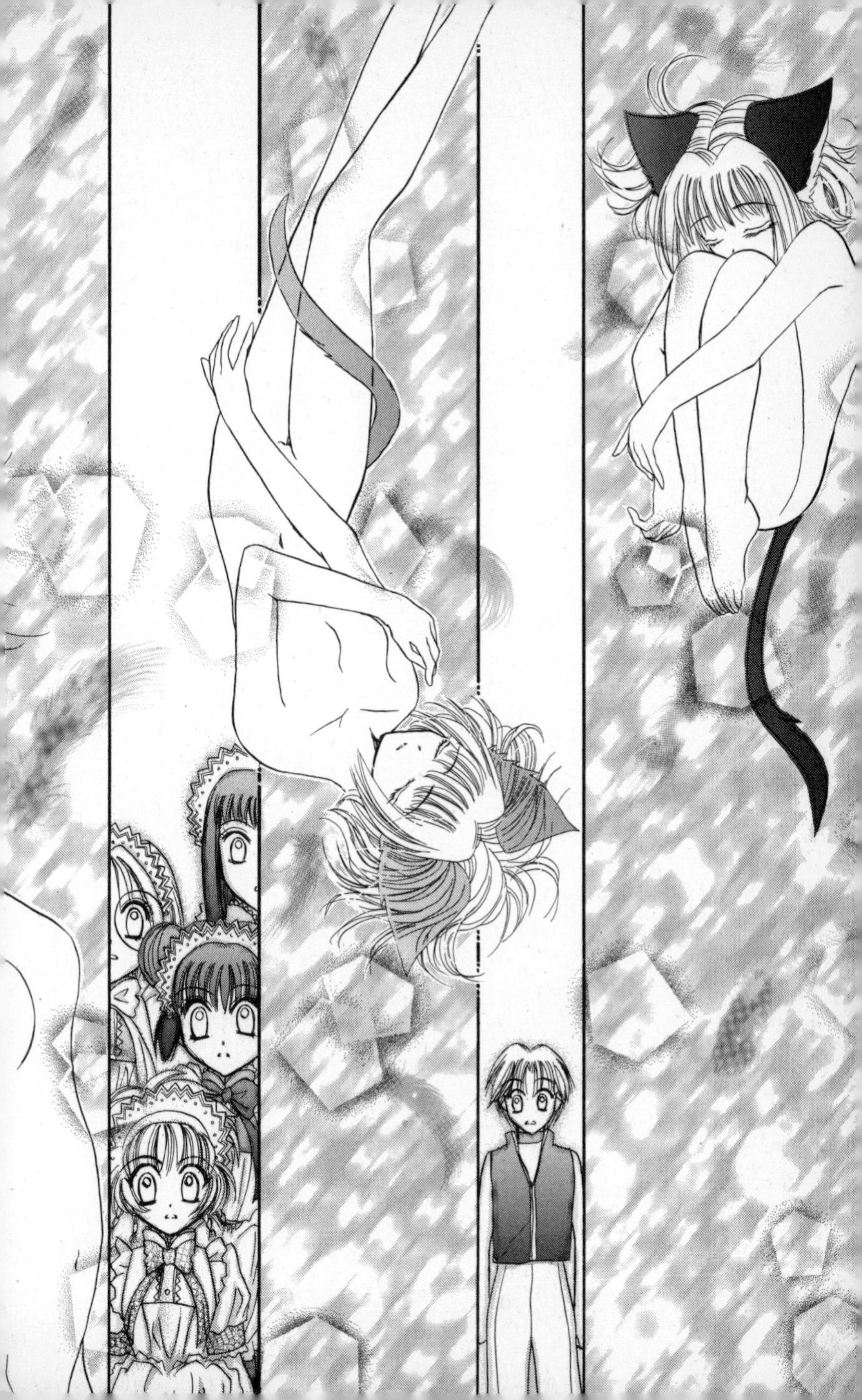

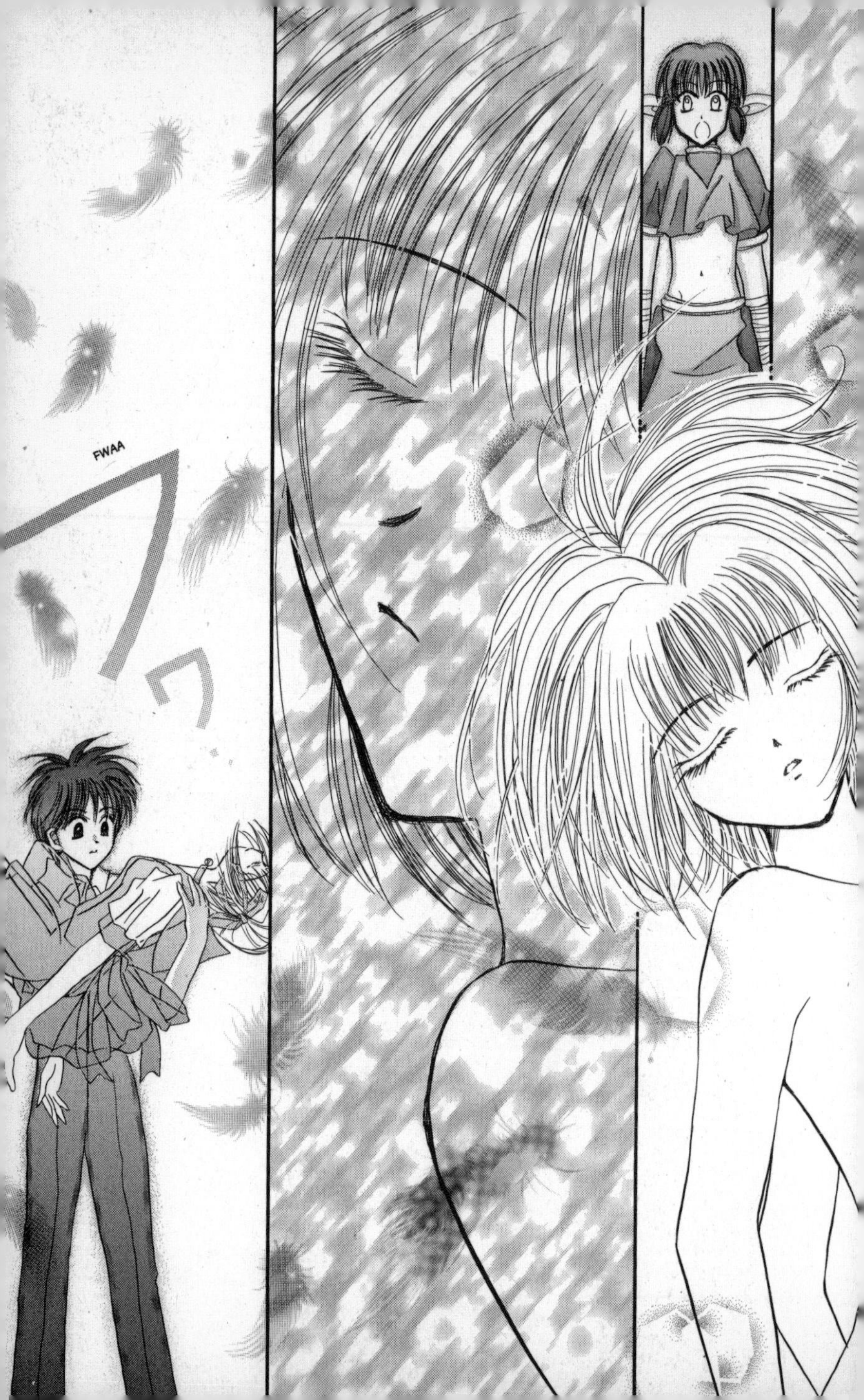
FWAA

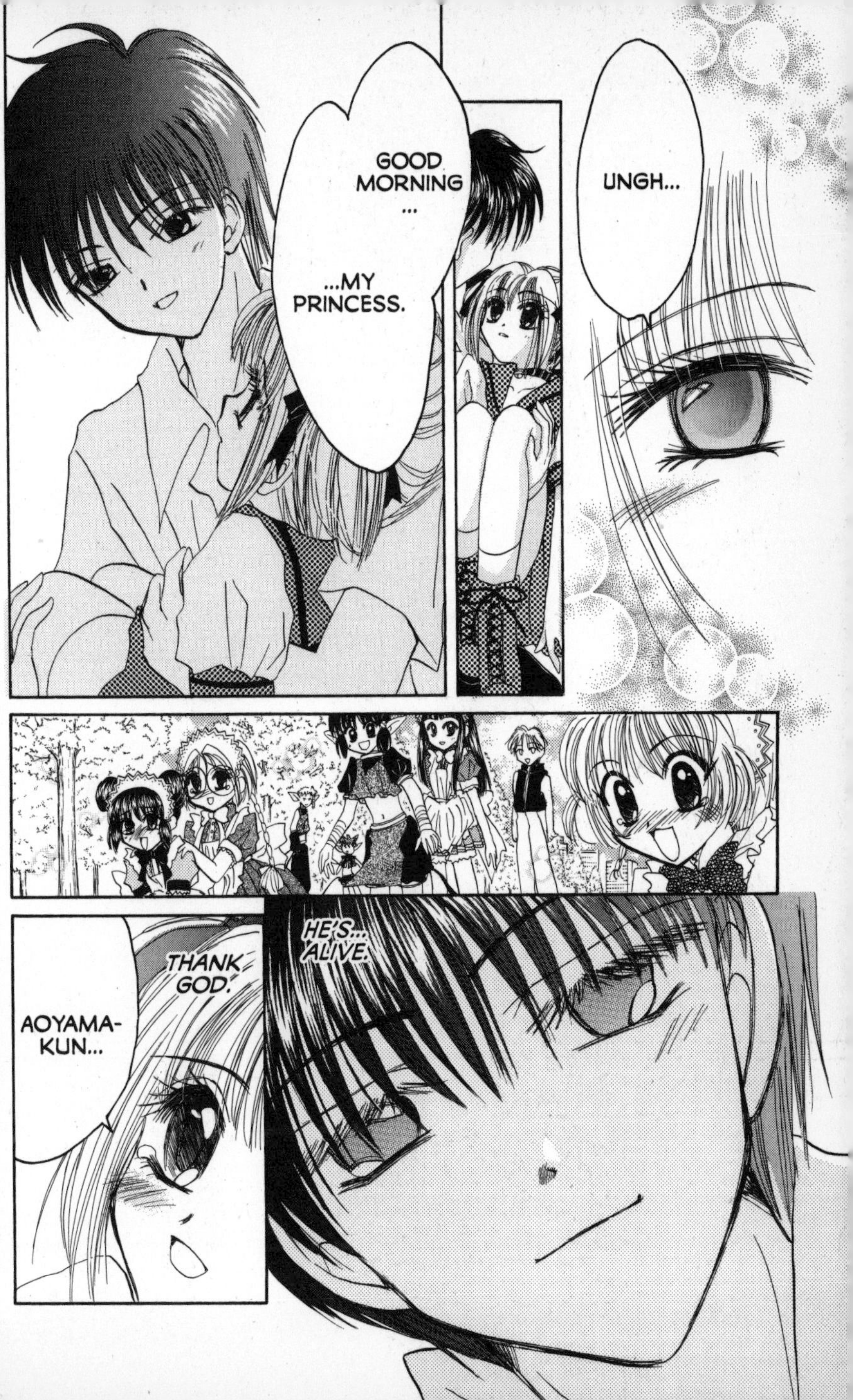
UNGH...
GOOD MORNING ...
...MY PRINCESS.
HE'S... ALIVE.
THANK GOD.
AOYAMA-KUN...

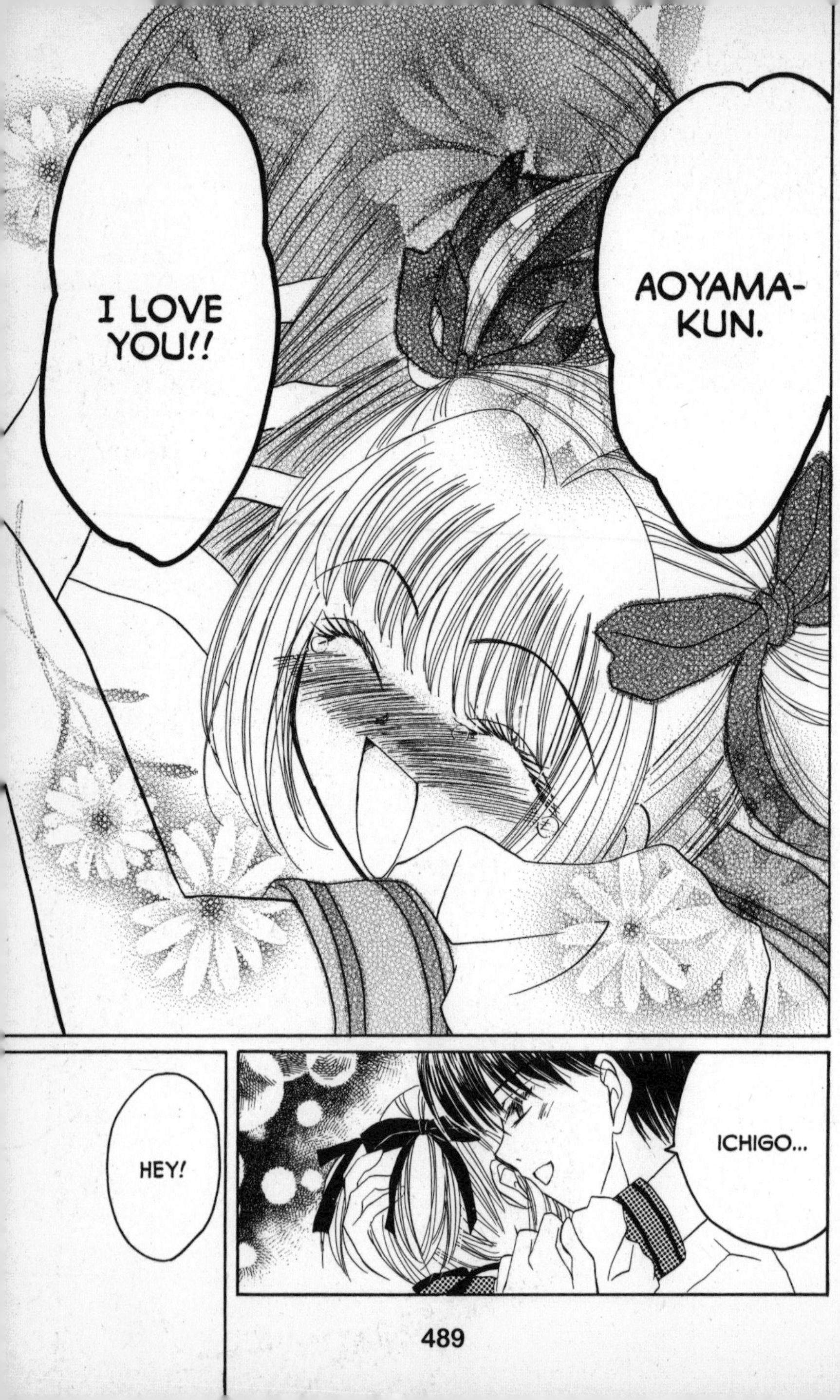
AOYAMA-KUN.
I LOVE YOU!!
ICHIGO...
HEY!

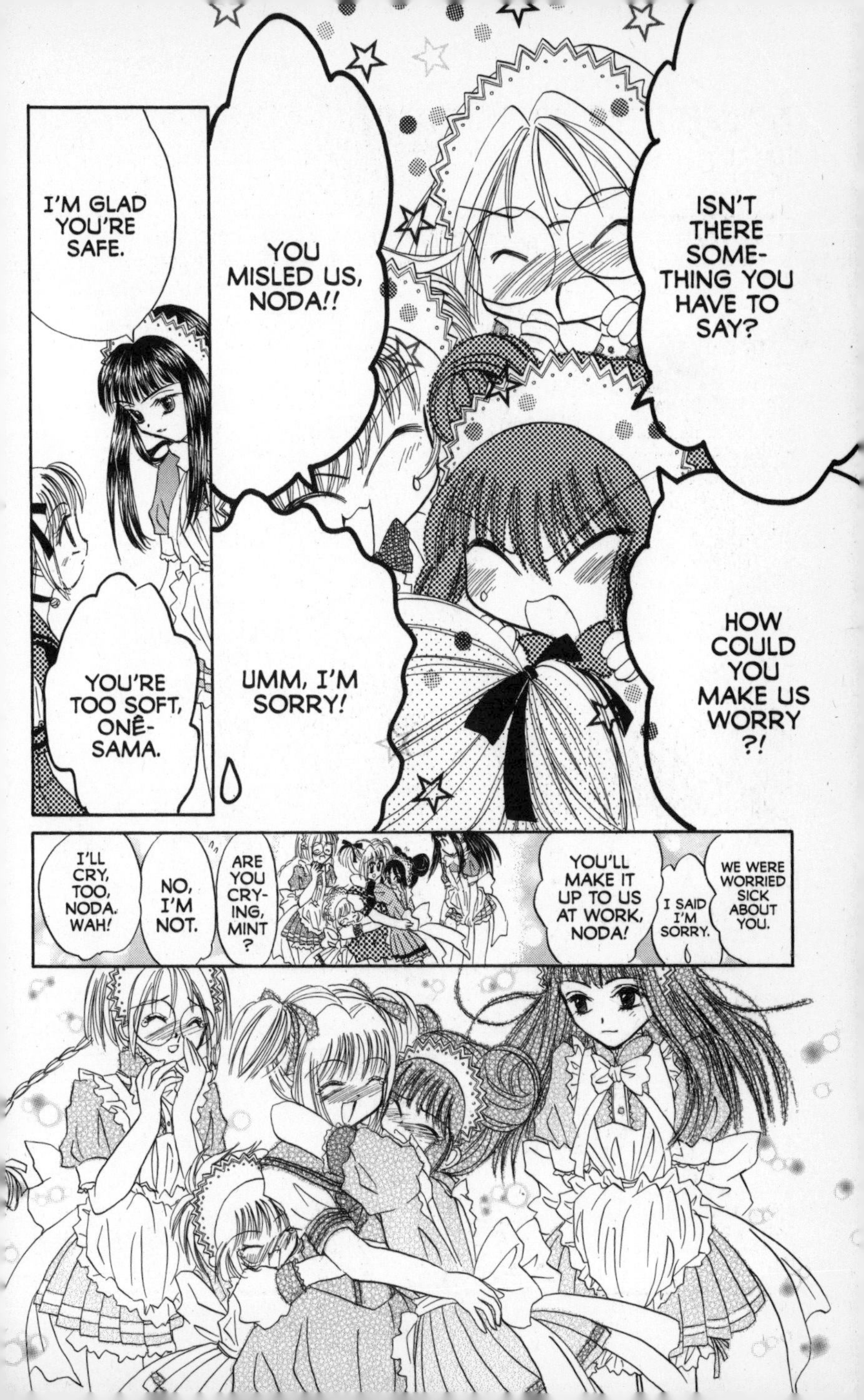
ISN'T THERE SOME-THING YOU HAVE TO SAY?
YOU MISLED US, NODA!!
HOW COULD YOU MAKE US WORRY ?!
UMM, I'M SORRY!
I'M GLAD YOU'RE SAFE.
YOU'RE TOO SOFT, ONÊ-SAMA.
WE WERE WORRIED SICK ABOUT YOU.
I SAID I'M SORRY.
YOU'LL MAKE IT UP TO US AT WORK, NODA!
ARE YOU CRY-ING, MINT ?
NO, I'M NOT.
I'LL CRY, TOO, NODA. WAH!

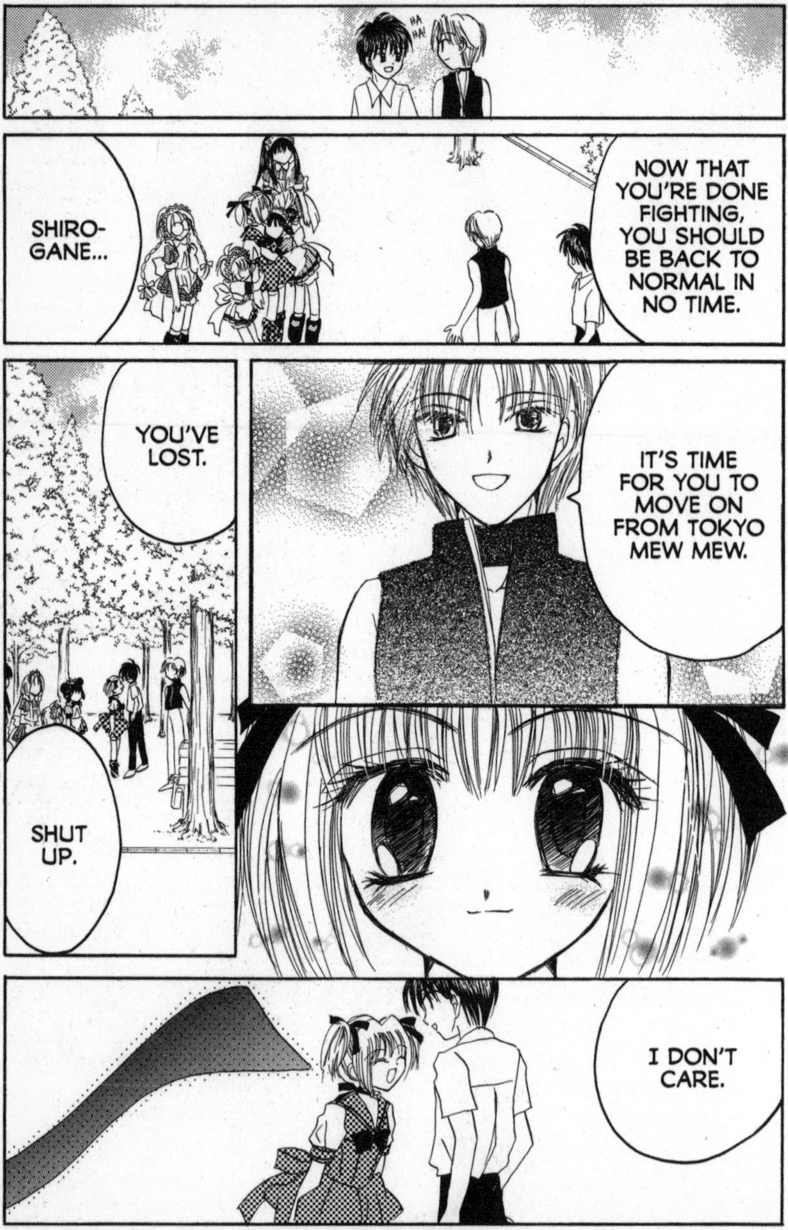
HA HA!
NOW THAT YOU'RE DONE FIGHTING, YOU SHOULD BE BACK TO NORMAL IN NO TIME.
SHIRO-GANE...
IT'S TIME FOR YOU TO MOVE ON FROM TOKYO MEW MEW.
YOU'VE LOST.
SHUT UP.
I DON'T CARE.

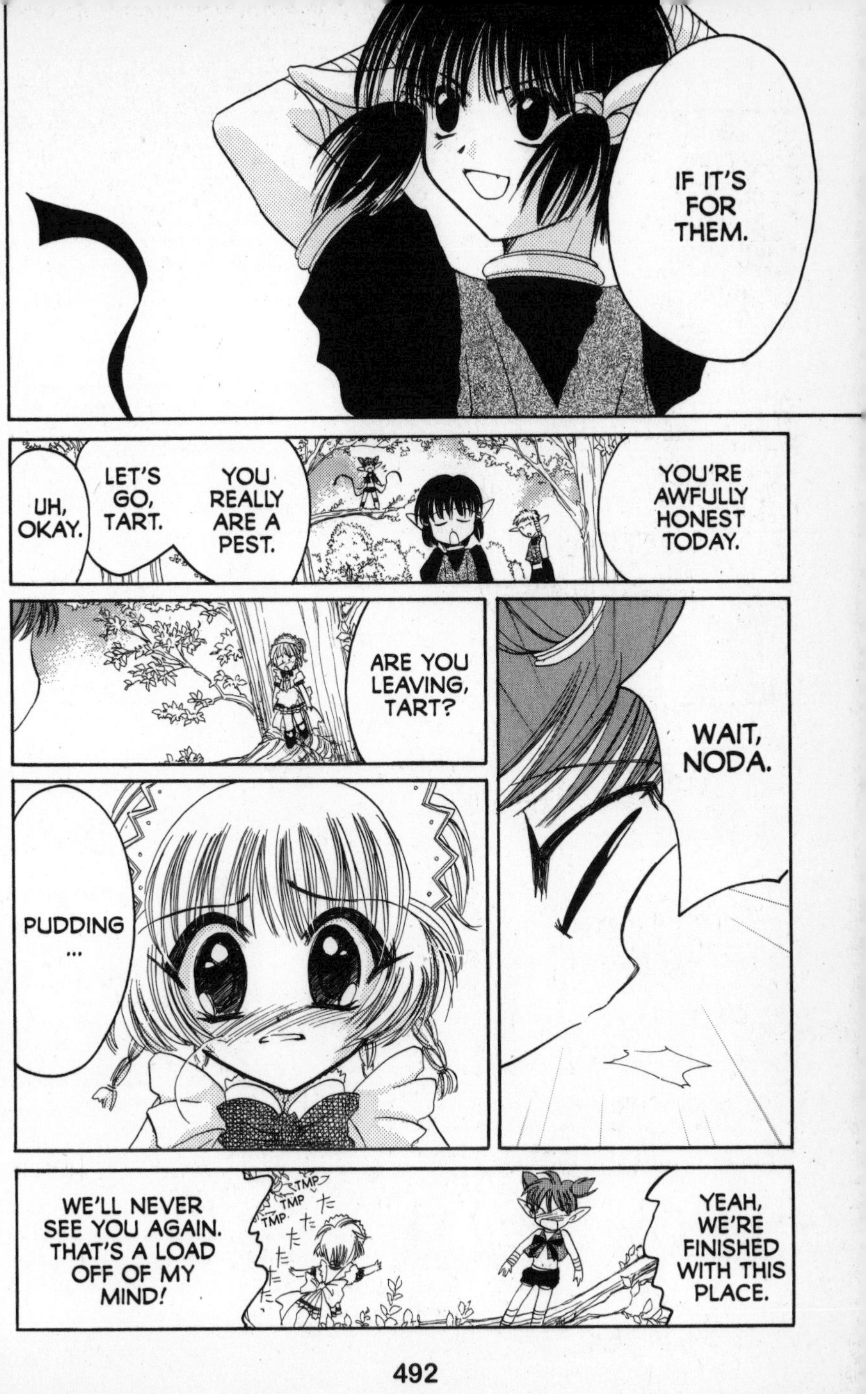

IF IT'S FOR THEM.
YOU'RE AWFULLY HONEST TODAY.
YOU REALLY ARE A PEST.
LET'S GO, TART.
UH, OKAY.
WAIT, NODA.
ARE YOU LEAVING, TART?
PUDDING ...
YEAH, WE'RE FINISHED WITH THIS PLACE.
TMP TMP TMP
たたたたた
WE'LL NEVER SEE YOU AGAIN. THAT'S A LOAD OFF OF MY MIND!

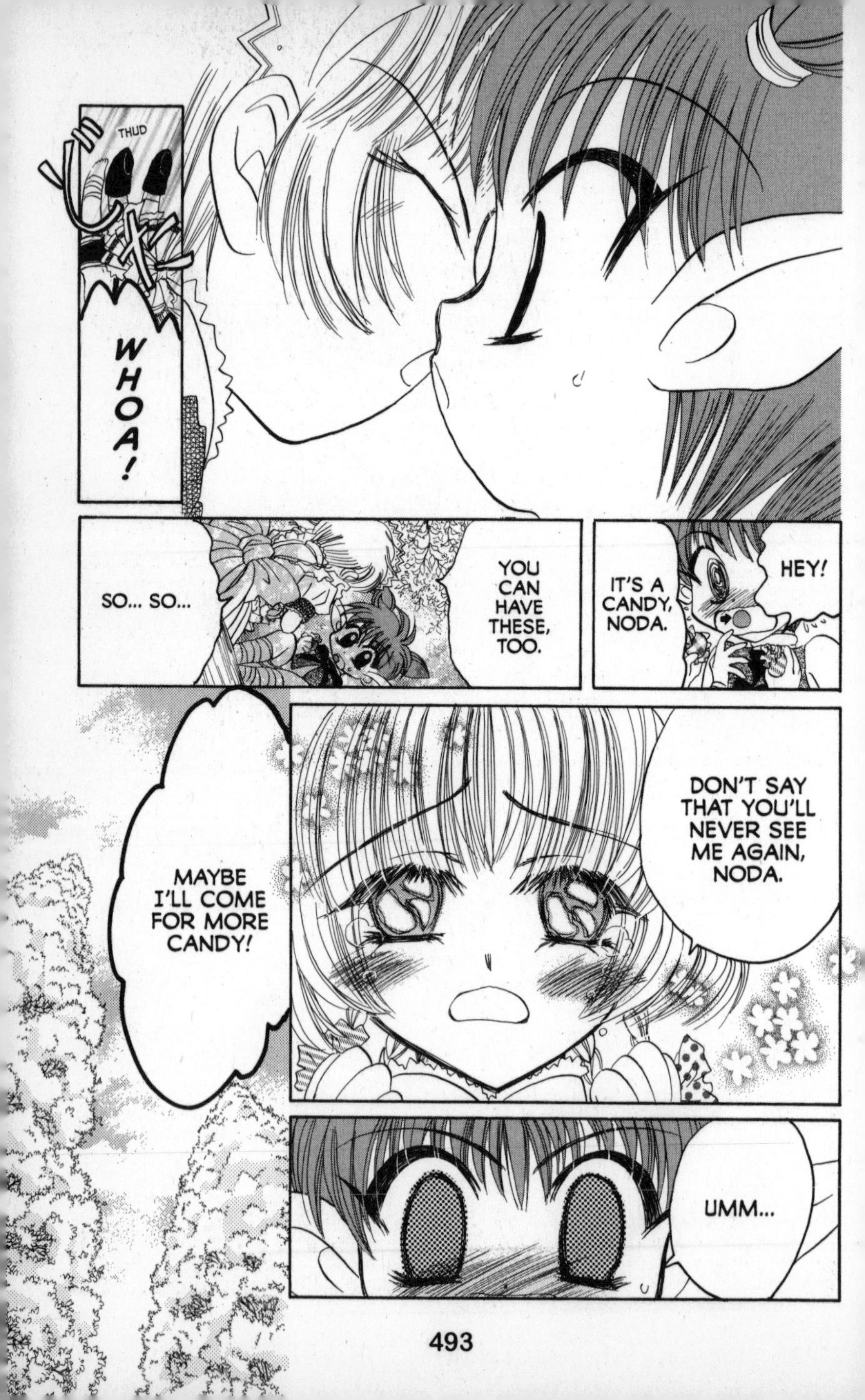
THUD
WHOA!
HEY!
IT'S A CANDY, NODA.
YOU CAN HAVE THESE, TOO.
SO... SO...
DON'T SAY THAT YOU'LL NEVER SEE ME AGAIN, NODA.
MAYBE I'LL COME FOR MORE CANDY!
UMM...

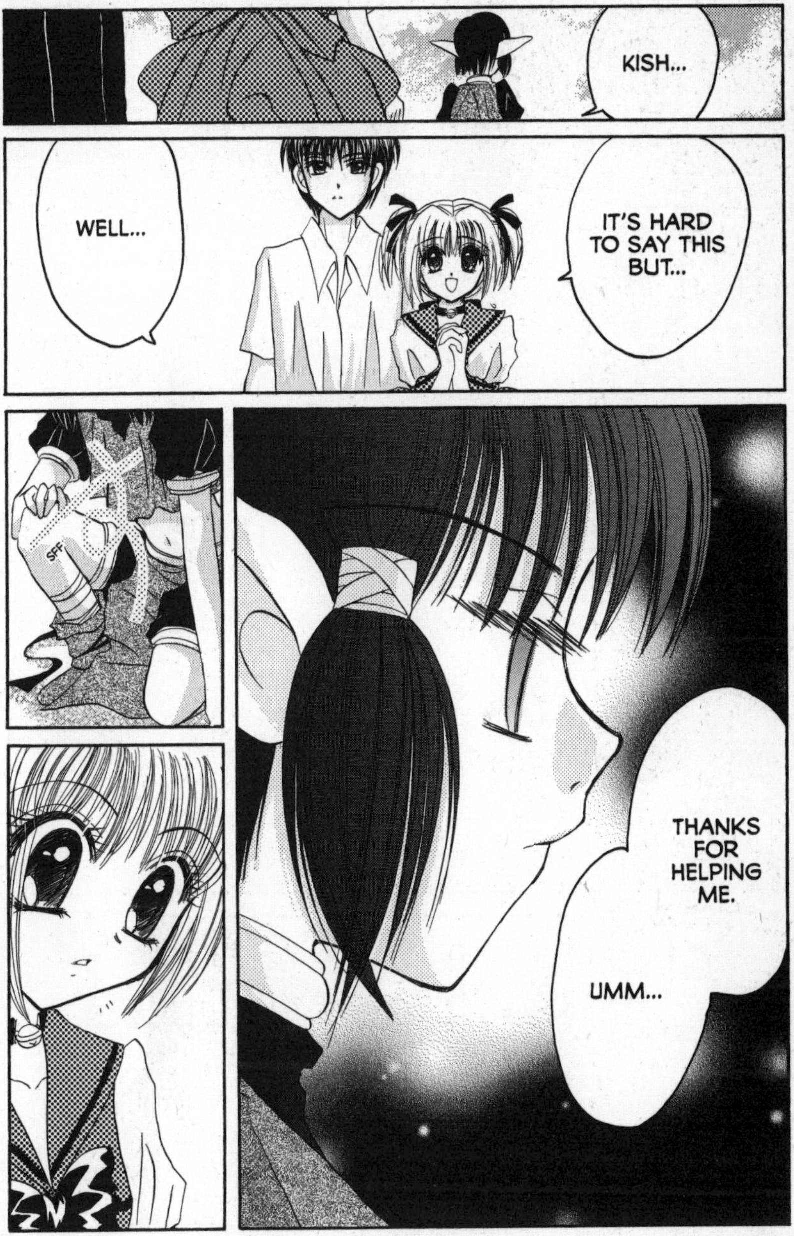
KISH...
IT'S HARD TO SAY THIS BUT...
WELL...
THANKS FOR HELPING ME.
UMM...
SFF

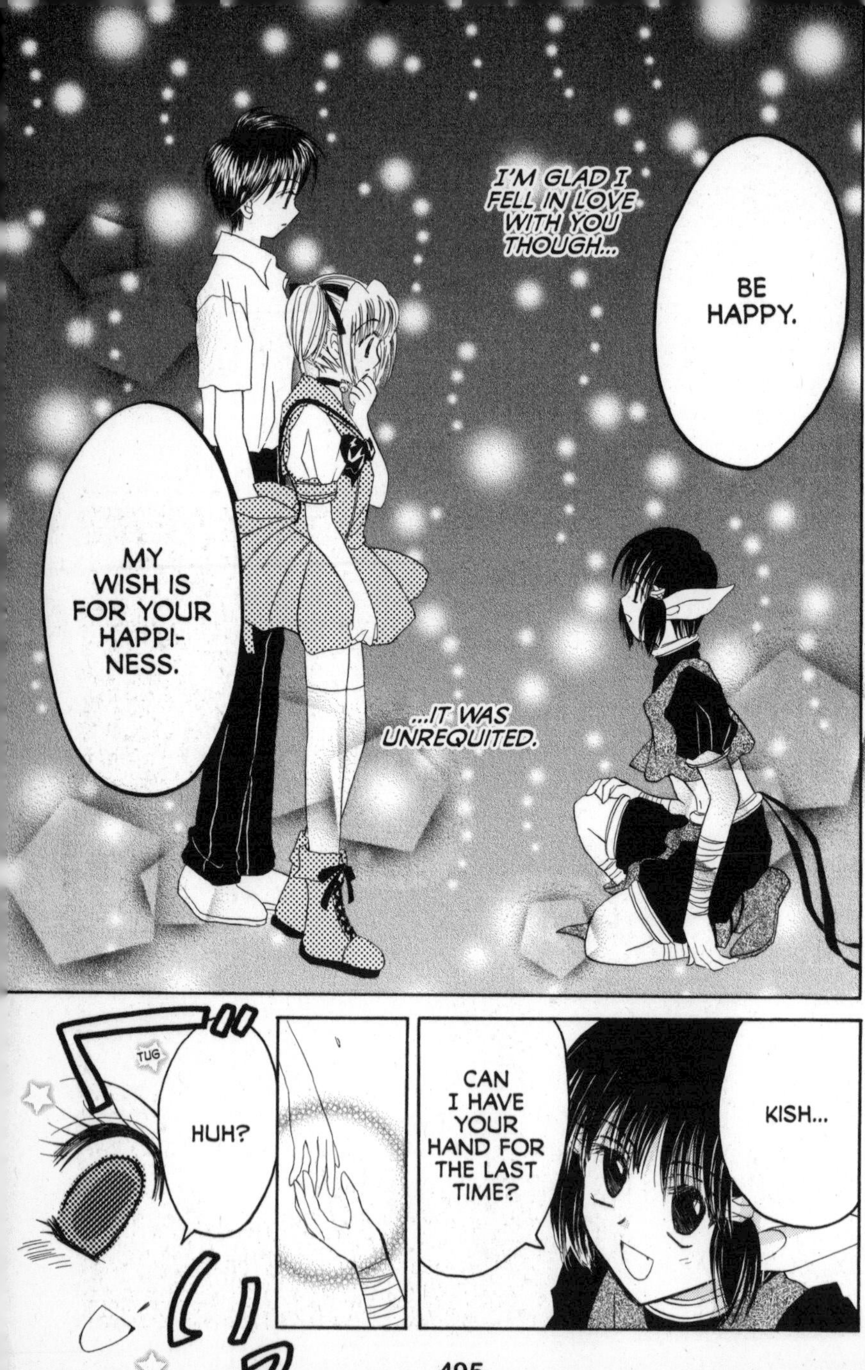
BE HAPPY.
I'M GLAD I FELL IN LOVE WITH YOU THOUGH...
MY WISH IS FOR YOUR HAPPI-NESS.
...IT WAS UNREQUITED.
KISH...
CAN I HAVE YOUR HAND FOR THE LAST TIME?
TUG
HUH?

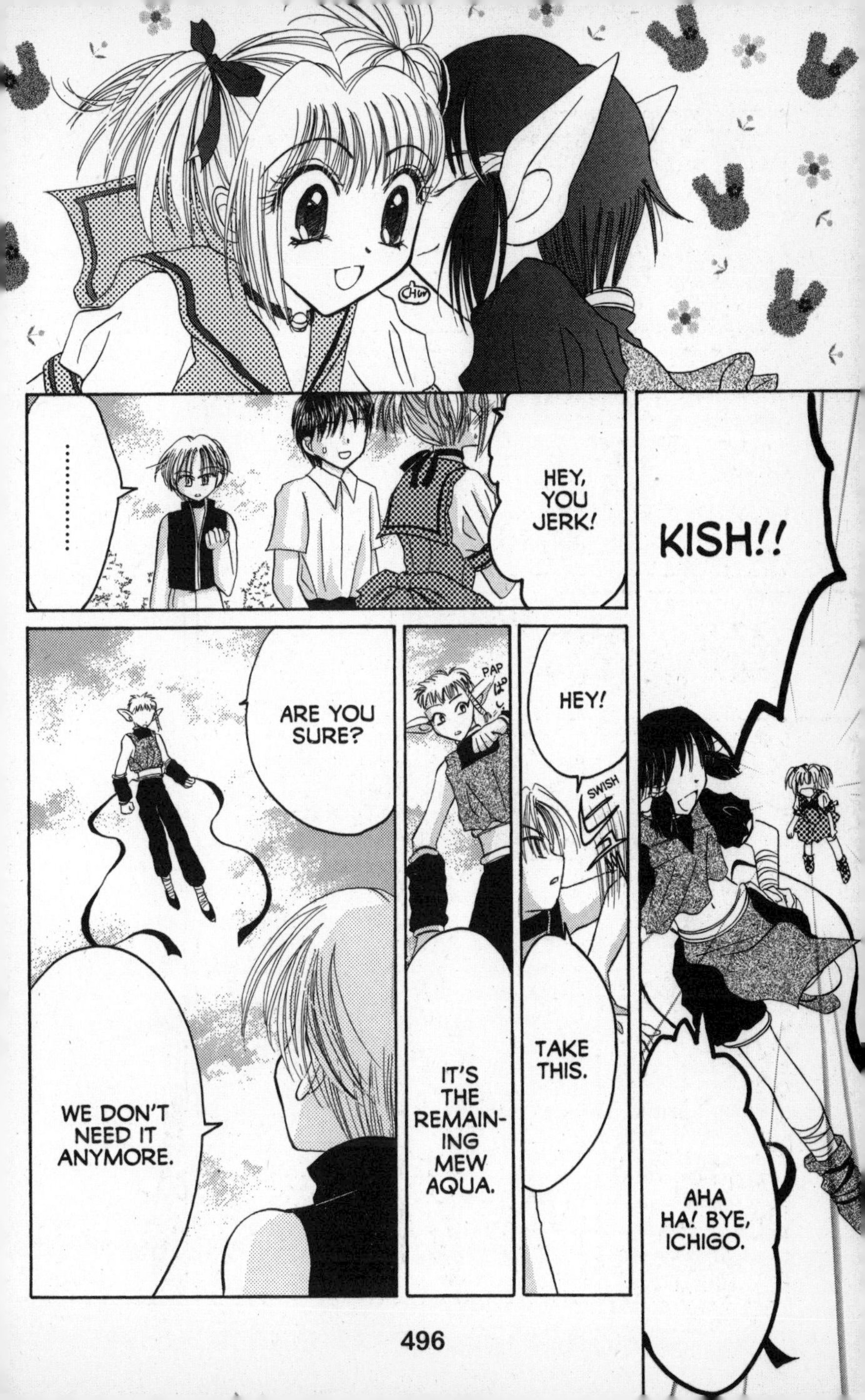
Chu
KISH!!
AHA HA! BYE, ICHIGO.
HEY, YOU JERK!
……………
HEY!
SWISH
TAKE THIS.
PAP
IT'S THE REMAINING MEW AQUA.
ARE YOU SURE?
WE DON'T NEED IT ANYMORE.

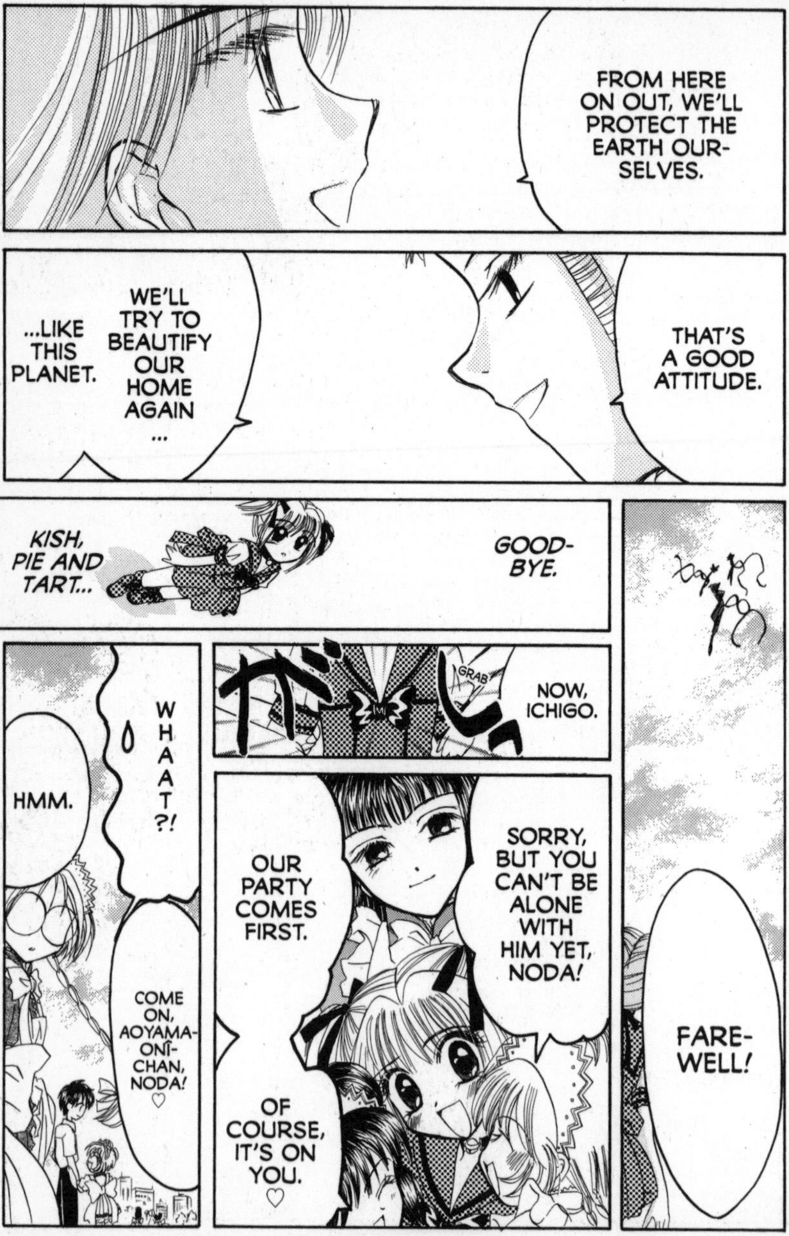
FROM HERE ON OUT, WE'LL PROTECT THE EARTH OUR-SELVES.
THAT'S A GOOD ATTITUDE.
WE'LL TRY TO BEAUTIFY OUR HOME AGAIN ...
...LIKE THIS PLANET.
FARE-WELL!
GOOD-BYE.
KISH, PIE AND TART...
GRAB
NOW, ICHIGO.
SORRY, BUT YOU CAN'T BE ALONE WITH HIM YET, NODA!
OUR PARTY COMES FIRST.
OF COURSE, IT'S ON YOU. ♡
WHAAAT?!
HMM.
COME ON, AOYAMA-ONÎ-CHAN, NODA! ♡

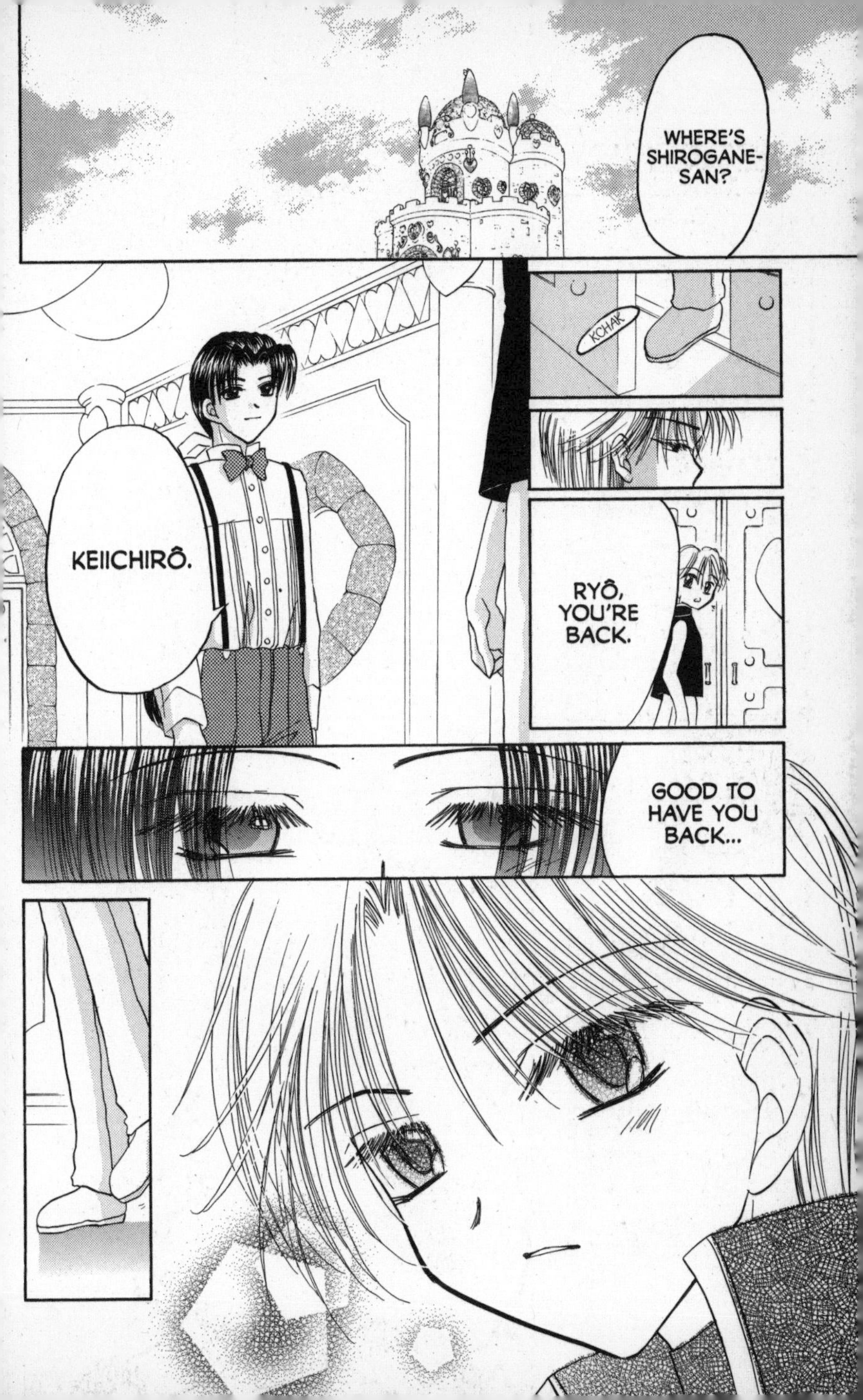
WHERE'S SHIROGANE-SAN?
KOCHAK
RYÔ, YOU'RE BACK.
KEIICHIRÔ.
GOOD TO HAVE YOU BACK...

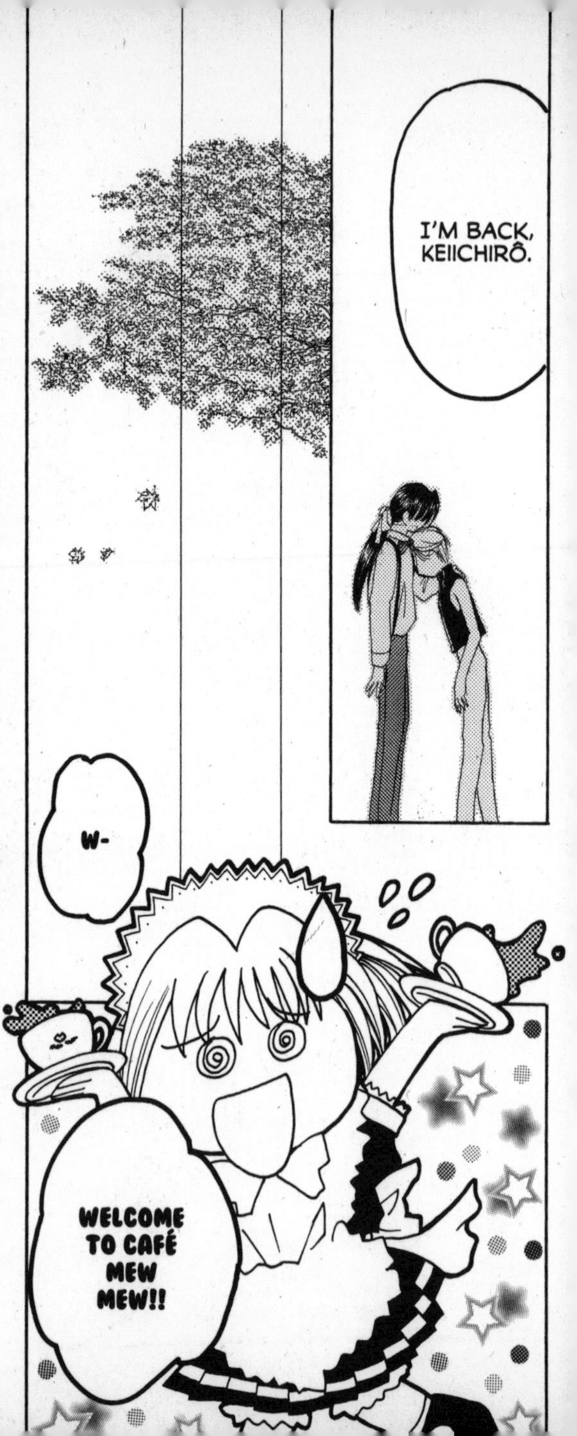
I'M BACK, KEIICHIRÔ.
W-
WELCOME TO CAFÉ MEW MEW!!

TOKYO HAM HAM

ART BY CHIEF MATSUMOTO, ARRANGED BY MIA IKUMI

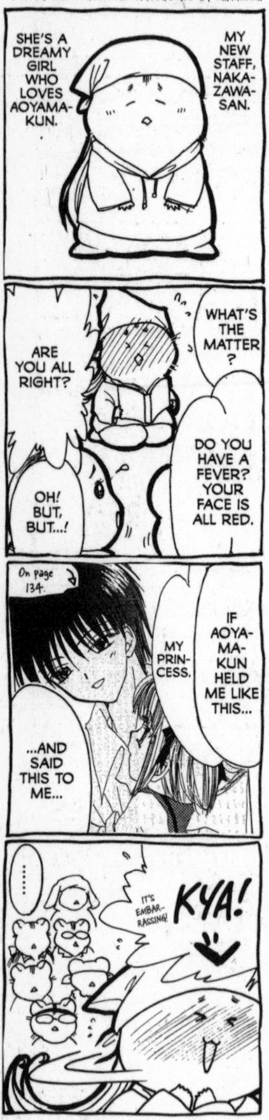
MY NEW STAFF, NAKAZAWA-SAN.
SHE'S A DREAMY GIRL WHO LOVES AOYAMA-KUN.
WHAT'S THE MATTER?
ARE YOU ALL RIGHT?
DO YOU HAVE A FEVER? YOUR FACE IS ALL RED.
OH! BUT, BUT...!
On page 134.
IF AOYAMA-KUN HELD ME LIKE THIS...
MY PRINCESS.
...AND SAID THIS TO ME...
KYA!
IT'S EMBARRASSING!
......

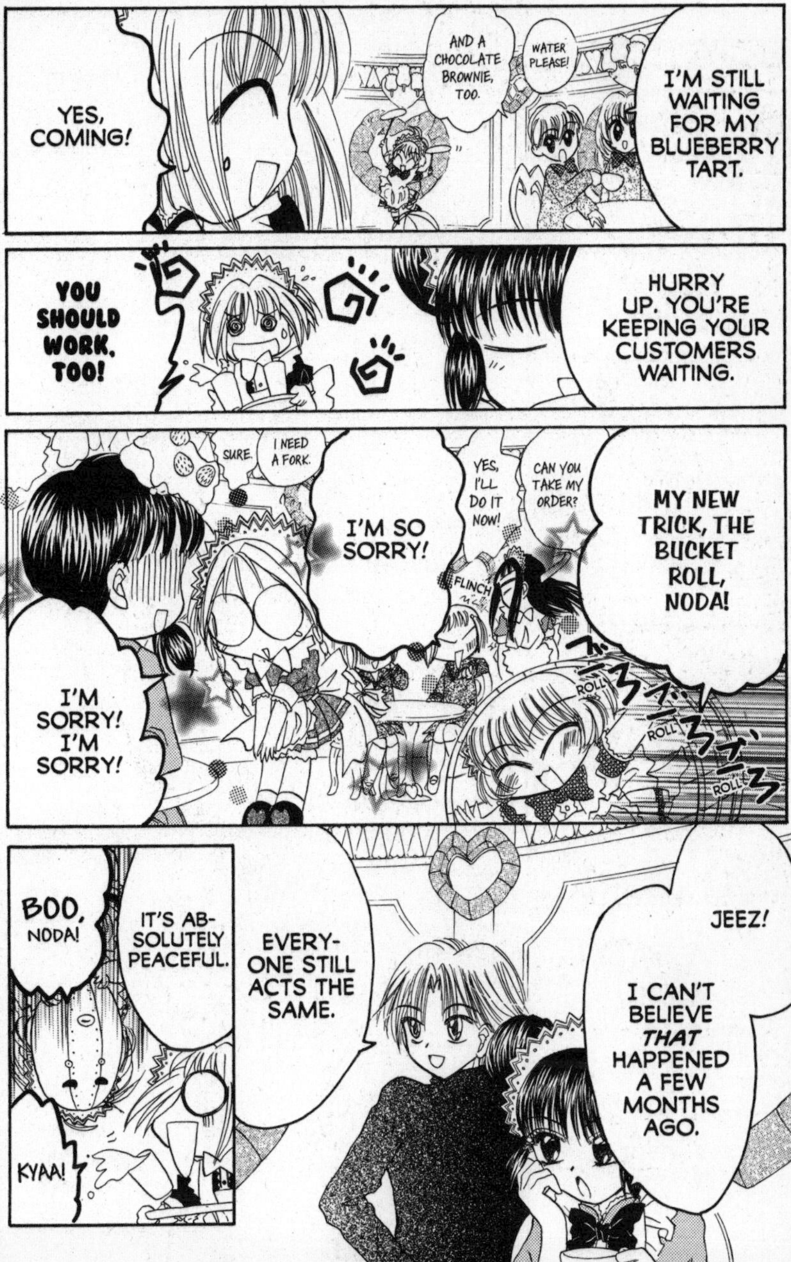
I'M STILL WAITING FOR MY BLUEBERRY TART.
WATER PLEASE!
AND A CHOCOLATE BROWNIE, TOO.
YES, COMING!
HURRY UP. YOU'RE KEEPING YOUR CUSTOMERS WAITING.
YOU SHOULD WORK, TOO!
MY NEW TRICK, THE BUCKET ROLL, NODA!
ROLL
ROLL
ROLL
CAN YOU TAKE MY ORDER?
YES, I'LL DO IT NOW!
FLINCH
I NEED A FORK.
SURE.
I'M SO SORRY!
I'M SORRY! I'M SORRY!
JEEZ!
I CAN'T BELIEVE *THAT* HAPPENED A FEW MONTHS AGO.
EVERY-ONE STILL ACTS THE SAME.
IT'S AB-SOLUTELY PEACEFUL.
BOO, NODA!
KYAA!

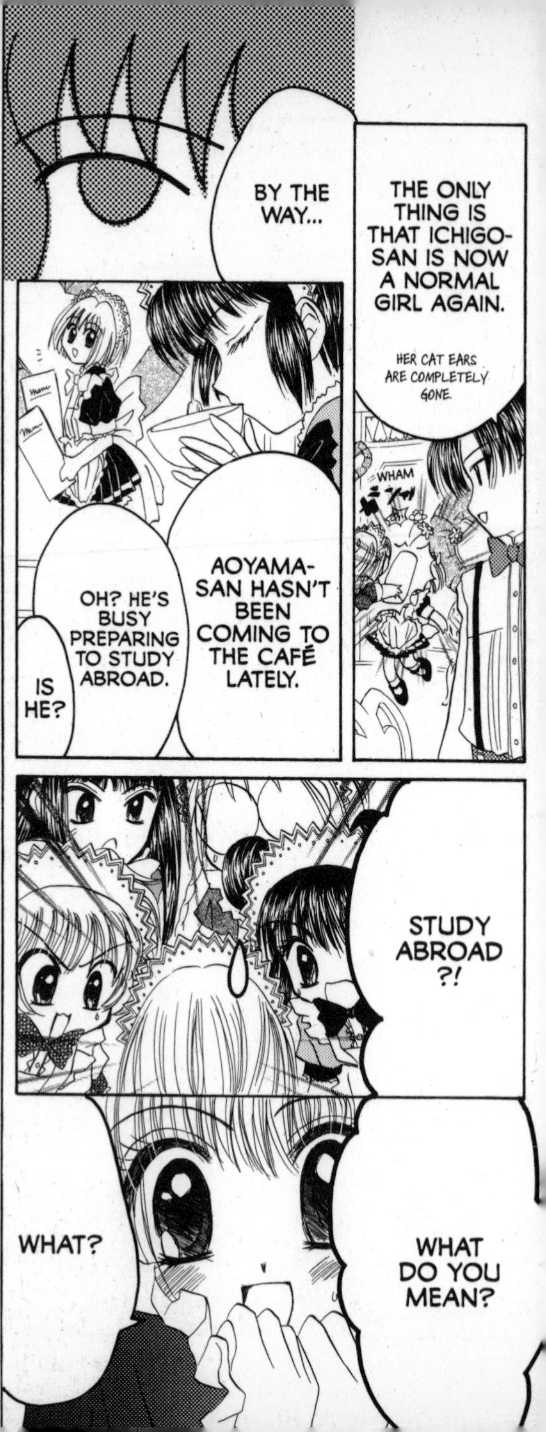
THE ONLY THING IS THAT ICHIGO-SAN IS NOW A NORMAL GIRL AGAIN.
HER CAT EARS ARE COMPLETELY GONE.
WHAM
BY THE WAY...
AOYAMA-SAN HASN'T BEEN COMING TO THE CAFÉ LATELY.
OH? HE'S BUSY PREPARING TO STUDY ABROAD.
IS HE?
STUDY ABROAD ?!
WHAT DO YOU MEAN?
WHAT?

TOKYO HAM HAM

ART BY CHIEF MATSUMOTO, ARRANGED BY MIA IKUMI

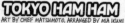

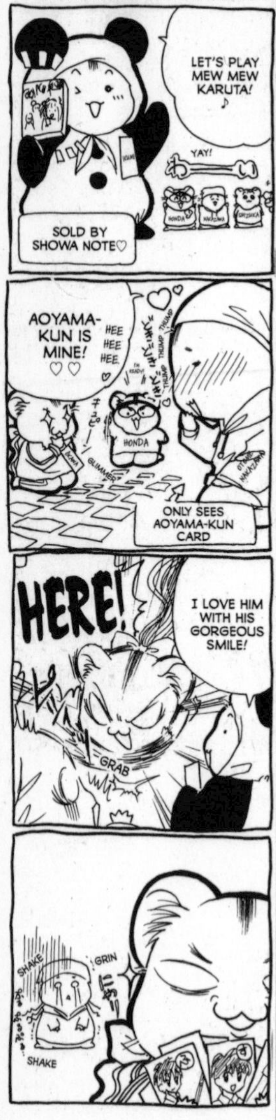
LET'S PLAY MEW MEW KARUTA! ♪
YAY!
HONDA
SOLD BY SHOWA NOTE♡
AOYAMA-KUN IS MINE! ♡♡
HEE HEE HEE.
THUMP THUMP
HONDA
GLIMMER
ONLY SEES AOYAMA-KUN CARD
HERE!
I LOVE HIM WITH HIS GORGEOUS SMILE!
GRAB
SHAKE
GRIN
SHAKE

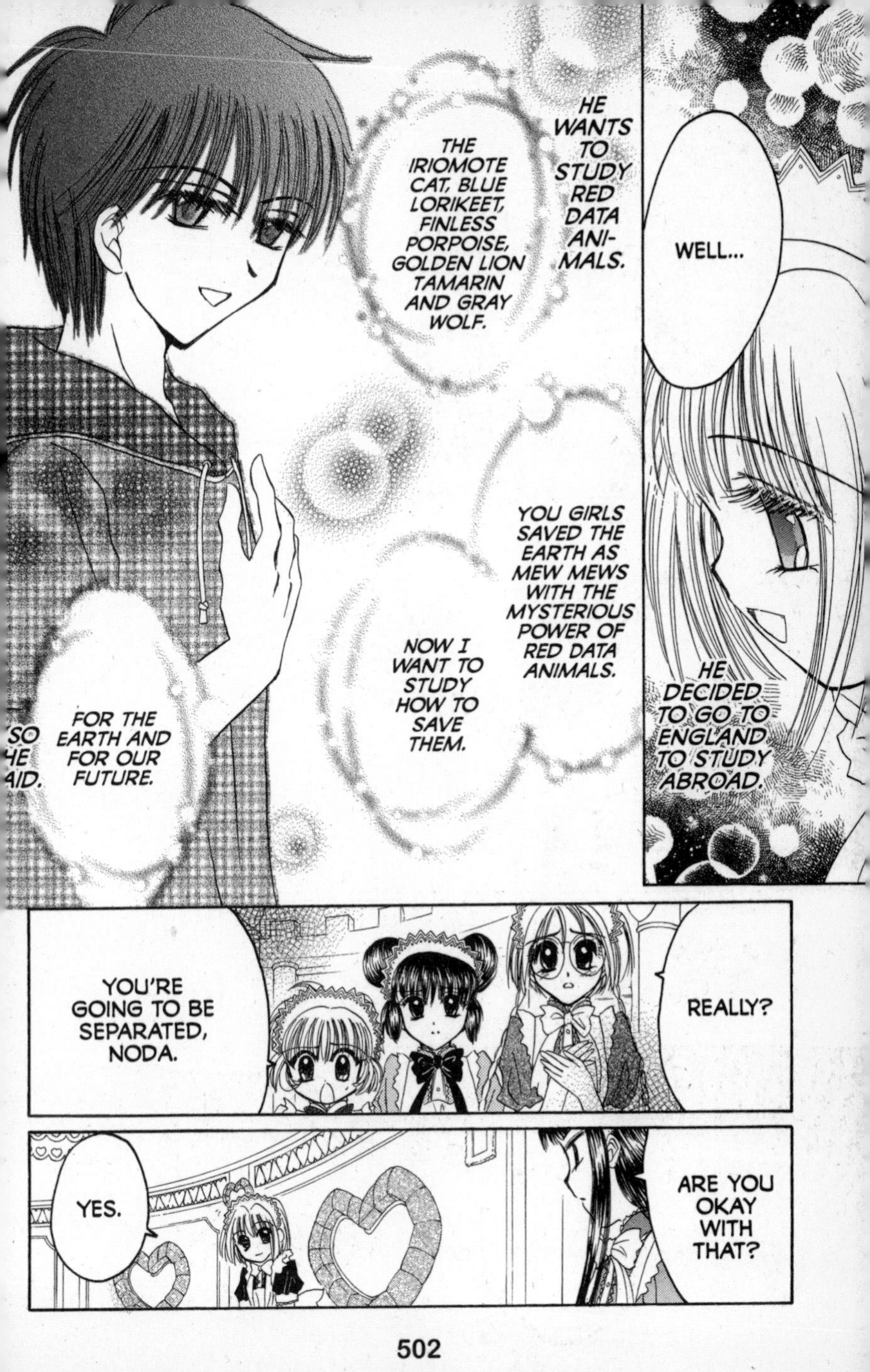
WELL...
HE DECIDED TO GO TO ENGLAND TO STUDY ABROAD.
HE WANTS TO STUDY RED DATA ANIMALS.
THE IRIOMOTE CAT, BLUE LORIKEET, FINLESS PORPOISE, GOLDEN LION TAMARIN AND GRAY WOLF.
YOU GIRLS SAVED THE EARTH AS MEW MEWS WITH THE MYSTERIOUS POWER OF RED DATA ANIMALS.
NOW I WANT TO STUDY HOW TO SAVE THEM.
FOR THE EARTH AND FOR OUR FUTURE.
REALLY?
YOU'RE GOING TO BE SEPARATED, NODA.
ARE YOU OKAY WITH THAT?
YES.

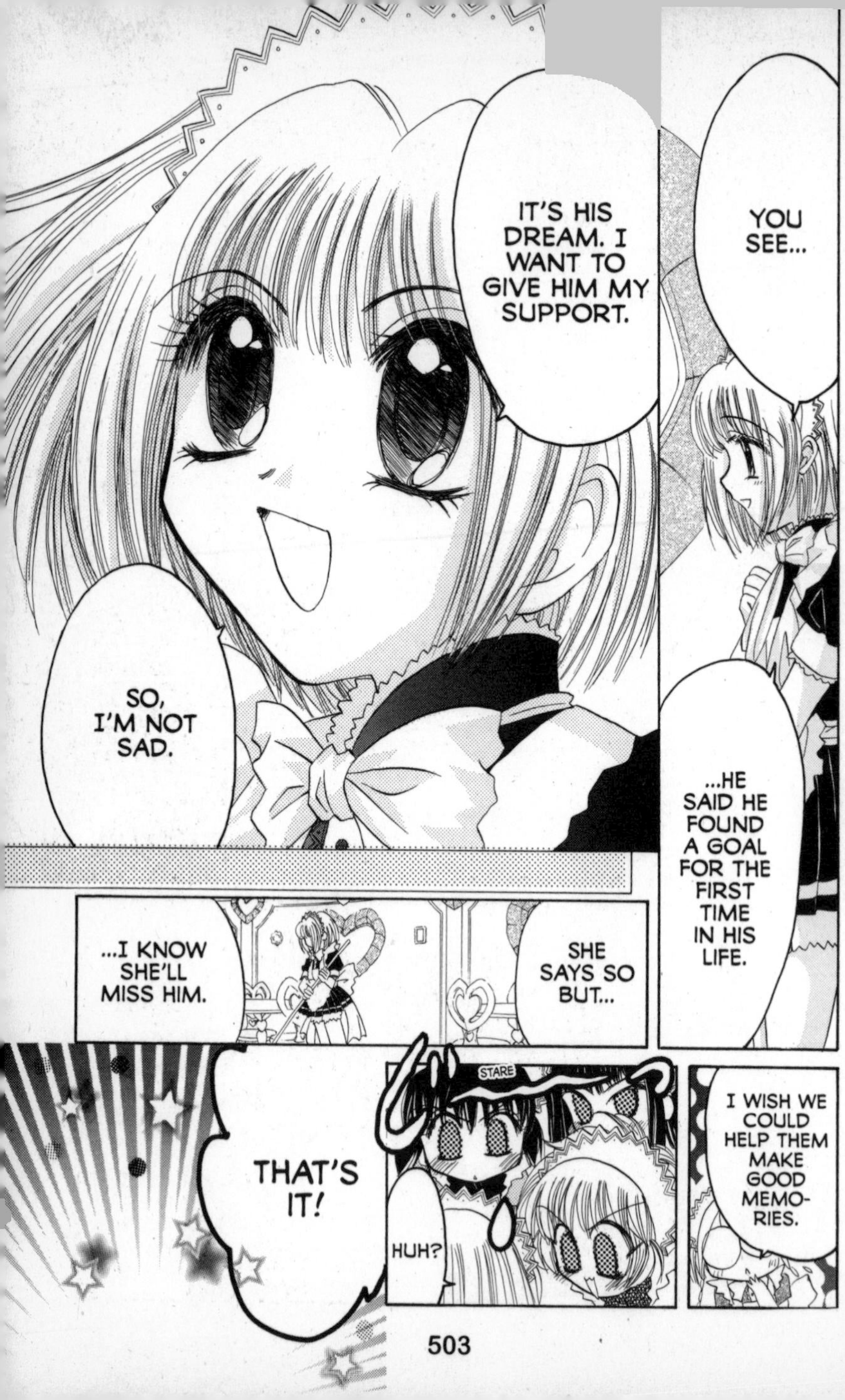
YOU SEE...
...HE SAID HE FOUND A GOAL FOR THE FIRST TIME IN HIS LIFE.
IT'S HIS DREAM. I WANT TO GIVE HIM MY SUPPORT.
SO, I'M NOT SAD.
SHE SAYS SO BUT...
...I KNOW SHE'LL MISS HIM.
I WISH WE COULD HELP THEM MAKE GOOD MEMORIES.
STARE
HUH?
THAT'S IT!

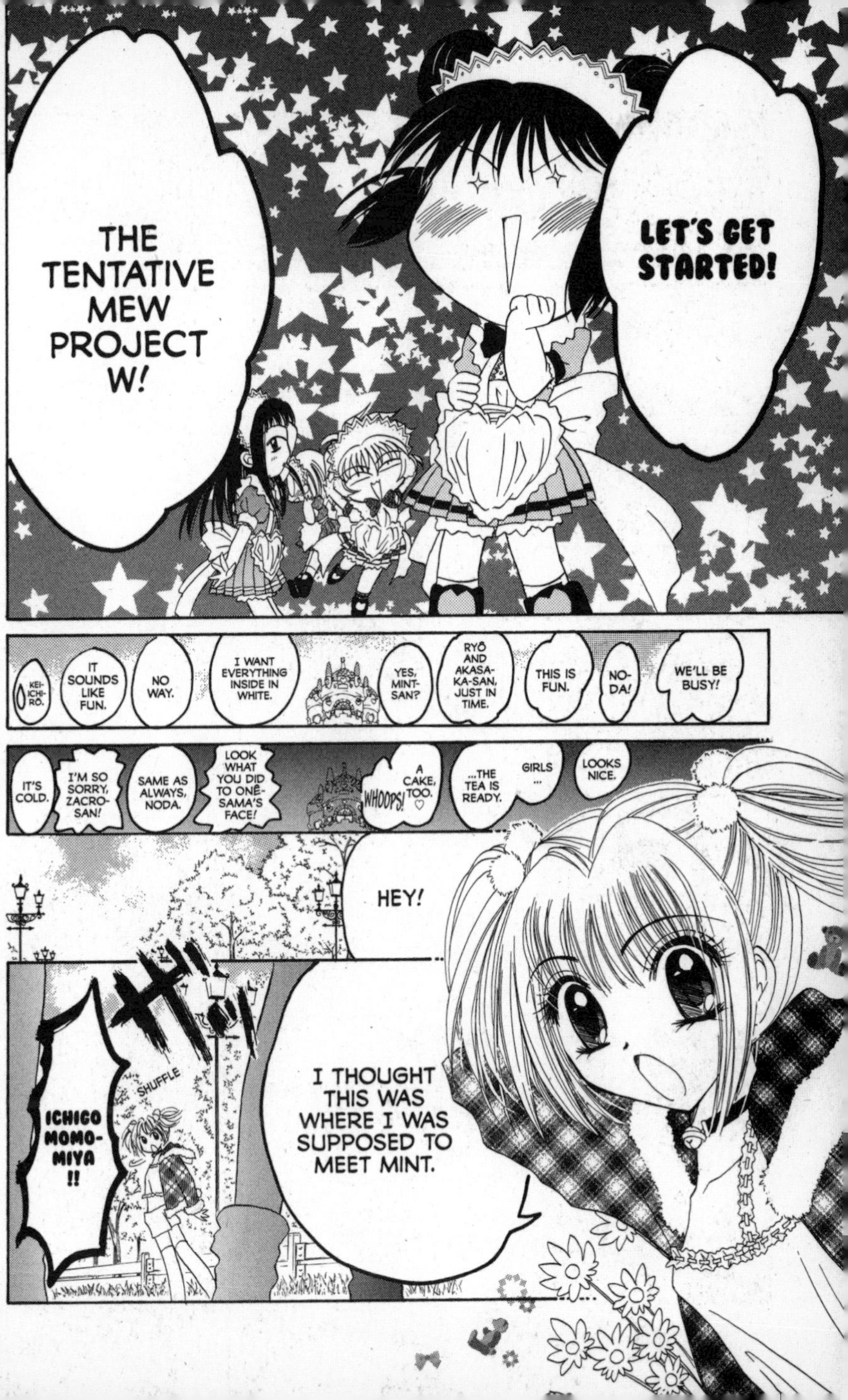
LET'S GET STARTED!
THE TENTATIVE MEW PROJECT W!
WE'LL BE BUSY!
NO-DA!
THIS IS FUN.
RYŌ AND AKASA-KA-SAN, JUST IN TIME.
YES, MINT-SAN?
I WANT EVERYTHING INSIDE IN WHITE.
NO WAY.
IT SOUNDS LIKE FUN.
KEI-ICHI-RŌ.
LOOKS NICE.
GIRLS ...
...THE TEA IS READY.
A CAKE, TOO. ♡
WHOOPS!
LOOK WHAT YOU DID TO ONĒ-SAMA'S FACE!
SAME AS ALWAYS, NODA.
I'M SO SORRY, ZACRO-SAN!
IT'S COLD.
HEY!
I THOUGHT THIS WAS WHERE I WAS SUPPOSED TO MEET MINT.
SHUFFLE
ICHIGO MOMO-MIYA !!

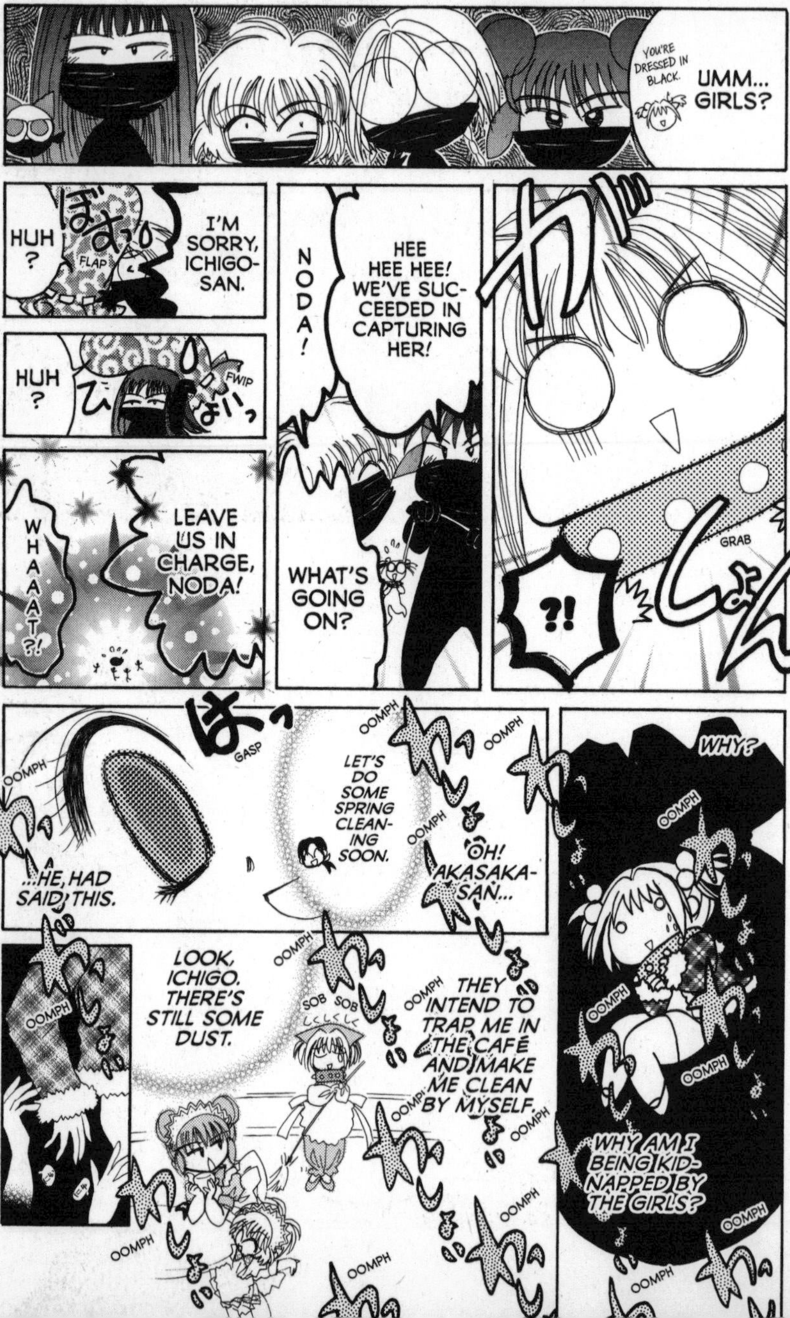
UMM... GIRLS?
YOU'RE DRESSED IN BLACK.
?!
GRAB
HEE HEE HEE! WE'VE SUC-CEEDED IN CAPTURING HER!
NODA!
WHAT'S GOING ON?
I'M SORRY, ICHIGO-SAN.
HUH?
FLAP
HUH?
FWIP
LEAVE US IN CHARGE, NODA!
WHAAAAT?!
WHY?
OOMPH
WHY AM I BEING KID-NAPPED BY THE GIRLS?
GASP
OOMPH
LET'S DO SOME SPRING CLEAN-ING SOON.
OH! AKASAKA-SAN...
...HE HAD SAID THIS.
OOMPH
THEY INTEND TO TRAP ME IN THE CAFÉ AND MAKE ME CLEAN BY MYSELF.
SOB SOB
LOOK, ICHIGO. THERE'S STILL SOME DUST.
OOMPH

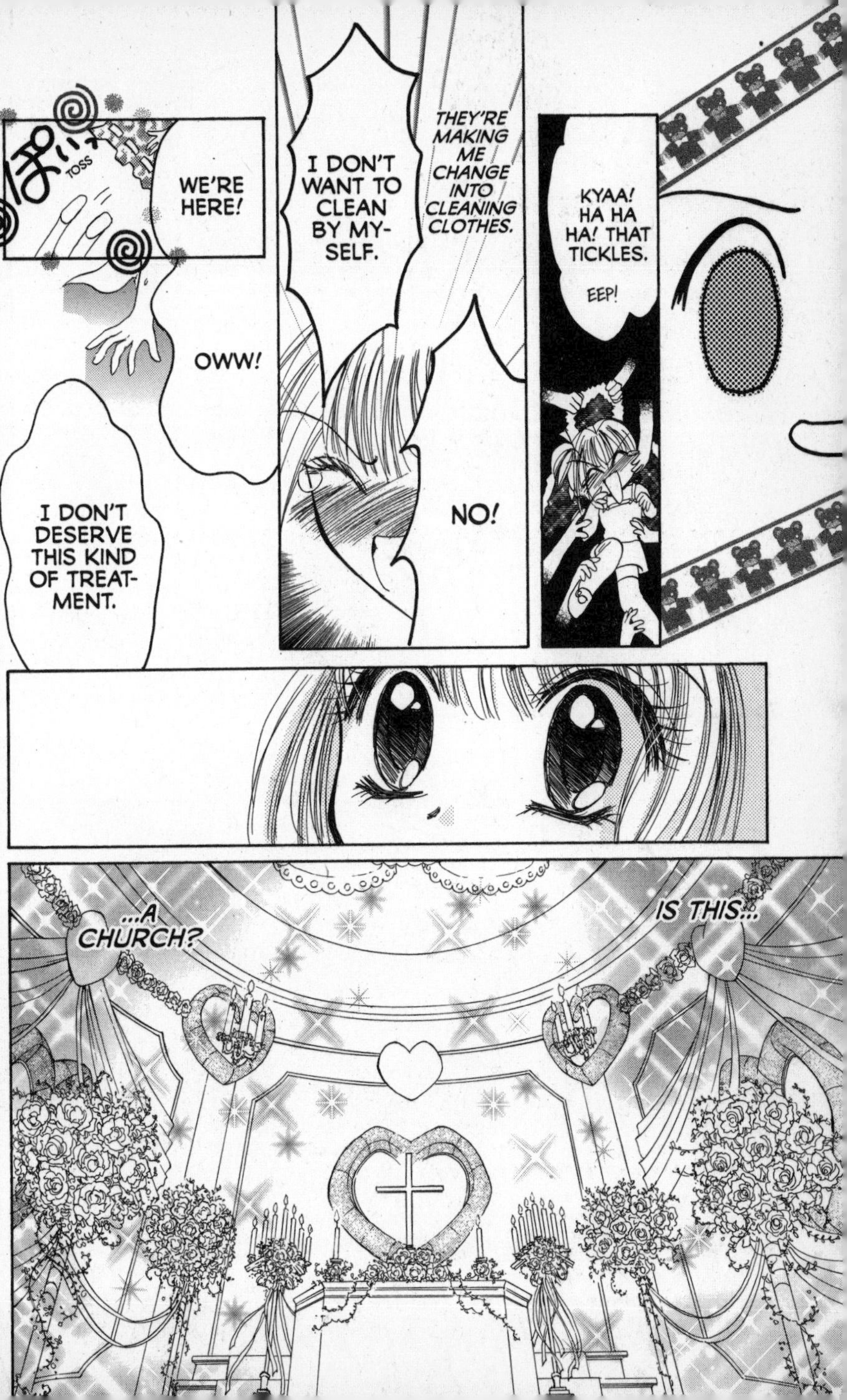
KYAA! HA HA HA! THAT TICKLES.
EEP!
THEY'RE MAKING ME CHANGE INTO CLEANING CLOTHES.
I DON'T WANT TO CLEAN BY MY-SELF.
NO!
ぽいっ
TOSS
WE'RE HERE!
OWW!
I DON'T DESERVE THIS KIND OF TREAT-MENT.
IS THIS...
...A CHURCH?

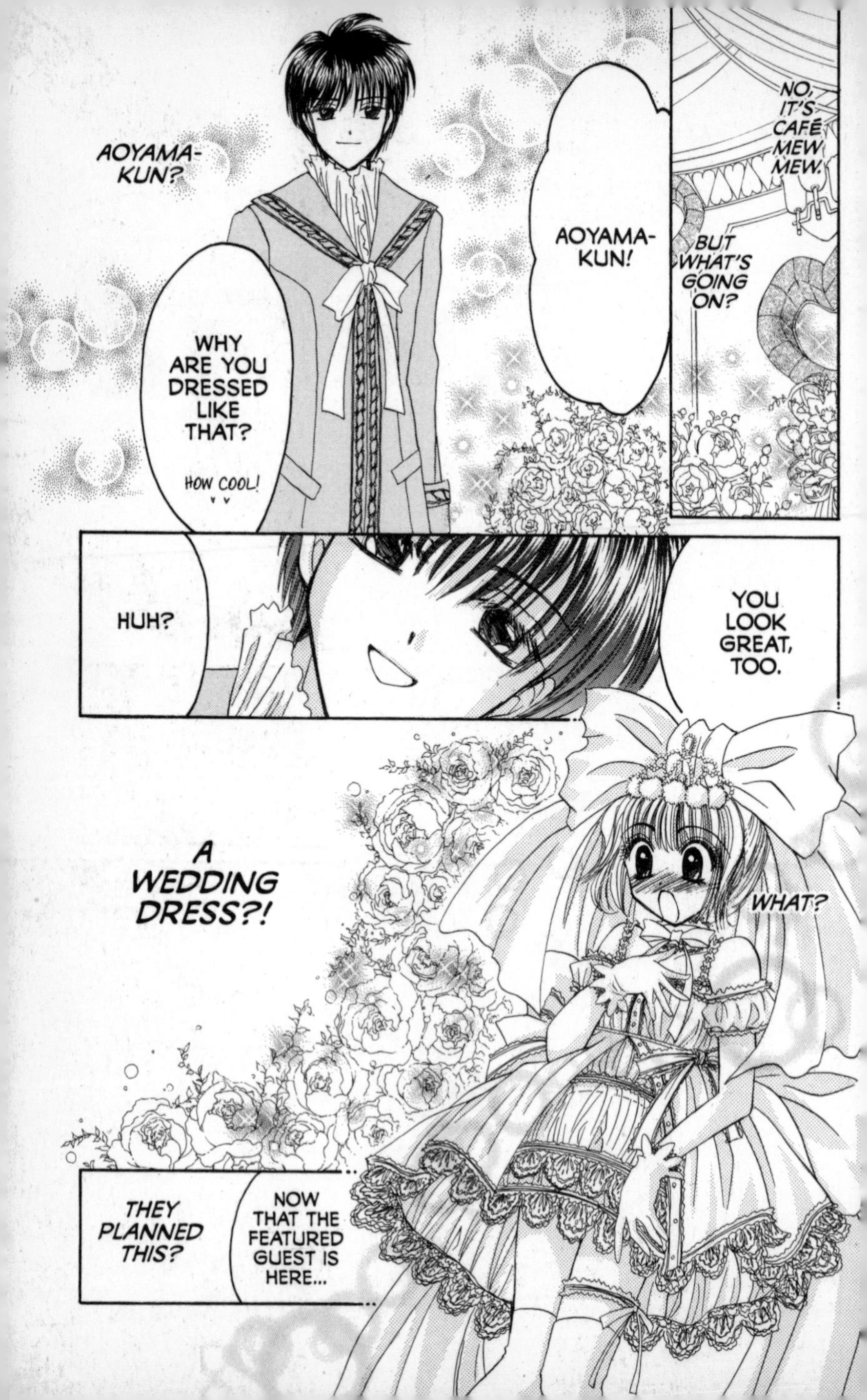
NO, IT'S CAFÉ MEW MEW.
BUT WHAT'S GOING ON?
AOYAMA-KUN!
AOYAMA-KUN?
WHY ARE YOU DRESSED LIKE THAT?
HOW COOL!
YOU LOOK GREAT, TOO.
HUH?
WHAT?
A WEDDING DRESS?!
NOW THAT THE FEATURED GUEST IS HERE...
THEY PLANNED THIS?

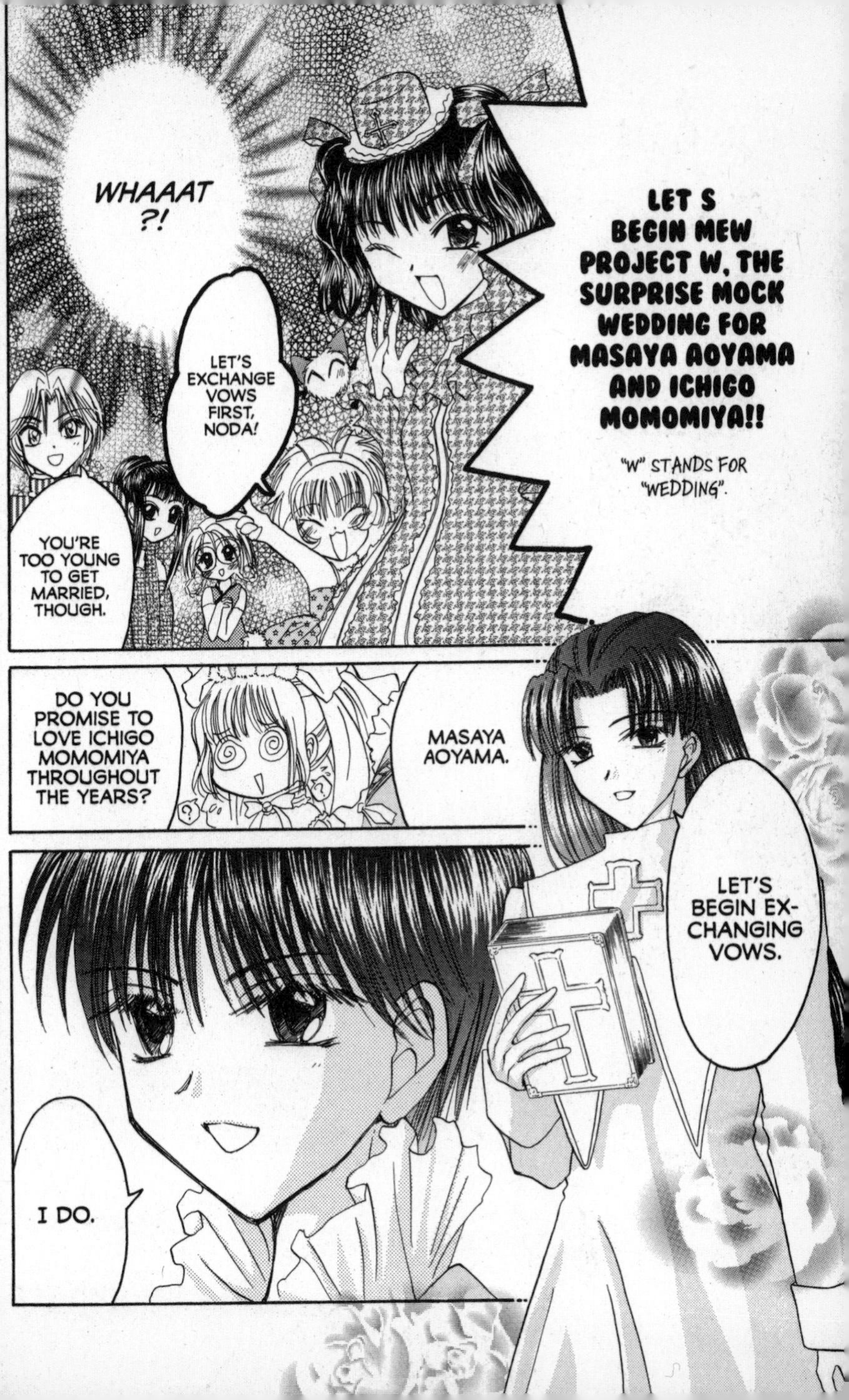
LET S BEGIN MEW PROJECT W, THE SURPRISE MOCK WEDDING FOR MASAYA AOYAMA AND ICHIGO MOMOMIYA!!
"W" STANDS FOR "WEDDING".
WHAAAT ?!
LET'S EXCHANGE VOWS FIRST, NODA!
YOU'RE TOO YOUNG TO GET MARRIED, THOUGH.
LET'S BEGIN EX-CHANGING VOWS.
MASAYA AOYAMA.
DO YOU PROMISE TO LOVE ICHIGO MOMOMIYA THROUGHOUT THE YEARS?
I DO.

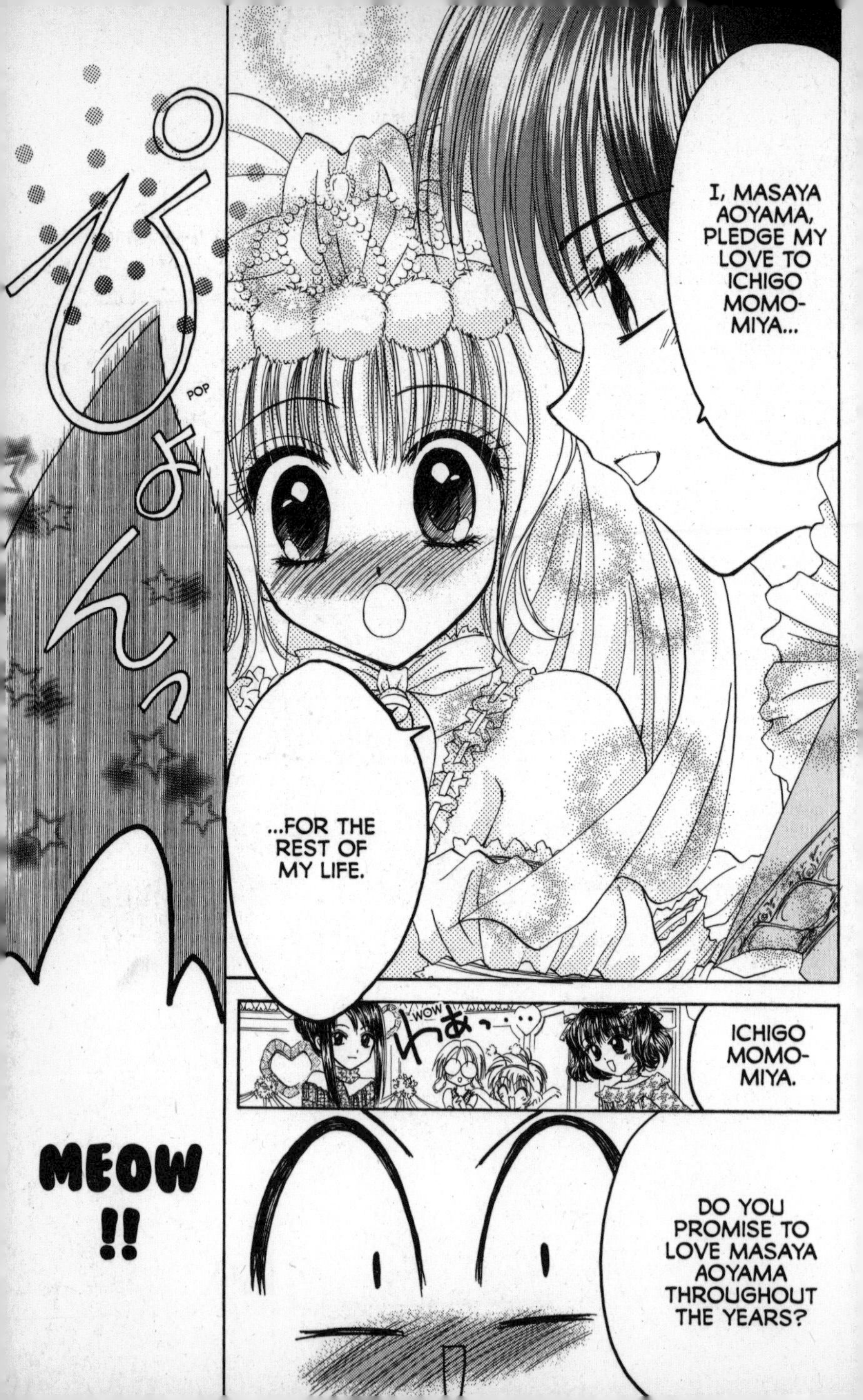
I, MASAYA AOYAMA, PLEDGE MY LOVE TO ICHIGO MOMO-MIYA...
...FOR THE REST OF MY LIFE.
ICHIGO MOMO-MIYA.
WOW
DO YOU PROMISE TO LOVE MASAYA AOYAMA THROUGHOUT THE YEARS?
POP
MEOW !!

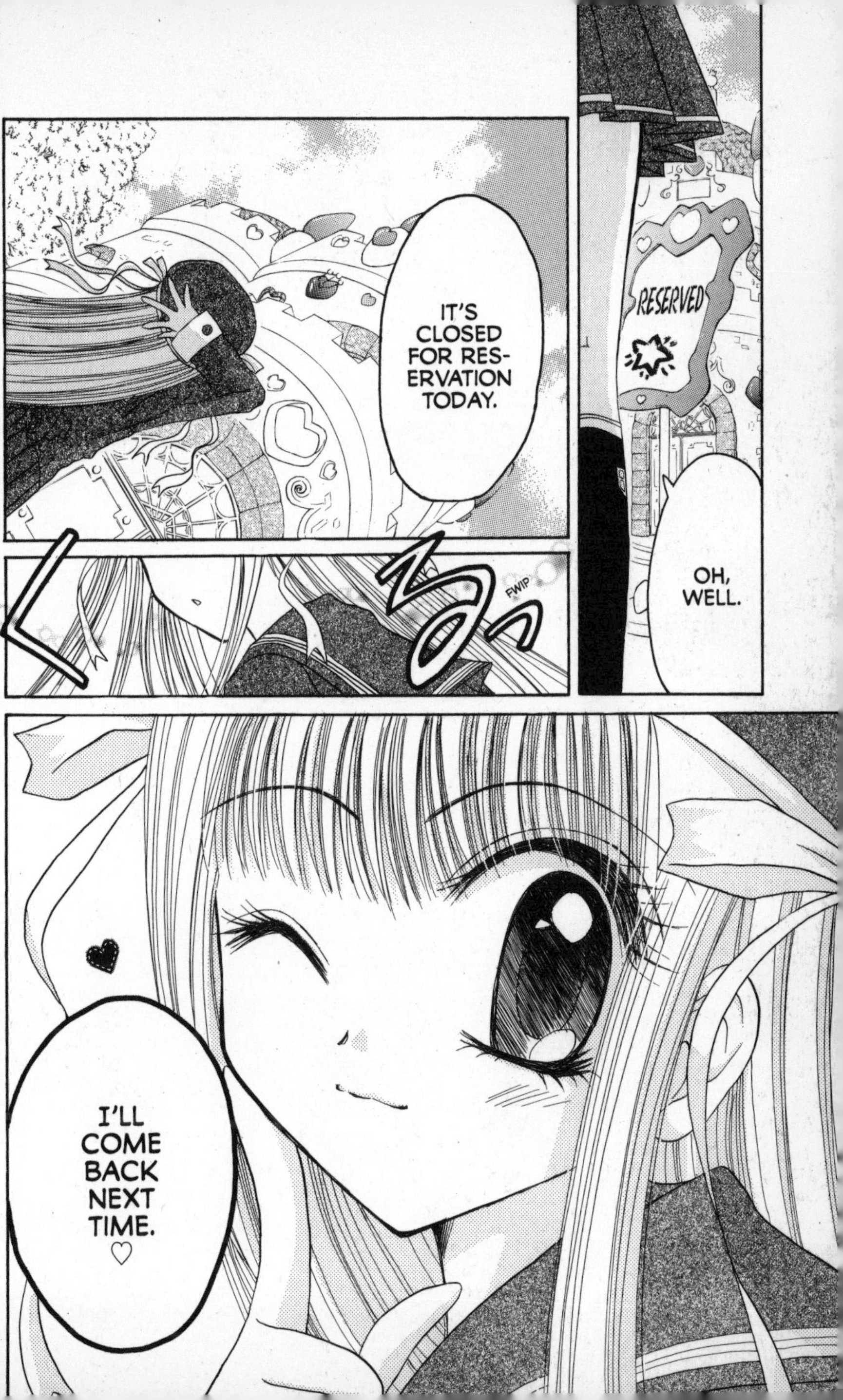
RESERVED
OH, WELL.
IT'S CLOSED FOR RES-ERVATION TODAY.
FWIP
I'LL COME BACK NEXT TIME. ♡

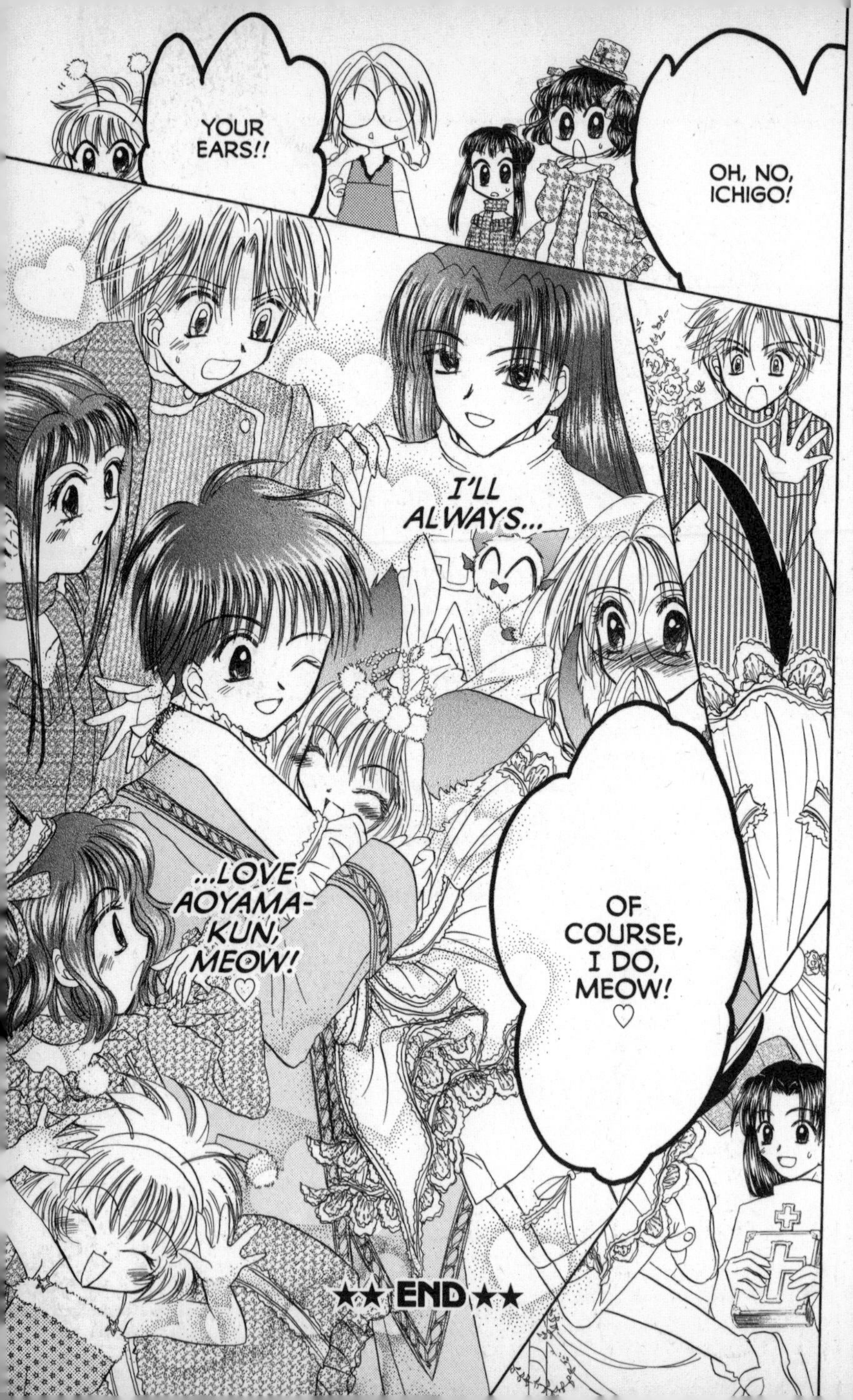
OH, NO, ICHIGO!
YOUR EARS!!
I'LL ALWAYS...
...LOVE AOYAMA-KUN, MEOW! ♡
OF COURSE, I DO, MEOW! ♡
★★ END ★★

ABOUT VOLUME 7
REIKO YOSHIDA

吉田玲子

FOR SOME REASON, I KEPT WRITING STORIES WITH CATS. I THOUGHT THAT THIS MUST BE FATE, SO I FINALLY GOT A CAT. SINCE HIS BREEDER WAS IN OSAKA, THE THREE-MONTH OLD KITTEN FLEW ON A PLANE TO MY HOUSE. HE'S A SCOTTISH FOLD CAT WITH LOPPED-EARS. HE'S WHITE AND BEIGE SO I NAMED HIM GINGER.

IT TURNS OUT THAT HE'S A RAMBUNCTIOUS CAT. THE OTHER DAY, HE LOCKED ME OUT OF MY HOUSE. IT SEEMS THAT HE KNOCKED THE DOOR BAR DOWN AS HE JUMPED. UNABLE TO DO ANYTHING ABOUT IT, I CALLED A LOCKSMITH TO UNLATCH IT FOR ME. HE'S WREAKED HAVOC BY PUTTING HOLES IN MY SWEATER, RIPPING UP MY UNDERWEAR AND DESTROYING MY BATH MAT. ON TOP OF THAT, HE'S A VERY SPOILED BOY. HE ALWAYS GREETS ME AT THE DOOR, JUMPS ON MY LAP, LICKS MY FINGERS DURING WORK AND FOLLOWS ME TO THE BATHROOM. HE'S A TROUBLEMAKER, BUT I FIND HIM ADORABLE WHEN HE SITS AND STARES AT ME WITH HIS ROUND EYES.

I THINK I'VE REALIZED WHY ALL THE BOYS FELL IN LOVE WITH ICHIGO. KITTY PURRS AND CUDDLES ARE POWERFUL. YOU SHOULD TRY THEM WHEN YOU GET A BOYFRIEND. A SMUG PERSIAN, AN ENERGETIC AMERICAN SHORTHAIR, A NOBLE RUSSIAN BLUE, A GRACEFUL ABYSSINIAN OR A PLUSHY RAGDOLL. PURSUE THE CAT OF YOUR CHOICE!

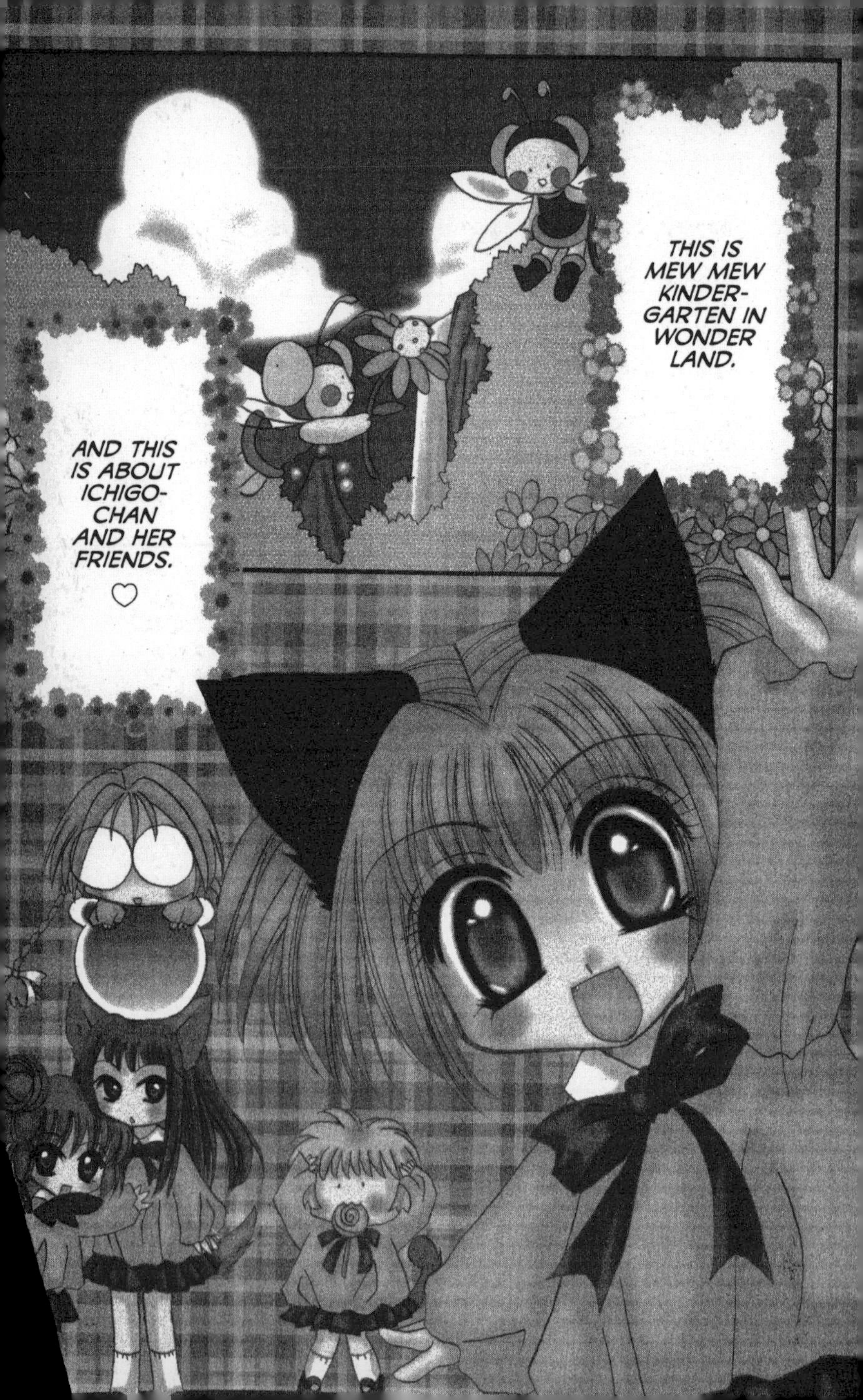
THIS IS MEW MEW KINDER-GARTEN IN WONDER LAND.
AND THIS IS ABOUT ICHIGO-CHAN AND HER FRIENDS. ♡

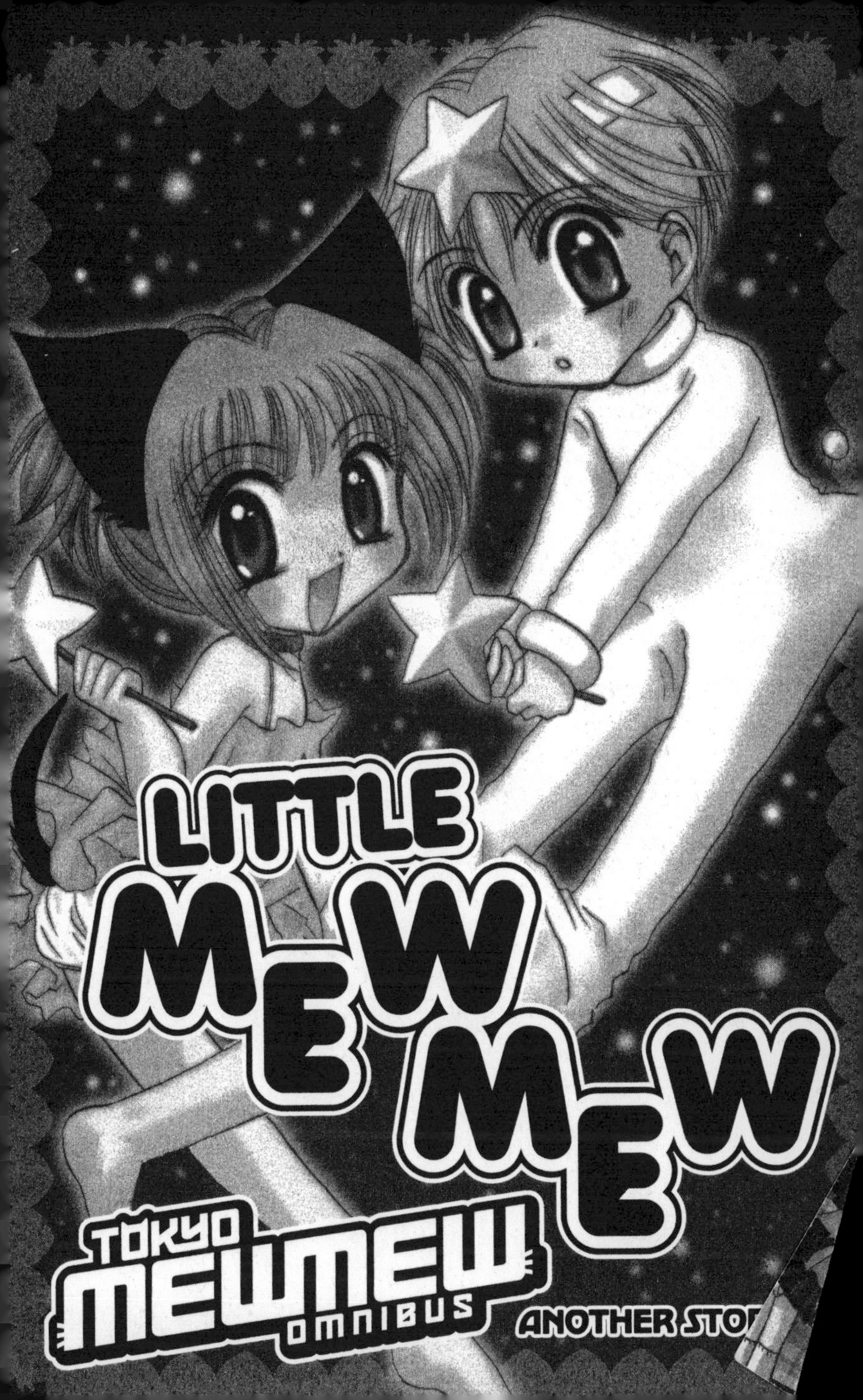
LITTLE MEW MEW
TOKYO MEWMEW OMNIBUS
ANOTHER STO

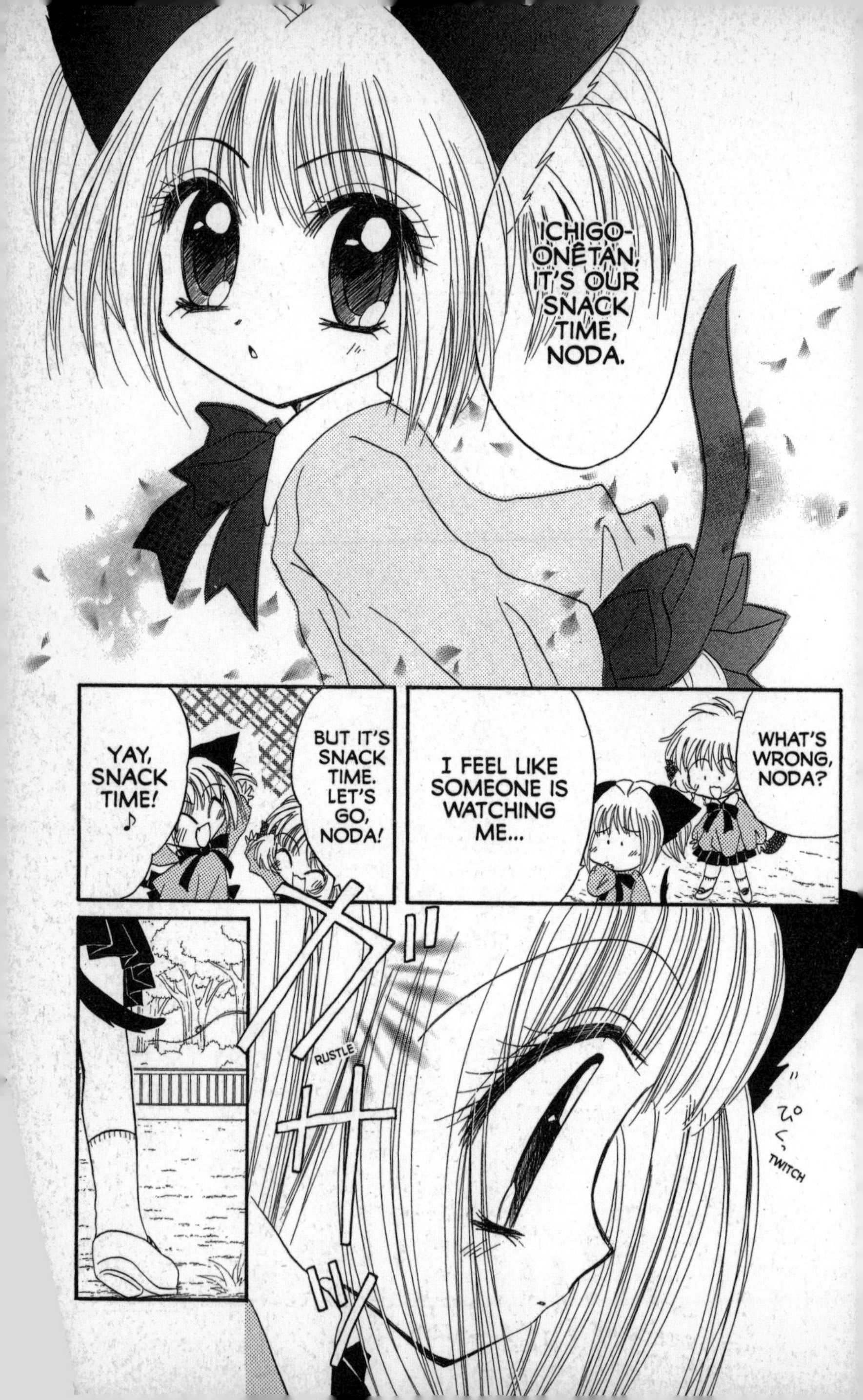
ICHIGO-ONÊTAN, IT'S OUR SNACK TIME, NODA.
WHAT'S WRONG, NODA?
I FEEL LIKE SOMEONE IS WATCHING ME...
BUT IT'S SNACK TIME. LET'S GO, NODA!
YAY, SNACK TIME! ♪
ぴく
TWITCH
RUSTLE

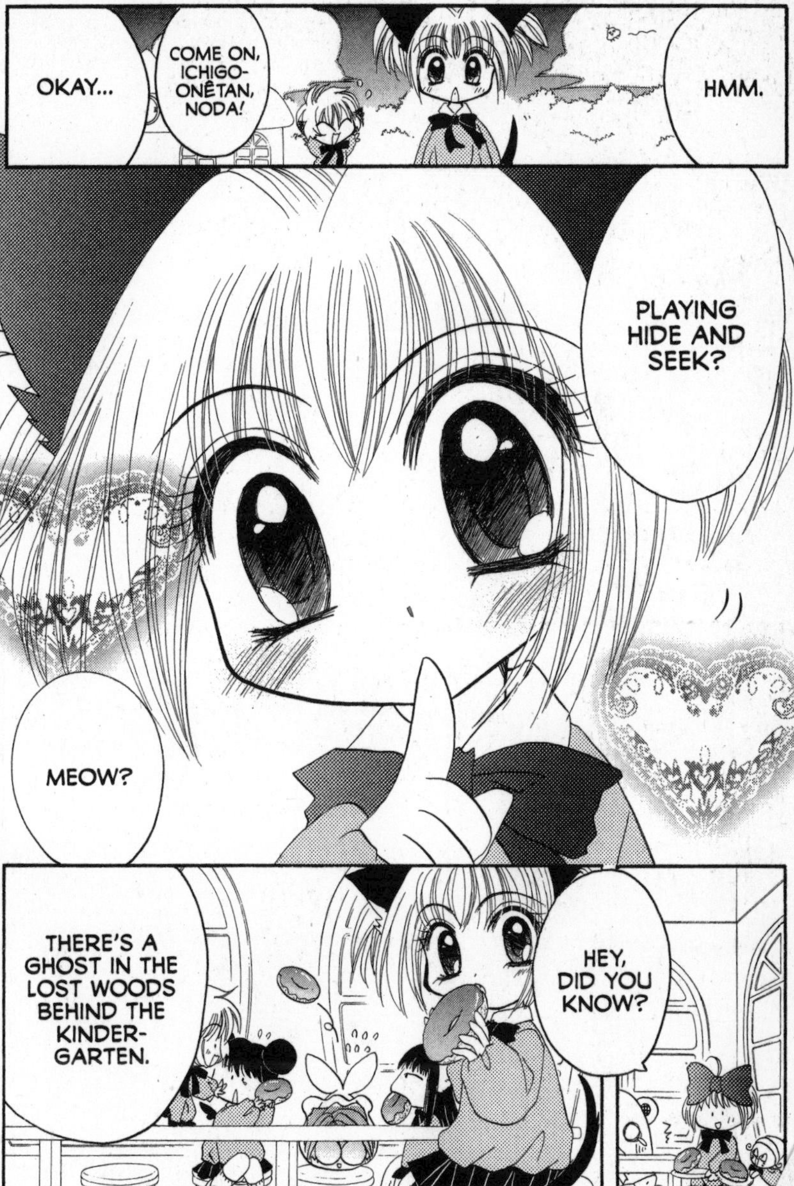
HMM.
COME ON, ICHIGO-ONÊTAN, NODA!
OKAY...
PLAYING HIDE AND SEEK?
MEOW?
HEY, DID YOU KNOW?
THERE'S A GHOST IN THE LOST WOODS BEHIND THE KINDER-GARTEN.

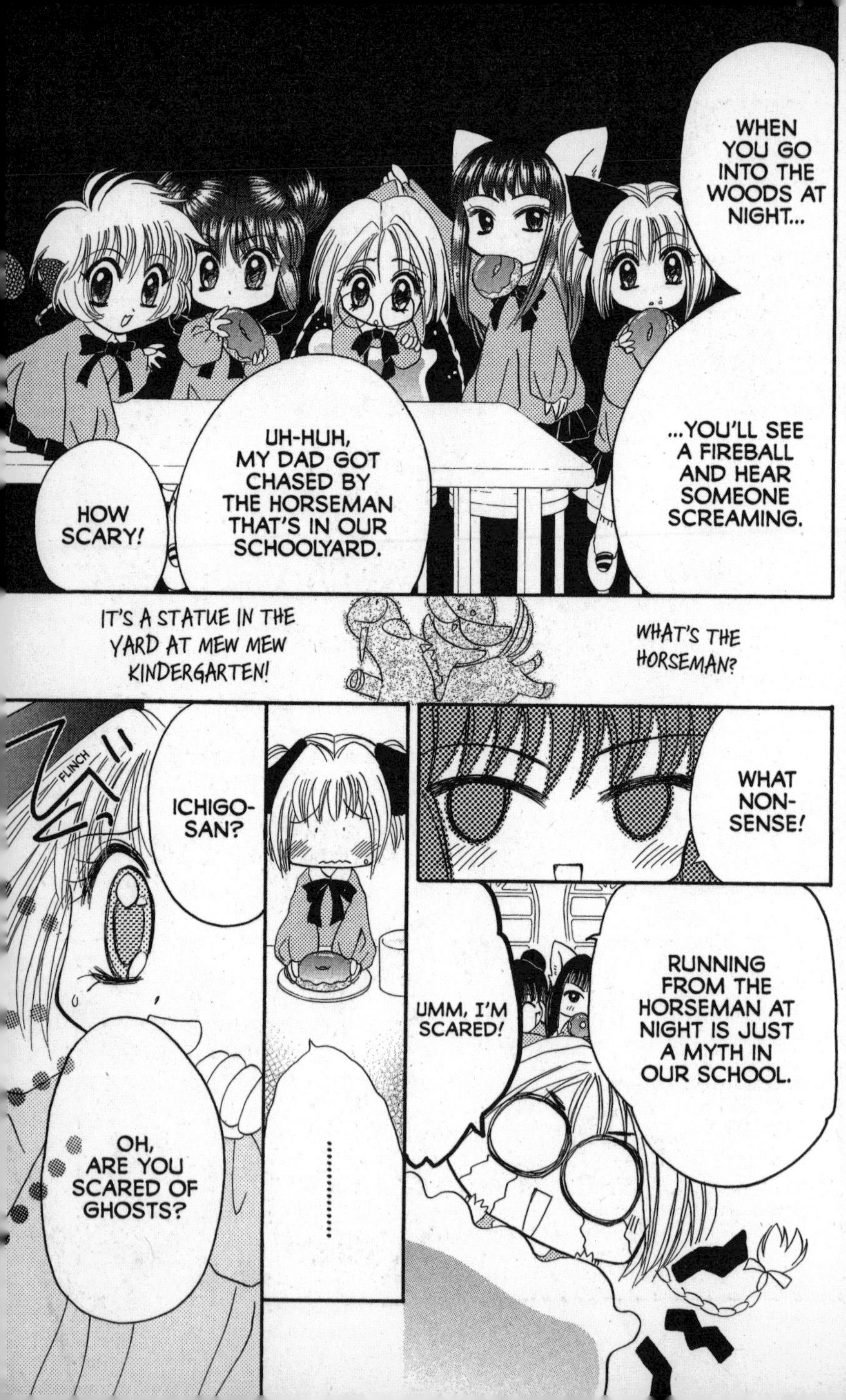
WHEN YOU GO INTO THE WOODS AT NIGHT...
...YOU'LL SEE A FIREBALL AND HEAR SOMEONE SCREAMING.
UH-HUH, MY DAD GOT CHASED BY THE HORSEMAN THAT'S IN OUR SCHOOLYARD.
HOW SCARY!
WHAT'S THE HORSEMAN?
IT'S A STATUE IN THE YARD AT MEW MEW KINDERGARTEN!
WHAT NON-SENSE!
RUNNING FROM THE HORSEMAN AT NIGHT IS JUST A MYTH IN OUR SCHOOL.
UMM, I'M SCARED!
....
ICHIGO-SAN?
FLINCH
OH, ARE YOU SCARED OF GHOSTS?

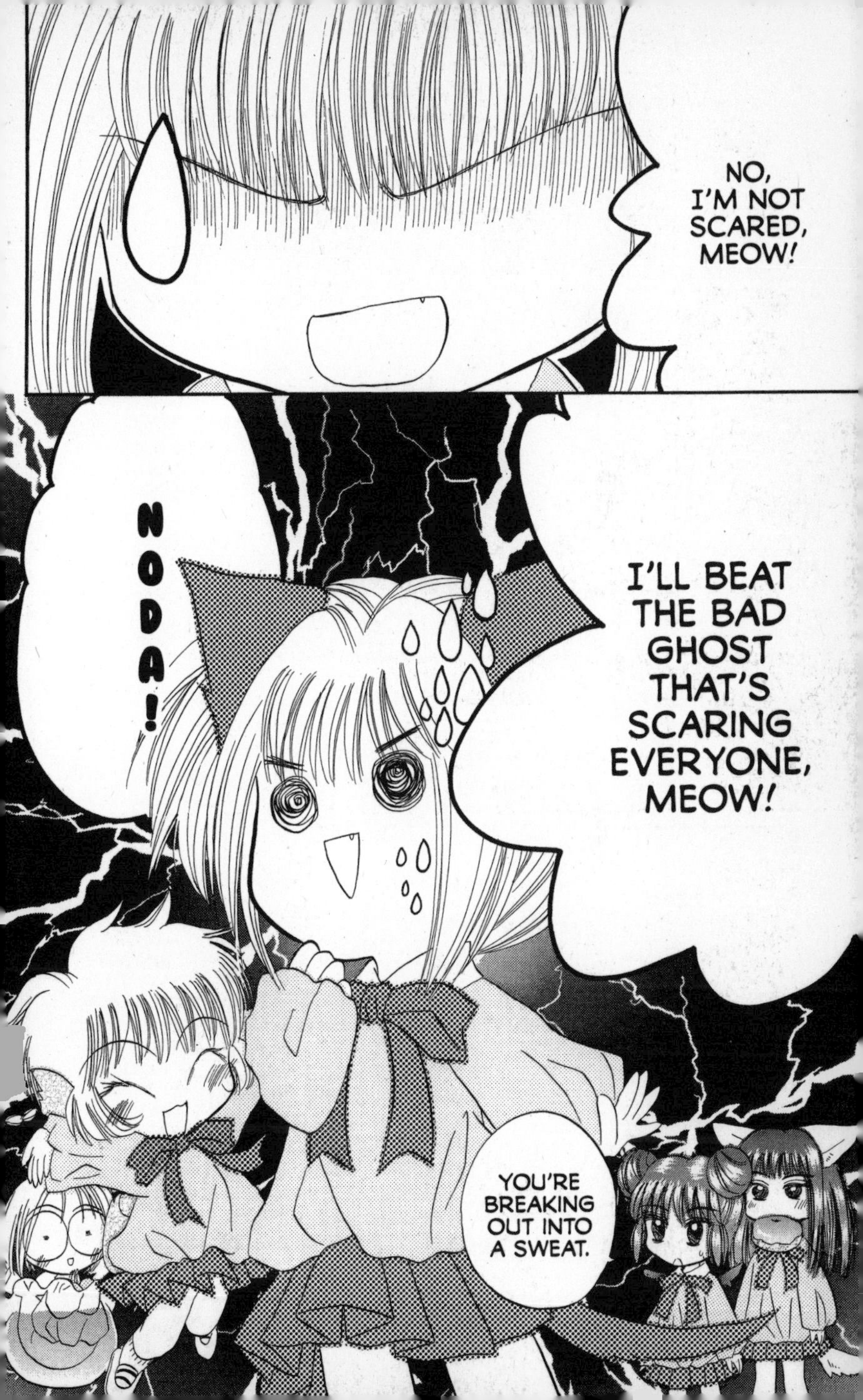
NO, I'M NOT SCARED, MEOW!
I'LL BEAT THE BAD GHOST THAT'S SCARING EVERYONE, MEOW!
NODA!
YOU'RE BREAKING OUT INTO A SWEAT.

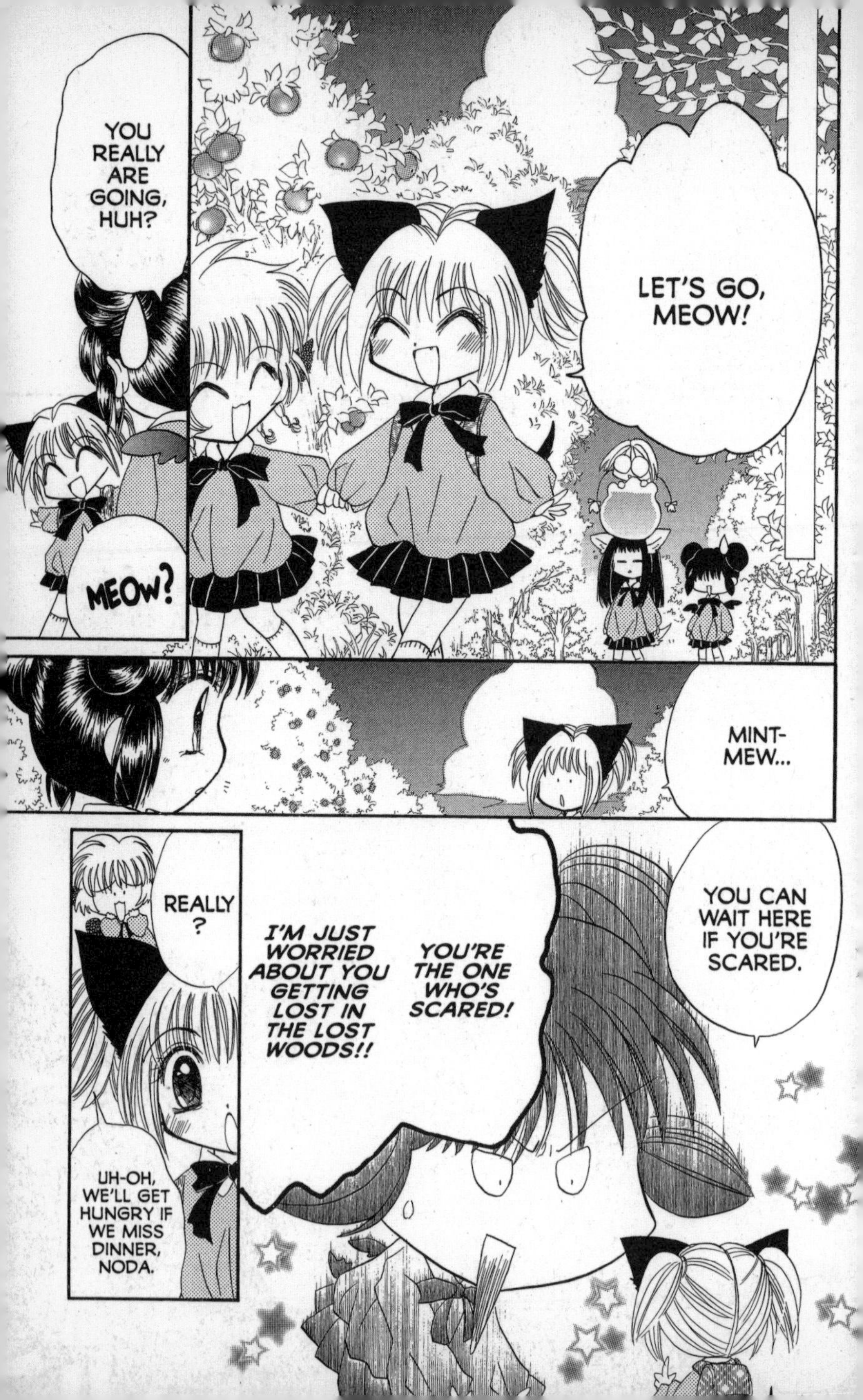
LET'S GO, MEOW!
YOU REALLY ARE GOING, HUH?
MEOW?
MINT-MEW...
YOU CAN WAIT HERE IF YOU'RE SCARED.
YOU'RE THE ONE WHO'S SCARED!
I'M JUST WORRIED ABOUT YOU GETTING LOST IN THE LOST WOODS!!
REALLY?
UH-OH, WE'LL GET HUNGRY IF WE MISS DINNER, NODA.

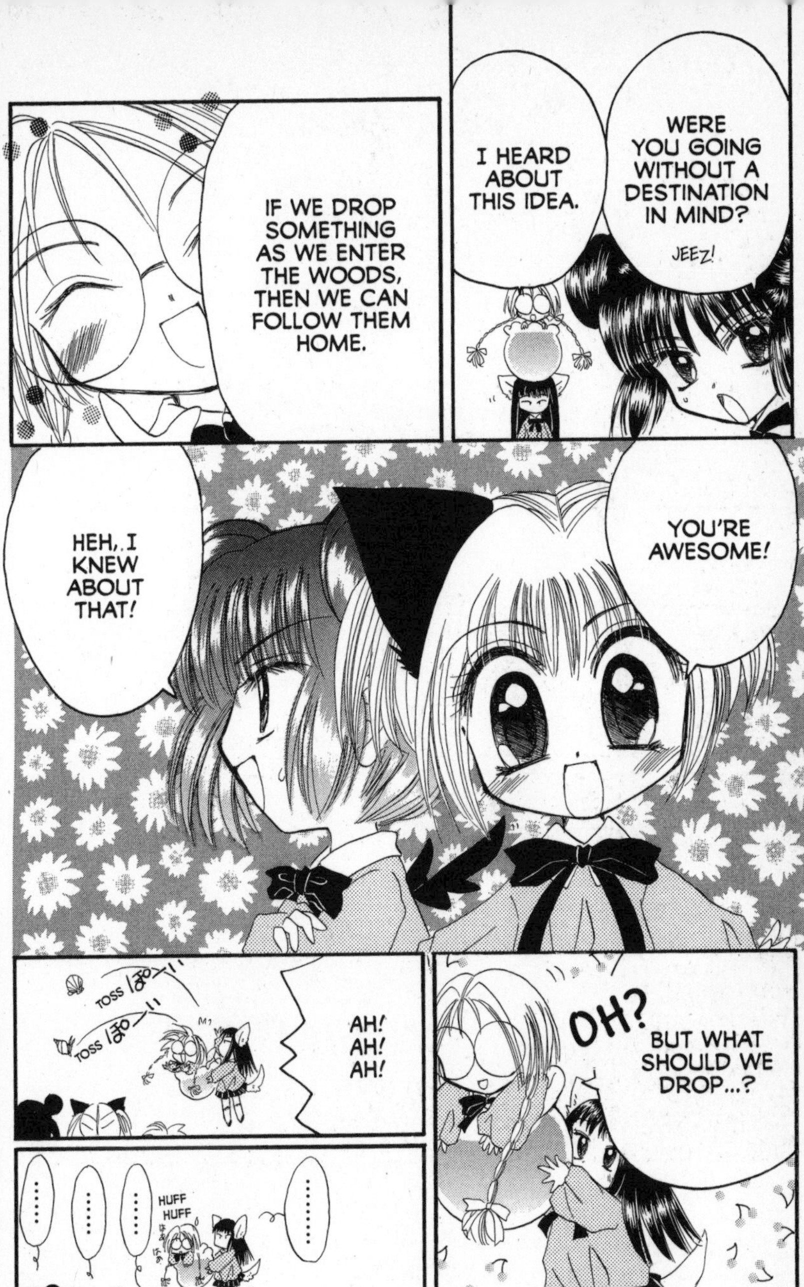
WERE YOU GOING WITHOUT A DESTINATION IN MIND?
JEEZ!
I HEARD ABOUT THIS IDEA.
IF WE DROP SOMETHING AS WE ENTER THE WOODS, THEN WE CAN FOLLOW THEM HOME.
YOU'RE AWESOME!
HEH, I KNEW ABOUT THAT!
OH?
BUT WHAT SHOULD WE DROP...?
AH! AH! AH!
TOSS
TOSS
......
HUFF HUFF
......
......
......

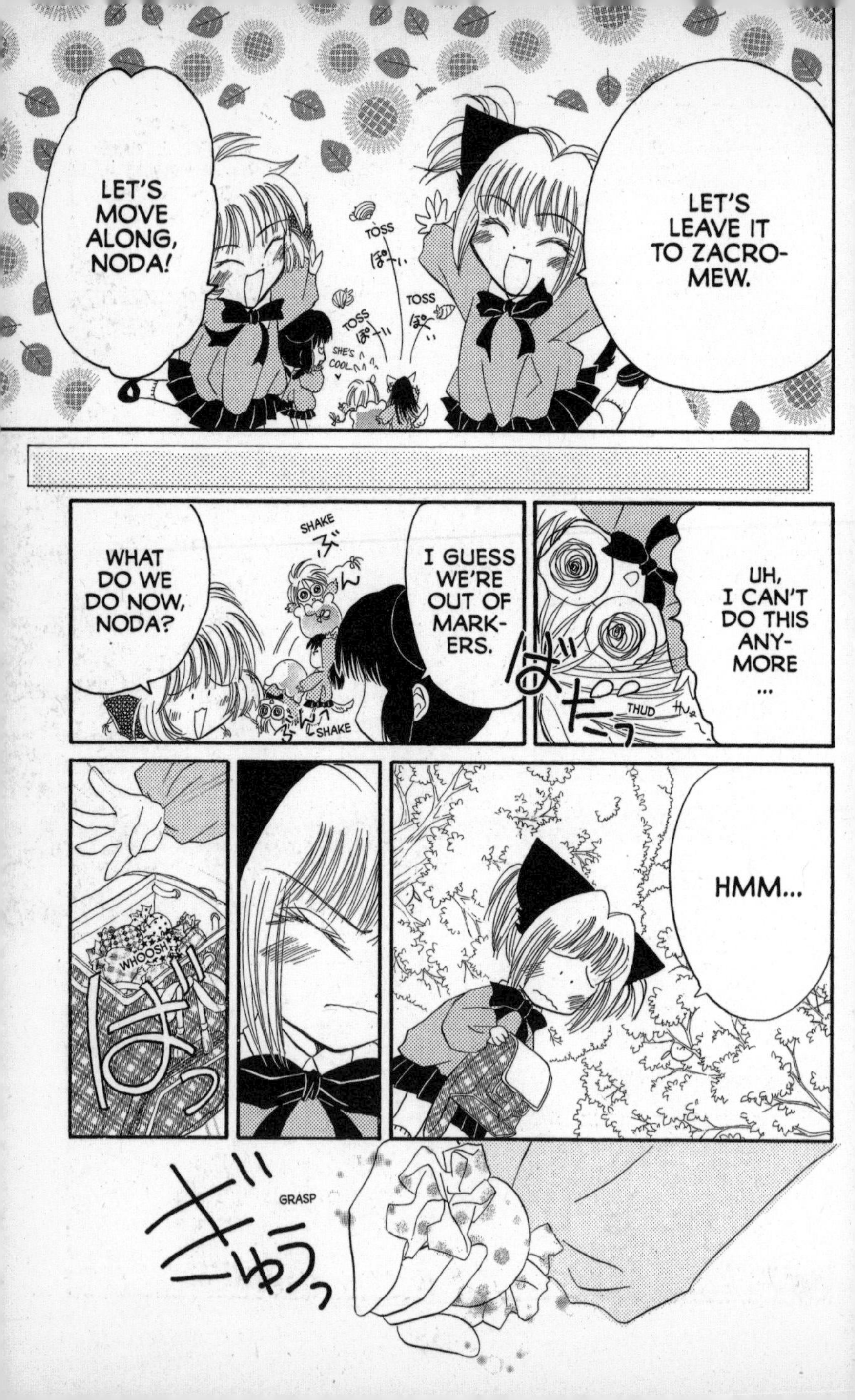
LET'S LEAVE IT TO ZACRO-MEW.
TOSS
TOSS
TOSS
SHE'S COOL
LET'S MOVE ALONG, NODA!
UH, I CAN'T DO THIS ANYMORE ...
THUD
I GUESS WE'RE OUT OF MARKERS.
SHAKE
SHAKE
WHAT DO WE DO NOW, NODA?
HMM...
WHOOSH
GRASP

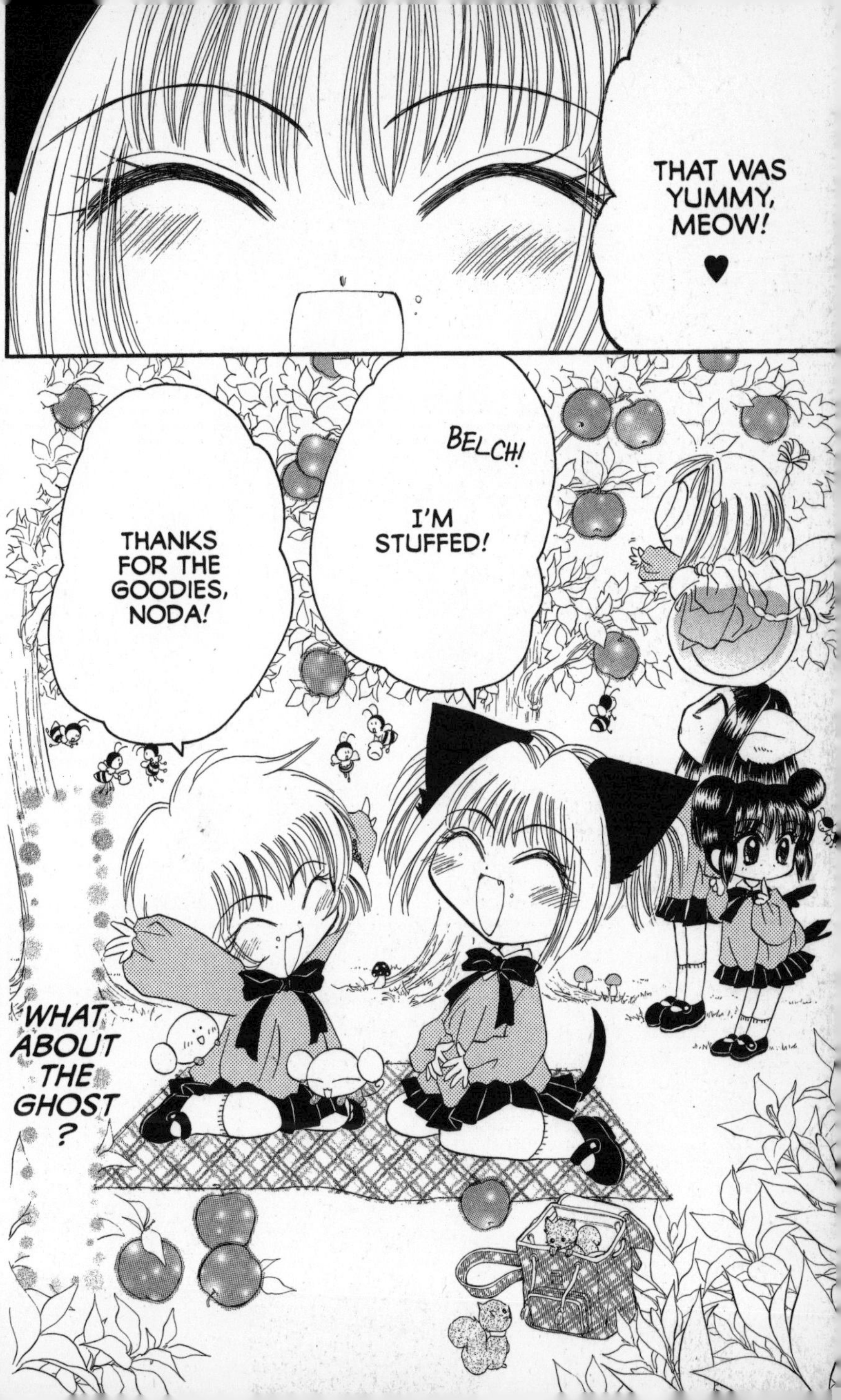
THAT WAS YUMMY, MEOW! ♥
BELCH!
I'M STUFFED!
THANKS FOR THE GOODIES, NODA!
WHAT ABOUT THE GHOST?

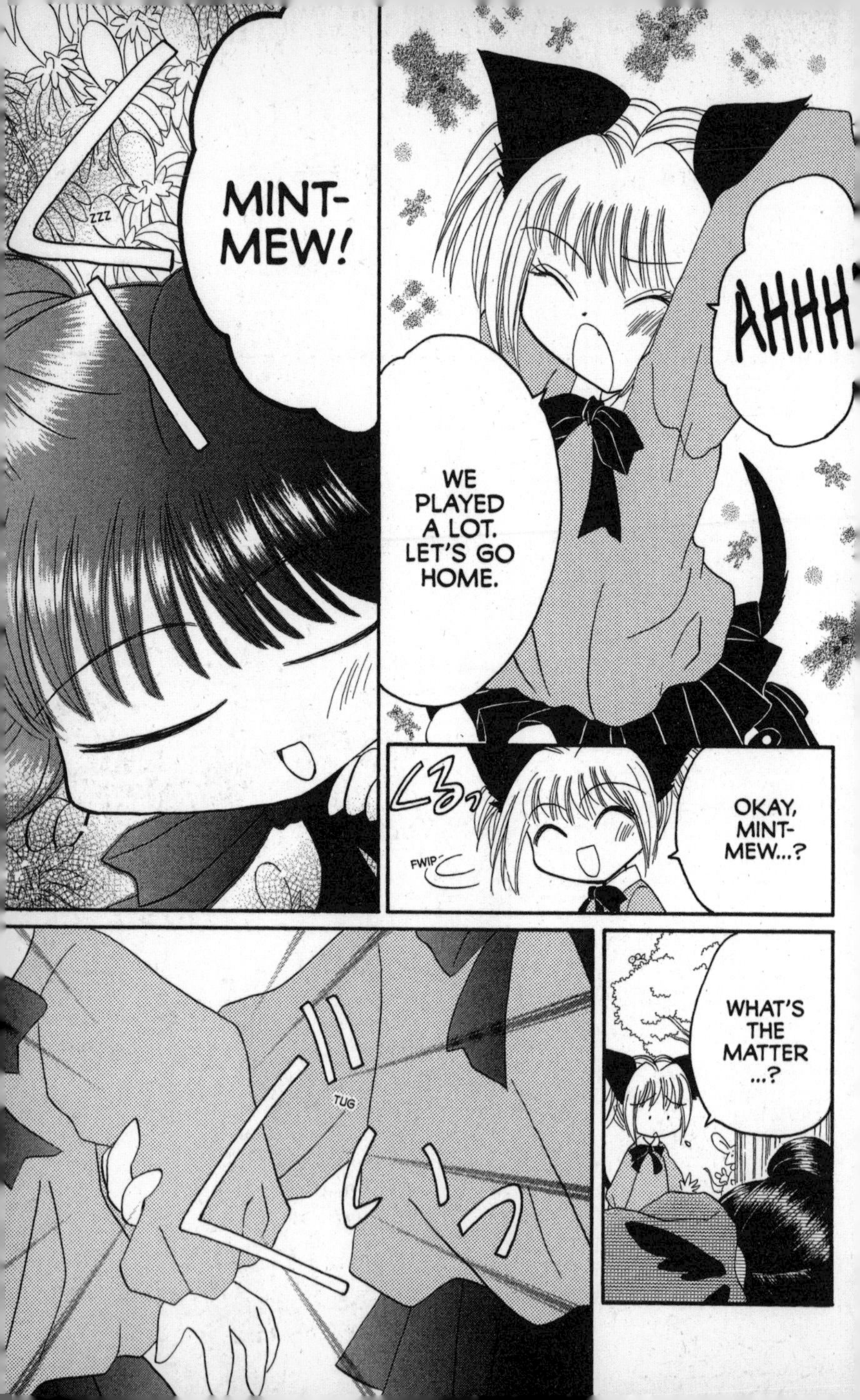
AHHH
WE PLAYED A LOT. LET'S GO HOME.
OKAY, MINT-MEW...?
くるっ
FWIP
MINT-MEW!
ZZZ
WHAT'S THE MATTER ...?
TUG
くいっ

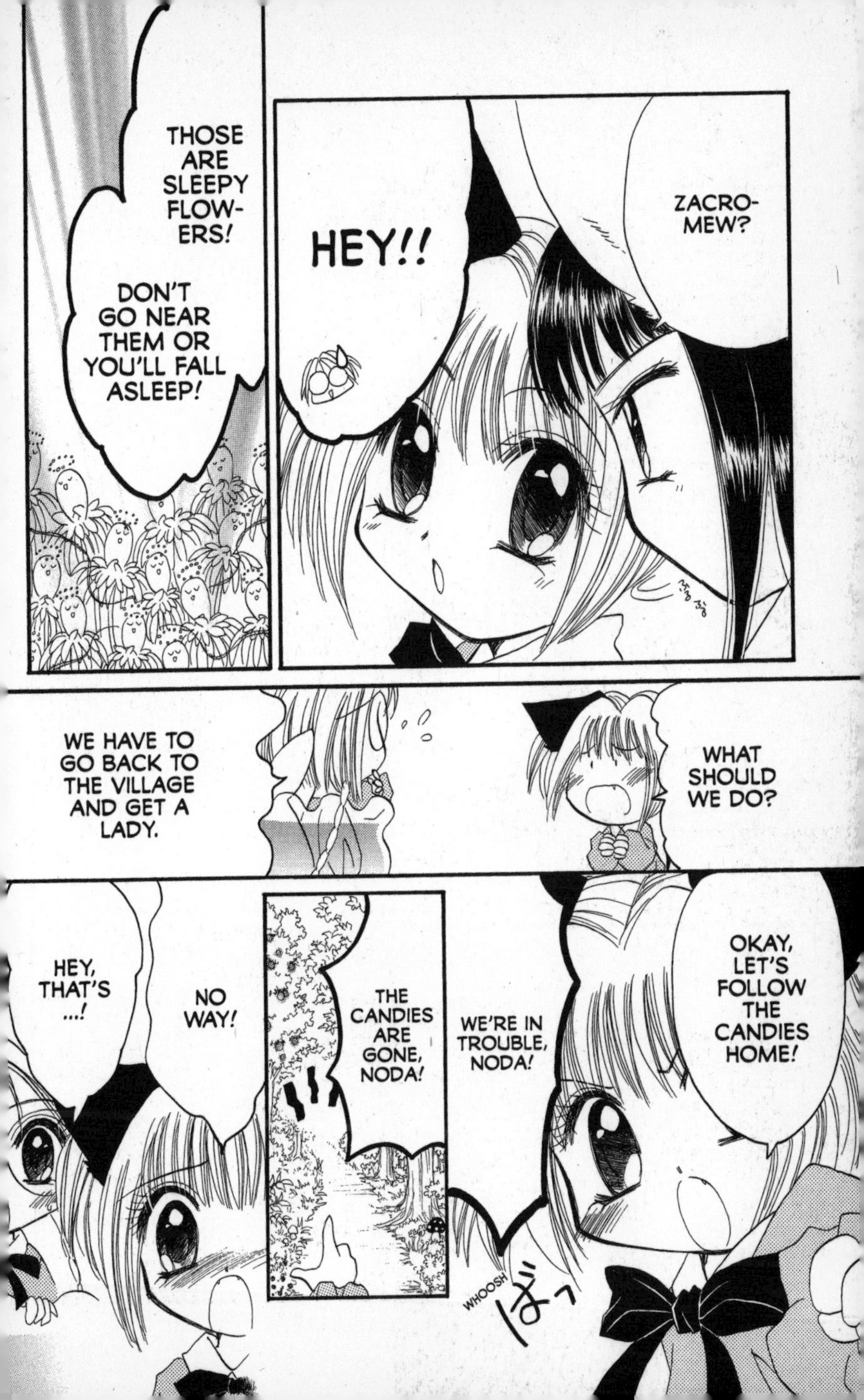
ZACRO-MEW?
HEY!!
THOSE ARE SLEEPY FLOWERS!
DON'T GO NEAR THEM OR YOU'LL FALL ASLEEP!
WHAT SHOULD WE DO?
WE HAVE TO GO BACK TO THE VILLAGE AND GET A LADY.
OKAY, LET'S FOLLOW THE CANDIES HOME!
WE'RE IN TROUBLE, NODA!
WHOOSH
THE CANDIES ARE GONE, NODA!
NO WAY!
HEY, THAT'S ...!

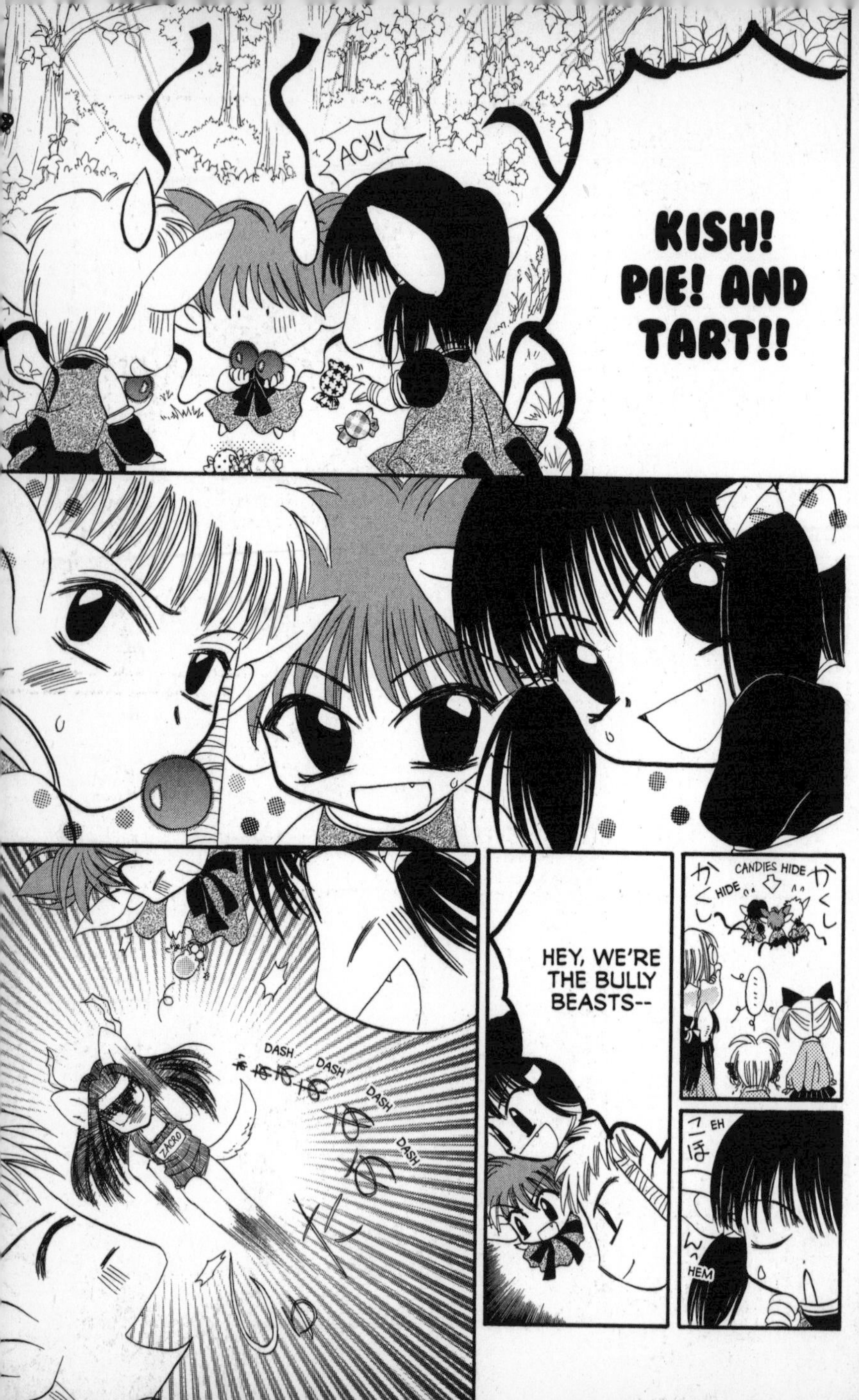

KISH! PIE! AND TART!!
ACK!
かくし
CANDIES HIDE
HIDE
かくし
...
EH
HEM
HEY, WE'RE THE BULLY BEASTS--
DASH
DASH
DASH
DASH
ZACRO

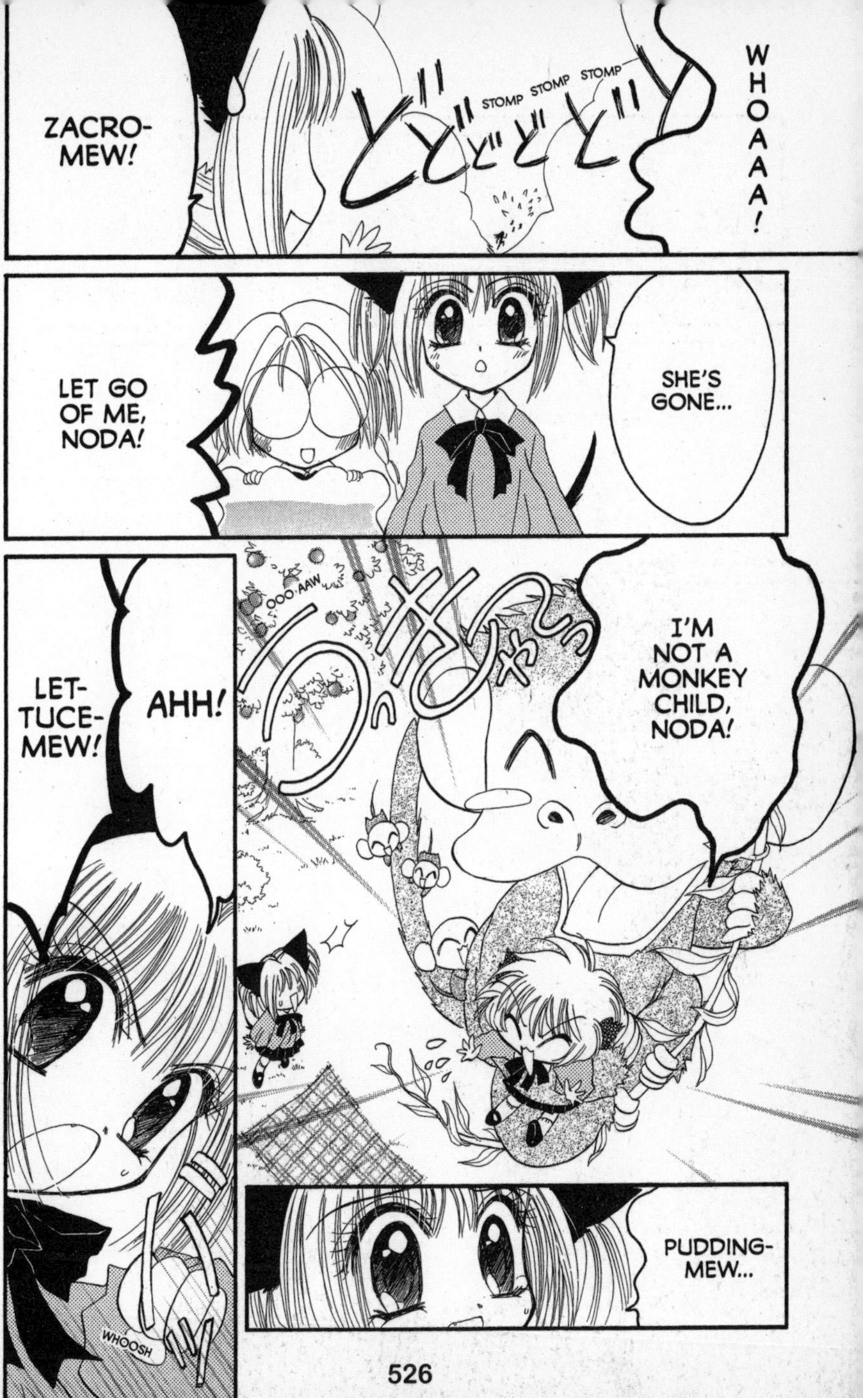
WHOAAAA!
STOMP STOMP STOMP
ZACRO-MEW!
SHE'S GONE...
LET GO OF ME, NODA!
I'M NOT A MONKEY CHILD, NODA!
OOO-AAW
PUDDING-MEW...
AHH!
LET-TUCE-MEW!
WHOOSH

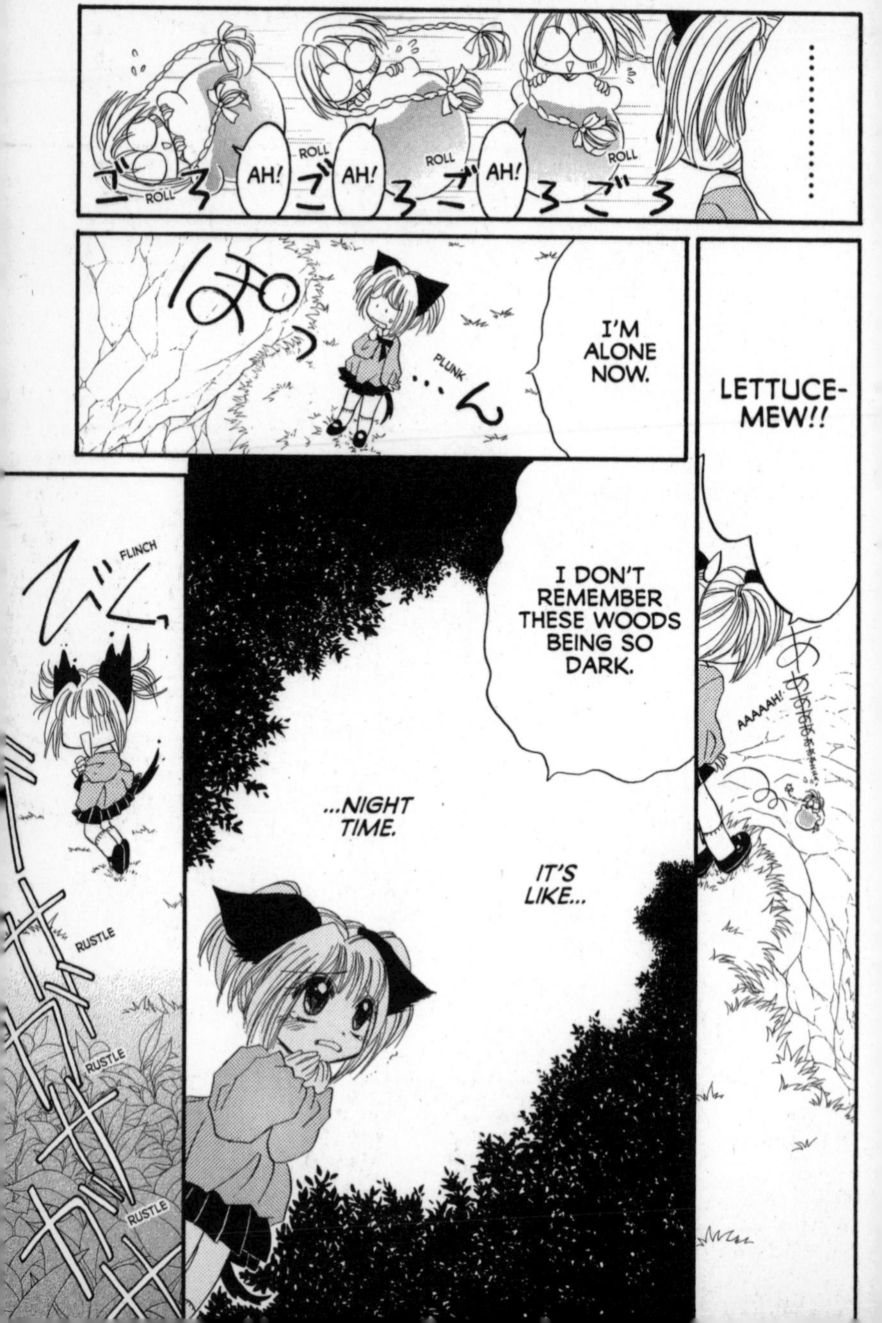

......
ROLL
AH!
ROLL
AH!
ROLL
AH!
ROLL
LETTUCE-MEW!!
AAAAAH!
I'M ALONE NOW.
PLUNK
I DON'T REMEMBER THESE WOODS BEING SO DARK.
IT'S LIKE...
...NIGHT TIME.
FLINCH
RUSTLE
RUSTLE
RUSTLE

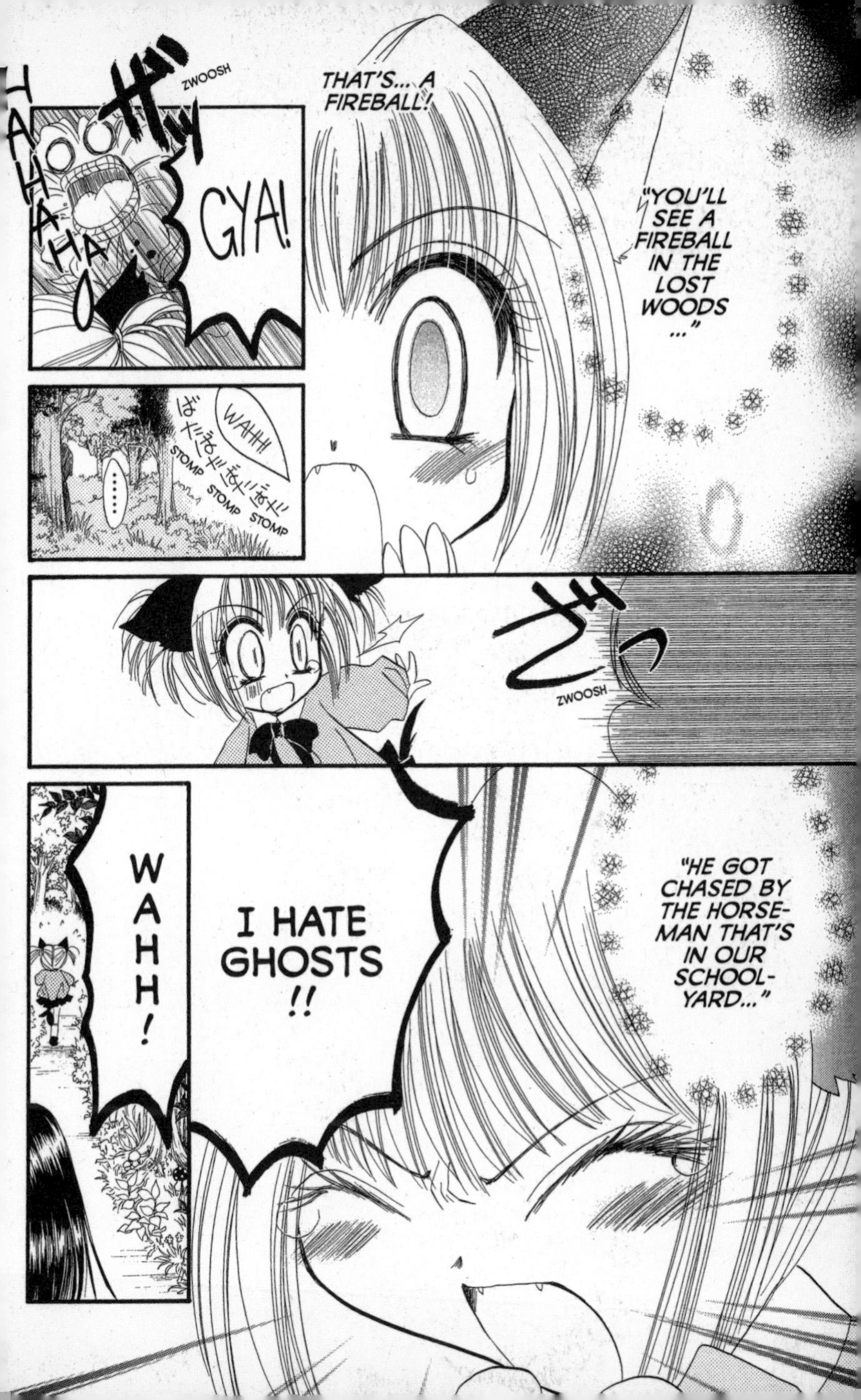
"YOU'LL SEE A FIREBALL IN THE LOST WOODS..."
THAT'S... A FIREBALL!
ZWOOSH
GYA!
HAHAHA
WAHH!
......
STOMP
STOMP
STOMP
ZWOOSH
"HE GOT CHASED BY THE HORSE-MAN THAT'S IN OUR SCHOOL-YARD..."
I HATE GHOSTS!!
WAHH!

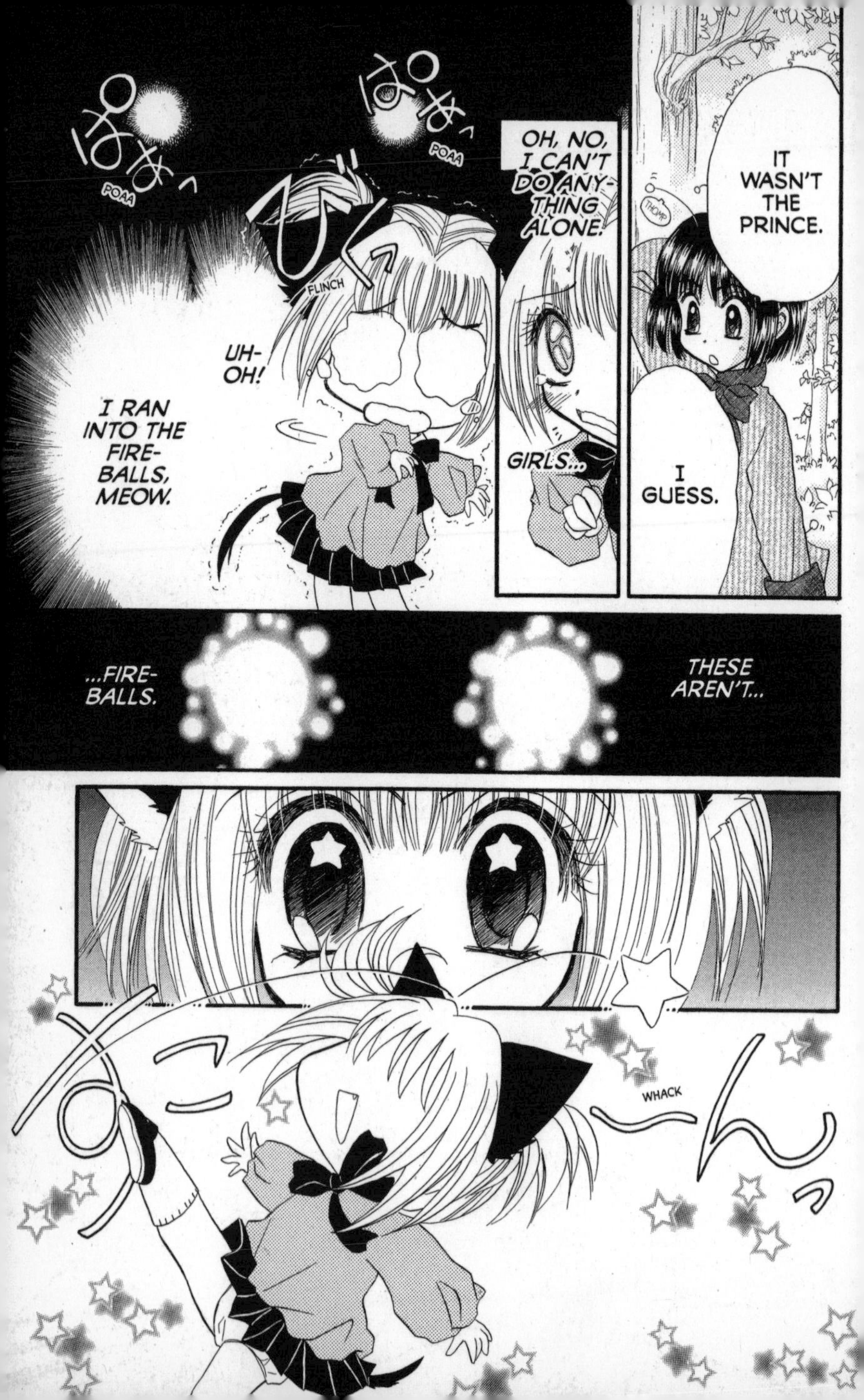
IT WASN'T THE PRINCE.
THOMP
I GUESS.
OH, NO, I CAN'T DO ANYTHING ALONE.
GIRLS...
POAA
POAA
FLINCH
UH-OH!
I RAN INTO THE FIREBALLS, MEOW.
THESE AREN'T...
...FIREBALLS.
WHACK

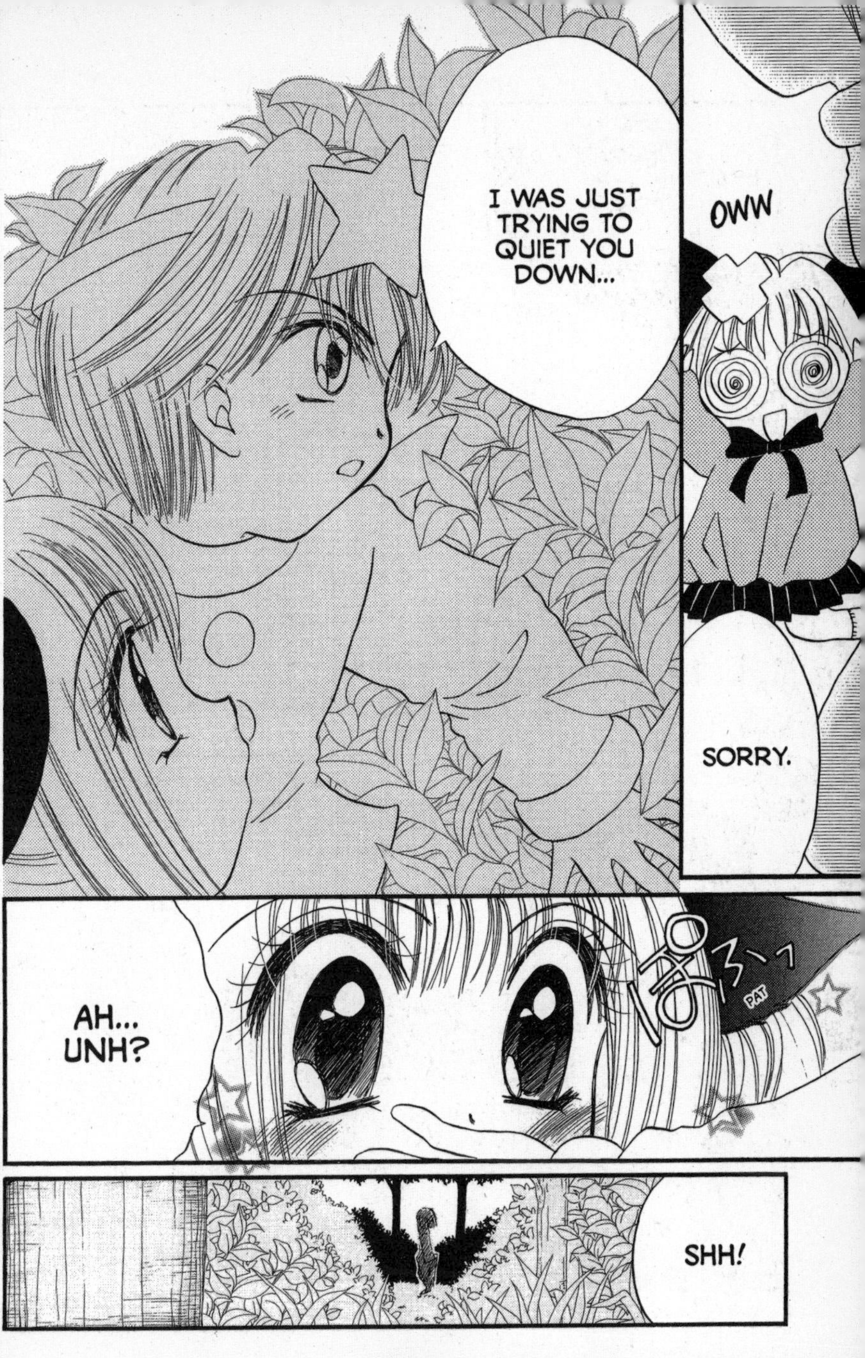
OWW
SORRY.
I WAS JUST TRYING TO QUIET YOU DOWN...
PAT
AH... UNH?
SHH!

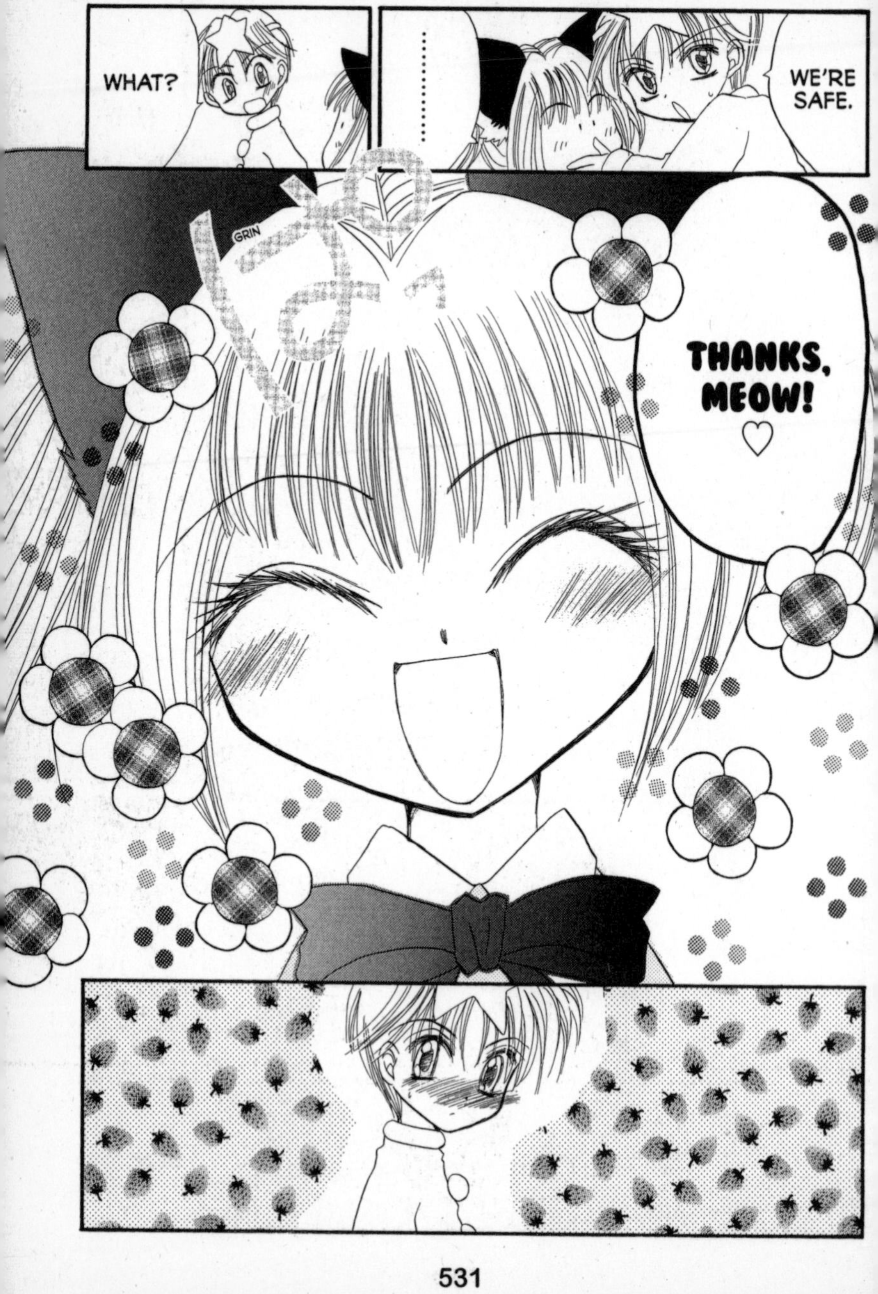
WE'RE SAFE.
......
WHAT?
THANKS, MEOW! ♡
GRIN

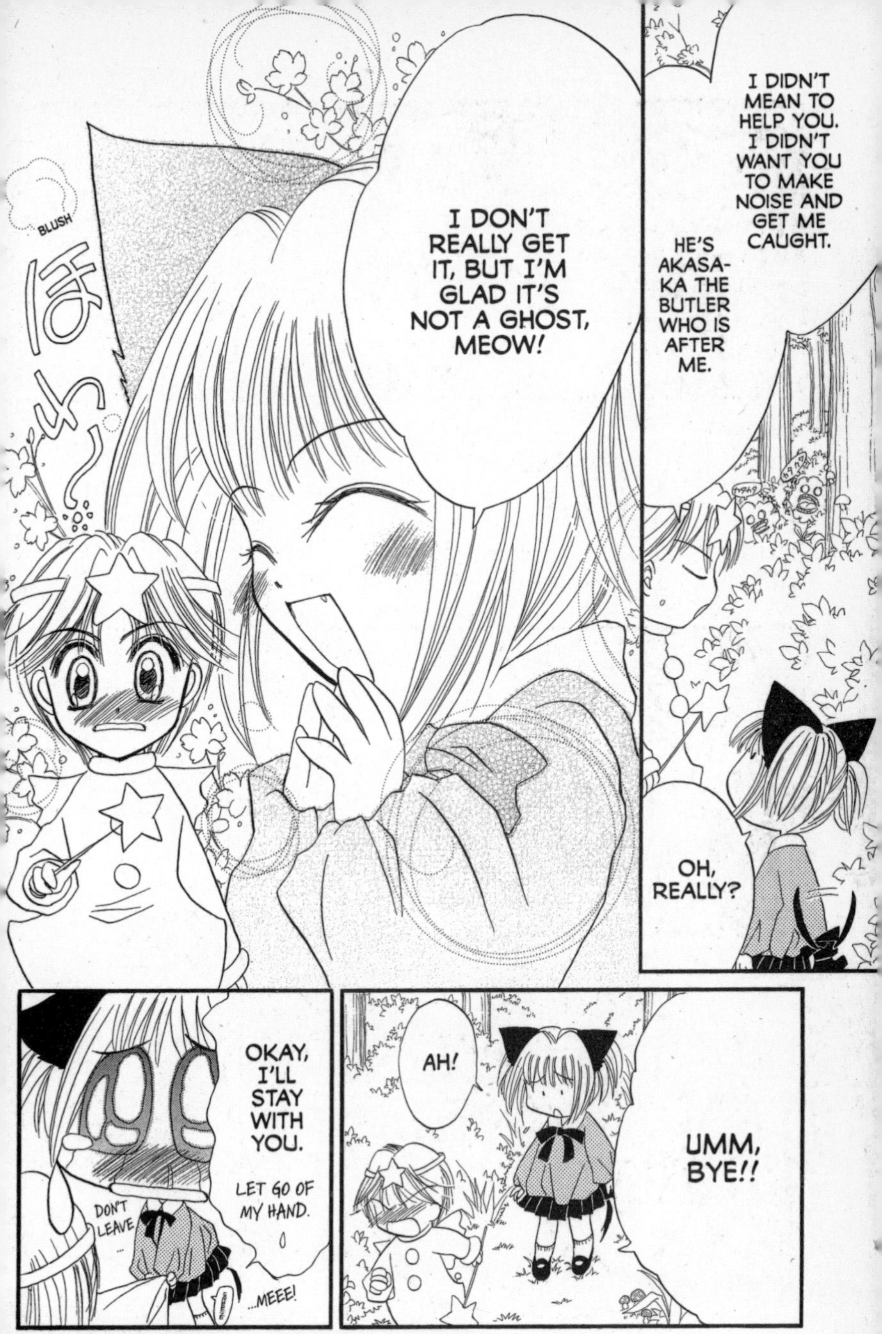
I DIDN'T MEAN TO HELP YOU. I DIDN'T WANT YOU TO MAKE NOISE AND GET ME CAUGHT.
HE'S AKASAKA THE BUTLER WHO IS AFTER ME.
OH, REALLY?
I DON'T REALLY GET IT, BUT I'M GLAD IT'S NOT A GHOST, MEOW!
BLUSH
ほわ
AH!
UMM, BYE!!
OKAY, I'LL STAY WITH YOU.
LET GO OF MY HAND.
DON'T LEAVE...
...MEEE!

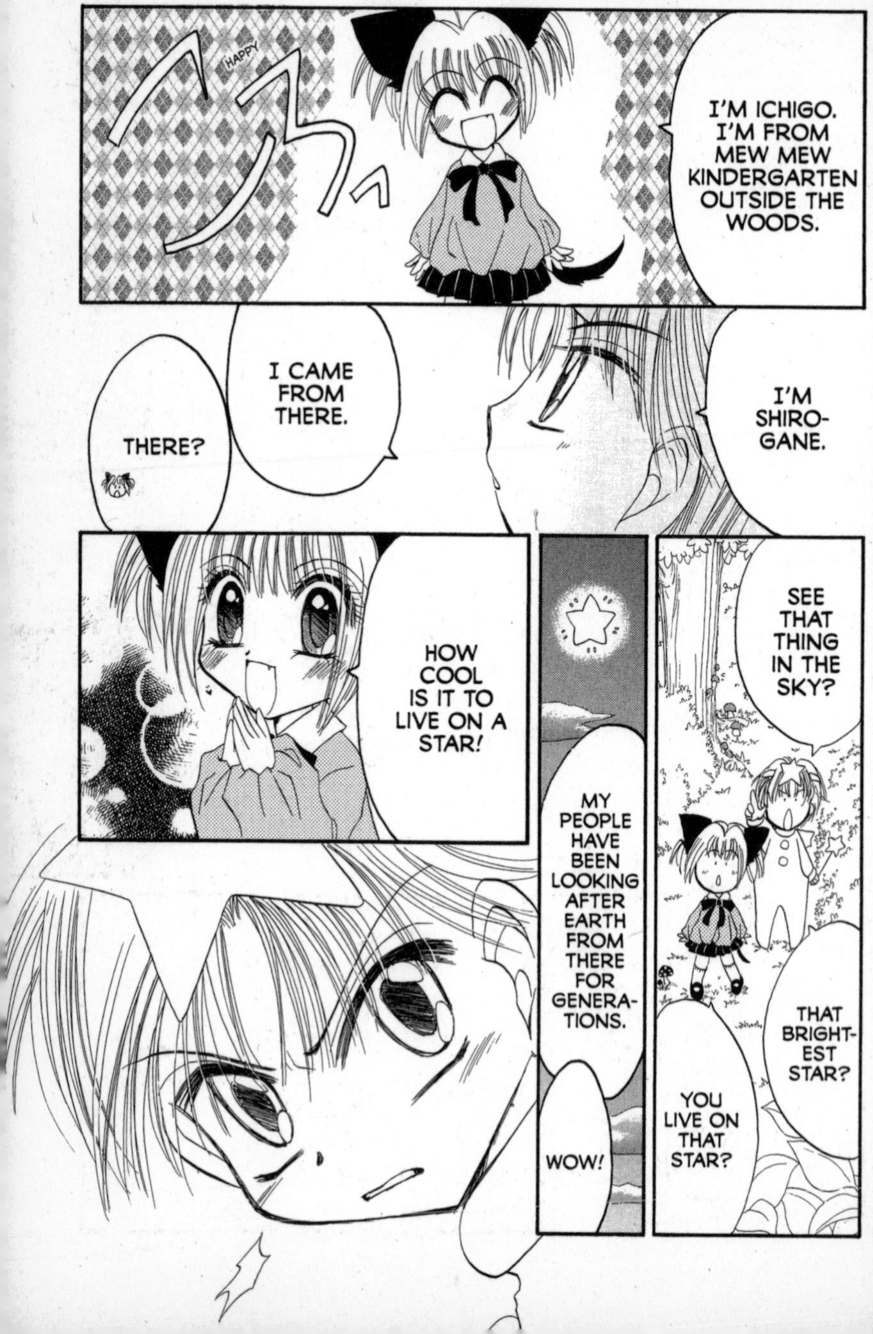
I'M ICHIGO. I'M FROM MEW MEW KINDERGARTEN OUTSIDE THE WOODS.
HAPPY
I'M SHIRO-GANE.
I CAME FROM THERE.
THERE?
SEE THAT THING IN THE SKY?
THAT BRIGHT-EST STAR?
YOU LIVE ON THAT STAR?
MY PEOPLE HAVE BEEN LOOKING AFTER EARTH FROM THERE FOR GENERA-TIONS.
WOW!
HOW COOL IS IT TO LIVE ON A STAR!

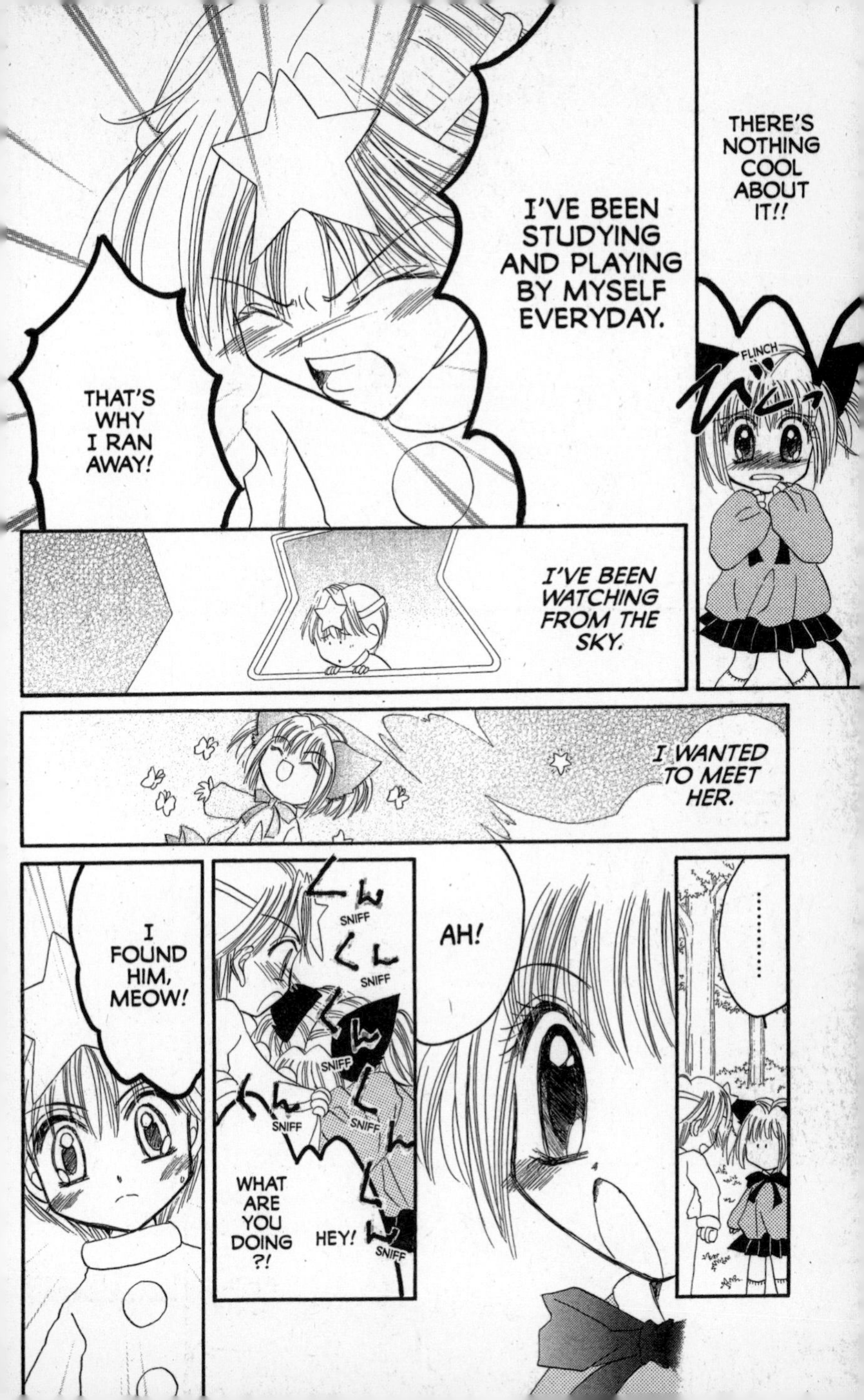
THERE'S NOTHING COOL ABOUT IT!!
FLINCH
I'VE BEEN STUDYING AND PLAYING BY MYSELF EVERYDAY.
THAT'S WHY I RAN AWAY!
I'VE BEEN WATCHING FROM THE SKY.
I WANTED TO MEET HER.
……
AH!
SNIFF
SNIFF
SNIFF
SNIFF
SNIFF
SNIFF
HEY!
WHAT ARE YOU DOING?!
I FOUND HIM, MEOW!

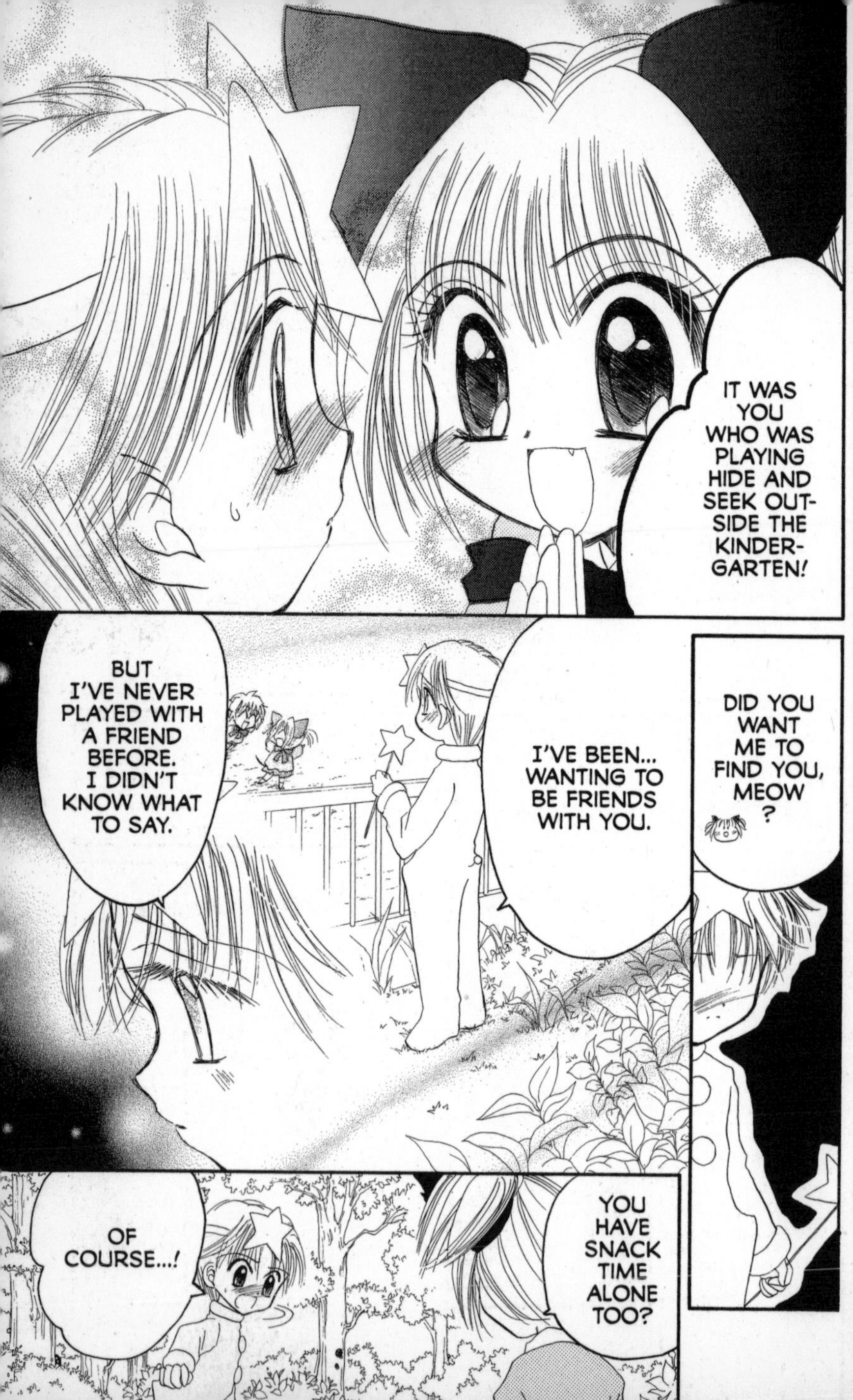

IT WAS YOU WHO WAS PLAYING HIDE AND SEEK OUT-SIDE THE KINDER-GARTEN!
DID YOU WANT ME TO FIND YOU, MEOW?
I'VE BEEN... WANTING TO BE FRIENDS WITH YOU.
BUT I'VE NEVER PLAYED WITH A FRIEND BEFORE. I DIDN'T KNOW WHAT TO SAY.
YOU HAVE SNACK TIME ALONE TOO?
OF COURSE...!

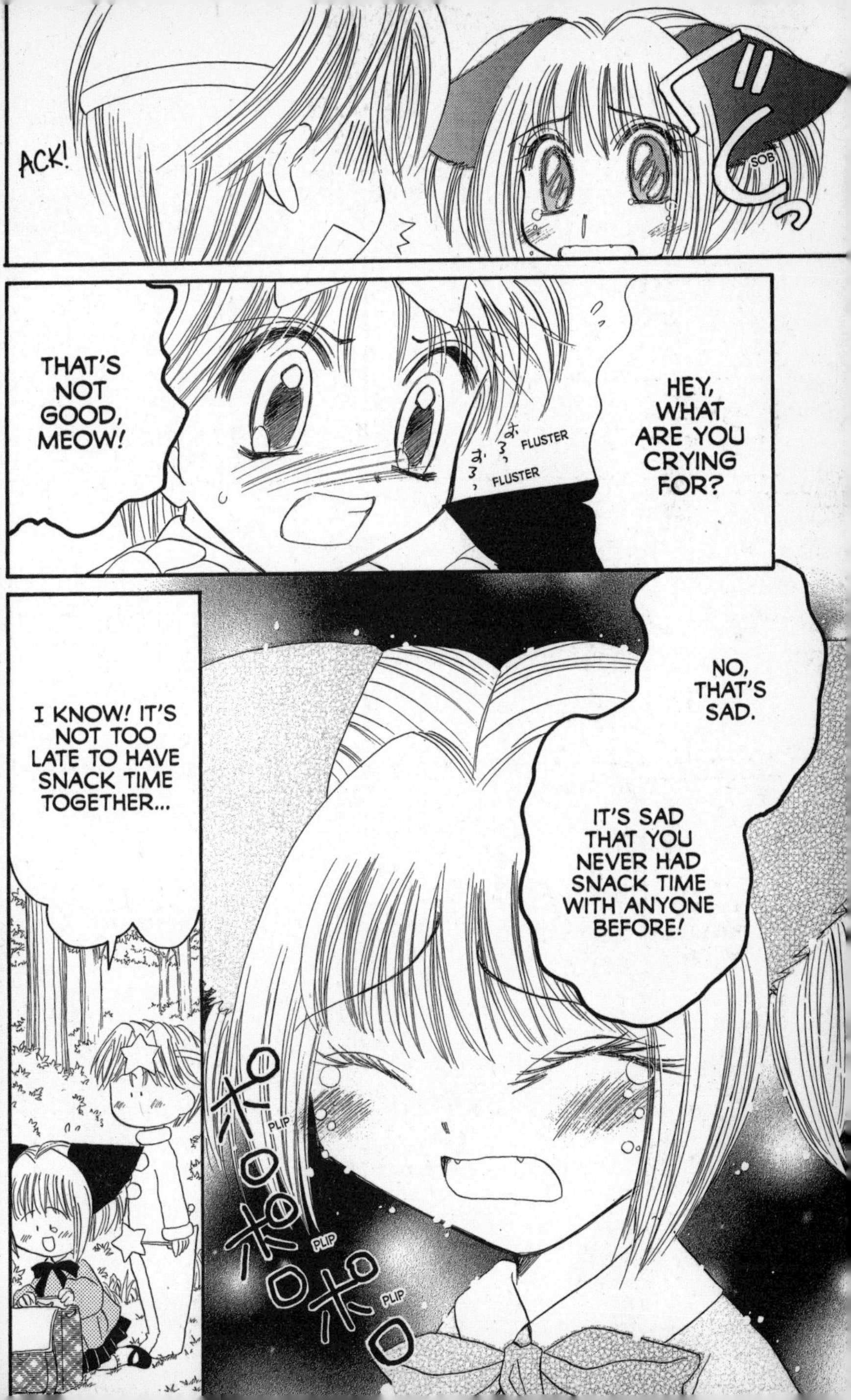
SOB
ACK!
HEY, WHAT ARE YOU CRYING FOR?
FLUSTER
FLUSTER
THAT'S NOT GOOD, MEOW!
NO, THAT'S SAD.
IT'S SAD THAT YOU NEVER HAD SNACK TIME WITH ANYONE BEFORE!
PLIP
PLIP
PLIP
I KNOW! IT'S NOT TOO LATE TO HAVE SNACK TIME TOGETHER...

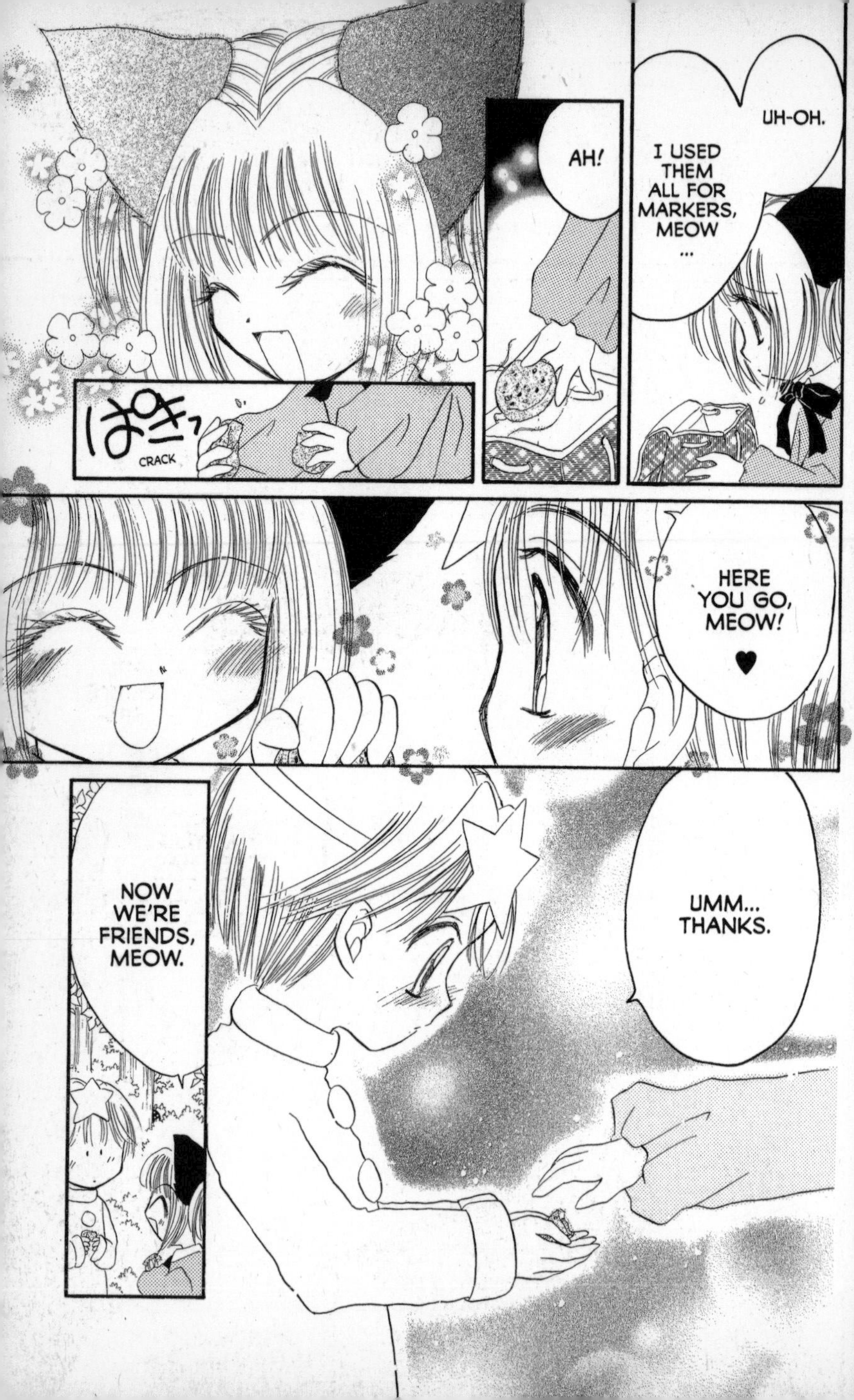
UH-OH.
I USED THEM ALL FOR MARKERS, MEOW ...
AH!
ぱきっ
CRACK
HERE YOU GO, MEOW! ♥
UMM... THANKS.
NOW WE'RE FRIENDS, MEOW.

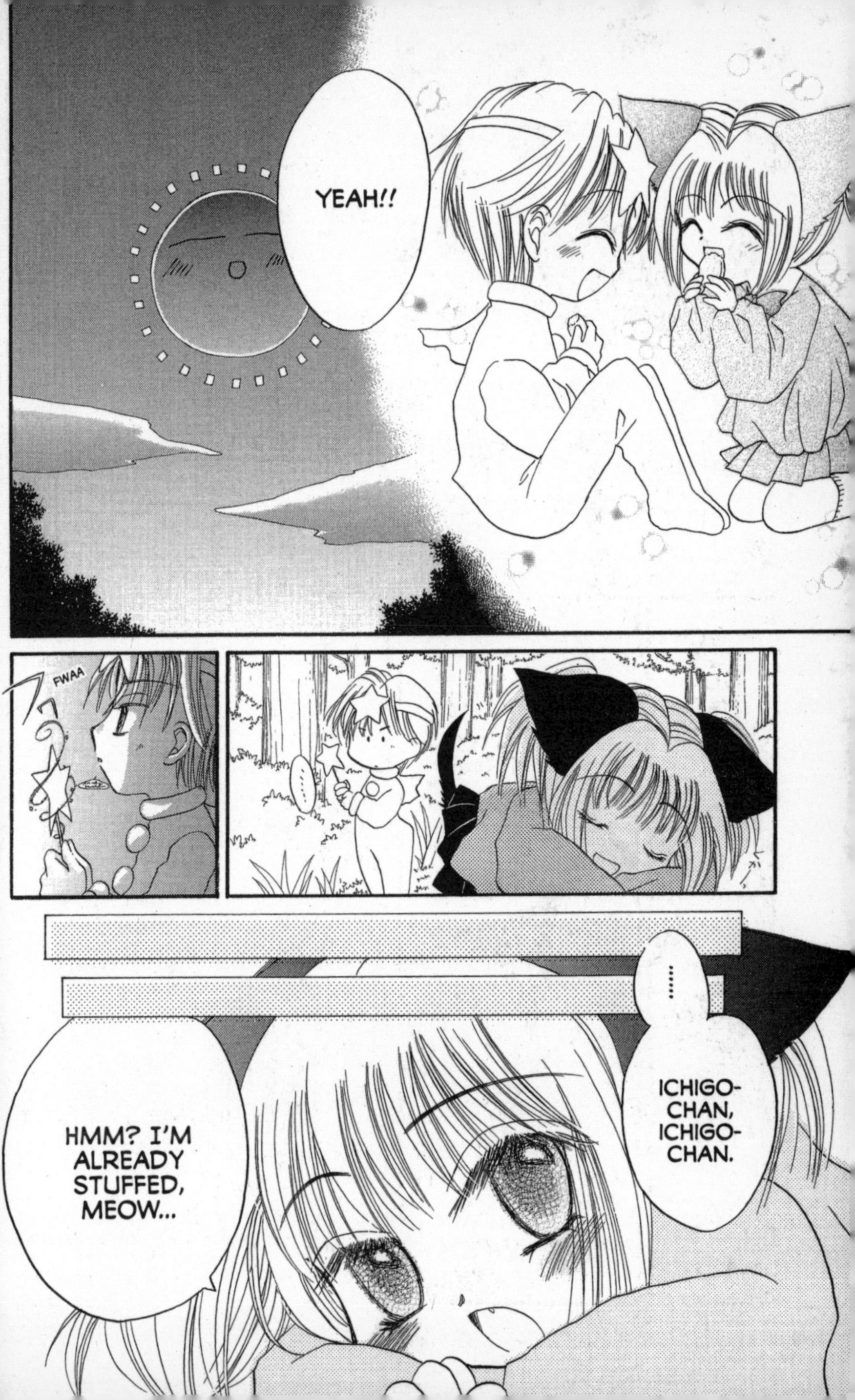
YEAH!!
......
FWAA
......
ICHIGO-CHAN, ICHIGO-CHAN.
HMM? I'M ALREADY STUFFED, MEOW...

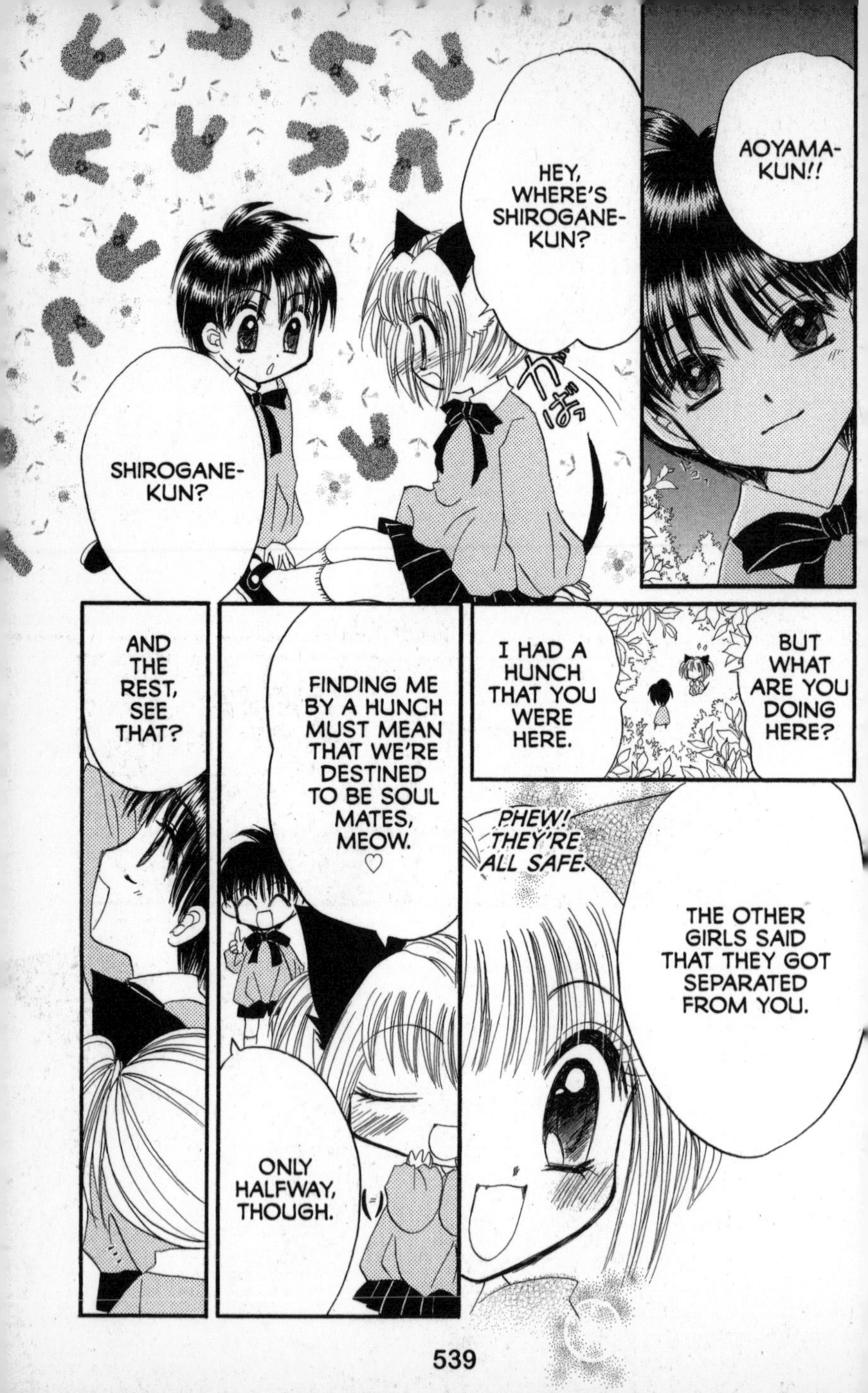
AOYAMA-KUN!!
HEY, WHERE'S SHIROGANE-KUN?
SHIROGANE-KUN?
BUT WHAT ARE YOU DOING HERE?
I HAD A HUNCH THAT YOU WERE HERE.
THE OTHER GIRLS SAID THAT THEY GOT SEPARATED FROM YOU.
PHEW! THEY'RE ALL SAFE.
FINDING ME BY A HUNCH MUST MEAN THAT WE'RE DESTINED TO BE SOUL MATES, MEOW. ♡
ONLY HALFWAY, THOUGH.
AND THE REST, SEE THAT?

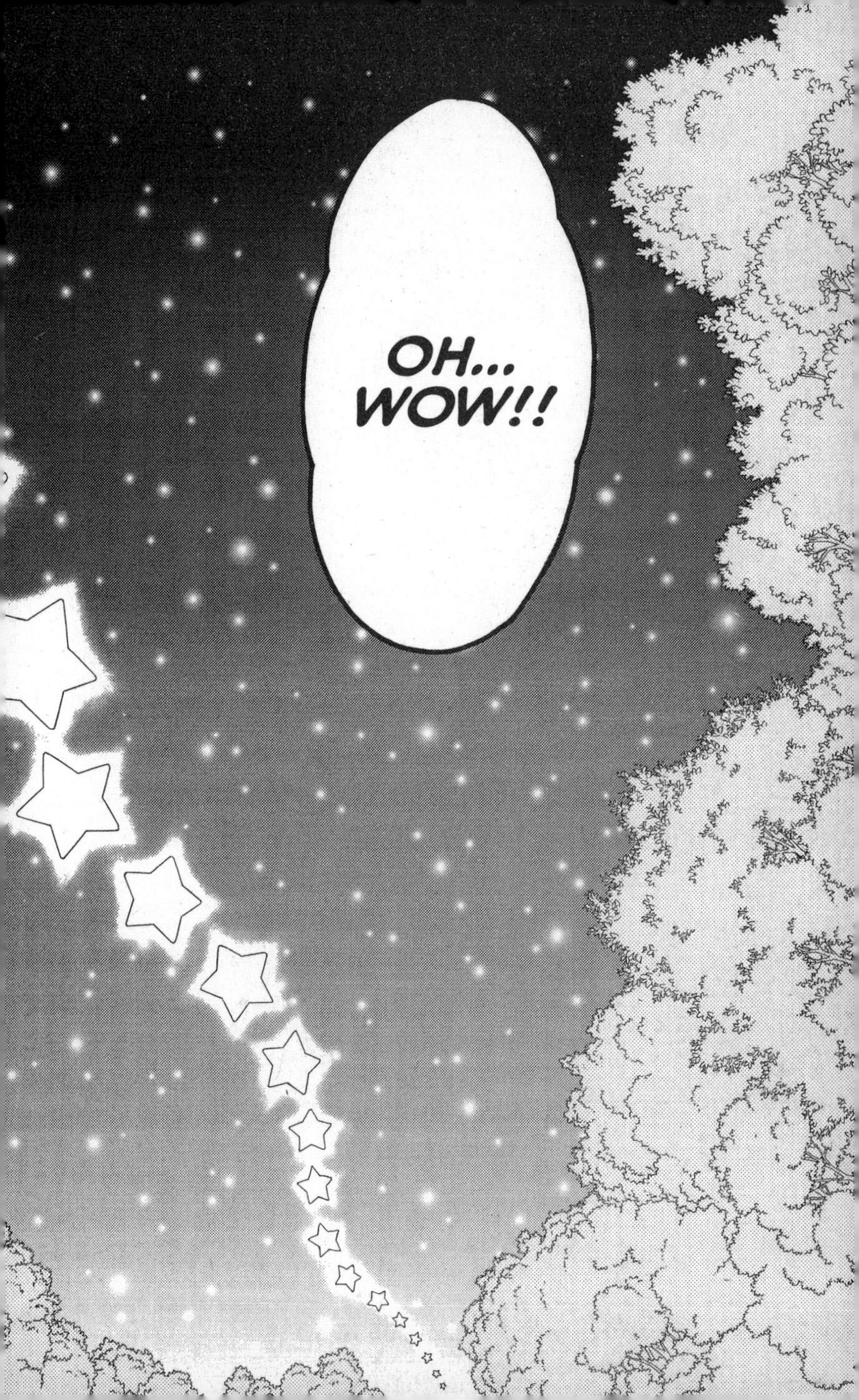
OH... WOW!!

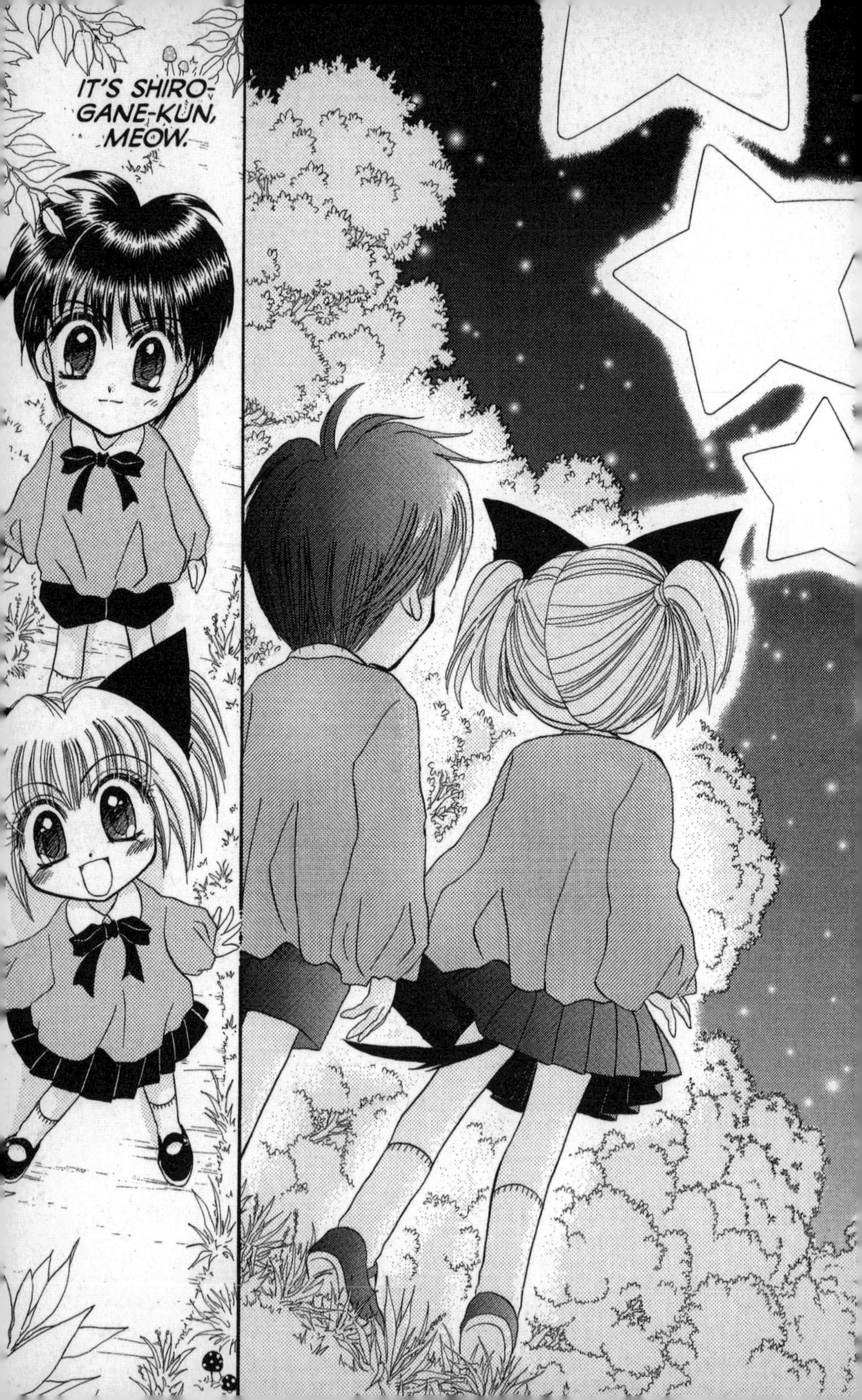
IT'S SHIRO-GANE-KUN, MEOW.

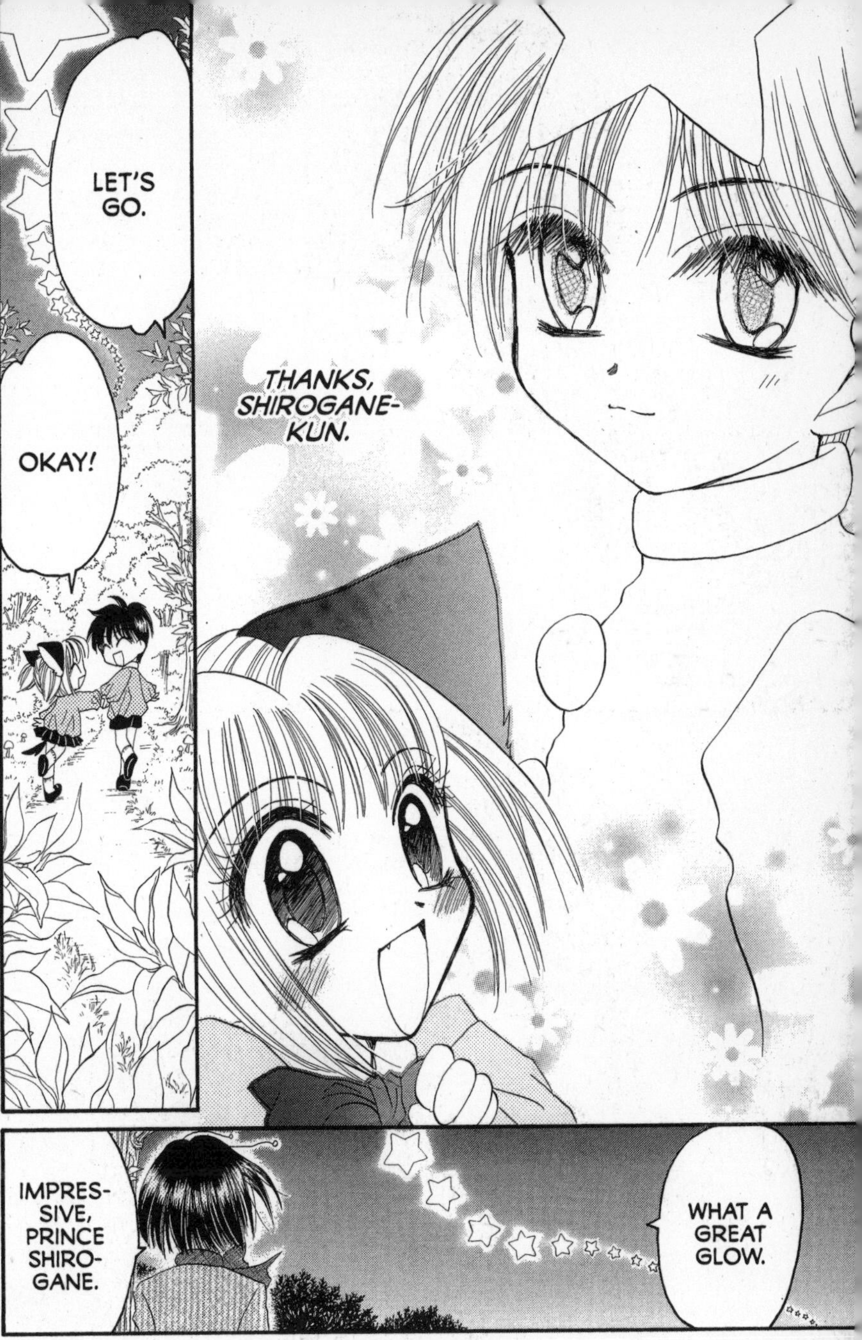
THANKS, SHIROGANE-KUN.
LET'S GO.
OKAY!
WHAT A GREAT GLOW.
IMPRESSIVE, PRINCE SHIROGANE.

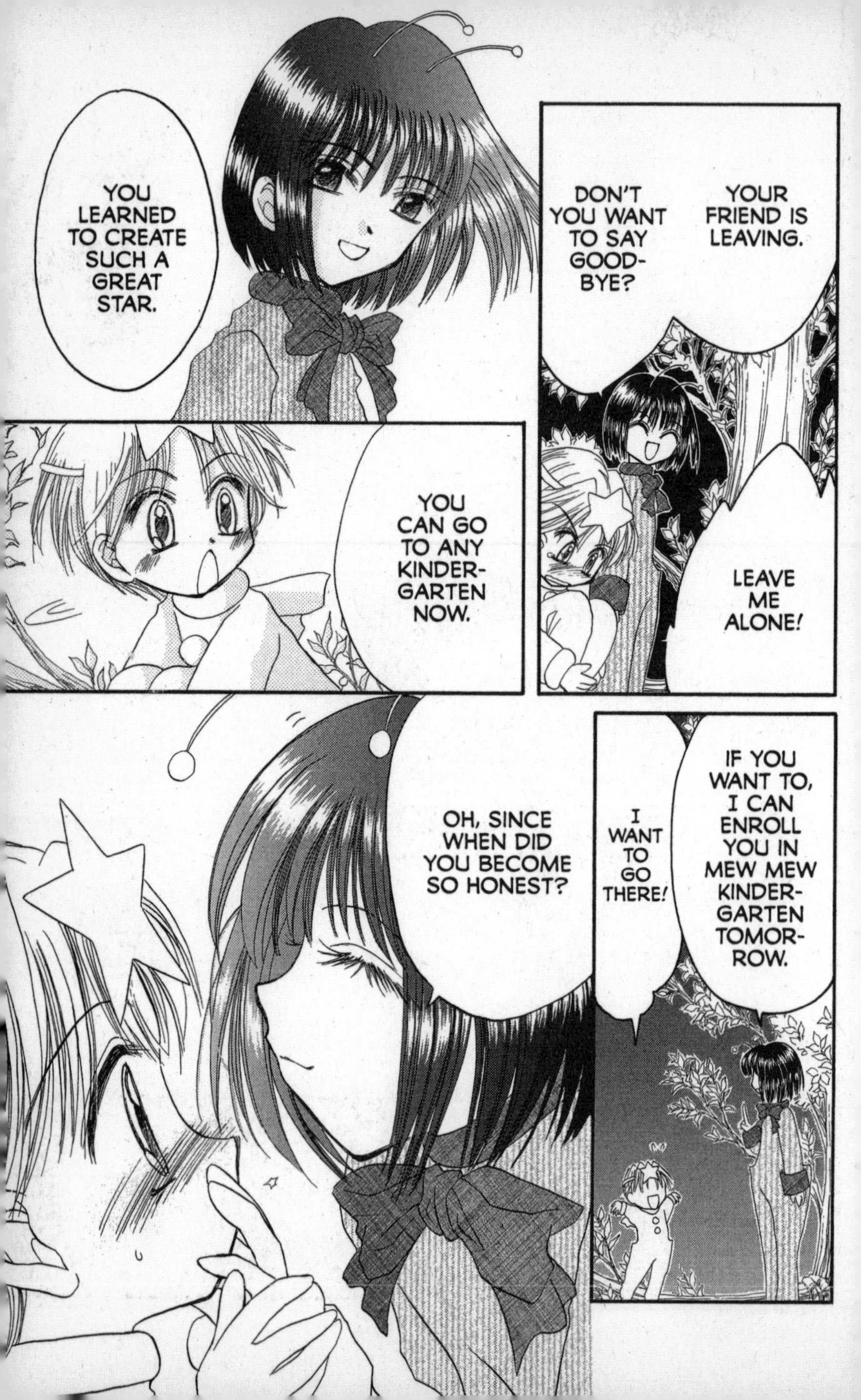
YOUR FRIEND IS LEAVING.
DON'T YOU WANT TO SAY GOOD-BYE?
LEAVE ME ALONE!
YOU LEARNED TO CREATE SUCH A GREAT STAR.
YOU CAN GO TO ANY KINDER-GARTEN NOW.
IF YOU WANT TO, I CAN ENROLL YOU IN MEW MEW KINDER-GARTEN TOMOR-ROW.
I WANT TO GO THERE!
OH, SINCE WHEN DID YOU BECOME SO HONEST?

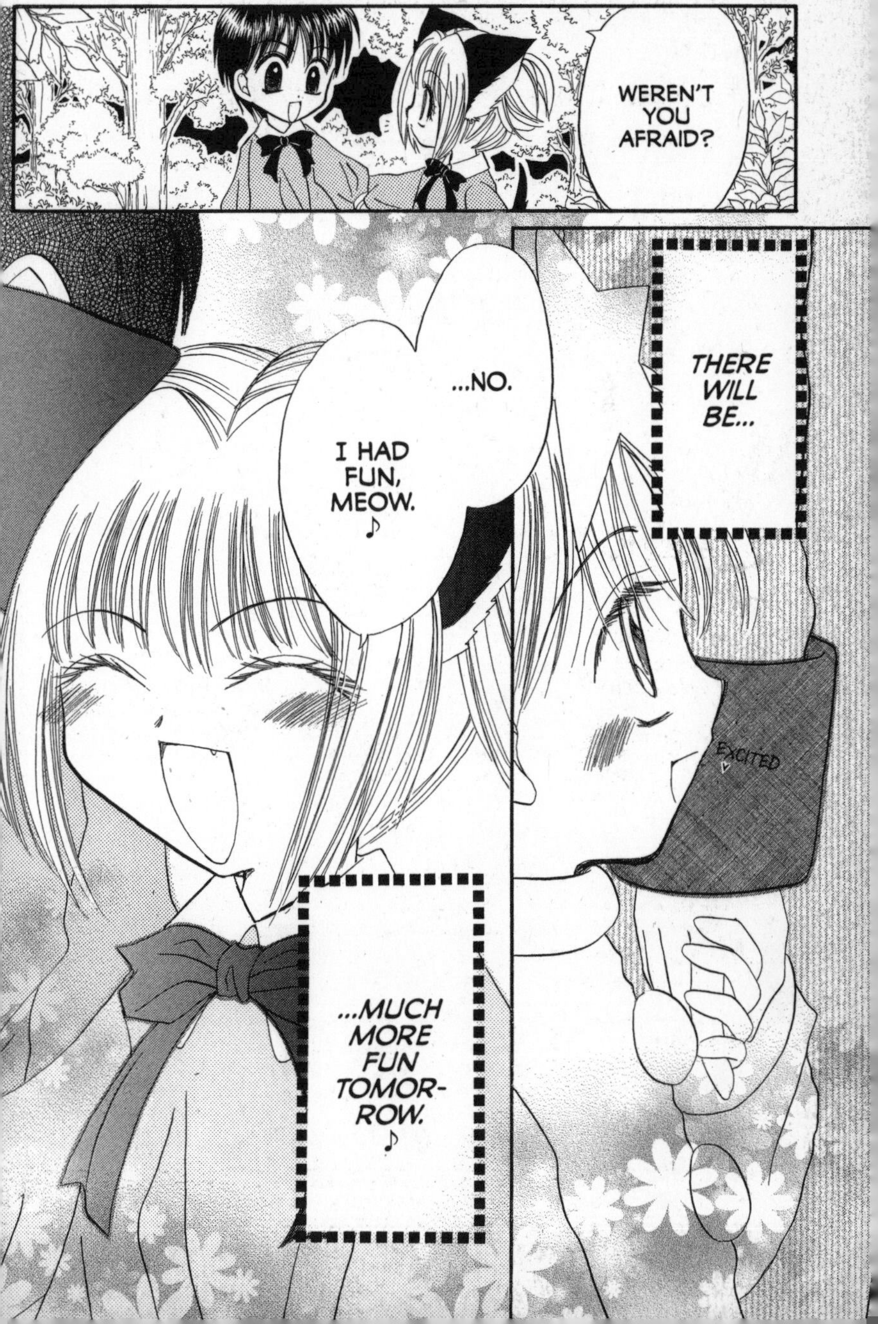
WEREN'T YOU AFRAID?
...NO.
I HAD FUN, MEOW. ♪
THERE WILL BE...
EXCITED ♪
...MUCH MORE FUN TOMORROW. ♪

Special: Tokyo Mew Mew Anime Messages

Hisayo Mochizuki as Pudding Fong, noda!

Ooh ahh → Ahh →

I play, noda!

This is Saki Nakajima as Ichigo Momomiya, meow.

We'll do our best, meow! We serve the people for their future, meow. ♥

Got it from Aoyama-kun.

This is Yumi Kakazu as Mint Aizawa. I'm studying impersonation at the studio.

Whatcha sayin'?!

Do I sound like her?

I'm Kumi Sakuma as Lettuce Midorikawa.

I want to fall in love, too.

Lettuce

Just kidding! By Sakuma.

I'm Junko Noda as Zacro Fujiwara and Masha. Friends are not bad to have.

This is Hikaru Midorikawa as Keiichirô Akasaka.

I'll escort you next time. ♥

I'm Megumi Ogata as Masaya Aoyama.

"Because you're my cat." (laughs) It's too much!!

DING DING

Ice

This is Kôichi Tohchika as Ryô Shirogane.

Do you like money? Me? I'm rich. Come to Café Mew Mew. We now have frozen treats.

Owner.

It's me, Katsuyuki Konishi as Shintarô Momomiya (Dad).

"Love ya ♥ Sakura! ♥

"Love ya ♥ Shin-chan! ♥

This is Nobutoshi Kanna as Pie!

"You've got the spirit." "I want your spirit next time."

I'm Kiyomi Asai as Tart. I'll strive to be mischievous! I love pranks!

"We'll metamorphose together!"

SMACK

This is Takako Honda as Sakura Momomiya (Mom).

This is Daisuke Sakaguchi as Kish.

Maybe I'll cheat on Ichigo since she won't take notice of me.

Chimera Frog

These messages are courtesy of the regular cast of the Tokyo Mew Mew anime. Thank you for your support!

Yo, This is Ikumi!

It's been a while and nice to meet you. This is Ikumi.
I present you Tokyo Mew Mew Volume 5.

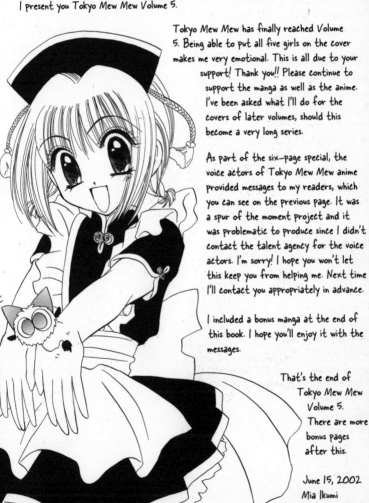

Tokyo Mew Mew has finally reached Volume 5. Being able to put all five girls on the cover makes me very emotional. This is all due to your support! Thank you!! Please continue to support the manga as well as the anime. I've been asked what I'll do for the covers of later volumes, should this become a very long series.

As part of the six-page special, the voice actors of Tokyo Mew Mew anime provided messages to my readers, which you can see on the previous page. It was a spur of the moment project and it was problematic to produce since I didn't contact the talent agency for the voice actors. I'm sorry! I hope you won't let this keep you from helping me. Next time I'll contact you appropriately in advance.

I included a bonus manga at the end of this book. I hope you'll enjoy it with the messages.

That's the end of Tokyo Mew Mew Volume 5. There are more bonus pages after this.

June 15, 2002
Mia Ikumi

Bunny's Dandelion

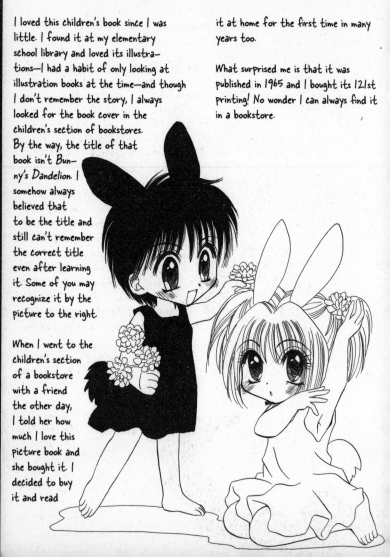

I loved this children's book since I was little. I found it at my elementary school library and loved its illustrations—I had a habit of only looking at illustration books at the time—and though I don't remember the story, I always looked for the book cover in the children's section of bookstores. By the way, the title of that book isn't *Bunny's Dandelion*. I somehow always believed that to be the title and still can't remember the correct title even after learning it. Some of you may recognize it by the picture to the right.

When I went to the children's section of a bookstore with a friend the other day, I told her how much I love this picture book and she bought it. I decided to buy it and read it at home for the first time in many years too.

What surprised me is that it was published in 1965 and I bought its 121st printing! No wonder I can always find it in a bookstore.

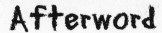

Afterword

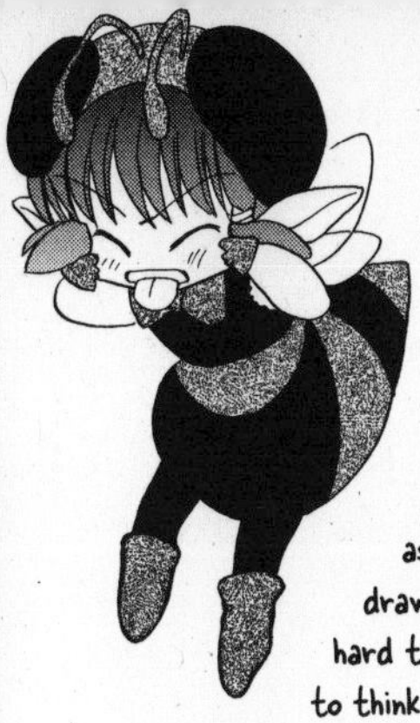

The power of one's voice is amazing. I watched it make the pictures come to life. I attended the recording of the first episode and was very impressed. Although I had to get back to work the next day, something amazing happened.

My characters were talking with the help of the voice actors as if it were magic. You can't expect a picture to move or be drawn by itself, but there's something different about it! It's hard to explain, but the characters speak in their own words. Come to think of it, I couldn't really explain how it's different when a voice actor asked me. The best description would be that they came to life. When I create dialogue for the characters, not only do I think of the way they talk but the expression they make and how they behave as well. Putting these on a piece of paper isn't exactly easy, but I feel fortunate to have this heartfelt experience through Tokyo Mew Mew.

Although this job is a lot of fun, I have to work very hard! I really, really, really have to do my best. That's all I can say for now.

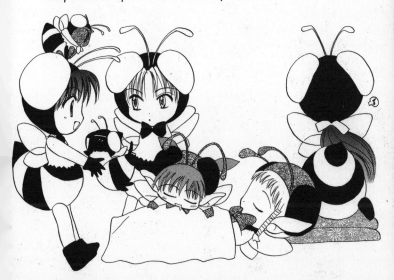

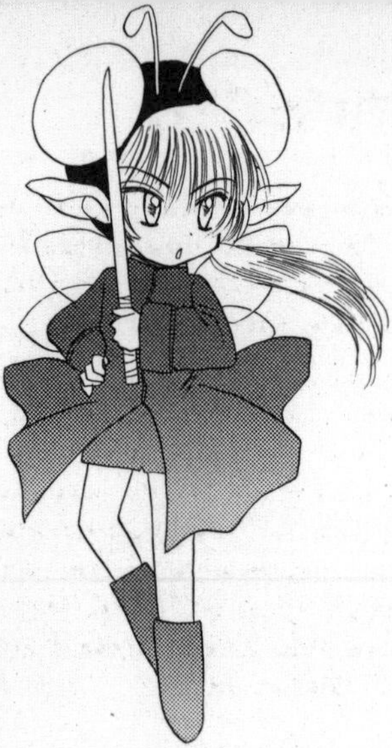

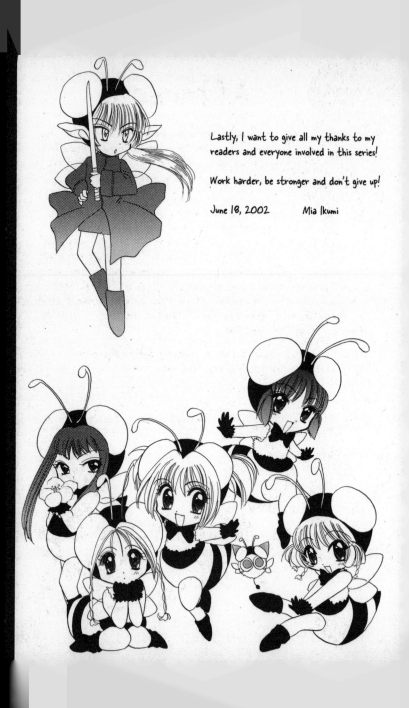

Lastly, I want to give all my thanks to my readers and everyone involved in this series!

Work harder, be stronger and don't give up!

June 18, 2002 Mia Ikumi

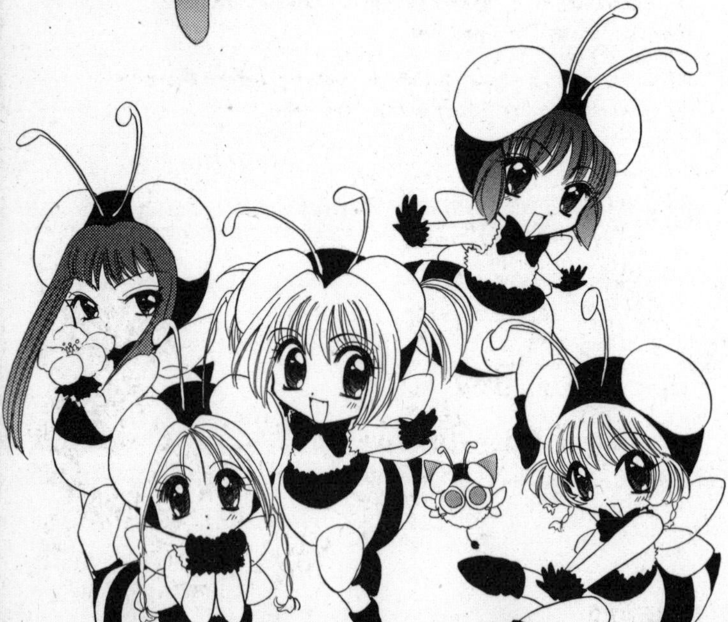

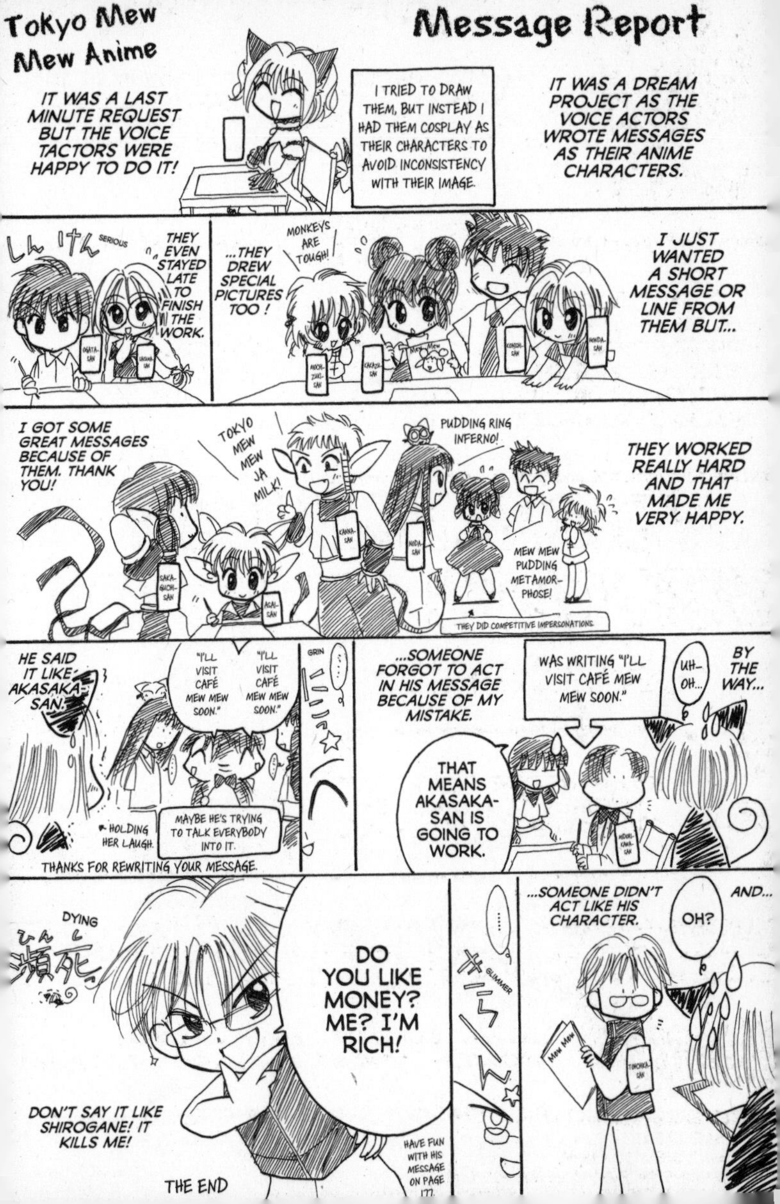
Tokyo Mew Mew Anime Message Report
IT WAS A DREAM PROJECT AS THE VOICE ACTORS WROTE MESSAGES AS THEIR ANIME CHARACTERS.
I TRIED TO DRAW THEM, BUT INSTEAD I HAD THEM COSPLAY AS THEIR CHARACTERS TO AVOID INCONSISTENCY WITH THEIR IMAGE.
IT WAS A LAST MINUTE REQUEST BUT THE VOICE TACTORS WERE HAPPY TO DO IT!
I JUST WANTED A SHORT MESSAGE OR LINE FROM THEM BUT...
MONKEYS ARE TOUGH!
...THEY DREW SPECIAL PICTURES TOO!
THEY EVEN STAYED LATE TO FINISH THE WORK.
しんけん
SERIOUS
THEY WORKED REALLY HARD AND THAT MADE ME VERY HAPPY.
PUDDING RING INFERNO!
MEW MEW PUDDING METAMORPHOSE!
TOKYO MEW MEW JA MILK!
I GOT SOME GREAT MESSAGES BECAUSE OF THEM. THANK YOU!
THEY DID COMPETITIVE IMPERSONATIONS.
BY THE WAY...
UH-OH...
WAS WRITING "I'LL VISIT CAFÉ MEW MEW SOON."
...SOMEONE FORGOT TO ACT IN HIS MESSAGE BECAUSE OF MY MISTAKE.
THAT MEANS AKASAKA-SAN IS GOING TO WORK.
GRIN
HE SAID IT LIKE AKASAKA-SAN.
"I'LL VISIT CAFÉ MEW MEW SOON."
"I'LL VISIT CAFÉ MEW MEW SOON."
HOLDING HER LAUGH.
MAYBE HE'S TRYING TO TALK EVERYBODY INTO IT.
THANKS FOR REWRITING YOUR MESSAGE.
AND...
OH?
...SOMEONE DIDN'T ACT LIKE HIS CHARACTER.
GLIMMER
HAVE FUN WITH HIS MESSAGE ON PAGE 177.
DO YOU LIKE MONEY? ME? I'M RICH!
DYING
ひんし
瀕死
DON'T SAY IT LIKE SHIROGANE! IT KILLS ME!
THE END

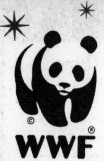

WWF PROTECTS NATURAL AREAS IN THE WORLD.

WWF, RECOGNIZED BY ITS PANDA LOGO, IS AN INTERNATIONAL NATURE CONSERVATION GROUP AND IS ACTIVE IN ABOUT 100 COUNTRIES. THEIR GOAL IS TO CONSERVE AN ENVIRONMENTALLY-FRIENDLY PLANET FOR ANIMALS.

WWF'S MAIN ACTIVITIES

- PROTECT ENDANGERED SPECIES SUCH AS TIGERS AND THE GIANT PANDA.
- PROTECT HABITATS INCLUDING FORESTS AND CORAL REEFS.
- EDUCATE CHILDREN ABOUT THE BEAUTY AND IMPORTANCE OF NATURE AS WELL AS GLOBAL ENVIRONMENTAL ISSUES SUCH AS GLOBAL WARMING AND CLIMATIC DISRUPTION.

TOKYO MEW MEW SUPPORTS WWF, TOO!

(1 YEN* FROM EVERY KODANSHA COMIC BOOK IS DONATED TO WWF.)

YOU'RE HELPING TO PROTECT ANIMALS WORLDWIDE BY PURCHASING THIS BOOK. ♡

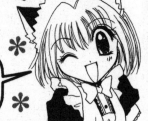

MEMBERSHIP IS REQUIRED AT WWF JAPAN. LET'S JOIN AND SUPPORT THEM. (JUNIOR MEMBERSHIP IS AVAILABLE TO THOSE UNDER 20.) ANNUAL MEMBERSHIP DUE IS 1,500 YEN*.

PRIVI-LEGES
- A WWF ORIGINAL KEY CHAIN AND A MEMBERSHIP CARD.
- QUARTERLY PANDA NEWS, A NATURE CONSERVATION NEWSLETTER.

CONTACT HERE IF YOU'RE INTERESTED.

WWF JAPAN
MEW MEW DIVISION
NIHONSEIMEI AKABANEBASHI BLDG. 6F
3-1-14 SHIBA MINATO-KU, TOKYO 105-0014
PHONE: 03-3769-1241 FAX: 03-3769-1717
FOR DETAILED INFORMATION, PLEASE VISIT WEBSITE: HTTP://WWW.WWF.OR.JP/

*1 YEN IS ABOUT ¢0.01, 1,500 YEN IS ABOUT $19.50.

Yo, This is Ikumi!

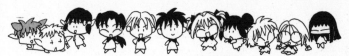

It's been a while or welcome new readers. I'm Ikumi. I present you Tokyo Mew Mew Volume 6.

Can you believe we're up to Volume 6? We've released four books this year! This is all due to your support. Thank you. I worked very hard on this volume. included a few illustrations of costumes that missed the grand prize in the contest as well as my comments on the original standalone manga and the first exhibition of my names (laughs). I also have a few words on Ringo Akai-chan, the original character of the PlayStation game. I hope you enjoy them! ♪

The illustration above is from the back cover of the anime script. I drew illustrations of the anime staff at the voice actors' request. The cross-dressed male characters in Pink House style I did for

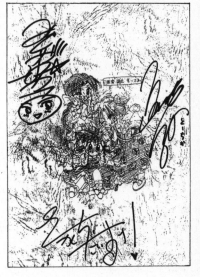

Kôichi Tohchika-san, who voiced Shirogane. I tried to draw them in my mind's image of each voice actor (laughs). Besides my assistants, I had been reluctant to bother them at work for their autographs. I really wanted them to sign this illustration, so I took advantage of my position. I'm sorry! Don't you think it's cool that it seems as if it's been signed by the cross-dressed characters? I am abusing my power. Ha ha ha! It's now one of my most treasured souvenirs (laughs). When I told Tohchika-san that I couldn't read his autograph, he kindly added furigana (laughs). Thank you! ☆

Other requests I received were: Lettuce madly in love with Kish from Daisuke Sakaguchi-san who voiced the role and liked Lettuce; Pudding, Zacro, Lettuce and Mint eating a strawberry from Yumi Kakazu-san who voiced Mint—I'll get it to you soon; Lettuce as the heart of head of lettuce or Pudding as a pudding cup from Katsuyuki Konishi-san as Shintarô Momomiya—how should I draw this?—etc. I hope I'll get a chance to show other illustrations too.

Sleeping Princess in Berry Forest ♥

This was my first work as a manga creator. Other than the tones done by a friend, I did the rest myself. I remember taking one month to create a name and another month to draw the manga in those days. I'm very impressed with my meticulous work (laughs).

I expected to seriously revise this manga and have it published in a book, but it wasn't necessary as I took time and effort to create a good manga. It doesn't seem like my work after all these years. I must say I love this manga. This may sound stupid, but I feel it was drawn with genuine feelings and with a pure heart. Am I corrupted now? I doubt I can create anything like it again. I really love this manga creator from the past.

I drew the illustration to the right today. My art doesn't seem to have changed drastically, but I think it has somewhat developed.

The boy's name is Yôta, which was asked about in many fan letters. I'm glad to finally be able to announce it. Shirogane before the Tokyo Mew Mew serialization looked like Yôta. I personally like this character as well as Kotori, who reminds me of a dog. I think it's unique to work on a girl with a dog-like personality. I hope I can create a manga like this again.

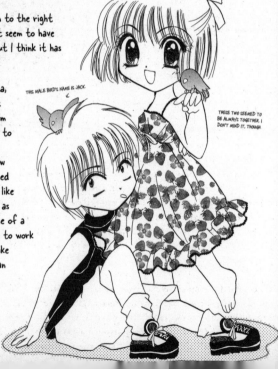

THIS MALE BIRD'S NAME IS JACK.
THESE TWO SEEMED TO BE ALWAYS TOGETHER. I DON'T MIND IT, THOUGH.

Unveiling Ikumi's Story-☆boards

Storyboards, also known as page layouts, are sketches of how panels will break down on the page. The storyboards get finalized after an editor's approval.

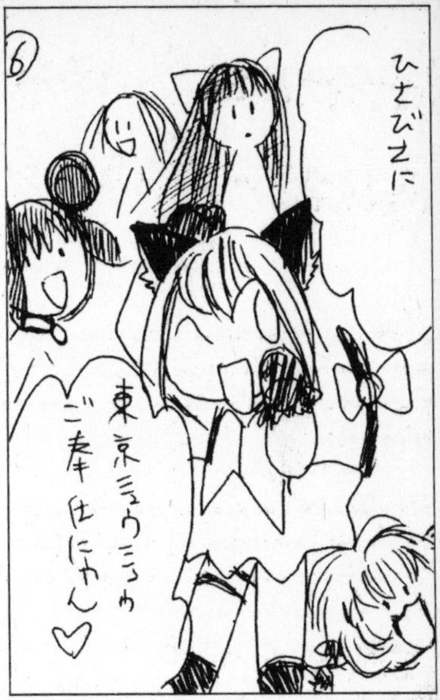
6
ひさびさに
東京ミュウミュウ
ご奉仕にゃん♡

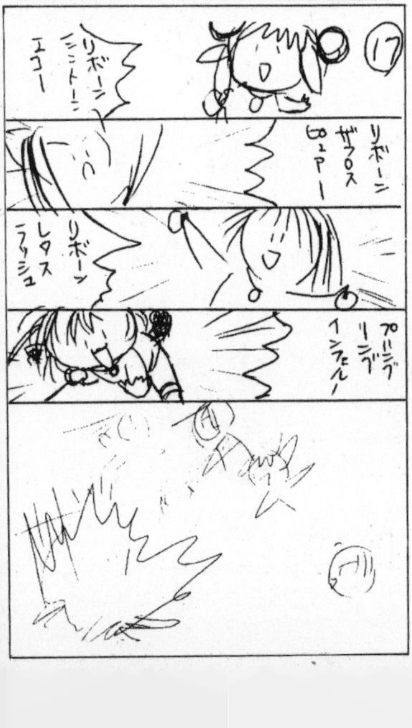
17
リボーン
ミントー
エコー
リボーン
ザクロス
ピュアー
リボーン
レタス
ラッシュ
プリン
リング
インフェルノ

These are storyboards for pages 98 and 99 in Volume 6, which are my favorite. I shouldn't be concerned about details for something that doesn't get revealed to the public, but I can't help worrying about them (laughs). This is what a storyboard looks like and I love how it resembles a picture book.

My art becomes rougher as I keep redo-ing the storyboards. I hope I don't have to revise them so that I can release them as storyboard Mew Mew someday. Maybe not. Aha ha!

I think Deep Blue looked like this at the end in the finalized version (laughs). I hope you enjoyed this glimpse into the production of Tokyo Mew Mew.

Here's Ringo Akai-chan ☆

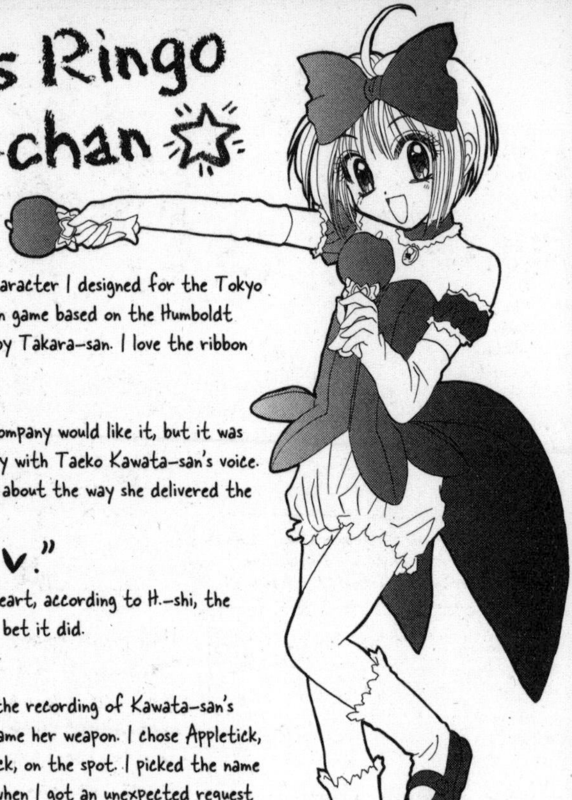

This is the original character I designed for the Tokyo Mew Mew PlayStation game based on the Humboldt penguin as requested by Takara-san. I love the ribbon on her head.

I wasn't sure if the company would like it, but it was well received, especially with Taeko Kawata-san's voice. The staff was crazy about the way she delivered the line,

"On^-chan. ♥."

It struck everyone's heart, according to H.-shi, the manager at Takara. I bet it did.
Hee hee! ♪

When I went to visit the recording of Kawata-san's song, I was asked to name her weapon. I chose Appletick, a pun on apple and stick, on the spot. I picked the name for Mew Berry Rod when I got an unexpected request at the recording studio too. I have a talent for names (laughs).

The other original character, Gateau-san, was created based on Takara-san's image of Kish's friend who is aristrocratic and intelligent. His favorite phrase is, "Do this or that," in Ryûtaro Okiayu's voice. I'm glad to hear that Okiayu-san, the voice actor, wanted to voice this role.

I hope the video game is released by the time this book comes out. I can't wait! ♥ I heard you can hear plenty of voice actors from the anime series talk.

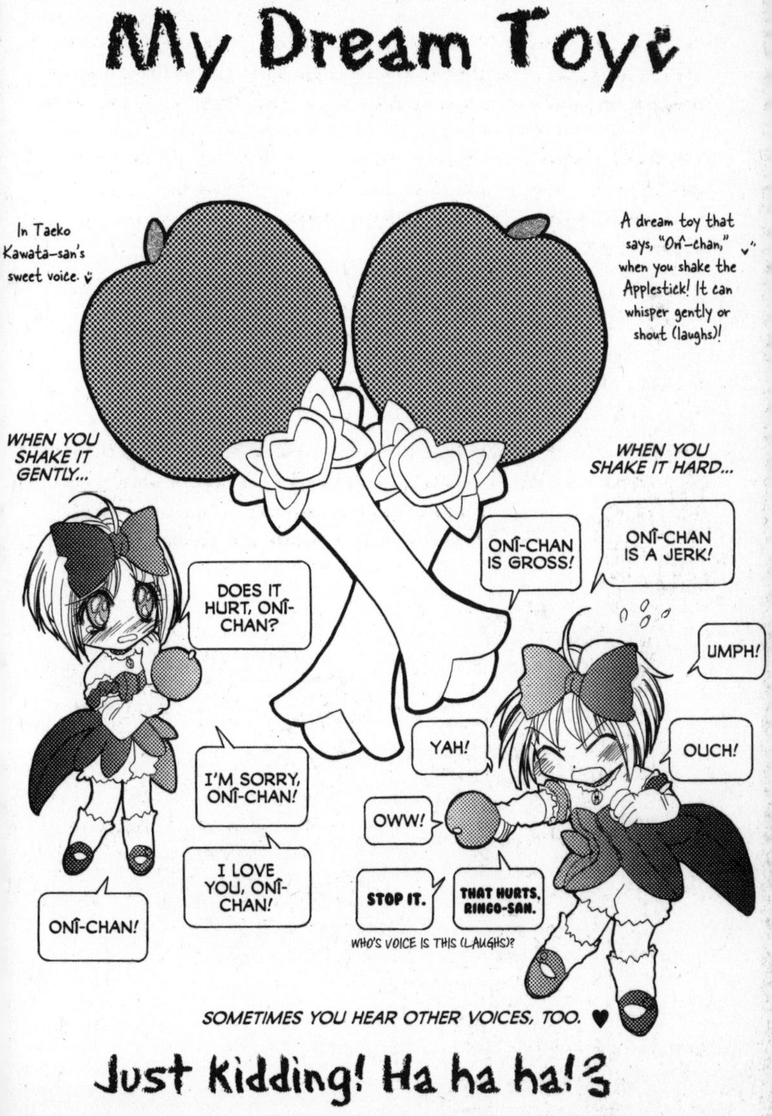
My Dream Toy
A dream toy that says, "Onî-chan," when you shake the Applestick! It can whisper gently or shout (laughs)!
In Taeko Kawata-san's sweet voice.
WHEN YOU SHAKE IT HARD...
ONÎ-CHAN IS A JERK!
ONÎ-CHAN IS GROSS!
UMPH!
OUCH!
YAH!
OWW!
THAT HURTS, RINGO-SAN.
STOP IT.
WHO'S VOICE IS THIS (LAUGHS)?
WHEN YOU SHAKE IT GENTLY...
DOES IT HURT, ONÎ-CHAN?
I'M SORRY, ONÎ-CHAN!
I LOVE YOU, ONÎ-CHAN!
ONÎ-CHAN!
SOMETIMES YOU HEAR OTHER VOICES, TOO.
Just Kidding! Ha ha ha!

Afterword

I know I've said this before but I like Ringo a lot. The more I draw her, the more I like her. It'd be nice if she appeared regularly in the manga. Can she? I get a good response to her from people around me. What do you think? Maybe, maybe not. ☆

I'm in a good mood now, but not due to anything in particular. In fact some bad things happened to me. I think I'm on a runner's high, the euphoric feeling that occurs when you push to the limit when you exercise (laughs). Maybe it's coming from working so hard non—stop.

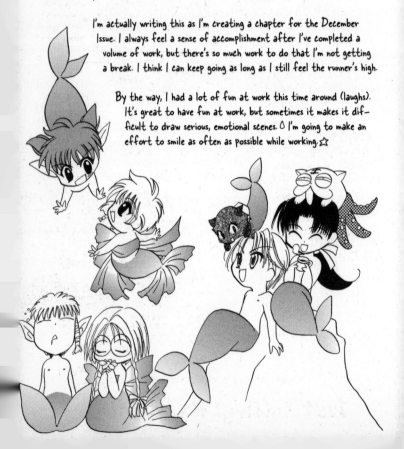

I'm actually writing this as I'm creating a chapter for the December Issue. I always feel a sense of accomplishment after I've completed a volume of work, but there's so much work to do that I'm not getting a break. I think I can keep going as long as I still feel the runner's high.

By the way, I had a lot of fun at work this time around (laughs). It's great to have fun at work, but sometimes it makes it difficult to draw serious, emotional scenes. ◊ I'm going to make an effort to smile as often as possible while working. ☆

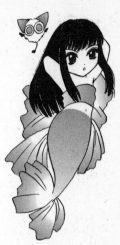

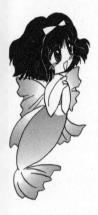

Lastly, many thanks
to the people who created this
manga with me or were
involved in this project, my
readers and my supporters!

I love people who try hard,
so I won't give up, either. ☆

October 11, 2002   Mia Ikumi

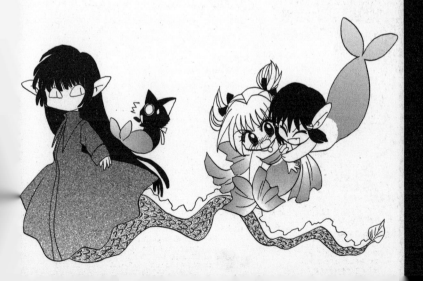

Tokyo Mew Mew Complete Celebration:
Staff Introduction Hamster Style!

THIS IS THE STAFF OF TOKYO MEW MEW MANGA AND IT'S NON-FICTITIOUS ALTER-EGO HAMSTERS.

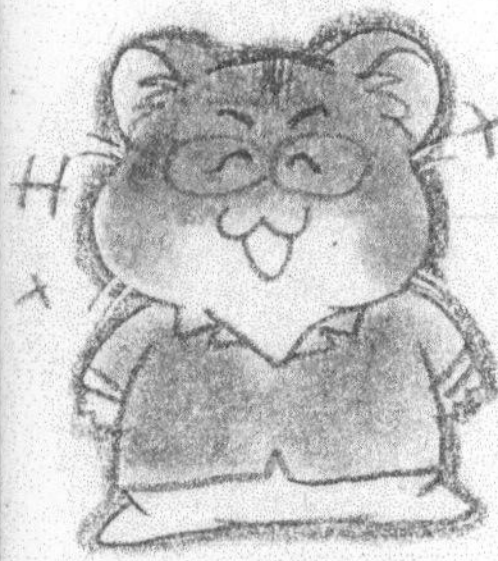

CHIEF MATSUMOTO

DRAWS BACKGROUNDS. AMUSES EVERYONE WITH WEIRD MOVES AND JOKES. WEAKENS AT THE WORD, "RAMEN."

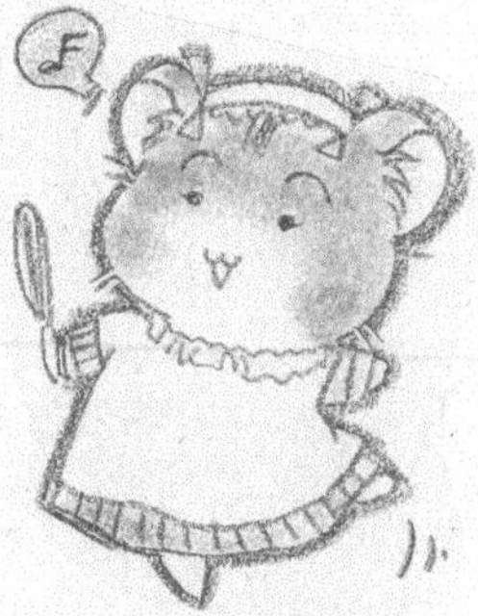

MIA IKUMI

MAINLY HANDLES ART. GOOD AT WEARING WEIRD CLOTHES CASUALLY. LOVES TO WEAR COSTUMES IN THE WINTER.

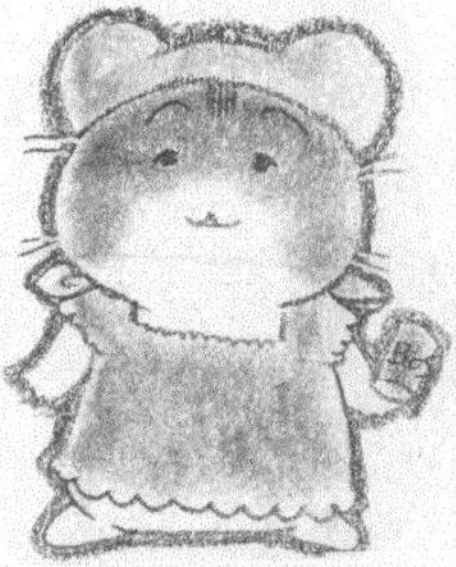

BLACK KANASHIRO (SUGAR-FREE)

HANDLES DIFFICULT TASKS. HELPFUL BUT COMES AND GOES LIKE THE WIND. HAS A DARK PERSONALITY.

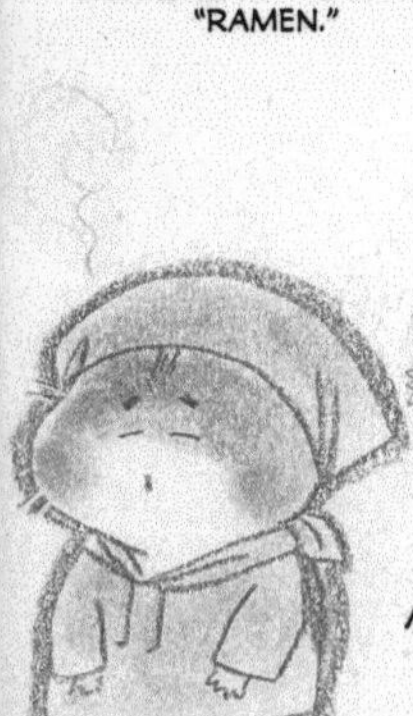

OTOME NAKAZAWA

HANDLES INKING AND DOING DISHES. A MYSTERIOUS GIRL WHO LOVES AOYAMA-KUN.

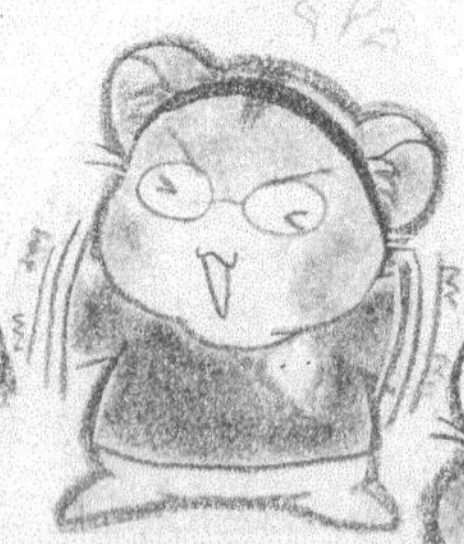

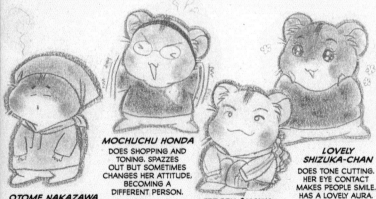

MOCHUCHU HONDA

DOES SHOPPING AND TONING. SPAZZES OUT BUT SOMETIMES CHANGES HER ATTITUDE, BECOMING A DIFFERENT PERSON.

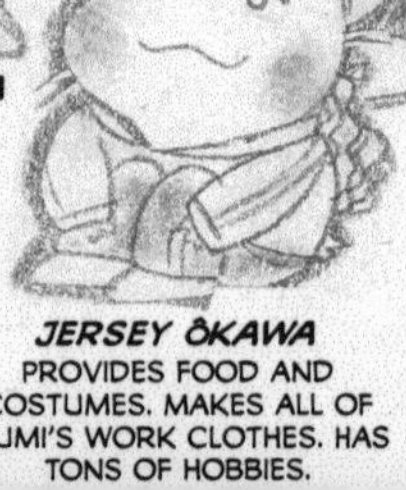

JERSEY ŌKAWA

PROVIDES FOOD AND COSTUMES. MAKES ALL OF IKUMI'S WORK CLOTHES. HAS TONS OF HOBBIES.

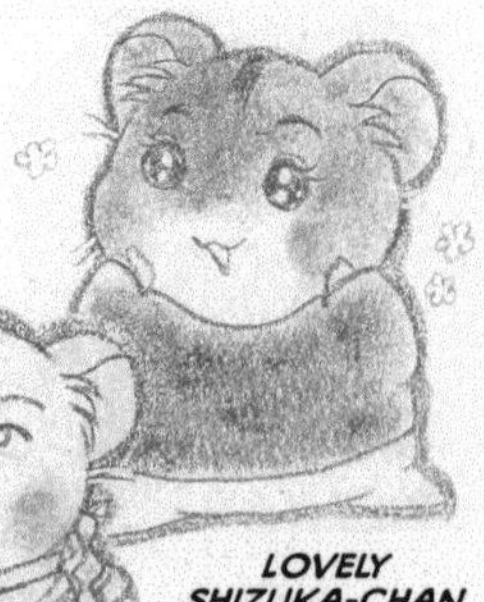

LOVELY SHIZUKA-CHAN

DOES TONE CUTTING. HER EYE CONTACT MAKES PEOPLE SMILE. HAS A LOVELY AURA.

Afterword

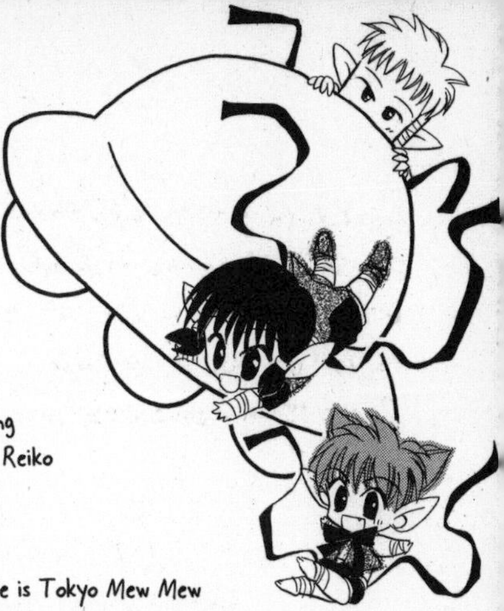

At last, this is the final volume of Tokyo Mew Mew. It seems to have gone by fast yet slow at the same time. People say that about experiences a lot but I think it's especially true in this case. I feel like I've experienced lots of good times and bad times in a short period. I think I've gained something in my life (laughs). Anyway, I want to thank Reiko Yoshida-san for developing the scenario!

I'll be starting a new series soon and its title is Tokyo Mew Mew a La Mode. It's the sequel to Tokyo Mew Mew, in which the world is still thriving! I'm able to do this because of you. Actually I'm working on the first chapter right now. It isn't just any sequel because I'm aiming for a cuter, hyper and fun manga. I think I drew far too much detail to my liking, but I also think that it brought me to a whole new world of Mew Mew, which made me excited. I hope you'll read the new Tokyo Mew Mew series, Tokyo Mew Mew a La Mode! Coming soon! ✩ by Ramens

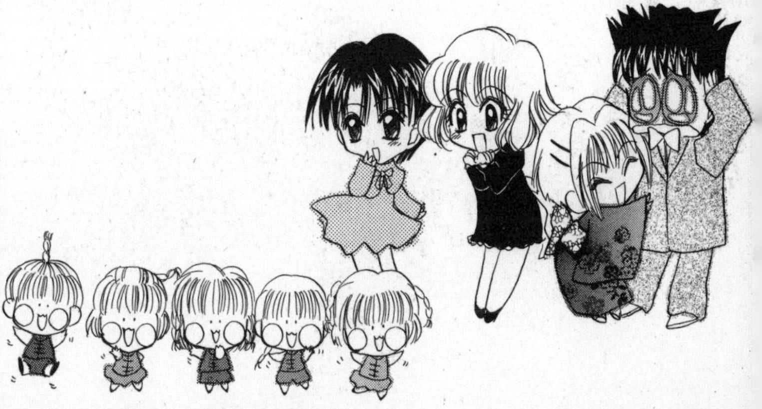

Lastly, many thanks to the people who
created this manga with me or were
involved in this project, my readers,
supporters and my beloved
Tokyo Mew Mew characters!

Thank you and
job well done!

February 7, 2003 at 2:20 AM   Mia Ikumi

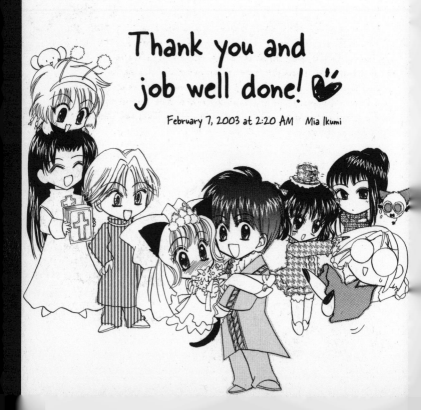

TRANSLATION NOTES

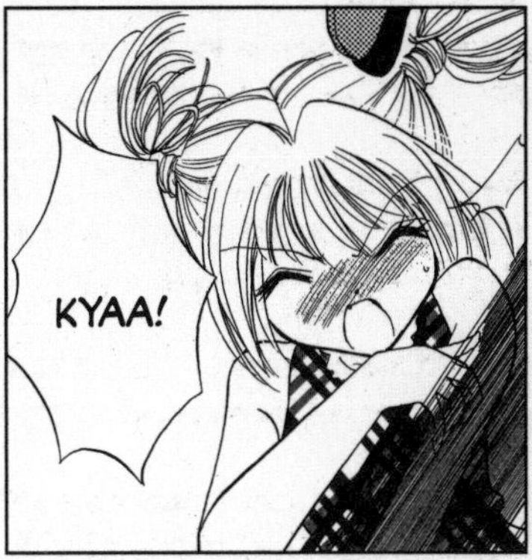
KYAA!

Kyaa and *Gyaa*
Kyaa is a girlish scream. Although it can be used when a character is frightened or surprised, it's usually heard as a scream of delight. *Gyaa* nearly always indicates real fright, embarrassment or pain, and hardly ever has a good meaning.

Ichigo and Strawberry
Ichigo's name means "strawberry" in Japanese.

Last Names
Each character's last name represents a color: Momomiya for *momoiro* or "pink," Aizawa for *aiiro* or "blue," Midorikawa for *midori* or "green," Fujiwara for *fujiiro* or "purple" and Fong means "yellow" in Chinese.

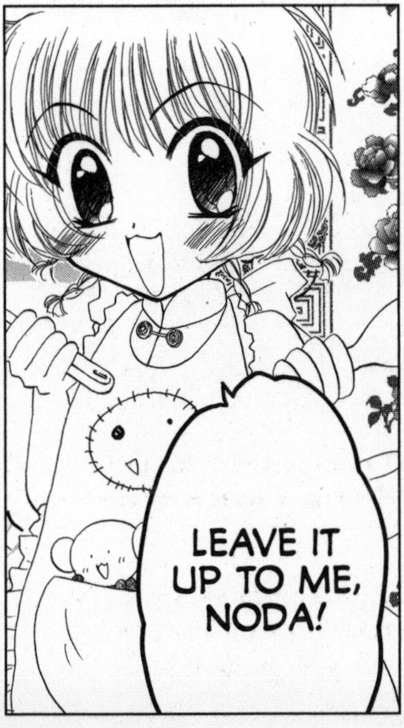
LEAVE IT UP TO ME, NODA!

Na no da
Pudding has a habit of ending all her lines of dialogue with the word Na no da, which literally means "it is that." While it is has no particular meaning in the way Pudding uses it, she applies it to her statement to put more emphasis.

Onêsama and onêchan
Onêsama and onêchan literally mean "older sister" as well as an older female deserving of great respect. While onêsama refers to someone of great prestige, onêchan expresses someone endearing to the speaker.

Men and Ippon, page 16
Men is a vertical strike to the head in kendo, a Japanese martial art of swordfighting. Ippon means "one point" in which a fighter must hit one of eight

valid targets to earn a point in a match.

An incentive trip, page 35
Japanese companies tend to recognize their employees as quasi-family members and invite them to an overnight trip every year.

A four-koma manga, page 37
A four-koma, or *yonkoma*, is a four-panel manga format that runs vertically, and is typically used for a gag manga.

Mille crepe, page 64
Mille crepe is a French cake made of many layers of crepes and cream filling.

Two plus two equals death, page 152
Tart is actually saying two plus two equals *shi*. The Japanese word *shi* means "four" as well as "death," despite being written differently in kanji, the Japanese script. The number four is considered unlucky in Japan for this reason.

Shôten, page 172
Shôten is a long-running Japanese TV comedy show. On the air since 1966, it features six comedians competing for the best joke. It's well-known for its catchy theme music.

Hai, page 264
Hai is a kendo term that means "yes."

Nattô, page 299
Nattô is a Japanese fermented food made from soy beans that is usually eaten with rice. It has a challenging taste, a strong smell, and a slimy texture.

Nakayoshi, page 299
Nakayoshi is a monthly shôjo Manga magazine.

Edokko, page 307
Edokko, literally meaning a "child of Edo," refers to a trueborn Tokyo native, known for being cheerful and headstrong and having a strong sense of justice.

Tamaya, page 315
People shout *Tamaya* or *Kagiya* to express delight at a fireworks display in Japan. They were rival firework makers that competed in an annual fireworks festival in the early 1800s. People would shout their names to show support.

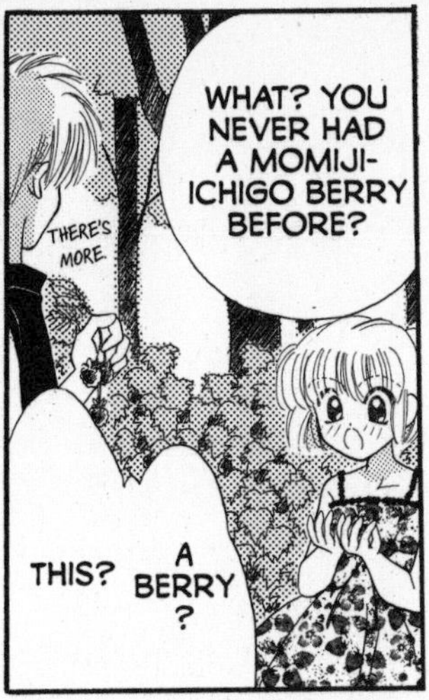
WHAT? YOU NEVER HAD A MOMIJI-ICHIGO BERRY BEFORE?
THERE'S MORE.
A BERRY?
THIS?

Odaiba, page 233
Odaiba is a seaport district located on an artificial island in Tokyo Bay.

Momiji-ichigo berry, page 334
Momiji-ichigo or Japanese maple raspberry grows on thorny shrubs with leaves that resemble maple leaves.

Pink House, page 355
Pink House is a well-known gothic lolita fashion label in Japan.

Furigana, page 158
Furigana is a small hiragana phonetics printed next to kanji characters.

Takara-san, page 361
The creator is referring to Takara Co., Ltd., a Japanese toy company that also develops video games.

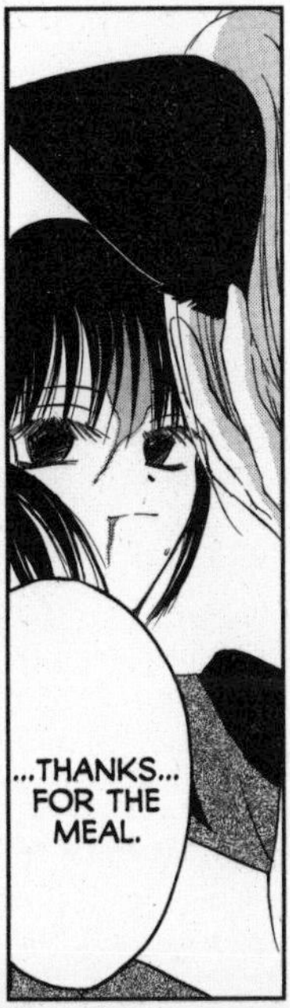
...THANKS... FOR THE MEAL.

Thanks for the meal, page 431
In Japan, people have a custom of saying *gochisôsama* or "thank you for the meal" at the end of the meal to express their gratitude towards people who made it possible.

Karuta, page 502
Karuta, originated from a Portuguese word, carte, which means "card", is a Japanese matching card game. There are two types of cards in katura, *yomifuda* or "reading cards" with a poem or a phrase and *torifuda* or "grabbing cards", which consist of the first syllable of the phrase and the image corresponding to *yomifuda*. One player reads a poem or a phrase on *yomifuda*, and the other player(s) try to find and grab *torifuda* that is associated with it. The basic rule of the game is to grab as many *torifuda* before anyone.

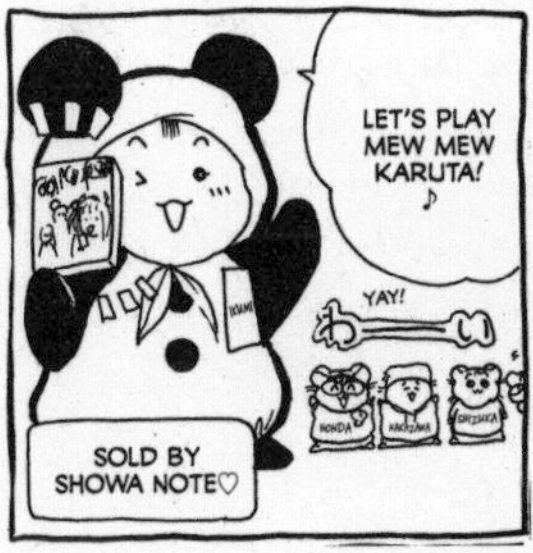
LET'S PLAY MEW MEW KARUTA! ♪
YAY!
SOLD BY SHOWA NOTE♡

Showa Note, page 321
Showa Note is a Japanese stationary company.

Thanks for the goodies, page 342
Like Kish on page 76, Pudding actually says *gochisôsama* to thank Ichigo for providing them snacks.

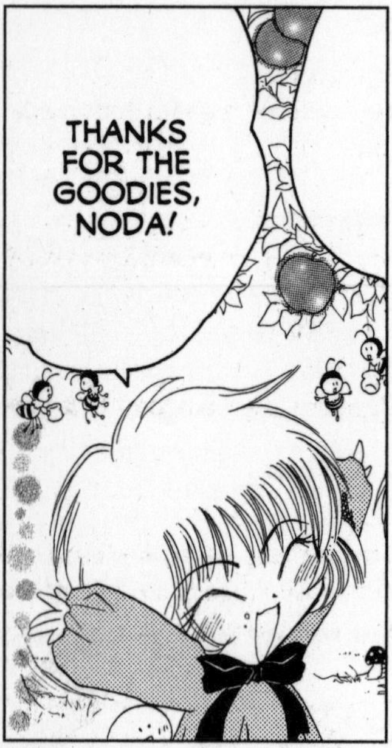
THANKS FOR THE GOODIES, NODA!

HONORIFICS EXPLAINED

Throughout the Kodansha Comics books, you will find Japanese honorifics left intact in the translations. For those not familiar with how the Japanese use honorifics and, more important, how they differ from American honorifics, we present this brief overview.

Politeness has always been a critical facet of Japanese culture. Ever since the feudal era, when Japan was a highly stratified society, use of honorifics—which can be defined as polite speech that indicates relationship or status—has played an essential role in the Japanese language. When addressing someone in Japanese, an honorific usually takes the form of a suffix attached to one's name (example: "Asuna-san"), is used as a title at the end of one's name, or appears in place of the name itself (example: "Negi-sensei," or simply "Sensei!").

Honorifics can be expressions of respect or endearment. In the context of manga and anime, honorifics give insight into the nature of the relationship between characters. Many English translations leave out these important honorifics and therefore distort the feel of the original Japanese. Because Japanese honorifics contain nuances that English honorifics lack, it is our policy at Kodansha Comics not to translate them. Here, instead, is a guide to some of the honorifics you may encounter in Kodansha Comics books.

-san: This is the most common honorific and is equivalent to Mr., Miss, Ms., or Mrs. It is the all-purpose honorific and can be used in any situation where politeness is required.

-sama: This is one level higher than "-san" and is used to confer great respect.

-dono: This comes from the word "tono," which means "lord." It is an even higher level than "-sama" and confers utmost respect.

-kun: This suffix is used at the end of boys' names to express familiarity or endearment. It is also sometimes used by men among friends, or when addressing someone younger or of a lower station.

-chan: This is used to express endearment, mostly toward girls. It is also used for little boys, pets, and even among lovers. It gives a sense of childish cuteness.

Bozu: This is an informal way to refer to a boy, similar to the English terms "kid" and "squirt."

Sempai/Senpai: This title suggests that the addressee is one's senior in a group or organization. It is most often used in a school setting, where underclassmen refer to their upperclassmen as "sempai." It can also be used in the workplace, such as when a newer employee addresses an employee who has seniority in the company.

Kohai: This is the opposite of "sempai" and is used toward underclassmen in school or newcomers in the workplace. It connotes that the addressee is of a lower station.

Sensei: Literally meaning "one who has come before," this title is used for teachers, doctors, or masters of any profession or art.

-[blank]: This is usually forgotten in these lists, but it is perhaps the most significant difference between Japanese and English. The lack of honorific means that the speaker has permission to address the person in a very intimate way. Usually, only family, spouses, or very close friends have this kind of permission. Known as yobisute, it can be gratifying when someone who has earned the intimacy starts to call one by one's name without an honorific. But when that intimacy hasn't been earned, it can be very insulting.

The Pretty Guardians are back!

Kodansha Comics is proud to present *Sailor Moon* with all new translations.

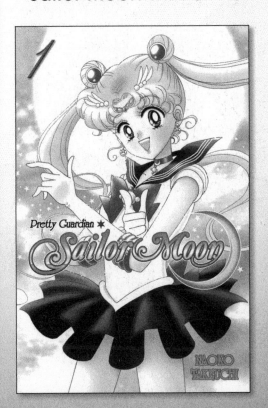

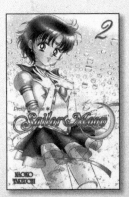

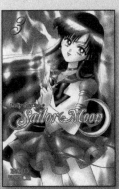

For more information, go to **www.kodanshacomics.com**

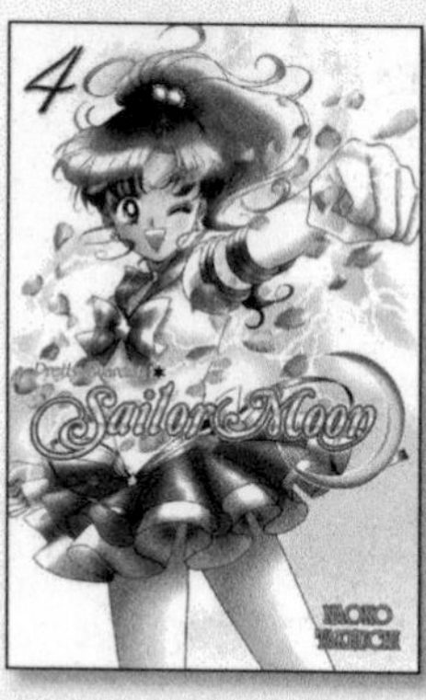
4
Pretty Guardian
Sailor Moon
NAOKO TAKEUCHI
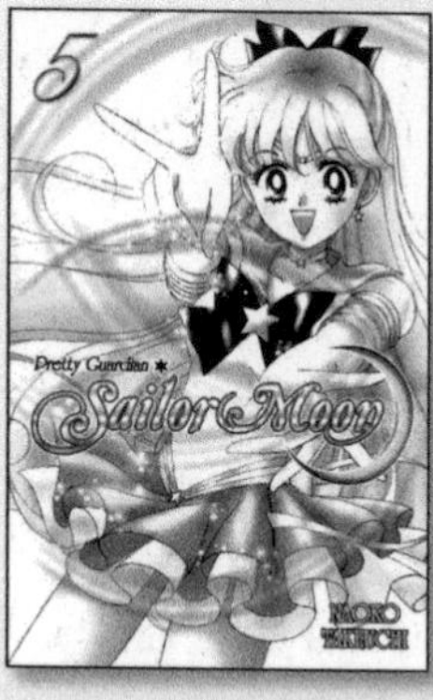
5
Pretty Guardian
Sailor Moon
NAOKO TAKEUCHI
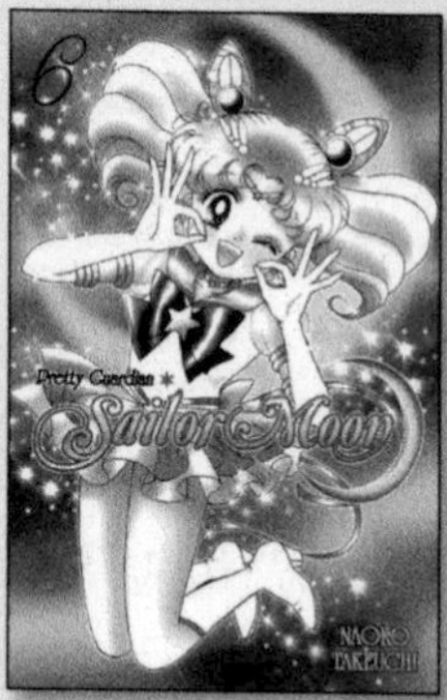
6
Pretty Guardian
Sailor Moon
NAOKO TAKEUCHI
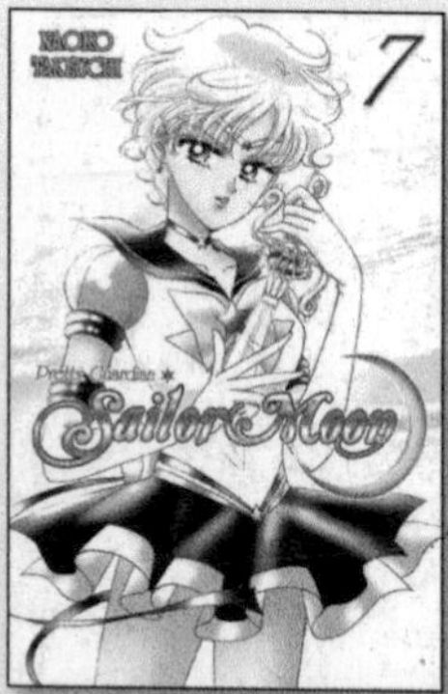
NAOKO TAKEUCHI
7
Pretty Guardian
Sailor Moon
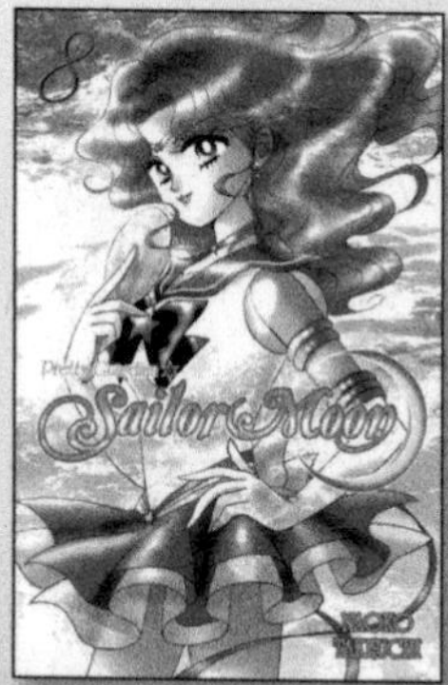
8
Sailor Moon
NAOKO TAKEUCHI
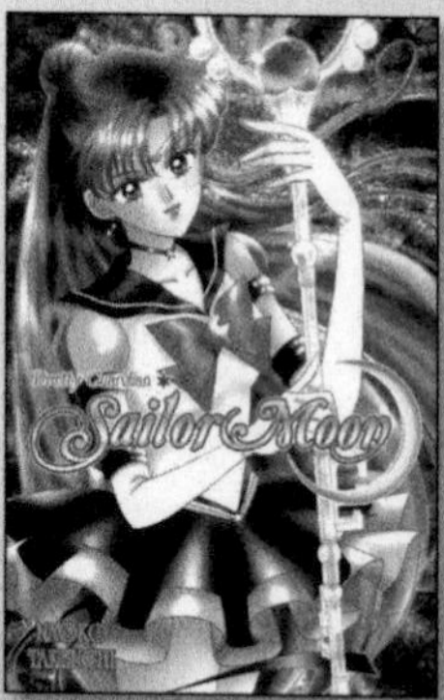
Sailor Moon
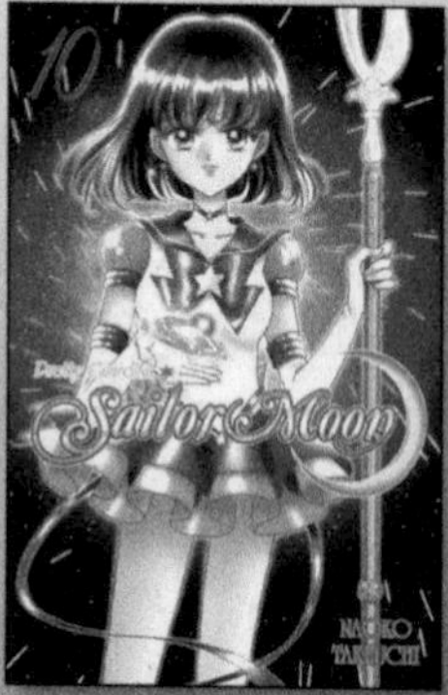
10
Sailor Moon
NAOKO TAKEUCHI
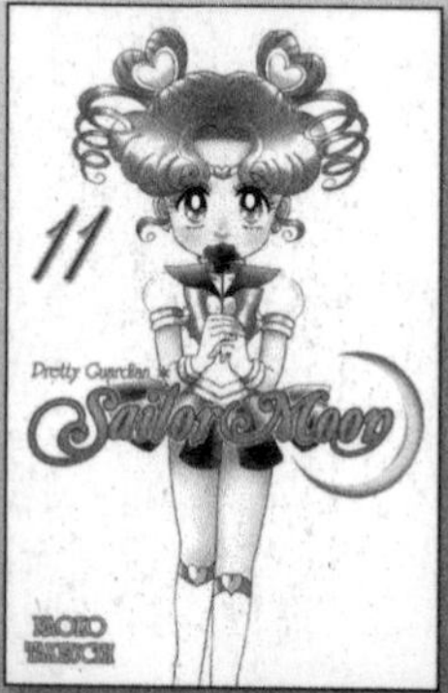
11
Pretty Guardian
Sailor Moon
NAOKO TAKEUCHI
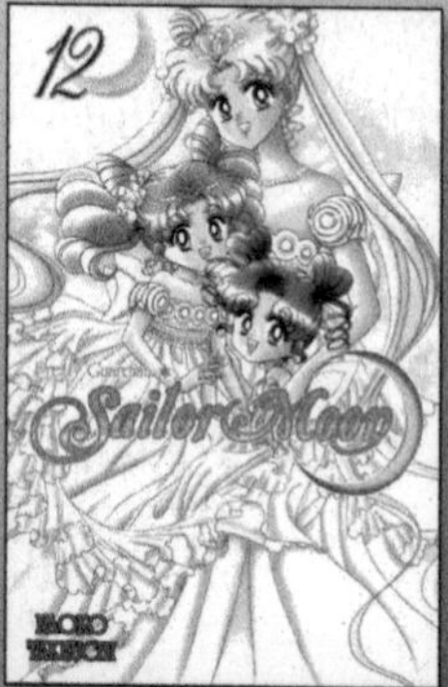
12
Sailor Moon
NAOKO TAKEUCHI

KC
KODANSHA
COMICS

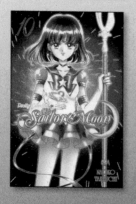

ANIMAL LAND

BY MAKOTO RAIKU

In a world of animals, where the strong eat the weak, Monoko the tanuki stumbles across a strange creature the likes of which has never been seen before–a human baby! While the newborn has no claws or teeth to protect itself, it does have the special ability to speak to and understand all different animals. Can the gift of speech between species change the balance of power in a land where the weak must always fear the strong?

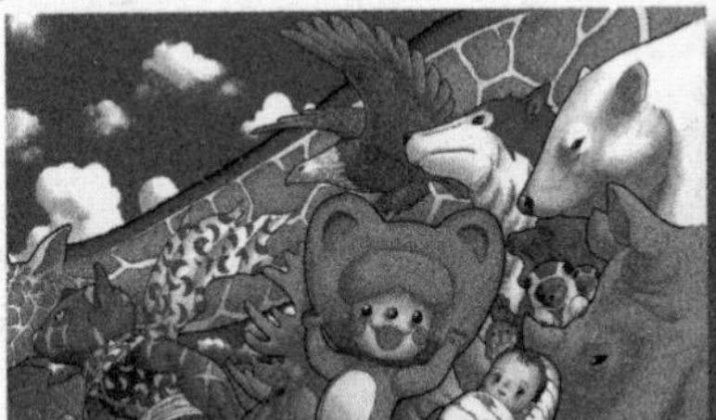
ANIMAL LAND 1
MAKOTO RAIKU

Ages 13+

KC KODANSHA COMICS

VISIT KODANSHACOMICS.COM TO:

- View release date calendars for upcoming volumes
- Find out the latest about upcoming Kodansha Comics series

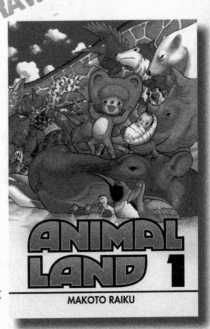

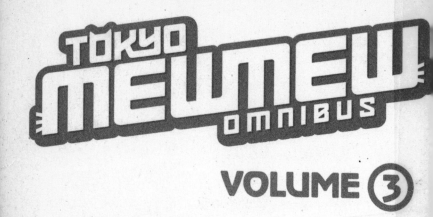

TOKYO MEWMEW OMNIBUS

VOLUME 3

Story by Reiko Yoshida
Art by Mia Ikumi

Translated by Elina Ishikawa
Lettered by AndWorld Design

KC KODANSHA COMICS

CONTENTS